MODELING THE PSYCHOPATHOLOGICAL DIMENSIONS OF SCHIZOPHRENIA

MODELING THE PSYCHOPATHOLOGICAL DIMENSIONS OF SCHIZOPHRENIA

FROM MOLECULES TO BEHAVIOR

Edited by

MIKHAIL V. PLETNIKOV
Johns Hopkins University School of Medicine
Baltimore, MD, USA

JOHN L. WADDINGTON
Royal College of Surgeons in Ireland
Dublin, Ireland

ELSEVIER

AMSTERDAM • BOSTON • HEIDELBERG • LONDON
NEW YORK • OXFORD • PARIS • SAN DIEGO
SAN FRANCISCO • SINGAPORE • SYDNEY • TOKYO

Academic Press is an imprint of Elsevier

Academic Press is an imprint of Elsevier
125 London Wall, London EC2Y 5AS, UK
525 B Street, Suite 1800, San Diego, CA 92101-4495, USA
225 Wyman Street, Waltham, MA 02451, USA
The Boulevard, Langford Lane, Kidlington, Oxford OX5 1GB, UK

ISBN: 978-0-12-800981-9

British Library Cataloguing-in-Publication Data
A catalogue record for this book is available from the British Library

Library of Congress Cataloging-in-Publication Data
A catalog record for this book is available from the Library of Congress

For information on all Academic Press publications
visit our website at http://store.elsevier.com/

Working together
to grow libraries in
developing countries

www.elsevier.com • www.bookaid.org

Typeset by TNQ Books and Journals
www.tnq.co.in

Printed and bound in the United Kingdom

Contents

I

FROM CLINICAL DIMENSIONS TO ANIMAL MODELS

Clinical and Pathological Aspects

Animal Models of Psychotic Disorders: Dimensional Approach

II

NEUROBIOLOGY OF PSYCHOTIC DISORDERS

Non-Genetic Models

18. Genetic Rat Models for Schizophrenia
BART A. ELLENBROEK AND TIM KARL

Gene–Gene and Gene–Environment Models

19. Modeling Gene–Gene Interactions in Schizophrenia
E. VON CHEONG AND COLM M.P. O'TUATHAIGH

20. Modeling Gene–Environment Interaction in Schizophrenia
YAN JOUROUKHIN, ROSS McFARLAND, YAVUZ AYHAN
AND MIKHAIL V. PLETNIKOV

21. Rodent Models of Multiple Environmental Exposures with Relevance to Schizophrenia
URS MEYER

Cell Models

22. Synaptic Abnormalities and Neuroplasticity
Molecular Mechanisms of Cognitive Dysfunction in Genetic Mouse Models of Schizophrenia
RUOQI GAO, THERON A. RUSSELL AND PETER PENZES

23. hiPSC Models Relevant to Schizophrenia
BRIGHAM J. HARTLEY, YOAV HADAS AND
KRISTEN J. BRENNAND

Contributors

Tursun Alkam   Department of Regional Pharmaceutical Care and Sciences, Graduate School of Pharmaceutical Sciences, Meijo University, Nagoya, Japan; Department of Basic Medical Sciences, College of Osteopathic Medicine of the Pacific, Western University of Health Sciences, Pomona, CA, USA

Yavuz Ayhan   Department of Psychiatry and Behavioral Sciences, Johns Hopkins University School of Medicine, Baltimore, MD, USA; Department of Psychiatry, Faculty of Medicine, Hacettepe University, Sihhiye, Ankara, Turkey

Philipp S. Baumann   Center for Psychiatric Neuroscience, Centre Hospitalier Universitaire Vaudois and University of Lausanne (CHUV-UNIL), Prilly-Lausanne, Switzerland; Department of Psychiatry, Centre Hospitalier Universitaire Vaudois and University of Lausanne (CHUV-UNIL), Prilly-Lausanne, Switzerland; Service of General Psychiatry, Centre Hospitalier Universitaire Vaudois and University of Lausanne (CHUV-UNIL), Prilly-Lausanne, Switzerland

Jean-Martin Beaulieu   Department of Psychiatry and Neuroscience, Faculty of Medicine, Laval University, Québec City, QC, Canada; Institut universitaire en santé mentale de Québec, Québec City, QC, Canada

Catherine Belzung   INSERM 930 and Université François Rabelais de Tours, UFR Sciences et Techniques, Tours, France

A. Berry   Behavioural Neuroscience Section, Department of Cell Biology and Neurosciences, Istituto Superiore di Sanità, Rome, Italy

Kristen J. Brennand   Department of Psychiatry, Icahn School of Medicine at Mount Sinai, New York, NY, USA

Alan S. Brown   Department of Psychiatry, Columbia University College of Physicians and Surgeons, New York State Psychiatric Institute, New York, NY, USA; Department of Epidemiology, Columbia University Mailman School of Public Health, New York, NY, USA

John P. Bruno   Department of Psychology, The Ohio State University, Columbus, OH, USA; Department of Neuroscience, The Ohio State University, Columbus, OH, USA

Daniel Chang   Department of Psychiatry and Behavioral Sciences, The Johns Hopkins University School of Medicine, Baltimore, MD, USA

F. Cirulli   Behavioural Neuroscience Section, Department of Cell Biology and Neurosciences, Istituto Superiore di Sanità, Rome, Italy

Michel Cuénod   Center for Psychiatric Neuroscience, Centre Hospitalier Universitaire Vaudois and University of Lausanne (CHUV-UNIL), Prilly-Lausanne, Switzerland; Department of Psychiatry, Centre Hospitalier Universitaire Vaudois and University of Lausanne (CHUV-UNIL), Prilly-Lausanne, Switzerland

Luka Culig   INSERM 930 and Université François Rabelais de Tours, UFR Sciences et Techniques, Tours, France

Angela J. Dean   Queensland Brain Institute, University of Queensland, Brisbane, QLD, Australia; Institute for Social Science Research, University of Queensland, Brisbane, QLD, Australia

Arsime Demjaha   Institute of Psychiatry, Psychosis & Neuroscience, London, UK

Lieve Desbonnet   School of Life Sciences, University of Glasgow, Glasgow, UK

Sofia M. Dibble   Departments of Neuroscience, Psychiatry and Psychology, University of Pittsburgh, Pittsburgh, PA, USA

Kim Q. Do   Center for Psychiatric Neuroscience, Centre Hospitalier Universitaire Vaudois and University of Lausanne (CHUV-UNIL), Prilly-Lausanne, Switzerland; Department of Psychiatry, Centre Hospitalier Universitaire Vaudois and University of Lausanne (CHUV-UNIL), Prilly-Lausanne, Switzerland

Yijuan Du   Departments of Neuroscience, Psychiatry and Psychology, University of Pittsburgh, Pittsburgh, PA, USA

Bart A. Ellenbroek   Victoria University of Wellington, Wellington, New Zealand

Darryl W. Eyles   Queensland Brain Institute, University of Queensland, Brisbane, QLD, Australia; Queensland Centre for Mental Health Research, Wacol, QLD, Australia

Gohar Fakhfouri   Department of Psychiatry and Neuroscience, Faculty of Medicine, Laval University, Québec City, QC, Canada; Institut universitaire en santé mentale de Québec, Québec City, QC, Canada

Kevin C.F. Fone   School of Life Sciences, Queens Medical Centre, University of Nottingham, Nottingham, UK

Margot Fournier   Center for Psychiatric Neuroscience, Centre Hospitalier Universitaire Vaudois and University of Lausanne (CHUV-UNIL), Prilly-Lausanne, Switzerland; Department of Psychiatry, Centre Hospitalier Universitaire Vaudois and University of Lausanne (CHUV-UNIL), Prilly-Lausanne, Switzerland

Papaleo Francesco   Department of Neuroscience and Brain Technologies, Istituto Italiano di Tecnologia, Genova, Italy

Raul R. Gainetdinov   Department of Neuroscience and Brain Technologies, Istituto Italiano di Tecnologia, Genova, Italy; Institute of Translational Biomedicine, St. Petersburg State University, St. Petersburg, Russia; Skolkovo Institute of Science and Technology (Skoltech), Skolkovo, Moscow Region, Russia

Ruoqi Gao   Department of Physiology, Northwestern University Feinberg School of Medicine, Chicago, IL, USA; Department of Psychiatry and Behavioral Sciences, Northwestern University Feinberg School of Medicine, Chicago, IL, USA

Emmy Gavrilidis   The Monash Alfred Psychiatry Research Centre, The Alfred and Monash University Central Clinical School, Monash University, Melbourne, VIC, Australia

Anthony A. Grace   Departments of Neuroscience, Psychiatry and Psychology, University of Pittsburgh, Pittsburgh, PA, USA

Yoav Hadas   Department of Psychiatry, Icahn School of Medicine at Mount Sinai, New York, NY, USA

Brigham J. Hartley   Department of Psychiatry, Icahn School of Medicine at Mount Sinai, New York, NY, USA

Noboru Hiroi   Department of Psychiatry and Behavioral Sciences, Albert Einstein College of Medicine, Bronx, NY, USA; Department of Genetics, Albert Einstein College of Medicine, Bronx, NY, USA; Dominick P. Purpura Department of Neuroscience, Albert Einstein College of Medicine, Bronx, NY, USA

Elaine Y. Hsiao   Division of Biology & Biological Engineering, California Institute of Technology, Pasadena, CA, USA

Huiping Huang   Department of Neuroscience and Brain Technologies, Istituto Italiano di Tecnologia, Genova, Italy

Yan Jouroukhin   Department of Psychiatry and Behavioral Sciences, Johns Hopkins University School of Medicine, Baltimore, MD, USA

Shin-ichi Kano   Department of Psychiatry and Behavioral Sciences, The Johns Hopkins University School of Medicine, Baltimore, MD, USA

Tim Karl   Neuroscience Research Australia, Randwick, NSW, Australia; School of Medical Sciences, University of New South Wales, Sydney, NSW, Australia; Schizophrenia Research Institute, Darlinghurst, NSW, Australia

Håkan Karlsson   Department of Neuroscience, Karolinska Institutet, Stockholm, Sweden

Jivan Khlghatyan   Department of Psychiatry and Neuroscience, Faculty of Medicine, Laval University, Québec City, QC, Canada; Institut universitaire en santé mentale de Québec, Québec City, QC, Canada

Brian P. Kirby   School of Pharmacy, Royal College of Surgeons in Ireland, Dublin, Ireland

Jayashri Kulkarni   The Monash Alfred Psychiatry Research Centre, The Alfred and Monash University Central Clinical School, Monash University, Melbourne, VIC, Australia

Poppy H.L. Lamberton   Department of Infectious Disease Epidemiology, School of Public Health, Imperial College Faculty of Medicine, London, UK

Florence S. Lau   Department of Clinical Psychology, Teachers College, Columbia University, New York, NY, USA

Brian Lo   Department of Psychiatry and Behavioral Sciences, The Johns Hopkins University School of Medicine, Baltimore, MD, USA

Natalia Malkova   Division of Biology & Biological Engineering, California Institute of Technology, Pasadena, CA, USA

Francesca Managó   Department of Neuroscience and Brain Technologies, Istituto Italiano di Tecnologia, Genova, Italy

Glenn A. McConkey   School of Biology, Faculty of Biological Sciences, University of Leeds, Leeds, UK

Ross McFarland   Department of Psychiatry and Behavioral Sciences, Johns Hopkins University School of Medicine, Baltimore, MD, USA; Department of Molecular Microbiology and Immunology, Johns Hopkins Bloomberg School of Public Health, Baltimore, MD, USA

Urs Meyer   Physiology and Behavior Laboratory, ETH Zurich, Zurich, Switzerland

Aline Monin   Center for Psychiatric Neuroscience, Centre Hospitalier Universitaire Vaudois and University of Lausanne (CHUV-UNIL), Prilly-Lausanne, Switzerland; Department of Psychiatry, Centre Hospitalier Universitaire Vaudois and University of Lausanne (CHUV-UNIL), Prilly-Lausanne, Switzerland

Paula M. Moran   School of Psychology, University of Nottingham, Nottingham, UK

Robin M. Murray   Institute of Psychiatry, Psychosis & Neuroscience, London, UK

Toshitaka Nabeshima   Department of Regional Pharmaceutical Care and Sciences, Graduate School of Pharmaceutical Sciences, Meijo University, Nagoya, Japan; NPO, Japanese Drug Organization of Appropriate Use and Research, Nagoya, Japan

Akira Nishi   Department of Psychiatry and Behavioral Sciences, Albert Einstein College of Medicine, Bronx, NY, USA; Department of Psychiatry, Course of Integrated Brain Sciences, Medical Informatics, Institute of Health Biosciences, University of Tokushima Graduate School, Tokushima, Japan

Francesca M. Notarangelo   Department of Psychiatry, Maryland Psychiatric Research Center, University of Maryland School of Medicine, Baltimore, MD, USA

Colm M.P. O'Tuathaigh   School of Medicine, Brookfield Health Sciences Complex, University College Cork, Cork, Ireland

Peter Penzes   Department of Physiology, Northwestern University Feinberg School of Medicine, Chicago, IL, USA; Department of Psychiatry and Behavioral Sciences, Northwestern University Feinberg School of Medicine, Chicago, IL, USA

Mikhail V. Pletnikov   Department of Psychiatry and Behavioral Sciences, Johns Hopkins University School of Medicine, Baltimore, MD, USA; Solomon H Snyder Department of Neuroscience, Johns Hopkins University School of Medicine, Baltimore, MD, USA; Department of Molecular and Comparative Pathobiology, Johns Hopkins University School of Medicine, Baltimore, MD, USA; Department of Molecular Microbiology and Immunology, Johns Hopkins Bloomberg School of Public Health, Baltimore, MD, USA

Ana Pocivavsek Department of Psychiatry, Maryland Psychiatric Research Center, University of Maryland School of Medicine, Baltimore, MD, USA

Susan B. Powell Department of Psychiatry, University of California San Diego, La Jolla, CA, USA; Research Service, VA San Diego Healthcare System, La Jolla, CA, USA

Mark Rafter School of Life Sciences, Queens Medical Centre, University of Nottingham, Nottingham, UK

Theron A. Russell Department of Physiology, Northwestern University Feinberg School of Medicine, Chicago, IL, USA; Department of Psychiatry and Behavioral Sciences, Northwestern University Feinberg School of Medicine, Chicago, IL, USA

Robert Schwarcz Department of Psychiatry, Maryland Psychiatric Research Center, University of Maryland School of Medicine, Baltimore, MD, USA

Emily G. Severance Department of Pediatrics, Johns Hopkins University School of Medicine, Baltimore, MD, USA

Ilya Sukhanov Department of Neuroscience and Brain Technologies, Istituto Italiano di Tecnologia, Genova, Italy

Neal R. Swerdlow Department of Psychiatry, University of California San Diego, La Jolla, CA, USA

E. Von Cheong School of Medicine, Brookfield Health Sciences Complex, University College Cork, Cork, Ireland

John L. Waddington Molecular and Cellular Therapeutics, Royal College of Surgeons in Ireland, Dublin, Ireland; Jiangsu Key Laboratory of Translational Research & Therapy for Neuro-Psychiatric-Disorders and Department of Pharmacology, College of Pharmaceutical Sciences, Soochow University, Suzhou, China

Joanne P. Webster Department of Pathology and Pathogen Biology, Centre for Emerging, Endemic and Exotic Diseases (CEEED), Royal Veterinary College, University of London, London, UK; Department of Infectious Disease Epidemiology, School of Public Health, Imperial College Faculty of Medicine, London, UK

Roisin Worsley The Monash Alfred Psychiatry Research Centre, The Alfred and Monash University Central Clinical School, Monash University, Melbourne, VIC, Australia

Wei-Li Wu Division of Biology & Biological Engineering, California Institute of Technology, Pasadena, CA, USA

Hui-Qiu Wu Department of Psychiatry, Maryland Psychiatric Research Center, University of Maryland School of Medicine, Baltimore, MD, USA

Robert H. Yolken Department of Pediatrics, Johns Hopkins University School of Medicine, Baltimore, MD, USA

Preface

Psychotic illness presents many challenges because of its complex life course and multifactorial origins; these involve contributions from diverse genetic, epigenetic, and environmental factors that result in a disorder of abnormal brain development and disconnectivity. For model systems to advance in their heuristic import, they must reflect these evolving concepts, with a particular focus on: (1) Psychotic illness as a dimensional construct that involves several domains of psychopathology and dysfunction that are disrespectful to our current nosology; these intersect with a yet broader range of psychopathologies and dysfunctions that are associated with a range of other neurodevelopmental disorders classically considered outside the psychosis spectrum. (2) Increasing evidence for not only psychopathological, but also genetic, environmental and pathobiological overlap between schizophrenia, bipolar disorder, and other neuropsychiatric disorders in which psychosis can occur. (3) Psychotic illness not as a point of onset of a disorder but rather as a stage in the trajectory of a disorder that is manifested throughout the lifespan, including prediagnostic manifestations that may be the harbingers of a psychotic diagnosis. Preclinical and clinical scientists who work in the area of model systems for psychotic illness need to factor these challenges into their approaches. This volume is the first comprehensive review of such models that reflects this new perspective.

Mikhail V. Pletnikov, Baltimore, USA
John L. Waddington, Dublin, Ireland
May 2015

FROM CLINICAL DIMENSIONS TO ANIMAL MODELS

Clinical and Pathological Aspects

Overview of Schizophrenia: Dimensions of Psychopathology

Arsime Demjaha, Robin M. Murray

Institute of Psychiatry, Psychosis & Neuroscience, London, UK

THE INADEQUACY OF DIAGNOSTIC CATEGORIES

The purpose of diagnosis in psychiatry, as in any other medical specialty, is to encapsulate clinical information in a most concise way, shed light on the underlying etiology and pathophysiology of the disorder, and form the basis for treatment guidance. The importance of an accurate diagnostic system is particularly relevant to psychiatry where diagnostic tests or precise biological markers are nonexistent, and consequently clinicians have to rely on descriptive psychopathology and its interpretation to diagnose patients. For most of the nineteenth century, psychiatrists mostly regarded psychosis as a unitary disorder (Griesinger, 1882). However, in the center of psychiatry, early German academic clinicians delineated catatonia, hebephrenia, and paranoid psychoses on the basis of their different clinical presentations (Kahlbaum, 1863). Out on the periphery, Thomas Clouston, the first clinical lecturer in the University of Edinburgh, took a different approach, describing adolescent psychosis on the basis that it had neurodevelopmental origins (Clouston, 1892). Nevertheless, it was Kraepelin's work on the dementia praecox and manic depression dichotomy that led to the categorical approach to diagnosis and accordingly classifying patients in distinct and mutually exclusive groups (Kraepelin, 1971). However, clinicians know, only too well, that frequently patients do not fall precisely into either category and over the decades it became clear that classifying schizophrenia into distinct subcategories does not fully capture the phenomenological complexity of the disorder. Moreover, these categories are not heritable, lack diagnostic stability and validity (Tandon et al., 2013), and clear demarcation is complicated by evident clinical, genetic, neurobiological, and biological overlap (Demjaha et al., 2012), which hinders progress in elucidating the precise mechanisms underlying schizophrenia. Thus, the adequacy of categorical conceptual models that have dominated the classification systems of psychosis has been increasingly questioned with an increasing view that the phenomenology of psychosis may be best conceptualized by several symptom dimensions, known also as "factors" (Arndt, Alliger, & Andreasen, 1991; Crow, 1980; Liddle, 1987; Lindenmayer, Grochowski, & Hyman, 1995; Malla, Norman, Williamson, Cortese, & Diaz, 1993; van Os et al., 1996).

Interestingly, before statistical identification of underlying dimensions, Carl Schneider (1942), in line with modern psychopathologists, took a different approach to diagnosis advocating the use of "symptom complexes" that represent constellations of symptoms that tend to naturally occur together, have different pathophysiological underpinning, can cooccur or exist independently, and are not necessarily specific to schizophrenia. He proposed three symptom complexes akin to the "psychosis," "disorganization," and "negative" modern dimensions described in a later section.

PSYCHOPATHOLOGICAL DIMENSIONS—A CHALLENGE TO CATEGORICAL APPROACH TO DIAGNOSIS

The dimensional model suggests that psychotic symptoms are likely to cluster in certain symptom groups more often than by chance alone, but unlike distinct categories, they do not impose boundaries, but can coexist in the same patient (Allardyce, Gaebel, Zielasek, & van Os, 2007). Further, dimensions, classify symptoms and not patients, as is the case with categories, and are empirically derived using sophisticated statistical methods such as factor analysis. Many factor analytic studies of symptom profiles have identified multidimensional models within schizophrenia (Bilder, Mukherjee, Rieder, & Pandurangi, 1985; Brown & White, 1992; Liddle, 1987; Peralta & Cuesta, 2001). The introduction of the positive and negative syndromes (Andreasen & Olsen, 1982; Crow, 1980; Strauss, 1973) not only attracted major attention in clinical settings, but also became a focus of both biological and clinical research, particularly stimulating extensive research in schizophrenic phenomenology and identifying underlying dimensional structure. The positive–negative model, even though radical in its own right and instrumental in the development of important assessing scales, was soon criticized for lacking stability over time (Marneros, Diester, & Rohde, 1991); in addition, for being categorical in nature hence not accounting for a patient group presenting with mixed symptoms (Peralta & Cuesta, 2004; Peralta, de Leon, & Cuesta, 1992), highlighting a need for a shift to a more

adequate multidimensional approach. Thus, the factor analysis of positive and negative symptoms led to emergence of the popular three syndromic model of schizophrenia that, in addition to negative (avolition, affective flattening, and alogia) and psychotic (delusions and hallucinations) symptom domains, identified also a disorganized symptom dimension comprising thought disorder, bizarre behavior, and often inappropriate affect (Bilder et al., 1985; Liddle, 1987). The disorganization dimension has been considerably less replicated or stable, particularly in studies considering a wider range of symptoms, but it has often emerged, and its existence confirmed in meta-analytic work (Grube, Bilder, & Goldman, 1998; Smith, Mar, & Turoff, 1998). Those faithful to the positive–negative dichotomy held that disorganization dimension is a part of positive symptomatology (Andreasen, Arndt, Alliger, Miller, & Flaum, 1995), whereas some others demonstrated its strong correlations with negative syndrome (Dollfus & Everitt, 1998; Peralta & Cuesta, 1994). The model, although highly reproducible (Table 1), was further criticized for being too simplistic, in particular,

TABLE 1   Factor Analysis Studies That Have Identified Three-Dimensional Models[a]

Study	No. of Patients	Rating Scale	Diagnosis/Stage of Illness	FA Method	Dimensions Identified
Minas et al. (1992)	114	SAPS-SANS	Chronic Sz	Multidimensional scaling	Psychosis, disorganization, negative
Malla et al. (1993)	155	SAPS-SANS	Chronic Sz	EFA	Psychosis, disorganization, negative
Murphy, Burke, Bray, Walsh, and Kendler (1994)	169	SCID-SANS	Chronic Sz	EFA	Psychosis, disorganization, negative
Bell et al. (1994)	149	SAPS-SANS	Chronic Sz	CFA	Psychosis, disorganization, negative
Andreasen et al. (1995)	243	SAPS-SANS	Chronic Sz schizophreniform disorder	EFA	Psychosis, disorganization, negative
Maziade et al. (1995)	138	SAPS-SANS	Chronic Sz	EFA	Psychosis, disorganization, negative
Gureje, Aderibigbe, and Obikoya (1995)	60	SANS-BPRS	Recent onset psychosis	EFA	Psychosis, disorganization, negative
Johnstone and Frith (1996)	329	Krawiecka scale	Chronic Sz	PCA	Poverty, disorganization, positive
Peralta, Cuesta, and Farre (1997)	314	SAPS-SANS	Chronic Sz	EFA	Psychosis, disorganization, negative
Ratakonda et al. (1998)	221	SAPS-SANS	Chronic Sz	EFA	Psychosis, disorganization, negative
Hori et al. (1999)	258	Manchester scale	Chronic Sz	EFA	Psychosis, disorganization, negative
Peralta and Cuesta (2000)	159	SAPS-SANS	Recent-onset psychosis	EFA	Psychosis, disorganization, negative

BPRS, brief psychiatric rating scale; CFA, confirmatory factor analysis; EFA, exploratory factor analysis; FA, factor analysis; SAPS, scale for the assessment of positive symptoms; SANS, scale for the assessment of negative symptoms; SCID, structured clinical interview for DSM-III-R; Sz, schizophrenia.
[a]Only studies that have included number of patients (n ≥ 100) were included.

for failing to account for the whole range of psychotic symptoms and consisting of roughly delineated and narrow dimensions. Subsequent studies have investigated samples of patients with all forms of psychosis yielding more complex, but also conflicting dimensional patterns with varied structures across studies, incorporating manic, depressive, anxiety, social dysfunction, and cognitive dimensions (Dollfus & Everitt, 1998; Kitamura, Okazaki, Fujinawa, Yoshino, & Kasahara, 1995; Lindenmayer et al., 1995; McGorry, Bell, Dudgeon, & Jackson, 1998; Peralta & Cuesta, 2001).

The identified dimensions have proved to be stable in terms of several demographic and clinical parameters. Thus, the stability of individual psychopathological dimensions in both patients who received antipsychotic treatment and the un-medicated ones as well as in responders and nonresponders was demonstrated (Czobor & Volavka, 1996; Lindenmayer et al., 1995). In addition, it was shown that the underlying structure of symptoms did not differ as a function of the age, gender, severity of illness, chronicity, or cognitive impairment status (Leonard White, Harvey, Opler, & Lindenmayer, 1997; Peralta & Cuesta, 2005; White, Harvey, Parrella, & Sevy, 1994). Finally, the multidimensional model emerged in all stages of psychotic illness ranging from the at-risk mental state (Demjaha, Mccabe, & Murray, 2012; Hawkins et al., 2004), FEP (Demjaha et al., 2009; McGorry et al., 1998; Russo et al., 2014) to chronic schizophrenia (Liddle, Ngan, Duffield, Kho, & Warren, 2002; Lindenmayer et al., 1995).

Although empirically established, the dimensional approach has also attracted criticism, raising concerns about its validity, particularly in terms of the lack of a consensus on a precise dimensional model, the chronological stability of dimensions, specificity to a certain disorder, and whether there is a clear demarcation between dimensions regarding etiology, pathophysiology, treatment response, and clinical outcome.

THE NEED FOR A PRECISE DIMENSIONAL MODEL

The main issue with the dimensional representation of psychopathology pertains to the lack of a single precise dimensional model (i.e., there is no as yet consensus in the field regarding the number and composition of specific dimensions as importantly emphasized by Peralta and Cuesta in their comprehensive review (Peralta & Cuesta, 2001), which impedes their effective use in both clinical and research settings. A decade on, studies continue to yield varied dimensional structures that is a consequence of sampling different patient populations and the use of different rating scales, factor analysis methods, and varying definitions for depression and

negative symptoms across different studies, which will invariably affect the number and the internal structure of distinct dimensions.

The use of different rating scales has a particular effect on a number of identified dimensions. Thus, the factor analysis of Scale for Assessing Positive Symptoms and Scale for Assessing Negative Symptoms one of the most frequently used scales comprising more than 50 items, yielded large factorial solutions often comprising 9 (Minas et al., 1992), 10 (Toomey et al., 1997), and even 11 dimensions (Peralta & Cuesta, 1999). The emergence of large factorial solutions (i.e., large number of dimensions) prompted phenomenologists to examine whether the dimensional model assumes hierarchical order, in other words, whether these dimensions are correlated or can further be divided into more basic components. Accordingly, the dimensional structure could be organized hierarchically where elementary or big and clear dimensions assume higher order but more complex ones or "fine grained dimensions" are assigned a lower order. This is well-illustrated in Peralta and Cuesta's work, which proposed that hierarchical approach may assist with organizing emerging complex dimensional structures (Cuesta & Peralta, 2001) (see Figure 1). Most recently, Russo et al. (2014) have replicated a hierarchical structure of dimensions and thus identified six first-order factors: mania, negative, disorganization, depression, hallucinations, and delusions (Russo et al., 2014). The division of positive symptoms into delusions and hallucinations is neurobiologically intriguing. It has been shown that different types of positive symptoms are related to different patterns of regional cerebral blood flow (Sabri et al., 1997), and more specifically that hallucinations but not delusions are associated with reduced left superior temporal lobe gyrus volume (Flaum et al., 1995). These studies illustrate that by using symptom dimensions at a more fine-grained level, external correlates of dimensions could be more precisely detectable (Cuesta & Peralta, 2001).

Overall, accumulating evidence suggests that a pentagonal model comprising positive (reality distortion), negative (psychomotor retardation), disorganization, and depressive and manic dimensions, which is highly replicated, best encapsulates the constellation of psychotic symptoms and unique patient's manifestation of illness (Demjaha et al., 2009; Lindenmayer et al., 1995) (Table 2). However, this model has failed to show an adequate fit by confirmatory factor analysis (van der Gaag, Cuijpers, et al., 2006; Lykouras et al., 2000).

Not only the composition, but also the terminology of individual psychopathological dimensions, differs greatly across the studies. For instance, authors have called the same dimension "psychomotor poverty" and "negative," or "positive" and "reality distortion."

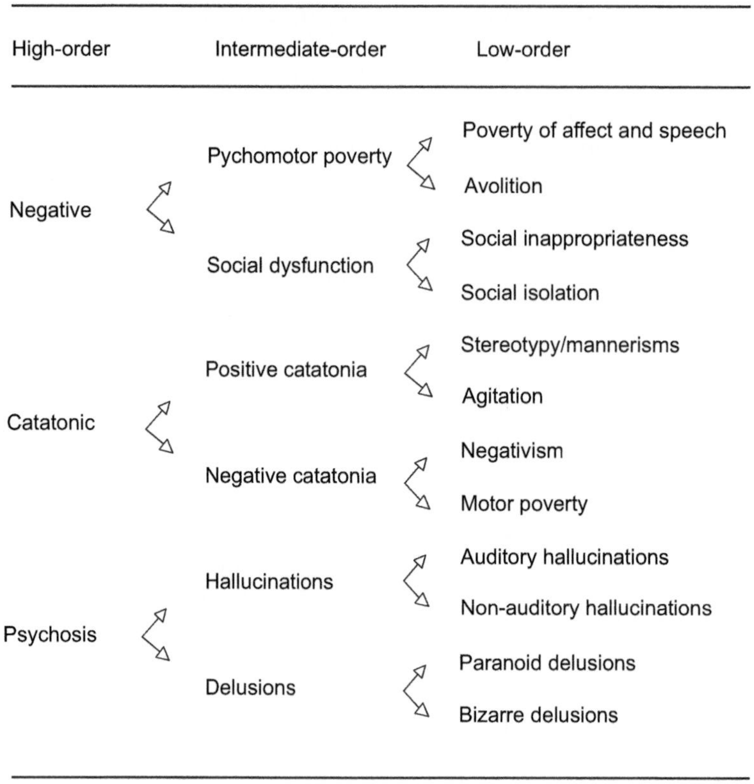

High-order	Intermediate-order	Low-order

Negative
- Pychomotor poverty
  - Poverty of affect and speech
  - Avolition
- Social dysfunction
  - Social inappropriateness
  - Social isolation

Catatonic
- Positive catatonia
  - Stereotypy/mannerisms
  - Agitation
- Negative catatonia
  - Negativism
  - Motor poverty

Psychosis
- Hallucinations
  - Auditory hallucinations
  - Non-auditory hallucinations
- Delusions
  - Paranoid delusions
  - Bizarre delusions

FIGURE 1   Simplified illustration of hierarchical ordering of dimensions. *Reproduced with kind permission from Schizophrenia Research (Cuesta & Peralta, 2001).*

TABLE 2   Factor Analysis Studies That Have Identified Five-Dimensional Models[a]

Study	No. of Patients	Rating Scale	Diagnosis/Stage of Illness	FA Method	Dimensions Identified
Lindström and Knorring (1993)	120	PANSS	Chronic Sz	PCA	Negative, positive, excitement, cognitive, depression/anxiety
Lindenmayer, Bernstein-Hyman, and Grochowski (1994)	240	PANSS	Chronic Sz	PCA	Negative, positive, excitement, cognitive, depression/anxiety
Kitamura et al. (1995)	584	Checklist	Chronic Sz	EFA	Psychosis, negative, catatonia, mania, depression
Lindenmayer et al. (1995)	517	PANSS	Chronic Sz	PCA	Negative, positive, cognitive, excitement and depression
Cardno et al. (1996)	102	OCPPI	Chronic Sz	EFA	paranoid, disorganization, negative. bizarre delusions, hallucinations
Marder, Davis, and Chouinard (1997)	513	PANSS	Chronic Sz	PCA	Negative, positive, disorganized, uncontrolled hostility/excitement, anxiety/depression
White et al. (1997)	1233	PANSS	Chronic Sz	PCA	Positive, negative, dysphoric mood, activation, and autistic preoccupation
Lancon, Aghababian, Llorca, and Auquier (1998)	205	PANSS	Chronic Sz	PCA	Negative, positive, excited, depressive, cognitive
Nakaya et al. (1999)	100	PANSS	Chronic Sz, schizophreniform disorder	CFA	Positive, negative, disorganization, excitement, and relational dimensions
Jim van Os et al. (1999)	706	OCPPI	Chronic Sz	PCA	Psychosis, disorganization, negative, mania, depression
Lancon, Auquier, Nayt, and Reine (2000)	324	PANSS	Chronic Sz	PCA	Negative, positive, excitation, depression, cognition

TABLE 2 Factor Analysis Studies That Have Identified Five-Dimensional Models[a]—cont'd

Study	No. of Patients	Rating Scale	Diagnosis/Stage of Illness	FA Method	Dimensions Identified
Lykouras et al. (2000)	258	PANSS	Chronic Sz	PCA	Negative, excitement, depression, positive, cognitive impairment
Mass, Schoemig, Hitschfeld, Wall, and Haasen (2000)	253	PANSS	Chronic Sz	PCA	Hostile excitement; negative, cognitive, positive depression
Wolthaus et al. (2000)	138	PANSS	Recent-onset schizophrenia	PCA	Positive, negative, depression, agitation-excitement and disorganization component
Wickham et al. (2001)	155	OCPPI	Chronic Sz schizoaffective, PUO	EFA	Depressive, manic, reality distortion, disorganization, psychomotor poverty
Liddle et al. (2002)	155	SSPI	Acute or persistent psychotic illness	PCA	Negative, psychomotor excitation, disorganization, reality distortion, anxiety and depression
Emsley, Rabinowitz, and Torreman (2003)	535	PANSS	Recent-onset SZ, schizophreniform disorder schizoaffective disorder	PCA	Negative, positive, disorganized (or cognitive), excited, anxiety/depression
Lee, Harris, Loughland, and Williams (2003)	105	PANSS	Chronic Sz	PCA	Psychomotor poverty, disorganization, reality distortion, excitement, and depression
Dikeos et al. (2006)	191	OPCRIT	Chronic Sz, mood disorders with psychosis, schizoaffective disorder, OPI	PCA	Mania, reality distortion, depression, disorganization, negative
van der Gaag, Hoffman, et al. (2006)	5769	PANSS	Chronic Sz FEP	CFA	Positive symptoms, negative symptoms, disorganization, excitement, emotional distress
Allardyce et al. (2007)	464	OPCRIT	Schizophrenia, schizoaffective disorder, delusional disorder, mania, DIPD, UPD	EFA	Manic, disorganization, depressive, delusional, hallucinations
Demjaha et al. (2009)	536	SCAN	FEP	EFA	Reality distortion, negative, disorganization, mania, depression
Demjaha et al. (2012)	122	CAARMS	ARMS	EFA	Negative, anxiety, disorganization/cognitive, self-harm, manic

CAARMS, comprehensive assessment of the at-risk mental state; CFA, confirmatory factor analysis; DIPD, drug-induced psychotic disorder; EFA, exploratory factor analysis; FA, factor analysis; FEP, first-episode psychosis; OCCPI, operational criteria checklist for psychotic illness; OPCRIT, operational checklist for psychotic symptoms; OPI, other psychotic illnesses; PANSS, positive and negative syndrome scale; PCA, principal component analysis; SCAN, schedules for clinical assessment in neuropsychiatry; UPD, unspecified psychotic disorder; Sz, schizophrenia.
[a]Only studies that have included number of patients (n ≥ 100) were included.

Obviously, this warrants some attention, clarification, and ultimately consensus on the most adequate nosology. It is clear, therefore, that an adequate dimensional model describing more accurately the underlying structure of psychotic psychopathology is missing.

SPECIFICITY TO DISORDER

Several studies have examined whether the identified schizophrenic dimensions are specific to this disorder, which is of crucial importance to both research and clinical domains. The majority of studies have demonstrated the presence of three-dimensional model in affective psychosis, schizophreniform, and schizoaffective disorder (Klimidis, Stuart, Minas, Copolov, & Singh, 1993; Maziade et al., 1995; Peralta, Cuesta, & Farre, 1997; Ratakonda, Gorman, Yale, & Amador, 1998). Further, Peralta and Cuesta (2001) have established the same symptom structure in schizophrenia and in a variety of other psychotic disorders, which led them to suggest that dimensions could be studied irrespective of diagnostic category and should be examined in relation to psychosis. Additionally, Demjaha et al. (2009)

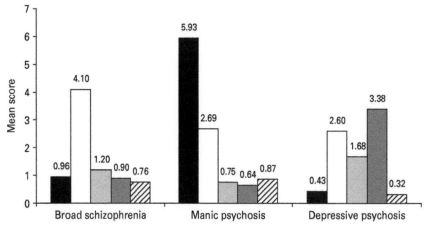

FIGURE 2   Symptom dimension scores cut across, and are evident in all diagnostic groups. ■, manic; □, reality distortion; ▣, negative; ▪, depressive; ▨, disorganization. *Reproduced with kind permission from Psychological Medicine (Demjaha et al 2009).*

have demonstrated that the symptom dimensions are evident in several diagnostic groups, specifically broad schizophrenia, manic psychosis, and depressive psychosis (Figure 2).

CHRONOLOGICAL STABILITY OF DIMENSIONS

Establishing the stability of factor structure across time is essential to demonstrate their validity and has relevant theoretical and clinical implications. The evidence supporting the stability of symptom dimensions is conflicting, which again could be related to rating scales used or inherent to longitudinal designs. Although several studies, particularly those of a shorter follow-up (Goldman, Tandon, Liberzon, Goodson, & Greden, 1991; Nakaya, Suwa, Komahashi, & Ohmori, 1999), but also a few more long-term ones (Salokangas, 1997), found that dimensional structure varied over time, there are several studies that support longitudinal stability of symptom dimensions (Arndt, Andreasen, Flaum, Miller, & Nopoulos, 1995; Dingemans, Linszen, Nugter, & Scholte, 1995; Rey et al., 1994). A recent large first-episode psychosis study, which was the first to examine the stability of dimensional structure in patients from the outset of their illness over the 5- to 10-year follow-up, demonstrated that the structure of identified dimensions at the baseline remained consistent and did not change over time (Russo et al., 2014). The evidence, however, regarding stability of specific dimensions is more consistent. Thus, from all identified dimensions, the negative one appears to chronologically be the most stable, whereas the disorganization dimension, on the other hand, is particularly unpredictable (Arndt et al., 1995; Dollfus & Petit, 1995; Nakaya et al., 1999).

DIFFERENTIAL ASSOCIATIONS OF DIMENSIONS WITH BIOLOGICAL AND CLINICAL PARAMETERS

The validity of a new diagnostic classificatory system is best determined by investigating whether this system can discriminate satisfactory between various neurobiological and clinical factors (Robins & Guze, 1970).

A growing amount of literature provides evidence for distinct cerebral correlates of each symptom dimension (Chua et al., 1997; Liddle, Friston, Frith, & Frackowiak, 1992). Chua et al. (1997) have thus shown that psychomotor poverty (negative) dimension was negatively correlated with the relative volume of the left ventro-medial prefrontal gray matter, whereas disorganization was positively correlated with the volumes of both the hippocampus and the parahippocampal gyrus bilaterally. More recently, Koutsouleris and colleagues using cross-sectional and conjunctional voxel-based morphometry examined gray matter density differences between 175 schizophrenic patients and 177 matched healthy controls and found distinct pattern of neuroanatomical correlations. In their study, negative symptoms were characterized by alterations in frontal and temporal regions as well as limbic and subcortical structures. The disorganized symptom dimension was associated with bilateral gray matter changes in temporal, medial prefrontal, and insular cortices, whereas positive symptoms scores were correlated with left perisylvian regions and extended thalamic gray matter losses (Koutsouleris et al., 2008). Further, the negative dimension has been in several studies clearly associated with an excess of neurological soft signs (Arango, Kirkpatrick, & Buchanan, 2000; Boks, Liddle, Burgerhof, Knegtering, & Bosch, 2004; Demjaha et al., 2009; Wong, Voruganti, Heslegrave, & Awad, 1997) and minor physical anomalies (O'Callaghan et al., 1995), but no other dimensions.

Furthermore, genetic twin studies have revealed that the greater the number of negative symptoms in a twin with schizophrenia, the greater the likelihood that another twin will be affected with the illness (Dworkin & Lenzenweger, 1984). Family studies have confirmed that the negative, disorganization, and manic dimensions were familial, which supports their use in the demarcation of homogeneous subsets for genetic studies (Wickham et al., 2001). However, in their meta-analytic work of the studies on affected sibling pairs, Rietkerk et al. (2008) documented genetic contribution to disorganization dimension only, and neither to negative or reality distortion dimensions, and consequently concluded that: "only the disorganization symptom dimension may provide an useful alternative phenotype for genetic research" (Rietkerk et al., 2008).

Studies that have examined neurocognitive deficits in schizophrenia have also observed distinct correlations with specific dimensions. Accordingly, the negative dimension has been shown to be associated with neurocognitive deficits, but affective and the positive dimensions have not. Specifically, the negative symptom dimension was found to be associated with generally poor cognitive function, and intelligence, executive function, memory, sustained-attention and sensory-motor function as well as poor premorbid functioning, whereas disorganized symptom dimension correlated with decreased intelligence, attention span, and sensory-motor function (Basso, Nasrallah, Olson, & Bornstein, 1998; Brown & White, 1992; Kravariti et al., 2012; Norman et al., 1997). The positive symptom dimension, on the other hand, was not related to any deficits (Nieuwenstein, Aleman, & de Haan, 2001).

The negative and positive symptom dimensions appeared in one study to follow independent clinical course over time (Eaton, Thara, Federman, Melton, & Liang, 1995). However in another, both negative and positive as well as disorganization dimensions were associated with chronic course and deterioration from premorbid functioning (Wickham et al., 2001). Manic dimension has been consistently across studies associated with an acute mode of onset, compulsory admission, and shorter duration of untreated psychosis (DUP) (Demjaha et al., 2009), whereas negative dimension has been associated with insidious onset (Dikeos et al., 2006; Fenton & McGlashan, 1991; Ratakonda et al., 1998), longer DUP (Edwards, McGorry, Waddell, & Harrigan, 1999; Larsen, Moe, Vibe-Hansen, & Johannessen, 2000; Malla et al., 2002), and poor functional outcome (Milev, Ho, Arndt, & Andreasen, 2005).

Reality distortion was associated in a number of studies with a longer DUP (Edwards et al., 1999; Larsen et al., 2000; Malla et al., 2002). Moreover, reality distortion along with depressive symptoms was associated with higher level of urbanicity, which was not observed for disorganization (Oher et al., 2014). Disorganization, on the other hand, was shown to be related to compulsory admission (Demjaha et al., 2009), but insignificant or no associations with depressive dimension were reported (Demjaha et al., 2009; Dikeos et al., 2006; Guerra et al., 2002). Finally, no dimension in particular has been associated with gender or age (Demjaha et al., 2009; Guerra et al., 2002; McIntosh et al., 2001).

Taken together, although there is evidence to show differential associations of specific dimension's scores and various biological and clinical variables, the findings across studies lack consistency; therefore, further research is needed to make any definitive conclusions regarding the true external validity of dimensional representation of psychosis.

CATEGORIES OR DIMENSIONS, OR BOTH?

In spite of these limitations to the use of dimensions, in an attempt to best conceptualize psychopathological classification, phenomenologists have focused on the comparative clinical utility of traditional diagnostic constructs and psychopathological dimensions. Although several studies have assumed the superiority of dimensional approach (van Os et al., 1996; Strauss, 1973), most recent studies have concluded that the concomitant use of both approaches may best conceptualize the richness of psychopathology and provide the most useful description of psychotic patients; hence, this approach may be most clinically useful. For example, Demjaha et al. (2009), in their large first-episode study, demonstrated that both diagnostic categories and dimensions independently explained various clinical characteristics and risk factors for psychosis, with dimensions performing marginally better. However, when dimensions were added to diagnosis, a significant increase in the amount of variability explained was observed, indicating that psychopathological dimensions provide additional information to that contained in diagnostic categories, particularly with regard to clinical parameters. Two earlier studies have concordantly concluded that the simultaneous use of both models could be most clinically informative (Allardyce, McCreadie, Morrison, & van Os, 2007; Dikeos et al., 2006). Thus, in later years, the trend from viewing diagnostic categories and dimensional model as competing diagnostic systems has moved to regarding them both as complementary suggesting that because dimensions provide additional quantitative measures, their use in clinical practice would facilitate appropriate intervention at a more appropriate time (Jablensky & Kendell, 2002). It has been proposed that dimensional measures can be derived from rating scales such as the Positive and Negative Syndrome Scale (Allardyce, McCreadie, et al., 2007; Kay, Flszbein, & Opfer, 1987).

CONCLUSION

More than 30 years of extensive research has no doubt provided evidence of existence of several psychopathological dimensions that, particularly when added to diagnostic categories, hold promise of encapsulating the whole range of psychotic symptoms. Despite, consecutive evidence indicating the simultaneous use of both diagnostic models, the Diagnostic and Statistical Manual of Mental Disorders, 5th edition, does not denote such a paradigm shift. This is in part because we still do not have a precise dimensional model, which precludes its more prominent integration in new diagnostic manuals and clinical practice as well as its use in research. And, although studies have provided evidence in support of validity of dimensions, the findings are inconsistent and conflicting, and more research is needed to establish equal or a greater validity than that of existing nosological symptoms.

Therefore, there is an urgent need in the field to develop a precise and uniform dimensional model. One of the major challenges in psychiatry is the attempt to link psychopathological dimensions to underlying neurobiological mechanisms. If we disentangle the complex heterogeneity of psychotic symptoms and provide refined and accurate constructs of psychopathology, we will be more likely to solve the etiological and pathophysiological heterogeneity of schizophrenia, which in turn will lead to more effective treatment and better outcome for our patients. In doing so, we do not need another study that yielded yet another dimensional structure the way it is currently done; instead, we need a consensus from the leaders in the field on first which rating scale to use or even to develop a new one first, which hopefully will account for all psychopathology, unlike the Positive and Negative Syndrome Scale and some others that omit important symptoms. This is perquisite in deriving dimensions that are more theoretically and clinically meaningful. Second, the same methodology in extracting factors at the same stage of illness should be universally used, which would hopefully yield more consistent factorial structure and help to establish its validity.

Important issue pertains to the level at which dimensions can be incorporated into diagnostic categories. Unsurprisingly, as rightly emphasized by Peralta and Cuesta, the accurately delineated dimensions would generate the data needed to formulate a "bottom-up" structural organization for the diagnostic categories (Peralta & Cuesta, 2007). For instance, patients scoring high on the dimensions of positive, negative, and disorganization symptoms, may qualify more for a schizophrenia diagnosis, whereas those scoring high on the positive and manic symptom dimensions are more likely to be given a diagnosis of bipolar disorder (van Os & Kapur, 2009).

Overall, more and urgent research is required to disentangle accurately the underlying nature of psychopathological symptoms. Once we generate a precise and valid dimensional model, we can have confidence in accelerating neurobiological research and ultimately develop effective intervention for both prevention and cure of devastating illnesses such as schizophrenia and other psychotic disorders.

References

Allardyce, J., Gaebel, W., Zielasek, J., & van Os, J. (2007). Deconstructing psychosis conference February 2006: the validity of schizophrenia and alternative approaches to the classification of psychosis. *Schizophrenia Bulletin, 33*(4), 863–867.

Allardyce, J., McCreadie, R. G., Morrison, G., & van Os, J. (2007). Do symptom dimensions or categorical diagnoses best discriminate between known risk factors for psychosis? *Social Psychiatry and Psychiatric Epidemiology, 42*(6), 429–437.

Andreasen, N. C., Arndt, S., Alliger, R., Miller, D., & Flaum, M. (1995). Symptoms of schizophrenia: methods, meanings, and mechanisms. *Archives of General Psychiatry, 52*(5), 341–351.

Andreasen, N. C., & Olsen, S. (1982). Negative v positive schizophrenia: definition and validation. *Archives of General Psychiatry, 39*(7), 789.

Arango, C., Kirkpatrick, B., & Buchanan, R. W. (2000). Neurological signs and the heterogeneity of schizophrenia. *American Journal of Psychiatry, 157*(4), 560–565.

Arndt, S., Alliger, R. J., & Andreasen, N. C. (1991). The distinction of positive and negative symptoms. The failure of a two-dimensional model. *The British Journal of psychiatry, 158*(3), 317–322.

Arndt, S., Andreasen, N. C., Flaum, M., Miller, D., & Nopoulos, P. (1995). A longitudinal study of symptom dimensions in schizophrenia: prediction and patterns of change. *Archives of General Psychiatry, 52*(5), 352–360.

Basso, M. R., Nasrallah, H. A., Olson, S. C., & Bornstein, R. A. (1998). Neuropsychological correlates of negative, disorganized and psychotic symptoms in schizophrenia. *Schizophrenia Research, 31*(2), 99–111.

Bell, R. C., Low, L. H., Jackson, H. J., Dudgeon, P. L., Copolov, D. L., & Singh, B. S. (1994). Latent trait modelling of symptoms of schizophrenia. *Psychological Medicine, 24*(02), 335–345.

Bilder, R. M., Mukherjee, S., Rieder, R. O., & Pandurangi, A. K. (1985). Symptomatic and neuropsychological components of defect states. *Schizophrenia Bulletin, 11*(3), 409.

Boks, M. P. M., Liddle, P. F., Burgerhof, J. G. M., Knegtering, R., & Bosch, R.-J. (2004). Neurological soft signs discriminating mood disorders from first episode schizophrenia. *Acta Psychiatrica Scandinavica, 110*(1), 29–35.

Brown, K. W., & White, T. (1992). Syndromes of chronic schizophrenia and some clinical correlates. *The British Journal of Psychiatry, 161*(3), 317–322.

Cardno, A. G., Jones, L. A., Murphy, K. C., Asherson, P., Scott, L. C., Williams, J., et al. (1996). Factor analysis of schizophrenic symptoms using the OPCRIT checklist. *Schizophrenia Research, 22*(3), 233–239.

Chua, S. E., Wright, I. C., Poline, J. B., Liddle, P. F., Murray, R. M., Frackowiak, R. S., et al. (1997). Grey matter correlates of syndromes in schizophrenia. A semi-automated analysis of structural magnetic resonance images. *The British Journal of Psychiatry, 170*(5), 406–410.

Clouston, T. S. (1892). *Mental diseases. Clinical lectures on mental diseases.*

Crow, T. J. (1980). Molecular pathology of schizophrenia: more than one disease process? *British Medical Journal, 280*(6207), 66.

Cuesta, M. J., & Peralta, V. (2001). Integrating psychopathological dimensions in functional psychoses: a hierarchical approach. *Schizophrenia Research, 52*(3), 215–229.

Czobor, P., & Volavka, J. (1996). Dimensions of the brief psychiatric rating scale: an examination of stability during haloperidol treatment. *Comprehensive Psychiatry, 37*(3), 205–215.

Demjaha, A., Morgan, K., Morgan, C., Landau, S., Dean, K., Reichenberg, A., et al. (2009). Combining dimensional and categorical representation of psychosis: the way forward for DSM-V and ICD-11? *Psychological Medicine, 39*(12), 1943–1955. http://dx.doi.org/10.1017/S0033291709990651.

Demjaha, A., MacCabe, J. H., & Murray, R. M., (2012). How genes and environmental factors determine the different neurodevelopmental trajectories of schizophrenia and bipolar disorder. *Schizophrenia bulletin, 38*(2), 209–214.

Dikeos, D. G., Wickham, H., McDonald, C., Walshe, M., Sigmundsson, T., Bramon, E., et al. (2006). Distribution of symptom dimensions across Kraepelinian divisions. *The British Journal of Psychiatry, 189*(4), 346–353.

Dingemans, P. M., Linszen, D. H., Nugter, M. A., & Scholte, W. F. (1995). Dimensions and subtypes of recent-onset schizophrenia: a longitudinal analysis. *The Journal of Nervous and Mental Disease, 183*(11), 681–687.

Dollfus, S., & Everitt, B. (1998). Symptom structure in schizophrenia: two-, three- or four-factor models? *Psychopathology, 31*(3), 120–130.

Dollfus, S., & Petit, M. (1995). Principal-component analyses of PANSS and SANS-SAPS in schizophrenia: their stability in an acute phase. *European Psychiatry, 10*(2), 97–106.

Dworkin, R. H., & Lenzenweger, M. F. (1984). Symptoms and the genetics of schizophrenia: implications for diagnosis. *The American Journal of Psychiatry, 41*, 1541–1546.

Eaton, W. W., Thara, R., Federman, B., Melton, B., & Liang, K. Y. (1995). Structure and course of positive and negative symptoms in schizophrenia. *Archives of General Psychiatry, 52*(2), 127–134.

Edwards, J., McGorry, P. D., Waddell, F. M., & Harrigan, S. M. (1999). Enduring negative symptoms in first-episode psychosis: comparison of six methods using follow-up data. *Schizophrenia Research, 40*(2), 147–158.

Emsley, R., Rabinowitz, J., & Torreman, M. (2003). The factor structure for the Positive and Negative Syndrome Scale (PANSS) in recent-onset psychosis. *Schizophrenia Research, 61*(1), 47–57.

Fenton, W. S., & McGlashan, T. H. (1991). Natural history of schizophrenia subtypes: II. Positive and negative symptoms and long-term course. *Archives of General Psychiatry, 48*(11), 978–986.

Flaum, M., O'Leary, D. S., Swayze, II, Victor, W., Miller, D. D., Arndt, S., et al. (1995). Symptom dimensions and brain morphology in schizophrenia and related psychotic disorders. *Journal of Psychiatric Research, 29*(4), 261–276.

van der Gaag, M., Cuijpers, A., Hoffman, T., Remijsen, M., Hijman, R., de Haan, L., et al. (2006). The five-factor model of the Positive and Negative Syndrome Scale I: confirmatory factor analysis fails to confirm 25 published five-factor solutions. *Schizophrenia Research, 85*(1), 273–279.

van der Gaag, M., Hoffman, T., Remijsen, M., Hijman, R., de Haan, L., van Meijel, B., et al. (2006). The five-factor model of the Positive and Negative Syndrome Scale II: a ten-fold cross-validation of a revised model. *Schizophrenia Research, 85*(1), 280–287.

Goldman, R. S., Tandon, R., Liberzon, I., Goodson, J., & Greden, J. F. (1991). Stability of positive and negative symptom constructs during neuroleptic treatment in schizophrenia. *Psychopathology, 24*(4), 247–252.

Griesinger, W. (1882). *Mental pathology and therapeutics* (Vol. 69). W. Wood & Company.

Grube, B. S., Bilder, R. M., & Goldman, R. S. (1998). Meta-analysis of symptom factors in schizophrenia. *Schizophrenia Research, 31*(2), 113–120.

Guerra, A., Fearon, P., Sham, P., Jones, P., Lewis, S., Mata, I., et al. (2002). The relationship between predisposing factors, premorbid function and symptom dimensions in psychosis: an integrated approach. *European Psychiatry, 17*(6), 311–320.

Gureje, O., Aderibigbe, Y. A., & Obikoya, O. (1995). Three syndromes in schizophrenia: validity in young patients with recent onset of illness. *Psychological Medicine, 25*(04), 715–725.

Hawkins, K. A., McGlashan, T. H., Quinlan, D., Miller, T. J., Perkins, D. O., Zipursky, R. B., et al. (2004). Factorial structure of the Scale of Prodromal Symptoms. *Schizophrenia Research, 68*(2), 339–347.

Hori, A., Tsunashima, K., Watanabe, K., Takekawa, Y., Ishihara, I., Terada, T., et al. (1999). Symptom classification of schizophrenia changes with the duration of illness. *Acta Psychiatrica Scandinavica, 99*(6), 447–452.

Jablensky, A., & Kendell, R. E. (2002). Criteria for assessing a classification in psychiatry. *Psychiatric Diagnosis and Classification, 1.*

Johnstone, E. C., & Frith, C. D. (1996). Validation of three dimensions of schizophrenic symptoms in a large unselected sample of patients. *Psychological Medicine, 26*(04), 669–679.

Kahlbaum, K. L. (1863). *Die Gruppierung der psychischen Krankheiten und die Eintheilung der Seelenstörungen: Entwurf einer historisch-kritischen Darstellung der bisherigen Eintheilungen und Versuch zur Anbahnung einer empirisch-wissenschaftlichen Grundlage der Psychiatrie als klinischer Disciplin.* Kafemann.

Kay, S. R., Flszbein, A., & Opfer, L. A. (1987). The positive and negative syndrome scale (PANSS) for schizophrenia. *Schizophrenia Bulletin, 13*(2), 261.

Kitamura, T., Okazaki, Y., Fujinawa, A., Yoshino, M., & Kasahara, Y. (1995). Symptoms of psychoses. A factor-analytic study. *The British Journal of Psychiatry, 166*(2), 236–240.

Klimidis, S., Stuart, G. W., Minas, I. H., Copolov, D. L., & Singh, B. S. (1993). Positive and negative symptoms in the psychoses: re-analysis of published SAPS and SANS global ratings. *Schizophrenia Research, 9*(1), 11–18.

Koutsouleris, N., Gaser, C., Jäger, M., Bottlender, R., Frodl, T., Holzinger, S., et al. (2008). Structural correlates of psychopathological symptom dimensions in schizophrenia: a voxel-based morphometric study. *Neuroimage, 39*(4), 1600–1612.

Kraepelin, E. (1971). *Dementia praecox and paraphrenia.* Krieger Publishing Company.

Kravariti, E., Russo, M., Vassos, E., Morgan, K., Fearon, P., Zanelli, J. W., et al. (2012). Linear and non-linear associations of symptom dimensions and cognitive function in first-onset psychosis. *Schizophrenia Research, 140*(1–3), 221–231. http://dx.doi.org/10.1016/j.schres.2012.06.008.

Lancon, C., Aghababian, V., Llorca, P. M., & Auquier, P. (1998). Factorial structure of the Positive and Negative Syndrome Scale (PANSS): a forced five-dimensional factor analysis. *Acta Psychiatrica Scandinavica, 98*(5), 369–376.

Lancon, C., Auquier, P., Nayt, G., & Reine, G. (2000). Stability of the five-factor structure of the Positive and Negative Syndrome Scale (PANSS). *Schizophrenia Research, 42*(3), 231–239.

Larsen, T. K., Moe, L. C., Vibe-Hansen, L., & Johannessen, J. O. (2000). Premorbid functioning versus duration of untreated psychosis in 1 year outcome in first-episode psychosis. *Schizophrenia Research, 45*(1), 1–9.

Lee, K. H., Harris, A. W., Loughland, C. M., & Williams, L. M. (2003). The five symptom dimensions and depression in schizophrenia. *Psychopathology, 36*(5), 226–233.

Liddle, P. F. (1987). The symptoms of chronic schizophrenia. A re-examination of the positive-negative dichotomy. *The British Journal of Psychiatry, 151*(2), 145–151.

Liddle, P. F., Ngan, E. T. C., Duffield, G., Kho, K., & Warren, A. J. (2002). Signs and Symptoms of Psychotic Illness (SSPI): a rating scale. *The British Journal of Psychiatry, 180*(1), 45–50.

Liddle, P. F., Friston, K. J., Frith, C. D., & Frackowiak, R. S. J. (1992). Cerebral blood flow and mental processes in schizophrenia. *Journal of the Royal Society of Medicine, 85*(4), 224–227.

Lindenmayer, J.-P., Bernstein-Hyman, R., & Grochowski, S. (1994). A new five factor model of schizophrenia. *Psychiatric Quarterly, 65*(4), 299–322.

Lindenmayer, J.-P., Grochowski, S., & Hyman, R. B. (1995). Five factor model of schizophrenia: replication across samples. *Schizophrenia Research, 14*(3), 229–234.

Lindström, E., & Knorring, L. Von (1993). Principal component analysis of the Swedish version of the Positive and Negative Syndrome Scale for schizophrenia. *Nordic Journal of Psychiatry, 47*(4), 257–263.

Lykouras, L., Oulis, P., Psarros, K., Daskalopoulou, E., Botsis, A., Christodoulou, G. N., et al. (2000). Five-factor model of schizophrenic psychopathology: how valid is it? *European Archives of Psychiatry and Clinical Neuroscience, 250*(2), 93–100.

Malla, A. K., Norman, R. M., Williamson, P., Cortese, L., & Diaz, F. (1993). Three syndrome concept of schizophrenia: a factor analytic study. *Schizophrenia Research, 10*(2), 143–150.

Malla, A. K., Norman, R. M. G., Manchanda, R., Ahmed, M. R., Scholten, D., Harricharan, R., et al. (2002). One year outcome in first episode psychosis: influence of DUP and other predictors. *Schizophrenia Research, 54*(3), 231–242.

Marder, S. R., Davis, J. M., & Chouinard, G. (1997). The effects of risperidone on the five dimensions of schizophrenia derived by factor analysis: combined results of the North American trials. *Journal of Clinical Psychiatry, 58*, 538–546.

Marneros, A., Diester, A., & Rohde, A. (1991). *Long-term investigation in stability of positive/negative distinction. Negative vs Positive Schizophrenia.* Berlin: Springer.

Mass, R., Schoemig, T., Hitschfeld, K., Wall, E., & Haasen, C. (2000). Psychopathological syndromes of schizophrenia: evaluation of the dimensional structure of the positive and negative syndrome scale. *Schizophrenia Bulletin, 26*(1), 167–177.

Maziade, M., Roy, M.-A., Martinez, M., Cliche, D., Fournier, J.-P., Garneau, Y., et al. (1995). Negative, psychoticism, and disorganized dimensions in patients with familial schizophrenia or bipolar disorder: continuity and discontinuity between the major psychoses. *The American Journal of Psychiatry, 152*, 1458–1463.

McGorry, P. D., Bell, R. C., Dudgeon, P. L., & Jackson, H. J. (1998). The dimensional structure of first episode psychosis: an exploratory factor analysis. *Psychological Medicine, 28*(04), 935–947.

McIntosh, A. M., Forrester, A., Lawrie, S. M., Byrne, M., Harper, A., Kestelman, J. N., et al. (2001). A factor model of the functional psychoses and the relationship of factors to clinical variables and brain morphology. *Psychological Medicine, 31*(01), 159–171.

Milev, P., Ho, B.-C., Arndt, S., & Andreasen, N. C. (2005). Predictive values of neurocognition and negative symptoms on functional outcome in schizophrenia: a longitudinal first-episode study with 7-year follow-up. *American Journal of Psychiatry, 162*(3), 495–506.

Minas, I. H., Stuart, G. W., Klimidis, S., Jackson, H. J., Singh, B. S., & Copolov, D. L. (1992). Positive and negative symptoms in the psychoses: multidimensional scaling of SAPS and SANS items. *Schizophrenia Research, 8*(2), 143–156.

Murphy, B. M., Burke, J. G., Bray, J. C., Walsh, D., & Kendler, K. S. (1994). An analysis of the clinical features of familial schizophrenia. *Acta Psychiatrica Scandinavica, 89*(6), 421–427.

Nakaya, M., Suwa, H., Komahashi, T., & Ohmori, K. (1999). Is schizophrenic symptomatology independent of the phase of the illness? *Psychopathology, 32*(1), 23–29.

Nieuwenstein, M. R., Aleman, A., & de Haan, E. H. F. (2001). Relationship between symptom dimensions and neurocognitive functioning in schizophrenia: a meta-analysis of WCST and CPT studies. *Journal of Psychiatric Research, 35*(2), 119–125.

Norman, R. M., Malla, A. K., Morrison-Stewart, S. L., Helmes, E., Williamson, P. C., Thomas, J., et al. (1997). Neuropsychological correlates of syndromes in schizophrenia. *The British Journal of Psychiatry, 170*(2), 134–139.

O'Callaghan, E., Buckley, P., Madigan, C., Redmond, O., Stack, J. P., Kinsella, A., et al. (1995). The relationship of minor physical anomalies and other putative indices of developmental disturbance in schizophrenia to abnormalities of cerebral structure on magnetic resonance imaging. *Biological Psychiatry, 38*(8), 516–524.

Oher, F. J., Demjaha, A., Jackson, D., Morgan, C., Dazzan, P., Morgan, K., et al. (2014). The effect of the environment on symptom dimensions in the first episode of psychosis: a multilevel study. *Psychological Medicine,* 1–12. http://dx.doi.org/10.1017/S0033291713003188.

van Os, J., Fahy, T. A., Jones, P., Harvey, I., Sham, P., Lewis, S., et al. (1996). Psychopathological syndromes in the functional psychoses: associations with course and outcome. *Psychological Medicine, 26*(01), 161–176.

van Os, J., Gilvarry, C., Bale, R., Van Horn, E., Tattan, T., & White, I. (1999). A comparison of the utility of dimensional and categorical representations of psychosis. *Psychological Medicine, 29*(03), 595–606.

van Os, J., & Kapur, S. (2009). Schizophrenia. *The Lancet, 374*(9690), 635–645.

Peralta, V., & Cuesta, M. J. (1994). Psychometric properties of the positive and negative syndrome scale (PANSS) in schizophrenia. *Psychiatry Research, 53*(1), 31–40.

Peralta, V., & Cuesta, M. J. (2000). Duration of illness and structure of symptoms in schizophrenia. *Psychological Medicine, 30*(2), 481–483.

Peralta, V., & Cuesta, M. J. (1999). Dimensional structure of psychotic symptoms: an item-level analysis of SAPS and SANS symptoms in psychotic disorders. *Schizophren Research, 38*(1), 13–26.

Peralta, V., & Cuesta, M. J. (2001). How many and which are the psychopathological dimensions in schizophrenia? Issues influencing their ascertainment. *Schizophren Research, 49*(3), 269–285.

Peralta, V., & Cuesta, M. J. (2004). The deficit syndrome of the psychotic illness. A clinical and nosological study. *European Archives of Psychiatry and Clinical Neuroscience, 254*(3), 165–171. http://dx.doi.org/10.1007/s00406-004-0464-7.

Peralta, V., de Leon, J., & Cuesta, M. J. (1992). Are there more than two syndromes in schizophrenia? A critique of the positive-negative dichotomy. *British Journal of Psychiatry, 161*, 335–343.

Peralta, V., & Cuesta, M. J. (2005). The underlying structure of diagnostic systems of schizophrenia: a comprehensive polydiagnostic approach. *Schizophrenia Research, 79*(2), 217–229.

Peralta, V., & Cuesta, M. J. (2007). A dimensional and categorical architecture for the classification of psychotic disorders. *World Psychiatry, 6*(2), 100.

Peralta, V., Cuesta, M. J., & Farre, C. (1997). Factor structure of symptoms in functional psychoses. *Biological Psychiatry, 42*(9), 806–815.

Ratakonda, S., Gorman, J. M., Yale, S. A., & Amador, X. F. (1998). Characterization of psychotic conditions: use of the domains of psychopathology model. *Archives of General Psychiatry, 55*(1), 75–81.

Rey, E.-R., Bailer, J., Bräuer, W., Händel, M., Laubenstein, D., & Stein, A. (1994). Stability trends and longitudinal correlations of negative and positive syndromes within a three-year follow-up of initially hospitalized schizophrenics. *Acta Psychiatrica Scandinavica, 90*(6), 405–412.

Rietkerk, T., Boks, M. P. M., Sommer, I. E., Liddle, P. F., Ophoff, R. A., & Kahn, R. S. (2008). The genetics of symptom dimensions of schizophrenia: review and meta-analysis. *Schizophrenia Research, 102*(1), 197–205.

Robins, E., & Guze, S. B. (1970). Establishment of diagnostic validity in psychiatric illness: its application to schizophrenia. *American Journal of Psychiatry, 126*(7), 983–987.

Russo, M., Levine, S. Z., Demjaha, A., Di Forti, M., Bonaccorso, S., Fearon, P., et al. (2014). Association between symptom dimensions and categorical diagnoses of psychosis: a cross-sectional and longitudinal investigation. *Schizophrenia Bulletin, 40*(1), 111–119. http://dx.doi.org/10.1093/schbul/sbt055.

Sabri, O., Erkwoh, R., Schreckenberger, M., Owega, A., Sass, H., & Buell, U. (1997). Correlation of positive symptoms exclusively to hyperperfusion or hypoperfusion of cerebral cortex in never-treated schizophrenics. *The Lancet, 349*(9067), 1735–1739.

Salokangas, R. K. R. (1997). Structure of schizophrenic symptomatology and its changes over time: prospective factor-analytical study. *Acta Psychiatrica Scandinavica, 95*(1), 32–39.

Schneider, C. (1942). Die heuristische Bedeutung der neuen Lehre. In *Die Schizophrenen Symptomverbände* (pp. 189–201). Springer.

Smith, D. A., Mar, C. M., & Turoff, B. K. (1998). The structure of schizophrenic symptoms: a meta-analytic confirmatory factor analysis. *Schizophrenia Research, 31*(1), 57–70.

Strauss, J. S. (1973). Diagnostic models and the nature of psychiatric disorder. *Archives of General Psychiatry, 29*(4), 445–449.

Tandon, R., Gaebel, W., Barch, D. M., Bustillo, J., Gur, R. E., Heckers, S., et al. (2013). Definition and description of schizophrenia in the DSM-5. *Schizophrenia Research, 150*(1), 3–10.

Toomey, R., Kremen, W. S., Simpson, J. C., Samson, J. A., Seidman, L. J., Lyons, M. J., et al. (1997). Revisiting the factor structure for positive and negative symptoms: evidence from a large heterogeneous group of psychiatric patients. *American Journal of Psychiatry, 154*(3), 371–377.

White, L., Harvey, P. D., Parrella, M., & Sevy, S. (1994). Empirical assessment of the factorial structure of clinical symptoms in schizophrenic patients: symptom structure in geriatric and nongeriatric samples. *New Trends in Experimental & Clinical Psychiatry, 10*, 75–83.

White, L., Harvey, P. D., Opler, L., & Lindenmayer, J. P. (1997). Empirical assessment of the factorial structure of clinical symptoms in schizophrenia. *Psychopathology, 30*(5), 263–274.

Wickham, H., Walsh, C., Asherson, P., Taylor, C., Sigmundson, T., Gill, M., et al. (2001). Familiality of symptom dimensions in schizophrenia. *Schizophrenia Research, 47*(2), 223–232.

Wolthaus, J. E. D., Dingemans, P. M. A. J., Schene, A. H., Linszen, D. H., Knegtering, H., Holthausen, E. A. E., et al. (2000). Component structure of the positive and negative syndrome scale (PANSS) in patients with recent-onset schizophrenia and spectrum disorders. *Psychopharmacology, 150*(4), 399–403.

Wong, A. H. C., Voruganti, L. N. P., Heslegrave, R. J., & Awad, A. G. (1997). Neurocognitive deficits and neurological signs in schizophrenia. *Schizophrenia Research, 23*(2), 139–146.

2

A Review of the Epidemiology of Schizophrenia

Alan S. Brown*,§, *Florence S. Lau*¶

*Department of Psychiatry, Columbia University College of Physicians and Surgeons, New York State Psychiatric Institute, New York, NY, USA; §Department of Epidemiology, Columbia University Mailman School of Public Health, New York, NY, USA; ¶Department of Clinical Psychology, Teachers College, Columbia University, New York, NY, USA

INTRODUCTION

Schizophrenia is a globally pervasive neuropsychiatric disorder with an approximate prevalence of 1% in any given adult population (Lauriello, Bustillo, & Keith, 2005) and a mean annual incidence rate of 0.2 per 1000 with a range of 0.04–0.58 per 1000 people (Eaton, 1999). In terms of incidence across countries, a study conducted by the World Health Organization has found contrasting results. In studies of narrowly defined schizophrenia, the incidence rate did not differ significantly across societies, but when schizophrenia was more broadly defined, the highest incident rates occurred in developing countries compared to industrialized countries (Jablensky et al., 1992). In addition, this study found a higher incidence of catatonic schizophrenia in developing countries.

Schizophrenia is characterized by cognitive, behavioral, and emotional abnormalities, including positive symptoms (e.g., delusions, hallucinations, catatonic behavior, disorganized speech) and negative symptoms (e.g., alogia, affective flattening, amotivation) (Buchanan & Carpenter, 2005). Furthermore, chronically disturbed cognition has been observed in several domains such as executive function, attention, and verbal fluency and causes considerable impairment in level of functioning (Gold & Green, 2005). Although research on the etiologies of this neuropsychiatric disorder is still in an early phase, the general consensus is that environmental risk factors, susceptibility genes, and their interaction lead to the eventual development of schizophrenia, and that much of the liability to schizophrenia is initiated by insults that occur during different windows of brain development, from the prenatal period up to adolescence. The neurodevelopmental hypothesis of schizophrenia suggests that these insults are most detrimental during certain critical periods of vulnerability (Piper et al., 2012). These insults' origins are believed to alter the neurodevelopmental trajectory of specific neurotransmitters and other molecules, synapses, cells, brain regions, and neural circuits and networks, leading to pathophysiologic and neuromorphologic alterations and ultimately behavioral outcomes characteristic of the disorder.

In this chapter, we review findings of specific environmental factors that have been found to contribute to schizophrenia. We will primarily focus on environmental insults that play a significant role during the prenatal and childhood phases of life, examining in particular infection, nutrition, cannabis use, advanced paternal age, immigration, and childhood trauma. We will then consider the diathesis-stress model in which genetic and environmental factors interact to influence the development of schizophrenia. Finally, we offer potential recommendations and interventions that are feasible at present which might help to prevent or mitigate the severity of schizophrenia and discuss future directions for research in this area of work.

EVIDENCE FOR ENVIRONMENTAL FACTORS IN SCHIZOPHRENIA

Schizophrenia is a heritable disorder. Early research on schizophrenia was dominated by twin, family, and adoption studies (Lowing, Mirsky, & Pereira, 1983; Reiss, 1976; Tienari et al., 1987). More recently, linkage and genome-wide association studies have identified chromosomal regions and genetic variants, both inherited and de novo, which are related to an increased risk of the disorder (Fromer et al., 2014).

Handbook of Behavioral Neuroscience
http://dx.doi.org/10.1016/B978-0-12-800981-9.00002-X

Despite the importance that genetics has on the development of schizophrenia, environmental risk factors have emerged as potentially important in the etiology of this disorder. Twin studies have found a concordance rate of approximately 50–60% in monozygotic (MZ) twins, which falls well short of complete concordance (McGuffin, Owen, & Farmer, 1995). Furthermore, this concordance rate is skewed by the fact that MZ twins generally share a similar in utero environment as well as greater similarities in the postnatal environment.

In a study that examined the difference in concordance rates within only MZ twins, Davis, Phelps, and Bracha (1995) found that there was a difference in these rates when comparing monochorionic and dichorionic MZ twins, the latter of whom have separate placentae and fetal circulation. In monochorionic MZ twins, who share a greater in utero environment almost from conception, the concordance rate of schizophrenia is 60%, whereas it is only 11% in dichorionic twins. Hence, this study supports an environmental role in the development of schizophrenia, even within MZ twin pairs.

Next we discuss major environmental risk factors that have been identified to date for schizophrenia and the evidence supporting their relationship with the disorder.

Prenatal Infection

A role of prenatal infection in schizophrenia is supported by several lines of research. Initial studies have found an increased risk of schizophrenia in children born during the winter and spring months, potentially reflective of respiratory infections in particular, and birth in urban settings, where infections can spread more rapidly (for a review, see Brown & Derkits, 2010).

More recent studies have focused on birth cohorts comprising children all born within the same time period and in which records of maternal infection, psychiatric illnesses, and related records were maintained throughout the pregnancy and during the early life of the child. These allow for long-term assessment to the diagnosis of schizophrenia; comparison of psychiatric and other outcomes among subjects with prospectively documented infection with those considered to be free of infection. Some cohorts capitalize on biological samples from the pregnancy and the fetus that were also stored. These samples have been used to serologically confirm antibodies to infection.

Next we review results of select studies of specific prenatal infections and schizophrenia (for a review, see Brown and Derkits, 2010).

Influenza

Because influenza is so prominent during the winter and the spring months, investigators began to examine the psychiatric outcomes of children born during influenza epidemics (Brown & Derkits, 2010). In the earliest studies, some were able to find a link between being born during an influenza epidemic and developing schizophrenia during adulthood, whereas others failed to replicate these results. These studies were limited in that it was possible that a significant proportion of the mothers did not have influenza at the time of pregnancy because individuals in these studies were included merely because they were pregnant during the time of the influenza exposure rather than being confirmed with influenza during pregnancy.

Therefore, researchers used birth cohort studies to document maternal influenza exposure during the pregnancy by relying on documented records and biomarkers prospectively collected during pregnancy. These subjects were linked to registries that contained data on psychiatric outcome. In some studies, the patients were interviewed, whereas in others, the registry diagnoses were used. One such study was conducted by Brown et al. (2004) using the birth cohort of the Child Health and Development Study, born between 1959 and 1967 in Alameda County, California, and followed by the Kaiser Foundation Health Plan. Strengths of this study included documentation and availability of maternal serum drawn during the pregnancy, psychiatric diagnoses based on structured interviews and reviews of psychiatric records of the offspring, and regular follow-up of the cohort. Quantification of influenza antibody in these specimens led to the finding that among mothers who were exposed to influenza during the first half of gestation, there was a threefold elevation in the risk of developing schizophrenia. If the exposure occurred during the first trimester of pregnancy, the risk was increased sevenfold. However, if the exposure to influenza was in the second half of gestation, there was no increased risk for schizophrenia.

These results correspond with those that have emerged from an increasing number of animal studies, including those on rodents and rhesus monkeys, of influenza and of maternal immune activation. These studies demonstrated that both of these immunologic exposures, particularly during early-to-middle gestation, were related to neurobiological and behavioral outcomes that are analogous to those found in schizophrenia or related psychoses (Bauman et al., 2014; Meyer, Yee, & Feldon, 2007; Vuillermot, Webber, Feldon, & Meyer, 2010).

Rubella

Researchers have also tested the risk of schizophrenia in a birth cohort exposed to the rubella virus. Rubella was one of the first known teratogens, with a spectrum of effects on congenital development including mental retardation, deafness, and cataracts as well as a 20% risk of miscarriage (Siegel, Fuerst, & Guinee, 1971). These findings suggested that rubella might also lead to long-term developmental consequences, such as schizophrenia, that may not be immediately apparent at birth.

Brown et al. (2001) investigated a birth cohort in which pregnant women were diagnosed as having had prenatal exposure to the rubella virus by clinical signs and confirmatory serological testing. In a longitudinal follow-up of the infants in this cohort, the authors found that more than 20% of the exposed children later developed schizophrenia or schizophrenia spectrum disorders. Much like the results found for influenza, the correlation was strongest when mothers were exposed to rubella during the first 2 months of pregnancy.

One hypothesis for how rubella affects the developing fetus is by altering the neurodevelopmental trajectory of the child, as this study found that approximately 90% of the rubella-exposed children who eventually developed schizophrenia spectrum disorders had increased neuromotor and/or behavioral abnormalities during childhood as well as a decline in intelligence quotient over time. This finding was in contrast to a much smaller proportion of these childhood neurodevelopmental abnormalities in those whose mothers were exposed to rubella during pregnancy, but who did not eventually develop these disorders.

Herpes Simplex Virus Type 2

Another viral infection with detrimental effects on infants is herpes simplex virus type 2 (HSV-2), a sexually transmitted virus which is transmitted to the infant from the mother as the fetus passes through the birth canal. Similar to rubella, HSV-2 causes abnormal neurological development and other related developmental consequences (Whitley, 2006).

One study that has examined the link between maternal HSV-2 infection and schizophrenia in offspring was by Buka, Tsuang, Torrey, Klebanoff, Bernstein, et al. (2001). Elevated levels of maternal immunoglobulin G (IgG) antibody associated with HSV-2 were linked to a higher risk of psychosis in those mothers' offspring. A larger follow-up study by Buka, Cannon, Torrey, and Yolken (2008) again found a higher risk of psychosis and an even higher risk of schizophrenia-related psychosis in offspring whose mothers tested positive for exposure to HSV-2 during pregnancy. This risk was particularly elevated in mothers who engaged in risky sexual practices during pregnancy, such as frequent sexual encounters without contraception. This was a particular strength of the study (Brown & Derkits, 2010).

Cytokines and Other Inflammatory Biomarkers

Cytokines, which encompass a family of soluble polypeptides, represent markers of prenatal infection and inflammatory conditions. Cytokines orchestrate the immune response to the presence of infections and other noxious insults and therefore play an essential role as part of the immune system. Hence, cytokine elevations may indicate exposure to a number of different types of infections during pregnancy.

In examining the connection between elevated levels of maternal cytokines and the development of schizophrenia in the offspring, Brown, Hooton, et al. (2005) found a twofold increase in levels of the pro-inflammatory cytokine interleukin-8 during the second and early third trimesters of pregnancies of offspring who later developed schizophrenia compared with control pregnancies. A second study by Buka, Tsuang, Torrey, Klebanoff, Wagner, et al. (2001) found that the mothers of children who developed psychosis later in life had higher levels of the pro-inflammatory cytokine tumor necrosis factor-α at the time of birth. Elevated cytokine levels have also been associated with other conditions such as a higher body mass index (BMI) (Schaefer et al., 2000) and preeclampsia (Cannon, Jones, & Murray, 2002), both of which have also been associated with schizophrenia (Brown, Michaeline, & Susser, 2005). Hence, cytokine levels may not necessarily indicate maternal prenatal infection, but can be an important indicator of other insults to the fetus and newborn. In the most recent study of a prenatal inflammatory biomarker and schizophrenia, Canetta et al. (2014) demonstrated that elevated maternal C-reactive protein measured during pregnancy in archived serum specimens is associated with an increased risk of schizophrenia in offspring from a Finnish national birth cohort.

Toxoplasma gondii

Nonviral or bacterial infections also have detrimental effects on fetal development. *Toxoplasma gondii* is an intracellular parasite that can increase the risk of schizophrenia in infants whose mothers were exposed to this pathogen during pregnancy (Brown, Schaefer, et al., 2005). Levels of *T. gondii* IgG antibody in archived maternal sera were greater than twice as high in mothers of children who developed schizophrenia compared with mothers of control offspring. *Toxoplasma gondii* has also been linked to congenital central nervous system (CNS) abnormalities and delays in neurological development, which supports its biological plausibility for increasing the risk for schizophrenia (Dukes, Luft, Durack, Scheld, & Whitley, 1997).

In a second study, which used *T. gondii* IgG antibody measurements on filter paper blood spots collected from newborns (first week of life), Mortensen et al. (2007) found that *T. gondii* IgG levels were higher in those who later developed schizophrenia compared with controls. This antibody most likely originated from the mother rather than the child, because the antibody crosses the placenta and *T. gondii* infection is highly unlikely in the first week of life. A more recent study of IgG levels measured in neonatal dried blood spots by Blomstrom et al. (2012) again associated higher levels of *T. gondii* IgG with later schizophrenia. These findings support the original results of Brown, Schaefer, et al. (2005).

Maternal Infection and the Pathobiology of Schizophrenia

Evidence from our group indicates that prenatal infection can have pathobiological consequences that are observed in schizophrenia, including effects on neurocognition. A study by Brown et al. (2009) investigated the relationship in schizophrenia patients between having had prenatal exposure to influenza or toxoplasmosis and subsequent performance on neurocognitive measures, including the Wisconsin Card Sorting Test and the Trail Making Test, part B. Schizophrenia patients who were exposed to maternal infection during gestation committed significantly more errors on the Wisconsin Card Sorting Test and needed significantly more time to complete the Trail Making Test, part B test. Furthermore, the patients showed deficient abilities on figural fluency, sequencing of letters and numbers, and backwards digit span, suggesting that prenatal infection may affect cognitive abilities, specifically set-shifting function, and that there may be associated abnormal physiological changes in the brain.

A study by Ellman et al. (2012) linked mothers who had anemia to an increased deficiency in neuromotor functions and intellectual difficulties in schizophrenia patients but not in controls. Schizophrenia offspring of mothers with lower hemoglobin values throughout pregnancy had a significant decrease in scores on the Grooved Pegboard test, the Finger Tapping test, and the Wechsler Adult Intelligent Scales. These results suggest that having a liability to schizophrenia make offspring more vulnerable to the negative cognitive effects of decreased maternal hemoglobin values.

Prenatal Nutrition

Deficient prenatal nutrition has also been implicated as a leading candidate risk factor in the etiology of schizophrenia. Some of the first studies on the effects of prenatal nutrition on the later development of schizophrenia were conducted on individuals who were born or in gestation during the Dutch Hunger Winter of 1944–1945 (Hoek, Brown, & Susser, 1997). This was a severe famine resulting from a blockade of the Netherlands by the Nazi regime. This led to thousands of deaths as well as deceased fertility and infant mortality. Because the caloric content of the rations and psychiatric outcomes were well documented and the famine was considered relatively time-limited, this was an opportunity to study the effects of prenatal nutrition on a cohort that was exposed to nutritional deficiency during specific periods of gestation.

This series of studies reported that the timing of the exposure may determine the type of psychiatric disorder that eventually develops, and that exposure to famine and malnutrition earlier in gestation may lead to more severe psychiatric disorders including schizophrenia and schizoid personality disorder (Hoek et al., 1997; Susser et al., 1996). Specifically, these studies found an increased risk of schizophrenia and schizophrenia spectrum disorders, as well as schizoid personality disorder, among those exposed to the peak of the famine during conception and early gestation. The authors of the study suggest that these findings might be explained by direct effects of protein caloric malnutrition, by micronutrient deficiency, or an unknown cooccurring factor. In a related study, Brown, van Os, Driessens, Hoek, and Susser (2000) demonstrated that the risk of developing unipolar or bipolar major affective disorder requiring hospitalization was higher in the subjects exposed to this famine during the second trimester and highest in those exposed during the third trimester. This study not only supports the earlier findings that prenatal malnutrition can have severe effects on psychiatric disorders, but also suggests that the timing of exposure to malnutrition may modify the type of psychiatric disorder that results.

The authors also found that early gestational exposure to the Dutch famine was associated with congenital abnormalities of the CNS, which is concordant with earlier work on this cohort and with the finding that exposure to famine during this period was also related to an increased risk of schizophrenia. Specifically, researchers found an increased rate of neural tube defects among the children who were in gestation during the famine. Interestingly, neural tube defects are related to prenatal folate deficiency, which is common during pregnancy, suggesting that this micronutrient may be a viable candidate risk factor for schizophrenia. Other nutrients related to neural tube defects and the folate metabolic cascade are vitamins B12 and B6. The lack of folate and of these vitamins causes maternal hyperhomocysteinemia (Penner & Brown, 2007). In the birth cohort of the Child Health and Development Study, we found a significant elevation in maternal homocysteine during pregnancy in cases of schizophrenia compared with matched controls (Brown et al., 2007). Elevated homocysteine levels may lead to an increased risk of schizophrenia by interfering with the development of N-methyl-D-aspartate receptors and leading to glutamatergic deficits (Picker & Coyle, 2005).

Low levels of prenatal vitamin D in the pregnant mother have also been associated with schizophrenia (McGrath, Eyles, & Mowry, 2003). Although prenatal vitamin D deficiency can be caused by maternal malnutrition, it is also related to seasonal fluctuations resulting in daily length of light exposure or migration to geographical regions with colder climates and less sunlight. Insufficient levels of vitamin D have been found in animal models to correspond to biological abnormalities seen in schizophrenia, and it is hypothesized that lack of vitamin D affects cell growth and proliferation and alters the immune system response in both the developing fetus as well as in adult brain.

Iron is another important nutrient that is essential for brain development and functioning. Prenatal iron deficiency or a lack of iron in the early stages of life may lead to permanent neurological and behavioral abnormalities from childhood, extending into adulthood. A study by Insel, Schaefer, McKeague, Susser, and Brown (2008) investigated the effect of maternal iron deficiency on the relative risk of developing schizophrenia or schizophrenia spectrum disorders during adulthood in the Child Health and Development Study birth cohort. The authors found that low maternal hemoglobin (in the anemic range), a robust marker of iron that was prospectively documented in all members of the cohort, was associated with a nearly fourfold increased risk of schizophrenia spectrum disorders in their offspring, adjusting for many covariates.

In an attempt to replicate the findings of this study, Sorensen, Nielsen, Pedersen, and Mortensen (2011) examined a cohort of Danish births from 1978 to 1998. The authors found that the individuals whose mothers had been diagnosed with anemia during pregnancy had a 1.60-fold increased risk for developing schizophrenia. Further research is required to identify plausible mechanisms by which prenatal iron deficiency modulates the risk of schizophrenia. Finally, new research has found that maternal iron deficiency may interact with prenatal infection and immune activation to contribute to schizophrenia-like behavior in rat offspring (Harvey & Boksa, 2014).

Additional nutritional risk factors for schizophrenia include maternal vitamin A deficiency (Bao et al., 2012) and excess docosahexaenoic acid (Harper et al., 2011).

McClellan, Susser, and King (2006) have suggested that lack of proper prenatal nutrition could lead to de novo mutations in the genes responsible for promoting healthy brain development. A developing fetus requires proper nutrients, as they are responsible for protecting, synthesizing, and repairing DNA (Ames, 2001). An excess of mutations in the genes that are critical to brain development could result in impairments in both brain structure and function. The timing of origin of these mutations is also essential because the fetus is most vulnerable during early gestation from the high cell division rate at this time; mutations that appear during or around the time of conception can lead to an exponential growth of mutant cells (Paashuis-Lew & Heddle, 1998).

Malnutrition could also lead to epigenetic changes in genes responsible for proper fetal development. Notably, folate is a known methylator of genes, because gene methylation generally represses gene expression (Yu et al., 2014), its absence may act to increase gene expression. The consequences may depend upon the gestational time period of exposure. For example, in a study by Heijmans et al. (2008), infants who were in gestation during the Dutch Hunger Winter displayed epigenetic changes in the insulin-like growth factor 2 gene compared with same-sex siblings who were unexposed during gestation. These and other epigenetic differences could be a mediator between prenatal malnutrition and the expression of genes related not only to fetal growth, but also neuropsychiatric development.

Prenatal and perinatal malnutrition may also modify fetal brain development through physiologic mechanisms that are implicated in schizophrenia. As an example, maternal iron deficiency is known to diminish myelination (Wu et al., 2008), and animal, postmortem, and neuroimaging studies support myelin deficits in schizophrenia (Flynn et al., 2003; Zhang et al., 2012).

Another finding related to prenatal nutrition and schizophrenia is the association between high maternal BMI and schizophrenia among offspring. In this study, conducted on the Child Health and Development Study birth cohort, mothers with a BMI greater than 30 were three times as likely to give birth to offspring who later developed schizophrenia (Schaefer et al., 2000). Furthermore, Solomon et al. (1997) found that gestational diabetes is correlated with high BMI as well as with the obstetric complications seen among infants who later develop schizophrenia. In addition, elevated BMI is associated with increased inflammation (Kitahara et al., 2014), which has also been associated with schizophrenia (Canetta et al., 2014). Hence, high BMI may lead to obstetric complications (Crane, Wojtowycz, Dye, Aubry, & Artal, 1997), or inflammation, which then increase the risk of the development of schizophrenia in the offspring (Cannon et al., 2002). This work has particularly important implications for public health as the obesity epidemic has become an increasing problem in industrialized countries (Güngör, 2014).

Paternal Age

Advanced paternal age has been identified as a risk factor for schizophrenia. In a seminal study, Malaspina et al. (2001) reported this finding on a single large birth cohort in Israel, the Jerusalem Perinatal Cohort. The authors found that advanced paternal age was correlated with the risk of schizophrenia beginning as early as 25 years of age. The risk of schizophrenia increased rapidly as paternal age advanced, with a relative risk of 2 in offspring of men who were 45–49 years old at time of birth of the child and nearly 3 in offspring of men older than 50. Advanced maternal age was not associated with schizophrenia and the paternal age finding persisted following adjustment for maternal age. In addition, the finding persisted after accounting for length of marriage as well as family history of schizophrenia and other psychiatric illnesses. The finding has been replicated by many groups throughout the world (Brown et al., 2002; Dalman & Allebeck, 2002; El-Saadi et al., 2004; Tsuchiya et al., 2005).

This finding has been hypothesized to result from de novo genetic mutations that are highly correlated with older paternal age (Kong et al., 2012; Malaspina et al., 2001). Unlike ova, spermatogonia undergo an exponentially rising number of cell divisions as paternal age increases. After a male experiences puberty, spermatogonia experience approximately 23 divisions per year, leading to about 200 divisions by age 20 and 660 by age 40 (Malaspina et al., 2001). This rapidly increasing number of cell divisions as paternal age advances, accompanied by deficits in DNA repair mechanisms, may be at least partially responsible for the increase in de novo mutations. Indeed, many studies have identified a significant excess of copy number variants in schizophrenia, including de novo mutations, and several are associated with very high risks of the disorder (Rippey et al., 2013; Merikangas et al., 2014; Luo et al., 2014). In an Icelandic cohort of fathers and offspring, Kong et al. (2012) found that the age of the father at conception of the offspring was the driving force behind the diversity in mutation rate of single nucleotide polymorphisms, with paternally derived mutations doubling every 16.5 years. Furthermore, they found that the father's age explained nearly all of the de novo mutations remaining after accounting for random variation.

An excess of de novo mutations would at least partially explain why schizophrenia persists in the population despite a reduction in reproductive fitness in this disorder. Parenthetically, inherited genetic variants for schizophrenia are expected to have been subject to negative selection pressures. Consequently, it has been argued that if new genes for schizophrenia were not introduced, the disorder should have either disappeared, or become rarer over time.

Cannabis Use

Cannabis, a drug prepared from the plant *Cannabis sativa* (including marijuana, resin, and "skunk"), is used widely throughout the world and is especially popular in North America, Western Europe, West and Central Africa, and Oceania (United Nations Office on Drugs and Crime, 2009). Several studies within the past decade have investigated the effect of continuous use of cannabis on psychotic illnesses, specifically schizophrenia. Zammit, Allebeck, Andreasson, Lundberg, and Lewis (2002) in Sweden found that those who smoked cannabis had a twofold increased risk of developing schizophrenia within 15 years. In addition, the researchers also found a dose–response relationship; subjects who used cannabis more heavily (over 50 reported occasions) were six times as likely to develop schizophrenia compared to those who did not use cannabis at all.

Subsequent studies were carried out in different countries, which confirmed the results found in the Zammit et al. (2002) study, showing that those clinically dependent on cannabis by 18 years of age had an increased risk of later developing psychotic symptoms (Fergusson, Horwood, & Swain-Campbell, 2003). Cannabis users were also more likely to develop schizophreniform disorder (Arseneault et al., 2002), and the dose–response relationship found in the first study was confirmed (Henquet et al., 2005).

Experimental studies have also been conducted in order to assess the effect of cannabis use on schizophrenia. D'Souza et al. (2004) administered varying levels of the main ingredient in cannabis to healthy individuals with a history of cannabis exposure (but not abuse) and found that the subjects in the study displayed both positive and negative symptoms associated with schizophrenia, although all symptoms disappeared by about 3 h. D'Souza et al. (2005) conducted a follow-up study in which they followed the same protocol, but with clinically stable schizophrenia patients. Again, they found brief increases in positive symptoms, even if the patients were already taking antipsychotics.

More recent studies have focused on the mechanisms behind the schizophrenia–cannabis interaction. Epstein and Kumra (2014) tested the effect of cannabis on executive control of attention and cognitive function by comparing scores on the Attention Network Test among people with early-onset schizophrenia (EOS) and cannabis use disorder, only EOS, only cannabis use disorder, and controls. They found that the first group in particular had less efficient executive control of attention compared with those who had only EOS. They also found a smaller right caudal anterior cingulate cortex in subjects with EOS and cannabis use disorder. However, it is presently unclear whether this means that the smaller cortex surface leads to deficits in self-regulation and heavy cannabis use or if the direction of causation is in the opposite direction. More recent studies have suggested gene–environment correlation between cannabis use and schizophrenia in that the increased risk of schizophrenia after heavy and consistent cannabis use may be moderated by a shared gene that may explain part of the association (Power et al., 2014).

In support of the previous study by Power et al. (in press), a second study by Giordano, Ohlsoon, Sundquist, Sundquist, and Kendler (2015) found that the relationship between cannabis use or abuse and schizophrenia may not be as strong as believed. The authors found that as the degree of shared genetic and environmental factors increased (beginning with first cousins to full siblings), the relationship between schizophrenia and cannabis abuse decreased, although it remained significant even in full sibling pairs.

Immigration Status

First- and second-generation migrants have a higher risk of schizophrenia (Selten, Cantor-Graae, & Kahn, 2007). This idea was originally presented in a paper by Odegaard (1932), who found that Norwegian immigrants in the United States were more likely to be admitted to the hospital for schizophrenia compared with Norwegians born in the United States or those who still lived in Norway. Cantor-Graae and Selten (2005) followed up on this idea, finding a higher incidence of schizophrenia among subjects in the United Kingdom who originally had an African Caribbean background; individuals in the Netherlands with a Surinamese, Dutch Antillean, or Moroccan background; and subjects of various ethnic backgrounds in Denmark. In addition, subjects who immigrated from a developing country were more likely to develop schizophrenia than those from a developed country.

In the 2007 paper, Selten et al. reaffirmed this finding from the 2005 meta-analysis (Cantor-Graae & Selten, 2005). The authors found a relative risk for schizophrenia of 2.7 among first-generation migrants and a relative risk of 4.5 among second-generation migrants. They found an especially high risk of schizophrenia for migrants in Europe from countries with high black populations; this finding was replicated in further studies (Dealberto, 2010). Dealberto (2010) suggested that vitamin D deficiency in dark-skinned individuals might be responsible for this higher rate of schizophrenia. Cantor-Graae and Selten (2005) proposed an alternative explanation for their findings, namely the experience of social defeat, which they define as a subordinate position in society or an outsider status. The authors suggested that the chronic experience of social defeat through high competition in jobs, housing, and other aspects of life leads to increased sensitivity in the mesolimbic dopamine system. In support of this theory, the authors observed that immigrant groups who suffer from a low socioeconomic status in a highly competitive atmosphere have the highest risks for schizophrenia, although this association may be due to social selection rather than social causation. In addition, people with dark skin often have to endure higher levels of racism and ethnic discrimination. Further proposed explanations or contributing factors involve an ethnic disadvantage in the immigrants' new home countries, an increase risk of schizophrenia in those living in urban settings, unemployment, poor housing conditions, and general social adversity.

Birthplace and Residence

The risk of schizophrenia is influenced by the place of birth and childhood residence, specifically in urban versus rural locations. Studies have consistently shown that being raised in an urban setting leads to a higher risk of developing schizophrenia and that this risk is related to the level of urbanicity in a dose–response relationship (March et al., 2008). In addition, a large study by Mortensen et al. (1999) found that birth in an urban setting is related to schizophrenia risk, with a twofold increased risk in those born in the capital of Denmark compared with those born in the rural regions. Pedersen and Mortensen (2001) also found that the timing of exposure to urban settings was related to schizophrenia, but that being raised in an urban setting was a greater risk factor than being born in an urban area. Further evidence indicated that family-level and individual-level exposure to urbanicity were important in the relationship between degree of urbanization and the development of schizophrenia (Pedersen & Mortensen, 2006). Finally, a recent study by Sariaslan et al. (2015) found that population density as measured when the subject was 15 years of age was a predictor of later schizophrenia.

However, in a more recent meta-analysis of four studies by Vassos, Pedersen, Murray, Collier, and Lewis (2012), including the 1999 study by Mortensen et al., the authors found that the timing of exposure to urbanicity in an individual's life did not change the relationship with schizophrenia. Potential explanations included individual or family characteristics, selective migration, a greater risk of being exposed to infections or pollutants, an insufficient diet, or a poor social environment. In addition, the authors point to social fragmentation and deprivation as a possible explanation.

Socioeconomic Status

Two different hypotheses have been generated and tested to account for the relationship between low socioeconomic status and schizophrenia (Dohrenwend et al., 1992). The first is social causation, which proposes that schizophrenia is due to the environmental disadvantages that people with a low socioeconomic must endure. An alternative hypothesis, social drift, argues that individuals with schizophrenia tend to move from higher to lower socioeconomic status because of the debilitating symptoms that accompany the illness. A full discussion of this question has been well covered in other references (Dohrenwend et al., 1992; Kwok, in press) and will therefore be only briefly discussed here.

Studies have found conflicting evidence, ranging from no link between socioeconomic status and schizophrenia (Hare, Price, & Slater, 1972; Timms, 1998) to the finding that those with schizophrenia are more likely to originate from a higher social class (Makikyro et al., 1997; Mulvany et al., 2001). More recently, Wicks, Hjern, and Dalman (2010) and Wicks, Hjern, Gunnell, Lewis, and Dalman (2005) have examined the risk of developing psychosis resulting from social adversity. Several indicators of low socioeconomic status during childhood were related to a greater risk for psychosis and schizophrenia, including rented apartments, single-parent households, unemployment, and social welfare benefits. The risks increased with the number of indicators present; individuals with four indicators of low social status had a 2.7-fold higher risk of schizophrenia compared with individuals who did not have any. In a second study, on a group of children raised by adoptive parents, adoptees whose nonbiological families were disadvantaged, measured by unemployment, living in apartments, or a single-parent household, had an increased risk for psychosis. Among those who also had a genetic liability for psychosis, the risk was much higher.

Childhood Abuse

Morgan and Fisher (2007), in a review of several studies, reported that subjects with psychotic disorders were more likely to have experienced childhood trauma. Although the work was important, the reviewed studies had certain limitations. The authors did not control for the various kinds of abuse (e.g., physical, sexual, psychological) and the studies generally had small numbers of subjects. Moreover, only a small number of studies examined subjects who were children or adolescents at that time, and there was a mixture of inpatient and outpatient samples of which there was only a minority with a diagnosis of psychosis. In addition, the studies that investigated subjects with a diagnosis of psychosis did not always focus specifically on schizophrenia. Finally, there were variations between studies in how childhood trauma was defined and measured, and studies did not always account for comorbid disorders and illnesses.

More recent studies have found a link between childhood sexual abuse and schizophrenia as well as positive symptoms in psychotic patients, specifically auditory hallucinations (Sheffield, Williams, Blackford, & Heckers, 2013). Patients with auditory hallucinations had the greatest level of abuse, specifically sexual abuse. A second study found that an overwhelming majority of patients with schizophrenia spectrum disorders had experienced at least one stressful or traumatic event in their lifetime, and the group had experienced a median of seven traumatic events (O'Hare, Shen, & Sherrer, 2013). Although this study examined schizophrenia specifically rather than psychotic symptoms in general, it did not distinguish abuse from other types of traumatic events.

Despite these initial findings, however, Spataro, Mullen, Burgess, Wells, and Moss (2004) noted that positive symptoms, including hallucinations, can be seen in cases of posttraumatic stress disorder, and for individuals who have experienced any kind of child abuse, schizophrenia symptoms may be confounded with symptoms of posttraumatic stress disorder, which can be a comorbid diagnosis. Therefore, although child abuse may be a risk factor for schizophrenia, there may not be a causal connection between them.

INFECTIONS AFTER BIRTH

In addition to the large body of evidence suggesting that prenatal infections give rise to an increased risk of schizophrenia, some mixed evidence has suggested a link between certain infections in those who already have developed schizophrenia (Yolken & Torrey, 2008). Torrey, Bartko, Lun, and Yolken (2007) found a twofold increased risk of schizophrenia in those with *T. gondii* infections; these findings have been replicated by some other groups. The direction of causation, however, is unclear. One study that attempted to address this, by Niebuhr et al. (2008), found that toxoplasma IgG antibodies in archived serum specimens of the US military drawn within 6 months of diagnosis were associated with a modest increase in risk of schizophrenia, although this relationship was not found in serum drawn before the 6 months leading up to diagnosis.

Amminger et al. (2007) found that subjects with more severe positive psychotic symptoms (although without a diagnosis of schizophrenia) were more likely to be seropositive for toxoplasma IgG, and the more severe the symptoms, the higher the level of IgG antibody. Finally, cytomegalovirus has been investigated as a possible risk factor for schizophrenia postnatally, but there have been mixed results (for a review, see Brown & Derkits, 2010).

Dalman et al. (2008) examined records of hospital admissions for CNS infections in children between birth and 12 years of age for nonaffective psychiatric illnesses from 14 years of age onwards for all the children born within a cohort in Sweden. These infections were further divided into bacterial versus viral infections and then divided more specifically into named illnesses such as the mumps virus and cytomegalovirus. A slightly higher risk for both nonaffective psychotic illnesses and schizophrenia was found to be associated with viral CNS infections, specifically the mumps virus and cytomegalovirus, but not with bacterial infection.

Some studies have examined whether antibiotic or antiviral medications that treat cytomegalovirus or *T. gondii* improve the severity of psychotic symptoms (Dickerson, Boronow, Stallings, Origoni, & Yolken, 2003; Dickerson, Stallings, Boronow, Origoni, & Yolken, 2009).

These two studies have produced positive and negative results, respectively. One possible reason for these conflicting findings is that the neuropathology may have been treated too late to be reversible with antibiotics.

GENE–ENVIRONMENT INTERACTION

It is unlikely that the environmental exposures reviewed here act alone to cause psychopathology. Rather, many investigators have proposed integrative, or diathesis–stress models, that incorporate genetic influences, including interactions between genetic mutations and environmental factors. According to this model, by interacting with genetic influences, these environmental factors impact development of the brain during critical periods and trigger the onset of psychotic syndromes such as schizophrenia (Brown, 2011; Brown & Derkits, 2010; van Os, Kenis, & Rutten, 2010). Various environmental influences act on sensitive subgroups of the population with a genetic predisposition to such environmental effects (van Os, Rutten, & Poulton, 2008).

This vulnerability is especially salient during critical periods of neuronal and brain development (Arnsten, 2009). Furthermore, repeated exposure to these insults has been associated with more severe psychotic symptoms, especially in those who experienced adversity early in life who become more sensitive to environmental stress in adulthood, possibly from altered dopamine activity in the brain (Glaser, van Os, Portegijs, & Myin-Germeys, 2006).

One example of a gene–environment interaction is provided by a potential relationship between the genes that encode the major histocompatibility complex class I proteins, which have been associated with schizophrenia in genome-wide association studies (Walters et al., 2013) and prenatal infection (McAllister, 2014). These proteins are necessary for proper functioning of not only T lymphocytes, but also synaptic function. It has been suggested that individuals with these mutations are more sensitive to the effects of a prenatal infection or other environmental events that activate the immune system (Brown & Derkits, 2010). According to this hypothesis, this aberrant immune response subsequently leads to a greater degree of modification of major histocompatibility complex class I function, leading to abnormal synaptic function, which is abnormal in schizophrenia (Stephan, Baldeweg, & Friston, 2006). In this way, major histocompatibility complex molecules might be one of many mediators between genetic and environmental contributions to schizophrenia.

Recent work by Kannan, Sawa, and Pletnikov (2013) on mouse models of gene–environment interaction has supported the diathesis-stress model. The authors found an interaction between psychological stress and the Disrupted-in-Schizophrenia-1, a genetic candidate for schizophrenia, in producing neurochemical and behavioral deficits. Other studies have found interaction effects between specific genes and stressors such as immune activation (Vuillermot et al., 2012) and cannabis use (Behan et al., 2012). In a recent study of interaction between environmental events, Giovanoli et al. (2013) demonstrated that exposure in mice to prenatal infection, combined with trauma during peripuberty, leads to pathological effects on behavior and neurochemistry during adulthood.

Intervention and Prevention

One of the key implications of research on environmental factors in schizophrenia is a potential role in prevention. Primary prevention includes interventions that attempt to reduce the incidence of schizophrenia by providing feasible interventions either to the general public ("universal prevention") or to specifically targeted populations (Gordon, 1983; Mrazek & Haggerty, 1994). Secondary prevention aims to avert serious symptomatology by means of early intervention at the first stage of pathology. Tertiary prevention aims to provide the most efficient treatment and rehabilitation to subjects already diagnosed with the disorder to prevent future relapse.

One metric used to assess the potential impact of a preventive approach is the population attributable risk, which is an estimate of the number of cases of a disease that could be prevented in a population if a certain risk factor was completely eliminated from that population (Brown & McGrath, 2010). Related to the population attributable risk is the number needed to prevent. This is a measure of the number of people from whom a specific risk factor would need to be removed to prevent a single new case of a disease.

Another factor that is used in decisions on prevention and intervention is risk assessment. The Global Burden of Disease project uses risk assessment to comparatively examine disorders to ascertain which have the greatest public impact. This allows policy makers to decide upon appropriate allocations of funding for proper treatment and prevention of different disorders (Murray & Lopez, 1996), taking public safety and known risks of the intervention or research into account.

At least some prenatal infections are preventable. We had found that the population attributable risk for exposure to influenza, *T. gondii*, and genital infections was about 30% (Brown & Derkits, 2010), meaning that if each of these infections were entirely eliminated from the pregnant population that we studied, nearly one-third of cases of schizophrenia could be eliminated. Although it is not feasible to entirely eliminate these infections and the findings were calculated only from estimates from our cohort studies, and thus may vary by population, this suggests that preventive efforts may lead to a sizable reduction in the incidence of schizophrenia.

With regard to influenza, vaccination is readily available in developed countries and continually updated to reflect new strains that come into existence every year. Maternal influenza is a potential risk factor not only for schizophrenia in the offspring, but also for other abnormal outcomes of the pregnancy, such as bipolar disorder (see the discussion in the next section) as well as fetal mortality (Zaman et al., 2008). Therefore, pregnant women have been identified as a population that should be targeted for influenza vaccination (Centers for Disease Control and Prevention (CDC), 2013). We have also argued that women planning a pregnancy and/or of reproductive age should consider influenza vaccination (Brown & Derkits, 2010). Furthermore, it might be prudent to increase efforts for influenza vaccination among the wider population to control the spread of the virus to pregnant women and to newborn infants.

Toxoplasma gondii is also preventable. Most individuals become infected with this parasite by ingesting oocyst-infected soil or water, eating contaminated food that is undercooked, or lacking proper hygienic measures when changing cat litter boxes (Elmore et al., 2010). Therefore, by using safety precautions such as handwashing after contact with soil, using gloves when changing cat litter boxes as well as thorough cooking practices, the incidence of *T. gondii* may be reduced in the population. Furthermore, all of these recommendations can be implemented with little or no cost.

Genital and reproductive infections, which are usually sexually transmitted infections may be difficult to control in the population, but general education about the risks of unsafe sex and use of condoms reduce the frequency of new cases of sexually transmitted infections in communities (Vivancos, Abubakar, Phillips-Howard, & Hunter, 2013). Furthermore, a vaccine has been developed for a specific sexually transmitted infection called human papillomavirus; universally vaccinating children against human papillomavirus may prevent patients from developing as they grow older and become sexually active (Deleré et al., 2014). Furthermore, prompt and proper treatment of those already infected with sexually transmitted infections may reduce the impact of the infection or cure it completely, should treatment be timely enough.

Prevention of prenatal malnutrition may be more challenging than preventing certain prenatal infections, given that protein-calorie malnutrition is commonly caused by social adversity or factors that require great effort to control. However, micronutrient deficiencies in the pregnant population are more readily preventable through improved obstetric counseling, education, and preventive interventions. For example, considerable proportions of the pregnant population do not receive adequate quantities of vitamins such as folic acid (Ray, Singh, & Burrows, 2004) or vitamin D (Bodnar et al., 2007), deficiencies of which have been implicated in schizophrenia (see the discussion in the prenatal malnutrition section) and that can be eliminated by taking prenatal vitamins.

Finally, risk factors such as cannabis use are widespread and difficult to control; indeed, some US states are beginning to overturn these laws and marijuana is legal in many other countries (Palamar, Ompad, & Petkova, 2014). One potential avenue of intervention might involve counseling on the effects of cannabis use among individuals with a family history of schizophrenia.

FUTURE DIRECTIONS

We suggest several directions for future work in this area. First, in addition to replicating previous associations, a significant priority should be given to the identification of new environmental exposures that may be involved in the pathogenesis of schizophrenia. Translational research on animal models as well as emerging work in clinical neuroscience will have an important role to play in this regard in that this work is expected to identify novel candidates for testing in epidemiologic studies. A second key issue is to use this work for the identification of common pathophysiologic pathways. As an example, we and other groups aim to examine how effects of prenatal infections are mediated through inflammatory pathways such as cytokines and C-reactive protein. Third, it will be key to study developmental trajectories, as revealed by several approaches including neurocognitive testing and neuroimaging. This will allow for relating risk factors identified from epidemiologic studies with pathobiologic processes in schizophrenia. Fourth, this work has significant future implications for genetics and epigenetics. Regarding genetics, we expect that future work will allow for the discovery of interactions between environmental exposures and susceptibility genes, or allow for the identification of new susceptibility genes by studying subjects with a common environmental exposure that plays a causal role. A related avenue of exploration is epigenetics: As discussed previously, it is likely that environmental exposures exert their influences via effects on the epigenome, and this may be one mechanism by which gene–environment interactions operate. Fifth, as discussed previously, this work could have significant potential for future public health interventions aimed at prevention of the environmental exposures and may help to stimulate responsible agencies, including those of governmental and nongovernmental organizations to develop feasible prevention strategies. Sixth, it will be critical to assess whether the environmental exposures that are related to schizophrenia may be risk factors for other psychiatric disorders. Our group has demonstrated, for example, that maternal influenza may be a risk factor for bipolar disorder with psychotic features among offspring (Canetta et al., 2014) and that elevated maternal C-reactive protein is a risk factor for both autism (Brown et al., 2014) and for schizophrenia (Canetta et al., 2014).

CONCLUSION

Epidemiologic studies of schizophrenia have revealed increasing evidence that environmental factors at key periods of life increase vulnerability to the disorder. These factors include infection, malnutrition, cannabis use, and social factors such as migration, childhood trauma, and socioeconomic status. These effects have been supported by an expanding literature on these same risks in animal models and by new research on the clinical pathobiology of schizophrenia. Although still in its infancy, it is likely that interactions between genetic and environmental, and between different environmental exposures, account for a considerable risk of the disorder. Implications of these studies include preventive approaches, and offer suggestions for future research that may capitalize on emerging findings from translational research.

References

Ames, B. (2001). DNA damage from micronutrient deficiencies is likely to be a major cause of cancer. *Mutation Research, 475*(1–2), 7–20.

Amminger, G. P., McGorry, P. D., Berger, G. E., Wade, D., Yung, A. R., Phillips, L. J., et al. (2007). Antibodies to infectious agents in individuals at ultra-high risk for psychosis. *Biological Psychiatry, 61,* 1215–1217.

Arnsten, A. F. (2009). Stress signaling pathways that impair prefrontal cortex structure and function. *Nature Reviews Neuroscience, 10,* 410–422.

Arseneault, L., Cannon, M., Poulton, R., Murray, R., Caspi, A., & Moffitt, T. E. (2002). Cannabis use in adolescence and risk for adult psychosis: longitudinal prospective study. *British Medical Journal, 325,* 1212–1213.

Bao, Y., Ibram, G., Blaner, W. S., Quesenberry, C. P., Shen, L., McKeague, I. W., et al. (2012). Low maternal retinol as a risk factor for schizophrenia in adult offspring. *Schizophrenia Research, 137*(1–3), 159–165.

Bauman, M. D., Losif, A.-M., Smith, S. E. P., Bregere, C., Amaral, D. G., & Patterson, P. H. (2014). Activation of the maternal immune system during pregnancy alters behavioral development of rhesus monkey offspring. *Biological Psychiatry, 75,* 332–341.

Behan, A. T., Hryniewiecka, M., O'Tuathaigh, C. M., Kinsella, A., Cannon, M., Karayiorgou, M., et al. (2012). Chronic adolescent exposure to delta-9-tetrahydrocannabinol in COMT mutant mice: impact on indices of dopaminergic, endocannabinoid and GABAergic pathways. *Neuropsychopharmacology, 37*(7), 1773–1783.

Blomstrom, A., Karlsson, H., Wicks, S., Yang, S., Yoken, R. H., & Dalman, C. (2012). Maternal antibodies to infectious agents and risk for non-affective psychoses in the offspring – a matched case-control study. *Schizophrenia Research, 140*(1–3), 25–30.

Bodnar, L. M., Simhan, H. N., Powers, R. W., Frank, M. P., Cooperstein, E., & Roberts, J. M. (2007). High prevalence of vitamin D insufficiency in black and white pregnant women residing in the northern United States and their neonates. *Journal of Nutrition, 137,* 447–452.

Brown, A. S. (2011). The environment and susceptibility to schizophrenia. *Progress in Neurobiology, 93,* 23–58.

Brown, A. S., & Derkits, E. J. (2010). Prenatal infection and schizophrenia: a review of epidemiologic and translational studies. *American Journal of Psychiatry, 167*(3), 261–280.

Brown, A. S., & McGrath, J. J. (2010). The prevention of schizophrenia. *Schizophrenia Bulletin, 37*(2), 257–261.

Brown, A. S., Begg, M. D., Gravenstein, S., Schaefer, C. A., Wyatt, R. J., Bresnahan, M. A., et al. (2004). Serologic evidence for prenatal influenza in the etiology of schizophrenia. *Archives of General Psychiatry, 61,* 774–780.

Brown, A. S., Bottiglieri, T., Schaefer, C. A., Quesenberry, C. P., Jr., Liu, L., Bresnahan, M., et al. (2007). Elevated prenatal homocysteine levels as a risk factor for schizophrenia. *Archives of General Psychiatry, 64*(1), 31–39.

Brown, A. S., Cohen, P., Harkavy-Friedman, J., Babulas, V., Malaspina, D., Gorman, J. M., et al. (2001). Prenatal rubella, premorbid abnormalities, and adult schizophrenia. *Biological Psychiatry, 49*(6), 473–486.

Brown, A. S., Hooton, J., Schaefer, C. A., Zhang, H., Petkova, E., Babulas, V., et al. (2005). Elevated maternal interleukin-8 levels and risk of schizophrenia in adult offspring. *American Journal of Psychiatry, 161,* 889–895.

Brown, A. S., Michaeline, B., & Susser, E. S. (2005). Schizophrenia: environmental epidemiology. In B. J. Sadock, & V. A. Sadock (Eds.), *Kaplan & Sadock's comprehensive textbook of psychiatry* (pp. 1371–1380). Philadelphia: Lippincott Williams & Wilkins.

Brown, A. S., van Os, J., Driessens, C., Hoek, H. W., & Susser, E. S. (2000). Further evidence of relation between prenatal famine and major affective disorder. *American Journal of Psychiatry, 157*(2), 190–195.

Brown, A. S., Schaefer, C. A., Quesenberry, C. P., Jr., Liu, L., Babulas, V. P., & Susser, E. S. (2005). Maternal exposure to toxoplasmosis and risk of schizophrenia in adult offspring. *American Journal of Psychiatry, 162,* 767–773.

Brown, A. S., Schaefer, C. A., Wyatt, R. J., Begg, M. D., Goetz, R., Bresnahan, M. A., et al. (2002). Paternal age and risk of schizophrenia in adult offspring. *American Journal of Psychiatry, 159,* 1528–1533.

Brown, A. S., Sourander, A., Hinkka-Yli-Salomaki, S., McKeague, I. W., Sundvall, J., & Surcel, H. M. (2014). Elevated maternal C-reactive protein and autism in a national birth cohort. *Molecular Psychiatry, 19*(2), 259–264.

Brown, A. S., Vinogradov, S., Kremen, W. S., Poole, J. H., Deicken, R. F., Penner, J. D., et al. (2009). Prenatal exposure to maternal infection and executive dysfunction in adult schizophrenia. *American Journal of Psychiatry, 166*(6), 683–690.

Buchanan, R. W., & Carpenter, W. T. (2005). Concept of schizophrenia. In B. J. Sadock, & V. A. Sadock (Eds.), *Kaplan & Sadock's comprehensive textbook of psychiatry* (pp. 1329–1345). Philadelphia: Lippincott Williams & Wilkins.

Buka, S. L., Cannon, T. D., Torrey, E. F., & Yolken, R. H. (2008). Maternal exposure to herpes simplex virus and risk of psychosis among adult offspring. *Biological Psychiatry, 63,* 809–815.

Buka, S. L., Tsuang, M. T., Torrey, E. F., Klebanoff, M. A., Bernstein, D., & Yolken, R. H. (2001). Maternal infections and subsequent psychosis among offspring. *Archives of General Psychiatry, 58,* 1032–1037.

Buka, S. L., Tsuang, M. T., Torrey, E. F., Klebanoff, M. A., Wagner, R. L., & Yolken, R. H. (2001). Maternal cytokine levels during pregnancy and adult psychosis. *Brain, Behavior, and Immunity, 15,* 411–420.

Canetta, S., Sourander, A., Surcel, H. M., Hinkka-Yli-Salomaki, S., Leiviska, J., Kellendonk, C., et al. (2014). Elevated maternal C-reactive protein and increased risk of schizophrenia in a national birth cohort. *American Journal of Psychiatry, 171*(9), 960–968.

Cannon, M., Jones, P., & Murray, R. (2002). Obstetric complications and schizophrenia: historical and meta-analytic review. *American Journal of Psychiatry, 159*(7), 1080–1092.

Cantor-Graae, E., & Selten, J. P. (2005). Schizophrenia and migration: a meta-analysis and review. *American Journal of Psychiatry, 162*(1), 12–24.

Centers for Disease Control and Prevention. (2013). *Vaccines for pregnant women.* Retrieved from http://www.cdc.gov/vaccines/adults/rec-vac/pregnant.html.

Crane, S., Wojtowycz, M., Dye, T., Aubry, R., & Artal, R. (1997). Association between prepregnancy obesity and the risk of cesarean delivery. *Obstetrics and Gynecology, 89*(2), 213–216.

D'Souza, D. C., Abi-Saab, W. M., Madonick, S., Forselius-Bielen, K., Doersch, A., Braley, G., et al. (2005). Delta-9-tetrahydrocannabinol effects in schizophrenia: implications for cognition, psychosis, and addiction. *Biological Psychiatry, 57*, 294–608.

D'Souza, D. C., Perry, E., MacDougall, L., Ammerman, Y., Cooper, T., Wu, Y. T., et al. (2004). The psychotomimetic effects of intravenous delta-9-tetrahydrocannabinol in healthy individuals: implications for psychosis. *Neuropsychopharmacology, 29*, 1558–1572.

Dalman, C., & Allebeck, P. (2002). Paternal age and schizophrenia: further support for an association. *American Journal of Psychiatry, 159*(9), 1591–1592.

Dalman, C., Allebeck, P., Gunnell, D., Harrison, G., Kristensson, K., Lewis, G., et al. (2008). Infections in the CNS during childhood and the risk of subsequent psychotic illness: a cohort study of more than one million Swedish subjects. *American Journal of Psychiatry, 165*, 59–65.

Davis, J. O., Phelps, J. A., & Bracha, H. S. (1995). Prenatal development of monozygotic twins and concordance for schizophrenia. *Schizophrenia Bulletin, 21*(3), 357–366.

Dealberto, M.-J. (2010). Ethnic origin and increased risk for schizophrenia in immigrants to countries of recent and longstanding immigration. *Acta Psychiatrica Scandinavica, 121*, 325–339.

Deleré, Y., Wichmann, O., Klug, S. J., van der Sande, M., Terhardt, M., Zepp, F., et al. (2014). The efficacy and duration of vaccine protection against human papillomavirus: a systematic review and meta-analysis. *Deutsches Ärzteblatt International, 111*(35–36), 584–591.

Dickerson, F. B., Boronow, J. J., Stallings, C. R., Origoni, A., & Yolken, R. (2003). Reduction of symptoms by valacyclovir in cytomegalovirus-seropositive individuals with schizophrenia. *American Journal of Psychiatry, 160*, 2234–2236.

Dickerson, F. B., Stallings, C. R., Boronow, J. J., Origoni, A., & Yolken, R. (2009). A double-blind trial of adjunctive azithromycin in individuals with schizophrenia who are seropositive for *Toxoplasma gondii*. *Schizophrenia Research, 112*, 198–199.

Dohrenwend, B. P., Levav, I., Shrout, P. E., Schwartz, S., Naveh, G., Link, B. G., et al. (1992). Socioeconomic status and psychiatric disorders: the causation-selection issue. *Science, 255*, 946–952.

Dukes, C. S., Luft, B. J., Durack, D. T., Scheld, W. M., & Whitley, R. J. (1997). Toxoplasmosis. In W. M. Scheld, R. J. Whitley, & D. T. Durack (Eds.), *Infections of the central nervous system* (pp. 785–806). Philadelphia: Lippincott-Raven.

Eaton, W. W. (1999). Evidence for universality and uniformity of schizophrenia around the world: assessment and implications. In W. F. Gattaz, & H. Hafner (Eds.), *Search for the causes of schizophrenia* (4th ed.). Berlin: Springer-Verlag.

Ellman, L. M., Vinogradov, S., Kremen, W. S., Poole, J. H., Kern, D. M., Deicken, R. F., et al. (2012). Low maternal hemoglobin during pregnancy and diminished neuromotor and neurocognitive performance in offspring with schizophrenia. *Schizophrenia Research, 138*(1), 81–87.

Elmore, S. A., Jones, J. L., Conrad, P. A., Patton, S., Lindsay, D. S., & Dubey, J. P. (2010). *Toxolasma gondii*: epidemology, feline clinical aspects, and prevention. *Trends in Parasitology, 26*(4), 190–196.

El-Saadi, O., Pedersen, C. B., McNeil, T. F., Saha, S., Welham, J., O'Callaghan, E., et al. (2004). Paternal and maternal age as risk factors for psychosis: findings from Denmark, Sweden and Australia. *Schizophrenia Research, 67*(2–3), 227–236.

Epstein, K. A., & Kumra, S. (2014). Executive attention impairment in adolescents with schizophrenia who have used cannabis. *Schizophrenia Research, 157*(1–3), 48–54.

Fergusson, D. M., Horwood, L. J., & Swain-Campbell, N. R. (2003). Cannabis dependence and psychotic symptoms in young people. *Psychological Medicine, 33*.

Flynn, S. W., Lang, D. J., Mackay, A. L., Goghari, V., Vavasour, I. M., Whittall, K. P., et al. (2003). Abnormalities of myelination in schizophrenia detected in vivo with MRI, and post-mortem with analysis of oligodendrocyte proteins. *Molecular Psychiatry, 8*, 811–820.

Fromer, M., Pocklington, A. J., Kavanagh, D. H., Williams, H. J., Dwyer, S., Gormley, P., et al. (2014). De novo mutation in schizophrenia implicate synaptic network. *Nature, 506*(7487), 179–184.

Giovanoli, S., Engler, H., Engler, A., Richetto, J., Voget, M., Willi, R., et al. (2013). Stress in puberty unmasks latent neuropathological consequences of prenatal immune activation in mice. *Science, 339*(6123), 1095–1099.

Giordano, G. N., Ohlsoon, H., Sundquist, K., Sundquist, J., & Kendler, K. S. (2015). The association between cannabis abuse and subsequent schizophrenia: a Swedish national co-relative control study. *Psychological Medicine, 45*(2), 407–414.

Glaser, J. P., van Os, J., Portegijs, P. J., & Myin-Germeys, I. (2006). Childhood trauma and emotional reactivity to daily life stress in adult frequent attenders in general practitioners. *Journal of Psychosomatic Research, 61*, 229–236.

Gold, J. M., & Green, M. F. (2005). Schizophrenia: cognition. In B. J. Sadock, & V. A. Sadock (Eds.), *Kaplan & Sadock's comprehensive textbook of psychiatry* (pp. 1436–1448). Philadelphia: Lippincott Williams & Wilkins.

Gordon, R. (1983). An operational classification of disease prevention. *Public Health Reports, 98*, 107–109.

Güngör, N. K. (2014). Overweight and obesity in children and adolescents. *Journal of Clinical Research in Pediatric Endocrinology, 6*(3), 129–143.

Hare, E. H., Price, J. S., & Slater, E. (1972). Parenthal social class in psychiatric patients. *British Journal of Psychiatry, 121*, 515–534.

Harper, K., Hibbeln, J. R., Deckelbaum, R., Bresnahan, M., Quesenberry, C. A., Schaefer, C. A., et al. (2011). Maternal serum docosahexaenoic acid and schizophrenia spectrum disorders in adult offspring. *Schizophrenia Research, 128*(1–3), 30–36.

Harvey, L., & Boksa, P. (2014). Additive effects of maternal iron deficiency and prenatal immune activation on adult behaviors in rat offspring. *Brain, Behavior, and Immunity, 40*, 27–37.

Heijmans, B., Tobi, E., Stein, A., Putter, H., Blauw, G., Susser, E., et al. (2008). Persistent epigenetic differences associated with prenatal exposure to famine in humans. *Proceedings of the National Academy of Sciences of the United States of America, 105*(44), 17046–17049.

Henquet, C., Krabbendam, L., Spauwen, J., Kaplan, C., Lieb, R., Wittchen, H. U., et al. (2005). Prospective cohort study of cannabis use, predisposition for psychosis, and psychotic symptoms in young people. *British Medical Journal, 330*, 11.

Hoek, H. W., Brown, A. S., & Susser, E. (1997). The Dutch famine and schizophrenia spectrum disorders. *Social Psychiatry and Psychiatric Epidemiology, 33*(8), 373–379.

Insel, B. J., Schaefer, C. A., McKeague, I. W., Susser, E. S., & Brown, A. S. (2008). Maternal iron deficiency and the risk of schizophrenia in offspring. *Archives of General Psychiatry, 65*(10), 1136–1144.

Jablensky, A., Sartorius, N., Ernberg, G., Anker, M., Korten, A., Cooper, J. E., et al. (1992). Schizophrenia: manifestations, incidence and course in different cultures. A World Health Organization ten-country study. *Psychological Medicine Monograph Supplement, 20*, 1–97.

Kannan, G., Sawa, A., & Pletnikov, M. V. (2013). Mouse models of gene–environment interactions in schizophrenia. *Neurobiology of Disease, 57*, 5–11.

Kitahara, C. M., Trabert, B., Katki, H. A., Chaturvedi, A. K., Kemp, T. J., Pinto, L. A., et al. (2014). Body mass index, physical activity, and serum markers of inflammation, immunity, and insulin resistance. *Cancer Epidemiology, Biomarkers & Prevention, 23*(12), 2840–2849.

Kong, A., Frigge, M. L., Masson, G., Besenbacher, S., Sulem, P., Magnusson, G., et al. (2012). Rate of de novo mutations and the importance of father's age to disease risk. *Nature, 488*, 471–475.

Kwok, W. Is there evidence that social class at birth increases risk of psychosis? A systematic review. *International Journal of Social Psychiatry*, in press.

Lauriello, J., Bustillo, J. R., & Keith, S. J. (2005). Schizophrenia: scope of the problem. In B. J. Sadock, & V. A. Sadock (Eds.), *Kaplan & Sadock's comprehensive textbook of psychiatry* (pp. 1345–1354). Philadelphia: Lippincott Williams & Wilkins.

Lowing, P. A., Mirsky, A. F., & Pereira, R. (1983). The inheritance of schizophrenia spectrum disorders: a reanalysis of the Danish adoptee study data. *American Journal of Psychiatry, 140*(9), 1167–1171.

Luo, X., Huang, L., Han, L., Luo, Z., Hu, F., Tieu, R., et al. (2014). Systematic prioritization and integrative analysis of copy number variations in schizophrenia reveal key schizophrenia susceptibility genes. *Schizophrenia Bulletin, 40*(6), 1285–1299.

Makikyro, T., Isohanni, M., Moring, J., Oja, H., Hakko, H., Jones, P., et al. (1997). Is a child's risk of early onset schizophrenia increased in the highest social class? *Schizophrenia Research, 23*, 245–252.

Malaspina, D., Harlap, S., Fennig, S., Heiman, D., Nahon, D., Feldman, D., et al. (2001). Advancing paternal age and the risk of schizophrenia. *Archives of General Psychiatry, 58*, 361–386.

March, D., Hatch, S. L., Morgan, C., Kirkbride, J. B., Bresnahan, M., Fearon, P., et al. (2008). Psychosis and place. *Epidemiologic Reviews, 30*, 84–100.

McAllister, A. K. (2014). Major histocompatibility complex I in brain development and schizophrenia. *Biological Psychiatry, 75*, 262–268.

McClellan, J., Susser, E., & King, M. (2006). Maternal famine, de novo mutations, and schizophrenia. *Journal of the American Medical Association, 296*(5), 582–584.

McGrath, J., Eyles, D., & Mowry, B. (2003). Low maternal vitamin D as a risk factor for schizophrenia: a pilot study using banked sera. *Schizophrenia Research, 63*(1–2), 73–78.

McGuffin, P., Owen, M. J., & Farmer, A. E. (1995). Genetic basis of schizophrenia. *Lancet, 346*(8976), 678–682.

Merikangas, A. S., Segurado, R., Cormican, P., Heron, E. A., Anney, R. J., Moore, S., et al. (2014). The phenotypic manifestations of rare CNVs in schizophrenia. *Schizophrenia Research, 158*(1–3), 255–260.

Meyer, U., Yee, B. K., & Feldon, J. (2007). The neurodevelopmental impact of prenatal infections at different times of pregnancy: the earlier the worse? *Neuroscientist, 13*(3), 241–256.

Morgan, C., & Fisher, H. (2007). Environment and schizophrenia: environmental factors in schizophrenia: childhood trauma—a critical review. *Schizophrenia Bulletin, 33*, 3–10.

Mortensen, P. B., Norgaard-Pedersen, B., Waltoft, B. L., Sorensen, T. L., Hougaard, D., Torrey, E. F., et al. (2007). *Toxoplasma gondii* as a risk factor for early-onset schizophrenia: analysis of filter paper blood samples obtained at birth. *Biological Psychiatry, 61*, 688–693.

Mortensen, P. B., Pedersen, C. B., Westergaard, T., Wohlfahrt, J., Ewald, H., Mors, O., et al. (1999). Effects of family history and place and season of birth on the risk of schizophrenia. *New England Journal of Medicine, 340*, 603–608.

Mrazek, P. J., & Haggerty, R. J. (1994). *Reducing risk for mental Disorders: Frontiers for preventive intervention research*. Washington, DC: National Academic Press.

Mulvany, F., O'Callaghan, E., Takei, N., Byrne, M., Fearon, P., & Larkin, C. (2001). Effect of social class at birth on risk and presentation of schizophrenia: case–control study. *British Medical Journal, 323*, 1398–1401.

Murray, C. J., & Lopez, A. D. (1996). *The global Burden of disease*. Boston, MA: Harvard School of Public Health.

Niebuhr, D. W., Millikan, A. M., Cowan, D. N., Yolken, R., Li, Y., & Weber, N. S. (2008). Selected infectious agents and risk of schizophrenia among U.S. military personnel. *American Journal of Psychiatry, 165*, 99–106.

O'Hare, T., Shen, C., & Sherrer, M. (2013). Differences in trauma and posttraumatic stress symptoms in clients with schizophrenia spectrum and major mood disorders. *Psychiatry Research, 205*(1–2), 85–89.

Odegaard, O. (1932). Emigration and insanity. *Acta Psychiatrica et Neurologica Scandinavica, Supplementum, 4*, 1–206.

Paashuis-Lew, Y., & Heddle, J. (1998). Spontaneous mutation during fetal development and post-natal growth. *Mutagenesis, 13*(6), 613–617.

Palamar, J. J., Ompad, D. C., & Petkova, E. (2014). Correlates of intentions to use cannabis among US high school seniors in the case of cannabis legalization. *International Journal of Drug Policy, 25*, 424–435.

Pedersen, C. B., & Mortensen, P. B. (2001). Evidence of a dose–response relationship between urbanicity during upbringing and schizophrenia risk. *Archives of General Psychiatry, 58*, 1039–1046.

Pedersen, C. B., & Mortensen, P. B. (2006). Are the cause(s) responsible for urban–rural differences in schizophrenia risk rooted in families or in individuals? *American Journal of Epidemiology, 163*, 971–978.

Penner, J. D., & Brown, A. S. (2007). Prenatal infectious and nutritional factors and risk of adult schizophrenia. *Expert Review of Neurotherapeutics, 7*(7), 797–805.

Picker, J. D., & Coyle, J. T. (2005). Do maternal folate and homocysteine levels play a role in neurodevelopmental processes that increase risk for schizophrenia? *Harvard Review of Psychiatry, 13*(4), 197–205.

Piper, M., Beneyto, M., Burne, T. H., Eyles, D. W., Lewis, D. A., & McGrath, J. J. (2012). The neurodevelopmental hypothesis of schizophrenia: convergent clues from epidemiology and neuropathology. *Psychiatric Clinics of North America, 35*(3), 571–584.

Power, R. A., Verweij, K. J., Zuhair, M., Montgomery, G. W., Henders, A. K., Heath, A. C., et al. (2014). Genetic predisposition to schizophrenia associated with increased use of cannabis. *Molecular Psychiatry, 19*, 1201–1204.

Ray, J. G., Singh, G., & Burrows, R. F. (2004). Evidence for suboptimal use of periconceptional folic acid supplements globally. *BJOG, 111*(5), 399–408.

Reiss, D. (1976). The family and schizophrenia. *American Journal of Psychiatry, 133*(2), 181–185.

Rippey, C., Walsh, T., Gulsuner, S., Brodsky, M., Nord, A. S., Gasperini, M., et al. (2013). Formation of chimeric genes by copy-number variation as a mutational mechanism in schizophrenia. *American Journal of Human Genetics, 93*(4), 697–710.

Sariaslan, A., Larsson, H., D'Onofrio, B., Langstrom, N., Fazel, S., & Lichtenstein, P. (2015). Does population density and neighborhood deprivation predict schizophrenia? A nationwide Swedish family-based study of 2.4 million individuals. *Schizophrenia Bulletin, 41*(2), 494–502.

Schaefer, C., Brown, A., Wyatt, R., Kline, J., Begg, M., Bresnahan, M., et al. (2000). Maternal prepregnant body mass and risk of schizophrenia in adult offspring. *Schizophrenia Bulletin, 26*(2), 275–286.

Selten, J.-P., Cantor-Graae, E., & Kahn, R. S. (2007). Migration and schizophrenia. *Current Opinion in Psychiatry, 20*, 111–115.

Sheffield, J. M., Williams, L. E., Blackford, J. U., & Heckers, S. (2013). Childhood sexual abuse increases risk of auditory hallucinations in psychotic disorders. *Comprehensive Psychiatry, 54*(7), 1098–1104.

Siegel, M., Fuerst, H. T., & Guinee, V. F. (1971). Rubella epidemicity and embryopathy: results of a long-term prospective study. *American Journal of Diseases of Children, 121*(6), 469–473.

Solomon, C., Willett, W., Carey, V., Rich-Edwards, J., Hunter, D., Colditz, G., et al. (1997). A prospective study of pregravid determinants of gestational diabetes mellitus. *Journal of the American Medical Association, 278*(13), 1078–1083.

Sorensen, H. J., Nielsen, P. R., Pedersen, C. B., & Mortensen, P. B. (2011). Association between prepartum maternal iron deficiency and offspring risk of schizophrenia: population-based cohort study with linkage of Danish national registers. *Schizophrenia Bulletin, 37*(5), 982–987.

Spataro, J., Mullen, P. E., Burgess, P. M., Wells, D. L., & Moss, S. A. (2004). Impact of child sexual abuse on mental health: prospective study in males and females. *British Journal of Psychiatry, 184*, 416–421.

Stephan, K. E., Baldeweg, T., & Friston, K. J. (2006). Synaptic plasticity and dysconnection in schizophrenia. *Biological Psychiatry, 59*, 929–939.

Susser, E., Neugebauer, R., Hoek, H. W., Brown, A. S., Lin, S., Labovitz, D., et al. (1996). Schizophrenia after prenatal famine. Further evidence. *Archives of General Psychiatry, 53*(1), 25–31.

Tienari, P., Sorri, A., Lahti, I., Naarala, M., Wahlberg, K. E., Moring, J., et al. (1987). Genetic and psychosocial factors in schizophrenia: the Finnish adoptive family study. *Schizophrenia Bulletin, 13*(3), 477–484.

Timms, D. (1998). Gender, social mobility and psychiatric diagnoses. *Society Science & Medicine, 46*, 1235–1247.

Torrey, E. F., Bartko, J. J., Lun, Z. R., & Yolken, R. H. (2007). Antibodies to *Toxoplasma gondii* in patients with schizophrenia: a meta-analysis. *Schizophrenia Bulletin, 33*, 729–736.

Tsuchiya, K. J., Takagai, S., Kawai, M., Matsumoto, H., Nakamura, K., Minabe, Y., et al. (2005). Advanced paternal age associated with an elevated risk for schizophrenia in offspring in a Japanese population. *Schizophrenia Research, 76*(2–3), 337–342.

United Nations Office on Drugs and Crime. (2009). *UNODC world drug report 2009*. New York: United Nations.

van Os, J., Kenis, G., & Rutten, B. P. F. (2010). The environment and schizophrenia. *Nature, 468*, 203–212.

van Os, J., Rutten, B. P., & Poulton, R. (2008). Gene-environment interactions in schizophrenia: review of epidemiological findings and future directions. *Schizophrenia Bulletin, 34*, 1066–1082.

Vassos, E., Pedersen, C. B., Murray, R. M., Collier, D. A., & Lewis, C. M. (2012). Meta-analysis of the association of urbanicity with schizophrenia. *Schizophrenia Bulletin, 38*(6), 1118–1123.

Vivancos, R., Abubakar, I., Phillips-Howard, P., & Hunter, P. R. (2013). School-based sex education is associated with reduced risky sexual behaviour and sexually transmitted infections in young adults. *Public Health, 127*(1), 53–57.

Vuillermot, S., Joodmardi, E., Perlmann, T., Ogren, S. O., Feldon, J., & Meyer, U. (2012). Prenatal immune activation interacts with genetic Nurr1 deficiency in the development of attentional impairments. *Journal of Neuroscience, 32*(2), 436–451.

Vuillermot, S., Webber, L., Feldon, J., & Meyer, U. (2010). A longitudinal examination of the neurodevelopmental impact of prenatal immune activation in mice reveals primary defects in dopaminergic development relevant to schizophrenia. *Journal of Neuroscience, 30*(4), 1270–1287.

Walters, J. T., Rujescu, D., Franke, B., Giegling, I., Vásquez, A. A., Hargreaves, A., et al. (2013). The role of the major histocompatibility complex region in cognition and brain structure: a schizophrenia GWAS follow-up. *American Journal of Psychiatry, 170*(8), 877–885.

Whitley, R. J. (2006). Herpes simplex virus infections. In J. S. Remington, J. O. Klein, C. B. Wilson, & C. J. Baker (Eds.), *Infectious diseases of the fetus and newborn infant* (6th ed.) (pp. 425–446). Philadelphia: Elsevier Saunders.

Wicks, S., Hjern, A., & Dalman, C. (2010). Social risk or genetic liability for psychosis? A study of children born in Sweden and reared by adoptive parents. *American Journal of Psychiatry, 167*(10), 1240–1246.

Wicks, S., Hjern, A., Gunnell, D., Lewis, G., & Dalman, C. (2005). Social adversity in childhood and the risk of developing psychosis: a national cohort study. *American Journal of Psychiatry, 162*, 1652–1657.

Wu, L.-L., Zhang, L., Shao, J., Qin, Y.-F., Yang, R.-W., & Zhao, Z.-Y. (2008). Effect of perinatal iron deficiency on myelination and associated behaviors in rat pups. *Behavioural Brain Research, 188*(2), 263–270.

Yolken, R. H., & Torrey, E. F. (2008). Are some cases of psychosis caused by microbial agents? A review of the evidence. *Molecular Psychiatry, 13*, 470–479.

Yu, X., Liu, R., Zhao, G., Zheng, M., Chen, J., & Wen, J. (2014). Folate supplementation modifies CCAAT/enhancer-binding protein α methylation to mediate differentiation of preadipocytes in chickens. *Poultry Science, 93*(10), 2596–2603.

Zaman, K., Roy, E., Arifeen, S. E., Rahman, M., Raqib, R., Wilson, E., et al. (2008). Effectiveness of maternal influenza immunization in mothers and infants. *New England Journal of Medicine, 359*(15), 1555–1564.

Zammit, S., Allebeck, P., Andreasson, S., Lundberg, L., & Lewis, G. (2002). Self reported cannabis use as a risk factor for schizophrenia in Swedish conscripts of 1969: historical cohort study. *British Medical Journal, 325*, 1199.

Zhang, R., He, J., Zhu, S., Zhang, H., Wang, H., Adilijiang, A., et al. (2012). Myelination deficit in a phencyclidine-induced neurodevelopmental model of schizophrenia. *Brain Research, 1469*, 136–143.

Animal Models of Psychotic Disorders: Dimensional Approach

3

Modeling Dimensions of Psychopathology: Integration with the Epidemiology and Pathobiology of Psychotic Illness

John L. Waddington[*],[§]

[*]Molecular and Cellular Therapeutics, Royal College of Surgeons in Ireland, Dublin, Ireland; [§]Jiangsu Key Laboratory of Translational Research & Therapy for Neuro-Psychiatric-Disorders and Department of Pharmacology, College of Pharmaceutical Sciences, Soochow University, Suzhou, China

INTRODUCTION

A diversity of genetic and environmental factors appears to determine the origins of psychotic illness and influence its complex life course (Brown, 2011; Hall, Trent, Thomas, O'Donovan, & Owen, 2015; van Os & Kapur, 2009). Although the term *psychotic illness* implies a broader concept of psychosis that transcends a single diagnostic category, the bulk of our evidence base derives from studies in schizophrenia. On this basis, current theorizing posits a neurodevelopmental disorder of high heritability with important environmental modifiers across infancy, childhood, adolescence, and into maturity in which the emergence of diagnostic symptoms represents the outcome of a pathobiological process that has its origins in the earliest stages of brain development (Rapoport, Giedd, & Gogtay, 2012; Waddington, Hennessy, O'Tuathaigh, Owoeye, & Russell, 2012); thereafter, the extent to which the subsequent life course and underlying pathobiology does or does not reflect an active, morbid process remains controversial and constitutes a major research front (Anderson et al., 2015; Fusar-Poli et al., 2013; Kobayashi et al., 2014; Rund, 2014; Van Haren, Cahn, Hulshoff Pol, & Kahn, 2013; Zipursky, Reilly, & Murray, 2013).

It remains challenging that psychosis can be manifested under no less than 11 diagnostic categories in addition to schizophrenia (schizoaffective disorder, schizophreniform disorder, delusional disorder, brief psychotic disorder, bipolar disorder, major depressive disorder, substance-induced psychotic disorder, psychotic disorder due to a general medical condition, substance-induced mood disorder, mood disorder due to a general medical condition, psychotic disorder not otherwise specified) (American Psychiatric Association, 1994, 2013). Increasing recognition of the breadth of psychopathology in schizophrenia and of clinical, genetic, and pathobiological overlap, not only with the enigma of schizoaffective disorder (Jager, Haack, Becker, & Frasch, 2011; Malaspina et al., 2013) (commonly conflated with schizophrenia), but also with bipolar disorder (Cardno & Owen, 2014; Hill et al., 2013; Ivleva et al., 2013; Tamminga et al., 2013), has been extended to major depressive disorder with psychotic features (Swartz & Shorter, 2007; Waddington & Buckley, 2013). Most recently, such overlap has been further extended to developmental disorders not usually considered within the realm of psychotic illness, such as autism spectrum disorder and attention-deficit hyperactivity disorder (Cross-Disorder Group of the Psychiatric Genomics Consortium, 2013a, 2013b; Gratten, Wray, Keller, & Visscher, 2014). Given such disrespect to prevailing nosology, current evidence suggests that these diagnostic categories may reflect arbitrary points of intersection along dimensions of psychopathology, dysfunction, and pathobiology (Demjaha et al., 2009; van Os & Kapur, 2009; Owen, 2014; Waddington et al., 2012).

Handbook of Behavioral Neuroscience
http://dx.doi.org/10.1016/B978-0-12-800981-9.00003-1

It should be recognized that psychotic illness is not defined by the onset of psychotic symptoms; rather, such symptoms reflect a stage in the trajectory of a disorder that is manifested throughout the lifespan: from the neurological and psychosocial/intellectual deficits of infancy, childhood, and adolescence that are evident on a population basis (but are too subtle to be of individual diagnostic utility), through to the increasing emergence of prediagnostic psychopathologies that are captured in terms such as "ultra high risk" and "attenuated psychosis syndrome" that can be (but are not necessarily) the harbingers of subsequent transition to a psychotic diagnosis (Brown, 2011; Carpenter & van Os, 2011; Howes & Murray, 2014; Insel, 2010; Linscott & van Os, 2013; Waddington et al., 2012).

To advance understanding of psychotic illness through model systems in terms of increased validity and heightened heuristics requires recognition and incorporation of this evolving clinical landscape.

MODELING DIMENSIONS OF PSYCHOPATHOLOGY

In accordance with long-standing convention, the most widely used psychometric instrument for the assessment of psychotic illness, the Positive and Negative Syndrome Scale (Kay, Fiszbein, & Opler, 1987) involves 30 items that are commonly aggregated into three primary domains: positive, negative, and general psychopathology. Although the more recent advances in psychopathology outlined previously have resulted in an expanding concept of dimensionality, investigators using model systems require those dimensions to be capable of assessment in animals; yet many human psychopathologies are intrinsically beyond nonhuman expression, whereas others are captured indirectly via indices that challenge isomorphic/homologous representation (Low & Hardy, 2007; van den Buuse, 2010; O'Tuathaigh, Desbonnet, & Waddington, 2014; Papaleo, Lipska, & Weinberger, 2011).

One widely entertained elaboration (van Os & Kapur, 2009; Tandon et al., 2013) posits five dimensions: psychotic (positive) symptoms, negative symptoms, depression, mania, and cognitive impairment. Although each of these five domains has been evaluated in animal models, they have been applied in what have been conceptualized previously as distinct contexts; for example, positive and negative symptoms have been studied most commonly in the context of modeling psychotic disorder, whereas depression and mania have been studied most commonly in the context of modeling affective disorder, with cognitive impairment studied in a wide context, from models of Alzheimer's disease through to a broad range of neuropsychiatric disorders, among which schizophrenia is but one part.

Furthermore, the same model may be "claimed" to reflect a different dimension according to the context in which it is applied: for example, does an animal model of anhedonia reflect the negative symptom of psychotic illness or the affective psychopathology of depression? (Belzung, 2014; O'Tuathaigh et al., 2014; O'Tuathaigh, Kirby, Moran, & Waddington, 2010). Such challenges reflect the clinical reality that it can be difficult to distinguish phenomenologically between negative and depressive symptoms; for example, do higher negative symptom scores in major depressive disorder with psychotic features reflect increasing prominence of negative symptoms or greater severity of depression or some combination thereof? (Owoeye et al., 2013).

For model studies to advance in their heuristic and translational import, they must reflect evolving concepts of the illness they seek to address. Therefore, in the context of psychotic illness, they should consider not only the modeling of positive symptoms (van den Buuse, 2010), negative symptoms (O'Tuathaigh et al., 2014), and cognitive impairment (Papaleo et al., 2011), but also affective symptoms (depression and mania: Neumann et al., 2011; Young, Henry, & Geyer 2011) in a manner that reflects our understanding of psychotic illness beyond conventional diagnostic categories. However, it would be unrealistic, on practical and fiscal grounds, to expect *every* contemporary study using a whole-animal model to evaluate, compare, and contrast indices relating to *each* of these five dimensions of psychopathology. Therefore, there are and will inevitably continue to be gaps in the evolving literature. Nevertheless, the field will not advance unless these dimensions are recognized and evaluated in such model systems. The heuristic would be for any differential effect of specific etiological/pathophysiological manipulations across these dimensions to be resolved and, ideally, related to pathobiological processes in a manner that can be back translated to studies in living patients.

MODELING DIMENSIONS OF PSYCHOPATHOLOGY IN THE CONTEXT OF THE EPIDEMIOLOGY OF PSYCHOTIC ILLNESS

A person presenting clinically with a first psychotic episode, most commonly in early adulthood, is an individual with psychopathology and dysfunctionality that is occurring in juxtaposition with other such individuals, who may be similar—but no two of whom are identical in their clinical presentation and setting. These cases are occurring among a population, such that factors distinguishing cases from noncases can be studied to establish the epidemiology of the disorder at issue and identify risk factors for caseness. Over the past 25 years, multiple studies have identified a diversity of environmental risk factors for psychosis (Brown, 2011; Meyer-Lindenberg & Tost, 2012; Waddington et al., 2012) on a background of high heritability and increasing but still incomplete understanding of the genes involved (Gratten et al., 2014; Schizophrenia Working Group of the Psychiatric Genomics Consortium, 2014). On this basis, risk for psychotic illness is likely to involve a combination not only of common alleles of small effect and/or rare, penetrant or de novo mutations of large effect, but also this diversity of environmental risk factors that may operate (1) independently, (2) additively, or (3) via "true" interactions between genes (G) and environmental risk factors (E), that is, $G \times E$ interaction (European Network of National Networks Studying Gene–Environment Interactions in Schizophrenia, 2014; McGrath, Mortensen, Visscher, & Wray, 2013; van Os, Kenis, & Rutten, 2010; O'Tuathaigh & Waddington, 2015).

Such putative phenomena are the subject of increasing investigation, most commonly in the form of the exposure of a mutant mouse, at a given point in development/maturation, to a biological or psychological environmental adversity, where each of the mutated gene and environmental adversity have been associated clinically with risk for schizophrenia (Kannan, Sawa, & Pletnikov, 2013; O'Tuathaigh & Waddington, 2015). However, although genotype is essentially fixed in an individual (subject to epigenetic regulation; Dempster, Viana, Pidsley, & Mill, 2013; Pishva et al., 2014), it can vary in a diverse manner between those who are affected and unaffected by psychotic illness, indicating a polygenic disorder (Gratten et al., 2014; Schizophrenia Working Group of the Psychiatric Genomics Consortium, 2014); furthermore, the range of environmental exposures implicated is large and can vary across the developmental/maturational timeline of psychotic illness, from early prenatal/postnatal adversities, through psychosocial stressors during childhood/adolescence, to substance abuse (Brown, 2011; Meyer-Lindenberg & Tost, 2012; Pishva et al., 2014; Waddington et al., 2012). Therefore, any simple *one gene–one environmental exposure–one time point* model is likely to be incomplete. However, although model studies can in theory isolate individual gene effects and deploy specific, experimentally controlled environmental interventions on multiple occasions, the logistical challenges in conducting studies that involve a broader range of genes, environmental exposures, and time points are immense.

Nevertheless, such approaches, although in their infancy, are emerging. In our own study, mice mutant for the schizophrenia risk gene *neuregulin 1* (G) were exposed to two environmental manipulations: maternal immune activation via prenatal exposure to polyinosinic:polycytidylic acid (E_1) and postnatal cross-fostering to an alternate dam (E_2); groups of both sexes having various permutations and combinations

of genetic mutation and environmental manipulations were then assessed, in young adulthood and, in some instances, also in adolescence, using procedures related to positive symptoms (parameters of activity, prepulse inhibition), negative symptoms (sociability, social novelty preference), and cognitive impairment (spatial working memory). The results indicated that, in relation to positive symptom indices, activity parameters were regulated primarily by G and by $E_1 \times E_2$ interactions, whereas prepulse inhibition was regulated by G, E_1, and E_2 and by $E_1 \times E_2$ and $G \times E_1 \times E_2$ interactions; in relation to negative symptom indices, sociability was regulated by E2 and by $G \times E_1$ and $E_1 \times E_2$ interactions, whereas social novelty preference was regulated by G and E_1 and by $G \times E_2$ interactions; in relation to the index of cognitive impairment, spatial working memory was regulated by G and E_1 and by $G \times E_1$ interactions; some of these regulatory effects differed according to whether assessments were made in adolescence versus young adulthood and in males versus females (O'Leary et al., 2014).

These findings suggest that concepts of $G \times E$ interaction in risk for psychotic illness should be elaborated to multiple interactions that involve individual genes interacting with diverse biological and psychosocial environmental factors over early life, to differentially influence particular domains of psychopathology, sometimes over specific stages of development and sometimes in a manner that can differ between the sexes. Such complex studies have yet to be extended beyond the positive/negative symptom/cognition domains to include the affective psychopathologies of depression and mania.

MODELING DIMENSIONS OF PSYCHOPATHOLOGY IN THE CONTEXT OF THE PATHOBIOLOGY OF PSYCHOTIC ILLNESS

Over the past decade, our concepts of the pathobiology of psychotic illness have moved from abnormalities and/or dysfunctions in individual brain regions, in terms of neuropathology, structural/functional neuroimaging, and neuropsychology, to developmentally determined disconnectivity in one or more brain network(s) that mediate the complex psychopathology and dysfunctionality of psychosis (Bastos-Leite et al., 2015; Fitzsimmons, Kubicki, & Shenton, 2013; van den Heuvel & Fornito, 2014; Orliac et al., 2013; Pettersson-Yeo, Allen, Benetti, McGuire, & Mechelli, 2011; Waddington et al., 2012); these concepts, deriving primarily from studies in schizophrenia, appear to generalize across diagnostic boundaries (Kumar et al., 2015) and to those showing subclinical psychotic experiences, whether at the level of "ultra high risk" (Wotruba et al., 2014) or more generally among the population at large (Orr, Turner, & Mittal, 2014).

Whole-animal models of psychotic illness had a primary origin in the effects of psychotomimetic drugs, a relationship that has stood the test of time and is subject to continuing evolution (Pratt, Winchester, Dawson, & Morris, 2012; Neill, Harte, Haddad, Lydal, & Dwyer, 2014). Models based on understanding the pathobiology of psychosis have a somewhat shorter history that was given impetus by findings from a new generation of neuroimaging and neuropathological studies that, for the first time, indicated replicable abnormalities in individual brain regions that could then be disrupted in animals by a variety of procedures. The first generation of such studies derived from clinical findings on what appeared to be neurodevelopmental rather than neurodegenerative changes in the temporal and frontal lobes and their interrelationships, with a particular focus on the hippocampus (Hyde & Weinberger, 1990). These initial insights were followed by studies seeking to disrupt hippocampal integrity and assess the functional consequences thereof, among which the rat neonatal ventral hippocampal lesion model (Lipska et al., 1993) has become the most thoroughly characterized (Tseng, Chambers, & Lipska, 2009).

In this model, ibotenic acid lesions of the ventral hippocampus at postnatal day 7 result in the emergence of hyperresponsivity to pharmacological or environmental stimuli known to provoke release of dopamine (DA) in the mesocorticolimbic DAergic system, that is, hyperactivity in response to the DA-releasing psychotomimetic amphetamine, enhanced sensitivity to the N-methyl-D-aspartate glutamate antagonist psychotomimetic phencyclidine, hyperreactivity to stress, disruption to sensorimotor gating in terms of prepulse inhibition, and deficits in latent inhibition; these effects, involving behaviors held to relate to positive, psychotic symptoms, emerge only during the postpubertal period and are sensitive to amelioration by antipsychotics. However, such lesions also result in prepubertal deficits in social interactions, behaviors held to relate to negative symptoms, when those related to psychotic symptoms have yet to emerge; these social deficits endure into the postpubertal period and are insensitive to amelioration by antipsychotics. Additionally, such lesions result in the postpubertal emergence of long-lasting deficits in working memory tasks, particularly the capacity to acquire and retain information in tests of spatial and avoidance learning; these behaviors are held to relate to the cognitive dysfunction of psychotic illness (Tseng et al., 2009).

In overview, on separate assessment of behaviors related to three dimensions of psychopathology, those for positive symptoms (postpubertal emergence), negative symptoms (prepubertal emergence), and cognitive impairment (prepubertal emergence) show longitudinal profiles that, in general terms and subject to the imprecision of assessment at limited time points, mirror the clinical characteristics of schizophrenia and related psychotic illness. Although behaviors related to affective psychopathology (depression and mania) have yet to be investigated systematically, some findings are suggestive in this regard (Bhardwaj, Tse, Ryan, Wong, & Srivastava, 2014). Aspects of this profile vary with lesion timing, differ between male versus female rats, and are influenced by both genetic background and environmental variables such as maternal care, periadolescent social impoverishment, and other psychosocial stressors. Mechanistically, aspects of this profile consequent to neonatal ventral hippocampal lesions are influenced by subsequent lesioning of the prefrontal cortex; when supplemented by a broader range of behavioral and cellular indices, the model indicates early disruption of limbic inputs to frontal corticostriatal circuits that alters development of mesocortical DAergic control of excitatory and inhibitory neurotransmission, with such control being critical for expression of mature brain function that normally emerges during late adolescence (Tseng et al., 2009).

CONCLUSIONS

Although these findings are complementary to some current concepts of schizophrenia pathobiology, it should be emphasized that they involve permanent destruction of one or more brain regions when no such lesions are present in schizophrenia itself, with network involvement presumptive on indirect indices. Thus, most of the more recently introduced models considered in this volume involve disruption to the brain, particularly to brain development, via either environmental (biological or psychosocial) or genetic manipulations that are more specifically related, and are in some instances isomorphic/homologous, to factors associated with clinical risk for psychotic illness. For example, it is now possible to disrupt limbic and cortical connectivity via genetic mutation and to investigate resultant phenotypes at numerous levels, from cellular organization, through both short- and long-range connectivity and associated electrophysiological changes, to behaviors related to distinct dimensions of psychopathology (Runker et al., 2011).

In a previous era, it was common to believe that a "valid" animal model of schizophrenia, involving a unitary manipulation such as treatment with a psychotomimetic drug or a circumscribed lesion, should reproduce "all" aspects of the condition (each of positive/negative symptoms and cognitive impairment). However, there is increasing recognition that each domain of psychopathology in psychotic illness may have its own pathobiological substrate, involving developmentally determined disconnectivities in one or more brain networks (Waddington et al., 2012); this is complementary to the US National Institute of Mental Health's Research Domain

Criteria initiative, which involves the development of a research-based classification system for mental disorders that is informed by the genetics, physiology, and neural circuitry underpinning biobehavioral constructs that cut across current diagnostic categories (Cuthbert & Insel, 2013). Increasing recognition of such heuristics for psychotic illness extends not only to genetic, but also to psychopathological and functional overlap with autism spectrum disorder (Hommer & Swedo, 2015) and attention deficit-hyperactivity disorder (Jandl, Steyer, & Kaschka, 2012).

Just as model systems have to keep pace with and reflect increasing knowledge on the epidemiology and pathobiology of psychotic illness, they have to keep pace also with still-evolving knowledge on psychopathology and associated dysfunction that is no longer accommodated easily by discrete categories of disease.

Acknowledgments

The authors' studies were supported by Science Foundation Ireland Principal Investigator Grant 07/IN.1/B960.

References

American Psychiatric Association. (1994). *Diagnostic and statistical manual of mental disorders* (4th ed.). Washington, DC: American Psychiatric Association.

American Psychiatric Association. (2013). *Diagnostic and statistical manual of mental disorders* (5th ed.). Washington, DC: American Psychiatric Association.

Anderson, K. K., Rodrigues, M., Mann, K., Voineskos, A., Mulsant, B. H., George, T. P., et al. (2015). Minimal evidence that untreated psychosis damages brain structures: a systematic review. *Schizophrenia Research, 162*, 222–233.

Bastos-Leite, A. J., Ridgway, G. R., Silveira, C., Norton, A., Reis, S., & Friston, K. J. (2015). Dysconnectivity within the default mode in first-episode schizophrenia: a stochastic dynamic causal modelling study with functional magnetic resonance imaging. *Schizophrenia Bulletin, 41*, 144–153.

Belzung, C. (2014). Innovative drugs to treat depression: did animal models fail to be predictive or did clinical trials fail to detect effects? *Neuropsychopharmacology, 39*, 1041–1051.

Bhardwaj, S. K., Tse, Y. C., Ryan, R., Wong, T. P., & Srivastava, L. K. (2014). Impaired adrenergic-mediated plasticity of prefrontal cortical glutamate synapses in rats with developmental disruption of the ventral hippocampus. *Neuropsychopharmacology, 39*, 2963–2973.

Brown, A. S. (2011). The environment and susceptibility to schizophrenia. *Progress in Neurobiology, 93*, 23–58.

van den Buuse, M. (2010). Modeling the positive symptoms of schizophrenia in genetically modified mice: pharmacology and methodology aspects. *Schizophrenia Bulletin, 36*, 246–270.

Cardno, A. G., & Owen, M. J. (2014). Genetic relationships between schizophrenia, bipolar disorder, and schizoaffective disorder. *Schizophrenia Bulletin, 40*, 504–515.

Carpenter, W. T., & van Os, J. (2011). Should attenuated psychosis syndrome be a DSM-5 diagnosis? *American Journal of Psychiatry, 168*, 460–463.

Cross-Disorder Group of the Psychiatric Genomics Consortium. (2013a). Identification of risk loci with shared effects on five major psychiatric disorders: a genome-wide analysis. *Lancet, 381*, 1371–1379.

Cross-Disorder Group of the Psychiatric Genomics Consortium. (2013b). Genetic relationship between five psychiatric disorders estimated from genome-wide SNPs. *Nature Genetics, 45*, 984–994.

Cuthbert, B. N., & Insel, T. R. (2013). Toward the future of psychiatric diagnosis: the seven pillars of RDoC. *BioMed Central Medicine, 11*, 126.

Demjaha, A., Morgan, K., Morgan, C., Landau, S., Dean, K., Reichenberg, A., et al. (2009). Combining dimensional and categorical representation of psychosis: the way forward for DSM-V and ICD-11? *Psychological Medicine, 39*, 1943–1955.

Dempster, E., Viana, J., Pidsley, R., & Mill, J. (2013). Epigenetic studies of schizophrenia: progress, predicaments, and promises for the future. *Schizophrenia Bulletin, 39*, 11–16.

European Network of National Networks studying Gene-Environment Interactions in Schizophrenia (EU-GEI), van Os, J., Rutten, B. P., Myin-Germeys, I., Delespaul, P., Viechtbauer, W., van Zelst, C., et al. (2014). Identifying gene-environment interactions in schizophrenia: contemporary challenges for integrated, large-scale investigations. *Schizophrenia Bulletin, 40*, 729–736.

Fitzsimmons, J., Kubicki, M., & Shenton, M. E. (2013). Review of functional and anatomical brain connectivity findings in schizophrenia. *Current Opinion in Psychiatry, 26*, 172–187.

Fusar-Poli, P., Smieskova, R., Kempton, M. J., Ho, B. C., Adreasen, N. C., & Borgwardt, S. (2013). Progressive brain changes in schizophrenia related to antipsychotic treatment? A meta-analysis of longitudinal MRI studies. *Neuroscience and Biobehavioral Reviews, 37*, 1680–1691.

Gratten, J., Wray, N. R., Keller, M. C., & Visscher, P. M. (2014). Large-scale genomics unveils the genetic architecture of psychiatric disorders. *Nature Neuroscience, 17*, 782–790.

Hall, J., Trent, S., Thomas, K. L., O'Donovan, M. C., & Owen, M. J. (2015). Genetic risk for schizophrenia: convergence on synaptic pathways involved in plasticity. *Biological Psychiatry, 77*, 52–58.

van den Heuvel, M. P., & Fornito, A. (2014). Brain networks in schizophrenia. *Neuropsychology Review, 24*, 32–48.

Hill, S. K., Reilly, J. L., Gold, J. M., Bishop, J. R., Gershon, E. S., Tamminga, C. A., et al. (2013). Neuropsychological impairments in schizophrenia and psychotic bipolar disorder: findings from the Bipolar-Schizophrenia Network on Intermediate Phenotypes (B-SNIP) study. *American Journal of Psychiatry, 170*, 1275–1284.

Hommer, R. E., & Swedo, S. E. (2015). Schizophrenia and autism – related disorders. *Schizophrenia Bulletin, 41*, 313–314.

Howes, O. D., & Murray, R. M. (2014). Schizophrenia: an integrated sociodevelopmental-cognitive model. *Lancet, 383*, 1677–1687.

Hyde, T. M., & Weinberger, D. R. (1990). The brain in schizophrenia. *Seminars in Neurology, 10*, 276–286.

Insel, T. (2010). Rethinking schizophrenia. *Nature, 468*, 187–193.

Ivleva, E. I., Bidesi, A. S., Keshavan, M. S., Pearlson, G. D., Meda, S. A., Dodig, D., et al. (2013). Gray matter volume as an intermediate phenotype for psychosis: Bipolar-Schizophrenia Network on Intermediate Phenotypes (B-SNIP). *American Journal of Psychiatry, 170*, 1285–1296.

Jäger, M., Haack, S., Becker, T., & Frasch, K. (2011). Schizoaffective disorder – an ongoing challenge for psychiatric nosology. *European Psychiatry, 26*, 159–165.

Jandl, M., Steyer, J., & Kaschka, W. P. (2012). Adolescent attention deficit hyperactivity disorder and susceptibility to psychosis in adulthood: a review of the literature and a phenomenological case report. *Early Intervention in Psychiatry, 6*, 11–20.

Kannan, G., Sawa, A., & Pletnikov, M. V. (2013). Mouse models of gene-environment interactions in schizophrenia. *Neurobiology of Disease, 57*, 5–11.

Kay, S. R., Fiszbein, A., & Opler, L. A. (1987). The positive and negative syndrome scale (PANSS) for schizophrenia. *Schizophrenia Bulletin, 13*, 261–276.

Kobayashi, H., Isohanni, M., Jaaskelainen, E., Miettunen, J., Veijola, J., Haapea, M., et al. (2014). Linking the developmental and degenerative theories of schizophrenia: association between infant development and adult cognitive decline. *Schizophrenia Bulletin, 40*, 1319–1327.

Kumar, J., Iwabuchi, S., Oowise, S., Balain, V., Palaniyappan, L., & Liddle, P. F. (2015). Shared white-matter dysconnectivity in schizophrenia and bipolar disorder with psychosis. *Psychological Medicine, 45*, 759–770.

Linscott, R. J., & van Os, J. (2013). An updated and conservative systematic review and meta-analysis of epidemiological evidence on psychotic experiences in children and adults: on the pathway from proneness to persistence to dimensional expression across mental disorders. *Psychological Medicine, 43*, 1133–1149.

Lipska, B. K., Jaskiw, G. E., Weinberger, D. R. (1993). Postpubertal emergence of hyperresponsiveness to stress and to amphetamine after neonatal excitotoxic hippocampal damage: a potential animal model of schizophrenia. *Neuropsychopharmacology, 9*, 67–75.

Low, N. C., & Hardy, J. (2007). What is a schizophrenic mouse? *Neuron, 54*, 348–349.

Malaspina, D., Owen, M. J., Heckers, S., Tandon, R., Bustillo, J., Schultz, S., et al. (2013). Schizoaffective disorder in the DSM-5. *Schizophrenia Research, 150*, 21–25.

McGrath, J. M., Mortensen, P. B., Visscher, P. M., & Wray, N. R. (2013). Where GWAS and epidemiology meet: opportunities for the simultaneous study of genetic and environmental risk factors in schizophrenia. *Schizophrenia Bulletin, 39*, 955–959.

Meyer-Lindenberg, A., & Tost, H. (2012). Neural mechanisms of social risk for psychiatric disorders. *Nature Neuroscience, 15*, 663–668.

Neill, J. C., Harte, M. K., Haddad, P. M., Lydal, E. S., & Dwyer, D. M. (2014). Acute and chronic effects of NMDA receptor antagonists in rodents, relevance to negative symptoms of schizophrenia: a translational link to humans. *European Neuropsychopharmacology, 24*, 822–835.

Neumann, I. D., Wegener, G., Homberg, J. R., Cohen, H., Slattery, D. A., Zohar, J., et al. (2011). Animal models of depression and anxiety: what do they tell us about human condition? *Progress in Neuropsychopharmacology and Biological Psychiatry, 35*, 1357–1375.

O'Leary, C., Desbonnet, L., Clarke, N., Petit, E., Tighe, O., Lai, D., et al. (2014). Phenotypic effects of maternal immune activation and early postnatal milieu in mice mutant for the schizophrenia risk gene neuregulin-1. *Neuroscience, 277*, 294–305.

Orliac, F., Naveau, M., Joliot, M., Delcroix, N., Razafimandimby, A., Brazo, P., et al. (2013). Links among resting-state default-mode network, salience network, and symptomatology in schizophrenia. *Schizophrenia Research, 148*, 74–80.

Orr, J. M., Turner, J. A., & Mittal, V. A. (2014). Widespread brain dysconnectivity associated with psychotic-like experiences in the general population. *NeuroImage Clinical, 4*, 343–351.

van Os, J., & Kapur, S. (2009). Schizophrenia. *Lancet, 374*, 635–645.

van Os, J., Kenis, G., & Rutten, B. P. (2010). The environment and schizophrenia. *Nature, 468*, 203–212.

O'Tuathaigh, C. M., Desbonnet, L., & Waddington, J. L. (2014). Genetically modified mice related to schizophrenia and other psychoses: seeking phenotypic insights into the pathobiology and treatment of negative symptoms. *European Neuropsychopharmacology, 24*, 800–821.

O'Tuathaigh, C. M., Kirby, B. P., Moran, P. M., & Waddington, J. L. (2010). Mutant mouse models: genotype-phenotype relationships to negative symptoms in schizophrenia. *Schizophrenia Bulletin, 36*, 271–288.

O'Tuathaigh, C. M., & Waddington, J. L. (2015). Closing the translational gap between mutant mouse models and the clinical reality of psychotic illness. *Neuroscience and Biobehavioral Reviews.* http://dx.doi.org/10.1016/j.neubiorev.2015.01.016 pii:S0149-7634(15)00018-4 [Epub ahead of print].

Owen, M. J. (2014). New approaches to psychiatric diagnostic classification. *Neuron, 84*, 564–571.

Owoeye, O., Kingston, T., Scully, P. J., Baldwin, P., Browne, D., Kinsella, A., Russell, V., O'Callaghan, E., Waddington, J. L. (2013). Epidemiological and clinical characterization following a first psychotic episode in major depressive disorder: comparisons with schizophrenia and bipolar I disorder in the Cavan-Monaghan First Episode Psychosis Study (CAMFEPS). *Schizophrenia Bulletin, 39*, 756–765.

Papaleo, F., Lipska, B. K., & Weinberger, D. R. (2011). Mouse models of genetic effects on cognition: relevance to schizophrenia. *Neuropharmacology, 62*, 1204–1220.

Pettersson-Yeo, W., Allen, P., Benetti, S., McGuire, P., & Mechelli, A. (2011). Dysconnectivity in schizophrenia: where are we now? *Neuroscience and Biobehavioral Reviews, 35*, 1110–1124.

Pishva, E., Kenis, G., van den Hove, D., Lesch, K., Boks, M. P., van Os, J., et al. (2014). The epigenome and postnatal environmental influences in psychotic disorders. *Social Psychiatry and Psychiatric Epidemiology, 49*, 337–348.

Pratt, J., Winchester, C., Dawson, N., & Morris, B. (2012). Advancing schizophrenia drug discovery: optimizing rodent models to bridge the translational gap. *Nature Reviews Drug Discovery, 11*, 560–579.

Rapoport, J. L., Giedd, J. N., & Gogtay, N. (2012). Neurodevelopmental model of schizophrenia: update 2012. *Molecular Psychiatry, 17*, 1228–1238.

Rund, B. R. (2014). Does active psychosis cause neurobiological pathology? A critical review of the neurotoxicity hypothesis. *Psychological Medicine, 44*, 1577–1590.

Runker, A. E., O'Tuathaigh, C., Dunleavy, M., Morris, D. W., Little, G. E., Corvin, A. P., et al. (2011). Mutation of semaphorin-6A disrupts limbic and cortical connectivity and models neurodevelopment psychopathology. *PLoS One, 6*, e26488.

Schizophrenia Working Group of the Psychiatric Genomics Consortium. (2014). Biological insights from 108 schizophrenia-associated genetic loci. *Nature, 511*, 421–427.

Swartz, C. M., & Shorter, E. (2007). *Psychotic depression.* Cambridge: Cambridge University Press.

Tamminga, C. A., Ivleva, E. I., Keshavan, M. S., Pearlson, G. D., Clementz, B. A., Witte, B., et al. (2013). Clinical phenotypes of psychosis in the Bipolar-Schizophrenia Network on Intermediate Phenotypes (B-SNIP). *American Journal of Psychiatry, 170*, 1263–1274.

Tandon, R., Gaebel, W., Barch, D. M., Bustillo, J., Gur, R. E., Heckers, D., et al. (2013). Definition and description of schizophrenia in the DSM-5. *Schizophrenia Research, 150*, 3–10.

Tseng, K. Y., Chambers, R. A., & Lipska, B. K. (2009). The neonatal ventral hippocampal lesion as a heuristic neurodevelopmental model of schizophrenia. *Behavioural Brain Research, 204*, 295–305.

Van Haren, N. E., Cahn, W., Hulshoff Pol, H. E., & Kahn, R. S. (2013). Confounders of excessive brain volume loss in schizophrenia. *Neuroscience and Biobehavioral Reviews, 37*, 2418–2423.

Waddington, J. L., & Buckley, P. F. (2013). Psychotic depression: an underappreciated window to explore the dimensionality and pathobiology of psychosis. *Schizophrenia Bulletin, 39*, 754–755.

Waddington, J. L., Hennessy, R. J., O'Tuathaigh, C. M. P., Owoeye, O., & Russell, V. (2012). Schizophrenia and the lifetime trajectory of psychotic illness: developmental neuroscience and pathobiology, redux. In A. S. Brown, & P. H. Patterson (Eds.), *The origins of schizophrenia* (pp. 3–21). New York: Columbia University Press.

Wotruba, D., Michels, L., Buechler, R., Metzler, S., Theodoridou, A., Gerstenberg, M., et al. (2014). Aberrant coupling within and across the default mode, task-positive, and salience network in subjects at risk for psychosis. *Schizophrenia Bulletin, 40*, 1095–1104.

Young, Y. W., Henry, B. L., & Geyer, M. A. (2011). Predictive animal models of mania: hits, misses and future directions. *British Journal of Pharmacology, 164*, 1263–1284.

Zipursky, R. B., Reilly, T. J., & Murray, R. M. (2013). The myth of schizophrenia as a progressive brain disease. *Schizophrenia Bulletin, 39*, 1363–1372.

Modeling the Positive Symptoms of Schizophrenia

Tursun Alkam*,¶, Toshitaka Nabeshima*,§

*Department of Regional Pharmaceutical Care and Sciences, Graduate School of Pharmaceutical Sciences, Meijo University, Nagoya, Japan; §NPO, Japanese Drug Organization of Appropriate Use and Research, Nagoya, Japan; ¶Department of Basic Medical Sciences, College of Osteopathic Medicine of the Pacific, Western University of Health Sciences, Pomona, CA, USA

List of Abbreviations

5-HT-2AR Serotonin-2A receptors
5-HTP 5-Hydroxytryptophan
AF Arcuate fasciculi
AHC Amygdala–hippocampal complex
AMP Amphetamine
AVHs Auditory verbal hallucinations
CB1R Cannabinoid CB1 receptors
CBF Cerebral blood flow
CT Computerized tomography
D2R Dopamine D2 receptors
DA Dopamine
DAT Dopamine transporter
DOI 2,5-Dimethoxy-4-iodoamphetamine
DTIs Diffusion tensor images
FA Fractional anisotropy
GABA-AR Gamma-aminobutyric acid A receptors
GM Gray matter
HTR Head-twitch response
LSD Lysergic acid diethylamide
METH Methamphetamine
MRI Magnetic resonance imaging
NMDAR N-methyl-D-aspartate receptors
PCP Phencyclidine
PET Positron emission tomography
PFC Prefrontal cortex
PPI Prepulse inhibition
STG Superior temporal gyrus
THC Δ9-Tetrahydrocannabinol
VBM Magnetic resonance voxel-based morphometry
VHs Visual hallucinations
WM Working memory

INTRODUCTION

Diagnostic criteria of schizophrenia are updated in Diagnostic and Statistical Manual of Mental Disorders-5 (DSM-5) by the American Psychiatric Association in 2013. Accordingly, to be diagnosed as schizophrenia, the patient should have two or more of the following characteristic symptoms, including delusions, hallucinations, disorganized speech, grossly disorganized or catatonic behavior, negative symptoms (i.e., diminished emotional expression) during a 1-month period (or less if successfully treated), and have social/occupational dysfunction during a 6-month period (Tandon et al., 2013). Among the characteristic symptoms, delusions, hallucinations, and disorganized speech are conventionally regarded as the core "positive symptoms" diagnosed with high reliability and might reasonably be considered necessary for a reliable diagnosis of schizophrenia (Tandon et al., 2013).

A delusion is a false belief that indicates an abnormality in the affected person's content of thought (Kiran & Chaudhury, 2009). Delusions are distorted false beliefs such as someone is plotting against you or a movie character is giving you commands. A person with a delusion will hold firmly to the belief regardless of evidence to the contrary (Kiran & Chaudhury, 2009). Delusions have particular significance for the diagnosis of schizophrenia, and are common in several psychiatric conditions (Blackwood, Howard, Bentall, & Murray, 2001; Kiran & Chaudhury, 2009).

A hallucination is a fake and involuntary perception with seemingly real quality in the absence of actual stimulus. Hallucinations differ from delusions in which an actual stimulus is distortedly interpreted and given some bizarre significance. A delusion might also be an attempt to explain a hallucinatory experience (Kiran & Chaudhury, 2009).

Disorganized speech is a demonstration of thought disorder or illogical thought processes that make speech poorly organized. With disorganized speech, the topic slips from one to the next (e.g., jumping from idea to idea) and it is difficult to communicate. Schizophrenic communication disturbances reflect specific cognitive deficits in the areas of working memory (WM) and attention (Docherty et al., 1996). Disorganized speech is associated with poor goal maintenance and with a task that included both goal maintenance and verbal WM storage demands (Becker, Cicero, Cowan, & Kerns, 2012). There is also a trend for poorer performance on WM tasks to be associated with hallucinations (Berenbaum, Kerns, Vernon, & Gomez, 2008).

Currently, we do not have any established knowledge in the field of disorganized speech, hallucinations, and delusions to help answer the questions about the relationships.

DELUSIONS AND HALLUCINATIONS

Although the positive symptoms are related closely to one another in occurrence, hallucinations are the mostly studied symptoms across the species. Hallucinations and delusions are almost inseparable symptoms in schizophrenia. The diagnosis of schizophrenia can be made with just one symptom including either auditory hallucinations or bizarre delusions, because 96% patients with auditory hallucination have delusions, and 88–99% patients with bizarre delusion have hallucinations (Shinn, Heckers, & Ongur, 2013).

Therefore, in this chapter, we will mainly focus on hallucination, briefly on delusions, to understand the modeling of positive symptoms of schizophrenia.

Delusions

Delusions result from abnormalities in how brain circuits identify hierarchical predictions and how they compute and respond to prediction mismatches. Defects in these fundamental brain mechanisms can weaken perception, memory, and social learning. As a result, individuals develop delusions and experience an internal and external world that healthy individuals would find difficult to comprehend (Corlett, Taylor, Wang, Fletcher, &

Krystal, 2010). Recent advances in computational neuroscience have led us to consider the delusions as the disturbance in error-dependent updating of inferences and beliefs about the world (Fletcher & Frith, 2009). Considering that the brain constructs hierarchical causal models of the external world, the failure to maintain the excitatory to inhibitory balance results in hallucinations as well as in the formation and subsequent consolidation of delusional beliefs (Jardri & Deneve, 2013). Indeed, the consequence of excitatory to inhibitory imbalance in a hierarchical neural network is equated to a pathological form of causal inference called "circular belief propagation." In circular belief propagation, prior beliefs are misinterpreted as sensory observations and sensory observations are misinterpreted as prior beliefs. The circular inference explains the emergence of erroneous percepts and the patient's overconfidence when facing probabilistic choices and the learning of "unshakable" causal relationships between unrelated events, which are all known to be associated with schizophrenia (Jardri & Deneve, 2013). It is suggested that hippocampal sensory gating deficits, disturbed frontolimbic balance, and DAergic dysregulation in limbic areas such as the amygdala in interaction with prefrontal cortex (PFC) and temporal cortex play an important role in the pathogenesis of positive symptoms (Javanbakht, 2006; Pankow, Knobel, Voss, & Heinz, 2012). Structural magnetic resonance imaging (MRI) in schizophrenia has convincingly demonstrated reductions in volumes of the amygdala–hippocampal complex and other limbic and paralimbic structures (Ganzola, Maziade, & Duchesne, 2014; Lawrie, Whalley, Job, & Johnstone, 2003). The amygdala–hippocampal complex in the medial temporal lobe is linked to independent memory systems, each with unique characteristic functions in context processing which is impaired in schizophrenia (Cohen, Barch, Carter, & Servan-Schreiber, 1999; Phelps, 2004). The amygdala can modulate both the encoding and the storage of hippocampal-dependent memories. The hippocampal complex, by forming episodic representations of the emotional significance and interpretation of events (including relationships between unrelated events), can influence the amygdala response when emotional stimuli are encountered (Phelps, 2004). Interrelation between amygdala and hippocampus may play a role in hippocampal sensory gating deficits in the pathogenesis of positive psychotic symptoms (Javanbakht, 2006). Although functional MRI studies suggest that WM performance depends upon the capacity of PFC to suppress bottom-up amygdala signals during emotional arousal, WM is found facilitated after basolateral amygdala damage (Morgan, Terburg, Thornton, Stein, & van Honk, 2012). WM is a vital cognitive capacity without which meaningful thinking and logical reasoning would be impossible (Morgan et al., 2012), and disruption of meaningful thinking and logical reasoning lead to delusions.

Molecular genetic analysis of delusional patients suggests dopamine (DA) signal transmission is increased in delusional patients (Morimoto et al., 2002). Decreased DA transporter (DAT) expressions in DAergic terminals are observed in the amygdala of subjects with schizophrenia (Markota, Sin, Pantazopoulos, Jonilionis, & Berretta, 2014). The decrease in DAT disrupts DA uptake, leading to increased DAergic synaptic transmission. These findings support hyper-DAergic hypothesis for delusion and the effectiveness of DA receptor blockers for delusions in schizophrenia (Corlett et al., 2010; Correll & Kane, 2014; Huber, Kirchler, Karner, & Pycha, 2007; Morimoto et al., 2002).

Hallucinations

Hallucinations have been described for more than two millennia, yet their causes remain unclear (Weiss & Heckers, 1999). Hallucinations remain as one of the most intriguing phenomena in psychopathology, specifically in schizophrenia (Allen, Laroi, McGuire, & Aleman, 2008; Weiss & Heckers, 1999). Hallucinations are a person's false but vivid and substantial perception of things in the absence of apparent stimulus and created by the awake mind. Not all people who experience hallucinations have a psychotic disorder. A hallucination may be a sensory experience in which a person can see (visual hallucination), hear (auditory hallucination), smell (olfactory hallucination), taste (gustatory hallucination), and feel (tactile hallucination or somatic hallucination), something that is not at all present at the time of perception. Among those, auditory hallucinations are by far the most common, followed by visual hallucinations, and then by tactile and olfactory or gustatory hallucinations in schizophrenia (Mueser, Bellack, & Brady, 1990).

It has been generally suggested that abnormal cerebral excitation and a lack of normal cerebral inhibition may play primary roles in the generation of hallucinations. Recent advances in structural neuroimaging is sensory modality-specific activation in cerebral areas that are involved in normal sensory processing associated with hallucinations (Weiss & Heckers, 1999). Neural activation in these sensory processing areas may be specifically related to distinct phenomenological features of the hallucinatory experiences (Braun, Dumont, Duval, Hamel-Hebert, & Godbout, 2003; Weiss & Heckers, 1999).

In a systematic review of structural neuroimaging studies, which applied computed tomography or MRI, the consistent relationships are observed between hallucinations (in the visual, auditory, and somatic aspects) and brain lesions in people (Braun et al., 2003). The lesion is practically always located in the brain pathway of the sensory modality of the hallucination and implied that compensatory overactivation of the nearby brain tissue as causative in hallucination. It is suggested that the lesioned tissue must have contained a predominance of inhibitory overexcitatory neurons for the sensory modality in question (Braun et al., 2003).

Visual Hallucinations

Visual hallucinations (VHs) are false visual sensory perceptions in the absence of external stimuli and one of the primary diagnostic criteria for schizophrenia (Cummings & Miller, 1987; Norton & Corbett, 2000). VHs also occur in diverse clinical circumstances including ophthalmologic diseases, neurologic disorders, and idiopathic psychiatric illnesses (Cummings & Miller, 1987). VHs may occur up to 32% in schizophrenia patients (Bracha, Wolkowitz, Lohr, Karson, & Bigelow, 1989; Mueser et al., 1990).

Brain activity related to VHs is found in higher visual areas corresponding to the content of the hallucinations (faces, bodies, scenes) and the hippocampus. The hippocampal activity is related to the retrieval of visual images from memory and that sensory cortex activity is related to the vividness of the perceptual experience (Oertel et al., 2007). Limbic areas, which involved in retrieval from long-term memory, and category-specific visual areas also contribute to the generation of VHs in schizophrenia. Electrocortical stimulation of temporo-occipital or parieto-occipital regions can produce VHs (Penfield & Perot, 1963). Although VHs are typically produced along the visual pathway, the temporal or subthalamic nucleus stimulation is also reported to produce VHs (Diederich, Alesch, & Goetz, 2000; Penfield & Perot, 1963). Recent evidence from molecular, pharmacological, and neuroimaging studies suggests a crucial role for serotonin 2A receptors (5-HT-2AR) in visual processing and the pathogenesis of VHs by increasing cortical excitability and altering the coherence of visual-evoked cortical responses in polysynaptic sensory circuits (Kometer, Schmidt, Jancke, & Vollenweider, 2013; Moreau, Amar, Le Roux, Morel, & Fossier, 2010). Activation of 5-HT-2AR may induce a processing mode in which stimulus-driven cortical excitation is overwhelmed by spontaneous neuronal excitation through the modulation of alpha-oscillations that play active inhibitory role in information processing (Kometer et al., 2013).

Auditory Hallucinations

In many ancient cultures, the experience of hearing voices (auditory verbal hallucinations, AVHs) were thought to be either sign of divine inspiration or evidence of demonic possession, depending on the content. Today, however, AVHs are often regarded as an abnormal experience and a sign of mental illness (Allen et al., 2008;

Weiss & Heckers, 1999). AVHs have been noted in normal as well as schizophrenic people in different cultures (Carpenter, Strauss, & Bartko, 1973; Chaudhury, 2010; Klemperer, 1992; Sartorius, Shapiro, Kimura, & Barrett, 1972). In the general population, some people who do not fulfill any criteria for specific psychotic or neurologic disorders may report auditory hallucination under undesired external stimulations (Chaudhury, 2010; Daalman et al., 2011). AVHs remain one of the most intriguing phenomena in psychopathology and are the cardinal symptom for the diagnosis of schizophrenia (Allen et al., 2008; Plaze et al., 2011). More than 70% of schizophrenic patients suffer from AVHs, which are unpleasant and distressing (Sartorius et al., 1986; Stephane, Barton, & Boutros, 2001).

Phenomenological studies in auditory hallucinations identified independent dimensions in auditory hallucinations including spatial location, language complexity, and impairments in monitoring of inner speech and the subsequent self-other misattribution (Gaser, Nenadic, Volz, Buchel, & Sauer, 2004; McGuire et al., 1995; Plaze et al., 2011). A predisposition to AVHs is associated with a failure to activate areas concerned with the monitoring of inner speech (McGuire et al., 1995). The fundamental mechanism for AVHs in schizophrenia is speech generation/perception pathology, which results from abnormal activation of speech production (Broca) and speech perception (Wernicke) areas (Stephane et al., 2001). The impaired self-monitoring or misattribution of self-generated inner speech or thoughts to external sources is one of the main difficulties in schizophrenia patients with AVHs. The misattribution of self-generated inner speech occurs even in healthy individuals with high levels of psychotic-like experiences (Allen, Freeman, Johns, & McGuire, 2006). Schizophrenia patients with AVHs are prone to misidentifying their own verbal material as alien or nonself (Allen et al., 2004). AVHs may be mediated by a distributed network of cortical and subcortical areas (Shergill, Brammer, Williams, Murray, & McGuire, 2000). Disrupted connectivity between frontal and temporoparietal language areas gives rise to impairments in monitoring of inner speech and the misattribution of this inner speech (McGuire et al., 1995; de Weijer et al., 2011). The brain regions that involve in language production and verbal monitoring include inferior frontal gyrus and superior temporal gyrus (STG) contribute to the misattribution processes. These regions are implicated in the genesis and/or persistence of AVHs through cortical intercorrelations between frontotemporal regions, supporting the critical role of this network in the pathophysiology of hallucinations (Garcia-Marti et al., 2008; Modinos et al., 2009). Brain structural imaging studies are shedding light on the understanding of anatomical contributors of AVHs in schizophrenia (Allen et al., 2008; Allen et al., 2012; Plaze et al., 2011).

NEUROIMAGING STUDIES ON POSITIVE SYMPTOMS

Brain Structures

Advanced neuroimaging techniques in the past 2 decades have improved our understanding on what is happening in the brain of those who experience AVHs, particularly in patients with schizophrenia (Allen et al., 2008, 2012). The fundamental mechanism for AVHs in schizophrenia is speech generation pathology, which results from abnormal activation of speech production (Broca) and speech perception (Wernicke) areas (Stephane et al., 2001). The Broca area is a region in the inferior frontal gyrus of (usually) the left hemisphere of the human brain with functions linked to speech production (Nixon, Lazarova, Hodinott-Hill, Gough, & Passingham, 2004). The Wernicke area is located in the posterior section of the STG in the left cerebral hemisphere and encircles the auditory cortex. MRI study of young schizophrenic patients demonstrates smaller volume of the STG, and the shrinkage of the left STG is strongly and selectively correlated with severity of AVHs (Barta, Pearlson, Powers, Richards, & Tune, 1990; Flaum et al., 1995). High-spatial-resolution MRI study on patients with first-episode schizophrenia found significantly (progressively) decreased gray matter volume over time in the left STG compared with healthy comparison subjects (Kasai et al., 2003). However, the relationship between the presence and characteristics of cerebral structural abnormalities with the intensity and phenomenology of auditory hallucinations needs to be analyzed by means of magnetic resonance voxel-based morphometry (VBM) method (Garcia-Marti et al., 2008; Neckelmann et al., 2006). The procedure in VBM involves spatially normalizing high-resolution images from all the subjects in the study into the same stereotactic space, followed by segmenting the gray matter from the spatially normalized images and characterizing regional cerebral volume and tissue concentration differences in structural MRIs (Ashburner & Friston, 2000; Good et al., 2001). In a VBM study on gray matter volume differences in the whole brain volume between a group of schizophrenia patients with AVHs and a healthy control group, significant gray matter volume reductions in the schizophrenia patient group in the left STG, the left middle frontal gyrus, and in the right cuneus are noticed (Neckelmann et al., 2006). Areas of gray matter volume reduction that correlated negatively with hallucinations are found in the STG, left thalamus, and left and right cerebellum. It is proposed that significant reductions in gray matter volume may be instrumental in generating spontaneous neuronal activity that is associated with speech perception experiences in the absence of an external acoustic stimulus that may cause hallucinations (Neckelmann et al., 2006).

In a more sensitive VBM method, reductions of gray matter concentration in schizophrenia patients with AVHs are observed in bilateral insula, bilateral STG, and left amygdala (Garcia-Marti et al., 2008), whereas gray matter volume in the left inferior frontal gyrus is positively correlated with severity of AVHs (Modinos et al., 2009).

Brain Regional Activity and Connectivity

The coupling of brain cell function to the vascular system is the basis for a number of functional neuroimaging methods relevant for human studies. These methods map specific localized brain activation through a vascular response such as an increase in cerebral blood flow (CBF) or a change in blood oxygenation (Villringer & Dirnagl, 1995). In a study using single photon emission computed tomography neuroimaging, schizophrenic AVHs were associated with increased regional CBF during verbal memory activation (Busatto et al., 1995). A recent study using magnetic resonance arterial spin labeling, which is a technique that provides a direct quantitative measure of CBF, demonstrate that schizophrenia patients with AVHs have significantly higher CBF (tonic hyperactivity) in a predefined region, the left STG compared with healthy controls and compared with global CBF (Homan et al., 2013). Reversing hyperactivity (decreasing CBF) in the primary auditory cortex (Heschl gyrus and the STG) via treatment with transcranial magnetic stimulation is correlated with the decrease in AVHs, supporting its crucial role in triggering AVHs and contributing to the physical quality of the false perceptions (Kindler et al., 2013). Further, the findings of continuously increased CBF in the left STG in patients with AVH has also been shown for patients with AVH of epileptic etiology (Hauf et al., 2013), supporting the relevance of left STG activation (speech perception areas) in the genesis of AVHs. However, both increased and decreased patterns of regional CBF are associated with different types of hallucinations and make it difficult to make CBF as a feature trait in hallucinations (Izumi, Terao, Ishino, & Nakamura, 2002; Okada, Suyama, Oguro, Yamaguchi, & Kobayashi, 1999; Sabri et al., 1997).

White matter abnormalities in schizophrenia may offer important clues to a better understanding of the disconnectivity associated with AVHs (Seok et al., 2007). Diffusion tensor images and MRI studies on hallucinating schizophrenic patients showed that white matter density is significantly increased in the left inferior longitudinal fasciculus. The decreased fractional anisotropy value of the left frontal part of the left superior longitudinal fasciculus is positively correlated with the severity score of AVHs in the hallucinating patient group, suggesting that disrupted connectivity in the left frontotemporal area may contribute to the development of auditory hallucinations in schizophrenia (Seok et al., 2007).

Disrupted connectivity between frontal and temporoparietal language areas, which may contribute to the misattribution of inner speech, should be reflected in the microstructure of the arcuate fasciculi, the main connection between frontal and temporoparietal language areas (de Weijer et al., 2011). To examine the connectivity, diffusion tensor images are used to compute fractional anisotropy and to reconstruct the fiber bundles of interest, whereas the magnetic transfer imaging scans are used to compute magnetic transfer ratio values. Schizophrenia patients with chronic severe hallucinations showed a general decrease in fractional anisotropy and significant increase in compute magnetic transfer ratio values for all bundles. These changes in the arcuate fasciculi in patients with AVHs suggest increased free water concentrations, probably caused by degraded integrity of the axons or the supportive glia cells. The disintegrated fiber integrity in the connection between frontal and temporoparietal language areas in schizophrenia patients may explain why patients do not recognize the self-produced words instead of attributing them to an external source (de Weijer et al., 2011). Recently, a functional connectivity study, using resting-state functional MRI on the primary auditory cortex, which is located on the Heschl gyrus, found neural circuit abnormalities are associated more specifically with AVHs (Shinn, Baker, Cohen, & Ongur, 2013). Schizophrenia patients with AVHs vulnerability showed increased left Heschl gyrus functional connectivity with left inferior frontal gyrus (Broca area) and left lateral STG, and showed decreased functional connectivity with right hippocampal formation and mediodorsal thalamus compared with patients without AVHs experiences (Shinn, Baker, et al., 2013). Abnormal interactions between left Heschl gyrus and regions involved in speech/language, memory, and the weak monitoring of self-generated sounds may contribute to vulnerability of suffering AVHs (Shinn, Baker, et al., 2013).

It is obvious that neuroimaging and connectivity studies are in broad agreement with a general abnormal connectivity within and between the left and right frontotemporal regions including both gray and white matter that involve in speech generation, speech perception, and memory (Benetti et al., 2013; Tracy & Shergill, 2013).

DELUSIONAL AND HALLUCINOGENIC SIGNALING

Delusions and hallucinations in healthy human subjects can be induced by natural occurring or man-made hallucinogens (Johnson, Richards, & Griffiths, 2008; Schultes, 1969). Hallucinogens have been adored and hated since prehistory; however, the exact mechanisms of hallucinogen-induced hallucinations are not yet understood.

Accumulating evidence suggests that a disturbance of the fine balance among the complex network involving multiple transmitter receptor systems is responsible for hallucinatory symptoms of schizophrenia. Research findings suggest that hallucinogens work by temporarily disrupting cellular communication at a neurotransmitter signaling level by at least six different pharmacological pathways including activation of dopamine D2 receptors (D2R), 5-HT-2AR, cannabinoid CB-1 receptors (CB-1R), gamma-aminobutyric acid A receptors (GABA-AR), and blockage of muscarinic receptors as well as N-methyl-D-aspartate receptors (NMDAR).

Dopamine Signaling through Dopamine D2 Receptors

DA hypothesis of schizophrenic hallucinations (auditory) is provided by the studies of psychostimulant drugs such as amphetamine (AMP) or methamphetamine (METH). AMP or METH is used primarily to enhance mental power and mood. During World War II, AMP or METH was used extensively to stimulate the fighting spirits of soldiers in Japan (Yui, Ikemoto, Ishiguro, & Goto, 2000). However, shortly after the release of postwar military stores of METH during reconstruction of the country, there was a sharp increase in the number of patients (about 200,000 patients) with MAP psychosis that indistinguishable from acute or chronic schizophrenia (Shimazono & Matsushima, 1995; Yui et al., 2000). The situation in Japan presents an opportunity to examine the etiology of MAP psychosis in relation to the pathophysiology of schizophrenia (Yui et al., 2000). Both AMP and METH increase DA signaling and cause addiction. METH increases the concentration of working DA in the synaptic cleft by reversing the transport direction of the DAT and also by decreasing the membrane-associated DAT in the presynaptic neurons (Miller, 2011; Xie & Miller, 2009). AMP, on the other hand, increases extracellular concentrations of DA and also induces psychotic behaviors in humans and monkeys, similar to the positive symptoms such as hallucination, seen in schizophrenia patients (Lieberman, Kane, & Alvir, 1987; Nielsen, Lyon, & Ellison, 1983). The DA system is one of the best known and most completely mapped neurotransmitter systems in the brain (Bjorklund & Dunnett, 2007). Neurons in the ventral tegmental area synthesize and release DA into the nucleus accumbens and the PFC, whereas neurons in the substantia nigra synthesize and release DA into the striatum (Bjorklund & Dunnett, 2007). DAergic systems project preferentially to striatal, frontal, and limbic areas, leading to the general concept that specificity might be related to localized dysfunction within those regions and preserved function elsewhere. The positive symptoms of schizophrenia are a direct result of too much DA neuronal firing originating in the midbrain

and allowing excessive DA release and activity in limbic structures (hyper-DAergic state), whereas negative symptoms are associated with hypo-DAergic state in the frontal-cortical terminal fields of mesocortical DA neurons (Schwartz, Sachdeva, & Stahl, 2012; Stahl, 2007). Molecular imaging studies have also generated important in vivo insights into the DA hypothesis in the etiology of schizophrenic hallucinations (Howes et al., 2009; Iyo et al., 1993). In a quantitative autoradiography study in normal human brain tissue, the majority of the D2R-enriched bands are observed in the lateral and inferior aspects of the STG, less frequently on the lateral surface of the inferior temporal gyrus and the parahippocampal cortices, whereas they are absent from primary auditory cortex (Goldsmith & Joyce, 1996). In the schizophrenic brain, disrupted pattern of D2R such as reduced concentrations of D2R in the supragranular layers and elevated concentrations of D2R in the granular layer in isocortical regions of the temporal lobe has been reported (Goldsmith, Shapiro, & Joyce, 1997). The anatomical localization of D2R, in auditory and speech association cortices and auditory–visual association areas, mirrors the presumed sites underlying hallucinations in schizophrenia. Further, in a functional and structural neuroimaging study, striatal D2R density is found significantly higher in the striatum in schizophrenic group than in the normal group by positron emission tomography (PET) scanning, and left STG volume is found significantly smaller in the schizophrenic group than in the normal group MRI scanning (Tune et al., 1996). Thus, the inverse relationship between STG volume and striatal D2R density lend support to the involvement of increased D2R signaling in functional connectivity of the striatum to the temporal cortex. In agreement, all currently licensed antipsychotic drugs block striatal D2/3R in vivo and that D2/3R occupancy above a threshold is required for antipsychotic treatment response (Howes et al., 2009). Increases in the level of DA as well as the number of D2R are observed in schizophrenia compared with control subjects (Abi-Dargham et al., 2000; Seeman & Kapur, 2000). Blockade of the disrupted distribution of D2R in hallucination association cortices is a likely mechanism for the clinical efficacy of D2R antagonists in reducing hallucinations and delusions (Goldsmith et al., 1997).

Serotonin Signaling through Serotonin 2A Receptors

The classical hallucinogens such as psychedelics include wide variety of substances with different chemical structures, but show remarkably similar effects including VHs. Psychedelics include naturally occurring psilocybin (in mushrooms) and synthetic lysergic acid diethylamide (LSD). The recreational use of LSD by counterculture youths in the Western world during the 1960s led to a focused study on psychedelics. The people who use either LSD or psilocybin suffer from incidence of psychosis that are identical to those of schizophrenia patients (Keeler, 1965; Vardy & Kay, 1983). Extensive behavioral and neuroimaging data show that these hallucinogens stimulate 5-HT-2AR, especially those expressed on neocortical pyramidal cells. Activation of 5-HT-2AR also leads to increased cortical glutamate levels presumably by a presynaptic receptor-mediated release from thalamic afferents (Nichols, 2004). By genetically expressing 5-HT-2AR only in the cortex, it has been shown that 5-HT-2AR-regulated pathways on cortical neurons are sufficient to mediate the signaling pattern and behavioral response to hallucinogens. Hallucinogenic and nonhallucinogenic 5-HT-2AR agonists both regulate signaling in the same 5-HT-2AR-expressing cortical neurons. However, the signaling and behavioral responses to the hallucinogens are distinct (Gonzalez-Maeso et al., 2007). Recent evidence suggests that activation of 5-HT-2AR may lead to the formation of VHs by increasing cortical excitability and altering visual-evoked cortical responses (Kometer et al., 2013).

Cannabinoid Signaling through CB-1 Receptors

The world's oldest and most widely used recreational drug cannabis (also known as marijuana or hashish) is also the most controversial drug because of its medicinal use. The hallucinations occur in cannabis-intoxicated healthy individuals tend to be visual and/or auditory in nature (van Os et al., 2002; Stefanis et al., 2004). In a study on a community sample of 880 adolescents, lifetime cannabis use and the frequency of cannabis use (in the past year) are associated with the experience of auditory and VHs (Hides et al., 2009). The major psychoactive substance in marijuana is Δ9-tetrahydrocannabinol (THC) (Hollister, 1974). Intravenous injection of THC in healthy and psychiatrically well individuals produces transient behavioral symptoms including hallucinations similar to those seen in schizophrenia (D'Souza et al., 2004; Morrison et al., 2009). Studying the psychoactive effects of cannabis led to the discovery of endocannabinoids (produced by the mammalian body) and cannabinoid receptors (Devane, Dysarz, Johnson, Melvin, & Howlett, 1988). Endocannabinoids work as retrograde messengers and contribute to short- and long-term modulation of synaptic transmission via presynaptic cannabinoid receptors. It is generally accepted that CB-1R mediates the effects of endocannabinoid both in excitatory and inhibitory synapses (Kawamura et al., 2006). A study using PET and the D2/D3R ligand [11C]raclopride found THC can induce DA release in the striatum of healthy human subjects (Bossong et al., 2009). CB-1R is abundantly expressed in brain regions targeted by the efferent terminals of the DAergic neurons and functionally interacts with both

cortical and striatal neurons that express D2R (Fitzgerald, Shobin, & Pickel, 2012). CBR agonists upregulate and enhance 5-HT-2AR activity, whereas CB-1R knock-out mice display impaired functionality of 5-HT-2AR (Hill, Sun, Tse, & Gorzalka, 2006; Mato et al., 2007). Thus, the involvement of the endogenous cannabinoid system in the regulation of neurotransmitter systems that are essential for the genesis of schizophrenia, supports the "cannabinoid hypothesis" in the neurobiological mechanisms of hallucinations in schizophrenia (Fernandez-Espejo, Viveros, Nunez, Ellenbroek, & Rodriguez de Fonseca, 2009; Muller-Vahl & Emrich, 2008).

Cholinergic Signaling through Muscarinic Receptors

The cholinergic system is one of the most important modulatory neurotransmitter systems in the brain and controls activities that depend on selective attention, which are an essential component of conscious awareness that monitors delusional and hallucinatory information processing (Perry, Walker, Grace, & Perry, 1999). Increased understanding of the role of acetylcholine in the human brain and its relationship to other neurotransmitter systems has led to a rapidly growing interest in the cholinergic system in schizophrenia (Berman, Talmage, & Role, 2007; Hyde & Crook, 2001). The cholinergic involvement in VHs and delusions are initially understood from the observations of subjects with dementia with Lewy bodies who manifest reductions in neocortical acetylcholine-related activity (McKeith et al., 1996; Sarter & Bruno, 1998). It is suggested that muscarinic acetylcholine receptors activation in the cortex is involved in restraining the contents of the discrete subconscious sensory events. In the absence of cortical acetylcholine, the understimulated muscarinic acetylcholine receptors allow currently irrelevant intrinsic and subconscious sensory information to be amplified and expressed as delusions and hallucinations (Perry & Perry, 1995). In hallucinating patients with Lewy body dementia or with Alzheimer's disease, the extensive loss of cortical acetylcholine allows irrelevant information to enter "conscious awareness" and thus leads to delusions and hallucinations (Perry et al., 1999; Sarter & Bruno, 1998). This is consistent with the ability of muscarinic-receptor antagonists, such as scopolamine and atropine, administered medically, recreationally, or ritualistically to induce VHs and other perceptual disturbances (Fisher, 1991; Perry & Perry, 1995; Warburton, Wesnes, Edwards, & Larrad, 1985). Increasing the levels of acetylcholine by treatments with reversible cholinesterase inhibitors ameliorates delusions and VHs in Alzheimer's and schizophrenia patients (Cummings, Gorman, & Shapira, 1993; Patel, Attard, Jacobsen, & Shergill, 2010). The density and expression of muscarinic receptors are reduced in hippocampal formation, PFC, and STG in schizophrenic patients (Crook, Tomaskovic-Crook, Copolov, & Dean, 2000; Crook, Tomaskovic-Crook, Copolov, & Dean, 2001; Deng & Huang, 2005; Mancama, Arranz, Landau, & Kerwin, 2003; Scarr, Sundram, Keriakous, & Dean, 2007). These reports support the involvement of muscarinic acetylcholine system in the pathogenesis of positive symptoms of schizophrenia (Dean, 2012; Foster, Jones, & Conn, 2012; Raedler, Bymaster, Tandon, Copolov, & Dean, 2007).

Gamma-Aminobutyric Acid A Signaling through Gamma-Aminobutyric Acid A Receptors

GABA is the principal inhibitory neurotransmitter throughout the nervous system, and it plays an important role in regulating neuronal excitability. GABA-AR agonists can cause hallucinations depending on functional selectivity. Certain hallucinogenic amanita mushrooms, including amanita muscaria, are reported to cause visual and auditory hallucinations (Brvar, Mozina, & Bunc, 2006; Magdalan & Antonczyk, 2007). The main psychoactive constituent of these mushrooms is identified as muscimol (Halpern, 2004; Tsujikawa et al., 2006). Muscimol is one of the most potent agonist ligands at the GABA-AR. Muscimol binds to the GABA-binding site on the GABA-AR complex. An agonist of GABA-AR, zolpidem, is used for insomnia and sleep disorder as prescription medicine. Overdose or misuse of zolpidem is reported to induce hallucination in patients (Kummer et al., 2012; Manfredi et al., 2010; Singh & Loona, 2013).

Investigations of postmortem brain from schizophrenic patients have revealed a preferential increase in bicuculline-sensitive 3H-muscimol binding on neuronal cell bodies of layers II and III of superficial layers of cingulate cortex, and in layers II, III, V, and VI of PFC in the schizophrenic cases (Benes, Vincent, Alsterberg, Bird, & SanGiovanni, 1992; Benes, Vincent, Marie, & Khan, 1996). Because information processing depends on corticocortical integration in outer layers I–III, a disturbance of inhibitory activity in these superficial layers of limbic cortex is suggested to contribute to the defective associative function (including delusions and hallucinations) seen in schizophrenia (Benes et al., 1992). The alteration in inhibition of pyramidal neurons contributes to a diminished capacity for the gamma-frequency-synchronized neuronal activity that is required for normal working memory function (Lewis, Hashimoto, & Volk, 2005), which is important in the control of delusional and hallucinatory information processing. In a quantitative autoradiography study to investigate the binding of the agonist [(3)H] muscimol to GABA-AR in the brain of schizophrenia patients, a significant increase in binding of [(3)H] muscimol is observed in the STG, suggesting

an increase of GABA-AR densities in the STG of schizophrenia patients (Deng & Huang, 2006). The STG, which connects to the hippocampus, amygdala, and neocortical association areas in the PFC, is involved in the pathology of AVHs. Recent advances in mouse genetics, neuroimaging, and electrophysiology techniques in schizophrenia study suggest perturbed functions of GABAergic interneurons of the cerebral cortex may underlie key symptoms of the disease (Benes & Berretta, 2001; Chen et al., 2014; Inan, Petros, & Anderson, 2013). These reports suggest the involvement of the increased inhibitory GABA-signaling through GABA-AR in the pathophysiology of delusions and hallucinations of schizophrenia.

Glutamate Signaling through NMDAR

Dissociative hallucinogenic side effects of recreational drug phencyclidine (PCP), which was marketed in the late 1950s, improved our understanding on the etiology of schizophrenic hallucinations. A broad range of schizophrenia-like symptomatology, including cognitive, positive, and negative symptoms in healthy volunteers, was observed after using PCP and another dissociative drug, ketamine (Cohen, Rosenbaum, Luby, & Gottlieb, 1962; Davies & Beech, 1960; Krystal et al., 1994; Luby, Cohen, Rosenbaum, Gottlieb, & Kelley, 1959). PCP, at submicromolar serum concentrations, interacts selectively with a specific binding site (PCP receptor), which is associated with the NMDAR and induces noncompetitive inhibition of NMDAR-mediated neurotransmission (Javitt & Zukin, 1991). NMDAR are primarily responsible for excitatory neurotransmitter in the brain. As opposed to DA receptors, NMDAR are widely distributed throughout the brain, including cortical and subcortical brain regions. Sensory dysfunction predicts impairments in higher order cognitive functions such as auditory or visual emotion recognition (Javitt, Zukin, Heresco-Levy, & Umbricht, 2012). PCP induces a schizophrenia-like psychosis by blocking neurotransmission at NMDAR and supports the hypoglutame (hypofunctional NMDAR) hypothesis of schizophrenia (Coyle, 2012; Javitt et al., 2012; Nabeshima, Mouri, Murai, & Noda, 2006). Other NMDAR antagonists such as the dissociative anesthetic ketamine also induce PCP-like neurobehavioral effects by inhibiting NMDAR (Javitt & Zukin, 1991). Studies agree that hypofunction of NMDAR leads to secondary DAergic dysregulation that may result in hallucination in schizophrenia. Normally, descending corticobrainstem glutamate neurons tonically excite mesocortical DA pathway (increase DA release) and also tonically inhibit the mesolimbic DA pathway (decrease DA release through inhibitory GABA interneurons). When NMDAR are hypofunctional in corticobrainstem glutamate neurons, a disinhibited and thus hyperactive mesolimbic DA pathway may result in hallucinatory experience, whereas a disinhibited mesocortical DA pathway may result in negative and cognitive symptoms of schizophrenia (Stahl, 2007). The hypofunction of NMDAR represents a convergence point possibly for progression and insistence of positive symptoms of schizophrenia (Snyder & Gao, 2013).

METHODS TO INVESTIGATE POSITIVE SYMPTOM-RELATED BEHAVIORS IN ANIMAL MODELS

Hallucinations and delusions are known to humans who can linguistically communicate with nonself about what they have heard and have seen. Although hallucinations in the healthy state might be unique to humans, the pathological hallucinations can be produced in animals by hallucinogens. The induced hallucination in animals (which cannot linguistically communicate with us) can be detected by observing the changes in their behaviors that may result from the experience of hallucinations during the experimental time-frame. The specificity of the hallucination-related behavioral changes should never be seen in response to other nonhallucinogenic drugs in theory. Although higher animals such as cats and monkeys show hallucination-like behaviors such as visual tracking of invisible objects or abortive grooming (Jacobs, Trulson, & Stern, 1976; Jacobs, Trulson, & Stern, 1977; Nielsen et al., 1983), they are not specific responses to hallucinogens (Marini & Sheard, 1981). The drug discrimination study, which applies standard two-lever operant procedures for rats, is proposed to detect a classical hallucinogen from saline (Hirschhorn & Winter, 1971). Although the drug discrimination studies have been proven to be quite useful for the investigation of addictive properties of hallucinogens and nonhallucinogens and hallucinogen-trained animals provide a functional behavioral model of 5-HT2R activation, it does not represent an animal model of hallucinogenic activity (Glennon, 1991; May et al., 2009). Despite the absence of hallucinatory behavior in animal models of schizophrenia, hallucinogen-associated behavioral studies have yielded important insights into the linkage between hallucinogenic molecules and schizophrenia, both in pharmacological and transgenic models, and have helped to identify receptor targets and interactions that could be exploited in the development of new therapeutic agents (Halberstadt & Geyer, 2013b; Marcotte, Pearson, & Srivastava, 2001; Nabeshima et al., 2006; Niwa et al., 2010; Young, Zhou, & Geyer, 2010). There is still no any specific method to exclusively investigate delusional or hallucinatory behaviors in rodent animal models. Nevertheless, several methods are being applied to investigate the hallucinogen-related behaviors in context with the confirmed hallucinogenic (delusional) molecules.

Here, we introduce the most commonly used behavioral methods which have been used to study the effects of hallucinogens as well as hallucination-related molecules.

Prepulse Inhibition of Startle Response

Schizophrenia patients and their relatives show deficits in prepulse inhibition (PPI) of startle responses, a phenomenon that measures an early stage of information processing (preattentional sensorimotor gating), and are seen as a feature for schizophrenia spectrum disorders (Cadenhead, Swerdlow, Shafer, Diaz, & Braff, 2000; Wynn et al., 2004). PPI refers to the ability of a weak prestimulus (nonstartling, the prepulse) to transiently inhibit the response to a closely following strong sensory stimulus (the startle stimulus, the pulse) (Kumari et al., 2008; Stitt, Hoffman, & Marsh, 1973; Zangrando et al., 2013). The PPI is impaired in a number of psychopathological disorders involving cortico-striato-pallido-pontine circuits that exhibits impaired gating of sensory, cognitive, or motor information (Braff, Geyer, & Swerdlow, 2001). In schizophrenia patients, the presence of auditory hallucinations is positively associated with a marked PPI deficit if the patients are not able to control their occurrence and thus are unable to dismiss them. Hearing voices with a high degree of negative content is associated with high mean startle amplitude in patients with current auditory hallucinations (Kumari et al., 2008). This supports the notion that auditory hallucinations in patients with schizophrenia are theorized to result from impaired monitoring of inner speech, the inability to consciously ignore them appears to be associated with a sensorimotor gating deficit (Kumari et al., 2008; McGuire et al., 1995).

Animal studies of PPI provide strong support for a loss of sensory gating with increased DA activity in the mesolimbic system and involvement of the 5-HTergic system in the modulation of startle habituation (Geyer & Braff, 1987; Geyer, Swerdlow, Mansbach, & Braff, 1990; Swerdlow, Braff, Taaid, & Geyer, 1994). PPI is also widely used to study the action mechanism of hallucinogens such as PCP (Takahashi et al., 2006), LSD (Halberstadt & Geyer, 2010), THC (Nagai et al., 2006), and METH (Arai et al., 2008) in mouse models. Activation of 5-HT-2AR is involved in PCP-induced disruption of PPI of the acoustic startle in rats (Yamada, Harano, Annoh, Nakamura, & Tanaka, 1999). PPI is also applied to test the role of genetic susceptibility factors for schizophrenia such as Disrupted-in-Schizophrenia-1 (Niwa et al., 2010), immune activation during pregnancy (Ozawa et al., 2006), and neuregulin 1 (Hong, Wonodi, Stine, Mitchell, & Thaker, 2008) in mouse models.

Thanks to the consistent application of PPI in schizophrenic patients and related animal models as a reproducible measure of sensorimotor gating, it can be used to monitor the animal modeling of schizophrenia and therapeutic effects of candidate drugs to control hallucinations. Although the PPI methods are described in all research publications involved, the protocol for the measurement of startle response, PPI, and habituation in rats and mice are also reported exclusively with detailed trouble shooting information (Geyer & Swerdlow, 2001; Valsamis & Schmid, 2011).

Locomotor Activity

Locomotor activity does not represent any hallucinatory behavior in any species. Although hallucinogenic drugs cause visual hallucination-like behaviors and increased locomotor activities (maybe because of the chasing of the invisible objects they are seeing) in monkeys and cats (Jacobs et al., 1976, 1977; Nielsen et al., 1983), the relationship between them needs to be addressed. Single or repeated exposure to drugs of abuse in animal models can also induce long-lasting increased locomotor response—the locomotor sensitization (Mizoguchi et al., 2007; Robinson & Berridge, 1993; Valjent et al., 2010). However, in combination with PPI in schizophrenia models, locomotor activity may help to examine the involvement of DAergic and 5-HTergic system in PPI deficiency that can result from auditory hallucination (Geyer & Braff, 1987; Kumari et al., 2008; Nabeshima et al., 2006; Niwa et al., 2010). The activation of D2R and 5-HT-2AR is associated with hallucination in humans (Goldsmith et al., 1997; Kometer et al., 2013; Tune et al., 1996) and hyperlocomotion in animal models of hallucinogens (Aoyama, Kase, & Borrelli, 2000; Halberstadt, Powell, & Geyer, 2013; Nabeshima, Kitaichi, & Noda, 1996). Therefore, locomotor activity is necessary to monitor the D2R and 5-HT-2AR signaling systems in the animal models of hallucination.

Locomotor activity is evaluated by placing an animal into the center of an open-field arena and allowing exploring for a preferred time. Activity in the open field can be quantified by direct observational techniques and automated monitoring. Total distance of locomotion, movement time, and movement speed are easily measured by a computer-based automated monitoring system. Protocols for measurement of locomotor activity using photocell-based automated monitoring systems are available with detailed information (Pierce & Kalivas, 2007).

Head-Twitch Response

Hallucinogens induce head-twitch response (HTR) in rodents; however, it may not represent any hallucinatory behavior. The HTR is a rapid side-to-side violent head-shaking movement that occurs in mice and rats only after administration of hallucinogens such as LSD, PCP, 5-hydroxytryptophan, 2,5-dimethoxy-4-iodoamphetamine, and 5-HT-2AR agonist (Corne, Pickering, & Warner, 1963; Keller & Umbreit, 1956; Nabeshima, Ishikawa, Yamaguchi, Furukawa, & Kameyama, 1987a; Nabeshima, Ishikawa, Yamaguchi, Furukawa, & Kameyama, 1987b; Willins & Meltzer, 1997). HTR does not occur in normal untreated mice and rats, but does occur in mice and rats in response to 5-HT-2AR activation; selective 5-HT-2AR antagonists block the HTR induced by hallucinogens (Willins & Meltzer, 1997). It is confirmed that 5-HT-2AR is essential for HTR generation by hallucinogens, because 5-HT-2AR knock-out mice do not react with HTR after treatment with hallucinogens (Gonzalez-Maeso et al., 2007; Gonzalez-Maeso et al., 2003). Interestingly, the other known hallucinogenic cannabinoids including THC inhibit 5-HT-2AR-mediated HTR, whereas selective cannabinoid CB-1R antagonist produces robust frequencies of HTR in mice (Darmani, 2001; Darmani & Pandya, 2000; Janoyan, Crim, & Darmani, 2002). Nevertheless, HTR is not only seen as an indicative of some hallucinogenic receptor activity in animal models (Corne & Pickering, 1967; Nabeshima et al., 1987b), it is also useful for studying the hallucinogenic signaling pathways in schizophrenia. However, it is not clear whether the 5-HT-2AR-mediated HTR in rodents is associated with 5-HT-2AR-mediated auditory hallucinations or VHs in humans because they cannot be induced in the same species. A recent study reported that a magnetometer coil can be used to detect HTR induced by hallucinogens (Halberstadt & Geyer, 2013a). Magnetometer-based HTR detection may provide a high-throughput, semiautomated assay for this behavior, and offer several advantages over traditional assessment methods (Halberstadt & Geyer, 2013a).

Y-Maze Test and Water-Finding Test

The Y-maze test is widely used for the evaluation of WM (or short-term memory) and requires immediate sequential association of movements and different visual stimuli (Nabeshima et al., 1994; Yamada et al., 1996). The water-finding test is used to evaluate WM as well as latent learning (Nabeshima et al., 1994). This test examines the capability of a mouse to associate a provided clue (the location, which is briefly explored in the training session) with the desired object (the water, in a test session after 24 h). The latent learning is an associate learning which is essential for correctly matching the prior beliefs with the novel observations and understand causal relationships between related events. The learning of causal relationships between unrelated events is seen as the impairment of associative learning and associated with the delusion in schizophrenia (Jardri & Deneve, 2013). Hallucinogenic drugs such as METH and PCP induce impairments of latent learning, WM, and PPI in mouse models of schizophrenia in relation with DA hypothesis (Mouri et al., 2007; Nabeshima et al., 2006; Nabeshima et al., 1994). Therefore, any impairment in the water-finding test may provide a clue for delusional information processing in mouse models.

WM enables us to hold the contents of our conscious awareness, even in the absence of real sensory input, by maintaining an active representation of information for a brief period (Courtney, Petit, Haxby, & Ungerleider, 1998). Auditory hallucinations are mediated by D2R activation, which also improves WM (Tarantino, Sharp, Geyer, Meves, & Young, 2011). Thus, abnormally overactive WM may support hallucinations that occur in the absence of real sensory input. On the other hand, impairment in WM disrupts logical reasoning and leads to the formation as well as the persistence of delusional ideation (Broome et al., 2012). Delusions are also difficult to model in animals, given that they involve dysfunctions of consciousness and reality monitoring and cognition. However, the Y-maze or water-finding test may help evaluate the delusion- or hallucination-related cognitive state in animal models in the context of related pathology.

Cued and Contextual Fear Conditioning

The role of the amygdala and hippocampus in the acquisition and consolidation of contextual representations is well confirmed in rodents during studies of conditioned fear responses to a cue and to context. Fear conditioning to either a cue or a context represents a form of associative learning (Curzon, Rustay, & Browman, 2009). Because the delusion in schizophrenia originates from "unshakable" causal relationships between unrelated events (Jardri & Deneve, 2013), testing the abnormality in associative response to a cue (a tone paired with foot-shock) and a context (background present during the tone-paired foot-shock) may represent how the animals miscompute and illogically reason the causal relationship of events. Of course, one should be careful to interpret the data because they are also implicated in associative fear memory. This method is widely used and the detailed protocol and methods of data analysis for cued and contextual fear conditioning in rodents are well reported (Curzon et al., 2009).

CONCLUSION

Despite the consistent findings in structural imaging and functional/connectivity studies to support anatomical origin of positive symptoms of schizophrenia, the underlying pathophysiological causes are still not fully understood (Steinmann, Leicht, & Mulert, 2014). Therefore, various approaches such as pharmacological,

genetic, and epigenetic manipulations should be applied to model the symptoms and find a target for therapeutic intervention.

Currently approved typical and atypical antipsychotics are D2R-antagonists with different affinity (with the exception of aripiprazole, which is a partial D2R agonist). Atypical antipsychotics also act as 5-HT-2AR antagonists with high affinity. Unfortunately, these medications cannot selectively target the D2R or 5-HT-2AR in pathways that involve in positive symptoms of schizophrenia, and blocking these receptors in other pathways can cause a wide range of adverse effects. Although DA theory is dominating our understanding of schizophrenia, a single neurotransmitter is less likely responsible for the genesis of the positive symptoms of the disease. To avoid the D2R blockade-related side effects, current understanding of research leads the drug development strategy to other hypothesis of schizophrenia to target related receptors. Obviously, animal models that are specific to positive symptoms as well as the underlying pin-point pathology are anticipated to develop better antipsychotics. Integration of the anatomical knowledge such as positive symptom-associated brain structures that, obtained from schizophrenic neuroimaging studies, with the positive symptom-associated receptors, obtained from hallucinogen studies, may facilitate the modeling of positive symptoms in animal models.

Future research on the modeling of positive symptoms in schizophrenia should focus on a better combination of region- and receptor-specific neurochemical and pharmacological basis of positive symptoms in animal models.

References

Abi-Dargham, A., Rodenhiser, J., Printz, D., Zea-Ponce, Y., Gil, R., Kegeles, L. S., et al. (2000). Increased baseline occupancy of D2 receptors by dopamine in schizophrenia. *Proceedings of the National Academy of Sciences of the United States of America, 97*, 8104–8109.

Allen, P., Freeman, D., Johns, L., & McGuire, P. (2006). Misattribution of self-generated speech in relation to hallucinatory proneness and delusional ideation in healthy volunteers. *Schizophrenia Research, 84*, 281–288.

Allen, P., Laroi, F., McGuire, P. K., & Aleman, A. (2008). The hallucinating brain: a review of structural and functional neuroimaging studies of hallucinations. *Neuroscience & Biobehavioral Reviews, 32*, 175–191.

Allen, P., Modinos, G., Hubl, D., Shields, G., Cachia, A., Jardri, R., et al. (2012). Neuroimaging auditory hallucinations in schizophrenia: from neuroanatomy to neurochemistry and beyond. *Schizophrenia Bulletin, 38*, 695–703.

Allen, P. P., Johns, L. C., Fu, C. H., Broome, M. R., Vythelingum, G. N., & McGuire, P. K. (2004). Misattribution of external speech in patients with hallucinations and delusions. *Schizophrenia Research, 69*, 277–287.

Aoyama, S., Kase, H., & Borrelli, E. (2000). Rescue of locomotor impairment in dopamine D2 receptor-deficient mice by an adenosine A2A receptor antagonist. *Journal of Neuroscience, 20*, 5848–5852.

Arai, S., Takuma, K., Mizoguchi, H., Ibi, D., Nagai, T., Takahashi, K., et al. (2008). Involvement of pallidotegmental neurons in methamphetamine- and MK-801-induced impairment of prepulse inhibition of the acoustic startle reflex in mice: reversal by GABAB receptor agonist baclofen. *Neuropsychopharmacology, 33*, 3164–3175.

Ashburner, J., & Friston, K. J. (2000). Voxel-based morphometry—the methods. *Neuroimage, 11*, 805–821.

Barta, P. E., Pearlson, G. D., Powers, R. E., Richards, S. S., & Tune, L. E. (1990). Auditory hallucinations and smaller superior temporal gyral volume in schizophrenia. *American Journal of Psychiatry, 147*, 1457–1462.

Becker, T. M., Cicero, D. C., Cowan, N., & Kerns, J. G. (2012). Cognitive control components and speech symptoms in people with schizophrenia. *Psychiatry Research, 196*, 20–26.

Benes, F. M., & Berretta, S. (2001). GABAergic interneurons: implications for understanding schizophrenia and bipolar disorder. *Neuropsychopharmacology, 25*, 1–27.

Benes, F. M., Vincent, S. L., Alsterberg, G., Bird, E. D., & SanGiovanni, J. P. (1992). Increased GABAA receptor binding in superficial layers of cingulate cortex in schizophrenics. *Journal of Neuroscience, 12*, 924–929.

Benes, F. M., Vincent, S. L., Marie, A., & Khan, Y. (1996). Up-regulation of GABAA receptor binding on neurons of the prefrontal cortex in schizophrenic subjects. *Neuroscience, 75*, 1021–1031.

Benetti, S., Pettersson-Yeo, W., Allen, P., Catani, M., Williams, S., Barsaglini, A., et al. (2013). auditory verbal hallucinations and brain dysconnectivity in the Perisylvian language network: a multimodal investigation. *Schizophrenia Bulletin.*

Berenbaum, H., Kerns, J. G., Vernon, L. L., & Gomez, J. J. (2008). Cognitive correlates of schizophrenia signs and symptoms: I. Verbal communication disturbances. *Psychiatry Research, 159*, 147–156.

Berman, J. A., Talmage, D. A., & Role, L. W. (2007). Cholinergic circuits and signaling in the pathophysiology of schizophrenia. *International Review of Neurobiology, 78*, 193–223.

Bjorklund, A., & Dunnett, S. B. (2007). Dopamine neuron systems in the brain: an update. *Trends in Neurosciences, 30*, 194–202.

Blackwood, N. J., Howard, R. J., Bentall, R. P., & Murray, R. M. (2001). Cognitive neuropsychiatric models of persecutory delusions. *American Journal of Psychiatry, 158*, 527–539.

Bossong, M. G., van Berckel, B. N., Boellaard, R., Zuurman, L., Schuit, R. C., Windhorst, A. D., et al. (2009). Delta 9-tetrahydrocannabinol induces dopamine release in the human striatum. *Neuropsychopharmacology, 34*, 759–766.

Bracha, H. S., Wolkowitz, O. M., Lohr, J. B., Karson, C. N., & Bigelow, L. B. (1989). High prevalence of visual hallucinations in research subjects with chronic schizophrenia. *American Journal of Psychiatry, 146*, 526–528.

Braff, D. L., Geyer, M. A., & Swerdlow, N. R. (2001). Human studies of prepulse inhibition of startle: normal subjects, patient groups, and pharmacological studies. *Psychopharmacology (Berl), 156*, 234–258.

Braun, C. M., Dumont, M., Duval, J., Hamel-Hebert, I., & Godbout, L. (2003). Brain modules of hallucination: an analysis of multiple patients with brain lesions. *Journal of Psychiatry Neuroscience, 28*, 432–449.

Broome, M. R., Day, F., Valli, I., Valmaggia, L., Johns, L. C., Howes, O., et al. (2012). Delusional ideation, manic symptomatology and working memory in a cohort at clinical high-risk for psychosis: a longitudinal study. *European Psychiatry, 27*, 258–263.

Brvar, M., Mozina, M., & Bunc, M. (2006). Prolonged psychosis after Amanita muscaria ingestion. *Wiener Klinische Wochenschrift, 118*, 294–297.

Busatto, G. F., David, A. S., Costa, D. C., Ell, P. J., Pilowsky, L. S., Lucey, J. V., et al. (1995). Schizophrenic auditory hallucinations are associated with increased regional cerebral blood flow during verbal memory activation in a study using single photon emission computed tomography. *Psychiatry Research, 61*, 255–264.

Cadenhead, K. S., Swerdlow, N. R., Shafer, K. M., Diaz, M., & Braff, D. L. (2000). Modulation of the startle response and startle laterality in relatives of schizophrenic patients and in subjects with schizotypal personality disorder: evidence of inhibitory deficits. *American Journal of Psychiatry, 157*, 1660–1668.

Carpenter, W. T., Jr., Strauss, J. S., & Bartko, J. J. (1973). Flexible system for the diagnosis of schizophrenia: report from the WHO International Pilot Study of Schizophrenia. *Science, 182*, 1275–1278.

Chaudhury, S. (2010). Hallucinations: clinical aspects and management. *Industrial Psychiatry Journal, 19*, 5–12.

Chen, C. M., Stanford, A. D., Mao, X., Abi-Dargham, A., Shungu, D. C., Lisanby, S. H., et al. (2014). GABA level, gamma oscillation, and working memory performance in schizophrenia. *NeuroImage: Clinical, 4*, 531–539.

Cohen, B. D., Rosenbaum, G., Luby, E. D., & Gottlieb, J. S. (1962). Comparison of phencyclidine hydrochloride (Sernyl) with other drugs. Simulation of schizophrenic performance with phencyclidine hydrochloride (Sernyl), lysergic acid diethylamide (LSD-25), and amobarbital (Amytal) sodium; II. Symbolic and sequential thinking. *Archives of General Psychiatry, 6*, 395–401.

Cohen, J. D., Barch, D. M., Carter, C., & Servan-Schreiber, D. (1999). Context-processing deficits in schizophrenia: converging evidence from three theoretically motivated cognitive tasks. *Journal of Abnormal Psychology, 108*, 120–133.

Corlett, P. R., Taylor, J. R., Wang, X. J., Fletcher, P. C., & Krystal, J. H. (2010). Toward a neurobiology of delusions. *Progress in Neurobiology, 92*, 345–369.

Corne, S. J., & Pickering, R. W. (1967). A possible correlation between drug-induced hallucinations in man and a behavioural response in mice. *Psychopharmacologia, 11*, 65–78.

Corne, S. J., Pickering, R. W., & Warner, B. T. (1963). A method for assessing the effects of drugs on the central actions of 5-hydroxytryptamine. *British Journal of Pharmacological and Chemotherapy, 20*, 106–120.

Correll, C. U., & Kane, J. M. (2014). Schizophrenia: mechanism of action of current and novel treatments. *Journal of Clinical Psychiatry, 75*, 347–348.

Courtney, S. M., Petit, L., Haxby, J. V., & Ungerleider, L. G. (1998). The role of prefrontal cortex in working memory: examining the contents of consciousness. *Philosophical Transactions of the Royal Society of London Series B: Biological Sciences, 353*, 1819–1828.

Coyle, J. T. (2012). NMDA receptor and schizophrenia: a brief history. *Schizophrenia Bulletin, 38*, 920–926.

Crook, J. M., Tomaskovic-Crook, E., Copolov, D. L., & Dean, B. (2000). Decreased muscarinic receptor binding in subjects with schizophrenia: a study of the human hippocampal formation. *Biological Psychiatry, 48*, 381–388.

Crook, J. M., Tomaskovic-Crook, E., Copolov, D. L., & Dean, B. (2001). Low muscarinic receptor binding in prefrontal cortex from subjects with schizophrenia: a study of Brodmann's areas 8, 9, 10, and 46 and the effects of neuroleptic drug treatment. *American Journal of Psychiatry, 158*, 918–925.

Cummings, J. L., Gorman, D. G., & Shapira, J. (1993). Physostigmine ameliorates the delusions of Alzheimer's disease. *Biological Psychiatry, 33*, 536–541.

Cummings, J. L., & Miller, B. L. (1987). Visual hallucinations. Clinical occurrence and use in differential diagnosis. *Western Journal of Medicine, 146*, 46–51.

Curzon, P., Rustay, N. R., & Browman, K. E. (2009). Cued and contextual fear conditioning for rodents. In J. J. Buccafusco (Ed.), *Methods of behavior analysis in neuroscience* (2nd ed.). Boca Raton, FL.

Daalman, K., van Zandvoort, M., Bootsman, F., Boks, M., Kahn, R., & Sommer, I. (2011). Auditory verbal hallucinations and cognitive functioning in healthy individuals. *Schizophrenia Research, 132*, 203–207.

Darmani, N. A. (2001). Cannabinoids of diverse structure inhibit two DOI-induced 5-HT(2A) receptor-mediated behaviors in mice. *Pharmacology, Biochemistry and Behavior, 68*, 311–317.

Darmani, N. A., & Pandya, D. K. (2000). Involvement of other neurotransmitters in behaviors induced by the cannabinoid CB1 receptor antagonist SR 141716A in naive mice. *Journal of Neural Transmission, 107*, 931–945.

Davies, B. M., & Beech, H. R. (1960). The effect of 1-arylcylohexylamine (Sernyl) on twelve normal volunteers. *Journal of Mental Science, 106*, 912–924.

Dean, B. (2012). Selective activation of muscarinic acetylcholine receptors for the treatment of schizophrenia. *Current Pharmaceutical Biotechnology, 13*, 1563–1571.

Deng, C., & Huang, X. F. (2005). Decreased density of muscarinic receptors in the superior temporal gyrusin schizophrenia. *Journal of Neuroscience Research, 81*, 883–890.

Deng, C., & Huang, X. F. (2006). Increased density of GABAA receptors in the superior temporal gyrus in schizophrenia. *Experimental Brain Research, 168*, 587–590.

Devane, W. A., Dysarz, F. A., 3rd, Johnson, M. R., Melvin, L. S., & Howlett, A. C. (1988). Determination and characterization of a cannabinoid receptor in rat brain. *Molecular Pharmacology, 34*, 605–613.

Diederich, N. J., Alesch, F., & Goetz, C. G. (2000). Visual hallucinations induced by deep brain stimulation in Parkinson's disease. *Clinical Neuropharmacology, 23*, 287–289.

Docherty, N. M., Hawkins, K. A., Hoffman, R. E., Quinlan, D. M., Rakfeldt, J., & Sledge, W. H. (1996). Working memory, attention, and communication disturbances in schizophrenia. *Journal of Abnormal Psychology, 105*, 212–219.

D'Souza, D. C., Perry, E., MacDougall, L., Ammerman, Y., Cooper, T., Wu, Y. T., et al. (2004). The psychotomimetic effects of intravenous delta-9-tetrahydrocannabinol in healthy individuals: implications for psychosis. *Neuropsychopharmacology, 29*, 1558–1572.

Fernandez-Espejo, E., Viveros, M. P., Nunez, L., Ellenbroek, B. A., & Rodriguez de Fonseca, F. (2009). Role of cannabis and endocannabinoids in the genesis of schizophrenia. *Psychopharmacology (Berl), 206*, 531–549.

Fisher, C. M. (1991). Visual hallucinations on eye closure associated with atropine toxicity. A neurological analysis and comparison with other visual hallucinations. *Canadian Journal of Neurological Science, 18*, 18–27.

Fitzgerald, M. L., Shobin, E., & Pickel, V. M. (2012). Cannabinoid modulation of the dopaminergic circuitry: implications for limbic and striatal output. *Progress in Neuro-Psychopharmacology and Biological Psychiatry, 38*, 21–29.

Flaum, M., O'Leary, D. S., Swayze, V. W., 2nd, Miller, D. D., Arndt, S., & Andreasen, N. C. (1995). Symptom dimensions and brain morphology in schizophrenia and related psychotic disorders. *Journal of Psychiatry Research, 29*, 261–276.

Fletcher, P. C., & Frith, C. D. (2009). Perceiving is believing: a Bayesian approach to explaining the positive symptoms of schizophrenia. *Nature Reviews Neuroscience, 10*, 48–58.

Foster, D. J., Jones, C. K., & Conn, P. J. (2012). Emerging approaches for treatment of schizophrenia: modulation of cholinergic signaling. *Discovery Medicine, 14*, 413–420.

Ganzola, R., Maziade, M., & Duchesne, S. (2014). Hippocampus and amygdala volumes in children and young adults at high-risk of schizophrenia: research synthesis. *Schizophrenia Research, 156*, 76–86.

Garcia-Marti, G., Aguilar, E. J., Lull, J. J., Marti-Bonmati, L., Escarti, M. J., Manjon, J. V., et al. (2008). Schizophrenia with auditory hallucinations: a voxel-based morphometry study. *Progress in Neuro-Psychopharmacology and Biological Psychiatry, 32*, 72–80.

Gaser, C., Nenadic, I., Volz, H. P., Buchel, C., & Sauer, H. (2004). Neuroanatomy of "hearing voices": a frontotemporal brain structural abnormality associated with auditory hallucinations in schizophrenia. *Cerebral Cortex, 14*, 91–96.

Geyer, M. A., & Braff, D. L. (1987). Startle habituation and sensorimotor gating in schizophrenia and related animal models. *Schizophrenia Bulletin, 13*, 643–668.

Geyer, M. A., & Swerdlow, N. R. (2001). Measurement of startle response, prepulse inhibition, and habituation. *Current Protocols in Neuroscience*. Chapter 8, Unit 8.7.

Geyer, M. A., Swerdlow, N. R., Mansbach, R. S., & Braff, D. L. (1990). Startle response models of sensorimotor gating and habituation deficits in schizophrenia. *Brain Research Bulletin, 25*, 485–498.

Glennon, R. A. (1991). Discriminative stimulus properties of hallucinogens and related designer drugs. *NIDA Research Monograph, 25*, 25–44.

Goldsmith, S. K., & Joyce, J. N. (1996). Dopamine D2 receptors are organized in bands in normal human temporal cortex. *Neuroscience, 74*, 435–451.

Goldsmith, S. K., Shapiro, R. M., & Joyce, J. N. (1997). Disrupted pattern of D2 dopamine receptors in the temporal lobe in schizophrenia. A postmortem study. *Archives of General Psychiatry, 54*, 649–658.

Gonzalez-Maeso, J., Weisstaub, N. V., Zhou, M., Chan, P., Ivic, L., Ang, R., et al. (2007). Hallucinogens recruit specific cortical 5-HT(2A) receptor-mediated signaling pathways to affect behavior. *Neuron, 53*, 439–452.

Gonzalez-Maeso, J., Yuen, T., Ebersole, B. J., Wurmbach, E., Lira, A., Zhou, M., et al. (2003). Transcriptome fingerprints distinguish hallucinogenic and nonhallucinogenic 5-hydroxytryptamine 2A receptor agonist effects in mouse somatosensory cortex. *Journal of Neuroscience, 23*, 8836–8843.

Good, C. D., Johnsrude, I. S., Ashburner, J., Henson, R. N., Friston, K. J., & Frackowiak, R. S. (2001). A voxel-based morphometric study of ageing in 465 normal adult human brains. *NeuroImage, 14*, 21–36.

Halberstadt, A. L., & Geyer, M. A. (2010). LSD but not lisuride disrupts prepulse inhibition in rats by activating the 5-HT(2A) receptor. *Psychopharmacology (Berl), 208*, 179–189.

Halberstadt, A. L., & Geyer, M. A. (2013a). Characterization of the head-twitch response induced by hallucinogens in mice: detection of the behavior based on the dynamics of head movement. *Psychopharmacology (Berl), 227*, 727–739.

Halberstadt, A. L., & Geyer, M. A. (2013b). Serotonergic hallucinogens as translational models relevant to schizophrenia. *International Journal of Neuropsychopharmacology, 16*, 2165–2180.

Halberstadt, A. L., Powell, S. B., & Geyer, M. A. (2013). Role of the 5-HT(2) A receptor in the locomotor hyperactivity produced by phenylalkylamine hallucinogens in mice. *Neuropharmacology, 70*, 218–227.

Halpern, J. H. (2004). Hallucinogens and dissociative agents naturally growing in the United States. *Pharmacology & Therapeutics, 102*, 131–138.

Hauf, M., Wiest, R., Schindler, K., Jann, K., Dierks, T., Strik, W., et al. (2013). Common mechanisms of auditory hallucinations-perfusion studies in epilepsy. *Psychiatry Research, 211*, 268–270.

Hides, L., Lubman, D. I., Buckby, J., Yuen, H. P., Cosgrave, E., Baker, K., et al. (2009). The association between early cannabis use and psychotic-like experiences in a community adolescent sample. *Schizophrenia Research, 112*, 130–135.

Hill, M. N., Sun, J. C., Tse, M. T., & Gorzalka, B. B. (2006). Altered responsiveness of serotonin receptor subtypes following long-term cannabinoid treatment. *International Journal of Neuropsychopharmacology, 9*, 277–286.

Hirschhorn, I. D., & Winter, J. C. (1971). Mescaline and lysergic acid diethylamide (LSD) as discriminative stimuli. *Psychopharmacologia, 22*, 64–71.

Hollister, L. E. (1974). Structure-activity relationships in man of cannabis constituents, and homologs and metabolites of delta9-tetrahydrocannabinol. *Pharmacology, 11*, 3–11.

Homan, P., Kindler, J., Hauf, M., Walther, S., Hubl, D., & Dierks, T. (2013). Repeated measurements of cerebral blood flow in the left superior temporal gyrus reveal tonic hyperactivity in patients with auditory verbal hallucinations: a possible trait marker. *Frontiers in Human Neuroscience, 7*, 304.

Hong, L. E., Wonodi, I., Stine, O. C., Mitchell, B. D., & Thaker, G. K. (2008). Evidence of missense mutations on the neuregulin 1 gene affecting function of prepulse inhibition. *Biological Psychiatry, 63*, 17–23.

Howes, O. D., Egerton, A., Allan, V., McGuire, P., Stokes, P., & Kapur, S. (2009). Mechanisms underlying psychosis and antipsychotic treatment response in schizophrenia: insights from PET and SPECT imaging. *Current Pharmaceutical Design, 15*, 2550–2559.

Huber, M., Kirchler, E., Karner, M., & Pycha, R. (2007). Delusional parasitosis and the dopamine transporter. A new insight of etiology? *Medical Hypotheses, 68*, 1351–1358.

Hyde, T. M., & Crook, J. M. (2001). Cholinergic systems and schizophrenia: primary pathology or epiphenomena? *Journal of Chemical Neuroanatomy, 22*, 53–63.

Inan, M., Petros, T. J., & Anderson, S. A. (2013). Losing your inhibition: linking cortical GABAergic interneurons to schizophrenia. *Neurobiology of Disease, 53*, 36–48.

Iyo, M., Nishio, M., Itoh, T., Fukuda, H., Suzuki, K., Yamasaki, T., et al. (1993). Dopamine D2 and serotonin S2 receptors in susceptibility to methamphetamine psychosis detected by positron emission tomography. *Psychiatry Research, 50*, 217–231.

Izumi, Y., Terao, T., Ishino, Y., & Nakamura, J. (2002). Differences in regional cerebral blood flow during musical and verbal hallucinations. *Psychiatry Research, 116*, 119–123.

Jacobs, B. L., Trulson, M. E., & Stern, W. C. (1976). An animal behavior model for studying the actions of LSD and related hallucinogens. *Science, 194*, 741–743.

Jacobs, B. L., Trulson, M. E., & Stern, W. C. (1977). Behavioral effects of LSD in the cat: proposal of an animal behavior model for studying the actions of hallucinogenic drugs. *Brain Research, 132*, 301–314.

Janoyan, J. J., Crim, J. L., & Darmani, N. A. (2002). Reversal of SR 141716A-induced head-twitch and ear-scratch responses in mice by delta 9-THC and other cannabinoids. *Pharmacology, Biochemistry and Behavior, 71*, 155–162.

Jardri, R., & Deneve, S. (2013). Circular inferences in schizophrenia. *Brain, 136*, 3227–3241.

Javanbakht, A. (2006). Sensory gating deficits, pattern completion, and disturbed fronto-limbic balance, a model for description of hallucinations and delusions in schizophrenia. *Medical Hypotheses, 67*, 1173–1184.

Javitt, D. C., & Zukin, S. R. (1991). Recent advances in the phencyclidine model of schizophrenia. *American Journal of Psychiatry, 148*, 1301–1308.

Javitt, D. C., Zukin, S. R., Heresco-Levy, U., & Umbricht, D. (2012). Has an angel shown the way? Etiological and therapeutic implications of the PCP/NMDA model of schizophrenia. *Schizophrenia Bulletin, 38*, 958–966.

Johnson, M., Richards, W., & Griffiths, R. (2008). Human hallucinogen research: guidelines for safety. *Journal of Psychopharmacology, 22*, 603–620.

Kasai, K., Shenton, M. E., Salisbury, D. F., Hirayasu, Y., Lee, C. U., Ciszewski, A. A., et al. (2003). Progressive decrease of left superior temporal gyrus gray matter volume in patients with first-episode schizophrenia. *American Journal of Psychiatry, 160*, 156–164.

Kawamura, Y., Fukaya, M., Maejima, T., Yoshida, T., Miura, E., Watanabe, M., et al. (2006). The CB1 cannabinoid receptor is the major cannabinoid receptor at excitatory presynaptic sites in the hippocampus and cerebellum. *Journal of Neuroscience, 26*, 2991–3001.

Keeler, M. H. (1965). Similarity of schizophrenia and the psilocybin syndrome as determined by objective methods. *International Journal of Neuropsychiatry, 1*, 630–634.

Keller, D. L., & Umbreit, W. W. (1956). Permanent alteration of behavior in mice by chemical and psychological means. *Science, 124*, 723–724.

Kindler, J., Homan, P., Jann, K., Federspiel, A., Flury, R., Hauf, M., et al. (2013). Reduced neuronal activity in language-related regions after transcranial magnetic stimulation therapy for auditory verbal hallucinations. *Biological Psychiatry, 73*, 518–524.

Kiran, C., & Chaudhury, S. (2009). Understanding delusions. *Industrial Psychiatry Journal, 18*, 3–18.

Klemperer, F. (1992). Ghosts, visions, and voices. *BMJ, 305*, 1518–1519.

Kometer, M., Schmidt, A., Jancke, L., & Vollenweider, F. X. (2013). Activation of serotonin 2A receptors underlies the psilocybin-induced effects on alpha oscillations, N170 visual-evoked potentials, and visual hallucinations. *Journal of Neuroscience, 33*, 10544–10551.

Krystal, J. H., Karper, L. P., Seibyl, J. P., Freeman, G. K., Delaney, R., Bremner, J. D., et al. (1994). Subanesthetic effects of the noncompetitive NMDA antagonist, ketamine, in humans. Psychotomimetic, perceptual, cognitive, and neuroendocrine responses. *Archives of General Psychiatry, 51*, 199–214.

Kumari, V., Peters, E. R., Fannon, D., Premkumar, P., Aasen, I., Cooke, M. A., et al. (2008). Uncontrollable voices and their relationship to gating deficits in schizophrenia. *Schizophrenia Research, 101*, 185–194.

Kummer, L., Rzewuska, M., Sienkiewicz-Jarosz, H., Mierzejewski, P., Bienkowski, P., & Samochowiec, J. (2012). Zolpidem misuse in two women with no psychiatric history: a crucial role of pleasant visual hallucinations. *Journal of Neuropsychiatry and Clinical Neurosciences, 24*, E32.

Lawrie, S. M., Whalley, H. C., Job, D. E., & Johnstone, E. C. (2003). Structural and functional abnormalities of the amygdala in schizophrenia. *Annals of the New York Academy of Sciences, 985*, 445–460.

Lewis, D. A., Hashimoto, T., & Volk, D. W. (2005). Cortical inhibitory neurons and schizophrenia. *Nature Reviews Neuroscience, 6*, 312–324.

Lieberman, J. A., Kane, J. M., & Alvir, J. (1987). Provocative tests with psychostimulant drugs in schizophrenia. *Psychopharmacology (Berl), 91*, 415–433.

Luby, E. D., Cohen, B. D., Rosenbaum, G., Gottlieb, J. S., & Kelley, R. (1959). Study of a new schizophrenomimetic drug; sernyl. *AMA Archives of Neurology and Psychiatry, 81*, 363–369.

Magdalan, J., & Antonczyk, A. (2007). *Amanita pantherina* poisoning or brain stroke? *Przeglad Lekarski, 64*, 341–343.

Mancama, D., Arranz, M. J., Landau, S., & Kerwin, R. (2003). Reduced expression of the muscarinic 1 receptor cortical subtype in schizophrenia. *American Journal of Medical Genetics Part B Neuropsychiatric Genetics, 119B*, 2–6.

Manfredi, G., Kotzalidis, G. D., Lazanio, S., Savoja, V., Talamo, A., Koukopoulos, A. E., et al. (2010). Command hallucinations with self-stabbing associated with zolpidem overdose. *Journal of Clinical Psychiatry, 71*, 92–93.

Marcotte, E. R., Pearson, D. M., & Srivastava, L. K. (2001). Animal models of schizophrenia: a critical review. *Journal of Psychiatry & Neuroscience, 26*, 395–410.

Marini, J. L., & Sheard, M. H. (1981). On the specificity of a cat behavior model for the study of hallucinogens. *European Journal of Pharmacology, 70*, 479–487.

Markota, M., Sin, J., Pantazopoulos, H., Jonilionis, R., & Berretta, S. (2014). Reduced dopamine transporter expression in the amygdala of subjects diagnosed with schizophrenia. *Schizophrenia Bulletin*.

Mato, S., Aso, E., Castro, E., Martin, M., Valverde, O., Maldonado, R., et al. (2007). CB1 knockout mice display impaired functionality of 5-HT1A and 5-HT2A/C receptors. *Journal of Neurochemistry, 103*, 2111–2120.

May, J. A., Sharif, N. A., Chen, H. H., Liao, J. C., Kelly, C. R., Glennon, R. A., et al. (2009). Pharmacological properties and discriminative stimulus effects of a novel and selective 5-HT2 receptor agonist AL-38022A [(S)-2-(8,9-dihydro-7H-pyrano[2,3-g]indazol-1-yl)-1-methylethylamine]. *Pharmacology, Biochemistry and Behavior, 91*, 307–314.

McGuire, P. K., Silbersweig, D. A., Wright, I., Murray, R. M., David, A. S., Frackowiak, R. S., et al. (1995). Abnormal monitoring of inner speech: a physiological basis for auditory hallucinations. *Lancet, 346*, 596–600.

McKeith, I. G., Galasko, D., Kosaka, K., Perry, E. K., Dickson, D. W., Hansen, L. A., et al. (1996). Consensus guidelines for the clinical and pathologic diagnosis of dementia with Lewy bodies (DLB): report of the consortium on DLB international workshop. *Neurology, 47*, 1113–1124.

Miller, G. M. (2011). The emerging role of trace amine-associated receptor 1 in the functional regulation of monoamine transporters and dopaminergic activity. *Journal of Neurochemistry, 116*, 164–176.

Mizoguchi, H., Yamada, K., Niwa, M., Mouri, A., Mizuno, T., Noda, Y., et al. (2007). Reduction of methamphetamine-induced sensitization and reward in matrix metalloproteinase-2 and -9-deficient mice. *Journal of Neurochemistry, 100*, 1579–1588.

Modinos, G., Vercammen, A., Mechelli, A., Knegtering, H., McGuire, P. K., & Aleman, A. (2009). Structural covariance in the hallucinating brain: a voxel-based morphometry study. *Journal of Psychiatry & Neuroscience, 34*, 465–469.

Moreau, A. W., Amar, M., Le Roux, N., Morel, N., & Fossier, P. (2010). Serotoninergic fine-tuning of the excitation-inhibition balance in rat visual cortical networks. *Cerebral Cortex, 20*, 456–467.

Morgan, B., Terburg, D., Thornton, H. B., Stein, D. J., & van Honk, J. (2012). Paradoxical facilitation of working memory after basolateral amygdala damage. *PLoS One, 7*, e38116.

Morimoto, K., Miyatake, R., Nakamura, M., Watanabe, T., Hirao, T., & Suwaki, H. (2002). Delusional disorder: molecular genetic evidence for dopamine psychosis. *Neuropsychopharmacology, 26*, 794–801.

Morrison, P. D., Zois, V., McKeown, D. A., Lee, T. D., Holt, D. W., Powell, J. F., et al. (2009). The acute effects of synthetic intravenous delta9-tetrahydrocannabinol on psychosis, mood and cognitive functioning. *Psychological Medicine, 39*, 1607–1616.

Mouri, A., Noda, Y., Noda, A., Nakamura, T., Tokura, T., Yura, Y., et al. (2007). Involvement of a dysfunctional dopamine-D1/N-methyl-D-aspartate-NR1 and Ca2+/calmodulin-dependent protein kinase II pathway in the impairment of latent learning in a model of schizophrenia induced by phencyclidine. *Molecular Pharmacology, 71*, 1598–1609.

Mueser, K. T., Bellack, A. S., & Brady, E. U. (1990). Hallucinations in schizophrenia. *Acta Psychiatrica Scandinavica, 82*, 26–29.

Muller-Vahl, K. R., & Emrich, H. M. (2008). Cannabis and schizophrenia: towards a cannabinoid hypothesis of schizophrenia. *Expert Review of Neurotherapeutics, 8*, 1037–1048.

Nabeshima, T., Ishikawa, K., Yamaguchi, K., Furukawa, H., & Kameyama, T. (1987a). Phencyclidine-induced head-twitch response in rats treated chronically with methysergide. *European Journal of Pharmacology, 133*, 319–328.

Nabeshima, T., Ishikawa, K., Yamaguchi, K., Furukawa, H., & Kameyama, T. (1987b). Phencyclidine-induced head-twitch responses as 5-HT2 receptor-mediated behavior in rats. *Neuroscience Letters, 76*, 335–338.

Nabeshima, T., Kitaichi, K., & Noda, Y. (1996). Functional changes in neuronal systems induced by phencyclidine administration. *Annals of the New York Academy of Sciences, 801*, 29–38.

Nabeshima, T., Mouri, A., Murai, R., & Noda, Y. (2006). Animal model of schizophrenia: dysfunction of NMDA receptor-signaling in mice following withdrawal from repeated administration of phencyclidine. *Annals of the New York Academy of Sciences, 1086*, 160–168.

Nabeshima, T., Nakayama, S., Ichihara, K., Yamada, K., Shiotani, T., & Hasegawa, T. (1994). Effects of nefiracetam on drug-induced impairment of latent learning in mice in a water finding task. *European Journal of Pharmacology, 255*, 57–65.

Nagai, H., Egashira, N., Sano, K., Ogata, A., Mizuki, A., Mishima, K., et al. (2006). Antipsychotics improve delta9-tetrahydrocannabinol-induced impairment of the prepulse inhibition of the startle reflex in mice. *Pharmacology, Biochemistry and Behavior, 84*, 330–336.

Neckelmann, G., Specht, K., Lund, A., Ersland, L., Smievoll, A. I., Neckelmann, D., et al. (2006). Mr morphometry analysis of grey matter volume reduction in schizophrenia: association with hallucinations. *International Journal of Neuroscience, 116*, 9–23.

Nichols, D. E. (2004). Hallucinogens. *Pharmacology & Therapeutics, 101*, 131–181.

Nielsen, E. B., Lyon, M., & Ellison, G. (1983). Apparent hallucinations in monkeys during around-the-clock amphetamine for seven to fourteen days. Possible relevance to amphetamine psychosis. *Journal of Nervous and Mental Disease, 171*, 222–233.

Niwa, M., Kamiya, A., Murai, R., Kubo, K., Gruber, A. J., Tomita, K., et al. (2010). Knockdown of DISC1 by in utero gene transfer disturbs postnatal dopaminergic maturation in the frontal cortex and leads to adult behavioral deficits. *Neuron, 65*, 480–489.

Nixon, P., Lazarova, J., Hodinott-Hill, I., Gough, P., & Passingham, R. (2004). The inferior frontal gyrus and phonological processing: an investigation using rTMS. *Journal of Cognitive Neuroscience, 16*, 289–300.

Norton, J. W., & Corbett, J. J. (2000). Visual perceptual abnormalities: hallucinations and illusions. *Seminars in Neurology, 20*, 111–121.

Oertel, V., Rotarska-Jagiela, A., van de Ven, V. G., Haenschel, C., Maurer, K., & Linden, D. E. (2007). Visual hallucinations in schizophrenia investigated with functional magnetic resonance imaging. *Psychiatry Research, 156*, 269–273.

Okada, K., Suyama, N., Oguro, H., Yamaguchi, S., & Kobayashi, S. (1999). Medication-induced hallucination and cerebral blood flow in Parkinson's disease. *Journal of Neurology, 246*, 365–368.

van Os, J., Bak, M., Hanssen, M., Bijl, R. V., de Graaf, R., & Verdoux, H. (2002). Cannabis use and psychosis: a longitudinal population-based study. *American Journal of Epidemiology, 156*, 319–327.

Ozawa, K., Hashimoto, K., Kishimoto, T., Shimizu, E., Ishikura, H., & Iyo, M. (2006). Immune activation during pregnancy in mice leads to dopaminergic hyperfunction and cognitive impairment in the offspring: a neurodevelopmental animal model of schizophrenia. *Biological Psychiatry, 59*, 546–554.

Pankow, A., Knobel, A., Voss, M., & Heinz, A. (2012). Neurobiological correlates of delusion: beyond the salience attribution hypothesis. *Neuropsychobiology, 66*, 33–43.

Patel, S. S., Attard, A., Jacobsen, P., & Shergill, S. (2010). Acetylcholinesterase Inhibitors (AChEI's) for the treatment of visual hallucinations in schizophrenia: a case report. *BMC Psychiatry, 10*, 68.

Penfield, W., & Perot, P. (1963). The brain's record of auditory and visual experience. A final summary and discussion. *Brain, 86*, 595–696.

Perry, E., Walker, M., Grace, J., & Perry, R. (1999). Acetylcholine in mind: a neurotransmitter correlate of consciousness? *Trends in Neurosciences, 22*, 273–280.

Perry, E. K., & Perry, R. H. (1995). Acetylcholine and hallucinations: disease-related compared to drug-induced alterations in human consciousness. *Brain and Cognition, 28*, 240–258.

Phelps, E. A. (2004). Human emotion and memory: interactions of the amygdala and hippocampal complex. *Current Opinion in Neurobiology, 14*, 198–202.

Pierce, R. C., & Kalivas, P. W. (2007). Locomotor behavior. *Current Protocols in Neuroscience*. Chapter 8, Unit 8.1.

Plaze, M., Paillere-Martinot, M. L., Penttila, J., Januel, D., de Beaurepaire, R., Bellivier, F., et al. (2011). "Where do auditory hallucinations come from?"–a brain morphometry study of schizophrenia patients with inner or outer space hallucinations. *Schizophrenia Bulletin, 37*, 212–221.

Raedler, T. J., Bymaster, F. P., Tandon, R., Copolov, D., & Dean, B. (2007). Towards a muscarinic hypothesis of schizophrenia. *Molecular Psychiatry, 12*, 232–246.

Robinson, T. E., & Berridge, K. C. (1993). The neural basis of drug craving: an incentive-sensitization theory of addiction. *Brain Research. Brain Research Reviews, 18*, 247–291.

Sabri, O., Erkwoh, R., Schreckenberger, M., Owega, A., Sass, H., & Buell, U. (1997). Correlation of positive symptoms exclusively to hyperperfusion or hypoperfusion of cerebral cortex in never-treated schizophrenics. *Lancet, 349*, 1735–1739.

Sarter, M., & Bruno, J. P. (1998). Cortical acetylcholine, reality distortion, schizophrenia, and Lewy body dementia: too much or too little cortical acetylcholine? *Brain and Cognition, 38*, 297–316.

Sartorius, N., Jablensky, A., Korten, A., Ernberg, G., Anker, M., Cooper, J. E., et al. (1986). Early manifestations and first-contact incidence of schizophrenia in different cultures. A preliminary report on the initial evaluation phase of the WHO Collaborative Study on determinants of outcome of severe mental disorders. *Psychological Medicine, 16*, 909–928.

Sartorius, N., Shapiro, R., Kimura, M., & Barrett, K. (1972). WHO international pilot study of schizophrenia. *Psychological Medicine, 2,* 422–425.

Scarr, E., Sundram, S., Keriakous, D., & Dean, B. (2007). Altered hippocampal muscarinic M4, but not M1, receptor expression from subjects with schizophrenia. *Biological Psychiatry, 61,* 1161–1170.

Schultes, R. E. (1969). Hallucinogens of plant origin. *Science, 163,* 245–254.

Schwartz, T. L., Sachdeva, S., & Stahl, S. M. (2012). Glutamate neurocircuitry: theoretical underpinnings in schizophrenia. *Frontiers in Pharmacology, 3,* 195.

Seeman, P., & Kapur, S. (2000). Schizophrenia: more dopamine, more D2 receptors. *Proceedings of the National Academy of Sciences of the United States of America, 97,* 7673–7675.

Seok, J. H., Park, H. J., Chun, J. W., Lee, S. K., Cho, H. S., Kwon, J. S., et al. (2007). White matter abnormalities associated with auditory hallucinations in schizophrenia: a combined study of voxel-based analyses of diffusion tensor imaging and structural magnetic resonance imaging. *Psychiatry Research, 156,* 93–104.

Shergill, S. S., Brammer, M. J., Williams, S. C., Murray, R. M., & McGuire, P. K. (2000). Mapping auditory hallucinations in schizophrenia using functional magnetic resonance imaging. *Archives of General Psychiatry, 57,* 1033–1038.

Shimazono, Y., & Matsushima, E. (1995). Behavioral and neuroimaging studies on schizophrenia in Japan. *Psychiatry and Clinical Neurosciences, 49,* 3–11.

Shinn, A. K., Baker, J. T., Cohen, B. M., & Ongur, D. (2013). Functional connectivity of left Heschl's gyrus in vulnerability to auditory hallucinations in schizophrenia. *Schizophrenia Research, 143,* 260–268.

Shinn, A. K., Heckers, S., & Ongur, D. (2013). The special treatment of first rank auditory hallucinations and bizarre delusions in the diagnosis of schizophrenia. *Schizophrenia Research, 146,* 17–21.

Singh, G. P., & Loona, N. (2013). Zolpidem-induced hallucinations: a brief case report from the Indian subcontinent. *Indian Journal of Psychological Medicine, 35,* 212–213.

Snyder, M. A., & Gao, W. J. (2013). NMDA hypofunction as a convergence point for progression and symptoms of schizophrenia. *Frontiers in Cellular Neuroscience, 7,* 31.

Stahl, S. M. (2007). Beyond the dopamine hypothesis to the NMDA glutamate receptor hypofunction hypothesis of schizophrenia. *CNS Spectrums, 12,* 265–268.

Stefanis, N. C., Delespaul, P., Henquet, C., Bakoula, C., Stefanis, C. N., & Van Os, J. (2004). Early adolescent cannabis exposure and positive and negative dimensions of psychosis. *Addiction, 99,* 1333–1341.

Steinmann, S., Leicht, G., & Mulert, C. (2014). Interhemispheric auditory connectivity: structure and function related to auditory verbal hallucinations. *Frontiers in Human Neuroscience, 8,* 55.

Stephane, M., Barton, S., & Boutros, N. N. (2001). Auditory verbal hallucinations and dysfunction of the neural substrates of speech. *Schizophrenia Research, 50,* 61–78.

Stitt, C. L., Hoffman, H. S., & Marsh, R. (1973). Modification of the rat's startle reaction by termination of antecedent acoustic signals. *Journal of Comparative and Physiological Psychology, 84,* 207–215.

Swerdlow, N. R., Braff, D. L., Taaid, N., & Geyer, M. A. (1994). Assessing the validity of an animal model of deficient sensorimotor gating in schizophrenic patients. *Archives of General Psychiatry, 51,* 139–154.

Takahashi, M., Kakita, A., Futamura, T., Watanabe, Y., Mizuno, M., Sakimura, K., et al. (2006). Sustained brain-derived neurotrophic factor up-regulation and sensorimotor gating abnormality induced by postnatal exposure to phencyclidine: comparison with adult treatment. *Journal of Neurochemistry, 99,* 770–780.

Tandon, R., Gaebel, W., Barch, D. M., Bustillo, J., Gur, R. E., Heckers, S., et al. (2013). Definition and description of schizophrenia in the DSM-5. *Schizophrenia Research, 150,* 3–10.

Tarantino, I. S., Sharp, R. F., Geyer, M. A., Meves, J. M., & Young, J. W. (2011). Working memory span capacity improved by a D2 but not D1 receptor family agonist. *Behavioural Brain Research, 219,* 181–188.

Tracy, D. K., & Shergill, S. S. (2013). Mechanisms underlying auditory hallucinations-understanding perception without stimulus. *Brain Science, 3,* 642–669.

Tsujikawa, K., Mohri, H., Kuwayama, K., Miyaguchi, H., Iwata, Y., Gohda, A., et al. (2006). Analysis of hallucinogenic constituents in *Amanita* mushrooms circulated in Japan. *Forensic Science International, 164,* 172–178.

Tune, L., Barta, P., Wong, D., Powers, R. E., Pearlson, G., Tien, A. Y., et al. (1996). Striatal dopamine D2 receptor quantification and superior temporal gyrus: volume determination in 14 chronic schizophrenic subjects. *Psychiatry Research, 67,* 155–158.

Valjent, E., Bertran-Gonzalez, J., Aubier, B., Greengard, P., Herve, D., & Girault, J. A. (2010). Mechanisms of locomotor sensitization to drugs of abuse in a two-injection protocol. *Neuropsychopharmacology, 35,* 401–415.

Valsamis, B., & Schmid, S. (2011). Habituation and prepulse inhibition of acoustic startle in rodents. *Journal of Visualized Experiments,* e3446.

Vardy, M. M., & Kay, S. R. (1983). LSD psychosis or LSD-induced schizophrenia? A multimethod inquiry. *Archives of General Psychiatry, 40,* 877–883.

Villringer, A., & Dirnagl, U. (1995). Coupling of brain activity and cerebral blood flow: basis of functional neuroimaging. *Cerebrovascular and Brain Metabolism Reviews, 7,* 240–276.

Warburton, D. M., Wesnes, K., Edwards, J., & Larrad, D. (1985). Scopolamine and the sensory conditioning of hallucinations. *Neuropsychobiology, 14,* 198–202.

de Weijer, A. D., Mandl, R. C., Diederen, K. M., Neggers, S. F., Kahn, R. S., Hulshoff Pol, H. E., et al. (2011). Microstructural alterations of the arcuate fasciculus in schizophrenia patients with frequent auditory verbal hallucinations. *Schizophrenia Research, 130,* 68–77.

Weiss, A. P., & Heckers, S. (1999). Neuroimaging of hallucinations: a review of the literature. *Psychiatry Research, 92,* 61–74.

Willins, D. L., & Meltzer, H. Y. (1997). Direct injection of 5-HT2A receptor agonists into the medial prefrontal cortex produces a head-twitch response in rats. *Journal of Pharmacology and Experimental Therapeutics, 282,* 699–706.

Wynn, J. K., Dawson, M. E., Schell, A. M., McGee, M., Salveson, D., & Green, M. F. (2004). Prepulse facilitation and prepulse inhibition in schizophrenia patients and their unaffected siblings. *Biological Psychiatry, 55,* 518–523.

Xie, Z., & Miller, G. M. (2009). A receptor mechanism for methamphetamine action in dopamine transporter regulation in brain. *Journal of Pharmacology and Experimental Therapeutics, 330,* 316–325.

Yamada, K., Hiramatsu, M., Noda, Y., Mamiya, T., Murai, M., Kameyama, T., et al. (1996). Role of nitric oxide and cyclic GMP in the dizocilpine-induced impairment of spontaneous alternation behavior in mice. *Neuroscience, 74,* 365–374.

Yamada, S., Harano, M., Annoh, N., Nakamura, K., & Tanaka, M. (1999). Involvement of serotonin 2A receptors in phencyclidine-induced disruption of prepulse inhibition of the acoustic startle in rats. *Biological Psychiatry, 46,* 832–838.

Young, J. W., Zhou, X., & Geyer, M. A. (2010). Animal models of schizophrenia. *Current Topics in Behavioral Neurosciences, 4,* 391–433.

Yui, K., Ikemoto, S., Ishiguro, T., & Goto, K. (2000). Studies of amphetamine or methamphetamine psychosis in Japan: relation of methamphetamine psychosis to schizophrenia. *Annals of the New York Academy of Sciences, 914,* 1–12.

Zangrando, J., Carvalheira, R., Labbate, G., Medeiros, P., Longo, B. M., Melo-Thomas, L., et al. (2013). Atypical antipsychotic olanzapine reversed deficit on prepulse inhibition of the acoustic startle reflex produced by microinjection of dizocilpine (MK-801) into the inferior colliculus in rats. *Behavioural Brain Research, 257,* 77–82.

5

Animal Models of Psychotic Disorders: Dimensional Approach Modeling Negative Symptoms

Brian P. Kirby

School of Pharmacy, Royal College of Surgeons in Ireland, Dublin, Ireland
E-mail: bkirby@rcsi.ie

INTRODUCTION

Schizophrenia is a complex psychiatric disorder, affecting up to 1% of the world's population, expressing characteristic domains of symptomatology, generally split into positive, negative, and cognitive symptoms (Kane, 1996). The positive symptoms are commonly regarded as additions to normal behavior (thought disorder, visual and auditory hallucinations, and delusions), whereas the negative symptoms represent deficits in normal healthy functioning (anhedonia, alogia, avolition, asociality, and blunted affect) and the cognitive symptoms are impaired working memory, attention, and executive function (Andreasen, 1995; Kirkpatrick & Fischer, 2006). Because schizophrenia is a heterogeneous condition, not all patients will suffer from the same symptoms; this can determine the success or failure of pharmacological treatment (Dawe, Hwang, & Tan, 2009). From recent interview studies on patients, using newer (Clinical Assessment Interview for Negative Symptoms) (Kring, Gur, Blanchard, Horan, & Reise, 2013) and older (Scale for the Assessment of Negative Symptoms, SANS) (Andreasen, 1982) interview methods, two broad domains of symptoms cover the negative symptoms, namely motivation/pleasure and expression. Indeed, these two domains may better cover the putative underlying mechanisms (Blanchard & Cohen, 2006; Kring & Elis, 2013).

From the point of view of treatment, the use of antipsychotic medication has resulted in clinical benefit, but this has not always produced improvement in functional outcomes (Robinson, Woerner, McMeniman, Mendelowitz, & Bilder, 2004). The negative symptoms of schizophrenia appear to have the most detrimental effect on the functioning of the patient and their long-term quality of life (Milev, Ho, Arndt, & Andreasen, 2005). This, coupled with the fact that the pharmacological treatments, although effective for positive symptoms, generally lack efficacy against the negative symptoms, means that there is a gap in the treatment profile for patients (Rosenbaum et al., 2012). The impact of second-generation antipsychotic drugs, which were meant to be more effective at treating the negative symptoms, has been further questioned with evidence to show that any change in negative symptoms may actually be mediated through a reduction in positive symptoms (Subotnik et al., 2014). Sadly, studies show that those with least functional improvement are the patients with the most marked negative symptoms (Ho, Nopoulos, Flaum, Arndt, & Andreasen, 1998; Milev et al., 2005).

Although efforts are ongoing to develop effective treatment regimens for patients with dominant negative symptoms, the results are not encouraging. Novel techniques such as repetitive transcranial magnetic stimulation have been investigated but have shown mixed results. One study has shown an improvement in the Positive and Negative Syndrome Scale, whereas results from a different group showed no improvement in Positive and Negative Syndrome Scale (Dlabac-de Lange et al., 2014; Zhao et al., 2014).

MODELING SYMPTOMATOLOGY

One method to address the clinical need for treatments is through the development of animal models that better represent the negative symptoms and through rigorous validation of these models. However, there are a number of difficulties with this, many of which are detailed in this section, not least of which is the representation of behaviors in animals that are uniquely human. Coupled with this is our limited (though admittedly improving) knowledge of the development of and pathophysiological changes in schizophrenia.

There is ample evidence that there are particular areas of the brain affected in patients with schizophrenia. The key areas involved, particularly in relation to the negative symptoms, appear to be the ventral striatum and prefrontal cortex. Indeed, in patients with predominant negative symptoms, cerebral blood flow imaging has shown hypofrontality (Pinkham et al., 2011), and other imaging studies have shown decreased activation of the ventral striatum was associated with negative symptoms (Menon, Anagnoson, Glover, & Pfefferbaum, 2001). Further work showed a negative correlation between the negative symptom, anhedonia, and dorsomedial prefrontal cortex metabolism (Park et al., 2009). Lesions of the medial prefrontal cortex result in a lack of spontaneity and reduced ability to initiate movement and speech, further underlining the importance of this region in schizophrenia (Fuster, 2001). There also appear to be differences in the connectivity between brain regions in schizophrenia patients. Positron emission tomography studies have shown fewer functional interactions between brain areas, particularly between thalamic and cortical regions, when comparing schizophrenia patients and controls (Volkow, Fowler, Ding, Wang, & Gatley, 1998). Morphological changes have also been shown in patients. In a study of first-episode, antipsychotic-naive patients, there were changes in the morphology of the orbitofrontal cortex. Compared with controls, the schizophrenia patients showed increased volumes of the orbitofrontal cortex, which correlated with the severity of negative symptoms (Lacerda et al., 2007).

The most enduring hypothesis to explain schizophrenia is the dopamine hypothesis, which suggests that raised dopamine levels, hyperdopaminergia, are responsible for the production of the symptoms of schizophrenia (Lau, Wang, Hsu, & Liu, 2013; Seeman, 1987). Indeed, amphetamine-induced psychosis, which can present as hallucinations and delusions similar to the positive symptoms, has been well-known for many years and underpins the dopamine hypothesis (Snyder, 1973). However, the situation is not as clear-cut because studies have shown that there appear to be behavior-specific changes in functioning of different areas of the brain, particularly the dorsolateral prefrontal cortex (Weinberger, Berman, & Illowsky, 1988). Hypofunction in this region may result in disinhibition and hyperdopaminergia in limbic regions (Weinberger, 1987). Despite the ample evidence in support of the dopamine hypothesis, recent work has shown that prefrontal cortical regions display hypodopaminergia (Howes & Kapur, 2009). Furthermore,

excess dopamine levels were not able to account for the negative and cognitive symptoms displayed by patients (Thaker & Carpenter, 2001). So, despite the fact that the majority of pharmacological treatments for schizophrenia mediate their effects through dopamine, the presented evidence necessitated a revision of the dopamine hypothesis to account for these observations.

It has become increasingly apparent that the glutamatergic system also has an important role to play in schizophrenia. The anesthetic, phencyclidine (PCP), which is an antagonist at the N-methyl-D-aspartate (NMDA) glutamate receptor, has long been known to produce effects in humans that resemble those of schizophrenia, both positive and negative symptoms, and early positron emission tomography scans of PCP abusers showed temporal and frontal lobe alterations similar to those seen in patients with schizophrenia (Hertzmann, Reba, & Kotlyarov, 1990; Rainey & Crowder, 1975). Similarly, ketamine, if given to healthy humans, will produce paranoia, hallucinations, and thought and cognitive impairments (Krystal et al., 1994). This evidence has resulted in the development of the glutamate hypothesis of schizophrenia (Malhotra et al., 1996). It has been proposed that as part of the glutamate hypothesis, there is chronic overrelease of glutamate, resulting in NMDA receptor hypofunction in patients with schizophrenia and this would lead to the behavioral symptoms and morphological changes in patients' brains (Olney, Newcomer, & Farber, 1999). Furthermore, there is molecular evidence also supporting NMDA receptor dysfunction in schizophrenia, with, for example, reduced levels of dysbindin and its messenger RNA in the hippocampus and the dorsolateral prefrontal cortex and polymorphisms of DTNBP1, which encodes dysbindin (Talbot et al., 2004; Voisey et al., 2010; Weickert et al., 2004).

Although both dopaminergic agonists and glutamatergic (NMDA) antagonists effectively replicate psychotic symptoms, it is the latter group that is better able to produce the negative (and cognitive) symptoms of schizophrenia. As a result, much emphasis has now been placed on the role of glutamate, and glutamatergic hypofunction, in the development of treatments for schizophrenia. This focus on glutamate is particularly concerned with the NMDA receptor because this is the site of action of PCP and ketamine.

Further support for this comes from the identification of the role of a number of the schizophrenia risk genes. There is evidence that Dysbindin, DISC1, and COMT are all involved in the dysfunction of the glutamatergic neurotransmission (Harrison & Weinberger, 2005; Wirgenes et al., 2009). Furthermore, neuregulin-1, through its receptor, erbB4, inhibits prefrontal cortical NMDA receptors in humans, and patients with schizophrenia have been shown to have increased interactions between erbB4 and the postsynaptic density protein, PSD-95 (Hahn et al., 2006): all of which strengthens the glutamatergic hypothesis of schizophrenia. In addition, clozapine, which does show some efficacy in treating the negative symptoms, results in downregulation of the GLT-1 glutamate transporter resulting in raised levels of glutamate in the cerebral cortex, whereas haloperidol, a first-generation antipsychotic, is ineffective because it does not affect glutamate levels in the prefrontal cortex (Mouri, Noda, Enomoto, & Nabeshima, 2007).

To further complicate matters, another symptom domain, affective symptoms, overlaps with the negative symptoms. There is clear evidence that patients with schizophrenia can also suffer from affective symptoms such as anxiety, suicidality, and depression. These form part of the spectrum of symptoms, and patients with schizophrenia have increased risk of developing depression compared with the general population, with depressive patients being at a higher risk for developing schizophrenia (Buckley, Miller, Lehrer, & Castle, 2009; Hafner et al., 2005; an der Heiden, Konnecke, Maurer, Ropeter, & Hafner, 2005). This relationship between the two disorders suggests that there may be commonalities in both their pathophysiology and etiology. Indeed, gene-wide association studies have shown shared genetic risk factors for both schizophrenia and depression (Cross-Disorder Group of the Psychiatric Genomics, 2013). Similarly, dysfunction in one neurotransmitter system, dopamine, could lead to downstream disruption of other systems and ultimately contribute to the development of, among others, affective symptoms (Hafner et al., 2005). As a result, some of the negative symptoms overlap with depressive symptoms, such as anhedonia, which can lead to overlap in modeling of the different symptom groups in schizophrenia.

Schizophrenia is particularly complex as it is a neurodevelopmental disorder with susceptibility affected by both genetic and environmental factors. However, as mentioned previously and as highlighted by many groups (Cognitive Neuroscience Treatment Research to Improve Cognition in Schizophrenia Initiative and the Measurement and Treatment Research to Improve Cognition in Schizophrenia (MATRICS) program among others), better animal models are required to better understand the pathophysiology of schizophrenia and to allow the identification of novel targets and treatments for schizophrenia (Carter & Barch, 2007; Marder & Fenton, 2004). One of the most important steps in this process is the validation of the putative animal models.

MODEL VALIDITY

There are clearly a number of issues when attempting to construct a model for schizophrenia, not least of which are the symptomatic domains and the changes in neuroanatomy and neurochemistry that occur in the patient. One way to develop a better model is to carefully validate the model ensuring that, as close as possible, the negative symptoms are represented. Broadly speaking, any effective animal model for the negative symptoms should show face validity, construct validity, and predictive validity. Face validity means that the animals mimic (as much as possible) the negative symptoms of schizophrenia seen in patients. Construct validity ensures there is a theoretical rationale to the model with representative pathophysiology. Finally, predictive validity ensures that existing and novel treatments are detected or predicted using the model.

Given the nature of the negative symptoms described previously, it is clear that it will be very difficult to construct a model that expresses all of the genetic, etiological, and neurobehavioral traits of schizophrenia patients. Indeed, the final factor, predictive validity, although arguably the most important, is the most challenging for negative symptoms because there is no known, consistently effective, therapeutic agent. Often the paradigm used is a modest response to clozapine or sometimes amisulpride and a lack of response to first-generation antipsychotics, such as haloperidol, neither of which is a robust mechanism.

However, the situation regarding face validity for animal models of negative symptoms is more positive. Although we do not fully understand the etiology of schizophrenia, we can directly measure, for example, asociality through social interaction of mice or rats (Trezza, Campolongo, & Vanderschuren, 2011; Trezza, Damsteegt, Achterberg, & Vanderschuren, 2011) and this can be manipulated through pharmacological, developmental, and genetic means (Moser, 2014; Neill, Harte, Haddad, Lydall, & Dwyer, 2014; O'Tuathaigh, Desbonnet, & Waddington, 2014).

MODELING TECHNIQUES

Despite the difficulty in validating a model of schizophrenia, many techniques have been used to develop such models and are based broadly on the different hypotheses of schizophrenia and observations of patients. It has been estimated by Carpenter and Koenig that there are more than 20 different animal models of schizophrenia (Carpenter & Koenig, 2008) and this number continues to rise. These generally fall within a number of categories, namely genetic models, lesion models, neurodevelopmental models, and pharmacological models. However, given the heterogeneous nature of schizophrenia, it is unlikely that any one model will display all of the required characteristics. To be an appropriate, comprehensive model for schizophrenia, the animal would need to show postpubertal onset, with a loss of hippocampal and cortical connectivity and functioning. In addition, there should be neurotransmitter abnormalities with changes to dopamine and glutamate levels and behavioral changes such as social withdrawal, an abnormal response to rewards, and impairment in cognition.

Other considerations when developing a model of schizophrenia are that the behaviors to be measured must be consistently represented across species and be mediated through the same neural circuits. This all lends to the construct validity of the model as described previously. However, many of the behavioral measures used are more aligned with face validity.

The neurodevelopment models exploit the fact that epidemiological studies have shown that environmental insults to the neonate, such as maternal stress or malnutrition, infections, and obstetric complications during birth, can all increase the risk of developing schizophrenia later on in life (Brown, 2006). One such model is the prenatal infection model, whereby administration of polyinosine-polycytidylic acid (poly I:C), during the gestational period, elicits a viral-like immune response. This results in offspring with long-term structural brain abnormalities coupled with behavioral and cognitive changes that are akin to schizophrenia (Meyer & Feldon, 2009, 2010). Indeed, the time of administration of poly I:C during gestation seems to affect the symptoms produced, with later administration times being more associated with the negative symptoms (Meyer, Feldon, & Yee, 2009).

Similarly, exposure of pregnant rodents to MAM, an antimitotic agent, produces long-term structural changes in the brain and behavioral changes in the offspring (Moore, Jentsch, Ghajarnia, Geyer, & Grace, 2006). Interestingly, like the poly I:C model, the time of administration to the pregnant rodent (between gestational day 14 and 17) also appears to impact the spectrum abnormalities expressed with later times (GD17) appearing to most closely represent schizophrenia (Balduini, Elsner, Lombardelli, Peruzzi, & Cattabeni, 1991; Fiore et al., 1999).

The earliest pharmacological models were built on the foundation of the dopamine hypothesis and hyperfunction of the mesolimbic dopaminergic system. For example, chronic amphetamine, resulting in sensitization, and subsequent acute amphetamine challenge produced exaggerated hyperactivity. The antipsychotic agents, haloperidol and clozapine, were able to reverse this sensitization (Meng, Feldpaush, & Merchant, 1998). However, amphetamine administration was not able to mimic the negative symptoms of schizophrenia (Sams-Dodd, 1998a, 1998b). This is a distinct limitation of the chronic amphetamine model, though it is in line with the current hypotheses of schizophrenia and in accordance with observations in humans (Javitt & Zukin, 1991).

Other pharmacological models involve the acute or subchronic administration of substances such as PCP or ketamine. In comparison to the earlier models, the use of PCP or ketamine is better able to elicit a spectrum of symptoms including positive, negative, and cognitive symptoms. They are also consistent with observations in humans of delusions, hallucinations, social withdrawal,

and alogia (Cohen, Rosenbaum, Luby, & Gottlieb, 1962; Krystal et al., 1994; Luby, Cohen, Rosenbaum, Gottlieb, & Kelley, 1959). Although the PCP model has the advantage that it induces positive and negative symptoms, it is generally only used acutely, or subchronically, to produce these symptoms, whereas schizophrenia is a chronic condition (Ellenbroek & Cools, 2000).

The lesion models involve the lesioning of a specific area of the brain in an attempt to modify the neural architecture in a similar way to schizophrenia. The neonatal ventral hippocampal lesion model involves the administration of ibotenic acid to the ventral hippocampus and the timing of the lesion is critical, in a similar manner to the neurodevelopmental models. This results in postpubertal changes in the prefrontal cortex and nucleus accumbens with concomitant changes in behavior (Tseng, Chambers, & Lipska, 2009). The behavioral changes from a ventral hippocampal lesion develop over time, but many of the abnormalities associated with schizophrenia are present by postnatal day 56 (Lipska, Jaskiw, & Weinberger, 1993; Lipska et al., 1995; Lipska & Weinberger, 1993).

The group of animal models of schizophrenia that is most rapidly developing is the genetic model, particularly the so-called risk factor models. It is well established from twin studies that there is a significant heritability in schizophrenia (Cardno et al., 1999; Kendler et al., 1993). The majority of the genes identified that are in some way disrupted in schizophrenia are involved in glutamatergic or dopaminergic function, neuronal plasticity, or synaptogenesis (Harrison & Weinberger, 2005). There are in excess of 1000 studies regarding the putative susceptibility genes for schizophrenia with more published annually (Allen et al., 2008). However, several of these risk genes have been explored in more detail than others and in some cases have displayed abnormal functioning of glutamate and/or dopamine, resulting in pathophysiological and behavioral changes representative of schizophrenia (Arguello & Gogos, 2010; Kirby, Waddington, & O'Tuathaigh, 2010; O'Tuathaigh, Kirby, Moran, & Waddington, 2010). For example, using a mutant mouse with a heterozygous deletion of the TM domain of neuregulin-1, O'Tuathaigh and coworkers demonstrated intact mnemonic processes, but impaired social novelty behavior, thereby underlining its role as a schizophrenia risk gene (O'Tuathaigh, Harte, et al., 2010).

MODELING THE NEGATIVE SYMPTOMS

Anhedonia

Anhedonia has long been suggested to be a core symptom of schizophrenia and was one of the symptoms described by Kraepelin in his original presentation of patients with dementia praecox (schizophrenia) (Kraepelin, 1971). Anhedonia can be defined as a lack of feeling pleasure, and in patients it can be assessed using the SANS anhedonia-asociality subscale. This scale examines the negative symptoms of anhedonia and asociality using interest in activities that may be sexual or recreational in addition to measures of intimacy, closeness, and relationships with friends.

Although many regions in the brain have a role in emotion and feelings of pleasure, studies in schizophrenia patients have highlighted a few areas. Reduced activity and responsiveness of the amygdala and striatum are thought to lead to anhedonia through a failure to respond to positive stimuli (Dowd & Barch, 2010). This reduced ventral striatal activity has also been seen in healthy subjects (Wacker, Dillon, & Pizzagalli, 2009). In addition, dopamine and, particularly, the mesolimbic to striatal dopaminergic projections, have an important role in reward prediction and incentivization (Berridge, 2004; Schultz, Dayan, & Montague, 1997).

However, to be able to assess its presence in animals, one needs to be able to measure when animals are pleased, or hedonic. Generally, animal behavior that is initiated voluntarily and then repeated is accepted to fulfill this. The most commonly used paradigm to measure anhedonia and a reduction in reward function, is a decrease in the sucrose consumption or preference relative to control, whereby the rodent is presented with a choice of consuming water or sucrose solutions of increasing concentrations (Cryan & Mombereau, 2004; Willner, Muscat, & Papp, 1992).

Many of the different models used in schizophrenia have examined sucrose consumption and preference. Recent research using the poly I:C model, administered late in gestation, showed that prenatal immune stimulation resulted in a reduction in sucrose preference compared with controls, which was indicative of anhedonic behavior (Bitanihirwe, Peleg-Raibstein, Mouttet, Feldon, & Meyer, 2010). However, the relevance of the sucrose preference test has been questioned. Work by Brady, McCallum, Glick, and O'Donnell (2008), using a progressive ratio schedule to examine motivation and effort, showed that rats that had undergone neonatal ventral hippocampal lesions worked harder in attaining their goal than control rats (Brady et al., 2008). This is contrary to the traditional thinking whereby the animal that is anhedonic would be expected to have a lower breaking point than a control animal.

However, recent evidence has somewhat confused matters and the measurement of anhedonia. Work by Horan et al. has shown that schizophrenia may not actually be associated with a reduced ability to experience pleasure, but rather with deficits in other aspects of the reward system (Horan, Kring, & Blanchard, 2006). This can be linked to animal work that has shown that dopaminergic

projections to the dorsal and ventral striatum mediate reward prediction (Berridge, 2004). Indeed, prediction of reward, in addition to the reward stimulus itself, is associated with dopaminergic neurons in the ventral tegmental area and the substantia nigra (Schultz, 2007).

Reports have shown that schizophrenia patients are indeed able to experience pleasure (Heerey & Gold, 2007), suggesting patients may not be anhedonic. Given this, it seems that schizophrenia may be more closely linked to deficits in anticipatory pleasure rather than the ability to experience the pleasure of a particular activity (Cohen & Minor, 2010) or that patients may be unable (or have a reduced ability) to use pleasurable memories to guide current behavior (Simpson, Waltz, Kellendonk, & Balsam, 2012).

Although this is an important development in the understanding of the symptomatology of schizophrenia, it does not help the development of a valid animal model of anhedonia and argues against the applicability of sucrose consumption as a measure. However, this does suggest that an effective model of avolition may fulfill a dual role.

Avolition

Avolition, which can be described as a reduced motivation to commence or continue goal-directed behaviors, is a key negative symptom of schizophrenia. Although, as described previously, consummatory pleasure, or liking something, is only modestly, if at all, compromised in patients with schizophrenia, there is ample evidence that wanting a reward and initiating action to acquire the reward are significantly impacted (Foussias, Agid, Fervaha, & Remington, 2014).

Evidence exists that people with schizophrenia appear have reduced participation in goal-directed behaviors because they perceive there will be less pleasure associated with the behavior when compared with controls (Gard, Kring, Gard, Horan, & Green, 2007). This links closely with mounting evidence that schizophrenic patients are impaired in value computation (Brown et al., 2013; Gold et al., 2012). This reduction in goal-directed behavior is thought to be linked to the functioning of the lateral prefrontal cortex (Braver & Cohen, 1999; Miller & Cohen, 2001). Studies in healthy volunteers using functional magnetic resonance imaging, examined the responses to anticipation of a reward and the actual receiving of that reward. Anticipation of reward resulted in activation in the ventral striatum, whereas reward (compared to nonreward) resulted in activation in the ventromedial frontal cortex (Knutson, Fong, Adams, Varner, & Hommer, 2001). The authors suggested that this work showed that although ascending dopamine projections are involved, reward and anticipation of reward activate distinct regions of the brain.

In an effort to develop an animal model of avolition, effort computation has been examined. Effort computation is the calculation of the work (or effort) required to acquire a reward or particular outcome and this is thought to involve dopaminergic projections from the nucleus accumbens and other forebrain areas to the dorsal anterior cingulate cortex. Research has demonstrated that lesions of the anterior cingulate cortex (ACC) or the medial prefrontal cortex in rats results in the preference of a low reward/low effort choice to a higher reward/higher effort option (Rudebeck et al., 2007; Rudebeck, Walton, Smyth, Bannerman, & Rushworth, 2006; Salamone, Correa, Farrar, & Mingote, 2007; Walton, Bannerman, & Rushworth, 2002; Walton, Rudebeck, Bannerman, & Rushworth, 2007). However, there is evidence to suggest that this may not be replicated in mice, therefore suggesting a species difference in performance (Solinsky & Kirby, 2013). It must be noted that results obtained in mice have the potential to differ from those in rats due to species differences (Asan et al., 2005). Much of the data that is available on the connections between brain regions has been obtained using rats. Studies examining brain connectivity comparing rats and mice found most connections to be present in the latter, but the extent of these can differ and some may be absent (Yilmazer-Hanke, 2008).

This, of course, also limits the potential of using this particular paradigm in the risk gene models of schizophrenia as they generally involve the use of mice. However, using a different model, dopamine D2 receptor overexpressing mice showed a motivational impairment in cost/benefit computations for the value of future rewards, which was reversed when the transgene was switched off (Ward et al., 2012). Furthermore, work with a transgenic model expressing a dominant negative DISC-1 showed behavioral deficits linked to the functioning of the prefrontal cortex, including progressive ration performance and social interaction (Johnson et al., 2013).

Social Withdrawal

Social withdrawal or asociality is one of the primary negative symptoms of schizophrenia and has a significant impact on functioning of the patient (Puig et al., 2008). Of all of the negative symptoms of schizophrenia, social withdrawal and asociality are the most widely studied in animal models. This is likely due to the relative ease with which asociality can be measured in rodents (using social interaction, for example) and thus provides a valid and quantifiable model. This, however, is not to undermine the importance of asociality as a symptom of schizophrenia as it causes significant behavioral impairment in patients, meaning they often live alone, with few social contacts and in general avoid

social interaction. Indeed, social withdrawal is often still present in periods of remission from the disease (Bellack, Morrison, Wixted, & Mueser, 1990).

Unlike avolition described above, it is more difficult to identify specific brain areas and structures that are involved in asociality as there is significant overlap with structures involved in social cognition and, as a concept, asociality is linked to both social cognition and avolition. Despite this, through the use of animal models, it has been possible to learn about the neurobiology of social interaction. The key neurotransmitters linked with schizophrenia are dopamine and glutamate and there is evidence to show there may also be a role for acetylcholine and noradrenaline and even neuropeptides may be involved (Adkins-Regan, 2009; Javitt, 2007; Snyder, Aghajanian, & Matthysse, 1972; Thomsen, Christensen, Hansen, Redrobe, & Mikkelsen, 2009). Similar to the other negative symptoms, areas of the forebrain, amygdala, frontal cortex, and hippocampus, have been implicated in asociality (Becker, Grecksch, Bernstein, Hollt, & Bogerts, 1999; Fernandez Espejo, 2003; File, James, & MacLeod, 1981). These studies, among others, have served to support the validity the social interaction paradigms for the examination of the negative symptoms of schizophrenia.

Social interaction tasks generally examine the behavior of an animal when exposed to an unfamiliar conspecific and the subsequent range of social and asocial responses (Neill et al., 2010). However, although social interaction impairment offers good face validity as a model of schizophrenia, there is also a caveat in that the impairment may be as a result of a number of changes, both cognitive and emotional. To overcome this, different tests of asociality should be employed, such as social approach/avoidance, aggression and social cognition (Arguello & Gogos, 2006).

Impairment in social interaction, such as social withdrawal and social isolation, can be induced by many of the different techniques for modeling schizophrenia in animals, including neonatal lesions, administration of PCP or ketamine or with knock-out mice. For example, a single administration of PCP can cause social withdrawal, which is amenable to treatment with clozapine but does not respond to treatment with haloperidol (Sams-Dodd, 1996). Interestingly, however, repeated administration of amphetamine does not produce social interaction deficits (Sams-Dodd, 1998a). Similarly, MK-801, an NMDA receptor antagonist, has shown deficits in social behavior in some studies following both acute and sub-chronic dosing (Matsuoka et al., 2005; Rung, Carlsson, Ryden Markinhuhta, & Carlsson, 2005), whereas others have failed to show enduring behavioral changes, albeit using different dosing regiments (Sams-Dodd, 2004).

The schizophrenia risk gene models have also shown good ability to produce deficits in the different social interaction tasks. Models with mutations (including knockout, overexpression, hypomorphs) in risk genes such as DISC-1, dysbindin (sdy mouse), NR1, and DAT have all shown deficits in social affiliation (Clapcote et al., 2007; Duncan et al., 2004; Feng et al., 2008; Rodriguiz, Chu, Caron, & Wetsel, 2004), whereas others have shown either no deficit, COMT (Babovic et al., 2008), or a mixed profile depending on the test used, neuregulin-1 (O'Tuathaigh et al., 2007, 2008).

This, and the other models of schizophrenia that induce social withdrawal and isolation, has the drawback that they lack neuroanatomical comparability (Dawe et al., 2009). Also, it must be remembered that the social interaction deficit may be present as a result of other negative symptoms manifesting in the animal.

Alogia

Although alogia is a negative symptom in its own right, it is very hard to dissociate this from many of the other symptoms as they are all interlinked. Alogia may hasten a patients withdrawal from social interaction, thereby exacerbating another negative symptom. Speech deficits have long been known to be linked with schizophrenia and studies have routinely found, for example reduced speech and verbal fluency in schizophrenia patients when compared to controls (Allen, Liddle, & Frith, 1993; Rochester & Martin, 1979). Recent functional magnetic resonance imaging studies have shown functionally altered language pathways in schizophrenia (Rapp & Steinhauser, 2013), and this may include reduced activation of networks including the frontotemporal regions and the thalamus (Kumari et al., 2010).

Poverty of speech is arguably the most difficult of negative symptoms to model in animals. However, rodents use other forms of communication, which it may be possible to study. These forms include olfactory and tactile modes of communication, such as mutual grooming (Dunbar, 2010). However, potentially, more promising is the possibility of measuring ultrasonic vocalizations that are emitted during different tests, including social interaction. Chabout and colleagues looked at this test and how acoustic communication was used by mice during the task (Chabout, Cressant, Hu, Edeline, & Granon, 2013). Other investigators have shown that mice exposed to prenatal lipopolysaccharide showed reduced number and duration of ultrasonic vocalizations on postnatal days and subsequently showed impaired nest-seeking behavior (Baharnoori, Bhardwaj, & Srivastava, 2012). The measurement of ultrasonic vocalizations as a model of negative symptoms in schizophrenia may be useful but a direct link with alogia in humans should only be made with caution.

Blunted Affect

The lack of emotional response to stimuli is another hallmark of schizophrenia in patients. As one of the negative symptoms, emotional flattening has a significant effect on outcome in patients. Work by Gur and colleagues in patients demonstrated a relationship between blunted affect and functional outcome, but with the caveat that the patients with blunted affect generally displayed more pronounced negative symptoms (Gur et al., 2006). With a diversity of imaging studies, it has been difficult to pinpoint areas of the brain associated with processing emotional stimuli in schizophrenia patients. However, a meta-analysis has demonstrated that, curiously, during emotional processing, some areas of the schizophrenic brain not normally associated with emotion show increased activation. This was contrasted with reduced activation in brain areas normally active during emotion such as the anterior cingulate cortex and the dorsal medial frontal cortex (Taylor et al., 2012). Studies looking at the emotional impact of facial stimuli have shown altered limbic activity. Functional magnetic resonance imaging studies have shown weaker deactivation of the medial prefrontal cortex (including the anterior cingulate cortex, which is involved in processing negative emotion) and reduced activation of the left cerebellum when viewing faces (Mothersill et al., 2014).

Although it is not possible to directly measure the emotional state of a rodent, many of the different test paradigms allow recording the expression of a motivational state. Tests examining locomotor behavior, social interaction, or reward-seeking behavior give a sense of the emotionality of a rodent. However, these are not direct measures and can be interpreted in different ways (Barnes, Der-Avakian, & Markou, 2014; Wilson & Koenig, 2014). It is known from human studies that ketamine, an NMDA receptor antagonist, will produce emotional blunting (Abel et al., 2003); subsequently, in 2007, Pietersen et al. published work showing the development of a model for emotional blunting—"the diminished ability to respond to emotionally salient stimuli." This group posited that because hypofunction is central to schizophrenia hypotheses, perhaps the negative symptoms are linked to hypofunction of the amygdala. The work showed that following ketamine-induced hypoactivation of the amygdala, the effects of fear conditioning were inhibited and animals froze less than the control animals. This does, however, require further validation as a model for emotional blunting.

CONCLUSIONS

Patients with predominant negative symptoms respond poorly to the currently available antipsychotic treatments. Potentially one reason for this is the concentration primarily on reversing symptoms instead of trying to understand and tackle the neurodevelopmental changes that occur. Better understanding of both the pathological changes and the symptoms themselves should allow the identification of novel targets.

Although the symptoms of schizophrenia are split into positive, negative, and cognitive, within each group there can be some difficulty distinguishing between symptoms. Horan et al. (2006) discussed the difficulty in distinguishing between two particular negative symptoms, namely anhedonia and amotivation. The group looked at, among others, the SANS scale, the current standard for assessment of negative symptoms, and concluded that as assessment of anhedonia is combined with participation in social activities, the SANS rating may appropriately show "a social performance deficit more than a fundamental hedonic capacity deficit" (Horan et al., 2006). In a similar way, many of the other negative symptoms may be difficult to distinguish or may not be mutually exclusive. The difficulties of modeling alogia are clear, but, for example, a patient with avolition may show social withdrawal as a result, meaning the symptoms are often interlinked. Furthermore, as described previously, our understanding of deficits in the reward systems of the brain and anhedonia is now showing a potential dissociation meaning anhedonia may not be as important a symptom of schizophrenia as it had previously been.

The overlap in both the symptoms and modeling of them is also apparent when one considers the affective symptoms. Some of the models for depressive symptoms are also used as models for the negative symptoms, meaning the lines between the two are blurred. Certainly anhedonia can be included under both symptom groups, and the sucrose preference test is more commonly used as a model of depression. Although we know that in patients with schizophrenia the ability to experience pleasure is intact, it seems that other aspects of the reward system are deficient. Therefore, a model of avolition, rather than anhedonia, may be more appropriate as a negative symptom model per se. Patients with schizophrenia and marked negative symptoms show reduced selection of high-effort choices (Barch, Treadway, & Schoen, 2014; Gold et al., 2013). Also, factor analyses have shown that avolition and apathy (in addition to blunted affect) are strong predictors of functional outcome in schizophrenia patients (Strauss et al., 2013).

Other issues that are affecting our modeling of schizophrenia and the ability to draw conclusions from the existing models are the inconsistencies in different studies. Depending on the research group using the model, different doses of drugs (e.g., PCP or ketamine) are administered, over different time periods, in different strains of mice or rats and subsequently different testing protocols are used. Coupled with this the widespread evidence of gender differences in mice, including the mice mutant for schizophrenia risk genes (O'Tuathaigh et al., 2006), one must wonder therefore, why in most cases male mice or rats are used.

Despite these concerns, many of the models described here (and in the subsequent chapters) effectively model many of the negative symptoms, though again, there are caveats with their use. For example, although the ketamine model does show good representation of many of the changes that occur as a result of schizophrenia, there is no neurodevelopmental or genetic element to the model. Given that this is a key element to schizophrenia in humans, this represents a limitation of the ketamine model. However, the genetic models are also not the answer, the so-called schizophrenia risk genes, such as disrupted in schizophrenia-1 (DISC-1) and neuregulin-1 are not exclusively linked with schizophrenia and have also been associated with bipolar disorder and autism, respectively (Marballi, Cruz, Thompson, & Walss-Bass, 2012; Szczepankiewicz, 2013).

Alternatively, the poly I:C model, which has an etiological basis and is neurodevelopmental, displays many of the symptoms of schizophrenia and in addition shows long-term neurochemical changes in different neurotransmitter systems (Bitanihirwe et al., 2010). One of the particular advantages of the neurodevelopmental models is that they allow the investigation of behavioral and/or neurochemical changes in animals that have not been exposed to pharmacological agents. However, as a counterpoint to that, the poly I:C model only captures the cytokine-associated acute phase responses rather than a full immune response triggered by viral infection, which must be borne in mind when using the model (Meyer & Feldon, 2012).

All of this argues for a more combined approach to the development and use of models for the negative symptoms. For example, combining the ketamine (or another pharmacological) model with either a neonatal lesion model or a risk gene model or other viable combinations (there are many), may result in a more valid model, allowing more clear identification of the negative symptoms and lead to the development of novel molecular targets and increasingly effective treatments. It must be remembered though, that given the range of changes that occur in patients with schizophrenia it is unlikely any animal model will ever display all of the characteristic symptoms of patients with schizophrenia. This is particularly true when one considers the uncertain influence of gene × gene and gene × environment interactions. Therefore, when it comes to modeling, we are, to some extent, developing models for schizophrenia rather than models of schizophrenia.

References

Abel, K. M., Allin, M. P., Kucharska-Pietura, K., David, A., Andrew, C., Williams, S., et al. (2003). Ketamine alters neural processing of facial emotion recognition in healthy men: an fMRI study. *Neuroreport, 14*(3), 387–391. http://dx.doi.org/10.1097/01.wnr.0000058031.29600.31.

Adkins-Regan, E. (2009). Neuroendocrinology of social behavior. *ILAR Journal, 50*(1), 5–14.

Allen, H. A., Liddle, P. F., & Frith, C. D. (1993). Negative features, retrieval processes and verbal fluency in schizophrenia. *British Journal of Psychiatry, 163*, 769–775.

Allen, N. C., Bagade, S., McQueen, M. B., Ioannidis, J. P., Kavvoura, F. K., Khoury, M. J., et al. (2008). Systematic meta-analyses and field synopsis of genetic association studies in schizophrenia: the SzGene database. *Nature Genetics, 40*(7), 827–834. http://dx.doi.org/10.1038/ng.171.

Andreasen, N. C. (1982). Negative symptoms in schizophrenia. Definition and reliability. *Archives of General Psychiatry, 39*(7), 784–788.

Andreasen, N. C. (1995). Symptoms, signs, and diagnosis of schizophrenia. *Lancet, 346*(8973), 477–481.

Arguello, P. A., & Gogos, J. A. (2006). Modeling madness in mice: one piece at a time. *Neuron, 52*(1), 179–196. http://dx.doi.org/10.1016/j.neuron.2006.09.023.

Arguello, P. A., & Gogos, J. A. (2010). Cognition in mouse models of schizophrenia susceptibility genes. *Schizophrenia Bulletin, 36*(2), 289–300. http://dx.doi.org/10.1093/schbul/sbp153.

Asan, E., Yilmazer-Hanke, D. M., Eliava, M., Hantsch, M., Lesch, K. P., & Schmitt, A. (2005). The corticotropin-releasing factor (CRF)-system and monoaminergic afferents in the central amygdala: investigations in different mouse strains and comparison with the rat. *Neuroscience, 131*(4), 953–967. http://dx.doi.org/10.1016/j.neuroscience.2004.11.040.

Babovic, D., O'Tuathaigh, C. M., O'Connor, A. M., O'Sullivan, G. J., Tighe, O., Croke, D. T., et al. (2008). Phenotypic characterization of cognition and social behavior in mice with heterozygous versus homozygous deletion of catechol-O-methyltransferase. *Neuroscience, 155*(4), 1021–1029. http://dx.doi.org/10.1016/j.neuroscience.2008.07.006.

Baharnoori, M., Bhardwaj, S. K., & Srivastava, L. K. (2012). Neonatal behavioral changes in rats with gestational exposure to lipopolysaccharide: a prenatal infection model for developmental neuropsychiatric disorders. *Schizophrenia Bulletin, 38*(3), 444–456. http://dx.doi.org/10.1093/schbul/sbq098.

Balduini, W., Elsner, J., Lombardelli, G., Peruzzi, G., & Cattabeni, F. (1991). Treatment with methylazoxymethanol at different gestational days: two-way shuttle box avoidance and residential maze activity in rat offspring. *Neurotoxicology, 12*(4), 677–686.

Barch, D. M., Treadway, M. T., & Schoen, N. (2014). Effort, anhedonia, and function in schizophrenia: reduced effort allocation predicts amotivation and functional impairment. *Journal of Abnormal Psychology, 123*(2), 387–397. http://dx.doi.org/10.1037/a0036299.

Barnes, S. A., Der-Avakian, A., & Markou, A. (2014). Anhedonia, avolition, and anticipatory deficits: assessments in animals with relevance to the negative symptoms of schizophrenia. *European Neuropsychopharmacology, 24*(5), 744–758. http://dx.doi.org/10.1016/j.euroneuro.2013.10.001.

Becker, A., Grecksch, G., Bernstein, H. G., Hollt, V., & Bogerts, B. (1999). Social behaviour in rats lesioned with ibotenic acid in the hippocampus: quantitative and qualitative analysis. *Psychopharmacology (Berlin), 144*(4), 333–338.

Bellack, A. S., Morrison, R. L., Wixted, J. T., & Mueser, K. T. (1990). An analysis of social competence in schizophrenia. *British Journal of Psychiatry, 156*, 809–818.

Berridge, K. C. (2004). Motivation concepts in behavioral neuroscience. *Physiology & Behavior, 81*(2), 179–209. http://dx.doi.org/10.1016/j.physbeh.2004.02.004.

Bitanihirwe, B. K., Peleg-Raibstein, D., Mouttet, F., Feldon, J., & Meyer, U. (2010). Late prenatal immune activation in mice leads to behavioral and neurochemical abnormalities relevant to the negative symptoms of schizophrenia. *Neuropsychopharmacology, 35*(12), 2462–2478. http://dx.doi.org/10.1038/npp.2010.129.

Blanchard, J. J., & Cohen, A. S. (2006). The structure of negative symptoms within schizophrenia: implications for assessment. *Schizophrenia Bulletin, 32*(2), 238–245. http://dx.doi.org/10.1093/schbul/sbj013.

Brady, A. M., McCallum, S. E., Glick, S. D., & O'Donnell, P. (2008). Enhanced methamphetamine self-administration in a neurodevelopmental rat model of schizophrenia. *Psychopharmacology (Berlin), 200*(2), 205–215. http://dx.doi.org/10.1007/s00213-008-1195-7.

Braver, T. S., & Cohen, J. D. (1999). Dopamine, cognitive control, and schizophrenia: the gating model. *Progress in Brain Research, 121*, 327–349.

Brown, A. S. (2006). Prenatal infection as a risk factor for schizophrenia. *Schizophrenia Bulletin, 32*(2), 200–202. http://dx.doi.org/10.1093/schbul/sbj052.

Brown, J. K., Waltz, J. A., Strauss, G. P., McMahon, R. P., Frank, M. J., & Gold, J. M. (2013). Hypothetical decision making in schizophrenia: the role of expected value computation and "irrational" biases. *Psychiatry Research, 209*(2), 142–149. http://dx.doi.org/10.1016/j.psychres.2013.02.034.

Buckley, P. F., Miller, B. J., Lehrer, D. S., & Castle, D. J. (2009). Psychiatric comorbidities and schizophrenia. *Schizophrenia Bulletin, 35*(2), 383–402. http://dx.doi.org/10.1093/schbul/sbn135.

Cardno, A. G., Marshall, E. J., Coid, B., Macdonald, A. M., Ribchester, T. R., Davies, N. J., et al. (1999). Heritability estimates for psychotic disorders: the Maudsley twin psychosis series. *Archives of General Psychiatry, 56*(2), 162–168.

Carpenter, W. T., & Koenig, J. I. (2008). The evolution of drug development in schizophrenia: past issues and future opportunities. *Neuropsychopharmacology, 33*(9), 2061–2079. http://dx.doi.org/10.1038/sj.npp.1301639.

Carter, C. S., & Barch, D. M. (2007). Cognitive neuroscience-based approaches to measuring and improving treatment effects on cognition in schizophrenia: the CNTRICS initiative. *Schizophrenia Bulletin, 33*(5), 1131–1137. http://dx.doi.org/10.1093/schbul/sbm081.

Chabout, J., Cressant, A., Hu, X., Edeline, J. M., & Granon, S. (2013). Making choice between competing rewards in uncertain vs. safe social environment: role of neuronal nicotinic receptors of acetylcholine. *Frontiers in Human Neuroscience, 7*, 468. http://dx.doi.org/10.3389/fnhum.2013.00468.

Clapcote, S. J., Lipina, T. V., Millar, J. K., Mackie, S., Christie, S., Ogawa, F., et al. (2007). Behavioral phenotypes of Disc1 missense mutations in mice. *Neuron, 54*(3), 387–402. http://dx.doi.org/10.1016/j.neuron.2007.04.015.

Cohen, A. S., & Minor, K. S. (2010). Emotional experience in patients with schizophrenia revisited: meta-analysis of laboratory studies. *Schizophrenia Bulletin, 36*(1), 143–150. http://dx.doi.org/10.1093/schbul/sbn061.

Cohen, B. D., Rosenbaum, G., Luby, E. D., & Gottlieb, J. S. (1962). Comparison of phencyclidine hydrochloride (Sernyl) with other drugs. Simulation of schizophrenic performance with phencyclidine hydrochloride (Sernyl), lysergic acid diethylamide (LSD-25), and amobarbital (Amytal) sodium; II. Symbolic and sequential thinking. *Archives of General Psychiatry, 6*, 395–401.

Cross-Disorder Group of the Psychiatric Genomics, C. (2013). Identification of risk loci with shared effects on five major psychiatric disorders: a genome-wide analysis. *Lancet, 381*(9875), 1371–1379. http://dx.doi.org/10.1016/S0140-6736(12)62129-1.

Cryan, J. F., & Mombereau, C. (2004). In search of a depressed mouse: utility of models for studying depression-related behavior in genetically modified mice. *Molecular Psychiatry, 9*(4), 326–357. http://dx.doi.org/10.1038/sj.mp.4001457.

Dawe, G. S., Hwang, E. H., & Tan, C. H. (2009). Pathophysiology and animal models of schizophrenia. *Annals, Academy of Medicine, Singapore, 38*(5), 425–426.

Dlabac-de Lange, J. J., Bais, L., van Es, F. D., Visser, B. G., Reinink, E., Bakker, B., et al. (2014). Efficacy of bilateral repetitive transcranial magnetic stimulation for negative symptoms of schizophrenia: results of a multicenter double-blind randomized controlled trial. *Psychological Medicine*, 1–13. http://dx.doi.org/10.1017/S0033291714002360.

Dowd, E. C., & Barch, D. M. (2010). Anhedonia and emotional experience in schizophrenia: neural and behavioral indicators. *Biological Psychiatry, 67*(10), 902–911. http://dx.doi.org/10.1016/j.biopsych.2009.10.020.

Dunbar, R. I. (2010). The social role of touch in humans and primates: behavioural function and neurobiological mechanisms. *Neuroscience & Biobehavioral Reviews, 34*(2), 260–268. http://dx.doi.org/10.1016/j.neubiorev.2008.07.001.

Duncan, G. E., Moy, S. S., Perez, A., Eddy, D. M., Zinzow, W. M., Lieberman, J. A., et al. (2004). Deficits in sensorimotor gating and tests of social behavior in a genetic model of reduced NMDA receptor function. *Behavioural Brain Research, 153*(2), 507–519. http://dx.doi.org/10.1016/j.bbr.2004.01.008.

Ellenbroek, B. A., & Cools, A. R. (2000). Animal models for the negative symptoms of schizophrenia. *Behavioural Pharmacology, 11*(3–4), 223–233.

Feng, Y. Q., Zhou, Z. Y., He, X., Wang, H., Guo, X. L., Hao, C. J., et al. (2008). Dysbindin deficiency in sandy mice causes reduction of snapin and displays behaviors related to schizophrenia. *Schizophrenia Research, 106*(2–3), 218–228. http://dx.doi.org/10.1016/j.schres.2008.07.018.

Fernandez Espejo, E. (2003). Prefrontocortical dopamine loss in rats delays long-term extinction of contextual conditioned fear, and reduces social interaction without affecting short-term social interaction memory. *Neuropsychopharmacology, 28*(3), 490–498. http://dx.doi.org/10.1038/sj.npp.1300066.

File, S. E., James, T. A., & MacLeod, N. K. (1981). Depletion in amygdaloid 5-hydroxytryptamine concentration and changes in social and aggressive behaviour. *Journal of Neural Transmission, 50*(1), 1–12.

Fiore, M., Talamini, L., Angelucci, F., Koch, T., Aloe, L., & Korf, J. (1999). Prenatal methylazoxymethanol acetate alters behavior and brain NGF levels in young rats: a possible correlation with the development of schizophrenia-like deficits. *Neuropharmacology, 38*(6), 857–869.

Foussias, G., Agid, O., Fervaha, G., & Remington, G. (2014). Negative symptoms of schizophrenia: clinical features, relevance to real world functioning and specificity versus other CNS disorders. *European Neuropsychopharmacology, 24*(5), 693–709. http://dx.doi.org/10.1016/j.euroneuro.2013.10.017.

Fuster, J. M. (2001). The prefrontal cortex–an update: time is of the essence. *Neuron, 30*(2), 319–333.

Gard, D. E., Kring, A. M., Gard, M. G., Horan, W. P., & Green, M. F. (2007). Anhedonia in schizophrenia: distinctions between anticipatory and consummatory pleasure. *Schizophrenia Research, 93*(1–3), 253–260. http://dx.doi.org/10.1016/j.schres.2007.03.008.

Gold, J. M., Strauss, G. P., Waltz, J. A., Robinson, B. M., Brown, J. K., & Frank, M. J. (2013). Negative symptoms of schizophrenia are associated with abnormal effort-cost computations. *Biological Psychiatry, 74*(2), 130–136. http://dx.doi.org/10.1016/j.biopsych.2012.12.022.

Gold, J. M., Waltz, J. A., Matveeva, T. M., Kasanova, Z., Strauss, G. P., Herbener, E. S., et al. (2012). Negative symptoms and the failure to represent the expected reward value of actions: behavioral and computational modeling evidence. *Archives of General Psychiatry, 69*(2), 129–138. http://dx.doi.org/10.1001/archgenpsychiatry.2011.1269.

Gur, R. E., Kohler, C. G., Ragland, J. D., Siegel, S. J., Lesko, K., Bilker, W. B., et al. (2006). Flat affect in schizophrenia: relation to emotion processing and neurocognitive measures. *Schizophrenia Bulletin, 32*(2), 279–287. http://dx.doi.org/10.1093/schbul/sbj041.

Hafner, H., Maurer, K., Trendler, G., an der Heiden, W., Schmidt, M., & Konnecke, R. (2005). Schizophrenia and depression: challenging the paradigm of two separate diseases–a controlled study of schizophrenia, depression and healthy controls. *Schizophrenia Research, 77*(1), 11–24. http://dx.doi.org/10.1016/j.schres.2005.01.004.

Hahn, C. G., Wang, H. Y., Cho, D. S., Talbot, K., Gur, R. E., Berrettini, W. H., et al. (2006). Altered neuregulin 1-erbB4 signaling contributes to NMDA receptor hypofunction in schizophrenia. *Nature Medicine, 12*(7), 824–828. http://dx.doi.org/10.1038/nm1418.

Harrison, P. J., & Weinberger, D. R. (2005). Schizophrenia genes, gene expression, and neuropathology: on the matter of their convergence. *Molecular Psychiatry, 10*(1), 40–68. http://dx.doi.org/10.1038/sj.mp.4001558 image 45.

Heerey, E. A., & Gold, J. M. (2007). Patients with schizophrenia demonstrate dissociation between affective experience and motivated behavior. *Journal of Abnormal Psychology, 116*(2), 268–278. http://dx.doi.org/10.1037/0021-843X.116.2.268.

an der Heiden, W., Konnecke, R., Maurer, K., Ropeter, D., & Hafner, H. (2005). Depression in the long-term course of schizophrenia. *European Archives of Psychiatry and Clinical Neuroscience, 255*(3), 174–184. http://dx.doi.org/10.1007/s00406-005-0585-7.

Hertzmann, M., Reba, R. C., & Kotlyarov, E. V. (1990). Single photon emission computed tomography in phencyclidine and related drug abuse. *American Journal of Psychiatry, 147*(2), 255–256.

Ho, B. C., Nopoulos, P., Flaum, M., Arndt, S., & Andreasen, N. C. (1998). Two-year outcome in first-episode schizophrenia: predictive value of symptoms for quality of life. *American Journal of Psychiatry, 155*(9), 1196–1201.

Horan, W. P., Kring, A. M., & Blanchard, J. J. (2006). Anhedonia in schizophrenia: a review of assessment strategies. *Schizophrenia Bulletin, 32*(2), 259–273. http://dx.doi.org/10.1093/schbul/sbj009.

Howes, O. D., & Kapur, S. (2009). The dopamine hypothesis of schizophrenia: version III–the final common pathway. *Schizophrenia Bulletin, 35*(3), 549–562. http://dx.doi.org/10.1093/schbul/sbp006.

Javitt, D. C. (2007). Glutamate and schizophrenia: phencyclidine, N-methyl-D-aspartate receptors, and dopamine-glutamate interactions. *International Review of Neurobiology, 78*, 69–108. http://dx.doi.org/10.1016/S0074-7742(06)78003-5.

Javitt, D. C., & Zukin, S. R. (1991). Recent advances in the phencyclidine model of schizophrenia. *American Journal of Psychiatry, 148*(10), 1301–1308.

Johnson, A. W., Jaaro-Peled, H., Shahani, N., Sedlak, T. W., Zoubovsky, S., Burruss, D., et al. (2013). Cognitive and motivational deficits together with prefrontal oxidative stress in a mouse model for neuropsychiatric illness. *Proceedings of the National Academy of Sciences of the United States of America, 110*(30), 12462–12467. http://dx.doi.org/10.1073/pnas.1307925110.

Kane, J. M. (1996). Schizophrenia. *New England Journal of Medicine, 334*(1), 34–41. http://dx.doi.org/10.1056/NEJM199601043340109.

Kendler, K. S., McGuire, M., Gruenberg, A. M., Spellman, M., O'Hare, A., & Walsh, D. (1993). The Roscommon family study. II. The risk of nonschizophrenic nonaffective psychoses in relatives. *Archives of General Psychiatry, 50*(8), 645–652.

Kirby, B. P., Waddington, J. L., & O'Tuathaigh, C. M. (2010). Advancing a functional genomics for schizophrenia: psychopathological and cognitive phenotypes in mutants with gene disruption. *Brain Research Bulletin, 83*(3–4), 162–176. http://dx.doi.org/10.1016/j.brainresbull.2009.09.010.

Kirkpatrick, B., & Fischer, B. (2006). Subdomains within the negative symptoms of schizophrenia: commentary. *Schizophrenia Bulletin, 32*(2), 246–249. http://dx.doi.org/10.1093/schbul/sbj054.

Knutson, B., Fong, G. W., Adams, C. M., Varner, J. L., & Hommer, D. (2001). Dissociation of reward anticipation and outcome with event-related fMRI. *Neuroreport, 12*(17), 3683–3687.

Kraepelin, E. (1971). *Dementia praecox and paraphrenia.* Huntington, NY: Robert E. Krieger Publishing.

Kring, A. M., & Elis, O. (2013). Emotion deficits in people with schizophrenia. *Annual Review of Clinical Psychology, 9,* 409–433. http://dx.doi.org/10.1146/annurev-clinpsy-050212-185538.

Kring, A. M., Gur, R. E., Blanchard, J. J., Horan, W. P., & Reise, S. P. (2013). The clinical assessment interview for negative symptoms (CAINS): final development and validation. *American Journal of Psychiatry, 170*(2), 165–172. http://dx.doi.org/10.1176/appi.ajp.2012.12010109.

Krystal, J. H., Karper, L. P., Seibyl, J. P., Freeman, G. K., Delaney, R., Bremner, J. D., et al. (1994). Subanesthetic effects of the noncompetitive NMDA antagonist, ketamine, in humans. Psychotomimetic, perceptual, cognitive, and neuroendocrine responses. *Archives of General Psychiatry, 51*(3), 199–214.

Kumari, V., Fannon, D., Ffytche, D. H., Raveendran, V., Antonova, E., Premkumar, P., et al. (2010). Functional MRI of verbal self-monitoring in schizophrenia: performance and illness-specific effects. *Schizophrenia Bulletin, 36*(4), 740–755. http://dx.doi.org/10.1093/schbul/sbn148.

Lacerda, A. L., Hardan, A. Y., Yorbik, O., Vemulapalli, M., Prasad, K. M., & Keshavan, M. S. (2007). Morphology of the orbitofrontal cortex in first-episode schizophrenia: relationship with negative symptomatology. *Progress in Neuro-Psychopharmacology & Biological Psychiatry, 31*(2), 510–516. http://dx.doi.org/10.1016/j.pnpbp.2006.11.022.

Lau, C. I., Wang, H. C., Hsu, J. L., & Liu, M. E. (2013). Does the dopamine hypothesis explain schizophrenia? *Reviews in the Neurosciences, 24*(4), 389–400. http://dx.doi.org/10.1515/revneuro-2013-0011.

Lipska, B. K., Jaskiw, G. E., & Weinberger, D. R. (1993). Postpubertal emergence of hyperresponsiveness to stress and to amphetamine after neonatal excitotoxic hippocampal damage: a potential animal model of schizophrenia. *Neuropsychopharmacology, 9*(1), 67–75. http://dx.doi.org/10.1038/npp.1993.44.

Lipska, B. K., Swerdlow, N. R., Geyer, M. A., Jaskiw, G. E., Braff, D. L., & Weinberger, D. R. (1995). Neonatal excitotoxic hippocampal damage in rats causes post-pubertal changes in prepulse inhibition of startle and its disruption by apomorphine. *Psychopharmacology (Berlin), 122*(1), 35–43.

Lipska, B. K., & Weinberger, D. R. (1993). Delayed effects of neonatal hippocampal damage on haloperidol-induced catalepsy and apomorphine-induced stereotypic behaviors in the rat. *Brain Research Developmental Brain Research, 75*(2), 213–222.

Luby, E. D., Cohen, B. D., Rosenbaum, G., Gottlieb, J. S., & Kelley, R. (1959). Study of a new schizophrenomimetic drug; sernyl. *AMA Archives of Neurology & Psychiatry, 81*(3), 363–369.

Malhotra, A. K., Pinals, D. A., Weingartner, H., Sirocco, K., Missar, C. D., Pickar, D., et al. (1996). NMDA receptor function and human cognition: the effects of ketamine in healthy volunteers. *Neuropsychopharmacology, 14*(5), 301–307. http://dx.doi.org/10.1016/0893-133X(95)00137-3.

Marballi, K., Cruz, D., Thompson, P., & Walss-Bass, C. (2012). Differential neuregulin 1 cleavage in the prefrontal cortex and hippocampus in schizophrenia and bipolar disorder: preliminary findings. *PLoS One, 7*(5), e36431. http://dx.doi.org/10.1371/journal.pone.0036431.

Marder, S. R., & Fenton, W. (2004). Measurement and treatment research to improve cognition in schizophrenia: NIMH MATRICS initiative to support the development of agents for improving cognition in schizophrenia. *Schizophrenia Research, 72*(1), 5–9. http://dx.doi.org/10.1016/j.schres.2004.09.010.

Matsuoka, T., Sumiyoshi, T., Tanaka, K., Tsunoda, M., Uehara, T., Itoh, H., et al. (2005). NC-1900, an arginine-vasopressin analogue, ameliorates social behavior deficits and hyperlocomotion in MK-801-treated rats: therapeutic implications for schizophrenia.

Brain Research, 1053(1–2), 131–136. http://dx.doi.org/10.1016/j.brainres.2005.06.035.

Meng, Z. H., Feldpaush, D. L., & Merchant, K. M. (1998). Clozapine and haloperidol block the induction of behavioral sensitization to amphetamine and associated genomic responses in rats. *Brain Research Molecular Brain Research, 61*(1–2), 39–50.

Menon, V., Anagnoson, R. T., Glover, G. H., & Pfefferbaum, A. (2001). Functional magnetic resonance imaging evidence for disrupted basal ganglia function in schizophrenia. *American Journal of Psychiatry, 158*(4), 646–649.

Meyer, U., & Feldon, J. (2009). Prenatal exposure to infection: a primary mechanism for abnormal dopaminergic development in schizophrenia. *Psychopharmacology (Berlin), 206*(4), 587–602. http://dx.doi.org/10.1007/s00213-009-1504-9.

Meyer, U., & Feldon, J. (2010). Epidemiology-driven neurodevelopmental animal models of schizophrenia. *Progress in Neurobiology, 90*(3), 285–326. http://dx.doi.org/10.1016/j.pneurobio.2009.10.018.

Meyer, U., & Feldon, J. (2012). To poly(I: C) or not to poly(I: C): advancing preclinical schizophrenia research through the use of prenatal immune activation models. *Neuropharmacology, 62*(3), 1308–1321. http://dx.doi.org/10.1016/j.neuropharm.2011.01.009.

Meyer, U., Feldon, J., & Yee, B. K. (2009). A review of the fetal brain cytokine imbalance hypothesis of schizophrenia. *Schizophrenia Bulletin, 35*(5), 959–972. http://dx.doi.org/10.1093/schbul/sbn022.

Milev, P., Ho, B. C., Arndt, S., & Andreasen, N. C. (2005). Predictive values of neurocognition and negative symptoms on functional outcome in schizophrenia: a longitudinal first-episode study with 7-year follow-up. *American Journal of Psychiatry, 162*(3), 495–506. http://dx.doi.org/10.1176/appi.ajp.162.3.495.

Miller, E. K., & Cohen, J. D. (2001). An integrative theory of prefrontal cortex function. *Annual Review of Neuroscience, 24,* 167–202. http://dx.doi.org/10.1146/annurev.neuro.24.1.167.

Moore, H., Jentsch, J. D., Ghajarnia, M., Geyer, M. A., & Grace, A. A. (2006). A neurobehavioral systems analysis of adult rats exposed to methylazoxymethanol acetate on E17: implications for the neuropathology of schizophrenia. *Biological Psychiatry, 60*(3), 253–264. http://dx.doi.org/10.1016/j.biopsych.2006.01.003.

Moser, P. (2014). Evaluating negative-symptom-like behavioural changes in developmental models of schizophrenia. *European Neuropsychopharmacology, 24*(5), 774–787. http://dx.doi.org/10.1016/j.euroneuro.2013.11.004.

Mothersill, O., Morris, D. W., Kelly, S., Rose, E. J., Bokde, A., Reilly, R., et al. (2014). Altered medial prefrontal activity during dynamic face processing in schizophrenia spectrum patients. *Schizophrenia Research, 157*(1–3), 225–230. http://dx.doi.org/10.1016/j.schres.2014.05.023.

Mouri, A., Noda, Y., Enomoto, T., & Nabeshima, T. (2007). Phencyclidine animal models of schizophrenia: approaches from abnormality of glutamatergic neurotransmission and neurodevelopment. *Neurochemistry International, 51*(2–4), 173–184. http://dx.doi.org/10.1016/j.neuint.2007.06.019.

Neill, J. C., Barnes, S., Cook, S., Grayson, B., Idris, N. F., McLean, S. L., et al. (2010). Animal models of cognitive dysfunction and negative symptoms of schizophrenia: focus on NMDA receptor antagonism. *Pharmacology & Therapeutics, 128*(3), 419–432. http://dx.doi.org/10.1016/j.pharmthera.2010.07.004.

Neill, J. C., Harte, M. K., Haddad, P. M., Lydall, E. S., & Dwyer, D. M. (2014). Acute and chronic effects of NMDA receptor antagonists in rodents, relevance to negative symptoms of schizophrenia: a translational link to humans. *European Neuropsychopharmacology, 24*(5), 822–835. http://dx.doi.org/10.1016/j.euroneuro.2013.09.011.

O'Tuathaigh, C. M., Babovic, D., O'Sullivan, G. J., Clifford, J. J., Tighe, O., Croke, D. T., et al. (2007). Phenotypic characterization of spatial cognition and social behavior in mice with 'knockout' of the schizophrenia risk gene neuregulin 1. *Neuroscience, 147*(1), 18–27. http://dx.doi.org/10.1016/j.neuroscience.2007.03.051.

O'Tuathaigh, C. M., Desbonnet, L., & Waddington, J. L. (2014). Genetically modified mice related to schizophrenia and other psychoses: seeking phenotypic insights into the pathobiology and treatment of negative symptoms. *European Neuropsychopharmacology, 24*(5), 800–821. http://dx.doi.org/10.1016/j.euroneuro.2013.08.009.

O'Tuathaigh, C. M., Harte, M., O'Leary, C., O'Sullivan, G. J., Blau, C., Lai, D., et al. (2010). Schizophrenia-related endophenotypes in heterozygous neuregulin-1 'knockout' mice. *European Journal of Neuroscience, 31*(2), 349–358. http://dx.doi.org/10.1111/j.1460-9568.2009.07069.x.

O'Tuathaigh, C. M., Kirby, B. P., Moran, P. M., & Waddington, J. L. (2010). Mutant mouse models: genotype-phenotype relationships to negative symptoms in schizophrenia. *Schizophrenia Bulletin, 36*(2), 271–288. http://dx.doi.org/10.1093/schbul/sbp125.

O'Tuathaigh, C. M., O'Connor, A. M., O'Sullivan, G. J., Lai, D., Harvey, R., Croke, D. T., et al. (2008). Disruption to social dyadic interactions but not emotional/anxiety-related behaviour in mice with heterozygous 'knockout' of the schizophrenia risk gene neuregulin-1. *Progress in Neuro-Psychopharmacology & Biological Psychiatry, 32*(2), 462–466. http://dx.doi.org/10.1016/j.pnpbp.2007.09.018.

O'Tuathaigh, C. M., O'Sullivan, G. J., Kinsella, A., Harvey, R. P., Tighe, O., Croke, D. T., et al. (2006). Sexually dimorphic changes in the exploratory and habituation profiles of heterozygous neuregulin-1 knockout mice. *Neuroreport, 17*(1), 79–83.

Olney, J. W., Newcomer, J. W., & Farber, N. B. (1999). NMDA receptor hypofunction model of schizophrenia. *Journal of Psychiatric Research, 33*(6), 523–533.

Park, K. M., Kim, J. J., Seok, J. H., Chun, J. W., Park, H. J., & Lee, J. D. (2009). Anhedonia and ambivalence in schizophrenic patients with fronto-cerebellar metabolic abnormalities: a fluoro-d-glucose positron emission tomography study. *Psychiatry Investigation, 6*(2), 72–77. http://dx.doi.org/10.4306/pi.2009.6.2.72.

Pietersen, C. Y., Bosker, F. J., Doorduin, J., Jongsma, M. E., Postema, F., Haas, J. V., et al. (2007). An animal model of emotional blunting in schizophrenia. *PLoS One, 2*(12), e1360. http://dx.doi.org/10.1371/journal.pone.0001360.

Pinkham, A., Loughead, J., Ruparel, K., Wu, W. C., Overton, E., Gur, R., et al. (2011). Resting quantitative cerebral blood flow in schizophrenia measured by pulsed arterial spin labeling perfusion MRI. *Psychiatry Research, 194*(1), 64–72. http://dx.doi.org/10.1016/j.pscychresns.2011.06.013.

Puig, O., Penades, R., Gasto, C., Catalan, R., Torres, A., & Salamero, M. (2008). Verbal memory, negative symptomatology and prediction of psychosocial functioning in schizophrenia. *Psychiatry Research, 158*(1), 11–17. http://dx.doi.org/10.1016/j.psychres.2007.04.017.

Rainey, J. M., Jr., & Crowder, M. K. (1975). Prolonged psychosis attributed to phencyclidine: report of three cases. *American Journal of Psychiatry, 132*(10), 1076–1078.

Rapp, A. M., & Steinhauser, A. E. (2013). Functional MRI of sentence-level language comprehension in schizophrenia: a coordinate-based analysis. *Schizophrenia Research, 150*(1), 107–113. http://dx.doi.org/10.1016/j.schres.2013.07.019.

Robinson, D. G., Woerner, M. G., McMeniman, M., Mendelowitz, A., & Bilder, R. M. (2004). Symptomatic and functional recovery from a first episode of schizophrenia or schizoaffective disorder. *American Journal of Psychiatry, 161*(3), 473–479.

Rochester, S. R., & Martin, J. R. (1979). *Crazy talk: A study of the discourse of schizophrenic speakers.* New York: Plenum.

Rodriguiz, R. M., Chu, R., Caron, M. G., & Wetsel, W. C. (2004). Aberrant responses in social interaction of dopamine transporter knockout mice. *Behavioural Brain Research, 148*(1–2), 185–198.

Rosenbaum, B., Harder, S., Knudsen, P., Koster, A., Lindhardt, A., Lajer, M., et al. (2012). Supportive psychodynamic psychotherapy versus treatment as usual for first-episode psychosis: two-year outcome. *Psychiatry, 75*(4), 331–341. http://dx.doi.org/10.1521/psyc.2012.75.4.331.

Rudebeck, P. H., Walton, M. E., Millette, B. H., Shirley, E., Rushworth, M. F., & Bannerman, D. M. (2007). Distinct contributions of frontal areas to emotion and social behaviour in the rat. *European Journal of Neuroscience, 26*(8), 2315–2326. http://dx.doi.org/10.1111/j.1460-9568.2007.05844.x.

Rudebeck, P. H., Walton, M. E., Smyth, A. N., Bannerman, D. M., & Rushworth, M. F. (2006). Separate neural pathways process different decision costs. *Nature Neuroscience, 9*(9), 1161–1168. http://dx.doi.org/10.1038/nn1756.

Rung, J. P., Carlsson, A., Ryden Markinhuhta, K., & Carlsson, M. L. (2005). (+)-MK-801 induced social withdrawal in rats; a model for negative symptoms of schizophrenia. *Progress in Neuro-Psychopharmacology & Biological Psychiatry, 29*(5), 827–832. http://dx.doi.org/10.1016/j.pnpbp.2005.03.004.

Salamone, J. D., Correa, M., Farrar, A., & Mingote, S. M. (2007). Effort-related functions of nucleus accumbens dopamine and associated forebrain circuits. *Psychopharmacology (Berlin), 191*(3), 461–482. http://dx.doi.org/10.1007/s00213-006-0668-9.

Sams-Dodd, F. (1996). Phencyclidine-induced stereotyped behaviour and social isolation in rats: a possible animal model of schizophrenia. *Behavioural Pharmacology, 7*(1), 3–23.

Sams-Dodd, F. (1998a). Effects of continuous D-amphetamine and phencyclidine administration on social behaviour, stereotyped behaviour, and locomotor activity in rats. *Neuropsychopharmacology, 19*(1), 18–25. http://dx.doi.org/10.1016/S0893-133X(97)00200-5.

Sams-Dodd, F. (1998b). A test of the predictive validity of animal models of schizophrenia based on phencyclidine and D-amphetamine. *Neuropsychopharmacology, 18*(4), 293–304. http://dx.doi.org/10.1016/S0893-133X(97)00161-9.

Sams-Dodd, F. (2004). (+) MK-801 and phencyclidine induced neurotoxicity do not cause enduring behaviours resembling the positive and negative symptoms of schizophrenia in the rat. *Basic & Clinical Pharmacology & Toxicology, 95*(5), 241–246. http://dx.doi.org/10.1111/j.1742-7843.2004.pto950507.x.

Schultz, W. (2007). Multiple dopamine functions at different time courses. *Annual Review of Neuroscience, 30*, 259–288. http://dx.doi.org/10.1146/annurev.neuro.28.061604.135722.

Schultz, W., Dayan, P., & Montague, P. R. (1997). A neural substrate of prediction and reward. *Science, 275*(5306), 1593–1599.

Seeman, P. (1987). Dopamine receptors and the dopamine hypothesis of schizophrenia. *Synapse, 1*(2), 133–152. http://dx.doi.org/10.1002/syn.890010203.

Simpson, E. H., Waltz, J. A., Kellendonk, C., & Balsam, P. D. (2012). Schizophrenia in translation: dissecting motivation in schizophrenia and rodents. *Schizophrenia Bulletin, 38*(6), 1111–1117. http://dx.doi.org/10.1093/schbul/sbs114.

Snyder, S. H. (1973). Amphetamine psychosis: a "model" schizophrenia mediated by catecholamines. *American Journal of Psychiatry, 130*(1), 61–67.

Snyder, S. H., Aghajanian, G. K., & Matthysse, S. (1972). Prospects for research on schizophrenia. V. Pharmacological observations, drug-induced psychoses. *Neurosciences Research Program Bulletin, 10*(4), 430–445.

Solinsky, C., & Kirby, B. P. (2013). Medial prefrontal cortex lesions in mice do not impair effort-based decision making. *Neuropharmacology, 65*, 223–231. http://dx.doi.org/10.1016/j.neuropharm.2012.10.005.

Strauss, G. P., Horan, W. P., Kirkpatrick, B., Fischer, B. A., Keller, W. R., Miski, P., et al. (2013). Deconstructing negative symptoms of schizophrenia: avolition-apathy and diminished expression clusters predict clinical presentation and functional outcome. *Journal of Psychiatric Research, 47*(6), 783–790. http://dx.doi.org/10.1016/j.jpsychires.2013.01.015.

Subotnik, K. L., Ventura, J., Gretchen-Doorly, D., Hellemann, G. S., Agee, E. R., Casaus, L. R., et al. (2014). The impact of second-generation antipsychotic adherence on positive and negative symptoms in recent-onset schizophrenia. *Schizophrenia Research, 159*(1), 95–100. http://dx.doi.org/10.1016/j.schres.2014.07.008.

Szczepankiewicz, A. (2013). Evidence for single nucleotide polymorphisms and their association with bipolar disorder. *Neuropsychiatric Disease and Treatment, 9*, 1573–1582. http://dx.doi.org/10.2147/NDT.S28117.

Talbot, K., Eidem, W. L., Tinsley, C. L., Benson, M. A., Thompson, E. W., Smith, R. J., et al. (2004). Dysbindin-1 is reduced in intrinsic, glutamatergic terminals of the hippocampal formation in schizophrenia. *Journal of Clinical Investigation, 113*(9), 1353–1363. http://dx.doi.org/10.1172/JCI20425.

Taylor, S. F., Kang, J., Brege, I. S., Tso, I. F., Hosanagar, A., & Johnson, T. D. (2012). Meta-analysis of functional neuroimaging studies of emotion perception and experience in schizophrenia. *Biological Psychiatry, 71*(2), 136–145. http://dx.doi.org/10.1016/j.biopsych.2011.09.007.

Thaker, G. K., & Carpenter, W. T., Jr. (2001). Advances in schizophrenia. *Nature Medicine, 7*(6), 667–671. http://dx.doi.org/10.1038/89040.

Thomsen, M. S., Christensen, D. Z., Hansen, H. H., Redrobe, J. P., & Mikkelsen, J. D. (2009). Alpha(7) nicotinic acetylcholine receptor activation prevents behavioral and molecular changes induced by repeated phencyclidine treatment. *Neuropharmacology, 56*(6–7), 1001–1009. http://dx.doi.org/10.1016/j.neuropharm.2009.02.003.

Trezza, V., Campolongo, P., & Vanderschuren, L. J. (2011). Evaluating the rewarding nature of social interactions in laboratory animals. *Developmental Cognitive Neuroscience, 1*(4), 444–458. http://dx.doi.org/10.1016/j.dcn.2011.05.007.

Trezza, V., Damsteegt, R., Achterberg, E. J., & Vanderschuren, L. J. (2011). Nucleus accumbens mu-opioid receptors mediate social reward. *Journal of Neuroscience, 31*(17), 6362–6370. http://dx.doi.org/10.1523/JNEUROSCI.5492-10.2011.

Tseng, K. Y., Chambers, R. A., & Lipska, B. K. (2009). The neonatal ventral hippocampal lesion as a heuristic neurodevelopmental model of schizophrenia. *Behavioural Brain Research, 204*(2), 295–305. http://dx.doi.org/10.1016/j.bbr.2008.11.039.

Voisey, J., Swagell, C. D., Hughes, I. P., Connor, J. P., Lawford, B. R., Young, R. M., et al. (2010). A polymorphism in the dysbindin gene (DTNBP1) associated with multiple psychiatric disorders including schizophrenia. *Behavioral and Brain Functions, 6*, 41. http://dx.doi.org/10.1186/1744-9081-6-41.

Volkow, N. D., Fowler, J. S., Ding, Y. S., Wang, G. J., & Gatley, S. J. (1998). Positron emission tomography radioligands for dopamine transporters and studies in human and nonhuman primates. *Advances in Pharmacology, 42*, 211–214.

Wacker, J., Dillon, D. G., & Pizzagalli, D. A. (2009). The role of the nucleus accumbens and rostral anterior cingulate cortex in anhedonia: integration of resting EEG, fMRI, and volumetric techniques. *Neuroimage, 46*(1), 327–337. http://dx.doi.org/10.1016/j.neuroimage.2009.01.058.

Walton, M. E., Bannerman, D. M., & Rushworth, M. F. (2002). The role of rat medial frontal cortex in effort-based decision making. *Journal of Neuroscience, 22*(24), 10996–11003.

Walton, M. E., Rudebeck, P. H., Bannerman, D. M., & Rushworth, M. F. (2007). Calculating the cost of acting in frontal cortex. *Annals of the New York Academy of Sciences, 1104*, 340–356. http://dx.doi.org/10.1196/annals.1390.009.

Ward, R. D., Simpson, E. H., Richards, V. L., Deo, G., Taylor, K., Glendinning, J. I., et al. (2012). Dissociation of hedonic reaction to reward and incentive motivation in an animal model of the negative symptoms of schizophrenia. *Neuropsychopharmacology, 37*(7), 1699–1707. http://dx.doi.org/10.1038/npp.2012.15.

Weickert, C. S., Straub, R. E., McClintock, B. W., Matsumoto, M., Hashimoto, R., Hyde, T. M., et al. (2004). Human dysbindin (DTNBP1) gene expression in normal brain and in schizophrenic prefrontal cortex and midbrain. *Archives of General Psychiatry, 61*(6), 544–555. http://dx.doi.org/10.1001/archpsyc.61.6.544.

Weinberger, D. R. (1987). Implications of normal brain development for the pathogenesis of schizophrenia. *Archives of General Psychiatry, 44*(7), 660–669.

Weinberger, D. R., Berman, K. F., & Illowsky, B. P. (1988). Physiological dysfunction of dorsolateral prefrontal cortex in schizophrenia. III. A new cohort and evidence for a monoaminergic mechanism. *Archives of General Psychiatry, 45*(7), 609–615.

Willner, P., Muscat, R., & Papp, M. (1992). An animal model of anhedonia. *Clinical Neuropharmacology, 15*(Suppl. 1 Pt A), 550A–551A.

Wilson, C. A., & Koenig, J. I. (2014). Social interaction and social withdrawal in rodents as readouts for investigating the negative symptoms of schizophrenia. *European Neuropsychopharmacology, 24*(5), 759–773. http://dx.doi.org/10.1016/j.euroneuro.2013.11.008.

Wirgenes, K. V., Djurovic, S., Agartz, I., Jonsson, E. G., Werge, T., Melle, I., et al. (2009). Dysbindin and d-amino-acid-oxidase gene polymorphisms associated with positive and negative symptoms in schizophrenia. *Neuropsychobiology, 60*(1), 31–36. http://dx.doi.org/10.1159/000235799.

Yilmazer-Hanke, D. M. (2008). Morphological correlates of emotional and cognitive behaviour: insights from studies on inbred and outbred rodent strains and their crosses. *Behavioural Pharmacology, 19*(5–6), 403–434. http://dx.doi.org/10.1097/FBP.0b013e32830dc0de.

Zhao, S., Kong, J., Li, S., Tong, Z., Yang, C., & Zhong, H. (2014). Randomized controlled trial of four protocols of repetitive transcranial magnetic stimulation for treating the negative symptoms of schizophrenia. *Shanghai Archives of Psychiatry, 26*(1), 15–21. http://dx.doi.org/10.3969/j.issn.1002-0829.2014.01.003.

I. FROM CLINICAL DIMENSIONS TO ANIMAL MODELS

6

Modeling Cognitive Impairment

Francesca Managó[a], Huiping Huang[a], Papaleo Francesco

Department of Neuroscience and Brain Technologies, Istituto Italiano di Tecnologia, Genova, Italy

COGNITIVE DYSFUNCTIONS IN SCHIZOPHRENIA AND MOUSE MODELS

Schizophrenia is a debilitating and chronic psychiatric disorder defined by three clusters of clinical features, namely positive symptoms, negative symptoms, and cognitive deficits (Lewis & Gonzalez-Burgos, 2006). Despite the fact that the presence and severity of these symptoms is very heterogeneous between the affected patients (Ross, Margolis, Reading, Pletnikov, & Coyle, 2006; Thaker & Carpenter, 2001), the full-blown appearance of all these behavioral abnormalities typically start to occur in late adolescence or early adulthood (Minzenberg & Carter, 2012; Thaker & Carpenter, 2001). However, strong evidence suggests that cognitive impairments might be detectable earlier in life (Elvevag & Goldberg, 2000; Goldman-Rakic, 1994; Owens & Johnstone, 2006). Furthermore, cognitive symptoms tend to be long-lasting traits of the illness and have been found to be key prognostic factors for the long-term effects of the disease such as the level of functional capability, social, and occupational ability and quality of life (Green, 1996; Green & Nuechterlein, 1999). Thus, cognitive deficits, depriving patients of the qualities needed to thrive in society, are nowadays considered among the main source of disability, having the most critical impact on public health because of combined economic and social costs (Mueser & McGurk, 2004). This is made even more dramatic because, in contrast to positive symptoms, cognitive deficits are still relatively unaffected by currently available medications (Keefe et al., 2007; Minzenberg & Carter, 2012; Miyamoto, Duncan, Marx, & Lieberman, 2005), with up to one-third of patients not even responding to medications (Javitt & Coyle, 2004). Critically, the development of novel treatments is severely hampered by an incomplete understanding of the heterogeneity, risk factors, and neural circuitry underlying the disease (Fava et al., 2014). This gap is extremely challenging to fill as clinical studies must deal with the complexity of human genetic/clinical heterogeneity and with the uncontrollable impact of gene–gene, gene–environment, and gene–environment–drug treatments interactions.

Mouse models can allow for selective control and modulation of all these confounding factors, on top of which, there is the advantage of cutting-edge genetic tools nowadays available for this animal species. For example, mouse models allow for strict control of environmental conditions, genetic background, sex-dependent effects, sample size, and developmental factors. Most importantly, the available tools in mouse genetics (e.g., classical, time- and site-specific conditional knockouts/knockins and transgenics, ENU, CRISPR, TALENs, ZFNs) can enable the establishment of a causal relationship between genetic variations and cognitive (dys)functions. Indeed, the mammal *mus musculus* is proving to be a very valuable animal model in improving our understanding of the nature of complex cognitive impairments in schizophrenia, the related implications of specific molecular/cellular pathways as well as neural circuits and, finally, can be effectively used to generate and screen mechanism-based treatments. However, to address all of these, cognitive studies in mice must be accurately developed and used to closely mimic human conditions. Furthermore, keeping in mind that a mouse model cannot recapitulate all the behavioral, genetic, and anatomical features of a human patient with schizophrenia, mouse-generated findings must be integrated with clinical evidence to directly translate their validity

[a] These authors contributed equally to this work.

Handbook of Behavioral Neuroscience
http://dx.doi.org/10.1016/B978-0-12-800981-9.00006-7

and predictivity. For example, a lack or inappropriate use of valid translational models has contributed to many global pharma companies withdrawing from the neuroscience research field (Nutt & Goodwin, 2011). In this chapter, we will illustrate the cognitive impairments presently believed to be hallmarks of schizophrenia and the most relevant corresponding tasks suggested to be used in animal models. In particular, the cognitive domains that we will specifically address are executive control, working memory, attention, and social cognition as these are the cognitive functions most frequently found to be altered in patients with schizophrenia (Barch & Ceaser, 2012; Ross et al., 2006).

EXECUTIVE CONTROL

Abnormalities in executive control have long been thought to be a hallmark cognitive characteristic of schizophrenia (Kerns, Nuechterlein, Braver, & Barch, 2008; Weinberger, Berman, & Zec, 1986). The term "executive function" can be defined as a "higher order" control over a set of cognitive abilities aiming to maximize performance in a particular situation. This includes the ability to monitor and change behavior as required, and to plan and/or adapt future behavior when faced with novel tasks and situations. On an experimental level, "executive control" can be difficult to assess and evaluate as, by definition, it is a high-level ability that influences more basic cognitive skills like attention, memory, and flexibility. Moreover, an executive function deficit does not always imply a poorer performance in one of the basic cognitive capabilities controlled.

To assess executive control abilities measuring rule generation and selection, so-called "attentional set-shifting tasks" are commonly used. A traditional and widely used task is the Wisconsin Card Sorting Task (WCST; Figure 1(A)) (Berg, 1948; Eling, Derckx, & Maes, 2008), whereas a more recent and refined task is the "intra- and extradimensional attentional set-shifting" (ID/ED; Figure 1(B)) of the Cambridge Neuropsychological Test Automated Battery (CANTAB) (Barnett et al., 2010; Roberts, Robbins, & Everitt, 1988). These tasks are based on the use of compound stimuli that differ in, at least, two perceptual dimensions. For example, in the WCST, the subject is presented with cards that can vary in the number, color, and shape of their stimuli (e.g., one red circle, four yellow triangles, two green stars). The subject must then understand the correct sorting rule in relation to the examiner's feedback in each trial (i.e., the examiner just state if the choice made is correct or not). Once the subject understands and keeps following the correct relevant dimension (e.g., color) while ignoring the other stimulus dimensions, he or she will be tested without instruction to find the new correct response with a different

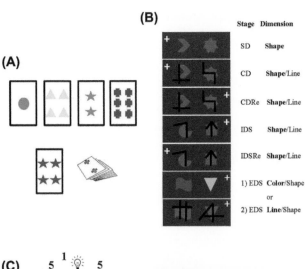

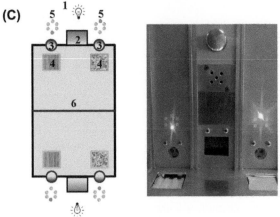

FIGURE 1 **Attentional set-shifting tasks.** (A) Wisconsin Card Sorting Test (WCST) for humans: Four stimulus cards are shown to a subject characterized by three different dimensions (colors, shapes, and numbers). The subject is required to match the cards according to the correct dimension of the three shown. For example, if the rule is color, the subject needs to place the blue four stars under the blue six crosses. The test ends when the subjects finish matching 128 cards. (B) The Cambridge Neuropsychological Test Automated Battery ID/ED task for humans: in this computerized version, the dimensions are shapes, colors, and lines. In this example, the correct dimension is reported in bold and the "+" indicates the correct response in each stage. The subject goes through different stages: simple discrimination (SD), compound discrimination (CD), compound discrimination reversal (CDRe), intradimensional shift (IDS), intradimensional shift reversal (IDSRe), and extradimensional shift (EDS). Two or three dimensions can be used for this task: in the first case, in the EDS stage, the dimensions shown are the same as in the previous stages, but the previously relevant dimension will now be irrelevant, and the irrelevant the relevant one; in the second case, a new dimension is introduced as the relevant one and the previously relevant dimension becomes the irrelevant one. (C) Automated two-chambered ID/ED Operon task for mice (Scheggia et al., 2014). On the left is a schematic representation of the task: the apparatus consists of two identical chambers divided by a transparent sliding door (6). The chambers are characterized by a house light (1), food dispenser (2), two nose-poke holes (the choice action to make) in which the odor stimuli are also delivered (3), a pair of tactile stimuli (4) and lights (5). Odors, lights, and tactile stimuli are switched on or placed in the required position just before the start of a trial while the test mouse is in the other chamber. On the right is a photo of one side of the apparatus.

category (e.g., shift from color to shape). A similar conceptual construct is used in the computerized ID/ED task (Figure 1(B)). In the first simple discrimination (SD) stage, the subject must discriminate between two exemplars from the same dimension (e.g., shape). Then, a second but irrelevant dimension (e.g., lines) is introduced in the compound discrimination (CD) stage. Typically, the successive stage consists of a reversal exercise (CDRe), where the exemplars and the relevant/irrelevant dimensions are unchanged but the subject has to learn that the previously correct stimulus is now incorrect. Following there is an intradimensional shift (IDS), where novel exemplars from each dimension are presented, but with the same relevant dimension being rewarded. Finally, the subject is exposed to the critical extradimensional shift (EDS) stage, in which he or she needs to shift the attention from the previously reinforced dimension (in this example, shape) (1) to the previously irrelevant dimension (in this example, line) or (2) to another new stimulus dimension (e.g., color). Thus, the EDS measures the ability to apply a new strategy that involves shifting from a previously formed cognitive set. This latter stage is analogous to the category shift of the WCST (Roberts et al., 1988). After the EDS stage another reversal stage (i.e., EDSRe) might be added. Reversal stages assess a very elementary form of set-shifting, determining whether the subject can shift from a previously rewarded cue to the previously not-rewarded choice. Moreover, consecutive reversal stages before the EDS (i.e., CDRe and IDSRe) also serve to reinforce the cognitive attentional-set challenged by the EDS stage and to prevent conditioning to unintended aspects of the stimulus. Similarly, the IDS stage serves as an internal control and also to strengthen the formation of a cognitive attentional set. Thus, compared with the WCST, the ID/ED task incorporates the metrics to compare cognitive set formation and shifting abilities challenging three main forms of cognitive flexibility: the intradimensional shift, the extradimensional shift, and the reversal learning. Moreover, playing with two or three different dimensions allows for the differentiation of two distinct cognitive mechanisms during the most challenging EDS stage. The first one is the inability to release attention from a relevant perceptual dimension (i.e., perseveration, also called "stuck-in-set"; best studied using three distinct dimensions). The second is the inability to reengage attention to a previously irrelevant dimension (i.e., "learned irrelevance"; assessed using only two dimensions).

Patients with schizophrenia have pronounced difficulties in performing the WCST and the CANTAB ID/ED (Owen, Roberts, Polkey, Sahakian, & Robbins, 1991; Weinberger et al., 1986). In particular, they are consistently impaired in the EDS stage (Ceaser et al., 2008; Elliott, McKenna, Robbins, & Sahakian, 1995; Pantelis et al., 1999; Turner et al., 2004). This is very similar to subjects with lesions of the frontal lobe who show deficits

in solving the EDS but not the IDS stage (Owen et al., 1993). In agreement, the EDS deficits in schizophrenia have been associated with physiological dysfunction of a specific region of the frontal lobe, the dorsolateral prefrontal cortex (DLPFC) (Weinberger et al., 1986). More specifically, patients with schizophrenia seem to show EDS impairments because of a high level of stuck-in-set perseveration (Perry & Braff, 1998), which has also been associated with dorsolateral PFC dysfunction (Owen et al., 1993; Sandson & Albert, 1984). Furthermore, neuroimaging studies (regional cerebral blood flow and functional magnetic resonance imaging) have associated stuck-in-set perseverative scores with reduced activity within the PFC, whereas other types of perseveration, such as recurrent or continuous, fail to correlate with PFC activity (Nagahama et al., 2001; Nagahama, Okina, Suzuki, Nabatame, & Matsuda, 2005). In conclusion, not only would an EDS impairment be useful as a sensitive measure of schizophrenia-related executive control deficit, but the stuck-in-set perseveration could be a true parameter of frontal dysfunction in schizophrenia.

The various components of the WCST and ID/ED tasks have been successfully modified and adapted in animal models. Consistent with frontal lobe patients (Owen et al., 1993), lesion studies in nonhuman primates and in rodents have demonstrated that the PFC has a functional homology to human lateral PFC (Birrell & Brown, 2000; Bissonette et al., 2008; Dias, Robbins, & Roberts, 1996). Damage of the lateral (in primates) or medial (in rodents) PFC impairs set-shifting abilities while sparing reversal learning. Conversely, lesions of the orbitofrontal cortex in humans (Rahman, Sahakian, Hodges, Rogers, & Robbins, 1999), monkeys (Dias et al., 1996), rats (McAlonan & Brown, 2003), and mice (Bissonette et al., 2008) impair the reversal learning stages but not the EDS. These data suggest a double dissociation or functional specialization between the PFC and orbitofrontal cortex (Bissonette et al., 2008; Brown & Bowman, 2002; Dias et al., 1996; Robbins, 2007). Moreover, humans, monkeys, and mice have been shown to exhibit qualitatively similar patterns of performance in attentional set-shifting tasks. That is, superior IDS performance compared with EDS, and progressive improvement of performance in serial reversal learning (Roberts et al., 1988; Scheggia, Bebensee, Weinberger, & Papaleo, 2014). Thus, the neural substrates that control the cognitive functions assessed by attentional set-shifting tasks seem conserved between humans, monkeys, rats, and mice.

The first example of an effective ID/ED attentional set-shifting task in rodents was developed in rats (Birrell & Brown, 2000). This "digging version" task involves the use of two cups filled with sawdust to retrieve food reward. The cup can be distinguished by three different dimensions: odor, outer texture, and the digging medium. Exactly as in humans and monkeys, rats go through a series of consecutive discriminations including the SD (where just one dimension is presented; e.g., odor), the CD (where a second distracting dimension is introduced; e.g., digging medium), the reversal (where the relevant and irrelevant dimensions are unchanged, whereas the previously incorrect cue is now correct), the IDS (where all cues are changed but the relevant and irrelevant dimensions remain unchanged), and the EDS (where all the pairs of cues are again changed but now the previously irrelevant dimension becomes relevant; e.g., digging medium). Successively, this task has been also implemented in mice and validated with genetically modified mice, pharmacological, and lesion studies (Bissonette et al., 2008; Papaleo et al., 2008). However, despite the validity and effectiveness of the rodents' digging version of the attentional set-shifting task, several limitations are dampening their use and application in translational studies relevant to psychiatric diseases. In particular, the presence of the food reinforcer inside the choice stimulus cups could result in an ambiguous interpretation of animal responses and potential bias in choice making (Gilmour et al., 2013). Moreover, this digging version set-shifting task is manually intensive and time-consuming, limiting its reliability, replicability, standardization, and application to large-scale genetic and/or drug-screening studies. With the intent to develop an automated task for rodents, a touchscreen visual discrimination paradigm using line and shape as dimensions (Brigman, Bussey, Saksida, & Rothblat, 2005), similar to the ID/ED task used in humans and monkeys, has been proposed. Again, in this task, mice go through the SD, CD, IDS, and EDS stages. However, after a very long training, although the rodents are able to learn the SD and CD stages, this touchscreen paradigm was not able to effectively reveal the expected difference in performance between the IDS and EDS stages. This is not in line with the behavioral results found in equivalent tasks in humans and monkeys, as well as in the rodent digging version. More recently, another work has attempted to use a touchscreen ID/ED paradigm for mice (Dickson, Calton, & Mittleman, 2014). However, the lengthy training, the important differences in dimensional salience of the compound stimuli, and a pattern of performance between successive IDS stages and between IDS and EDS stages discordant with human studies again proved that touchscreen setups might not be optimal to study executive control in mice. In contrast, a novel automated two-chamber ID/ED Operon task for rodents that overcomes the major limitations of the previous manual versions and of the first attempts of automation has been recently successfully validated, demonstrating strict analogies to the humans' WCST and ID/ED tasks (Figure 1(C)) (Scheggia et al., 2014). In this new setup, mice quickly learn (in an average of 7 days) to perform the complete consecutive series of SD, CD, CDRe, IDS, IDSRe, IDS2, IDS2Re, EDS, and EDSRe stages. Importantly, in this automated

test, three different dimensions with equivalent salience are available (i.e., lights, odors, and textures), allowing for selective assessment of stuck-in-set or "learned irrelevance" switching abilities. Furthermore, this novel operant-based task presents several advantages over previously used ID/ED tasks for rodents: (1) it has less labor-intensive procedures; (2) it eliminates any source of subjectivity in the measured parameters; (3) it eliminates potential experimental bias resulting from reinforcement-related cues; (4) it avoids arbitrary environmental conditions; (5) it allows manipulation of multiple dimensions with a large range of different stimuli; and (6) it allows for large-scale mouse studies for genetic, pharmacologic, and neuronal screenings relevant to schizophrenia.

Notwithstanding their effectiveness and relevance to schizophrenia, there are still only few examples of application of these tasks to schizophrenia-relevant mouse models. For example, transgenic mice over-expressing the human catechol-O-methyltransferase-Val polymorphism (COMT Val-tg), simulating human genetic conditions leading to relative increased COMT activity, have shown a selective impairment in their EDS ability (Papaleo et al., 2008). Conversely, genetic conditions of reduced COMT activity, which translate into increased cortical dopamine, produce a selective improvement on EDS abilities in mice (Scheggia et al., 2014). These results closely parallel findings in healthy humans and patients with schizophrenia showing that COMT Val carriers have impaired performance and a higher number of perseverative errors in the EDS phase of the WCST and/or the CANTAB ID/ED task compared with individuals with two copies of the COMT Met allele (Egan et al., 2001; Joober et al., 2002; Malhotra et al., 2002; Mattay et al., 2003). Furthermore, the schizophrenia-relevant animal model of chronic administration of phencyclidine, shows selective EDS impairments in the attentional set-shifting tasks in both mice and rats (Egerton, Reid, McKerchar, Morris, & Pratt, 2005; Scheggia et al., 2014). The reasons of the paucity of current studies employing attentional set-shifting tasks in mouse models of schizophrenia might reside in their complexity and difficult setup. However, we consider these as the most refined and translationally valid paradigms able to give an accurate and relevant information to model cognitive impairments in schizophrenia.

WORKING MEMORY

Impairments in working memory are among the most consistent cognitive deficits observed in patients with schizophrenia (Castner, Goldman-Rakic, & Williams, 2004; Forbes, Carrick, McIntosh, & Lawrie, 2009; Keefe et al., 1995). This term refers to the type of memory that is active and relevant only for a short period, on the scale of seconds, while performing complex tasks such as reasoning, comprehension, and learning. The concept of working memory evolved from that of short-term memory and now it stands at the interface between perceptual processes and long-term memory formation. The major components of working memory, as suggested by Baddeley's model (Baddeley, 2010), are (1) a short-term storage buffer for visuospatial information that provides a virtual environment for physical simulation, calculation, visualization, and optical memory recall; (2) a short-term storage buffer for verbal information; (3) a central executive component that is responsible for response selection and for coordinating the outputs of different short-term memory buffers; and (4) an episodic buffer, in which complex multimodal events are integrated and stored online. In this model, the maintenance of specific information is governed by the buffer systems, whereas the regulation and coordination of this information (i.e., updating and maintenance of task goals, management of interference, and manipulation and transformations of stored content) are handled by the central executive processes.

One of the most commonly used neurocognitive paradigms to test working memory functions in patients with schizophrenia has been the n-back task because this has been often coupled with functional neuroimaging studies (Callicott et al., 2000). "n-back" refers to how far back the subject has to recall in the sequence of presented stimuli (usually visuospatial, but can be also auditory or olfactory). In the first phase of this task, the subject is presented with a non–memory-guided control condition (0-back) that simply requires identifying the stimulus currently seen. Then, in the working memory condition, the task requires recollection of a stimulus seen one stimulus (1-back) or two stimuli before (2-back), while continuing to encode additional incoming stimuli. Other working memory paradigms that have been extensively used in patients with schizophrenia are the spatial delayed response tasks (Barch, Moore, Nee, Manoach, & Luck, 2012). In these tasks, subjects are required to remember the position of five objects (i.e., dots). During each trial, five dots appear sequentially (1 second each) with very little interstimulus intervals. Then, after a retention interval, a probe stimulus appears for 1 s and the subject has to indicate whether this stimulus was at one of the memorized locations.

Patients with schizophrenia show deficits in all subprocesses of working memory (Forbes et al., 2009; Lee & Park, 2005). In particular, several functional magnetic resonance imaging studies applied to the n-back and delayed match-to-sample tasks consistently converge, indicating that while performing working memory paradigms patients with schizophrenia present an abnormal activation of the PFC (Anticevic, Repovs, & Barch, 2013; Callicott & Weinberger, 1999; Weinberger et al., 2001).

To date, more emphasis is being put on the investigation of working memory neuronal networks and on how genetic vulnerability might influence the developmental trajectory of working memory deficits in schizophrenia. Indeed, variations in different schizophrenia-candidate genes have been observed to influence working memory functions in schizophrenia (Harrison & Weinberger, 2005; Rasetti & Weinberger, 2011). These include, but not only, functional polymorphisms in COMT (Egan et al., 2001), genetic variations in the Neuregulin 1 gene, its receptor ERBB4 (Nicodemus et al., 2010), and in the dysbindin-1 gene (Donohoe et al., 2007).

There are numerous working memory tasks that have been employed and validated in rodents to reliably measure the maintenance of visuospatial information with high translational efficacy (Dudchenko, 2004; Kellendonk et al., 2006; Papaleo, Burdick, Callicott, & Weinberger, 2014; Papaleo, Lipska, & Weinberger, 2012). For example, the T-maze discrete paired-trial variable-delay alternation task (Aultman & Moghaddam, 2001; Kellendonk et al., 2006; Papaleo et al., 2008), the eight-arm radial maze "delayed nonmatch to sample" or "win-shift" (Seamans, Floresco, & Phillips, 1995; Seamans & Phillips, 1994), the eight-arm maze "random foraging task" (Floresco, Seamans, & Phillips, 1997; Seamans et al., 1995), the odor span tasks (Dudchenko, 2004; Young, Kerr, et al., 2007), and some paradigms of delayed matching and delay nonmatching to sample position operant conditioning tasks (Dunnett, 1993) are considered the most effective and valid paradigms. In general, the tasks that bear close resemblance to the human delayed response tasks are the ones adopting the delayed nonmatch to position rule. These tasks involve an initial "sample" or "forced run" phase in which the rodent is exposed to a visual target or an arm of the maze. Subsequently, in the "choice" phase that is run after a variable delay, the subject is simultaneously presented with the original sample (the "match") and another visual target or arm (the "nonmatch"). These pairs of phases must be presented repeatedly but, importantly, with randomly changing cues presented in the sample phase. Thus, the working memory construct is based on the fact that the tested rodent is required to integrate information held online (the sample phase) with the learned rule (nonmatch or match to sample).

Importantly, mouse studies adopting these paradigms indicate that schizophrenia-susceptibility genes might alter working memory functions through their modulation of the dopaminergic and/or glutamatergic systems in the PFC. This provides supporting biological validity to the indications derived in functional magnetic resonance imaging studies in patients with schizophrenia. For example, transgenic mice overexpressing the human COMT Val variant (that has been suggested as a weak risk factor for schizophrenia) show working memory deficits in a discrete paired-trial variable-delay T-maze task (Papaleo et al., 2008). COMT Val-tg mice have increased COMT enzyme activity and possibly decreased dopamine in the PFC compared with their control littermates. Conversely, mice with reduced levels of COMT show improved working memory performance in this same task compared with wild-type mice (Papaleo et al., 2008). This was true only for male subjects, as reported by equivalent working memory data in mice and humans (Sannino et al., 2014). Furthermore, mice overexpressing the D2 receptors selectively in the striatum (another mouse model with relevance to schizophrenia) show impaired acquisition of the discrete paired-trial alternation T-maze working memory task because of changes in dopamine metabolism and D1 receptor activation in the PFC (Kellendonk et al., 2006). Of note, these deficits persist in these D2 mutant mice even after the transgene is switched off in adulthood, indicating developmental dysfunctions produced by the striatal upregulation of the D2 receptors. These findings help to reshape the current dopamine hypothesis of schizophrenia, pointing to a functional role played by the PFC-striatal loop, possibly arising already from developmental stages. In relation to the glutamatergic system, mice lacking the NR2A subunit of the NMDA receptors have shown impairments in a spatial non-matching-to-place T-maze task (Bannerman et al., 2008). Similarly, genetic downregulation in mice of another subunit of the NMDA receptors, namely the NR1, produced working memory impairments (Gandal et al., 2012). Thus, these results suggest an important role of NMDA-dependent glutamate transmission in working memory abnormalities found in schizophrenia. Further support for the dopamine and glutamate implications in working memory deficits found in schizophrenia come from mice with genetic modifications of the dysbindin-1 gene. Indeed, genetically modified mice with decreased dysbindin-1 showed altered working memory functions with different patterns of effects depending on the cognitive load that could be ascribed to either alterations of the dopamine and/or glutamate systems (Karlsgodt et al., 2011; Papaleo & Weinberger, 2011; Papaleo, Yang, et al., 2012). In agreement, dysbindin-1 has been recently shown to participate in a genetic interaction with COMT that modulates working memory functions dependent on the medial PFC (Papaleo et al., 2014). In particular, although dysbindin-1 reduction resulted in a faster acquisition of a working memory task, this same reduction in a background of reduced COMT gene in the same subject results in marked cognitive disadvantages. Notably, these mouse studies faithfully predicted the COMT*dysbindin-1–dependent effects on the modulation of PFC physiological responses in humans performing the n-back working memory task (Papaleo et al., 2014). Thus, dysbindin-1 reduction may represent

a direct genetic bridge between the dopamine and glutamate schizophrenia-related signaling systems, and the molecular mechanism of dysbindin as a psychosis risk gene may involve this bridge. Furthermore, the strict agreement between human and mouse studies (e.g., Papaleo et al., 2014; Sannino et al., 2014) highlights the potential of accurately combining mouse–human studies for true translational medicine.

ATTENTION

Abnormalities in attentional processes are fundamental cognitive deficits in schizophrenia, with evidence suggesting that lack of selection of relevant information may be a cause of impairment also in the other cognitive domains (Gold & Thaker, 2002; Zvyagintsev, Parisi, Chechko, Nikolaev, & Mathiak, 2013). A broad definition of the term "attention" is the ability to select a subset of the available information for preferential processing, while ignoring competing information (Smid, de Witte, Homminga, & van den Bosch, 2006). However, there are different forms of attentional processes: (1) sustained attention (vigilance; i.e., the capacity to allocate informational processing resources over an extended period); (2) selective/focused attention (i.e., the ability to preferentially attend to a subset of stimuli while ignoring others); and (3) divided attention (i.e., the capacity to monitor and respond to multiple stimuli simultaneously according to the demands of the situation) (Millan et al., 2012).

The processes most studied in schizophrenia are selective attention and sustained attention. Notably, mounting evidence suggests that patients with schizophrenia have an intact implementation of information selection (i.e., unaltered sustained attention), while being impaired in the control of information selection (i.e., switching the focus of attention) and broad monitoring (Hahn et al., 2012; Luck & Gold, 2008; Nuechterlein, Luck, Lustig, & Sarter, 2009; Smid, Martens, de Witte, & Bruggeman, 2013). This might be due to the fact that, in contrast to sustained attention (in which competing information are absent or minimal), the other forms of attentional processes require additional control mechanisms that enable flexibility and selective integration of different information.

Several paradigms are available to measure attentional processes. Here, we briefly describe few of them that proved to be relevant in clinical studies of schizophrenia. The Continuous Performance Test (CPT), a visual vigilance task, has been used extensively to measure selective attentional or vigilance deficits in patients with schizophrenia (Cornblatt, Risch, Faris, Friedman, & Erlenmeyer-Kimling, 1988; Gold & Thaker, 2002; Nuechterlein & Dawson, 1984). In the basic CPT task, subjects are exposed to a rapid presentation of continuously changing stimuli (e.g., letters, auditory tones), and are required to respond only to an infrequent target stimulus (typically 10–20% of total stimulus presentations), while withholding any response following noncue targets or cues followed by a distractor. Subjects might be monitoring for a single target (e.g., a letter C) or a target sequence (e.g., letters A, B, C) (Gold & Thaker, 2002; Nuechterlein & Dawson, 1984). Variants of the task such as the CPT Identical Pairs (Cornblatt et al., 1988) and the A-X CPT versions (Servan-Schreiber, Cohen, & Steingard, 1996) have been shown to be especially relevant to schizophrenia.

The Stroop task is another test of selective attention based on the interference effect (MacLeod, 1991; Stroop, 1935; Zvyagintsev et al., 2013). In this task, subjects are presented with words written with inks of different colors and instructed either to name the ink color and ignore the word or, at other times, read the word and ignore the color. When the ink color and word form are incompatible, there is a slowing of responses because of interference from the highly overlearned read-the-word rule (Luck & Gold, 2008). Patients with schizophrenia show significantly stronger Stroop interference compared with healthy subjects, resulting from selective attention deficits and/or impaired rule selection abilities (Barch, Carter, Hachten, Usher, & Cohen, 1999; Henik & Salo, 2004; Luck & Gold, 2008; Perlstein, Carter, Barch, & Baird, 1998).

The Spatial Attentional Resource Allocation Task (SARAT) has been described and validated as a tool for manipulating the size of the attentional focus in space (Hahn, Ross, & Stein, 2006). In short, this task requires subjects to fixate on a central circle (divided into four quarters (four cues)) that would predict the location of one of four peripheral target stimuli. One, two, three, or all four possible cues can be turned on simultaneously (Hahn et al., 2006). In this way, predictability of the target location is varied across trials. Thus, subjects are required to continuously allocate attention to cued locations in anticipation of a target engaging the ability to spread attention across a variety of locations and the ability to focus the attention (Hahn et al., 2012, 2006). In summary, this task has been developed to investigate and distinguish selective attention from broad monitoring. In particular, patients with schizophrenia show a substantial impairment in the ability to distribute attention broadly, but are unimpaired at focusing attention on one location and withdrawing attention from others (Hahn et al., 2012). These studies suggest that visuospatial attentional deficits in schizophrenia arise because of the presence of distractors and when broad monitoring of cues is required.

Preclinically, discrete elements of attentional processes such as sustained and focused attention, impulse control, perseverative and reactivity-related functions can be effectively studied in rodents. For example, a cognitive test allowing the concomitant examination of multiple cognitive measures such as attention, impulse

control, processing speed and cognitive flexibility is the 5-Choice Serial Reaction Time Task (Carli, Robbins, Evenden, & Everitt, 1983; Robbins, 2002; Robbins, Muir, Killcross, & Pretsell, 1993). Succinctly, in this task, the animal is required to simultaneously monitor five light stimuli (either over or inside five nose-poke holes) positioned on one wall of an operant chamber; when one of the light stimuli is illuminated, to respond with a nose poke in the corresponding location. Food or liquid reinforcements are delivered at a dispenser situated at the opposite wall of the chamber following a correct response. This task has been often used in animal models relevant to schizophrenia (Amitai & Markou, 2009; Carli, Calcagno, Mainolfi, Mainini, & Invernizzi, 2011; Le Pen, Grottick, Higgins, & Moreau, 2003; Paine & Carlezon, 2009; Papaleo, Erickson, Liu, Chen, & Weinberger, 2012; Young, Crawford, et al., 2007). Indeed, the advantages of the 5-Choice Serial Reaction Time Task, including, for example, a low within- and between-subject variance, possibility to detect impairments as well as improvements, complete automation, concomitant registration of different behaviors/measures, high versatility to flexibly and selectively manipulate the testing parameters (e.g., increasing intertrial interval, decreasing stimulus duration) (Amitai & Markou, 2011; Robbins, 2002). Furthermore, the stable baselines of performance of the rodents in this task have made it useful in the assessment of repeated effects of systemically administered drugs, particularly as performance often returns to baseline quite rapidly (Robbins, 2002).

The Distractor Condition Sustained Attention Task is another operant attention task that has been first developed as a signal-detection task in rodents. Here animals are required to indicate the appearance of a signal (e.g., a brief focal light illumination) by pressing the correct lever in a series of discrete trials under distractor conditions (e.g., flashing house light) and under standard (without distractor) conditions (Bushnell, 1999; McGaughy & Sarter, 1995; Mohler, Meck, & Williams, 2001; Nuechterlein et al., 2009). Thereafter, this task has been redesigned and validated for use in humans, thus exhibiting clinical translatability (Demeter, Sarter, & Lustig, 2008). This task is now being applied to patients with schizophrenia (Demeter, Guthrie, Taylor, Sarter, & Lustig, 2013). In particular, in agreement with previous literature (Bowen et al., 1994; Ford, Pfefferbaum, & Roth, 1992; Grillon, Courchesne, Ameli, Geyer, & Braff, 1990; Melcher et al., 2013; Oltmanns, 1978; Oltmanns & Neale, 1975), results of studies using this task provide confirmation that patients with schizophrenia are more vulnerable to distraction than healthy controls.

The Distractor Condition Sustained Attention Task is a good example of effective and useful translational research that might have important implications in the study of cognitive impairments in schizophrenia.

Similarly, based on the proven utility of the SARAT paradigm in distinguishing deficits in selective attention from broad monitoring alterations relevant to schizophrenia, additional tasks with this translatable value will prove to be highly useful. Unfortunately, as yet, no preclinical paradigms equivalent to SARAT exist.

SOCIAL COGNITION

In recent years, there has been growing consensus that abnormalities in social cognition form part of the core symptoms in schizophrenia (Billeke & Aboitiz, 2013; Millan, Fone, Steckler, & Horan, 2014). Social cognition can be generally defined as the ability to construct mental representations of others, oneself, and relations between others and oneself and to use these representations to guide social behavior and facilitate skillful social interactions (Adolphs, 2001; Sergi et al., 2007). In schizophrenia, deficits in social cognition are correlated with neurocognitive impairments and negative symptoms and thus also play an important role in the functional outcome of patients (Brune, 2005; Brune, Abdel-Hamid, Lehmkamper, & Sonntag, 2007; Couture, Penn, & Roberts, 2006; Sergi et al., 2007). Furthermore, social cognitive impairments as well as other cognitive deficits, are poorly ameliorated by currently available antipsychotics (Brune, 2005; Kucharska-Pietura & Mortimer, 2013; Millan et al., 2014). The progression of social cognitive impairment in schizophrenia is still unclear; whether it is present at the start of illness, whether it exists before the onset of illness, whether the degree of impairment progressively decreases or increases, or whether such changes apply across multiple social cognitive domains (Green & Leitman, 2008). Indeed, to better conceptualize social cognitive impairment, and in agreement with the Measurement and Treatment Research to Improve Cognition in Schizophrenia and Cognitive Neuroscience Treatment Research to Improve Cognition in Schizophrenia guidelines (Carter, Barch, Gur, Pinkham, & Ochsner, 2009; Green et al., 2008), social skill domains can be categorized into five main areas: emotional processing, social perception, social knowledge, theory of mind, and attributional bias (Green & Horan, 2010; Green & Leitman, 2008; Green, Olivier, Crawley, Penn, & Silverstein, 2005). Emotional processing refers to the ability to identify, facilitate, understand, and manage emotions (Green et al., 2008). Social perception involves the capacity to identify roles, rules, and contexts in a social setting (Billeke & Aboitiz, 2013). Social knowledge refers to an awareness of the roles, rules, and goals that characterize social situations and guide social interactions (Green et al., 2008). Theory of mind is the ability to infer the mental state of others (i.e., their beliefs, desires, dispositions, knowledge, intentions, and future behavior) (Green et al., 2008; Millan & Bales, 2013).

Finally, attribution bias reflects the way people tend to infer the cause of particular positive and negative events (i.e., context-sensitive regulation) (Billeke & Aboitiz, 2013; Green et al., 2008). Clinical studies have shown that patients with schizophrenia display impairments in all the social cognition domains: emotion processing (Archer, Hay, & Young, 1994; Pollard, Hellewell, & William Deakin, 1995), social perception (Corrigan & Green, 1993a; Toomey, Schuldberg, Corrigan, & Green, 2002), social knowledge (Corrigan & Addis, 1995; Penn, Ritchie, Francis, Combs, & Martin, 2002), theory of mind (Greig, Bryson, & Bell, 2004; Roncone et al., 2002), and attributional bias (Green & Horan, 2010; Green et al., 2005). These deficits can be uncovered by a wide range of psychological tests that measure social skills (a few examples are listed in Table 1).

Because of the high complexity and multidimensionality of the measures used to study social cognition in humans, it is difficult to find perfectly matched replica tasks in mouse models. Nonetheless, mice are also a social species that exhibit complex social behaviors. For example, measures of social abilities can be deduced from home cage observations such as maternal/parental behaviors, colony formation/hierarchy, interactions between peers, nest-building, sleeping together in the nest, or resting in group huddles (Green et al., 2005; Millan & Bales, 2013).

The basic assessment of social interaction abilities in rodents involves measurements of specific behaviors such as sniffing, following, climbing on, ultrasonic vocalizations, allogrooming, fighting, and sexual behavior, whereas two unfamiliar adults freely interact in an open-field arena (File & Hyde, 1978; File & Seth, 2003; Huang et al., 2014; Silverman, Yang, Lord, & Crawley, 2010). Using this setting, many genetic, pharmacological, developmental, and neurobiological rodent models relevant to schizophrenia have shown perturbations in social interaction (Hida, Mouri, & Noda, 2013; Koros, Rosenbrock, Birk, Weiss, & Sams-Dodd, 2007; Millan & Brocco, 2008; Peleg-Raibstein, Feldon, & Meyer, 2012; Pratt, Winchester, Dawson, & Morris, 2012; Sams-Dodd, 1999). These social interaction abnormalities are usually interpreted to be relevant to the social withdrawal phenotypes associated with negative symptoms in schizophrenia.

Furthermore, there are available in rodents more specific paradigms that might recruit, to some extent, the animal's ability to encode, retrieve/recognize, and respond appropriately to social stimuli, testing domains such as: sociability (i.e., the motivation to interact with social over nonsocial stimuli); social recognition/memory (i.e., the ability to remember an individual and discriminate between individuals); and social motivation (i.e., motivation to perform an action to gain access to a social partner) (Millan & Bales, 2013; Silverman et al., 2010). These tasks could prove to be more relevant to the social cognitive constructs in humans.

TABLE 1 Measures of Social Cognition in Humans

Measure	Construct	Description	Indicator	Other Measures of the Same Construct
Mayer-Salovey-Caruso Emotional Intelligence Test (Mayer, Salovey, & Caruso, 2002)	Emotion perception and processing	A self-report instrument that consists of 141 items and eight ability subscales that assess four branches of emotion processing (identifying, using, understanding, and managing emotions).	Mayer-Salovey-Caruso Emotional Intelligence Test total score as well as the four branch scores.	Bell-Lysaker Emotion Recognition Test (Bell, Bryson, & Lysaker, 1997), Facial Emotion Identification Test (Kerr & Neale, 1993), Pictures of Facial Affect (Ekman & Friesen, 1976), Facial Emotion Discrimination Test (Kerr & Neale, 1993), Videotape Affect Perception Test (Bellack, Blanchard, & Mueser, 1996), Vocal Emotion Identification Test (Kerr & Neale, 1993), Vocal Affect Recognition (Nowicki & Duke, 1994), Prosody task (Pijnenborg, Withaar, Bosch, & Brouwer, 2007).
The Half-Profile of Nonverbal Sensitivity (Ambady, Hallahan, & Rosenthal, 1995; Rosenthal, Hall, DiMatteo, Rogers, & Archer, 1979)	Social perception and knowledge	110 videotaped 2-s scenes of facial expressions, voice intonations, and/or bodily gestures of a Caucasian female are shown to subjects who are then required to select which of two labels better describes a situation that would generate the social cue(s) after watching each scene.	Total number of correct items.	Situational Feature Recognition Test (Corrigan & Green, 1993b), Schema Component Sequencing Task (Corrigan & Addis, 1995), Social Cue Recognition Task (Corrigan & Green, 1993), Social Stimuli Sequencing Task (Corrigan, Wallace, & Green, 1992), Wechsler Adult Intelligence Scale comprehension (Wechsler, 1987).
Hinting task (Corcoran, Mercer, & Frith, 1995)	Theory of mind (mental state reasoning/decoding)	10 short stories involving the interaction of two people, each one ending with a character dropping an obvious hint are read to the subject. The subject is then asked about the meaning of the character's statements.	Two marks are given for a correct answer to the first question, one mark for a correct answer following a second, more obvious hint (which is given to the subject when he or she fails to correctly answer the first question) and 0 for an incorrect response to both hints.	The Awareness of Social Inference Test (McDonald, Flanagan, & Rollins, 2002), Eyes Test (Baron-Cohen, Wheelwright, Hill, Raste, & Plumb, 2001).
The Ambiguous Intentions Hostility Questionnaire (Combs, Penn, Wicher, & Waldheter, 2007)	Attribution biases	Subjects read a series of vignettes describing social situations and answer questions about the intentions of the characters and how subjects themselves would respond to the situation.	Ambiguous situations are scored and three summary scores are computed: hostility bias, aggression bias, and a composite "blame" score (average of Intentionality, Anger, and Blame item ratings).	Internal, Personal, and Situational Attributions Questionnaire (Kinderman & Bentall, 1996)

Sociability is commonly tested using a three-chambered setup where rodents are presented and can chose to interact with a social stimulus (an unknown conspecific, a partner, etc.), with no stimulus (an empty chamber), or with a socially neutral stimulus (an inanimate object) (Crawley, 2000; Kaidanovich-Beilin, Lipina, Vukobradovic, Roder, & Woodgett, 2011; Moy et al., 2007; Roullet & Crawley, 2011; Young, Gobrogge, Liu, & Wang, 2011). It is argued that these tasks are relevant to social "drive" (i.e., motivation to engage in social interactions in

I. FROM CLINICAL DIMENSIONS TO ANIMAL MODELS

humans) (Millan & Bales, 2013). Animal models relevant to schizophrenia such as the rat neonatal hippocampal lesion model (Lipska, 2004), mice with mutations in the Neuregulin-1 and Disrupted in Schizophrenia-1 (*DISC1*) genes have been found to exhibit sociability deficits in these paradigms (Li et al., 2007; O'Tuathaigh et al., 2007).

Tests assessing social recognition/memory abilities take advantage of the natural tendency of rodents to explore more unfamiliar versus familiar conspecifics. Thus, a widely used procedure is the "habituation/dishabituation" paradigm in which the tested subject is first repeatedly exposed to the same stimulus animal (resulting in progressively shorter investigation times), and then exposed to a novel unfamiliar animal (renewed interest indicated by increased exploration time) (Dluzen & Kreutzberg, 1993; Huang et al., 2014; Winslow & Camacho, 1995). Alternatively, in the social (novelty) discrimination procedure, the test subject is first exposed to a conspecific and, after a short delay, in the second trial, it is simultaneously exposed to the previously explored animal and with a second novel conspecific. Various animal models relevant to schizophrenia have shown disrupted social recognition/discrimination measured in these tasks. For example, (1) neonatal exposure to phencyclidine and neonatal immune activation (Boulay et al., 2008; Ibi et al., 2010; Meffre et al., 2012); (2) genetic disruption of *DISC-1* or microtubules (Begou et al., 2008; Ibi et al., 2010); and (3) subchronic interference with NMDA receptor-mediated transmission by ketamine (Gao, Elmer, Adams-Huet, & Tamminga, 2009; Millan et al., 2007).

Social motivation is generally tested in operant chambers, where a rodent is trained to press a lever with access to a conspecific as a social reinforcer (Evans et al., 1994). However, so far no animal models relevant to schizophrenia have been tested in these paradigms.

Despite their extensive use and important utility, the currently available tasks in rodents to assess social cognitive functions relevant to schizophrenia are still limited in their equivalence to human clinical tasks. For example, evaluation of social cognitive processes such as theory of mind, facial perception/recognition, and gaze-following can be tested in nonhuman primates (Machado & Nelson, 2011; Millan & Bales, 2013), but are not yet, and perhaps never will be, be doable in mice or rats. This will require consistent efforts in the field with a clear aim to prove the predictive translational validity of novel and more refined social cognitive tasks in rodents.

CONCLUSIONS AND FUTURE DIRECTIONS

Nowadays schizophrenia is considered a neurodevelopmental disorder (Insel, 2010; Lewis & Levitt, 2002; Weinberger, 1987), with its cognitive impairments appearing before the onset of full symptomatology. Thus, early detection and early intervention of cognitive deficits could be potentially more effective in mitigating or reversing the pathological trajectories and ultimately the life quality of individuals with schizophrenia vulnerability. In this context, mouse studies allow early investigations and testing of early interventions/treatments from conception to adulthood, strictly controlling any environmental and genetic factors. This can be done only following a stringent translational approach and using appropriate tasks as discussed in detail in this chapter. Notably, almost the totality of the cognitive tasks described above have been adopted and validated only in adult mice and rats. Therefore, future work will be required to develop and validate similar tasks for "infant," "prepubertal," and "adolescent" rodents. These future behavioral tools, when in place, combined with available advanced tools to finely examine mouse brain development (with a range of highly efficient genetic, imaging, neural, and electrophysiological techniques), will provide unique and strong advantages in the schizophrenia field.

The PFC has been consistently shown as an essential hub orchestrating "higher order" cognitive functions (Goldman-Rakic, Muly, & Williams, 2000; Robbins & Roberts, 2007). As we have discussed, these same "higher order" cognitive functions are the most affected in schizophrenia. In agreement, the PFC and its brain networks have been constantly indicated as a crucial brain substrate of the abnormalities found in schizophrenia. This includes findings from neuropsychological/cognitive assessments (Goldberg & Weinberger, 1988; Goldberg, Weinberger, Berman, Pliskin, & Podd, 1987; Keefe et al., 1995; Pantelis et al., 2009; Weickert et al., 2000), neuroimaging (Callicott et al., 2000; Weinberger et al., 1986), and electrophysiological studies (Abrams & Taylor, 1979; Guenther et al., 1988; Tauscher, Fischer, Neumeister, Rappelsberger, & Kasper, 1998). In particular, additional evidence shows a reduced activation of the dorsolateral PFC and abnormal synaptic organization and architecture of the same brain area in patients with a diagnosis of schizophrenia while performing cognitive tasks (Callicott & Weinberger, 1999; Weinberger et al., 1986; Weinberger et al., 2001). Additionally, physiological abnormalities have been found in other brain areas anatomically connected to the PFC, such as the temporal and parietal cortices but also striatum and thalamus (Andreasen et al., 1996; Andreasen, Paradiso, & O'Leary, 1998; Callicott et al., 2000; Fletcher et al., 1998). Skepticism obviously exists when considering a direct comparison between the highly complex structure/function of the human PFC with the less evolved rodent counterpart. We certainly agree that we are not a mouse and that our brains might not work in exactly the same way. Despite this, when a mechanistic prediction based on appropriately designed mouse study can be confirmed in human studies, as has been implemented now more often (e.g. Papaleo et al., 2014; Sannino et al., 2014; Soliman et al., 2010; Young et al., 2013), we have proof of the power and utility of these preclinical studies.

In conclusion, a true concerted and synergistic effort between clinical and preclinical studies focused on the complexity of cognitive (dys)functions in schizophrenia constitute the much-needed step forward. This could indeed help to finally solve the causes of schizophrenia development, paving the way for more efficient, and possibly personalized, therapeutic strategies to ameliorate cognitive/schizophrenia-related impairments.

References

Abrams, R., & Taylor, M. A. (1979). Differential EEG patterns in affective disorder and schizophrenia. *Archives of General Psychiatry, 36,* 1355–1358.

Adolphs, R. (2001). The neurobiology of social cognition. *Current Opinion in Neurobiology, 11,* 231–239.

Ambady, N., Hallahan, M., & Rosenthal, R. (1995). On judging and being judged accurately in zero-acquaintance situations. *Journal of Personality and Social Psychology, 69,* 518–529.

Amitai, N., & Markou, A. (2009). Increased impulsivity and disrupted attention induced by repeated phencyclidine are not attenuated by chronic quetiapine treatment. *Pharmacology Biochemistry and Behavior, 93,* 248–257.

Amitai, N., & Markou, A. (2011). Comparative effects of different test day challenges on performance in the 5-choice serial reaction time task. *Behavioral Neuroscience, 125,* 764–774.

Andreasen, N. C., O'Leary, D. S., Cizadlo, T., Arndt, S., Rezai, K., Ponto, L. L., et al. (1996). Schizophrenia and cognitive dysmetria: a positron-emission tomography study of dysfunctional prefrontal-thalamic-cerebellar circuitry. *Proceedings of the National Academy of Sciences of the United States of America, 93,* 9985–9990.

Andreasen, N. C., Paradiso, S., & O'Leary, D. S. (1998). "Cognitive dysmetria" as an integrative theory of schizophrenia: a dysfunction in cortical-subcortical-cerebellar circuitry? *Schizophrenia Bulletin, 24,* 203–218.

Anticevic, A., Repovs, G., & Barch, D. M. (2013). Working memory encoding and maintenance deficits in schizophrenia: neural evidence for activation and deactivation abnormalities. *Schizophrenia Bulletin, 39,* 168–178.

Archer, J., Hay, D. C., & Young, A. W. (1994). Movement, face processing and schizophrenia: evidence of a differential deficit in expression analysis. *British Journal of Clinical Psychology, 33,* 517–528.

Aultman, J. M., & Moghaddam, B. (2001). Distinct contributions of glutamate and dopamine receptors to temporal aspects of rodent working memory using a clinically relevant task. *Psychopharmacology (Berl), 153,* 353–364.

Baddeley, A. (2010). Working memory. *Current Biology, 20,* R136–R140.

Bannerman, D. M., Niewoehner, B., Lyon, L., Romberg, C., Schmitt, W. B., Taylor, A., et al. (2008). NMDA receptor subunit NR2A is required for rapidly acquired spatial working memory but not incremental spatial reference memory. *Journal of Neuroscience, 28,* 3623–3630.

Barch, D. M., Carter, C. S., Hachten, P. C., Usher, M., & Cohen, J. D. (1999). The "benefits" of distractibility: mechanisms underlying increased Stroop effects in schizophrenia. *Schizophrenia Bulletin, 25,* 749–762.

Barch, D. M., & Ceaser, A. (2012). Cognition in schizophrenia: core psychological and neural mechanisms. *Trends in Cognitive Sciences, 16,* 27–34.

Barch, D. M., Moore, H., Nee, D. E., Manoach, D. S., & Luck, S. J. (2012). CNTRICS imaging biomarkers selection: working memory. *Schizophrenia Bulletin, 38,* 43–52.

Barnett, J. H., Robbins, T. W., Leeson, V. C., Sahakian, B. J., Joyce, E. M., & Blackwell, A. D. (2010). Assessing cognitive function in clinical trials of schizophrenia. *Neuroscience & Biobehavioral Reviews, 34,* 1161–1177.

Baron-Cohen, S., Wheelwright, S., Hill, J., Raste, Y., & Plumb, I. (2001). The "Reading the Mind in the Eyes" Test revised version: a study with normal adults, and adults with Asperger syndrome or high-functioning autism. *Journal of Child Psychology and Psychiatry, 42,* 241–251.

Begou, M., Volle, J., Bertrand, J. B., Brun, P., Job, D., Schweitzer, A., et al. (2008). The stop null mice model for schizophrenia displays [corrected] cognitive and social deficits partly alleviated by neuroleptics. *Neuroscience, 157,* 29–39.

Bell, M., Bryson, G., & Lysaker, P. (1997). Positive and negative affect recognition in schizophrenia: a comparison with substance abuse and normal control subjects. *Psychiatry Research, 73,* 73–82.

Bellack, A. S., Blanchard, J. J., & Mueser, K. T. (1996). Cue availability and affect perception in schizophrenia. *Schizophrenia Bulletin, 22,* 535–544.

Berg, E. A. (1948). A simple objective technique for measuring flexibility in thinking. *Journal of General Psychology, 39,* 15–22.

Billeke, P., & Aboitiz, F. (2013). Social cognition in schizophrenia: from social stimuli processing to social engagement. *Frontiers in Psychiatry, 4.*

Birrell, J. M., & Brown, V. J. (2000). Medial frontal cortex mediates perceptual attentional set shifting in the rat. *Journal of Neuroscience, 20,* 4320–4324.

Bissonette, G. B., Martins, G. J., Franz, T. M., Harper, E. S., Schoenbaum, G., & Powell, E. M. (2008). Double dissociation of the effects of medial and orbital prefrontal cortical lesions on attentional and affective shifts in mice. *Journal of Neuroscience, 28,* 11124–11130.

Boulay, D., Pichat, P., Dargazanli, G., Estenne-Bouhtou, G., Terranova, J. P., Rogacki, N., et al. (2008). Characterization of SSR103800, a selective inhibitor of the glycine transporter-1 in models predictive of therapeutic activity in schizophrenia. *Pharmacology Biochemistry and Behavior, 91,* 47–58.

Bowen, L., Wallace, C. J., Glynn, S. M., Nuechterlein, K. H., Lutzker, J. R., & Kuehnel, T. G. (1994). Schizophrenic individuals' cognitive functioning and performance in interpersonal interactions and skills training procedures. *Journal of Psychiatric Research, 28,* 289–301.

Brigman, J. L., Bussey, T. J., Saksida, L. M., & Rothblat, L. A. (2005). Discrimination of multidimensional visual stimuli by mice: intra- and extradimensional shifts. *Behavioral Neuroscience, 119,* 839–842.

Brown, V. J., & Bowman, E. M. (2002). Rodent models of prefrontal cortical function. *Trends in Neurosciences, 25,* 340–343.

Brune, M. (2005). Emotion recognition, 'theory of mind,' and social behavior in schizophrenia. *Psychiatry Research, 133,* 135–147.

Brune, M., Abdel-Hamid, M., Lehmkamper, C., & Sonntag, C. (2007). Mental state attribution, neurocognitive functioning, and psychopathology: what predicts poor social competence in schizophrenia best? *Schizophrenia Research, 92,* 151–159.

Bushnell, P. J. (1999). Detection of visual signals by rats: effects of signal intensity, event rate, and task type. *Behavioural Processes, 46,* 141–150.

Callicott, J. H., Bertolino, A., Mattay, V. S., Langheim, F. J., Duyn, J., Coppola, R., et al. (2000). Physiological dysfunction of the dorsolateral prefrontal cortex in schizophrenia revisited. *Cerebral Cortex, 10,* 1078–1092.

Callicott, J. H., & Weinberger, D. R. (1999). Neuropsychiatric dynamics: the study of mental illness using functional magnetic resonance imaging. *European Journal of Radiology, 30,* 95–104.

Carli, M., Calcagno, E., Mainolfi, P., Mainini, E., & Invernizzi, R. W. (2011). Effects of aripiprazole, olanzapine, and haloperidol in a model of cognitive deficit of schizophrenia in rats: relationship with glutamate release in the medial prefrontal cortex. *Psychopharmacology (Berl)*, *214*, 639–652.

Carli, M., Robbins, T. W., Evenden, J. L., & Everitt, B. J. (1983). Effects of lesions to ascending noradrenergic neurones on performance of a 5-choice serial reaction task in rats; implications for theories of dorsal noradrenergic bundle function based on selective attention and arousal. *Behavioural Brain Research*, *9*, 361–380.

Carter, C. S., Barch, D. M., Gur, R., Pinkham, A., & Ochsner, K. (2009). CNTRICS final task selection: social cognitive and affective neuroscience-based measures. *Schizophrenia Bulletin*, *35*, 153–162.

Castner, S. A., Goldman-Rakic, P. S., & Williams, G. V. (2004). Animal models of working memory: insights for targeting cognitive dysfunction in schizophrenia. *Psychopharmacology (Berl)*, *174*, 111–125.

Ceaser, A. E., Goldberg, T. E., Egan, M. F., McMahon, R. P., Weinberger, D. R., & Gold, J. M. (2008). Set-shifting ability and schizophrenia: a marker of clinical illness or an intermediate phenotype? *Biological Psychiatry*, *64*, 782–788.

Combs, D. R., Penn, D. L., Wicher, M., & Waldheter, E. (2007). The Ambiguous Intentions Hostility Questionnaire (AIHQ): a new measure for evaluating hostile social-cognitive biases in paranoia. *Cognitive Neuropsychiatry*, *12*, 128–143.

Corcoran, R., Mercer, G., & Frith, C. D. (1995). Schizophrenia, symptomatology and social inference: investigating "theory of mind" in people with schizophrenia. *Schizophrenia Research*, *17*, 5–13.

Cornblatt, B. A., Risch, N. J., Faris, G., Friedman, D., & Erlenmeyer-Kimling, L. (1988). The Continuous Performance Test, identical pairs version (CPT-IP): I. New findings about sustained attention in normal families. *Psychiatry Research*, *26*, 223–238.

Corrigan, P. W., & Addis, I. B. (1995). The effects of cognitive complexity on a social sequencing task in schizophrenia. *Schizophrenia Research*, *16*, 137–144.

Corrigan, P. W., & Green, M. F. (1993a). Schizophrenic patients' sensitivity to social cues: the role of abstraction. *American Journal of Psychiatry*, *150*, 589–594.

Corrigan, P. W., & Green, M. F. (1993b). The Situational Feature Recognition Test: a measure of schema comprehension for schizophrenia. *International Journal of Methods in Psychiatric Research*, *3*, 29–35.

Corrigan, P. W., Wallace, C. J., & Green, M. F. (1992). Deficits in social schemata in schizophrenia. *Schizophrenia Research*, *8*, 129–135.

Couture, S. M., Penn, D. L., & Roberts, D. L. (2006). The functional significance of social cognition in schizophrenia: a review. *Schizophrenia Bulletin*, *32*, 17.

Crawley, J. (2000). *What's wrong with my mouse? Behavioral phenotyping of transgenic and knockout mice*. New York: Wiley-Liss.

Demeter, E., Guthrie, S. K., Taylor, S. F., Sarter, M., & Lustig, C. (2013). Increased distractor vulnerability but preserved vigilance in patients with schizophrenia: evidence from a translational sustained attention task. *Schizophrenia Research*, *144*, 136–141.

Demeter, E., Sarter, M., & Lustig, C. (2008). Rats and humans paying attention: cross-species task development for translational research. *Neuropsychology*, *22*, 787–799.

Dias, R., Robbins, T. W., & Roberts, A. C. (1996). Primate analogue of the Wisconsin Card Sorting Test: effects of excitotoxic lesions of the prefrontal cortex in the marmoset. *Behavioral Neuroscience*, *110*, 872–886.

Dickson, P. E., Calton, M. A., & Mittleman, G. (2014). Performance of C57BL/6J and DBA/2J mice on a touchscreen-based attentional set-shifting task. *Behavioural Brain Research*, *261*, 158–170.

Dluzen, D. E., & Kreutzberg, J. D. (1993). 1-Methyl-4-phenyl-1,2,3,6-tetrahydropyridine (MPTP) disrupts social memory/recognition processes in the male mouse. *Brain Research*, *609*, 98–102.

Donohoe, G., Morris, D. W., Clarke, S., McGhee, K. A., Schwaiger, S., Nangle, J. M., et al. (2007). Variance in neurocognitive performance is associated with dysbindin-1 in schizophrenia: a preliminary study. *Neuropsychologia*, *45*, 454–458.

Dudchenko, P. A. (2004). An overview of the tasks used to test working memory in rodents. *Neuroscience & Biobehavioral Reviews*, *28*, 699–709.

Dunnett, S. B. (1993). Operant delayd matching and non-matching to position in rats. In A. Sahgal (Ed.), *Behavioural neuroscience: A practical approach* (Vol. 1) (pp. 123–136). Oxford, UK: IRL Press.

Egan, M. F., Goldberg, T. E., Kolachana, B. S., Callicott, J. H., Mazzanti, C. M., Straub, R. E., et al. (2001). Effect of COMT Val108/158 Met genotype on frontal lobe function and risk for schizophrenia. *Proceedings of the National Academy of Sciences of the United States of America*, *98*, 6917–6922.

Egerton, A., Reid, L., McKerchar, C. E., Morris, B. J., & Pratt, J. A. (2005). Impairment in perceptual attentional set-shifting following PCP administration: a rodent model of set-shifting deficits in schizophrenia. *Psychopharmacology (Berl)*, *179*, 77–84.

Ekman, P., & Friesen, W. (1976). *Pictures of facial affect*. Palo Alto, CA: Consulting Psychologists.

Eling, P., Derckx, K., & Maes, R. (2008). On the historical and conceptual background of the Wisconsin Card Sorting Test. *Brain and Cognition*, *67*, 247–253.

Elliott, R., McKenna, P. J., Robbins, T. W., & Sahakian, B. J. (1995). Neuropsychological evidence for frontostriatal dysfunction in schizophrenia. *Psychological Medicine*, *25*, 619–630.

Elvevag, B., & Goldberg, T. E. (2000). Cognitive impairment in schizophrenia is the core of the disorder. *Critical Reviews in Neurobiology*, *14*, 1–21.

Evans, M. J., Duvel, A., Funk, M. L., Lehman, B., Sparrow, J., Watson, N. T., et al. (1994). Social reinforcement of operant behavior in rats: a methodological note. *Journal of the Experimental Analysis of Behavior*, *62*, 149–156.

Fava, G. A., Tossani, E., Bech, P., Berrocal, C., Chouinard, G., Csillag, C., et al. (2014). Emerging clinical trends and perspectives on comorbid patterns of mental disorders in research. *International Journal of Methods in Psychiatric Research*, *23*(Suppl. 1), 92–101.

File, S. E., & Hyde, J. R. (1978). Can social interaction be used to measure anxiety? *British Journal of Pharmacology*, *62*, 19–24.

File, S. E., & Seth, P. (2003). A review of 25 years of the social interaction test. *European Journal of Pharmacology*, *463*, 35–53.

Fletcher, P. C., McKenna, P. J., Frith, C. D., Grasby, P. M., Friston, K. J., & Dolan, R. J. (1998). Brain activations in schizophrenia during a graded memory task studied with functional neuroimaging. *Archives of General Psychiatry*, *55*, 1001–1008.

Floresco, S. B., Seamans, J. K., & Phillips, A. G. (1997). Selective roles for hippocampal, prefrontal cortical, and ventral striatal circuits in radial-arm maze tasks with or without a delay. *Journal of Neuroscience*, *17*, 1880–1890.

Forbes, N. F., Carrick, L. A., McIntosh, A. M., & Lawrie, S. M. (2009). Working memory in schizophrenia: a meta-analysis. *Psychological Medicine*, *39*, 889–905.

Ford, J. M., Pfefferbaum, A., & Roth, W. (1992). P3 and Schizophreniaa. *Annals of the New York Academy of Sciences*, *658*, 146–162.

Gandal, M. J., Sisti, J., Klook, K., Ortinski, P. I., Leitman, V., Liang, Y., et al. (2012). GABAB-mediated rescue of altered excitatory-inhibitory balance, gamma synchrony and behavioral deficits following constitutive NMDAR-hypofunction. *Translational Psychiatry*, *2*, e142.

Gao, X. M., Elmer, G. I., Adams-Huet, B., & Tamminga, C. A. (2009). Social memory in mice: disruption with an NMDA antagonist and attenuation with antipsychotic drugs. *Pharmacology Biochemistry and Behavior*, *92*, 236–242.

Gilmour, G., Arguello, A., Bari, A., Brown, V. J., Carter, C., Floresco, S. B., et al. (2013). Measuring the construct of executive control in schizophrenia: defining and validating translational animal paradigms for discovery research. *Neuroscience & Biobehavioral Reviews*, *37*, 2125–2140.

Gold, J. M., & Thaker, G. K. (2002). Current progress in schizophrenia research: cognitive phenotypes of schizophrenia: attention. *Journal of Nervous and Mental Disease*, *190*, 638–639.

Goldberg, T. E., & Weinberger, D. R. (1988). Probing prefrontal function in schizophrenia with neuropsychological paradigms. *Schizophrenia Bulletin, 14*, 179–183.

Goldberg, T. E., Weinberger, D. R., Berman, K. F., Pliskin, N. H., & Podd, M. H. (1987). Further evidence for dementia of the prefrontal type in schizophrenia? A controlled study of teaching the Wisconsin Card Sorting Test. *Archives of General Psychiatry, 44*, 1008–1014.

Goldman-Rakic, P. S. (1994). Working memory dysfunction in schizophrenia. *Journal of Neuropsychiatry & Clinical Neurosciences, 6*, 348–357.

Goldman-Rakic, P. S., Muly, E. C., 3rd, & Williams, G. V. (2000). D(1) receptors in prefrontal cells and circuits. *Brain Research Brain Research Reviews, 31*, 295–301.

Green, M. F. (1996). What are the functional consequences of neurocognitive deficits in schizophrenia? *American Journal of Psychiatry, 153*, 321–330.

Green, M. F., & Horan, W. P. (2010). Social Cognition in Schizophrenia. *Current Directions in Psychological Science, 19*, 243–248.

Green, M. F., & Leitman, D. I. (2008). Social cognition in schizophrenia. *Schizophrenia Bulletin, 34*, 670–672.

Green, M. F., & Nuechterlein, K. H. (1999). Should schizophrenia be treated as a neurocognitive disorder? *Schizophrenia Bulletin, 25*, 309–319.

Green, M. F., Olivier, B., Crawley, J. N., Penn, D. L., & Silverstein, S. (2005). Social cognition in schizophrenia: recommendations from the measurement and treatment research to improve cognition in schizophrenia new approaches conference. *Schizophrenia Bulletin, 31*, 882–887.

Green, M. F., Penn, D. L., Bentall, R., Carpenter, W. T., Gaebel, W., Gur, R. C., et al. (2008). Social cognition in schizophrenia: an NIMH workshop on definitions, assessment, and research opportunities. *Schizophrenia Bulletin, 34*, 1211–1220.

Greig, T. C., Bryson, G. J., & Bell, M. D. (2004). Theory of mind performance in schizophrenia: diagnostic, symptom, and neuropsychological correlates. *Journal of Nervous and Mental Disease, 192*, 12–18.

Grillon, C., Courchesne, E., Ameli, R., Geyer, M. A., & Braff, D. L. (1990). Increased distractibility in schizophrenic patients: electrophysiologic and behavioral evidence. *Archives of General Psychiatry, 47*, 171–179.

Guenther, W., Davous, P., Godet, J. L., Guillibert, E., Breitling, D., & Rondot, P. (1988). Bilateral brain dysfunction during motor activation in type II schizophrenia measured by EEG mapping. *Biological Psychiatry, 23*, 295–311.

Hahn, B., Robinson, B. M., Harvey, A. N., Kaiser, S. T., Leonard, C. J., Luck, S. J., et al. (2012). Visuospatial attention in schizophrenia: deficits in broad monitoring. *Journal of Abnormal Psychology, 121*, 119–128.

Hahn, B., Ross, T. J., & Stein, E. A. (2006). Neuroanatomical dissociation between bottom-up and top-down processes of visuospatial selective attention. *Neuroimage, 32*, 842–853.

Harrison, P. J., & Weinberger, D. R. (2005). Schizophrenia genes, gene expression, and neuropathology: on the matter of their convergence. *Molecular Psychiatry, 10*, 40–68; Image 45.

Henik, A., & Salo, R. (2004). Schizophrenia and the stroop effect. *Behavioral and Cognitive Neuroscience Reviews, 3*, 42–59.

Hida, H., Mouri, A., & Noda, Y. (2013). Behavioral phenotypes in schizophrenic animal models with multiple combinations of genetic and environmental factors. *Journal of Pharmacological Sciences, 121*, 185–191.

Huang, H., Michetti, C., Busnelli, M., Manago, F., Sannino, S., Scheggia, D., et al. (2014). Chronic and acute intranasal oxytocin produce divergent social effects in mice. *Neuropsychopharmacology, 39*, 1102–1114.

Ibi, D., Nagai, T., Koike, H., Kitahara, Y., Mizoguchi, H., Niwa, M., et al. (2010). Combined effect of neonatal immune activation and mutant DISC1 on phenotypic changes in adulthood. *Behavioural Brain Research, 206*, 32–37.

Insel, T. R. (2010). Rethinking schizophrenia. *Nature, 468*, 187–193.

Javitt, D. C., & Coyle, J. T. (2004). Decoding schizophrenia. *Scientific American, 290*, 48–55.

Joober, R., Gauthier, J., Lal, S., Bloom, D., Lalonde, P., Rouleau, G., et al. (2002). Catechol-O-methyltransferase Val-108/158-Met gene variants associated with performance on the Wisconsin Card Sorting Test. *Archives of General Psychiatry, 59*, 662–663.

Kaidanovich-Beilin, O., Lipina, T., Vukobradovic, I., Roder, J., & Woodgett, J. R. (2011). Assessment of social interaction behaviors. *Journal of Visualized Experiments, 25*.

Karlsgodt, K. H., Robleto, K., Trantham-Davidson, H., Jairl, C., Cannon, T. D., Lavin, A., et al. (2011). Reduced dysbindin expression mediates N-methyl-D-aspartate receptor hypofunction and impaired working memory performance. *Biological Psychiatry, 69*, 28–34.

Keefe, R. S., Bilder, R. M., Davis, S. M., Harvey, P. D., Palmer, B. W., Gold, J. M., CATIE Investigators, & Neurocognitive Working Group., et al. (2007). Neurocognitive effects of antipsychotic medications in patients with chronic schizophrenia in the CATIE Trial. *Archives of General Psychiatry, 64*, 633–647.

Keefe, R. S., Roitman, S. E., Harvey, P. D., Blum, C. S., DuPre, R. L., Prieto, D. M., et al. (1995). A pen-and-paper human analogue of a monkey prefrontal cortex activation task: spatial working memory in patients with schizophrenia. *Schizophrenia Research, 17*, 25–33.

Kellendonk, C., Simpson, E. H., Polan, H. J., Malleret, G., Vronskaya, S., Winiger, V., et al. (2006). Transient and selective overexpression of dopamine D2 receptors in the striatum causes persistent abnormalities in prefrontal cortex functioning. *Neuron, 49*, 603–615.

Kerns, J. G., Nuechterlein, K. H., Braver, T. S., & Barch, D. M. (2008). Executive functioning component mechanisms and schizophrenia. *Biological Psychiatry, 64*, 26–33.

Kerr, S. L., & Neale, J. M. (1993). Emotion perception in schizophrenia: specific deficit or further evidence of generalized poor performance? *Journal of Abnormal Psychology, 102*, 312–318.

Kinderman, P., & Bentall, R. P. (1996). A new measure of causal locus: the internal, personal and situational attributions questionnaire. *Personality and Individual Differences, 20*, 261–264.

Koros, E., Rosenbrock, H., Birk, G., Weiss, C., & Sams-Dodd, F. (2007). The selective mGlu5 receptor antagonist MTEP, similar to NMDA receptor antagonists, induces social isolation in rats. *Neuropsychopharmacology, 32*, 562–576.

Kucharska-Pietura, K., & Mortimer, A. (2013). Can antipsychotics improve social cognition in patients with schizophrenia? *CNS Drugs, 27*, 335–343.

Le Pen, G., Grottick, A. J., Higgins, G. A., & Moreau, J. L. (2003). Phencyclidine exacerbates attentional deficits in a neurodevelopmental rat model of schizophrenia. *Neuropsychopharmacology, 28*, 1799–1809.

Lee, J., & Park, S. (2005). Working memory impairments in schizophrenia: a meta-analysis. *Journal of Abnormal Psychology, 114*, 599–611.

Lewis, D. A., & Gonzalez-Burgos, G. (2006). Pathophysiologically based treatment interventions in schizophrenia. *Nature Medicine, 12*, 1016–1022.

Lewis, D. A., & Levitt, P. (2002). Schizophrenia as a disorder of neurodevelopment. *Annual Review of Neuroscience, 25*, 409–432.

Li, W., Zhou, Y., Jentsch, J. D., Brown, R. A., Tian, X., Ehninger, D., et al. (2007). Specific developmental disruption of disrupted-in-schizophrenia-1 function results in schizophrenia-related phenotypes in mice. *Proceedings of the National Academy of Sciences of the United States of America, 104*, 18280–18285.

Lipska, B. K. (2004). Using animal models to test a neurodevelopmental hypothesis of schizophrenia. *Journal of Psychiatry & Neuroscience, 29*, 282–286.

Luck, S. J., & Gold, J. M. (2008). The construct of attention in schizophrenia. *Biological Psychiatry, 64*, 34–39.

Machado, C. J., & Nelson, E. E. (2011). Eye-tracking with nonhuman primates is now more accessible than ever before. *American Journal of Primatology, 73*, 562–569.

I. FROM CLINICAL DIMENSIONS TO ANIMAL MODELS

MacLeod, C. M. (1991). Half a century of research on the Stroop effect: an integrative review. *Psychological Bulletin, 109*, 163–203.

Malhotra, A. K., Kestler, L. J., Mazzanti, C., Bates, J. A., Goldberg, T., & Goldman, D. (2002). A functional polymorphism in the COMT gene and performance on a test of prefrontal cognition. *American Journal of Psychiatry, 159*, 652–654.

Mattay, V. S., Goldberg, T. E., Fera, F., Hariri, A. R., Tessitore, A., Egan, M. F., et al. (2003). Catechol O-methyltransferase val158-met genotype and individual variation in the brain response to amphetamine. *Proceedings of the National Academy of Sciences of the United States of America, 100*, 6186–6191.

Mayer, J. D., Salovey, P., & Caruso, D. R. (2002). *Mayer-Salovey-Caruso Emotional Intelligence Test (MSCEIT) user's manual*. Toronto, Canada: MHS Publishers.

McAlonan, K., & Brown, V. J. (2003). Orbital prefrontal cortex mediates reversal learning and not attentional set shifting in the rat. *Behavioural Brain Research, 146*, 97–103.

McDonald, S., Flanagan, S., & Rollins, J. (2002). *The Awareness of Social Inference Test*. Suffolk, UK: Thames Valley Test Company, Ltd.

McGaughy, J., & Sarter, M. (1995). Behavioral vigilance in rats: task validation and effects of age, amphetamine, and benzodiazepine receptor ligands. *Psychopharmacology (Berl), 117*, 340–357.

Meffre, J., Chaumont-Dubel, S., Mannoury la Cour, C., Loiseau, F., Watson, D. J., Dekeyne, A., et al. (2012). 5-HT(6) receptor recruitment of mTOR as a mechanism for perturbed cognition in schizophrenia. *EMBO Molecular Medicine, 4*, 1043–1056.

Melcher, T., Wolter, S., Falck, S., Wild, E., Wild, F., Gruber, E., et al. (2013). Common and disease-specific dysfunctions of brain systems underlying attentional and executive control in schizophrenia and bipolar disorder. *European Archives of Psychiatry and Clinical Neuroscience, 24*, 24.

Millan, M. J., Agid, Y., Brune, M., Bullmore, E. T., Carter, C. S., Clayton, N. S., et al. (2012). Cognitive dysfunction in psychiatric disorders: characteristics, causes and the quest for improved therapy. *Nature Reviews Drug Discovery, 11*, 141–168.

Millan, M. J., & Bales, K. L. (2013). Towards improved animal models for evaluating social cognition and its disruption in schizophrenia: the CNTRICS initiative. *Neuroscience & Biobehavioral Reviews, 37*, 2166–2180.

Millan, M. J., & Brocco, M. (2008). Cognitive impairment in schizophrenia: a review of developmental and genetic models, and procognitive profile of the optimised D(3) > D(2) antagonist, S33138. *Therapie, 63*, 187–229.

Millan, M. J., Di Cara, B., Dekeyne, A., Panayi, F., De Groote, L., Sicard, D., et al. (2007). Selective blockade of dopamine D(3) versus D(2) receptors enhances frontocortical cholinergic transmission and social memory in rats: a parallel neurochemical and behavioural analysis. *Journal of Neurochemistry, 100*, 1047–1061.

Millan, M. J., Fone, K. C., Steckler, T., & Horan, W. P. (2014). Negative symptoms of schizophrenia: clinical characteristics, pathophysiological substrates, experimental models and prospects for improved treatment. *European Neuropsychopharmacology, 24*, 645–692.

Minzenberg, M. J., & Carter, C. S. (2012). Developing treatments for impaired cognition in schizophrenia. *Trends in Cognitive Sciences, 16*, 35–42.

Miyamoto, S., Duncan, G. E., Marx, C. E., & Lieberman, J. A. (2005). Treatments for schizophrenia: a critical review of pharmacology and mechanisms of action of antipsychotic drugs. *Molecular Psychiatry, 10*, 79–104.

Mohler, E. G., Meck, W. H., & Williams, C. L. (2001). Sustained attention in adult mice is modulated by prenatal choline availability. *International Journal of Comparative Psychology, 14*.

Moy, S. S., Nadler, J. J., Young, N. B., Perez, A., Holloway, L. P., Barbaro, R. P., et al. (2007). Mouse behavioral tasks relevant to autism: phenotypes of 10 inbred strains. *Behavioural Brain Research, 176*, 4–20.

Mueser, K. T., & McGurk, S. R. (2004). Schizophrenia. *Lancet, 363*, 2063–2072.

Nagahama, Y., Okada, T., Katsumi, Y., Hayashi, T., Yamauchi, H., Oyanagi, C., et al. (2001). Dissociable mechanisms of attentional control within the human prefrontal cortex. *Cerebral Cortex, 11*, 85–92.

Nagahama, Y., Okina, T., Suzuki, N., Nabatame, H., & Matsuda, M. (2005). The cerebral correlates of different types of perseveration in the Wisconsin Card Sorting Test. *Journal of Neurology, Neurosurgery, and Psychiatry, 76*, 169–175.

Nicodemus, K. K., Law, A. J., Radulescu, E., Luna, A., Kolachana, B., Vakkalanka, R., et al. (2010). Biological validation of increased schizophrenia risk with NRG1, ERBB4, and AKT1 epistasis via functional neuroimaging in healthy controls. *Archives of General Psychiatry, 67*, 991–1001.

Nowicki, S., Jr., & Duke, M. (1994). Individual differences in the nonverbal communication of affect: the diagnostic analysis of nonverbal accuracy scale. *Journal of Nonverbal Behavior, 18*, 9–35.

Nuechterlein, K. H., & Dawson, M. E. (1984). Information processing and attentional functioning in the developmental course of schizophrenic disorders. *Schizophrenia Bulletin, 10*, 160–203.

Nuechterlein, K. H., Luck, S. J., Lustig, C., & Sarter, M. (2009). CNTRICS final task selection: control of attention. *Schizophrenia Bulletin, 35*, 182–196.

Nutt, D., & Goodwin, G. (2011). ECNP Summit on the future of CNS drug research in Europe 2011: report prepared for ECNP by David Nutt and Guy Goodwin. *European Neuropsychopharmacology, 21*, 495–499.

O'Tuathaigh, C. M., Babovic, D., O'Sullivan, G. J., Clifford, J. J., Tighe, O., Croke, D. T., et al. (2007). Phenotypic characterization of spatial cognition and social behavior in mice with 'knockout' of the schizophrenia risk gene neuregulin 1. *Neuroscience, 147*, 18–27.

Oltmanns, T. F. (1978). Selective attention in schizophrenic and manic psychoses: the effect of distraction on information processing. *Journal of Abnormal Psychology, 87*, 212–225.

Oltmanns, T. F., & Neale, J. M. (1975). Schizophrenic performance when distractors are present: attentional deficit or differential task difficulty? *Journal of Abnormal Psychology, 84*, 205–209.

Owen, A. M., Roberts, A. C., Hodges, J. R., Summers, B. A., Polkey, C. E., & Robbins, T. W. (1993). Contrasting mechanisms of impaired attentional set-shifting in patients with frontal lobe damage or Parkinson's disease. *Brain, 116*(Pt 5), 1159–1175.

Owen, A. M., Roberts, A. C., Polkey, C. E., Sahakian, B. J., & Robbins, T. W. (1991). Extra-dimensional versus intra-dimensional set shifting performance following frontal lobe excisions, temporal lobe excisions or amygdalo-hippocampectomy in man. *Neuropsychologia, 29*, 993–1006.

Owens, D. G., & Johnstone, E. C. (2006). Precursors and prodromata of schizophrenia: findings from the Edinburgh High Risk Study and their literature context. *Psychological Medicine, 36*, 1501–1514.

Paine, T. A., & Carlezon, W. A., Jr. (2009). Effects of antipsychotic drugs on MK-801-induced attentional and motivational deficits in rats. *Neuropharmacology, 56*, 788–797.

Pantelis, C., Barber, F. Z., Barnes, T. R., Nelson, H. E., Owen, A. M., & Robbins, T. W. (1999). Comparison of set-shifting ability in patients with chronic schizophrenia and frontal lobe damage. *Schizophrenia Research, 37*, 251–270.

Pantelis, C., Wood, S. J., Proffitt, T. M., Testa, R., Mahony, K., Brewer, W. J., et al. (2009). Attentional set-shifting ability in first-episode and established schizophrenia: relationship to working memory. *Schizophrenia Research, 112*, 104–113.

Papaleo, F., Burdick, M. C., Callicott, J. H., & Weinberger, D. R. (2014). Epistatic interaction between COMT and DTNBP1 modulates prefrontal function in mice and in humans. *Molecular Psychiatry, 19*, 311–316.

Papaleo, F., Crawley, J. N., Song, J., Lipska, B. K., Pickel, J., Weinberger, D. R., et al. (2008). Genetic dissection of the role of catechol-O-methyltransferase in cognition and stress reactivity in mice. *Journal of Neuroscience, 28*, 8709–8723.

Papaleo, F., Erickson, L., Liu, G., Chen, J., & Weinberger, D. R. (2012). Effects of sex and COMT genotype on environmentally modulated cognitive control in mice. *Proceedings of the National Academy of Sciences of the United States of America, 109,* 20160–20165.

Papaleo, F., Lipska, B. K., & Weinberger, D. R. (2012). Mouse models of genetic effects on cognition: relevance to schizophrenia. *Neuropharmacology, 62,* 1204–1220.

Papaleo, F., & Weinberger, D. R. (2011). Dysbindin and Schizophrenia: it's dopamine and glutamate all over again. *Biological Psychiatry, 69,* 2–4.

Papaleo, F., Yang, F., Garcia, S., Chen, J., Lu, B., Crawley, J. N., et al. (2012). Dysbindin-1 modulates prefrontal cortical activity and schizophrenia-like behaviors via dopamine/D2 pathways. *Molecular Psychiatry, 17,* 85–98.

Peleg-Raibstein, D., Feldon, J., & Meyer, U. (2012). Behavioral animal models of antipsychotic drug actions. *Handbook of Experimental Pharmacology, 212,* 361–406.

Penn, D. L., Ritchie, M., Francis, J., Combs, D., & Martin, J. (2002). Social perception in schizophrenia: the role of context. *Psychiatry Research, 109,* 149–159.

Perlstein, W. M., Carter, C. S., Barch, D. M., & Baird, J. W. (1998). The Stroop task and attention deficits in schizophrenia: a critical evaluation of card and single-trial Stroop methodologies. *Neuropsychology, 12,* 414–425.

Perry, W., & Braff, D. L. (1998). A multimethod approach to assessing perseverations in schizophrenia patients. *Schizophrenia Research, 33,* 69–77.

Pijnenborg, G. H., Withaar, F. K., Bosch, R. J., & Brouwer, W. H. (2007). Impaired perception of negative emotional prosody in schizophrenia. *Clinical Neuropsychology, 21,* 762–775.

Pollard, V. B., Hellewell, J. S. E., & William Deakin, J. F. (1995). Performance of schizophrenic subjects on tests of recognition memory, perception and face processing. *Schizophrenia Research, 15,* 122.

Pratt, J., Winchester, C., Dawson, N., & Morris, B. (2012). Advancing schizophrenia drug discovery: optimizing rodent models to bridge the translational gap. *Nature Reviews Drug Discovery, 11,* 560–579.

Rahman, S., Sahakian, B. J., Hodges, J. R., Rogers, R. D., & Robbins, T. W. (1999). Specific cognitive deficits in mild frontal variant frontotemporal dementia. *Brain, 122*(Pt 8), 1469–1493.

Rasetti, R., & Weinberger, D. R. (2011). Intermediate phenotypes in psychiatric disorders. *Current Opinion in Genetics and Development, 21,* 340–348.

Robbins, T. W., Muir, J. L., Killcross, A. S., & Pretsell, D. O. (1993). Methods for assessing attention and stimulus control in the rat. *Behavioural Neuroscience: A Practical Approach, 1,* 13–47.

Robbins, T. W. (2002). The 5-choice serial reaction time task: behavioural pharmacology and functional neurochemistry. *Psychopharmacology (Berl), 163,* 362–380.

Robbins, T. W. (2007). Shifting and stopping: fronto-striatal substrates, neurochemical modulation and clinical implications. *Philosophical Transactions of the Royal Society of London Series B: Biological Sciences, 362,* 917–932.

Robbins, T. W., & Roberts, A. C. (2007). Differential regulation of fronto-executive function by the monoamines and acetylcholine. *Cerebral Cortex, 17*(Suppl. 1), i151–160.

Roberts, A. C., Robbins, T. W., & Everitt, B. J. (1988). The effects of intradimensional and extradimensional shifts on visual discrimination learning in humans and non-human primates. *Quarterly Journal of Experimental Psychology B, 40,* 321–341.

Roncone, R., Falloon, I. R., Mazza, M., De Risio, A., Pollice, R., Necozione, S., et al. (2002). Is theory of mind in schizophrenia more strongly associated with clinical and social functioning than with neurocognitive deficits? *Psychopathology, 35,* 280–288.

Rosenthal, R., Hall, J. A., DiMatteo, M. R., Rogers, P. L., & Archer, D. (1979). *Sensitivity to nonverbal communication: The PONS test.* Johns Hopkins University Press Baltimore.

Ross, C. A., Margolis, R. L., Reading, S. A. J., Pletnikov, M., & Coyle, J. T. (2006). Neurobiology of schizophrenia. *Neuron, 52,* 139–153.

Roullet, F. I., & Crawley, J. N. (2011). Mouse models of autism: testing hypotheses about molecular mechanisms. *Current Topics in Behavioral Neuroscience, 7,* 187–212.

Sams-Dodd, F. (1999). Phencyclidine in the social interaction test: an animal model of schizophrenia with face and predictive validity. *Reviews in the Neuroscience, 10,* 59–90.

Sandson, J., & Albert, M. L. (1984). Varieties of perseveration. *Neuropsychologia, 22,* 715–732.

Sannino, S., Gozzi, A., Cerasa, A., Piras, F., Scheggia, D., Manago, F., et al. (2014). COMT genetic reduction produces sexually divergent effects on cortical anatomy and working memory in mice and humans. *Cerebral Cortex.*

Scheggia, D., Bebensee, A., Weinberger, D. R., & Papaleo, F. (2014). The ultimate intra-/extra-dimensional attentional set-shifting task for mice. *Biological Psychiatry, 75,* 660–670.

Seamans, J. K., Floresco, S. B., & Phillips, A. G. (1995). Functional differences between the prelimbic and anterior cingulate regions of the rat prefrontal cortex. *Behavioral Neuroscience, 109,* 1063–1073.

Seamans, J. K., & Phillips, A. G. (1994). Selective memory impairments produced by transient lidocaine-induced lesions of the nucleus accumbens in rats. *Behavioral Neuroscience, 108,* 456–468.

Sergi, M. J., Rassovsky, Y., Widmark, C., Reist, C., Erhart, S., Braff, D. L., et al. (2007). Social cognition in schizophrenia: relationships with neurocognition and negative symptoms. *Schizophrenia Research, 90,* 316–324.

Servan-Schreiber, D., Cohen, J. D., & Steingard, S. (1996). Schizophrenic deficits in the processing of context. A test of a theoretical model. *Archives of General Psychiatry, 53,* 1105–1112.

Silverman, J. L., Yang, M., Lord, C., & Crawley, J. N. (2010). Behavioural phenotyping assays for mouse models of autism. *Nature Reviews Neuroscience, 11,* 490–502.

Smid, H. G., de Witte, M. R., Homminga, I., & van den Bosch, R. J. (2006). Sustained and transient attention in the continuous performance task. *Journal of Clinical and Experimental Neuropsychology, 28,* 859–883.

Smid, H. G., Martens, S., de Witte, M. R., & Bruggeman, R. (2013). Inflexible minds: impaired attention switching in recent-onset schizophrenia. *PLoS One, 8.*

Soliman, F., Glatt, C. E., Bath, K. G., Levita, L., Jones, R. M., Pattwell, S. S., et al. (2010). A genetic variant BDNF polymorphism alters extinction learning in both mouse and human. *Science, 327,* 863–866.

Stroop, J. R. (1935). Studies of interference in serial verbal reactions. *Journal of Experimental Psychology, 18,* 643–662.

Tauscher, J., Fischer, P., Neumeister, A., Rappelsberger, P., & Kasper, S. (1998). Low frontal electroencephalographic coherence in neuroleptic-free schizophrenic patients. *Biological Psychiatry, 44,* 438–447.

Thaker, G. K., & Carpenter, W. T., Jr. (2001). Advances in schizophrenia. *Nature Medicine, 7,* 667–671.

Toomey, R., Schuldberg, D., Corrigan, P., & Green, M. F. (2002). Nonverbal social perception and symptomatology in schizophrenia. *Schizophrenia Research, 53,* 83–91.

Turner, D. C., Clark, L., Pomarol-Clotet, E., McKenna, P., Robbins, T. W., & Sahakian, B. J. (2004). Modafinil improves cognition and attentional set shifting in patients with chronic schizophrenia. *Neuropsychopharmacology, 29,* 1363–1373.

Wechsler, D. (1987). *WMS-R: Wechsler Memory Scale-Revised: Manual.* San Antonio: Psychological Corporation.

Weickert, T. W., Goldberg, T. E., Gold, J. M., Bigelow, L. B., Egan, M. F., & Weinberger, D. R. (2000). Cognitive impairments in patients with schizophrenia displaying preserved and compromised intellect. *Archives of General Psychiatry, 57,* 907–913.

Weinberger, D. R. (1987). Implications of normal brain development for the pathogenesis of schizophrenia. *Archives of General Psychiatry, 44,* 660–669.

I. FROM CLINICAL DIMENSIONS TO ANIMAL MODELS

Weinberger, D. R., Berman, K. F., & Zec, R. F. (1986). Physiologic dysfunction of dorsolateral prefrontal cortex in schizophrenia. I. Regional cerebral blood flow evidence. *Archives of General Psychiatry*, *43*, 114–124.

Weinberger, D. R., Egan, M. F., Bertolino, A., Callicott, J. H., Mattay, V. S., Lipska, B. K., et al. (2001). Prefrontal neurons and the genetics of schizophrenia. *Biological Psychiatry*, *50*, 825–844.

Winslow, J. T., & Camacho, F. (1995). Cholinergic modulation of a decrement in social investigation following repeated contacts between mice. *Psychopharmacology (Berl)*, *121*, 164–172.

Young, J. W., Crawford, N., Kelly, J. S., Kerr, L. E., Marston, H. M., Spratt, C., et al. (2007). Impaired attention is central to the cognitive deficits observed in alpha 7 deficient mice. *European Neuropsychopharmacology*, *17*, 145–155.

Young, J. W., Geyer, M. A., Rissling, A. J., Sharp, R. F., Eyler, L. T., Asgaard, G. L., et al. (2013). Reverse translation of the rodent 5C-CPT reveals that the impaired attention of people with schizophrenia is similar to scopolamine-induced deficits in mice. *Translational Psychiatry*, *3*, e324.

Young, J. W., Kerr, L. E., Kelly, J. S., Marston, H. M., Spratt, C., Finlayson, K., et al. (2007). The odour span task: a novel paradigm for assessing working memory in mice. *Neuropharmacology*, *52*, 634–645.

Young, K. A., Gobrogge, K. L., Liu, Y., & Wang, Z. (2011). The neurobiology of pair bonding: insights from a socially monogamous rodent. *Frontiers in Neuroendocrinology*, *32*, 53–69.

Zvyagintsev, M., Parisi, C., Chechko, N., Nikolaev, A. R., & Mathiak, K. (2013). Attention and multisensory integration of emotions in schizophrenia. *Frontiers in Human Neuroscience*, *7*.

7

Modeling Affective Symptoms of Schizophrenia

Luka Culig, Catherine Belzung

INSERM 930 and Université François Rabelais de Tours, UFR Sciences et Techniques, Tours, France

INTRODUCTION

The description of schizophrenia as a disorder including positive (delusions, hallucinations) as well as affective/negative symptoms (anhedonia, avolition, emotional flattening) became quite classical and is generally agreed upon among psychiatrists. Negative symptoms have similarities with features of major depression: for example, anhedonia is considered a core symptom of this disease. Even if the treatments currently available target the positive rather than the affective symptoms, negative symptoms have historically been the focus of much attention. Bleuler, who coined the term "schizophrenia," considered emotional blunting and decrease in emotional expression to be a part of its core symptoms. Interestingly, these symptoms are most prevalent before pharmacological treatment has been started: they develop in more than 50% of these patients (Johnson, 1981), in around 25% of patients during the 6 months after discharge, and in 4–25% in patients in the chronic phase of the illness (Leff, 1990). Although this increases the need for the medication to be effective against both the positive and negative symptoms, most of the available drugs have very limited efficacy against negative symptoms, even with the advent of new-generation atypical antipsychotics (Gardner, Baldessarini, & Waraich, 2005). In addition, managing negative symptoms of schizophrenia is especially important not only because they worsen psychosocial functioning, but also because they frequently occur before suicide attempts or suicide itself. Considering the severity of impact of negative symptoms on patients and the limitations of currently available medication, improving the pharmacological therapies is an urgently required step in managing the illness. One of the ways through which they might be improved involves research on animal models.

Social withdrawal, affective flattening, lack of motivation (avolition), and the inability to experience pleasure (anhedonia) comprise the affective symptoms found in schizophrenia which can be (and have been) modeled in animals to a certain extent. Because these affective symptoms are so similar in nature to the core symptoms of depression, one would think that for testing them in schizophrenia models, behavioral readouts already used in animal models of major depression (early maternal separation, chronic corticosterone administration, social defeat, and unpredictable chronic mild stress) could be relevant (Table 1) (Belzung, 2014).

However, it is to be highlighted here that the affective symptoms—even if transnosographic—observed in schizophrenic patients might be quite different from depressive symptoms: they are not triggered by the same causes and do not respond to treatment with the same drugs. It is to be considered that animal models of depression are validated by similarity with the etiology of depression and sensitivity to antidepressants and thus might not be well suited for the evaluation of negative symptoms in schizophrenia. In this chapter, our main focus will be on two of those symptoms—anhedonia and social interaction—and the assays designed to assess behavior related to them. In humans, it is considered that the loss of social desire is a symptom which overlaps both negative and affective symptom domains (Morrissette & Stahl, 2011). In animal models, social defects are considered as a separate symptom, but avolition or social anhedonia might contribute to them, which connects the symptoms and places them under the same umbrella (Barnes, Der-Avakian, & Markou, 2014). Further, in animal models of depression, several assays have been designed that assess anhedonia, and these tests have already been used in the context of animal models of schizophrenia. Additionally, modeling avolition will

TABLE 1   Different Readouts Enabling Depression-Like Behavior in Rodents to Be Assessed

Depression-Related Phenotype	Test	References
Resignation	Forced swimming	Porsolt et al. (1978)
	Tail suspension	Steru et al. (1985)
Avolition	Grooming behavior in the splash test	Santarelli et al. (2003)
	Nest building in the nest test	Nollet, Le Guisquet, and Belzung (2013)
	Decrease in coat state score	Nollet et al. (2013)
Anhedonia	Sucrose preference	Willner, Towell, Sampson, Sophokleous, and Muscat (1987)
	Cookie test	Surget et al. (2011)
	Intracranial self-stimulation	Moreau et al. (1992)
Anxiety	Novelty-induced suppression of feeding behavior	Dulawa and Hen (2005)
Irritability	Resident-intruder test	Mineur, Prasol, Belzung, and Crusio (2003)

Modified from Belzung (2014).

also be briefly discussed because it has recently come under a spotlight as one of the core symptoms of schizophrenia dissociated from hedonic features.

ANHEDONIA

Anhedonia (Greek: an-, "without" and hēdonē, "pleasure"), as its name suggest, is a term describing the inability or diminished capacity to feel pleasure in all usual and pleasant activities as well as withdrawal from them (Kollias et al., 2008). It was coined by Ribot in 1896, when he used it to describe the following condition:

> The state of anhedonia, if I may coin a new word to pair off with analgesia," he writes, "has been very little studied, but it exists. A young girl was smitten with a liver disease which for some time altered her constitution. She felt no longer any affection for her father and mother. She would have played with her doll, but it was impossible to find the least pleasure in the act. The same things which formerly convulsed her with laughter entirely failed to interest her now. Esquirol observed the case of a very intelligent magistrate who was also a prey to hepatic disease. Every emotion appeared dead within him. He manifested neither perversion nor violence, but complete absence of emotional reaction. If he went to the theatre, which he did out of habit, he could find no pleasure there. The thought of his house, of his home, of his wife, and of his absent children moved him as little, he said, as a theorem of Euclid. *James (1985)*

Anhedonia has since been described as a schizophrenic symptom by many authors, suggesting that it could be a central defect in the illness. However, as already mentioned, anhedonia has also been associated with major depression. In humans, several scales have been used to evaluate depressive symptomatology in schizophrenia, but most of them were not originally developed for this intention. The Calgary Depression Scale for Schizophrenia has been specifically designed for individuals with schizophrenia and it has excellent psychometric properties, internal consistency, interrater reliability, sensitivity, specificity, and discriminant and convergent validity (Addington, Shah, Liu, & Addington, 2014). The scores obtained by using this scale correlate with both physical anhedonia and social anhedonia ratings, which are usually assessed with the scales designed to assess specific domains of anhedonia: the Physical Anhedonia Scale and the Social Anhedonia Scale (Kollias et al., 2008). However, for obvious reasons, it is not possible to apply these tests to animals, so different behavioral tests have been developed to assess anhedonia in rodents.

One of the tests for evaluating anhedonia in rodents is the sucrose preference test, which has been originally designed to assess loss of motivation for pleasurable activity in animal models of depression. It emerged from the observation that the animals exposed to chronic stress (which triggers depressive-like states) failed to increase their fluid consumption of and preference for sweet solutions (saccharin or sucrose added to drinking water), linking this deficit to hedonic disturbances of depression (Katz, 1982). Originally, the protocol consisted of exposing rats to a 21-day-long stress protocol, which caused a decrease of sucrose intake. It has been postulated that this decreased sensitivity to reward might reflect the inability to experience pleasure, and is now considered as a test for the consummatory component of anhedonia (Der-Avakian & Markou, 2012). Since then, the protocol has been adjusted to obtain a closer analogy to the human situation by using milder stressors and extending the duration of exposure to stress (Willner et al., 1987). This regime shows the gradual development of anhedonia through the course of several weeks of stress exposure.

The general procedure for carrying out the test consists of presenting the rodents (each in separate cage) with two tubes, one of which contains plain drinking water, whereas the other one usually contains a 1–4% (depending on the protocol) sucrose solution. Sometimes, a concentration as high as 10% can be used (Clapcote et al, 2007). Before the start of the test itself, animals are habituated to the presence of these bottles. Usually, both bottles contain just drinking water in the habituation phase, which lasts for 1–3 days. After habituation, animals are exposed to a bottle containing sucrose solution and a bottle containing drinking water and the intake from both of them is measured on a daily basis. This phase usually lasts for 4 days. During testing, the position of the bottles is switched daily to reduce any confound produced by a side bias. Rodents typically develop a strong preference for the solution containing sucrose and consume more liquid from that bottle. Sucrose preference is calculated as a percentage of consumed sucrose solution of the total amount of liquid drunk. A decrease of sucrose preference taken as the criterion for anhedonia depends on the experimental procedure as well as mouse strain and other factors (Pothion, Bizot, Trovero, & Belzung, 2004). However, recent research questions the validity of this readout and a review of the literature show that the effects of chronic unpredictable mild stress, measured as a decrease in consumption of or preference for sweet solutions, are less reliably observed in several laboratories (Nielsen, Arnt, & Sánchez, 2000; Willner, 1997).

A more recent behavioral paradigm has been developed for testing anhedonia in animals. It is based on the motivation for consuming a palatable stimulus—a chocolate cookie; hence, it was named the cookie test (Surget et al., 2011). It is based on the conflict between the drive for the stimulus and the neophobic behavior of the animal.

The cookie test is carried out in a device containing three aligned chambers of the same size; only the colors of the walls and the floor are different between the chambers. The first chamber is white, the second gray, and the third one black. Animals are initially familiarized with a chocolate cookie 4.5 weeks before the testing; 1 h before the testing all the regular food is removed from the cage lid. Then, a small amount of the cookie is placed at the center of the black chamber and the animal is placed in the white chamber. Each session lasts for 5 min and the cookie consumption is recorded (Nollet et al., 2013). A reduction of the cookie consumption may be interpreted as anhedonia, a habituation deficit, or a combination of both effects. The importance of the "hedonic" feature of the stimulus has been shown in a control experiment where the cookie was replaced with a regular food pellet, resulting in almost zero consumption of it. However, although validated, the cookie test does not directly evaluate the sensitivity to reward in animals, which can be accomplished by using the intracranial self-stimulation (ICSS) paradigm that has been developed by Olds and Milner in 1954.

The ICSS paradigm enables animals with implanted electrodes in certain reward areas of their brain to self-administer weak electrical pulses. Such (self-)stimulation can have strong reinforcing properties and thus the self-stimulation threshold can be used as an index of the hedonic/anhedonic state of the animal (Nielsen et al., 2000). The areas that are commonly targeted for stimulation in this paradigm correspond to either the medial forebrain bundle, which is thought to play an important role in the integration of reward and pleasure, or the lateral hypothalamus (Barnes et al., 2014). ICSS is well known to be a useful paradigm for use in the study of rewards and anhedonia because it reflects the direct activation of brain reward systems. Typically, animals self administer the current by pressing the lever and two measures are used to study anhedonia: the lever-pressing rate and stimulation threshold (Ellenbroek & Cools, 2000). It shares a common theoretical basis with the sucrose preference paradigm by interpreting the attenuated self-stimulation behavior (reduction in lever pressing or increased stimulation threshold) as a measure of anhedonia. However, one of the greatest limitations of this methodology is that the performance assessed may be contaminated by other processes, such as motor function, which affects the ability of the animal to perform the action and thus hinders the ability to provide a measure of reward function independent of the motor ability (Markou & Koob, 1992). When used to assess anhedonia in animal models of depression, it was shown that ICSS has variable sensitivity to antidepressants and a high intrastrain variability in rate and frequency responses to ICSS (McArthur & Borsini, 2006).

SOCIAL INTERACTION

Unlike other affective symptoms, such as flattened affect or apathy, measuring social interactions in animals is relatively straightforward, which is an important reason for the considerable use of social interaction tests (Neill et al., 2010). However, one of the caveats of using social interaction tests with genetic models of schizophrenia is the problematic interpretation of such results because the manipulation used could affect the olfactory system, which is a critical determinant of social interaction in rodents (O'Tuathaigh, Kirby, Moran, & Waddington, 2010). The interpretation of the tests is further complicated in more general terms because some protocols (e.g., resident-intruder) assess the range of behaviors more closely related to aggression, whereas some protocols (such as social choice) could be interpreted to assess either social anhedonia or anxious behavior. Some of the most common approaches of assessing social interactions, especially in regards to schizophrenia, are (1) social approach-avoidance, (2) social choice, and (3) social dominance-aggression.

The social approach-avoidance approach consists of placing two unfamiliar animals in a novel environment and measuring either the distance between them or the time that the animals spend in a defined (and species-specific) element of active social interaction. The assessment is usually conducted with the help of recording equipment and object tracking software (Sams-Dodd, 1995a) or it can be done manually or by using photocell beam breaks, which activate every time an animal crosses from one chamber to the other (Nadler et al., 2004). Using photocells and automated analysis eliminates the labor-intensive and tedious aspects of manual scoring and thus minimizes the observer fatigue and increases the consistency of results across experiments and laboratories. In addition, automating one aspect of the scoring (basic behaviors) enables the researchers to score more interesting and complex behaviors, such as investigative sniffing, biting, and pinning. This kind of methodology not only provides an objective methodology for scoring social interactions, but also increases the consistency of results across experiments and laboratories. One of the considerations to have in mind when interpreting the results of this dyadic paradigm in schizophrenia-related research is that the social encounter can be initiated by either mouse (which is not the case in some other paradigms). Also, because the test is carried out in a novel environment, the social behavior could be modulated by the response to novelty, which is in turn modulated by the treatment or the genotype of the animal. Overall, it is considered that this paradigm is well suited for assessing negative-like symptoms of schizophrenia (Ellenbroek & Cools, 2000).

Social choice is one of commonly used paradigms to test interest to engage in social interaction and is used in many animal models associated with impairments in social behavior including not just schizophrenia, but also autism and other psychiatric disorders linked with anxiety-related behaviors (Sankoorikal, Kaercher, Boon, Lee, & Brodkin, 2006). The test is performed in an apparatus consisting of three interconnected chambers with two wire enclosures that are occupied differently, depending on what is studied. The tested animal is placed in the apparatus and left to freely explore chambers and, if sociability is studied, one of the wire enclosures is left empty, whereas an unfamiliar conspecific is placed in the other enclosure. To study preference for social novelty, an unfamiliar conspecific is placed in one of the enclosures, whereas a familiar conspecific is placed in the second enclosure. As mentioned, one of the advantages of the social choice paradigm is that only the tested mouse can initiate social encounters. However, when exploring sociability, one caveat to keep in mind is that the behavior may be influenced by the test animal's appraisal of each conspecific in terms of social status or aggression. Also, when examining preference for social novelty, which assesses social recognition memory, it is important to control for phenotypic or treatment effects on olfaction because social recognition heavily relies on olfactory sensory control. The interpretation of the social choice approach is debatable because a lower interest in social interaction could be ambiguous and considered a result of lowered pleasure/reward response from social interactions (social anhedonia) or a result of anxiety-like behavior (or both in varying proportions).

When exploring aggressive behavior, a paradigm called social dominance-aggression is used. There are two approaches that are commonly used, both of them employ a dyadic interaction. The first one involves a neutral setting, so the behavior is assessed when both animals are placed in a clean and unfamiliar cage, similar to the social approach-avoidance paradigm. The second approach, called the resident–intruder test, consists of placing one animal (intruder), usually smaller and nonaggressive, into the home cage of the animal being tested (resident) and observing them for a defined time (until the first attack, or with a time limit if a full offensive behavioral repertoire is of interest) or until the researcher needs to intervene because of ethical considerations. This paradigm can be used for studying aggression, defensive behavior, violence, and social stress, and interestingly because a tool to assess the predisposition for stress-induced anhedonia, which is associated with submissive behavior in the resident-intruder test (Strekalova, Spanagel, Bartsch, Henn, & Gass, 2004). The resident–intruder test is used in animal models of depression because a significant part of clinically depressed patients report irritability as one of the symptoms. It has its value as an antidepressant screening test because it has been shown that some mouse strains exhibit increased aggressive behavior after unpredictable chronic mild stress that can be reversed by treatment with compounds with antidepressant effects (Mineur et al., 2003; Nollet et al., 2012). In conclusion, although some researchers suggest that submissive behavior in the resident–intruder test is an indicator of predisposition to stress-induced anhedonia, it can also be considered that this paradigm is more valuable for assessing negative-like symptoms and aggression.

AVOLITION

Avolition is a term describing lack of motivation and is considered to be the core symptom of schizophrenia since its earliest description by Kraepelin and Bleuler (Bleuler, 1951; Kraepelin, 1919). Patients can experience pleasure, but they have a reduced outward expression of emotions and a decreased capacity to anticipate whether the pursuit or achievement of a goal will be pleasurable. Currently, some researchers consider avolition (rather than anhedonia) to be a core symptom of the disorder (Pratt, Winchester, Dawson, & Morris, 2012). This is due to the findings that indicate a detachment between hedonic reaction to rewarding stimuli and motivated behavior in patients with schizophrenia. The majority of the present-day literature is indicative of relatively unimpaired subjective hedonic reaction to rewarding stimuli, but impaired incentive motivation (Ward et al., 2012).

Avolition is assessed by operant assays, such as progressive-ratio tasks, in which the animal has to work (press a lever or poke their nose into an aperture an increasing number of time over successive trials) to obtain a food reward—for instance, a weak solution of sucrose. The breaking point is defined as the number of lever presses at which the animal stops pressing the lever, which indicates that the rewarding value is lower than the effort the animal is willing to make to obtain the reward (Ellenbroek & Cools, 2000). In theory, if animals were to perceive less reward or be less motivated to work for the reward, they would have a lower breaking point (quitting sooner) than control rats, so the breaking point is taken as an index of avolition. The main differences between the progressive-ratio task as a measure of avolition and ICSS as a measure of anhedonia are summarized in Figure 1.

The translational potential of these tests might be substantial, but has yet to be fully exploited. The progressive-ratio task is already used in the research of depression where it has an important role of differentiating between consummatory and motivational anhedonia (Treadway & Zald, 2011). In addition to the progressive-ratio task paradigm, some researchers consider the increased immobility time in the forced swimming test (FST) to be a measure of avolition, but the interpretation of this paradigm is questionable (Noda, Kamei, Mamiya, Furukawa, & Nabeshima, 2000). There are also certain tests used in the research of depression, particularly in response to stress, which can be used to detect deficits in motivation. One such test is the splash test, which is used to measure spontaneous grooming behavior. In this test, the mouse is placed in a "splash cage" and "splashed" with a sprayer containing a 10% sucrose solution on its dorsal region and then returned to its home cage. The animal initiates grooming behavior because of the viscosity of the solution, which soils the fur. The latency to initiate first grooming behavior is measured as well

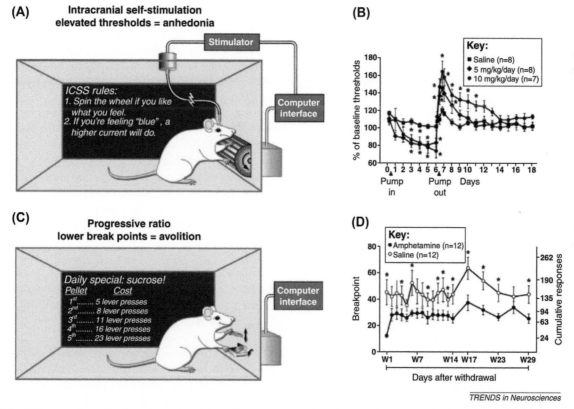

FIGURE 1 Differences between the progressive-ratio task as a measure of avolition and intracranial self-stimulation (ICSS) as a measure of anhedonia. (A) ICSS enables animals with implanted electrodes in their brain reward areas (for example, medial forebrain bundle or lateral hypothalamus) to administer weak electrical pulses; such self-stimulation has strong reinforcing properties at particular current intensities. The threshold that supports self-stimulation is ascertained by varying the intensity of the current. If the intensity of the current required to elicit a behavioral response is increased, an anhedonic state of the animal is suggested. (B) The reward threshold is increased after withdrawal from chronic amphetamine for up to 5 days in rats. "Pump in/out" marks the initiation/termination of exposure to amphetamine. (C) The progressive-ratio schedule of reinforcement can be used to assess avolition. Animals have to work (press the lever) to obtain a food reward (for example, sucrose pellets or weak sucrose solution), with each new pellet "costing" more lever presses. The animals will eventually stop pressing the lever, a point that is called the breaking point, and indicates that the rewarding value is lower than the effort the animal is willing to make to obtain the reward. A lower breaking point (quitting sooner) is interpreted as an index of avolition or decreased motivation to obtain the reward. (D) The break point for a sucrose pellet is decreased after withdrawal from chronic amphetamine exposure for up to 29 days in rats. *Modified from Der-Avakian & Markou (2012).*

as the frequency and the duration of grooming over a 5-min period. The test provides a direct quantitative measure of grooming behavior, which serves as an index of self-care and motivational behavior. It is considered that a decrease in grooming frequency corresponds with some symptoms of depression, such as apathetic behavior. A test that can be used to assess spontaneous motivation is the nest building test, which exploits the fact that nest building is an ethologically well-preserved behavior in rodents and that nests have important roles for small rodents, such as heat conservation, shelter, and in reproduction. Mice are, because of their small size, especially vulnerable to heat loss, so both male and female mice build nests spontaneously. The nest building test is carried out in individual cages for each animal, and one cotton nestlet is placed in each cage 1h before the beginning of the dark phase. The quality of the nest built by the animal is evaluated two times on a 5-point nest-rating scale 5 and 23h after nestlet has been provided. It is suggested that the deficits in nest building (lower scores) are related to self-neglect and social withdrawal, both of which might be relevant for assessing negative-like symptoms of schizophrenia (Pedersen, Sørensen, Parachikova, & Plath, 2014). Another ethological test used to assess motivation toward self-centered activities is the coat state test. The coat quality is a result of grooming behavior, and deterioration in the quality of the coat state can be related to a decrease in grooming and thus a deficiency in self-directed behavior. The coat state assessment is carried out weekly and multiple areas of the animal's body are assessed quantitatively (giving a score of 0 for smooth and shiny fur (good condition), 0.5 for slightly fluffy fur (moderate), and 1 (bad) for fluffy fur with slight staining). Stressed animals usually exhibit a worse score in coat state than nonstressed animals, and this change can be reversed with chronic administration of antidepressants.

ANIMAL MODELS OF SCHIZOPHRENIA

Most drugs used in the treatment of schizophrenia have been designed to treat positive symptoms. Since 1952, more than 50 antipsychotic drugs have been developed to treat schizophrenia and all of them act on the dopamine D_2 receptor, including clozapine, an atypical antipsychotic with a superiority claim for treatment-resistant schizophrenia (Carpenter & Koenig, 2007). Given the efficacy and the targets of the current antipsychotic medication, it is crucial to develop new and more efficient therapeutic strategies, but also relevant and useful animal models for preclinical testing (Flint & Shifman, 2008; Nagai, Bi, & Amada, 2011).

It has been estimated that more than 20 different animal models of schizophrenia have been developed, but all of them can be placed into one of four distinct categories: developmental, drug-induced, genetic manipulation, or lesion models (Carpenter & Koenig, 2007). Most of them replicate aspects of the positive symptoms, and the development of more exhaustive models that better replicate the negative/affective symptoms is ongoing, but many of them need to be tested. The original animal models have been developed on the basis of the belief that dopamine dysfunction was a key feature in the pathophysiology of schizophrenia, but as the understanding of the disease widened in regards to the genetic basis to the disease and the potential involvement of glutamate, animal models that explore their relationship to the disease have been developed (Jones, Watson, & Fone, 2011). We will briefly describe the most used models.

PHARMACOLOGICAL MODELS

Amphetamine Model of Schizophrenia

The amphetamine model of schizophrenia is based on the theory that hyperfunction of the mesolimbic dopamine system underlies schizophrenia, so attempts have been made to mimic this property with pharmaceutical manipulation of the dopamine system (Jones et al., 2011). In humans, amphetamine-induced psychosis has been described as consisting of auditory hallucinations and persecutory delusions, which bear resemblance to the positive symptoms of schizophrenia.

In animal models, chronic treatment with amphetamine induces a persistent sensitization in rats, suggesting changes in prefrontal function similar to those seen in schizophrenia, but not memory impairments similar to those seen in schizophrenia (Featherstone, Rizos, Kapur, & Fletcher, 2008). Preadministration of a low dose of haloperidol, a first-generation antipsychotic, or clozapine, a second-generation antipsychotic, prevents the induction of sensitization (Meng, Feldpausch, & Merchant, 1998). However, the model was not so successful in regards to negative symptoms because chronic amphetamine administration did not induce deficits in social interaction in rats, which is used to model certain aspects of negative symptoms (Sams-Dodd, 1995b). It has also failed to induce prolonged immobility in the FST, which could model some aspects of the negative symptomatology (Borsini, Volterra, & Meli, 1986; Noda, Yamada, Furukawa, & Nabeshima, 1995). This failure to induce negative symptoms in animals is in accordance with data in humans suggesting that negative symptoms are unrelated to a hyperdopaminergic state, and with the fact that some patients with predominately negative symptoms respond poorly or fail to respond to treatment with dopamine antagonists (Javitt & Zukin, 1991; Marcotte, Pearson, & Srivastava, 2001). To conclude, chronic amphetamine administration is able to induce positive-like symptoms of schizophrenia, but does not replicate the negative symptoms.

Phencyclidine Model of Schizophrenia

It has been hypothesized that the dysfunction of the glutamatergic system is involved in the etiology of schizophrenia (Carlsson, Hansson, Waters, & Carlsson, 1997). More specifically, N-methyl-D-aspartatereceptor (NMDA) receptors, which bind glutamate, have been implicated in the pathogenesis of schizophrenia by several lines of evidence, which include postmortem studies of schizophrenic patients (Mouri, Nagai, Ibi, & Yamada, 2013).

Phencyclidine (PCP), which acts predominately on glutamatergic NMDA receptors, can perhaps more faithfully mimic non paranoid schizophrenia, particularly when it includes negative symptoms (Marcotte et al., 2001). In humans, PCP rekindles and exacerbates the positive symptoms in both stabilized and acute schizophrenic patients; in healthy volunteers, it produces psychotic symptoms accompanied by progressive withdrawal and poverty of speech, which resemble the negative symptoms of schizophrenia (Jones et al., 2011). Because of these schizophrenia-like symptoms in humans, PCP has been used to produce a pharmacological rodent model of schizophrenia.

Both acute and chronic treatment with PCP have been used in animal models and both produce similar symptoms, such as hyperlocomotion, prepulse inhibition (PPI) deficits, social deficits, working memory impairments, extradimensional shifting impairment, latent learning impairment, and object recognition memory impairment (Mouri et al., 2013). However, it has been proposed that the effects of chronic administration may better mimic the symptoms of schizophrenia (Jentsch & Roth, 1999). Early positron emission tomography scans suggested that PCP abuse in humans was associated with deficits in the temporal and frontal lobes, which is similar to the changes seen in schizophrenic patients (Hertzmann, Reba, & Kotlyarov, 1990). Although many findings support claims of face and predictive validity, one criticism of the chronic PCP model is the lack of construct validity in regards to the neurodevelopmental origin of schizophrenia because PCP is administered to adult rats (Jones et al., 2011; Marcotte et al., 2001). However, there has been attempts to address this issue with the neonatal PCP model of schizophrenia, in which rat or mouse pups start receiving PCP on postnatal day 7 (Nakatani-Pawlak, Yamaguchi, Tatsumi, Mizoguchi, & Yoneda, 2009; Rajagopal, 2011).

Other Pharmacological Models

Besides the dopaminergic and the glutamatergic systems, the serotoninergic (5-HT) and GABAergic systems have also been implicated in schizophrenia. They will be mentioned briefly because their relevance is still difficult to establish and because the behavioral deficits they produce are less relevant for examining affective symptoms in schizophrenia.

It is believed that lysergic acid diethylamide (LSD) and mescaline, both psychedelic hallucinogenic drugs, act on 5-HT2A receptors to elicit their effects, and a polymorphism of the 5-HT2A receptor gene is reported to be a minor risk factor for schizophrenia. Clozapine, an atypical antipsychotic, has a relatively high affinity for the 5-HT2A receptor, which supports a role of the 5-HT system in schizophrenia. Both LSD and mescaline affect startle habituation and PPI of startle, but also behavioral abnormalities such as scratching, forepaw treading, head twitches, and lower lip retraction (Gobira, Ropke, Aguiar, Crippa, & Moreira, 2013; Marcotte et al., 2001). Although there are strong implications of the 5-HT system in schizophrenia, hard evidence for a primary dysfunction of it is lacking. Contrary to the situation in schizophrenia, repeated administration of LSD leads to behavioral tolerance in both humans and rodents, which is one of the things that make the assessment of the relevance of LSD administration elusive. Hence, the construct validity of this model is difficult to establish (Marcotte et al., 2001).

GABA is a major inhibitory neurotransmitter, and the GABAergic system has been implicated in schizophrenia on the basis on both theoretical considerations and experimental data. Its involvement with the disease is supposed because of its interaction with the dopaminergic system. In animal studies, it has been shown that picrotoxin, a $GABA_A$ receptor antagonist, reduces PPI of startle in rats and haloperidol, an antipsychotic drug, antagonized this effect (Japha & Koch, 1999). However, further studies are needed to examine the relevance of GABAergic models of schizophrenia, especially having in mind that there is a lack of reported GABA-induced behavioral deficits related to schizophrenia-like symptoms.

LESION MODELS

There is a collection of evidence, ranging from epidemiological and brain imaging to neuropathological data, which suggests that schizophrenia may be a developmental disorder in which one inherits or sustains a brain insult early in life, but expresses it in adulthood (Lewis & Levitt, 2002). Because of this, some lesion models could also be considered as overlapping with developmental models because the lesion could be applied during development. In fact, this also applies to the category of genetic models. However, to conform with the other literature, we will follow the standard typology in which any lesion, including the neonatal lesion, is considered to fall under the umbrella of lesion models as is the case with genetic models.

Neonatal Ventral Hippocampal Lesions

Twin studies have shown that genetic factor plays a substantial role in the development of schizophrenia and a batch of studies indicates that some of the genes involved play a role in early brain development (Mouri et al., 2013; Sullivan, Kendler, & Neale, 2003).

Most of the research has focused on lesions of the rodent ventral hippocampus (that is functionally equivalent to the human anterior hippocampus), which is not surprising because this region has a major role in regulating subcortical dopamine (Marcotte et al., 2001). A neurodevelopmental model of schizophrenia in which lesions of the ventral hippocampus are created in neonatal rodents (PND 7, a period of central nervous system development that overlaps the human third-trimester "brain growth spurt") has been used to create abnormalities in animals in early adulthood, which resemble those found in schizophrenia (Dawe, Hwang, & Tan, 2009; Pratt et al., 2012). In addition to enhanced locomotor activity in a novel environment, PPI, and working memory deficits, exaggerated hyperlocomotion in response to amphetamines and dizocilpine, the model also shows social deficits and increased aggressiveness (Marcotte et al., 2001; Mouri et al., 2013). These deficits are ameliorated after antipsychotic medication, but the deficits in social interaction are present both pre- and postpubertally and clozapine had no effects on them (Sams-Dodd, Lipska, & Weinberger, 1997). In addition, even if deficits in the hippocampal pyramidal neurons have been observed in schizophrenic patients, their brain does not show any signs of a lesion comparable with the ones elicited in rodents by this neonatal ablation and thus although the model may be used to test the efficacy of antipsychotic drugs, some researchers do not consider it to be a really accurate model of schizophrenia (Dawe et al., 2009).

DEVELOPMENTAL MODELS

Gestational Methylazoxymethanol Acetate

Methylazoxymethanol acetate (MAM) is an antimitotic and antiproliferative agent used to specifically target neuroblast proliferation in the central nervous system (Cattabeni & Di Luca, 1997). Administration of MAM to pregnant rat dams interferes with the development of specific brain regions in the offspring and leads to morphological and cytological alterations resembling those seen in schizophrenia postmortem brains (Hradetzky et al., 2012). The behavioral alterations caused by MAM are dependent on the day of administration, which range usually from gestational day (GD) 14 to GD17. As MAM administration at or before GD15 produces a too broad disruption of brain morphology and behavior to provide a useful model of the specific changes seen in schizophrenia, the recommended strategy is to use GD17 MAM (Jones et al., 2011). MAM treatment on GD17 is likely to have a substantial impact on the brain structures that are actively developing at that time, which includes the hippocampus. The peak of proliferation in this region occurs on GD17, and MAM administration at that time decreases the thickness of the hippocampus, but also of the thalamus and of several cortical regions—the same structures which are morphologically altered in schizophrenia (Flagstad et al., 2004).

Behavioral studies of MAM-treated rats exhibit a range of deficits, from being unable to ignore irrelevant stimuli and sensorimotor gating deficits to social withdrawal (Hradetzky et al., 2012). They are highly dependent on the day of MAM administration and are beyond the scope of this chapter, but more detail is available in the review article by Jones et al. (2011). Peculiarly, there is a lack of studies exploring behavioral deficits in the GD17 model and there are no studies in which a pharmacological reversal of the deficits was attempted. Hence, although the model has construct validity, reasonable face validity, the predictive validity is unknown because there have been no attempts to detect existing antipsychotic drugs or novel procognitive compounds that might be helpful in treating schizophrenia (Jones et al., 2011).

Early Environmental Manipulations

Postweaning Social Isolation

Rats have a defined social organization within colonies, and the hierarchy they develop within the colony has a crucial impact on their development. In the social isolation model, rat pups that are isolated into separate cages after weaning exhibit behavioral deficits at adulthood and also altered brain development (Fone & Porkess, 2008). These changes remain unaltered after the animals are re-socialized with the colony later in life (Pascual, Zamora-León, & Valero-Cabré, 2006).

The behavioral deficits caused by the model include spontaneous locomotor hyperactivity, enhanced responses to novelty (neophobia), sensorimotor gating deficits, cognitive impairments, and heightened anxiety states and aggression (Jones et al., 2011). Although some of the symptoms resemble those found in schizophrenia, they largely belong to positive symptoms. Placing the animal in a mildly aversive novel arena may produce useful readouts with high predictive validity to test drug reversal of the positive symptoms of schizophrenia, given that existing antipsychotic drugs are able reverse them (Jones et al., 2011). However, in terms of negative symptoms, in the social interaction task, it has been found that isolating the male (but not female) animals increased adult social interaction (Ferdman, Murmu, Bock, Braun, & Leshem, 2007). In terms of increased aggressive behavior, it was successfully reversed with tricyclic antidepressants, but the predictive validity for modeling negative symptoms using treatments effective on these symptoms is unknown (Porkess, 2008).

Some other weaknesses of this model also include the relative fragility of behavioral effects that can be reversed by repeated handling or with exposure to too many other tests during the developmental period and the long duration and associated cost of the experiments. However, the duration is combated by the relative ease of executing the protocol because it is a pure environmental model without any physical interaction to the animal. In addition, the model can also be complemented with other interventions that could potentially improve the paradigm, as we will discuss when describing genetic models of schizophrenia (Jones et al., 2011).

Other Early Environmental Manipulations

In addition to gestational MAM and postweaning social isolation, there are other developmental models that cause alterations that bear resemblance to some symptoms of schizophrenia. To list all of them is beyond the scope of this chapter, but we will briefly mention the main principles behind these early-life interventions.

One of the models is based on maternal immune activation at a critical developmental window during gestation, which is usually achieved through systemic administration of viral- or bacterial-like immune activating agents or through maternal exposure to a viral infection (Meyer & Feldon, 2010). These environmental challenges fall in the category of maternal infections and/or immune challenges. Other epidemiological factors that can be modeled are maternal stress, maternal nutritional deficiency, and obstetric complications, and each of them can be modeled experimentally in different ways. For example, the experimental systems used to model maternal stress range from maternal exposure to repeated restraint stress to maternal dexamethasone treatment, and obstetric complications can be modeled with neonatal anoxia exposure, birth by cesarean section, etc. (Meyer & Feldon, 2010). The main principle behind all these interventions is simple: there are

findings that suggest that the etiology of schizophrenia involves abnormal neurodevelopmental processes, which result from exposure to prenatal and/or perinatal environmental insults, before the illness is clinically expressed. Thus, just like in other neurodevelopmental models, the goal is to induce a disruption in early brain development, which leads to neurodevelopmental consequences, and then to study the alterations in behavior, neurochemistry, and neuroanatomy in adult animals. In regards to negative symptoms of schizophrenia, some of the models discussed display certain negative features of schizophrenia. One of the powerful animal neurodevelopmental models for (but not limited to) negative symptoms of schizophrenia uses late prenatal polyinosine-polycytidylic (poly I:C) exposure to induce behavioral and neurochemical abnormalities in mice. Poly I:C is a synthetic analog of double-stranded RNA that simulates viral infections and elicits a viral-like response in mammals (Fortier et al., 2004). In this model, animals exhibit reduced social interaction and anhedonic behavior in a sucrose preference test as well as reduced prefrontal and hippocampal dopamine and glutamate levels (Bitanihirwe et al., 2010).

GENETIC MODELS

Studies have demonstrated that schizophrenia has a high (80%) heritability rate. Twin studies have shown that genetic factors play a substantial role in the development of schizophrenia, with a heritability rate close to 80%. Although no single genetic alteration is responsible for a complex disorder such as schizophrenia, many genes have been associated with an increased risk of schizophrenia. Most of the genes disrupted have an effect on neurotransmission, neuronal plasticity, and functioning of synapses (Harrison & Weinberger, 2005). Most of genetic models have been developed to replicate the changes in messenger RNA and proteins that are observed in schizophrenia, and many different genetic models have been created, but only a selection of them will be discussed here because describing all of them would be far beyond the scope of this chapter.

Disrupted-in-Schizophrenia 1

Disrupted-in-schizophrenia 1 (DISC1) is one of the earliest genes discovered to be involved in the development of schizophrenia. The product of the gene is a synaptic protein that has many roles in pre- and postnatal neuronal development, including regulating the proliferation of neuronal progenitor cells and axon elongation (Jaaro-Peled, 2009). To date, seven DISC1 models have been created (Kellendonk, Simpson, & Kandel, 2009).

However, because the development of a knockout DISC1 has proved difficult, various alternative approaches that create a (partial) loss of function of DISC1 have been used. Although some of the behavioral alterations in DISC1 mice resemble symptoms of schizophrenia, one should have in mind that the level of similarity on both the nucleotide and amino acid level is only 60% between human and mouse DISC1, which prompts for caution when discussing DISC1 mouse models (Ma et al., 2002).

Some of the pathological changes in this model that are reminiscent of schizophrenia are enlarged lateral ventricles, reduced cortical thickness, and partial agenesis of the corpus callosum (Jaaro-Peled, Ayhan, Pletnikov, & Sawa, 2010). In terms of changes in behavior, the results are mixed because some groups have found differences in PPI, spontaneous locomotor activity, and social interaction, whereas others have reported no significant difference (Jones et al., 2011). In regards to anhedonia, the sucrose preference test has been used, and some models (such as Q31L) show decreased consumption of sucrose, whereas some others (such as L100P) do not (Clapcote et al., 2007). One possible explanation for these differences might be associated with the method of generating these transgenic animals, or by differences in strains, gender, or different methodologies and environments. Additionally, it is interesting to note that DISC1 is also a candidate gene for depression, so the phenotype displayed is of interest even if it is not clearly attributed to a specific disease (Jaaro-Peled, 2009).

Neuregulin 1 and ErbB4

Neuregulin 1 (NRG1) and its receptor, ErbB4, are also considered to be candidate "risk" genes for schizophrenia because recent studies identified variations in them to be associated with the disorder. NRG1 has many important roles in the development and functioning of the nervous system, including (but not limited to) both excitatory and inhibitory neurotransmission, synaptic plasticity, axon guidance, and myelination (Mei & Xiong, 2008). Although heterozygous knockout mice were found to be healthy and fertile, homozygous knockout of NRG1 is lethal in mice, and embryos die of cardiac arrest (Stefansson & Petursson, 2002). The heterozygous or conditional knockout mice that were developed have different "schizophrenia-like" alterations, depending on the mechanism through which they regulate neuregulin–ErbB4 signaling (Jones et al., 2011). Some of these models include a heterozygous deletion of the EGF-like domain [Nrg1(ΔEGF)$^{+/-}$], a heterozygous deletion of the transmembrane domain of NRG1 [Nrg1(ΔTM)$^{+/-}$], and so forth.

Because of this, the clinical picture is not as clear, also in terms of negative symptoms. For example, Nrg1(ΔEGF)$^{+/-}$ mice show robust deficits in social interaction, but Nrg1(ΔTM)$^{+/-}$ mice show normal social interaction. Transgenic animals in which erbB

signaling in oligodendrocytes was blocked by expression of a dominant negative erbB receptor showed reduced social interaction, suggesting that the erbB signaling may be involved in the negative symptoms of schizophrenia (Roy et al., 2007). In addition, the construct validity of most of these models is questionable because the clinical manifestations of schizophrenia are associated with NRG1 hyperfunction, and not hypofunction, which is the result of a heterozygous deletion used in most models (Jones et al., 2011). It is interesting to note that despite having two transgenic models which model NRG1 hyperfunction instead of hypofunction, there is a substantial overlap in the traits observed, including increased locomotor activity, reduced PPI, and a decrease in social behavior (Kato et al., 2010). However, the exact mechanisms underlying the phenotype observed have not been explained and the controversy of the similarity of effects between hyper- and hypomorphic models remains to be explained.

Other Genetic Models

Several other genetic models are being developed, but because it is difficult or even impossible to replicate the entire genetic architecture underlying a complex disorder such as schizophrenia in a single model, they differ in both the quality and the quantity of observed behavioral alterations reminiscent of schizophrenia (Pratt et al., 2012). These genetic models include the calcineurin conditional knockout mice, dysbindin mutant mice, reelin disrupted mice (also called reeler mice), and dopamine-related and glutamate-related knockout mice such as dopamine receptor knockout mice (Carpenter & Koenig, 2007; Pratt et al., 2012). However, despite their number, these genetic models do not seem to capture the spectrum of schizophrenia-related phenotypes (Carpenter & Koenig, 2007). In addition, some genetic models (notably, homozygous deletions) create artificial voids in protein expression that do not exist in patients, but recently more selective strategies are attempting to address this concern.

In summary, because permanently disrupting a single gene potentially involved with schizophrenia is unlikely to encompass the complex nature of the disorder, particularly because of the complex gene–gene and gene–environment interactions, more complex models are being developed. These models use inducible and tissue-specific knockout techniques to address the confounds related to compensatory mechanisms by selectively (both temporally and spatially) modulating genes of interest (Pratt et al., 2012). In addition, they may be potentially further enhanced by combining them with already existing environmental or pharmacological models of the disease, possibly increasing their translational value by modeling the disorder more accurately and combating the overly simplistic attempts to focus on single genes as causes of the disease. One such example is a model combining maternal immune activation with poly I:C with DISC1 mutant mice, which exhibited an enhanced schizophrenia-like phenotype (Abazyan et al., 2010). New models such as these could open up new pharmacological avenues to treat schizophrenia, possibly even through separate therapeutic development targeting the different domains of the disorder.

AFFECTIVE ASSAYS IN MODELS OF SCHIZOPHRENIA

Because the behavioral phenotype can be assessed by using different paradigms and because of the sheer number of diverse animal models used to model schizophrenia, there is no simple relationship among the symptom, the assay, and the model. We have briefly touched upon this when describing different animal models, but we will share a broader overview with more detail, and focused on affective assays.

As mentioned previously, managing the negative symptoms of schizophrenia is still an unmet clinical need that prompts improvements in modeling these deficits. Although there has been considerable progress in the past several years, there are still challenges in applying these models to better understand the pathobiology of negative symptoms in schizophrenia (O'Tuathaigh et al., 2010). One of the biggest issues is that the large majority of data is related to deficits in social behavior, which does not clearly relate to affective symptomatology but rather to negative symptoms in a more general way, whereas the data relevant for anhedonia are scarce, and the body of work relating avolition and schizophrenia is even more limited in scope. In addition, even the data related to social behavior, which is by far most extensively studied, suffer from some problems. In various mutant lines, different tests related to sociability and aggression have been (and still are) used, and things are complicated by the problematic interpretation of these tests as the manipulation itself might affect the olfactory system, which is a crucial element of social interaction in rodents. There are also issues with replication of results because the "same" strain in the same "test" can, for poorly understood reasons, generate different results (O'Tuathaigh et al., 2010).

The results of behavioral phenotyping for various manipulations of rodents and the effects of antipsychotic administration (where an attempt has been made) are summarized in Table 2. Because our goal is to provide a broad overview, it was not feasible to include every model and assay, but rather we selected the models and assays that are representative, so that for each affective symptom we present the results from the four main categories of models: pharmaceutical, lesion, developmental, and genetic (and their combinations).

In terms of anhedonia, because there is no research relating the animal models of schizophrenia and the cookie test, we have focused on the results gained from the sucrose preference test and ICSS. The models should lead to a decrease in sucrose or saccharine preference, a reduction in intracranial self-stimulation, and an increased threshold for self-stimulation. The results are mixed; some models, such as the maternal immune challenge with poly I:C in mice, DISC1 mutant (Q31L mouse), neonatal ventral hippocampus lesion, and acute PCP and MK-801 in rats all show a decreased preference for a sucrose (or saccharine) solution. However, other models, such as postweaning social isolation and subchronic PCP in rats, along with dopamine receptor knockout mice and the DISC1 mutant (L100P mouse) showed no difference regarding sucrose preference.

Regarding the effects of antipsychotics, it is important to bear in mind that all available antipsychotics have only limited efficacy in alleviating negative symptoms (see the previous section) and display quite variable effects according to the class of drugs investigated. Indeed, first-generation antipsychotics such as chlorpromazine or haloperidol have poor efficacy when compared with second-generation antipsychotics such as clozapine, olanzapine, risperidone, or quetiapine (see, for example, Hartling et al., 2012). Indeed, this is found in most readouts because haloperidol did not reverse anhedonia in the PCP and MK 801 models or aggressive behavior in the neonatal ventral hippocampus lesion model. In some cases, haloperidol even worsened the negative symptoms, as found in the clinic. For example, acute haloperidol produced an overall decrease in sucrose consumption in both PCP-pretreated and control groups and further decreased the breaking point in both PCP-treated rats and control groups (Wiley & Compton, 2004). The sole study in which haloperidol reversed the schizophrenia model-induced impairments used the amphetamine administration model. Indeed, haloperidol reversed the effects of amphetamine in regards to the threshold of self-stimulation. But this effect is probably just trivial because amphetamine and haloperidol act on dopaminergic transmission in opposite directions. Therefore, if we consider that an animal model should mimic the clinical situation, a lack of effect on negative/affective symptoms with haloperidol cannot really be considered a failure of the model to achieve predictive validity. It rather strengthens the relevance of the model.

Regarding second-generation antipsychotics, they showed ability to counteract affective symptoms in schizophrenia models when administered chronically. For example, chronic (but not acute) clozapine reversed anhedonia in the MK-801 model and in the acute PCP model. Second-generation antipsychotic reversal has also been attempted in the chronic mild stress model, which is not a model of schizophrenia, but a naturalistic paradigm of a hostile environment that can induce anhedonia. It has been shown that quetiapine causes a complete recovery from absence of sucrose preference. It has also been found that many antipsychotics per se are able to reduce

TABLE 2 Models Used to Assess Affective Symptoms in Schizophrenia and Antipsychotic Reversal

Affective Symptom	Animal Model	Assessing Paradigm	Measure	Effect of AP	Reference
Anhedonia	Maternal immune challenge (mouse)	Sucrose preference	↓	NA	Bitanihirwe, Peleg-Raibstein, Mouttet, Feldon, and Meyer (2010)
	Neonatal ventral hippocampus lesion (rat)	Saccharine preference	↓	NA	Le Pen, Gaudet, Mortas, Mory, and Moreau (2002)
	Postweaning social isolation (rat)	Sucrose preference	±	NA	Hall, Humby, Wilkinson, and Robbins (1997)
	Acute PCP (rat)	Sucrose preference	↓	NA	Baird, Turgeon, Wallman, and Hulick (2008)
		Sucrose preference	↓	+ (subchronic clozapine) - (acute clozapine, haloperidol)	Turgeon and Hulick (2007)
		ICSS	↑Threshold	NA	Spielewoy and Markou (2003)
	Acute MK-801 (rat)	Sucrose preference	↓	+ (clozapine) - (haloperidol)	Vardigan, Huszar, McNaughton, Hutson, and Uslaner (2010)
	Subchronic PCP (rat)	Sucrose preference	±	NA	Jenkins, Harte, and Reynolds (2010)
	Amphetamine (rat)	ICSS	↑Stimulation↓threshold	- Stimulation	Wauquier (1979)
		ICSS	↓Stimulation↑threshold	+ (haloperidol)	Barrett and White (1980)
	Chronic mild stress (rat)	Sucrose preference	↓	+ (quetiapine)	Orsetti et al. (2007)
	DISC1 mutant (Q31L mouse)	Sucrose preference	↓	NA	Clapcote et al. (2007)
	DISC1 mutant (L100P mouse)	Sucrose preference	±		
	Dopamine receptor knockout (mouse)	Sucrose preference	±	NA	El-Ghundi, O'Dowd, Erclik, and George (2003)
Avolition	Repeated PCP (mouse)	Forced swimming test	↑Immobility	+ (clozapine, AD-5423) - (haloperidol)	Nagai, Noda, Une, and Furukawa (2003), Noda et al. (1995)
	Methamphetamine (mouse)		±	NA	
	Repeated PCP (rat)	Progressive-ratio task	±	- (clozapine) ↓ (haloperidol)	Wiley and Compton (2004)
	Chronic amphetamine (rat)	Progressive-ratio task	↓Break point	NA	Der-Avakian and Markou (2010)
	DISC1 mutant (Q31L mouse)	Forced swimming test	↑Immobility	+ (bupropion) - (rolipram)	Clapcote et al. (2007)
	DISC1 mutant (truncated C-terminal, mouse)	Forced swimming test	↑Immobility	NA	Hikida et al. (2007)
	DISC1 mutant + maternal immune challenge (mouse)	Forced swimming test	↑Immobility	NA	Abazyan et al. (2010)
	Hippocampal lesion (rat)	Progressive-ratio task	↑Break point	NA	Schmelzeis and Mittleman (1996)
	Dopamine receptor knockout (mouse)	Progressive-ratio task	↓Break point	NA	El-Ghundi et al. (2003)
	Striatal dopamine D_2 receptor overexpression (mouse)	Progressive-ratio task	↓Break point	NA	Drew et al. (2007)

Domain	Model	Assay	Effect	AP	Reference
Social interaction	Gestational MAM (rat)	Social interaction test	↓ Interaction	NA	Flagstad et al. (2004), Le Pen et al. (2006)
	Prenatal stress (rat)	Social interaction test	↓ Interaction	+ (oxytocin)	Lee, Brady, Shapiro, Dorsa, and Koenig (2007)
	Maternal immune challenge (mouse)	Social interaction test	↓ Interaction	NA	Bitanihirwe et al. (2010)
		Social choice	↓ Preference	NA	Smith, Li, Garbett, Mirnics, and Patterson (2007)
	Prenatal restraint stress (mouse)	Social interaction in a novel environment	↓ Interaction	+ (clozapine), + (valproate)	Matrisciano et al. (2013)
	Postweaning social isolation (rat)	Social interaction test	↑ Interaction (in males)	NA	Ferdman et al. (2007)
	Neonatal ventral hippocampus lesion (rat)	Social interaction test	↓ Interaction	± (clozapine)	Sams-Dodd et al. (1997)
			↑ Aggression	↓ (clozapine) ± (haloperidol)	Becker (2003)
	Acute amphetamine (rat)	Social interaction test	±	NA	Sams-Dodd (1995b)
	Repeated amphetamine (rat)	Social interaction test	±	NA	Der-Avakian and Markou, 2010, Sams-Dodd (1998)
	Acute PCP (rat)	Social interaction test	↓ Interaction	NA	Sams-Dodd (1995b)
	Repeated PCP (mouse)	Social interaction test	↓ Interaction	+ (risperidone with galantamine)	Wang et al. (2007)
	DISC1 mutant (Q31L)	Social interaction test	↓ Interaction	NA	Clapcote et al. (2007)
	DISC1 mutant (L100P)		±		
	DISC1 mutant (truncated N-terminal, mouse)	Social interaction test	↓ Interaction	NA	Pletnikov et al. (2008)
	DISC1 mutant (truncated C-terminal, mouse)	Social interaction test	±	NA	Hikida et al. (2007)
	NRG1 overexpression (transgenic mouse)	Resident-intruder test	↓ Interaction ↑ aggression	NA	Kato et al. (2010)
	NRG1 TM-domain heterozygous mutant (mouse)	Social interaction test	↓ Interaction	NA	O'Tuathaigh et al. (2007), O'Tuathaigh et al. (2008)
		Social choice	↓ Preference		
		Resident-intruder test	↑ Aggression		
	DISC1 mutant + maternal immune challenge (mouse)	Social choice	↓ Time sniffing live mouse	NA	Abazyan et al. (2010)

↓, decrease; ↑, increase; ±, no change; +, reversal of the induced effect; -, no drug-induced reversal; AP, antipsychotics; ICSS, intracranial self-stimulation; MAM, methylazoxymethanol acetate; NA, not applicable; PCP, phencyclidine.

I. FROM CLINICAL DIMENSIONS TO ANIMAL MODELS

intracranial self-stimulation, which may be related to their ability to induce extrapyramidal side effects that are often very hard to differentiate from the negative symptoms of schizophrenia (Ellenbroek & Cools, 2000).

Most of the data available regarding avolition in schizophrenia assess this affective symptom by either progressive-ratio tasks or the FST. Some researchers (Strekalova et al., 2004) consider the FST to be a measure of anhedonia, whereas some (Corbett, 1999) use it as a measure of avolition. Significant criticisms have been made regarding the interpretation of the FST, and most antipsychotics do not affect behavior during FST (Borsini et al., 1986; Ellenbroek & Cools, 2000). Even though that modeling and assessing avolition is hard because it is difficult to determine if the results are caused by avolition or simply because of an overall reduction in motor performance, it is considered that the progressive-ratio task examines this dimension of the phenotype to an adequate degree. The models should lead to either an increase in immobility time in the FST or a lowered breaking point in the progressive-ratio task. In the progressive-ratio task, chronic amphetamine treatment in rats and dopamine receptor knockout and striatal dopamine D_2 receptor overexpression in mice leads to a lowered breaking point, whereas, interestingly, hippocampal lesions in rats lead to a higher breaking point. There is a lack of studies that attempt a reversal in the progressive-ratio task by antipsychotics in animal models of schizophrenia, but one group attempted an antipsychotic reversal in the repeated PCP model in rats and found that clozapine had no effect. Chronic methamphetamine in mice and repeated PCP in rats had no effects on the immobility time in the FST, whereas repeated PCP in rats did increase immobility time, which could be reversed by clozapine and AD-5423 (also an antipsychotic agent), but again, not haloperidol. Numerous genetic models of schizophrenia—such as the DISC1 mutant Q31L, DISC1 mutant with a truncated C-terminal, and a DISC1 mutant combined with maternal immune challenge—all exhibit increased immobility time and in the Q31L model a drug reversal has been attempted, where bupropion successfully reversed the immobility, whereas rolipram had no effect. However, it seems difficult to relate this to efficacy of these drugs in schizophrenic patients.

Unlike the lack of research regarding avolition and anhedonia, a substantial amount of literature is available regarding alterations in social behavior. Most models from all the four categories of animal models of schizophrenia (details in Table 2) exhibit social withdrawal and/or increased aggression. The models in which such an effect has not been observed include both acute and repeated amphetamine administration in rats and certain DISC1 mutants in mice (L100P and truncated C-terminal). Interestingly, in the postweaning social isolation, social behavior in males was increased after social isolation. It has been attempted to reverse these changes using

antipsychotic administration, and it has been shown that although clozapine can reverse the effects of prenatal restraint stress in mice in regards to social behavior, it elicited no effects in the neonatal ventral hippocampus lesions in rats. In the repeated PCP model in mice, risperidone with galantamine reversed social deficits. In regards to aggression, it was found to be increased in rats with neonatal ventral hippocampus lesions, mice with NRG1 overexpression, and mice who are NRG1 TM-domain heterozygous mutants. Clozapine (but not haloperidol) successfully decreased the aggressive behavior of rats with neonatal ventral hippocampus lesions. Finally, in some cases, these models have also been used to assess the effects of compounds that are not yet used in the treatment of schizophrenia, such as valproate or oxytocin. Indeed, valproate as well as oxytocin have been shown to reverse social interaction defects in the prenatal stress model, suggesting they could be used to treat some negative symptoms in schizophrenic patients.

CONCLUSION

Overall, the findings summarized here show that negative/affective symptoms have been poorly studied in animal models of schizophrenia. However, even if sparse, some data exist. It reveals that few animal models of schizophrenia recapitulate both anhedonia and avolition, which are the main features of affective symptoms in schizophrenia. In most cases, one of these two phenotypes was present, whereas the other one remained untested or was not detectable. For example, regarding the neonatal hippocampal lesion model, it induced decreased sucrose preference, which correlates with anhedonia, but it increased the breaking point in the progressive ratio, which is the reverse of the prediction. Pharmacological models yield the same results: amphetamine elicits contradictory results in the ICSS, even if it decreased the breaking point in the progressive ratio, acute PCP and acute MK 801 decreased sucrose preference but has not been tested in avolition readouts, repeated PCP decreased the breaking point but anhedonia had not been assessed. Similar findings are found with the genetic models, the sole exception being the DISC1 mutant (Q31L mouse) that exhibits both avolition and anhedonia. Because all these models have been able to detect positive-like symptoms of schizophrenia, one can suggest that, except for the DISC1 (Q31L) mouse, all models are not models of schizophrenia per se, but models inducing positive symptoms of schizophrenia. In this case, new models of schizophrenia, enabling detection of both kinds of symptoms, should be designed. Alternatively, it can be that the behavioral readouts used are not relevant for the schizophrenia-related negative symptoms and that new assays, rather than new models, should be developed or applied to better detect them. This particularly applies to avolition. Indeed, as seen from Table 1, several more ethological tests have been developed to assess avolition in animal models of depression, including assessment of coat state, grooming behavior, and nest building. Some of them have already been used also in the field of schizophrenia research. One can mention, for example, that subchronic PCP, genetic deletion of neurexin-1alpha, NMDA receptor deficiency, and early postnatal deficit in the NR1 subunits of the NMDA receptor in GABAergic cells of the hippocampus and the cortex, which have all been proposed as schizophrenia models, all induced nest building deficits (Belforte et al., 2010; Etherton, Blaiss, Powell, & Südhof, 2009; Halene et al., 2009; Pedersen et al., 2014). Such ethological assays should be included in the behavioral phenotyping of animal models of schizophrenia in a more systematic way and validated pharmacologically with treatments effective in achieving remission of the affective symptomatology in schizophrenic patients. Finally, some aspects of the affective symptomatology have been poorly tested in animal models of schizophrenia. This applies, for example, to emotional blunting, which is an important feature in schizophrenic patients. This is related to the fact that few assays measuring such phenotype are currently available, even if some authors proposed that poor response to classical fear condition can be considered a test of emotional blunting (Pietersen et al., 2007). Additional tests assessing emotional blunting should thus be designed.

References

Abazyan, B., Nomura, J., Kannan, G., Ishizuka, K., Tamashiro, K. L., Nucifora, F., et al. (2010). Prenatal interaction of mutant DISC1 and immune activation produces adult psychopathology. *Biological Psychiatry*, 68(12), 1172–1181. http://dx.doi.org/10.1016/j.biopsych.2010.09.022.

Addington, J., Shah, H., Liu, L., & Addington, D. (2014). Reliability and validity of the Calgary Depression Scale for Schizophrenia (CDSS) in youth at clinical high risk for psychosis. *Schizophrenia Research*, 153(1–3), 64–67. http://dx.doi.org/10.1016/j.schres.2013.12.014.

Baird, J., Turgeon, S., Wallman, A., & Hulick, V. (2008). Behavioral processes mediating phencyclidine-induced decreases in voluntary sucrose consumption. *Pharmacology, Biochemistry, and Behavior*, 88(3), 272–279.

Barnes, S. A., Der-Avakian, A., & Markou, A. (2014). Anhedonia, avolition, and anticipatory deficits: assessments in animals with relevance to the negative symptoms of schizophrenia. *European Neuropsychopharmacology: The Journal of the European College of Neuropsychopharmacology*, 24(5), 744–758. http://dx.doi.org/10.1016/j.euroneuro.2013.10.001.

Barrett, R. J., & White, D. K. (1980). Reward system depression following chronic amphetamine: antagonism by haloperidol. *Pharmacology, Biochemistry, and Behavior*, 13(4), 555–559. http://dx.doi.org/10.1016/0091-3057(80)90280-4.

Becker, A. (2003). Haloperidol and clozapine affect social behaviour in rats postnatally lesioned in the ventral hippocampus. *Pharmacology, Biochemistry, and Behavior*, 76(1), 1–8. http://dx.doi.org/10.1016/S0091-3057(03)00139-4.

Belforte, J. E., Zsiros, V., Sklar, E. R., Jiang, Z., Yu, G., Li, Y., et al. (2010). Postnatal NMDA receptor ablation in corticolimbic interneurons confers schizophrenia-like phenotypes. *Nature Neuroscience*, 13(1), 76–83. http://dx.doi.org/10.1038/nn.2447.

Belzung, C. (2014). Innovative drugs to treat depression: did animal models fail to be predictive or did clinical trials fail to detect effects? *Neuropsychopharmacology*, 39(5), 1041–1051. http://dx.doi.org/10.1038/npp.2013.342.

Bitanihirwe, B. K. Y., Peleg-Raibstein, D., Mouttet, F., Feldon, J., & Meyer, U. (2010). Late prenatal immune activation in mice leads to behavioral and neurochemical abnormalities relevant to the negative symptoms of schizophrenia. *Neuropsychopharmacology*, 35(12), 2462–2478. http://dx.doi.org/10.1038/npp.2010.129.

Bleuler, E. (1951). Dementia praecox or the group of schizophrenias. *Journal of the American Medical Association*, 145(9), 685. http://dx.doi.org/10.1001/jama.1951.02920270079043.

Borsini, F., Volterra, G., & Meli, A. (1986). Does the behavioral "despair" test measure "despair"? *Physiology & Behavior*, 38(3), 385–386. http://dx.doi.org/10.1016/0031-9384(86)90110-1.

Carlsson, A., Hansson, L. O., Waters, N., & Carlsson, M. L. (1997). Neurotransmitter aberrations in schizophrenia: new perspectives and therapeutic implications. *Life Sciences*, 61(2), 75–94.

Carpenter, W., & Koenig, J. (2007). The evolution of drug development in schizophrenia: past issues and future opportunities. *Neuropsychopharmacology*, 2061–2079. http://dx.doi.org/10.1038/sj.npp.1301639.

Cattabeni, F., & Di Luca, M. (1997). Developmental models of brain dysfunctions induced by targeted cellular ablations with methylazoxymethanol. *Physiological Reviews*, 77(1), 199–215.

Clapcote, S. J., Lipina, T. V., Millar, J. K., Mackie, S., Christie, S., Ogawa, F., et al. (2007). Behavioral phenotypes of Disc1 missense mutations in mice. *Neuron*, 54(3), 387–402. http://dx.doi.org/10.1016/j.neuron.2007.04.015.

Corbett, R. (1999). Animal models of negative symptoms M100907 antagonizes PCP-induced immobility in a forced swim test in Mice. *Neuropsychopharmacology*, 21(6), S211–S218. http://dx.doi.org/10.1016/S0893-133X(99)00128-1.

Dawe, G. S., Hwang, E. H., & Tan, C. H. (2009). Pathophysiology and animal models of schizophrenia. *Annals of the Academy of Medicine, Singapore*, 38(5), 425–426.

Der-Avakian, A., & Markou, A. (2010). Withdrawal from chronic exposure to amphetamine, but not nicotine, leads to an immediate and enduring deficit in motivated behavior without affecting social interaction in rats. *Behavioural Pharmacology*, 21(4), 359–368. http://dx.doi.org/10.1097/FBP.0b013e32833c7cc8.

Der-Avakian, A., & Markou, A. (2012). The neurobiology of anhedonia and other reward-related deficits. *Trends in Neurosciences*, 35(1), 68–77. http://dx.doi.org/10.1016/j.tins.2011.11.005.

Drew, M. R., Simpson, E. H., Kellendonk, C., Herzberg, W. G., Lipatova, O., Fairhurst, S., et al. (2007). Transient overexpression of striatal D_2 receptors impairs operant motivation and interval timing. *Journal of Neuroscience*, 27(29), 7731–7739. http://dx.doi.org/10.1523/JNEUROSCI.1736-07.2007.

Dulawa, S. C., & Hen, R. (2005). Recent advances in animal models of chronic antidepressant effects: the novelty-induced hypophagia test. *Neuroscience and Biobehavioral Reviews*, 29, 771–783.

El-Ghundi, M., O'Dowd, B. F., Erclik, M., & George, S. R. (2003). Attenuation of sucrose reinforcement in dopamine D1 receptor deficient mice. *European Journal of Neuroscience*, 17(4), 851–862. http://dx.doi.org/10.1046/j.1460-9568.2003.02496.x.

Ellenbroek, B. A., & Cools, A. R. (2000). Animal models for the negative symptoms of schizophrenia. *Behavioural Pharmacology*, 11(3–4), 223–233.

Etherton, M. R., Blaiss, C. A., Powell, C. M., & Südhof, T. C. (2009). Mouse neurexin-1α deletion causes correlated electrophysiological and behavioral changes consistent with cognitive impairments.

Proceedings of the National Academy of Sciences of the United States of America, 106(42), 17998–18003. http://dx.doi.org/10.1073/pnas.0910297106.

Featherstone, R. E., Rizos, Z., Kapur, S., & Fletcher, P. J. (2008). A sensitizing regimen of amphetamine that disrupts attentional set-shifting does not disrupt working or long-term memory. *Behavioural Brain Research, 189*(1), 170–179. http://dx.doi.org/10.1016/j.bbr.2007.12.032.

Ferdman, N., Murmu, R. P., Bock, J., Braun, K., & Leshem, M. (2007). Weaning age, social isolation, and gender, interact to determine adult explorative and social behavior, and dendritic and spine morphology in prefrontal cortex of rats. *Behavioural Brain Research, 180*(2), 174–182. http://dx.doi.org/10.1016/j.bbr.2007.03.011.

Flagstad, P., Mørk, A., Glenthøj, B. Y., van Beek, J., Michael-Titus, A. T., & Didriksen, M. (2004). Disruption of neurogenesis on gestational day 17 in the rat causes behavioral changes relevant to positive and negative schizophrenia symptoms and alters amphetamine-induced dopamine release in nucleus accumbens. *Neuropsychopharmacology, 29*(11), 2052–2064. http://dx.doi.org/10.1038/sj.npp.1300516.

Flint, J., & Shifman, S. (2008). Animal models of psychiatric disease. *Current Opinion in Genetics & Development, 18*(3), 235–240. http://dx.doi.org/10.1016/j.gde.2008.07.002.

Fone, K. C. F., & Porkess, M. V. (2008). Behavioural and neurochemical effects of post-weaning social isolation in rodents-relevance to developmental neuropsychiatric disorders. *Neuroscience and Biobehavioral Reviews.* http://dx.doi.org/10.1016/j.neubiorev.2008.03.003.

Fortier, M.-E., Kent, S., Ashdown, H., Poole, S., Boksa, P., & Luheshi, G. N. (2004). The viral mimic, polyinosinic: polycytidylic acid, induces fever in rats via an interleukin-1-dependent mechanism. *American Journal of Physiology. Regulatory, Integrative and Comparative Physiology, 287*(4), R759–R766. http://dx.doi.org/10.1152/ajpregu.00293.2004.

Gardner, D. M., Baldessarini, R. J., & Waraich, P. (2005). Modern antipsychotic drugs: a critical overview. *CMAJ: Canadian Medical Association Journal = Journal de l'Association Medicale Canadienne, 172*(13), 1703–1711. http://dx.doi.org/10.1503/cmaj.1041064.

Gobira, P. H., Ropke, J., Aguiar, D. C., Crippa, J. A. S., & Moreira, F. A. (2013). Animal models for predicting the efficacy and side effects of antipsychotic drugs. *Revista Brasileira de Psiquiatria (São Paulo, Brazil: 1999), 35*(Suppl. 2), S132–S139. http://dx.doi.org/10.1590/1516-4446-2013-1164.

Halene, T. B., Ehrlichman, R. S., Liang, Y., Christian, E. P., Jonak, G. J., Gur, T. L., et al. (2009). Assessment of NMDA receptor NR1 subunit hypofunction in mice as a model for schizophrenia. *Genes, Brain, and Behavior, 8*(7), 661–675. http://dx.doi.org/10.1111/j.1601-183X.2009.00504.x.

Hall, F. S., Humby, T., Wilkinson, L. S., & Robbins, T. W. (1997). The effects of isolation-rearing on sucrose consumption in rats. *Physiology & Behavior, 62*(2), 291–297.

Harrison, P. J., & Weinberger, D. R. (2005). Schizophrenia genes, gene expression, and neuropathology: on the matter of their convergence. *Molecular Psychiatry, 10*(1), 40–68. http://dx.doi.org/10.1038/sj.mp.4001558 image 5.

Hartling, L., Abou-Setta, A. M., Dursun, S., Mousavi, S. S., Pasichnyk, D., & Newton, A. S. (2012). Antipsychotics in adults with schizophrenia: comparative effectiveness of first-generation versus second-generation medications: a systematic review and meta-analysis. *Annals of Internal Medicine, 157*(7), 498–511. http://dx.doi.org/10.7326/0003-4819-157-7-201210020-00525.

Hertzmann, M., Reba, R. C., & Kotlyarov, E. V. (1990). Single photon emission computed tomography in phencyclidine and related drug abuse. *American Journal of Psychiatry, 147*(2), 255–256.

Hikida, T., Jaaro-Peled, H., Seshadri, S., Oishi, K., Hookway, C., Kong, S., et al. (2007). Dominant-negative DISC1 transgenic mice display schizophrenia-associated phenotypes detected by measures translatable to humans. *Proceedings of the National Academy of Sciences of the United States of America, 104*(36), 14501–14506. http://dx.doi.org/10.1073/pnas.0704774104.

Hradetzky, E., Sanderson, T. M., Tsang, T. M., Sherwood, J. L., Fitzjohn, S. M., Lakics, V., et al. (2012). The methylazoxymethanol acetate (MAM-E17) rat model: molecular and functional effects in the hippocampus. *Neuropsychopharmacology, 37*(2), 364–377. http://dx.doi.org/10.1038/npp.2011.219.

Jaaro-Peled, H. (2009). Gene models of schizophrenia: DISC1 mouse models. *Progress in Brain Research, 179*, 75–86. http://dx.doi.org/10.1016/S0079-6123(09)17909-8.

Jaaro-Peled, H., Ayhan, Y., Pletnikov, M. V., & Sawa, A. (2010). Review of pathological hallmarks of schizophrenia: comparison of genetic models with patients and nongenetic models. *Schizophrenia Bulletin, 36*(2), 301–313. http://dx.doi.org/10.1093/schbul/sbp133.

James, W. (1985). *The varieties of religious experience* (Vol. 13, P. 669).

Japha, K., & Koch, M. (1999). Picrotoxin in the medial prefrontal cortex impairs sensorimotor gating in rats: reversal by haloperidol. *Psychopharmacology, 144*(4), 347–354.

Javitt, D. C., & Zukin, S. R. (1991). Recent advances in the phencyclidine model of schizophrenia. *American Journal of Psychiatry, 148*(10), 1301–1308.

Jenkins, T. A., Harte, M. K., & Reynolds, G. P. (2010). Effect of subchronic phencyclidine administration on sucrose preference and hippocampal parvalbumin immunoreactivity in the rat. *Neuroscience Letters, 471*(3), 144–147. http://dx.doi.org/10.1016/j.neulet.2010.01.028.

Jentsch, J. D., & Roth, R. H. (1999). The neuropsychopharmacology of phencyclidine: from NMDA receptor hypofunction to the dopamine hypothesis of schizophrenia. *Neuropsychopharmacology.* http://dx.doi.org/10.1016/S0893-133X(98)00060-8.

Johnson, D. A. (1981). Studies of depressive symptoms in schizophrenia. *British Journal of Psychiatry, 139*(2), 89–101. http://dx.doi.org/10.1192/bjp.139.2.89.

Jones, C., Watson, D., & Fone, K. (2011). Animal models of schizophrenia. *British Journal of Pharmacology, 164*(4), 1162–1194. http://dx.doi.org/10.1111/j.1476-5381.2011.01386.x.

Kato, T., Kasai, A., Mizuno, M., Fengyi, L., Shintani, N., Maeda, S., et al. (2010). Phenotypic characterization of transgenic mice overexpressing neuregulin-1. *PLoS One, 5*(12), e14185. http://dx.doi.org/10.1371/journal.pone.0014185.

Katz, R. J. (1982). Animal model of depression: pharmacological sensitivity of a hedonic deficit. *Pharmacology, Biochemistry, and Behavior, 16*(6), 965–968.

Kellendonk, C., Simpson, E. H., & Kandel, E. R. (2009). Modeling cognitive endophenotypes of schizophrenia in mice. *Trends in Neurosciences, 32*(6), 347–358. http://dx.doi.org/10.1016/j.tins.2009.02.003.

Kollias, C. T., Kontaxakis, V. P., Havaki-Kontaxaki, B. J., Stamouli, S., Margariti, M., & Petridou, E. (2008). Association of physical and social anhedonia with depression in the acute phase of schizophrenia. *Psychopathology, 41*(6), 365–370. http://dx.doi.org/10.1159/000152378.

Kraepelin, E. (1919). *Dementia praecox and paraphrenia.* Chicago: Chicago Medical Book Co.

Leff, J. (1990). Depressive symptoms in the course of schizophrenia. In L. E. DeLisi (Ed.), *Depression in Schizophrenia.* Washington, DC: American Psychiatric Press.

Le Pen, G., Gaudet, L., Mortas, P., Mory, R., & Moreau, J.-L. (2002). Deficits in reward sensitivity in a neurodevelopmental rat model of schizophrenia. *Psychopharmacology, 161*(4), 434–441. http://dx.doi.org/10.1007/s00213-002-1092-4.

Le Pen, G., Gourevitch, R., Hazane, F., Hoareau, C., Jay, T. M., Krebs, M.-O., et al. (2006). Peri-pubertal maturation after developmental disturbance: a model for psychosis onset in the rat. *Neuroscience, 143*(2), 395–405. http://dx.doi.org/10.1016/j.neuroscience.2006.08.004.

Lee, P. R., Brady, D. L., Shapiro, R. A., Dorsa, D. M., & Koenig, J. I. (2007). Prenatal stress generates deficits in rat social behavior: reversal by oxytocin. *Brain Research, 1156*, 152–167. http://dx.doi.org/10.1016/j.brainres.2007.04.042.

Lewis, D. A., & Levitt, P. (2002). Schizophrenia as a disorder of neurodevelopment. *Annual Review of Neuroscience, 25*, 409–432. http://dx.doi.org/10.1146/annurev.neuro.25.112701.142754.

Ma, L., Liu, Y., Ky, B., Shughrue, P. J., Austin, C. P., & Morris, J. A. (2002). Cloning and characterization of Disc1, the mouse ortholog of DISC1 (Disrupted-in-Schizophrenia 1). *Genomics, 80*(6), 662–672. http://dx.doi.org/10.1006/geno.2002.7012.

Marcotte, E. R., Pearson, D. M., & Srivastava, L. K. (2001). Animal models of schizophrenia: a critical review. *Journal of Psychiatry and Clinical Neuroscience, 26*(5), 395–410.

Markou, A., & Koob, G. F. (1992). Construct validity of a self-stimulation threshold paradigm: effects of reward and performance manipulations. *Physiology & Behavior, 51*(1), 111–119.

Matrisciano, F., Tueting, P., Dalal, I., Kadriu, B., Grayson, D. R., Davis, J. M., et al. (2013). Epigenetic modifications of GABAergic interneurons are associated with the schizophrenia-like phenotype induced by prenatal stress in mice. *Neuropharmacology, 68*, 184–194. http://dx.doi.org/10.1016/j.neuropharm.2012.04.013.

McArthur, R., & Borsini, F. (2006). Animal models of depression in drug discovery: a historical perspective. *Pharmacology, Biochemistry, and Behavior, 84*(3), 436–452. http://dx.doi.org/10.1016/j.pbb.2006.06.005.

Mei, L., & Xiong, W. (2008). Neuregulin 1 in neural development, synaptic plasticity and schizophrenia. *Nature Reviews Neuroscience, 9*(6), 437–452. http://dx.doi.org/10.1038/nrn2392.Neuregulin.

Meng, Z. H., Feldpaush, D. L., & Merchant, K. M. (1998). Clozapine and haloperidol block the induction of behavioral sensitization to amphetamine and associated genomic responses in rats. *Brain Research. Molecular Brain Research, 61*(1–2), 39–50.

Meyer, U., & Feldon, J. (2010). Epidemiology-driven neurodevelopmental animal models of schizophrenia. *Progress in Neurobiology, 90*(3), 285–326. http://dx.doi.org/10.1016/j.pneurobio.2009.10.018.

Mineur, Y. S., Prasol, D. J., Belzung, C., & Crusio, W. E. (2003). Agonistic behavior and unpredictable chronic mild stress in mice. *Behavior Genetics, 33*(5), 513–519.

Moreau, J. L., Jenck, F., Martin, J. R., Mortas, P., & Haefely, W. E. (1992). Antidepressant treatment prevents chronic unpredictable mild stress-induced anhedonia as assessed by ventral tegmentum self-stimulation behavior in rats. *European Neuropsychopharmacology, 2*, 43–49.

Morrissette, D. A., & Stahl, S. M. (2011). Affective symptoms in schizophrenia. *Drug Discovery Today: Therapeutic Strategies, 8*(1–2), 3–9. http://dx.doi.org/10.1016/j.ddstr.2011.10.005.

Mouri, A., Nagai, T., Ibi, D., & Yamada, K. (2013). Animal models of schizophrenia for molecular and pharmacological intervention and potential candidate molecules. *Neurobiology of Disease, 53*, 61–74. http://dx.doi.org/10.1016/j.nbd.2012.10.025.

Nadler, J. J., Moy, S. S., Dold, G., Trang, D., Simmons, N., Perez, A., et al. (2004). Automated apparatus for quantitation of social approach behaviors in mice. *Genes, Brain, and Behavior, 3*(5), 303–314. http://dx.doi.org/10.1111/j.1601-183X.2004.00071.x.

Nagai, T., Ibi, D., & Yamada, K. (2011). Animal model for schizophrenia that reflects gene-environment interactions. *Biological & Pharmaceutical Bulletin, 34*(9), 1364–1368. http://dx.doi.org/10.1016/j.bbr.2009.04.010.

Nagai, T., Noda, Y., Une, T., Furukawa, K., Furukawa, H., Kan, Q. M., & Nabeshima, T. (2003). Effect of AD-5423 on animal models of schizophrenia: phencyclidine-induced behavioral changes in mice. *Neuroreport, 14*(2), 269–272. http://dx.doi.org/10.1097/00001756-200302100-00023.

Nakatani-Pawlak, A., Yamaguchi, K., Tatsumi, Y., Mizoguchi, H., & Yoneda, Y. (2009). Neonatal phencyclidine treatment in mice induces behavioral, histological and neurochemical abnormalities in adulthood. *Biological & Pharmaceutical Bulletin, 32*(9), 1576–1583.

Neill, J. C., Barnes, S., Cook, S., Grayson, B., Idris, N. F., McLean, S. L., et al. (2010). Animal models of cognitive dysfunction and negative symptoms of schizophrenia: focus on NMDA receptor antagonism. *Pharmacology & Therapeutics, 128*(3), 419–432. http://dx.doi.org/10.1016/j.pharmthera.2010.07.004.

Nielsen, C. K., Arnt, J., & Sánchez, C. (2000). Intracranial self-stimulation and sucrose intake differ as hedonic measures following chronic mild stress: interstrain and interindividual differences. *Behavioural Brain Research, 107*(1–2), 21–33.

Noda, Y., Kamei, H., Mamiya, T., Furukawa, H., & Nabeshima, T. (2000). Repeated phencyclidine treatment induces negative symptom-like behavior in forced swimming test in mice: imbalance of prefrontal serotonergic and dopaminergic functions. *Neuropsychopharmacology, 23*(4), 375–387. http://dx.doi.org/10.1016/S0893-133X(00)00138-X.

Noda, Y., Yamada, K., Furukawa, H., & Nabeshima, T. (1995). Enhancement of immobility in a forced swimming test by subacute or repeated treatment with phencyclidine: a new model of schizophrenia. *British Journal of Pharmacology, 116*(5), 2531–2537.

Nollet, M., Gaillard, P., Tanti, A., Girault, V., Belzung, C., & Leman, S. (2012). Neurogenesis-independent antidepressant-like effects on behavior and stress axis response of a dual orexin receptor antagonist in a rodent model of depression. *Neuropsychopharmacology, 37*(10), 2210–2221. http://dx.doi.org/10.1038/npp.2012.70.

Nollet, M., Le Guisquet, A.-M., & Belzung, C. (June 2013). Models of depression: unpredictable chronic mild stress in mice. *Current Protocols in Pharmacology*. http://dx.doi.org/10.1002/0471141755.ph0565s61 Chapter 5: Unit 5.65.

Orsetti, M., Canonico, P. L., Dellarole, A., Colella, L., Di Brisco, F., & Ghi, P. (2007). Quetiapine prevents anhedonia induced by acute or chronic stress. *Neuropsychopharmacology, 32*(8), 1783–1790. http://dx.doi.org/10.1038/sj.npp.1301291.

O'Tuathaigh, C. M. P., Babovic, D., O'Sullivan, G. J., Clifford, J. J., Tighe, O., Croke, D. T., et al. (2007). Phenotypic characterization of spatial cognition and social behavior in mice with "knockout" of the schizophrenia risk gene neuregulin 1. *Neuroscience, 147*(1), 18–27. http://dx.doi.org/10.1016/j.neuroscience.2007.03.051.

O'Tuathaigh, C. M. P., Kirby, B. P., Moran, P. M., & Waddington, J. L. (2010). Mutant mouse models: genotype-phenotype relationships to negative symptoms in schizophrenia. *Schizophrenia Bulletin, 36*(2), 271–288. http://dx.doi.org/10.1093/schbul/sbp125.

O'Tuathaigh, C. M. P., O'Connor, A.-M., O'Sullivan, G. J., Lai, D., Harvey, R., Croke, D. T., et al. (2008). Disruption to social dyadic interactions but not emotional/anxiety-related behaviour in mice with heterozygous "knockout" of the schizophrenia risk gene neuregulin-1. *Progress in Neuro-Psychopharmacology & Biological Psychiatry, 32*(2), 462–466. http://dx.doi.org/10.1016/j.pnpbp.2007.09.018.

Pascual, R., Zamora-León, S. P., & Valero-Cabré, A. (2006). Effects of postweaning social isolation and re-socialization on the expression of vasoactive intestinal peptide (VIP) and dendritic development in the medial prefrontal cortex of the rat. *Acta Neurobiologiae Experimentalis, 66*(1), 7–14.

Pedersen, C. S., Sørensen, D. B., Parachikova, A. I., & Plath, N. (2014). PCP-induced deficits in murine nest building activity: employment of an ethological rodent behavior to mimic negative-like symptoms of schizophrenia. *Behavioural Brain Research, 273C*, 63–72. http://dx.doi.org/10.1016/j.bbr.2014.07.023.

Pietersen, C. Y., Bosker, F. J., Doorduin, J., Jongsma, M. E., Postema, F., Haas, J. V., et al. (2007). An animal model of emotional blunting in schizophrenia. *PLoS One, 2*(12), e1360. http://dx.doi.org/10.1371/journal.pone.0001360.

I. FROM CLINICAL DIMENSIONS TO ANIMAL MODELS

Pletnikov, M. V., Ayhan, Y., Nikolskaia, O., Xu, Y., Ovanesov, M. V., Huang, H., et al. (2008). Inducible expression of mutant human DISC1 in mice is associated with brain and behavioral abnormalities reminiscent of schizophrenia. *Molecular Psychiatry*, *13*(2), 173–186. http://dx.doi.org/10.1038/sj.mp.4002079 115.

Porkess, M. (2008). *The impact of social isolation on rat behaviour*.

Porsolt, R. D., Anton, G., Blavet, N., & Jalfre, M. (1978). Behavioural despair in rats: a new model sensitive to antidepressant treatments. *European Journal of Pharmacology*, *47*, 379–391.

Pothion, S., Bizot, J.-C., Trovero, F., & Belzung, C. (2004). Strain differences in sucrose preference and in the consequences of unpredictable chronic mild stress. *Behavioural Brain Research*, *155*(1), 135–146. http://dx.doi.org/10.1016/j.bbr.2004.04.008.

Pratt, J., Winchester, C., Dawson, N., & Morris, B. (2012). Advancing schizophrenia drug discovery: optimizing rodent models to bridge the translational gap. *Nature Reviews Drug Discovery*, *11*(7), 560–579. http://dx.doi.org/10.1038/nrd3649.

Rajagopal, L. (2011). *Neonatal phencyclidine (PCP) induced deficits in rats: A behavioural investigation of relevance to schizophrenia*. School of Pharmacy.

Roy, K., Murtie, J. C., El-Khodor, B. F., Edgar, N., Sardi, S. P., Hooks, B. M., et al. (2007). Loss of erbB signaling in oligodendrocytes alters myelin and dopaminergic function, a potential mechanism for neuropsychiatric disorders. *Proceedings of the National Academy of Sciences of the United States of America*, *104*(19), 8131–8136. http://dx.doi.org/10.1073/pnas.0702157104.

Sams-Dodd, F. (1995a). Automation of the social interaction test by a video-tracking system: behavioural effects of repeated phencyclidine treatment. *Journal of Neuroscience Methods*, *59*(2), 157–167.

Sams-Dodd, F. (1995b). Distinct effects of D-amphetamine and phencyclidine on the social behaviour of rats. *Behavioural Pharmacology*. http://dx.doi.org/10.1097/00008877-199501000-00009.

Sams-Dodd, F. (1998). Effects of continuous D-amphetamine and phencyclidine administration on social behaviour, stereotyped behaviour, and locomotor activity in rats. *Neuropsychopharmacology*, *19*(1), 18–25.

Sams-Dodd, F., Lipska, B. K., & Weinberger, D. R. (1997). Neonatal lesions of the rat ventral hippocampus result in hyperlocomotion and deficits in social behaviour in adulthood. *Psychopharmacology*, *132*(3), 303–310.

Sankoorikal, G. M. V., Kaercher, K. A., Boon, C. J., Lee, J. K., & Brodkin, E. S. (2006). A mouse model system for genetic analysis of sociability: C57BL/6J versus BALB/cJ inbred mouse strains. *Biological Psychiatry*, *59*(5), 415–423. http://dx.doi.org/10.1016/j.biopsych.2005.07.026.

Santarelli, L., Saxe, M., Gross, C., Surget, A., Battaglia, F., Dulawa, S., et al. (2003). Requirement of hippocampal neurogenesis for the behavioral effects of antidepressants. *Science*, *301*, 805–809.

Schmelzeis, M. C., & Mittleman, G. (1996). The hippocampus and reward: effects of hippocampal lesions on progressive-ratio responding. *Behavioral Neuroscience*, *110*, 1049–1066. http://dx.doi.org/10.1037/0735-7044.110.5.1049.

Smith, S. E. P., Li, J., Garbett, K., Mirnics, K., & Patterson, P. H. (2007). Maternal immune activation alters fetal brain development through interleukin-6. *Journal of Neuroscience*, *27*(40), 10695–10702. http://dx.doi.org/10.1523/JNEUROSCI.2178-07.2007.

Spielewoy, C., & Markou, A. (2003). Withdrawal from chronic phencyclidine treatment induces long-lasting depression in brain reward function. *Neuropsychopharmacology*, *28*(6), 1106–1116. http://dx.doi.org/10.1038/sj.npp.1300124.

Stefansson, H., & Petursson, H. (2002). Neuregulin 1 and susceptibility to schizophrenia. *American Journal of Human Genetics*, 877–892.

Steru, L., Chermat, R., Thierry, B., & Simon, P. (1985). The tail suspension test: a new method for screening antidepressants in mice. *Psychopharmacology (Berl)*, *85*, 367–370.

Strekalova, T., Spanagel, R., Bartsch, D., Henn, F. A., & Gass, P. (2004). Stress-induced anhedonia in mice is associated with deficits in forced swimming and exploration. *Neuropsychopharmacology*, *29*(11), 2007–2017. http://dx.doi.org/10.1038/sj.npp.1300532.

Sullivan, P. F., Kendler, K. S., & Neale, M. C. (2003). Schizophrenia as a complex trait: evidence from a meta-analysis of twin studies. *Archives of General Psychiatry*, *60*(12), 1187–1192. http://dx.doi.org/10.1001/archpsyc.60.12.1187.

Surget, A., Tanti, A., Leonardo, E. D., Laugeray, A., Rainer, Q., Touma, C., et al. (2011). Antidepressants recruit new neurons to improve stress response regulation. *Molecular Psychiatry*, *16*(12), 1177–1188. http://dx.doi.org/10.1038/mp.2011.48.

Treadway, M. T., & Zald, D. H. (2011). Reconsidering anhedonia in depression: lessons from translational neuroscience. *Neuroscience and Biobehavioral Reviews*, *35*(3), 537–555. http://dx.doi.org/10.1016/j.neubiorev.2010.06.006.

Turgeon, S. M., & Hulick, V. C. (2007). Differential effects of acute and subchronic clozapine and haloperidol on phencyclidine-induced decreases in voluntary sucrose consumption in rats. *Pharmacology, Biochemistry, and Behavior*, *86*(3), 524–530. http://dx.doi.org/10.1016/j.pbb.2007.01.014.

Vardigan, J. D., Huszar, S. L., McNaughton, C. H., Hutson, P. H., & Uslaner, J. M. (2010). MK-801 produces a deficit in sucrose preference that is reversed by clozapine, D-serine, and the metabotropic glutamate 5 receptor positive allosteric modulator CDPPB: relevance to negative symptoms associated with schizophrenia? *Pharmacology, Biochemistry, and Behavior*, *95*(2), 223–229. http://dx.doi.org/10.1016/j.pbb.2010.01.010.

Wang, D., Noda, Y., Zhou, Y., Nitta, A., Furukawa, H., & Nabeshima, T. (2007). Synergistic effect of galantamine with risperidone on impairment of social interaction in phencyclidine-treated mice as a schizophrenic animal model. *Neuropharmacology*, *52*(4), 1179–1187. http://dx.doi.org/10.1016/j.neuropharm.2006.12.007.

Ward, R. D., Simpson, E. H., Richards, V. L., Deo, G., Taylor, K., Glendinning, J. I., et al. (2012). Dissociation of hedonic reaction to reward and incentive motivation in an animal model of the negative symptoms of schizophrenia. *Neuropsychopharmacology*, *37*(7), 1699–1707. http://dx.doi.org/10.1038/npp.2012.15.

Wauquier, A. (1979). International review of neurobiology Volume 21. *International review of neurobiology* (Vol. 21). Elsevier. http://dx.doi.org/10.1016/S0074-7742(08)60643-1 pp. 335–403.

Wiley, J., & Compton, A. (2004). Progressive ratio performance following challenge with antipsychotics, amphetamine, or NMDA antagonists in adult rats treated perinatally with phencyclidine. *Psychopharmacology*, *177*, 170–177. http://dx.doi.org/10.1007/s00213-004-1936-1.Progressive.

Willner, P. (1997). Validity, reliability and utility of the chronic mild stress model of depression: a 10-year review and evaluation. *Psychopharmacology*, *134*(4), 319–329.

Willner, P., Towell, A., Sampson, D., Sophokleous, S., & Muscat, R. (1987). Reduction of sucrose preference by chronic unpredictable mild stress, and its restoration by a tricyclic antidepressant. *Psychopharmacology*, *93*(3), 358–364. http://dx.doi.org/10.1007/BF00187257.

NEUROBIOLOGY OF PSYCHOTIC DISORDERS

Non-Genetic Models

8

Dysregulation of Dopamine Systems in a Developmental Disruption Model of Schizophrenia: Implications for Pathophysiology, Treatment, and Prevention

Sofia M. Dibble, Yijuan Du, Anthony A. Grace

Departments of Neuroscience, Psychiatry and Psychology, University of Pittsburgh, Pittsburgh, PA, USA

Schizophrenia is a complex, uniquely human disorder. Nonetheless, significant insight into the pathophysiology of schizophrenia has been obtained by studying systems that have been shown in imaging and postmortem studies to play a significant role in this disorder. Among these are the dopamine system, the hippocampus, and the prefrontal cortex (Bogerts, 1997; Laurelle, Frankle, Narendran, Kegeles, & Abi-Dargham, 2005; Tan, Callicott, & Weinberger, 2007). However, to best understand the disease process, it is most rigorous to study these systems and their alterations in an animal model of this disease. Although it is clear that a precise model that replicates all features of the human condition is not likely to be produced, studies based on disruption of development, in which an insult occurring early in life sets into motion a series of changes in the brain that ultimately lead to pathology in these systems, have been a promising avenue of investigation. In this chapter, we review the evidence for schizophrenia as a developmental disorder, discuss one of the more powerful models that has been used by us and others to investigate the development of pathophysiological changes that mimic many aspects of schizophrenia in humans, and build upon this model to predict what therapeutic avenues could be employed to address the treatment and ultimately prevention of schizophrenia in susceptible individuals.

SCHIZOPHRENIA AS A NEURODEVELOPMENTAL DISORDER

There are multiple systems that appear pathologically altered in the postmortem brain of schizophrenia patients. However, in contrast to major neurodegenerative diseases such as Parkinson's and Alzheimer's disease in which massive degeneration and abnormal deposits are qualitatively apparent, the brain alterations observed in schizophrenia are more subtle and require quantitative analyses (Bogerts, 1993). Given the obvious limitations of postmortem analysis, it is difficult to pinpoint when these neuroanatomical abnormalities arise, but multiple lines of evidence point to an early neurodevelopmental, rather than a late neurodegenerative, origin of the disease. For instance, reactive gliosis, a hallmark sign of degeneration in the postmortem brain, is essentially absent from schizophrenia postmortem tissue (Arnold, 1999). The first psychotic episode is typically during young adulthood (van der Welf et al., 2014), and furthermore, the cognitive symptoms of schizophrenia can be identified retrospectively to exhibit an onset in childhood (Ambelas, 1992; Fuller et al., 2002). The disease does not progress precipitously after its onset, nor in proportion to neuron loss as in Parkinson's or Alzheimer's disease; instead, the disease is said to have a "critical period" in which positive symptoms manifest but stabilize afterward (Crumlish et al., 2009). Schizophrenia is also associated with gestational abnormalities. Gyri/sulci formations that typically develop in the later trimesters are disrupted in schizophrenia (for review, Bogerts, 1993). Altered placement of neurons in schizophrenia postmortem tissue has been reported and interpreted as disrupted migration in cortical and limbic areas (Akbarian, Bunny, et al., 1993; Akbarian, Viñuela, et al., 1993). Other developmental abnormalities, such as low-set ears, have been reported (Lane et al., 1997). Primary risk factors in individuals who ultimately develop schizophrenia include maternal complications during pregnancy (such as malnutrition, viral infection, or diabetes) or complications during delivery—such as fetal distress or premature membrane rupture (Boog, 2004; Cannon, Jones, & Murray, 2002; O'Callaghan et al., 1992). Finally, several schizophrenia-associated genes play critical roles in normal neurodevelopment; for instance, neuregulin 1 and its receptor tyrosine kinase ErbB4, Disrupted-in-Schizophrenia 1, and Nitric Oxide Synthase 1 Adaptor Protein play critical roles in the radial and/or tangential migration of cortical neurons (Carrel et al., 2014; Kamiya et al., 2005; Mei & Xiong, 2008; Steinecke, Gampe, Valkova, Kaether, & Boltz, 2012).

Altogether, a multifaceted approach in the study of schizophrenia has revealed a multitude of risk factors in the genetic as well as in utero and early life domains. Although the schizophrenic population is certainly heterogeneous with respect to risk factors, these varying risk factors may converge by altering similar neuroanatomical substrates, thereby similarly disrupting brain processes at the systems level. During midgestation, limbic brain regions implicated in schizophrenia are rapidly growing and are especially vulnerable to perturbation by risk factors. This is clearly demonstrated in the methylazoxymethanol (MAM)-17 rodent model described in this chapter, in which a single prenatal disruption leads to a constellation of symptoms consistent with that observed in schizophrenia patients. In this model, embryonic neurogenesis is transiently disrupted on gestational day (GD) 17 via acute administration of the mitotoxin MAM, which leads to aberrant methylation of DNA. We should emphasize to those unfamiliar with this model that accidental MAM exposure is exceedingly rare and therefore is not an environmental factor for the emergence of schizophrenia. Rather, it appears that by producing cytoarchitectural abnormalities in areas such as the hippocampus, MAM-17 treatment engenders schizophrenia-like circuit abnormalities that ultimately give rise to hyperdopaminergia and behavioral deficits. Thus, this model is ideal for exploring the link between altered embryonic neurogenesis and the emergence of a schizophrenia-like phenotype in the adult.

CELLULAR MECHANISMS OF PRENATAL MAM EXPOSURE

Interest in the compound methylazoxymethanol arose in the 1960s as a part of a study of Guam neurodegenerative disease (Matusomo & Strong, 1963). Part of the indigenous diet held suspect were two toxins found in cycad seed flour: BMAA and cycasin (Brimer, 2011; Spencer et al., 1987). When consumed, cycasin (methylazoxymethanol β-D-glucoside) is hydrolyzed into two components: glucose and the aglycone, MAM (Brimer, 2011). Whether Guam neurodegenerative disease is truly caused by cycasin exposure remains controversial (Cox & Sacks, 2002), but the inquiry lead to the discovery and isolation of MAM, the investigation of its cellular effects in different tissues, and, finally, its use as an antiproliferative agent in studying the neurodevelopment of laboratory animals.

Like X-irradiation, MAM administration interferes with neurogenesis. A decrease in the number of hippocampal neurons incorporating bromodeoxyuridine (BrdU), indicative of DNA replication during proliferation, is observed when BrdU and MAM are coadministered on E16 or E17 (Hoareau, Hazane, Le Pen, & Krebs, 2006); even beyond embryogenesis, in the case of adult neurogenesis, MAM treatment dramatically decreases BrdU labeling in the hippocampus (Shors et al., 2001). Although the effects of X-irradiation and MAM are comparable in the brain, MAM has the distinct advantage of preferentially interfering with neurogenesis while sparing peripheral organs and causing few bodily malformations (Rodier, 1986). In vivo administration of MAM induces apoptosis of progenitor cells; for example, administering MAM during the rapid proliferation of cerebellar granule cells within the external granular layer results in apoptosis in this proliferative zone, as inferred by ribosomal degradation and ultrastructural analysis (Lafarga et al., 1997). The selective vulnerability of actively dividing neurons to MAM compared with nondividing neurons and dividing astrocytes has also been observed in vitro (Cattaneo, Reinach, Caputi, Cattabeni, & Di Luca, 1995). Nonetheless, cell degeneration is not restricted to proliferative zones. Signs of degeneration such as chromatin aggregation have been found in cortex 24 h after MAM administration (Bassanini et al., 2007).

The molecular action underlying MAM's antiproliferative effects is DNA guanine methylation at the N^7 and O^6 positions, and both types of adducts contribute to the neurotoxic effects of MAM (for a review, see Kisby, Kabel, Hugon, & Spencer, 1999). The formation of the N^7- and O^6-meG adducts by MAM can be reversed by separate repair mechanisms, involving the enzymes apurinic/apyrimidinic endonuclease and O^6-methylguanine methyltransferase, such that expression levels of these enzymes can dramatically affect repair processes and the longevity of DNA adducts (Gelman et al., 1994; Kisby et al., 2009; Shiraishi, Sakumi, & Sekiguchi, 2000; for a review, see Fu, Calvo, & Samson, 2012). Thus, the surprising paucity of O^6-methylguanine methyltransferase activity in the brain compared with other organs (Kaina, Christmann, Naumann, & Roos, 2007) can explain, at least in part, why the brain is most susceptible to DNA alkylating agents like MAM and why the reversal of O^6-meG adducts is especially inefficient in nervous tissue compared with other organs (Kleihues & Bucheler, 1977).

It is thought that the accumulation of uncorrected O^6-meG adducts makes subsequent cell death more likely; the finding that graded doses (0, 14, 22, and 30 mg/kg) of MAM delivered on GD15 produce graded effects on brain size is consistent with this mechanism (Dambska, Haddad, Kozlowski, Lee, & Shek, 1982). Regarding MAM's antiproliferative effects, dividing cells undergoing DNA replication in S-phase are well positioned to undergo apoptosis when sufficiently burdened by DNA adducts. The mechanistic details underlying this phenomenon are thoroughly described elsewhere (Fu et al., 2012; Noonan, Shah, Yaffe, Lauffenburger, & Samson, 2012), although we summarize briefly here. In a cell undergoing DNA replication in S-phase, uncorrected O^6-meG adducts change the affinity of the associated guanine, resulting in a consistent nucleotide mismatch with thymine; mismatch repair mechanisms deployed during S-phase cannot remedy the mismatch in the usual way since the O^6-meG adducts bind thymine strictly. Ultimately, mismatch repair mechanisms leave nicks and single-strand breaks that will cause problems for the replication machinery and initiate apoptotic signaling should another S-phase be encountered. In this way, cell cycle plays a determinant role in MAM's neurotoxic effects. To summarize the effects of MAM, Rodier (1986) explains that although MAM is not an antimitotic agent in a strict sense (e.g., it does not interfere with mitotic spindle formation), dividing neural precursors has an enhanced vulnerability to MAM and die in its presence rendering MAM a selective antiproliferative agent.

The notion that a threshold level of DNA damage needs to be realized before apoptotic pathways are commenced implies the existence of neurons that survive MAM exposure but remain MAM-compromised. Consistent with this, although an immediate degeneration event is apparent in cortex 2 days after administration (Bassanini et al., 2007), it has been shown that N^7-meG adducts remain detectable in cerebral tissue in the 30-day-old rat after MAM prenatal administration (Kisby et al., 1999); furthermore, the O^6-meG adducts caused by N-nitrosomethylurea, an alkylating agent very similar to MAM, are detectable in brain tissue for at least 180 days following the acute injection and, by extrapolation, the authors estimated that the return to undetectable levels would require one year (Kleihues & Bucheler,

1977). Delivering MAM at GD15, Dambska et al. (1982) observed periventricular nodular heterotopias—abnormal clusters of neurons that failed to migrate from the periventricular region. They also reported other abnormalities as well such as aberrant myelinated bundles, hippocampal ectopias—in which pyramidal neurons are found in nonpyramidal layers, decreases in spine density, and altered morphology. Because direct application of MAM to neurons in vitro causes neurites and axons to retract permanently (Hoffman, Boyne, Levitt, & Fischer, 1996)—that is, the effect outlasts MAM exposure—the neurons with abnormal morphologies and placements could be MAM-compromised.

MAM exposure has additional subtle yet widespread effects on the integrity of the neural tissue. For example, Bassanini et al. (2007) report subdural enlargement and cortical edema that subsided 4 days after injection at GD15, suggesting that inflammatory processes may contribute to the MAM mechanism. In the same study, MAM exposure was found to alter vasculogenesis and angiogenesis, resulting in vessels that were less dense, abnormally branched, and contacted by unusual clusters of neurons. The authors demonstrated that in vitro, MAM inhibits VEGF signaling and angiogenesis directly. These observations imply a sparse exchange of oxygen, nutrients, and metabolites in the cortex as well as vessel-associated growth cues. Potentially contributing to inflammatory responses, MAM administration on PD5 activates cerebellar Bergmann glial cell phagocytosis of injured neuron precursors (Lafarga, Andres, Calle, & Berciano, 1998); furthermore, the cortical density of microglia is increased until adulthood following MAM treatment at GD17 (Ciaroni, Buffi, Ambrogini, Cecchini, & Del Grande, 1996). Thus, apart from its antiproliferative effects, there are several known avenues by which MAM may alter the milieu of expanding structures: impairing blood flow and the associated nutrient–waste exchange, transient edema, and increases in glial density and activity.

EFFECTS OF PRENATAL MAM EXPOSURE ON CORTICAL DEVELOPMENT

Because a slight change in the time point of MAM administration (e.g., E14 vs E15) can determine, with high reliability, what structures are affected (e.g., disruption of particular cortical layers), MAM's neurotoxic effects are assumed to occur within a short time frame (Cattabeni & Di Luca, 1997). A recent study reported a longer-than-expected MAM half-life of 32 h in the fetal brain following an in utero injection of MAM acetate (Bassanini et al., 2007); however, it is unclear how low MAM concentrations must drop before its antiproliferative actions cease; in fact, MAM has a steep dose–response curve: at 12 mg/kg MAM has no effect, whereas it is lethal at 25 mg/kg (Rodier, 1986). Regardless, MAM's temporal precision is sufficient in producing qualitatively different neuroanatomical and behavioral effects at different stages of embryogenesis, making it a valuable tool in the studying the timetable of brain development.

MAM exerts its maximal effects on cerebral cortex on GD14 and 15, when neurogenesis of cortical neurons is greatest; this results in dramatic microcephaly and a dramatic imbalance between the major neurotransmitters (glutamate and gamma-aminobutyric acid (GABA)) and neuromodulators (dopamine, norepinephrine, serotonin; Johnston, Grzanna, & Coyle, 1979; Jonsson & Hallman, 1981; Rodier, 1986). Venturing to generate a brain with more moderate hyperdopaminergia and fewer global abnormalities, Moore et al. (2006) compared the effects of MAM administration (22 mg/kg, intraperitoneal) on GD15 and GD17, with the prediction that administration at the later time point would not disturb peak corticogenesis occurring at GD 14–15, making reductions in brain size less severe. Indeed, MAM-17 treatment produced brains with more subtle volume reductions, affecting chiefly limbic cortical areas (medial prefrontal cortex (mPFC), hippocampus, and parahippocampus) and mediodorsal thalamus without affecting sensorimotor areas or cerebellum (Moore, Jentsch, Ghajarnia, Geyer, & Grace, 2006). The mPFC, nucleus accumbens, and hippocampus were approximately 20% less massive in MAM-17 rats than controls (Moore et al., 2006), and the reductions in hippocampal mass and volume have also been reported by others (Chin et al., 2011; Featherstone, Rizos, Nobrega, Kapur, & Fletcher, 2007). Thinning of cortices was associated with increased cell packing, indicating a loss of neuropil (Moore et al., 2006), although unusual dispersion of neurons has been reported for entorhinal, perirhinal, and retrosplenial cortices (Gourevitch, Rocher, Le Pen, Krebs, & Jay, 2004). Pyramidal cells are more diffuse and disorganized (Flagstad et al., 2004; Gourevitch et al., 2004; Moore et al., 2006). Enlargement of lateral and third ventricles, a recognized feature in schizophrenia patients (Mueser & McGurk, 2004), is also reported in MAM rats when a larger dose is administered on GD17; this larger dose (25 mg/kg) also makes the hippocampal-specific ablations qualitatively obvious (Chin et al., 2011; Le Pen et al., 2006).

These limbic abnormalities induced by a prenatal insult resemble those observed in schizophrenia. The human ventromedial temporal lobe (hippocampus, amygdala, and the parahippocampal gyrus) and its major cortical target, the heteromodal association cortex—including the dorsolateral prefrontal cortex (DLPFC)—are abnormal in schizophrenia, and abnormalities tend to be greater in the left hemisphere, perhaps predisposing left-side language centers to aberrant activation during auditory hallucinations (Bogerts, 1997). One of the most robust findings in schizophrenia patients is reduced *hippocampal* volume (~5%) both in magnetic resonance imaging and postmortem studies as well as reduced volume of cortical targets of hippocampal projections (Bogerts, 1997; Heckers & Konradi, 2002; Steen, Mull, McClure, Hamer, & Lieberman, 2006); smaller neuron size has also been reported (Benes et al., 1991). A wide array of neurochemical abnormalities has been found in postmortem hippocampal tissue; proteins important in glutamatergic, GABAergic, and neuromodulatory signaling and synapse maintenance have all been implicated (Lisman et al., 2008). There is also evidence for functional deviations in the hippocampus: the comorbidity of temporal lobe epilepsy with schizophrenia has been an important clue in associating hippocampal hyperactivity with psychosis (Harrison, 2004); basal hippocampal blood flow (Tamminga, Stan, & Wagner, 2010), and metabolism (Medoff, Holcomb, Lahti, & Tamminga, 2001) are elevated in schizophrenia; furthermore, hippocampal Blood Oxygenation Level Dependent (BOLD) response is reduced during a variety of cognitive tasks among schizophrenic patients, is not properly recruited by saccadic eye movements, and responds differentially to drugs like nicotine (Tamminga et al., 2010).

In addition, functional imaging work has brought cortical, especially prefrontal, abnormalities to the forefront of schizophrenia research. In particular, DLPFC dysfunction has been correlated with cognitive symptoms and is a predictor of long-term outcome (Winterer & Weinberger, 2004). The obvious strength of this technique, the ability to probe diverse cognitive processes in real time, is a double-edged sword because the diversity of tasks employed has generated conflicting results. Nonetheless, a pattern is emerging: when asked to perform prefrontal-dependent cognitive tasks *beyond* their abilities resulting in poor performance, schizophrenia patients fail to recruit prefrontal cortex to the same extent as controls; cognitive tasks that are difficult but *doable* for this population tend to activate the prefrontal cortex more than healthy controls, suggesting that cognitive processing in the DLPFC is "inefficient" among schizophrenics (Weinberger & Berman, 1996). Genetic screens and postmortem analyses have also implicated prefrontal cortex in schizophrenia. For example, there is evidence for reduced dopamine neuromodulation in prefrontal cortex, and a deficient D1:D2 receptor ratio has been proposed; if D1 receptors do facilitate working memory by enhancing the formation of stable, persistently active ensembles, then a decreased D1:D2 ratio may contribute to working memory impairments (Winterer & Weinberger, 2004); this is consistent with hypotheses of prefrontal dopaminergic abnormalities that arose from animal studies. Atrophy in the DLPFC has also been observed, in terms of soma size, dendritic lengths, spine densities, and terminal marker proteins (Volk & Lewis, 2010).

Although it is clear now that the hippocampus and DLPFC are involved in schizophrenia, identifying specific cell types or microcircuits that drive pathological symptoms is an ongoing endeavor. There is increasing evidence that interneuron dysfunction drives both prefrontal and hippocampal pathology in schizophrenia. A decrease in the density of nonpyramidal, but not pyramidal, neurons has been found in CA2 (Benes, Kwok, Vincent, & Todtenkopf, 1998); Zhang and Reynolds (2002) compared the hippocampal densities of parvalbumin, calretinin, and calbindin interneurons and found a decrease in the parvalbumin populations in schizophrenia patients across all subfields. In parallel, magnetic resonance imaging studies parsing pyramidal and nonpyramidal changes found reductions in the volume of hippocampal white matter (strata oriens, radiatum, lacunosum-moleculare), but not the pyramidal layer, have been shown to drive the total volume reduction (Heckers & Konradi, 2002). In *neocortex*, layer-specific decreases in nonpyramidal neurons of the anterior cingulate and prefrontal cortex have been reported, but attempts to show changes in density of specific interneuron subtypes has yielded mixed results (Benes & Berretta, 2001). It has been suggested that DLPFC parvalbumin-containing neurons are hypofunctional in schizophrenia because they contain lower GAD67 messenger RNA levels (Lewis, Hashimoto, & Volk, 2005). Because it is well established that parvalbumin interneurons in cortical areas are fast-spikers that contribute to gamma oscillations (Buszaki & Wang, 2012), parvalbumin hypofunction may give rise to reductions in evoked gamma oscillations during cognitive tasks (Lewis et al., 2005).

Given that parvalbumin interneurons are implicated in schizophrenia, immunohistochemical analyses of MAM-17 brain tissue was performed, revealing a decreased density of parvalbumin-positive interneurons in the adult MAM-17 ventral (but not dorsal) hippocampus, mPFC, and anterior cingulate; furthermore, the decrease in parvalbumin staining correlated with fear-evoked gamma in these regions (Lodge, Behrens, & Grace, 2009). Using a larger dose at GD17, Penschuck et al. (2006) observed decreased hippocampal staining for parvalbumin (but not calretinin or calbindin) in the dorsal hippocampus and found no change in mPFC. The larger dose may explain discrepancies in dorsal hippocampus, but reason for the mPFC discrepancy is unclear. Given the activity-dependence of parvalbumin expression, these studies do not address whether the reduction in parvalbumin staining reflects a change in protein expression or a loss of the interneurons that typically express parvalbumin. Taking advantage of the fact that parvalbumin-containing interneurons also express substance P receptors constitutively, Gill and Grace

(2014) determined that there were fewer of the substance P-expressing *cell type* in the ventral dentate as early as PN27 but there appeared to be a loss of parvalbumin *content* in the dorsal dentate and dorsal/ventral CA3 fields. Whether this ventral dentate loss is attributed to a disruption of parvalbumin-containing interneurons' proliferation or migration to the hippocampus during embryogenesis, to necrosis or apoptosis of hippocampal parvalbumin interneurons at a later time as suggested by the oxidative stress models (Steullet et al., 2010), to impaired adult neurogenesis or a combination of these events remains unresolved. For instance, although it is true that MAM-17 treatment reduces gestational neurogenesis (Hoareau et al., 2006), the identity of the affected cell types remains unknown. Notably, parvalbumin-staining increases during adolescence in both the hippocampus and prefrontal cortex of normal rats (Caballero, Diah, & Tseng, 2013), but this increase in hippocampal parvalbumin protein levels across postnatal development is blunted in MAM rats, beginning as early as PN25 and lasting through adulthood (Chen, Perez, & Lodge, 2014).

SUBCORTICAL HYPERDOPAMINERGIA IN MAM: BEHAVIORAL CORRELATES, DIRECT MEASURES, AND HIPPOCAMPAL INVOLVEMENT

Although dopamine abnormalities do not account for all symptoms of schizophrenia, there is abundant, long-standing evidence that subcortical hyperdopaminergia is highly correlated with psychosis (Howes & Kapur, 2009). Psychostimulants that artificially elevate dopaminergic signaling cause psychosis in healthy subjects and furthermore, acute, low-dose psychostimulant exposure that is insufficient to induce psychotic symptoms in healthy subjects has been shown to exacerbate psychosis in schizophrenia patients, suggesting that active endogenous dopaminergic activity and psychostimulant-induced dopaminergic activity can have an additive effect in schizophrenia (Lieberman, Kinon, & Loebel, 1990). Studies employing the radiolabeled dopamine precursors [^{11}C]-L-dopa and 6-[^{18}F]-dopa to measure synthesis and storage of presynaptic dopamine indicate greater dopamine synthesis in psychotic schizophrenic patients (reviewed in Howes & Kapur, 2009). Schizophrenic patients, compared with healthy controls, also show an increase in baseline extracellular dopamine as measured by D_2 receptor radioligand displacement (Abi-Dargham et al., 2000). Using the same method, psychostimulant-induced increases in positive symptoms is associated with enhanced mesolimbic dopamine release; moreover, response to challenge is correlated with the phase of illness, being pronounced at onset and relapse phases but not remission (Laruelle & Abi-Dargham, 1999).

Similarly, a significant feature of MAM-17 rats is their heightened locomotor responses to psychostimulants such as phencyclidine (Moore et al., 2006; Penschuck, Flagstad, Didriksen, Leist, & Michael-Titus, 2006), amphetamine (Flagstad et al., 2004; Moore et al., 2006), MK-801 (Le Pen, Jay, & Krebs, 2011), and ketamine (Phillips, Cotel, et al., 2012). The enhanced response to amphetamine among MAM-17 rats corresponds to an increase in amphetamine-evoked dopamine efflux in the nucleus accumbens, whereas, in contrast, basal dopamine levels appear either normal or decreased (Flagstad et al., 2004).

A reasonable hypothesis stemming from these microdialysis results is that baseline dopamine activity is intact or diminished in the MAM-17 model, whereas stimulant/stimulus-induced dopamine activity is exaggerated. Dopamine neurons do exhibit two distinct firing patterns: when not in a hyperpolarized state of quiescence, dopamine neurons can fire tonically (single spikes at irregular intervals) or phasically (in bursts), the latter of which is thought to be a neural correlate of salient stimuli (reviewed in Grace, Floresco, Goto, & Lodge, 2007). However, the hypothesis that tonic activity does not contribute to amphetamine-induced dopamine efflux was not supported by further testing. Floresco, West, Ash, Moore, and Grace (2003) observed that distinct afferents to the ventral tegmental area (VTA) could be manipulated to independently alter tonic and phasic firing. In one manipulation, VTA dopaminergic neurons were transitioned from quiescence to tonic firing by inactivating inhibitory ventral pallidal inputs. In a second manipulation, dopaminergic neurons were transitioned from tonic firing to phasic firing by activating the pedunculopontine tegmentum. Surprisingly, the first manipulation evoked greater dialysate dopamine than the second, emphasizing the contribution that tonic firing can have to the amphetamine response (Floresco et al., 2003).

We now know that MAM-17 animals exhibit an increase in tonic dopaminergic neuron firing. In the normal anesthetized (Grace et al., 2007) or awake (Freeman, Meltzer, & Bunney, 1985) rat, it is estimated that about 50% of dopaminergic neurons are in the hyperpolarized, quiescent state. In contrast, the number of active neurons in the MAM-17 animal is roughly twice that of controls, so that nearly all dopaminergic neurons are spontaneously active (Lodge & Grace, 2007). This has been directly measured in anesthetized MAM-17 rats by lowering glass electrodes nine times through the VTA in a preset pattern and counting the number of active dopamine neurons encountered; in this preparation, dopamine neurons can be estimated with 90% accuracy based on waveform and firing characteristics

(Ungless & Grace, 2012). By driving GABAergic projections from the accumbens to the ventral pallidum, the ventral hippocampus (vHPC) can inhibit the ventral pallidum, thereby disinhibiting dopaminergic neurons and increasing tonic firing in the VTA (Floresco, Todd, & Grace, 2001; Floresco et al., 2003). Activating vHPC of SAL-17 animals increases the number of spontaneously active neurons in the VTA but has no effect in MAM-17 animals, presumably because of a ceiling effect; on the other hand, tetrodotoxin (TTX) inactivation of the vHPC normalizes the number of spontaneously active neurons in the VTA in MAM-17 animals but has no effect in saline controls (Lodge & Grace, 2007), suggesting that the vHPC contributes substantially more to baseline dopaminergic activity in MAM-17 than in saline animals.

What is the function of tonic dopamine neuron firing? Studies show that when an organism is exposed to a behaviorally salient stimulus, there is an activation of burst firing of dopamine neurons (Schultz, 1998). This is driven by the pedunculopontine tegmentum (PPTg); a region known to show activation to conditioned stimuli (Pan & Hyland, 2005). However, for a dopamine neuron to burst-fire in response to glutamatergic input, it must be already depolarized and tonically firing; otherwise, there is a magnesium block of the N-methyl-D-aspartate receptor (NMDA) channel and no change in dopamine neuron state occurs (Grace et al., 2007). Thus, the fraction of dopamine neurons that are in a depolarized, tonic firing state before PPTg activation determines the extent of burst-firing on the population level upon activation (Figure 1). If PPTg-driven burst-firing is the behaviorally salient signal of the dopamine system, then the amplitude of this signal depends on the number of dopamine neurons engaged in tonic firing, with more firing neurons producing a larger phasic response (Lodge & Grace, 2006). In the case of the MAM-17 rat and presumably the schizophrenia patient, an increase in the number of dopamine neurons firing would render the system hyperresponsive to stimuli, potentially leading to a state of aberrant salience (Kapur, 2003). Indeed, the increase in fluorodopa uptake in the striatum of schizophrenia patients (reviewed in Howes & Kapur, 2009), which is indicative of increased number of active terminals, is consistent with the increase in tonic dopamine neuron firing observed in the MAM-17 rat.

Excessive hippocampal drive of the dopamine system observed in MAM-17 is consistent with data from schizophrenia patients. For instance, psychosis is correlated with hyperactivity in the limbic hippocampus (Medoff et al., 2001; Molina et al., 2003; Schobel et al., 2009). Among ultra-high-risk individuals, increased presynaptic indices of dopaminergic function correlated with alterations in hippocampal glutamate levels (Stone et al., 2010). Last, excessive hippocampal drive is consistent with the loss of parvalbumin interneurons in the

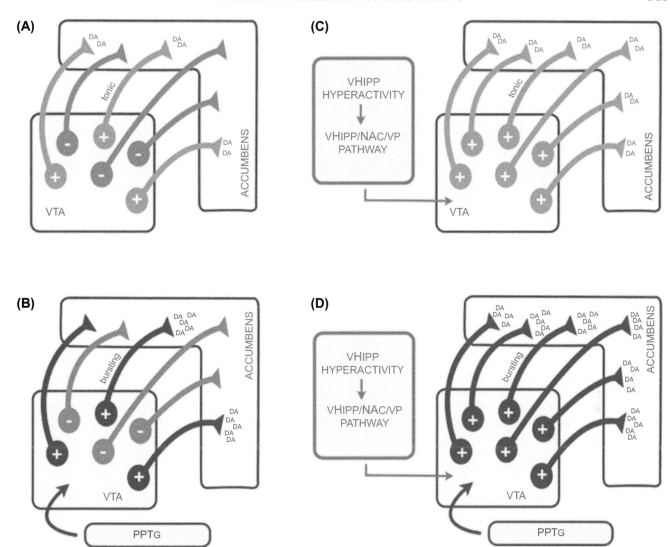

FIGURE 1 A hyperpolarized (−) dopamine neuron is quiescent (depicted in gray), but when depolarized (+), it can fire either in tonic mode (brown) or in phasic mode (red). (A) In an unaroused state, about 50% of dopamine neurons are tonic firing while the rest are quiescent. (B) When an arousing sensory stimulus activates ascending glutamatergic afferents to ventral tegmental area (VTA) (here, pedunculopontine tegmentum, PPTg), already depolarized VTA neurons will transition to a bursting state in an N-methyl-ᴅ-aspartate receptor–dependent manner, increasing synaptic dopamine release. (C) In the MAM-17 animal, the number of dopamine neurons firing in tonic mode is increased. This is due to hippocampal hyperactivity, which activates accumbens (NAc) neurons, inhibiting ventral pallidal (VP) neurons, thereby disinhibiting dopaminergic neurons, and releasing them from a quiescent state. (D) Having a greater number of tonically active dopamine neurons at baseline means that more neurons can burst fire in response to ascending activation, resulting in augmented dopamine efflux.

MAM-17 animals (Lodge et al., 2009; Penschuck et al., 2006), similar to the postmortem observations in schizophrenia brains (Zhang & Reynolds, 2002).

PRODROMAL HYPERSENSITIVITY TO STRESS IN MAM-17

Psychological stress has long believed to be a risk factor in the onset and development of multiple psychiatric disorders, including schizophrenia. Schizophrenia subjects may not necessarily experience more traumatic life events but feel life events as being more uncontrollable

and intolerable (Thompson, Pogue-Geile, & Grace, 2004; van Winkel, Stefanis, & Myin-Germeys, 2008). This is consistent with reports of elevated basal cortisol and impaired dexamethasone suppression among schizophrenic patients (for a review, Walker & Diforio, 1997). In accordance with this model, MAM rats are more vulnerable to stress exposure. Following saline injection, a mildly stressful event, these rats exhibit a greater increase in locomotor activity (Flagstad et al., 2004; Le Pen et al., 2006). In addition, stress has a greater impact on their synaptic plasticity; minor levels of stress exposure impair hippocampal-mPFC long-term potentiation in MAM rats but not in controls (Goto & Grace, 2006).

Given the putative influence of stress on disease onset, it is natural to examine the effects of stress in the prodromal phase, a critical period in the disease that has been the focus of many studies over the past decade. High-risk individuals for schizophrenia can be identified based on genetic background, family history, and structured interviews that reliably evaluate psychosis risk, including the Structured Interview for Psychosis Risk Syndromes (Miller et al., 2003) and the Comprehensive Assessment of At-Risk Mental States (Miller et al., 2003; Straub & Weinberger, 2006; Sullivan, Kendler, & Neale, 2003; Yung et al., 2005). Among individuals identified as at-risk for schizophrenia, measures of situational anxiety, emotion and affect, and tolerance to stress are predictive of psychosis onset (Owens, Miller, Lawrie, & Johnstone, 2005; Yung et al., 2005). In the prodromal phase, altered cortisol levels are associated with "subthreshold" levels of paranoid suspicion (Corcoran et al., 2012) and conceptual disorganization (Devylder et al., 2013).

In MAM-17 rats, hypersensitivity to stress is also observed before the emergence of behavioral hyper-responsivity to psychostimulants. Prepubertal MAM-17 rats exhibit a higher level of anxiety as measured in an elevated plus maze (Du & Grace, 2013). They emit a greater than 22 kHz vocalization, which reflects affective state, following foot shock and exhibit more freezing behavior (Zimmerman, Bellaire, Ewing, & Grace, 2013). In addition, plasma corticosterone levels in response to foot shock exposure are blunted (Zimmerman et al., 2013). This is significant, given that a substantial corticosterone response is necessary for adaptation to stressors (McEwen & Gianaros, 2010; Rao, Anilkumar, McEwen, & Chattarji, 2012).

These observations are consistent with abnormalities in vHPC function. In addition to its role in hyperdopaminergia, the vHPC is involved in emotional processing. Unlike the dorsal aspect, vHPC is dispensable for spatial memory tasks such as the Morris water maze, but lesions interfere with fear conditioning to a tone and decrease anxiety-like behavior in the elevated plus maze (Fanselow & Dong, 2010). Importantly, its activation curtails both stressor-induced and circadian corticosteroid elevations (Herman & Mueller, 2006). In response to a stressor, autonomic nervous system responses and the hypothalamic–pituitary–adrenal axis response are triggered by the hypothalamic paraventricular nucleus; in turn, the vHPC extends glutamatergic projections to the bed nucleus of the stria terminalis and multiple hypothalamic nuclei that inhibit the paraventricular nucleus (Ulrich-Lai & Herman, 2009). The vHPC is also laden with glucocorticoid receptors and is thus fully equipped to provide feedback inhibition on the hypothalamic–pituitary–adrenal axis (Herman & Mueller, 2006). Altogether, the blunted corticosteroid response reported in MAM-17 rats is consistent with a hyperactive hippocampus

(Zimmerman et al., 2013). Furthermore, activation of dentate parvalbumin neurons is implicated in exercise-induced resilience toward aversive, stressful events in normal mice, and enhancement of inhibitory processes in vHPC artificially creates resilience (Schoenfeld, Rada, Pieruzzini, Hsueh, & Gould, 2013), such that the loss of these neurons in MAM-17 may reasonably contribute to their hypersensitivity to stress.

Thus, the vHPC may be a critical locus where stress-related circuitry can contribute to MAM-17 hyperdopaminergic phenotype. Testing the hypothesis that stress can induce hyperdopaminergia via the vHPC, Valenti, Lodge, and Grace (2011) demonstrated that acute restraint, a psychogenic stressor that induces c-fos expression in mPFC and ventral (but not dorsal) hippocampus, also increases spontaneous activity of dopaminergic VTA neurons. The authors also found stress to increase AMPH-induced locomotion, and both the increases in dopaminergic activity and locomotion were reversed by TTX inactivation of vHPC.

Finally, addressing the contribution of stress to the adolescent onset of the MAM-17 behavioral phenotype, Du and Grace (2013) found that administering the antianxiety drug diazepam to alleviate stress hypersensitivity in peripubertal MAM-17 rats prevented the development of hyperactivity of VTA dopamine neurons and hypersensitivity to amphetamine in adulthood. Altogether, these results support the application of the two-hit hypothesis to the MAM-17 model, in which the coincidence of MAM-17 neuroanatomical alterations (say, parvalbumin neuron dysfunction) and stressors are required for the emergence of hyperdopaminergia. However, the emergence of hyperdopaminergia appears to be a gradual, not step-function, process. VTA recordings in anesthetized MAM-17 rats indicate that a hyperdopaminergic state is present even during preadolescence; hypersensitivity between preadolescent MAM-17 and SAL-17 can be observed with high doses of amphetamine (Chen et al., 2014). Thus, one should bear in mind that defining the onset of a phenotype does depend on how that phenotype tested, both in animal models and the clinic.

SENSORIMOTOR GATING DEFICITS IN MAM-17

An abrupt, salient stimulus (such as an intense light, touch, or loud sound) causes a reflexive muscle contraction, referred to as the "startle response." This is measured as an eye-blink response in humans and a whole-body flinch in rodents (Braff, 2010). The startle response is neurologically a reflex; auditory, tactile, and vestibular sensory signals are routed through sensory pathways to the caudal portion of the pontine reticular nucleus, which in turn commands motoneurons that elicit the startle (reviewed in Fendt, Li, & Yeomans, 2001). If the startle stimulus is immediately preceded (30–500 ms prior) by a less-salient stimulus (termed a "prepulse"), the startle response is attenuated—an effect termed prepulse inhibition (PPI). Lesion studies have identified brain areas that do not participate in the startle response but do modulate PPI, indicating that the reflexive startle pathway is extrinsically gated (Fendt et al., 2001; Swerdlow, Geyer, & Braff, 2001).

PPI disruptions in schizophrenia patients were first reported in the late 1970s. In contrast to the higher order deficits reported in schizophrenia patients, PPI deficits are remarkably robust in unmedicated schizophrenia patients across the spectrum and in their nonafflicted relatives, making PPI deficits especially tractable for study (Braff, 2010). Furthermore, although individuals adapt their startle responses across multiple presentations, PPI does not adapt readily, allowing repeated testing in the same individual (Braff, 2010). Although there is no evidence that PPI deficits themselves contribute to clinical symptoms, PPI is correlated with positive symptoms (Perry & Braff, 1994) and is normalized most reliably by atypical antipsychotics (Kumari & Sharma, 2002). Altogether, PPI deficits seem to reflect alterations in the neural systems that also underlie positive symptoms.

Unlike thought disorder and psychosis, PPI can be studied in lower mammals. In this endeavor, it has been repeatedly shown that amphetamine and dopamine receptor agonists can induce PPI deficits, similar to the human case. A vast array of higher ordered brain areas—including mPFC, hippocampus, amygdala, nucleus accumbens, mediodorsal thalamus—have also been shown to be capable of influencing PPI (Swerdlow et al., 2001), and it has been suggested that the normally functioning basal ganglia, via the substantia nigra pars reticulata—its GABAergic output region—may inhibit pontine reticular nucleus following a prepulse (Koch, Fendt, & Kretschmer, 2000). Especially in light of increasing evidence of PPI deficits in psychiatric disorders other than schizophrenia (Kohl, Heekeren, Klosterkotter, & Kuhn, 2013), PPI deficits may be a common result of multiple basal ganglia-related abnormalities.

MAM-17 animals show adolescent-onset PPI deficits (Hazane, Krebs, Jay, & Le Pen, 2009; Moore et al., 2006), consistent with the hyperdopaminergia. Although we have emphasized aberrant hippocampal regulation of dopamine in MAM-17 animals, hippocampal contributions to PPI may be more complex and may involve other neuromodulators or other brain structures such as amygdala. Activation of the vHPC with infusions of NMDA, picrotoxin, or carbachol generates PPI deficits, but so does inactivation by TTX and muscimol (reviewed in Bast & Feldon, 2003). Clozapine (but not haloperidol) reverses PPI deficits in rats with vHPC NMDA microinfusions (Zhang, Pouzet, Jongen-Rêlo, Weiner, & Feldon,

1999) despite the fact that haloperidol can counter the dopamine efflux elicited by this manipulation. Nonetheless, given that haloperidol's effects diametrically differ between MAM-17 animals and those allowed to develop normally (Valenti, Cifelli, Gill, & Grace, 2011), it remains possible that haloperidol may be effective in reversing PPI deficits in the MAM-17 model—but this awaits experimental testing.

DEFICITS IN PREFRONTAL-DEPENDENT BEHAVIORS AND ABERRANT PREFRONTAL ACTIVITY

Impairments in both declarative and working memory are psychological features of schizophrenia, and some forms are dependent on prefrontal function (Tamminga et al., 2010; Tan et al., 2007). Similar impairments have been observed in MAM-17 animals. In the rat, the hippocampus is well known to encode place information essential for navigation and foraging. Although hippocampal–accumbens connectivity is sufficient for exploratory foraging behavior, hippocampal–prefrontal connectivity is critical for successful foraging guided by short-term memory (Floresco, Seamans, & Phillips, 1997). The delay-interposed radial maze learning task is used to test memory-guided foraging. In this task, all arms are baited but some arms of the maze are blocked during the animal's initial exploration; after a delay during which the blockades are removed, animals are placed again into the maze and are expected to visit the novel, still-baited arms. Compared with controls, MAM-17 rats perform poorly with a 30-min, but not 5-min delay interposed, which is consistent with the poorer performance of schizophrenia patients with heavy working memory load (Gourevitch et al., 2004). The spontaneous alternation test is a well-established spatial working test that measures the tendency of an animal to explore an entire radial maze with optimal efficiency and has been shown to also require an intact PFC and hippocampus (Lalonde, 2002). MAM-17 rats were less likely to alternate between arms, suggesting deficits in spatial working memory (Hazane et al., 2009). However, in this same study, MAM-17 rats also showed impaired Morris water maze performance, indicating that impairments in spatial learning may also play a role in these deficits.

Behavioral flexibility is also mediated by the rodent prefrontal cortex and is limited in MAM-17 animals, further implicating prefrontal malfunction (Ragozzino, 2007). For instance, although the initial associational learning is not impaired, MAM-17 rats require a greater number of trials to switch strategies in a y-maze task as well as in extradimensional set-shifting (Featherstone et al., 2007; Moore et al., 2006) in which attention must be shifted to previously ignored attributes of the presented stimuli. This task was designed as the rodent analogue to the Wisconsin card-sorting task, in which schizophrenia patients fail to use feedback to shift attention between suit and value between two card decks. Impairment of MAM-17 rats in reversal learning has also been reported in a water maze task (Flagstad et al., 2005). These deficits in extradimensional set shifting and reversal learning are due to a perseverative behavior (Gastambide et al., 2012).

In contrast, purely attention deficits can be measured using the five-choice serial reaction time task, where the animal must maintain attention across five LEDs and nose-poke at the appropriate port when the associated LED activates. Featherstone et al. (2007) used this paradigm as the rodent analogue to the Continuous Performance Task, in which human participants must respond to each stimulus presentation with a key press. In both versions, omitted trials are interpreted as failures in sustaining attention. Schizophrenia patients show Continuous Performance Task impairments, suggesting deficits in attentional vigilance. Notably, the intensity of the stimulus can influence the results, such that ambiguous stimuli that require more deliberate attention to resolve are typically better for detecting differences between schizophrenic patients and controls. MAM-17 animals are capable of sustained attention—as measured by response accuracy and omissions—in the five-choice serial reaction time task even when stimuli flicker very briefly. Although attention appears intact, MAM-17 animals demonstrated more impulsive-like premature responding (Featherstone et al., 2007) in this paradigm. The behavioral inhibition that occurs when an animal bears in mind an intention to act during a delay period but must wait to execute the action is thought to be mediated by prefrontal cortex. This executive behavioral inhibition can be measured in a task in which subjects are rewarded only when their response rate is sufficiently slow; MAM-17 animals are impaired in this task (Featherstone et al., 2007).

In the MAM-17 prefrontal cortex, there is electrophysiological evidence of alterations in local circuitry that could give rise to aberrant activity. For example, the ability of basolateral amygdala stimulation and hippocampal stimulation to recruit inhibitory processes in the mPFC is attenuated and enhanced, respectively, in MAM-17 animals, suggesting that MAM-17 treatment alters the strength of afferent inputs to mPFC (Esmaeli & Grace, 2013). Phencyclidine, an NMDA receptor antagonist that can preferentially obstruct interneuron activation, also disturbs amygdalar recruitment of inhibitory processes when given to normal animals, mimicking the effects of MAM-17 treatment (Esmaeli & Grace, 2013); this suggests that hypofunction of the interneuron class that the amygdala innervates (Gabbott, Warner, & Busby, 2006) may mediate the changes observed in MAM-17

rats (Esmaeli & Grace, 2013). Dopamine neuromodulation in the mPFC is also altered by MAM-17 exposure; VTA stimulation has opposite short-latency effects on mPFC neuron depolarization in MAM-17 and SAL-17 animals, with VTA stimulation producing long-lasting depolarizations in MAM-17 rats only (Lavin, Moore, & Grace, 2005). MAM-17 animals also exhibit increases in psychostimulant-induced norepinephrine release in the prefrontal cortex (Lena, Chessel, Le Pen, Krebs, & Garcia, 2007).

The normal gating mechanisms that regulate prefrontal activity are disrupted in MAM-17. Because these gating mechanisms are theorized to gate afferent input based on contextual relevance (Tseng & O'Donnell, 2005), their disruption in MAM-17 animals likely contributes their cognitive impairments mentioned above as well as impairments in hippocampal-dependent fear conditioning (Lodge, Behrens, & Grace, 2009). Normally, cortical and striatal neurons exhibit a bistable resting membrane potential in vivo, alternating between a DOWN state (a lower membrane potential) and an UP state (a higher membrane potential), where the difference between these two states is approximately 8–22 mV (Lewis & O'Donnell, 2000; O'Donnell & Grace, 1995). During DOWN states, neurons are markedly less excitable than in UP states, such that spiking is confined to the UP states. Thus, any afferent input endowed with the ability to modulate the DOWN-to-UP state transition will be able to designate which neural ensembles are excitable at a given time. For example, in the accumbens, the hippocampal input has this unique ability (O'Donnell & Grace, 1995). In the prefrontal cortex, bistability occurs spontaneously but VTA "burst" stimulation can evoke UP states in most neurons (Lewis & O'Donnell, 2000). In the MAM-17 rat, PFC and NAc neurons tend to exist in a sustained (monostable) depolarized state (Moore et al., 2006), consistent with hippocampal hyperactivity and hyperdopaminergia in these animals. As a consequence, prefrontal neurons exhibit higher spontaneous firing rates (Lavin et al., 2005) and less time-variant firing patterns (Goto & Grace, 2006), functional gating is lost and the system is poised to respond to a number of stimuli in an unfiltered manner (Moore et al., 2006).

FUNCTIONAL DISCONNECTION WITHIN LIMBIC CIRCUITS

Disconnection theories of schizophrenia emphasize that prefrontal cortex interacts with other brain areas in a hierarchical manner and it is the disruption of these interactions that leads to impaired mental function. One method of probing interactions across brain areas is to stimulate in one region and record in another in the anesthetized animal; in this method, causative relationships are clear. Using this method, alterations in limbic circuitry of MAM-17 rats have been found. For instance, the hippocampal–prefrontal pathway in MAM-17 rats can be potentiated by high-frequency stimulation (HFS) of the fimbria but not in controls (Belujon, Patton, & Grace, 2014; Goto & Grace, 2006). Given the reduced prefrontal parvalbumin staining in MAM-17 (Lodge & Grace, 2009), it is possible that a loss of mPFC inhibitory tone and/or hippocampal feedforward inhibition in MAM-17 enhances LTP in this paradigm. Another possibility is that hippocampal–prefrontal potentiation varies as a function of prefrontal dopamine in an inverted-U relationship, so that if hippocampal stimulation evokes different amounts of dopamine in MAM-17 and SAL-17 animals, the outcome could be qualitatively affected; this view is consistent with the effects of stressing (which likely evokes prefrontal dopamine) MAM-17 and SAL-17 animals before LTP induction (Goto & Grace, 2006). However, the plastic changes mediating this effect could theoretically occur in any circuit in which mPFC and fimbria both participate. Altered plasticity in the MAM-17 model is also observed in the nucleus accumbens. Fimbria HFS potentiates and depresses the hippocampal–striatal pathway in SAL-17 and MAM-17, respectively (Belujon et al., 2014). Intriguingly, inactivation of the mPFC before fimbria HFS does not eliminate the MAM-17 and SAL-17 differences but instead yields an inverted result—that is, fimbria HFS subsequently depresses and potentiates the hippocampal–striatal pathway in SAL and MAM-17, respectively (Beljuon et al., 2014). From this study, three things become evident: first, mPFC dramatically influences the directionality of hippocampal–striatal plasticity; second, the influence of mPFC over hippocampal–striatal plasticity is qualitatively different in MAM-17 and SAL-17; and third, though a site of pathology, mPFC is not the sole source of circuit malfunction, because in its absence, new abnormalities are unmasked.

A second method of probing regional interactions is passive recording from two or more regions during different brain states. Electroencephalogram recordings during sleep in MAM-17 animals reveal abnormal hippocampal–prefrontal relationships. It is believed that during sleep, memories are replayed and consolidated (Wilson & McNaughton, 1994). This has been shown by the rapid reactivation of memory-associated place cells during hippocampal ripples—short-lasting, high-frequency events. These bursts of activity tend to be followed by spindles (7–14 Hz events, lasting 1–4 s) in the neocortex (Siapas & Wilson, 1998). However, this association between hippocampal ripples and neocortical spindles is disturbed in MAM-17 rats (Phillips, Bartsch, et al., 2012). These rats also exhibit fragmented non–rapid eye movement and reduced delta wave activity.

How much these impairments in sleep may contribute to cognitive malfunction remains unexplored.

OSCILLATORY ACTIVITIES IN MAM

Neural oscillations are a fundamental mechanism for enabling coordinated activity during normal brain function. Impaired gamma oscillations, theta and other slow oscillations, and coherence among regions have been reported by many studies on schizophrenia patients, and are associated with impaired cognitive functions (for a review, see Uhlhaas & Singer, 2010). In MAM-17 rats, gamma oscillations in the hippocampus and mPFC are impaired in response to a conditioned tone. In addition, the deficits in oscillations are correlated with loss of parvalbumin staining in the hippocampus and mPFC (Lodge et al., 2009). The loss of parvalbumin interneurons may be the cause of an impaired gamma band response to a conditioned tone associated with impaired performance in a latent inhibition paradigm (Lodge et al., 2009). Because parvalbumin-containing interneurons are known to participate in the gamma-band synchronization (Buzsáki & Wang, 2012; Sohal, Zhang, Yizhar, & Deisseroth, 2009), it has been hypothesized that the GABAergic deficits in parvalbumin population observed in postmortem studies could underlie impairments in gamma oscillations observed in schizophrenia (Lewis et al., 2005). Thus, the MAM-17 model, displaying both gamma and parvalbumin impairment, can serve as a good platform for studying this relationship further. Decreased gamma oscillations in visual but not motor cortex of MAM rats in response to NMDA receptor antagonists has also been reported, which correlates with decreased parvalbumin density in the visual but not motor cortex (Phillips, Cotel, et al., 2012). Awake MAM rats also deficit in the power of theta oscillations in the mediodorsal thalamic nucleus (Ewing & Grace, 2013), and reductions in delta and low gamma have been observed in cortex under anesthesia (Goto & Grace, 2006).

SOCIAL WITHDRAWAL IN MAM

Social withdrawal is frequency observed in schizophrenia patients as a negative symptom (Mueser & McGurk, 2004). Behaviors of social interaction are examined in MAM rats by placing two unfamiliar rats that have received identical prenatal treatment in an open chamber. MAM rats spend less time near each other and engage in less active social interaction. In addition, this deficit in social interaction occurs both in pre- and postpuberty (Flagstad et al., 2004; Hazane et al., 2009; Le Pen et al., 2006).

ANTIPSYCHOTIC DRUG ACTIONS IN MAM

It is unclear how antipsychotics achieve their therapeutic effect. Antipsychotic drugs exert rapid therapeutic action during the first days of administration, but the maximal antipsychotic action requires weeks to develop (Kapur and Seeman, 2001). Although antipsychotics are primarily dopamine D2 receptor antagonists, dopamine receptor antagonism alone cannot account for the delayed maximal efficacy and the lack of tolerance development. Studying how antipsychotics alter dopamine activity over time in normal rats has been useful in elucidating the mechanims underlying the delayed therapeutic effect. Acute administration to control rats of either first- or second-generation drugs leads to an initial increase of dopamine system activity, driven in part by circuit-level compensatory mechanisms, whereas a decrease in dopamine firing emerges after chronic, 3-week antipsychotic administration. One mechanism that could explain the shift from increased to decreased dopamine activity is depolarization block of the dopamine neurons (Grace, Bunney, Moore, & Todd, 1997). Depolarization block requires a threshold of activation to be reached, which takes time to accrue. In control rats, depolarization block can only be induced after a 3 week chronic administration.

However, studies on antipsychotic actions using normal rats only recapitulate the long-term actions of antipsychotics - the delayed maximal efficacy and lack of tolerance - but do not mimic the rapid onset of antipsychotic actions. In contrast, the response of MAM-treated rats to antipsychotics, as measured by dopamine system activity, parallels that of patients. In MAM-17 rats, the dopamine system is already in a hyperactive state (Lodge & Grace, 2007). As a consequence, the added excitatory effects of the antipsychotic drug ushers dopamine neurons into depolarization block more quickly. Indeed, dopamine firing is reduced immediately by an acute administration of a first- or second-generation antipsychotic drug and is further decreased by repeated administration (Valenti, Ciefelli, et al, 2011). Altogether, it appears that antipsychotic drugs are effective in reducing dopamine neuron hyperactivity. However, it is doing so not by restoring dopamine system to a normal condition, but instead, by inducing depolarization block, an offsetting pathological condition.

TESTING NOVEL TREATMENT IN THE MAM MODEL

Dopamine plays an essential role in pathophysiology of schizophrenia; the neural circuits that we have highlighted here suggest that the hippocampus, rather than the dopaminergic nuclei themselves, is the source of aberrant dopaminergic activity (Lodge & Grace, 2007). As described previously, antipsychotic drugs work by inducing depolarization block in dopamine neurons without reversing pathological activity in the hippocampus. Thus, it is not surprising that although antipsychotic drugs have revolutionized the treatment of schizophrenia, they are not very effective in treating nonpsychotic symptoms and can produce untoward side effects (Lieberman et al., 2005).

Novel treatment targeting the hippocampus has been shown effective in reversing schizophrenia phenotypes in MAM-17 rats. Treating GABAergic dysfunction selectively is difficult, given that GABA synapses represent 30% of the synapses in the brain. However, the subtypes of $GABA_A$ receptors are pharmacologically distinct and do not show an equal distribution. In particular, the distribution of the α5 subunit of the $GABA_A$ receptor is relatively confined in the hippocampus (Heldt & Ressler, 2007). Indeed, both systemic and hippocampal local administration of a $GABA_A$ α5-positive allosteric modulator to MAM-17 rats normalizes hippocampal function, dopamine hyperactivity, and the augmented locomotor response to amphetamine (Gill, Lodge, Cook, Aras, & Grace, 2011). In addition, hippocampal deep brain stimulation that is thought to decrease hippocampal activity restores dopamine system hyperactivity, auditory evoked potentials in mPFC, nucleus accumbens, mediodorsal thalamic nucleus, and vHPC as well as behavioral hypersensitivity to amphetamine and deficits in attentional set-shifting (Ewing & Grace, 2013; Perez, Shah, Asher, & Lodge, 2013). Vagus nerve stimulation that effectively reverse dopamine neuron hyperactivity and hyperresponsivity to amphetamine is also thought to suppress hippocampal activity in MAM-17 rats via an unknown mechanism (Perez, Carreno, Frazer, & Lodge, 2014).

However, when evaluating novel treatments in clinical trials, caution should be taken when evaluating their effects on schizophrenia patients who had been exposed to antipsychotic drugs for years and only briefly withdrawn. Gill, Cook, Poe, and Grace (2014) demonstrate the impact of withdrawal from repeated antipsychotic treatment on MAM-17 rats. Following withdrawal from 3 weeks of haloperidol administration, MAM-17 and normal rats similarly show a decrease in dopamine population activity; thus, the plastic changes induced by haloperidol (e.g., dopamine supersensitivity) that gives rise to depolarization block in dopamine neurons remain even in the absence of haloperidol. Dopamine supersensitivity is evidenced by a heightened sensitivity to amphetamine in haloperidol-withdrawn rats. Unlike haloperidol-withdrawn SAL-17 rats, dopamine supersensitivity in withdrawn MAM-17 rats is not mitigated by systemic treatment with α5-positive allosteric modulator, known to normalize the electrophysiological and behavioral abnormalities of dopamine system in previously untreated MAM-17 rats (Gill et al., 2011). Thus, prior antipsychotic exposure may interfere with the effects of novel drugs.

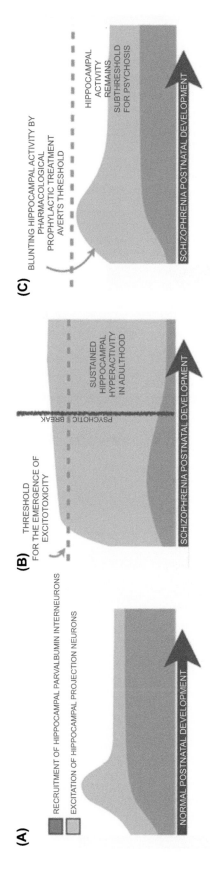

FIGURE 2 In the methylazoxymethanol (MAM)-17 model, *peripubertal* administration of diazepam for 10days has surprisingly long-lasting effects, preventing the hyperdopaminergia and elevated anxiety-like behavior normally associated with adulthood in this animal model (Du & Grace, 2013). The mechanism for this long-lasting change is unclear. Perhaps, during adolescence, glutamatergic signaling in the hippocampus is heightened, which is eventually compensated by increased recruitment of parvalbumin (and other) interneurons. Thus, there may be a sensitive period in normal development (A) in which the hippocampus is especially excitable. If interneurons are lacking from the onset, as in schizophrenia and MAM-17, this elevated excitability may lead to long-lasting excitotoxic damage, leading in turn to long-lasting hippocampal hyperactivity (B). However, prophylactic treatment with diazepam, which enhances GABAergic signaling, during the sensitive period will sufficiently reduce hippocampal activity and avert excitotoxic levels (C).

II. NEUROBIOLOGY OF PSYCHOTIC DISORDERS

MAM-E17 AS A MODEL TO STUDY DEVELOPMENTAL TRAJECTORY

We began this chapter discussing schizophrenia as having early neurodevelopmental, rather than late neurodegenerative origins. However, if prenatal events (in addition to the appropriate genetic background) determine whether an individual develops schizophrenia, why do the positive symptoms not appear until adolescence? This remains an open question. A benefit of a neurodevelopment disruption model such as the MAM model is its use as a system to examine potential neurophysiological alterations across development that may have relevance to the adolescent onset of psychosis. On the one hand, perhaps the schizophrenia pathology is present at birth but is either compensated by mechanisms present only in childhood (certain GABAergic receptors or ion gradients, for example) or is triggered by processes that are negligible until adolescence (e.g., hormonal changes, cortical myelination). On the other hand, perinatal events may cause a small disruption in the brain that grows with time via some feedforward, degenerative event or collection of events (e.g., oxidative stressors, excitotoxic damage, impaired repair processes). The plausibility of any of these hypotheses can be tested in the MAM-17 model by exploring whether it can influence the adolescent onset of MAM-17 psychostimulant hypersensitivity or deficits in PPI.

Studying the MAM-17 directly is also producing new data that challenge our current understanding of the model and may uncover important clues to adolescent onset. For example, we previously thought that heightened VTA activity arose during puberty in the MAM-17 model, but there is evidence that the dopamine activity is already augmented before puberty (Chen et al., 2014). Thus, the emergence of hyperdopaminergia may be more gradual than initially expected. This is consistent with a gradual change in parvalbumin expression (Chen et al., 2014; Gill & Grace, 2014). Referring back to the clinical literature, abnormal cerebral blood volume increases and hypermetabolism observed in the hippocampus of *at-risk* human subjects (Schobel et al., 2013; Schobel et al., 2009) as well as a correlated increased fluorodopa uptake and hippocampal glutamate levels in *ultra-high-risk* patients (Stone et al., 2010) is indicative of a hyperactivity of hippocampus in the prodromal period.

We know precious little about the prodromal and critical periods, during which schizophrenia symptoms appear and worsen before stabilizing, although it has recently become a focal point of research (Phillips, Yung, Yuen, Pantelis, & McGorry, 2002). Prevention or early intervention might be a highly effective approach to schizophrenia given that the duration of untreated schizophrenia correlates with a worsened prognosis in patients (Hill et al., 2012). Interestingly, the emergence of phenotypes in MAM-17 rats parallels disease progression in schizophrenia patients–namely hypersensitivity to psychostimulants and deficits in PPI occurs only after puberty, whereas social withdrawal and cognitive deficits are present both before and after puberty. Furthermore, studies on MAM rats before adulthood have indicated that peri-adolescent intervention can have long-lasting protective effects in the adult (Figure 2; Du & Grace, 2013), making MAM-17 a promising model in which to determine the nature of the critical period and to develop strategies for early treatment and prevention of schizophrenia.

References

Abi-Dargham, A., Rodenhiser, J., Printz, D., Zea-Ponce, Y., Gil, R., Kegeles, L. S., et al. (2000). Increased baseline occupancy of D_2 receptors by dopamine in schizophrenia. *Proceedings of the National Academy of Sciences of the United States of America, 97*(14), 8104–8109.

Akbarian, S., Bunney, W. E., Potkin, S. G., Wigal, S. B., Hagman, J. O., Sandman, C. A., et al. (1993). Altered distribution of nicotinamide-adenine dinucleotide phosphate-diaphorase cells in frontal lobe of schizophrenics implies disturbances of cortical development. *Archives of General Psychiatry, 50,* 169–177.

Akbarian, S., Viñuela, A., Kim, J. J., Potkin, S. G., Bunney, W. E., & Jones, E. G. (1993). Distorted distribution of nicotinamide-adenine dinucleotide phosphate-diaphorase neurons in temporal lobe of schizophrenics implies anomalous cortical development. *Archives of General Psychiatry, 50,* 178–187.

Ameblas, A. (1992). Preschizophrenics: Adding to the evidence, sharpening the focus. *British Journal of Psychiatry, 160,* 401–404.

Arnold, S. E. (1999). Neurodevelopmental abnormalities in schizophrenia: insights from neuropathology. *Development and Psychopathology, 11,* 439–456.

Bassanini, S., Hallene, K., Battaglia, G., Finardi, A., Santaguida, S., Cipolla, M., et al. (2007). Early cerebrovascular and parenchymal events following prenatal exposure to the putative neurotoxin methylazoxymethanol. *Neurobiology of Disease, 26*(2), 481–495.

Bast, T., & Feldon, J. (2003). Hippocampal modulation of sensorimotor processes. *Progress in Neurobiology, 70*(4), 319–345.

Belujon, P., Patton, M. H., & Grace, A. A. (2014). Role of the prefrontal cortex in altered hippocampal-accumbens synaptic plasticity in a developmental animal model of schizophrenia. *Cerebral Cortex, 24*(4), 968–977.

Benes, F. M., & Berretta, S. (2001). GABAergic interneurons: implications for understanding schizophrenia and bipolar disorder. *Neuropsychopharmacology, 25*(1), 1–27.

Benes, F. M., Kwok, E. W., Vincent, S. L., & Todtenkopf, M. S. (1998). A reduction of nonpyramidal cells in sector CA2 of schizophrenics and manic depressives. *Biological Psychiatry, 44,* 88–97.

Benes, F. M., McSparren, J., Bird, E. D., SanGiovanni, J. P., & Vincent, S. L. (1991). Deficits in small interneurons in prefrontal and cingulate cortices of schizophrenic and schizoaffective patients. *Archives of General Psychiatry, 48*(11), 996–1001.

Benes, F. M., Sorensen, I., & Bird, E. D. (1991). Reduced neuronal size in posterior hippocampus of schizophrenic patients. *Schizophrenia Bulletin, 17*(4), 597–608.

Bogerts, B. (1993). Recent advances in the neuropathology of schizophrenia. *Schizophrenia Bulletin, 19*(2), 431–445.

Bogerts, B. (1997). The temporolimbic system theory of positive schizophrenic symptoms. *Schizophrenia Bulletin, 23*(3), 423–435.

Boog, G. (2004). Obstetrical complications and subsequent schizophrenia in adolescent and young adult offsprings: is there a relationship? *European Journal of Obstetrics & Gynecology and Reproductive Biology, 114*(2), 130–136.

Braff, D. L. (2010). Prepulse inhibition of the startle reflex: a window on the brain in schizophrenia. In N. R. Swerdlow (Ed.), *Behavioral neurobiology of schizophrenia and its treatment* (pp. 349–371). New York: Springer-Verlag Berlin Heidelberg.

Brimer, L. (2011). *Chemical food safety*. Cambridge: CAB International.

Buzsáki, G., & Wang, X.-J. (2012). Mechanisms of gamma oscillations. *Annual Review of Neuroscience, 13*(18), 203–225.

Caballero, A., Diah, K. C., & Tseng, K. Y. (2013). Region-specific upregulation of parvalbumin-, but not calretinin-positive cells in the ventral hippocampus during adolescence. *Hippocampus, 23*(12), 1331–1336.

Cannon, M., Jones, P. B., & Murray, R. M. (2002). Obstetric complications and schizophrenia: historical and meta-analytic review. *American Journal of Psychiatry, 159*(7), 1080–1092.

Carrel, D., Hernandez, K., Kwon, M., Mau, C., Trivedi, M. P., Brzustowicz, L. M., et al. (2014). Nitric oxide synthase 1 adaptor protein, a protein implicated in schizophrenia, controls radial migration of cortical neurons. *Biological Psychiatry, 29*(25), 8248–8258.

Cattabeni, F., & Di Luca, M. (1997). Developmental models of brain dysfunctions induced by targeted cellular ablations with methylazoxymethanol. *Physiological Reviews, 77*(1), 199–215.

Cattaneo, E., Reinach, B., Caputi, A., Cattabeni, F., & Di Luca, M. (1995). Selective in vitro blockade of neuroepithelial cells proliferation by methylazoxymethanol, a molecule capable of inducin long lasting functional impairments. *Journal of Neuroscience Research, 41*(5), 640–647.

Chen, L., Perez, S. M., & Lodge, D. J. (2014). An augmented dopamine system function is present prior to puberty in the methylazoxymethanol acetate rodent model of schizophrenia. *Developmental Neurobiology, 74*(9), 907–917.

Chin, C. L., Curzon, P., Schwartz, A. J., O'Connor, E. M., Rueter, L. E., Fox, G. B., et al. (2011). Structural abnormalities revealed by magnetic resonance imaging in rats prenatally exposed to methylazoxymethanol acetate parallel cerebral pathology in schizophrenia. *Synapse, 65*, 393–403.

Ciaroni, S., Buffi, O., Ambrogini, P., Cecchini, T., & Del Grande, P. (1996). Quantitative changes in neuron and glial cells of neocortex following prenatal exposure to methylazoxymethanol. *Journal für Hirnforschung, 37*(4), 537–546.

Corcoran, C. M., Smith, C., McLaughlin, D., Auther, A., Malaspina, D., & Cornblatt, B. (2012). HPA axis function and symptoms in adolescents at clinical high risk for schizophrenia. *Schizophrenia Research, 135*, 170–174.

Cox, P. A., & Sacks, O. W. (2002). Cycad neurotoxins, consumption of flying foxes, and ALS-PDC disease in Guam. *Neurology, 58*(6), 956–959.

Crumlish, N., Whitty, P., Clarke, M., Browne, S., Kamali, M., Gervin, M., et al. (2009). Beyond the critical period: longitudinal study of 8-year outcome in first-episode non-affective psychosis. *British Journal of Psychiatry, 194*(1), 18–24.

Dambska, M., Haddad, R., Kozlowski, P. B., Lee, M. H., & Shek, J. (1982). Telencephalic cytoarchitectonics in the brains of rats with graded degrees of microencephaly. *Acta Neuropathologica, 58*, 203–209.

Devylder, J. E., Ben-David, S., Schobel, S. A., Kimhy, D., Malaspina, D., & Corcoran, C. M. (2013). Temporal association of stress sensitivity and symptoms in individuals at clinical high risk for psychosis. *Psychological Medicine, 43*(2), 259–268.

Du, Y., & Grace, A. A. (2013). Peripubertal diazepam administration prevents the emergence of dopamine system hyperresponsivity in the MAM developmental disruption model of schizophrenia. *Neuropsychopharmacology, 38*(10), 1881–1888.

Esmaeili, B., & Grace, A. A. (2013). Afferent drive of medial prefrontal cortex by hippocampus and amygdala is altered in MAM-treated rats: evidence for interneuron dysfunction. *Neuropsychopharmacology, 38*(10), 1871–1880.

Ewing, S. G., & Grace, A. A. (2013). Deep brain stimulation of the ventral hippocampus restores deficits in processing of auditory evoked potentials in a rodent developmental disruption model of schizophrenia. *Schizophrenia Research, 143*(2–3), 377–383.

Fanselow, M. S., & Dong, H. W. (2010). Are the dorsal and ventral hippocampus functionally distinct structures? *Neuron, 65*(1), 7–19.

Featherstone, R. E., Rizos, Z., Nobrega, J. N., Kapur, S., & Fletcher, P. J. (2007). Gestational methylazoxymethanol acetate treatment impairs select cognitive functions: parallels to schizophrenia. *Neuropsychopharmacology, 32*(2), 483–492.

Fendt, M., Li, L., & Yeomans, J. S. (2001). Brain stem circuits mediating prepulse inhibition of the startle reflex. *Psychopharmacology (Berl), 156*(2–3), 216–224.

Flagstad, P., Glenthoj, B. Y., & Didriksen, M. (2005). Cognitive deficits caused by late gestational disruption of neurogenesis in rats: a preclinical model of schizophrenia. *Neuropsychopharmacology, 30*(2), 250–260.

Flagstad, P., Mork, A., Glenthoj, B. Y., van Beek, J., Michael-Titus, A. T., & Didriksen, M. (2004). Disruption of neurogenesis on gestational day 17 in the rat causes behavioral changes relevant to positive and negative schizophrenia symptoms and alters amphetamine-induced dopamine release in nucleus accumbens. *Neuropsychopharmacology, 29*(11), 2052–2064.

Floresco, S. B., Seamans, J. K., & Phillips, A. G. (1997). Selective roles for hippocampal, prefrontal cortical, and ventral striatal circuits in radial-arm maze task with or without a delay. *Journal of Neuroscience, 17*(5), 1880–1890.

Floresco, S. B., Todd, C. L., & Grace, A. A. (2001). Glutamatergic afferents from the hippocampus to the nucleus accumbens regulate activity of ventral tegmental area dopamine neurons. *Journal of Neuroscience, 21*(13), 4915–4922.

Floresco, S. B., West, A. R., Ash, B., Moore, H., & Grace, A. A. (2003). Afferent modulation of dopamine neuron firing differentially regulates tonic and phasic dopamine transmission. *Nature Neuroscience, 6*(9), 968–973.

Freeman, A. S., Meltzer, L. T., & Bunney, B. S. (1985). Firing properties of substantia nigra dopaminergic neurons in freely moving rats. *Life Sciences, 36*(20), 1983–1994.

Fu, D., Calvo, J. A., & Samson, L. D. (2012). Balancing repair and tolerance of DNA damage caused by alkylating agents. *Nature Reviews Cancer, 12*(2), 104–120.

Fuller, R., Nopoulos, P., Arndt, S., O'Leary, D., Ho, B.-C., & Andreasen, N. C. (2002). Longitudinal assessment of premorbid cognitive functioning in patients with schizophrenia through examination of standardized scholastic test performance. *American Journal of Psychiatry, 159*(7), 1183–1189.

Gabbott, P. L., Warner, T. A., & Busby, S. J. (2006). Amygdala input monosynaptically innervates parvalbumin immunoreactive local circuit neurons in rat medial prefrontal cortex. *Neuroscience, 139*(3), 1039–1048.

Gastambide, F., Cotel, M. C., Gilmour, G., O'Neill, M. J., Robbins, T. W., & Tricklebank, M. D. (2012). Selective remediation of reversal learning deficits in the neurodevelopmental MAM model of schizophrenia by a novel mGlu5 positive allosteric modulator. *Neuropsychopharmacology, 37*(4), 1057–1066.

Gelman, S. L., Zaidi, N. H., Dumenco, L. L., Allay, E., Fan, C. Y., Liu, L., et al. (1994). Alkyltransferase trangenic mice: probes of chemical carcinogenesis. *Mutation Research, 307*, 541–555.

Gill, K. M., Cook, J. M., Poe, M. M., & Grace, A. A. (2014). Prior antipsychotic drug treatment prevents response to novel antipsychotic agent in the methylazoxymethanol acetate model of schizophrenia. *Schizophrenia Bulletin, 40*(2), 341–350.

Gill, K. M., & Grace, A. A. (2014). Corresponding decrease in neuronal markers signals progressive parvalbumin neuron loss in MAM schizophrenia model. *International Journal of Neuropsychopharmacology, 17*(10), 1609–1619.

Gill, K. M., Lodge, D. J., Cook, J. M., Aras, S., & Grace, A. A. (2011). A novel α5GABA(A)R-positive allosteric modulator reverses hyperactivation of the dopamine system in the MAM model of schizophrenia. *Neuropsychopharmacology, 36*(9), 1903–1911.

Goto, Y., & Grace, A. A. (2006). Alterations in medial prefrontal cortical activity and plasticity in rats with disruption of cortical development. *Biological Psychiatry, 60*(11), 1259–1267.

Gourevitch, R., Rocher, C., Le Pen, G., Krebs, M. O., & Jay, T. M. (2004). Working memory deficits in adult rats after prenatal disruption of neurogenesis. *Behavioural Pharmacology, 15*(4), 287–292.

Grace, A., Bunney, B. S., Moore, H., & Todd, C. L. (1997). Dopamine-cell depolarization block as a model for the therapeutic actions of antipsychotic drugs. *TINS, 20*(1), 31–37.

Grace, A. A., Floresco, S. B., Goto, Y., & Lodge, D. J. (2007). Regulation of firing of dopaminergic neurons and control of goal-directed behaviors. *Trends in Neuroscience, 30*(5), 220–227.

Harrison, P. J. (2004). The hippocampus in schizophrenia: a review of the neuropathological evidence and its pathophysiological implications. *Psychopharmacology (Berl), 174*, 151–162.

Hazane, F., Krebs, M.-O., Jay, T. M., & Le Pen, G. (2009). Behavioral perturbations after prenatal neurogenesis disturbance in female rat. *Neurotoxicity Research, 15*, 311–320.

Heckers, S., & Konradi, C. (2002). Hippocampal neurons in schizophrenia. *Journal of Neural Transmission, 109*, 891–905.

Heldt, S. A., & Ressler, K. J. (2007). Forebrain and midbrain distribution of major benzodiazepine-sensitive GABA(A) receptor subunits in the adult C57 mouse as assessed with in situ hybridization. *Neuroscience, 150*, 370–385.

Herman, J. P., & Mueller, N. K. (2006). Role of the ventral subiculum in stress integration. *Behavioural Brain Research, 174*, 215–224.

Hill, M., Crumlish, N., Clarke, M., Whitty, P., Owens, E., Renwick, L., et al. (2012). Prospective relationship of duration of untreated psychosis to psychopathology and functional outcome over 12 years. *Schizophrenia Research, 141*, 215–221.

Hoareau, C., Hazane, F., Le Pen, G., & Krebs, M.-O. (2006). Postnatal effect of embryonic neurogenesis disturbance on reelin level in organotypic cultures of rat hippocampus. *Brain Research, 1097*, 43–51.

Hoffman, J. R., Boyne, L. J., Levitt, P., & Fischer, I. (1996). Short exposure to methylazoxymethanol causes a long-term inhibition of axonal outgrowth from cultured embryonic rat hippocampal neurons. *Journal of Neuroscience Research, 46*, 349–359.

Howes, O. D., & Kapur, S. (2009). The dopamine hypothesis of schizophrenia: version III – the final common pathway. *Schizophrenia Bulletin, 35*(3), 549–562.

Johnston, M. V., Grzanna, R., & Coyle, J. T. (1979). Methylazoxymethanol treatment of fetal rats results in abnormally dense noradrenergic innervation of neocortex. *Science, 203*(4378), 369–371.

Jonsson, G., & Hallman, H. (1981). Effects of prenatal methylazoxymethanol treatment on the development of central monoamine neurons. *Brain Research, 254*(4), 513–530.

Kaina, B., Christmann, M., Naumann, S., & Roos, W. P. (2007). MGMT: key node in the battle against genotoxicity, carcinogenicity and apoptosis induced by alkylating agents. *DNA Repair (Amst), 6*(8), 1079–1099.

Kamiya, A., Kubo, K., Tomoda, T., Takaki, M., Youn, R., Ozeki, Y., et al. (2005). A schizophrenia-associated mutation of DISC1 perturbs cerebral cortex development. *Nature Cell Biology, 7*(12), 1167–1178.

Kapur, S. (2003). Psychosis as a state of aberrant salience: a framework linking biology, phenomenology, and pharmacology in schizophrenia. *American Journal of Psychiatry, 160*(1), 13–23.

Kapur, S., & Seeman, P. (2001). Does fast dissociation from the dopamine D_2 receptor explain the action of atypical antipsychotics? a new hypothesis. *American Journal of Psychiatry, 158*(3), 360–369.

Kisby, G. E., Kabel, H., Hugon, J., & Spencer, P. (1999). Damage and repair of nerve cell DNA in toxic stress. *Drug Metabolism Reviews, 31*(3), 589–618.

Kisby, G. E., Olivas, A., Park, T., Churchwell, M., Doerge, D., Samson, L. D., et al. (2009). DNA repair modulates the vulnerability of the developing brain to alkylating agents. *DNA Repair (Amst), 8*(3), 400–412.

Kleihues, P., & Bucheler, J. (1977). Long-term persistence of O^6-methylguanine in rat brain DNA. *Nature, 269*, 625–626.

Koch, M., Fendt, M., & Kretschmer, B. D. (2000). Role of the substantia nigra pars reticulata in sensorimotor gating measured by prepulse inhibition of startle in rats. *Behavioural Brain Research, 117*, 153–162.

Kohl, S., Heekeren, K., Klosterkotter, J., & Kuhn, J. (2013). Prepulse inhibition in psychiatric disorders – apart from schizophrenia. *Journal of Psychiatric Research, 47*(4), 445–452.

Kumari, V., & Sharma, T. (2002). Effects of typical and atypical antipsychotics on prepulse inhibition in schizophrenia: a critical evaluation of current evidence and directions for future research. *Psychopharmacology (Berl), 162*(2), 97–101.

Lafarga, M., Andres, M. A., Calle, E., & Berciano, M. T. (1998). Reactive gliosis of immature Bergmann glia and microglial cell activation in response to cell death of granule cell precursors induced by methylazoxymethanol treatment in developing rat cerebellum. *Anatomy and Embryology (Berl), 198*(2), 111–122.

Lafarga, M., Lerga, A., Andres, M. A., Polanco, J. I., Calle, E., & Berciano, M. T. (1997). Apoptosis induced by methylazoxymethanol in developing rat cerebellum: organization of the cell nucleus and its relationship to DNA and rDNA degradation. *Cell and Tissue Research, 289*, 25–38.

Lalonde, R. (2002). The neurobiological basis of spontaneous alternation. *Neuroscience & Biobehavioral Reviews, 26*, 91–104.

Lane, A., Kinsella, A., Murphy, P., Byrne, M., Keenan, J., Colgan, K., et al. (1997). The anthropometric assessment of dysmorphic features in schizophrenia as an index of its developmental origins. *Psychological Medicine, 27*, 1155–1164.

Laruelle, M., & Abi-Dargham, A. (1999). Dopamine as the win of the psychotic fire: new evidence from brain imaging studies. *Journal of Psychopharmacology, 13*(4), 358–371.

Laurelle, M., Frankle, W. G., Narendran, R., Kegeles, L. S., & Abi-Dargham, A. (2005). Mechanism of action of antipsychotic drugs: from dopamine D_2 receptor antagonism to glutamate NMDA facilitation. *Clinical Therapetuics, 27*, S16–S24.

Lavin, A., Moore, H. M., & Grace, A. A. (2005). Prenatal disruption of neocortical development alters prefrontal cortical neuron responses to dopamine in adult rats. *Neuropsychopharmacology, 30*(8), 1426–1435.

Le Pen, G., Gourevitch, R., Hazane, F., Hoareau, C., Jay, T. M., & Krebs, M.-O. (2006). Peri-pubertal maturation after developmental disturbance: a model for psychosis onset in the rat. *Neuroscience, 143*(2), 395–405.

Le Pen, G., Jay, T. M., & Krebs, M.-O. (2011). Effect of antipsychotics on spontaneous hyperactivity and hypersensitivity to MK-801-induced hyperactivity in rats prenatally exposed to methylazoxymethanol. *Journal of Psychopharmacology, 25*(6), 822–835.

Lena, I., Chessel, A., Le Pen, G., Krebs, M.-O., & Garcia, R. (2007). Alterations in prefrontal glutamatergic and noradrenergic systems following MK-801 administration in rats prenatally exposed to methylazoxymethanol at gestational day 17. *Psychopharmacology (Berl), 192*(3), 373–383.

Lewis, B. L., & O'Donnell, P. (2000). Ventral tegmental area afferents to prefrontal cortex maintain membrane potential 'up' states in pyramidal neurons via D1 dopamine receptors. *Cerebral Cortex, 10*(12), 1168–1175.

Lewis, D. A., Hashimoto, T., & Volk, D. W. (2005). Cortical inhibitory neurons and schizophrenia. *Nature Reviews Neuroscience, 6*(4), 312–324.

Lieberman, J. A., Kinon, B. J., & Loebel, A. D. (1990). Dopaminergic mechanisms in idiopathic and drug-induced psychoses. *Schizophrenia Bulletin, 16*(1), 97–110.

Lieberman, J. A., Stroup, T. S., McEvoy, J. P., Swartz, M. S., Rosenheck, R. A., Perkins, D. O., et al. (2005). Effectiveness of antipsychotic drugs in patients with chronic schizophrenia. *New England Journal of Medicine, 353*(12), 1209–1223.

Lisman, J. E., Coyle, J. T., Green, R. W., Javitt, D. C., Benes, F. M., Heckers, S., et al. (2008). Circuit-based framework for understanding neurotransmitter and risk gene interactions in schizophrenia. *Trends in Neurosciences, 31*(5), 234–242.

Lodge, D. J., Behrens, M. M., & Grace, A. A. (2009). A loss of parvalbumin-containing interneurons is associated with diminished oscillatory activity in an animal model of schizophrenia. *Journal of Neuroscience, 29*(8), 2344–2354.

Lodge, D. J., & Grace, A. A. (2006). The hippocampus modulates dopamine neuron responsivity by regulating the intensity of phasic neuron activation. *Neuropsychopharmacology, 31*, 1356–1361.

Lodge, D. J., & Grace, A. A. (2007). Aberrant hippocampal activity underlies the dopamine dysregulation in an animal model of schizophrenia. *Journal of Neuroscience, 27*(42), 11424–11430.

Matsumoto, H., & Strong, F. M. (1963). The occurrence of methylazoxymethanol in *Cycas circinalids* L. *Archives of Biochemistry and Biophysics, 101*, 299–310.

McEwen, B. S., & Gianaros, P. J. (2010). Central role of the brain in stress and adaptation: links to socioeconomic status, health, and disease. *Annals of the New York Academy of Sciences, 1186*, 190–222.

Medoff, D. R., Holcomb, H. H., Lahti, A. C., & Tamminga, C. A. (2001). Probing the human hippocampus using rCBF: contrasts in schizophrenia. *Hippocampus, 11*, 543–550.

Mei, L., & Xiong, W.-C. (2008). Neuregulin 1 in neural development, synaptic plasticity and schizophrenia. *Nature Reviews Neuroscience, 9*, 437–453.

Miller, T. J., McGlashan, T. H., Rosen, J. L., Cadenhead, K., Ventura, J., McFarlane, W., et al. (2003). Prodromal assessment with the structured interview for prodromal symptoms and the scale of prodromal symptoms: predictive validity, interrater reliability, and training to reliability. *Schizophrenia Bulletin, 29*(4), 703–715.

Molina, V., Reig, S., Pascau, J., Sanz, J., Sarramea, F., Gispert, J. D., et al. (2003). Anatomical and functional cerebral variables associated with basal symptoms but not risperidone response in minimally treated schizophrenia. *Psychiatric Research: Neuroimaging, 124*, 164–175.

Moore, H., Jentsch, J. D., Ghajarnia, M., Geyer, M. A., & Grace, A. A. (2006). A neurobehavioral systems analysis of adult rats exposed to methylazoxymethanol acetate on E17: implications for the neuropathology of schizophrenia. *Biological Psychiatry, 60*, 253–264.

Mueser, K. T., & McGurk, S. R. (2004). Schizophrenia. *Lancet, 363*, 2063–2072.

Noonan, E. M., Shah, D., Yaffe, M. B., Lauffenburger, D. A., & Samson, L. D. (2012). O⁶-methylguanine DNA lesions induce an intra-S-phase arrest from which cells exit into apoptosis governed by early and late multi-pathway signaling network activation. *Integrative Biology, 4*, 1237–1255.

O'Callaghan, E., Gibson, T., Colohan, H. A., Buckley, P., Walshe, D. G., Larkin, C., et al. (1992). Risk of schizophrenia in adults born after obstetric complications and their association with early onset of illness: a controlled study. *BMJ, 305*(6864), 1256–1259.

O'Donnell, P., & Grace, A. A. (1995). Synaptic interactions among excitatory afferents to nucleus accumbens neurons: hippocampal gating of prefrontal cortical input. *Journal of Neuroscience, 15*(5), 3622–3639.

Owens, D. G. C., Miller, P., Lawrie, S. M., & Johnstone, E. C. (2005). Pathogenesis of schizophrenia: a psychopathological perspective. *British Journal of Psychiatry, 186*, 386–393.

Pan, W.-X., & Hyland, B. I. (2005). Pedunculopontine tegmental nucleus controls conditioned responses of midbrain dopamine neurons in behaving rats. *Journal of Neuroscience, 25*(19), 4725–4732.

Penschuck, S., Flagstad, P., Didriksen, M., Leist, M., & Michael-Titus, A. T. (2006). Decrease in parvalbumin-expressing neurons in the hippocampus and increased phencyclidine-induced locomotor activity in the rat methylazoxymethanol (MAM) model of schizophrenia. *European Journal of Neuroscience, 23*(1), 279–284.

Perez, S. M., Carreno, F. R., Frazer, A., & Lodge, D. J. (2014). Vagal nerve stimulation reverses aberrant dopamine system function in the methylazoxymethanol acetate rodent model of schizophrenia. *Journal of Neuroscience, 34*(28), 9261–9267.

Perez, S. M., Shah, A., Asher, A., & Lodge, D. J. (2013). Hippocampal deep brain stimulation reverses physiological and behavioural deficits in a rodent model of schizophrenia. *International Journal of Neuropsychopharmacology, 16*(6), 1331–1339.

Perry, W., & Braff, D. L. (1994). Information-processing deficits and thought disorder in schizophrenia. *American Journal of Psychiatry, 151*(3), 363–367.

Phillips, K. G., Bartsch, U., McCarthy, A. P., Edgar, D. M., Tricklebank, M. D., Wafford, K. A., et al. (2012). Decoupling of sleep-dependent cortical and hippocampal interactions in a neurodevelopmental model of schizophrenia. *Neuron, 76*(3), 526–533.

Phillips, K. G., Cotel, M. C., McCarthy, A. P., Edgar, D. M., Tricklebank, M., O'Neill, M. J., et al. (2012). Differential effects of NMDA antagonists on high frequency and gamma EEG oscillations in a neurodevelopmental model of schizophrenia. *Neuropharmacology, 62*(3), 1359–1370.

Phillips, L. J., Yung, A. R., Yuen, H. P., Pantelis, C., & McGorry, P. D. (2002). Prediction and prevention of transition to psychosis in young people at incipient risk for schizophrenia. *American Journal of Medical Genetics, 114*, 929–937.

Ragozzino, M. E. (2007). The contribution of the medial prefrontal cortex, orbitofrontal cortex, and dorsomedial striatum to behavioral flexibility. *Annals of the New York Academy of Sciences, 1121*, 355–375.

Rao, R. P., Anilkumar, S., McEwen, B. S., & Chattarji, S. (2012). Glucocorticoids protect against the delayed behavioral and cellular effects of acute stress on the amygdala. *Biological Psychiatry, 72*(6), 466–475.

Rodier, P. M. (1986). Behavioral effects of antimitotic agents administered during neurogenesis. In E. P. Riley, & C. V. Vorhees (Eds.), *Handbook of behavioral teratology* (pp. 185–209). New York: Plenum Press.

Schobel, S. A., Chaudhury, N. H., Khan, U. A., Paniagua, B., Styner, M. A., Asllani, I., et al. (2013). Imaging patients with psychosis and a mouse model establishes a spreading pattern of hippocampal dysfunction and implicates glutamate as a driver. *Neuron, 78*(1), 81–93.

Schobel, S. A., Lewandowski, N. M., Corcoran, C. M., Moore, H., Brown, T., Malaspina, D., et al. (2009). Differential targeting of the CA1 subfield of the hippocampal formation by schizophrenia and related psychotic disorders. *Archives of General Psychiatry, 66*(9), 938–946.

Schoenfeld, T. J., Rada, P., Pieruzzini, P. R., Hsueh, B., & Gould, E. (2013). Physical exercise prevents stress-induced activation of granule neurons and enhances local inhibitory mechanisms in the dentate gyrus. *Journal of Neuroscience, 33*(18), 7770–7777.

Schultz, W. (1998). Predictive reward signal of dopamine neurons. *Journal of Neurophysiology, 80*, 1–27.

Shiraishi, A., Sakumi, K., & Sekiguchi, M. (2000). Increased susceptibility to chemotherapeutic alkylating agents of mice deficient in DNA repair methyltransferase. *Carcinogenesis, 21*(10), 1879–1883.

Shors, T. J., Miesegaes, G., Beylin, A., Zhao, M., Rydel, T., & Gould, E. (2001). Neurogenesis in the adult is involved in the formation of trace memories. *Nature, 410*, 372–376.

Siapas, A. G., & Wilson, M. A. (1998). Coordinated interactions between hippocampal ripples and cortical spindles during slow-wave sleep. *Neuron, 21*(5), 1123–1128.

II. NEUROBIOLOGY OF PSYCHOTIC DISORDERS

Sohal, V. S., Zhang, F., Yizhar, O., & Deisseroth, K. (2009). Parvalbumin neurons and gamma rhythms enhance cortical circuit performance. *Nature, 459*(7247), 698–702.

Spencer, P. S., Nunn, P. B., Hugon, J., Ludolph, A. C., Roy, D. N., & Ross, S. M. (1987). Guam amyotrophic lateral sclerosis-parkinsonism-dementia linked to a plant excitant neurotoxin. *Science, 237*(4814), 517–522.

Steen, R. G., Mull, C., McClure, R., Hamer, R. M., & Lieberman, J. A. (2006). Brain volume in first-episode schizophrenia. *British Journal of Psychiatry, 188*, 510–518.

Steinecke, A., Gampe, C., Valkova, C., Kaether, C., & Boltz, J. (2012). Disrupted-in-schizophrenia 1 (DISC1) is necessary for the correct migration of cortical interneurons. *Journal of Neuroscience, 32*(2), 738–745.

Steullet, P., Cabungcal, J.-H., Kulak, A., Kraftsik, R., Chen, Y., Dalton, T. P., et al. (2010). Redox dysregulation affects the ventral but not dorsal hippocampus: impairment of parvalbumin neurons, gamma oscillations, and related behaviors. *Journal of Neuroscience, 30*(7), 2547–2558.

Stone, J. M., Howes, O. D., Egerton, A., Kambeitz, J., Allen, P., Lythgoe, D. J., et al. (2010). Altered relationship between hippocampal glutamate levels and striatal dopamine function in subjects at ultra high risk of psychosis. *Biological Psychiatry, 68*, 599–602.

Straub, R. E., & Weinberger, D. R. (2006). Schizophrenia genes – famine to feast. *Biological Psychiatry, 60*, 81–83.

Sullivan, P. F., Kendler, K. S., & Neale, M. C. (2003). Schizophrenia as a complex trait. *Archives of General Psychiatry, 60*, 1187–1192.

Swerdlow, N. R., Geyer, M. A., & Braff, D. L. (2001). Neural circuit regulation of prepulse inhibition of startle in the rat: current knowledge and future challenges. *Psychopharmacology (Berl), 156*, 194–215.

Tamminga, C. A., Stan, A. D., & Wagner, A. D. (2010). The hippocampal formation in schizophrenia. *American Journal of Psychiatry, 167*(10), 1178–1193.

Tan, H.-Y., Callicott, J. H., & Weinberger, D. R. (2007). Dysfunctional and compensatory prefrontal cortical systems, genes and the pathogenesis of schizophrenia. *Cerebral Cortex, 17*, i171–i181.

Thompson, J. L., Pogue-Geile, M. F., & Grace, A. A. (2004). Developmental pathology, dopamine, and stress: a model for the age of onset of schizophrenia symptoms. *Schizophrenia Bulletin, 30*(4), 875–900.

Tseng, K. Y., & O'Donnell, P. (2005). Dopaminergic modulation of cortical and striatal UP states. In J. P. Bolam, C. A. Ingham, & P. J. Magil (Eds.), *The Basal Ganglia VIII* (pp. 467–474). Singapore: Springer.

Uhlhaas, P. J., & Singer, W. (2010). Abnormal neural oscillations and synchrony in schizophrenia. *Nature Reviews Neuroscience, 11*, 100–113.

Ulrich-Lai, Y. M., & Herman, J. P. (2009). Neural regulation of endocrine and autonomic stress responses. *Nature Reviews Neuroscience, 10*, 397–409.

Ungless, M. A., & Grace, A. A. (2012). Are you or aren't you? Challenges associated with physiologically identifying dopamine neurons. *Trends in Neurosciences, 35*(7), 422–430.

Valenti, O., Cifelli, P., Gill, K. M., & Grace, A. A. (2011). Antipsychotic drugs rapidly induce dopamine neuron depolarization block in a developmental rat model of schizophrenia. *Journal of Neuroscience, 31*(34), 12330–12338.

Valenti, O., Lodge, D. J., & Grace, A. A. (2011). Aversive stimuli alter ventral tegmental area dopamine neuron activity via a common action in the ventral hippocampus. *Journal of Neuroscience, 31*(11), 4280–4289.

Volk, D. W., & Lewis, D. A. (2010). Prefrontal cortical circuits in schizophrenia. In N. Swerdlow (Ed.), *Behavioral neurobiology of schizophrenia and its treatment* (pp. 485–508). New York: Springer-Verlag Berlin Heidelberg.

Walker, E. F., & Diforio, D. (1997). Schizophrenia: a neural diathesis-stress model. *Psychological Review, 104*(4), 667–685.

van der Werf, M., Hanssen, M., Kohler, S., Verkaaik, M., Verhey, F. R., & Allardyce, J. (2014). Systematic review and collaborative recalculation of 133,693 incident cases of schizophrenia. *Psychological Medicine, 44*(1), 9–16.

Weinberger, D. R., & Berman, K. F. (1996). Prefrontal function in schizophrenia: confounds and controversies. *Philosophical Transactions of the Royal Society of London, 351*(1346), 1495–1503.

Wilson, M. A., & McNaughton, B. L. (1994). Reactivation of hippocampal ensemble memories during sleep. *Science, 265*(5172), 676–679.

van Winkel, R., Stefanis, N. C., & Myin-Germeys, I. (2008). Psychosocial stress and psychosis. A review of the neurobiological mechanisms and the evidence for gene-stress interaction. *Schizophrenia Bulletin, 34*(6), 1095–1105.

Winterer, G., & Weinberger, D. R. (2004). Genes, dopamine and cortical signal-to-noise ratio in schizophrenia. *Trends in Neuroscience, 27*(11), 683–690.

Yung, A. R., Yuen, H. P., McGorry, P. D., Phillips, L. J., Kelly, D., Dell'Olio, M., et al. (2005). Mapping the onset of psychosis: the comprehensive assessment of at-risk mental states. *Australian and New Zealand Journal of Psychiatry, 39*, 964–971.

Zhang, W., Pouzet, B., Jongen-Rêlo, A. L., Weiner, I., & Feldon, J. (1999). Disruption of prepulse inhibition following N-methyl-D-aspartate infusion into the ventral hippocampus is antagonized by clozapine but not by haloperidol: a possible model for the screening of atypical antipsychotics. *NeuroReport, 10*(12), 2533–2538.

Zhang, Z. J., & Reynolds, G. P. (2002). A selective decrease in the relative density of parvalbumin-immunoreactive neurons in the hippocampus in schizophrenia. *Schizophrenia Research, 55*, 1–10.

Zimmerman, E. C., Bellaire, M., Ewing, S. G., & Grace, A. A. (2013). Abnormal stress responsivity in a rodent developmental disruption model of schizophrenia. *Neuropsychopharmacology, 38*(11), 2131–2139.

9

Social Isolation Rearing and Sensorimotor Gating in Rat Models of Relevance to Schizophrenia: What We Know, and What We Do Not Know

Susan B. Powell*,§, *Neal R. Swerdlow**

*Department of Psychiatry, University of California San Diego, La Jolla, CA, USA; §Research Service, VA San Diego Healthcare System, La Jolla, CA, USA

SOCIAL ISOLATION REARING IN RATS

Social isolation rearing (SIR) of rodents is a developmental manipulation in which postweanling rats are raised to adulthood in single-housed cages, absent from social contact with other rats. Raising postweanling animals in single-housed conditions deprives them of social interactions during a developmental period in which play behavior emerges (Einon & Morgan, 1977). One consequence of SIR is that animals are deprived of stimuli critical to behavioral and neurobiological development (reviewed in Hall, 1998). This environmental manipulation leads to profound and enduring effects on behavior, immune function, and brain development. Some of the long-term alterations in brain function and behavior that emerge after SIR are reminiscent of abnormalities exhibited in developmentally linked brain disorders such as schizophrenia (Geyer, Wilkinson, Humby, & Robbins, 1993; Powell & Geyer, 2002).

The consequences of SIR are investigated to understand the impact of aberrant social development on the adult brain and behavior, as a model for abnormal brain development and its behavioral consequences in different clinical conditions. There are at least two potentially overlapping pathways by which the effects of SIR might be relevant to the etiology of developmental brain disorders, and *we do not yet know the degree to which the neurobiological and behavioral effects of the experimentally induced SIR model has on one, both, or neither of these pathways.*

First, as a chronic developmental stressor, SIR allows us to study the biological impact of sustained stress in early life. Sustained early life stress has been implicated as a predisposing factor in many different forms of psychopathology. For example, chronic stress-induced immune activation might have direct or indirect neurotoxic effects that degrade specific neural circuits and thereby contribute to the conversion to psychosis in predisposed individuals; by studying mechanisms and neural targets of SIR-induced immune activation, we might identify potentially neuroprotective interventions that could be applied to biomarker-identified vulnerable individuals.

Second, pre- and postpubertal social withdrawal and isolation are primary manifestations of certain brain disorders, including some forms of schizophrenia. These primary symptoms might then have secondary biological consequences, through the loss of normal, neurostimulatory social interactions. To the degree that experimentally and symptomatically imposed social isolation both result in the loss of a normal neurostimulatory environmental social structure (e.g., cues, learning, circadian entrainment, etc.), SIR might inform us about the potentially lifelong neural and behavioral *consequences* of symptomatic social withdrawal and impaired social cognition in schizophrenia and related developmental brain disorders.

Clearly, these two pathways—stress-induced neurotoxicity and isolation-induced loss of

---

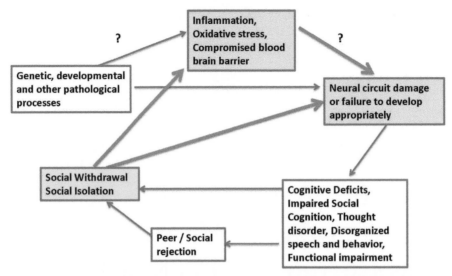

FIGURE 1 **Hypothesized role of social isolation in the developmental pathophysiology of schizophrenia.** The schematic is a hypothetical framework for the role of social withdrawal and social isolation in the course of illness of schizophrenia. Represented here are the proposed pathways in which social isolation exerts its effects on neural circuits and, conversely, how cognitive deficits, functional impairments, and peer/social rejection contribute to social isolation. This framework suggests that psychosocial adversity during early life can both (1) trigger chronic stress cascades and (2) be a consequence of the functional impairment resulting from premorbid social cognitive deficits in mental illness. Red arrows indicate effects of adolescent SIR studied in model organisms without premorbid pathology (e.g., rat SIR; reviewed in this chapter). A "?" indicates the putative, but as yet unknown, biological mechanisms (e.g., immune, metabolic) through which SIR may mediate its effects on neural circuits relevant to disease pathology.

neurostimulation—might converge at multiple levels. For example, psychosocial adversity during early life can clearly both (1) trigger chronic stress cascades and (2) be a consequence of the functional impairment resulting from premorbid social cognitive deficits in mental illness (Figure 1).

Neurobiological Consequences of SIR

SIR rats exhibit profound abnormalities in behavior, drug responses, and neurochemistry compared to rats reared in social groups (cf., Fone & Porkess, 2008; Hall, 1998; Powell, 2010; Powell & Geyer, 2002). These abnormalities include evidence for dopamine hyperreactivity: (1) increased behavioral sensitivity to dopamine agonists (Bowling & Bardo, 1994; Jones, Hernandez, Kendall, Marsden, & Robbins, 1992; Jones, Marsden, & Robbins, 1990; Sahakian, Robbins, Morgan, & Iversen, 1975), (2) reduced responsivity to dopamine antagonists (Sahakian, Robbins, & Iversen, 1977), (3) elevated basal and amphetamine-stimulated dopamine release in the nucleus accumbens (NAC) and/or dorsal striatum (Hall et al., 1998; Han, Wang, Shao, & Li, 2011; Jones et al., 1992; Möller, Du Preez, Viljoen, Berk, Emsley, et al., 2013; Yorgason, España, Konstantopoulos, Weiner, & Jones, 2013), (4) elevated dopamine concentrations (Jones et al., 1992) and altered dopamine turnover (Blanc et al., 1980) in the frontal cortex, and (5) increased firing activity of dopamine neurons (Fabricius et al., 2010).

In addition to alterations in dopamine function, SIR rats display abnormalities in the hippocampus, thalamus, and frontal cortex. For example, SIR rats have an increased density of 5-HT1A receptors in the hippocampus (Del-Bel, Joca, Padovan, & Guimaraes, 2002; Preece, Dalley, Theobald, Robbins, & Reynolds, 2004). SIR rats have reduced synaptophysin immunoreactivity in the dentate gyrus (Varty, Marsden, & Higgins, 1999); synaptophysin is a synapse-specific protein involved in neurotransmitter release, and its expression is reduced within certain hippocampal subfields in schizophrenia (Eastwood & Harrison, 1995). There is also evidence of reduced BDNF in the hippocampus (Scaccianoce et al., 2006) and decreased spine density in SIR rats (Silva-Gomez, Rojas, Juarez, & Flores, 2003). Loss of parvalbumin (PV)-positive GABA interneurons observed in SIR rats (Harte, Powell, Swerdlow, Geyer, & Reynolds, 2007; Schiavone et al., 2009) may reproduce some features of cellular abnormalities reported in the hippocampus and frontal cortex of schizophrenia patients (Reynolds, Abdul-Monim, Neill, & Zhang, 2004; Reynolds & Beasley, 2001). Metabolic abnormalities in the hippocampus and thalamus after SIR were reported by Bonab et al. (2012).

We might expect that postweaning manipulations would have greatest effects on later-developing brain structures such as the prefrontal cortex (PFC). Abnormalities in the PFC detected in SIR rats include the following: (1) abnormal firing of PFC pyramidal cells upon dopamine stimulation from VTA neurons (Peters & O'Donnell, 2005);

(2) decreased PFC volume (Day-Wilson, Jones, Southam, Cilia, & Totterdell, 2006; Schubert, Porkess, Dashdorj, Fone, & Auer, 2009); (3) decreased PFC dendritic arborization (Pascual, Zamora-Leon, & Valero-Cabre, 2006; Silva-Gomez et al., 2003); and (4) decreased basal dopamine turnover in the infralimbic part of the medial prefrontal cortex (Heidbreder et al., 2000) and depressed immediate early gene expression (Levine et al., 2007). Neurochemical perturbations after SIR in other limbic-forebrain regions include (1) increased basal dopamine turnover in the amygdaloid complex; (2) decreased basal turnover of serotonin in the nucleus accumbens (Heidbreder et al., 2000); and (3) evidence of increased oxidative stress (increased superoxide dismutase activity, decreased oxidized:reduced glutathione ratio and increased lipid peroxidation) in limbic cortico-striatal circuitry (Möller, Du Preez, Emsley, & Harvey, 2011).

No clear unifying mechanism has been established as the cause of the widespread pathology that follows SIR. That the neural consequences of SIR are identified across widely distributed brain regions (e.g., hippocampus, amygdala, PFC, and nucleus accumbens, among others) and levels of cellular function indicate that this developmental manipulation reproduces the broadly distributed pathological findings in developmental brain disorders such as schizophrenia (cf., Swerdlow, 2011) raises the possibility that these consequences reflect one or more processes with diffuse cerebral impact, such as alterations in immune function (e.g., Levine et al., 2008; Wellen & Hotamisligil, 2005) or changes in the blood–brain barrier (e.g., Osburg et al., 2002; Quagliarello, Wispelwey, Long, & Scheld, 1991). Indeed, inflammatory cytokines have been reported to be activated by SIR (e.g., Lukasz et al., 2013; Möller, Du Preez, Viljoen, Berk, Emsley, et al., 2013), and SIR impairs such basic somatic mechanisms as wound healing (Detillion, Craft, Glasper, Prendergast, & DeVries, 2004; Glasper & Devries, 2005; Levine et al., 2008). Recently, a clear role for nicotinamide adenosine dinucleotide phosphate oxidase 2 (Nox2)-dependent oxidative mechanisms in the SIR model was demonstrated (Schiavone et al., 2009). Corroborating our earlier work (Harte et al., 2007), Schiavone et al. (2009) reported decreased PV immunoreactivity in the brains of SIR rats, which was associated with elevations in Nox2. The decrease in PV-staining and deficits in novel object recognition were blocked by treatment with the Nox2 inhibitor apocynin in SIR rats (Schiavone et al., 2009). While there are large knowledge gaps to fill in this area, it is not inconceivable that such changes—which in some cases re-create reported inflammatory disturbances in schizophrenia (cf., Meyer, 2013)—might have more far-reaching effects on systemic processes that could influence a broad range of neural functions, from metabolic alterations (Kern, Ranganathan, Li, Wood, & Ranganathan, 2001; Park, Park, & Yu, 2005; Wellen & Hotamisligil, 2005) to neurotoxic deviations in trytophan metabolism (cf., Muller, Myint, & Schwarz, 2011; Silver et al., 1992) to dysregulation of the gut–brain microbiome (Bercik & Collins, 2014).

Behavioral Consequences

Given the widely distributed neural changes after SIR, it is not surprising that SIR rats exhibit a broad range of behavioral disturbances; in fact, it is beyond the scope of this review to catalog these changes in a comprehensive way. The behavioral "nonspecificity" of this experimental manipulation is supported by the fact that SIR is associated with abnormalities ranging from unconditioned, simple motor activity to more complex tasks of learning and memory. One challenge in understanding such a diffuse behavioral profile is that behavioral measures do not reflect unitary processes, and it is highly likely that SIR-induced disturbances across multiple behaviors reflect shared mechanisms at both neural and behavioral levels. Nonetheless, because reports generally describe disturbances in a very limited subset of these measures, *there is no simple way to identify sources of shared variance or hierarchical structure among these behavioral disturbances.* In some cases, SIR-relevant phenotypes can be dissociated (e.g., see below, PPI and startle magnitude), while in others, there is like substantial mechanistic overlap (e.g., deficits in different learning-based tasks).

SIR rats show elevated levels and slowed habituation of locomotor activity in novel environments (Hall, 1998; Jones et al., 1990; Jones, Robbins, & Marsden, 1989; Lapiz, Mateo, Parker, & Marsden, 2000; Paulus, Bakshi, & Geyer, 1998; Sahakian et al., 1975; Varty, Paulus, Braff, & Geyer, 2000), increased investigatory behavior (e.g., rearings, holepokes; Lapiz et al., 2000; Paulus et al., 1998), and an increased preference for a novel environment (Hall, Humby, Wilkinson, & Robbins, 1997). Additionally, SIR rats show increased anxiety-like behavior in both the elevated plus maze and a variety of open-field assays (Da Silva, Ferreira, Carobrez Ade, & Morato, 1996; Hori et al., 2014; McCool & Chappell, 2009; Molina-Hernandez, Tellez-Alcantara, & Perez-Garcia, 2001; Wright, Upton, & Marsden, 1991), deficits in fear learning (Weiss, Pryce, Jongen-Relo, Nanz-Bahr, & Feldon, 2004), impaired recognition memory (e.g., novel object recognition; Bianchi et al., 2006; McLean et al., 2010), increased aggression (Wongwitdecha & Marsden, 1996), impulsivity (Zeeb, Wong, & Winstanley, 2013) and reactivity to novelty (Gentsch, Lichtsteiner, Frischknecht, Feer, & Siegfried, 1988; Hall et al., 1997), reduced spatial memory (Quan, Tian, Xu, Zhang, & Yang, 2010), and cognitive inflexibility as demonstrated by deficits in reversal learning (Amitai et al., 2013; Krech, Rosenzweig, & Bennett, 1962;

Schrijver, Pallier, Brown, & Wurbel, 2004; Schrijver & Wurbel, 2001) and extradimensional set-shifting tasks (McLean et al., 2010; Schrijver & Wurbel, 2001).

In some cases, SIR paradigms that do not elicit robust behavioral disturbances still produce rats with an enhanced sensitivity to the behavioral effects of psychoactive drugs. For example, Lim, Taylor, and Malone (2012) reported that SIR rats exhibited normal locomotor levels and novel object recognition at baseline; in contrast, SIR (but not socially housed rats) exhibited hyperactivity and impaired NOR if they had received a low dose of the NMDA antagonist, MK-801, during postnatal days 7–10. A number of reports have also documented that SIR-induced behavioral (and systemic) disturbances can be prevented or reversed by pharmacological (e.g., clozapine; Möller, Du Preez, Viljoen, Berk, Emsley, et al., 2013; oxytocin; Vitalo et al., 2009), behavioral (e.g., tickling; Hori et al., 2014), and environmental manipulations (e.g., environmental enrichment; Vitalo et al., 2009).

REDUCED PREPULSE INHIBITION AFTER SIR

One behavioral measure that has been extensively studied in SIR rats is prepulse inhibition of the acoustic startle response (PPI). PPI is a laboratory-based operational measure of sensorimotor gating in which a weak prepulse inhibits the magnitude of a startle response to an intense, abrupt "pulse" occurring 30–120 ms later. PPI is easily studied in laboratory animals, using stimulus parameters and equipment for stimulus delivery and response acquisition that are similar or identical to those used in humans (cf., Swerdlow, Weber, Qu, Light, & Braff, 2008).

Perhaps the main reason that PPI has been so extensively studied across species is that Braff et al. (1978) reported that schizophrenia patients exhibited deficient PPI: prepulses did not generate full levels of inhibition in these patients, compared to matched healthy comparison subjects. Indeed, since Braff et al.'s original finding, PPI deficits in schizophrenia or "prodromal" patients have been detected in over 40 PubMed reports (cf., Swerdlow et al., 2014). However, reduced PPI is not specific to patients with schizophrenia: it has also been detected in patients with Huntington's disease (Swerdlow, Paulsen, et al., 1995; Valls-Sole, Munoz, & Valldeoriola, 2004), obsessive compulsive disorder (Ahmari, Risbrough, Geyer, & Simpson, 2012; Hoenig, Hochrein, Quednow, Maier, & Wagner, 2005; Swerdlow, Benbow, Zisook, Geyer, & Braff, 1993), nocturnal enuresis (Ornitz, Hanna, & de Traversay, 1992), Asperger's syndrome (McAlonan et al., 2002), 22q11 syndrome (Sobin, Kiley-Brabeck, & Karayiorgou, 2005), Kleinfelter syndrome (van Rijn, Swaab, Magnee, van Engeland, & Kemner,

2011), Fragile-X syndrome (Frankland et al., 2004), blepharospasm (Gomez-Wong, Marti, Tolosa, & Valls-Sole, 1998), and Tourette syndrome (Castellanos et al., 1996; Swerdlow et al., 2001). Nonetheless, PPI deficits in schizophrenia patients are highly heritable (Greenwood et al., 2007), associated with specific genes (Greenwood et al., 2011; Greenwood, Light, Swerdlow, Radant, & Braff, 2012), sensitive to second-generation antipsychotics (e.g., Swerdlow et al., 2006; Swerdlow et al., 2014) and related to global function in these patients (Swerdlow et al., 2006).

Geyer et al. (1993) first reported that SIR rats show deficits in PPI; this finding has been reproduced by many different groups (Bristow, Landon, Saywell, & Tricklebank, 1995; Cilia, Hatcher, Reavill, & Jones, 2005; Cilia, Reavill, Hagan, & Jones, 2001; Powell, Swerdlow, Pitcher, & Geyer, 2002; Swerdlow et al., 2013; Varty & Higgins, 1995; Wilkinson et al., 1994). Equally clear from the onset has been that the PPI-reducing effects of SIR are "fragile" (e.g., Weiss, Feldon, & Domeney, 1999), with different groups reporting paradigmatic differences that impact the magnitude and consistency of SIR-induced PPI deficits. *The basis for this fragility is not well understood, and the longitudinal and labor-intensive nature of the SIR paradigm is not fully conducive to the types of controlled, parametric analyses that might clarify the variable effects of SIR on PPI.* Some factors have been associated with differential effects of SIR on PPI, as noted briefly below, but the mechanisms by which these factors moderate SIR effects remain obscure. The difficulty in consistently reproducing SIR-induced PPI deficits is similar to the difficulty observed with other developmental models of relevance to schizophrenia such as prenatal stress, maternal immune activation, and maternal toxins (e.g., methylazoxymethanol acetate, MAM) in terms of reproducibility and consistency of effects across laboratories (Powell, 2010).

Methodological and Parametric Considerations

1. Timing: Deficits in PPI produced by SIR are developmentally specific in that they only appear when social isolation occurs early, during the postnatal period, and not in rats isolated as adults (Wilkinson et al., 1994). In a typical SIR paradigm, rats are isolated postweaning (typically pnd 24–28), and PPI is tested in early adulthood, e.g., pnd 53–63. Earlier weaning (e.g., pnd 21) does not enhance and may hinder the development of SIR-induced PPI deficits (Cilia, Hatcher, et al., 2005), though in some cases, persistent SIR-induced PPI deficits are detected after only 2 weeks of postweaning SIR (Liu, Kao, & Tung, 2011). In some cases, PPI deficits in SIR rats have been detected early in adulthood, but they have faded with both age and repeated testing

(e.g., Swerdlow et al., 2013). In other cases, PPI deficits in SIR rats have been found to be repeatable (Powell et al., 2002) and persistent throughout later adulthood (Cilia, Hatcher, et al., 2005; Cilia et al., 2001). Among parametric manipulations tested for their impact on the development of SIR-induced PPI deficits, these deficits are prevented by rat handling (Krebs-Thomson, Giracello, Solis, & Geyer, 2001; Rosa et al., 2005; Sciolino et al., 2010) and are no longer detected after subjecting rats to other experimental measures (e.g., activity monitoring; Domeney & Feldon, 1998) or electrophysiological measures (e.g., Swerdlow et al., 2013) but are not enhanced by concomitant stressors such as water deprivation (Powell et al., 2002).

2. Sex: SIR-induced PPI deficits are alternately reported only in male rats (e.g., Swerdlow et al., 2013), only in female rats (e.g., Powell, Risbrough, & Geyer, 2003), or in both male and female rats (e.g., Powell et al., 2002), though often with preferential effects displayed by one or the other sex. It is worth noting that studies differing in the magnitude of SIR-induced PPI deficits across male and female rats also differ in the strain of rat, and no systematic comparisons have attempted to disentangle these two factors.

3. Strain and species: Several studies have detected strain differences in the magnitude or even presence of SIR-induced PPI deficits in rats. Varty and Geyer (1998) reported SIR-induced PPI deficits in Sprague Dawley and Fischer rats, but not Lewis rats. Wistar, Long Evans, Lister hooded, and Buffalo rats all exhibit SIR-induced PPI deficits, though deficits in Wistars tend to be easily interrupted (Domeney & Feldon, 1998) or even absent in some studies (Weiss, Di Iorio, Feldon, & Domeney, 2000), those in Long Evans rats tend to favor female over males (Powell et al., 2002), and those in Buffalo rats were detected exclusively in males (Swerdlow et al., 2013). More recent studies have also shown that several different mouse strains that exhibit SIR-induced PPI deficits (e.g., ddY, 129T2, C57BL/6) (Dai et al., 2004; Sakaue, Ago, Baba, & Matsuda, 2003; Varty, Powell, Lehmann-Masten, Buell, & Geyer, 2006; although see Pietropaolo, Singer, Feldon, & Yee, 2008). Strain differences in SIR-induced PPI deficits are expected based on the proposed gene × environment interactions that modulate complex behavior. Strain-specific effects of an environmental manipulation such as SIR are similar to strain differences observed in response to dopamine agonists (Rigdon, 1990; Swerdlow et al., 2000; Swerdlow, Shoemaker, Auerbach, et al., 2004; Swerdlow, Shoemaker, Crain, et al., 2004; Swerdlow, Shoemaker, Platten, et al., 2004; Swerdlow et al., 2003) as well as epistatic interactions in which gene deletion has different effects on PPI and other behaviors depending on the background mouse strain (e.g., FMR1 KO mice; Pietropaolo, Guilleminot, Martin, D'Amato, & Crusio, 2011; Spencer et al., 2011).

In laboratory animals and humans, social interaction is essential for pair bonding, parental care, and cooperation (Trezza, Campolongo, & Vanderschuren, 2011). Conceptually, one would predict that SIR might have the greatest impact on PPI and other measures of brain function in species that rely most heavily on social contact after being weaned from the mother. To date, however, these effects of SIR on PPI have only been tested systematically in rats and mice, and there is no clear relationship between levels of positive social contact (typically rat > mice) versus aggression (typically mice > rats) and the magnitude of SIR-induced PPI deficits. One report describes differential development of PPI among human infants born to mothers who reported more vs. less social isolation during pregnancy (Huggenberger, Suter, Blumenthal, & Schachinger, 2013).

4. Startle magnitude: Two other startle phenotypes that appear to be variably impacted by SIR are startle reflex magnitude and habituation. Startle magnitude is often (e.g., Heidbreder et al., 2000) but not always potentiated in SIR rats (e.g., Cilia, Hatcher, et al., 2005; five out of 19 SIR cohorts exhibited enhanced startle; but see Roncada et al., 2009), and these effects are dissociated from changes in PPI. In some cases, startle potentiation is detected after SIR while PPI remains unchanged; for example, we detected potentiated startle in both male and female SIR Buffalo rats, while PPI deficits were evident only in males (Swerdlow et al., 2013). Importantly, changes in startle magnitude can often confound the interpretation of changes in PPI (cf., Swerdlow et al., 2000), and in cases where both measures are impacted by SIR, it has been possible to demonstrate that these effects were independent (Cilia, Hatcher, et al., 2005; Swerdlow et al., 2013). SIR-potentiated startle is thought to be regulated by interacting neuropeptide systems, with a prominent role of corticotropin-releasing factor activity in the shell of the nucleus accumbens (Nair, Gutman, Davis, & Young, 2005). In addition to increased startle magnitude, SIR also has been associated with slower rates of startle habituation (for reviews, see Geyer, Krebs-Thomson, Braff, & Swerdlow, 2001; Geyer et al., 1993; Powell & Geyer, 2002; Weiss & Feldon, 2001).

5. The "unknowns": Chronic developmental manipulations present many methodological complexities, and for SIR, these are multiplied by

the known sensitivity of SIR effects to environmental stimulation. Thus, it is likely, though untested, that variability in the magnitude of SIR effects on PPI and other phenotypes across laboratories might reflect evanescent factors such as the following: (1) the proximity and (2) olfactory and acoustic insulation of individually housed relative to socially housed rats, both in the rat colony and when rodents are moved for laboratory testing, (3) patterns and styles of animal handling during changes in cage bedding, water, and food, or health maintenance, and weight checks, etc. For example, the degree to which testing chambers are cleaned of olfactory signals between tests of socially housed and SIR rats might conceivably impact the robustness of SIR-induced behavioral changes. Weiss et al. (1999) reported that Wistar rats housed in grid floor cages did not show SIR-induced PPI deficits, whereas those housed in sawdust bedding did show SIR-induced PPI deficits. While investigators strive to control and document many of these methodological variables, in truth, it is very difficult to maintain such methods with perfect consistency over 8–16 weeks of animal housing, care, and testing, particularly when designs generally call for contemporaneous housing, care, and testing of both socially reared and SIR groups; moreover, variations from such protocols are likely to happen "invisibly" in the vast majority of hours during which SIR rats are being maintained by individuals other than the senior investigators and authors of the SIR reports.

Neural Substrates of SIR-Induced PPI Deficits

Systemic Pharmacology

Many studies report the "reversal" of SIR-induced PPI deficits by systemic drug administration, though in truth, many fewer studies have actually demonstrated such a "reversal." A *reversal* of SIR effects can only be demonstrated when the same SIR cohorts are tested under two order-balanced conditions (i.e., a within-subject cross-over design), and the SIR effects are detected in one but not the other condition. In fact, many studies of acute pharmacological effects on SIR-induced PPI deficits use a *between-subject design* in which PPI after active drug administration in one group of SIR rats is compared to PPI after placebo administration in a second group of SIR rats. In this design, the absence (or reduction) in SIR-induced PPI deficits after active drug treatment is most clearly interpreted as a blockade (or diminution) of the expression of these deficits, rather than a "reversal" per se. One reason for the use of this between-subject design is that repeated testing of SIR rats (required for a within-subject assessment of two or more drug doses) is often associated with a weakening of SIR effects on PPI

(e.g., Dashti, Aboutaleb, & Shahbazi, 2013). Using this within-subject cross-over design, reversals of SIR-induced PPI deficits have been demonstrated with an alpha7 nicotinic receptor agonist (Cilia, Cluderay, et al., 2005), the histamine H3 receptor antagonist GSK207040 (Southam et al., 2009), and the 5-HT2A/D4 antagonists (Geyer et al., 1999).

To our knowledge, absent from the literature are studies assessing the ability of a drug to prevent the *development* of SIR-induced PPI deficits. This approach has been used to demonstrate the ability of handling, environmental enrichment, and even oxytocin to prevent the behavioral and immunological effects of SIR in rats (e.g., Vitalo et al., 2009) and the ability of the Nox2 inhibitor apocynin to prevent the decrease in PV-staining and deficits in novel object recognition in SIR rats (Schiavone et al., 2009), but to our knowledge has not been attempted with pharmacologic interventions and SIR-induced PPI deficits. From a perspective of modeling preventative interventions to protect vulnerable individuals from pathological consequences of developmental stressors, such an approach would seem particularly powerful (Powell, Risbrough, et al., 2003).

Nonetheless, a substantial literature does demonstrate that expression of SIR-induced PPI deficits can be blocked or diminished by acute pharmacologic challenge. In fact, a long list of drugs with very diverse pharmacologic properties can prevent or reduce the expression of SIR-induced PPI deficits in rats, including typical antipsychotics (Geyer et al., 1993; Varty & Higgins, 1995), atypical antipsychotics (Bakshi, Swerdlow, Braff, & Geyer, 1998; but see also Barr, Powell, Markou, & Geyer, 2006; Cilia et al., 2001; Varty & Higgins, 1995), and the glycine/NMDA receptor antagonist, L-701,324 (Bristow et al., 1995). In mice, the pharmacology of SIR-induced PPI deficits is equally diverse, with these deficits being blocked by the acetylcholinesterase (AChE) inhibitors galantamine (Koda et al., 2008), the 5HT1A receptor agonist, osemozotan (Sakaue et al., 2003), and the metabotropic glutamate 2/3 receptor agonist MGS0028 (Ago et al., 2012). Clearly, the heterogeneous pharmacology of drugs capable of preventing the expression of SIR effects on PPI argues against any single locus of neural dysregulation as a basis for these deficits.

Additionally, the pharmacological blockade or reversal of SIR-induced PPI deficits shows at least some specificity to antipsychotics or putative antipsychotics. To assess the specificity of this predictive model, PPI has been measured in isolation-reared rats after acute treatments with selected nonantipsychotic psychoactive drugs. Isolation rearing-induced deficits in PPI are not blocked by the anxiolytic diazepam (Nakato, Morita, Wanibuchi, & Yamaguchi, 1997; Varty & Higgins, 1995) or the antidepressant amitriptyline (Nakato et al., 1997). One pitfall with the use of SIR as a screen for novel antipsychotic drugs is that it is costly and time-consuming. Although the model has several benefits over pharmacologically induced deficits in PPI (Geyer et al., 2001; Varty & Higgins, 1995), individual investigators need to determine the cost/benefit ratio when assessing its use as a screening tool. Additionally, as with most environmental and many pharmacological manipulations, isolation-rearing effects on PPI are dependent on the strain, the handling procedures, and the caging conditions (see above), which may be problematic in establishing a pharmacological screen.

Relevant Associated Neural Changes

In rats, PPI is regulated by interconnected limbic-forebrain structures and their projections to lower pontine circuitry, likely including the pedunculopontine nucleus (cf., Swerdlow et al., 2008). Many of the brain regions that exhibit identifiable changes after SIR are among those known to regulate PPI, including the hippocampus (Caine, Geyer, & Swerdlow, 1991; Caine, Geyer, & Swerdlow, 1992; Swerdlow, Lipska, et al., 1995), amygdala (Swerdlow, Caine, & Geyer, 1992; Wan & Swerdlow, 1997), PFC (Bubser & Koch, 1994; Swerdlow, Lipska, et al., 1995), thalamus (Kodsi & Swerdlow, 1997; Wolf et al., 2010), and nucleus accumbens (Swerdlow, Braff, Geyer, & Koob, 1986; Swerdlow, Braff, Masten, & Geyer, 1990). Clearly, SIR-induced changes in these brain regions would likely contribute to the observed PPI deficits in SIR rats; in fact, it would seem plausible that changes within multiple different levels of interconnected limbic cortico-striato-pallido-pontine (CSPP) circuitry might result from SIR, and that the phenotype of reduced PPI in SIR rats might reflect the integrated impact of these circuit changes on structures that ultimately mediate PPI, that is, determine the inhibitory impact of the lead stimulus on the startle reflex, somewhere within the pontine tegmentum (Koch, Kungel, & Herbert, 1993; Swerdlow et al., 1992; Swerdlow & Geyer, 1993). The hypothesis that this CSPP circuitry might mediate PPI deficits produced by a number of disparate experimental manipulations—developmental and otherwise—has been supported by several reports (e.g., Risterucci et al., 2005).

Of course, this parsimonious hypothesis—that SIR-induced PPI deficits reflect SIR-induced changes in one or more levels of limbic CSPP circuitry—*has never been tested, and it may even be premature to claim that it is supported by strong inference.* As described above, the "fragile" nature of SIR-induced PPI deficits makes it difficult to test specific neural mechanisms as the basis for behavioral changes that are somewhat unpredictable in magnitude and durability (e.g., Dashti et al., 2013). In truth, while we have accumulated evidence for the variability of the SIR-induced PPI phenotype, the consistency and robustness of SIR-induced changes in any particular level or levels of limbic CSPP circuitry has not been tested in

a manner that allows a systematic matching of neural changes and PPI deficits, though studies focused on correlations of SIR-disrupted PPI and neural changes within a single brain region have been reported (e.g., Harte et al., 2007). More generally, if we believe that SIR triggers consistent changes in a specific brain substrate, for example, the hippocampus, it is unclear how such consistent changes could explain SIR-induced PPI deficits that are much less consistent. Presumably, in cohorts where SIR-induced PPI deficits are not detected (e.g., female Buffalo rats; Swerdlow et al., 2013), we would expect that the PPI-relevant SIR-induced neural changes would also not be detected, or at least would be less marked, compared to cohorts where such PPI deficits are robust. Given the multiplicity of SIR-induced circuit changes, it would seem equally possible that cohorts not exhibiting SIR-induced PPI deficits might have changes in multiple levels of limbic CSPP circuitry, with "downstream" changes that compensate for the potentially PPI-disruptive effects of "upstream" changes (e.g., Forcelli, West, Murnen, & Malkova, 2012; Swerdlow, Braff, & Geyer, 1990). And, given the number of reports of strain difference in SIR-induced PPI phenotypes (above), as well as strain differences in PPI and its regulation by specific forebrain substrates (e.g., Shilling, Saint Marie, Shoemaker, & Swerdlow, 2008; Swerdlow, Breier, & Saint Marie, 2011), it seems plausible that PPI deficits in different rat strains might reflect distinct SIR-induced changes within PPI-regulatory circuitry. Thus, the search for a "final common substrate" explaining SIR-induced PPI deficits in different experimental cohorts—strain, sexes, species, etc.—might not ultimately be productive.

Perhaps more importantly, the notion that SIR-induced PPI deficits reflect dysregulation within an integrated circuit suggests the possibility that these deficits might be reversed by interventions that may not directly impact the "primary" insult. Thus, SIR-induced PPI deficits can be blocked by dopamine antagonists (e.g., Bakshi et al., 1998) and by mesolimbic dopamine depletion (Powell, Geyer, et al., 2003), and yet elevated mesolimbic dopamine activity is equivocal in SIR rats (no change: Howes, Dalley, Morrison, Robbins, & Everitt, 2000; Leng, Feldon, & Ferger, 2004; elevations: Fabricius et al., 2010; Han et al., 2011; Möller, Du Preez, Viljoen, Berk, & Harvey, 2013; Yorgason et al., 2013); similarly, SIR-induced PPI deficits can be blocked by systemic administration of an alpha-7 nicotinic receptor agonist (Cilia, Cluderay, et al., 2005), but there is no evidence that SIR disrupts normal functions of alpha-7 nicotinic receptors. In some cases, indirect association implicates specific circuit-level changes with SIR-induced PPI deficits: for example, SIR causes changes in endocannabinoid signaling across a number of levels of CSPP circuitry (Sciolino et al., 2010), only some of which (e.g., PFC) are prevented by frequent handling that also prevents SIR-induced PPI deficits.

Similarly, SIR triggers increased measures of oxidative stress in limbic cortico-striatal circuitry and aberrant tryptophan metabolism, and both of these changes as well as SIR-induced PPI deficits are reversed by the atypical antipsychotic clozapine (Möller et al., 2011; Möller, Du Preez, Viljoen, Berk, Emsley, et al., 2013). These examples suggest very specific mechanisms for normalized PPI in SIR rats (handling-induced changes in PFC endocannabinoid systems, and clozapine-induced normalization of a cortico-striatal redox disequilibrium reflecting aberrant tryptophan metabolism shifted toward quinolinic acid production). But the more plausible explanation for behavioral changes after a pervasive developmental stressor is that (1) they reflect the dysregulation of widely distributed and interconnected neural circuits; (2) because it involves multiple different nodes or "hubs" of neural activity, this circuit dysregulation manifests itself in complex and multifaceted behavioral phenotypes; and (3) some of these phenotypes (including reduced PPI) can be moderated via interventions targeting different levels of, and substrates within, this circuitry.

Gene Expression

Consistent with the heterogeneous behavioral and neural effects of SIR in rats, and the many different pharmacological targets capable of moderating SIR-induced changes in PPI, the list of alterations in gene expression after SIR, and particularly those associated with PPI deficits, is long and diverse. Reductions in nonspecific, immediate, early gene expression in the PFC have been reported (Levine et al., 2008; Wall, Fischer, & Bland, 2012), as have reductions in more specific forms of gene expression, including mRNA relevant to glutamate (Turnock-Jones et al., 2009; Zhao et al., 2009), endocannabinoid (Robinson, Loiacono, Christopoulos, Sexton, & Malone, 2010), and serotonin function (Martin et al., 2010).

Our recent findings (Swerdlow et al., 2013) suggest that even when SIR does not change the absolute levels of gene expression in the PFC and ventral striatum, the functional consequences of that expression (reflecting the integrated output of a larger circuitry) can change. Thus, after SIR that disrupted PPI in male Buffalo rats, absolute expression levels of seven PPI- and schizophrenia-associated genes in the PFC and nucleus accumbens did not differ in SIR versus socially reared rats. However, in SIR rats (and not in socially reared rats), these expression levels in the PFC correlated significantly and positively with PPI, and expression levels in the nucleus accumbens correlated significantly and negatively with PPI. Based on evidence suggesting that region-specific expression levels in these genes tracked levels of regional cellular activation (Swerdlow et al., 2012), we interpreted these findings to indicate that higher PFC activity was associated with sparing of PPI after SIR, while within the

nucleus accumbens, relative quiescence was associated with sparing of PPI. Presumably, these relationships of regional activity to post-SIR PPI would be mediated via downstream effects within CSPP circuitry.

RELEVANCE TO DEFICIENT SENSORIMOTOR GATING IN SCHIZOPHRENIA?

As noted above, PPI deficits are detected in a number of different brain disorders, and different models with construct validity for these disorders have been shown to produce rodents that also exhibit impaired PPI. For example, mice transgenic for the Huntington gene (Carter et al., 1999) and knock-outs for histidine decarboxylase (Castellan Baldan et al., 2014) both exhibit impaired PPI, recapitulating the PPI deficits detected in patients with Huntington's disease and Tourette syndrome, respectively, which are each associated with these genetic "lesions." In each case, these models offer a relatively specific mechanism for the observed PPI phenotype, with potential homology to the human condition.

By contrast, it is very likely that SIR-induced PPI deficits relate to those detected in schizophrenia in a manner that is much less direct, and via mechanisms with more diffuse and dispersed effects on CSPP and other circuitry. Perhaps the facts that both schizophrenia and SIR are associated with (1) a developmental insult; (2) an overlapping, widely distributed neuropathology; and (3) a specific behavioral deficit—reduced PPI—supports the hypothesis that SIR-induced PPI deficits in rats is a model with construct validity for PPI deficits detected in schizophrenia patients. Certainly, the chronic stress and deprivation of social stimulation imparted by SIR may have naturalistic similarities to the sustained developmental stress and symptomatic social isolation that characterize schizophrenia. But the intermediate steps between these two psychological processes and reduced PPI in schizophrenia remain obscure. Indeed, compared to SIR, other developmental models yielding PPI deficits in rodents, for example, in utero immune activation (Meyer, Feldon, Schedlowski, & Yee, 2005), hypoxia (Vaillancourt & Boksa, 2000), or neonatal lesions (Lipska et al., 1995) are closer to specific biological mechanisms with potential etiological ties to schizophrenia. Nonetheless, some of these models—particularly those related to immune activation—may ultimately be informative about potential biological mechanisms for SIR-induced PPI deficits. In fact, elevations in oxidative stress pathways appear across several neurodevelopmental models including maternal immune activation (cf., Boksa, 2010), neonatal ventral hippocampal lesions (Cabungcal et al., 2014), and SIR (Möller et al., 2011; Möller, Du Preez, Viljoen,

Berk, Emsley, et al., 2013; Schiavone et al., 2009) and, hence, may provide a common underlying mechanisms for several models of dysfunctional brain development (Powell, Sejnowski, & Behrens, 2012).

As noted above, even if SIR-induced PPI deficits do model PPI deficits in schizophrenia, *it remains unclear whether the basis for this model reflects the primary cause of the disorder, e.g., neurotoxic effects of stress/immune activation or secondary effects of symptomatic social isolation*. We know that schizophrenia patients experience social isolation: in both retrospective and prospective studies, social isolation is a nonspecific symptom that appears early in the course of schizophrenia (Hafner et al., 2003; Møller & Husby, 2000) and in those at a genetic risk for schizophrenia (Dworkin et al., 1991; Dworkin, Lewis, Cornblatt, & Erlenmeyer-Kimling, 1994). Social withdrawal and isolation are thought to increase disease risk and conversion to psychosis in prodromal patients (Addington, Penn, Woods, Addington, & Perkins, 2008). Indeed, social functioning, among other factors, predicts conversion to psychosis in patients at a high risk of developing psychosis (Cannon et al., 2008). And conversely, therapies that strengthen social skills enhance function in schizophrenia patients (Granholm, Holden, Link, & McQuaid, 2014). No studies to date have reported the relationship of premorbid social function to postconversion PPI levels in schizophrenia patients.

One finding highlighting the complex causal relationship between social isolation and the expression of PPI deficits comes from studies of healthy, socially reared adult Wistar rats, in which high levels of PPI predicted high levels of social interaction, and low levels of PPI predicted low levels of social interactions (Goktalay, Kayir, Ulusoy, & Uzbay, 2014); neither levels of PPI nor social interaction was associated with anxiety-like traits, assessed by elevated plus maze. Thus, low trait levels of social interaction—presumably associated with reduced socially generated neurostimulation, but presumably *not* associated with stress-induced inflammatory brain injury or other pathological events—were accompanied by low levels of PPI. Clearly, this connection of trait social interactions and PPI might reflect a third phenotype, for example, two ends of the normal distribution of basal forebrain oxytocin expression or amygdala activity levels, but this finding, to the degree that it has cross-species validity, suggests that we do not need to implicate pathological changes in brain circuitry as a mechanism linking the expression of low PPI and low social activity. In a related observation, oxytocin, which increases social interactions in rats, increases PPI in rat strains with low "trait" PPI levels (Feifel, Shilling, & Belcher, 2012). Again, social interactions and low PPI can be linked mechanistically without the need to invoke pathological processes caused by the stress associated with developmental social isolation.

CONCLUSIONS

SIR-induced PPI deficits in rodents remains an attractive heuristic model for how a "naturalistic," nonpharmacological, and nonlesion developmental intervention can generate a very specific behavioral phenotype expressed by patients with schizophrenia. Reduced PPI is one of many behavioral deficits in SIR rats, and there is no simple way to identify sources of shared variance or hierarchical structure among these behavioral disturbances. SIR-induced PPI deficits are expressed to varying degrees across studies and are often diminished or eliminated by interventions like handling or repeated testing; the basis for this "fragility" is not well understood. SIR has widely dispersed neural consequences for which no clear unifying mechanism has yet been established. Moreover, with SIR-induced changes identified at many levels of PPI-regulatory circuitry, no single SIR-induced "lesion" is known to be causative to reduced PPI after SIR. At a very basic level, it remains unclear whether the basis for reduced PPI after SIR reflects a process that might be linked to the primary pathology underlying a brain disorder, for example, neurotoxic effects of stress/immune activation, or that it, instead, is a secondary effect of symptoms, such as impaired social function and consequent social isolation. Some findings from animal studies suggest that low PPI and low social interactions may be traits linked even within normal cohorts, independent of any brain pathology, but suggestive that they may be co-varying traits representing normal variations in underlying neural circuitry. Whether, and how, this normal association of reflexive and social traits is relevant to the behavioral effects of SIR in rats, or to the behavioral consequences of symptomatic social withdrawal in schizophrenia, is worthy of future consideration.

Acknowledgments

This work was supported by MH091407, MH042228, MH059803, MH094320, and Veteran's Affairs VISN 22 MIRECC.

References

Addington, J., Penn, D., Woods, S. W., Addington, D., & Perkins, D. O. (2008). Social functioning in individuals at clinical high risk for psychosis. *Schizophrenia Research*, *99*(1–3), 119–124.

Ago, Y., Araki, R., Yano, K., Kawasaki, T., Chaki, S., Nakazato, A., et al. (2012). The selective metabotropic glutamate 2/3 receptor agonist MGS0028 reverses isolation rearing-induced abnormal behaviors in mice. *Journal of Pharmaceutical Sciences*, *118*(2), 295–298.

Ahmari, S. E., Risbrough, V. B., Geyer, M. A., & Simpson, H. B. (2012). Impaired sensorimotor gating in unmedicated adults with obsessive-compulsive disorder. *Neuropsychopharmacology*, *37*(5), 1216–1223.

Amitai, N., Young, J. W., Higa, K., Sharp, R. F., Geyer, M. A., & Powell, S. B. (2013). Isolation rearing effects on probabilistic learning and cognitive flexibility in rats. *Cognitive, Affective, & Behavioral Neuroscience*.

Bakshi, V. P., Swerdlow, N. R., Braff, D. L., & Geyer, M. A. (1998). Reversal of isolation rearing-induced deficits in prepulse inhibition by Seroquel and olanzapine. *Biological Psychiatry, 43*(6), 436–445.

Barr, A. M., Powell, S. B., Markou, A., & Geyer, M. A. (2006). Iloperidone reduces sensorimotor gating deficits in pharmacological models, but not a developmental model, of disrupted prepulse inhibition in rats. *Neuropharmacology, 51*(3), 457–465.

Bercik, P., & Collins, S. M. (2014). The effects of inflammation, infection and antibiotics on the microbiota-gut-brain axis. *Advances in Experimental Medicine and Biology, 817*, 279–289.

Bianchi, M., Fone, K. F., Azmi, N., Heidbreder, C. A., Hagan, J. J., & Marsden, C. A. (2006). Isolation rearing induces recognition memory deficits accompanied by cytoskeletal alterations in rat hippocampus. *European Journal of Neuroscience, 24*(10), 2894–2902.

Blanc, G., Herve, D., Simon, H., Lisoprawski, A., Glowinski, J., & Tassin, J. P. (1980). Response to stress of mesocortico-frontal dopaminergic neurones in rats after long-term isolation. *Nature, 284*(5753), 265–267.

Boksa, P. (2010). Effects of prenatal infection on brain development and behavior: a review of findings from animal models. *Brain, Behavior, and Immunity, 24*(6), 881–897.

Bonab, A. A., Fricchione, J. G., Gorantla, S., Vitalo, A. G., Auster, M. E., Levine, S. J., et al. (2012). Isolation rearing significantly perturbs brain metabolism in the thalamus and hippocampus. *Neuroscience, 223*, 457–464.

Bowling, S. L., & Bardo, M. T. (1994). Locomotor and rewarding effects of amphetamine in enriched, social, and isolate reared rats. *Pharmacology, Biochemistry and Behavior, 48*(2), 459–464.

Braff, D., Stone, C., Callaway, E., Geyer, M., Glick, I., & Bali, L. (1978). Prestimulus effects on human startle reflex in normals and schizophrenics. *Psychophysiology, 15*(4), 339–343.

Bristow, L. J., Landon, L., Saywell, K. L., & Tricklebank, M. D. (1995). The glycine/NMDA receptor antagonist, L-701,324 reverses isolation-induced deficits in prepulse inhibition in the rat. *Psychopharmacology (Berl), 118*(2), 230–232.

Bubser, M., & Koch, M. (1994). Prepulse inhibition of the acoustic startle response of rats is reduced by 6-hydroxydopamine lesions of the medial prefrontal cortex. *Psychopharmacology (Berl), 113*(3–4), 487–492.

Cabungcal, J.-H., Counotte, D. S., Lewis, E. M., Tejeda, H. A., Piantadosi, P., Pollock, C., et al. (2014). Juvenile antioxidant treatment prevents adult deficits in a developmental model of schizophrenia. *Neuron, 83*(5), 1073–1084.

Caine, S. B., Geyer, M. A., & Swerdlow, N. R. (1991). Carbachol infusion into the dentate gyrus disrupts sensorimotor gating of startle in the rat. *Psychopharmacology (Berl), 105*(3), 347–354.

Caine, S. B., Geyer, M. A., & Swerdlow, N. R. (1992). Hippocampal modulation of acoustic startle and prepulse inhibition in the rat. *Pharmacology, Biochemistry and Behavior, 43*(4), 1201–1208.

Cannon, T. D., Cadenhead, K., Cornblatt, B., Woods, S. W., Addington, J., Walker, E., et al. (2008). Prediction of psychosis in youth at high clinical risk: a multisite longitudinal study in North America. *Archives of General Psychiatry, 65*(1), 28–37.

Carter, R. J., Lione, L. A., Humby, T., Mangiarini, L., Mahal, A., Bates, G. P., et al. (1999). Characterization of progressive motor deficits in mice transgenic for the human Huntington's disease mutation. *Journal of Neuroscience, 19*(8), 3248–3257.

Castellan Baldan, L., Williams, K. A., Gallezot, J. D., Pogorelov, V., Rapanelli, M., Crowley, M., et al. (2014). Histidine decarboxylase deficiency causes tourette syndrome: parallel findings in humans and mice. *Neuron, 81*(1), 77–90.

Castellanos, F. X., Fine, E. J., Kaysen, D., Marsh, W. L., Rapoport, J. L., & Hallett, M. (1996). Sensorimotor gating in boys with Tourette's syndrome and ADHD: preliminary results. *Biological Psychiatry, 39*(1), 33–41.

Cilia, J., Cluderay, J., Robbins, M., Reavill, C., Southam, E., Kew, J., et al. (2005). Reversal of isolation-rearing-induced PPI deficits by an α7 nicotinic receptor agonist. *Psychopharmacology, 182*(2), 214–219.

Cilia, J., Hatcher, P. D., Reavill, C., & Jones, D. N. (2005). Long-term evaluation of isolation-rearing induced prepulse inhibition deficits in rats: an update. *Psychopharmacology (Berl), 180*(1), 57–62.

Cilia, J., Reavill, C., Hagan, J. J., & Jones, D. N. (2001). Long-term evaluation of isolation-rearing induced prepulse inhibition deficits in rats. *Psychopharmacology (Berl), 156*(2–3), 327–337.

Da Silva, N. L., Ferreira, V. M., Carobrez Ade, P., & Morato, G. S. (1996). Individual housing from rearing modifies the performance of young rats on the elevated plus-maze apparatus. *Physiology & Behavior, 60*(6), 1391–1396.

Dai, H., Okuda, H., Iwabuchi, K., Sakurai, E., Chen, Z., Kato, M., et al. (2004). Social isolation stress significantly enhanced the disruption of prepulse inhibition in mice repeatedly treated with methamphetamine. *Annals of the New York Academy of Sciences, 1025*, 257–266.

Dashti, S., Aboutaleb, N., & Shahbazi, A. (2013). The effect of leptin on prepulse inhibition in a developmental model of schizophrenia. *Neuroscience Letters, 555*, 57–61.

Day-Wilson, K. M., Jones, D. N. C., Southam, E., Cilia, J., & Totterdell, S. (2006). Medial prefrontal cortex volume loss in rats with isolation rearing-induced deficits in prepulse inhibition of acoustic startle. *Neuroscience, 141*(3), 1113–1121.

Del-Bel, E. A., Joca, S. R., Padovan, C. M., & Guimaraes, F. S. (2002). Effects of isolation-rearing on serotonin-1A and M1-muscarinic receptor messenger RNA expression in the hipocampal formation of rats. *Neuroscience Letters, 332*(2), 123–126.

Detillion, C. E., Craft, T. K., Glasper, E. R., Prendergast, B. J., & DeVries, A. C. (2004). Social facilitation of wound healing. *Psychoneuroendocrinology, 29*(8), 1004–1011.

Domeney, A., & Feldon, J. (1998). The disruption of prepulse inhibition by social isolation in the Wistar rat: how robust is the effect? *Pharmacology, Biochemistry and Behavior, 59*(4), 883–890.

Dworkin, R. H., Bernstein, G., Kaplansky, L. M., Lipsitz, J. D., Rinaldi, A., Slater, S. L., et al. (1991). Social competence and positive and negative symptoms: a longitudinal study of children and adolescents at risk for schizophrenia and affective disorder. *American Journal of Psychiatry, 148*(9), 1182–1188.

Dworkin, R. H., Lewis, J. A., Cornblatt, B. A., & Erlenmeyer-Kimling, L. (1994). Social competence deficits in adolescents at risk for schizophrenia. *Journal of Nervous and Mental Disease, 182*(2), 103–108.

Eastwood, S. L., & Harrison, P. J. (1995). Decreased synaptophysin in the medial temporal lobe in schizophrenia demonstrated using immunoautoradiography. *Neuroscience, 69*(2), 339–343.

Einon, D. F., & Morgan, M. J. (1977). A critical period for social isolation in the rat. *Developmental Psychobiology, 10*(2), 123–132.

Fabricius, K., Helboe, L., Fink-Jensen, A., Wörtwein, G., Steiniger-Brach, B., & Sotty, F. (2010). Increased dopaminergic activity in socially isolated rats: an electrophysiological study. *Neuroscience Letters, 482*(2), 117–122.

Feifel, D., Shilling, P. D., & Belcher, A. M. (2012). The effects of oxytocin and its analog, carbetocin, on genetic deficits in sensorimotor gating. *European Neuropsychopharmacology, 22*(5), 374–378.

Fone, K. C., & Porkess, M. V. (2008). Behavioural and neurochemical effects of post-weaning social isolation in rodents-relevance to developmental neuropsychiatric disorders. *Neuroscience & Biobehavioral Reviews, 32*(6), 1087–1102.

Forcelli, P. A., West, E. A., Murnen, A. T., & Malkova, L. (2012). Ventral pallidum mediates amygdala-evoked deficits in prepulse inhibition. *Behavioral Neuroscience, 126*(2), 290–300.

Frankland, P. W., Wang, Y., Rosner, B., Shimizu, T., Balleine, B. W., Dykens, E. M., et al. (2004). Sensorimotor gating abnormalities in young males with fragile X syndrome and Fmr1-knockout mice. *Molecular Psychiatry, 9*(4), 417–425.

Gentsch, C., Lichtsteiner, M., Frischknecht, H. R., Feer, H., & Siegfried, B. (1988). Isolation-induced locomotor hyperactivity and hypoalgesia in rats are prevented by handling and reversed by resocialization. *Physiology & Behavior, 43*(1), 13–16.

Geyer, M. A., Krebs-Thomson, K., Braff, D. L., & Swerdlow, N. R. (2001). Pharmacological studies of prepulse inhibition models of sensorimotor gating deficits in schizophrenia: a decade in review. *Psychopharmacology (Berl), 156*(2–3), 117–154.

Geyer, M. A., Swerdlow, N. R., Lehmann-Masten, V., Teschendorf, H. J., Traut, M., & Gross, G. (1999). Effects of LU-111995 in three models of disrupted prepulse inhibition in rats. *Journal of Pharmacology and Experimental Therapeutics, 290*(2), 716–724.

Geyer, M. A., Wilkinson, L. S., Humby, T., & Robbins, T. W. (1993). Isolation rearing of rats produces a deficit in prepulse inhibition of acoustic startle similar to that in schizophrenia. *Biological Psychiatry, 34*(6), 361–372.

Glasper, E. R., & Devries, A. C. (2005). Social structure influences effects of pair-housing on wound healing. *Brain, Behavior, and Immunity, 19*(1), 61–68.

Goktalay, G., Kayir, H., Ulusoy, G. K., & Uzbay, T. (2014). Social interaction of rats is related with baseline prepulse inhibition level. *Neuroscience Letters, 582*, 125–129.

Gomez-Wong, E., Marti, M. J., Tolosa, E., & Valls-Sole, J. (1998). Sensory modulation of the blink reflex in patients with blepharospasm. *Archives of Neurology, 55*(9), 1233–1237.

Granholm, E., Holden, J., Link, P. C., & McQuaid, J. R. (2014). Randomized clinical trial of cognitive behavioral social skills training for schizophrenia: improvement in functioning and experiential negative symptoms. *Journal of Consulting and Clinical Psychology*.

Greenwood, T. A., Braff, D. L., Light, G. A., Cadenhead, K. S., Calkins, M. E., Dobie, D. J., et al. (2007). Initial heritability analyses of endophenotypic measures for schizophrenia: the consortium on the genetics of schizophrenia. *Archives of General Psychiatry, 64*(11), 1242–1250.

Greenwood, T. A., Lazzeroni, L. C., Murray, S. S., Cadenhead, K. S., Calkins, M. E., Dobie, D. J., et al. (2011). Analysis of 94 candidate genes and 12 endophenotypes for schizophrenia from the consortium on the genetics of schizophrenia. *American Journal of Psychiatry*.

Greenwood, T. A., Light, G. A., Swerdlow, N. R., Radant, A. D., & Braff, D. L. (2012). Association analysis of 94 candidate genes and schizophrenia-related endophenotypes. *PLoS One, 7*(1), e29630.

Hafner, H., Maurer, K., Loffler, W., an der Heiden, W., Hambrecht, M., & Schultze-Lutter, F. (2003). Modeling the early course of schizophrenia. *Schizophrenia Bulletin, 29*(2), 325–340.

Hall, F. S. (1998). Social deprivation of neonatal, adolescent, and adult rats has distinct neurochemical and behavioral consequences. *Critical Reviews in Neurobiology, 12*(1–2), 129–162.

Hall, F. S., Humby, T., Wilkinson, L. S., & Robbins, T. W. (1997). The effects of isolation-rearing on preference by rats for a novel environment. *Physiology & Behavior, 62*(2), 299–303.

Hall, F. S., Wilkinson, L. S., Humby, T., Inglis, W., Kendall, D. A., Marsden, C. A., et al. (1998). Isolation rearing in rats: pre- and post-synaptic changes in striatal dopaminergic systems. *Pharmacology, Biochemistry and Behavior, 59*(4), 859–872.

Han, X., Wang, W., Shao, F., & Li, N. (2011). Isolation rearing alters social behaviors and monoamine neurotransmission in the medial prefrontal cortex and nucleus accumbens of adult rats. *Brain Research, 1385*, 175–181.

Harte, M. K., Powell, S. B., Swerdlow, N. R., Geyer, M. A., & Reynolds, G. P. (2007). Deficits in parvalbumin and calbindin immunoreactive cells in the hippocampus of isolation reared rats. *Journal of Neural Transmission, 114*(7), 893–898.

Heidbreder, C. A., Weiss, I. C., Domeney, A. M., Pryce, C., Homberg, J., Hedou, G., et al. (2000). Behavioral, neurochemical and endocrinological characterization of the early social isolation syndrome. *Neuroscience, 100*(4), 749–768.

Hoenig, K., Hochrein, A., Quednow, B. B., Maier, W., & Wagner, M. (2005). Impaired prepulse inhibition of acoustic startle in obsessive-compulsive disorder. *Biological Psychiatry, 57*(10), 1153–1158.

Hori, M., Yamada, K., Ohnishi, J., Sakamoto, S., Furuie, H., Murakami, K., et al. (2014). Tickling during adolescence alters fear-related and cognitive behaviors in rats after prolonged isolation. *Physiology & Behavior, 131*, 62–67.

Howes, S. R., Dalley, J. W., Morrison, C. H., Robbins, T. W., & Everitt, B. J. (2000). Leftward shift in the acquisition of cocaine self-administration in isolation-reared rats: relationship to extracellular levels of dopamine, serotonin and glutamate in the nucleus accumbens and amygdala-striatal FOS expression. *Psychopharmacology (Berl), 151*(1), 55–63.

Huggenberger, H. J., Suter, S. E., Blumenthal, T. D., & Schachinger, H. (2013). Maternal social stress modulates the development of prepulse inhibition of startle in infants. *Developmental Cognitive Neuroscience, 3*, 84–90.

Jones, G. H., Hernandez, T. D., Kendall, D. A., Marsden, C. A., & Robbins, T. W. (1992). Dopaminergic and serotonergic function following isolation rearing in rats: study of behavioural responses and postmortem and in vivo neurochemistry. *Pharmacology, Biochemistry and Behavior, 43*(1), 17–35.

Jones, G. H., Marsden, C. A., & Robbins, T. W. (1990). Increased sensitivity to amphetamine and reward-related stimuli following social isolation in rats: possible disruption of dopamine-dependent mechanisms of the nucleus accumbens. *Psychopharmacology (Berl), 102*(3), 364–372.

Jones, G. H., Robbins, T. W., & Marsden, C. A. (1989). Isolation-rearing retards the acquisition of schedule-induced polydipsia in rats. *Physiology & Behavior, 45*(1), 71–77.

Kern, P. A., Ranganathan, S., Li, C., Wood, L., & Ranganathan, G. (2001). Adipose tissue tumor necrosis factor and interleukin-6 expression in human obesity and insulin resistance. *American Journal of Physiology. Endocrinology and Metabolism, 280*(5), E745–E751.

Koch, M., Kungel, M., & Herbert, H. (1993). Cholinergic neurons in the pedunculopontine tegmental nucleus are involved in the mediation of prepulse inhibition of the acoustic startle response in the rat. *Experimental Brain Research, 97*(1), 71–82.

Koda, K., Ago, Y., Kawasaki, T., Hashimoto, H., Baba, A., & Matsuda, T. (2008). Galantamine and donepezil differently affect isolation rearing-induced deficits of prepulse inhibition in mice. *Psychopharmacology (Berl), 196*(2), 293–301.

Kodsi, M. H., & Swerdlow, N. R. (1997). Regulation of prepulse inhibition by ventral pallidal projections. *Brain Research Bulletin, 43*(2), 219–228.

Krebs-Thomson, K., Giracello, D., Solis, A., & Geyer, M. A. (2001). Postweaning handling attenuates isolation-rearing induced disruptions of prepulse inhibition in rats. *Behavioural Brain Research, 120*(2), 221–224.

Krech, D., Rosenzweig, M. R., & Bennett, E. L. (1962). Relations between chemistry and problem-solving among rats raised in enriched and impoverished environments. *Journal of Comparative and Physiological Psychology, 55*, 801–807.

Lapiz, M. D., Mateo, Y., Parker, T., & Marsden, C. (2000). Effects of noradrenaline depletion in the brain on response on novelty in isolation-reared rats. *Psychopharmacology (Berl), 152*(3), 312–320.

Leng, A., Feldon, J., & Ferger, B. (2004). Long-term social isolation and medial prefrontal cortex: dopaminergic and cholinergic neurotransmission. *Pharmacology, Biochemistry and Behavior, 77*(2), 371–379.

Levine, J. B., Leeder, A. D., Parekkadan, B., Berdichevsky, Y., Rauch, S. L., Smoller, J. W., et al. (2008). Isolation rearing impairs wound healing and is associated with increased locomotion and decreased immediate early gene expression in the medial prefrontal cortex of juvenile rats. *Neuroscience, 151*(2), 589–603.

Levine, J. B., Youngs, R. M., MacDonald, M. L., Chu, M., Leeder, A. D., Berthiaume, F., et al. (2007). Isolation rearing and hyperlocomotion are associated with reduced immediate early gene expression levels in the medial prefrontal cortex. *Neuroscience, 145*(1), 42–55.

Lim, A. L., Taylor, D. A., & Malone, D. T. (2012). A two-hit model: behavioural investigation of the effect of combined neonatal MK-801 administration and isolation rearing in the rat. *Journal of Psychopharmacology*, 26(9), 1252–1264.

Lipska, B. K., Swerdlow, N. R., Geyer, M. A., Jaskiw, G. E., Braff, D. L., & Weinberger, D. R. (1995). Neonatal excitotoxic hippocampal damage in rats causes post-pubertal changes in prepulse inhibition of startle and its disruption by apomorphine. *Psychopharmacology (Berl)*, 122(1), 35–43.

Liu, Y. P., Kao, Y. C., & Tung, C. S. (2011). Critical period exists in the effects of isolation rearing on sensorimotor gating function but not locomotor activity in rat. *Progress in Neuro-Psychopharmacology & Biological Psychiatry*, 35(4), 1068–1073.

Lukasz, B., O'Sullivan, N. C., Loscher, J. S., Pickering, M., Regan, C. M., & Murphy, K. J. (2013). Peripubertal viral-like challenge and social isolation mediate overlapping but distinct effects on behaviour and brain interferon regulatory factor 7 expression in the adult Wistar rat. *Brain, Behavior, and Immunity*, 27(1), 71–79.

Martin, S., Lino-de-Oliveira, C., Joca, S. R., Weffort de Oliveira, R., Echeverry, M. B., Da Silva, C. A., et al. (2010). Eag 1, Eag 2 and Kcnn3 gene brain expression of isolated reared rats. *Genes, Brain and Behavior*, 9(8), 918–924.

McAlonan, G. M., Daly, E., Kumari, V., Critchley, H. D., van Amelsvoort, T., Suckling, J., et al. (2002). Brain anatomy and sensorimotor gating in Asperger's syndrome. *Brain*, 125(Pt 7), 1594–1606.

McCool, B. A., & Chappell, A. M. (2009). Early social isolation in male Long-Evans rats alters both appetitive and consummatory behaviors expressed during operant ethanol self-administration. *Alcoholism: Clinical and Experimental Research*, 33(2), 273–282.

McLean, S., Grayson, B., Harris, M., Protheroe, C., Woolley, M., & Neill, J. (2010). Isolation rearing impairs novel object recognition and attentional set shifting performance in female rats. *Journal of Psychopharmacology*, 24(1), 57–63.

Meyer, U. (2013). Developmental neuroinflammation and schizophrenia. *Progress in Neuro-Psychopharmacology & Biological Psychiatry*, 42, 20–34.

Meyer, U., Feldon, J., Schedlowski, M., & Yee, B. K. (2005). Towards an immuno-precipitated neurodevelopmental animal model of schizophrenia. *Neuroscience & Biobehavioral Reviews*, 29(6), 913–947.

Molina-Hernandez, M., Tellez-Alcantara, P., & Perez-Garcia, J. (2001). Isolation rearing induced fear-like behavior without affecting learning abilities of Wistar rats. *Progress in Neuro-Psychopharmacology & Biological Psychiatry*, 25(5), 1111–1123.

Möller, M., Du Preez, J. L., Emsley, R., & Harvey, B. H. (2011). Isolation rearing-induced deficits in sensorimotor gating and social interaction in rats are related to cortico-striatal oxidative stress, and reversed by sub-chronic clozapine administration. *European Neuropsychopharmacology*, 21(6), 471–483.

Möller, M., Du Preez, J. L., Viljoen, F. P., Berk, M., Emsley, R., & Harvey, B. H. (2013). Social isolation rearing induces mitochondrial, immunological, neurochemical and behavioural deficits in rats, and is reversed by clozapine or N-acetyl cysteine. *Brain, Behavior, and Immunity*, 30, 156–167.

Möller, M., Du Preez, J. L., Viljoen, F. P., Berk, M., & Harvey, B. H. (2013). N-Acetyl cysteine reverses social isolation rearing induced changes in cortico-striatal monoamines in rats. *Metabolic Brain Disease*, 28(4), 687–696.

Møller, P., & Husby, R. (2000). The initial prodrome in schizophrenia: searching for naturalistic core dimensions of experience and behavior. *Schizophrenia Bulletin*, 26(1), 217–232.

Muller, N., Myint, A. M., & Schwarz, M. J. (2011). Kynurenine pathway in schizophrenia: pathophysiological and therapeutic aspects. *Current Pharmaceutical Design*, 17(2), 130–136.

Nair, H. P., Gutman, A. R., Davis, M., & Young, L. J. (2005). Central oxytocin, vasopressin, and corticotropin-releasing factor receptor densities in the basal forebrain predict isolation potentiated startle in rats. *Journal of Neuroscience*, 25(49), 11479–11488.

Nakato, K., Morita, T., Wanibuchi, F., & Yamaguchi, T. (1997). Antipsychotics restored, but antidepressants and anxiolytics did not restore prepulse inhibition (PPI) deficits in isolation-reared rats, an animal model of schizophrenia. *Society for Neuroscience Abstract*, 23, 1855.

Ornitz, E. M., Hanna, G. L., & de Traversay, J. (1992). Prestimulation-induced startle modulation in attention-deficit hyperactivity disorder and nocturnal enuresis. *Psychophysiology*, 29(4), 437–451.

Osburg, B., Peiser, C., Domling, D., Schomburg, L., Ko, Y. T., Voigt, K., et al. (2002). Effect of endotoxin on expression of TNF receptors and transport of TNF-alpha at the blood–brain barrier of the rat. *American Journal of Physiology. Endocrinology and Metabolism*, 283(5), E899–E908.

Park, H. S., Park, J. Y., & Yu, R. (2005). Relationship of obesity and visceral adiposity with serum concentrations of CRP, TNF-alpha and IL-6. *Diabetes Research and Clinical Practice*, 69(1), 29–35.

Pascual, R., Zamora-Leon, S. P., & Valero-Cabre, A. (2006). Effects of postweaning social isolation and re-socialization on the expression of vasoactive intestinal peptide (VIP) and dendritic development in the medial prefrontal cortex of the rat. *Acta Neurobiologiae Experimentalis (Wars)*, 66(1), 7–14.

Paulus, M. P., Bakshi, V. P., & Geyer, M. A. (1998). Isolation rearing affects sequential organization of motor behavior in post-pubertal but not pre-pubertal Lister and Sprague-Dawley rats. *Behavioural Brain Research*, 94(2), 271–280.

Peters, Y. M., & O'Donnell, P. (2005). Social isolation rearing affects prefrontal cortical response to ventral tegmental area stimulation. *Biological Psychiatry*, 57(10), 1205–1208.

Pietropaolo, S., Guilleminot, A., Martin, B., D'Amato, F. R., & Crusio, W. E. (2011). Genetic-background modulation of core and variable autistic-like symptoms in Fmr1 knock-out mice. *PLoS One*, 6(2), e17073.

Pietropaolo, S., Singer, P., Feldon, J., & Yee, B. K. (2008). The postweaning social isolation in C57BL/6 mice: preferential vulnerability in the male sex. *Psychopharmacology (Berl)*, 197(4), 613–628.

Powell, S. B. (2010). Models of neurodevelopmental abnormalities in schizophrenia. *Current Topics in Behavioral Neurosciences*, 4, 435–481.

Powell, S. B., & Geyer, M. A. (2002). Developmental markers of psychiatric disorders as identified by sensorimotor gating. *Neurotoxicity Research*, 4(5–6), 489–502.

Powell, S. B., Geyer, M. A., Preece, M. A., Pitcher, L. K., Reynolds, G. P., Swerdlow, N. R. (2003). Dopamine depletion of the nucleus accumbens reverses isolation-induced deficits in prepulse inhibition in rats. *Neuroscience*, 119, 233–240.

Powell, S. B., Risbrough, V. B., & Geyer, M. A. (2003). Potential use of animal models to examine antipsychotic prophylaxis for schizophrenia. *Clinical Neuroscience Research*, 3, 289–296.

Powell, S. B., Sejnowski, T. J., & Behrens, M. M. (2012). Behavioral and neurochemical consequences of cortical oxidative stress on parvalbumin-interneuron maturation in rodent models of schizophrenia. *Neuropharmacology*, 62(3), 1322–1331.

Powell, S. B., Swerdlow, N. R., Pitcher, L. K., & Geyer, M. A. (2002). Isolation rearing-induced deficits in prepulse inhibition and locomotor habituation are not potentiated by water deprivation. *Physiology & Behavior*, 77(1), 55–64.

Preece, M. A., Dalley, J. W., Theobald, D. E., Robbins, T. W., & Reynolds, G. P. (2004). Region specific changes in forebrain 5-hydroxytryptamine1A and 5-hydroxytryptamine2A receptors in isolation-reared rats: an in vitro autoradiography study. *Neuroscience*, 123(3), 725–732.

Quagliarello, V. J., Wispelwey, B., Long, W. J., Jr., & Scheld, W. M. (1991). Recombinant human interleukin-1 induces meningitis and blood–brain barrier injury in the rat. Characterization and comparison with tumor necrosis factor. *Journal of Clinical Investigation*, 87(4), 1360–1366.

Quan, M. N., Tian, Y. T., Xu, K. H., Zhang, T., & Yang, Z. (2010). Post weaning social isolation influences spatial cognition, prefrontal cortical synaptic plasticity and hippocampal potassium ion channels in Wistar rats. *Neuroscience*, 169(1), 214–222.

Reynolds, G. P., Abdul-Monim, Z., Neill, J. C., & Zhang, Z. J. (2004). Calcium binding protein markers of GABA deficits in schizophrenia–postmortem studies and animal models. *Neurotoxicity Research*, 6(1), 57–61.

Reynolds, G. P., & Beasley, C. L. (2001). GABAergic neuronal subtypes in the human frontal cortex–development and deficits in schizophrenia. *Journal of Chemical Neuroanatomy*, 22(1–2), 95–100.

Rigdon, G. C. (1990). Differential effects of apomorphine on prepulse inhibition of acoustic startle reflex in two rat strains. *Psychopharmacology (Berl)*, 102(3), 419–421.

van Rijn, S., Swaab, H., Magnee, M., van Engeland, H., & Kemner, C. (2011). Psychophysiological markers of vulnerability to psychopathology in men with an extra X chromosome (XXY). *PLoS One*, 6(5), e20292.

Risterucci, C., Jeanneau, K., Schoppenthau, S., Bielser, T., Kunnecke, B., von Kienlin, M., et al. (2005). Functional magnetic resonance imaging reveals similar brain activity changes in two different animal models of schizophrenia. *Psychopharmacology (Berl)*, 180(4), 724–734.

Robinson, S. A., Loiacono, R. E., Christopoulos, A., Sexton, P. M., & Malone, D. T. (2010). The effect of social isolation on rat brain expression of genes associated with endocannabinoid signaling. *Brain Research*, 1343, 153–167.

Roncada, P., Bortolato, M., Frau, R., Saba, P., Flore, G., Soggiu, A., et al. (2009). Gating deficits in isolation-reared rats are correlated with alterations in protein expression in nucleus accumbens. *Journal of Neurochemistry*, 108(3), 611–620.

Rosa, M. L., Silva, R. C., Moura-de-Carvalho, F. T., Brandao, M. L., Guimaraes, F. S., Bel, D., et al. (2005). Routine post-weaning handling of rats prevents isolation rearing-induced deficit in prepulse inhibition. *Brazilian Journal of Medical and Biological Research*, 38(11), 1691–1696.

Sahakian, B. J., Robbins, T. W., & Iversen, S. D. (1977). The effects of isolation rearing on exploration in the rat. *Animal Learning & Behavior*, 5, 193–198.

Sahakian, B. J., Robbins, T. W., Morgan, M. J., & Iversen, S. D. (1975). The effects of psychomotor stimulants on stereotypy and locomotor activity in socially deprived and control rats. *Brain Research*, 84(2), 195–205.

Sakaue, M., Ago, Y., Baba, A., & Matsuda, T. (2003). The 5-HT1A receptor agonist MKC-242 reverses isolation rearing-induced deficits of prepulse inhibition in mice. *Psychopharmacology (Berl)*, 170(1), 73–79.

Scaccianoce, S., Del Bianco, P., Paolone, G., Caprioli, D., Modafferi, A. M., Nencini, P., et al. (2006). Social isolation selectively reduces hippocampal brain-derived neurotrophic factor without altering plasma corticosterone. *Behavioural Brain Research*, 168(2), 323–325.

Schiavone, S., Sorce, S., Dubois-Dauphin, M., Jaquet, V., Colaianna, M., Zotti, M., et al. (2009). Involvement of NOX2 in the development of behavioral and pathologic alterations in isolated rats. *Biological Psychiatry*, 66(4), 384–392.

Schrijver, N. C., Pallier, P. N., Brown, V. J., & Wurbel, H. (2004). Double dissociation of social and environmental stimulation on spatial learning and reversal learning in rats. *Behavioural Brain Research*, 152(2), 307–314.

Schrijver, N. C., & Wurbel, H. (2001). Early social deprivation disrupts attentional, but not affective, shifts in rats. *Behavioral Neuroscience*, 115(2), 437–442.

Schubert, M. I., Porkess, M. V., Dashdorj, N., Fone, K. C., & Auer, D. P. (2009). Effects of social isolation rearing on the limbic brain: a combined behavioral and magnetic resonance imaging volumetry study in rats. *Neuroscience*, 159(1), 21–30.

Sciolino, N. R., Bortolato, M., Eisenstein, S. A., Fu, J., Oveisi, F., Hohmann, A. G., et al. (2010). Social isolation and chronic handling alter endocannabinoid signaling and behavioral reactivity to context in adult rats. *Neuroscience*, 168(2), 371–386.

Shilling, P. D., Saint Marie, R. L., Shoemaker, J. M., & Swerdlow, N. R. (2008). Strain differences in the gating-disruptive effects of apomorphine: relationship to gene expression in nucleus accumbens signaling pathways. *Biological Psychiatry*, 63(8), 748–758.

Silva-Gomez, A., Rojas, D., Juarez, I., & Flores, G. (2003). Decreased dendritic spine density on prefrontal cortical and hippocampal pyramidal neurons in postweaning social isolation rats. *Brain Research*, 983(1–2), 128–136.

Silver, R. M., McKinley, K., Smith, E. A., Quearry, B., Harati, Y., Sternberg, E. M., et al. (1992). Tryptophan metabolism via the kynurenine pathway in patients with the eosinophilia-myalgia syndrome. *Arthritis & Rheumatology*, 35(9), 1097–1105.

Sobin, C., Kiley-Brabeck, K., & Karayiorgou, M. (2005). Lower prepulse inhibition in children with the 22q11 deletion syndrome. *American Journal of Psychiatry*, 162(6), 1090–1099.

Southam, E., Cilia, J., Gartlon, J. E., Woolley, M. L., Lacroix, L. P., Jennings, C. A., et al. (2009). Preclinical investigations into the antipsychotic potential of the novel histamine H3 receptor antagonist GSK207040. *Psychopharmacology (Berl)*, 201(4), 483–494.

Spencer, C. M., Alekseyenko, O., Hamilton, S. M., Thomas, A. M., Serysheva, E., Yuva-Paylor, L. A., et al. (2011). Modifying behavioral phenotypes in Fmr1KO mice: genetic background differences reveal autistic-like responses. *Autism Research*, 4(1), 40–56.

Swerdlow, N. R. (2011). Are we studying and treating schizophrenia correctly? *Schizophrenia Research*, 130(1–3), 1–10.

Swerdlow, N. R., Benbow, C. H., Zisook, S., Geyer, M. A., & Braff, D. L. (1993). A preliminary assessment of sensorimotor gating in patients with obsessive compulsive disorder. *Biological Psychiatry*, 33(4), 298–301.

Swerdlow, N. R., Braff, D. L., & Geyer, M. A. (1990). GABAergic projection from nucleus accumbens to ventral pallidum mediates dopamine-induced sensorimotor gating deficits of acoustic startle in rats. *Brain Research*, 532(1–2), 146–150.

Swerdlow, N. R., Braff, D. L., Geyer, M. A., & Koob, G. F. (1986). Central dopamine hyperactivity in rats mimics abnormal acoustic startle response in schizophrenics. *Biological Psychiatry*, 21(1), 23–33.

Swerdlow, N. R., Braff, D. L., Masten, V. L., & Geyer, M. A. (1990). Schizophrenic-like sensorimotor gating abnormalities in rats following dopamine infusion into the nucleus accumbens. *Psychopharmacology (Berl)*, 101(3), 414–420.

Swerdlow, N. R., Breier, M. R., & Saint Marie, R. L. (2011). Probing the molecular basis for an inherited sensitivity to the startle-gating disruptive effects of apomorphine in rats. *Psychopharmacology (Berl)*, 216(3), 401–410.

Swerdlow, N. R., Caine, S. B., & Geyer, M. A. (1992). Regionally selective effects of intracerebral dopamine infusion on sensorimotor gating of the startle reflex in rats. *Psychopharmacology (Berl)*, 108(1–2), 189–195.

Swerdlow, N. R., & Geyer, M. A. (1993). Prepulse inhibition of acoustic startle in rats after lesions of the pedunculopontine tegmental nucleus. *Behavioral Neuroscience*, 107(1), 104–117.

Swerdlow, N. R., Karban, B., Ploum, Y., Sharp, R., Geyer, M. A., & Eastvold, A. (2001). Tactile prepuff inhibition of startle in children with Tourette's syndrome: in search of an "fMRI-friendly" startle paradigm. *Biological Psychiatry*, 50(8), 578–585.

Swerdlow, N. R., Light, G. A., Cadenhead, K. S., Sprock, J., Hsieh, M. H., & Braff, D. L. (2006). Startle gating deficits in a large cohort of patients with schizophrenia: relationship to medications, symptoms, neurocognition, and level of function. *Archives of General Psychiatry*, 63(12), 1325–1335.

Swerdlow, N. R., Light, G. A., Sprock, J., Calkins, M. E., Green, M. F., Greenwood, T. A., et al. (2014). Deficient prepulse inhibition in schizophrenia detected by the multi-site COGS. *Schizophrenia Research*, 152(2–3), 503–512.

Swerdlow, N. R., Light, G. A., Trim, R. S., Breier, M. R., Hines, S. R., & Powell, S. B. (2013). Forebrain gene expression predicts deficits in sensorimotor gating after isolation rearing in male rats. *Behavioural Brain Research*.

Swerdlow, N. R., Lipska, B. K., Weinberger, D. R., Braff, D. L., Jaskiw, G. E., & Geyer, M. A. (1995). Increased sensitivity to the sensorimotor gating-disruptive effects of apomorphine after lesions of medial prefrontal cortex or ventral hippocampus in adult rats. *Psychopharmacology (Berl)*, 122(1), 27–34.

Swerdlow, N. R., Martinez, Z. A., Hanlon, F. M., Platten, A., Farid, M., Auerbach, P., et al. (2000). Toward understanding the biology of a complex phenotype: rat strain and substrain differences in the sensorimotor gating-disruptive effects of dopamine agonists. *Journal of Neuroscience, 20*(11), 4325–4336.

Swerdlow, N. R., Paulsen, J., Braff, D. L., Butters, N., Geyer, M. A., & Swenson, M. R. (1995). Impaired prepulse inhibition of acoustic and tactile startle response in patients with Huntington's disease. *Journal of Neurology, Neurosurgery and Psychiatry, 58*(2), 192–200.

Swerdlow, N. R., Shilling, P. D., Breier, M., Trim, R. S., Light, G. A., & Marie, R. S. (2012). Fronto-temporal-mesolimbic gene expression and heritable differences in amphetamine-disrupted sensorimotor gating in rats. *Psychopharmacology (Berl), 224*(3), 349–362.

Swerdlow, N. R., Shoemaker, J. M., Auerbach, P. P., Pitcher, L., Goins, J., & Platten, A. (2004). Heritable differences in the dopaminergic regulation of sensorimotor gating. II. Temporal, pharmacologic and generational analyses of apomorphine effects on prepulse inhibition. *Psychopharmacology (Berl), 174*(4), 452–462.

Swerdlow, N. R., Shoemaker, J. M., Crain, S., Goins, J., Onozuka, K., & Auerbach, P. P. (2004). Sensitivity to drug effects on prepulse inhibition in inbred and outbred rat strains. *Pharmacology, Biochemistry and Behavior, 77*(2), 291–302.

Swerdlow, N. R., Shoemaker, J. M., Platten, A., Pitcher, L., Goins, J., & Auerbach, P. P. (2004). Heritable differences in the dopaminergic regulation of sensorimotor gating. I. Apomorphine effects on startle gating in albino and hooded outbred rat strains and their F1 and N2 progeny. *Psychopharmacology (Berl), 174*(4), 441–451.

Swerdlow, N. R., Shoemaker, J. M., Platten, A., Pitcher, L., Goins, J., & Crain, S. (2003). Heritable differences in the effects of amphetamine but not DOI on startle gating in albino and hooded outbred rat strains. *Pharmacology, Biochemistry and Behavior, 75*(1), 191–197.

Swerdlow, N. R., Weber, M., Qu, Y., Light, G. A., & Braff, D. L. (2008). Realistic expectations of prepulse inhibition in translational models for schizophrenia research. *Psychopharmacology (Berl), 199*(3), 331–388.

Trezza, V., Campolongo, P., & Vanderschuren, L. J. (2011). Evaluating the rewarding nature of social interactions in laboratory animals. *Developmental Cognitive Neuroscience, 1*(4), 444–458.

Turnock-Jones, J. J., Jennings, C. A., Robbins, M. J., Cluderay, J. E., Cilia, J., Reid, J. L., et al. (2009). Increased expression of the NR2A NMDA receptor subunit in the prefrontal cortex of rats reared in isolation. *Synapse, 63*(10), 836–846.

Vaillancourt, C., & Boksa, P. (2000). Birth insult alters dopamine-mediated behavior in a precocial species, the guinea pig. Implications for schizophrenia. *Neuropsychopharmacology, 23*(6), 654–666.

Valls-Sole, J., Munoz, J. E., & Valldeoriola, F. (2004). Abnormalities of prepulse inhibition do not depend on blink reflex excitability: a study in Parkinson's disease and Huntington's disease. *Clinical Neurophysiology, 115*(7), 1527–1536.

Varty, G. B., & Geyer, M. A. (1998). Effects of isolation rearing on startle reactivity, habituation, and prepulse inhibition in male Lewis, Sprague-Dawley, and Fischer F344 rats. *Behavioral Neuroscience, 112*(6), 1450–1457.

Varty, G. B., & Higgins, G. A. (1995). Examination of drug-induced and isolation-induced disruptions of prepulse inhibition as models to screen antipsychotic drugs. *Psychopharmacology (Berl), 122*(1), 15–26.

Varty, G. B., Marsden, C. A., & Higgins, G. A. (1999). Reduced synaptophysin immunoreactivity in the dentate gyrus of prepulse inhibition-impaired isolation-reared rats. *Brain Research, 824*(2), 197–203.

Varty, G. B., Paulus, M. P., Braff, D. L., & Geyer, M. A. (2000). Environmental enrichment and isolation rearing in the rat: effects on locomotor behavior and startle response plasticity. *Biological Psychiatry, 47*(10), 864–873.

Varty, G. B., Powell, S. B., Lehmann-Masten, V., Buell, M. R., & Geyer, M. A. (2006). Isolation rearing of mice induces deficits in prepulse inhibition of the startle response. *Behavioural Brain Research, 169*(1), 162–167.

Vitalo, A., Fricchione, J., Casali, M., Berdichevsky, Y., Hoge, E. A., Rauch, S. L., et al. (2009). Nest making and oxytocin comparably promote wound healing in isolation reared rats. *PLoS One, 4*(5), e5523.

Wall, V. L., Fischer, E. K., & Bland, S. T. (2012). Isolation rearing attenuates social interaction-induced expression of immediate early gene protein products in the medial prefrontal cortex of male and female rats. *Physiology & Behavior, 107*(3), 440–450.

Wan, F. J., & Swerdlow, N. R. (1997). The basolateral amygdala regulates sensorimotor gating of acoustic startle in the rat. *Neuroscience, 76*(3), 715–724.

Weiss, I. C., Di Iorio, L., Feldon, J., & Domeney, A. M. (2000). Strain differences in the isolation-induced effects on prepulse inhibition of the acoustic startle response and on locomotor activity. *Behavioral Neuroscience, 114*(2), 364–373.

Weiss, I. C., & Feldon, J. (2001). Environmental animal models for sensorimotor gating deficiencies in schizophrenia: a review. *Psychopharmacology (Berl), 156*(2–3), 305–326.

Weiss, I. C., Feldon, J., & Domeney, A. M. (1999). Isolation rearing-induced disruption of prepulse inhibition: further evidence for fragility of the response. *Behavioural Pharmacology, 10*(2), 139–149.

Weiss, I. C., Pryce, C. R., Jongen-Relo, A. L., Nanz-Bahr, N. I., & Feldon, J. (2004). Effect of social isolation on stress-related behavioural and neuroendocrine state in the rat. *Behavioural Brain Research, 152*(2), 279–295.

Wellen, K. E., & Hotamisligil, G. S. (2005). Inflammation, stress, and diabetes. *Journal of Clinical Investigation, 115*(5), 1111–1119.

Wilkinson, L. S., Killcross, S. S., Humby, T., Hall, F. S., Geyer, M. A., & Robbins, T. W. (1994). Social isolation in the rat produces developmentally specific deficits in prepulse inhibition of the acoustic startle response without disrupting latent inhibition. *Neuropsychopharmacology, 10*(1), 61–72.

Wolf, R., Matzke, K., Paelchen, K., Dobrowolny, H., Bogerts, B., & Schwegler, H. (2010). Reduction of prepulse inhibition (PPI) after neonatal excitotoxic lesion of the ventral thalamus in pubertal and adult rats. *Pharmacopsychiatry, 43*(3), 99–109.

Wongwitdecha, N., & Marsden, C. A. (1996). Effects of social isolation rearing on learning in the Morris water maze. *Brain Research, 715*(1–2), 119–124.

Wright, I. K., Upton, N., & Marsden, C. A. (1991). Resocialisation of isolation-reared rats does not alter their anxiogenic profile on the elevated X-maze model of anxiety. *Physiology & Behavior, 50*(6), 1129–1132.

Yorgason, J. T., España, R. A., Konstantopoulos, J. K., Weiner, J. L., & Jones, S. R. (2013). Enduring increases in anxiety-like behavior and rapid nucleus accumbens dopamine signaling in socially isolated rats. *European Journal of Neuroscience, 37*(6), 1022–1031.

Zeeb, F. D., Wong, A. C., & Winstanley, C. A. (2013). Differential effects of environmental enrichment, social-housing, and isolation-rearing on a rat gambling task: dissociations between impulsive action and risky decision-making. *Psychopharmacology (Berl), 225*(2), 381–395.

Zhao, X., Sun, L., Jia, H., Meng, Q., Wu, S., Li, N., et al. (2009). Isolation rearing induces social and emotional function abnormalities and alters glutamate and neurodevelopment-related gene expression in rats. *Progress in Neuro-Psychopharmacology & Biological Psychiatry, 33*(7), 1173–1177.

10

Glutamate Pharmacological Models Relevant to Schizophrenia and Psychosis: Can a Receptor Occupancy Normalization Approach Reduce the Gap between Animal and Human Experiments?

Mark Rafter*, Kevin CF. Fone*, Paula M. Moran[§]

*School of Life Sciences, Queens Medical Centre, University of Nottingham, Nottingham, UK; [§]School of Psychology, University of Nottingham, Nottingham, UK

Recent pharmacological approaches to modeling schizophrenia have focused on behavioral and neural effects of glutamatergic drugs. Pharmacological approaches had previously focused on two categories of drugs that produce psychosis-like symptoms: drugs that increase dopamine transmission (agonists or transporter blockers) and hallucinogens (e.g., Lysergic acid diethylamide (LSD)). Dopamine-modulating drugs have been reviewed extensively in this regard as these effects have played a key role in the formulation of the pivotal dopamine hypothesis of schizophrenia in the 1970s and its subsequent revisions (Howes, McCutcheon, & Stone, 2015; Lieberman, Kane, & Alvir, 1987; Moran, O'Tuathaigh, Papaleo, & Waddington, 2014). Hallucinogenic drugs, which interact with serotonin 5-HT2A receptors, have recently been re-evaluated in this context following some neglect since the 1970s (e.g., Halberstadt, 2015; Hanks & Gonzalez-Maeso, 2013; Martin, Marona-Lewicka, Nichols, & Nichols, 2014). However, there is increasing evidence that glutamate abnormality is central to the pathophysiology of schizophrenia and may represent an alternative therapeutic target to dopamine and serotonin.

Drugs that block the N-methyl-D-aspartate receptor (NMDA-R) have been known to induce "schizophrenia-like" symptoms in healthy individuals since the 1960s, when it was reported that subanesthetic doses of phencyclidine (PCP) consistently produced symptoms such as affective flattening, depersonalization, derealization, avolition, thought disorganization, and perseveration (Davies & Beech, 1960; Luby, Cohen, Rosenbaum, Gottlieb, & Kelley, 1959). Similar controlled observations have since been made with other NMDA-R antagonists such as ketamine (Krystal, Karper, Seibyl, et al., 1994), CGS-19,755 (Grotta et al., 1995), and traxoprodil (Preskorn et al., 2008).

This review will first give an overview of which human behaviors are affected by acute NMDA-R antagonism and how this might relate to symptom dimensions in schizophrenia. It will then integrate physiological findings to propose a model of how NMDA-R antagonists induce these behavioral changes and discuss how accurately the acute NMDA-R antagonism model in rodents translates to human conditions. Finally, we evaluate whether emphasis on the pharmacokinetics and pharmacodynamics of NMDA-R antagonists in published studies may help to differentiate between the diversity of effects they have been reported to produce, to potentially explain discrepancies between animal and human findings, and help to guide future studies. Specifically, for the studies reviewed here, we have made every effort to calculate an estimated global receptor occupancy (RO_{est})

of NMDA-Rs given the dose and administration time point each study uses, based on the receptor occupancy normalization approach of Shaffer et al.[1] (Shaffer, Osgood, Smith, Liu, & Trapa, 2014).

BEHAVIORAL EFFECTS IN HUMANS

NMDA-R antagonists were initially developed as general anesthetics and to have anesthetic effects when administered at doses sufficient to cause blockade of at least 70% of the brain's NMDA-Rs (Domino et al., 1982). However, it was observed that once consciousness was regained, patients frequently displayed psychotic symptoms (Knox, Bovill, Clarke, & Dundee, 1970). As a consequence, investigators have used ketamine to model schizophrenia, since it possesses a safer clinical profile than PCP. There does appear to be good concordance between some of the positive symptoms of schizophrenia and the behavioral effects of ketamine. The Brief Psychiatric Rating Scale (BPRS) is widely used to measure dimensions of positive symptoms such as behavioral activation, conceptual disorganization, hallucinatory behavior, hostility–suspiciousness, and unusual thought content. It has been shown that within 10 min of an intravenous ketamine infusion (equivalent to ~10% brain NMDA-R blockade) there is a significant increase in all of these symptoms (Krystal et al., 1994), and this finding has been widely replicated at numerous doses (Abel, Allin, Hemsley, & Geyer, 2003; Deakin et al., 2008; Lahti, Weiler, Tamara, Parwani, & Tamminga, 2001; Malhotra et al., 1996; Newcomer et al., 1999) (see Table 1). In addition, ketamine augments BPRS measured symptoms in schizophrenia patients at doses with occupancy as low as 8% RO_{est} (Lahti et al., 2001).

A core positive symptom of schizophrenia is delusionality (Kapur, 2003), which among other explanations is proposed to arise from a "jumping to conclusions" bias in schizophrenia (Moritz & Woodward, 2005). On probabilistic sampling tasks, schizophrenia patients consistently make fewer samples than healthy controls before making a confident decision (Moritz & Woodward, 2005). However, ketamine infused with a RO_{est} of 25% or 35% has no effect on this task (Evans et al., 2012).

Disturbances in sense of agency are common in schizophrenia, with patients frequently reporting the insertion of thoughts and external control of their actions

(Voss et al., 2010). In healthy volunteers, ketamine at 35% RO_{est} is able to enhance the rubber hand illusion (Morgan et al., 2011). Self-reports of a perception of limb disownership have also occurred at 32% RO_{est} (Pomarol-Clotet et al., 2006).

Cognitive and perceptual fragmentation has been proposed as a basic, bottom-up disturbance that precedes delusion formation in schizophrenia (Uhlhaas & Mishara, 2007), with patients seemingly unable to contextualize whole scenes and instead focusing on these "fragments" in an incorrect order. Similar subjective effects have been reported with ketamine at a wide range of doses, with significantly higher scores of "visionary restructuralization" on a Five-dimension Altered States of Consciousness (5D-ASC) scale (Studerus, Gamma, & Vollenweider, 2010).

RELATING TO NEGATIVE SYMPTOMS OF SCHIZOPHRENIA

Ketamine at 10% RO_{est} significantly increases three key negative BPRS symptoms: blunted affect, emotional withdrawal, and motor retardation (Krystal et al., 1994). Ketamine also increases dissociative symptoms on the Clinician-Administered Dissociative States Scale (CADSS) at this dose, and it increases "disembodiment" on the OAV scale at a range of doses (Studerus et al., 2010). These findings are widely replicated (see Table 1). For example, ketamine increased social withdrawal and blunted effect on the Positive and Negative Symptoms Scale (PANSS), at 23% RO_{est} (Driesen et al., 2013). It also significantly increased affective flattening, avolition, and anhedonia—but not alogia or attention—at 16% RO_{est}, but not at 4% RO_{est} (Newcomer et al., 1999). Despite these effects, ketamine is abused as a recreational drug (Morris & Wallach, 2014), and one study found that participants reported liking and desire of the drug at doses of 21–35% RO_{est} (Morgan, Mofeez, Brandner, Bromley, & Curran, 2004), although there was also a higher rating of discontentedness. On the 5D-ASC scale, ketamine has been reported to induce both blissful and dreadful states (Studerus et al., 2010). Likewise, ketamine has been shown to have antianhedonic effects in depressed patients at doses similar to those producing anhedonia in healthy participants, although this effect persists long after elimination of the drug and, therefore, may

---

[1] To estimate the percentage of receptor occupancy (RO%) by ketamine, first the unbound plasma concentration ($C_{p,u}$) was calculated using Eqn (1), with Molecular Weight (MW) equalling 237.725 g/mol and plasma unbound fraction equalling 0.71 for humans (0.64 for rats). The receptor occupancy (RO%) was then calculated using Eqn (2), with an assumed I_{max} of 100% and IC_{50} of 1420 nM (Shaffer et al., 2014).

$$C_{p,u} \ (nM) = (plasma\ concentration\ in\ nM/MW) \times 1000 \times plasma\ unbound\ fraction. \tag{1}$$

$$RO\% = \left(C_{p,u} \times I_{max} \right) / \left(C_{p,u} + IC_{50} \right). \tag{2}$$

TABLE 1 Behavioral Effects Resembling Symptoms of Schizophrenia Upon Ketamine Administration

Symptom	Effect	Dose; (Plasma)	Time Point (mins)	%RO$_{est}$	Task/Measure	n	Effect in Schizophrenia
POSITIVE SYMPTOMS							
Psychosis	↑(Krystal et al., 1994)	0.5mg/kg	T+10-80	10-35	BPRS	18	↑(Lahti et al., 2001)
	↑(Abel, Allin, Hemsley, et al., 2003)	0.5mg/kg	T+35	30		20	
	↑(Lahti et al., 2001)	0.3mg/kg bolus; (80ng/mL)	T+20	14		18	
	↑(Malhotra et al., 1996)	0.77mg/kg	T+55			15	
	↑(Newcomer et al., 1999)	(90ng/mL)	T+30	16		15	
Delusionality	↔(Evans et al., 2012)	(150ng/mL)		24	Beads task	16	↑(Evans et al., 2012)
		(250ng/mL)		34		16	
Referential ideation	↑(Corlett et al., 2006)	(210ng/mL)		31	PSE	15	↑(Owens, Miller, Lawrie, & Johnstone, 2005)
Self-monitoring abnormalities	↑(Morgan et al., 2011)	(258ng/mL)		35	Rubber hand illusion	15	↑(Thakkar, Nichols, McIntosh, & Park, 2011)
Visionary restructuralization	↑(Studerus et al., 2010)	0.24-0.72mg/kg[a]	T+25-120		5D-ASC	109	↑(Uhlhaas & Mishara, 2007)
NEGATIVE SYMPTOMS							
Dissociation	↑(Krystal et al., 1994)	0.5mg/kg	T+10-80	10-35	CADSS	19	↑(Peralta & Cuesta, 1994)
	↑(Studerus et al., 2010)	0.24-0.72mg/kg[a]	T+25-120		5D-ASC	109	
Social withdrawal, blunted affect	↑(Driesen et al., 2013)	0.58mg/kg; (140ng/mL)		23	PANSS	22	
Anhedonia, avolition, blunted affect	↑(Newcomer et al., 1999)	(90ng/mL)	T+30	16	SANS	15	
	↔(Newcomer et al., 1999)	(20ng/mL)		4		15	
	↑(Radant et al., 1998)	(100-200ng/mL)	T+0-120	17-30		10	
COGNITIVE SYMPTOMS							
Sustained attention	↓(Krystal et al., 1994)	0.5mg/kg	T+20-80	17-35	Visual CPT	14	↓(Nuechterlein et al., 2004)
	↓(Malhotra et al., 1996)	0.77mg/kg	T+55		Verbal CPT	15	
	↔(Newcomer et al., 1999)	(90ng/mL)		16	Stroop task	15	
					Visual CPT	15	
	↔(Oranje et al., 2000)	(130ng/mL)		21	Auditory CPT	18	

Continued

II. NEUROBIOLOGY OF PSYCHOTIC DISORDERS

TABLE 1   Behavioral Effects Resembling Symptoms of Schizophrenia Upon Ketamine Administration—cont'd

Symptom	Effect	Dose; (Plasma)	Time Point (mins)	%RO$_{est}$	Task/Measure	n	Effect in Schizophrenia
Verbal fluency	↔(Abel, Allin, Hemsley, et al., 2003)	0.5 mg/kg	T+35	30	FAS fluency	20	↓(Nuechterlein et al., 2004)
	↔(Rowland, Astur, et al., 2005)	0.27 mg/kg	T+45			9	
	↓(Krystal et al., 1994)	0.5 mg/kg	T+20–80	17–35		15	
	↔(Newcomer et al., 1999)	(90 ng/mL)		16		15	
Verbal working memory (WM)	↓(Krystal et al., 1994)	0.5 mg/kg	T+10	10	10 min delay	16	↓(Forbes et al., 2009)
	↓(Malhotra et al., 1996)	0.77 mg/kg	T+55	>35	2+ min delay	15	
	↔(Abel, Allin, Hemsley, et al., 2003)	0.5 mg/kg	T+35	30	Digit span	20	
	↔(Rowland, Astur, et al., 2005)	0.27 mg/kg	T+45			9	
	↓(Newcomer et al., 1999)	0.05 mg/kg		3	30 min delay	15	
Visual WM	↓(Honey et al., 2008)	(100 ng/mL)		17	n-back	14	
Spatial WM	↓(Rowland, Astur, et al., 2005)	0.27 mg/kg	T+45	16	Virtual maze	8	
	↔(Newcomer et al., 1999)	(90 ng/mL)			120s delay	15	
	↔(Honey et al., 2004)	(50 ng/mL) (100 ng/mL)	T+5	10–17	7s delay, manipulation	12	
Verbal episodic memory	↓(Honey, Honey, Sharar, et al., 2005)	(50 ng/mL)	T+210	5–7	Encoding	12	↓(Fletcher & Honey, 2006)
	↔(Honey, Honey, O'Loughlin, et al., 2005)	(100 ng/mL)		6–8		12	
	↔(Honey, Honey, Sharar, et al., 2005)	(50 ng/mL)	T+60	10–17	Retrieval	12	
	↔(Honey, Honey, O'Loughlin, et al., 2005)	(100 ng/mL)		10–17		12	
Impulsivity	↔(Morgan et al., 2004)	0.4 mg/kg (130 ng/mL)	T+50	21	Hayling task part B errors	18	↑(Chan et al., 2012)
	↑(Morgan et al., 2004)	0.8 mg/kg (260 ng/mL)		35		18	
Attentional set shifting	↓(Krystal et al., 1994)	0.5 mg/kg	T+20–80	17–35	WCST	19	↓(Leeson et al., 2009)
	↓(Krystal et al., 2000)	0.87 mg/kg	T+40	>30		15	

SANS: Scale for the assessment of negative symptoms; 5D-ASC: Five-dimension altered states of consciousness scale; PSE: Present state examination; FAS: Spontaneous production of words beginning with F, A, and S; WM: Working memory.

aThis study used S-Ketamine; therefore, the dose was multiplied by 1.5 to obtain the racemate equivalent (based on Vollenweider, Leenders, Øye, et al. (1997)).

be the result of a separate mechanism (Lally et al., 2014; Luckenbaugh et al., 2014; Murrough et al., 2013).

RELATING TO COGNITIVE SYMPTOMS OF SCHIZOPHRENIA

Impairments in working memory (WM) and episodic memory are some of the most consistent findings in schizophrenia (Al-Uzri et al., 2006; Aleman, Hijman, de Haan, & Kahn, 1999; Forbes, Carrick, McIntosh, & Lawrie, 2009; Silver, Feldman, Bilker, & Gur, 2003). Patients also display attentional deficits on the Continuous Performance Task (CPT) (Cornblatt & Keilp, 1994), impulsivity (Ouzir, 2013), impairments in verbal fluency tasks (Bokat & Goldberg, 2003), reversal learning tasks (Leeson et al., 2009), and cognitive inflexibility on the Wisconsin Card Sort Test (WCST) (Li, 2004).

In a verbal WM task, there was no effect of ketamine 10 or 90 min after administration (RO_{est} of 10% and 15%, respectively) on immediate or postdistraction word recall, but a significant impairment of 10 min delayed recall only at the 10 min time point. These doses also impaired performance on a visual CPT, a verbal fluency task, and the WCST (Krystal et al., 1994). Similarly, a marginally higher dose of ketamine was able to impair verbal attention, recall, and recognition (Malhotra et al., 1996). Interestingly, 30 min after cessation of infusion, a deficit in verbal recall persisted despite no residual impairment in attention and recognition, and a subsidence of psychotic and dissociative symptoms. These specific postacute effects may be a result of plasticity in response to the acute pharmacological effects, or they may be a result of the less potent but longer acting metabolite norketamine (acting at very low receptor occupancies).

Ketamine significantly decreased paragraph recall after a 30 min delay at doses as low as 0.05 mg/kg (3% RO_{est}), however a visual WM task with a distracting 3.5 min delay was unimpaired at this dose, but impaired at 16% RO_{est} (Newcomer et al., 1999). A multiple trial visuospatial WM task with a 2 min delay was unimpaired at 17% RO_{est} (Honey et al., 2008), and a multi-trial verbal/spatial WM task that involved manipulation of letters into alphabetical order was also unimpaired by ketamine at 10% and 17% RO_{est} (Honey et al., 2004).

In an episodic memory task, ketamine at doses of 10–17% RO_{est} had no effect on retrieval of a 90 word list encoded prior to infusion (60 min earlier) (Honey, Honey, O'Loughlin, et al., 2005; Honey, Honey, Sharar, et al., 2005). However, when a second list was encoded before cessation of the infusion, retrieval was impaired 90 min later (5–7% RO_{est}) (Honey, Honey, Sharar, et al., 2005), although these authors failed to replicate this finding in a later study (Honey, Honey, O'Loughlin, et al., 2005).

People with schizophrenia also display impulsivity on the Hayling sentence completion task (Chan et al., 2012), which requires withholding an obvious verbal response. Ketamine increased impulsivity at 35% but not 21% RO_{est} (Morgan et al., 2004). Meanwhile, ketamine also impairs attentional set shifting on the WCST at doses of 0.5 and 0.87 mg/kg (Krystal et al., 2004, 1994).

Overall, it appears that low doses of ketamine selectively impair performance during tasks with a high cognitive load (especially containing a verbal component), which may be dependent on circuitry that requires fine-tuned signal-to-noise ratios to function optimally, such as in the dorsolateral prefrontal cortex (Arnsten, Wang, & Paspalas, 2012) (discussed later).

OTHER EFFECTS

It should be noted that participant withdrawal due to nausea and vomiting is common in ketamine studies. This may be important as cognitive deficits could be due to a nonspecific malaise effect, and co-treatments that apparently ameliorate these "deficits" may be working via a nonspecific antiemetic effect. In addition, ketamine has been reported to induce oculomotor saccade disruptions and nystagmus at higher doses, which may be relevant to ataxia in animal models. Ketamine also has wide use as an analgesic (Persson, 2013), and this effect occurs at ≥5% RO_{est} (Sprenger et al., 2006).

NEUROBIOLOGY OF NMDA-R ANTAGONISM

Glutamate is the main excitatory neurotransmitter in the brain, and it can bind to either metabotropic receptors (mGluRs) or three classes of ionotropic receptor: the AMPA, NMDA, and kainate receptors. Of these, NMDA-Rs, AMPA-Rs (mostly postsynaptic), and $mGluR_{2/3}$-Rs (presynaptic) appear to be the most important in the pathophysiology of psychosis. Although no conclusive theory exists as to how NMDA-R antagonists induce their behavioral effects, it is known that they decrease the firing rate of inhibitory interneurons and increase the firing rate of excitatory pyramidal cells (Homayoun & Moghaddam, 2007). This then leads to glutamate release and postsynaptic AMPA-R stimulation, both of which are required for the psychotomimetic effects of NMDA-R antagonists (Deakin et al., 2008; Baker et al., 2008; Hiyoshi, Marumo, et al., 2014; Krystal et al., 2005; Moghaddam, Adams, Verma, & Daly, 1997; Moghaddam & Adams, 1998) and serotonergic hallucinogens (Benneyworth et al., 2007; Lee, Chiang, Chiu, Chan, & Chen, 2014; Zhang & Marek, 2008). The shift in NMDA:AMPA balance is proposed to decrease the signal-to-noise ratio of cortical neuronal ensembles (Jackson, Homayoun, & Moghaddam, 2004), which leads to an increase in resting state (Gonzalez-Burgos & Lewis, 2012) but a decrease in evoked (Tatard-Leitman et al., 2015) gamma oscillatory power, and it decreases "top-down" predictive coding of sensory information Moran, Jones, Blockeel, Adams, Stephan, & Friston, 2014. Subcortically, these changes lead to an aberrant increase in phasic mesolimbic and mesocortical dopamine signalling (Bartsch et al., 2015; Lodge & Grace, 2011). Figure 1 describes these findings.

This neurobiology is similar to that proposed by theories of schizophrenia based upon disruptions of excitatory/inhibitory balance (Anticevic et al., 2012; Nakazawa et al., 2012; Pavão, Tort, & Amaral, 2015; Weickert et al., 2013). However, abnormalities of gamma oscillations (Kocsis, Brown, McCarley, & Hajos, 2013; Uhlhaas, 2013; Uhlhaas & Singer, 2010) and brain connectivity (Whitfield-Gabrieli & Ford, 2012) in schizophrenia are more equivocal in direction—resting-state activity may be increased in the early stages of the disease but decreased in the chronic disease (see Anticevic et al., 2015 and Adell, Jiménez-Sánchez, López-Gil, & Romón, 2012), whilst evoked activity may depend on task demands. In addition, although aberrant increases in mesolimbic dopamine signalling are extremely well replicated in schizophrenia, mesocortical dopamine signaling appears to be decreased (Howes & Kapur, 2009), and both these phenomena may be a result of hypoactivity in the prefrontal cortex (Meyer-Lindenberg et al., 2002; Sesack & Carr, 2002). This may be due to developmental alterations prior to adulthood in the aforementioned circuitry (Lewis, Hashimoto, & Volk, 2005; Uhlhaas, 2013).

LINKING NMDA-R HYPOFUNCTION AND SCHIZOPHRENIA

These pathophysiological changes have been suggested to be responsible for a number of neurobiological and behavioral phenomena relevant to schizophrenia such as the following:

- Impaired "corollary discharge" or "efference copy" between cortical areas (Fletcher & Frith, 2009), causing attribution of self-generated thoughts/actions to external sources, for example, auditory hallucinations, thought insertion, and experiences of passivity
- Misattribution of salience to irrelevant stimuli (Kapur, 2003), causing persistence of bizarre thoughts, paranoia, delusions of ideation, and distractibility of irrelevant information in working memory
- Disruption of the top-down versus bottom-up signal processing balance (Jardri & Denève, 2013), causing weak sensory evidence to be reverberated and thus overweighed as strong prior evidence. This leads to the "jumping to conclusions" phenomenon and strengthens the belief of delusions.
- Aberrant "delay cell" firing in the dorsolateral PFC (Wang et al., 2013), causing working memory deficits
- Abnormal dorsolateral PFC activity and connectivity (Goghari et al., 2010) and abnormal activity in Broca's area (Lahti et al., 2005), causing disorganized behavior and speech
- Impaired hippocampal recruitment, leading to spatial working memory deficits (Folley, Astur, Jagannathan, Calhoun, & Pearlson, 2010)

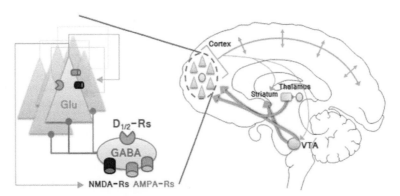

FIGURE 1   In the cortex (left), individual parvalbumin-expressing basket interneurons (green) can simultaneously hyperpolarize over a thousand (Cobb, Buhl, Halasy, Paulsen, & Somogyi, 1995) excitatory pyramidal cells (orange). These interneurons are critical for synchronized activity of pyramidal neurons in the gamma frequency range (>40 Hz). At psychotomimetic doses, it is proposed that NMDA-R antagonists preferentially target the inhibitory reticular thalamic nucleus (Dawson et al., 2013; Stone et al., 2008; Troyano-Rodriguez et al., 2014), leading to disinhibition of thalamocortical neurons and cortical glutamate release. This glutamate then binds to AMPA-Rs on basket cells, driving gamma oscillations (Gonzalez-Burgos & Lewis, 2012). The global NMDA-to-AMPA shift causes failures in top-down monitoring, leading to aberrant VTA activity and subsequent *potentiation* of cortical (Aalto et al., 2005; Deutch, Tam, Freeman, Bowers, & Roth, 1987) and striatal dopamine release (Adams, Bradberry, & Moghaddam, 2002; Kegeles et al., 2000). In concordance with this theory, drugs that block AMPA-Rs or presynaptic glutamate release attenuate the effects of NMDA-R antagonists and other psychotomimetics such as 5-HT$_{2A}$ receptor agonists (see text for references). D$_{1/2}$-Rs:dopamine D1 and D2 receptors; Glu: glutamate; VTA: ventral tegmental area.

- Inability to mentally represent the value of rewards in frontostriatal circuits (Gold, Waltz, Prentice, Morris, & Heerey, 2008), causing motivational deficits and anhedonia
- Disrupted deactivation of resting-state brain networks and activation of task-positive networks (Anticevic et al., 2012; Whitfield-Gabrieli et al., 2009), leading to task inefficiency and aberrant salience

Relating to Positive Symptoms

Many studies have made physiological measurements simultaneously with behavioral measurements when administering ketamine (see Table 2). One of the most consistent findings is a global increase in cortical activation, as measured by glucose utilization (Långsjö et al., 2003; Vollenweider, Leenders, Scharfetter, et al., 1997), blood oxygen level-dependent (BOLD) activity (De Simoni et al., 2013; Deakin et al., 2008), high-frequency oscillatory power (Hong et al., 2010), and global brain connectivity (reviewed in Anticevic et al. (2013))—all occurring at doses in the range of 10% to 40% RO_{est} and sufficient to produce psychosis and dissociation. However, in chronic schizophrenia, there appears to be a decrease in most of these markers (see Table 2). One hypothesis for this is that the hyperactivated prefrontal cortical state is only present during early psychosis, as a result of the brain remodeling cognitive frameworks to account for aberrant perceptions (Andreou et al., 2015).

Ketamine has been shown to increase glutamate levels in the PFC and anterior cingulate cortex (ACC) at 24% RO_{est}, which correlated with psychosis scores (Stone et al., 2012), although another study found no effect of a 40 min 0.5 mg/kg infusion (17–35% RO_{est}) (Taylor, Tiangga, Mhuircheartaigh, & Cowen, 2012). Another study found an increase in ACC glutamine with 0.27 mg/kg ketamine, but there was no correlation with positive or negative symptoms (Rowland, Bustillo, et al., 2005). In concordance with these findings, ketamine increases resting-state blood flow to the ACC at 22% RO_{est} (Långsjö et al., 2003), and in another study at 0.3 mg/kg (Holcomb, Lahti, Medoff, Weiler, & Tamminga, 2001), which also found a correlation with psychosis. Ketamine at 0.25 mg/kg also increases BOLD activity in the posterior cingulate cortex (PCC), which correlates with positive symptoms (Deakin et al., 2008). In general, these findings agree with findings in unmedicated schizophrenia patients, who display increased glutamate levels in the ACC (Poels et al., 2014) and increased resting-state blood flow to the ACC, which correlates with their positive symptoms (Lahti et al., 2005).

The effect of ketamine on dopamine release is unclear. Numerous studies have looked at D_2/D_3 receptor binding in the striatum using positron emission tomography (PET), inferring that a decrease in binding equates

to increased dopamine release (Rabiner, 2007). Early studies found decreased binding at doses as low as 16% RO_{est} (Breier et al., 1998), and a study using a high dose of S-ketamine (>50% RO_{est}) found a correlation between ventral striatal dopamine release and positively reinforcing effects (Vollenweider, Vontobel, Øye, Hell, & Leenders, 2000). However, other studies with more robust measurement methodology found no effect of ketamine at doses producing 23%, 29%, and 38% RO_{est} (Aalto et al., 2002; Kegeles et al., 2000, 2002). One study found that ketamine at 41% RO_{est} was only able to significantly increase dopamine release in the PCC, but it found significant correlations between individual positive symptom severity and dopamine release in the ACC and dorsolateral PFC (Aalto et al., 2005). Overall, this may corroborate previous evidence that disturbances in ACC and PCC activity correlate with psychosis.

Sensorimotor gating deficits are considered a reliable, quantitative endophenotype in schizophrenia (Swerdlow, Weber, Qu, Light, & Braff, 2008). However, ketamine has been shown to either have no effect (van Berckel et al., 1998) or actually enhance sensorimotor gating at a wide range of doses (Abel, Allin, Hemsley, et al., 2003; Heekeren et al., 2007). Mismatch negativity (MMN) is an evoked electrophysiological response that occurs when a stimulus deviates from its predictable nature. MMN disruptions are well replicated in schizophrenia (Umbricht & Krljes, 2005). Ketamine has been shown to disrupt MMN at various doses (although see Oranje et al., 2000), and this disruption correlates with alterations in consciousness (Heekeren et al., 200; Schmidt et al., 2012; Umbricht, Koller, Vollenweider, & Schmid, 2002).

Auditory hallucinations in schizophrenia typically display as monotone voices, using short dialogue that can be a running commentary on what the person is doing, or it is often critical of the person. It has been proposed that these hallucinations arise from disconnectivity in the right hemisphere homologue of Broca's area (Sommer et al., 2008). Although ketamine reliably alters auditory perception, it does not consistently induce auditory hallucinations in participants, although it has been proposed that if the auditory illusions induced by acute ketamine were sustained for a long enough period, hallucinations would precipitate (Corlett, Honey, Krystal, & Fletcher, 2011).

The neural correlates of delusionality have been measured using associative learning tasks that purposely induce prediction errors on specific trials (Corlett et al., 2004; Moran, Owen, Crookes, Al-Uzri, & Reveley, 2008; Moran, Rouse, Cross, Corcoran, & Schürmann, 2012). In healthy individuals, a violation in expected feedback leads to increased BOLD activity in the right lateral prefrontal cortex (rPFC), whereas nonviolation leads to no change in rPFC activity. In schizophrenia, the violation-evoked rPFC activity is attenuated, and there is also an

TABLE 2 Neurophysiological Effects of Ketamine and Their Relationship to Schizophrenia

Biomarker	Effect	Dose (Plasma)	Time Point (mins)	%RO$_{est}$	Task/Measure	n	Effect in Schizophrenia
RESTING STATE							
PFC glucose utilization	↑(Vollenweider, Leenders, Scharfetter, et al., 1997)	(557 ng/mL)	Mean	54	PET	10	↓(Siegel et al., 1993)
	↑(Vollenweider, Leenders, Øye, et al., 1997)	(570 ng/mL)[a]	Mean	55	PET	10	
PFC blood flow	↔(Långsjö et al., 2003)	(37 ng/mL)	Mean	7	PET	9	↓(Liddle et al., 1992)
	↑(Långsjö et al., 2003)	(132 ng/mL)		22		10	
PFC connectivity	↑(De Simoni et al., 2013)	(75 ng/mL)		14	BOLD		↓(Hill et al., 2004)
	↑(Anticevic et al., 2015)	0.58 mg/kg; (121 ng/mL)		20	BOLD		↑High-risk, Early ↓Chronic
DMN connectivity next day	↓(Scheidegger et al., 2012)	0.375 mg/kg[a]	T+24h	0	BOLD	17	↑(Whitfield-Gabrieli et al., 2009)
ACC blood flow	↑(Långsjö et al., 2003)	(132 ng/mL)	Mean	22	PET	9	↑(Lahti et al., 2005)
	↑(Holcomb et al., 2001)	0.3 mg/kg bolus	T+6–26		PET	13	
ACC glutamine	↑(Rowland et al., 2005b)	0.27 mg/kg	T+10	17–35	MRS	9	↑Unmedicated (Poels et al., 2014) ↓Chronic (Marsman et al., 2013)
ACC/PFC glutamate	↔(Taylor et al., 2012)	0.5 mg/kg	T+5, 20, 40		MRS	8	
	↑(Stone et al., 2012)	(150 ng/mL)	T+25	24	MRS	13	
OFC activity	↓(Deakin et al., 2008)	0.25 mg/kg	T+0–8		BOLD	12	
PCC activity	↓(Deakin et al., 2008)						
PCC dopamine	↑(Aalto et al., 2005)	(325 ng/mL)	T+20–80	41	PET	8	
Striatal dopamine	↔(Rabiner, 2007)	Wide range			PET	50	↑(Howes & Kapur, 2009)
EVOKED							
PFC gamma power	↑(Hong et al., 2010)	0.3 mg/kg bolus	T+0–20		ERP	10	↓(Spencer, Salisbury, Shenton, & McCarley, 2008)
MMN disruption	↑(Umbricht et al., 2002)	0.9 mg/kg			ERP	20	↑(Umbricht & Krljes, 2005)
	↑(Schmidt et al., 2012)	10 mg bolus + titrated infusion				19	
	↑(Heekeren et al., 2008)	0.5 mg/kg[a]	T+20–50			9	
	↑(Heekeren et al., 2008)	1 mg/kg[a]				9	
	↔(Oranje et al., 2000)	(130 ng/mL)		21		18	

TABLE 2 Neurophysiological Effects of Ketamine and Their Relationship to Schizophrenia—cont'd

Biomarker	Effect	Dose (Plasma)	Time Point (mins)	%RO$_{est}$	Task/Measure	n	Effect in Schizophrenia
Sensorimotor gating	↑(Abel, Allin, Hemsley, et al., 2003)	0.5 mg/kg	T+40	30	Prepulse inhibition	20	↓(Swerdlow et al., 2008)
	↑(Heekeren et al., 2007)	0.5 mg/kg[a]	T+35	>30		10	
	↑(Heekeren et al., 2007)	1 mg/kg[a]		>30		10	
	↔(van Berckel et al., 1998)	0.3 mg/kg (130 ng/mL)	T+40	21		18	
TASK-RELATED							
PFC disruption during PE processing	↑(Corlett et al., 2006)	(88 ng/mL)		16	BOLD	15	↑(Corlett et al., 2007)
Striatal disruption	↔(Corlett et al., 2006)						
PFC activity during WM	↑(Honey et al., 2004)	(50 ng/mL) (100 ng/mL)	T+5	11–17	BOLD	12	↑High-risk (Yaakub et al., 2013), ↓Early (Tan, Choo, Fones, & Chee, 2005), Chronic (Cannon et al., 2005)
DMN-TPN orthogonality during WM	↓(Anticevic et al., 2012)	(183 ng/mL)		28	BOLD	19	↓(Whitfield-Gabrieli et al., 2009)
PFC activity during episodic memory retrieval	↓(Honey, Honey, O'Loughlin, et al., 2005)	(100 ng/mL)	T+60	17	BOLD	12	↓(Ragland et al., 2009)
Amygdala response to emotional faces	↓(Abel, Allin, Kucharska-Pietura, et al., 2003)	0.5 mg/kg	T+20–60		BOLD	8	↓(Gur et al., 2002) ↑(Kosaka et al., 2002)
Oculomotor disruption	↑(Schmechtig et al., 2013)	(100 ng/mL)	T+10	17	Eye-tracking	17	↑(Ettinger et al., 2006)
	↑(Radant et al., 1998)	(100–200 ng/mL)	T+0–120	17–30		10	

PET: positron emission tomography; ERP: event-related potential; MRS: magnetic resonance spectroscopy; PE: prediction error; WM: working memory.
[a]This study used S-Ketamine; therefore, the dose was multiplied by 1.5 to obtain the racemate equivalent (based on Vollenweider, Leenders, Øye, et al. (1997)).

increase in rPFC to unsurprising feedback (Corlett et al., 2007). Ketamine at 16% RO_{est} replicates this phenotype veraciously (Corlett, Honey, Aitken, et al., 2006).

Relating to Negative Symptoms

The neurophysiological substrates of negative symptoms are much less clear than with positive symptoms, since there are no known pharmacological targets for negative symptoms. Some studies have shown an inverse relationship between apathy/anhedonia symptoms and ventral striatal activation during reward anticipation (reviewed in Barch and Dowd (2010)). There have also been reports of orbitofrontal cortex (OFC) volume inversely correlating with negative symptoms (Baaré et al., 1999; Gur et al., 2000), and this brain region is known to be important for assigning value to stimuli (Wallis, 2006).

One study found that—with 0.25 mg/kg ketamine—the decrease in BOLD activity in the OFC correlated with dissociative symptoms on the CADSS (Deakin et al., 2008). Another study using a dose of 23% RO_{est} could not find any region-specific changes in global connectivity that correlated with negative symptoms, but it did find that increases in anterior striatum connectivity appeared to prevent negative symptom formation (Driesen et al., 2013) (and a separate group made a similar finding; Dandash et al., 2015). Another study found that a high dose of ketamine (55% RO_{est}) caused significant increases in dissociation, which correlated with increased prefrontal glucose metabolism (Vollenweider, Leenders, Øye, Hell, & Angst, 1997); however, this change also correlates with many other symptoms and is unlikely to be specific to dissociation. An increase in apathy was correlated with increased glucose metabolism in the left insula and bilateral parietal cortices. Meanwhile, a study using a low dose of S-ketamine (0.1 mg/kg) found a decrease in the occipitoparietal BOLD response and EEG amplitude to the P300 response during a visual oddball task (Musso et al., 2011), which correlated with negative symptoms. Another study found that the BOLD response in the amygdala to emotional faces was attenuated with 0.5 mg/kg ketamine (Abel, Allin, Kucharska-Pietura, et al., 2003), which may reflect affective flattening.

Relating to Cognitive Symptoms

There are many studies that have investigated cognitive task-evoked brain activity in schizophrenia. Most consistently, abnormalities in the prefrontal cortex are detected (Arnsten et al., 2012; Minzenberg, Laird, Thelen, Carter, & Glahn, 2009; Potkin et al., 2009; Ragland et al., 2009).

In a multiple trial working memory task, ketamine was shown to decrease the efficiency of dorsolateral PFC circuit activity at 10% and 17% RO_{est} (Honey et al., 2004). Specifically, ketamine significantly increased dorsolateral PFC circuit activity during manipulation trials at a low WM load compared to placebo. In another study, it was found that ketamine at 28% RO_{est} impaired working memory, which correlated with a failure to deactivate the default mode network (DMN) and activate the task-positive network (TPN, including dorsolateral PFC) during the encoding and delay periods (Anticevic et al., 2012). Computational modeling suggested this effect was induced by NMDA-R hypofunction on inhibitory interneurons.

In an episodic memory task, ketamine was shown to attenuate the left PFC BOLD response during retrieval of deeply encoded episodic memories at 17% RO_{est} (Honey, Honey, O'Loughlin, et al., 2005), meanwhile there was an increase in right hippocampal and bilateral PFC response. During placebo infusion, activation of these regions was seen during presentation of unfamiliar items. These findings may be related to aberrant right PFC signaling seen during error processing (Corlett et al., 2007).

Summary

In summary, although acute NMDA-R antagonism is a useful model of psychosis that also mimics the negative and cognitive symptoms of schizophrenia, there are clearly some discrepancies with the chronic disorder. Numerous theories of schizophrenia have been proposed that may account for this, mostly revolving around neurodevelopmental alterations in up- or downstream circuitry (Do, Cabungcal, Frank, Steullet, & Cuenod, 2009; Insel, 2010). It has been reported that children are much less susceptible to the psychotomimetic effects of ketamine (Bergman, 1999), which may have relevance to the observation that schizophrenia only emerges after adolescence (Uhlhaas, 2013).

There are many caveats to consider when comparing the "healthy human ketamine model" to schizophrenia. First, most ketamine studies are conducted on adults with above average intelligence and no history of psychiatric disease. It is possible that NMDA-R antagonists produce different effects in pathological brains, although in the few studies where ketamine was administered to people with schizophrenia, similar effects were noted. Second, schizophrenia is a very heterogeneous disorder, and within the literature, methodologies are also heterogeneous. For example, the samples recruited vary in age, duration of illness, medication status, and smoking status—factors that have been shown to affect many measures. Third, treatment effects are measured in a range of ways across the literature. Ketamine studies are usually cross-over trials with repeated measures, where each participant is compared to themselves on or off treatment. Schizophrenia studies are almost always

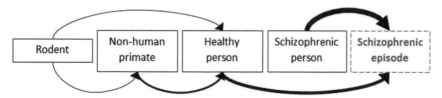

FIGURE 2   How NMDA-R antagonists are used to model schizophrenia. Black boxes represent the agent being administered the drug. Black arrows represent the addition of the drug and what it attempts to model, with arrow width representing the putative validity of the model.

compared between cohorts. Fourth, caution should be taken when interpreting subtle findings from ketamine studies, since although the majority are double-blinded, most researchers and participants are able to determine which treatment has been administered, given the profound effects of ketamine and lack of effects of placebo. Therefore, some of the effects induced by NMDA-R antagonists may be the result of prior expectations (e.g., many participants in one study thought they received the hallucinogen psilocybin rather than dextromethorphan, citing knowledge of the lab's previous studies on psilocybin (Reissig et al., 2012)). Thus, it is important for studies to include active placebos, such as psilocybin or midazolam (Haile et al., 2014), although use of the latter has been criticized for its absence of psychedelic effects (Neuroskeptic, 2014). It may be that behavioral and neurophysiological reactions to ketamine are partly the result of surprise at—or a stress response to—the sheer novelty of the experience of a profoundly altered state of consciousness (although this could be part of the psychotic process nonetheless), although some authors have found reliable effects across two sessions (De Simoni et al., 2013), which tempers this suggestion.

RODENT MODELING OF HUMAN NMDA-R ANTAGONISM

Acute NMDA-R antagonism in rodents has been proposed to be a representative model of human NMDA-R antagonism (see Figure 2). As rodent models generally encompass a more diverse range of drugs than human models, the pharmacology of different NMDA-R antagonists and the neurophysiological and behavioral effects of these compounds at relevant doses will be overviewed.

DIVERSITY OF NMDA-R ANTAGONISTS

NMDA-Rs are composed of four subunits made up of a mixture of NR1, NR2, and NR3 subunits (see Figure 3). Activation (cation influx) requires the following: voltage-dependent removal of the Mg^{2+} blockade, agonist binding to the glutamate binding site (NR2 subunit), and co-agonist binding to the glycine binding site

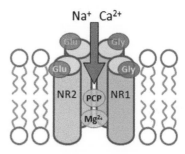

FIGURE 3   A simplified schematic of the NMDA receptor. After voltage-dependent release of Mg^{2+} and glutamate/glycine co-binding, the NMDA receptor opens, and drugs binding to the PCP site can enter the channel and prevent cation influx. Antagonists can bind to the glutamate site, glycine site, or an allosteric site (not shown).

(NR1 subunit). NMDA-R antagonists may bind to any of these sites and allosteric sites further still (Monaghan & Jane, 2009). As a result, there are numerous subclasses of NMDA-R antagonist, and the degree to which they mimic psychosis mostly depends on their binding site and dissociation kinetics (see Table 3).

The most psychotomimetic NMDA-R antagonists are those that bind to the PCP binding site and possess a slow dissociation rate. However, most NMDA-R antagonists can produce psychotomimetic effects at high enough doses (Tricklebank, Singh, Oles, Preston, & Iversen, 1989) (with the possible exception of glycine antagonists (Koek & Colpaert, 1990)), which implies that nonspecific NMDA-R blockade is sufficient to produce this effect rather than some unique temporal effect of ion channel blockers.

It should be noted that there is subunit heterogeneity across the brain. The NR2C subunit is mostly found in the cerebellum, midbrain, and brain stem (Monyer, Burnashev, Laurie, Sakmann, & Seeburg, 1994). NMDA-Rs containing the NR2C subunit also possess a less potent Mg^{2+} block. MK-801 has equal affinity for the NR2A, NR2B, and NR2C subunits, and yet it is more likely to induce ataxia than memantine (Parsons et al., 1995), which has a subunit selectivity profile of NR2C > NR2B >> NR2A (Dravid et al., 2007). This may be explained by the slower on–off kinetics of MK-801 at NR2C-containing channels (Monaghan & Larsen, 1997), which presumably causes a greater disturbance of cerebellar signaling.

Some studies have reported that blockade of NR2A-containing receptors is sufficient to produce

TABLE 3   Classes of NMDA-R Antagonist

Drug	Binding Site	Dissociation Rate (Mealing, Lanthorn, Murray, Small, & Morley, 1999)	Psychotomimetic Potential (Kornhuber & Weller, 1997)
CGS-19755	Glutamate site (NR2 nonspecific)	N/A	Low
NVP-AAM077	Allosteric site (NR2A specific)	N/A	Equivocal (Chaperon et al., 2003; Kocsis, 2012)
Ifenprodil, traxoprodil	Allosteric site (NR2B specific)	N/A	Low
7-chloro kynurenic acid	Glycine site	N/A	Very low (Koek & Colpaert, 1990)
PCP	Ion channel (also known as the "PCP binding site"	Slow	Very high
Ketamine		Slow	
MK-801		Slow	
Dextrorphan		Slow	
Memantine		Fast	Low
Lanicemine		Very fast	Very low

Reviewed in Paoletti and Neyton (2007).

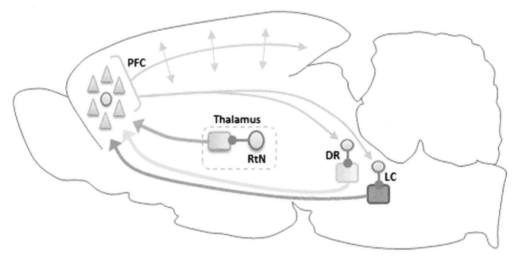

FIGURE 4   Increased release of glutamate (orange), serotonin (yellow), and noradrenaline (purple) in cortical areas is a widely replicated finding with NMDA-R antagonist administration (see Table 2). Dawson and others found that a high subanaesthetic dose* of ketamine decreased glucose metabolism in the thalamus, dorsal raphé nucleus (DR), and locus coeruleus (LC), whilst increasing metabolism in the PFC (another widely replicated finding). They propose that ketamine blocks tonically active NR2C-containing NMDA-Rs on interneurons (green) in the reticular thalamic nucleus (RtN), DR, and LC, leading to disinhibition of projection neurons from these nuclei. * >83% RO_{est} based on mouse data from Lord et al. (2013).

psychotomimetic effects (Kocsis, 2012), whereas others have reported that NR2A blockade is not psychotomimetic (Chaperon, Müller, Auberson, Tricklebank, & Neijt, 2003), and that NR2B blockade is sufficient (Chaperon et al., 2003; Gilmour et al., 2009; Nicholson, Mansbach, Menniti, & Balster, 2007). Meanwhile, others have suggested that NR2B blockade is not psychotomimetic (Higgins, Ballard, Huwyler, Kemp, & Gill, 2003), or that neither is sufficient, and both must be antagonized (Jiménez-Sánchez et al., 2014). Most of these studies fail to titrate for global NMDA-R blockade given the doses used, and therefore, it remains to be determined whether

these are specific effects or just the result of an overall lower level of NMDA-R blockade with subunit selective antagonists.

Another hypothesis, proposed by Dawson, Morris, and Pratt (2013), is that selective blockade of NR2C-containing NMDA-Rs leads to increased prefrontal glutamate, serotonin, and noradrenaline release (see Figure 4), and this contributes to the psychotomimetic effects. It is uncertain how NR2C antagonism leads to monoamine release, as one study found that systemic ketamine-induced 5-HT release was dependent on AMPA-R stimulation in the dorsal raphé, but that intra-raphé infusion of ketamine had no effect (albeit at a very low dose) (Nishitani et al., 2014). Similarly, noradrenaline release by ketamine was dependent on AMPA-R stimulation (Lorrain, Schaffhauser, et al., 2003).

Adding to the complexity, (S)-ketamine and (R)-ketamine are equally effective in stimulating 5-HT and noradrenaline release, but (R)-ketamine is much less effective in stimulating dopamine release (Tso, Blatchford, Callado, McLaughlin, & Stamford, 2004). It is well established that (S)-ketamine is more psychotomimetic (Vollenweider, Leenders, Øye, et al., 1997), and relative to (R)-ketamine, it has a higher affinity for the NR2C subunit and much lower affinity for the NR2A subunit (Dravid et al., 2007).

The importance of the monoamine releasing effects of NMDA-R antagonists is questionable, given the mixed findings in humans (see Table 2). Dopamine D2 receptor antagonists fail to attenuate the psychotomimetic effects (Krystal et al., 1999), whilst atypical antipsychotics (which possess high 5-HT2A receptor affinity) attenuate some of the subjective effects (Malhotra et al., 1997) and neurophysiological changes (Doyle et al., 2013), although it is unclear whether this is a nonspecific effect due to the intrinsic sedative nature of 5-HT2A antagonists (Distler, 1990).

Some NMDA receptor antagonists also possess affinity for other targets, such as sigma receptors, opioid receptors, and monoamine transporters. However, ketamine and PCP require doses tenfold higher than those required to induce anaesthesia to bind to these receptors (Roth et al., 2013), and therefore, they are not relevant to models of psychosis. We cannot exclude the possibility that metabolites display much higher, relevant affinities for these targets (Morris & Wallach, 2014), but these would be expected to have a delayed onset with intravenous administration, and therefore do not fit with the rapid onset of psychotomimetic effects. It has also been reported that PCP, ketamine, and MK-801 display nanomolar in vitro affinity for the D_2 receptor in its high affinity state (D_2^{High}), and that this correlates with psychotomimetic potency (Seeman, Ko, & Tallerico, 2005); however, others have failed to replicate many of the findings from this lab (Fell et al., 2009; Jordan et al., 2006; Odagaki & Toyoshima, 2006; Roth et al., 2013), and since D2 antagonists fail to attenuate most of the psychotomimetic effects of NMDA-R antagonists (Krystal et al., 1999) and because the psychotomimetic potential of NMDA-R antagonists correlates with their NMDA-R affinity (Ginski & Witkin, 1994) (although see Stone et al., 2008), it is proposed that in vitro D_2^{High} affinity is irrelevant to models of psychosis.

Based on clinical and preclinical literature (see Table 4), it is proposed that NMDA-R antagonists optimally produce schizophrenia-like symptoms within a certain dose window. To decrease complications when additionally

TABLE 4 NMDA-R Antagonist Dose–Response Relationships

	Dose of Racemic Ketamine (mg/kg)			
Human (i.v.)	0.1–0.6	0.3–0.8	>0.8	1–4
NMDA-RO	~10–30%	~30–80%		>80%
Rat (i.p.)	3–10	10–30	30–50	>80
Behavior	Mild	Moderate	Severe	General anesthesia
	Analgesia, cognitive impairment, dissociation, psychosis, ataxia			
Target	Higher cortical areas	+Midbrain areas, limbic system, cerebellum		+Arousal nuclei, thalamus PCs
References	Sinner and Graf (2008), Subramaniam, Subramaniam, and Steinbrook (2004), Bergman (1999), Green, Knight, Precious, and Simpkin (1981), Radant et al. (1998)			

analyzing the time course effects, this review will only focus on this dosage window and disregard higher doses that induce anesthesia.

NMDA-R ANTAGONIST BEHAVIORAL EFFECTS IN RODENTS

In this evaluation of the literature, an effort has been made to only include studies using relevant doses. For ketamine, this includes any dose up to 30 mg/kg i.p. or 20 mg/kg s.c. (Shaffer et al., 2014). For PCP, this includes any dose up to 10 mg/kg i.p. or 5 mg/kg s.c. (Kalinichev et al., 2008), and for MK-801 up to 0.2 mg/kg i.p. or s.c. These maximal doses attain >70% RO_{est} (Shaffer et al., 2014), which is far in excess of any human schizophrenia modeling study. In addition, Hiyoshi, Kambe, Karasawa, and Chaki (2014) found an inverse-U dose–response effect of ketamine, PCP, and MK-801 on gamma oscillations, with peak effect occurring at (all s.c.) 20, 5, and 0.2 mg/kg, respectively. This implies that above these doses, anesthetic effects begin to predominate.

REPRESENTING POSITIVE SYMPTOMS

The most commonly measured rodent behavioral phenotype for positive symptoms is locomotor activity. Any drug that increases striatal dopamine release will increase locomotor activity (LMA) (Ikemoto, 2002), and aberrant increases in striatal dopamine signalling are considered to be the cause of aberrant salience, which leads to psychosis (Kapur, 2003). All of the psychotomimetic NMDA-R antagonists cause a dose-dependent increase in LMA at subanesthetic doses (see Table 5); however, there have been some nuanced findings at higher doses.

TABLE 5 Behavioral Effects Resembling Positive Symptoms of Schizophrenia upon Administration of NMDA-R Antagonists to Rodents

Symptom	Effect	Drug	Dose (mg/kg)	Route	Time Point (mins)	Task/Measure	References
Psychosis	↕	MK-801	0.03	s.c.	T+0–120	Locomotor boxes (LABORAS™)	Castagné et al. (2012)
	↑		0.1				
	↑		0.3				
	↕	Ketamine	3	s.c.	T+0–120		
	↑		10	s.c.	T+0–40		
	↑		30	s.c.	T+20–80		
	↑	PCP	5	i.p.	T+4–80	Locomotor boxes	Suzuki et al. (2002)
	↕	S-Ketamine	10	s.c.	T+0–300	Locomotor boxes	Phillips et al. (2012)
	↑	MK-801	0.1	s.c.	T+10–180		
	↑	PCP	2.5	s.c.	T+10–200		
	↕	Ketamine	5	i.p.	T+15–30	Locomotor boxes (no habituation period prior to dosing)	Kotermanski et al. (2013)
	↓		10		or		
	↓		20		T+45–60		
	↓		40				
	↑	MK-801	0.1	i.p.	T+40–220	Locomotor boxes (no habituation)	Daya et al. (2014)
	↑		0.5				
	↑	Ketamine	3	s.c.	T+0–15	Locomotor boxes	Ma and Leung (2014)
	↕	Ketamine	25	i.p.	T+0–40	Locomotor boxes	Razoux et al. (2006)
	↑	MK-801	0.01–0.03	s.c.	T+10	Locomotor boxes	Higgins et al. (2003)
	↑		0.1–0.3				
	↕	Ketamine	30	i.p.	T+30–60	Open field (no habituation)	Danysz et al. (1994)
	↕	PCP	1				
	↕		3				
	↑		10				
	↕	MK-801	0.1				
	↑		0.2		T+30–45		
	↑		0.3		T+30–60		

TABLE 5 Behavioral Effects Resembling Positive Symptoms of Schizophrenia upon Administration of NMDA-R Antagonists to Rodents—cont'd

Symptom	Effect	Drug	Dose (mg/kg)	Route	Time Point (mins)	Task/Measure	References
Stereotypy and ataxia	↑	Ketamine	2.5	s.c.	T+20–80	Observation scoring	Pinault (2008)
	↑	MK-801	0.16	s.c.	T+20–90+		Danysz et al. (1994)
	↑	PCP	10	i.p.	T+35–50		
	↑	MK-801	0.2	i.p.			Kos et al. (2006)
	↕	Ketamine	12.5	i.p.	T+5–15		
	↑		25				
	↑		33				
	↑	Ketamine	25	i.p.	T+0–40		Razoux et al. (2006)
	↕	MK-801	0.03	s.c.	T+10		Higgins et al. (2003)
	↑		0.1–0.3				
Sensorimotor gating	→	Ketamine	10	s.c.	T+0	Prepulse inhibition of the acoustic startle response	Kos et al. (2006)
	→		20				
	→		40				
	→	Ketamine	3	s.c.	T+0		Ma and Leung (2014)
	→	Ketamine	10	s.c.	T+5		Nikiforuk et al. (2013)
	→	MK-801	0.1	i.p.	T+15		Daya et al. (2014)
	→		0.5				
	↕	PCP	1	i.p.	T+15		Ma et al. (2004)
	→		3				
	→		5				
	↕	MK-801	0.03	s.c.	T+10		Higgins et al. (2003)
	→		0.1–0.3				
Aberrant salience—latent inhibition	↔/↓/↑	PCP	0.5–8.6	i.p. or s.c.	Range	Various—Conditioned emotional response, taste aversion, avoidance response	Moser et al. (2000)
		Ketamine	25–50				Weiner and Arad (2009)
		MK-801	0.05–1				

II. NEUROBIOLOGY OF PSYCHOTIC DISORDERS

This is most likely due to the fact that stereotypy and ataxia are prominent, so gross measures such as ambulation decrease, but mobility is still increased (Castagné, Wolinsky, Quinn, & Virley, 2012). Stereotypy is another behavioral phenotype induced by increases in striatal dopamine signaling (Delfs & Kelley, 1990). NMDA-R antagonists have been shown to increase stereotypy at moderate to high doses (Danysz, Essmann, Bresink, & Wilk, 1994; Higgins et al., 2003; Kos et al., 2006; Pinault, 2008).

As mentioned previously, sensorimotor gating deficits are a common phenotype in schizophrenia, though in human models, NMDA-R antagonist administration leads to enhanced sensorimotor gating. In rodents, however, NMDA-R antagonists consistently impair sensorimotor gating, as measured by prepulse inhibition of the auditory startle response (Daya et al., 2014; Kos et al., 2006; Ma, Shen, Rajakumar, & Leung, 2004).

A number of behavioral models taken from associative learning have also been investigated in animals. Latent inhibition refers to a phenomenon whereby an agent finds it harder to associate outcomes with a stimulus that has been preexposed without an outcome, compared to a stimulus that has had no preexposure. In acute, unmedicated schizophrenia, latent inhibition appears to be disrupted, explaining why attention is paid to irrelevant stimuli (Weiner, 2003). However, in chronic schizophrenia (and especially in those with strong negative symptoms), latent inhibition appears to be enhanced, which may explain the phenotypes of perseveration and motivational anhedonia (Weiner, 2003). A recent study in schizotypy has suggested that whether enhancement or reduction is seen may depend on whether the tasks used contain learned irrelevance or conditioned inhibition confounds (Granger, Moran, Buckley, & Haselgrove, submitted for publication); this hypothesis remains to be tested in patients, however. In rodents, NMDA-R antagonists have been reported either to enhance, to impair, or to have no effect on latent inhibition (reviewed in Moser, Hitchcock, Lister, and Moran (2000) and Weiner and Arad (2009)). Which effect is seen is dependent on the behavioral manipulations used that differ in their sensitivities to glutamatergic manipulation but are generally reversible by antipsychotic drugs. Thus, high levels of latent inhibition are not disrupted by NMDA-R antagonists; this procedure is, however, disrupted by dopaminergic drugs such as D-amphetamine (Bay-Richter et al., 2013), which together with genetic data suggest a more dopaminergic-based behavioral process (Bay-Richter et al., 2009). In experimental conditions where latent inhibition is rendered low in controls by reducing stimulus exposures, NMDA-R antagonists can reverse this low latent inhibition (termed abnormally persistent latent inhibition). This abnormally persistent latent inhibition is sensitive to antipsychotic drug treatment (Weiner & Arad, 2009). Thus, differing effects of NMDA-R antagonists in latent inhibition reflect their interaction with different categories of behavioral abnormality that differ vis-à-vis their relative dopamine versus glutamate sensitivity.

REPRESENTING NEGATIVE SYMPTOMS

One of the most widely used behavioral assays in animal models of depression is the forced swim test or tail suspension test. These tests restrain an animal in inescapable conditions and measure its "helplessness" (immobility time). This may be relevant to the symptom of amotivation in schizophrenia. NMDA-R antagonists consistently decrease immobility on these tests, which some authors claim indicates an antidepressant effect. However, it is most likely a confound from the increase in LMA these drugs cause; although selective antagonists for GluN2A or GluN2B decrease immobility without increasing open field locomotor activity, unlike nonselective antagonists that increase both (Jiménez-Sánchez et al., 2014). It should be noted that NMDA-R antagonists have been shown to decrease immobility long after excretion and at quite low doses (Autry et al., 2011; Li et al., 2010; Maeng et al., 2008) (see Table 6), which may be a true antidepressant effect resulting from AMPA-R mediated synaptic changes (Koike, Iijima, & Chaki, 2011; Li et al., 2010). In addition, they improve learned helplessness in escapable shock assays (Autry et al., 2011), although another study found this effect occurred only after three daily doses (Belujon & Grace, 2014).

NMDA-R antagonists are also able to improve measures of anhedonia, such as novelty-suppressed feeding (Autry et al., 2011; Li et al., 2010), which is sensitive to chronic dosing of traditional antidepressants (Cryan, Markou, & Lucki, 2002). Although this test is also sensitive to anxiolytic compounds, and given that ketamine had no effect on appetitive behavior toward sucrose (Autry et al., 2011), this is a more likely explanation for this behavior. However, in other studies investigating gustatory anhedonia, NMDA-R antagonists generally have been found to have no effect at a range of doses and time points (Garcia et al., 2009; Shin et al., 2014). One study found increased sucrose consumption with low doses of PCP and MK-801 (Lydall, Gilmour, & Dwyer, 2010), but as the dose was increased, there was no effect, until at higher doses a decrease occurred that was due to nonspecific motor impairment.

Anhedonia can also be measured using intracranial self-stimulation (ICSS), which is considered a direct measure of the pleasure response and is insatiable (Wise, 2002). Facilitation of ICSS indicates an increased motivational state and is reliably produced by acute

TABLE 6 Behavioral Effects Resembling Negative Symptoms of Schizophrenia upon Administration of NMDA-R Antagonists to Rodents

Symptom	Effect	Drug	Dose (mg/kg)	Route	Time Point (mins)	Task/Measure	References
Amotivation/apathy	↓	Ketamine	3	i.p.	T+30min	Immobility time on the forced swim test/tail suspension test	Autry et al. (2011)
					T+3h		
					T+1day		
					T+7days		
	↓	Ketamine	10	i.p.	T+30		Li et al. (2010)
	↓	Ketamine	5	i.p.	T+10		Da Silva et al. (2010)
	↓		10				
	↓		20				
	↕	Ketamine	12.5	i.p.	T+30		Kos et al. (2006)
	↕		25				
	↕		33				
	↕	Ketamine	30	i.p.	T+24h		Chindo, Adzu, Yahaya, and Gamaniel (2012)
	↓	MK-801	0.05	i.p.?	T+30		Maeng et al. (2008)
	↓		0.1				
	↓		0.2				
Learned helplessness	↓	Ketamine	3	i.p.	T+30	Latency to escape shocks	Autry et al. (2011)
	↕	Ketamine	5	i.p.	T+20 or T+120		Belujon and Grace (2014)
Anhedonia/anxiety	↓	Ketamine	3	i.p.	T+30	Novelty-suppressed feeding	Autry et al. (2011)
	↕				T+3days		
	↓	Ketamine	10	i.p.	T+30		Li et al. (2010)

Continued

TABLE 6   Behavioral Effects Resembling Negative Symptoms of Schizophrenia upon Administration of NMDA-R Antagonists to Rodents—cont'd

Symptom	Effect	Drug	Dose (mg/kg)	Route	Time Point (mins)	Task/Measure	References
Anhedonia	↔	Ketamine	3	i.p.	T+30	Sucrose/saccharin consumption tests	Autry et al. (2011)
	↕	Ketamine	10	i.p.	T+30		Shin et al. (2014)
	↕	Ketamine	15	i.p.	T+60		Garcia et al. (2009)
	↓	PCP	0.25	s.c.	T+30		Lydall et al. (2010)
	↕		0.5				
	↕		1				
	↑		2.5				
	↕	MK-801	0.0125	s.c.	T+30		
	↓		0.025				
	↓		0.05				
	↑		0.1				
	↕	Ketamine	1	i.p.	T+10	Change in ICSS responding at a range of stimulation frequencies	Hillhouse et al. (2014)
	↕		3.2				
	↑		5.6				
	↑		10				
	↕	MK-801	0.032	i.p.	T+15		
	↓		0.1				
	⇄		0.18				
	↑		0.32				
	↑	Ketamine	5.6	i.p	T+10–100		
	↑		10		T+10–100		
	↓	MK-801	0.18	i.p	T+10–100		
	↑		0.32		T+10–30		
	⇄				T+100		
	↑				T+300		
	↓	PCP	2.5	i.p.	T+0–60		Carlezon and Wise (1993)
	↓		5		T+0–90		
	↑	PCP	2	s.c.	T+30		Amitai et al. (2009)

Social interaction test	Drug	Dose	Route	T	Social anhedonia
Daya et al. (2014)	MK-801	0.1	i.p.	T+0–15	↑
		0.5			↑
Nikiforuk et al. (2013)	Ketamine	20	i.p.	T+30	↑
Baker et al. (2008)	PCP	3	s.c.	T+60	↑
Georgiadou et al. (2014)	S-Ketamine	8	i.p.	T+30	↑
Sallinen et al. (2013)	PCP	1–2	s.c.	T+45	↑
Koros et al. (2006)	PCP	0.5–4	s.c.	T+45	↑
	MK-801	0.03	s.c.	T+45	↕
	MK-801	0.06–0.25			↑
	Ketamine	2	s.c.	T+30	↕
		4–16			↑
Morales et al. (2013)	MK-801	0.01	i.p.	T+30	→
		0.03			↕

administration of reinforcing drugs (Bauer, Banks, Blough, & Negus, 2013). Meanwhile, suppression of ICSS indicates motivational anhedonia and is produced by withdrawal from these drugs (Epping-Jordan, Watkins, Koob, & Markou, 1998; Markou & Koob, 1991). One study found mixed effects of NMDA-R antagonists, with ketamine-decreasing ICSS responding at higher doses but MK-801 showing facilitation of ICSS at moderate doses and suppression of ICSS at higher doses (Hillhouse, Porter, & Negus, 2014). This may have been due to task disengagement as the effect disappeared with chronic dosing, and it was not present during the later stages. The authors noted that this also occurs with morphine, but unlike ketamine, once sedation subsides, ICSS thresholds decrease (Altarifi & Negus, 2011). Another study found that PCP at moderate doses (2.5–5 mg/kg i.p.) facilitated ICSS at lower stimulation frequencies (Carlezon & Wise, 1993). Meanwhile, slightly higher doses (2 mg/kg s.c., equivalent to ~6 mg/kg i.p.) suppressed ICSS responding (Amitai, Semenova, & Markou, 2009). These authors noted the variability of PCP on ICSS, stating that they found facilitation with doses of 0.3–0.9 mg/kc s.c., no change with 1.3 mg/kg, and suppression with 2–2.5 mg/kg.

In contrast to some of the antidepressant effects previously mentioned, NMDA-R antagonists decrease social interaction in rodents, which may represent social anhedonia (Baker et al., 2008; Daya et al., 2014; Nikiforuk et al., 2013). The doses used in these studies were quite high and have been shown to cause motor impairment and task disengagement in operant tasks, which together suggest an increase in dissociative symptoms. Other studies have avoided this effect by administering NMDA-R antagonists on the days prior to testing, which is known to induce tolerance to the motor effects but retain some of the more subtle behavioral effects (although stereotypy still remains (Koros, Rosenbrock, Birk, Weiss, & Sams-Dodd, 2006)). These studies still report a decrease in social interaction, and cover a wide range of dosages, implying that NMDA-R antagonists consistently produce a socially isolating phenotype (Georgiadou, Grivas, Tarantilis, & Pitsikas, 2014; Koros et al., 2006). One exception to this was in a study using a low dose of MK-801 (0.01 mg/kg) in adolescent rats, where an increase in social interaction was observed (Morales, Varlinskaya, & Spear, 2013).

Overall, NMDA-R antagonists seem to mimic the negative symptoms of schizophrenia when administered in the moderate-to-high dose range. It should be noted that all of the effects described are in "normal" animals, and that in stressed animals, NMDA-R antagonists consistently produce antianhedonic effects in the low-to-moderate dose range (Autry et al., 2011; Belujon & Grace, 2014; Koike et al., 2011; Shin et al., 2014).

However, these effects are persistent upon elimination of the drug (Donahue, Muschamp, Russo, Nestler, & Carlezon, 2014; Li et al., 2011; Maeng et al., 2008), and may therefore represent a mechanism distinct from psychosis.

Representing Cognitive Symptoms

There are many rodent assays that measure cognitive deficits relevant to schizophrenia. Here, we will focus on attention, episodic memory, working memory, and cognitive flexibility (see Table 7), all of which have been shown to be affected in human NMDA-R antagonist models.

The most commonly used assay for measuring attention in rodents is the 5-choice serial reaction time task (5-CSRTT). PCP has been shown to impair accuracy on this task in a dose-dependent manner (Amitai, Semenova, & Markou, 2007). This study found an increased latency to respond and no change in latency to collect reward, dismissing impulsivity, and motor impairment as potential confounds. Meanwhile, other studies found similar effects with MK-801 (Higgins, Ballard, Enderlin, Haman, & Kemp, 2005) and ketamine (Nikiforuk & Popik, 2014; Smith et al., 2011).

Episodic memory can be assessed in rodents using maze tasks, novel object recognition (NOR) tasks, and novel location recognition (NLR) tasks. One study found that low doses of ketamine were able to impair novel object and NLR, regardless of whether administered prior to or after acquisition (Pitsikas, Boultadakis, & Sakellaridis, 2008). Another study found that a low dose of MK-801 impaired NOR when given 20 min prior to acquisition, irrespective of whether the delay between the acquisition phase and the recognition phase was 1.5 or 24 h (De Lima, Laranja, Bromberg, Roesler, & Schröder, 2005). Meanwhile, MK-801 has been shown to impair water maze learning when administered at a range of time points and dosages (Åhlander et al., 1999).

NMDA-R antagonists consistently produce impairments in working memory tasks. MK-801 at high doses caused rats to make more retroactive arm entries in an eight-arm radial maze (Daya et al., 2014). On a four-arm alternation task, ketamine was only able to impair performance at a very high subanesthetic dose (Kotermanski, Johnson, & Thiels, 2013), and MK-801 actually improved performance at a low dose, but impaired it at moderate-to-high doses (Jackson et al., 2004). Meanwhile, on a delayed nonmatching to sample lever task, a moderately high dose (0.1 mg/kg) of MK-801 perturbed performance at delays of 4–32 s, but not 0 s, implying a specific deficit in working memory (Bonaventure et al., 2011). Other studies have also found dose-dependent effects of MK-801, PCP, and ketamine (Higgins et al., 2005; Kos et al., 2006; Smith et al., 2011;

TABLE 7 Behavioral Effects Resembling Cognitive Symptoms of Schizophrenia upon Administration of NMDA-R Antagonists to Rodents

Symptom	Effect	Drug	Dose (mg/kg)	Route	Time Point (mins)	Task/Measure	References
Sustained attention	↕	PCP	1.5	s.c.	T+30	5-CSRTT percentage correct	Amitai et al. (2007)
	→		2.25				
	→		3				
	↕	MK-801	0.03	s.c.	T+10		Higgins et al. (2005)
	→		0.06				
	→		0.1				
	↕	Ketamine	3	i.p.	T+45		Nikiforuk and Popik (2014)
	→		10				
	→	PCP	1–3	s.c.	T+30		Smith et al. (2011)
	↕	MK-801	0.025–0.05	s.c.	T+30		
	→	MK-801	0.1				
	→	S-Ketamine	2.5–10	s.c.	T+5		
	↕	MK-801	0.03	s.c.	T+10		Higgins et al. (2003)
	→		0.06				
	↕	Ketamine	2–4	i.p.	T+10	Lever pressing task	Nelson et al. (2002)
	↕	Ketamine	0.3	i.p.	Acq: T+20; T+42	NOR/NLR—drugged during acquisition	Pitsikas et al. (2008)
	→		1–3				
	↕		0.3		Acq: T−2; T+22	NOR/NLR—drugged during retrieval	
	→		1–3				
Episodic memory	↕	MK-801	0.001	i.p.	Acq: T+20; T+110/T+24 h	NOR—drugged during acquisition	De Lima et al. (2005)
	→		0.01–0.1				
	→		0.1		Acq: T−5; T+110/T+24 h	NOR—drugged after acquisition	
	↕	MK-801	0.01	i.p. or s.c.	range	Water maze latency to platform	Åhlander et al. (1999)
	→		0.05–0.1				

Continued

II. NEUROBIOLOGY OF PSYCHOTIC DISORDERS

TABLE 7　Behavioral Effects Resembling Cognitive Symptoms of Schizophrenia upon Administration of NMDA-R Antagonists to Rodents—cont'd

Symptom	Effect	Drug	Dose (mg/kg)	Route	Time Point (mins)	Task/Measure	References
Working memory	↓	MK-801	0.1	i.p.	T+5	Eight-arm radial maze	Daya et al. (2014)
			0.5				
	↕	Ketamine	5–20	i.p.	T+15 or T+45	Four-arm maze spontaneous alternation	Kotermanski et al. (2013)
	↓		40				
	↑	MK-801	0.01	i.p.	T+40		Jackson et al. (2004)
	↓		0.05				
	↓		0.1				
	↓	MK-801	0.1	i.p.	T+10	Delayed matching/nonmatching to sample	Bonaventure et al. (2011)
	↕	MK-801	0.01–0.1	i.p.	T+15		Willmore et al. (2001)
	↓		0.2				
	↕	PCP	0.5–2	i.p.	T+15		Higgins et al. (2005)
	↓		4–8				
	↕	MK-801	0.03	s.c.	T+10		
	↓		0.06				
	↓		0.1				
	↕	Ketamine	3–18	i.p.	T+10		Kos et al. (2006)
	↓		30				
	↕	PCP	0.5–1	s.c.	T+30		Smith et al. (2011)
	↓		2–2.5				
	↕	MK-801	0.025	s.c.	T+30		
	↓		0.05				
	↕	S-Ketamine	2.5	s.c.	T+5		
	↓		5–10				
	↕	MK-801	0.03	s.c.	T+10		Higgins et al. (2003)
	↓		0.06–0.1				

Domain	Effect	Drug	Dose	Route	Time	Task	Reference
Reversal learning	→	PCP	2.5	s.c.	T+210	Bowl digging task—reversal phases	Gastambide et al. (2013)
	↕	S-Ketamine	10	s.c.	T+150		Kos et al. (2011)
	↕	Ketamine	10–20	i.p.	T+50		
	↕	Ketamine	3–10	s.c.	T+180		Nikiforuk et al. (2010)
	↕	Ketamine	10	s.c.	T+24h		Nikiforuk et al. (2013)
	↕	MK-801	0.025–0.075	s.c.	T+60	Instrumental conditioning task	De Bruin et al. (2013)
	↕	PCP	0.5	s.c.	T+75		
	→	PCP	1–2		T+30		
	↕	PCP	0.5	s.c.	T+30		Fellini et al.
	→	PCP	1		T+30		
Attentional set shifting	→	PCP	2.58	i.p.	T+24h	Bowl digging task—extradimensional shift phases	Egerton et al. (2005)
	→	PCP	2.5	s.c.	T+300		Gastambide et al. (2013)
	→	S-Ketamine	10	s.c.	T+240		Kos et al. (2011)
	→	Ketamine	10–20	i.p.	T+50		
	↕	Ketamine	10		T+180		
	↕	Ketamine	3	s.c.	T+24h		Nikiforuk et al. (2010)
	→	Ketamine	10		T+60		
	→	Ketamine	10	s.c.	T+75		Nikiforuk et al. (2013)
	→	MK-801	0.03	i.p.	T+35	Plus maze set shifting task	Jones et al. (2014)
	→	MK-801	0.1				
Contextual discrimination	→	PCP	1.5	i.p.	T+30	Instrumental conditioning task	Large et al. (2011)
	↕	PCP	1	i.p.	T+30		Idris et al. (2005)
	→	PCP	1.5–2				

Willmore, LaVecchia, & Wiley, 2001); however, many of these studies find impairments at delays below 1 s, which may imply motor impairment or biased responding.

NMDA-R antagonists have been tested in assays for cognitive flexibility, such as the bowl digging task, which requires hungry animals to discriminate between smells and textures to determine where a food reward is; or instrumental tasks, where animals are required to make a specific action to receive a reward. In one study, a high dose of PCP impaired reversal learning, whilst a moderate dose of ketamine did not (Gastambide, Mitchell, Robbins, Tricklebank, & Gilmour, 2013); however, the pharmacokinetic data show that PCP levels were still notable during the task, whereas ketamine levels were very low at this time point. Other bowl digging studies have also failed to produce reversal learning deficits with ketamine at low to high doses (Kos, Nikiforuk, Rafa, & Popik, 2011; Nikiforuk, Gołembiowska, & Popik, 2010). In an operant task, administration of low-to-moderate doses of MK-801 before each of the five testing sessions had no effect on the acquisition of a reversed rule, whilst moderate doses of PCP did slow the acquisition of the reversal (De Bruin et al., 2013). Intriguingly though, MK-801 did increase perseveration during extinction to a similar degree as PCP at these doses. In a touch screen visual discrimination task, low doses of PCP impaired the acquisition of a reversal without affecting performance of a pre-learned discrimination (Fellini, Kumar, Gibbs, Steckler, & Talpos, 2014).

Although the findings with reversal learning are equivocal, NMDA-R antagonists have been shown to consistently impair attentional set shifting at a range of doses and with pretreatment times sufficient to avoid motor confounds (Egerton, Reid, McKerchar, Morris, & Pratt, 2005; Gastambide et al., 2013; Kos et al., 2011; Nikiforuk et al., 2010, 2013). MK-801 was also shown to impair set shifting on a plus maze discrimination task (Jones et al., 2014). In contextual discrimination tasks, in which an animal has to implement different pre-learned rules depending on the context of the task, NMDA-R antagonists often impair performance (Idris, Repeto, Neill, & Large, 2005; Large et al., 2011).

It could be argued that many of the deficits previously mentioned are all the result of task impulsivity, as NMDA-R antagonists are known to cause behavioral "speeding." However, across dosages, there was little evidence for a specific effect on cognitive impulsivity (i.e., decreased response latencies to task-relevant cues in the absence of decreased latencies in task initiation or reward collection) (Amitai et al., 2007; Kos et al., 2006). Another argument is that the deficits are induced by task disengagement and, therefore, are not specific. This is clearly a problem at the higher dosages and shorter pretreatment times where omissions are often increased

(Gastambide et al., 2013; Kos et al., 2006; Nelson, Burk, Bruno, & Sarter, 2002), probably reflecting a dissociative state.

Overall, it appears that NMDA-R antagonists are effective at impairing attention and memory in rodents at doses that produce little motor impairment. Reversal learning is usually unaffected on the bowl digging task, which is reliant on goal-directed circuitry and often has "discovery" trials where the rodent can make errors that are not counted toward performance. Performance on instrumental reversal tasks is often impaired; and these tasks rely more on implicit/habitual circuitry and do not have "discovery" trials; therefore, they are more sensitive at detecting impaired performance. Extradimensional set shifting is consistently impaired, even when the NMDA-R antagonist is administered 24 h prior at a moderately low dose.

NMDA-R Antagonist Physiological Effects in Rodents

As in humans, NMDA-R antagonists have been consistently shown to increase cortical activation in rodents (see Table 8), as measured by resting oxygen (Finnerty, Bolger, Pålsson, & Lowry, 2013; Li et al., 2014), glucose (Finnerty et al., 2013), glutamate (Bonaventure et al., 2011; Uslaner et al., 2012), and dopamine levels (Adams & Moghaddam, 1998; Bonaventure et al., 2011; Lorrain, Baccei, Bristow, Anderson, & Varney, 2003b), along with single unit firing (Jackson et al., 2004; Suzuki, Jodo, Takeuchi, Niwa, & Kayama, 2002) and gamma oscillatory power (reviewed in Hunt and Kasicki (2013)). Studies have also shown an increase in hippocampal gamma power (Ma & Leung, 2014) that correlates with disruption of sensorimotor gating (Ma et al., 2004). Furthermore, ketamine-induced ECoG gamma power correlated with stereotypy/ataxia ratings, but dopamine agonists induced stereotypy without affecting gamma power, implying that this is an upstream biomarker (Pinault, 2008). In addition, MK-801 provoked PFC pyramidal neuron firing at low-to-high doses, which correlated with stereotypy scores but had no relationship to working memory performance (Jackson et al., 2004).

Resting-state spike activity has been shown to be increased in the ACC and OFC (Wood, Kim, & Moghaddam, 2012), but gamma power was only increased in the ACC and not the OFC, which may be relevant to the finding in humans that ketamine increases BOLD response in the ACC but decreases it in the OFC (Deakin et al., 2008).

Regarding the meso-accumbens pathway, NMDA-R antagonists have generally been shown to increase activity. Nucleus accumbens (NAc) oxygen levels were increased with moderate-to-high doses of ketamine (Li et al., 2014); meanwhile, gamma power (Hunt, Raynaud,

Continued

TABLE 8 Neurophysiological Effects Induced by Acute NMDA-R Antagonist Administration in Rodents

Biomarker	Effect	Drug	Dose (mg/kg)	Route	Time point (mins)	Measure	References
PFC oxygen levels	↑	S-Ketamine	5–10	s.c.	T+10–40	Oxygen amperometry	Li et al. (2014)
	↑		25		T+10–80		Finnerty et al. (2013)
PFC glucose levels	↑	PCP	10	i.p.	T+10–180		Finnerty et al. (2013)
	↑	PCP	10	i.p.	T+40–240	Glucose amperometry	Finnerty et al. (2013)
PFC glucose utilization	↑	Ketamine	30	i.p.	T+1	Glucose radiography	Dawson et al. (2013)
PFC glutamate levels	↑	MK-801	0.1	i.p.	T+5–60+	Glutamate amperometry	Bonaventure et al. (2011)
	↑	MK-801	0.23	s.c.	T+30–180		Uslaner et al. (2012)
	↔	S-Ketamine	15	i.p.			Stan et al. (2014)
	↔	Ketamine	10	i.p.	T+120–180	Microdialysis—HLPC	Nikiforuk et al. (2010)
	↑	Ketamine	18	s.c.	T+60–180+		Lorrain et al. (2003b)
	↔	PCP	1	s.c.	T+0–140		Baker et al. (2008)
	↑		3		T+20–140		
PFC activity	↑	PCP	5	i.p.	T+10–80	Single unit firing	Suzuki et al. (2002)
	↔	MK-801	0.01	i.p.	T+0–120		Jackson et al. (2004)
	↔		0.05				
			0.1		T+30–120+		
	↑	Ketamine	2.5	s.c.	T+2–30	ECoG gamma power	Pinault (2008)
	↑		5		T+2–50		
	↑		10		T+2–70+		
	↑	MK-801	0.08	s.c.	T+15–70+		
	↑		0.16		T+15–70+		
PFC dopamine	↑	Ketamine	2.5	s.c.	T+15		Kulikova et al. (2012)
	↑	MK-801	0.1	i.p.	T+30–105+	Microdialysis—HLPC	Bonaventure et al. (2011)
	↔	Ketamine	10	i.p.	T+120–180		Nikiforuk et al. (2010)
	↑	Ketamine	18	s.c.	T+20–60		Lorrain et al. (2003b)
	↑	Ketamine	30	i.p.	T+20–100		Verma and Moghaddam (1996)
	↑	PCP	2.5	i.p.	T+20–100		Jentsch, Sanchez, Elsworth, and Roth (2008)
	↑	PCP	5	i.p.	T+20–140		Adams and Moghaddam (1998)

TABLE 8 Neurophysiological Effects Induced by Acute NMDA-R Antagonist Administration in Rodents—cont'd

Biomarker	Effect	Drug	Dose (mg/kg)	Route	Time point (mins)	Measure	References
Hippocampal activity	↑	Ketamine	3	s.c.	T+5–10	EEG gamma power	Ma and Leung (2014)
	↕	PCP	1	i.p.	T+15	EEG gamma power during PPI task	Ma et al. (2004)
	↑	PCP	3–5	i.p.			
ACC activity	↑	MK-801	0.1	i.p.	T+10–100+	Single unit firing	Wood et al. (2012)
	↑				T+20–100+	LFP gamma power	
OFC activity	↑	MK-801	0.1	i.p.	T+20–100+	Single unit firing	
	↕				T+0–100	LFP gamma power	
Visual cortex activity	↑	S-Ketamine	10	s.c.	T+10–60	LFP gamma power	Phillips et al. (2012)
	↑	MK-801	0.1	s.c.	T+10–150	LFP gamma power	
	↑	PCP	2.5	s.c.	T+20–220	LFP gamma power	
NAc activity	↕	Ketamine	10	i.p.	T+0–60	LFP gamma power	Hunt et al. (2006)
	↑		25		T+2–40		
NAc oxygen levels	↑	S-Ketamine	5–10	s.c.	T+10–40	Oxygen amperometry	Li et al. (2014)
	↑		25		T+10–100		
NAc glutamate	↕	Ketamine	25	i.p.	T+10–140	Microdialysis	Razoux et al. (2006)
NAc dopamine	↕	Ketamine	10–25	s.c.	T+0–120	Microdialysis—HPLC	Littlewood et al. (2006)
	↕	Ketamine	30	i.p.	T+0–120		Verma and Moghaddam (1996)
	↑	PCP	2.5	s.c.	T+20–60		Carboni, Imperato, Perezzani, and Di Chiara (1989)
	↑		5		T+20–100		
	↑	MK-801	0.1	s.c.	T+20–180+		Mathé, Nomikos, Hygge Blakeman, and Svensson (1999)
	↕	MK-801	0.1	i.p.	T+0–180		Hatip-Al-Khatib, Mishima, Iwasaki, and Fujiwara (2001)
VTA activity	↕	Ketamine	5	i.p.	T+20	Population activity	Belujon and Grace (2014)
	↑				T+120		
	↑	Ketamine	5	i.p.	T+20	Burst firing/firing rate	
	↕				T+120		
Evoked activity (thalamocortical)	↓	Ketamine	2.5	s.c.	T+15	ECoG gamma power	Kulikova et al. (2012)
Evoked glutamate (hippocampus)	↕	S-Ketamine	15	i.p.	T+30	Glutamate amperometry	Stan et al. (2014)
	↓				T+120		
Parvalbumin expression (RtN)	↓	PCP	2.58	i.p.	T+24h	mRNA expression	Egerton et al. (2005)

& Garcia, 2006) and glutamate (Razoux, Garcia, & Léna, 2006) were only increased at high doses. Population activity of dopamine neurons in the VTA was unchanged during the acute phase of the drug, but then they increased at the 2 h time point, which may be related to effects on synaptic plasticity (Belujon & Grace, 2014). Meanwhile, the *firing rate* of those neurons was increased during the acute phase, and it had subsided by the 2 h mark.

The effect on accumbal dopamine levels is unclear. Studies using PCP appear to more consistently report increases, whereas ketamine and MK-801 do not (especially at lower doses). Meanwhile, prefrontal cortex dopamine levels are more consistently increased by ketamine at similar dosages, and in the same animals (Verma & Moghaddam, 1996). It should be stated that dopamine is more tightly regulated in the striatum, with far higher reuptake rates via the dopamine transporter compared to the prefrontal cortex (Schmitz, Benoit-Marand, Gonon, & Sulzer, 2003; Sesack, Hawrylak, Matus, Guido, & Levey, 1998), which may mean that microdialysis (which has a low temporal resolution) is less effective at detecting increases in striatal dopamine compared to prefrontal dopamine.

There is also evidence of decreased signal-to-noise ratios with NMDA-R antagonists, as basal thalamocortical gamma power was increased, but evoked power was decreased (Kulikova et al., 2012). In another paper, evoked glutamate release in the subiculum (hippocampus) was decreased at the 2 h mark, but not during the acute phase (Stan, Alvarsson, Branzell, Sousa, & Svenningsson, 2014).

Overall, NMDA-R antagonists appear to produce similar physiological effects in rodents as they do in humans.

CONCLUSION AND SYNTHESIS

In this chapter, we have summarized how the acute effects of NMDA-R antagonists in humans and rodents might relate to the symptom dimensions of schizophrenia. Careful consideration of the dose and measurement time points is essential if rodents are to be used as a representative model of humans.

Depending on the desired symptom dimension that is to be most accurately modeled, different doses and time points are appropriate. High doses and early time points may be most relevant for measurements relevant to gross positive symptoms, such as locomotor activity and stereotypy induced by striatal dopamine release. These symptoms should be susceptible to amelioration by typical antipsychotics (D_2 antagonists). Measurement of any other phenotypes is discouraged, since NMDA-R antagonists severely disturb serotonergic, noradrenergic, and cholinergic signaling at these doses (Dawson

et al., 2013), which may help to explain why a plethora of drugs acting on these pathways have been shown to produce antipsychotic and/or procognitive effects in these models but have failed to translate to humans (Bubser et al., 2014; Harkin, Morris, Kelly, O'Donnell, & Leonard, 2001; Lieberman et al., 2008; Meltzer, Horiguchi, & Massey, 2011; Sallinen et al., 2013; Stuchlík, Petrásek, & Vales, 2009; Wallace & Porter, 2011).

Low-to-moderate doses might be most relevant for modeling aberrant associative learning and cognitive deficits, providing the task does not have a substantial motor requirement. Given that these doses do not reliably induce striatal dopamine release, typical antipsychotics may not ameliorate these effects (although they may interfere with prefrontal dopamine signalling).

Low doses and late time points should be used for measurements that may be confounded by motor impairment, such as social interaction, maze navigation, or digging tasks. These measures represent negative and cognitive symptoms that are not remedied by typical or atypical antipsychotics in schizophrenia or human NMDA-R antagonist models, and therefore, these drugs should have no ameliorative effect in rodent models.

Modeling other negative symptoms such as amotivation and anhedonia in rodents may prove difficult given the antianhedonic and motivating effects of NMDA-R antagonists. It is possible that laboratory rodents are more sensitive to these effects since they live in a deprived environment compared to healthy humans, and that rodents living in enriched environments may be more representative of healthy humans, and therefore more susceptible to the anhedonic effects of ketamine. The use of sucrose consumption assays is also questionable, given that consummatory anhedonia is not altered in schizophrenia or depression (Der-Avakian & Markou, 2012). Measuring motivational anhedonia is more desirable, such as via progressive ratio schedules.

An ideal study design would use multiple doses of a psychotomimetic NMDA-R antagonist, in conjunction with a vehicle control and a non-psychotomimetic NMDA-R antagonist (such as lanicemine). For testing new compounds with ameliorative potential, potentiators of $mGluR_{2/3}$ signaling or lamotrigine should be used as a positive control, since these compounds are most effective at attenuating the behavioral and physiological effects of NMDA-R antagonists in humans (Doyle et al., 2013; Krystal et al., 2005) and rodents (Gozzi et al., 2007; Jones et al., 2011; Large et al., 2011; Moghaddam & Adams, 1998; Quarta & Large, 2011). Interpretative control measurements should be made to eliminate motor impairment or task disengagement as confounds (e.g., latencies and omissions, respectively).

A key consideration is that acute NMDA-R antagonism does not equate to chronic schizophrenia, but that it may induce a state of psychosis similar to that seen early in the disorder. For example, mGluR$_{2/3}$ agonists are effective at attenuating the effects of a single administration of NMDA-R antagonist, but they showed no efficacy in a large-scale trial in schizophrenia patients (Hopkins, 2013). Although a positive allosteric modulator of mGluR$_2$ proved more effective (possibly by avoiding agonism-induced mGluR$_2$ downregulation), it would be over simplistic to assume that any compound that attenuates the effects of acute NMDA-R antagonism will show efficacy in schizophrenia. Rather, the acute NMDA-R antagonist model should be further understood to probe the mechanisms of psychopathology that may hold new potential treatment targets, irrespective of whether they are pharmacologically, behaviorally, or neurotechnologically based. Rather than replacing earlier approaches focusing on dopamine and serotonin, use of glutamatergic models is likely to further understanding of how abnormalities in these neural systems interact, both with each other and with genetic and environmental factors to produce the behavioral symptoms associated with a diagnosis of schizophrenia.

References

Aalto, S., Hirvonen, J., Kajander, J., Scheinin, H., Någren, K., Vilkman, H., et al. (2002). Ketamine does not decrease striatal dopamine D2 receptor binding in man. *Psychopharmacology (Berlin), 164*, 401–406.

Aalto, S., Ihalainen, J., Hirvonen, J., Kajander, J., Scheinin, H., Tanila, H., et al. (2005). Cortical glutamate–dopamine interaction and ketamine-induced psychotic symptoms in man. *Psychopharmacology (Berlin), 182*, 375–383.

Abel, K. M., Allin, M. P. G., Hemsley, D. R., & Geyer, M. A. (2003). Low dose ketamine increases prepulse inhibition in healthy men. *Neuropharmacology, 44*, 729–737.

Abel, K. M., Allin, M. P. G., Kucharska-Pietura, K., David, A., Andrew, C., Williams, S., et al. (2003). Ketamine alters neural processing of facial emotion recognition in healthy men: an fMRI study. *Neuroreport, 14*, 387–391.

Adams, B., & Moghaddam, B. (1998). Corticolimbic dopamine neurotransmission is temporally dissociated from the cognitive and locomotor effects of phencyclidine. *Journal of Neuroscience, 18*, 5545–5554.

Adams, B. W., Bradberry, C. W., & Moghaddam, B. (2002). NMDA antagonist effects on striatal dopamine release: microdialysis studies in awake monkeys. *Synapse, 43*, 12–18.

Adell, A., Jiménez-Sánchez, L., López-Gil, X., & Romón, T. (2012). Is the acute NMDA receptor hypofunction a valid model of schizophrenia? *Schizophrenia Bulletin, 38*, 9–14.

Åhlander, M., Misane, I., Schött, P. A., & Ögren, S. O. (1999). A behavioral analysis of the spatial learning deficit induced by the NMDA receptor antagonist MK-801 (dizocilpine) in the rat. *Neuropsychopharmacology, 21*, 414–426.

Al-Uzri, M. M., Reveley, M. A., Owen, L., Bruce, J., Frost, S., Mackintosh, D., et al. (2006). Measuring memory impairment in community-based patients with schizophrenia. Case-control study. *British Journal of Psychiatry Journal of Mental Science, 189*, 132–136.

Aleman, A., Hijman, R., de Haan, E. H., & Kahn, R. S. (1999). Memory impairment in schizophrenia: a meta-analysis. *American Journal of Psychiatry, 156*, 1358–1366.

Altarifi, A. A., & Negus, S. S. (2011). Some determinants of morphine effects on intracranial self-stimulation in rats: dose, pretreatment time, repeated treatment, and rate dependence. *Behavioural Pharmacology, 22*, 663–673.

Amitai, N., Semenova, S., & Markou, A. (2009). Clozapine attenuates disruptions in response inhibition and task efficiency induced by repeated phencyclidine administration in the intracranial self-stimulation procedure. *European Journal of Pharmacology, 602*, 78–84.

Amitai, N., Semenova, S., & Markou, A. (2007). Cognitive-disruptive effects of the psychotomimetic phencyclidine and attenuation by atypical antipsychotic medications in rats. *Psychopharmacology (Berlin), 193*, 521–537.

Andreou, C., Nolte, G., Leicht, G., Polomac, N., Hanganu-Opatz, I. L., Lambert, M., et al. (2015). Increased resting-state gamma-band connectivity in first-episode schizophrenia. *Schizophrenia Bulletin, 41*, 930–939.

Anticevic, A., Cole, M. W., Repovs, G., Savic, A., Driesen, N. R., Yang, G., et al. (2013). Connectivity, pharmacology, and computation: toward a mechanistic understanding of neural system dysfunction in schizophrenia. *Frontiers in Psychiatry, 4*, 169.

Anticevic, A., Corlett, P. R., Cole, M. W., Savic, A., Gancsos, M., Tang, Y., et al. (2015). NMDA receptor antagonist effects on prefrontal cortical connectivity better model early than chronic schizophrenia. *Biological Psychiatry, 77*, 569–580.

Anticevic, A., Gancsos, M., Murray, J. D., Repovs, G., Driesen, N. R., Ennis, D. J., et al. (2012). NMDA receptor function in large-scale anticorrelated neural systems with implications for cognition and schizophrenia. *Proceedings of the National Academy of Sciences of the United States of America, 109*, 16720–16725.

Arnsten, A. F. T., Wang, M. J., & Paspalas, C. D. (2012). Neuromodulation of thought: flexibilities and vulnerabilities in prefrontal cortical network synapses. *Neuron, 76*, 223–239.

Autry, A. E., Adachi, M., Nosyreva, E., Na, E. S., Los, M. F., Cheng, P., et al. (2011). NMDA receptor blockade at rest triggers rapid behavioral antidepressant responses. *Nature, 475*, 91–95.

Baaré, W. F., Hulshoff Pol, H. E., Hijman, R., Mali, W. P., Viergever, M. A., & Kahn, R. S. (1999). Volumetric analysis of frontal lobe regions in schizophrenia: relation to cognitive function and symptomatology. *Biological Psychiatry, 45*, 1597–1605.

Baker, D. A., Madayag, A., Kristiansen, L. V., Meador-Woodruff, J. H., Haroutunian, V., & Raju, I. (2008). Contribution of cystine-glutamate antiporters to the psychotomimetic effects of phencyclidine. *Neuropsychopharmacology, 33*, 1760–1772.

Barch, D. M., & Dowd, E. C. (2010). Goal Representations and motivational drive in schizophrenia: the role of prefrontal–striatal interactions. *Schizophrenia Bulletin, 36*, 919–934.

Bartsch, J. C., Fidzinski, P., Huck, J. H. J., Hörtnagl, H., Kovacs, R., Liotta, A., et al. (2015). Enhanced dopamine-dependent hippocampal plasticity after single MK-801 application. *Neuropsychopharmacology, 40*, 987–995.

Bauer, C. T., Banks, M. L., Blough, B. E., & Negus, S. S. (2013). Use of intracranial self-stimulation to evaluate abuse-related and abuse-limiting effects of monoamine releasers in rats. *British Journal of Pharmacology, 168*, 850–862.

Bay-Richter, C., O'Callaghan, M. J., Mathur, N., O'Tuathaigh, C. M. P., Heery, D. M., Fone, K. C. F., et al. (2013). D-amphetamine and antipsychotic drug effects on latent inhibition in mice lacking dopamine D2 receptors. *Neuropsychopharmacology: Official Publication of American College of Neuropsychopharmacology, 38*, 1512–1520.

Bay-Richter, C., O'Tuathaigh, C. M. P., O'Sullivan, G., Heery, D. M., Waddington, J. L., & Moran, P. M. (2009). Enhanced latent inhibition in dopamine receptor-deficient mice is sex-specific for the D1 but not D2 receptor subtype: implications for antipsychotic drug action. *International Journal of Neuropsychopharmacology: Official Science Journal of College International Neuropsychopharmacology CINP, 12*, 403–414.

Belujon, P., & Grace, A. A. (2014). Restoring mood balance in depression: ketamine reverses deficit in dopamine-dependent synaptic plasticity. *Biological Psychiatry, 76*, 927–936.

Benneyworth, M. A., Xiang, Z., Smith, R. L., Garcia, E. E., Conn, P. J., & Sanders-Bush, E. (2007). A selective positive allosteric modulator of metabotropic glutamate receptor subtype 2 blocks a hallucinogenic drug model of psychosis. *Molecular Pharmacology, 72*, 477–484.

van Berckel, B. N. M., Oranje, B., van Ree, J. M., Verbaten, M. N., & Kahn, R. S. (1998). The effects of low dose ketamine on sensory gating, neuroendocrine secretion and behavior in healthy human subjects. *Psychopharmacology (Berlin), 137*, 271–281.

Bergman, S. A. (1999). Ketamine: review of its pharmacology and its use in pediatric anesthesia. *Anesthesia Progress, 46*, 10–20.

Bokat, C. E., & Goldberg, T. E. (2003). Letter and category fluency in schizophrenic patients: a meta-analysis. *Schizophrenia Research, 64*, 73–78.

Bonaventure, P., Aluisio, L., Shoblock, J., Boggs, J. D., Fraser, I. C., Lord, B., et al. (2011). Pharmacological blockade of serotonin 5-HT7 receptor reverses working memory deficits in rats by normalizing cortical glutamate neurotransmission. *PLoS One, 6*, e20210.

Breier, A., Adler, C. M., Weisenfeld, N., Su, T.-P., Elman, I., Picken, L., et al. (1998). Effects of NMDA antagonism on striatal dopamine release in healthy subjects: application of a novel PET approach. *Synapse, 29*, 142–147.

Bubser, M., Bridges, T. M., Dencker, D., Gould, R. W., Grannan, M., Noetzel, M. J., et al. (2014). Selective activation of M4 muscarinic acetylcholine receptors reverses MK-801-induced behavioral impairments and enhances associative learning in rodents. *ACS Chemical Neuroscience, 5*, 920–942.

Cannon, T. D., Glahn, D. C., Kim, J., Van Erp, T. G. M., Karlsgodt, K., Cohen, M. S., et al. (2005). Dorsolateral prefrontal cortex activity during maintenance and manipulation of information in working memory in patients with schizophrenia. *Archives of General Psychiatry, 62*, 1071–1080.

Carboni, E., Imperato, A., Perezzani, L., & Di Chiara, G. (1989). Amphetamine, cocaine, phencyclidine and nomifensine increase extracellular dopamine concentrations preferentially in the nucleus accumbens of freely moving rats. *Neuroscience, 28*, 653–661.

Carlezon, W. A., Jr., & Wise, R. A. (1993). Phencyclidine-induced potentiation of brain stimulation reward: acute effects are not altered by repeated administration. *Psychopharmacology (Berlin), 111*, 402–408.

Castagné, V., Wolinsky, T., Quinn, L., & Virley, D. (2012). Differential behavioral profiling of stimulant substances in the rat using the LABORAS™ system. *Pharmacology Biochemistry and Behavior, 101*, 553–563.

Chan, K. K. S., Xu, J. Q., Liu, K. C. M., Hui, C. L. M., Wong, G. H. Y., & Chen, E. Y. H. (2012). Executive function in first-episode schizophrenia: a three-year prospective study of the hayling sentence completion test. *Schizophrenia Research, 135*, 62–67.

Chaperon, F., Müller, W., Auberson, Y. P., Tricklebank, M. D., & Neijt, H. C. (2003). Substitution for PCP, disruption of prepulse inhibition and hyperactivity induced by N-methyl-D-aspartate receptor antagonists: preferential involvement of the NR2B rather than NR2A subunit. *Behavioural Pharmacology, 14*, 477–487.

Chindo, B. A., Adzu, B., Yahaya, T. A., & Gamaniel, K. S. (2012). Ketamine-enhanced immobility in forced swim test: a possible animal model for the negative symptoms of schizophrenia. *Progress in Neuro-Psychopharmacology & Biological Psychiatry, 38*, 310–316.

Cobb, S. R., Buhl, E. H., Halasy, K., Paulsen, O., & Somogyi, P. (1995). Synchronization of neuronal activity in hippocampus by individual GABAergic interneurons. *Nature, 378*, 75–78.

Corlett, P. R., Aitken, M. R. F., Dickinson, A., Shanks, D. R., Honey, G. D., Honey, R. A. E., et al. (2004). Prediction error during retrospective revaluation of causal associations in humans: fMRI evidence in favor of an associative model of learning. *Neuron, 44*, 877–888.

Corlett, P. R., Honey, G. D., Aitken, M. F., et al. (2006). Frontal responses during learning predict vulnerability to the psychotogenic effects of ketamine: linking cognition, brain activity, and psychosis. *Archives of General Psychiatry, 63*, 611–621.

Corlett, P. R., Honey, G. D., Krystal, J. H., & Fletcher, P. C. (2011). Glutamatergic model psychoses: prediction error, learning, and inference. *Neuropsychopharmacology, 36*, 294–315.

Corlett, P. R., Murray, G. K., Honey, G. D., Aitken, M. R. F., Shanks, D. R., Robbins, T. W., et al. (2007). Disrupted prediction-error signal in psychosis: evidence for an associative account of delusions. *Brain, 130*, 2387–2400.

Cornblatt, B. A., & Keilp, J. G. (1994). Impaired attention, genetics, and the pathophysiology of schizophrenia. *Schizophrenia Bulletin, 20*, 31–46.

Cryan, J. F., Markou, A., & Lucki, I. (2002). Assessing antidepressant activity in rodents: recent developments and future needs. *Trends in Pharmacological Sciences, 23*, 238–245.

Da Silva, F. C. C., do Carmo de Oliveira Cito, M., da Silva, M. I. G., Moura, B. A., de Aquino Neto, M. R., Feitosa, M. L., et al. (2010). Behavioral alterations and pro-oxidant effect of a single ketamine administration to mice. *Brain Research Bulletin, 83*, 9–15.

Dandash, O., Harrison, B. J., Adapa, R., Gaillard, R., Giorlando, F., Wood, S. J., et al. (2015). Selective augmentation of striatal functional connectivity following NMDA receptor antagonism: implications for psychosis. *Neuropsychopharmacology, 40*, 622–631.

Danysz, W., Essmann, U., Bresink, I., & Wilk, R. (1994). Glutamate antagonists have different effects on spontaneous locomotor activity in rats. *Pharmacology Biochemistry and Behavior, 48*, 111–118.

Davies, B. M., & Beech, H. R. (1960). The effect of 1-Arylcyclohexylamine (Sernyl) on twelve normal volunteers. *British Journal of Psychiatry, 106*, 912–924.

Dawson, N., Morris, B. J., & Pratt, J. A. (2013). Subanaesthetic ketamine treatment alters prefrontal cortex connectivity with thalamus and ascending subcortical systems. *Schizophrenia Bulletin, 39*, 366–377.

Daya, R. P., Bhandari, J. K., Hui, P. A., Tian, Y., Farncombe, T., & Mishra, R. K. (2014). Effects of MK-801 treatment across several pre-clinical analyses including a novel assessment of brain metabolic function utilizing PET and CT fused imaging in live rats. *Neuropharmacology, 77*, 325–333.

De Bruin, N. M. W. J., van Drimmelen, M., Kops, M., van Elk, J., Wetering, M. M., & Schwienbacher, I. (2013). Effects of risperidone, clozapine and the 5-HT6 antagonist GSK-742457 on PCP-induced deficits in reversal learning in the two-lever operant task in male Sprague Dawley rats. *Behavioural Brain Research, 244*, 15–28.

De Lima, M. N. M., Laranja, D. C., Bromberg, E., Roesler, R., & Schröder, N. (2005). Pre- or post-training administration of the NMDA receptor blocker MK-801 impairs object recognition memory in rats. *Behavioural Brain Research, 156*, 139–143.

De Simoni, S., Schwarz, A. J., O'Daly, O. G., Marquand, A. F., Brittain, C., Gonzales, C., et al. (2013). Test–retest reliability of the BOLD pharmacological MRI response to ketamine in healthy volunteers. *NeuroImage, 64*, 75–90.

Deakin, J. F. W., Lees, J., McKie, S., Hallak, J. E. C., Williams, S. R., & Dursun, S. M. (2008). Glutamate and the neural basis of the subjective effects of ketamine: a pharmaco–magnetic resonance imaging study. *Archives of General Psychiatry, 65*, 154–164.

Delfs, J. M., & Kelley, A. E. (1990). The role of D1 and D2 dopamine receptors in oral stereotypy induced by dopaminergic stimulation of the ventrolateral striatum. *Neuroscience, 39*, 59–67.

Der-Avakian, A., & Markou, A. (2012). The neurobiology of anhedonia and other reward-related deficits. *Trends in Neurosciences, 35*, 68–77.

Deutch, A. Y., Tam, S.-Y., Freeman, A. S., Bowers, M. B., Jr., & Roth, R. H. (1987). Mesolimbic and mesocortical dopamine activation induced by phencyclidine: contrasting pattern to striatal response. *European Journal of Pharmacology, 134*, 257–264.

II. NEUROBIOLOGY OF PSYCHOTIC DISORDERS

Distler, A. (1990). Clinical aspects during therapy with the serotonin antagonist ketanserin. *Clinical Physiology and Biochemistry*, 8(Suppl. 3), 64–80.

Do, K. Q., Cabungcal, J. H., Frank, A., Steullet, P., & Cuenod, M. (2009). Redox dysregulation, neurodevelopment, and schizophrenia. *Current Opinion in Neurobiology*, 19, 220–230.

Domino, E. F., Zsigmond, E. K., Domino, L. E., Domino, K. E., Kothary, S. P., & Domino, S. E. (1982). Plasma levels of ketamine and two of its metabolites in surgical patients using a gas chromatographic mass fragmentographic assay. *Anesthesia & Analgesia*, 61, 87–92.

Donahue, R. J., Muschamp, J. W., Russo, S. J., Nestler, E. J., & Carlezon, W. A., Jr. (2014). Effects of striatal ΔFosB overexpression and ketamine on social defeat stress–induced anhedonia in mice. *Biological Psychiatry*, 76, 550–558.

Doyle, O. M., Simoni, S. D., Schwarz, A. J., Brittain, C., O'Daly, O. G., Williams, S. C. R., et al. (2013). Quantifying the attenuation of the ketamine pharmacological magnetic resonance imaging response in humans: a validation using antipsychotic and glutamatergic agents. *Journal of Pharmacology and Experimental Therapeutics*, 345, 151–160.

Dravid, S. M., Erreger, K., Yuan, H., Nicholson, K., Le, P., Lyuboslavsky, P., et al. (2007). Subunit-specific mechanisms and proton sensitivity of NMDA receptor channel block. *Journal of Physiology*, 581, 107–128.

Driesen, N. R., McCarthy, G., Bhagwagar, Z., Bloch, M., Calhoun, V., D'Souza, D. C., et al. (2013). Relationship of resting brain hyperconnectivity and schizophrenia-like symptoms produced by the NMDA receptor antagonist ketamine in humans. *Molecular Psychiatry*, 18, 1199–1204.

Egerton, A., Reid, L., McKerchar, C. E., Morris, B. J., & Pratt, J. A. (2005). Impairment in perceptual attentional set-shifting following PCP administration: a rodent model of set-shifting deficits in schizophrenia. *Psychopharmacology (Berlin)*, 179, 77–84.

Epping-Jordan, M. P., Watkins, S. S., Koob, G. F., & Markou, A. (1998). Dramatic decreases in brain reward function during nicotine withdrawal. *Nature*, 393, 76–79.

Ettinger, U., Picchioni, M., Hall, M.-H., Schulze, K., Toulopoulou, T., Landau, S., et al. (2006). Antisaccade performance in monozygotic twins discordant for schizophrenia: the Maudsley twin study. *American Journal of Psychiatry*, 163, 543–545.

Evans, S., Almahdi, B., Sultan, P., Sohanpal, I., Brandner, B., Collier, T., et al. (2012). Performance on a probabilistic inference task in healthy subjects receiving ketamine compared with patients with schizophrenia. *Journal of Psychopharmacology Oxford England*, 26, 1211–1217.

Fell, M. J., Perry, K. W., Falcone, J. F., Johnson, B. G., Barth, V. N., Rash, K. S., et al. (2009). In vitro and in vivo evidence for a lack of interaction with dopamine D2 receptors by the metabotropic glutamate 2/3 receptor agonists 1S,2S,5R,6S-2-Aminobicyclo[3.1.0]hexane-2,6-bicarboxylate Monohydrate (LY354740) and (−)-2-Oxa-4-aminobicyclo[3.1.0] Hexane-4,6-dicarboxylic acid (LY379268). *Journal of Pharmacology and Experimental Therapeutics*, 331, 1126–1136.

Fellini, L., Kumar, G., Gibbs, S., Steckler, T., & Talpos, J. (2014). Reevaluating the PCP challenge as a pre-clinical model of impaired cognitive flexibility in schizophrenia. *European Neuropsychopharmacology*, 24, 1836–1849.

Finnerty, N. J., Bolger, F. B., Pålsson, E., & Lowry, J. P. (2013). An investigation of hypofrontality in an animal model of schizophrenia using real-time microelectrochemical sensors for glucose, oxygen, and nitric oxide. *ACS Chemical Neuroscience*, 4, 825–831.

Fletcher, P. C., & Frith, C. D. (2009). Perceiving is believing: a Bayesian approach to explaining the positive symptoms of schizophrenia. *Nature Reviews Neuroscience*, 10, 48–58.

Fletcher, P. C., & Honey, G. D. (2006). Schizophrenia, ketamine and cannabis: evidence of overlapping memory deficits. *Trends in Cognitive Sciences*, 10, 167–174.

Folley, B. S., Astur, R., Jagannathan, K., Calhoun, V. D., & Pearlson, G. D. (2010). Anomalous neural circuit function in schizophrenia during a virtual Morris water task. *NeuroImage*, 49, 3373–3384.

Forbes, N. F., Carrick, L. A., McIntosh, A. M., & Lawrie, S. M. (2009). Working memory in schizophrenia: a meta-analysis. *Psychologie Medicale*, 39, 889–905.

Garcia, L. S. B., Comim, C. M., Valvassori, S. S., Réus, G. Z., Stertz, L., Kapczinski, F., et al. (2009). Ketamine treatment reverses behavioral and physiological alterations induced by chronic mild stress in rats. *Progress in Neuro-Psychopharmacology & Biological Psychiatry*, 33, 450–455.

Gastambide, F., Mitchell, S. N., Robbins, T. W., Tricklebank, M. D., & Gilmour, G. (2013). Temporally distinct cognitive effects following acute administration of ketamine and phencyclidine in the rat. *European Neuropsychopharmacology*, 23, 1414–1422.

Georgiadou, G., Grivas, V., Tarantilis, P. A., & Pitsikas, N. (2014). Crocins, the active constituents of *Crocus Sativus* L., counteracted ketamine–induced behavioral deficits in rats. *Psychopharmacology (Berlin)*, 231, 717–726.

Gilmour, G., Pioli, E. Y., Dix, S. L., Smith, J. W., Conway, M. W., Jones, W. T., et al. (2009). Diverse and often opposite behavioral effects of NMDA receptor antagonists in rats: implications for "NMDA antagonist modelling" of schizophrenia. *Psychopharmacology (Berlin)*, 205, 203–216.

Ginski, M. J., & Witkin, J. M. (1994). Sensitive and rapid behavioral differentiation of N-methyl-D-aspartate receptor antagonists. *Psychopharmacology (Berlin)*, 114, 573–582.

Goghari, V. M., Sponheim, S. R., & MacDonald, A. W., III (2010). The functional neuroanatomy of symptom dimensions in schizophrenia: a qualitative and quantitative review of a persistent question. *Neuroscience & Biobehavioral Reviews*, 34, 468–486.

Gold, J. M., Waltz, J. A., Prentice, K. J., Morris, S. E., & Heerey, E. A. (2008). Reward processing in schizophrenia: a deficit in the representation of value. *Schizophrenia Bulletin*, 34, 835–847.

Gonzalez-Burgos, G., & Lewis, D. A. (2012). NMDA receptor hypofunction, parvalbumin-positive neurons, and cortical gamma oscillations in schizophrenia. *Schizophrenia Bulletin*, 38, 950–957.

Gozzi, A., Large, C. H., Schwarz, A., Bertani, S., Crestan, V., & Bifone, A. (2007). Differential effects of antipsychotic and glutamatergic agents on the phMRI response to phencyclidine. *Neuropsychopharmacology*, 33, 1690–1703.

Granger, K. T., Moran P. M., Buckley M., Haselgrove, M. Enhanced latent inhibition in high schizotypy individuals: controls for conditioned inhibition and learned irrelevance. *Behavioural Brain Research*, submitted for publication.

Green, C. J., Knight, J., Precious, S., & Simpkin, S. (1981). Ketamine alone and combined with diazepam or xylazine in laboratory animals: a 10 year experience. *Laboratory Animals*, 15, 163–170.

Grotta, J., Clark, W., Coull, B., Pettigrew, L. C., Mackay, B., Goldstein, L. B., et al. (1995). Safety and tolerability of the glutamate antagonist CGS 19755 (Selfotel) in patients with acute ischemic stroke. Results of a phase IIa randomized trial. *Stroke: A Journal of Cerebral Circulation*, 26, 602–605.

Gur, R. E., Cowell, P. E., Latshaw, A., Turetsky, B. I., Grossman, R. I., Arnold, S. E., et al. (2000). Reduced dorsal and orbital prefrontal gray matter volumes in schizophrenia. *Archives of General Psychiatry*, 57, 761–768.

Gur, R. E., McGrath, C., Chan, R. M., Schroeder, L., Turner, T., Turetsky, B. I., et al. (2002). An fMRI study of facial emotion processing in patients with schizophrenia. *American Journal of Psychiatry*, 159, 1992–1999.

Haile, C. N., Murrough, J. W., Iosifescu, D. V., Chang, L. C., Jurdi, R. K. A., Foulkes, A., et al. (2014). Plasma brain derived neurotrophic factor (BDNF) and response to ketamine in treatment-resistant depression. *International Journal of Neuropsychopharmacology: Official Science Journal of College International Neuropsychopharmacology CINP*, 17, 331–336.

Halberstadt, A. L. (2015). Recent advances in the Neuropschopharmacology of serotonergic hallucinogens. *Behavioural Brain Research*, 277, 99–120.

Hanks, J. B., & Gonzalez-Maeso (2013). Animla mdoels of serotonergic psychedelics. *ACS Chemical Neuroscience*, 33–42.

Harkin, A., Morris, K., Kelly, J. P., O'Donnell, J. M., & Leonard, B. E. (2001). Modulation of MK-801-induced behaviour by noradrenergic agents in mice. *Psychopharmacology (Berlin)*, *154*, 177–188.

Hatip-Al-Khatib, I., Mishima, K., Iwasaki, K., & Fujiwara, M. (2001). Microdialysates of amines and metabolites from core nucleus accumbens of freely moving rats are altered by dizocilpine. *Brain Research*, *902*, 108–118.

Heekeren, K., Daumann, J., Neukirch, A., Stock, C., Kawohl, W., Norra, C., et al. (2008). Mismatch negativity generation in the human 5HT2A agonist and NMDA antagonist model of psychosis. *Psychopharmacology (Berlin)*, *199*, 77–88.

Heekeren, K., Neukirch, A., Daumann, J., Stoll, M., Obradovic, M., Kovar, K.-A., et al. (2007). Prepulse inhibition of the startle reflex and its attentional modulation in the human S-ketamine and N,N-dimethyltryptamine (DMT) models of psychosis. *Journal of Psychopharmacology (Oxford)*, *21*, 312–320.

Higgins, G. A., Ballard, T. M., Enderlin, M., Haman, M., & Kemp, J. A. (2005). Evidence for improved performance in cognitive tasks following selective NR2B NMDA receptor antagonist pre-treatment in the rat. *Psychopharmacology (Berlin)*, *179*, 85–98.

Higgins, G. A., Ballard, T. M., Huwyler, J., Kemp, J. A., & Gill, R. (2003). Evaluation of the NR2B-selective NMDA receptor antagonist Ro 63-1908 on rodent behaviour: evidence for an involvement of NR2B NMDA receptors in response inhibition. *Neuropharmacology*, *44*, 324–341.

Hill, K., Mann, L., Laws, K. R., Stephenson, C. M. E., Nimmo-Smith, I., & McKenna, P. J. (2004). Hypofrontality in schizophrenia: a meta-analysis of functional imaging studies. *Acta Psychiatrica Scandinavica*, *110*, 243–256.

Hillhouse, T. M., Porter, J. H., & Negus, S. S. (2014). Dissociable effects of the noncompetitive NMDA receptor antagonists ketamine and MK-801 on intracranial self-stimulation in rats. *Psychopharmacology (Berlin)*, *231*, 2705–2716.

Hiyoshi, T., Kambe, D., Karasawa, J., & Chaki, S. (2014). Differential effects of NMDA receptor antagonists at lower and higher doses on basal gamma band oscillation power in rat cortical electroencephalograms. *Neuropharmacology*, *85*, 384–396.

Hiyoshi, T., Marumo, T., Hikichi, H., Tomishima, Y., Urabe, H., Tamita, T., et al. (2014). Neurophysiologic and antipsychotic profiles of TASP0433864, a novel positive allosteric modulator of metabotropic glutamate 2 receptor. *Journal of Pharmacology and Experimental Therapeutics*, *351*, 642–653.

Holcomb, H. H., Lahti, A. C., Medoff, D. R., Weiler, M., & Tamminga, C. A. (2001). Sequential regional cerebral blood flow brain scans using PET with H215O demonstrate ketamine actions in CNS dynamically. *Neuropsychopharmacology*, *25*, 165–172.

Homayoun, H., & Moghaddam, B. (2007). NMDA receptor hypofunction produces opposite effects on prefrontal cortex interneurons and pyramidal neurons. *Journal of Neuroscience*, *27*, 11496–11500.

Honey, G. D., Corlett, P. R., Absalom, A. R., Lee, M., Pomarol-Clotet, E., Murray, G. K., et al. (2008). Individual differences in psychotic effects of ketamine are predicted by brain function measured under placebo. *Journal of Neuroscience*, *28*, 6295–6303.

Honey, G. D., Honey, R. A. E., O'Loughlin, C., Sharar, S. R., Kumaran, D., Suckling, J., et al. (2005). Ketamine disrupts frontal and hippocampal contribution to encoding and retrieval of episodic memory: an fMRI study. *Cerebral Cortex*, *15* New York, NY: 1991.

Honey, G. D., Honey, R. A. E., Sharar, S. R., Turner, D. C., Pomarol-Clotet, E., Kumaran, D., et al. (2005). Impairment of specific episodic memory processes by sub-psychotic doses of ketamine: the effects of levels of processing at encoding and of the subsequent retrieval task. *Psychopharmacology (Berlin)*, *181*, 445–457.

Honey, R., Honey, G., O'Loughlin, C., Sharar, S., Kumaran, D., Bullmore, E., et al. (2004). Acute ketamine administration alters the brain responses to executive demands in a verbal working memory task: an fMRI study. *Neuropsychopharmacology: Official Publication of American College of Neuropsychopharmacology*, *29*.

Hong, L. E., Summerfelt, A., Buchanan, R. W., O'Donnell, P., Thaker, G. K., Weiler, M. A., et al. (2010). Gamma and delta neural oscillations and association with clinical symptoms under subanesthetic ketamine. *Neuropsychopharmacology*, *35*, 632–640.

Hopkins, C. R. (2013). Is there a path forward for mGlu2 positive allosteric modulators for the treatment of schizophrenia? *ACS Chemical Neuroscience*, *4*, 211–213.

Howes, O. D., & Kapur, S. (2009). The dopamine hypothesis of Schizophrenia: version III—the final common pathway. *Schizophrenia Bulletin*, *35*, 549–562.

Howes, O. D., McCutcheon, & Stone, J. (2015). Glutamate and dopamine in schizophrenia: an update for the 21st century. *Journal of Psychopharmacology*, *29*, 97–115.

Hunt, M. J., & Kasicki, S. (2013). A systematic review of the effects of NMDA receptor antagonists on oscillatory activity recorded in vivo. *Journal of Psychopharmacology (Oxford)*, *27*, 972–986.

Hunt, M. J., Raynaud, B., & Garcia, R. (2006). Ketamine dose-dependently induces high-frequency oscillations in the nucleus accumbens in freely moving rats. *Biological Psychiatry*, *60*, 1206–1214.

Idris, N. F., Repeto, P., Neill, J. C., & Large, C. H. (2005). Investigation of the effects of lamotrigine and clozapine in improving reversal-learning impairments induced by acute phencyclidine and d-amphetamine in the rat. *Psychopharmacology (Berlin)*, *179*, 336–348.

Ikemoto, S. (2002). Ventral striatal anatomy of locomotor activity induced by cocaine, D-amphetamine, dopamine and D1/D2 agonists. *Neuroscience*, *113*, 939–955.

Insel, T. R. (2010). Rethinking schizophrenia. *Nature*, *468*, 187–193.

Jackson, M. E., Homayoun, H., & Moghaddam, B. (2004). NMDA receptor hypofunction produces concomitant firing rate potentiation and burst activity reduction in the prefrontal cortex. *Proceedings of the National Academy of Sciences of the United States of America*, *101*, 8467–8472.

Jardri, R., & Denève, S. (2013). Circular inferences in schizophrenia. *Brain*, *136*, 3227–3241.

Jentsch, J. D., Sanchez, D., Elsworth, J. D., & Roth, R. H. (2008). Clonidine and guanfacine attenuate phencyclidine-induced dopamine overflow in rat prefrontal cortex: mediating influence of the alpha-2A adrenoceptor subtype. *Brain Research*, *1246*, 41–46.

Jiménez-Sánchez, L., Campa, L., Auberson, Y. P., & Adell, A. (2014). The role of GluN2A and GluN2B subunits on the effects of NMDA receptor antagonists in modeling schizophrenia and treating refractory depression. *Neuropsychopharmacology*, *39*, 2673–2680.

Jones, K. M., McDonald, I. M., Bourin, C., Olson, R. E., Bristow, L. J., & Easton, A. (2014). Effect of alpha7 nicotinic acetylcholine receptor agonists on attentional set-shifting impairment in rats. *Psychopharmacology (Berlin)*, *231*, 673–683.

Jones, N. C., Reddy, M., Anderson, P., Salzberg, M., O'Brien, T. J., & Pinault, D. (2011). Acute administration of typical and atypical antipsychotics reduces EEG gamma power, but only the preclinical compound LY379268 reduces the ketamine-induced rise in gamma power. *International Journal of Neuropsychopharmacology*, *15*, 657–668.

Jordan, S., Chen, R., Fernalld, R., Johnson, J., Regardie, K., Kambayashi, J., et al. (2006). In vitro biochemical evidence that the psychotomimetics phencyclidine, ketamine and dizocilpine (MK-801) are inactive at cloned human and rat dopamine D2 receptors. *European Journal of Pharmacology*, *540*, 53–56.

Kalinichev, M., Robbins, M. J., Hartfield, E. M., Maycox, P. R., Moore, S. H., Savage, K. M., et al. (2008). Comparison between intraperitoneal and subcutaneous phencyclidine administration in Sprague–Dawley rats: a locomotor activity and gene induction study. *Progress in Neuro-Psychopharmacology & Biological Psychiatry*, *32*, 414–422.

Kapur, S. (2003). Psychosis as a state of aberrant salience: a framework linking biology, phenomenology, and pharmacology in schizophrenia. *American Journal of Psychiatry*, *160*, 13–23.

Kegeles, L. S., Abi-Dargham, A., Zea-Ponce, Y., Rodenhiser-Hill, J., Mann, J. J., Van Heertum, R. L., et al. (2000). Modulation of amphetamine-induced striatal dopamine release by ketamine in humans: implications for schizophrenia. *Biological Psychiatry*, *48*, 627–640.

Kegeles, L. S., Martinez, D., Kochan, L. D., Hwang, D.-R., Huang, Y., Mawlawi, O., et al. (2002). NMDA antagonist effects on striatal dopamine release: positron emission tomography studies in humans. *Synapse, 43,* 19–29.

Knox, J. W. D., Bovill, J. G., Clarke, R. S. J., & Dundee, J. W. (1970). Clinical studies of induction agents XXXVI: ketamine. *British Journal of Anaesthesia, 42,* 875–885.

Kocsis, B. (2012). Differential role of NR2A and NR2B subunits in N-methyl-D-aspartate receptor antagonist-induced aberrant cortical gamma oscillations. *Biological Psychiatry, 71,* 987–995.

Kocsis, B., Brown, R. E., McCarley, R. W., & Hajos, M. (2013). Impact of ketamine on neuronal network dynamics: translational modeling of schizophrenia-relevant deficits. *CNS Neuroscience & Therapeutics, 19,* 437–447.

Koek, W., & Colpaert, F. C. (1990). Selective blockade of N-methyl-D-aspartate (NMDA)-induced convulsions by NMDA antagonists and putative glycine antagonists: relationship with phencyclidine-like behavioral effects. *Journal of Pharmacology and Experimental Therapeutics, 252,* 349–357.

Koike, H., Iijima, M., & Chaki, S. (2011). Involvement of AMPA receptor in both the rapid and sustained antidepressant-like effects of ketamine in animal models of depression. *Behavioural Brain Research, 224,* 107–111.

Kornhuber, J., & Weller, M. (1997). Psychotogenicity and N-methyl-D-aspartate receptor antagonism: implications for neuroprotective pharmacotherapy. *Biological Psychiatry, 41,* 135–144.

Koros, E., Rosenbrock, H., Birk, G., Weiss, C., & Sams-Dodd, F. (2006). The selective mGlu5 receptor antagonist MTEP, similar to NMDA receptor antagonists, induces social isolation in rats. *Neuropsychopharmacology, 32,* 562–576.

Kos, T., Nikiforuk, A., Rafa, D., & Popik, P. (2011). The effects of NMDA receptor antagonists on attentional set-shifting task performance in mice. *Psychopharmacology (Berlin), 214,* 911–921.

Kos, T., Popik, P., Pietraszek, M., Schäfer, D., Danysz, W., Dravolina, O., et al. (2006). Effect of 5-HT3 receptor antagonist MDL 72222 on behaviors induced by ketamine in rats and mice. *European Neuropsychopharmacology, 16,* 297–310.

Kosaka, H., Omori, M., Murata, T., Iidaka, T., Yamada, H., Okada, T., et al. (2002). Differential amygdala response during facial recognition in patients with schizophrenia: an fMRI study. *Schizophrenia Research, 57,* 87–95.

Kotermanski, S. E., Johnson, J. W., & Thiels, E. (2013). Comparison of behavioral effects of the NMDA receptor channel blockers memantine and ketamine in rats. *Pharmacology Biochemistry and Behavior, 109,* 67–76.

Krystal, J. H., Abi-Saab, W., Perry, E., D'Souza, D. C., Liu, N., Gueorguieva, R., et al. (2005). Preliminary evidence of attenuation of the disruptive effects of the NMDA glutamate receptor antagonist, ketamine, on working memory by pretreatment with the group II metabotropic glutamate receptor agonist, LY354740, in healthy human subjects. *Psychopharmacology (Berlin), 179,* 303–309.

Krystal, J. H., Bennett, A., Abi-Saab, D., Belger, A., Karper, L. P., D'Souza, D. C., et al. (2000). Dissociation of ketamine effects on rule acquisition and rule implementation: possible relevance to NMDA receptor contributions to executive cognitive functions. *Biological Psychiatry, 47,* 137–143.

Krystal, J. H., D'Souza, D. C., Karper, L. P., Bennett, A., Abi-Dargham, A., Abi-Saab, D., et al. (1999). Interactive effects of subanesthetic ketamine and haloperidol in healthy humans. *Psychopharmacology (Berlin), 145,* 193–204.

Krystal, J. H., Karper, L. P., Seibyl, J. P., et al. (1994). Subanesthetic effects of the noncompetitive nmda antagonist, ketamine, in humans: psychotomimetic, perceptual, cognitive, and neuroendocrine responses. *Archives of General Psychiatry, 51,* 199–214.

Kulikova, S. P., Tolmacheva, E. A., Anderson, P., Gaudias, J., Adams, B. E., Zheng, T., et al. (2012). Opposite effects of ketamine and deep brain stimulation on rat thalamocortical information processing. *European Journal of Neuroscience, 36,* 3407–3419.

Lahti, A. C., Weiler, M. A., Holcomb, H. H., Tamminga, C. A., Carpenter, W. T., & McMahon, R. (2005). Correlations between rCBF and symptoms in two independent cohorts of drug-free patients with schizophrenia. *Neuropsychopharmacology, 31,* 221–230.

Lahti, A. C., Weiler, M. A., Tamara, M., Parwani, A., & Tamminga, C. A. (2001). Effects of ketamine in normal and schizophrenic volunteers. *Neuropsychopharmacology, 25,* 455–467.

Lally, N., Nugent, A. C., Luckenbaugh, D. A., Ameli, R., Roiser, J. P., & Zarate, C. A. (2014). Anti-anhedonic effect of ketamine and its neural correlates in treatment-resistant bipolar depression. *Translational Psychiatry, 4,* e469.

Långsjö, J. W., Kaisti, K. K., Aalto, S., Hinkka, S., Aantaa, R., Oikonen, V., et al. (2003). Effects of subanesthetic doses of ketamine on regional cerebral blood flow, oxygen consumption, and blood volume in humans. *Anesthesiology, 99,* 614–623.

Large, C. H., Bison, S., Sartori, I., Read, K. D., Gozzi, A., Quarta, D., et al. (2011). The efficacy of sodium channel blockers to prevent phencyclidine-induced cognitive dysfunction in the rat: potential for novel treatments for schizophrenia. *Journal of Pharmacology and Experimental Therapeutics, 338,* 100–113.

Lee, M.-Y., Chiang, C.-C., Chiu, H.-Y., Chan, M.-H., & Chen, H.-H. (2014). N-acetylcysteine modulates hallucinogenic 5-HT2A receptor agonist-mediated responses: behavioral, molecular, and electrophysiological studies. *Neuropharmacology, 81,* 215–223.

Leeson, V. C., Robbins, T. W., Matheson, E., Hutton, S. B., Ron, M. A., Barnes, T. R. E., et al. (2009). Discrimination learning, reversal, and set-shifting in first-episode schizophrenia: stability over six years and specific associations with medication type and disorganization syndrome. *Biological Psychiatry, 66,* 586–593.

Lewis, D. A., Hashimoto, T., & Volk, D. W. (2005). Cortical inhibitory neurons and schizophrenia. *Nature Reviews Neuroscience, 6,* 312–324.

Li, C.-S. R. (2004). Do schizophrenia patients make more perseverative than non-perseverative errors on the Wisconsin Card sorting test? A meta-analytic study. *Psychiatry Research, 129,* 179–190.

Li, J., Ishiwari, K., Conway, M. W., Francois, J., Huxter, J., Lowry, J. P., et al. (2014). Dissociable effects of antipsychotics on ketamine-induced changes in regional oxygenation and inter-regional coherence of low frequency oxygen fluctuations in the rat. *Neuropsychopharmacology, 39,* 1635–1644.

Li, N., Lee, B., Liu, R.-J., Banasr, M., Dwyer, J. M., Iwata, M., et al. (2010). mTOR-dependent synapse formation underlies the rapid antidepressant effects of NMDA antagonists. *Science, 329,* 959–964.

Li, N., Liu, R.-J., Dwyer, J. M., Banasr, M., Lee, B., Son, H., et al. (2011). Glutamate N-methyl-D-aspartate receptor antagonists rapidly reverse behavioral and synaptic deficits caused by chronic stress exposure. *Biological Psychiatry, 69,* 754–761.

Liddle, P. F., Friston, K. J., Frith, C. D., Hirsch, S. R., Jones, T., & Frackowiak, R. S. (1992). Patterns of cerebral blood flow in schizophrenia. *British Journal of Psychiatry, 160,* 179–186.

Lieberman, J. A., Bymaster, F. P., Meltzer, H. Y., Deutch, A. Y., Duncan, G. E., Marx, C. E., et al. (2008). Antipsychotic drugs: comparison in animal models of efficacy, neurotransmitter regulation, and neuroprotection. *Pharmacological Reviews, 60,* 358–403.

Lieberman, J. .A., Kane, J. .M., & Alvir, J. (1987). Provocative tests with psychostimulant drugs in schizophrenia. *Psychopharmacology (Berlin), 91,* 415–433.

Littlewood, C. L., Jones, N., O'Neill, M. J., Mitchell, S. N., Tricklebank, M., & Williams, S. C. R. (2006). Mapping the central effects of ketamine in the rat using pharmacological MRI. *Psychopharmacology (Berlin), 186,* 64–81.

Lodge, D. J., & Grace, A. A. (2011). Hippocampal dysregulation of dopamine system function and the pathophysiology of schizophrenia. *Trends in Pharmacological Sciences, 32*, 507–513.

Lord, B., Wintmolders, C., Langlois, X., Nguyen, L., Lovenberg, T., & Bonaventure, P. (2013). Comparison of the ex vivo receptor occupancy profile of ketamine to several NMDA receptor antagonists in mouse hippocampus. *European Journal of Pharmacology, 715*, 21–25.

Lorrain, D. S., Baccei, C. S., Bristow, L. J., Anderson, J. J., & Varney, M. A. (2003). Effects of ketamine and n-methyl-d-aspartate on glutamate and dopamine release in the rat prefrontal cortex: modulation by a group II selective metabotropic glutamate receptor agonist LY379268. *Neuroscience, 117*, 697–706.

Lorrain, D. S., Schaffhauser, H., Campbell, U. C., Baccei, C. S., Correa, L. D., Rowe, B., et al. (2003). Group II mGlu receptor activation suppresses norepinephrine release in the ventral hippocampus and locomotor responses to acute ketamine challenge. *Neuropsychopharmacology: Official Publication of American College of Neuropsychopharmacology, 28*, 1622–1632.

Luby, E. D., Cohen, B. D., Rosenbaum, G., Gottlieb, J. S., & Kelley, R. (1959). Study of a new schizophrenomimetic drug—sernyl. *AMA Archives of Neurology & Psychiatry, 81*, 363–369.

Luckenbaugh, D. A., Niciu, M. J., Ionescu, D. F., Nolan, N. M., Richards, E. M., Brutsche, N. E., et al. (2014). Do the dissociative side effects of ketamine mediate its antidepressant effects? *Journal of Affective Disorders, 159*, 56–61.

Lydall, E. S., Gilmour, G., & Dwyer, D. M. (2010). Analysis of licking microstructure provides no evidence for a reduction in reward value following acute or sub-chronic phencyclidine administration. *Psychopharmacology (Berlin), 209*, 153–162.

Ma, J., & Leung, L. S. (2014). Deep brain stimulation of the medial septum or nucleus accumbens alleviates psychosis-relevant behavior in ketamine-treated rats. *Behavioural Brain Research, 266*, 174–182.

Ma, J., Shen, B., Rajakumar, N., & Leung, L. S. (2004). The medial septum mediates impairment of prepulse inhibition of acoustic startle induced by a hippocampal seizure or phencyclidine. *Behavioural Brain Research, 155*, 153–166.

Maeng, S., Zarate, C. A., Jr., Du, J., Schloesser, R. J., McCammon, J., Chen, G., et al. (2008). Cellular mechanisms underlying the antidepressant effects of ketamine: role of α-amino-3-hydroxy-5-methylisoxazole-4-propionic acid receptors. *Biological Psychiatry, 63*, 349–352.

Malhotra, A. K., Adler, C. M., Kennison, S. D., Elman, I., Pickar, D., & Breier, A. (1997). Clozapine blunts N-methyl-D-aspartate antagonist-induced psychosis: a study with ketamine. *Biological Psychiatry, 42*, 664–668.

Malhotra, A. K., Pinals, D. A., Weingartner, H., Sirocco, K., David Missar, C., Pickar, D., et al. (1996). NMDA receptor function and human cognition: the effects of ketamine in healthy volunteers. *Neuropsychopharmacology, 14*, 301–307.

Markou, A., & Koob, G. F. (1991). Postcocaine anhedonia. An animal model of cocaine withdrawal. *Neuropsychopharmacology: Official Publication of American College of Neuropsychopharmacology, 4*, 17–26.

Marsman, A., van den Heuvel, M. P., Klomp, D. W. J., Kahn, R. S., Luijten, P. R., & Hulshoff Pol, H. E. (2013). Glutamate in schizophrenia: a focused review and meta-analysis of 1H-MRS studies. *Schizophrenia Bulletin, 39*, 120–129.

Martin, D. A., Marona-Lewicka, D., Nichols, D. E., & Nichols, C. D. (2014). Chronic LSD alters gene expression profiles in the mPFC relevant to schizophrenia. *Neuropharmacology, 83*, 1–8.

Mathé, J. M., Nomikos, G. G., Hygge Blakeman, K., & Svensson, T. H. (1999). Differential actions of dizocilpine (MK-801) on the mesolimbic and mesocortical dopamine systems: role of neuronal activity. *Neuropharmacology, 38*, 121–128.

Mealing, G. A. R., Lanthorn, T. H., Murray, C. L., Small, D. L., & Morley, P. (1999). Differences in degree of trapping of low-affinity uncompetitive N-methyl-D-aspartic acid receptor antagonists with similar kinetics of block. *Journal of Pharmacology and Experimental Therapeutics, 288*, 204–210.

Meltzer, H. Y., Horiguchi, M., & Massey, B. W. (2011). The role of serotonin in the NMDA receptor antagonist models of psychosis and cognitive impairment. *Psychopharmacology (Berlin), 213*, 289–305.

Meyer-Lindenberg, A., Miletich, R. S., Kohn, P. D., Esposito, G., Carson, R. E., Quarantelli, M., et al. (2002). Reduced prefrontal activity predicts exaggerated striatal dopaminergic function in schizophrenia. *Nature Neuroscience, 5*, 267–271.

Minzenberg, M. J., Laird, A. R., Thelen, S., Carter, C. S., & Glahn, D. C. (2009). Meta-analysis of 41 functional neuroimaging studies of executive function in schizophrenia. *Archives of General Psychiatry, 66*, 811–822.

Moghaddam, B., Adams, B., Verma, A., & Daly, D. (1997). Activation of glutamatergic neurotransmission by ketamine: a novel step in the pathway from NMDA receptor blockade to dopaminergic and cognitive disruptions associated with the prefrontal cortex. *Journal of Neuroscience: The Official Journal of the Society for Neuroscience, 17*, 2921–2927.

Moghaddam, B., & Adams, B. W. (1998). Reversal of phencyclidine effects by a group II metabotropic glutamate receptor agonist in rats. *Science, 281*, 1349–1352.

Monaghan, D. T., & Jane, D. E. (2009). Pharmacology of NMDA receptors. In A. M. Van Dongen (Ed.), *Biology of the NMDA receptor*. Boca Raton (FL): CRC Press.

Monaghan, D. T., & Larsen, H. (1997). NR1 and NR2 subunit contributions to N-methyl-d-aspartate receptor channel blocker pharmacology. *Journal of Pharmacology and Experimental Therapeutics, 280*, 614–620.

Monyer, H., Burnashev, N., Laurie, D. J., Sakmann, B., & Seeburg, P. H. (1994). Developmental and regional expression in the rat brain and functional properties of four NMDA receptors. *Neuron, 12*, 529–540.

Morales, M., Varlinskaya, E. I., & Spear, L. P. (2013). Low doses of the NMDA receptor antagonists, MK-801, PEAQX, and ifenprodil, induces social facilitation in adolescent male rats. *Behavioural Brain Research, 250*, 18–22.

Moran, P. M., O'Tuathaigh, C. M. P., Papaleo, F., & Waddington, J. L. (2014). Dopaminergic function in relation to genes associated with risk for schizophrenia: translational mouse models. *Progress in Brain Research, 211*, 79–112.

Moran, P. M., Owen, L., Crookes, A. E., Al-Uzri, M. M., & Reveley, M. A. (2008). Abnormal prediction error is associated with negative and depressive symptoms in schizophrenia. *Progress in Neuro-Psychopharmacology & Biological Psychiatry, 32*, 116–123.

Moran, P. M., Rouse, J. L., Cross, B., Corcoran, R., & Schürmann, M. (2012). Kamin blocking is associated with reduced medial-frontal gyrus activation: implications for prediction error abnormality in schizophrenia. *PloS One, 7*, e43905.

Moran, R. J., Jones, M. W., Blockeel, A. J., Adams, R. A., Stephan, K. E., & Friston, K. J. (2014). Losing control under ketamine: suppressed cortico-hippocampal drive following acute ketamine in rats. *Neuropsychopharmacology, 40*, 268–277.

Morgan, C. J. A., Mofeez, A., Brandner, B., Bromley, L., & Curran, H. V. (2004). Ketamine impairs response inhibition and is positively reinforcing in healthy volunteers: a dose–response study. *Psychopharmacology (Berlin), 172*, 298–308.

Morgan, H. L., Turner, D. C., Corlett, P. R., Absalom, A. R., Adapa, R., Arana, F. S., et al. (2011). Exploring the impact of ketamine on the experience of illusory body ownership. *Biological Psychiatry, 69*, 35–41.

Moritz, S., & Woodward, T. S. (2005). Jumping to conclusions in delusional and non-delusional schizophrenic patients. *British Journal of Clinical Psychology British Psychological Society, 44*, 193–207.

Morris, H., & Wallach, J. (2014). From PCP to MXE: a comprehensive review of the non-medical use of dissociative drugs. *Drug Testing and Analysis, 6,* 614–632.

Moser, P. C., Hitchcock, J. M., Lister, S., & Moran, P. M. (2000). The pharmacology of latent inhibition as an animal model of schizophrenia. *Brain Research Reviews, 33,* 275–307.

Murrough, J. W., Perez, A. M., Pillemer, S., Stern, J., Parides, M. K., aan het Rot, M., et al. (2013). Rapid and longer-term antidepressant effects of repeated ketamine infusions in treatment-resistant major depression. *Biological Psychiatry, 74,* 250–256.

Musso, F., Brinkmeyer, J., Ecker, D., London, M. K., Thieme, G., Warbrick, T., et al. (2011). Ketamine effects on brain function—simultaneous fMRI/EEG during a visual oddball task. *NeuroImage, 58,* 508–525.

Nakazawa, K., Zsiros, V., Jiang, Z., Nakao, K., Kolata, S., Zhang, S., et al. (2012). GABAergic interneuron origin of schizophrenia pathophysiology. *Neuropharmacology, 62,* 1574–1583.

Nelson, C. L., Burk, J. A., Bruno, J. P., & Sarter, M. (2002). Effects of acute and repeated systemic administration of ketamine on prefrontal acetylcholine release and sustained attention performance in rats. *Psychopharmacology (Berlin), 161,* 168–179.

Neuroskeptic. (2014). *Depression: Ketamine eyes hath seen the glory?.*

Newcomer, J. W., Farber, N. B., Jevtovic-Todorovic, V., Selke, G., Melson, A. K., Hershey, T., et al. (1999). Ketamine-induced NMDA receptor hypofunction as a model of memory impairment and psychosis. *Neuropsychopharmacology, 20,* 106–118.

Nicholson, K. L., Mansbach, R. S., Menniti, F. S., & Balster, R. L. (2007). The phencyclidine-like discriminative stimulus effects and reinforcing properties of the NR2B-selective N-methyl-D-aspartate antagonist CP-101 606 in rats and rhesus monkeys. *Behavioural Pharmacology, 18,* 731–743.

Nikiforuk, A., Gołembiowska, K., & Popik, P. (2010). Mazindol attenuates ketamine-induced cognitive deficit in the attentional set shifting task in rats. *European Neuropsychopharmacology, 20,* 37–48.

Nikiforuk, A., Kos, T., Fijal, K., Holuj, M., Rafa, D., & Popik, P. (2013). Effects of the selective 5-HT7 receptor antagonist SB-269970 and amisulpride on ketamine-induced schizophrenia-like deficits in rats. *PLoS One, 8.*

Nikiforuk, A., & Popik, P. (2014). The effects of acute and repeated administration of ketamine on attentional performance in the five-choice serial reaction time task in rats. *European Neuropsychopharmacology, 24,* 1381–1393.

Nishitani, N., Nagayasu, K., Asaoka, N., Yamashiro, M., Shirakawa, H., Nakagawa, T., et al. (2014). Raphe AMPA receptors and nicotinic acetylcholine receptors mediate ketamine-induced serotonin release in the rat prefrontal cortex. *International Journal of Neuropsychopharmacology: Official Science Journal of College International Neuropsychopharmacology CINP, 17,* 1321–1326.

Nuechterlein, K. H., Barch, D. M., Gold, J. M., Goldberg, T. E., Green, M. F., & Heaton, R. K. (2004). Identification of separable cognitive factors in schizophrenia. *Schizophrenia Research, 72,* 29–39.

Odagaki, Y., & Toyoshima, R. (2006). Dopamine D2 receptor-mediated G protein activation assessed by agonist-stimulated [35S]guanosine 5′-O-(γ-thiotriphosphate) binding in rat striatal membranes. *Progress in Neuro-Psychopharmacology & Biological Psychiatry, 30,* 1304–1312.

Oranje, B., van Berckel, B., Kemner, C., van Ree, J., Kahn, R. S., & Verbaten, M. N. (2000). The effects of a sub-anaesthetic dose of ketamine on human selective attention. *Neuropsychopharmacology, 22,* 293–302.

Ouzir, M. (2013). Impulsivity in schizophrenia: a comprehensive update. *Aggression and Violent Behavior, 18,* 247–254.

Owens, D. G. C., Miller, P., Lawrie, S. M., & Johnstone, E. C. (2005). Pathogenesis of schizophrenia: a psychopathological perspective. *British Journal of Psychiatry, 186,* 386–393.

Paoletti, P., & Neyton, J. (2007). NMDA receptor subunits: function and pharmacology. *Current Opinion in Pharmacology, 7,* 39–47.

Parsons, C. G., Quack, G., Bresink, I., Baran, L., Przegalinski, E., Kostowski, W., et al. (1995). Comparison of the potency, kinetics and voltage-dependency of a series of uncompetitive NMDA receptor antagonists in vitro with anticonvulsive and motor impairment activity in vivo. *Neuropharmacology, 34,* 1239–1258.

Pavão, R., Tort, A. B. L., & Amaral, O. B. (2015). Multifactoriality in psychiatric disorders: a computational study of schizophrenia. *Schizophrenia Bulletin, 41,* 980–988.

Peralta, V., & Cuesta, M. J. (1994). Psychometric properties of the positive and negative syndrome scale (PANSS) in schizophrenia. *Psychiatry Research, 53,* 31–40.

Persson, J. (2013). Ketamine in pain management. *CNS Neuroscience & Therapeutics, 19,* 396–402.

Phillips, K. G., Cotel, M. C., McCarthy, A. P., Edgar, D. M., Tricklebank, M., O'Neill, M. J., et al. (2012). Differential effects of NMDA antagonists on high frequency and gamma EEG oscillations in a neurodevelopmental model of schizophrenia. *Neuropharmacology, 62,* 1359–1370.

Pinault, D. (2008). N-Methyl d-aspartate receptor antagonists ketamine and MK-801 induce wake-related aberrant γ oscillations in the rat neocortex. *Biological Psychiatry, 63,* 730–735.

Pitsikas, N., Boultadakis, A., & Sakellaridis, N. (2008). Effects of sub-anesthetic doses of ketamine on rats' spatial and non-spatial recognition memory. *Neuroscience, 154,* 454–460.

Poels, E. M. P., Kegeles, L. S., Kantrowitz, J. T., Slifstein, M., Javitt, D. C., Lieberman, J. A., et al. (2014). Imaging glutamate in schizophrenia: review of findings and implications for drug discovery. *Molecular Psychiatry, 19,* 20–29.

Pomarol-Clotet, E., Honey, G. D., Murray, G. K., Corlett, P. R., Absalom, A. R., Lee, M., et al. (2006). Psychological effects of ketamine in healthy volunteers phenomenological study. *British Journal of Psychiatry, 189,* 173–179.

Potkin, S. G., Turner, J. A., Brown, G. G., McCarthy, G., Greve, D. N., Glover, G. H., et al. (2009). Working memory and DLPFC inefficiency in schizophrenia: the FBIRN study. *Schizophrenia Bulletin, 35,* 19–31.

Preskorn, S. H., Baker, B., Kolluri, S., Menniti, F. S., Krams, M., & Landen, J. W. (2008). An innovative design to establish proof of concept of the antidepressant effects of the NR2B subunit selective N-methyl-D-aspartate antagonist, CP-101,606, in patients with treatment-refractory major depressive disorder. *Journal of Clinical Psychopharmacology, 28,* 631–637.

Quarta, D., & Large, C. H. (2011). Effects of lamotrigine on PCP-evoked elevations in monoamine levels in the medial prefrontal cortex of freely moving rats. *Journal of Psychopharmacology (Oxford), 25,* 1703–1711.

Rabiner, E. A. (2007). Imaging of striatal dopamine release elicited with NMDA antagonists: is there anything there to be seen? *Journal of Psychopharmacology Oxford England, 21,* 253–258.

Radant, A. D., Bowdle, T. A., Cowley, D. S., Kharasch, E. D., & Roy-Byrne, P. P. (1998). Does ketamine-mediated N-methyl-D-aspartate receptor antagonism cause schizophrenia-like oculomotor abnormalities? *Neuropsychopharmacology, 19,* 434–444.

Ragland, J. D., Laird, A. R., Ranganath, C., Blumenfeld, R. S., Gonzales, S. M., & Glahn, D. C. (2009). Prefrontal activation deficits during episodic memory in schizophrenia. *American Journal of Psychiatry, 166,* 863–874.

Razoux, F., Garcia, R., & Léna, I. (2006). Ketamine, at a dose that disrupts motor behavior and latent inhibition, enhances prefrontal cortex synaptic efficacy and glutamate release in the nucleus accumbens. *Neuropsychopharmacology, 32,* 719–727.

Reissig, C. J., Carter, L. P., Johnson, M. W., Mintzer, M. Z., Klinedinst, M. A., & Griffiths, R. R. (2012). High doses of dextromethorphan, an NMDA antagonist, produce effects similar to classic hallucinogens. *Psychopharmacology (Berlin), 223,* 1–15.

Roth, B. L., Gibbons, S., Arunotayanun, W., Huang, X.-P., Setola, V., Treble, R., et al. (2013). The ketamine analogue methoxetamine and 3- and 4-methoxy analogues of phencyclidine are high affinity and selective ligands for the glutamate NMDA receptor. *PLoS One, 8.*

Rowland, L. M., Astur, R. S., Jung, R. E., Bustillo, J. R., Lauriello, J., & Yeo, R. A. (2005). Selective cognitive impairments associated with NMDA receptor blockade in humans. *Neuropsychopharmacology, 30*, 633–639.

Rowland, L. M., Bustillo, J. R., Mullins, P. G., Jung, R. E., Lenroot, R., Landgraf, E., et al. (2005). Effects of ketamine on anterior cingulate glutamate metabolism in healthy humans: a 4-T proton MRS study. *American Journal of Psychiatry, 162*, 394–396.

Sallinen, J., Holappa, J., Koivisto, A., Kuokkanen, K., Chapman, H., Lehtimäki, J., et al. (2013). Pharmacological characterisation of a structurally novel α2C -adrenoceptor antagonist ORM-10921 and its effects in neuropsychiatric models. *Basic & Clinical Pharmacology & Toxicology, 113*, 239–249.

Scheidegger, M., Walter, M., Lehmann, M., Metzger, C., Grimm, S., Boeker, H., et al. (2012). Ketamine decreases resting state functional network connectivity in healthy Subjects: implications for antidepressant drug action. *PLoS One, 7*.

Schmechtig, A., Lees, J., Perkins, A., Altavilla, A., Craig, K. J., Dawson, G. R., et al. (2013). The effects of ketamine and risperidone on eye movement control in healthy volunteers. *Translational Psychiatry, 3*, e334.

Schmidt, A., Bachmann, R., Kometer, M., Csomor, P. A., Stephan, K. E., Seifritz, E., et al. (2012). Mismatch negativity encoding of prediction errors predicts s-ketamine-induced cognitive impairments. *Neuropsychopharmacology, 37*, 865–875.

Schmitz, Y., Benoit-Marand, M., Gonon, F., & Sulzer, D. (2003). Presynaptic regulation of dopaminergic neurotransmission. *Journal of Neurochemistry, 87*, 273–289.

Seeman, P., Ko, F., & Tallerico, T. (2005). Dopamine receptor contribution to the action of PCP, LSD and ketamine psychotomimetics. *Molecular Psychiatry, 10*, 877–883.

Sesack, S. R., & Carr, D. B. (2002). Selective prefrontal cortex inputs to dopamine cells: implications for schizophrenia. *Physiology & Behavior, 77*, 513–517.

Sesack, S. R., Hawrylak, V. A., Matus, C., Guido, M. A., & Levey, A. I. (1998). Dopamine axon varicosities in the prelimbic division of the rat prefrontal cortex exhibit sparse immunoreactivity for the dopamine transporter. *Journal of Neuroscience, 18*, 2697–2708.

Shaffer, C. L., Osgood, S. M., Smith, D. L., Liu, J., & Trapa, P. E. (2014). Enhancing ketamine translational pharmacology via receptor occupancy normalization. *Neuropharmacology, 86*, 174–180.

Shin, I.-J., Son, S. U., Park, H., Kim, Y., Park, S. H., Swanberg, K., et al. (2014). Preclinical evidence of rapid-onset antidepressant-like effect in radix polygalae extract. *PLoS One, 9*.

Siegel, B. V., Buchsbaum, M. S., Bunney, W. E., Gottschalk, L. A., Haier, R. J., Lohr, J. B., et al. (1993). Cortical-striatal-thalamic circuits and brain glucose metabolic activity in 70 unmedicated male schizophrenic patients. *American Journal of Psychiatry, 150*, 1325–1336.

Silver, H., Feldman, P., Bilker, W., & Gur, R. C. (2003). Working memory deficit as a core neuropsychological dysfunction in schizophrenia. *American Journal of Psychiatry, 160*, 1809–1816.

Sinner, B., & Graf, B. M. (2008). Ketamine. In P. D. h c J. Schüttler, & P. D. D. H. Schwilden (Eds.), *Modern anesthetics* (pp. 313–333). Springer Berlin Heidelberg.

Smith, J. W., Gastambide, F., Gilmour, G., Dix, S., Foss, J., Lloyd, K., et al. (2011). A comparison of the effects of ketamine and phencyclidine with other antagonists of the NMDA receptor in rodent assays of attention and working memory. *Psychopharmacology (Berlin), 217*, 255–269.

Sommer, I. E. C., Diederen, K. M. J., Blom, J.-D., Willems, A., Kushan, L., Slotema, K., et al. (2008). Auditory verbal hallucinations predominantly activate the right inferior frontal area. *Brain, 131*, 3169–3177.

Spencer, K. M., Salisbury, D. F., Shenton, M. E., & McCarley, R. W. (2008). γ-Band auditory steady-state responses are impaired in first episode psychosis. *Biological Psychiatry, 64*, 369–375.

Sprenger, T., Valet, M., Woltmann, R., Zimmer, C., Freynhagen, R., Kochs, E. F., et al. (2006). Imaging pain modulation by subanesthetic s-(+)-ketamine. *Anesthesia & Analgesia, 103*, 729–737.

Stan, T. L., Alvarsson, A., Branzell, N., Sousa, V. C., & Svenningsson, P. (2014). NMDA receptor antagonists ketamine and Ro25-6981 inhibit evoked release of glutamate in vivo in the subiculum. *Translational Psychiatry, 4*, e395.

Stone, J. M., Dietrich, C., Edden, R., Mehta, M. A., De Simoni, S., Reed, L. J., et al. (2012). Ketamine effects on brain GABA and glutamate levels with 1H-MRS: relationship to ketamine-induced psychopathology. *Molecular Psychiatry, 17*, 664–665.

Stone, J. M., Erlandsson, K., Arstad, E., Squassante, L., Teneggi, V., Bressan, R. A., et al. (2008). Relationship between ketamine-induced psychotic symptoms and NMDA receptor occupancy—a [123I]CNS-1261 SPET study. *Psychopharmacology (Berlin), 197*, 401–408.

Stuchlík, A., Petrásek, T., & Vales, K. (2009). Effect of alpha(1)-adrenergic antagonist prazosin on behavioral alterations induced by MK-801 in a spatial memory task in Long-Evans rats. *Physiological Research Academia Scientiarum Bohemoslovaca, 58*, 733–740.

Studerus, E., Gamma, A., & Vollenweider, F. X. (2010). Psychometric evaluation of the altered states of consciousness rating scale (OAV). *PLoS One, 5*, e12412.

Subramaniam, K., Subramaniam, B., & Steinbrook, R. A. (2004). Ketamine as adjuvant analgesic to opioids: a quantitative and qualitative systematic review. *Anesthesia & Analgesia*, 482–495.

Suzuki, Y., Jodo, E., Takeuchi, S., Niwa, S., & Kayama, Y. (2002). Acute administration of phencyclidine induces tonic activation of medial prefrontal cortex neurons in freely moving rats. *Neuroscience, 114*, 769–779.

Swerdlow, N. R., Weber, M., Qu, Y., Light, G. A., & Braff, D. L. (2008). Realistic expectations of prepulse inhibition in translational models for schizophrenia research. *Psychopharmacology (Berlin), 199*, 331–388.

Tan, H.-Y., Choo, W.-C., Fones, C. S. L., & Chee, M. W. L. (2005). fMRI study of maintenance and manipulation processes within working memory in first-episode schizophrenia. *American Journal of Psychiatry, 162*, 1849–1858.

Tatard-Leitman, V. M., Jutzeler, C. R., Suh, J., Saunders, J. A., Billingslea, E. N., Morita, S., et al. (2015). Pyramidal cell selective ablation of N-methyl-D-aspartate receptor 1 causes increase in cellular and network excitability. *Biological Psychiatry, 77*, 556–568.

Taylor, M. J., Tiangga, E. R., Mhuircheartaigh, R. N., & Cowen, P. J. (2012). Lack of effect of ketamine on cortical glutamate and glutamine in healthy volunteers: a proton magnetic resonance spectroscopy study. *Journal of Psychopharmacology Oxford England, 26*, 733–737.

Thakkar, K. N., Nichols, H. S., McIntosh, L. G., & Park, S. (2011). Disturbances in body ownership in schizophrenia: evidence from the rubber hand illusion and case study of a spontaneous out-of-body experience. *PLoS One, 6*, e27089.

Tricklebank, M. D., Singh, L., Oles, R. J., Preston, C., & Iversen, S. D. (1989). The behavioural effects of MK-801: a comparison with antagonists acting non-competitively and competitively at the NMDA receptor. *European Journal of Pharmacology, 167*, 127–135.

Troyano-Rodriguez, E., Lladó-Pelfort, L., Santana, N., Teruel-Martí, V., Celada, P., & Artigas, F. (2014). Phencyclidine inhibits the activity of thalamic reticular gamma-aminobutyric acidergic neurons in rat brain. *Biological Psychiatry, 76*, 937–945.

Tso, M. M., Blatchford, K. L., Callado, L. F., McLaughlin, D. P., & Stamford, J. A. (2004). Stereoselective effects of ketamine on dopamine, serotonin and noradrenaline release and uptake in rat brain slices. *Neurochemistry International, 44*, 1–7.

Uhlhaas, P. J. (2013). Dysconnectivity, large-scale networks and neuronal dynamics in schizophrenia. *Current Opinion in Neurobiology, 23*, 283–290.

Uhlhaas, P. J., & Mishara, A. L. (2007). Perceptual anomalies in schizophrenia: integrating phenomenology and cognitive neuroscience. *Schizophrenia Bulletin, 33*, 142–156.

Uhlhaas, P. J., & Singer, W. (2010). Abnormal neural oscillations and synchrony in schizophrenia. *Nature Reviews Neuroscience, 11*, 100–113.

Umbricht, D., Koller, R., Vollenweider, F. X., & Schmid, L. (2002). Mismatch negativity predicts psychotic experiences induced by NMDA receptor antagonist in healthy volunteers. *Biological Psychiatry, 51*, 400–406.

Umbricht, D., & Krljes, S. (2005). Mismatch negativity in schizophrenia: a meta-analysis. *Schizophrenia Research, 76*, 1–23.

Uslaner, J. M., Smith, S. M., Huszar, S. L., Pachmerhiwala, R., Hinchliffe, R. M., Vardigan, J. D., et al. (2012). T-type calcium channel antagonism produces antipsychotic-like effects and reduces stimulant-induced glutamate release in the nucleus accumbens of rats. *Neuropharmacology, 62*, 1413–1421.

Verma, A., & Moghaddam, B. (1996). NMDA receptor antagonists impair prefrontal cortex function as assessed via spatial delayed alternation performance in rats: modulation by dopamine. *Journal of Neuroscience, 16*, 373–379.

Vollenweider, F. X., Leenders, K. L., Øye, I., Hell, D., & Angst, J. (1997a). Differential psychopathology and patterns of cerebral glucose utilisation produced by (S)- and (R)-ketamine in healthy volunteers using positron emission tomography (PET). *European Neuropsychopharmacology, 7*, 25–38.

Vollenweider, F. X., Leenders, K. L., Scharfetter, C., Antonini, A., Maguire, P., Missimer, J., et al. (1997b). Metabolic hyperfrontality and psychopathology in the ketamine model of psychosis using positron emission tomography (PET) and [18F]fluorodeoxyglucose (FDG). *European Neuropsychopharmacology, 7*, 9–24.

Vollenweider, F. X., Vontobel, P., Øye, I., Hell, D., & Leenders, K. L. (2000). Effects of (S)-ketamine on striatal dopamine: a [11C]raclopride PET study of a model psychosis in humans. *Journal of Psychiatric Research, 34*, 35–43.

Voss, M., Moore, J., Hauser, M., Gallinat, J., Heinz, A., & Haggard, P. (2010). Altered awareness of action in schizophrenia: a specific deficit in predicting action consequences. *Brain, 133*, 3104–3112.

Wallace, T. L., & Porter, R. H. P. (2011). Targeting the nicotinic alpha7 acetylcholine receptor to enhance cognition in disease. *Biochemical Pharmacology, 82*, 891–903.

Wallis, J. D. (2006). Evaluating apples and oranges. *Nature Neuroscience, 9*, 596–598.

Wang, M., Yang, Y., Wang, C.-J., Gamo, N. J., Jin, L. E., Mazer, J. A., et al. (2013). NMDA receptors subserve persistent neuronal firing during working memory in dorsolateral prefrontal cortex. *Neuron, 77*, 736–749.

Weickert, C. S., Fung, S. J., Catts, V. S., Schofield, P. R., Allen, K. M., Moore, L. T., et al. (2013). Molecular evidence of N-methyl-D-aspartate receptor hypofunction in schizophrenia. *Molecular Psychiatry, 18*, 1185–1192.

Weiner, I. (2003). The "two-headed" latent inhibition model of schizophrenia: modeling positive and negative symptoms and their treatment. *Psychopharmacology (Berlin), 169*, 257–297.

Weiner, I., & Arad, M. (2009). Using the pharmacology of latent inhibition to model domains of pathology in schizophrenia and their treatment. *Behavioural Brain Research, 204*, 369–386.

Whitfield-Gabrieli, S., & Ford, J. M. (2012). Default mode network activity and connectivity in psychopathology. *Annual Review of Clinical Psychology, 8*, 49–76.

Whitfield-Gabrieli, S., Thermenos, H. W., Milanovic, S., Tsuang, M. T., Faraone, S. V., McCarley, R. W., et al. (2009). Hyperactivity and hyperconnectivity of the default network in schizophrenia and in first-degree relatives of persons with schizophrenia. *Proceedings of the National Academy of Sciences of the United States of America, 106*, 1279–1284.

Willmore, C. B., LaVecchia, K. L., & Wiley, J. L. (2001). NMDA antagonists produce site-selective impairment of accuracy in a delayed nonmatch-to-sample task in rats. *Neuropharmacology, 41*, 916–927.

Wise, R. A. (2002). Brain reward circuitry: insights from unsensed incentives. *Neuron, 36*, 229–240.

Wood, J., Kim, Y., & Moghaddam, B. (2012). Disruption of prefrontal cortex large scale neuronal activity by different classes of psychotomimetic drugs. *Journal of Neuroscience, 32*, 3022–3031.

Yaakub, S. N., Dorairaj, K., Poh, J. S., Asplund, C. L., Krishnan, R., Lee, J., et al. (2013). Preserved working memory and altered brain activation in persons at risk for psychosis. *American Journal of Psychiatry, 170*, 1297–1307.

Zhang, C., & Marek, G. J. (2008). AMPA receptor involvement in 5-hydroxytryptamine2A receptor-mediated pre-frontal cortical excitatory synaptic currents and DOI-induced head shakes. *Progress in Neuro-Psychopharmacology & Biological Psychiatry, 32*, 62–71.

11

Modeling the Maternal Immune Activation Risk Factor for Schizophrenia

Natalia Malkova[a], Wei-Li Wu[a], Elaine Y. Hsiao

Division of Biology & Biological Engineering, California Institute of Technology, Pasadena, CA, USA

INTRODUCTION

Schizophrenia is a serious neurodevelopmental disorder afflicting approximately 1% of adults in the United States, with similar prevalence reported in other countries around the world. The disorder is characterized by negative, positive, and cognitive symptoms, including impaired social functioning, hallucinations, and disorganized thought. In addition to these core diagnostic areas, there are a variety of medical comorbidities associated with the disorder, including infectious, autoimmune, and metabolic diseases (Crump, Winkleby, Sundquist, & Sundquist, 2013; Eaton et al., 2006). The causes of schizophrenia are largely unknown, but believed to be contributed by a combination of both genetic and environmental risk factors. A meta-analyses of 12 twin studies reports that the concordance of schizophrenia among monozygotic versus dizygotic twins is 81% (Sullivan, Kendler, & Neale, 2003), indicating high heritability of the disorder and a role for both genes and environment in the etiology of schizophrenia. Consistent with this, a study finds that monozygotic twins sharing the same placenta (monochorionic) exhibit a 60% concordance rate compared with 10.7% concordance for monozygotic twins that do not share the same placenta (dichorionic) (Davis, Phelps, & Bracha, 1995). This suggests a significant role for the shared uterine environment in the etiopathogenesis of schizophrenia.

[a] Equal contribution.

MATERNAL INFECTION RISK FACTORS FOR SCHIZOPHRENIA

Several environmental factors have been identified to increase schizophrenia risk, many of which impact immunological status. Early life challenges, such as perinatal infection, nutrient deficiency, maternal stress, fetal hypoxia, obstetric complications, and advanced paternal age, are each associated with schizophrenia (Brown, 2011). Postnatal exposures to infection, trauma, and cannabis (Brown, 2011) are also implicated. Among these various factors, maternal infection, in particular, is strongly supported by large epidemiological, case, and animal studies as a significant environmental risk for schizophrenia (Brown, 2006; Brown & Patterson, 2011; Patterson, 2009). Prenatal exposures to influenza virus, rubella, toxoplasmosis, herpes simplex virus type 2, and other infections increase the risk of schizophrenia in the offspring (Brown, 2012b; Khandaker, Zimbron, Lewis, & Jones, 2013). In addition, maternal infection and increased inflammatory cytokines during pregnancy are linked with structural and functional brain changes in the offspring that are relevant to schizophrenia, such as increased ventricular volume, reduced cortical volume, and a presence of a cavum septum pellucidum, a marker for fetal neural maldevelopment (Ellman et al., 2010; Ellman, Yolken, Buka, Torrey, & Cannon, 2009; Fineberg & Ellman, 2013; Galarza, Merlo, Ingratta, Albanese, & Albanese, 2004). Moreover, the offspring of the mothers infected with influenza virus display decreased executive and cognitive functions in childhood and adulthood (Ellman et al., 2009).

Early evidence that maternal infection during pregnancy is associated with schizophrenia derives from population studies of the 1957 type A2 influenza epidemic. These early investigations are retrospective, based on documented data from the time of the particular epidemic, and perhaps not surprisingly, have yielded contradictory results (Mednick, Machon, Huttunen, & Bonett, 1988; Selten, Frissen, Lensvelt-Mulders, & Morgan, 2010). However, more recent studies based on birth cohort or nested case–control designs use serological assays, clinical examination of the mother, and longitudinal evaluation of the offspring to more effectively diagnose maternal infection (Brown, Begg, et al., 2004; Buka, Tsuang, Torrey, Klebanoff, Wagner, et al., 2001; Khandaker et al., 2013; Mortensen et al., 2010). Maternal exposure to influenza virus during first two trimesters of pregnancy, as measured by the presence of anti-influenza antibodies in maternal serum, increases the risk for schizophrenia in the offspring by three- to sevenfolds (Brown, Begg, et al., 2004). In addition, elevated levels of maternal immunoglobulin G antibodies to herpes simplex virus type 2 and *Toxoplasma gondii* are positively associated with increased schizophrenia susceptibility (Brown et al., 2005; Buka, Tsuang, Torrey, Klebanoff, Bernstein, et al., 2001). Moreover, various types of respiratory tract and reproductive infections are linked to an increased risk for schizophrenia in the offspring (Babulas, Factor-Litvak, Goetz, Schaefer, & Brown, 2006; Nielsen, Laursen, & Mortensen, 2013; Sorensen, Mortensen, Reinisch, & Mednick, 2009).

The diversity in the types of maternal infection that increase the risk for schizophrenia supports the notion that general activation of the maternal immune system, rather than a site- or pathogen-specific infection, is responsible. Consistent with this, pro-inflammatory factors are believed to mediate the effects of maternal immune activation (MIA) on abnormal neurodevelopment. Positive correlations between elevated maternal cytokine level and increased risk of schizophrenia are reported for tumor necrosis factor (TNF)-α and interleukin (IL)-8 (Brown, Hooton, et al., 2004; Buka, Tsuang, Torrey, Klebanoff, Wagner, et al., 2001). Many cytokines and cytokine receptors are expressed in the developing brain (Mousa, Seiger, Kjaeldgaard, & Bakhiet, 1999), where they play a key role in synaptic plasticity, neurogenesis, and gliogenesis (Deverman & Patterson, 2009).

MODELING MIA USING PRENATAL POLYINOSINE-POLYCYTIDYLIC INJECTIONS

Although the preponderance of human case and epidemiological studies link maternal infection and maternal inflammatory factors to the etiopathogenesis of schizophrenia, fundamental questions remain. For example, how does the timing or severity of immune activation during pregnancy influence neurodevelopment and postnatal brain function and behavior? In addition, how is maternal immune challenge relayed to the developing embryo and what are the molecular mechanisms underlying its effects?

Modeling the MIA risk factor in animal models is important for testing the hypotheses generated from epidemiological findings and enabling the investigation of the cellular and molecular underpinnings of schizophrenia-related endophenotypes. Several MIA models have been developed involving the infection of pregnant rodents or monkeys with influenza virus or the use of microbial antigens to induce an inflammatory response in the absence of a persistent infection. Most widely used are the synthetic double-stranded RNA, polyinosine-polycytidylic—poly (I:C)—that evokes an antiviral inflammatory response and the bacterial cell wall constituent, lipopolysaccharide, which evokes an antibacterial inflammatory response. Although these approaches differ in their specific molecular cascades of immune activation, the influenza infection, poly (I:C), and lipopolysaccharide models all similarly demonstrate that MIA in pregnant rodents or monkeys sufficiently yields offspring displaying behavioral and neuropathological abnormalities relevant to schizophrenia.

To be considered relevant to human pathology, animal models of schizophrenia should display three criteria of validity: construct, face, and predictive (Jones, Watson, & Fone, 2011; Macedo et al., 2012). Constructive validity means that the animal model should have an etiological basis that is relevant to the biological origins or risk factors for the human disorder. Face validity entails that the animal model should display symptoms that are homologous to those seen in the human disease, thereby enabling studies into the neurobiological bases of these schizophrenia-related symptoms. Predictive validity denotes the ability to reproduce in animal models pharmacological responses known to be effective for the human disorder.

Rodent models of MIA display face, construct and predictive validity for several behavioral, neuropathological, and biochemical abnormalities associated with schizophrenia (Table 1). For the poly (I:C) approach, pregnant rats or mice are injected with poly (I:C) during mid-gestation to yield offspring that display behavioral abnormalities that resemble common negative symptoms of schizophrenia, such as deficits in sensorimotor gating and information processing (Bitanihirwe, Peleg-Raibstein, Mouttet, Feldon, & Meyer, 2010; Smith, Li, Garbett, Mirnics, & Patterson, 2007). Sensorimotor gating refers to the ability to habituate to repetitious unimportant stimuli, and is known to be impaired in schizophrenic patients who cannot distinguish between specific stimuli and background noise (Light & Braff, 1999).

TABLE 1 Comparative Overview of Poly (I:C) Rodent Models and Their Validation for Animal Models of Psychiatric Disorders

Poly (I:C) Treatment	Behavioral Phenotype	Neurochemical and Structural Defects	Antipsychotic Treatment
Mouse, 20 mg/kg GD 9 (Shi, Fatemi, Sidwell, & Patterson, 2003)	PPI deficit		
Rat, 4 mg/kg GD 15 (Piontkewitz, Arad, & Weiner, 2011; Piontkewitz, Assaf, & Weiner, 2009; Piontkewitz et al., 2012; Zuckerman, Rehavi, Nachman, & Weiner, 2003; Zuckerman & Weiner, 2005)	LI deficit, APMH- and MK-801–induced hyperlocomotion	Enlargement of lateral ventricles; reduction of hippocampal volume; impaired neurogenesis, reduced capillarization and cell density in hippocampus; decreased number of hippocampal parvalbumin-containing GABAergic interneurons; increased KCl-induced dopamine release from striatum	CLZ (7.5 mg/mL/kg; PND 34–47) and RIS (0.045 or 1.2 mg/kg; PND 34–47) prevent enlargement of lateral ventricles and reduction of hippocampal volume; CLZ (7.5 mg/mL/kg; ND 34–47) (5 mg/kg; PND 35 or P90), HAL (0.1 mg/kg; PND 35 or 90) and RIS (0.045 or 1.2 mg/kg; PND 34–47) correct LI deficit and AMPH-induced hyperlocomotion; RIS (0.045 or 1.2 mg/kg; PND 34–47) prevents impaired neurogenesis, reduced capillarization and granular cell density in hippocampus and decreased number of hippocampal parvalbumin-containing GABAergic interneurons
Mouse, 5 or 10 mg/kg GD 9 (Meyer, Feldon, Schedlowski, & Yee, 2005; Meyer, Schwendener, Feldon, & Yee, 2006)	Deficits in PPI, LI, and spatial working memory; increased anxiety; amphetamine-induced hyperlocomotion	Elevation of fetal IL-1β	
Mouse, 5 mg/kg GD 12–17 (Ozawa et al., 2006)	Attenuated thigmotaxis; MAP-induced hyperlocomotion; PPI deficit; cognitive impairment in novel object recognition test	Increased dopamine turnover; decreased level of D2-like receptor in striatum	CLZ (5.0 mg/kg; P35D or P90D for 2 weeks) improves cognitive impairment
Mouse, 5 mg/kg GD 9 (Li et al., 2010; Meyer, Engler, Weber, Schedlowski, & Feldon, 2008; Meyer, Feldon, Schedlowski, & Yee, 2006; Meyer, Nyffeler, Yee, Knuesel, & Feldon, 2008; Shi et al., 2009; Winter et al., 2009)	PPI and LI deficit	Fetus: Reduction of prefrontal D1R; increase in the number of mesencephalic dopamine neurons; Adults: Increased level of dopamine in globus pallidus and prefrontal cortex; decreased level of serotonin in the hippocampus, nucleus accumbens and globus pallidus; reduction of taurine in the hippocampus; enlargement of lateral ventricles; decreased myelination	
Mouse, 5 mg/kg GD 17 (Bitanihirwe et al., 2010; Meyer, Feldon, et al., 2006; Meyer, Knuesel, Nyffeler, & Feldon, 2010; Meyer, Nyffeler, Yee, et al., 2008; Shi et al., 2009; Vuillermot, Weber, Feldon, & Meyer, 2010)	Impaired working memory; deficit in social interaction, anhedonic behavior, and alterations in the locomotor and stereotyped behavioral responses to APO	Reduction of hippocampal NMDAR; reduction of prefrontal reelin and parvalbumin-expressing neurons; increased number of midbrain dopamine cells; reduced hippocampal neurogenesis; expansion of 4th ventricle volume; reduced dopamine, glutamate, GABA, and glycine levels in prefrontal cortex and hippocampus	CLZ (5 mg/kg; PND 85–106) improves working memory deficits

Continued

TABLE 1   Comparative Overview of Poly (I:C) Rodent Models and Their Validation for Animal Models of Psychiatric Disorders—cont'd

Poly (I:C) Treatment	Behavioral Phenotype	Neurochemical and Structural Defects	Antipsychotic Treatment
Mouse, 20 mg/kg GD 12.5 (Ito, Smith, Hsiao, & Patterson, 2010; Smith et al., 2007)	Deficit in PPI, LL, increased anxiety, and decreased sociability. The behavioral effects are normalized by coadministration of anti–IL-6 antibodies. Perseverant behavior in the Morris water maze task and abnormal preference in the novel object recognition task	Abnormal hippocampal network; increased sensitivity to dopamine at distal CA1 synapses	
Mouse, 2 mg/kg GD 9 (Meyer, Spoerri, Yee, Schwarz, & Feldon, 2010)	PPI and LI deficit, hypersensitivity to AMPH		CLZ (15 mg/kg/day; PND 35–65) and FLX (20 mg/kg/day; PND 35–65) treatment normalizes PPI; CLZ (15 mg/kg/day; PND 35–65) and HAL (3 mg/kg/day; PND 35–65) treatment prevent LI deficit; HAL (3 mg/kg/day; PND 35–65) and FLX (20 mg/kg/day; PND 35–65) treatment attenuate high response to AMPH
Rat, 4 mg/kg GD 15 (Dickerson, Restieaux, & Bilkey, 2012; Dickerson, Wolff, & Bilkey, 2010)	PPI deficit	Disruption in long-range neuronal synchrony	CLZ (1 mg/kg or 5 mg/kg; <PND 150) ameliorates the deficit in theta frequency coherence between the prefrontal cortex and the hippocampus
Rat, 8 mg/kg GD 14 (Richtand et al., 2011; Richtand et al., 2012; Roenker et al., 2011)	Decreased response to the low dose of AMPH	NMDA hypofunction in prefrontal cortex	Paliperidone (0.01 mg/kg/day; PND 34–35) and RIS (0.01 mg/kg/day; PND 34–35) normalize basal extracellular glutamate; paliperidone (0.05 mg/kg/day; PND 35–70), RIS (0.45 mg/kg/day; PND 35–70), FLX (10 mg/kg/day; PND 35–70); and aripiprazole (0.66 mg/kg/day; PND 35–70) stabilize response to APMH
Mouse, 5 mg/kg GD 9 (Holloway et al., 2013)	High sensitivity to DOI; cognitive impairment on the T-maze task	Increased 5HT-2AR level but decreased mGlu2/3R level in frontal cortex	
Mouse, 5 mg/kg GD 10, 12, and 14 (Malkova, Gallagher, Yu, Jacobs, & Patterson, 2014)	PPI deficit, high sensitivity to DOI	Increased level of 5HT-2AR, RGS-4, and PLC-β 1 in the frontal cortex; greater DOI-induced brain activity	5-HTR antagonist ketanserin (2 mg/kg; 1 week; PND 56) diminishes DOI-induced stereotypic behavior

APMH, amphetamine; APO, apomorphine; CLZ, clozapine; DOI, 2,5-dimethoxy-4-iodoamphetamine; DR, dopamine receptor; FLX, fluoxetine; GABA, γ-aminobutyric acid; GD, gestational day; HAL, haloperidol; 5-HTR, serotonin receptor; IL, interleukin; LI, latent inhibition; MAP, methamphetamine; mGluR, metabotropic glutamate receptor; NMDA, N-methyl-D-aspartate receptor; PLC, phospholipase C; PND, postnatal day; PPI, prepulse inhibition of acoustic stimulus; RGS, regulator of G protein signaling; RIS, risperidone.

To measure sensorimotor gating in animals, the prepulse inhibition (PPI) task is used. A series of acoustic tones are presented, some of which are preceded by a lower intensity prepulse, and the startle response is recorded. PPI refers to the ability of the animal to inhibit its startle response to the primary pulse when it is preceded by a lower intensity prepulse. This assay in mice parallels the P50 auditory-evoked potential suppression task used to measure sensorimotor gating in humans.

Another method of evaluating sensorimotor gating is the latent inhibition (LI) assay (Swerdlow, Braff, Hartston, Perry, & Geyer, 1996). LI is a cross-species selective attention phenomenon and refers to the observation that organisms display reduced learning if they receive nonreinforced preexposure to the to-be-conditioned stimulus compared with a group without such preexposure. LI assesses an organism's ability to learn to ignore irrelevant stimuli and is known to be abnormal in patients with schizophrenia (Weiner & Arad, 2009). Inducing MIA in rodents also yields offspring with disrupted LI (Meyer et al., 2005; Meyer, Feldon, et al., 2006; Meyer, Spoerri, et al., 2010; Smith et al., 2007; Zuckerman et al., 2003).

In addition to abnormalities in sensorimotor gating, several long-term cognitive impairments are observed in MIA offspring. These include deficiencies in spatial working memory (Meyer et al., 2005; Meyer, Nyffeler, Yee, et al., 2008; Samuelsson, Jennische, Hansson, & Holmang, 2006), novel object recognition (Ito et al., 2010; Ozawa et al., 2006), discrimination reversal learning (Meyer, Nyffeler, Yee, et al., 2008; Zuckerman & Weiner, 2005), and performance in the T-maze task and water maze (Holloway et al., 2013; Ito et al., 2010).

Although the positive symptoms of schizophrenia, such as hallucinations, are arguably unique to humans, recent studies model hallucination-like activity in mice using the agonist for serotonin receptor 2A, 2,5-dimethoxy-4-iodoamphetamine (DOI) (Holloway et al., 2013; Malkova et al., 2014). Consistent with the elevated response to hallucinogenic drugs seen in schizophrenia, MIA offspring display increased brain activity and stereotypic behavior in response to DOI treatment. Manganese (Mn^2)-enhanced magnetic resonance imaging reveals that MIA offspring exhibit significantly higher DOI-induced brain activity in frontal, primary motor, and somatosensory cortices as well as caudate putamen, midbrain, and thalamus (Figure 1). Moreover, MIA offspring display DOI-induced Mn^{2+} accumulation in the parafascicular thalamic nucleus, one of the intralaminar nuclei of the dorsal thalamus that is known to play the role in the pathogenesis of the visual and auditory hallucinations (Delgado & Bogousslavsky, 2013). The high sensitivity to DOI seen in MIA offspring may be explained by the increased levels of serotonin receptor 2A and downstream signaling molecules seen in the unstimulated MIA prefrontal cortex (Holloway et al., 2013; Malkova et al., 2014). MIA offspring also exhibit higher levels of frontal pyramidal neurons, which are known to express serotonin receptor 2A (Fatemi et al., 2002).

Hyperlocomotion in response to amphetamine (APMH) and MK-801, an N-methyl-D-aspartate (NMDA) receptor antagonist, is also observed in MIA offspring and can be interpreted as a positive symptom for schizophrenia (Meyer, Schwendener, et al., 2006; Meyer, Spoerri, et al., 2010; Smith et al., 2007; Zuckerman et al., 2003). APMH is known to exacerbate psychotic symptoms in schizophrenia patients mimicking the well-documented subcortical dopamine hyperfunction in this disorder (Harrison, 2000a; Laruelle, 2014; Laruelle et al., 1996; Laruelle, Abi-Dargham, Gil, Kegeles, & Innis, 1999).

In addition to modeling schizophrenia-related behavioral abnormalities, maternal poly (I:C) injection in rodents results in several neuropathologies in the offspring that are relevant to schizophrenia. Importantly, MIA offspring exhibit a hallmark neuropathology of schizophrenia—an enlargement of lateral ventricles that is the result of the gray matter volume diminution (Piontkewitz et al., 2009, 2011; Shi et al., 2009).

Maternal poly (I:C) injection also leads to aberrations in the central dopamine system that are analogous to symptoms seen in schizophrenia (Laruelle, 2014). MIA offspring exhibit increased levels of dopaminergic neurons as well as dopamine receptors 1 and 2 in the midbrain (Vuillermot et al., 2010), higher sensitivity to dopamine at distal hippocampal CA1 synapses (Ito et al., 2010), and increased dopamine turnover in the striatum (Ozawa et al., 2006). MIA mice also display a reduction of hippocampal volume (Piontkewitz et al., 2009, 2011). Structural and functional abnormalities of the hippocampal are also seen in MIA offspring and in schizophrenic individuals (Harrison, 2000b, 2004). Maternal poly (I:C) injection yields offspring with abnormal hippocampal network organization (Dickerson et al., 2010, 2012; Ito et al., 2010), reduced hippocampal neurogenesis (Meyer, Knuesel, et al., 2010; Piontkewitz et al., 2012), decreased hippocampal volume, and reduced hippocampal capilarization and cell density (Piontkewitz et al., 2009, 2011, 2012). Furthermore, hippocampal levels of several neurotransmitters, including dopamine, γ-aminobutyric acid (GABA), glutamate and glycine, are decreased in MIA offspring (Bitanihirwe et al., 2010).

Overall, the MIA model exhibits strong face and constructive validity for behavioral, biochemical, and morphological symptoms of schizophrenia, rendering it a valuable tool for testing the efficacy of antipsychotic drugs and novel therapeutics for schizophrenia. Several known antipsychotic drugs have been applied to the MIA model and yielded positive effects on ameliorating

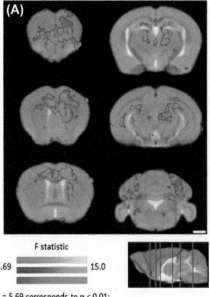

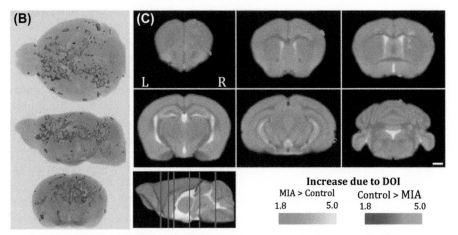

FIGURE 1   Magnetic resonance images demonstrate global brain activation by hallucinogen 2,5-dimethoxy-4-iodoamphetamine (DOI) in mice. (A) DOI stimulates the frontal, primary motor, and somatosensory cortices as well as caudate putamen and thalamic nuclei that are indicated in green. (B) Three-dimensional parametric map of the mouse brain demonstrating a DOI-induced signal increase in maternal immune activation (MIA) offspring (shown in red). (C) Specific coronal slices represent a DOI-induced signal increase in MIA offspring. LH, left hemisphere; RH, right hemisphere. *Credit: Natalia Malkova.*

schizophrenia-related symptoms. Acute treatment of MIA offspring with clozapine (CLZ), an atypical antipsychotic drug with high binding affinity for multiple neurotransmitter receptors (Pratt, Winchester, Dawson, & Morris, 2012), corrects abnormalities in LI (Piontkewitz et al., 2009; Zuckerman et al., 2003; Zuckerman & Weiner, 2005), PPI (Meyer, Spoerri, et al., 2010), and APMH-induced hyperlocomotion (Piontkewitz et al., 2009) in various MIA models. MIA offspring also exhibit improved cognitive behavior after subchronic CLZ treatment, as measured in the novel-object recognition test (Ozawa et al., 2006), wet T-maze (Zuckerman & Weiner, 2005), and alternative Morris water maze (Meyer, Knuesel, et al., 2010). In addition to conferring beneficial effects on behavior, chronic CLZ treatment during

periadolescence corrects several key neuropathologies in MIA offspring, including enlarged ventricles and reduced hippocampal volume (Piontkewitz et al., 2009). Interestingly, acute CLZ treatment also improves the abnormal synchronization of neural networks seen in MIA offspring, as measured by dose-dependent increases in theta frequency coherence between the prefrontal cortex and hippocampus (Dickerson et al., 2012).

Another drug that effectively treats symptoms in MIA offspring is risperidone (RIS), an atypical antipsychotic that activates dopamine and serotonin receptors (Pratt et al., 2012). Chronic postnatal RIS treatment corrects abnormalities in LI, rapid reversal learning, and APMH-induced hyperlocomotion in rat MIA offspring (Richtand et al., 2011). Magnetic resonance imaging analysis demonstrates that RIS treatment also prevents the enlargement of lateral ventricles and reduction of hippocampal volume in MIA offspring (Piontkewitz et al., 2011). Moreover, MIA-induced impairments in neurogenesis, hippocampal capillarization, granular cell density, levels of hippocampal parvalbumin-positive GABAergic interneurons, and levels of cortical extracellular glutamate (Roenker et al., 2011) are each improved by chronic RIS treatment (Piontkewitz et al., 2012).

Other atypical antipsychotic drugs, such as paliperidone (a serotonin receptor 2A receptor and dopamine receptor antagonist) and aripiprazole (a dopamine agonist) also effectively treat schizophrenia-related symptoms in MIA offspring. As with RIS, paliperidone treatment normalizes levels of extracellular glutamate in the prefrontal cortex of rats born to MIA mothers (Roenker et al., 2011). Both paliperidone and aripiprazole correct APMH-induced locomotion in the MIA model as well (Richtand et al., 2011, 2012). In addition, the typical antipsychotic and dopamine receptor agonist haloperidol (HAL) (Pratt et al., 2012) prevents abnormal LI behavior (Zuckerman et al., 2003) and AMPH-induced hyperlocomotion in MIA offspring (Meyer, Spoerri, et al., 2010). Interestingly, the selective serotonin reuptake inhibitor antidepressant fluoxetine (FLX) also exhibits therapeutic effects in the MIA model. Oral treatment with FLX during adolescence improves abnormalities in PPI and AMPH-induced hyperlocomotion in MIA offspring (Meyer, Spoerri, et al., 2010; Richtand et al., 2012).

Dietary choline supplementation is being increasingly explored as a potential treatment for schizophrenia-related symptoms, based on associations of schizophrenia with genetic disruptions alpha7 nicotinic acetylcholine receptor (α7nAChR) (Freedman et al., 1997; Leonard et al., 2002), decreased brain α7nAChR expression (Freedman, Adams, & Leonard, 2000), and maternal choline deficiency (Miwa, Freedman, & Lester, 2011; Ross et al., 2010). Moreover, stimulation of α7nAChR during the embryonic stage is important for the development of fetal brain inhibitory neurocircuits and sensorimotor gating behavior (Miwa et al., 2011; Ross et al., 2010). Interestingly, MIA offspring, which display abnormalities in sensorimotor gating, anxiety, sociability, and repetitive behavior, exhibit improved behavioral performance after perinatal choline supplementation (Wu, Adams, Chow, Stevens, & Patterson, in preparation). This is consistent with the finding that perinatal choline supplementation improves the deficient P50 sensorimotor gating behavior in the inbred DBA mouse strain (Stevens et al., 2008).

Overall, several known antipsychotic drugs exhibit therapeutic effects on the MIA model, supporting the predictive validity of the model for advancing studies on the neurobiological bases of drug treatment. The face, construct, and predictive validity of the MIA model render it useful for studying underlying mechanisms of disease etiopathogenesis and drug efficacy (Figure 2).

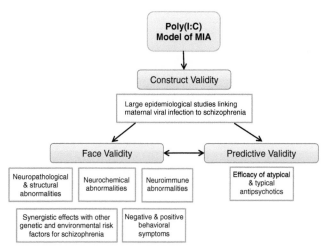

FIGURE 2   Construct, face, and predictive validity of the polyinosine-polycytidylic approach for maternal immune activation (MIA).

GENE–ENVIRONMENT INTERACTIONS

Although modeling MIA in animals is useful for studying maternal infection as a primary environmental risk factor for schizophrenia, it is important to note that maternal infection on its own is not *causal* for schizophrenia. That is, epidemiological studies indicate that maternal infection is associated with schizophrenia and increases the risk, or odds ratio, for schizophrenia in the offspring, but certainly, children born to mothers that experience infection during pregnancy do not necessarily develop schizophrenia. Schizophrenia is a complex, multifactorial disorder, believed to be caused by a combination of several genetic and environmental risk factors. In the context of MIA, it is plausible that maternal infection causes schizophrenia in the context of additional genetic susceptibility factors. An increasing number of studies are focused on so-called gene–environment interactions, and several reveal interesting interactions between MIA and known susceptibility genes for schizophrenia.

Interestingly, induction of MIA exacerbates several behavioral, neuropathological, and neurochemical abnormalities seen in mice overexpressing mutant human DISC1 (mhDISC1) (Abazyan et al., 2010). Disrupted-in-schizophrenia 1 (DISC1) is a prominent susceptibility gene for schizophrenia, which encodes a pleiotropic protein that regulates a variety of biological processes (Brandon et al., 2009; Brandon & Sawa, 2011). Gene–environment interactions are similarly seen with maternal poly (I:C) injection and point mutation of the DISC1 gene at L100P (*Disc1*-L100P$^{+/-}$) (Lipina, Zai, Hlousek, Roder, & Wong, 2013). Synergistic gene–environment interactions are also seen with MIA and the steroid hormone receptor Nurr1 (NR4A2). MIA induction in *Nurr1*$^{+/-}$ mice leads to hyperlocomotion, deficient PPI, and decreased sustained attention compared with control *Nurr1*$^{+/-}$ offspring (Vuillermot et al., 2012).

MIA also displays a synergistic interaction with the *CHRNA7* gene, which encodes for the alpha-7 acetylcholine receptor (α7nAChR). Mutations in *CHRNA7* are associated with an elevated risk for schizophrenia (Freedman et al., 1997). Recent studies demonstrate that offspring with reduced expression of α7nAChR are more vulnerable to prenatal poly (I:C) injection (Wu et al., in preparation).

ENVIRONMENT–ENVIRONMENT INTERACTIONS

MIA is being increasingly explored in the context of other environmental risk factors, wherein perinatal infection synergizes with postnatal challenges such as stress or drug exposure to precipitate schizophrenia-related endophenotypes. The notion that an additional postnatal insult potentiates detrimental effects of a prenatal environmental risk exposure is often referred to as the "two-hit hypothesis."

Postnatal stress is an environmental risk factor for schizophrenia (Brown, 2011) and has been studied in tandem with MIA in environment–environment interaction models. Combining prenatal immune challenge with postnatal restraint stress leads to synergistic effects on the development of deficient behavior and neuropathology (Deslauriers, Larouche, Sarret, & Grignon, 2013). A similar paradigm evaluating this two-hit hypothesis involves prenatal immune challenge followed by variable and unpredictable stress during peripubertal development (Giovanoli et al., 2013), where MIA and peripubertal stress produce synergistic effects on the development of abnormal behavior, microgliosis, and immune activation (Giovanoli et al., 2013). In addition, direct effects of MIA on abnormal maternal care can introduce postnatal stress on the developing offspring (Meyer, Nyffeler, Schwendener, et al., 2008; Meyer, Schwendener, et al., 2006; Richetto, Calabrese, Meyer, & Riva, 2013). Interestingly, cross-fostering control offspring to MIA surrogate mothers sufficiently leads to specific neurochemical abnormalities (Meyer, Nyffeler, Schwendener, et al., 2008; Richetto et al., 2013). This supports the two-hit hypothesis, suggesting that traumatizing postnatal experiences interact with MIA to precipitate the presentation of schizophrenia-related symptoms.

Abuse of drugs, such as cannabis, during adolescence is also linked to an increased risk for psychotic outcome and schizophrenia (Brown, 2011). In a rat model examining the synergistic effects of cannabis usage and MIA, offspring born to poly (I:C)-injected mothers that are exposed to cannabinoid display an elevated 5-HT1AR binding activity (Dalton, Verdurand, Walker, Hodgson, & Zavitsanou, 2012). This suggests that prenatal infection and adolescent cannabinoid exposure interact with

each other to modulate the brain serotonergic system. Hallucinogenic drug abuse also contributes to the onset of schizophrenia (Paparelli, Di Forti, Morrison, & Murray, 2011). MIA offspring display stronger DOI-induced behavioral responses and greater brain activity that can be explained by increased levels of 5HT-2A in the prefrontal cortex (Holloway et al., 2013; Malkova et al., 2014).

Overall, translating the maternal infection risk factor to animal models reveals that immune activation during pregnancy can perturb neurodevelopment in the offspring, and lead to the development of neuropathological and behavioral symptoms of schizophrenia. Furthermore, an increasing number of so-called gene–environment and environment–environment studies demonstrate that MIA interacts with genetic and environmental susceptibility factors for schizophrenia to potentiate schizophrenia-related abnormalities. Based on considerable construct, face and predictive validity for schizophrenia, animal models for maternal infection and MIA are useful for investigations into the molecular underpinnings of and treatments for schizophrenia-related symptoms.

NEONATAL POLY (I:C) MODEL

A challenge to translating the maternal infection risk factor to animal models is in accounting for species-dependent differences in physiological development. For example, glia proliferation and migration are known to reach a peak during the second trimester of pregnancy in humans, whereas in rodents this critical developmental period occurs during the early neonatal period (Nawa & Takei, 2006). This period is also known to be a critical time for neurogenesis in the hippocampus and for cortical synaptogenesis (Bayer, Altman, Russo, & Zhang, 1993). To account for disparity between the timing of brain development in humans versus rodents, many investigators use a modified MIA model, in which poly (I:C) is administered neonatally to better mimic brain development during the second trimester in humans (Ibi et al., 2009; Nagai, Yu, Kitahara, Nabeshima, & Yamada, 2012; Ribeiro et al., 2013). Neonatal mice or rats repeatedly injected with poly (I:C) during the first week of postnatal life (postnatal days 2–6 for mice and postnatal days 5–7 for rats, respectively) develop deficient PPI behavior (Ibi et al., 2009; Nagai et al., 2012; Ribeiro et al., 2013), increased anxiety impaired social behavior (Hida et al., 2014; Ibi et al., 2009; Nagai et al., 2012), and deficient memory (Ibi et al., 2009; Nagai et al., 2012; Ribeiro et al., 2013). Moreover, these animals display enhanced sensitivity to methamphetamine (MAP)-induced hyperactivity in adolescence (Hida et al., 2014), which could be interpreted as a schizophrenia-related positive symptom. Several neurophysiological abnormalities are observed in response to neonatal poly (I:C) injection, including decreased glutamate release (Ibi et al., 2009), microglial activation (Ribeiro et al., 2013), and oxidative stress (Ribeiro et al., 2013). Interestingly, CLZ treatment of adult rats exposed to neonatal immune challenge ameliorates microglial activation and signs of oxidative stress, and further reverses PPI and working memory deficits (Ribeiro et al., 2013). D-serine, an endogenous coagonist of NMDA receptors, is also effective in treating emotional and cognitive deficits in poly (I:C)–treated mice (Ribeiro et al., 2013).

Altogether, these results demonstrate that the neonatal poly (I:C) model displays strong face validity for behavioral and neuropathological symptoms of schizophrenia as well as some intriguing predictive validity. The behavioral abnormalities induced by neonatal poly (I:C) exposure are consistent with what is observed in maternal poly (I:C) models (Harvey & Boksa, 2012a; Ibi et al., 2009). Both paradigms lead to increased anxiety, impaired PPI, abnormal social interaction, deficient working memory, and glutamatergic hypofunction. The antipsychotic CLZ is effective in ameliorating particular schizophrenia-related phenotypes in both the maternal and neonatal poly (I:C) models. However, many behavioral and biochemical abnormalities that are reported for MIA remain to be assessed in the neonatal poly (I:C) models. Moreover, although neonatal immune challenge may better mimic construct validity in terms of the timing of brain development, there are several potential disadvantages of neonatal poly (I:C) injection compared with maternal poly (I:C) injection. First, neonatal rodents are directly exposed to the immune challenge with poly (I:C), whereas in case of MIA there is a combination of complex interactions between maternal, placental, and embryonic sites. Second, the immune response to poly (I:C) is likely different in pregnant females versus neonatal animals. The mature maternal immune system undergoes phasic changes in cellular function and cytokine profiles during pregnancy, and the immune system of neonatal animals is relatively immature; therefore, the cytokine response may vary under these two conditions. Third, daily injections and stress may contribute to the behavioral and biochemical abnormalities observed in the neonatal model. Fourth, early life infection can be an independent risk factor for schizophrenia and other neurodevelopmental disorders (Harvey & Boksa, 2012a). Taking this into account, replication of other behavioral phenotypes and morphological abnormalities reported for MIA models and schizophrenia patients as well as investigation of the role of the dopaminergic and serotonergic systems in the control of these changes will be a promising avenue for future studies in the neonatal poly (I:C) model.

MODELING MIA IN PRIMATES

The rodent MIA models allow scientists to investigate the mechanistic bases underlying how maternal infection impacts neurodevelopment and leads to the pathogenesis of symptoms relevant to schizophrenia. However, there are some obstacles to studying MIA in rodents, such as the need to account for differences between rodents and humans in behavioral presentation and brain development. The onset of key brain developmental events varies across humans, mice, and rats (Workman, Charvet, Clancy, Darlington, & Finlay, 2013) (Figure 3). Induction of MIA at gestational days (GD) 9–10 in mouse resembles the midphase of the human first trimester of gestation, wherein locus coeruleus development, Purkinje cell differentiation, and hippocampal neurogenesis occurs. Induction of MIA at GD 17 in mouse corresponds most similarly to the early second trimester in humans, during which the corpus callosum

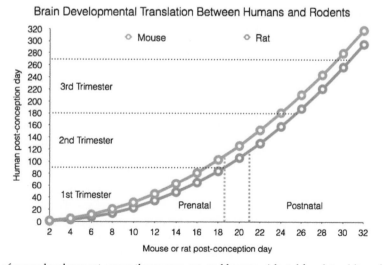

FIGURE 3 Trajectory of neurodevelopment across the mouse, rat, and human. *Adapted from* http://translatingtime.org/translate.

appears, and early hippocampal and cortical neurogenesis reach completion. As such, it is not surprising that variations in the timing of MIA exposure across various MIA models may yield differential effects on neurodevelopment and behavior. A caveat of rodent MIA models is that key neurodevelopmental events characteristic of the second trimester of human gestation occur postnatally in mice and rats. In addition, the lack of behavior complexity in rodents is a primary drawback to studying the role of MIA in predisposing for a human disease that is characterized by complex cognitive, social, and affective symptoms.

As an alternative to mice and rats, the rhesus monkey is a species that lives in a complicated, hierarchical social system. Rhesus monkeys exhibit complex facial expression and social gestures to communicate with conspecies, with developmental trajectories that better match those of humans (Capitanio & Emborg, 2008). A recent study translates the MIA model to nonhuman primates, where pregnant rhesus monkeys are injected with a modified form of poly (I:C), called poly (ICLC), which is stabilized with poly-L-lysine and thus adapted for use in primates. Pregnant monkeys intravenously injected with 0.25 mg/kg poly (ICLC) during the first trimester (GDs 43, 44, and 46) or second trimester (GDs 100, 101, and 103) yield behavioral abnormalities relevant to both autism and schizophrenia. Young MIA offspring display abnormal distress and self-soothing behaviors, such as tantrums, convulsive jerk, self-clasp, and infant crook tail. They also produce persistently increased motor stereotypic and self-directed behaviors and fewer contact "coo" calls than control offspring. Social behavior was similarly abnormal in a social approach assay, wherein the testing monkey is given the opportunity to interact with a novel conspecific monkey. Offspring born to mothers exposed to MIA during the first trimester of gestation display inappropriate social interactions, characterized by more duration spent with and in proximity to the unfamiliar monkey. Overall, this study demonstrates that injection of pregnant rhesus monkeys with modified poly (I:C) yields offspring that display several behavioral abnormalities relevant to neurodevelopmental disorders, including schizophrenia. Future studies aimed toward testing construct and predictive validity in the MIA monkey model will be of significant interest.

MIA AS A RISK FACTOR FOR AUTISM SPECTRUM DISORDER AND SCHIZOPHRENIA

Several large epidemiological studies reveal that maternal infection is associated with an increased risk for, not only schizophrenia, but also autism spectrum disorder (ASD) in the offspring. Consistent with this, there are several clinical and biological links between ASD and schizophrenia (Brown, 2012a). In fact, the term "autism" was first introduced by the Swiss psychiatrist Eugen Bleuler to describe social and communication impairments seen in schizophrenic individuals. In addition, enhanced anxiety and deficient sensorimotor gating are similarly seen in both disorders. Structural and functional abnormalities in the cerebellum, insular cortex, and fusiform gyrus are similar in both autistic and schizophrenic individuals (Cheung et al., 2010). Additionally, deficits in reelin, a neuronal protein involved in the control of neuronal connectivity and synaptic plasticity, are seen in both disorders (Folsom & Fatemi, 2013). These shared abnormalities may reflect common etiological mechanisms (Brown, 2012a).

Consistent with this, maternal poly (I:C) injection in mice results in symptoms that are relevant to either, or both, disorders. Importantly MIA yields offspring with the core diagnostic features of ASD—impaired communication, decreased social interaction, and stereotyped behaviors—as well as a hallmark neuropathology of ASD, a spatially restricted deficit in Purkinje cells. The hyperresponsiveness to hallucinogenic drugs and enlarged ventricles seen in MIA offspring may be more relevant to schizophrenia. The age of onset for particular phenotypes also recapitulate the human conditions, where ASD is diagnosed by 3 years of age, whereas schizophrenia most commonly diagnosed during adolescence. MIA offspring display decreased communication, a key symptom of ASD, as early as first week of postnatal development (Malkova, Yu, Hsiao, Moore, & Patterson, 2012), whereas schizophrenia-related behavioral phenotypes are seen later in adulthood (Meyer, Schwendener, et al., 2006; Vuillermot et al., 2010). There are also behavioral abnormalities in MIA offspring that are reported in both ASD and schizophrenia, such as elevated anxiety and deficient sensorimotor gating. Overall, consistent with maternal infection as a risk factor for both schizophrenia and ASD, the MIA model exhibits both symptoms in common between the disorders and symptoms that differentiate them.

That maternal poly (I:C) injection models phenotypes relevant to both schizophrenia and autism raises the interesting question of whether changes in the type, timing, route, or dosage of immune activation can skew the types or severity of neuropathological and behavioral abnormalities in the offspring. Interestingly, there is some evidence that poly (I:C) injections at different gestational stages are associated with distinctive psychopathological profiles in the adult offspring. MIA during early gestation yields offspring that exhibit suppressed spatial exploration, deficient sensorimotor gating, and disrupted latent inhibition, whereas MIA induced during late gestation yields offspring with potentiated MK-801 sensitivity, impaired working memory, and retarded reversal learning. Some behavioral phenotypes, such as potentiated AMPH sensitivity and loss of unconditioned stimulus-preexposure effect, are commonly observed with both MIA approaches (Meyer, Feldon, & Yee, 2009). MIA-induced neuropathologies also differ by timing of injection. MIA during early gestation yields offspring with reduced D1R and D2R expression in the medial prefrontal cortex, increased GABA$_A$-R subunit alpha 2 in the amygdala, and enhanced tyrosine hydroxylase in the nucleus accumbens, whereas MIA induction during late gestation results in offspring with reduced NR1 expression in the dorsal hippocampus, increased GABA$_A$-R subunit in the ventral hippocampus and reduced parvalbumin expression in the hippocampus. Reduced reelin and parvalbumin expression in the medial prefrontal cortex is commonly observed across both MIA approaches (Meyer et al., 2009). Overall, these studies suggest that early MIA results in behaviors that resemble positive symptoms of schizophrenia whereas injections at later time points yield impaired cognitive symptoms (Meyer, Feldon, et al., 2006; Meyer, Knuesel, et al., 2010; Meyer, Nyffeler, Schwendener, et al., 2008). Additional work on comparing ASD and schizophrenia related symptoms with changes in exposure to MIA will be of significant interest.

POTENTIAL MECHANISMS UNDERLYING THE EFFECTS OF MIA

Although several laboratories have investigated the face, construct, and predictive validity of MIA animal models, key questions regarding the molecular mechanisms linking MIA to abnormal neurodevelopment and behavior remain. Converging evidence highlights an important role for maternal cytokines in relaying the maternal immune response to the developing embryo. As a direct response to MIA, levels of pro-inflammatory cytokines, such as IL-6, TNF-α, and interferon (IFN)-γ, are elevated in maternal blood (Connor et al., 2012; Harvey & Boksa, 2012b; Meyer, Feldon, et al., 2006; O'Leary et al., 2014; Vuillermot et al., 2012), consistent with inflammation and reductions in maternal weight gain by 24h post-MIA (Dalton et al., 2012). Elevations in maternal pro-inflammatory cytokines are transient, declining by 48h post-MIA (Meyer, Engler, et al., 2008). Importantly, the cytokine IL-6 is critical for mediating the effects of poly (I:C)–induced MIA on offspring behavior (Smith et al., 2007). Coinjection of poly (I:C) with a blocking antibody against IL-6, or injection of poly (I:C) into IL-6 knockout mice, effectively prevents the development of abnormal PPI, anxiety, and sociability in MIA offspring. In contrast, maternal injection of recombinant IL-6 instead of poly (I:C) sufficiently yields offspring with behavioral abnormalities. Interestingly,

MIA-induced increases in IL-6 and TNF-α are significantly reduced after poly (I:C) injection into pregnant mice with genetic overexpression of IL-10 from macrophages (macIL-10tg) (Meyer, Murray, et al., 2008), highlighting a potential role for maternal macrophages in modulating the MIA response. Overall, the finding that IL-6 is both necessary and sufficient for mediating effects of MIA offers a direction for tracing the biological pathways that lead to abnormal brain development and behavior relevant to schizophrenia and ASD.

As the primary site of direct maternal–fetal interactions, the placenta plays an important role in translating the maternal response to MIA into the developing fetus. Shortly after MIA, pro-inflammatory cytokines are increased in the placenta, with corresponding activation of decidual immune cells (Hsiao & Patterson, 2011). Placental IL-6 is particularly elevated, and is critical for relaying the MIA response to fetally derived cells in the placenta. These effects of maternally derived placental IL-6 on activation of fetal trophoblast cells result in significant changes in levels of endocrine factors, such as insulin-like growth factor 1 and placental pro-lactin-like proteins. Increasing evidence suggests an important effect of placental physiology on neurodevelopment (Hsiao & Patterson, 2011, 2012), raising the important question of whether placental responses to MIA are required for downstream effects on fetal brain. Placental IL-6 signaling is particularly important, as conditional knockout of IL-6R in placental trophoblast cells sufficiently prevents downstream effects of MIA on fetal brain activation, behavior, and neuropathology.

In addition to impacting placental immune and endocrine responses, MIA induces rapid increases in levels of several cytokines and chemokines directly in the fetal brain. In particular, IL-1β, IL-4, IL-5, IL-6, IL-17, and IL-13, the chemokines MCP-1 and MIP1α, are elevated, suggesting that these factors confer deleterious effects of MIA on neurodevelopment (Abazyan et al., 2010; Arrode-Bruses & Bruses, 2012; Connor et al., 2012; Meyer, Nyffeler, Engler, et al., 2006; Meyer, Nyffeler, Schwendener, et al., 2008; Pratt, Ni, Ponzio, & Jonakait, 2013). In addition, chronic postnatal changes in brain cytokine levels are observed in MIA offspring, supporting the notion that early effects of MIA lead to prenatal programming of long-term neuroimmune dysfunction. Several cytokines are elevated in the prefrontal cortex of newly born mice, followed by decreases during early adolescence and further increase in the adulthood (Garay, Hsiao, Patterson, & McAllister, 2013). Several studies demonstrate that alterations in brain cytokine levels lead to abnormal behavioral development. For example, intracerebroventricular administration of IL-1β induces stress, anxiety-like behavior, and memory impairment, in addition to changes in neurotransmission

(Song, Manku, & Horrobin, 2008; Song, Phillips, Leonard, & Horrobin, 2004).

Global alterations in gene expression patterns are also detected in the fetal brain shortly after MIA. Several genes, including those encoding crystalline family proteins known to play important roles in developmental neurogenesis, are highly upregulated in the fetal brain by 3h post-MIA (Garbett, Hsiao, Kalman, Patterson, & Mirnics, 2012). Interestingly, increases in *Cryaa*, *Cryba1*, and *Crybb1* transcript are highly correlated with the severity of placental weight loss, suggesting a potential link between placental and fetal brain responses to MIA. Genes related to dopaminergic development, such as *Shh*, *Fgf8*, *Nurr1*, and *Pitx3*, are also altered in fetal brains after maternal poly (I:C) injection (Meyer, Engler, et al., 2008). Consistent with this, MIA offspring display elevated levels of dopamine transporter in the fetal ventral midbrain as well as increased tyrosine hydroxylase positive neurons in the ventral aspect of the fetal mesencephalic flexure. Fetal cholinergic activity is also elevated, with increased choline acetyltransferase activity in basal forebrain after maternal poly (I:C) injection (Pratt et al., 2013). In addition, MIA impairs cortical progenitor proliferation and the formation of the cortical laminar layer in the fetal brain (Soumiya, Fukumitsu, & Furukawa, 2011). Overall, activation of the maternal immune system during gestation induces a rapid response in the placental and fetal brain that leads to impaired neurodevelopment and lasting behavioral abnormalities relevant to both autism and schizophrenia.

IMMUNE ABNORMALITIES IN SCHIZOPHRENIA

The neuroimmunological abnormalities induced by the MIA model align well with increasing evidence that immune dysregulation plays an important role in the etiology and clinical manifestations of schizophrenia. Elevated levels of cytokines are detected in the cerebrospinal fluid, plasma, and sera of schizophrenic individuals, suggesting chronic immune dysfunction (Miller, Buckley, Seabolt, Mellor, & Kirkpatrick, 2011; Potvin et al., 2008; Song, Lv, Li, Hao, & Zhao, 2009). In addition, peripheral blood leukocytes isolated from schizophrenic individuals are hyperresponsive to in vitro stimulation, consistent with pro-inflammatory–like immune phenotypes in schizophrenia. Interestingly, a meta-analysis of 40 studies assessing blood and cerebrospinal fluid cytokines in schizophrenia and first-episode psychosis patients reveals that levels IL-1β, IL-6, and transforming growth factor-beta are increased in both states, and are normalized by antipsychotic treatment (Miller et al., 2011). Similarly, higher levels of IL-1β are in peripheral blood leukocytes from schizophrenic individuals, and this effect is ameliorated by treatment with risperidone (Song et al., 2009). These findings suggest that changes in cytokine levels contribute to or respond to changes in schizophrenia-related symptoms.

Alterations in immune-related genes are also detected by transcriptomic profiling of human postmortem brains from schizophrenic individuals (Arion, Unger, Lewis, Levitt, & Mirnics, 2007; Hwang et al., 2013; Saetre et al., 2007). In addition to alterations in brain cytokine gene expression (Dean et al., 2013; Rao, Kim, Harry, Rapoport, & Reese, 2013), cortical and hippocampal expression of *SERPINA3*, *IFITM2* and *IFITM3* is upregulated in schizophrenia (Arion et al., 2007; Saetre et al., 2007). *SERPINA3* encodes serpin peptidase inhibitor (alpha-1 antiproteinase, antitrypsin), which is widely expressed by immune cells during an inflammatory response. *IFITM 2* and *3* are interferon induced transmembrane proteins, synthesized as part of an antiviral proinflammatory immune response. TNF-β, IFN-α, and IFN-γ elevate expression of *SERPINA3*, *IFITM2*, and *IFITM3* in oligodendrocyte and endothelial cells (Saetre et al., 2007), suggesting a cascading effect of cytokine dysregulation on brain function.

Consistent with both peripheral and central immune abnormalities, brains of schizophrenic individuals also exhibit abnormal microglial and astrocyte physiology. Elevated microglial activation, as measured by expression of class II human leucocyte antigen (HLA-DR), is observed in the postmortem frontal cortex and hippocampus (Bayer, Buslei, Havas, & Falkai, 1999; Radewicz, Garey, Gentleman, & Reynolds, 2000; Steiner, Bielau, et al., 2008). Degenerative traits of microglia, including cytoplasm shrinkage, phagosomes, and process thinning, shortening, and fragmentation are seen in the schizophrenic frontal and temporal cortex (Wierzba-Bobrowicz et al., 2004; Wierzba-Bobrowicz, Lewandowska, Lechowicz, Stepien, & Pasennik, 2005). Furthermore, quantitative (R)-[(11)C]PK11195 positron emission tomography scan provides evidence of increased microglial activation in total gray matter of living schizophrenic individuals (van Berckel et al., 2008). In addition, elevated levels of the astrocyte marker, GFAP, are seen in the dorsal lateral prefrontal cortex (Rajkowska et al., 2002) and various subcortical regions (Barley, Dracheva, & Byne, 2009), whereas reduced levels of GFAP are reported for the anterior cingulate cortex and corpus callosum (Steffek, McCullumsmith, Haroutunian, & Meador-Woodruff, 2008; Webster, O'Grady, Kleinman, & Weickert, 2005; Williams et al., 2013). There is also evidence of altered astrocyte function, in which increases in the activation marker S100B are seen in dorsal lateral prefrontal cortex, particularly in paranoid schizophrenics (Steiner, Bernstein, et al., 2008).

IMMUNE-RELATED GENETIC RISK FACTORS FOR SCHIZOPHRENIA

Although several environmental risk factors for schizophrenia seem to converge on immune activation pathways, many immune-related genetic risk factors, including common gene variants, copy number variations, and short nucleotide polymorphisms, are also associated with schizophrenia. The most replicable site is on chromosome 6, which harbors specific haplotypes of immune genes, including those encoding major histocompatibility complex (MHC) proteins. Consistent with this, several large genome-wide studies have together identified over 450 schizophrenia-associated short nucleotide polymorphisms that map to the MHC locus (International Schizophrenia et al., 2009; Jia et al., 2012; Lee, Woon, Teo, & Sim, 2012; Michel, Schmidt, & Mirnics, 2012; Shi et al., 2009; Stefansson et al., 2009). In addition, a meta-analysis of data from genome-wide association studies significantly associates a region of linkage disequilibrium on chromosome 6p22.1–6p21.31 with schizophrenia (Shi et al., 2009). MHC1 is involved in different aspects of immunity, brain development, and synaptic plasticity (McAllister, 2014). Short nucleotide polymorphism rs6904-71, located in the MHC region, is associated with delayed episodic memory and decreased hippocampal volume in schizophrenia and healthy subjects (Walters et al., 2013). Interestingly, two protective HLA alleles, HLA-B*08:01 and DRB1*03:01, have been identified (Irish Schizophrenia Genomics & the Wellcome Trust Case Control, 2012). In searching for schizophrenia susceptibility genes in the class III region of the human MHC, three short nucleotide polymorphisms near the NOTCH4 locus are associated with schizophrenia-rs1009382, rs204887, and rs8283 (Wei & Hemmings, 2004). Mutations in stimulating factor receptor 2 alpha (*CSF2RA*), *IL3RA*, *IL1*, and the promoter haplotype for *TNFA* are also linked to schizophrenia (Katila, Hanninen, & Hurme, 1999; Lencz et al., 2007; Saviouk, Chow, Bassett, & Brzustowicz, 2005). Altogether, these findings suggest that genetic predisposition can contribute to the widespread immune dysregulation observed in schizophrenic individuals and further raises the interesting notion of convergent pathways by which immune-related environmental and genetic risk factors contribute to the etiopathology of schizophrenia.

CONCLUSION

Modeling MIA in animal models is a powerful approach for investigating the neurobiological underpinnings of schizophrenia and autism endophenotypes, and for further testing the efficacy of novel therapeutics in treating neuropathological, neurochemical, and behavioral features of disease. To date, several laboratories have validated the face, construct, and predictive validity of maternal poly (I:C) exposure on yielding offspring with schizophrenia-related symptoms. Studies aimed toward elucidating the mechanisms linking MIA to abnormal fetal neurodevelopment and further linking disruptions in early life brain development to later life behavioral abnormalities are warranted, and offer the exciting prospect of uncovering novel molecular targets for defined interventions. In light of increasing evidence for etiological and phenotypic overlap between schizophrenia and autism, the MIA model may serve as a useful tool for evaluating parallel and/or independent pathways for the etiopathogenesis of particular symptoms of disease. Moreover, MIA models are becoming increasingly valuable for the study of multifactorial contributions to schizophrenia by studying the effects of gene–environment and environment–environment interactions on manifesting or potentiating symptom severity.

References

Abazyan, B., Nomura, J., Kannan, G., Ishizuka, K., Tamashiro, K. L., Nucifora, F., et al. (2010). Prenatal interaction of mutant DISC1 and immune activation produces adult psychopathology. *Biological Psychiatry, 68*, 1172–1181.

Arion, D., Unger, T., Lewis, D. A., Levitt, P., & Mirnics, K. (2007). Molecular evidence for increased expression of genes related to immune and chaperone function in the prefrontal cortex in schizophrenia. *Biological Psychiatry, 62*, 711–721.

Arrode-Bruses, G., & Bruses, J. L. (2012). Maternal immune activation by poly I: C induces expression of cytokines IL-1beta and IL-13, chemokine MCP-1 and colony stimulating factor VEGF in fetal mouse brain. *Journal of Neuroinflammation, 9*, 83.

Babulas, V., Factor-Litvak, P., Goetz, R., Schaefer, C. A., & Brown, A. S. (2006). Prenatal exposure to maternal genital and reproductive infections and adult schizophrenia. *American Journal of Psychiatry, 163*, 927–929.

Barley, K., Dracheva, S., & Byne, W. (2009). Subcortical oligodendrocyte- and astrocyte-associated gene expression in subjects with schizophrenia, major depression and bipolar disorder. *Schizophrenia Research, 112*, 54–64.

Bayer, S. A., Altman, J., Russo, R. J., & Zhang, X. (1993). Timetables of neurogenesis in the human brain based on experimentally determined patterns in the rat. *Neurotoxicology, 14*, 83–144.

Bayer, T. A., Buslei, R., Havas, L., & Falkai, P. (1999). Evidence for activation of microglia in patients with psychiatric illnesses. *Neuroscience Letters, 271*, 126–128.

van Berckel, B. N., Bossong, M. G., Boellaard, R., Kloet, R., Schuitemaker, A., Caspers, E., et al. (2008). Microglia activation in recent-onset schizophrenia: a quantitative (R)-[11C]PK11195 positron emission tomography study. *Biological Psychiatry, 64*, 820–822.

Bitanihirwe, B. K., Peleg-Raibstein, D., Mouttet, F., Feldon, J., & Meyer, U. (2010). Late prenatal immune activation in mice leads to behavioral and neurochemical abnormalities relevant to the negative symptoms of schizophrenia. *Neuropsychopharmacology: Official Publication of the American College of Neuropsychopharmacology, 35*, 2462–2478.

Brandon, N. J., Millar, J. K., Korth, C., Sive, H., Singh, K. K., & Sawa, A. (2009). Understanding the role of DISC1 in psychiatric disease and during normal development. *Journal of Neuroscience: the Official Journal of the Society for Neuroscience, 29*, 12768–12775.

Brandon, N. J., & Sawa, A. (2011). Linking neurodevelopmental and synaptic theories of mental illness through DISC1. *Nature Reviews Neuroscience, 12*, 707–722.

Brown, A. S. (2006). Prenatal infection as a risk factor for schizophrenia. *Schizophrenia Bulletin, 32*, 200–202.

Brown, A. S. (2011). The environment and susceptibility to schizophrenia. *Progress in Neurobiology, 93*, 23–58.

Brown, A. S. (2012a). Epidemiologic studies of exposure to prenatal infection and risk of schizophrenia and autism. *Developmental Neurobiology, 72*, 1272–1276.

Brown, A. S. (2012b). Maternal infection and schizophrenia. In A. S. Brown, & P. H. Patterson (Eds.), *The origins of schizophrenia* (pp. 25–57). Columbia University Press.

Brown, A. S., Begg, M. D., Gravenstein, S., Schaefer, C. A., Wyatt, R. J., Bresnahan, M., et al. (2004). Serologic evidence of prenatal influenza in the etiology of schizophrenia. *Archives of General Psychiatry, 61*, 774–780.

Brown, A. S., Hooton, J., Schaefer, C. A., Zhang, H., Petkova, E., Babulas, V., et al. (2004). Elevated maternal interleukin-8 levels and risk of schizophrenia in adult offspring. *American Journal of Psychiatry, 161*, 889–895.

Brown, A. S., & Patterson, P. H. (2011). Maternal infection and schizophrenia: implications for prevention. *Schizophrenia Bulletin, 37*, 284–290.

Brown, A. S., Schaefer, C. A., Quesenberry, C. P., Jr., Liu, L., Babulas, V. P., & Susser, E. S. (2005). Maternal exposure to toxoplasmosis and risk of schizophrenia in adult offspring. *American Journal of Psychiatry, 162*, 767–773.

Buka, S. L., Tsuang, M. T., Torrey, E. F., Klebanoff, M. A., Bernstein, D., & Yolken, R. H. (2001). Maternal infections and subsequent psychosis among offspring. *Archives of General Psychiatry, 58*, 1032–1037.

Buka, S. L., Tsuang, M. T., Torrey, E. F., Klebanoff, M. A., Wagner, R. L., & Yolken, R. H. (2001). Maternal cytokine levels during pregnancy and adult psychosis. *Brain, Behavior, and Immunity, 15*, 411–420.

Capitanio, J. P., & Emborg, M. E. (2008). Contributions of non-human primates to neuroscience research. *Lancet, 371*, 1126–1135.

Cheung, C., Yu, K., Fung, G., Leung, M., Wong, C., Li, Q., et al. (2010). Autistic disorders and schizophrenia: related or remote? An anatomical likelihood estimation. *PLoS One, 5*, e12233.

Connor, C. M., Dincer, A., Straubhaar, J., Galler, J. R., Houston, I. B., & Akbarian, S. (2012). Maternal immune activation alters behavior in adult offspring, with subtle changes in the cortical transcriptome and epigenome. *Schizophrenia Research, 140*, 175–184.

Crump, C., Winkleby, M. A., Sundquist, K., & Sundquist, J. (2013). Comorbidities and mortality in persons with schizophrenia: a Swedish national cohort study. *American Journal of Psychiatry, 170*, 324–333.

Dalton, V. S., Verdurand, M., Walker, A., Hodgson, D. M., & Zavitsanou, K. (2012). Synergistic effect between maternal infection and adolescent cannabinoid exposure on serotonin 5HT1A receptor binding in the hippocampus: testing the "two hit" hypothesis for the development of schizophrenia. *ISRN Psychiatry, 2012*, 451865.

Davis, J. O., Phelps, J. A., & Bracha, H. S. (1995). Prenatal development of monozygotic twins and concordance for schizophrenia. *Schizophrenia Bulletin, 21*, 357–366.

Dean, B., Gibbons, A. S., Tawadros, N., Brooks, L., Everall, I. P., & Scarr, E. (2013). Different changes in cortical tumor necrosis factor-alpha-related pathways in schizophrenia and mood disorders. *Molecular Psychiatry, 18*, 767–773.

Delgado, M. G., & Bogousslavsky, J. (2013). 'Distorteidolias' – fantastic perceptive distortion. A new, pure dorsomedial thalamic syndrome. *European Neurology, 70*, 6–9.

Deslauriers, J., Larouche, A., Sarret, P., & Grignon, S. (2013). Combination of prenatal immune challenge and restraint stress affects prepulse inhibition and dopaminergic/GABAergic markers. *Progress in Neuro-Psychopharmacology & Biological Psychiatry, 45*, 156–164.

Deverman, B. E., & Patterson, P. H. (2009). Cytokines and CNS development. *Neuron, 64*, 61–78.

Dickerson, D. D., Restieaux, A. M., & Bilkey, D. K. (2012). Clozapine administration ameliorates disrupted long-range synchrony in a neurodevelopmental animal model of schizophrenia. *Schizophrenia Research, 135*, 112–115.

Dickerson, D. D., Wolff, A. R., & Bilkey, D. K. (2010). Abnormal long-range neural synchrony in a maternal immune activation animal model of schizophrenia. *Journal of Neuroscience: the Official Journal of the Society for Neuroscience, 30*, 12424–12431.

Eaton, W. W., Byrne, M., Ewald, H., Mors, O., Chen, C. Y., Agerbo, E., et al. (2006). Association of schizophrenia and autoimmune diseases: linkage of Danish national registers. *American Journal of Psychiatry, 163*, 521–528.

Ellman, L. M., Deicken, R. F., Vinogradov, S., Kremen, W. S., Poole, J. H., Kern, D. M., et al. (2010). Structural brain alterations in schizophrenia following fetal exposure to the inflammatory cytokine interleukin-8. *Schizophrenia Research, 121*, 46–54.

Ellman, L. M., Yolken, R. H., Buka, S. L., Torrey, E. F., & Cannon, T. D. (2009). Cognitive functioning prior to the onset of psychosis: the role of fetal exposure to serologically determined influenza infection. *Biological Psychiatry, 65*, 1040–1047.

Fatemi, S. H., Earle, J., Kanodia, R., Kist, D., Emamian, E. S., Patterson, P. H., et al. (2002). Prenatal viral infection leads to pyramidal cell atrophy and macrocephaly in adulthood: implications for genesis of autism and schizophrenia. *Cellular and Molecular Neurobiology, 22*, 25–33.

Fineberg, A. M., & Ellman, L. M. (2013). Inflammatory cytokines and neurological and neurocognitive alterations in the course of schizophrenia. *Biological Psychiatry, 73*, 951–966.

Folsom, T. D., & Fatemi, S. H. (2013). The involvement of Reelin in neurodevelopmental disorders. *Neuropharmacology, 68*, 122–135.

Freedman, R., Adams, C. E., & Leonard, S. (2000). The alpha7-nicotinic acetylcholine receptor and the pathology of hippocampal interneurons in schizophrenia. *Journal of Chemical Neuroanatomy, 20*, 299–306.

Freedman, R., Coon, H., Myles-Worsley, M., Orr-Urtreger, A., Olincy, A., Davis, A., et al. (1997). Linkage of a neurophysiological deficit in schizophrenia to a chromosome 15 locus. *Proceedings of the National Academy of Sciences of the United States of America, 94*, 587–592.

Galarza, M., Merlo, A. B., Ingratta, A., Albanese, E. F., & Albanese, A. M. (2004). Cavum septum pellucidum and its increased prevalence in schizophrenia: a neuroembryological classification. *Journal of Neuropsychiatry and Clinical Neurosciences, 16*, 41–46.

Garay, P. A., Hsiao, E. Y., Patterson, P. H., & McAllister, A. K. (2013). Maternal immune activation causes age- and region-specific changes in brain cytokines in offspring throughout development. *Brain, Behavior, and Immunity, 31*, 54–68.

Garbett, K. A., Hsiao, E. Y., Kalman, S., Patterson, P. H., & Mirnics, K. (2012). Effects of maternal immune activation on gene expression patterns in the fetal brain. *Translational Psychiatry, 2*, e98.

Giovanoli, S., Engler, H., Engler, A., Richetto, J., Voget, M., Willi, R., et al. (2013). Stress in puberty unmasks latent neuropathological consequences of prenatal immune activation in mice. *Science, 339*, 1095–1099.

Harrison, P. J. (2000a). Dopamine and schizophrenia–proof at last? *Lancet, 356*, 958–959.

Harrison, P. J. (2000b). Postmortem studies in schizophrenia. *Dialogues in Clinical Neuroscience, 2*, 349–357.

Harrison, P. J. (2004). The hippocampus in schizophrenia: a review of the neuropathological evidence and its pathophysiological implications. *Psychopharmacology, 174*, 151–162.

Harvey, L., & Boksa, P. (2012a). Prenatal and postnatal animal models of immune activation: relevance to a range of neurodevelopmental disorders. *Developmental Neurobiology, 72*, 1335–1348.

Harvey, L., & Boksa, P. (2012b). A stereological comparison of GAD67 and reelin expression in the hippocampal stratum oriens of offspring from two mouse models of maternal inflammation during pregnancy. *Neuropharmacology, 62*, 1767–1776.

Hida, H., Mouri, A., Ando, Y., Mori, K., Mamiya, T., Iwamoto, K., et al. (2014). Combination of neonatal PolyI: C and adolescent phencyclidine treatments is required to induce behavioral abnormalities with overexpression of GLAST in adult mice. *Behavioural Brain Research*, *258*, 34–42.

Holloway, T., Moreno, J. L., Umali, A., Rayannavar, V., Hodes, G. E., Russo, S. J., et al. (2013). Prenatal stress induces schizophrenia-like alterations of serotonin 2A and metabotropic glutamate 2 receptors in the adult offspring: role of maternal immune system. *Journal of Neuroscience: the Official Journal of the Society for Neuroscience*, *33*, 1088–1098.

Hsiao, E. Y., & Patterson, P. H. (2011). Activation of the maternal immune system induces endocrine changes in the placenta via IL-6. *Brain, Behavior, and Immunity*, *25*, 604–615.

Hsiao, E. Y., & Patterson, P. H. (2012). Placental regulation of maternal-fetal interactions and brain development. *Developmental Neurobiology*, *72*, 1317–1326.

Hwang, Y., Kim, J., Shin, J. Y., Kim, J. I., Seo, J. S., Webster, M. J., et al. (2013). Gene expression profiling by mRNA sequencing reveals increased expression of immune/inflammation-related genes in the hippocampus of individuals with schizophrenia. *Translational Psychiatry*, *3*, e321.

Ibi, D., Nagai, T., Kitahara, Y., Mizoguchi, H., Koike, H., Shiraki, A., et al. (2009). Neonatal polyI: C treatment in mice results in schizophrenia-like behavioral and neurochemical abnormalities in adulthood. *Neuroscience Research*, *64*, 297–305.

International Schizophrenia, C., Purcell, S. M., Wray, N. R., Stone, J. L., Visscher, P. M., O'Donovan, M. C., et al. (2009). Common polygenic variation contributes to risk of schizophrenia and bipolar disorder. *Nature*, *460*, 748–752.

Irish Schizophrenia Genomics, C., and the Wellcome Trust Case Control, C. (2012). Genome-wide association study implicates HLA-C*01:02 as a risk factor at the major histocompatibility complex locus in schizophrenia. *Biological Psychiatry*, *72*, 620–628.

Ito, H. T., Smith, S. E., Hsiao, E., & Patterson, P. H. (2010). Maternal immune activation alters nonspatial information processing in the hippocampus of the adult offspring. *Brain, Behavior, and Immunity*, *24*, 930–941.

Jia, P., Wang, L., Fanous, A. H., Chen, X., Kendler, K. S., International Schizophrenia, C., et al. (2012). A bias-reducing pathway enrichment analysis of genome-wide association data confirmed association of the MHC region with schizophrenia. *Journal of Medical Genetics*, *49*, 96–103.

Jones, C. A., Watson, D. J., & Fone, K. C. (2011). Animal models of schizophrenia. *British Journal of Pharmacology*, *164*, 1162–1194.

Katila, H., Hanninen, K., & Hurme, M. (1999). Polymorphisms of the interleukin-1 gene complex in schizophrenia. *Molecular Psychiatry*, *4*, 179–181.

Khandaker, G. M., Zimbron, J., Lewis, G., & Jones, P. B. (2013). Prenatal maternal infection, neurodevelopment and adult schizophrenia: a systematic review of population-based studies. *Psychological Medicine*, *43*, 239–257.

Laruelle, M. (2014). Schizophrenia: from dopaminergic to glutamatergic interventions. *Current Opinion in Pharmacology*, *14*, 97–102.

Laruelle, M., Abi-Dargham, A., van Dyck, C. H., Gil, R., D'Souza, C. D., Erdos, J., et al. (1996). Single photon emission computerized tomography imaging of amphetamine-induced dopamine release in drug-free schizophrenic subjects. *Proceedings of the National Academy of Sciences of the United States of America*, *93*, 9235–9240.

Laruelle, M., Abi-Dargham, A., Gil, R., Kegeles, L., & Innis, R. (1999). Increased dopamine transmission in schizophrenia: relationship to illness phases. *Biological Psychiatry*, *46*, 56–72.

Lee, K. W., Woon, P. S., Teo, Y. Y., & Sim, K. (2012). Genome wide association studies (GWAS) and copy number variation (CNV) studies of the major psychoses: what have we learnt? *Neuroscience and Biobehavioral Reviews*, *36*, 556–571.

Lencz, T., Morgan, T. V., Athanasiou, M., Dain, B., Reed, C. R., Kane, J. M., et al. (2007). Converging evidence for a pseudoautosomal cytokine receptor gene locus in schizophrenia. *Molecular Psychiatry*, *12*, 572–580.

Leonard, S., Gault, J., Hopkins, J., Logel, J., Vianzon, R., Short, M., et al. (2002). Association of promoter variants in the alpha7 nicotinic acetylcholine receptor subunit gene with an inhibitory deficit found in schizophrenia. *Archives of General Psychiatry*, *59*, 1085–1096.

Li, Q., Cheung, C., Wei, R., Cheung, V., Hui, E. S., You, Y., et al. (2010). Voxel-based analysis of postnatal white matter microstructure in mice exposed to immune challenge in early or late pregnancy. *NeuroImage*, *52*, 1–8.

Light, G. A., & Braff, D. L. (1999). Human and animal studies of schizophrenia-related gating deficits. *Current Psychiatry Reports*, *1*, 31–40.

Lipina, T. V., Zai, C., Hlousek, D., Roder, J. C., & Wong, A. H. (2013). Maternal immune activation during gestation interacts with Disc1 point mutation to exacerbate schizophrenia-related behaviors in mice. *Journal of Neuroscience: the Official Journal of the Society for Neuroscience*, *33*, 7654–7666.

Macedo, D. S., Araujo, D. P., Sampaio, L. R., Vasconcelos, S. M., Sales, P. M., Sousa, F. C., et al. (2012). Animal models of prenatal immune challenge and their contribution to the study of schizophrenia: a systematic review. *Brazilian Journal of Medical and Biological Research = Revista brasileira de pesquisas medicas e biologicas/Sociedade Brasileira de Biofisica [et al]*, *45*, 179–186.

Malkova, N. V., Gallagher, J. J., Yu, C. Z., Jacobs, R. E., & Patterson, P. H. (2014). Manganese-enhanced magnetic resonance imaging reveals increased DOI-induced brain activity in a mouse model of schizophrenia. *Proceedings of the National Academy of Sciences of the United States of America*, *111*, E2492–E2500.

Malkova, N. V., Yu, C. Z., Hsiao, E. Y., Moore, M. J., & Patterson, P. H. (2012). Maternal immune activation yields offspring displaying mouse versions of the three core symptoms of autism. *Brain, Behavior, and Immunity*, *26*, 607–616.

McAllister, A. K. (2014). Major histocompatibility complex I in brain development and schizophrenia. *Biological Psychiatry*, *75*, 262–268.

Mednick, S. A., Machon, R. A., Huttunen, M. O., & Bonett, D. (1988). Adult schizophrenia following prenatal exposure to an influenza epidemic. *Archives of General Psychiatry*, *45*, 189–192.

Meyer, U., Engler, A., Weber, L., Schedlowski, M., & Feldon, J. (2008). Preliminary evidence for a modulation of fetal dopaminergic development by maternal immune activation during pregnancy. *Neuroscience*, *154*, 701–709.

Meyer, U., Feldon, J., Schedlowski, M., & Yee, B. K. (2005). Towards an immuno-precipitated neurodevelopmental animal model of schizophrenia. *Neuroscience and Biobehavioral Reviews*, *29*, 913–947.

Meyer, U., Feldon, J., Schedlowski, M., & Yee, B. K. (2006). Immunological stress at the maternal-foetal interface: a link between neurodevelopment and adult psychopathology. *Brain, Behavior, and Immunity*, *20*, 378–388.

Meyer, U., Feldon, J., & Yee, B. K. (2009). A review of the fetal brain cytokine imbalance hypothesis of schizophrenia. *Schizophrenia Bulletin*, *35*, 959–972.

Meyer, U., Knuesel, I., Nyffeler, M., & Feldon, J. (2010). Chronic clozapine treatment improves prenatal infection-induced working memory deficits without influencing adult hippocampal neurogenesis. *Psychopharmacology*, *208*, 531–543.

Meyer, U., Murray, P. J., Urwyler, A., Yee, B. K., Schedlowski, M., & Feldon, J. (2008). Adult behavioral and pharmacological dysfunctions following disruption of the fetal brain balance between pro-inflammatory and IL-10-mediated anti-inflammatory signaling. *Molecular Psychiatry*, *13*, 208–221.

Meyer, U., Nyffeler, M., Engler, A., Urwyler, A., Schedlowski, M., Knuesel, I., et al. (2006). The time of prenatal immune challenge determines the specificity of inflammation-mediated brain and behavioral pathology. *Journal of Neuroscience: the Official Journal of the Society for Neuroscience*, *26*, 4752–4762.

Meyer, U., Nyffeler, M., Schwendener, S., Knuesel, I., Yee, B. K., & Feldon, J. (2008). Relative prenatal and postnatal maternal contributions to schizophrenia-related neurochemical dysfunction after in utero immune challenge. Neuropsychopharmacology: Official Publication of the American College of Neuropsychopharmacology, 33, 441–456.

Meyer, U., Nyffeler, M., Yee, B. K., Knuesel, I., & Feldon, J. (2008). Adult brain and behavioral pathological markers of prenatal immune challenge during early/middle and late fetal development in mice. Brain, Behavior, and Immunity, 22, 469–486.

Meyer, U., Schwendener, S., Feldon, J., & Yee, B. K. (2006). Prenatal and postnatal maternal contributions in the infection model of schizophrenia. Experimental Brain Research, 173, 243–257.

Meyer, U., Spoerri, E., Yee, B. K., Schwarz, M. J., & Feldon, J. (2010). Evaluating early preventive antipsychotic and antidepressant drug treatment in an infection-based neurodevelopmental mouse model of schizophrenia. Schizophrenia Bulletin, 36, 607–623.

Michel, M., Schmidt, M. J., & Mirnics, K. (2012). Immune system gene dysregulation in autism and schizophrenia. Developmental Neurobiology, 72, 1277–1287.

Miller, B. J., Buckley, P., Seabolt, W., Mellor, A., & Kirkpatrick, B. (2011). Meta-analysis of cytokine alterations in schizophrenia: clinical status and antipsychotic effects. Biological Psychiatry, 70, 663–671.

Miwa, J. M., Freedman, R., & Lester, H. A. (2011). Neural systems governed by nicotinic acetylcholine receptors: emerging hypotheses. Neuron, 70, 20–33.

Mortensen, P. B., Pedersen, C. B., Hougaard, D. M., Norgaard-Petersen, B., Mors, O., Borglum, A. D., et al. (2010). A Danish National Birth Cohort study of maternal HSV-2 antibodies as a risk factor for schizophrenia in their offspring. Schizophrenia Research, 122, 257–263.

Mousa, A., Seiger, A., Kjaeldgaard, A., & Bakhiet, M. (1999). Human first trimester forebrain cells express genes for inflammatory and anti-inflammatory cytokines. Cytokine, 11, 55–60.

Nagai, T., Yu, J., Kitahara, Y., Nabeshima, T., & Yamada, K. (2012). D-Serine ameliorates neonatal PolyI: C treatment-induced emotional and cognitive impairments in adult mice. Journal of Pharmacological Sciences, 120, 213–227.

Nawa, H., & Takei, N. (2006). Recent progress in animal modeling of immune inflammatory processes in schizophrenia: implication of specific cytokines. Neuroscience Research, 56, 2–13.

Nielsen, P. R., Laursen, T. M., & Mortensen, P. B. (2013). Association between parental hospital-treated infection and the risk of schizophrenia in adolescence and early adulthood. Schizophrenia Bulletin, 39, 230–237.

O'Leary, C., Desbonnet, L., Clarke, N., Petit, E., Tighe, O., Lai, D., et al. (2014). Phenotypic effects of maternal immune activation and early postnatal milieu in mice mutant for the schizophrenia risk gene neuregulin-1. Neuroscience.

Ozawa, K., Hashimoto, K., Kishimoto, T., Shimizu, E., Ishikura, H., & Iyo, M. (2006). Immune activation during pregnancy in mice leads to dopaminergic hyperfunction and cognitive impairment in the offspring: a neurodevelopmental animal model of schizophrenia. Biological Psychiatry, 59, 546–554.

Paparelli, A., Di Forti, M., Morrison, P. D., & Murray, R. M. (2011). Drug-induced psychosis: how to avoid star gazing in schizophrenia research by looking at more obvious sources of light. Frontiers in Behavioral Neuroscience, 5, 1.

Patterson, P. H. (2009). Immune involvement in schizophrenia and autism: etiology, pathology and animal models. Behavioural Brain Research, 204, 313–321.

Piontkewitz, Y., Arad, M., & Weiner, I. (2011). Risperidone administered during asymptomatic period of adolescence prevents the emergence of brain structural pathology and behavioral abnormalities in an animal model of schizophrenia. Schizophrenia Bulletin, 37, 1257–1269.

Piontkewitz, Y., Assaf, Y., & Weiner, I. (2009). Clozapine administration in adolescence prevents postpubertal emergence of brain structural pathology in an animal model of schizophrenia. Biological Psychiatry, 66, 1038–1046.

Piontkewitz, Y., Bernstein, H. G., Dobrowolny, H., Bogerts, B., Weiner, I., & Keilhoff, G. (2012). Effects of risperidone treatment in adolescence on hippocampal neurogenesis, parvalbumin expression, and vascularization following prenatal immune activation in rats. Brain, Behavior, and Immunity, 26, 353–363.

Potvin, S., Stip, E., Sepehry, A. A., Gendron, A., Bah, R., & Kouassi, E. (2008). Inflammatory cytokine alterations in schizophrenia: a systematic quantitative review. Biological Psychiatry, 63, 801–808.

Pratt, L., Ni, L., Ponzio, N. M., & Jonakait, G. M. (2013). Maternal inflammation promotes fetal microglial activation and increased cholinergic expression in the fetal basal forebrain: role of interleukin-6. Pediatric Research, 74, 393–401.

Pratt, J., Winchester, C., Dawson, N., & Morris, B. (2012). Advancing schizophrenia drug discovery: optimizing rodent models to bridge the translational gap. Nature Reviews Drug Discovery, 11, 560–579.

Radewicz, K., Garey, L. J., Gentleman, S. M., & Reynolds, R. (2000). Increase in HLA-DR immunoreactive microglia in frontal and temporal cortex of chronic schizophrenics. Journal of Neuropathology and Experimental Neurology, 59, 137–150.

Rajkowska, G., Miguel-Hidalgo, J. J., Makkos, Z., Meltzer, H., Overholser, J., & Stockmeier, C. (2002). Layer-specific reductions in GFAP-reactive astroglia in the dorsolateral prefrontal cortex in schizophrenia. Schizophrenia Research, 57, 127–138.

Rao, J. S., Kim, H. W., Harry, G. J., Rapoport, S. I., & Reese, E. A. (2013). Increased neuroinflammatory and arachidonic acid cascade markers, and reduced synaptic proteins, in the postmortem frontal cortex from schizophrenia patients. Schizophrenia Research, 147, 24–31.

Ribeiro, B. M., do Carmo, M. R., Freire, R. S., Rocha, N. F., Borella, V. C., de Menezes, A. T., et al. (2013). Evidences for a progressive microglial activation and increase in iNOS expression in rats submitted to a neurodevelopmental model of schizophrenia: reversal by clozapine. Schizophrenia Research, 151, 12–19.

Richetto, J., Calabrese, F., Meyer, U., & Riva, M. A. (2013). Prenatal versus postnatal maternal factors in the development of infection-induced working memory impairments in mice. Brain, Behavior, and Immunity, 33, 190–200.

Richtand, N. M., Ahlbrand, R., Horn, P., Stanford, K., Bronson, S. L., & McNamara, R. K. (2011). Effects of risperidone and paliperidone pre-treatment on locomotor response following prenatal immune activation. Journal of Psychiatric Research, 45, 1194–1201.

Richtand, N. M., Ahlbrand, R., Horn, P., Tambyraja, R., Grainger, M., Bronson, S. L., et al. (2012). Fluoxetine and aripiprazole treatment following prenatal immune activation exert longstanding effects on rat locomotor response. Physiology & Behavior, 106, 171–177.

Roenker, N. L., Gudelsky, G., Ahlbrand, R., Bronson, S. L., Kern, J. R., Waterman, H., et al. (2011). Effect of paliperidone and risperidone on extracellular glutamate in the prefrontal cortex of rats exposed to prenatal immune activation or MK-801. Neuroscience Letters, 500, 167–171.

Ross, R. G., Stevens, K. E., Proctor, W. R., Leonard, S., Kisley, M. A., Hunter, S. K., et al. (2010). Research review: cholinergic mechanisms, early brain development, and risk for schizophrenia. Journal of Child Psychology and Psychiatry, and Allied Disciplines, 51, 535–549.

Saetre, P., Emilsson, L., Axelsson, E., Kreuger, J., Lindholm, E., & Jazin, E. (2007). Inflammation-related genes up-regulated in schizophrenia brains. BMC Psychiatry, 7, 46.

Samuelsson, A. M., Jennische, E., Hansson, H. A., & Holmang, A. (2006). Prenatal exposure to interleukin-6 results in inflammatory neurodegeneration in hippocampus with NMDA/GABA(A) dysregulation and impaired spatial learning. American Journal of Physiology Regulatory, Integrative and Comparative Physiology, 290, R1345–R1356.

Saviouk, V., Chow, E. W., Bassett, A. S., & Brzustowicz, L. M. (2005). Tumor necrosis factor promoter haplotype associated with schizophrenia reveals a linked locus on 1q44. *Molecular Psychiatry, 10*, 375–383.

Selten, J. P., Frissen, A., Lensvelt-Mulders, G., & Morgan, V. A. (2010). Schizophrenia and 1957 pandemic of influenza: meta-analysis. *Schizophrenia Bulletin, 36*, 219–228.

Shi, L., Fatemi, S. H., Sidwell, R. W., & Patterson, P. H. (2003). Maternal influenza infection causes marked behavioral and pharmacological changes in the offspring. *Journal of Neuroscience: the Official Journal of the Society for Neuroscience, 23*, 297–302.

Shi, J., Levinson, D. F., Duan, J., Sanders, A. R., Zheng, Y., Pe'er, I., et al. (2009). Common variants on chromosome 6p22.1 are associated with schizophrenia. *Nature, 460*, 753–757.

Smith, S. E., Li, J., Garbett, K., Mirnics, K., & Patterson, P. H. (2007). Maternal immune activation alters fetal brain development through interleukin-6. *Journal of Neuroscience: the Official Journal of the Society for Neuroscience, 27*, 10695–10702.

Song, C., Manku, M. S., & Horrobin, D. F. (2008). Long-chain polyunsaturated fatty acids modulate interleukin-1beta-induced changes in behavior, monoaminergic neurotransmitters, and brain inflammation in rats. *Journal of Nutrition, 138*, 954–963.

Song, C., Phillips, A. G., Leonard, B. E., & Horrobin, D. F. (2004). Ethyl-eicosapentaenoic acid ingestion prevents corticosterone-mediated memory impairment induced by central administration of interleukin-1beta in rats. *Molecular Psychiatry, 9*, 630–638.

Song, X. Q., Lv, L. X., Li, W. Q., Hao, Y. H., & Zhao, J. P. (2009). The interaction of nuclear factor-kappa B and cytokines is associated with schizophrenia. *Biological Psychiatry, 65*, 481–488.

Sorensen, H. J., Mortensen, E. L., Reinisch, J. M., & Mednick, S. A. (2009). Association between prenatal exposure to bacterial infection and risk of schizophrenia. *Schizophrenia Bulletin, 35*, 631–637.

Soumiya, H., Fukumitsu, H., & Furukawa, S. (2011). Prenatal immune challenge compromises the normal course of neurogenesis during development of the mouse cerebral cortex. *Journal of Neuroscience Research, 89*, 1575–1585.

Stefansson, H., Ophoff, R. A., Steinberg, S., Andreassen, O. A., Cichon, S., Rujescu, D., et al. (2009). Common variants conferring risk of schizophrenia. *Nature, 460*, 744–747.

Steffek, A. E., McCullumsmith, R. E., Haroutunian, V., & Meador-Woodruff, J. H. (2008). Cortical expression of glial fibrillary acidic protein and glutamine synthetase is decreased in schizophrenia. *Schizophrenia Research, 103*, 71–82.

Steiner, J., Bernstein, H. G., Bielau, H., Farkas, N., Winter, J., Dobrowolny, H., et al. (2008). S100B-immunopositive glia is elevated in paranoid as compared to residual schizophrenia: a morphometric study. *Journal of Psychiatric Research, 42*, 868–876.

Steiner, J., Bielau, H., Brisch, R., Danos, P., Ullrich, O., Mawrin, C., et al. (2008). Immunological aspects in the neurobiology of suicide: elevated microglial density in schizophrenia and depression is associated with suicide. *Journal of Psychiatric Research, 42*, 151–157.

Stevens, K. E., Adams, C. E., Yonchek, J., Hickel, C., Danielson, J., & Kisley, M. A. (2008). Permanent improvement in deficient sensory inhibition in DBA/2 mice with increased perinatal choline. *Psychopharmacology, 198*, 413–420.

Sullivan, P. F., Kendler, K. S., & Neale, M. C. (2003). Schizophrenia as a complex trait: evidence from a meta-analysis of twin studies. *Archives of General Psychiatry, 60*, 1187–1192.

Swerdlow, N. R., Braff, D. L., Hartston, H., Perry, W., & Geyer, M. A. (1996). Latent inhibition in schizophrenia. *Schizophrenia Research, 20*, 91–103.

Vuillermot, S., Joodmardi, E., Perlmann, T., Ogren, S. O., Feldon, J., & Meyer, U. (2012). Prenatal immune activation interacts with genetic Nurr1 deficiency in the development of attentional impairments.

Journal of Neuroscience: the Official Journal of the Society for Neuroscience, 32, 436–451.

Vuillermot, S., Weber, L., Feldon, J., & Meyer, U. (2010). A longitudinal examination of the neurodevelopmental impact of prenatal immune activation in mice reveals primary defects in dopaminergic development relevant to schizophrenia. *Journal of Neuroscience: the Official Journal of the Society for Neuroscience, 30*, 1270–1287.

Walters, J. T., Rujescu, D., Franke, B., Giegling, I., Vasquez, A. A., Hargreaves, A., et al. (2013). The role of the major histocompatibility complex region in cognition and brain structure: a schizophrenia GWAS follow-up. *American Journal of Psychiatry, 170*, 877–885.

Webster, M. J., O'Grady, J., Kleinman, J. E., & Weickert, C. S. (2005). Glial fibrillary acidic protein mRNA levels in the cingulate cortex of individuals with depression, bipolar disorder and schizophrenia. *Neuroscience, 133*, 453–461.

Wei, J., & Hemmings, G. P. (2004). TNXB locus may be a candidate gene predisposing to schizophrenia. *American Journal of Medical Genetics, Part B: Neuropsychiatric Genetics: the Official Publication of the International Society of Psychiatric Genetics, 125B*, 43–49.

Weiner, I., & Arad, M. (2009). Using the pharmacology of latent inhibition to model domains of pathology in schizophrenia and their treatment. *Behavioural Brain Research, 204*, 369–386.

Wierzba-Bobrowicz, T., Lewandowska, E., Kosno-Kruszewska, E., Lechowicz, W., Pasennik, E., & Schmidt-Sidor, B. (2004). Degeneration of microglial cells in frontal and temporal lobes of chronic schizophrenics. *Folia Neuropathologica/Association of Polish Neuropathologists and Medical Research Centre, Polish Academy of Sciences, 42*, 157–165.

Wierzba-Bobrowicz, T., Lewandowska, E., Lechowicz, W., Stepien, T., & Pasennik, E. (2005). Quantitative analysis of activated microglia, ramified and damage of processes in the frontal and temporal lobes of chronic schizophrenics. *Folia Neuropathologica/Association of Polish Neuropathologists and Medical Research Centre, Polish Academy of Sciences, 43*, 81–89.

Williams, M. R., Hampton, T., Pearce, R. K., Hirsch, S. R., Ansorge, O., Thom, M., et al. (2013). Astrocyte decrease in the subgenual cingulate and callosal genu in schizophrenia. *European Archives of Psychiatry and Clinical Neuroscience, 263*, 41–52.

Winter, C., Djodari-Irani, A., Sohr, R., Morgenstern, R., Feldon, J., Juckel, G., et al. (2009). Prenatal immune activation leads to multiple changes in basal neurotransmitter levels in the adult brain: implications for brain disorders of neurodevelopmental origin such as schizophrenia. *International Journal of Neuropsychopharmacology/Official Scientific Journal of the Collegium Internationale Neuropsychopharmacologicum (CINP), 12*, 513–524.

Workman, A. D., Charvet, C. J., Clancy, B., Darlington, R. B., & Finlay, B. L. (2013). Modeling transformations of neurodevelopmental sequences across mammalian species. *Journal of Neuroscience: the Official Journal of the Society for Neuroscience, 33*, 7368–7383.

Wu, W. L., Adams, C. E., Chow, K. H., Stevens, K. E., & Patterson, P. H. The interaction between maternal immune activation and α7nAChR in regulating schizophrenia- and autism-like behaviors (in preparation).

Zuckerman, L., Rehavi, M., Nachman, R., & Weiner, I. (2003). Immune activation during pregnancy in rats leads to a postpubertal emergence of disrupted latent inhibition, dopaminergic hyperfunction, and altered limbic morphology in the offspring: a novel neurodevelopmental model of schizophrenia. *Neuropsychopharmacology: Official Publication of the American College of Neuropsychopharmacology, 28*, 1778–1789.

Zuckerman, L., & Weiner, I. (2005). Maternal immune activation leads to behavioral and pharmacological changes in the adult offspring. *Journal of Psychiatric Research, 39*, 311–323.

12

Etiological Environmental Models: Virus Infection Models

Håkan Karlsson

Department of Neuroscience, Karolinska Institutet, Stockholm, Sweden

BACKGROUND

Introduction

Animal models of human diseases are useful to understand the mechanisms underlying an association between an outcome/disease and an exposure (identified by clinical or epidemiological observations). In the case of schizophrenia and other neuropsychiatric disorders, the outcomes (symptoms) are difficult to model experimentally. With regard to environmental exposures conferring the risk for these outcomes, many of the associations are inconsistent and ill-defined. Before discussing the different virus infection models for schizophrenia, I will start by reviewing the existing literature for support of the hypothesis that infections, particularly virus infections, may *cause* schizophrenia.

Although the causal involvement of infections in chronic neuropsychiatric disorders is, as we shall see, far from established, it is well-known that several common (and uncommon) microbial infections can indeed cause central nervous system (CNS)-related symptoms, including psychotic features, in infected individuals. Usually these symptoms disappear as the infection is cleared. For example, Karl Menninger described several cases with schizophrenia-like symptoms in the aftermath of the Spanish flu in 1918–1919. Most of these, if not all, appeared to have recovered fully by the mid-1920s (Menninger, 1926). Additional examples are psychotic episodes in individuals infected with HIV (Dolder, Patterson, & Jeste, 2004), herpes virus (Oommen, Johnson, & Ray, 1982), or the spirochete *Borrelia burgdorferi* (Hess et al., 1999). Thus, a wide range of infectious agents targeting the brain are clearly capable of eliciting symptoms resembling some of those observed in patients with schizophrenia and other nonaffective psychoses.

Epidemiological Studies Associating Virus Infections with the Later Development of Schizophrenia

A large number of case–control studies have reported increased prevalence of a wide range of infections in patients with schizophrenia, previously reviewed (Karlsson, 2003), and more recently as part of a meta-analysis (Arias et al., 2012). Because these exposures were assessed after onset, often by several years, they may be confounded by disease-associated factors, such as differences in the lifestyle between cases and controls, rather than on a causal pathway. Prospective studies, however, have detected an association between exposures to infectious agents well before the onset of symptoms, which raises the possibility that these exposures in fact contribute to disease development later on (see the following sections).

Seasonality in the births of individuals with schizophrenia is an old and widely replicated observation dating back to the nineteenth century, reviewed elsewhere (Torrey, Torrey, & Peterson, 1977). The observed excess of births (10–15%) in the winter/spring months of individuals with schizophrenia not only indicates environmental influences but also indicates that such influences act already during gestation or early postnatal life. Several factors that show seasonal variation, such as sunlight, vitamin D, rainfall, and infections, have all been investigated for their involvement in the seasonality of schizophrenia births (Torrey et al., 1977). In 1988, Mednick et al. made the seminal observation of an association between the 1957 influenza A virus epidemic and an increase in births of individuals who would later be diagnosed with schizophrenia (Mednick, Machon, Huttunen, & Bonett, 1988). Subsequently, several studies replicated the association between gestational influenza and schizophrenia in offspring, whereas other studies failed to do so (reviewed in Munk-Jorgensen & Ewald, 2001). The study by Mednick et al. (1988) was based on a purely ecological association (i.e., the investigators did not assess whether the mothers of future cases were actually infected with the flu virus, only that they were living in an area exposed to the epidemic). In a later study, Brown et al. reported a sevenfold (but nonsignificant) increase in the odds of developing schizophrenia following exposure to maternal influenza A virus. The exposure was measured by hemagglutination inhibition assays on maternal sera detecting both immunoglobulin (Ig)M and IgG (Brown, Begg, et al., 2004). In a subsequent study, Brown et al. (2009) reported an association between gestational influenza A virus exposure and cognitive deficits among cases of schizophrenia or related psychoses. Moreover, Ellman, Yolken, Buka, Torrey, and Cannon (2009) measured IgG directed at influenza A or B viruses in maternal sera and cognitive performance at age 7 years among control cases with psychotic disease. Although cases exposed to maternal influenza B virus performed worse on the cognitive tests than unexposed cases already at age 7, the performance of exposed control children did not differ from unexposed controls, suggesting that genetic risk rendered the offspring more vulnerable to neurodevelopmental insults of the maternal infection (Ellman et al., 2009). Several other infections during pregnancy have been associated (significantly) with the later diagnosis of schizophrenia in offspring. These include rubella (Brown et al., 2001), measles (Torrey, Rawlings, & Waldman, 1988), *Toxoplasma gondii* (which is a parasite, not a virus) (Blomstrom et al., 2012; Brown et al., 2005; Mortensen et al., 2007), herpes simplex virus type 2 (HSV2) (Buka, Tsuang, Torrey, Klebanoff, Bernstein, et al., 2001; Mortensen et al., 2010), and cytomegalovirus (Blomstrom et al., 2012). For most of these, associations have been based on serological analyses of maternal sera or neonatal dried blood spots where maternal IgG, actively transported across the placental barrier to provide passive immunization of the fetus, can be measured by commercially available enzyme-linked immunosorbent assays. Such specific IgGs develop weeks after the initial exposure and persist for years. They are therefore not informative with regard to the timing of the maternal infection, which in the vast majority of cases probably occurred preconceptually.

Although rubella, *T. gondii*, and cytomegalovirus (CMV) are known teratogens following primary infection in pregnant women, rubella (and measles) are unlikely to contribute to current cases thanks to successful immunization programs in many, but not all, parts of the world (Centers for Disease Control & Prevention, 2009). For *Toxoplasma*, HSV-2, or CMV, such programs are not in place and these agents remain potential causes of neurodevelopmental disorders such as schizophrenia.

Because the reported associations are made with IgG and not IgM, it appears that chronic maternal infection rather than acute ones are of relevance for psychiatric outcomes in the offspring. Although these prevalent latent infections have generally been considered safe for the fetus, preconceptual CMV infections can reactivate during pregnancy to infect the fetus and cause long-term sequelae (Townsend et al., 2013). In fact, a recent report indicate that reactivated CMV is a significant and perhaps underdiagnosed cause of intrauterine growth restriction (Pereira et al., 2014), a pregnancy complication associated with several adverse outcomes, including schizophrenia (Abel et al., 2010; Nielsen, Mortensen, et al., 2013). More direct support for CMV in the etiology of neuropsychiatric disorders is suggested by the recent detection of CMV DNA in a larger than expected proportion of neonatal blood samples collected from children who were later diagnosed with autism (Sakamoto, Moriuchi, Matsuzaki, Motoyama, & Moriuchi, 2014). Such studies have so far not been conducted on neonatal samples from individuals who later developed schizophrenia and it is not known if the transmission of CMV or other infectious agents occur more often in these newborns.

Maternal Inflammation Rather than Infection?

The range of different infectious agents associated with schizophrenia pregnancies have led many researchers to propose that it is perhaps not transmission of the infectious agent that is causing schizophrenia in offspring but rather the maternal immune activation (MIA) that follows exposure to infectious agents. Indeed, experimental studies using rodents have consistently reported neurobehavioral disturbances in offspring to dams exposed to, not only viruses, but also lipopolysaccharides, polyinosine-polycytidylic (poly I:C), or cytokines that mimic some aspect of acute bacterial or viral infections. Molecular analyses of animals used in such experiments have suggested that interleukin-6 is a critical maternal mediator of the effects of MIA (Smith, Li, Garbett, Mirnics, & Patterson, 2007); see also the chapter on Maternal immune activation. In a comparison of MIA by influenza A virus infection, interleukin-6, or poly I:C, Garbett et al. report very different effects on the transcriptome in the fetal brains but also some interesting commonalities regarding crystalline gene expression that appeared to correlate with the degree of MIA elicited by the different exposures (Garbett, Hsiao, Kalman, Patterson, & Mirnics, 2012).

Direct clinical support for a MIA during pregnancy among women whose children will later develop schizophrenia or other psychoses is, however, currently provided by only two studies. These report on observations of elevated levels of tumor necrosis factor (TNF)-α (Buka, Tsuang, Torrey, Klebanoff, Wagner, et al., 2001) or interleukin-8 (Brown, Hooton, et al., 2004) in biobanked sera obtained at various time points during pregnancy from mothers whose children would later develop schizophrenia as compared with control mothers. Other investigated cytokines, including interleukin-6, were not detected at elevated levels in the sera from mothers of future cases (Brown, Hooton, et al., 2004; Buka, Tsuang, Torrey, Klebanoff, Wagner, et al., 2001). In addition, two recent studies have investigated cytokines and other markers of inflammation and innate immune activation in neonatal blood samples from cases of schizophrenia or other nonaffective psychoses and control individuals (Gardner, Dalman, Wicks, Lee, & Karlsson, 2013; Nielsen, Agerbo, et al., 2014). Neither of these found any signs of ongoing inflammation among the cases. Gardner et al., however, observed significantly reduced levels of several markers of innate immunity, including serum amyloid A and tissue plasminogen activator among newborns who would later on develop nonaffective psychoses (Gardner et al., 2013). Thus, although attractive and biologically plausible, the direct clinical support for MIA during pregnancy in the etiology of schizophrenia is currently weak.

Acute Infection during Pregnancy

With the exception of influenza A virus, few studies have investigated if acute infections occur more often in pregnancies resulting in schizophrenia births, see Table 1. In the largest study, to date, Nielsen and coworkers have reported a small but significant association between infections requiring hospitalization during pregnancy and the risk of schizophrenia in the offspring in Denmark (Nielsen, Laursen, & Mortensen, 2013). Upon

closer inspection, these authors found equally strong associations with both maternal and paternal infections at any time (i.e., also outside of pregnancy). The authors therefore suggest that it is not the acute infection during pregnancy per se, but a general familial vulnerability or sensitivity to (hospitalization for) infections that explains the association with schizophrenia. Nevertheless, Nielsen and coworkers observed a significant interaction between hospitalization during pregnancy and a diagnosis of psychotic illness in the mother (Nielsen, Laursen, et al., 2013). This finding suggests that infections during pregnancy may contribute to disease in the offspring only among certain mothers—for example, those with a vulnerability involving the innate immune system, as is often reported in patients with schizophrenia and other psychiatric conditions (reviewed in Drexhage et al., 2010). The finding by Nielsen and coworkers is in agreement with an earlier study by Clarke et al., who reported a synergistic interaction between family history of psychotic disorder and exposure to maternal infection during pregnancy (Clarke, Tanskanen, Huttunen, Whittaker, & Cannon, 2009). Weak but significant associations have more recently been made also between maternal infections during pregnancy and the development of autism in the offspring (Atladottir, Henriksen, Schendel, & Parner, 2012; Lee et al., 2014; Zerbo et al., 2013). More detailed analyses for potential interactions with parental disease or if associations with these childhood outcomes are observed also with infections outside pregnancy have so far not been reported. In conclusion, clinical and epidemiological studies conducted so far have so far not firmly established if acute *maternal* infections *during* pregnancy are indeed associated with risk for the later development of schizophrenia or other neuropsychiatric disorders in the offspring. Only two studies report interactions between infections during pregnancy and family history of psychotic disorders, but it is not known if this interaction is limited to the

TABLE 1 Register-Based Studies on the Association between Maternal Infections during Pregnancy and the Development of Schizophrenia or Schizophrenia Spectrum Disorders in the Offspring

Samples	Published Studies	Exposure	Type of Psychotic Disorder	Association with Psychotic Disorder
PDS, US cohort, N=7800	Brown et al. (2000)	Respiratory infection	SSD, n=58	**OR 2.1 (95% CI 1.0–4.4)**
	Babulas, Factor-Litvak, Goetz, Schaefer, and Brown, (2006)	Genital/reproductive infection (first trimester)	SSD, n=71	RR 0.9 (95% CI 0.2–3.7)
Finnish national cohort, N=23,400	Clarke et al. (2009)	Pyelonephritis	Schizophrenia, n=71	OR 1.5 (95% CI 0.9–2.4)
Danish cohort, N=7900	Sorensen, Mortensen, Reinisch, and Mednick (2009)	Viral infection Bacterial infection	Schizophrenia, n=153	OR 0.5 (95% CI 0.1–2.1) **OR 2.1 (95% CI 1.1–4.3)**
Danish national cohort, N=1,115,700	Nielsen, Laursen, et al. (2013)	Any infection	Schizophrenia, n=3700	**RR 1.2 (95% CI 1.0–1.4)**

CI, confidence interval; OR, odds ratio; PDS, prenatal determinants of schizophrenia; RR, relative risk; SSD, schizophrenia spectrum disorder. Bold indicates significant associations.

mother during pregnancy (Clarke et al., 2009; Nielsen, Laursen, et al., 2013).

Postnatal Infections

For schizophrenia, the risk associated with environmental exposures, including infections, is not necessarily limited to gestation. Postnatal infections may also be causally related to the later development of schizophrenia or merely a consequence of genetic liability to be hospitalized for infections not on the causal pathway to disease. Compared with pregnancy, far fewer studies on the role of infections have been conducted in the period between birth and onset of disease. An obvious limitation to such studies is the general lack of prospectively collected biological samples that can be analyzed for evidence of exposure during this period. Epidemiological studies using registered hospitalizations for infections during childhood, however, recently reported that hospitalization for any infection during childhood, between birth and age 13, was more common among those who would later develop nonaffective psychoses in Sweden (Blomstrom et al., 2013). Importantly, this finding was not explained by parental psychiatric history, adverse social factors, or hospitalizations for reasons other than infections or psychiatric care, which were all the more common among children who would later develop psychoses (Blomstrom et al., 2013). Analyses of different classes of agents and ages at hospitalization indicated the strongest associations between bacterial infections during early adolescence. Interestingly, we observed an association between childhood infections and previous maternal infections during pregnancy, suggesting that postnatal infections are not entirely independent of prenatal exposures. Whether this association is explained by shared genetic factors between mother and offspring or by programming of the fetal immune system by maternal infections during pregnancy is not known but is the subject of ongoing studies. An association between childhood infections (particularly bacterial) and the later development of schizophrenia, regardless of parental psychiatric illness, were also recently made in Denmark by Nielsen, Benros, and Mortensen (2014). In neither of these recent Scandinavian studies were CNS infections during childhood associated with psychosis risk, which contradicts some previous and smaller studies from Finland (Rantakallio, Jones, Moring, & Von Wendt, 1997), Sweden (Dalman et al., 2008), and Brazil (Abrahao, Focaccia, & Gattaz, 2005), but not from Israel (Weiser et al., 2010). Interestingly, a prospective serological study recently reported an association between Epstein-Barr virus exposure during childhood and the appearance of psychotic symptoms in the Avon Longitudinal Study of Parents and Children cohort (Khandaker, Stochl, Zammit, Lewis, & Jones, 2014), suggesting

that future studies on postnatal exposures will benefit from inclusion of biological samples that can be investigated for specific common exposures during childhood, or even at later time points, as exemplified by studies of individuals in the US armed forces (Niebuhr et al., 2011, 2008), which are not captured by hospital registers. In conclusion, recent data from large epidemiological studies find associations between infections during childhood and early adolescence and a later diagnosis of schizophrenia and related psychoses. These associations remain after adjusting for several, but probably not all, potential confounders, including parental psychiatric illness, suggesting childhood infections are independent risk factors for the later development of schizophrenia and other nonaffective psychoses.

EXPERIMENTAL MODELS EMPLOYING VIRUSES

Animal experiments involving infections in schizophrenia research have been carried out by inoculating experimental animals, including both rodents and monkeys with biological material, CSF, or brain tissue obtained from affected patients (Baker et al., 1983; Baker, Ridley, Crow, & Tyrrell, 1989; Kaufmann et al., 1988). In keeping with Henle-Koch's modified postulates (Evans, 1976), the purpose of these studies was to try to identify an infectious agent in schizophrenia by means of transmitting the agent to susceptible animals and monitoring them for signs of any infection ranging from very general signs such as weight loss to more subtle neurobehavioral symptoms. Despite very long observation periods allowing time for even a slow agent to exert its effects, these studies did not find any evidence in support of an infectious agent in schizophrenia (Baker et al., 1983, 1989; Kaufmann et al., 1988). Renewed interest was sparked in 2003 when Shi and coworkers in the late Paul Patterson's laboratory reported neurobehavioral abnormalities elicited in offspring to mice infected with the influenza A/NWS/33 virus during pregnancy (Shi, Fatemi, Sidwell, & Patterson, 2003). These offspring exhibited abnormal behavioral responses, including deficits in sensorimotor gating as measured by the prepulse inhibition test. These investigators were unable to detect the flu virus in fetal tissues and concluded that the maternal response to the infection, or to poly I:C, and not a congenital infection was responsible for the behavioral problems in the offspring (Shi et al., 2003). The effects of poly I:C injections into pregnant mice on the offspring have subsequently been replicated and extended in several independent studies and have provided the scientific basis for the hypothesis of MIA, not only in schizophrenia but also in autism and related conditions, recently reviewed in Knuesel et al. (2014). Models involving MIA are the subject of another chapter in this book and will not be further detailed here except where comparisons with viral infections are relevant.

Maternal or Neonatal Infection

As noted in the Introduction, it is far from clear that acute infections during pregnancy are more important than infections during postnatal life, at least based on epidemiological studies using medical registers. In fact, current studies indicate more solid associations with acute childhood infections requiring inpatient care than such infections among pregnant women. From an experimental point of view, it should also be noted that many of the developmental processes that occur during the third human trimester correspond to those occurring during the first week of postnatal life in mice (Rice & Barone, 2000). Moreover, the outcome of an experimental infection is determined, not only by the age of the exposed animal but also by the route of infection. Results of direct neonatal exposure, by for example intracranial injection of virus, is likely to differ from that of a congenital exposure. The outcome is also determined by the type of cell that is permissive for infection and on the type of damage that the infection does to that cell (Johnson, 1972). Regarding maternal infections, the virus does not necessarily have to reach the developing fetus to have detrimental influences. Infection of cells in the placenta can cause impairments in placental function and/or release of effector molecules acting on the developing fetal brain (Johnson, 1972). It should also be kept in mind that the rodent placenta differs structurally from the human placenta (Simmons et al., 2008) and any (or the lack of) effects observed in rodents cannot necessarily be extrapolated to the human situation. Moreover, experimental maternal infections tend to be performed in inbred strains with no genetic conflict between mother and fetus, which appear to impair placental function/fetal outcome (Madeja et al., 2011) and may contribute to differences between inbred and outbred strains, as was recently reported following MIA (Babri, Doosti, & Salari, 2013).

SPECIFIC EXPERIMENTAL INFECTIONS

Influenza A Virus

Influenza A virus is a global common exposure with seasonal variation. Influenza A viruses infect and replicate in cells in the respiratory epithelium. In addition to sickness symptoms, including hypersomnia during acute infection, cases with neurological complications are often reported during most, if not all, epidemics (Ekstrand, 2012). Such complications may indicate that

virus variants can reach and infect cells in the brain parenchyma, potentially eliciting damage to neuronal populations. For example, cases of encephalitis lethargica, or von Economo disease, that appeared in the wake of the 1918 influenza pandemic has long been suspected, but never proven, to be caused by the virus (reviewed in Reid, McCall, Henry, & Taubenberger, 2001). The observations of an association between the 1957 flu epidemic and an increase in schizophrenia births (Mednick et al., 1988) sparked an interest in the potential effects of gestational influenza A virus exposure on animal behavior related to neuropsychiatric disorders. Human isolates or strains can be easily adapted to infect and replicate to high titers in mouse lungs (Hirst, 1947). Passage of mouse-adapted strains in mouse brains also allow the isolation of neurovirulent strains (Ward, 1996). For example, two mouse adapted strains, both derived from the first human flu virus isolated in 1933 by Wilson-Smith (Smith, Andrewes, & Laidlaw, 1933), the A/33/NWS (Stuart-Harris, 1939) and A/33/WSN (Francis & Moore, 1940) strains were obtained by the 1940s following serial passages in rodent brains. Neurovirulent strains of influenza A virus target different brain regions depending on the route of inoculation (e.g., intracranial injection, intranasal instillation, intraperitoneal injection) (Reinacher, Bonin, Narayan, & Scholtissek, 1983). Following injection into the olfactory bulb of adult C57BL/6 mice, the A/WSN/33 strain appears to selectively target habenular, paraventricular thalamic, and brainstem monoaminergic neurons (Mori, Diehl, Chauhan, Ljunggren, & Kristensson, 1999). In the habenular and paraventricular thalamic areas, the infection caused an almost total loss of neurons. In these immunocompetent mice, virus proteins were cleared within 2 weeks (Mori et al., 1999). In a subsequent follow-up study of these animals were deficits in learning and increased anxiety levels (Beraki, Aronsson, Karlsson, Ogren, & Kristensson, 2005), suggesting that a transient infection can cause persistent changes in behaviors of relevance for neuropsychiatric disorders, tentatively by a "hit-and-run" mechanism. Similar injections into adult mice lacking functional cytotoxic T-cells because of an absence of major histocompatibility complex (MHC) class I expression following deletion of a transporter associated with antigen processing 1, $Tap1$, (i.e., $Tap1^{-/-}$ mice) results in virus persistence in the same regions for at least 17 months (Aronsson, Karlsson, Ljunggren, & Kristensson, 2001). This study indicates that an adaptive cytotoxic T-cell response is important for clearance of the virus and that the virus is able to persist and replicate at a low level in the absence of such a response.

To study the influence of the A/WSN/33 strain at earlier stages of development, we employed an intraperitoneal injection of neonatal mice with influenza A/WSN/33 virus (Asp, Beraki, Kristensson, Ogren, &

Karlsson, 2009; Asp, Holtze, Powell, Karlsson, & Erhardt, 2010). To investigate the role of adaptive immunity in the potential sequelae of this infection we used both wild-type C57BL/6 and $Tap1^{-/-}$ mice on the same genetic background. The virus reached both lungs and brains of the inoculated animals with similar kinetics. Interestingly, both strains efficiently cleared the infection with more or less complete clearance of viral RNA within 40 days (Asp et al., 2009). Interestingly, the animals with defects in their adaptive immunity exhibited a prolonged innate immune response compared with wild-type animals. With regard to neurobehavioral problems, only $Tap1^{-/-}$ mice exhibited learning difficulties (Asp et al., 2009) and deficits in sensorimotor gating (Asp et al., 2010) at 6 months of age. Following behavioral testing, the prefrontal cortex, a region implicated in learning, harbored reduced levels of transcripts encoding type III neuregulin, but not those encoding types I or II, in the affected animals compared with control animals. Such infected mice exhibited a transient activation of the kynurenine pathway of tryptophan degradation accompanied by a transient increase in kynurenic acid in the brain (Asp et al., 2010). In a subsequent study, some of the adult behavioral abnormalities induced by the neonatal influenza A virus infection were also observed following transient elevation of brain kynurenic acid during early postnatal life (Liu et al., 2014). The kynurenine pathway is activated in vivo by a range of agents targeting the CNS, including bacteria (Too et al., 2014), viruses(Asp et al., 2010; Eastman, Urbanska, Love, Kristensson, & Schwarcz, 1994; Holtze, Asp, Schwieler, Engberg, & Karlsson, 2008), and T. gondii (Notarangelo et al., 2014) as part of the innate immune response. This finding suggests that some of the long-term effects of infection during early life can be mediated by activation of the kynurenine pathway. Taken together, these studies indicate that mice with defects in adaptive immunity are at risk to develop molecular and neurobehavioral changes relevant for schizophrenia following a neonatal infection with a neurotropic strain of influenza A virus. Subsequent genome-wide association studies of schizophrenia consistently reported associations in the MHC region on chromosome 6 (reviewed in Corvin & Morris, 2014). Unfortunately, potential interactions between human genetic variation in the MHC region and environmental exposures, such as infections, in conferring schizophrenia risk remain largely unexplored (Kodavali et al., 2014).

Both the A/NWS/33 and the A/WSN/33 strains of influenza A virus have been used to infect pregnant mice in independent studies. The ability to cross the murine placenta appears to differ between the two strains, with the A/NWS/33 strain being unable to target the fetus (Shi, Tu, & Patterson, 2005), whereas the A/WSN/33 strain appears to be able to infect the placenta and target

the fetus, including the fetal brain following a maternal respiratory infection during pregnancy (Aronsson et al., 2002). Although congenital infection has been reported for other strains of influenza A virus in both human (McGregor, Burns, Levin, Burlington, & Meiklejohn, 1984; Yawn, Pyeatte, Joseph, Eichler, & Garcia-Bunuel, 1971) and rodent (Chen et al., 2009; Williams & Mackenzie, 1977) pregnancies, it is probably not a general feature (Irving et al., 2000). In our study (Aronsson et al., 2002), A/WSN/33 RNA was found to persist in the brain parenchyma for extended periods following congenital infection. We reported gene expression changes but no gross behavioral abnormalities in adult offspring to pregnant mice infected on gestational day 14 using a low dose of A/WSN/33 intranasally (Asp et al., 2005). Interestingly, the changes in gene expression were investigated in 3-month-old offspring and the ones verified could not be detected before postnatal day 60, suggesting multiple events occurring after gestational exposure resulting in persistent changes in adult offspring. Moreno and coworkers (Moreno et al., 2011) used a similar experimental setup but employed CD1 mice and instillation of A/WSN/33 on gestational day 9.5. They reported abnormal behavior relating to spontaneous locomotor activity, altered serotonin, and glutamate receptor densities in brains of adult offspring as well as altered responses to hallucinogens and MK-801, an N-methyl-D-aspartate receptor blocker in these animals (Moreno et al., 2011). These investigators were unable to detect the replicating virus in the lungs of exposed offspring but detected antibodies directed at the virus in 5% of exposed offspring. Fatemi and coworkers have conducted a series of studies using the influenza A/NWS/33 strain reporting behavioral and molecular effects of maternal infection on the offspring that in many aspects resemble those observed in patients with autism or schizophrenia (Fatemi et al., 2004; Fatemi, Cuadra, El-Fakahany, Sidwell, & Thuras, 2000; Fatemi, Earle, et al., 2002; Fatemi et al., 1999; Fatemi, Emamian, et al., 2002; Fatemi, Folsom, Reutiman, Abu-Odeh, et al., 2009; Fatemi, Folsom, Reutiman, Huang, et al., 2009; Fatemi, Pearce, Brooks, & Sidwell, 2005; Fatemi et al., 2008). These changes involve defective corticogenesis, reduced expression of structural proteins, and abnormal behavior that to some extent is normalized by antipsychotic medication. Because this strain does not target the fetus, the mechanisms responsible for the effects on the fetuses remained elusive. These investigators therefore went on to investigate if the virus maternal infection caused disturbances in placental function that in turn may affect the developing fetus. Following maternal intranasal instillation of a sublethal dose of influenza A/NWS/33 virus on day 7 of pregnancy, they reported changes in expression of several genes in both placentae and postnatal brains of exposed offspring compared with unexposed offspring (Fatemi et al., 2012) and recently reviewed in (Kneeland & Fatemi, 2013).

Other strains of influenza A virus have subsequently been used in maternal infections during pregnancy. Short and coworkers (Short et al., 2010) employed intranasal instillation of the human influenza A/Sydney/5/97 strain of the H3N2 serotype in pregnant rhesus monkeys during early third trimester. Virus was subsequently detected in nasal secretions along with the development of maternal IgM and IgG, the latter but not the former, also being detected in the blood of the newborn. Offspring to infected dams did not differ from control offspring in terms of gestational length, birth weight, or hypothalamic-pituitary-adrenal responses. Neuroimaging of offspring at 1 year of age, however, indicated reduced intracranial volumes and reduced white matter in cerebellum and cortical regions and amygdalae.

In conclusion, a large number of independent experimental influenza A virus infections during pregnancy conducted in different species consistently suggest that the offspring is at increased risk for subtle structural, molecular and neurobehavioral abnormalities. The experimental evidence indicate that these effects on the offspring can be mediated by both direct effects of the virus as well as indirect effects mediated by detrimental influences on the placenta or by an innate immune response to the infection. Experimental studies using mouse adapted neurotropic strains illustrate the importance of both innate and adaptive immune systems in clearing the virus following neonatal and adult exposures and indicate that postnatal exposures may also be associated with persistent neurobehavioral deficits of relevance for adult-onset schizophrenia. Moreover, experimental infections of rodents by human isolates suggest that neurotropism of influenza A virus is not uncommon (Li et al., 2011; Nishimura, Itamura, Iwasaki, Kurata, & Tashiro, 2000; Tanaka et al., 2003).

Herpes Viruses

Human herpes viruses are highly prevalent throughout the world and, following initial infection, can all establish life-long persistence characterized by episodes of latency with intermittent episodes of reactivation. Different herpes viruses have been proposed to contribute to chronic inflammatory (Owens, Gilden, Burgoon, Yu, & Bennett, 2011) neurodegenerative (Miklossy, 2011) CNS disorders as well as schizophrenia (Yolken, 2004). Despite the epidemiological associations between maternal (chronic) infections with the human herpes viruses, HSV-2, and CMV, and the development of schizophrenia in offspring, few experimental studies evaluating relevant animal behaviors have been conducted using murine herpes strains. Experimentation using human herpes simplex strains in animals is limited by the fact that these wild-type human simplex strains are usually highly lethal to rodents following intracranial injection.

In a series of experiments conducted during the 1970s, Lycke and Roos reported that before death, such animals exhibit changes in behavior along with changes in different neurotransmitter systems (Lycke & Roos, 1972, 1974, 1975). Using an attenuated and nonlethal mutant strain of HSV-1, Crnic and Pizer (1988) reported specific behavioral problems in adult animals following subcutaneous injections during the neonatal period. Virus targeted the brain in some but not all animals and appeared to be cleared by 20 days of age. Adult survivors exhibited hyperactivity but no cognitive impairments. Using another attenuated strain (F) of HSV-1, Engel and coworkers (Engel et al., 2000) infected neonatal rats on postnatal day 2 and observed deficits in sensorimotor gating using the prepulse inhibition test at 37–58 days of age. No other abnormalities in locomotor activity were observed in the infected animals compared with animals injected similarly with saline. Similar observations were made by Rothschild, O'Grady, and Wecker (1999) using neonatal rats injected subcutaneously with a different herpes virus, rat CMV. These investigators reported impairments in PPI at 120 days of age in infected rats compared with control-injected rats. No attempt was made however to study the kinetics of the infection and it was not known if the virus targeted the brain in this model. Mouse CMV has been reported to target both glial cells and neurons in the developing brain following peripheral injection, causing a lytic infection (reviewed in Tsutsui, Kosugi, & Kawasaki, 2005). Moreover, following such injection, mouse CMV can establish latency in infected neuronal cells and thus have the potential to cause disturbance in CNS function many years after infection (Tsutsui et al., 2005). In light of the recent studies suggesting a potential involvement of human CMV in the etiology of schizophrenia (Blomstrom et al., 2012) and the genetic associations with the MHC region, murine models employing murine CMV strains and mice with known genetic deletions involving the immune system deserve to be further explored. Murine CMV does not cause congenital infection in immunocompetent animals. Models employing human CMV (Tang et al., 2002) or murine CMV in immunodeficient mouse strains (Woolf, Jaquish, & Koehrn, 2007) have, however, been reported to recapitulate some aspects of congenital human disease, including infection of the fetal brain and fetal growth retardation. Long-term follow-up of such exposed offspring with regard to persistent behavioral abnormalities of relevance for neuropsychiatric disorders have not been reported.

Borna Disease Virus

Borna disease virus (BDV) is the infectious agent causing abnormal and stereotypical behavior and death, denoted Borna disease in infected animals, named after the German city of Borna where these symptoms in horses was first described in the 1880s. BDV is a nonsegmented negative-strand RNA virus (Lipkin, Briese, & Hornig, 2011). Following infection of neonatal rats by intracranial injection, BDV causes a persistent nonlytic infection that gradually spreads to neurons throughout the brain parenchyma. Interestingly, BDV appears to be selectively harmful only to certain subtypes of infected neurons. Cerebellar Purkinje cells in the cerebellum and granule cells of the dentate gyrus in the hippocampus appear to be particularly vulnerable to BDV and continue to degenerate (reviewed in Pletnikov, Moran, & Carbone, 2002). Thinning of the cortex during BDV infection has also been reported, suggesting a general neuronal loss during the infection (Hornig, Weissenbock, Horscroft, & Lipkin, 1999). The mechanisms underlying the observed neuronal loss are not completely elucidated but appear to involve endoplasmic reticulum stress (Williams & Lipkin, 2006). Neonatally infected rodents do not exhibit increased mortality and do not develop overt neurological disease but exhibit neurobehavioral abnormalities reminiscent of those observed in cases of autism or schizophrenia. These involve impairments in learning and memory (Rubin et al., 1999) and social interactions (Lancaster, Dietz, Moran, & Pletnikov, 2007). Although serological studies indicate that BDV can infect several mammalians, including not only horses but also sheep, cattle, rodents, and primates, it is not established if BDV can infect humans. Even more controversial are the studies associating antibodies directed at BDV to neuropsychiatric diseases in humans (Hornig et al., 2012). Regardless of its role in human disease, experimental BDV infections illustrate how a virus can lead to neurobehavioral abnormalities during a persistent, slowly progressing infection of the brain parenchyma. A recent report indicates that some rat strains are protected from neurodegeneration, but not from infection, and that susceptibility to disease in rats is dependent on host genetic factors (Wu et al., 2013). Interestingly, BDV-like sequences have been integrated into the genomes of several mammalian species, including human, during evolution (Horie et al., 2010). Although mammalian genomes are known to harbor large amounts of viral sequences, these were previously thought to be exclusively of retroviral origin. The human genome, for example, was reported to harbor two sequences with high similarity to the nucleocapsid (N) gene of BDV (Horie et al., 2010). These sequences contain fairly long open-reading frames, a 3′poly-A stretch and are flanked by target-site duplications indicating that they are pseudogenes originally generated by L1-encoded reverse transcriptase activity (Horie et al., 2010). Functionality of such sequences in squirrels was recently indicated by their interference with exogenous BDV replication (Fujino, Horie, Honda,

Merriman, & Tomonaga, 2014). Interestingly, reverse transcription of BDV transcripts was commonly detected de novo in infected brain tissues in bank voles, suggesting that somatic integrations into host DNA may occur in infected individuals (Kinnunen et al., 2011). Lack of detectable pathology in infected bank voles, despite widespread neuronal infection, along with detection of viral shedding in feces and urine, indicates that bank voles may be part of a natural reservoir for this virus (Kinnunen et al., 2011). If Borna virus or other, unknown, viruses with similar properties cause disease or contribute to human neuropsychiatric disease in the human population remain to be established.

Picornaviruses

Viruses in the picornavirus family are ubiquitous among humans and several are known to have neurotropic properties, such as enteroviruses, poliovirus, and Coxsackie viruses (Whitton, Cornell, & Feuer, 2005). For example, CNS involvement is often reported during epidemics of enterovirus 71 infections (Solomon et al., 2010). Chronic sequelae including cognitive deficits or schizophrenia, particularly among those infected at a young age, have been reported in long-term follow-up studies of infected individuals (Chamberlain et al., 1983; Rantakallio et al., 1997). Experimental infections of rodents with picornaviruses, such as Theiler murine encephalomyelitis virus (TMEV), report apoptosis in infected hippocampal neurons along with impaired spatial learning in the Morris' water maze in a model of acute and transient CNS infection. In this model, virus is not restricted to the hippocampus, and only a small number of hippocampal pyramidal neurons are in fact infected. The selective death of these neurons is caused by bystander effects involving excitotoxic neurotransmitter release and oxidative damage elicited by the infection (Buenz et al., 2009). Intracranial injection of neonatal mice with a sublethal dose of Coxsackie B3 virus on the other hand leads to selective targeting of the virus to dividing neural precursor cells resulting in reduced brain weight and cortical thinning along with a low level of viral persistence for several months (Ruller et al., 2012). Initiation of antiviral treatment (Ribavirin) during the persistent stage resulted in a recovery in brain weight suggesting that the slowly replicating stage contributed to the long-term sequelae and that the brain is able to recover from such adverse influences (Ruller et al., 2012). Behavioral testing of surviving animals was, however, not performed in this study. Meagher et al. reported that prior exposure to social stress exacerbates the outcome of acute experimental TMEV infections illustrating a plausible environment × environment interaction of relevance for neuropsychiatric outcomes (Meagher et al., 2007).

Human maternal–fetal transmission of members of the picornavirus family, such as enteroviruses, following infection during pregnancy may occur but is more often occurring neonatally (reviewed in Abzug, 2008). Emerging evidence indicates, however, that congenital infections with enteroviruses may be more common than has previously been thought, (Abzug, 2008). Experimental murine TMEV infections during early pregnancy result in placental infection and fetal transmission, whereas infections during later stages of pregnancy result in placental infection but no transmission to the fetus (see Abzug & Tyson, 2000 and references therein). The outcome of such infections with regard to behavior relevant for neuropsychiatric disorder is not known. An interesting observation, however, suggests that a maternal infection Coxsackie virus B4 during pregnancy renders the offspring more vulnerable to a subsequent infection with the same virus (Bopegamage et al., 2012). In their study, Bopegamage and coworkers focused on insular pancreatic damage in the offspring which was indeed reported as a consequence of the infection in pups although no trace of the virus was found in the pancreatic tissue. Brain pathology or behavioral abnormalities were however not addressed in this study of the diabetogenic potential of coxsackie B4 virus (Bopegamage et al., 2012).

Lymphocytic Choriomeningitis Virus

Lymphocytic choriomeningitis virus (LCMV) is a noncytolytic arenavirus for which the common mouse is the natural reservoir. Infected mice excrete virus in saliva, urine, and feces. Humans usually become infected by inhaling dust contaminated by virus particles. Infections usually causes mild symptoms including fever, headache, and vomiting, but up to one-third of infected individuals remain asymptomatic. Following temporary improvement, classical symptoms associated with the development of meningitis can occur (Bonthius, 2012). The virus is not thought to infect horizontally from human to human. LCMV is prevalent in many areas, and serological surveys in such areas indicate that approximately 5% of adult individuals have IgG directed at LCMV, indicating previous exposure. Experimental LCMV infection of adult mice using leads to generalized infection followed by T-cell–mediated clearance of virus within 2 weeks, whereas intracranial injection leads to a fatal disease within 6–8 days because of immune-mediated damage (reviewed in Kang & McGavern, 2008). In immune animals following adult exposure, low levels of persisting LCMV, strain WE, have been detected in the form of both DNA (Klenerman, Hengartner, & Zinkernagel, 1997) and RNA (Ciurea et al., 1999), of which at least the RNA form retains biological activity (Ciurea et al., 1999). In infected pregnant mice, congenital transmission occurs with no obvious pathology in the fetus. LCMV is nonlytic (i.e., it does not disrupt its host cell) and congenitally infected animals appear to develop tolerance to the virus, such animals shed large amounts of virus throughout their life (reviewed in Bonthius & Perlman, 2007). Hotchin and Seegal reported behavioral abnormalities in mice neonatally infected with LCMV, including increased latency in the open field, decrease in the current necessary to elicit a startle response, and a decrease in running wheel activity (Hotchin & Seegal, 1977). Neonatal infections of rats have illustrated how host age influences the outcome of the infection, indicating that the differences in gestational age at infection can explain the different pathologies seen in congenital human infections (Bonthius & Perlman, 2007). Immunohistochemical studies of neonatally infected rats indicate structural and functional abnormalities in the hippocampus that gradually evolve to result in severe loss of cells in the dentate gyrus. Pearce and coworkers reported that early infection causes defects of inhibitory GABAergic neurons that may be indirectly responsible for the later loss of neurons from uncontrolled excitation/disinhibition (Pearce, Valadi, Po, & Miller, 2000), resembling observations in TMEV-infected animals described in the previous section. Thus, the neonatal rat model of LCMV infection model illustrates that an infection during early life can elicit delayed structural and behavioral abnormalities.

Endogenous Retroviruses

The genomes of all investigated vertebrate species to date contain numerous retroviral elements (Hayward, Cornwallis, & Jern, 2014). These are remnants of previous germline integrations inherited by subsequent generations to become endogenous retroviruses (ERVs), a process that can currently be viewed in real-time in Koalas in western Australia (Stoye, 2006). Current estimates indicate that approximately 8% of the human and 10% of the mouse genomes are made up of ERV sequences. The vast majority, if not all, ERV integrations are replication-incompetent, meaning that such individual loci cannot, on their own, generate infectious particles that can cause further spread within the infected host or between susceptible individuals. Individual elements can, however, become transcriptionally active by exogenous cues acting on repressive chromatin and the retroviral promoter in the long terminal repeat region to generate messenger RNA (and retroviral proteins if open reading frames are intact) (Nellaker et al., 2006). In fact, a few such retroviral *env* genes have been adopted to become bona fide mammalian genes with key fusogenic functions reported in the mammalian placenta, such as syncytin-1, encoded by an element, *ERVWE1*, in the HERV-W family located on chromosome 7 (Mallet et al., 2004; Mi et al., 2000). Some exogenous virus infections, such as influenza A virus, can induce expression of *ERVWE1* and other elements in the HERV-W family also in extraplacental human cell types by removing repressive chromatin modifications and inducing expression of transcription enhancers acting on the long-terminal repeat region (Li et al., 2014). Similar effects of influenza A virus infection are also observed in extraplacental mouse cells in vitro (Asp, Nellaker, & Karlsson, 2007) and in vivo (Asp et al., 2005, 2007). HERV-W–encoded transcripts and proteins have been observed in the CNS as well as systemically in individuals with schizophrenia (Karlsson et al., 2001; Perron et al., 2012, 2008). The mechanisms underlying the generation of HERV-W transcription in schizophrenia and if they play any role in disease development is not known. Intriguingly, individual replication incompetent ERV loci in the mouse genome were recently reported to complement each other to allow generation of recombinant infectious virus particles (Young et al., 2012). Such particles were reported to infect susceptible animals both vertically and horizontally. Key roles for humoral adaptive immunity and translocation of components of the gut flora in the control and initiation such events in host animals were identified (Young et al., 2012). Behavioral testing, particularly with regard to cognitive function or sensory-motor gating, of naive animals infected by such viruses has not been reported.

CONCLUDING REMARKS

From the clinical studies conducted so far, it is not evident that acute maternal or early-life virus infections are risk factors of large effect in the general population. Recent large population-based register studies suggest that acute infections pose larger risk for the offspring among mother with a history of psychiatric disease, indicating perhaps that gene variants associated with psychiatric disease render the offspring more vulnerable to maternal infections. The true impact of infections is difficult to appreciate from such epidemiological studies because most infections do not warrant hospital admission or even in treatment at outpatient facilities for which register data are becoming available in some countries. Despite including a large number of individuals, maternal hospital treatment for infection during pregnancy is rare, and these types of studies are often underpowered to allow stratification by different maternal psychiatric diagnoses and by different types of infections. Postnatal infections are more common and large register-based studies from Scandinavia report significant associations with a later diagnosis of schizophrenia and other psychoses regardless of the differences in social class,

hospitalization for other causes, and parental psychiatric illnesses between case and control individuals. The serological studies conducted, to date, originate from the United States, Denmark, and Sweden and have focused on the role of "the usual suspects" (i.e., the TORCH agents well known to have teratogenic properties in terms of maternal exposures during pregnancy). These studies consistently report significant associations between IgG levels directed at *T. gondii*, and less consistently so with maternal IgG directed at HSV-2 and CMV. In addition to these, a single study report an association with antibodies directed at influenza A virus in maternal serum. Thus, many specific maternal infections remain to be investigated by serology and for evidence of maternal–fetal transmission. Future larger studies employing medical registers and biological samples from mothers and newborn children need to better identify specific risk factors in terms of genetic variants in both probands and their mothers and in terms of their interaction with specific infectious agents to cause neuropsychiatric disorders in children and adults.

The experimental models for schizophrenia that have employed virus infections reported to date are heavily biased toward influenza A virus. These include studies of infections during pregnancy in both mice and monkeys as well as neonatal and adult infections in mice. Taken together, these studies clearly suggest that influenza A virus infection can cause long-term abnormalities in molecular, structural, and behavioral outcomes relating to cognitive domains and sensorimotor gating in exposed animals by several different mechanisms. Other viral infections and combinations of exposures to infections during pre- and postnatal life are currently underinvestigated in terms of molecular, structural, and behavioral outcomes of relevance for chronic neuropsychiatric disorders and therefore warranted in future studies.

With the advent of next-generation sequencing of the human metagenome, from healthy individuals as well as from patients with schizophrenia or other disorders, novel viruses infecting humans will be discovered and their potential role in human disease will require investigations using rodents to establish pathogenetic mechanisms and identify novel avenues for prevention and treatment. As an example, Yolken and coworkers recently identified, by next-generation sequencing, a chlorovirus, thought to only infect green algae, in human oropharyngeal samples. The presence of viral DNA in throat swabs was associated with cognitive deficits among otherwise healthy individuals. Mice orally inoculated with the chlorovirus subsequently developed behavioral abnormalities relating to working memory and sensorimotor gating along with altered expression of synaptic plasticity and immune system genes in the hippocampus (Yolken et al., 2014).

References

Abel, K. M., Wicks, S., Susser, E. S., Dalman, C., Pedersen, M. G., Mortensen, P. B., et al. (2010). Birth weight, schizophrenia, and adult mental disorder: is risk confined to the smallest babies? *Archives of General Psychiatry*, *67*(9), 923–930. http://dx.doi.org/10.1001/archgenpsychiatry.2010.100.

Abrahao, A. L., Focaccia, R., & Gattaz, W. F. (2005). Childhood meningitis increases the risk for adult schizophrenia. *World Journal of Biological Psychiatry*, *6*(Suppl. 2), 44–48. http://dx.doi.org/10.1080/15622970510030063. pii:UV757435001U3M67.

Abzug, M. J. (2008). The enteroviruses: an emerging infectious disease? The real, the speculative and the really speculative. *Advances in Experimental Medicine and Biology*, *609*, 1–15. http://dx.doi.org/10.1007/978-0-387-73960-1_1.

Abzug, M. J., & Tyson, R. W. (2000). Picornavirus infection in early murine gestation: significance of maternal illness. *Placenta*, *21*(8), 840–846. http://dx.doi.org/10.1053/plac.2000.0577.

Arias, I., Sorlozano, A., Villegas, E., de Dios Luna, J., McKenney, K., Cervilla, J., et al. (2012). Infectious agents associated with schizophrenia: a meta-analysis. *Schizophrenia Research*, *136*(1–3), 128–136. http://dx.doi.org/10.1016/j.schres.2011.10.026.

Aronsson, F., Karlsson, H., Ljunggren, H.-G., & Kristensson, K. (2001). Persistence of the influenza A/WSN/33 virus RNA at midbrain levels of immunodefective mice. *Journal of Neurovirology*, *7*, 117–124.

Aronsson, F., Lannebo, C., Paucar, M., Brask, J., Kristensson, K., & Karlsson, H. (2002). Persistence of viral RNA in the brain of offspring to mice infected with influenza A/WSN/33 virus during pregnancy. *Journal of Neurovirology*, *8*(4), 353–357.

Asp, L., Beraki, S., Aronsson, F., Rosvall, L., Ogren, S. O., Kristensson, K., et al. (2005). Gene expression changes in brains of mice exposed to a maternal virus infection. *Neuroreport*, *16*(10), 1111–1115.

Asp, L., Beraki, S., Kristensson, K., Ogren, S. O., & Karlsson, H. (2009). Neonatal infection with neurotropic influenza A virus affects working memory and expression of type III Nrg1 in adult mice. *Brain, Behavior, and Immunity*, *23*(6), 733–741. http://dx.doi.org/10.1016/j.bbi.2009.04.004. pii:S0889-1591(09)00106-8.

Asp, L., Holtze, M., Powell, S. B., Karlsson, H., & Erhardt, S. (2010). Neonatal infection with neurotropic influenza A virus induces the kynurenine pathway in early life and disrupts sensorimotor gating in adult Tap1$^{-/-}$ mice. *International Journal of Neuropsychopharmacology*, *13*(4), 475–485. http://dx.doi.org/10.1017/S1461145709990253. pii:S1461145709990253.

Asp, L., Nellaker, C., & Karlsson, H. (2007). Influenza A virus transactivates the mouse envelope gene encoding syncytin B and its regulator, glial cells missing 1. *Journal of Neurovirology*, *13*(1), 29–37.

Atladottir, H. O., Henriksen, T. B., Schendel, D. E., & Parner, E. T. (2012). Autism after infection, febrile episodes, and antibiotic use during pregnancy: an exploratory study. *Pediatrics*, *130*(6), e1447–e1454. http://dx.doi.org/10.1542/peds.2012-1107.

Babri, S., Doosti, M. H., & Salari, A. A. (2013). Strain-dependent effects of prenatal maternal immune activation on anxiety- and depression-like behaviors in offspring. *Brain, Behavior, and Immunity*. http://dx.doi.org/10.1016/j.bbi.2013.12.003. pii:S0889-1591(13)00588-6.

Babulas, V., Factor-Litvak, P., Goetz, R., Schaefer, C. A., & Brown, A. S. (2006). Prenatal exposure to maternal genital and reproductive infections and adult schizophrenia. *American Journal of Psychiatry*, *163*(5), 927–929. http://dx.doi.org/10.1176/appi.ajp.163.5.927.

Baker, H. F., Ridley, R. M., Crow, T. J., Bloxham, C. A., Parry, R. P., & Tyrrell, D. A. (1983). An investigation of the effects of intracerebral injection in the marmoset of cytopathic cerebrospinal fluid from patients with schizophrenia or neurological disease. *Psychological Medicine*, *13*(3), 499–511.

Baker, H. F., Ridley, R. M., Crow, T. J., & Tyrrell, D. A. (1989). A reinvestigation of the behavioural effects of intracerebral injection in marmosets of cytopathic cerebrospinal fluid from patients with schizophrenia or neurological disease. *Psychological Medicine*, *19*(2), 325–329.

Beraki, S., Aronsson, F., Karlsson, H., Ogren, S. O., & Kristensson, K. (2005). Influenza A virus infection causes alterations in expression of synaptic regulatory genes combined with changes in cognitive and emotional behaviors in mice. *Molecular Psychiatry*, *10*(3), 299–308. http://dx.doi.org/10.1038/sj.mp.4001545.

Blomstrom, A., Karlsson, H., Svensson, A., Frisell, T., Lee, B. K., Dal, H., et al. (2013). Hospital admission with infection during childhood and risk for psychotic illness–a population-based cohort study. *Schizophrenia Bulletin*. http://dx.doi.org/10.1093/schbul/sbt195. pii:sbt195.

Blomstrom, A., Karlsson, H., Wicks, S., Yang, S., Yolken, R. H., & Dalman, C. (2012). Maternal antibodies to infectious agents and risk for non-affective psychoses in the offspring – a matched case-control study. *Schizophrenia Research*, *140*(1–3), 25–30. http://dx.doi.org/10.1016/j.schres.2012.06.035. pii:S0920-9964(12)00352-0.

Bonthius, D. J. (2012). Lymphocytic choriomeningitis virus: an underrecognized cause of neurologic disease in the fetus, child, and adult. *Seminars in Pediatric Neurology*, *19*(3), 89–95. http://dx.doi.org/10.1016/j.spen.2012.02.002.

Bonthius, D. J., & Perlman, S. (2007). Congenital viral infections of the brain: lessons learned from lymphocytic choriomeningitis virus in the neonatal rat. *PLoS Pathogens*, *3*(11), e149. http://dx.doi.org/10.1371/journal.ppat.0030149.

Bopegamage, S., Precechtelova, J., Marosova, L., Stipalova, D., Sojka, M., Borsanyiova, M., et al. (2012). Outcome of challenge with coxsackievirus B4 in young mice after maternal infection with the same virus during gestation. *FEMS Immunology and Medical Microbiology*, *64*(2), 184–190. http://dx.doi.org/10.1111/j.1574-695X.2011.00886.x.

Brown, A. S., Begg, M. D., Gravenstein, S., Schaefer, C. A., Wyatt, R. J., Bresnahan, M., et al. (2004). Serologic evidence of prenatal influenza in the etiology of schizophrenia. *Archives of General Psychiatry*, *61*(8), 774–780.

Brown, A. S., Cohen, P., Harkavy-Friedman, J., Babulas, V., Malaspina, D., Gorman, J. M., et al. (2001). A.E. Bennett Research Award. Prenatal rubella, premorbid abnormalities, and adult schizophrenia. *Biological Psychiatry*, *49*(6), 473–486.

Brown, A. S., Hooton, J., Schaefer, C. A., Zhang, H., Petkova, E., Babulas, V., et al. (2004). Elevated maternal interleukin-8 levels and risk of schizophrenia in adult offspring. *American Journal of Psychiatry*, *161*(5), 889–895.

Brown, A. S., Schaefer, C. A., Quesenberry, C. P., Jr., Liu, L., Babulas, V. P., & Susser, E. S. (2005). Maternal exposure to toxoplasmosis and risk of schizophrenia in adult offspring. *American Journal of Psychiatry*, *162*(4), 767–773.

Brown, A. S., Schaefer, C. A., Wyatt, R. J., Goetz, R., Begg, M. D., Gorman, J. M., et al. (2000). Maternal exposure to respiratory infections and adult schizophrenia spectrum disorders: a prospective birth cohort study. *Schizophrenia Bulletin*, *26*(2), 287–295.

Brown, A. S., Vinogradov, S., Kremen, W. S., Poole, J. H., Deicken, R. F., Penner, J. D., et al. (2009). Prenatal exposure to maternal infection and executive dysfunction in adult schizophrenia. *American Journal of Psychiatry*, *166*(6), 683–690. http://dx.doi.org/10.1176/appi.ajp.2008.08010089.

Buenz, E. J., Sauer, B. M., Lafrance-Corey, R. G., Deb, C., Denic, A., German, C. L., et al. (2009). Apoptosis of hippocampal pyramidal neurons is virus independent in a mouse model of acute neurovirulent picornavirus infection. *American Journal of Pathology*, *175*(2), 668–684. http://dx.doi.org/10.2353/ajpath.2009.081126.

Buka, S. L., Tsuang, M. T., Torrey, E. F., Klebanoff, M. A., Bernstein, D., & Yolken, R. H. (2001). Maternal infections and subsequent psychosis among offspring. *Archives of General Psychiatry*, *58*(11), 1032–1037.

Buka, S. L., Tsuang, M. T., Torrey, E. F., Klebanoff, M. A., Wagner, R. L., & Yolken, R. H. (2001). Maternal cytokine levels during pregnancy and adult psychosis. *Brain, Behavior, and Immunity*, *15*(4), 411–420.

Centers for Disease Control & Prevention. (2009). Progress toward measles elimination – European Region, 2005–2008. *Morbidity and Mortality Weekly Report, 58*(6), 142–145.

Chamberlain, R. N., Christie, P. N., Holt, K. S., Huntley, R. M., Pollard, R., & Roche, M. C. (1983). A study of school children who had identified virus infections of the central nervous system during infancy. *Child: Care, Health and Development, 9*(1), 29–47.

Chen, B. Y., Chang, H. H., Chen, S. T., Tsao, Z. J., Yeh, S. M., Wu, C. Y., et al. (2009). Congenital eye malformations associated with extensive periocular neural crest apoptosis after influenza B virus infection during early embryogenesis. *Molecular Vision, 15*, 2821–2828.

Ciurea, A., Klenerman, P., Hunziker, L., Horvath, E., Odermatt, B., Ochsenbein, A. F., et al. (1999). Persistence of lymphocytic choriomeningitis virus at very low levels in immune mice. *Proceedings of the National Academy of Sciences of the United States of America, 96*(21), 11964–11969.

Clarke, M. C., Tanskanen, A., Huttunen, M., Whittaker, J. C., & Cannon, M. (2009). Evidence for an interaction between familial liability and prenatal exposure to infection in the causation of schizophrenia. *American Journal of Psychiatry, 166*(9), 1025–1030. http://dx.doi.org/10.1176/appi.ajp.2009.08010031.

Corvin, A., & Morris, D. W. (2014). Genome-wide association studies: findings at the major histocompatibility complex locus in psychosis. *Biological Psychiatry, 75*(4), 276–283. http://dx.doi.org/10.1016/j.biopsych.2013.09.018.

Crnic, L. S., & Pizer, L. I. (1988). Behavioral effects of neonatal herpes simplex type 1 infection of mice. *Neurotoxicology and Teratology, 10*(4), 381–386.

Dalman, C., Allebeck, P., Gunnell, D., Harrison, G., Kristensson, K., Lewis, G., et al. (2008). Infections in the CNS during childhood and the risk of subsequent psychotic illness: a cohort study of more than one million Swedish subjects. *American Journal of Psychiatry, 165*(1), 59–65.

Dolder, C. R., Patterson, T. L., & Jeste, D. V. (2004). HIV, psychosis and aging: past, present and future. *AIDS, 18*(Suppl. 1), S35–S42.

Drexhage, R. C., Knijff, E. M., Padmos, R. C., Heul-Nieuwenhuijzen, L., Beumer, W., Versnel, M. A., et al. (2010). The mononuclear phagocyte system and its cytokine inflammatory networks in schizophrenia and bipolar disorder. *Expert Review of Neurotherapeutics, 10*(1), 59–76. http://dx.doi.org/10.1586/ern.09.144.

Eastman, C. L., Urbanska, E., Love, A., Kristensson, K., & Schwarcz, R. (1994). Increased brain quinolinic acid production in mice infected with a hamster neurotropic measles virus. *Experimental Neurology, 125*(1), 119–124. http://dx.doi.org/10.1006/exnr.1994.1015.

Ekstrand, J. J. (2012). Neurologic complications of influenza. *Seminars in Pediatric Neurology, 19*(3), 96–100. http://dx.doi.org/10.1016/j.spen.2012.02.004.

Ellman, L. M., Yolken, R. H., Buka, S. L., Torrey, E. F., & Cannon, T. D. (2009). Cognitive functioning prior to the onset of psychosis: the role of fetal exposure to serologically determined influenza infection. *Biological Psychiatry*.

Engel, J. A., Zhang, J., Bergstrom, T., Conradi, N., Forkstam, C., Liljeroth, A., et al. (2000). Neonatal herpes simplex virus type 1 brain infection affects the development of sensorimotor gating in rats. *Brain Research, 863*(1–2), 233–240.

Evans, A. S. (1976). Causation and disease: the Henle-Koch postulates revisited. *Yale Journal of Biology and Medicine, 49*(2), 175–195.

Fatemi, S. H., Araghi-Niknam, M., Laurence, J. A., Stary, J. M., Sidwell, R. W., & Lee, S. (2004). Glial fibrillary acidic protein and glutamic acid decarboxylase 65 and 67 kDa proteins are increased in brains of neonatal BALB/c mice following viral infection in utero. *Schizophrenia Research, 69*(1), 121–123. http://dx.doi.org/10.1016/s0920-9964(03)00175-0.

Fatemi, S. H., Cuadra, A. E., El-Fakahany, E. E., Sidwell, R. W., & Thuras, P. (2000). Prenatal viral infection causes alterations in nNOS expression in developing mouse brains. *Neuroreport, 11*(7), 1493–1496.

Fatemi, S. H., Earle, J., Kanodia, R., Kist, D., Emamian, E. S., Patterson, P. H., et al. (2002). Prenatal viral infection leads to pyramidal cell atrophy and macrocephaly in adulthood: implications for genesis of autism and schizophrenia. *Cellular and Molecular Neurobiology, 22*(1), 25–33.

Fatemi, S. H., Emamian, E. S., Kist, D., Sidwell, R. W., Nakajima, K., Akhter, P., et al. (1999). Defective corticogenesis and reduction in Reelin immunoreactivity in cortex and hippocampus of prenatally infected neonatal mice. *Molecular Psychiatry, 4*(2), 145–154.

Fatemi, S. H., Emamian, E. S., Sidwell, R. W., Kist, D. A., Stary, J. M., Earle, J. A., et al. (2002). Human influenza viral infection in utero alters glial fibrillary acidic protein immunoreactivity in the developing brains of neonatal mice. *Molecular Psychiatry, 7*(6), 633–640. http://dx.doi.org/10.1038/sj.mp.4001046.

Fatemi, S. H., Folsom, T. D., Reutiman, T. J., Abu-Odeh, D., Mori, S., Huang, H., et al. (2009). Abnormal expression of myelination genes and alterations in white matter fractional anisotropy following prenatal viral influenza infection at E16 in mice. *Schizophrenia Research, 112*(1–3), 46–53. http://dx.doi.org/10.1016/j.schres.2009.04.014.

Fatemi, S. H., Folsom, T. D., Reutiman, T. J., Huang, H., Oishi, K., & Mori, S. (2009). Prenatal viral infection of mice at E16 causes changes in gene expression in hippocampi of the offspring. *European Neuropsychopharmacology, 19*(9), 648–653. http://dx.doi.org/10.1016/j.euroneuro.2009.03.004.

Fatemi, S. H., Folsom, T. D., Rooney, R. J., Mori, S., Kornfield, T. E., Reutiman, T. J., et al. (2012). The viral theory of schizophrenia revisited: abnormal placental gene expression and structural changes with lack of evidence for H1N1 viral presence in placentae of infected mice or brains of exposed offspring. *Neuropharmacology, 62*(3), 1290–1298. http://dx.doi.org/10.1016/j.neuropharm.2011.01.011.

Fatemi, S. H., Pearce, D. A., Brooks, A. I., & Sidwell, R. W. (2005). Prenatal viral infection in mouse causes differential expression of genes in brains of mouse progeny: a potential animal model for schizophrenia and autism. *Synapse, 57*(2), 91–99. http://dx.doi.org/10.1002/syn.20162.

Fatemi, S. H., Reutiman, T. J., Folsom, T. D., Huang, H., Oishi, K., Mori, S., et al. (2008). Maternal infection leads to abnormal gene regulation and brain atrophy in mouse offspring: implications for genesis of neurodevelopmental disorders. *Schizophrenia Research, 99*(1–3), 56–70. http://dx.doi.org/10.1016/j.schres.2007.11.018.

Francis, T., & Moore, A. E. (1940). A study of the neurotropic tendency in strains of the virus of epidemic influenza. *Journal of Experimental Medicine, 72*(6), 717–728.

Fujino, K., Horie, M., Honda, T., Merriman, D. K., & Tomonaga, K. (2014). Inhibition of Borna disease virus replication by an endogenous bornavirus-like element in the ground squirrel genome. *Proceedings of the National Academy of Sciences of the United States of America, 111*(36), 13175–13180. http://dx.doi.org/10.1073/pnas.1407046111.

Garbett, K. A., Hsiao, E. Y., Kalman, S., Patterson, P. H., & Mirnics, K. (2012). Effects of maternal immune activation on gene expression patterns in the fetal brain. *Translational Psychiatry, 2*, e98. http://dx.doi.org/10.1038/tp.2012.24.

Gardner, R. M., Dalman, C., Wicks, S., Lee, B. K., & Karlsson, H. (2013). Neonatal levels of acute phase proteins and later risk of non-affective psychosis. *Translational Psychiatry, 19*(3), e228. http://dx.doi.org/10.1038/tp.2013.5.

Hayward, A., Cornwallis, C. K., & Jern, P. (2014). Pan-vertebrate comparative genomics unmasks retrovirus macroevolution. *Proceedings of the National Academy of Sciences of the United States of America*. http://dx.doi.org/10.1073/pnas.1414980112.

Hess, A., Buchmann, J., Zettl, U. K., Henschel, S., Schlaefke, D., Grau, G., et al. (1999). Borrelia burgdorferi central nervous system infection presenting as an organic schizophrenialike disorder. *Biological Psychiatry, 45*(6), 795.

Hirst, G. K. (1947). Studies on the mechanism of adaptation of influenza virus to mice. *Journal of Experimental Medicine, 86*(5), 357–366.

Holtze, M., Asp, L., Schwieler, L., Engberg, G., & Karlsson, H. (2008). Induction of the kynurenine pathway by neurotropic influenza A virus infection. *Journal of Neuroscience Research, 86*(16), 3674–3683. http://dx.doi.org/10.1002/jnr.21799.

Horie, M., Honda, T., Suzuki, Y., Kobayashi, Y., Daito, T., Oshida, T., et al. (2010). Endogenous non-retroviral RNA virus elements in mammalian genomes. *Nature, 463*(7277), 84–87. http://dx.doi.org/10.1038/nature08695.

Hornig, M., Briese, T., Licinio, J., Khabbaz, R. F., Altshuler, L. L., Potkin, S. G., et al. (2012). Absence of evidence for bornavirus infection in schizophrenia, bipolar disorder and major depressive disorder. *Molecular Psychiatry, 17*(5), 486–493. http://dx.doi.org/10.1038/mp.2011.179.

Hornig, M., Weissenbock, H., Horscroft, N., & Lipkin, W. I. (1999). An infection-based model of neurodevelopmental damage. *Proceedings of the National Academy of Sciences of the United States of America, 96*(21), 12102–12107.

Hotchin, J., & Seegal, R. (1977). Virus-induced behavioral alteration of mice. *Science, 196*(4290), 671–674.

Irving, W. L., James, D. K., Stephenson, T., Laing, P., Jameson, C., Oxford, J. S., et al. (2000). Influenza virus infection in the second and third trimesters of pregnancy: a clinical and seroepidemiological study. *British Journal of Obstetrics and Gynaecology, 107*, 1282–1289.

Johnson, R. T. (1972). Effects of viral infection on the developing nervous system. *New England Journal of Medicine, 287*(12), 599–604. http://dx.doi.org/10.1056/NEJM197209212871208.

Kang, S. S., & McGavern, D. B. (2008). Lymphocytic choriomeningitis infection of the central nervous system. *Frontiers in Bioscience, 13*, 4529–4543.

Karlsson, H. (2003). Viruses and schizophrenia, connection or coincidence. *Neuroreport, 14*(4), 535–542.

Karlsson, H., Bachmann, S., Schroder, J., McArthur, J., Torrey, E. F., & Yolken, R. H. (2001). Retroviral RNA identified in the cerebrospinal fluids and brains of individuals with schizophrenia. *Proceedings of the National Academy of Sciences of the United States of America, 98*(8), 4634–4639.

Kaufmann, C. A., Weinberger, D. R., Stevens, J. R., Asher, D. M., Kleinman, J. E., Sulima, M. P., et al. (1988). Intracerebral inoculation of experimental animals with brain tissue from patients with schizophrenia. Failure to observe consistent or specific behavioral and neuropathological effects. *Archives of General Psychiatry, 45*(7), 648–652.

Khandaker, G. M., Stochl, J., Zammit, S., Lewis, G., & Jones, P. B. (2014). Childhood Epstein-Barr Virus infection and subsequent risk of psychotic experiences in adolescence: a population-based prospective serological study. *Schizophrenia Research, 158*(1–3), 19–24. http://dx.doi.org/10.1016/j.schres.2014.05.019.

Kinnunen, P. M., Inkeroinen, H., Ilander, M., Kallio, E. R., Heikkila, H. P., Koskela, E., et al. (2011). Intracerebral Borna disease virus infection of bank voles leading to peripheral spread and reverse transcription of viral RNA. *PLoS One, 6*(8), e23622. http://dx.doi.org/10.1371/journal.pone.0023622.

Klenerman, P., Hengartner, H., & Zinkernagel, R. M. (1997). A non-retroviral RNA virus persists in DNA form. *Nature, 390*(6657), 298–301. http://dx.doi.org/10.1038/36876.

Kneeland, R. E., & Fatemi, S. H. (2013). Viral infection, inflammation and schizophrenia. *Progress in Neuro-Psychopharmacology Biological Psychiatry, 42*, 35–48. http://dx.doi.org/10.1016/j.pnpbp.2012.02.001.

Knuesel, I., Chicha, L., Britschgi, M., Schobel, S. A., Bodmer, M., Hellings, J. A., et al. (2014). Maternal immune activation and abnormal brain development across CNS disorders. *Nature Reviews Neurology, 10*(11), 643–660. http://dx.doi.org/10.1038/nrneurol.2014.187.

Kodavali, C. V., Watson, A. M., Prasad, K. M., Celik, C., Mansour, H., Yolken, R. H., et al. (2014). HLA associations in schizophrenia: are we re-discovering the wheel? *American Journal of Medical Genetics, Part B: Neuropsychiatric Genetics, 165B*(1), 19–27. http://dx.doi.org/10.1002/ajmg.b.32195.

Lancaster, K., Dietz, D. M., Moran, T. H., & Pletnikov, M. V. (2007). Abnormal social behaviors in young and adult rats neonatally infected with Borna disease virus. *Behavioural Brain Research, 176*(1), 141–148. http://dx.doi.org/10.1016/j.bbr.2006.06.013.

Lee, B. K., Magnusson, C., Gardner, R. M., Blomstrom, S., Newschaffer, C. J., Burstyn, I., et al. (2014). Maternal hospitalization with infection during pregnancy and risk of autism spectrum disorders. *Brain, Behavior, and Immunity*. http://dx.doi.org/10.1016/j.bbi.2014.09.001.

Li, J., Liu, B., Chang, G., Hu, Y., Zhan, D., Xia, Y., et al. (2011). Virulence of H5N1 virus in mice attenuates after in vitro serial passages. *Virology Journal, 8*, 93. http://dx.doi.org/10.1186/1743-422X-8-93.

Li, F., Nellaker, C., Sabunciyan, S., Yolken, R. H., Jones-Brando, L., Johansson, A. S., et al. (2014). Transcriptional de-repression of ERVWE1 following influenza A virus infection. *Journal of Virology*. http://dx.doi.org/10.1128/JVI.03628-13. pii:JVI.03628-13.

Lipkin, W. I., Briese, T., & Hornig, M. (2011). Borna disease virus – fact and fantasy. *Virus Research, 162*(1–2), 162–172. http://dx.doi.org/10.1016/j.virusres.2011.09.036.

Liu, X. C., Holtze, M., Powell, S. B., Terrando, N., Larsson, M. K., Persson, A., et al. (2014). Behavioral disturbances in adult mice following neonatal virus infection or kynurenine treatment – role of brain kynurenic acid. *Brain, Behavior, and Immunity, 36*, 80–89. http://dx.doi.org/10.1016/j.bbi.2013.10.010.

Lycke, E., & Roos, B. E. (1972). The monoamine metabolism in viral encephalitides of the mouse. II. Turnover of monoamines in mice infected with herpes simplex virus. *Brain Research, 44*(2), 603–613.

Lycke, E., & Roos, B. E. (1974). Influence of changes in brain monoamine metabolism on behaviour of herpes simplex-infected mice. *Journal of the Neurological Sciences, 22*(3), 277–289.

Lycke, E., & Roos, B. E. (1975). Virus infections in infant mice causing persistent impairment of turnover of brain catecholamines. *Journal of the Neurological Sciences, 26*(1), 49–60.

Madeja, Z., Yadi, H., Apps, R., Boulenouar, S., Roper, S. J., Gardner, L., et al. (2011). Paternal MHC expression on mouse trophoblast affects uterine vascularization and fetal growth. *Proceedings of the National Academy of Sciences of the United States of America, 108*(10), 4012–4017. http://dx.doi.org/10.1073/pnas.1005342108.

Mallet, F., Bouton, O., Prudhomme, S., Cheynet, V., Oriol, G., Bonnaud, B., et al. (2004). The endogenous retroviral locus ERVWE1 is a bona fide gene involved in hominoid placental physiology. *Proceedings of the National Academy of Sciences of the United States of America, 101*(6), 1731–1736.

McGregor, J. A., Burns, J. C., Levin, M. J., Burlington, B., & Meiklejohn, G. (1984). Transplacental passage of influenza A/Bangkok (H3N2) mimicking amniotic fluid infection syndrome. *American Journal of Obstetrics and Gynecology, 149*(8), 856–859.

Meagher, M. W., Johnson, R. R., Young, E. E., Vichaya, E. G., Lunt, S., Hardin, E. A., et al. (2007). Interleukin-6 as a mechanism for the adverse effects of social stress on acute Theiler's virus infection. *Brain, Behavior, and Immunity, 21*(8), 1083–1095. http://dx.doi.org/10.1016/j.bbi.2007.05.001.

Mednick, S. A., Machon, R. A., Huttunen, M. O., & Bonett, D. (1988). Adult schizophrenia following prenatal exposure to an influenza epidemic. *Archives of General Psychiatry, 45*(2), 189–192.

Menninger, K. (1926). Influenza and schizophrenia: an analysis of post-influenzal "dementia precox" as of 1918 and five years later. *American Journal of Psychiatry, 5*(4), 469–529.

Miklossy, J. (2011). Emerging roles of pathogens in Alzheimer disease. *Expert Reviews in Molecular Medicine, 13*, e30. http://dx.doi.org/10.1017/S1462399411002006.

Mi, S., Lee, X., Li, X., Veldman, G. M., Finnerty, H., Racie, L., et al. (2000). Syncytin is a captive retroviral envelope protein involved in human placental morphogenesis. *Nature, 403*(6771), 785–789.

Moreno, J. L., Kurita, M., Holloway, T., Lopez, J., Cadagan, R., Martinez-Sobrido, L., et al. (2011). Maternal influenza viral infection causes schizophrenia-like alterations of 5-HT(2)A and mGlu(2) receptors in the adult offspring. *Journal of Neuroscience, 31*(5), 1863–1872. http://dx.doi.org/10.1523/jneurosci.4230-10.2011.

Mori, I., Diehl, A. D., Chauhan, A., Ljunggren, H. G., & Kristensson, K. (1999). Selective targeting of habenular, thalamic midline and monoaminergic brainstem neurons by neurotropic influenza A virus in mice. *Journal of Neurovirology, 5*(4), 355–362.

Mortensen, P. B., Norgaard-Pedersen, B., Waltoft, B. L., Sorensen, T. L., Hougaard, D., Torrey, E. F., et al. (2007). *Toxoplasma gondii* as a risk factor for early-onset schizophrenia: analysis of filter paper blood samples obtained at birth. *Biological Psychiatry, 61*(5), 688–693.

Mortensen, P. B., Pedersen, C. B., Hougaard, D. M., Norgaard-Petersen, B., Mors, O., Borglum, A. D., et al. (2010). A Danish National Birth Cohort study of maternal HSV-2 antibodies as a risk factor for schizophrenia in their offspring. *Schizophrenia Research, 122*(1–3), 257–263. http://dx.doi.org/10.1016/j.schres.2010.06.010. pii:S0920-9964(10)01365-4.

Munk-Jorgensen, P., & Ewald, H. (2001). Epidemiology in neurobiological research: exemplified by the influenza-schizophrenia theory. *British Journal of Psychiatry. Supplement, 40*, s30–32.

Nellaker, C., Yao, Y., Jones-Brando, L., Mallet, F., Yolken, R. H., & Karlsson, H. (2006). Transactivation of elements in the human endogenous retrovirus W family by viral infection. *Retrovirology, 3*, 44.

Niebuhr, D. W., Li, Y., Cowan, D. N., Weber, N. S., Fisher, J. A., Ford, G. M., et al. (2011). Association between bovine casein antibody and new onset schizophrenia among US military personnel. *Schizophrenia Research, 128*(1–3), 51–55. http://dx.doi.org/10.1016/j.schres.2011.02.005. pii:S0920-9964(11)00085-5.

Niebuhr, D. W., Millikan, A. M., Cowan, D. N., Yolken, R., Li, Y., & Weber, N. S. (2008). Selected infectious agents and risk of schizophrenia among U.S. military personnel. *American Journal of Psychiatry, 165*(1), 99–106.

Nielsen, P. R., Agerbo, E., Skogstrand, K., Hougaard, D. M., Meyer, U., & Mortensen, P. B. (2014). Neonatal levels of inflammatory markers and later risk of schizophrenia. *Biological Psychiatry*. http://dx.doi.org/10.1016/j.biopsych.2014.07.013.

Nielsen, P. R., Benros, M. E., & Mortensen, P. B. (2014). Hospital contacts with infection and risk of schizophrenia: a population-based cohort study with linkage of Danish national registers. *Schizophrenia Bulletin, 40*(6), 1526–1532. http://dx.doi.org/10.1093/schbul/sbt200.

Nielsen, P. R., Laursen, T. M., & Mortensen, P. B. (2013). Association between parental hospital-treated infection and the risk of schizophrenia in adolescence and early adulthood. *Schizophrenia Bulletin, 39*(1), 230–237. http://dx.doi.org/10.1093/schbul/sbr149 sbr149.

Nielsen, P. R., Mortensen, P. B., Dalman, C., Henriksen, T. B., Pedersen, M. G., Pedersen, C. B., et al. (2013). Fetal growth and schizophrenia: a nested case-control and case-sibling study. *Schizophrenia Bulletin, 39*(6), 1337–1342. http://dx.doi.org/10.1093/schbul/sbs148.

Nishimura, H., Itamura, S., Iwasaki, T., Kurata, T., & Tashiro, M. (2000). Characterization of human influenza A (H5N1) virus infection in mice: neuro-, pneumo- and adipotropic infection. *Journal of General Virology, 81*(Pt 10), 2503–2510.

Notarangelo, F. M., Wilson, E. H., Horning, K. J., Thomas, M. A., Harris, T. H., Fang, Q., et al. (2014). Evaluation of kynurenine pathway metabolism in *Toxoplasma gondii*-infected mice: implications for schizophrenia. *Schizophrenia Research, 152*(1), 261–267. http://dx.doi.org/10.1016/j.schres.2013.11.011.

Oommen, K. J., Johnson, P. C., & Ray, C. G. (1982). Herpes simplex type 2 virus encephalitis presenting as psychosis. *American Journal of Medicine, 73*(3), 445–448.

Owens, G. P., Gilden, D., Burgoon, M. P., Yu, X., & Bennett, J. L. (2011). Viruses and multiple sclerosis. *Neuroscientist, 17*(6), 659–676. http://dx.doi.org/10.1177/1073858411386615.

Pearce, B. D., Valadi, N. M., Po, C. L., & Miller, A. H. (2000). Viral infection of developing GABAergic neurons in a model of hippocampal disinhibition. *Neuroreport, 11*(11), 2433–2438.

Pereira, L., Petitt, M., Fong, A., Tsuge, M., Tabata, T., Fang-Hoover, J., et al. (2014). Intrauterine growth restriction caused by underlying congenital cytomegalovirus infection. *Journal of Infectious Diseases, 209*(10), 1573–1584. http://dx.doi.org/10.1093/infdis/jiu019.

Perron, H., Hamdani, N., Faucard, R., Lajnef, M., Jamain, S., Daban-Huard, C., et al. (2012). Molecular characteristics of Human Endogenous Retrovirus type-W in schizophrenia and bipolar disorder. *Translational Psychiatry, 2*, e201. http://dx.doi.org/10.1038/tp.2012.125.

Perron, H., Mekaoui, L., Bernard, C., Veas, F., Stefas, I., & Leboyer, M. (2008). Endogenous retrovirus type W GAG and envelope protein antigenemia in serum of schizophrenic patients. *Biological Psychiatry, 64*(12), 1019–1023. http://dx.doi.org/10.1016/j.biopsych.2008.06.028. pii:S0006-3223(08)00836-6.

Pletnikov, M. V., Moran, T. H., & Carbone, K. M. (2002). Borna disease virus infection of the neonatal rat: developmental brain injury model of autism spectrum disorders. *Frontiers in Bioscience, 7*, d593–607.

Rantakallio, P., Jones, P., Moring, J., & Von Wendt, L. (1997). Association between central nervous system infections during childhood and adult onset schizophrenia and other psychoses: a 28-year follow-up. *International Journal of Epidemiology, 26*(4), 837–843.

Reid, A. H., McCall, S., Henry, J. M., & Taubenberger, J. K. (2001). Experimenting on the past: the enigma of von Economo's encephalitis lethargica. *Journal of Neuropathology & Experimental Neurology, 60*(7), 663–670.

Reinacher, M., Bonin, J., Narayan, O., & Scholtissek, C. (1983). Pathogenesis of neurovirulent influenza A virus infection in mice. Route of entry of virus into brain determines infection of different populations of cells. *Laboratory Investigation, 49*(6), 686–692.

Rice, D., & Barone, S., Jr. (2000). Critical periods of vulnerability for the developing nervous system: evidence from humans and animal models. *Environmental Health Perspectives, 108*(Suppl. 3), 511–533.

Rothschild, D. M., O'Grady, M., & Wecker, L. (1999). Neonatal cytomegalovirus exposure decreases prepulse inhibition in adult rats: implications for schizophrenia. *Journal of Neuroscience Research, 57*(4), 429–434.

Rubin, S. A., Sylves, P., Vogel, M., Pletnikov, M., Moran, T. H., Schwartz, G. J., et al. (1999). Borna disease virus-induced hippocampal dentate gyrus damage is associated with spatial learning and memory deficits. *Brain Research Bulletin, 48*(1), 23–30.

Ruller, C. M., Tabor-Godwin, J. M., Van Deren, D. A., Jr., Robinson, S. M., Maciejewski, S., Gluhm, S., et al. (2012). Neural stem cell depletion and CNS developmental defects after enteroviral infection. *American Journal of Pathology, 180*(3), 1107–1120. http://dx.doi.org/10.1016/j.ajpath.2011.11.016.

Sakamoto, A., Moriuchi, H., Matsuzaki, J., Motoyama, K., & Moriuchi, M. (2014). Retrospective diagnosis of congenital cytomegalovirus infection in children with autism spectrum disorder but no other major neurologic deficit. *Brain and Development*. http://dx.doi.org/10.1016/j.braindev.2014.03.016.

Shi, L., Fatemi, S. H., Sidwell, R. W., & Patterson, P. H. (2003). Maternal influenza infection causes marked behavioral and pharmacological changes in the offspring. *Journal of Neuroscience, 23*(1), 297–302.

Shi, L., Tu, N., & Patterson, P. H. (2005). Maternal influenza infection is likely to alter fetal brain development indirectly: the virus is not detected in the fetus. *International Journal of Developmental Neuroscience, 23*(2–3), 299–305. http://dx.doi.org/10.1016/j.ijdevneu.2004.05.005.

Short, S. J., Lubach, G. R., Karasin, A. I., Olsen, C. W., Styner, M., Knickmeyer, R. C., et al. (2010). Maternal influenza infection during pregnancy impacts postnatal brain development in the rhesus monkey. *Biological Psychiatry, 67*(10), 965–973. http://dx.doi.org/10.1016/j.biopsych.2009.11.026.

Simmons, D. G., Natale, D. R., Begay, V., Hughes, M., Leutz, A., & Cross, J. C. (2008). Early patterning of the chorion leads to the trilaminar trophoblast cell structure in the placental labyrinth. *Development, 135*(12), 2083–2091. http://dx.doi.org/10.1242/dev.020099.

Smith, W., Andrewes, C. H., & Laidlaw, P. P. (July 8, 1933). A virus obtained from influenza patients. *The Lancet, 1*, 66–68.

Smith, S. E., Li, J., Garbett, K., Mirnics, K., & Patterson, P. H. (2007). Maternal immune activation alters fetal brain development through interleukin-6. *Journal of Neuroscience, 27*(40), 10695–10702. http://dx.doi.org/10.1523/JNEUROSCI.2178-07.2007.

Solomon, T., Lewthwaite, P., Perera, D., Cardosa, M. J., McMinn, P., & Ooi, M. H. (2010). Virology, epidemiology, pathogenesis, and control of enterovirus 71. *Lancet Infectious Diseases, 10*(11), 778–790. http://dx.doi.org/10.1016/S1473-3099(10)70194-8.

Sorensen, H. J., Mortensen, E. L., Reinisch, J. M., & Mednick, S. A. (2009). Association between prenatal exposure to bacterial infection and risk of schizophrenia. *Schizophrenia Bulletin, 35*(3), 631–637. http://dx.doi.org/10.1093/schbul/sbn121.

Stoye, J. P. (2006). Koala retrovirus: a genome invasion in real time. *Genome Biology, 7*(11), 241. http://dx.doi.org/10.1186/gb-2006-7-11-241.

Stuart-Harris, C. H. (1939). A neurotropic strain of human influenza virus. *The Lancet,* 497–499.

Tanaka, H., Park, C. H., Ninomiya, A., Ozaki, H., Takada, A., Umemura, T., et al. (2003). Neurotropism of the 1997 Hong Kong H5N1 influenza virus in mice. *Veterinary Microbiology, 95*(1–2), 1–13.

Tang, J. L., Wang, M. L., Qiu, J. J., Wu, D., Hu, W., Shi, B. F., et al. (2002). Building a mouse model hallmarking the congenital human cytomegalovirus infection in central nervous system. *Archives of Virology, 147*(6), 1189–1195. http://dx.doi.org/10.1007/s00705-002-0797-3.

Too, L. K., McQuillan, J. A., Ball, H. J., Kanai, M., Nakamura, T., Funakoshi, H., et al. (2014). The kynurenine pathway contributes to long-term neuropsychological changes in experimental pneumococcal meningitis. *Behavioural Brain Research, 270*, 179–195. http://dx.doi.org/10.1016/j.bbr.2014.05.018.

Torrey, E. F., Rawlings, R., & Waldman, I. N. (1988). Schizophrenic births and viral diseases in two states. *Schizophrenia Research, 1*(1), 73–77.

Torrey, E. F., Torrey, B. B., & Peterson, M. R. (1977). Seasonality of schizophrenic births in the United States. *Archives of General Psychiatry, 34*(9), 1065–1070.

Townsend, C. L., Forsgren, M., Ahlfors, K., Ivarsson, S. A., Tookey, P. A., & Peckham, C. S. (2013). Long-term outcomes of congenital cytomegalovirus infection in Sweden and the United Kingdom. *Clinical Infectious Diseases, 56*(9), 1232–1239. http://dx.doi.org/10.1093/cid/cit018.

Tsutsui, Y., Kosugi, I., & Kawasaki, H. (2005). Neuropathogenesis in cytomegalovirus infection: indication of the mechanisms using mouse models. *Reviews in Medical Virology, 15*(5), 327–345. http://dx.doi.org/10.1002/rmv.475.

Ward, A. C. (1996). Neurovirulence of influenza A virus. *Journal of Neurovirology, 2*(3), 139–151.

Weiser, M., Werbeloff, N., Levine, A., Livni, G., Schreiber, S., Halperin, D., et al. (2010). CNS infection in childhood does not confer risk for later schizophrenia: a case-control study. *Schizophrenia Research, 124*(1–3), 231–235. http://dx.doi.org/10.1016/j.schres.2010.08.025. pii:S0920-9964(10)01496-9.

Whitton, J. L., Cornell, C. T., & Feuer, R. (2005). Host and virus determinants of picornavirus pathogenesis and tropism. *Nature Reviews Microbiology, 3*(10), 765–776. http://dx.doi.org/10.1038/nrmicro1284.

Williams, B. L., & Lipkin, W. I. (2006). Endoplasmic reticulum stress and neurodegeneration in rats neonatally infected with borna disease virus. *Journal of Virology, 80*(17), 8613–8626. http://dx.doi.org/10.1128/JVI.00836-06.

Williams, K., & Mackenzie, J. S. (1977). Influenza infections during pregnancy in the mouse. *The Journal of Hygiene (London), 79*(2), 249–257.

Woolf, N. K., Jaquish, D. V., & Koehrn, F. J. (2007). Transplacental murine cytomegalovirus infection in the brain of SCID mice. *Virology Journal, 4*, 26. http://dx.doi.org/10.1186/1743-422X-4-26.

Wu, Y. J., Schulz, H., Lin, C. C., Saar, K., Patone, G., Fischer, H., et al. (2013). Borna disease virus-induced neuronal degeneration dependent on host genetic background and prevented by soluble factors. *Proceedings of the National Academy of Sciences of the United States of America, 110*(5), 1899–1904. http://dx.doi.org/10.1073/pnas.1214939110.

Yawn, D. H., Pyeatte, J. C., Joseph, J. M., Eichler, S. L., & Garcia-Bunuel, R. (1971). Transplacental transfer of influenza virus. *JAMA, 216*(6), 1022–1023.

Yolken, R. (2004). Viruses and schizophrenia: a focus on herpes simplex virus. *Herpes, 11*(Suppl. 2), 83A–88A.

Yolken, R. H., Jones-Brando, L., Dunigan, D. D., Kannan, G., Dickerson, F., Severance, E., et al. (2014). Chlorovirus ATCV-1 is part of the human oropharyngeal virome and is associated with changes in cognitive functions in humans and mice. *Proceedings of the National Academy of Sciences of the United States of America, 111*(45), 16106–16111. http://dx.doi.org/10.1073/pnas.1418895111.

Young, G. R., Eksmond, U., Salcedo, R., Alexopoulou, L., Stoye, J. P., & Kassiotis, G. (2012). Resurrection of endogenous retroviruses in antibody-deficient mice. *Nature, 491*(7426), 774–778. http://dx.doi.org/10.1038/nature11599.

Zerbo, O., Qian, Y., Yoshida, C., Grether, J. K., Van de Water, J., & Croen, L. A. (2013). Maternal infection during pregnancy and autism spectrum disorders. *Journal of Autism and Developmental Disorders.* http://dx.doi.org/10.1007/s10803-013-2016-3.

13

Toward a Diathesis-Stress Model of Schizophrenia in a Neurodevelopmental Perspective

A. Berry, F. Cirulli

Behavioural Neuroscience Section, Department of Cell Biology and Neurosciences, Istituto Superiore di Sanità, Rome, Italy

Our fear of psychosis or disruptive behavior may keep us from seeing the heroic struggle that people with this disorder [schizophrenia] face just to survive amidst the internal chaos and panic that is part of this chronic illness. **Insel (2010)**

INTRODUCTION

Schizophrenia is a profoundly disabling and persistent psychiatric disorder that affects more than 21 million people worldwide based on the World Health Organization estimate. It is characterized by broad-range devastating symptoms that include those commonly defined as positive (hyperarousal, hallucinations, delusions, and racing thoughts) and negative (emotional flattening, social withdrawal, and apathy) in addition to cognitive impairment (lack of insight, disorganized thoughts, and attention and memory deficits), with auditory hallucination and paranoid delusions being among the most striking and disruptive (Tamminga & Holcomb, 2005). The first signs of the disease appear at adolescence or early adulthood, with men showing an anticipated onset compared with women, on average by 3–4 years (Hafner, Maurer, Loffler, & Riecher-Rossler, 1993), usually followed by a long-term course of social and professional disability. Indeed, decreased community functioning has been recently suggested to be a core symptom of schizophrenia together with somatic comorbidity (Rethelyi, Benkovits, & Bitter, 2013; Scott & Happell, 2011). This latter includes cardiovascular complications, metabolic syndrome, impaired

lung function (also from excessive cigarette smoking), and higher susceptibility to HIV, hepatitis, and tuberculosis leading to an overall increase in the management costs of these psychiatric patients who suffer from mortality rates—including suicide—2 to 2.5 times higher than the general population (Bradley & Dinan, 2010; Kelly et al., 2011; McEvoy et al., 2005; Mitchell & Lord, 2010; Ringen, Engh, Birkenaes, Dieset, & Andreassen, 2014; Saha, Chant, & McGrath, 2007; Weinmann, Read, & Aderhold, 2009).

As recently pointed out by Insel (2010), 100 years ago, there were large public institutions for mental illness, tuberculosis, and leprosy; nowadays, whereas prevalence of infectious diseases has in most cases been reduced, the burden of mental disability, and particularly of schizophrenia, has not changed, if not increased (Hegarty, Baldessarini, Tohen, Waternaux, & Oepen, 1994). In fact, notwithstanding a large number of research efforts to derive pharmacological and psychosocial treatments, schizophrenia still remains a puzzling syndrome with a very heterogeneous symptomatology and a mainly unknown multifactorial complex etiology.

Among psychiatric disorders, schizophrenia appears to be the most severe and the highest heritability, suggesting that genetic factors play a main role in the etiology of this disorder. Epidemiological studies on twins estimate its heritability at about 80% (Sullivan, Kendler, & Neale, 2003), whereas studies taking into account the family history provide a reliable estimate closer to 60% (Lichtenstein et al., 2009) or lower (Modinos et al., 2013; van Os, Kenis, & Rutten, 2010; Zuk, Hechter, Sunyaev, & Lander, 2012). Indeed, although several genes have been proposed as strong candidates playing a role in the etiopathogenesis of schizophrenia, only weak evidence of association with disease risk were found (Allen et al., 2008). Interestingly, many of these genes play a role during neuronal development being involved in cell migration and proliferation, axonal outgrowth, myelination, synaptogenesis, and apoptosis, suggesting a major role of neurodevelopmental insults (Fatemi & Folsom, 2009). Most intriguingly, schizophrenia has also been associated with genes of the major histocompatability complex on human chromosome 6, suggesting that major histocompatability complex proteins, in addition to their obvious role in immune response pathways, might also share an effect in neuronal development and synaptic plasticity (Shatz, 2009), further supporting the idea that immune challenges in critical developmental time might represent a risk factor for the onset of the disease (Knuesel et al., 2014).

The availability of new high-throughput genotyping technology has pushed genomic research to investigate beyond the risk conferred by single candidate genes by carrying out genome-wide association studies on psychiatric populations (Corvin, Craddock, & Sullivan, 2010). This approach on the one hand has identified common and rare variants showing reliable association with schizophrenia and on the other has provided highly replicable results among different studies. However, the risk associated with each common variant is comparable to that based on a candidate gene hypothesis (Modinos et al., 2013). As for rare variants (e.g., copy number variants), the risk effects are much higher but being so rare they can only account for a small proportion of the genetic vulnerability to schizophrenia (Consortium, 2008; Modinos et al., 2013; Stefansson et al., 2008). Thus, the picture emerging from this evidence is such that schizophrenia has a very complex genetic architecture that can only partially account for the onset of the disease.

This "missing heritability" calls into question the role of the environment as a main liability factor participating to the so-called "hidden heritability" of schizophrenia (van Dongen & Boomsma, 2013; van Os et al., 2010; Zuk et al., 2012). In this regard, adverse environments can be a source of stress provided by very different stimuli of biological or psychosocial nature that might occur early during the perinatal development of an organism and/or during subsequent life stages (as a further "hit" with additive effects on the genetic and/or the perinatal vulnerability) contributing to the etiology and course of the disease. Based on epidemiological studies, obstetric complications at birth (Cannon, Jones, & Murray, 2002; Mittal, Ellman, & Cannon, 2008), maternal stress (Khashan et al., 2008), maternal malnutrition (Brown & Susser, 2008), childhood abuse (or early traumatic events in general) (Arseneault et al., 2011; Varese

et al., 2012), urbanicity (Pedersen & Mortensen, 2006), minority or migrant status (Cantor-Graae & Selten, 2005), and cannabis use (Arseneault et al., 2002)—just to mention a few—appear as reliable risk factors playing causal roles in the etiopathogenesis of the disease. However, the neurobiological mechanisms underlying their effects on schizophrenia risk are mostly unknown. In addition, it must be emphasized that most of these risk factors show a poor outcome, if considered per se, are characterized by pleiotropic effects (being therefore not specific for schizophrenia) and are found to be associated with several other psychiatric conditions (Insel, 2010).

A widely accepted model takes into account both genetic and environmental risk factors in an integrative vulnerability view that considers schizophrenia as a neurodevelopmental (and also a neurodegenerative) disorder. This hypothesis, sustained by strong epidemiological and preclinical evidence, considers that multiple gene–environment interactions—and the deriving "epigenetic scars"—act as driving forces to reshape the brain circuitry (temporal and prefrontal cortical–thalamic–ventral striatal being the most affected pathways) during development (i.e., from prenatal life to adolescence) (Fatemi & Folsom, 2009; Feinberg, 1982; Insel, 2010; Lewis & Levitt, 2002; McGowan & Szyf, 2010; Murray, Jones, & O'Callaghan, 1991; Weinberger, 1987).

As briefly mentioned previously, many aspects of the environmental contribution to the neurodevelopmental origin of the disease can be broadly ascribed to stress. In this context, environmental stressors are no longer seen, just as the precipitants of conditions that will appear sooner or later during the life course of the individual or as exacerbating factors of an existing or dormant symptomatology, but rather as biologically active forces driving developmental trajectories through the interaction with a genotype leading to a unique vulnerable "epiphenotype." Thus, a crucial challenge in this field of research is trying to understand how stressors become integrated into the developmental program of an organism, leading to the specific brain functional and structural changes (e.g., hippocampal damage ventricular enlargement, altered cytoarchitecture, migration of neurons) and alterations in neurochemical parameters (dopamine (DA), glutamate, γ-amino butyric acid (GABA) serotonin, and brain-derived neurotrophic factor (BDNF)) characterizing the disease, and persisting into adult life. Understanding the biological mechanisms occurring during the early stages of life, including pre- and perinatal phases, can help to predict specific changes in brain development (architecture, connectivity, neurochemistry) underlying mental disability in a life-long perspective (Bateson et al., 2004).

Ultimately, health promotion might depend upon our ability to moderate or redirect the adverse effects of stress during specific developmental sensitive periods (time windows) through early intervention strategies.

STRESS AS A RISK FACTOR FOR PSYCHOPATHOLOGY

Mammalian development for most species relies upon a gradual process occurring before and after birth, leading to a continuous accumulation of small changes. This process results from the interaction between the individual genetic asset and the pre- and/or postnatal environment and is functional to the generation of very different phenotypes fitting with different environmental conditions promoting the successful perpetuation of the genotype and affecting both the existence of the individual and population biology (Bateson, 2001; Bateson et al., 2004; D'Udine & Alleva, 1980). During development, the organism shows increased plasticity allowing the individual to adjust to environmental changes; however, the bad side of this developmental flexibility is such that it provides "diathetic windows" for later diseases. The final outcome of the developmental program will depend, beyond the genetic asset of the individual, upon the stability of the environment that contributed to prime developmental trajectories (Bateson et al., 2004).

It is widely accepted that body-mind homeostasis is lost following exposure to chronic stress (or "allostatic load") (Bateson et al., 2004). The activation of stress systems results in an integrated repertoire of physiological responses that include the activation of the hypothalamic-pituitary-adrenal (HPA) axis and the secretion of adrenal stress hormones (glucocorticoids (GC)), increased heart rate and blood pressure, elevated blood sugar, and redirection of blood flow to the brain leading to increased vigilance and eventually ending up to a "fight or flight" coping strategy. The discrete activation of these systems results in a stress response, which is functional for organism to cope with an acute threat. However, an unwanted and prolonged response, such as during circumstances of chronic or overwhelming adversity, will lead to the overshooting of the system becoming harmful for the individual (Shonkoff, Boyce, & McEwen, 2009). Thus, it has been hypothesized that early in life, adverse events can shape the experience-dependent maturation of the neuroendocrine systems and corticolimbic circuitry underlying emotional functioning, leading to increased stress responses at adulthood (Meaney, 2001; Schore, 2000; Seckl & Meaney, 2004; Tronick & Reck, 2009). Schizophrenia patients with a history of childhood abuse are indeed characterized by a dysfunctional HPA axis (Read, Perry, Moskowitz, & Connolly, 2001). Likewise, Walker and Diforio suggest that prenatal stress by affecting HPA axis

development might lead to its overdrive and in turn to increased DA receptors and DA release that characterize the positive symptoms of the disease (for review see Read et al., 2001; Walker & Diforio, 1997). Moreover, early life abuse or neglect has been associated with abnormal development of those brain areas involved in emotional disorders including volume loss in hippocampus, corpus callosum, prefrontal cortex, altered symmetry in cortical regions, and reduced neuronal density and integrity in the anterior cingulate (Bremner et al., 1997; Carrion et al., 2001; De Bellis et al., 2002; Driessen et al., 2000; Stein, Koverola, Hanna, Torchia, & McClarty, 1997; Teicher et al., 2004).

In a mechanistic perspective, several theories have been put forward to describe how liability can become "embedded" into brain physiology: among others, a "cumulative stress" also known as the "two-hit" (or three-hit) hypothesis and a "mismatch hypothesis" are of main interest (Nederhof & Schmidt, 2012). According to the cumulative stress model, environmental stressful conditions lead to a "first hit" perturbing the early developmental trajectories of neurochemical pathways and neuronal circuits and providing a long-term vulnerable background. These same pathways may be targets also for a "second hit" of stress occurring in the adolescent or adult organism (often providing a triggering factor for the onset of the disease). The final outcome is therefore the result of cumulative hits during development (allostatic load), whereas individual susceptibility to early programming is provided by the genetic asset (three-hit model) (Daskalakis, Bagot, Parker, Vinkers, & de Kloet, 2013).

A different and somehow provocative idea, inspired from evolutionary theories, is the "mismatch hypothesis." According to this theory, individuals are more likely to be affected by a disease if a mismatch occurs between the environmental conditions experienced during early life developmental stages and the adult environment. Also in this case, the genotype provides the ground for environmental stress-related shaping effects on developing neurochemical pathways and neuronal brain circuits and for the selection of the most adapted phenotype. A reconciling and intriguing view proposes that specific genes or genetic variants (individual genetic asset) by increasing the individual plasticity, or programming sensitivity, may predispose an organism to be more vulnerable to stressful environmental conditions, also explaining the often observed inter-individual differences in the outcomes of stress (Belsky et al., 2009). Thus, the cumulative stress hypothesis should better apply to individuals characterized by a "genetic resiliency" to environmental programming, whereas the mismatch hypothesis applies to individuals characterized by "genetic plasticity" who experienced strong programming effects (Nederhof & Schmidt, 2012).

AN INTEGRATIVE NEURODEVELOPMENTAL APPROACH TO THE ETIOPATHOGENESIS OF SCHIZOPHRENIA

Schizophrenia is generally not diagnosed until adolescence or early adulthood, suggesting that this disease originates as the final outcome of some disruptive process acting on the immature brain of a developing organism ("neurodevelopmental hypothesis of schizophrenia" (Fatemi & Folsom, 2009; Harrison, 1997; Rehn & Rees, 2005)). Epidemiological studies have provided ample evidence for prenatal immune challenges (e.g., exposure to influenza viruses), obstetric complications—involving hypoxic events—prenatal maternal psychological stress, and maternal and fetal nutritional deficiency to be risk factors for the onset of schizophrenia later in life (see Rethelyi et al., 2013 and references therein). However, because not every individual develops the disease, the etiopathogenesis of schizophrenia likely involves interactions at multiple levels between genetic vulnerability and environmental factors taking place at different time points throughout the development of an organism to produce a very heterogeneous symptomatology. Thus, it has been hypothesized that an early insult might occur followed by a quiescent phase; the onset of the disease usually appears in late adolescence or early adulthood, a sensitive time characterized by a massive neuronal rearrangement (pruning). A possible explanation for this phenomenon is provided by the "developmental allostasis" hypothesis (Thompson & Levitt, 2010) i.e., a "lesion" early during development does not manifest until a much later developmental stage, when compensatory changes can no longer compensate. Alternatively, the developmental lesion influences pathways or regulatory processes, such as the fine balance of excitatory and inhibitory synapses in the prefrontal cortex, which may have only subtle effects until a fine tuning is required in late adolescence. Current data cannot distinguish between these two options, but either way a neurodevelopmental perspective implies the importance of timing and the opportunity for earlier intervention and prevention (Insel, 2010). This model is based on the occurrence of early abnormalities during the neurodevelopmental processes, well in advance of the disease onset. However, as pointed out by Limosin, all stages of proper brain development may be affected, from proliferation to the differentiation and migration processes, and then from dendritic and axonal growth to myelination, a process that continues at least until early adulthood, notably in the prefrontal cortex (Limosin, 2014).

Despite being one of the most accepted and exhaustive models, critics to the neurodevelopmental hypothesis of schizophrenia claim that it does not fully address the issues of the long time lapse between neurodevelopmental insult and the development of symptoms as well as the progressive clinical deterioration observed in some patients and evidence of progressive changes in certain ventricular and cortical brain structures (Bertolino et al., 1998; Lieberman, 1999). In this context, a further interesting vision integrates the neurodevelopmental approach with a neurodegenerative etiopathogenesis hypothesis of the onset of the disease, suggesting that one potential mechanism that could account for the progressive nature of schizophrenia is apoptosis, or programmed cell death, especially synaptic apoptosis, which is localized to distal neurites without inducing immediate neuronal death (Fatemi & Folsom, 2009; Jarskog, Glantz, Gilmore, & Lieberman, 2005; Mattson & Duan, 1999). However, a more accepted view implies that the changes in brain structure and morphology observed in postmortem tissues from schizophrenic patients account for an increased reduction of neuritic processes (dendrite and synapses) rather than loss of neuronal or glial cell bodies, a physiological phenomenon also known as "pruning," which characterizes adolescence and late adulthood. Thus, abnormal reduction in synaptic connectivity should result from developmental disruption of synaptogenic processes taking place during early developmental phases and/or of synaptic pruning during adolescence (Andersen, Thompson, Rutstein, Hostetter, & Teicher, 2000; Limosin, 2014; McGlashan & Hoffman, 2000).

ANIMAL MODELS OF SCHIZOPHRENIA

Being characterized by a very heterogeneous clinical symptomatology, and having a frank multigenic component, devising reliable animal models as useful tools to study schizophrenia has never been an easy task. In the past few decades, with the availability of new technologies, there has been great advancement in investigating susceptibility genes for schizophrenia leading to the identification of signaling cascades related to the pathophysiology of the disease. However, as mentioned previously, a direct cause–effect link is still complex to prove (Jaaro-Peled, Ayhan, Pletnikov, & Sawa, 2010). Nonetheless, the generation of specific animal models aimed at translating the human genetic mutations represents an important strategy to investigate the etiology and pathogenesis of schizophrenia, to identify new potential drug targets, and to test the efficacy of novel antipsychotic treatments. Endpoints assessed in animal models of schizophrenia are mainly related to changes in brain morphology, neurochemistry, or behavior (Boksa, 2004). So far several genetically modified mouse models have been generated that reproduce with good approximation some aspects of the pathology ranging from specific anatomical features to positive, negative, and cognitive symptoms characterizing the disease. Interestingly, several genetic mouse models for schizophrenia are based on the targeted disruption of genes involved in neurodevelopment and neuronal plasticity (e.g., reeler mice, heterozygous or inducible BDNF knock-out mice, DISC1 mutants, NCAM-deficient mice (Albrecht & Stork, 2012; Cash-Padgett & Jaaro-Peled, 2013; Chen, Lipska, & Weinberger, 2006; Sakata & Duke, 2014)), whereas others have been specifically generated in the search for vulnerability factors affecting the molecular pathways of the dopamine and glutamine neurotransmission systems most relevant to the disease—hyperdopaminergic and hypogluta-minergic hypotheses (e.g., Nrg1 knock-out mice characterized by deficit in the neurotrophic regulation of GABAergic and dopaminergic neurons, myelination, and N-methyl-D-aspartate (NMDA) receptor function; dopamine transporter and dopamine D1 and D2 receptors; DARPP-32 knockout mice, NMDA receptor subunit 1 and calcineurin knock-out mice; (Rethelyi et al., 2013) see also Chen et al. (2006) and references therein for a complete review). However, a comprehensive discussion of genetic models of schizophrenia is beyond the scope of this chapter and reference has been made in a dedicated chapter.

There is a large body of evidence that stress, especially experienced during early life phases, plays a pivotal role as a risk factor for the development of almost all psychiatric disorders ranging from posttraumatic stress disorder (Bremner, Southwick, Johnson, Yehuda, & Charney, 1993) and major depressive disorder (Heim & Nemeroff, 2001) to schizophrenia (van Os et al., 2010). However, despite decades of research in this field, questions related to which particular stressor or combination of stressful events are the most etiologically relevant and how they interact at different time points during life to forecast the development of psychopathology remain currently unanswered (Daskalakis et al., 2013). A traumagenic hypothesis of schizophrenia is based upon studies correlating early life stressful events to the development of the disease later in life (Limosin, 2014; Read et al., 2001). Nonetheless, this evidence is quite speculative, being based upon retrospective subjective reports. In addition, events leading to traumatic wounds with long-lasting consequences for one person can be perceived just as temporary obstacles for others. For obvious ethical reasons, the manipulation of the early environment for subsequent assessment of emotional state in humans is unfeasible. Thus, early life stress-based animal models are mandatory to understand how early adversities can affect behavioral and neurobiological features relevant to the disease and to establish and evaluate novel pharmacological approaches to treat schizophrenia patients.

Before the identification of genetic susceptibility factors for schizophrenia different approaches to model the disease were built around the administration of drugs (Ellenbroek & Cools, 2002)—often mimicking psychotic symptoms—or were aimed at dissecting out the neurodevelopmental risks of schizophrenia. As for drug-based models, these show some predictive or construct validity and have been instrumental to theorize three of the most prominent mechanistic assumptions of schizophrenia: the dopamine, serotonin, and glutamate hypothesis. These involve the administration of dopaminergic or serotonergic agonists to mimic positive symptoms or antagonist of the NMDA receptors to mimic the negative ones (Geyer & Moghaddam, 2002). As for neurodevelopmental models, they involve two very different approaches relying either on brain neurotoxic lesions (Lipska & Weinberger, 1993; Molteni, Lipska, Weinberger, Racagni, & Riva, 2001) or on environmental stressors at appropriate timing (Jaaro-Peled et al., 2010). The former class involves neonatal excitotoxic lesions of the ventral hippocampus able to produce postpubertal behavioral abnormalities, such as increased spontaneous, amphetamine-induced, and NMDA antagonist-induced locomotion (Lipska & Weinberger, 1993). By contrast, as for the developmental stress models, the most frequently used to assess long-term consequences on schizophrenia-related emotional and cognitive deficits range from prenatal maternal immune activation (Meyer, Feldon, Schedlowski, & Yee, 2006), obstetric complications (Boksa, 2004), and prenatal maternal psychological challenges (Baier, Katunar, Adrover, Pallares, & Antonelli, 2012; Kinnunen, Koenig, & Bilbe, 2003; Lee, Brady, Shapiro, Dorsa, & Koenig, 2007) to maternal vitamin D deficiency (Kesby et al., 2012), maternal deprivation (Ellenbroek, van den Kroonenberg, & Cools, 1998; Garner, Wood, Pantelis, & van den Buuse, 2007; Girardi, Zanta, & Suchecki, 2014), and social isolation rearing starting from weaning (Geyer, Wilkinson, Humby, & Robbins, 1993; Moller, Du Preez, Emsley, & Harvey, 2011).

This neurodevelopmental approach will be the focus of this chapter and the main emphasis will be given to rodents' models of perinatal stress resulting, at adult age, in behavioral deficits as well as in neuropathological features similar to those observed in brains of schizophrenia patients. The following sections will be devoted to dissect the mechanisms through which the stress system and its effectors can modulate brain function and behavior in a long-term perspective, paving the way for vulnerability to psychopathology. Interestingly, stress and the underlying changes of the neuroendocrine system appear both as causal factors and part of the symptomatology of the disease. In fact, it has been suggested that early life adversities by affecting HPA axis maturation might lead to its overdrive and, in turn, to increased DA receptors and DA release characterizing the positive symptoms of the disease (for a review, see Read et al., 2001; Walker & Diforio, 1997). In addition, psychotic disorders appear to be associated with increased HPA activity both at baseline and after stressful challenge; moreover, antipsychotic treatments reduce HPA activation, whereas stress and the consequent increase in circulating glucocorticoid hormones can exacerbate psychotic symptoms (Walker, Mittal, & Tessner, 2008). Thus, the role of the neuroendocrine system, and of the HPA axis in particular, will be described in the context of psychopathology. In addition, the role of dynamic epigenetic remodeling will be explored as a potential mechanism underlying the long-term programming effects of stress and as a promising target for environmental or pharmacological interventions.

MODELING SCHIZOPHRENIA WITH PRENATAL STRESS

Stress is any change of the internal or external milieu perturbing the maintenance of homeostasis. In complex organisms, it implies a coordinated set of intercellular signals and physiological and behavioral responses that result in avoidance or adaptation to the stressful stimulus. The activation of the neuroendocrine system (HPA axis) in response to stress, in the short run, is functional to adapt and maintain the homeostasis (allostasis = maintaining stability through changes). Yet, over prolonged times, it imposes a cost (allostatic load) that might affect growth, metabolism, reproduction, inflammatory/immune, and neuroendocrine responses (de Kloet, Joels, & Holsboer, 2005; Maccari & Morley-Fletcher, 2007; McEwen, 1998; Seckl, 2004).

During prenatal phases, the effects of environmental challenges are transmitted to the fetus, shaping developmental trajectories in a tissue-, time-, and challenge-specific fashion (Harris & Seckl, 2011). Thus, the allostatic load accumulated during early life phases can pervasively impact on animal's biology, setting the stage for the emergence of phenotypes vulnerable to the onset of many and different pathologies during adult life, including cardiovascular disease, type 2 diabetes, emotional disorders, and psychopathology, just to mention a few (Cirulli & Berry, 2013). As is often the case, the occurrence of the previously mentioned pathological conditions is not mutually exclusive and comorbid clinical frames can be observed involving the presence of metabolic, cardiovascular alterations, and psychiatric disorders, including schizophrenia, strengthening the hypothesis of a common origin for vulnerability to diseases (Engum, 2007; Fan et al., 2010; Fan, Wu, Shen, Ji, & Zhan, 2013; Leonard, Schwarz, & Myint, 2012; McEvoy et al., 2005).

Human epidemiological studies consistently provide evidence for an association between environmental challenges during pregnancy, altered fetal growth (often characterized by intrauterine growth restriction), and the development and occurrence of many pathological conditions later in life, findings that gave origin to the so-called "Barker hypothesis," also known as "developmental origins of adult disease" (Barker et al., 1993; Seckl, 1998). Interestingly, these associations seem independent from lifestyle-related risk factors (e.g., obesity, smoking, alcohol consumption, social class) (Harris & Seckl, 2011; Leon et al., 1996; Levine, Hennekens, & Jesse, 1994; Osmond, Barker, Winter, Fall, & Simmonds, 1993) and, as assessed in studies on twins, the genetic asset can just moderately account for this association (Baird et al., 2001; Bateson et al., 2004). Indeed, decreased weight at birth has been associated with cognitive disabilities, depression, schizophrenia, anxiety, attention deficit/hyperactivity disorder, and antisocial behaviors (Famularo & Fenton, 1994; Khashan et al., 2008; Raikkonen & Pesonen, 2009; Raikkonen et al., 2008; Wust, Entringer, Federenko, Schlotz, & Hellhammer, 2005). Several maternal complications have been specifically related to negative fetal outcomes, including preeclampsia, depression, diabetes, infection/inflammation, and obesity (Zammit et al., 2009), whereas maternal psychosocial stress results in altered fetal weight; insulin resistance; metabolic, immune, and endocrine function; and decreased cognitive performance (Entringer et al., 2010). With respect to schizophrenia, obstetric complications, both during pregnancy and at labor, are considered a main factor in the etiopathogenesis of this disease. These include diabetes, rhesus incompatibility, bleeding, preeclampsia, emergency cesarean section, uterine atony, and asphyxia. In this context, hypoxic/ischemic injury has been proposed as a reliable common mechanism leading to the later onset of the disease (Boksa, 2004; Cannon et al., 2002). In addition, maternal infection during pregnancy, prenatal stress, and prenatal malnutrition can be all considered as risk factors for schizophrenia (Brown, 2011; Brown & Susser, 2008; Knuesel et al., 2014).

Most of these mentioned causal links have been investigated in animal models of prenatal stress including restraint or chronic unpredictable stress in the third week of pregnancy—a time window during gestation particularly sensitive to stress in rodent models (Welberg, Seckl, & Holmes, 2001). Metabolic or immune challenges have been also used such as disruption of maternal metabolic pathways (chronic undernutrition, nutrient unbalance, maternal diabetes) (Harms, Eyles, McGrath, Mackay-Sim, & Burne, 2008; Johansson, Meyerson, & Eriksson, 1991; Palmer, Printz, Butler, Dulawa, & Printz, 2004) or viral/bacterial infections (Meyer, Schwendener, Feldon, & Yee, 2006) often providing insights into the mechanisms mediating the effects of maternal stress on the fetus and the behavioral abnormalities characterizing adult age and strengthening the conclusions deriving from human studies (Boksa, 2004; Koenig et al., 2005; Meyer & Feldon, 2009; Meyer & Feldon, 2010). As a result of these early challenges, several abnormal behaviors can be observed in the postpubertal offspring, such as increased anxiety and depressive-like behavior, impaired cognitive abilities, greater vulnerability to psychostimulants, disrupted circadian rhythm, and increased paradoxical sleep in addition to increased markers of brain inflammation and oxidative stress (Bilbo & Tsang, 2010; Darnaudery & Maccari, 2008; Koenig et al., 2005; Maccari & Morley-Fletcher, 2007; Vallee et al., 1999; Vallee et al., 1997). Most of these features, including pharmacological abnormalities, are consistent with a schizophrenia-like phenotype. In this regard, following prenatal restraint stress, both a potentiation of the locomotor response to novelty or amphetamine (Deminiere et al., 1992) and a facilitation of amphetamine sensitization (Henry et al., 1995) have been observed. These data appear overall in agreement with a dopaminergic hypothesis of schizophrenia and strongly suggest that prenatal psychophysical stressors can have long-term programming effects on the dopaminergic system as well as on the individual perception and responsivity to environmental stimuli leading to a hyperaroused phenotype.

In the search for specific behavioral markers to evaluate the validity of animal models of schizophrenia, many studies have reported a deficit in the sensorimotor gating of experimental subjects undergoing different prenatal insults as assessed in the prepulse inhibition of the startle reflex (PPI) and/or in the latent inhibition (LI) tests. The PPI refers to the reduction of an acoustic startle response upon preexposure to a weak, nonstartling stimulus, whereas LI is based on the phenomenon of reduced conditioning after preexposure to stimulus (Ellenbroek & Riva, 2003; Leumann, Feldon, Vollenweider, & Ludewig, 2002). The popularity of these experimental paradigms is related to clinical observations showing that schizophrenia patients are characterized by impairment in the ability to filter or "gate" irrelevant, intrusive sensory stimuli (Swerdlow, Weber, Qu, Light, & Braff, 2008). Worth noticing, the original face validity of the PPI paradigm derives from the observation that apomorphine, a dopamine agonist, disrupts PPI in rats while attenuating or abolishing LI (Leumann et al., 2002). As far as animal models of prenatal challenges are concerned, disrupted PPI is found in the offspring as a result of maternal immune challenges (Shi, Fatemi, Sidwell, & Patterson, 2003), chronic unpredictable stress (Koenig et al., 2005), and protein deprivation (Palmer et al., 2004) in mice and rats as well as a result of cesarean section in guinea pigs (Vaillancourt & Boksa, 2000). Worth noticing, alteration in the sensorimotor gating

have been also reported in animal models of postnatal stress mimicking traumatic adverse early experiences such as maternal deprivation or rearing in social isolation (Ellenbroek & Riva, 2003; Geyer et al., 1993). Thus, animal models of schizophrenia characterized by dysfunctional sensorimotor gating are generally considered robust and reliable also across species. However, despite specific changes in the PPI and LI being greeted with great enthusiasm when trying to model schizophrenia, data in the literature are overall conflicting varying upon the nature of the prenatal (or postnatal) stressor the selected animal model and the gender of the offspring (Patterson, 2012). These discrepancies should not be surprising because it must be emphasized that, taken alone, PPI and LI cannot be considered as diagnostic instruments in the clinical practice. In addition, there are many different disorders in which affected individuals show reduced PPI, on average, when compared with a normal population; moreover, not all schizophrenia patients are characterized by disrupted LI (Braff, Geyer, & Swerdlow, 2001; Weiner, 2003). Last but not least, several physiological conditions might affect the sensorimotor gating, including estrogens as well as pregnancy both in humans and in animal models (Jovanovic et al., 2004; Koch, 1998; Plappert, Rodenbucher, & Pilz, 2005; Swerdlow, Hartman, & Auerbach, 1997). To this aim, Bonsignore and coworkers have provided evidence that lactating rats, born under conditions of cesarean section and acute perinatal asphyxia, are characterized by a deficit in maternal care associated with increased arousal in the plus maze (a test of anxiety) as well as with increased freezing in the fear conditioning (an associative learning task involving a freezing response as the result of pairing an unconditioned stimulus—such as foot shock—with a conditioned stimulus a particular context and/or such a cue) (Bonsignore, Venerosi, Chiarotti, Alleva, & Cirulli, 2006). Thus it is possible to hypothesize that the long-term effect of obstetric complication on maternal arousal might reflect an overall inability of the mother to filter out irrelevant stimuli while caring for the offspring. This feature is of main adaptive value for the mother–infant dyad and has been found disrupted in schizophrenia (Boksa, 2004; Cirulli, Berry, & Alleva, 2003).

A different class of behavioral alterations related to the individual's hypofunctionality rather than to a hyperresponsiveness to environmental stimuli is that of negative symptoms. The negative symptoms of schizophrenia, that include anhedonia, affective flattening, and impaired social functioning (among others), represent core features of the disorder, accounting for much of the long-term morbidity and poor functional outcome (Insel, 2010; Limosin, 2014). Notwithstanding their prominence and prognostic value the research for effective and feasible animal models of these negative symptoms has not been completely successful (Ellenbroek & Cools, 2000; Moser, 2014). In fact, as pointed out by Ellenbroek and Cool, although an approach based on exogenous drug administration (psychomimetic drugs such as phencyclidine or amphetamine see also Geyer & Moghaddam, 2002) to mimic negative symptoms has led to weak or sometimes inconclusive results (with main reference to predictive validity), the growing consensus on the neurodevelopmental hypothesis of schizophrenia has started to call for different animal models where early life stressful events can account for the long-term behavioral changes observed (Ellenbroek & Cools, 2000)—also in the search of valid novel therapeutic approaches. In this regard, it is interesting to note that two very recent papers report comparable long-term effects on social behavior in the adolescent offspring as a result of different perinatal stressors such as prenatal restraint stress or maternal deprivation (Berry et al., 2015; Girardi et al., 2014). In particular, Girardi and coworkers found that adolescent rats that have experienced 24 h of maternal deprivation were characterized by reduced sociality and affective flattening (Girardi et al., 2014). Likewise, Berry and coworkers found that prenatally stressed rats, at adolescence showed not only a reduction in social interest and in affiliative behaviors but also decreased hippocampal expression levels of BDNF, a neurotrophin playing a pivotal role in neuronal development as well as synaptic plasticity, emotionality and cognitive abilities (Cirulli & Alleva, 2009). These effects were also associated to a specific change in the hippocampal *NKCC1/KCC2* ratio (two genes related to GABA signaling), suggesting an imbalance between neuronal inhibitory and excitatory mechanisms possibly related to an immature GABA system (Hyde et al., 2011). Most intriguingly, the authors also provide evidence that, for a prenatally stressed rat, the interaction with a nonstressed control subject leads to an improvement in sociality suggesting that the social environment could be exploited for nonpharmacological therapeutic intervention (Berry et al., 2015). In this regard, Luoni and coworkers showed that early treatment with lurasidone, an atypical multireceptor antipsychotic, prevents the observed reduction in BDNF levels in prenatally stressed rats (Luoni et al., 2014), further suggesting that an early therapeutic intervention (environmental, pharmacological, or, even better, a combination of the two) in vulnerable individuals, during critical developmental phases, has the potential to act on dynamic systems enhancing the expression of neuroplastic molecules in key brain regions, leading to long-term beneficial effects on brain function as well as enhanced resilience to stress-related disorders.

Exposure to prenatal stress in rodents results in increased responsiveness of the HPA axis to stress, though this overdrive of the neuroendocrine system may vary according to gender and to the nature or the intensity of the stressor (Maccari et al., 1995; Morley-Fletcher et al., 2003; Vallee et al., 1997). In addition, reduced levels of both mineralocorticoid and glucocorticoid receptors (the main receptors for the adrenal stress hormones cortisol and corticosterone) are found in the hippocampus of adult offspring, revealing a possible mechanism for the deficit of HPA axis feedback processes (Maccari et al., 1995). Moreover, a reduced hippocampal mineralocorticoid/glucocorticoid receptor ratio could also account for the disrupted circadian rhythmicity of corticosterone secretion, observed as a result of prenatal stress (Koehl et al., 1999). Likewise, it has been proposed that specific alterations related to the dopaminergic system (e.g., enhanced sensitivity to dopaminergic agonists in prenatally stressed rats) observed as a result of prenatal stress might be the result of a permanent reprogramming of the neuroendocrine system; in fact, there is ample evidence that DA synthesis, reuptake, and receptor sensitivity are, at least in part, under the control of the HPA axis. Most interestingly, it has been proposed that the neuroendocrine and the dopaminergic system might interact in a mutual synergistic fashion resulting in an increased vulnerability to stress and, in turn, in the onset of psychiatric disorders, such as schizophrenia (Baier et al., 2012; Deminiere et al., 1992; Walker & Diforio, 1997).

Several animal models of early manipulations have provided evidence that altered GC secretion and behavioral response occur earlier than the often-observed cognitive alterations that are mainly observed later in life, and these cognitive alterations could be one consequence of early HPA axis hyperactivity (Vallee et al., 1999; Viltart et al., 2006). Interestingly, the response of adult prenatally stressed female rats to an early stress is less evident, and despite showing hyperactivity in the HPA axis, females are characterized by reduced anxiety-like behavior and improved learning, suggesting an early effect of stress on hormonal systems with an impact on their "organizational effects." These preclinical studies are quite interesting particularly when considering that women with schizophrenia often show better premorbid functioning, a later onset, and better course of the disease, in addition to different structural brain abnormalities and cognitive deficits (Canuso & Pandina, 2007). By contrast, it has been proposed that greater premorbid behavioral dysfunction, earlier onset of symptoms, and poorer prognosis found in male patients can be triggered and/or exacerbated (in vulnerable individuals) by a hyperresponsive HPA axis (Walker & Diforio, 1997).

Apart from maternal psychophysical stress, which has been amply reviewed in this chapter, most of the animal models related to prenatal stress and mentioned previously (e.g., maternal infection, malnutrition and diabetes during pregnancy), have been shown to be associated with enhanced maternal glucocorticoid secretion (Boksa, 2004;

Koenig, Kirkpatrick, & Lee, 2002). Thus excessive prenatal exposure to GCs might indeed represent a common risk factor and a possible mechanism underlying vulnerability to schizophrenia.

COMMON MECHANISMS UNDERLYING PRENATAL ADVERSITIES ASSOCIATED WITH SCHIZOPHRENIA

A great body of evidence suggests that prenatal insults represent the main risk factors for developing schizophrenia later in life, and that exposure to a very different range of prenatal insults seems to converge to comparable effects on the fetal development, suggesting that some kind of "funneling effect" occurs during pregnancy (Cirulli & Berry, 2013). Given the prevalent effects of stress on the functionality of the HPA axis, this phenomenon should not be surprising providing a main link between the adaptation of the central nervous system to environmental challenges and peripheral behavioral, endocrine, and metabolic responses (Cirulli & Alleva, 2009; McEwen et al., 1992; McEwen, Brinton, & Sapolsky, 1988; Sapolsky, Krey, & McEwen, 1986).

The placenta is the main mother–fetus interface, a temporary structure that, for the growing fetus, performs the functions of several adult organs related to metabolism, respiration, excretion, and endocrine function. Most importantly, it handles stress signals from the mother to the fetus through the expression of specific transporters regulating the access of glucose, amino acids, vitamins, and ions required for growth and development (Bale et al., 2010; Fowden, Sferruzzi-Perri, Coan, Constancia, & Burton, 2009). In addition, the presence of the 11β-hydroxysteroid dehydrogenase type 2 (HSD2) enzyme, by acting as a shield, guarantees the rapid inactivation of maternal GCs (Edwards, Benediktsson, Lindsay, & Seckl, 1993; Meaney, Szyf, & Seckl, 2007). However, HSD2 provides only a partial barrier, allowing a moderate amount of maternal GCs to reach the fetus (Benediktsson, Calder, Edwards, & Seckl, 1997) promoting lung maturation (Ward, 1994) and brain development, remodeling axons and dendrites, and affecting cell survival (Meyer, 1983; Yehuda, Fairman, & Meyer, 1989). In fact, GCs are essential for the fetus to develop, they bind to GR and mineralocorticoid receptors that are widely expressed in the fetal tissues and in the placenta, acting as transcription factors to alter gene expression. Controlled fluctuations in the expression levels or in the functionality of HSD2 naturally occur during pregnancy to allow the correct amount of GCs to reach the fetus at the proper time for organs maturation. As a consequence, an incorrect activation of the HSD2 barrier can profoundly impact on the exposure of the fetus to GCs hormones and on its development.

Worth noticing, emotional stressors (Mairesse et al., 2007) and metabolic/nutritional challenges (Bertram, Trowern, Copin, Jackson, & Whorwood, 2001; Langley-Evans, 1997) have an equal potential to impact on the expression and/or activity of the HSD2 leading to high levels of GCs reaching the fetus, with a consequent effect on growth retardation and on developmental programming resulting in an increased vulnerability to diseases later in life (Benediktsson et al., 1997; Edwards et al., 1993; Seckl, 1998). In addition, in vitro studies using placental cells lines have also provided evidence that the activity of HSD2 can be downregulated by several other factors including hypoxia, catecholamines, and proinflammatory cytokines (Chisaka, Johnstone, Premyslova, Manduch, & Challis, 2005; Hardy & Yang, 2002; Homan, Guan, Hardy, Gratton, & Yang, 2006). Thus, hormonal signals of maternal status, including GCs, insulin-like growth factors, insulin, and leptin, are sensed by the placenta and transmitted to the fetus predominantly through effects on placental function.

A proper placental functionality is strictly related to successful birth. In this regard, it is interesting to note that preeclampsia-like conditions have been observed both in animal models of prenatal stress and in a model of gestational diabetes (Boksa, 2004; Ishihara, Hiramatsu, Masuyama, & Kudo, 2000; Takiuti, Kahhale, & Zugaib, 2002). These data are also in agreement with recent observations in mice that high-fat diet administration during pregnancy results in a pervasive impact on maternal physiology leading to a disrupted placental functionality in addition to increased pregnancy length and maternal emotionality often leading to increased mortality around the time of delivery (Bellisario et al., 2015) overall suggesting that obstetric complications per se might represent a risk factor for the later onset of diseases.

Despite this evidence, prenatal challenges certainly cannot act alone and interesting results from rodents' models have clearly proven that the maternal genetic asset can critically act in determining the developmental origin of health and diseases. A nice example is provided by two strains of rats selectively bred for high or low anxiety-related behavior. In particular, it has been shown that low anxiety-related behavior rats can modulate placental HSD2 in response to restraint stress during pregnancy protecting their offspring from the negative effects of a too high exposure to maternal GCs (Lucassen et al., 2009). Moreover, knock-out mice for the HSD2 enzyme are characterized by a reduced birth weight only on C57Bl/6J but not on the 129 × MF1 background (Holmes et al., 2006; Kotelevtsev et al., 1999). Thus, not only the fetal but also the maternal individual genetic asset can interact with the environment leading to a complex remodeling of the developing organism providing an "allostatic load," which results in long-term diathesis toward mental health.

ENVIRONMENTAL IMPACT ON THE EPIGENETIC SHAPING AND IMPLICATIONS FOR SCHIZOPHRENIA

Not every individual characterized with a vulnerable genetic background will develop schizophrenia. In fact, the etiopathogenesis of this disorder is quite complex, likely involving interactions at multiple levels between genetic susceptibility and environmental factors taking place at different time points throughout the development to produce a heterogeneous symptomatology. In this regard, the concept of epigenetics—that is the influence of the environment operating over or above the level of the genetic code—is well suited to describe gene by environment interactions, and it has been successfully applied to the neurodevelopmental hypothesis of psychiatric disorders. Indeed, the idea that a multitude of external or internal challenges can affect the genome during brain development is particularly intriguing in the context of the neurobiological models of schizophrenia (Akbarian, 2014). The most striking example, in this regard, is provided by monozygotic twins that are characterized by an identical genetic background but do not share the same pre- and postnatal experiences. Thus, specific environmental-driven changes in their epigenome can account for the often observed discordance in their prevalence of mental disorders, including schizophrenia (McDonald, Lewis, Murphy, O'Reilly, & Singh, 2003; Petronis et al., 2003; Tsujita et al., 1998).

Epigenetics is the study of heritable changes different from those provided by DNA sequence that include DNA methylation and histone modifications (methylation, acetylation, phosphorylation, and sumoylation) (Callinan & Feinberg, 2006). The state of modification of the histones defines the accessibility of the DNA to the transcription machinery necessary for gene function; inaccessible genes are relatively silent, whereas accessible genes are actively transcribed (Razin, 1998).

Interestingly, because genetic and epigenetic silencing could have similar phenotypic consequences, it can be hypothesized that a great part of the phenotypic variation observed in human populations might also result from differences in the long-term programming of gene function rather than the sequence per se (McGowan & Szyf, 2010). Thus, if the plasticity characterizing the developing organism is based on epigenetic mechanisms, disease-related outcomes might result from the disruptions of epigenetic processes elicited by internal or external stressful challenges during sensitive times. This epigenetic vision of brain plasticity might provide a mechanistic explanation for the long-term effects of adverse/stressful fetal, infant, and childhood environments and a growing body of preclinical evidence support this idea.

As already widely discussed, stress and the consequent allostatic load on the neuroendocrine system are both causal factors (early in life), as are elements contributing to the symptomatology of schizophrenia (later in life). Animal models have provided ample evidence for the contribution of early (positive or negative) environment/experiences to epigenetic alterations in stress responsiveness. As an example, Meaney and Szyf investigating epigenetic effects of maternal care in rats found that higher maternal care increases the expression of the glucocorticoid receptor in the hippocampus, while reducing hypothalamic corticotrophin- releasing hormone and HPA responsivity to stress (Francis & Meaney, 1999; Liu et al., 1997; Meaney & Szyf, 2005), providing a direct link between early experiences (maternal behavior) and DNA methylation in glucocorticoid receptor gene. Most intriguingly, the same authors also provided evidence that such early effects can be reversed by central infusion of methionine (a methyl donor), suggesting that these epigenomic modifications are potentially reversible later in life (Weaver et al., 2004; Weaver et al., 2005). By contrast, early life stress as provided by maternal separation has shown that low maternal care results in a DNA hypomethylation in the arginine-vasopressin neurons of the hypothalamic paraventricular nucleus resulting in a hyperactive HPA axis in adult mice offspring (Murgatroyd et al., 2009). Another early life stress model based on stressed, abusive rat dams has shown that pups reared under these conditions are characterized by reduced levels of BDNF expression in the prefrontal cortex, which correlates with DNA hypermethylation at the activity dependent exon IV promoter. These authors on the one hand provided evidence for the transgenerational effects of these epigenetic modifications; on the other hand, they were able to reverse this effect by infusing the DNA methylation inhibitor zebularine (Roth, Lubin, Funk, & Sweatt, 2009). More recently, it has been shown that prenatal stress in rats leads to a specific decrease in the expression of BDNF, possibly mediated by increased DNA methylation of BDNF exon IV (Boersma et al., 2014). These preclinical data are interesting not only because this neurotrophin may act as a neuroendocrine effector involved in the response to stress (Cirulli & Alleva, 2009), but also because a reduced expression of BDNF in pyramidal neurons, and of its receptor TrkB in GABAergic interneurons, might be responsible for changes in brain plasticity, as exemplified by decreased spine density observed in the brains of schizophrenia patients (Lewis, Hashimoto, & Volk, 2005).

Most of the studies just mentioned support the hypothesis that epigenetic modifications occurring during early life phases are potentially reversible also in predominantly postmitotic tissues, such as the brain

(McGowan & Szyf, 2010). In particular, it has been proposed that the DNA methylation pattern is the balance between methylation and demethylation reactions occurring as a result of physiological and environmental signals setting the stage for gene–environment interactions (Ramchandani, Bhattacharya, Cervoni, & Szyf, 1999; Weaver et al., 2004). Differently from the static architecture of the genome, this dynamic nature of the epigenome might provide a mechanism for reprogramming gene function in response to changes in lifestyle and/or to pharmacological interventions specifically targeting epigenetic mechanisms. As an example, valproic acid is a mood stabilizer showing some effects in alleviating psychotic symptoms (in adjunct to antipsychotics) in schizophrenia and, very interestingly, it acts as a histone deacetylase inhibitor (Phiel et al., 2001). Although the biological and behavioral effects of some epigenetic drugs such as histone deacetylase inhibitor have been characterized in the brain, the mechanisms underlying specificity in the gene targeted by these compounds, which are fundamental for an effective use in mental illnesses, are still being actively investigated.

All in all, identifying epigenetic changes accounting for behavioral pathological traits could have important implications for therapy because these mechanisms are potentially reversible (McGowan & Szyf, 2010). In this regard, in the future, building an epigenome map of the brain as a consequence of mental illness appears as an appealing strategy.

Acknowledgments

This work was supported by EU (FP7) Project DORIAN "Developmental Origin of Healthy and Unhealthy aging: the role of maternal obesity" (grant number 278603) and by ERA net-NEURON "Poseidon" and RF-2009-1498890 and Fondazione Cariplo 2014. The authors are grateful to Sara Capoccia e Veronica Bellisario and Pamela Panetta for their skillful help in retrieving and selecting bibliographic entries.

References

Akbarian, S. (2014). Epigenetic mechanisms in schizophrenia. *Dialogues in Clinical NeuroSciences, 16*(3), 405–417.

Albrecht, A., & Stork, O. (2012). Are NCAM deficient mice an animal model for schizophrenia? *Frontiers in Behavioral Neuroscience, 6*, 43.

Allen, N. C., Bagade, S., McQueen, M. B., Ioannidis, J. P., Kavvoura, F. K., Khoury, M. J., et al. (2008). Systematic meta-analyses and field synopsis of genetic association studies in schizophrenia: the SzGene database. *Nature Genetics, 40*(7), 827–834. http://dx.doi.org/10.1038/ng.171.

Andersen, S. L., Thompson, A. T., Rutstein, M., Hostetter, J. C., & Teicher, M. H. (2000). Dopamine receptor pruning in prefrontal cortex during the periadolescent period in rats. *Synapse, 37*(2), 167–169.

Arseneault, L., Cannon, M., Fisher, H. L., Polanczyk, G., Moffitt, T. E., & Caspi, A. (2011). Childhood trauma and children's emerging psychotic symptoms: a genetically sensitive longitudinal cohort study. *American Journal of Psychiatry, 168*(1), 65–72. http://dx.doi.org/10.1176/appi.ajp.2010.10040567.

Arseneault, L., Cannon, M., Poulton, R., Murray, R., Caspi, A., & Moffitt, T. E. (2002). Cannabis use in adolescence and risk for adult psychosis: longitudinal prospective study. *BMJ, 325*(7374), 1212–1213.

Baier, C. J., Katunar, M. R., Adrover, E., Pallares, M. E., & Antonelli, M. C. (2012). Gestational restraint stress and the developing dopaminergic system: an overview. *Neurotoxicity Research, 22*(1), 16–32.

Baird, J., Osmond, C., MacGregor, A., Snieder, H., Hales, C. N., & Phillips, D. I. (2001). Testing the fetal origins hypothesis in twins: the Birmingham twin study. *Diabetologia, 44*(1), 33–39.

Bale, T. L., Baram, T. Z., Brown, A. S., Goldstein, J. M., Insel, T. R., McCarthy, M. M., et al. (2010). Early life programming and neurodevelopmental disorders. *Biological Psychiatry, 68*(4), 314–319.

Barker, D. J., Gluckman, P. D., Godfrey, K. M., Harding, J. E., Owens, J. A., & Robinson, J. S. (1993). Fetal nutrition and cardiovascular disease in adult life. *Lancet, 341*(8850), 938–941.

Bateson, P. (2001). Fetal experience and good adult design. *International Journal of Epidemiology, 30*(5), 928–934.

Bateson, P., Barker, D., Clutton-Brock, T., Deb, D., D'Udine, B., Foley, R. A., et al. (2004). Developmental plasticity and human health. *Nature, 430*(6998), 419–421.

Bellisario, V., Panetta, P., Balsevich, G., Baumann, V., Noble, J., Raggi, C., Nathan, O., Berry, A., Seckl, J., Schmidt, M., Holmes, M., Cirulli, F. (2015). Maternal high-fat diet acts as a stressor increasing maternal glucocorticoids' signaling to the fetus and disrupting maternal behavior and brain activation in C57BL/6J mice. *Psychoneuroendocrinology, 24*(60), 138–150.

Belsky, J., Jonassaint, C., Pluess, M., Stanton, M., Brummett, B., & Williams, R. (2009). Vulnerability genes or plasticity genes? *Molecular Psychiatry, 14*(8), 746–754. http://dx.doi.org/10.1038/mp.2009.44.

Benediktsson, R., Calder, A. A., Edwards, C. R., & Seckl, J. R. (1997). Placental 11 beta-hydroxysteroid dehydrogenase: a key regulator of fetal glucocorticoid exposure. *Clinical Endocrinology (Oxford), 46*(2), 161–166.

Berry, A., Panetta, P., Luoni, A., Bellisario, V., Capoccia, S., Riva, M. A., Cirulli, F. (2015). Decreased Bdnf expression and reduced social behavior in periadolescent rats following prenatal stress. *Developmental Psychobiology, 57*(3), 365–373.

Bertolino, A., Kumra, S., Callicott, J. H., Mattay, V. S., Lestz, R. M., Jacobsen, L., et al. (1998). Common pattern of cortical pathology in childhood-onset and adult-onset schizophrenia as identified by proton magnetic resonance spectroscopic imaging. *American Journal of Psychiatry, 155*(10), 1376–1383.

Bertram, C., Trowern, A. R., Copin, N., Jackson, A. A., & Whorwood, C. B. (2001). The maternal diet during pregnancy programs altered expression of the glucocorticoid receptor and type 2 11beta-hydroxysteroid dehydrogenase: potential molecular mechanisms underlying the programming of hypertension in utero. *Endocrinology, 142*(7), 2841–2853.

Bilbo, S. D., & Tsang, V. (2010). Enduring consequences of maternal obesity for brain inflammation and behavior of offspring. *FASEB Journal, 24*(6), 2104–2115.

Boersma, G. J., Lee, R. S., Cordner, Z. A., Ewald, E. R., Purcell, R. H., Moghadam, A. A., et al. (2014). Prenatal stress decreases Bdnf expression and increases methylation of Bdnf exon IV in rats. *Epigenetics, 9*(3), 437–447. http://dx.doi.org/10.4161/epi.27558.

Boksa, P. (2004). Animal models of obstetric complications in relation to schizophrenia. *Brain Research. Brain Research Reviews, 45*(1), 1–17. http://dx.doi.org/10.1016/j.brainresrev.2004.01.001.

Bonsignore, L. T., Venerosi, A., Chiarotti, F., Alleva, E., & Cirulli, F. (2006). Acute perinatal asphyxia at birth has long-term effects on behavioural arousal and maternal behaviour in lactating rats. *Behavioural Brain Research, 172*(1), 54–62. http://dx.doi.org/10.1016/j.bbr.2006.04.010.

Bradley, A. J., & Dinan, T. G. (2010). A systematic review of hypo-thalamic-pituitary-adrenal axis function in schizophrenia: implications for mortality. *Journal of Psychopharmacology*, 24(4 Suppl.), 91–118.

Braff, D. L., Geyer, M. A., & Swerdlow, N. R. (2001). Human studies of prepulse inhibition of startle: normal subjects, patient groups, and pharmacological studies. *Psychopharmacology (Berl)*, 156(2–3), 234–258.

Bremner, J. D., Randall, P., Vermetten, E., Staib, L., Bronen, R. A., Mazure, C., et al. (1997). Magnetic resonance imaging-based measurement of hippocampal volume in posttraumatic stress disorder related to childhood physical and sexual abuse–a preliminary report. *Biological Psychiatry*, 41(1), 23–32.

Bremner, J. D., Southwick, S. M., Johnson, D. R., Yehuda, R., & Charney, D. S. (1993). Childhood physical abuse and combat-related posttraumatic stress disorder in Vietnam veterans. *American Journal of Psychiatry*, 150(2), 235–239.

Brown, A. S. (2011). The environment and susceptibility to schizophrenia. *Progress in Neurobiology*, 93(1), 23–58. http://dx.doi.org/10.1016/j.pneurobio.2010.09.003.

Brown, A. S., & Susser, E. S. (2008). Prenatal nutritional deficiency and risk of adult schizophrenia. *Schizophrenia Bulletin*, 34(6), 1054–1063. http://dx.doi.org/10.1093/schbul/sbn096.

Callinan, P. A., & Feinberg, A. P. (2006). The emerging science of epigenomics. *Human Molecular Genetics*, 15(Spec No 1), R95–R101.

Cannon, M., Jones, P. B., & Murray, R. M. (2002). Obstetric complications and schizophrenia: historical and meta-analytic review. *American Journal of Psychiatry*, 159(7), 1080–1092.

Cantor-Graae, E., & Selten, J. P. (2005). Schizophrenia and migration: a meta-analysis and review. *American Journal of Psychiatry*, 162(1), 12–24. http://dx.doi.org/10.1176/appi.ajp.162.1.12.

Canuso, C. M., & Pandina, G. (2007). Gender and schizophrenia. *Psychopharmacology Bulletin*, 40(4), 178–190.

Carrion, V. G., Weems, C. F., Eliez, S., Patwardhan, A., Brown, W., Ray, R. D., et al. (2001). Attenuation of frontal asymmetry in pediatric posttraumatic stress disorder. *Biological Psychiatry*, 50(12), 943–951.

Cash-Padgett, T., & Jaaro-Peled, H. (2013). DISC1 mouse models as a tool to decipher gene-environment interactions in psychiatric disorders. *Frontiers in Behavioral Neuroscience*, 7, 113.

Chen, J., Lipska, B. K., & Weinberger, D. R. (2006). Genetic mouse models of schizophrenia: from hypothesis-based to susceptibility gene-based models. *Biological Psychiatry*, 59(12), 1180–1188. http://dx.doi.org/10.1016/j.biopsych.2006.02.024.

Chisaka, H., Johnstone, J. F., Premyslova, M., Manduch, Z., & Challis, J. R. (2005). Effect of pro-inflammatory cytokines on expression and activity of 11beta-hydroxysteroid dehydrogenase type 2 in cultured human term placental trophoblast and human choriocarcinoma JEG-3 cells. *Journal of the Society for Gynecologic Investigation*, 12(5), 303–309. http://dx.doi.org/10.1016/j.jsgi.2005.02.003.

Cirulli, F., & Alleva, E. (2009). The NGF saga: from animal models of psychosocial stress to stress-related psychopathology. *Frontiers in Neuroendocrinology*, 30(3), 379–395.

Cirulli, F., & Berry, A. (2013). Early developmental trajectories of brain development: new directions in the search of early determinants of health and longevity. In G. Laviola, & S. Macrì (Eds.), *Adaptive and maladaptive aspects of developmental stress* (Vol. 3). New York: Springer.

Cirulli, F., Berry, A., & Alleva, E. (2003). Early disruption of the mother-infant relationship: effects on brain plasticity and implications for psychopathology. *Neuroscience & Biobehavioral Reviews*, 27, 73–82.

Consortium, I. S. (2008). Rare chromosomal deletions and duplications increase risk of schizophrenia. *Nature*, 455(7210), 237–241. http://dx.doi.org/10.1038/nature07239.

Corvin, A., Craddock, N., & Sullivan, P. F. (2010). Genome-wide association studies: a primer. *Psychological Medicine*, 40(7), 1063–1077. http://dx.doi.org/10.1017/S0033291709991723.

Darnaudery, M., & Maccari, S. (2008). Epigenetic programming of the stress response in male and female rats by prenatal restraint stress. *Brain Research Reviews*, 57(2), 571–585.

Daskalakis, N. P., Bagot, R. C., Parker, K. J., Vinkers, C. H., & de Kloet, E. R. (2013). The three-hit concept of vulnerability and resilience: toward understanding adaptation to early-life adversity outcome. *Psychoneuroendocrinology*, 38(9), 1858–1873.

De Bellis, M. D., Keshavan, M. S., Shifflett, H., Iyengar, S., Beers, S. R., Hall, J., et al. (2002). Brain structures in pediatric maltreatment-related posttraumatic stress disorder: a sociodemographically matched study. *Biological Psychiatry*, 52(11), 1066–1078.

Deminiere, J. M., Piazza, P. V., Guegan, G., Abrous, N., Maccari, S., Le Moal, M., et al. (1992). Increased locomotor response to novelty and propensity to intravenous amphetamine self-administration in adult offspring of stressed mothers. *Brain Research*, 586(1), 135–139.

van Dongen, J., & Boomsma, D. I. (2013). The evolutionary paradox and the missing heritability of schizophrenia. *American Journal of Medical Genetics Part B: Neuropsychiatric Genetics*, 162B(2), 122–136. http://dx.doi.org/10.1002/ajmg.b.32135.

Driessen, M., Herrmann, J., Stahl, K., Zwaan, M., Meier, S., Hill, A., et al. (2000). Magnetic resonance imaging volumes of the hippocampus and the amygdala in women with borderline personality disorder and early traumatization. *Archives of General Psychiatry*, 57(12), 1115–1122.

D'Udine, B., & Alleva, E. (1980). On the teleonomic study of maternal behaviour. In R. S. A. Muir (Ed.), *Dialectics of biology and society in the production of mind: The dialectics of biology group* (pp. 50–61). London: Allison and Busby.

Edwards, C. R., Benediktsson, R., Lindsay, R. S., & Seckl, J. R. (1993). Dysfunction of placental glucocorticoid barrier: link between fetal environment and adult hypertension? *Lancet*, 341(8841), 355–357.

Ellenbroek, B. A., & Cools, A. R. (2000). Animal models for the negative symptoms of schizophrenia. *Behavioural Pharmacology*, 11(3–4), 223–233.

Ellenbroek, B. A., & Cools, A. R. (2002). Apomorphine susceptibility and animal models for psychopathology: genes and environment. *Behavior Genetics*, 32(5), 349–361.

Ellenbroek, B. A., van den Kroonenberg, P. T., & Cools, A. R. (1998). The effects of an early stressful life event on sensorimotor gating in adult rats. *Schizophrenia Research*, 30(3), 251–260.

Ellenbroek, B. A., & Riva, A. (2003). Early maternal deprivation as an animal model for schizophrenia. *Clinical Neuroscience Research*, 3, 297–320.

Engum, A. (2007). The role of depression and anxiety in onset of diabetes in a large population-based study. *Journal of Psychosomatic Research*, 62(1), 31–38. http://dx.doi.org/10.1016/j.jpsychores.2006.07.009.

Entringer, S., Buss, C., Shirtcliff, E. A., Cammack, A. L., Yim, I. S., Chicz-DeMet, A., et al. (2010). Attenuation of maternal psychophysiological stress responses and the maternal cortisol awakening response over the course of human pregnancy. *Stress*, 13(3), 258–268.

Famularo, R., & Fenton, T. (1994). Early developmental history and pediatric posttraumatic stress disorder. *Archives of Pediatrics and Adolescent Medicine*, 148(10), 1032–1038.

Fan, X., Liu, E. Y., Freudenreich, O., Park, J. H., Liu, D., Wang, J., et al. (2010). Higher white blood cell counts are associated with an increased risk for metabolic syndrome and more severe psychopathology in non-diabetic patients with schizophrenia. *Schizophrenia Research*, 118(1–3), 211–217. http://dx.doi.org/10.1016/j.schres.2010.02.1028.

Fan, Z., Wu, Y., Shen, J., Ji, T., & Zhan, R. (2013). Schizophrenia and the risk of cardiovascular diseases: a meta-analysis of thirteen cohort studies. *Journal of Psychiatric Research*, 47(11), 1549–1556. http://dx.doi.org/10.1016/j.jpsychires.2013.07.011.

Fatemi, S. H., & Folsom, T. D. (2009). The neurodevelopmental hypothesis of schizophrenia, revisited. *Schizophrenia Bulletin*, 35(3), 528–548. http://dx.doi.org/10.1093/schbul/sbn187.

Feinberg, I. (1982). Schizophrenia: caused by a fault in programmed synaptic elimination during adolescence? *Journal of Psychiatric Research*, 17(4), 319–334.

Fowden, A. L., Sferruzzi-Perri, A. N., Coan, P. M., Constancia, M., & Burton, G. J. (2009). Placental efficiency and adaptation: endocrine regulation. *Journal of Physiology*, 587(Pt 14), 3459–3472.

Francis, D. D., & Meaney, M. J. (1999). Maternal care and the development of stress responses. *Current Opinion in Neurobiology*, 9, 128–134.

Garner, B., Wood, S. J., Pantelis, C., & van den Buuse, M. (2007). Early maternal deprivation reduces prepulse inhibition and impairs spatial learning ability in adulthood: no further effect of post-pubertal chronic corticosterone treatment. *Behavioural Brain Research*, 176(2), 323–332.

Geyer, M. A., & Moghaddam, B. (2002). Animal models relevant to schizophrenia disorders. In K. N. Davis, D. Charney, J. T. Coyle, & C. Nemeroff (Eds.), *Neuropsychopharmacology: The fifth generation of progress*. Philadelphia: Lippincott Williams & Wilkins.

Geyer, M. A., Wilkinson, L. S., Humby, T., & Robbins, T. W. (1993). Isolation rearing of rats produces a deficit in prepulse inhibition of acoustic startle similar to that in schizophrenia. *Biological Psychiatry*, 34(6), 361–372.

Girardi, C. E., Zanta, N. C., & Suchecki, D. (2014). Neonatal stress-induced affective changes in adolescent Wistar rats: early signs of schizophrenia-like behavior. *Frontiers in Behavioral Neuroscience*, 8, 319.

Hafner, H., Maurer, K., Loffler, W., & Riecher-Rossler, A. (1993). The influence of age and sex on the onset and early course of schizophrenia. *British Journal of Psychiatry*, 162, 80–86.

Hardy, D. B., & Yang, K. (2002). The expression of 11 beta-hydroxysteroid dehydrogenase type 2 is induced during trophoblast differentiation: effects of hypoxia. *Journal of Clinical Endocrinology & Metabolism*, 87(8), 3696–3701. http://dx.doi.org/10.1210/jcem.87.8.8720.

Harms, L. R., Eyles, D. W., McGrath, J. J., Mackay-Sim, A., & Burne, T. H. (2008). Developmental vitamin D deficiency alters adult behaviour in 129/SvJ and C57BL/6J mice. *Behavioural Brain Research*, 187(2), 343–350. http://dx.doi.org/10.1016/j.bbr.2007.09.032.

Harris, A., & Seckl, J. (2011). Glucocorticoids, prenatal stress and the programming of disease. *Hormones and Behavior*, 59(3), 279–289.

Harrison, P. J. (1997). Schizophrenia: a disorder of neurodevelopment? *Current Opinion in Neurobiology*, 7(2), 285–289.

Hegarty, J. D., Baldessarini, R. J., Tohen, M., Waternaux, C., & Oepen, G. (1994). One hundred years of schizophrenia: a meta-analysis of the outcome literature. *American Journal of Psychiatry*, 151(10), 1409–1416.

Heim, C., & Nemeroff, C. B. (2001). The role of childhood trauma in the neurobiology of mood and anxiety disorders: preclinical and clinical studies. *Biological Psychiatry*, 49, 1023–1039.

Henry, C., Guegant, G., Cador, M., Arnauld, E., Arsaut, J., Le Moal, M., et al. (1995). Prenatal stress in rats facilitates amphetamine-induced sensitization and induces long-lasting changes in dopamine receptors in the nucleus accumbens. *Brain Research*, 685(1–2), 179–186.

Holmes, M. C., Abrahamsen, C. T., French, K. L., Paterson, J. M., Mullins, J. J., & Seckl, J. R. (2006). The mother or the fetus? 11beta-hydroxysteroid dehydrogenase type 2 null mice provide evidence for direct fetal programming of behavior by endogenous glucocorticoids. *Journal of Neuroscience*, 26(14), 3840–3844.

Homan, A., Guan, H., Hardy, D. B., Gratton, R. J., & Yang, K. (2006). Hypoxia blocks 11beta-hydroxysteroid dehydrogenase type 2 induction in human trophoblast cells during differentiation by a time-dependent mechanism that involves both translation and transcription. *Placenta*, 27(8), 832–840. http://dx.doi.org/10.1016/j.placenta.2005.09.006.

Hyde, T. M., Lipska, B. K., Ali, T., Mathew, S. V., Law, A. J., Metitiri, O. E., et al. (2011). Expression of GABA signaling molecules KCC2, NKCC1, and GAD1 in cortical development and schizophrenia. *Journal of Neuroscience*, 31(30), 11088–11095. http://dx.doi.org/10.1523/JNEUROSCI.1234-11.2011.

Insel, T. R. (2010). Rethinking schizophrenia. *Nature*, 468(7321), 187–193.

Ishihara, G., Hiramatsu, Y., Masuyama, H., & Kudo, T. (2000). Streptozotocin-induced diabetic pregnant rats exhibit signs and symptoms mimicking preeclampsia. *Metabolism*, 49(7), 853–857. http://dx.doi.org/10.1053/meta.2000.6750.

Jaaro-Peled, H., Ayhan, Y., Pletnikov, M. V., & Sawa, A. (2010). Review of pathological hallmarks of schizophrenia: comparison of genetic models with patients and nongenetic models. *Schizophrenia Bulletin*, 36(2), 301–313. http://dx.doi.org/10.1093/schbul/sbp133.

Jarskog, L. F., Glantz, L. A., Gilmore, J. H., & Lieberman, J. A. (2005). Apoptotic mechanisms in the pathophysiology of schizophrenia. *Progress in Neuro-Psychopharmacology & Biological Psychiatry*, 29(5), 846–858.

Johansson, B., Meyerson, B., & Eriksson, U. J. (1991). Behavioral effects of an intrauterine or neonatal diabetic environment in the rat. *Biology of the Neonate*, 59(4), 226–235.

Jovanovic, T., Szilagyi, S., Chakravorty, S., Fiallos, A. M., Lewison, B. J., Parwani, A., et al. (2004). Menstrual cycle phase effects on prepulse inhibition of acoustic startle. *Psychophysiology*, 41(3), 401–406. http://dx.doi.org/10.1111/1469-8986.2004.00166.x.

Kelly, D. L., McMahon, R. P., Wehring, H. J., Liu, F., Mackowick, K. M., Boggs, D. L., et al. (2011). Cigarette smoking and mortality risk in people with schizophrenia. *Schizophrenia Bulletin*, 37(4), 832–838.

Kesby, J. P., O'Loan, J. C., Alexander, S., Deng, C., Huang, X. F., McGrath, J. J., et al. (2012). Developmental vitamin D deficiency alters MK-801-induced behaviours in adult offspring. *Psychopharmacology (Berl)*, 220(3), 455–463.

Khashan, A. S., Abel, K. M., McNamee, R., Pedersen, M. G., Webb, R. T., Baker, P. N., et al. (2008). Higher risk of offspring schizophrenia following antenatal maternal exposure to severe adverse life events. *Archives of General Psychiatry*, 65(2), 146–152. http://dx.doi.org/10.1001/archgenpsychiatry.2007.20.

Kinnunen, A. K., Koenig, J. I., & Bilbe, G. (2003). Repeated variable prenatal stress alters pre- and postsynaptic gene expression in the rat frontal pole. *Journal of Neurochemistry*, 86(3), 736–748.

de Kloet, E. R., Joels, M., & Holsboer, F. (2005). Stress and the brain: from adaptation to disease. *Nature Reviews Neuroscience*, 6(6), 463–475.

Knuesel, I., Chicha, L., Britschgi, M., Schobel, S. A., Bodmer, M., Hellings, J. A., et al. (2014). Maternal immune activation and abnormal brain development across CNS disorders. *Nature Reviews Neurology*, 10(11), 643–660.

Koch, M. (1998). Sensorimotor gating changes across the estrous cycle in female rats. *Physiology & Behavior*, 64(5), 625–628.

Koehl, M., Darnaudery, M., Dulluc, J., Van Reeth, O., Le Moal, M., & Maccari, S. (1999). Prenatal stress alters circadian activity of hypothalamo-pituitary-adrenal axis and hippocampal corticosteroid receptors in adult rats of both gender. *Journal of Neurobiology*, 40(3), 302–315.

Koenig, J. I., Elmer, G. I., Shepard, P. D., Lee, P. R., Mayo, C., Joy, B., et al. (2005). Prenatal exposure to a repeated variable stress paradigm elicits behavioral and neuroendocrinological changes in the adult offspring: potential relevance to schizophrenia. *Behavioural Brain Research*, 156(2), 251–261. http://dx.doi.org/10.1016/j.bbr.2004.05.030.

Koenig, J. I., Kirkpatrick, B., & Lee, P. (2002). Glucocorticoid hormones and early brain development in schizophrenia. *Neuropsychopharmacology*, 27(2), 309–318. http://dx.doi.org/10.1016/S0893-133X(01)00396-7.

Kotelevtsev, Y., Brown, R. W., Fleming, S., Kenyon, C., Edwards, C. R., Seckl, J. R., et al. (1999). Hypertension in mice lacking 11beta-hydroxysteroid dehydrogenase type 2. *Journal of Clinical Investigation*, 103(5), 683–689.

Langley-Evans, S. C. (1997). Hypertension induced by foetal exposure to a maternal low-protein diet, in the rat, is prevented by pharmacological blockade of maternal glucocorticoid synthesis. *Journal of Hypertension*, 15(5), 537–544.

Lee, P. R., Brady, D. L., Shapiro, R. A., Dorsa, D. M., & Koenig, J. I. (2007). Prenatal stress generates deficits in rat social behavior: reversal by oxytocin. *Brain Research, 1156*, 152–167.

Leon, D. A., Koupilova, I., Lithell, H. O., Berglund, L., Mohsen, R., Vagero, D., et al. (1996). Failure to realise growth potential in utero and adult obesity in relation to blood pressure in 50 year old Swedish men. *BMJ, 312*(7028), 401–406.

Leonard, B. E., Schwarz, M., & Myint, A. M. (2012). The metabolic syndrome in schizophrenia: is inflammation a contributing cause? *Journal of Psychopharmacology, 26*(5 Suppl.), 33–41. http://dx.doi.org/10.1177/0269881111431622.

Leumann, L., Feldon, J., Vollenweider, F. X., & Ludewig, K. (2002). Effects of typical and atypical antipsychotics on prepulse inhibition and latent inhibition in chronic schizophrenia. *Biological Psychiatry, 52*(7), 729–739.

Levine, R. S., Hennekens, C. H., & Jesse, M. J. (1994). Blood pressure in prospective population based cohort of newborn and infant twins. *BMJ, 308*(6924), 298–302.

Lewis, D. A., Hashimoto, T., & Volk, D. W. (2005). Cortical inhibitory neurons and schizophrenia. *Nature Reviews Neuroscience, 6*(4), 312–324. http://dx.doi.org/10.1038/nrn1648.

Lewis, D. A., & Levitt, P. (2002). Schizophrenia as a disorder of neurodevelopment. *Annual Review of Neuroscience, 25*, 409–432. http://dx.doi.org/10.1146/annurev.neuro.25.112701.142754.

Lichtenstein, P., Yip, B. H., Bjork, C., Pawitan, Y., Cannon, T. D., Sullivan, P. F., et al. (2009). Common genetic determinants of schizophrenia and bipolar disorder in Swedish families: a population-based study. *Lancet, 373*(9659), 234–239. http://dx.doi.org/10.1016/S0140-6736(09)60072-6.

Lieberman, J. A. (1999). Is schizophrenia a neurodegenerative disorder? A clinical and neurobiological perspective. *Biological Psychiatry, 46*(6), 729–739.

Limosin, F. (2014). Neurodevelopmental and environmental hypotheses of negative symptoms of schizophrenia. *BMC Psychiatry, 14*, 88.

Lipska, B. K., & Weinberger, D. R. (1993). Delayed effects of neonatal hippocampal damage on haloperidol-induced catalepsy and apomorphine-induced stereotypic behaviors in the rat. *Brain Research. Developmental Brain Research, 75*(2), 213–222.

Liu, D., Diorio, J., Tannenbaum, B., Caldji, C., Francis, D., Freedman, A., et al. (1997). Maternal care, hippocampal glucocorticoid receptors, and hypothalamic-pituitary-adrenal responses to stress. *Science, 277*, 1659–1662.

Lucassen, P. J., Bosch, O. J., Jousma, E., Kromer, S. A., Andrew, R., Seckl, J. R., et al. (2009). Prenatal stress reduces postnatal neurogenesis in rats selectively bred for high, but not low, anxiety: possible key role of placental 11beta-hydroxysteroid dehydrogenase type 2. *European Journal of Neuroscience, 29*(1), 97–103.

Luoni, A., Berry, A., Calabrese, F., Capoccia, S., Bellisario, V., Gass, P., et al. (2014). Delayed BDNF alterations in the prefrontal cortex of rats exposed to prenatal stress: preventive effect of lurasidone treatment during adolescence. *European Neuropsychopharmacology, 24*(6), 986–995. http://dx.doi.org/10.1016/j.euroneuro.2013.12.010.

Maccari, S., & Morley-Fletcher, S. (2007). Effects of prenatal restraint stress on the hypothalamus-pituitary-adrenal axis and related behavioural and neurobiological alterations. *Psychoneuroendocrinology, 32*(Suppl. 1), S10–S15.

Maccari, S., Piazza, P. V., Kabbaj, M., Barbazanges, A., Simon, H., & Le Moal, M. (1995). Adoption reverses the long-term impairment in glucocorticoid feedback induced by prenatal stress. *Journal of Neuroscience, 15*(1 Pt 1), 110–116.

Mairesse, J., Lesage, J., Breton, C., Breant, B., Hahn, T., Darnaudery, M., et al. (2007). Maternal stress alters endocrine function of the fetoplacental unit in rats. *American Journal of Physiology. Endocrinology and Metabolism, 292*(6), E1526–E1533.

Mattson, M. P., & Duan, W. (1999). "Apoptotic" biochemical cascades in synaptic compartments: roles in adaptive plasticity and neurodegenerative disorders. *Journal of Neuroscience Research, 58*(1), 152–166.

McDonald, P., Lewis, M., Murphy, B., O'Reilly, R., & Singh, S. M. (2003). Appraisal of genetic and epigenetic congruity of a monozygotic twin pair discordant for schizophrenia. *Journal of Medical Genetics, 40*(2), E16.

McEvoy, J. P., Meyer, J. M., Goff, D. C., Nasrallah, H. A., Davis, S. M., Sullivan, L., et al. (2005). Prevalence of the metabolic syndrome in patients with schizophrenia: baseline results from the Clinical Antipsychotic Trials of Intervention Effectiveness (CATIE) schizophrenia trial and comparison with national estimates from NHANES III. *Schizophrenia Research, 80*(1), 19–32.

McEwen, B. S. (1998). Protective and damaging effects of stress mediators. *New England Journal of Medicine, 338*(3), 171–179.

McEwen, B. S., Angulo, J., Cameron, H., Chao, H. M., Daniels, D., Gannon, M. N., et al. (1992). Paradoxical effects of adrenal steroids on the brain: protection versus degeneration. *Biological Psychiatry, 31*(2), 177–199.

McEwen, B. S., Brinton, R. E., & Sapolsky, R. M. (1988). Glucocorticoid receptors and behavior: implications for the stress response. *Advances in Experimental Medicine and Biology, 245*, 35–45.

McGlashan, T. H., & Hoffman, R. E. (2000). Schizophrenia as a disorder of developmentally reduced synaptic connectivity. *Archives of General Psychiatry, 57*(7), 637–648.

McGowan, P. O., & Szyf, M. (2010). The epigenetics of social adversity in early life: implications for mental health outcomes. *Neurobiology of Disease, 39*(1), 66–72. http://dx.doi.org/10.1016/j.nbd.2009.12.026.

Meaney, M. J. (2001). Maternal care, gene expression, and the transmission of individual differences in stress reactivity across generations. *Annual Review of Neuroscience, 24*, 1161–1192.

Meaney, M. J., & Szyf, M. (2005). Maternal care as a model for experience-dependent chromatin plasticity? *Trends in Neurosciences, 28*(9), 456–463.

Meaney, M. J., Szyf, M., & Seckl, J. R. (2007). Epigenetic mechanisms of perinatal programming of hypothalamic-pituitary-adrenal function and health. *Trends in Molecular Medicine, 13*(7), 269–277.

Meyer, J. S. (1983). Early adrenalectomy stimulates subsequent growth and development of the rat brain. *Experimental Neurology, 82*(2), 432–446.

Meyer, U., & Feldon, J. (2009). Prenatal exposure to infection: a primary mechanism for abnormal dopaminergic development in schizophrenia. *Psychopharmacology (Berl), 206*(4), 587–602. http://dx.doi.org/10.1007/s00213-009-1504-9.

Meyer, U., & Feldon, J. (2010). Epidemiology-driven neurodevelopmental animal models of schizophrenia. *Progress in Neurobiology, 90*(3), 285–326. http://dx.doi.org/10.1016/j.pneurobio.2009.10.018.

Meyer, U., Feldon, J., Schedlowski, M., & Yee, B. K. (2006). Immunological stress at the maternal-foetal interface: a link between neurodevelopment and adult psychopathology. *Brain, Behavior, and Immunity, 20*(4), 378–388.

Meyer, U., Schwendener, S., Feldon, J., & Yee, B. K. (2006). Prenatal and postnatal maternal contributions in the infection model of schizophrenia. *Experimental Brain Research, 173*(2), 243–257. http://dx.doi.org/10.1007/s00221-006-0419-5.

Mitchell, A. J., & Lord, O. (2010). Do deficits in cardiac care influence high mortality rates in schizophrenia? A systematic review and pooled analysis. *Journal of Psychopharmacology, 24*(4 Suppl.), 69–80.

Mittal, V. A., Ellman, L. M., & Cannon, T. D. (2008). Gene-environment interaction and covariation in schizophrenia: the role of obstetric complications. *Schizophrenia Bulletin, 34*(6), 1083–1094. http://dx.doi.org/10.1093/schbul/sbn080.

Modinos, G., Iyegbe, C., Prata, D., Rivera, M., Kempton, M. J., Valmaggia, L. R., et al. (2013). Molecular genetic gene-environment studies using candidate genes in schizophrenia: a systematic review. *Schizophrenia Research, 150*(2–3), 356–365. http://dx.doi.org/10.1016/j.schres.2013.09.010.

Moller, M., Du Preez, J. L., Emsley, R., & Harvey, B. H. (2011). Isolation rearing-induced deficits in sensorimotor gating and social interaction in rats are related to cortico-striatal oxidative stress, and reversed by sub-chronic clozapine administration. *European Neuropsychopharmacology, 21*(6), 471–483.

Molteni, R., Lipska, B. K., Weinberger, D. R., Racagni, G., & Riva, M. A. (2001). Developmental and stress-related changes of neurotrophic factor gene expression in an animal model of schizophrenia. *Molecular Psychiatry, 6*(3), 285–292.

Morley-Fletcher, S., Darnaudery, M., Koehl, M., Casolini, P., Van Reeth, O., & Maccari, S. (2003). Prenatal stress in rats predicts immobility behavior in the forced swim test. Effects of a chronic treatment with tianeptine. *Brain Research, 989*(2), 246–251.

Moser, P. (2014). Evaluating negative-symptom-like behavioural changes in developmental models of schizophrenia. *European Neuropsychopharmacology, 24*(5), 774–787. http://dx.doi.org/10.1016/j.euroneuro.2013.11.004.

Murgatroyd, C., Patchev, A. V., Wu, Y., Micale, V., Bockmuhl, Y., Fischer, D., et al. (2009). Dynamic DNA methylation programs persistent adverse effects of early-life stress. *Nature Neuroscience, 12*(12), 1559–1566.

Murray, R. M., Jones, P., & O'Callaghan, E. (1991). Fetal brain development and later schizophrenia. *Ciba Foundation Symposium, 156*, 155–163 discussion 163–70.

Nederhof, E., & Schmidt, M. V. (2012). Mismatch or cumulative stress: toward an integrated hypothesis of programming effects. *Physiology & Behavior, 106*(5), 691–700.

van Os, J., Kenis, G., & Rutten, B. P. (2010). The environment and schizophrenia. *Nature, 468*(7321), 203–212. http://dx.doi.org/10.1038/nature09563.

Osmond, C., Barker, D. J., Winter, P. D., Fall, C. H., & Simmonds, S. J. (1993). Early growth and death from cardiovascular disease in women. *BMJ, 307*(6918), 1519–1524.

Palmer, A. A., Printz, D. J., Butler, P. D., Dulawa, S. C., & Printz, M. P. (2004). Prenatal protein deprivation in rats induces changes in prepulse inhibition and NMDA receptor binding. *Brain Research, 996*(2), 193–201.

Patterson, P. H. (2012). Animal models of the maternal stress risk factor for schizophrenia. In A. S. Brown, & P. H. Patterson (Eds.), *The origins of schizophrenia*. New York: Columbia University Press.

Pedersen, C. B., & Mortensen, P. B. (2006). Urbanicity during upbringing and bipolar affective disorders in Denmark. *Bipolar Disorders, 8*(3), 242–247. http://dx.doi.org/10.1111/j.1399-5618.2006.00307.x.

Petronis, A., Gottesman, I. I., Kan, P., Kennedy, J. L., Basile, V. S., Paterson, A. D., et al. (2003). Monozygotic twins exhibit numerous epigenetic differences: clues to twin discordance? *Schizophrenia Bulletin, 29*(1), 169–178.

Phiel, C. J., Zhang, F., Huang, E. Y., Guenther, M. G., Lazar, M. A., & Klein, P. S. (2001). Histone deacetylase is a direct target of valproic acid, a potent anticonvulsant, mood stabilizer, and teratogen. *Journal of Biological Chemistry, 276*(39), 36734–36741. http://dx.doi.org/10.1074/jbc.M101287200.

Plappert, C. F., Rodenbucher, A. M., & Pilz, P. K. (2005). Effects of sex and estrous cycle on modulation of the acoustic startle response in mice. *Physiology & Behavior, 84*(4), 585–594. http://dx.doi.org/10.1016/j.physbeh.2005.02.004.

Raikkonen, K., & Pesonen, A. K. (2009). Early life origins of psychological development and mental health. *Scandinavian Journal of Psychology, 50*(6), 583–591.

Raikkonen, K., Pesonen, A. K., Heinonen, K., Kajantie, E., Hovi, P., Jarvenpaa, A. L., et al. (2008). Depression in young adults with very low birth weight: the Helsinki study of very-low-birth-weight adults. *Archives of General Psychiatry, 65*(3), 290–296.

Ramchandani, S., Bhattacharya, S. K., Cervoni, N., & Szyf, M. (1999). DNA methylation is a reversible biological signal. *Proceeding of the National Academy of Sciences of the United States of America, 96*(11), 6107–6112.

Razin, A. (1998). CpG methylation, chromatin structure and gene silencing-a three-way connection. *EMBO Journal, 17*(17), 4905–4908. http://dx.doi.org/10.1093/emboj/17.17.4905.

Read, J., Perry, B. D., Moskowitz, A., & Connolly, J. (2001). The contribution of early traumatic events to schizophrenia in some patients: a traumagenic neurodevelopmental model. *Psychiatry, 64*(4), 319–345.

Rehn, A. E., & Rees, S. M. (2005). Investigating the neurodevelopmental hypothesis of schizophrenia. *Clinical and Experimental Pharmacology and Physiology, 32*(9), 687–696. http://dx.doi.org/10.1111/j.1440-1681.2005.04257.x.

Rethelyi, J. M., Benkovits, J., & Bitter, I. (2013). Genes and environments in schizophrenia: the different pieces of a manifold puzzle. *Neuroscience & Biobehavioral Reviews, 37*(10 Pt 1), 2424–2437.

Ringen, P. A., Engh, J. A., Birkenaes, A. B., Dieset, I., & Andreassen, O. A. (2014). Increased mortality in schizophrenia due to cardiovascular disease – a non-systematic review of epidemiology, possible causes, and interventions. *Frontiers in Psychiatry, 5*, 137.

Roth, T. L., Lubin, F. D., Funk, A. J., & Sweatt, J. D. (2009). Lasting epigenetic influence of early-life adversity on the BDNF gene. *Biological Psychiatry, 65*(9), 760–769. http://dx.doi.org/10.1016/j.biopsych.2008.11.028.

Saha, S., Chant, D., & McGrath, J. (2007). A systematic review of mortality in schizophrenia: is the differential mortality gap worsening over time? *Archives of General Psychiatry, 64*(10), 1123–1131.

Sakata, K., & Duke, S. M. (2014). Lack of BDNF expression through promoter IV disturbs expression of monoamine genes in the frontal cortex and hippocampus. *Neuroscience, 260*, 265–275.

Sapolsky, R. M., Krey, L. C., & McEwen, B. S. (1986). The neuroendocrinology of stress and aging: the glucocorticoid cascade hypothesis. *Endocrine Reviews, 7*(3), 284–301.

Schore, A. N. (2000). Attachment and the regulation of the right brain. *Attachment & Human Development, 2*(1), 23–47.

Scott, D., & Happell, B. (2011). The high prevalence of poor physical health and unhealthy lifestyle behaviours in individuals with severe mental illness. *Issues in Mental Health Nursing, 32*(9), 589–597.

Seckl, J. R. (1998). Physiologic programming of the fetus. *Clinics in Perinatology, 25*(4), 939–962 vii.

Seckl, J. R. (2004). Prenatal glucocorticoids and long-term programming. *European Journal of Endocrinology, 151*(Suppl. 3), U49–U62.

Seckl, J. R., & Meaney, M. J. (2004). Glucocorticoid programming. *Annals of the New York Academy of Sciences, 1032*, 63–84.

Shatz, C. J. (2009). MHC class I: an unexpected role in neuronal plasticity. *Neuron, 64*(1), 40–45.

Shi, L., Fatemi, S. H., Sidwell, R. W., & Patterson, P. H. (2003). Maternal influenza infection causes marked behavioral and pharmacological changes in the offspring. *Journal of Neuroscience, 23*(1), 297–302.

Shonkoff, J. P., Boyce, W. T., & McEwen, B. S. (2009). Neuroscience, molecular biology, and the childhood roots of health disparities: building a new framework for health promotion and disease prevention. *JAMA, 301*(21), 2252–2259.

Stefansson, H., Rujescu, D., Cichon, S., Pietilainen, O. P., Ingason, A., Steinberg, S., et al. (2008). Large recurrent microdeletions associated with schizophrenia. *Nature, 455*(7210), 232–236. http://dx.doi.org/10.1038/nature07229.

Stein, M. B., Koverola, C., Hanna, C., Torchia, M. G., & McClarty, B. (1997). Hippocampal volume in women victimized by childhood sexual abuse. *Psychological Medicine, 27*(4), 951–959.

Sullivan, P. F., Kendler, K. S., & Neale, M. C. (2003). Schizophrenia as a complex trait: evidence from a meta-analysis of twin studies. *Archives of General Psychiatry*, 60(12), 1187–1192. http://dx.doi.org/10.1001/archpsyc.60.12.1187.

Swerdlow, N. R., Hartman, P. L., & Auerbach, P. P. (1997). Changes in sensorimotor inhibition across the menstrual cycle: implications for neuropsychiatric disorders. *Biological Psychiatry*, 41(4), 452–460. http://dx.doi.org/10.1016/S0006-3223(96)00065-0.

Swerdlow, N. R., Weber, M., Qu, Y., Light, G. A., & Braff, D. L. (2008). Realistic expectations of prepulse inhibition in translational models for schizophrenia research. *Psychopharmacology (Berl)*, 199(3), 331–388. http://dx.doi.org/10.1007/s00213-008-1072-4.

Takiuti, N. H., Kahhale, S., & Zugaib, M. (2002). Stress in pregnancy: a new Wistar rat model for human preeclampsia. *American Journal of Obstetrics & Gynecology*, 186(3), 544–550.

Tamminga, C. A., & Holcomb, H. H. (2005). Phenotype of schizophrenia: a review and formulation. *Molecular Psychiatry*, 10(1), 27–39. http://dx.doi.org/10.1038/sj.mp.4001563.

Teicher, M. H., Dumont, N. L., Ito, Y., Vaituzis, C., Giedd, J. N., & Andersen, S. L. (2004). Childhood neglect is associated with reduced corpus callosum area. *Biological Psychiatry*, 56(2), 80–85.

Thompson, B. L., & Levitt, P. (2010). Now you see it, now you don't—closing in on allostasis and developmental basis of psychiatric disorders. *Neuron*, 65(4), 437–439.

Tronick, E., & Reck, C. (2009). Infants of depressed mothers. *Harvard Review of Psychiatry*, 17(2), 147–156.

Tsujita, T., Niikawa, N., Yamashita, H., Imamura, A., Hamada, A., Nakane, Y., et al. (1998). Genomic discordance between monozygotic twins discordant for schizophrenia. *American Journal of Psychiatry*, 155(3), 422–424.

Vaillancourt, C., & Boksa, P. (2000). Birth insult alters dopamine-mediated behavior in a precocial species, the guinea pig. Implications for schizophrenia. *Neuropsychopharmacology*, 23(6), 654–666. http://dx.doi.org/10.1016/S0893-133X(00)00164-0.

Vallee, M., MacCari, S., Dellu, F., Simon, H., Le Moal, M., & Mayo, W. (1999). Long-term effects of prenatal stress and postnatal handling on age-related glucocorticoid secretion and cognitive performance: a longitudinal study in the rat. *European Journal of Neuroscience*, 11(8), 2906–2916.

Vallee, M., Mayo, W., Dellu, F., Le Moal, M., Simon, H., & Maccari, S. (1997). Prenatal stress induces high anxiety and postnatal handling induces low anxiety in adult offspring: correlation with stress-induced corticosterone secretion. *Journal of Neuroscience*, 17(7), 2626–2636.

Varese, F., Smeets, F., Drukker, M., Lieverse, R., Lataster, T., Viechtbauer, W., et al. (2012). Childhood adversities increase the risk of psychosis: a meta-analysis of patient-control, prospective- and cross-sectional cohort studies. *Schizophrenia Bulletin*, 38(4), 661–671. http://dx.doi.org/10.1093/schbul/sbs050.

Viltart, O., Mairesse, J., Darnaudery, M., Louvart, H., Vanbesien-Mailliot, C., Catalani, A., et al. (2006). Prenatal stress alters Fos protein expression in hippocampus and locus coeruleus stress-related brain structures. *Psychoneuroendocrinology*, 31(6), 769–780.

Walker, E., Mittal, V., & Tessner, K. (2008). Stress and the hypothalamic pituitary adrenal axis in the developmental course of schizophrenia. *Annual Review of Clinical Psychology*, 4, 189–216. http://dx.doi.org/10.1146/annurev.clinpsy.4.022007.141248.

Walker, E. F., & Diforio, D. (1997). Schizophrenia: a neural diathesis-stress model. *Psychological Review*, 104(4), 667–685.

Ward, R. M. (1994). Pharmacologic enhancement of fetal lung maturation. *Clinics in Perinatology*, 21(3), 523–542.

Weaver, I. C., Cervoni, N., Champagne, F. A., D'Alessio, A. C., Sharma, S., Seckl, J. R., et al. (2004). Epigenetic programming by maternal behavior. *Nature Neuroscience*, 7(8), 847–854.

Weaver, I. C., Champagne, F. A., Brown, S. E., Dymov, S., Sharma, S., Meaney, M. J., et al. (2005). Reversal of maternal programming of stress responses in adult offspring through methyl supplementation: altering epigenetic marking later in life. *Journal of Neuroscience*, 25(47), 11045–11054. http://dx.doi.org/10.1523/JNEUROSCI.3652-05.2005.

Weinberger, D. R. (1987). Implications of normal brain development for the pathogenesis of schizophrenia. *Archives of General Psychiatry*, 44(7), 660–669.

Weiner, I. (2003). The "two-headed" latent inhibition model of schizophrenia: modeling positive and negative symptoms and their treatment. *Psychopharmacology (Berl)*, 169(3–4), 257–297. http://dx.doi.org/10.1007/s00213-002-1313-x.

Weinmann, S., Read, J., & Aderhold, V. (2009). Influence of antipsychotics on mortality in schizophrenia: systematic review. *Schizophrenia Research*, 113(1), 1–11.

Welberg, L. A., Seckl, J. R., & Holmes, M. C. (2001). Prenatal glucocorticoid programming of brain corticosteroid receptors and corticotrophin-releasing hormone: possible implications for behaviour. *Neuroscience*, 104(1), 71–79.

Wust, S., Entringer, S., Federenko, I. S., Schlotz, W., & Hellhammer, D. H. (2005). Birth weight is associated with salivary cortisol responses to psychosocial stress in adult life. *Psychoneuroendocrinology*, 30(6), 591–598.

Yehuda, R., Fairman, K. R., & Meyer, J. S. (1989). Enhanced brain cell proliferation following early adrenalectomy in rats. *Journal of Neurochemistry*, 53(1), 241–248.

Zammit, S., Odd, D., Horwood, J., Thompson, A., Thomas, K., Menezes, P., et al. (2009). Investigating whether adverse prenatal and perinatal events are associated with non-clinical psychotic symptoms at age 12 years in the ALSPAC birth cohort. *Psychological Medicine*, 39(9), 1457–1467.

Zuk, O., Hechter, E., Sunyaev, S. R., & Lander, E. S. (2012). The mystery of missing heritability: genetic interactions create phantom heritability. *Proceedings of the National Academy of Sciences of the United States of America*, 109(4), 1193–1198. http://dx.doi.org/10.1073/pnas.1119675109.

14

The *Toxoplasma gondii* Model of Schizophrenia

Joanne P. Webster*,§, Poppy H.L. Lamberton§, Glenn A. McConkey¶

*Department of Pathology and Pathogen Biology, Centre for Emerging, Endemic and Exotic Diseases (CEEED), Royal Veterinary College, University of London, London, UK; §Department of Infectious Disease Epidemiology, School of Public Health, Imperial College Faculty of Medicine, London, UK; ¶School of Biology, Faculty of Biological Sciences, University of Leeds, Leeds, UK

INTRODUCTION

With increasing pressure and improved methodologies to understand transmissible agents, renewed recognition of infectious causation of both acute and chronic diseases from cancers to affective disorders is occurring. That certain infectious agents can cause psychiatric syndromes when they infect adult humans is now well-documented (Caroff, Mann, Gliatto, Sullivan, & Campbell, 2001). Of even greater interest, perhaps, is whether infectious agents' exposure of a developing fetus, newborn, or young child can cause psychiatric syndromes such as schizophrenia later in life (Mortensen et al., 2007). Schizophrenia is a severe and usually chronic mental health condition that presents a significant burden on individuals, their families, and society as a whole. Current antipsychotic medications are unable to effectively treat "positive symptoms" (hallucinations, delusions, thought disorders) in nearly 30% of the patient population and are not effective treatments for "negative symptoms" (emotional blunting, anhedonia, decreased motivation) or cognitive deficits (attention, memory and learning deficits). The etiology of schizophrenia is highly complex, with both genetic and environmental risk factors undoubtedly playing major, but as yet not fully understood, roles (Torrey, Bartko, & Yolken, 2012; Torrey & Yolken, 2003). Some of the key environmental risk factors proposed, to date, include cannabis use, pregnancy and birth complications, childhood adversities, urbanicity and immigration (first and second generation), particularly in certain ethnic groups, and infections of the central nervous system, particularly in early childhood

(Matheson, Shepherd, & Carr, 2014; Torrey & Yolken, 2014). An infectious etiology of schizophrenia was first proposed as early as 1896 (Editorial, 1896). The infectious agents proposed have been wide-ranging, with *Chlamydophila psittaci*, *Chlamydophila pneumoniae*, human endogenous retrovirus W, Borna disease virus, human herpesvirus 2, and, in particular, *Toxoplasma gondii*, being some of the most currently convincing examples (Carter, 2009; Kaushik, Lamberton, & Webster, 2012; Matheson et al., 2014).

Here we focus on the risk factors of *T. gondii* infection for schizophrenia, the potential mechanisms involved, and whether studies of *T. gondii* in rodents can serve as a valid model to study schizophrenia in humans. As with any model of human neuropsychiatric diseases, particularly those incorporating rodents and in this instance *T. gondii*–exposed rodents as a model for human schizophrenia, a valid and useful model must aim to optimize (1) face validity, that is, resemblance to the human symptoms; (2) construct validity, that is, similarity to the underlying causes of the disease; (3) predictive validity, that is, expected responses to treatments that are effective in the human disease; and (4) use ethically and epidemiologically appropriate host–parasite combinations and behavioral assays (Crawley, 2004; Webster, Kaushik, Bristow, & McConkey, 2013). We believe that the *T. gondii* rat model of schizophrenia, if used ethically and appropriately, provides a highly useful and promising tool to aid future research applicable to many, but of course not all, areas of human schizophrenia symptomology and ideal management.

TOXOPLASMA GONDII AS A CULPABLE PARASITE

Toxoplasma gondii, the causative agent of toxoplasmosis, is a highly successful apicomplexan protozoan capable of infecting all warm-blooded animals worldwide. Infection seroprevalence levels can be very high, with for example 20–80% prevalence in humans (Desmonts & Couvreur, 1974). Members of the cat family (*Felidae*) are the only definitive hosts of *T. gondii*, within which the parasite undergoes full gametogenesis and sexual reproduction within the intestinal epithelium, culminating in the generation of oocysts containing sporozoites that are shed in cat feces (Hutchison, Dunachie, Siim, & Work, 1969). In addition to congenital transmission, infection of intermediate (such as rodents and birds) or other secondary (such as humans and domestic livestock) hosts can occur following ingestion of oocysts (via contaminated soil, water, or food) or tissue cysts (through raw/undercooked infected meat, including via cannibalism) as well as potentially, under certain conditions, by sexual transmission. Within intermediate/secondary hosts the parasite undergoes asexual reproduction, characterized by rapidly dividing tachyzoites and the more slowly dividing bradyzoites. Bradyzoites encyst in the brain, heart, and other tissues, where they can potentially remain for the host's lifetime. Transmission to the feline definitive host occurs when an immunologically naive cat ingests an infected intermediate host through predation (and/or consumes contaminated meat). Because sexual reproduction of *T. gondii* can be accomplished only in felines, there are likely to be strong selective pressures on the parasite to evolve mechanisms to enhance transmission from the intermediate host to the definitive feline host. The predilection of *T. gondii* for the central nervous system (CNS) also places this parasite in a privileged position to alter host behavior (Webster, 2001, 2007).

Although the severe sequelae of congenital infections are well-known, until relatively recently, latent adult-acquired toxoplasmosis in immunocompetent humans and animals was generally considered to be asymptomatic. We know little, however, of the potential impact of this parasite on the host brain and, indeed, it is classified as a "neglected tropical disease" or "neglected parasitic infection" by the US Centers for Disease Control and Prevention (http://www.cdc.gov/parasites/npi/ Document CS245336A, 2014). Behavioral studies of wild animals with naturally occurring infections are, in particular, rare, although wild brown rats, *Rattus norvegicus*, on farmlands have been demonstrated to exhibit higher levels of activity and, at least under certain situations, an increased propensity to be trapped in cages, among *T. gondii*–infected individuals relative to their uninfected counterparts (Webster, 1994; Webster, Brunton, & Macdonald, 1994). Laboratory and/or experimentally controlled naturalistic studies on rats and mice have also shown that *T. gondii* infection is associated with a range of subtle behavioral alterations, many of which would facilitate parasite transmission from the infected intermediate host to the feline definitive host. For example, *T. gondii*–infected rodents exhibit an increase in activity and a decrease in predator vigilance behavioral traits (Berdoy, Webster, & Macdonald, 1995; Hay, Aitken, Hair, Hutchison, & Graham, 1984; Hay, Aitken, Hutchison, & Graham, 1983; Hutchison, Aitken, & Wells, 1980; Hutchison, Bradley, Cheyne, Wells, & Hay, 1980; Lamberton, Donnelly, & Webster, 2008; Webster, 1994, 2001, 2007; Webster et al., 1994; Webster, Lamberton, Donnelly, & Torrey, 2006). Moreover, although uninfected rats show a strong innate aversion to predator odor, *T. gondii* infection appears to subtly alter the rats' cognitive perception of cat predation risk, turning their innate aversion into a suicidal "fatal feline attraction" (Berdoy, Webster, & Macdonald, 2000; Vyas, Seon-Kyeong, Giacomini, Boothroyd, & Sapolsky, 2007; Webster et al., 2006). Such fatal feline attraction appears specific to a response to cat (urine) odor, with no difference observed between infected and uninfected rats in their responses to odors of nonpredatory mammals such as rabbit (Berdoy et al., 2000; Vyas, Seon-Kyeong, et al., 2007; Webster et al., 2006), nor contrasting potential predatory species odors such as mink (Lamberton et al., 2008) or dog (Kannan et al., 2010). There do, however, appear to be some differences between species of feline host, potentially in relation to their capacities as efficient definitive hosts (Kaushik, Knowles, & Webster, 2014). Overall, such rodent studies are consistent with the hypothesis that *T. gondii* specifically manipulates the behavior of its rodent, rat at least, intermediate host rather than simply causing a broad pathology or destruction of particular behavioral traits.

Within the feline definitive host itself some potential "general pathology" neurological signs have been reported, such as circling, head bobbing, atypical crying, and increased affectionate behavior, even though CNS toxoplasmosis in felines may be relatively uncommon—only 7–10% of cats postmortem with toxoplasmic symptoms have been reported to have apparent CNS involvement (Bowman, 2002; Dubey & Carpenter, 1993). In terms of secondary, nonintermediate hosts, although empirical studies are again rare, *T. gondii* appears to induce a range of behavioral alterations across host species. California sea otters with moderate to severe toxoplasmic encephalitis have been observed to be 3.7 times more likely to be attacked by sharks than their uninfected counterparts (Miller et al., 2004), suggesting that they may exhibit aberrant behavior similar to that displayed by infected intermediate host rodents, although as a "byproduct" of infection with no current adaptive advantage to the parasite in this host–predator combination. Human studies have also revealed a range of subtle behavioral alterations associated with *T. gondii* infection, many of which may be comparable to those observed among infected rodent intermediate hosts—such as increased activity, decreased reaction times, and altered personality profiles (Flegr, 2007, 2013; Flegr, Havlíček, Kodym, Maly, & Smahel, 2002; Flegr & Hrdy, 1994; Flegr et al., 2003; Webster, 2001). Furthermore, consistent with a possible impairment in psychomotor performance and/or enhanced risk-taking personality profiles, individuals with latent toxoplasmosis have reported a 2.65 times increased risk to be involved in a road traffic accident relative to the general population (Flegr et al., 2002), a result subsequently replicated by other groups (Flegr, Klose, Novotná, Berenreitterová, & Havlíček, 2009; Kocazeybeka et al., 2009; Yereli, Balcioğlu, & Ozbilgin, 2006). Another study, albeit significant only in a subset with lower socioeconomic status, linked *T. gondii* seropositivity with workplace accidents (Alvarado-Esquivel, Torres-Castorena, Liesenfeld, Estrada-Martínez, & Urbina-Álvarez, 2012). Even an equivalent of the fatal feline attraction phenomenon observed in infected rats (Berdoy et al., 2000) has been identified in humans, in which *T. gondii* positive humans showed altered questionnaire responses to the odors of the domestic cat (and of the brown hyena) (Flegr, Lenochova, Hodny, & Vondrova, 2011).

RELATIONSHIP BETWEEN *TOXOPLASMA GONDII* AND SCHIZOPHRENIA

Latent *T. gondii* infection in the human host may, in a small proportion of cases, have substantial health implications. Within humans infected with *T. gondii*, including immunocompetent adult hosts and/or those infected but asymptomatic at birth, severe pathologies, including meningoencephalitis (Kaushik, Mahajan, Sharma, Kaushik, & Kukreti, 2005), ocular abnormalities (Faucher et al., 2012), and *T. gondii*–related brain cancers (Thomas et al., 2011), have been reported. There is, furthermore, an ever-growing and convincing body of evidence concerning a potential relationship linking *T. gondii* infection with some forms of affective and neurological disorders in humans. Correlations have been found for obsessive-compulsive disorder (Miman et al., 2010), biopolar disorder (Pearce, Kruszon-Moran, & Jones, 2012), generalized-anxiety disorder (Gale, Brown, Berrett, Erickson, & Hedges, 2014), panic disorder (Gale et al., 2014; Yolken, Dickerson, & Torrey, 2009), Parkinson's disease (Miman et al., 2010), Alzheimer's disease (Kusbeci, Miman, Yaman, Aktepe, & Yazar, 2011), attempted suicide (Alvarado-Esquivel, Sanchez-Anguiano, Arnaud-Gil, et al., 2013; Arling et al., 2009; Ling, Lester, Mortensen, Langenberg, & Postolache, 2011; Pedersen, Mortensen, Norgaard-Pedersen, et al., 2012), lower cognitive scoring (Dickerson et al., 2014), and reduced memory in older individuals (Dickerson et al., 2014; Gajewski, Alkenstein, Hengstler, & Golka, 2014). The most substantial body of empirical evidence gathered, to date, relates to the potential association between *T. gondii* and some cases of schizophrenia in humans (Table 1). For example, there are similarities in the epidemiology of schizophrenia (Cichon et al., 2009) and toxoplasmosis (Johnson, Suzuki, & Mack, 2002) in which, for instance, both have been demonstrated to have strong familial associations, affecting multiple members of the same family. *Toxoplasma gondii* seroprevalence has also been directly positively correlated with (first incidence) schizophrenia in at least 39 studies to date (Mortensen et al., 2007; Torrey, Bartko, Lun, & Yolken, 2007; Torrey et al., 2012; Torrey, Rawlings, & Yolken, 2000; Torrey & Yolken, 2003; Yolken & Torrey, 2008). Indeed, meta-analyses assessing potential associations between different infectious agents and schizophrenia found a highly significant association with *T. gondii* infection (odds ratio (OR) = 2.70; 95% confidence interval, 1.34–4.42; $p = 0.005$) (Arias et al., 2012) and a stronger association between schizophrenia and detection of *T. gondii* antibodies (combined OR 2.73) than for schizophrenia and any human gene in a genome-wide linkage analysis study (OR ≤ 1.40) (Purcell et al., 2009). Further support for an association includes analyses of serum samples obtained from mothers shortly before or after giving birth that revealed a significantly raised proportion of immunoglobulin (Ig) M antibodies to *T. gondii* in those whose children went on to develop schizophrenia in later life (Torrey & Yolken, 2003). Individuals suffering from first-episode schizophrenia also have significantly elevated levels of IgG, IgM, and/or IgA class antibodies to *T. gondii*, within both serum and cerebral spinal fluid, compared with uninfected control subjects (Yolken et al., 2001). In a study of military personnel from whom serum specimens were available from periods of up to 11 years before the onset of their schizophrenia (180 individuals with schizophrenia and 532 matched controls), significantly increased levels of IgG antibodies to *T. gondii* were observed before the onset of schizophrenic illness (hazard ratio = 1.24, $p < 0.01$), with a peak in the 6 months before onset but seen as early as 3 years before the onset (Niebuhr, Millikan, Cowan, et al., 2008). A recent study also considered the epidemiological association between *T. gondii* and schizophrenia through the relatively novel perspective of estimating the population-attributable fraction for schizophrenia if *T. gondii* were assumed absent from within human populations (Smith, 2014). In particular, they calculated what would be the potential lifetime reduction in the risk of a diagnosis of schizophrenia if we could prevent human infection with *T. gondii*, using a modified parameter of the population-attributable fraction. Their estimated population-attributable fraction was 21.4% (within a potential range

TABLE 1   *Toxoplasma gondii* as a Causative Agent in Some Cases of Schizophrenia: Some Key Examples of Association

Neurological	Epidemiological	Pharmacological	Mechanistic
Toxoplasma gondii's persistent CNS infection and behavioral alterations observed in both infected animals and humans (Flegr, 2013; Webster et al., 2013).	Both *T. gondii* antibodies and schizophrenia risk associated with cat exposure in childhood (Torrey et al., 2000; Torrey & Yolken, 1995; Torrey & Yolken, in press).	*Toxoplasma gondii* antibodies are lower/reduced in patients undergoing antischizophrenia drug treatment (Leweke et al., 2004).	*Toxoplasma gondii* infection and schizophrenia characterized by significant differences in levels of homovanillic acid, norepinephrine, and in particular, altered dopamine (Stibbs, 1985; Torrey et al., 2000; Torrey & Yolken, 2003).
Neurological and psychiatric symptoms in some *T. gondii*–infected individuals (Kramer, 1966).	Countries with high levels of *T. gondii* infection also tend to have high levels of schizophrenia.	Antipsychotic drugs inhibit *T. gondii* replication in vitro (Jones-Brando, Torrey, & Yolken, 2003).	Dopamine D2 antagonists (e.g., haloperidol) can prevent development of *T. gondii*–induced behavioral alternations in rats (Webster et al., 2006).
Similar glial cells, especially astrocytes, are selectively affected.	Both *T. gondii* infection and schizophrenia have strong familial associations.	Antipsychotic drugs inhibit *T. gondii* replication in vivo (Webster et al., 2006).	Tyrosine phenylalanine hydroxylase encoded in the *T. gondii* genome that synthesizes L-DOPA, the precursor to dopamine (Gaskell, Smith, Pinney, Westhead, & McConkey, 2009).
	Both *T. gondii* infection and schizophrenia have significant gender associations.		Dopamine release is increased by *T. gondii* in vivo and in vitro (Prandovszky, Gaskell, Dubey, Webster, & McConkey, 2011).
Toxoplasma gondii–positive schizophrenia patients express more severe psychosis than *T. gondii*–negative patients.	*Toxoplasma gondii* increases risk of schizophrenia (odds ratio 2.73) > any gene for schizophrenia (odds ratio, 1.09).		
MRI reduction in brain gray matter "characteristic" of schizophrenia, only in patients with *T. gondii* (Horacek et al., 2011).	US military personnel *T. gondii* seroconversion 6 months–2 years before schizophrenia onset (hazard ratio = 1.24) (Niebuhr et al., 2008).		
Olfactory lobe alterations observed in both *T. gondii* infection and in certain neuropsychiatric disorders including schizophrenia (Prandota, 2014).	Serum samples obtained from mothers shortly before or after giving birth revealed a significantly raised proportion of IgM antibodies to *T. gondii* in those whose children subsequently develop schizophrenia in later life (Torrey & Yolken, 2003).		
	Individuals suffering from first-episode schizophrenia have significantly elevated levels of IgG, IgM, and/or IgA class antibodies to *T. gondii* antibodies, within both serum and cerebral spinal fluid compared with uninfected control subjects (Yolken et al., 2001).		

CNS, central nervous system; Ig, immunoglobulin.

of 13.7–30.6%), and the author thus proposed that, as it is estimated that schizophrenia in the United States, for instance, affects a minimum of 0.5% of the population (Wu, Shi, Birnbaum, Hudson, & Kessler, 2006), were *T. gondii* infection to be one of the most common causes of a diagnosis of schizophrenia, that would amount to more than 335,000 potentially preventable cases of schizophrenia in the United States over a single human lifetime (Smith, 2014)—if indeed *T. gondii* infection/exposure could be prevented and or infections cleared.

Although there are few drugs available that successfully clear the *T. gondii* bradyzoite stage within the CNS, studies have, however, demonstrated that *T. gondii* antibodies in patients with schizophrenia and treated with antipsychotic drugs are intermediate between those of schizophrenia patients never treated and those of

T. gondii–uninfected (or unaffected) control groups, with a significant reduction in those patients undergoing current drug treatment, thereby suggesting that antipsychotic treatment may reduce *T. gondii* infection levels (Leweke et al., 2004). Indeed, antipsychotic drugs used in the treatment of schizophrenia inhibit the replication of *T. gondii* tachyzoites *in vitro* (Goodwin, Strobl, & Lindsay, 2011; Jones-Brando et al., 2003) and *in vivo* (Webster et al., 2006). *Toxoplasma gondii*–infected/exposed rats treated with the same key antipsychotic or mood stabilizer drugs during the tachyzoite replicative stage of infection, in particular that of the dopamine D2 antagonist haloperidol (Webster et al., 2006) or the dopamine selective uptake inhibitor (GBR 12909 1-[2-[bis(4-fluorofenyl) metoxy]-etyl]-4-[3-fenylpropyl]piperazin) (Skallova, Kodym, Frynta, & Flegr, 2006), did not develop the potentially suicidal feline attraction or other predation-specific altered behavioral profiles displayed by their untreated but infected counterparts. There was also lower parasite establishment within the brains of these drug-treated infected rats relative to their untreated infected counterparts (Webster et al., 2006). Such results therefore raise the hypothesis that the antipsychotic and mood stabilizing activity of some medications used for patients with schizophrenia may at least be augmented through their inhibition of *T. gondii* replication, invasion, and/or subsequent modulatory impact in infected individuals.

SCHIZOPHRENIA, *TOXOPLASMA GONDII*, AND POTENTIAL SHARED MECHANISM(S) OF ACTION

Dopamine dysregulation has been a long-standing paradigm in schizophrenia, although the relationship remains unclear. Risk genes that have been identified may lead to downstream impairments in dopaminergic function. *Toxoplasma gondii* also alters dopamine levels in its infected host, potentially indicating a pathway through which *T. gondii* infection could confer a risk of developing schizophrenia. Raised or disrupted dopamine levels have been reported in both rodent and human *T. gondii* infections and within human patients with schizophrenia (Howes & Kapur, 2009; Prandovszky et al., 2011; Stibbs, 1985; Torrey & Yolken, 2003), together with other affective disorders such as obsessive-compulsive disorder, bipolar disorder, and in individuals with suicide attempts (Berk et al., 2007; Denys, Zohar, & Westenberg, 2004; Diehl & Gershon, 1992; Roy, Karoum, & Pollack, 1992). Research indicates that the parasite itself may actually be a source of this dopamine (Gaskell et al., 2009; Prandovszky et al., 2011). In mammals, dopamine is synthesized in two steps from its precursor amino acid tyrosine: tyrosine hydroxylase metabolism to produce L-DOPA then decarboxylation of

L-DOPA by aromatic L-amino acid decarboxylase to dopamine. In noradrenergic cells, dopamine is further metabolized to norepinephrine by dopamine beta-hydroxylase. *Toxoplasma gondii* was found to encode a protein with high homology, and showing similar catalytic properties, to the tyrosine hydroxylases found in mammals. This *T. gondii* ortholog synthesizes L-DOPA, the precursor to dopamine, as well as tyrosine, and is correlated with increased dopamine levels within *T. gondii* cysts in the rodent brain (Prandovszky et al., 2011). The degradation of tryptophan through the kynurenine pathway, which contains several neuroactive metabolites, including 3-hydroxykynurenine, quinolinic acid and kynurenic acid, has also been suggested as a potential mechanistic connection between *T. gondii* and the pathophysiology of schizophrenia. *Toxoplasma gondii* infection enhanced the production of kynurenine pathway metabolites in the brain in mice; however, during the first 2 months after infection, the kynurenine pathway changes did not reliably duplicate abnormalities seen in the brain of individuals with schizophrenia (Notarangelo et al., 2014).

SCHIZOPHRENIA RISK GENES AND POTENTIAL INTERACTIONS IN *TOXOPLASMA GONDII* INFECTION

Selected genetic marker studies and, more recently, genome-wide association studies (GWAS) have implicated a large number (>100) of genes potentially associated with schizophrenia. It is possible that specific schizophrenia-related genes may interact with *T. gondii* infection in the host exacerbating schizophrenic behaviors and/or the chance of them being induced. Variations in the associated genes range from rare alleles with a large effect to common alleles with less effect. Among those genes that have been correlated with schizophrenia are genes whose products are involved in cell connectivity, cell adhesion and myelination, neurotransmission, and cell metabolism (proliferation, apoptosis, transcription factors, and growth factors). The genes associated with the highest risk identified, to date, are DISC1 (disrupted-in-schizophrenia 1), TCF4 (transcription factor 4), MBP (myelin basic protein), and HSPA1B (heat shock 70 KDa protein 2). In addition, strong positive associations have been observed for neurotransmitter-related genes (COMT, DRD2, DTNBP1, GAD1, GRIA1, GRIN2B, HTR2A, SNAP-25, TNIK) and cell adhesion and connectivity genes (NCAM1, RELN) based on GWAS, and other expression data, and single nucleotide polymorphism data from both human and animal models (Ayalew et al., 2012). Because schizophrenia is a developmental disorder, genes regulated during cerebral cortex development have been implicated, such as regulation in genes encoding receptors and transporters with neurotransmission (DRD1, DRD1a, NOTCH2, and SLC1A2), gamma-aminobutyric acid (GABA) regulation (GAD1, DBI), and transcription factor NR4A2 with a role in dopaminergic neurones during subplate layer development (Hoerder-Suabedissen et al., 2013). Rare loss-of-function variants and copy number variants are strongly correlated with the phenotype of schizophrenia. An excess of rare novel loss-of-function variants in synaptic genes are correlated with both schizophrenia and autism spectrum disorders (Kenny et al., 2014), although, for example, neurexins (Nrxn1), involved in synaptic formation and maintenance, have copy number variations in the gene (also in autism spectrum disorder (Reichelt, Rodgers, & Clapcote, 2012)).

Drug-target gene network analysis of drugs approved for schizophrenia has also indicated genes in several pathways that may be positively associated with the disease. Bridge genes between the drug networks identified GRIN2A, GRIN3B, GRIN2C, GRIN2B, DRD1, and DRD2 representing the *N*-methyl-D-aspartate (NMDA) receptor family and dopamine receptors as potential biological factors correlated with schizophrenia (Putnam, Sun, & Zhao, 2011). Recently, a study identified 108 loci associated with schizophrenia using the GWAS (Group, 2014). Of the 108 loci, 75% include protein-coding genes (40% of which are monogenic). There were strong associations with genes involved in glutamatergic neurotransmission (DRD2), synaptic plasticity (GRM3, GRIN2A, SRR, GRIA1), and voltage-gated calcium channel subunits (CACNA1C, CACNB2, and CACNA1I). Associations were also enriched among genes encoding proteins that have important roles in immunity (Group, 2014). Hence, it is clear that there is a large range of genes affecting various systems, from catecholamines to neuronal connectivity as well as genes associated with immune responses that could interact with *T. gondii* during infection and facilitate schizophrenia.

The importance of genetic factors in schizophrenia has prompted the development of mutant (or drug-exposed) rodent models aimed to advance our understanding of biological mechanisms underlying schizophrenia symptomology and the neurological alterations involved in cognitive changes associated with schizophrenia. To date, no genetic mutant rodent models have incorporated environmental exposure to *T. gondii* as a (two-hit) cofactor, although there in an ever-gathering selection of mouse and rat models available to do so. Among the first rodent models of schizophrenia studied was the inbred mouse strain DBA/2J that exhibits higher stress and anxiety-related behavioral traits as well as a lower reward-seeking for substances including ethanol, nicotine, amphetamine, and morphine relative to the C57BL/6J inbred strain (Sarnyai, Jashar, & Olivier, 2015). DBA/2J mice also exhibited a significantly reduced prepulse inhibition of startle compared with several other mouse strains. Following the success of dopaminergic antagonists that target the dopamine receptor D2, such as haloperidol, to treat the symptoms of schizophrenia, mice that overexpress D2 receptors in the striatum (D2R-OE mice) were then also generated as a potential model of schizophrenia (Simpson, Waltz, Kellendonk, & Balsam, 2012). The D2R-OE mice exhibit a deficit in incentive motivation as observed by a decreased effort in appetite rewards that may result from an inability to assess the value of positive outcomes. Another example is the discovery that the mouse strain 129S6/SvEv, which exhibits deficits in cognitive functions, has at least a partially deleted DISC1 gene, a major risk-associated schizophrenia gene. Indeed, modifications in genes involved in cognitive dysfunction, a central feature of schizophrenia, have helped contribute to understanding cognitive processes (Papaleo, Lipska, & Weinberger, 2012). Neurological systems that have been scrutinized include dopaminergic transmission (e.g., genes D1, D2, D3, D4, D5, DAT, COMT, MAOA), GABAergic transmission (e.g., genes deltaGABA(A), GABA(B1), GAT1), glutamatergic (e.g., genes GluR, NR1, NR2A, NR2B, GRM2, GRM3, GLAST), acetylcholine (e.g., nAChR), calcium balance (e.g., genes CaMKII, neurogranin, CaMKK, CaMKIV), and schizophrenia risk-associated genes dysbindin (DTNBP1), neuregulin (NRG1), DISC1, reelin and proline dehydrogenase (PRODH). Genetic modifications within the stress-sensitive systems of corticotropin-releasing factor and brain-derived neurotrophic factor also exhibit cognitive alterations aligned with schizophrenia.

Several parallels have also been found between schizophrenia and dopaminergic-mutant mice. Studies of dopamine D2 and D3 receptor null mutant mice (−/−) find that the mice are deficient in their response to a T-maze spatial delayed alternation task, although the D2$^{-/-}$ mice performance may be inaccurate because these mice also have impaired locomotor activity. Overall, the genetic disruption of dopamine D2 and D3 receptor pathways appear to impact executive memory functions, analogous to schizophrenia. Mice lacking the dopamine transporter DAT are characterized by high extracellular dopamine levels and spontaneous hyperlocomotion and intriguingly, along with D2 knock-out (KO) mice, show some neurochemical changes in olfactory bulbs and olfactory deficits. Such increased dopamine, hyperlocomotion, and olfactory alterations may be similar to those same specific behavioral alterations observed in *T. gondii*–infected rodents. Changes in the neurotransmitter-related gene COMT, involved in the dopamine turnover, such as overexpressing human COMT Val variant, are generally not associated with disease, but overexpressors showed impairments in attention shifting in a prefrontal cortex dopamine-sensitive digging test (modeled on the human Wisconsin Card Sorting Test) similar to the effects of dopamine depletion in monkeys (Papaleo, Burdick, Callicott, & Weinberger, 2014).

GABA receptors also have been strongly implicated in schizophrenia, and findings in mutant mice suggest that the A and B receptors might have opposing roles in cognitive function based on studies of GABA transporters (GAT1-GAT4) involved in GABA neurotransmission termination. Changes in GAT1 expression in mice alter GABA concentrations in the hippocampus and affect learning and memory capabilities in tests such as the Morris water maze, passive avoidance, and contextual fear conditioning (Yu et al., 2013). *Toxoplasma gondii* has been shown to affect the host generation of GABA and glutamate, with differential effects depending on the strain of the organism (Fuks, Arrighi, Weidner, et al., 2012; Xiao, Li, Jones-Brando, & Yolken, 2013).

Although disruption of a gene provides a concrete test of the product's role in the brain, for etiologic validity, partial KOs and single-nucleotide substitutions are being pursued with testing in both hetero- and homozygous mice to mimic the features of schizophrenia. DISC1 is one of the genes with the highest association with schizophrenia and among the most studied in mouse models and is known to interact with the environmental factor stress (Gamo et al., 2013). DISC1 was identified by a pedigree analysis with members of the same family suffering from a variety of psychiatric disorders including schizophrenia, major depression, bipolar disorder, and adolescent conduct disorder and has been linked to autism. DISC1 regulates many aspects of development and function of the nervous system (Blackwood et al., 2001). Several DISC1 models in mice have been generated with different genetic manipulation, assays for characterizing, and behavior tests, complicating comparison between models (Cash-Padgett & Jaaro-Peled, 2013). Yet overall, these genetic models exhibit abnormalities relevant to schizophrenia and mood disorders such as synaptic deficits, dysfunction in the dopaminergic system, and cognitive and emotional behavioral deficits. Hence, although the selection of a particular mutant may grossly effect the results of testing and limit the application as a model of schizophrenia, clear gene × environment interactions can be observed (Niwa et al., 2013).

Many of the genes associated with schizophrenia, including those that closely regulate levels of nutrients in the blood as well as neurophysiological genes, also affect the lifecycle of *T. gondii*. Numerous schizophrenia susceptibility genes are partially responsible for membrane components that *T. gondii* binds to, directly before entering the host cell. The gene GNPAT codes for expression of proteins that metabolize glycerone-3-phosphate to acylclyceronephosphate, which parasites may

metabolize from the blood stream. Also, tryptophan is required by many parasites for growth, including *T. gondii*, and the gene that encodes tryptophan hydroxylase regulates serotonin levels. The gene coding for expression of NMDA receptors is very sensitive to concentrations of glutathione, which is depleted in cerebrospinal fluid and the brain in people with schizophrenia. This presents an advantage for *T. gondii* because fewer NMDA receptors to bind glutathione allows for more available glutathione, which activates an apyrase released by *T. gondii*, causing the parasite to leave the vacuole it is contained in. This results in *T. gondii* quickly using up the host cell's adenosine triphosphate and draining it of energy (Carter, 2009). Various other genes metabolize and provide ligands that *T. gondii* binds to, including PLA2, GALNT7, and B3GAT1, which may also be involved in interactions with schizophrenia or other disorders. In addition, an orthologous region to a gene found in rats that is associated with resistance to *T. gondii* (Toxo1) has been found in the human genome, including a gene ALOX12, which has recently been associated with susceptibility to human congenital toxoplasmosis (Cavaillès, Bisanz, et al., 2006; Cavaillès, Sergent, et al., 2006; Witola et al., 2014). Allelic variants of ALOX12 are also associated with diseases including schizophrenia, atherosclerosis, and cancers, although potential mechanisms had not been defined (Phillis, Horrocks, & Farooqui, 2006).

Further to the genes mentioned previously, the presence of cysts of *T. gondii* in the brain and spinal fluid induces immune response genes to increase production of proinflammatory cytokines, with diffusion to blood plasma and cerebrospinal fluid. Elevated levels of these cytokines in the blood plasma (e.g., tumor necrosis factor) and cerebrospinal fluid (e.g., interleukin-6) have been closely associated with suicidal behavior (Kaushik et al., 2012). Accumulating evidence indicates that neuronal major histocompatibility complex class I molecules do not simply function in an immune capacity, but also are crucial for normal brain development, neuronal differentiation, synaptic plasticity, and even behavior (Boulanger & Shatz, 2004). Expression of 15 immunomodulatory molecules have recently been observed to be significantly altered in individuals with schizophrenia and those with an at-risk mental status for psychosis compared with healthy controls (Hayes et al., 2014). These included interleukin-6 receptor, tumor necrosis factor-alpha, and angiotensin converting enzyme inversely correlated with *T. gondii* antibody titer in the cerebrospinal fluid, suggesting a possible involvement of *T. gondii* infection in the pathology (Hayes et al., 2014). Further understanding of these functions of immune proteins may well provide insights into how infections such as

T. gondii can contribute to the causation of mental illness (Kaushik et al., 2012; Mortensen et al., 2007).

GENE–ENVIRONMENT INTERACTIONS—"A > TWO-HIT *TOXOPLASMA GONDII* MODEL OF SCHIZOPHRENIA"

If *T. gondii* is involved in the etiology of some cases of schizophrenia, its synergy with genes may determine the person's brain development, immune response to infections, and response to other infectious agents (Torrey & Yolken, 2003). Infections, particularly in the fetal or neonatal period (Mortensen et al., 2007), in genetically predisposed individuals could present a scenario in which the combination have a high likelihood of developing characteristics of schizophrenia. There are many possibilities for how changes induced by *T. gondii* could interact with the host's genetic makeup to contribute to neurological disorders. Based on the observed changes in dopamine with infection, for example, there is potential for *T. gondii* to interact with alleles with differing catecholamine proteins such as COMT, dopamine receptors, and transporters. Alternatively, *T. gondii* may provide the dopamine changes that may complement genetic changes in connectivity such as Nrxn and NCAM1. Indeed, alterations in the expression of arginine vasopressin in the amygdala of rats infected with *T. gondii* were recently found (Hari Dass & Vyas, 2014). The vasopressinergic neurons were found to be more activated after exposure of infected rats to cat odor than uninfected rats. This could thereby potentially link with schizophrenia since vasopressin receptor expression has been shown to decrease in the amygdala following MK-801 treatment, an NMDA antagonist used as an animal model of schizophrenia (Tanaka et al., 2003).

Toxoplasma gondii may facilitate the action and/or interact with of other infectious agents such as endogenous retroviruses, in a form of "three hit" model for schizophrenia *T. gondii*, host genetics, and an additional coinfecting agent (Webster et al., 2013; Webster & McConkey, 2010). This may particularly be plausible as *T. gondii* is known to have the ability to activate retroviruses in animal model systems (Gazzinellim et al., 1996) and is also consistent with the observation that many persons with schizophrenia also exhibit increased retroviral activation within their central nervous systems (Karlsson et al., 2001). Interactions between autoimmune diseases, gastrointestinal infections, gut microbiomes, and schizophrenia have been recently reviewed elsewhere and further support the potential connections between multiple risk factors for inducing schizophrenia-associated behaviors (Severance, Yolken, & Eaton, in press; Stilling, Dinan, & Cryan, 2013).

FUTURE POTENTIAL *TOXOPLASMA GONDII* MODELS OF SCHIZOPHRENIA

Toxoplasma gondii can be successfully maintained in vitro and hence many studies on the parasite, such as those examining gene expression, can be performed without the need for animal infections. However, to fully elucidate the impact upon behavior, and the mechanisms involved, future studies, across a range of different host species and individuals, will remain essential. The choice of animal host to study, down to species, strain, gender, and past parasitic and behavioral histories clearly will have an effect on the outcome of any behavioral assay used, and in doing so should provide further key information regarding the evolution, mechanisms involved, and the behavioral outcome of infection (Webster et al., 2013). For instance, recent studies have revealed sex-specific changes in gene expression and behavior induced by chronic *T. gondii* infection in mice (Xiao et al., 2012). Similarly, *T. gondii* has been reported to increase testosterone levels in men but decrease levels in women (Flegr, Lindova, & Kodym, 2008). The associations with schizophrenia in humans is equally unclear. Recent studies have indicated that *T. gondii* is a risk factor for schizophrenia in women (Khademvatan, Khajeddin, Izadi, & Yousefi, 2014), although others observed elevated *T. gondii* antibody levels in males with schizophrenia, but not in women (Flegr et al., 2014). Furthermore, the gender of the person performing the laboratory experiments may also be important, and hence must be controlled for between experimental trials, with male olfactory cues inducing stress within the rodents, which may bias the subtle behavioral changes under investigation (Sorge et al., 2014). In a similar manner, the choice of the parasite used as well as the route and timing of infection may also influence the behavioral outcomes within such studies (Webster et al., 2013). Key parasite associated factors may plausibly relate to the route of infection, such as oocyst or tissue cyst (Webster, 2001; Webster & McConkey, 2010) or perhaps even sexually transmitted route, and recent development in serological diagnostics may not enable us to differential such routes of transmission in natural/wild-sourced studies (Hill, Coss, & Dubey, 2011). The timing of initial infection may also be important, whether congenital (and at which trimester), neonatal, prepubescent, or adult-acquired (Webster, 1994, 2001; Webster et al., 2013). Prepubescent infection may be particularly important in models of schizophrenia. The strain of *T. gondii* is also undoubtedly of paramount importance in terms of the clinical, behavioral, and ethical outcomes of infection. *Toxoplasma gondii* is composed of three major genotypes, types I, II, and III (previously estimated to encompass 94% of all isolates when combined), which have emerged as the dominant strains worldwide (Howe, Honore, Derouin, & Sibley, 1997).

Although type I strains tend to be fatal in mice, type II and III parasites are relatively avirulent and more readily form cysts and thereby establish chronic infections (Howe, Summers, & Sibley, 1996; Sibley & Boothroyd, 1992; Sibley, Mordue, Su, Robben, & Howe, 2002), which make the latter two strains more suitable for the study of behavioral changes with chronic infection. Type II and III strains also show higher expression of the parasite's tyrosine hydroxylase genes, proposed to be involved in behavioral changes, relative to type I strains (Gaskell et al., 2009; Prandovszky et al., 2011). Infection with type II also accounts for most human cases (60–80%) in Europe and North America (Ajzenberg et al., 2002; Ajzenberg et al., 2009; Peyron et al., 2006), although both types I and III are commonly found in Colombia (Peyron et al., 2006). However, it is critical to clarify that sampling has been largely biased toward parasites recovered from symptomatic humans and domestic animals, and hence relatively little is known about the majority of wild animal infections or even potentially those human infections with no apparent disease. A role for atypical genotypes in cases with severe host morbidity has, however, been indicated by the Californian sea otters populations suffering from increased mortality—where, although 40% were infected with the common zoonotic type II strain, 60% were infected with a genotype that possessed novel alleles at three genetic loci different from the alleles found in the standard types I–III (Miller et al., 2004). Furthermore, recent research suggests that such atypical strains, previously referred to as A and X, may designate together as a "type 12" (Khan et al., 2011), and this type 12 lineage may actually account for 46.7% (79/169) of isolates and are dominant among wildlife of North America (Dubey et al., 2011). One could thus perhaps postulate that future molecular typing studies could reveal different clinical and behavioral outcomes in human or other *T. gondii* infections in relation to whether the zoonotic infection route may be wildlife or domestic, and typical or atypical genotype. Even within the *T. gondii* type, however, different clinical and behavioral outcomes may be predicted. Within type II alone, variation in host cell gene expression (Hill, Gouffon, Saxton, & Su, 2012) and development (Diana et al., 2004), host immune and encephalitic response (Araujo & Slifer, 2003; Hill et al., 2012), parasite dissemination, reactivation and recrudescence (Saeij, Boyle, Grigg, Arrizabalaga, & Boothroyd, 2005), and impact on host behavior (Kannan et al., 2010) have all been reported between different strains. For example, although both Prugniaud (Pru) and ME49 have been reported to increase attraction to cat odor in mice at 2 months postinfection, in at least one study this behavior was no longer present with the ME49 strain at 7 months postinfection (Kannan et al., 2010). Prugniaud-infected mice in this study were also reported to have greater hyperactivity than their ME49-infected counterparts, although only the ME49-infected group showed impaired spatial working memory (Kannan et al., 2010).

It is strongly proposed that experiments with more "resistant" animals, such as rats, provide a superior model in which to study the behavior changes induced by *T. gondii*, from both an ethical and biological perspective in terms of their generalizability to humans, relative to the mouse model (Hrda, Votypka, & Kodym, 2000; Webster, 2007; Webster et al., 2013). In terms of future research into the *T. gondii* model of schizophrenia, several potentially useful rat in vivo models are already available that could plausibly provide valuable experimental tools to further test the hypotheses of causality. For example, one could propose the spontaneously hypertensive rat model of anxiety to further elucidate host from parasite associations in relation to generalized anxiety profiles. Prenatal exposure to various infectious agents has been linked to an increased risk of neurodevelopmental brain disorders, and specifically those associated with altered dopaminergic development. For example, there is recent evidence that rats born to mothers exposed to the viral mimic polyriboinosinic-polyribocytidylic acid in pregnancy provide a useful rodent model for human affective disorders such as schizophrenia (Vuillermot et al., 2012). Although admittedly previous studies found no significant difference in the hyperactivity profiles between adult-acquired and congenitally acquired *T. gondii* infections among rats (Webster, 1994), it may be fascinating to examine the impact of *T. gondii* on the resulting developmental, behavioral, and neurophysiological phenotypes among such polyriboinosinic-polyribocytidylic acid offspring—hence, a "two-step environmental–environmental (i.e., infection:infection) hit." Likewise, although there are no rodent models available as of yet for hallucinations, NMDA receptor antagonists, such as MK-801, can induce schizophrenia-like psychoses, together with other "positive symptoms," in rats (Brigman, Graybeal, & Holmes, 2010). Intriguingly, the effects of MK-801 on mouse behavior were found to parallel the effects of *T. gondii* infection on behavior (Nishikawa et al., 2013). The mechanism involves hyperactivity of mesolimbic dopamine neurons, although multiple brain regions and multiple neurotransmitter systems are affected (Seeman, 1987). Notably, Wang and colleagues also showed, using MK-801 administration in mice as their model of schizophrenia, that when such mice were also infected with *T. gondii*, they showed impaired learning relative to uninfected mice on certain "state of despair" task such as the forced swimming and tail suspension tests (Wang et al., 2013). Hence, one may predict future studies incorporating the additional exposure of *T. gondii* in such rodent models, ideally using ethically and phenotypically appropriate behavioral assays (Webster et al., 2013), may further provide valuable insights in to the mechanisms involved and potential phenotypic outcomes.

As raised previously, genetically engineered and naturally occurring mutant rodent models can also be particularly useful in providing requisite information about the neurodevelopmental, behavioral, and molecular consequences of dysregulation of specific genes, and hence the potential gene–environment interactions of infection with *T. gondii* on subsequent behavioral outcomes. At present, there are several relevant mouse models available that may be particularly useful for future *T. gondii* research, in particular those using KO mice involving dopamine (dopamine synthesis and/or regulation genes) (Kirby, Waddington, & O'Tuathaigh, 2010). Unfortunately, there are few KO rat models yet available, although several are underway and these will need to be validated, and their development is likely to prove extremely valuable for examining gene–environment interactions, particularly with the newly developed technologies. In particular, we may predict that, for example, the combination of such genetic (KO line) and environmental (*T. gondii* infection) factors not only exerts additive effects on behavioral traits such as locomotor hyperactivity and "fatal feline attraction," but further produces synergistic effects in the development of, for instance, impaired attentional shifting and sustained attention. Furthermore, we may predict that the combination of both these gene–environmental factors is necessary to trigger maldevelopment of the host dopamine system in these etio-pathological processes.

Future studies aimed to elucidate that mechanisms of action may also benefit from recent advancements in mutant *T. gondii* strain development. Within type I, for instance, new conditional mutant RH lines have recently been constructed via promoter replacement strategies that target genes encoding proteins that are conserved and unique to these Apicomplexan parasites (Sheiner et al., 2011). RH∆*hxgprt* and Pru∆*hxgprt* strains, for example, have been produced to provide parasites in which the selectable marker HXGPRT is used for gene insertion/replacement (Donald, Carter, Ullman, & Roos, 1996), although targeting specific *T. gondii* genes for KO has previously proved difficult because of a high frequency of nonhomologous recombination in the parasite. The production of RH∆*ku80*∆*hxgprt* (Fox, Ristuccia, Gigley, & Bzik, 2009) and also notably the type II Pru∆*ku80*∆*hxgprt* (Fox et al., 2011) has, however, greatly improved the efficiency of gene replacement by homologous recombination in *T. gondii* strains, thereby increasing the opportunity to investigate the contributions of individual *T. gondii* genes to behavioral modifications of the host. Indeed, within type II, and hence those lines particularly applicable for the "*T. gondii*-rat-manipulation-schizophrenia" model, key areas of interest will be parasites such as Pru lines with differential levels

of expression and/or KO of the tyrosine hydroxylase gene shown to be associated with dopamine metabolism (Gaskell et al., 2009; Prandovszky et al., 2011; Webster & McConkey, 2010).

In addition to replicating prior observations, novel approaches and tests are required, and there is no doubt that animal models can play an essential role in furthering this theoretically and applied area of research. However, if such animal studies are to be performed, it is imperative that they are performed appropriately, testing biologically and evolutionary applicable hypotheses, and equally importantly, in the most ethical and noninvasive manner possible, particularly considering today's 3Rs environment (Webster et al., 2013). When specifically testing hypotheses relating to the role of *T. gondii* in human affective disorders such as schizophrenia, the behavioral assays to be used are not necessarily the same as those for either studying schizophrenia alone or the impact of *T. gondii* on host behavior alone. Furthermore, when choosing such assays, one must consider that, in the absence of any true "schizophrenia rodent model," the behavioral repertoire of a rodent infected with *T. gondii* may well be altered but not necessarily in the same way as that of a human with schizophrenia. For instance, if considering selective benefits to the parasite of *T. gondii* in rodents, one should focus on behavioral traits specifically associated with enhanced predation rate (such as altered activity, feline attraction, altered neophobia profiles). On the other hand, if explicitly testing for the spectrum of traits relevant to schizophrenia, a different set of behavioral assays (such as working memory, selective attention, set shifting, social interaction, and psychophysiological measures) may be more appropriate. There are generally considered to be three groups of major symptoms of schizophrenia in humans: that of positive, negative and cognitive/executive. "Positive symptoms" are so-called because they add to the normal behavioral repertoire. Although there are no rodent models available as of yet for hallucinations, other "positive symptoms," such as psychomotor agitation and hyperresponsivity to psychotomimetic drugs, are modeled in rodents by testing locomotor responses and hyperactivity-inducing effects of psychostimulants (e.g., amphetamine) and other psychotomimetics (e.g., NMDA receptor antagonists dizocilpine/MK-801 or PCP) (Brigman et al., 2010). Thus one could perhaps propose that the increased activity observed in *T. gondii*–infected rat studies (Webster, 1994; Webster et al., 2013), be also useful as a "positive symptom" assay. Likewise, as the fatal feline attraction invoked by this parasite is not simply a reduction or removal of a behavioral trait, but instead a positive reversal of an innate behavior, an apparent "alteration of the mind of the rat in the face of predation" (Berdoy et al., 2000; Webster et al., 2006), one could perhaps also propose that altered fatal feline attraction behavioral assays may be another valuable behavioral assay relevant to both *T. gondii* epidemiology and evolution but also as a potential "positive symptom" indictor for further *T. gondii* models of schizophrenia.

"Negative symptoms" of schizophrenia are so-called because they subtract from the normal behavioral repertoire, and include blunted affect, social withdrawal, and loss of pleasure in normally rewarding activities (anhedonia). Various rodent assays for social behavior and anhedonia have been typically used to model other disorders such as anxiety (File, Zangrossi, & Andrews, 1993), autism (Crawley, 2004), and depression (Strekalova, Spanagel, Bartsch, Henn, & Gass, 2004), but may also lend themselves well to the study of similar behavioral abnormalities in rodent models of schizophrenia. However, although *T. gondii*–infected mice may suffer severe morbidity and hence may show equivalent "negative symptoms" as a result of generalized pathology, *T. gondii* does not generally induce any specific "negative symptoms" in rats, as can be illustrated by the normal social behavior and mating success between infected and uninfected rats maintained under naturalistic conditions (Berdoy et al., 1995). Nevertheless, the fact that the "pleasure/reward" system does appear to be altered in *T. gondii*–infected rodents, even if in perhaps an opposite direction to those related to schizophrenia in humans (i.e., some evidence of increased pleasure/fatal feline attraction) through increased sex drive (enhanced pleasure rather than loss of pleasure, again potentially associated with increased dopamine levels), there is an argument for use of these behavioral assays when examining the "*T. gondii*-rat-manipulation-schizophrenia model." For instance, in relation to modelling "negative symptoms," one could perhaps test for alterations between infected and uninfected rodents in terms of their preference or motivation to obtain rewarding substances, such as sucrose, even if the direction of response predicted may be different between rats and humans.

Abnormalities in cognition and executive functions are also a prominent feature of schizophrenia in humans and range from deficits in episodic memory, impaired attention, and sensorimotor gating, to impaired reversal learning and set-shifting. Learning and memory can certainly, and frequently is, assessed in rodents using a range of standard behavioral assays, such as that of the reference memory version of the Morris water maze. However, although impaired episodic memory is one of the strongest features of the cognitive profile of schizophrenia (Ranganath, Minzenberg, & Ragland, 2008), rodent models of this disease have generally not relied upon such measures, and indeed do not distinguish a model of schizophrenia from other conditions that are also characterized by memory deficits, e.g., Alzheimer's disease (Brigman et al., 2010). Furthermore, one could

perhaps particularly question their utility here for any *T. gondii* rat model of schizophrenia. This may be explained as, if *T. gondii* is selectively altering intermediate host behavior to alter the predation rate, one may predict there to be no selective advantage for this parasite to alter such traits—as with a cat the change of avoiding predation on encounter is likely to be all or none—and hence such assays are less relevant to understanding the epidemiology and evolution of such manipulation. Indeed, although there are some conflicting results, particularly in the early literature, indicating potential cognitive deficits in mice after infection with *T. gondii* (Piekarski, Zippelius, & Witting, 1978; Witting, 1979) found no difference between infected and uninfected individuals. Likewise, recent research, using C57BL/6 mice chronically infected with the avirulent *T. gondii* (ME49, a type II strain), found no impact of *T. gondii* infection on cognition (Gulinello et al., 2010). This again emphasizes how any potential rodent model for human neuropsychiatric diseases is unlikely ever to fully encompass all characteristic traits and deficits.

Other potential behavioral assays for both *T. gondii* and schizophrenia concern incorporating odor detection. Damage of the olfactory system has been indicated to be, at least in part, responsible for the development of depression and may be involved in other neuropsychiatric disorders including schizophrenia (Prandota, 2014). Although there are inconsistencies between studies, experimental exposure studies of *T. gondii* in rodents have revealed cysts in various regions of the brain, including the olfactory bulb (McConkey, Gaskell, Bristow, & Webster, 2013). Studies, to date, suggest that rodents infected with *T. gondii* do not, however, appear to have any general disruption of their odor/olfaction system—as they can, for instance, discriminate between feline and other predator and nonpredator odors and even between different concentrations of odor presented—and hence it appears rather their perception of cat odor is affected (Berdoy et al., 2000; Kannan et al., 2010; Lamberton et al., 2008; Vyas, Kim, & Sapolsky, 2007). Olfaction dysfunction is frequently observed in patients with schizophrenia, with the greatest impact on odor identification (Cohen, Brown, & Auster, 2012), which may thereby present a parallel to that observed in *T. gondii*–infected rodents. Thus, further examination of the subtle changes in odor-specific thresholds and identification deficits observed are warranted as part of the *T. gondii*-rat-manipulation-schizophrenia model and a range of standardized behavioral assays are available.

Cognitive flexibility is a critical executive function that can be broadly defined as the ability to adapt behaviors in response to changes in the environment. There are potentially useful noninvasive behavioral assays for these deficits in rodents available that could be highly applicable for a *T. gondii* model of schizophrenia. These include, among others, intradimensional/extradimensional digging tasks. During such assays, rodents are trained to dig for food reward using either olfactory (digging medium odor) or tactile (digging medium texture) cues. The rewarded cue in the same dimension is switched to test for intradimensional shifting. The rewarded cue can also be changed to a different dimension to test for extradimensional shifting. Likewise, the Wisconsin Card Sorting Task (WCST; Grant & Berg, 1948) has been one of the more commonly employed assays for impaired cognitive flexibility in schizophrenic patients, and analogous versions have been developed for use in rodents. In essence, these tasks involve the subject selecting between stimuli, which vary from one another in more than one perceptual dimension, and being reinforced for choosing a stimulus based upon one specific dimension alone (e.g., odor). During an "intradimensional shift," the form of the dimension the subject must choose is changed by the experimenter (e.g., from cinnamon to chocolate odor). In an "extradimensional shift," the correct dimension is changed altogether, such that choices must be guided by the new dimension (texture) while ignoring the previously rewarded dimension. In a rodent intradimensional shift/extradimensional shift analog of the Wisconsin Card Sorting Task, rats (Birrell & Brown, 2000) dig in sand to make choices based on the dimension of texture or smell, thereby providing another example of a potentially useful, biologically and ethically behavioral assay available and able to be incorporated into future research in this field.

GENERAL DISCUSSION

As we expand our knowledge of how the brain functions, it is important to understand the potential impact of infectious agents, particularly chronic neurological pathogens. Infectious diseases, and the immune response to infections, may influence behavior and, in some cases, be related to psychiatric disorders. *Toxoplasma gondii* is a common, chronic neural infection of humans and other animals. Several of these species, including humans, have considerably longer lifespans than a "natural" rodent intermediate hosts, and hence one could reasonably propose may be more susceptible to developing "unselected" pathological behavioral changes simply as a byproduct of their extended durations of infections. One of these potentially associated pathologies may thereby include schizophrenia in some humans. There seems little doubt that the subtle behavioral changes observed in rodents infected with *T. gondii* will be reflected by similar subtle behavioral changes in humans, and a convincing body of empirical evidence now exists in support of this. However, when it comes to considering animal infection models for human

severe behavioral alterations, such as those that occur within schizophrenia, the case is undoubtedly more complex. There is no doubt that animal, in particular rodent, models have been and continue to be useful in helping us understand aspects of schizophrenia—such as in terms of elucidating how current and potential future antipsychotic drugs work. Indeed, it was an understanding of the interaction of certain neuroleptics with dopamine receptors that was an instigator in formulating the still-maintained theory that schizophrenia involves some form of dysregulation of brain dopamine function (Creese, Burt, & Snyder, 1976; Seeman, 1987; Seeman, Lee, Chau-Wong, & Wong, 1976). However, we are unlikely to ever be able to reproduce the full phenotypic spectrum of a human psychiatric disorder such as schizophrenia in a rat or mouse (Arguello & Gogos, 2006). Schizophrenia is a highly heterogeneous disorder of myriad symptoms. The presentation of different symptoms and their severity varies considerably across patients. Nevertheless, although this complexity cannot be fully recapitulated in rodent models, specific symptom categories can be behaviorally modeled. A constructive starting point has been to demarcate schizophrenia-related phenotypes into the clinical categories of "positive," "negative," and cognitive/executive symptoms (Brigman et al., 2010). Of course, an essential step in clarifying the etiology of schizophrenia is understanding the gene–environment interactions contributing to this and associated disorders. In this context in particular, animal models will have a central and indispensable role in the process of elucidating the mechanisms involved and perhaps the epidemiology of certain causes of psychiatric disorders (Arguello & Gogos, 2006). For a better understanding of the synergy between genetic factors and environmental factors such as *T. gondii* in the pathogenesis of schizophrenia, we need to establish well-controlled analyses of gene–environment interactions.

CONCLUSIONS

Schizophrenia is a pervasive neuropsychiatric disease of uncertain, and probably multiple, audiologies that affects approximately 0.5–1% of the adult population in the United States and Europe (Wu et al., 2006). *Toxoplasma gondii* is a protozoan parasite of the CNS that affects approximately 20–80% of the adult population worldwide and approximately 30% in the United States and Europe (Dubey, 2010). Although there is an ever-gathering body of evidence supporting an association between the two (Table 1), can the simple difference in prevalence alone confound the potential for *T. gondii* as a valid model for schizophrenia? Our hypothesis suggests that the two are compatible, in that *T. gondii*, as an environmental stressor, can initiate or amplify behavioral deficits in rodent models, including genotype mutant models, of schizophrenia. We hypothesize that at least a "two-hit" or "three-or-more-hit" mode for development of schizophrenia and/or cognitive abnormalities could occur with interaction between *T. gondii* and the genotype of the individual. *Toxoplasma gondii* may thereby serve in gene–environment interactions with processes affected by schizophrenia risk genes potentiating and/or triggering a psychiatric disorder in susceptible individuals. We may now be gaining some insight into the behavioral changes observed within rats chronically infected with *T. gondii*, particularly because *T. gondii* can be associated with dopamine dysregulation and the parasite encodes a tyrosine hydroxylase. Based, at least in part, on the observation that compounds that elicit dopamine release, such as amphetamine, induce psychosis, whereas agents that block dopamine D2 receptors ameliorate psychotic symptoms, the dysregulation of dopamine has been the prevailing neurochemical hypothesis of schizophrenia. The interactions of genetic and environmental factors in the etiology of schizophrenia and other psychiatric disorders are undefined, but a gathering body of empirical evidence strongly supports a role for *T. gondii* in the interplay with genetic factors in some cases of schizophrenia etiology. Future research is now required to rigorously test whether *T. gondii* infection exacerbates behavioral deficits in rodent models of schizophrenia and interacts with three well-defined schizophrenia risk genes. Additional studies should be directed at the more detailed evaluation of exposure to *T. gondii* and other infectious agents during pregnancy and childhood. Future studies are needed to elucidate the critical periods for infection; the possible role of other specific infections; if, or to what extent, confounding genetic factors related to disease susceptibility may explain the association between *T. gondii* infection and schizophrenia; and to what extent gene–infection interactions are relevant to the causation of schizophrenia. Only when such factors are elucidated can we hope to have successful prevention and/or control of *T. gondii*–associated schizophrenia morbidity. A recent overview of the potential pathophysiological relationship between depression, suicide, and *T. gondii* infection provides guidelines for the screening, diagnosis, and treatment of depression for nurse practitioners (Hsu, Groer, & Beckie, 2014), and similar guidelines should become available for *T. gondii* and schizophrenia screening, diagnosis, and treatment. Understanding the neurological effects of *T. gondii* infection and potential interactions may suggest approaches to reduce schizophrenia burden potentially with implications for other neurological disorders and neuropathic infectious agents.

References

Ajzenberg, D., Cogné, N., Paris, L., Bessières, M. H., Thulliez, P., Filisetti, D., et al. (2002). *Toxoplasma gondii* isolates associated with human congenital toxoplasmosis, and correlation with clinical findings. *Journal of Infectious Diseases, 186*, 684–689.

Ajzenberg, D., Yera, H., Marty, P., Paris, L., Dalle, F., Menotti, J., et al. (2009). Genotype of 88 *Toxoplasma gondii* isolates associated with toxoplasmosis in immunocompromised patients and correlation with clinical findings. *Journal of Infectious Diseases, 199*, 1155–1167.

Alvarado-Esquivel, C., Sanchez-Anguiano, L. F., Arnaud-Gil, C. A., et al. (2013). *Toxoplasma gondii* infection and suicide attempts: a case-control study in psychiatric outpatients. *Journal of Nervous Mental Disorders, 201*, 948–952.

Alvarado-Esquivel, C., Torres-Castorena, A., Liesenfeld, O., Estrada-Martínez, S., & Urbina-Álvarez, J. (2012). High seroprevalence of *Toxoplasma gondii* infection in a subset of Mexican patients with work accidents and low socioeconomic status. *Parasites & Vectors, 5*.

Araujo, F. G., & Slifer, T. (2003). Different strains of *Toxoplasma gondii* induce different cytokine responses in CBA/Ca mice. *Infection and Immunity, 71*, 4171–4174.

Arguello, P. A., & Gogos, J. A. (2006). Modeling madness in mice: one piece at a time. *Neuron, 52*, 179–196.

Arias, I., Sorlozano, A., Villegas, E., de Dios Luna, J., McKenney, K., Cervilla, J., et al. (2012). Infectious agents associated with schizophrenia: a meta-analysis. *Schizophrenia Research, 136*, 128–136.

Arling, T. A., Yolken, R. H., Lapidus, M., Langenberg, P., Dickerson, F. B., Zimmerman, B. S., et al. (2009). *Toxoplasma gondii* antibody titers and history of suicide attempts in patients with recurrent mood disorders. *The Journal of Nervous and Mental Disease, 197*, 905–908.

Ayalew, M., Le-Niculescu, H., Levey, D. F., Jain, N., Changala, B., Patel, S. D., et al. (2012). Convergent functional genomics of schizophrenia: from comprehensive understanding to genetic risk prediction. *Molecular Psychiatry, 17*, 887–905.

Berdoy, M., Webster, J. P., & Macdonald, D. W. (1995). Parasite altered behaviour: is the effect of *Toxoplasma gondii* on *Rattus norvegicus* specific? *Parasitology, 111*, 403–409.

Berdoy, M., Webster, J. P., & Macdonald, D. W. (2000). Fatal attraction in *Toxoplasma*-infected rats: a case of parasite manipulation of its mammalian host. *Proceedings of the Royal Society (London) Series B, 267*, 267.

Berk, M., Dodd, S., Kauer-Sant'Anna, M., Malhi, G. S., Bourin, M., Kapczinski, F., et al. (2007). Dopamine dysregulation syndrome: implications for a dopamine hypothesis of bipolar disorder. *Acta Pscychiatrica Scandinavia, 434*, 41–49.

Birrell, J. M., & Brown, V. J. (2000). Medial frontal cortex mediates perceptual attentional set shifting in the rat. *Journal of Neuroscience, 20*(11), 4320–4324.

Blackwood, D. H., Fordyce, A., Walker, M. T., St Clair, D. M., Porteous, D. J., & Muir, W. J. (2001). Schizophrenia and affective disorders–cosegregation with a translocation at chromosome 1q42 that directly disrupts brain-expressed genes: clinical and P300 findings in a family. *American Journal of Human Genetics, 69*, 428–433.

Boulanger, L. M., & Shatz, C. J. (2004). Immune signalling in neural development, synaptic plasticity and disease. *Nature Reviews Neuroscience, 5*, 521–531.

Bowman, D. (2002). *Feline clinical parasitology*. IA: Iowa State University Press.

Brigman, J. L., Graybeal, C., & Holmes, A. (2010). Predictably irrational: assaying cognitive inflexibility in mouse models of schizophrenia. *Frontiers in Neuroscience, 4*, 19–28.

Caroff, S. N., Mann, S. C., Gliatto, M. F., Sullivan, K. A., & Campbell, E. C. (2001). Psychiatric manifestations of acute viral encephalitis. *Psychiatric Annals*, 193–204.

Carter, C. (2009). Schizophrenia susceptibility genes directly implicated in the life cycles of pathogens: cytomegalovirus, influenza, herpes simplex, rubella and *Toxoplasma gondii*. *Schizophrenia Bulletin, 35*, 1163–1182.

Cash-Padgett, T., & Jaaro-Peled, H. (2013). DISC1 mouse models as a tool to decipher gene-environment interactions in psychiatric disorders. *Frontiers in Behavioral Neuroscience, 7*, 113.

Cavaillès, P., Bisanz, C., Papapietro, O., Colacios, C., Sergent, V., Pipy, B., et al. (2006). The rat Toxo1 locus controls the outcome of the toxoplasmic infection according to a Mendelian mode. *Medical Science (Paris), 22*, 679–680.

Cavaillès, P., Sergent, V., Bisanz, C., Papapietro, O., Colacios, C., Mas, M., et al. (2006). The rat Toxo1 locus directs toxoplasmosis outcome and controls parasite proliferation and spreading by macrophage-dependent mechanisms. *Proceedings of the National Academy of Sciences of the United States of America, 103*, 744–749.

Cichon, S., Craddock, N., Daly, M., Faraone, S. V., Gejman, P. V., Kelsoe, J., & Psychiatric GWAS Consortium Coordinating Committee., et al. (2009). Genomewide association studies: history, rationale, and prospects for psychiatric disorders. *American Journal of Psychiatry, 166*, 540–556.

Cohen, A. S., Brown, L. A., & Auster, T. L. (2012). Olfaction, "olfiction," and the schizophrenia-spectrum: an updated meta-analysis on identification and acuity. *Schizophrenia Research, 135*, 152–157.

Crawley, J. N. (2004). Designing mouse behavioral tasks relevant to autistic-like behaviors. *Mental Retardation and Developmental Disabilities Research Reviews, 10*, 248–258.

Creese, I., Burt, D. R., & Snyder, S. H. (1976). Dopamine receptor binding predicts clinical and pharmacological potencies of antischizophrenic drugs. *Science, 192*, 481–483.

Denys, D., Zohar, J., & Westenberg, H. G. (2004). The role of dopamine in obsessive-compulsive disorder: preclinical and clinical evidence. *Journal of Clinical Psychiatry, 65*, 11–17.

Desmonts, G., & Couvreur, J. (1974). Congenital toxoplasmosis. A prospective study of 378 pregnancies. *New England Journal of Medicine, 290*.

Diana, J., Persat, F., Staquet, M. J., Assossou, O., Ferrandiz, J., Gariazzo, M. J., et al. (2004). Migration and maturation of human dendritic cells infected with *Toxoplasma gondii* depend on parasite strain type. *FEMS Immunology and Medical Microbiology, 42*, 321–331.

Dickerson, F., Stallings, C., Origoni, A., Katsafanas, E., Schweinfurth, L., et al. (2014). Antibodies to *Toxoplasma gondii* and cognitive functioning in schizophrenia, bipolar disorder, and nonpsychiatric controls. *Journal of Nervous and Mental Disorders, 202*, 589–593.

Diehl, D. J., & Gershon, S. (1992). The role of dopamine in mood disorders. *Comparative Pyschiatry, 33*, 115–120.

Donald, R. G., Carter, D., Ullman, B., & Roos, D. S. (1996). Insertional tagging, cloning, and expression of the *Toxoplasma gondii* hypoxanthine-xanthine-guanine phosphoribosyltransferase gene. Use as a selectable marker for stable transformation. *Journal of Biological Chemistry, 271*, 14010–14019.

Dubey, J. P. (2010). *Toxoplasmosis of humans and animals*.

Dubey, J. P., & Carpenter, J. L. (1993). Histologically confirmed clinical toxoplasmosis in cats: 100 cases (1952–1990). *Journal of the American Veterinary Medical Association, 203*, 1556–1566.

Dubey, J. P., Velmurugan, G. V., Rajendran, C., Yabsley, M. J., Thomas, N. J., Beckmen, K. B., et al. (2011). Genetic characterisation of *Toxoplasma gondii* in wildlife from North America revealed widespread and high prevalence of the fourth clonal type. *International Journal for Parasitology, 41*, 1139–1147.

Editorial. (1896). Is insanity due to a microbe? *Scientific American, 75*, 303–304.

Faucher, B., Garcia-Meric, P., Franck, J., Minodier, P., Francois, P., Gonnet, S., et al. (2012). Long-term ocular outcome in congenital toxoplasmosis: a prospective cohort of treated children. *Journal of Infectious Diseases, 64*, 104–109.

File, S. E., Zangrossi, H., & Andrews, N. (1993). Novel environment and cat odor change GABA and 5-HT release and uptake in the rat. *Pharmacology, Biochemistry and Behavior, 45*, 931–934.

Flegr, J. (2007). Effects of *Toxoplasma gondii* on human behaviour. *Schizophrenia Bulletin, 33*, 757–760.

Flegr, J. (2013). Influence of latent *Toxoplasma* infection on human personality, physiology and morphology: pros and cons of the *Toxoplasma*–human model in studying the manipulation hypothesis. *Journal of Experimental Biology, 216*, 127–133.

Flegr, J., Havlícek, J., Kodym, P., Maly, M., & Smahel, Z. (2002). Increased risk of traffic accidents in subjects with latent toxoplasmosis: a retrospective case-control study. *BMC Infectious Diseases, 2*, 1–6.

Flegr, J., & Hrdy, I. (1994). Influence of chronic toxoplasmosis on some human personality factors. *Folia Parasitologica, 41*, 121–126.

Flegr, J., Klose, J., Novotná, M., Berenreitterová, M., & Havlícek, J. (2009). Increased incidence of traffic accidents in *Toxoplasma*-infected military drivers and protective effect RhD molecule revealed by a large-scale prospective cohort study. *BMC Infectious Diseases, 9*.

Flegr, J., Lenochova, P., Hodny, Z., & Vondrova, M. (2011). Fatal attraction phenomenon in humans: cat odour attractiveness increased for *Toxoplasma*-infected men while decreased for infected women. *PLoS Neglected Tropical Diseases, 5*.

Flegr, J., Lindova, J., & Kodym, P. (2008). Sex-dependent toxoplasmosis-associated differences in testosterone concentration in humans. *Parasitology, 135*, 427–431.

Flegr, J., Preiss, M., Klose, J., Havlícek, J., Vitakova, M., & Kodym, P. (2003). Decreased level of psycholbiological factor novelty seeking and lower intelligence in men latently infected with the protozoan parasite *Toxoplasma gondii*. *Biological Psychology, 63*, 253–268.

Flegr, J., Priplatova, L., Hampl, R., Bicikovia, M., Ripova, D., et al. (2014). Difference of neuro- and immunomodulatory steroids and selected hormone and lipid concentrations between *Toxoplasma*-free and *Toxoplasma*-infected but not CMV-free and CMV-infected schizophrenia patients. *Neuro Endocrinology Letters, 35*, 20–27.

Fox, B. A., Falla, A., Rommereim, L. M., Tomita, T., Gigley, J., Mercier, C., et al. (2011). Type II *Toxoplasma gondii* KU80 knockout strains enable functional analysis of genes required for cyst development and latent infection. *Eukaryotic Cell, 10*, 1193–1206.

Fox, B. A., Ristuccia, J. G., Gigley, J. P., & Bzik, D. J. (2009). Efficient gene replacements in *Toxoplasma gondii* strains deficient for nonhomologous end joining. *Eukaryotic Cell, 8*, 520–529.

Fuks, J. M., Arrighi, R. B. G., Weidner, J. M., et al. (2012). GABAergic signaling is linked to a hypermigratory phenotype in dendritic cells infected by *Toxoplasma gondii*. *PLoS Pathogens, 8*, e1003051.

Gajewski, P. D., Alkenstein, M., Hengstler, J. G., & Golka, K. (2014). *Toxoplasma gondii* impairs memory in infected seniors. *Brain, Behavior, and Immunity, 36*, 193–199.

Gale, S. D., Brown, B. L., Berrett, A., Erickson, L. D., & Hedges, D. W. (2014). Association between latent toxoplasmosis and major depression, generalised anxiety disorder and panic disorder in human adults. *Folia Parasitologica (Praha), 61*, 285–292.

Gamo, N. J., Duque, A., Paspalas, C. D., Kata, A., Fine, R., Boven, L., et al. (2013). Role of disrupted in schizophrenia 1 (DISC1) in stress-induced prefrontal cognitive dysfunction. *Translational Psychiatry, 3*, e328.

Gaskell, E. A., Smith, J. E., Pinney, J. W., Westhead, D. R., & McConkey, G. A. (2009). A unique dual activity amino acid hydroxylase in *Toxoplasma gondii*. *PLoS One, 4*, e4801.

Gazzinellim, R. T., Sher, A., Cheever, A., Gerstberger, S., Martin, M. A., & Dickie, P. (1996). Infection of human immunodeficiency virus 1 transgenic mice with *Toxoplasma gondii* stimulates proviral transcription in macrophages in vivo. *Journal of Experimental Medicine, 183*, 1645–1655.

Goodwin, D. G., Strobl, J. S., & Lindsay, D. S. (2011). Evaluation of five antischizophrenic agents against *Toxoplasma gondii* in human cell cultures. *Journal of Parasitology, 97*, 148–151.

Grant, D. A., & Berg, E. A. (1948). A behavioural analysis of degree of reinforcement and ease of shifting to new responses in a Weigl-type card sorting problem *Journal of Experimental Psychology*, *38*, 404–411.

Group, S. W. (2014). Biological insights from 108 schizophrenia-associated genetic loci. *Nature*, *511*, 421.

Gulinello, M., Acquarone, M., Kim, J. H., Spray, D. C., Barbosa, H. S., Sellers, R., et al. (2010). Acquired infection with *Toxoplasma gondii* in adult mice results in sensorimotor deficits but normal cognitive behavior despite widespread brain pathology. *Microbes and Infection*, *12*, 528–537.

Hari Dass, S. A., & Vyas, A. (2014). *Toxoplasma gondii* infection reduces predator aversion in rats through epigenetic modulation in the host medial amygdala. *Molecular Ecology*.

Hay, J., Aitken, P. P., Hair, D. M., Hutchison, W. M., & Graham, D. I. (1984). The effect of congenital *Toxoplasma* infection on mouse activity and relative preference for exposed areas over a series of trials. *Annals of Tropical Medicine and Parasitology*, *78*, 611–618.

Hay, J., Aitken, P. P., Hutchison, W. M., & Graham, D. I. (1983). The effect of congenital and adult-acquired *Toxoplasma* infections on activity and responsiveness to novel stimulation in mice. *Annals of Tropical Medicine and Parasitology*, *77*, 483–495.

Hayes, L. N., Severance, E. G., Leek, J., Gressitt, K. L., Rohleder, C., Coughlin, J. M., et al. (2014). Inflammatory molecular signature associated with infectious agents in psychosis. *Schizophrenia Bulletin*, *40*, 963–972.

Hill, D., Coss, C., & Dubey, J. P. (2011). Identification of a sporozoite-specific antigen from *Toxoplasma gondii*. *Journal of Parasitology*, *97*, 328–337.

Hill, R. D., Gouffon, J. S., Saxton, A. M., & Su, C. (2012). Differential gene expression in mice infected with distinct *Toxoplasma* strains. *Infection and Immunity*, *80*, 968–974.

Hoerder-Suabedissen, A., Oeschgera, F. M., Krishnanb, M. L., Belgarda, T. G., Wang, W. Z., Lee, S., et al. (2013). Expression profiling of mouse subplate reveals a dynamic gene network and disease association with autism and schizophrenia. *Proceedings of the National Academy of Sciences of the United States of America*, *110*, 3555–3560.

Horacek, J., Flegr, J., Tintera, J., Verebova, K., Spaniel, F., Novak, T., et al. (2011). Latent toxoplasmosis reduces gray matter density in schizophrenia but not in controls: voxel-based-morphometry (VBM) study. *World Journal of Biologial Psychiatry*.

Howe, D. K., Honore, S., Derouin, F., & Sibley, L. D. (1997). Determination of genotypes of *Toxoplasma gondii* strains isolated from patients with toxoplasmosis. *Journal of Clinical Microbiology*, *35*, 1411–1414.

Howe, D. K., Summers, B. C., & Sibley, L. D. (1996). Acute virulence in mice is associated with markers on chromosome VIII in *Toxoplasma gondii*. *Infection and Immunity*, *64*, 5193–5198.

Howes, O. D., & Kapur, S. (2009). The dopamine hypothesis of schizophrenia: version III – the final common pathway. *Schizophrenia Bulletin*, *35*, 549–562.

Hrda, S., Votypka, J., & Kodym, P. (2000). Transient nature of *Toxoplasma gondii*-induced behavioural changes in mice. *Journal of Parasitology*, *86*, 657–663.

Hsu, P. C., Groer, M., & Beckie, T. (2014). New findings: depression, suicide, and *Toxoplasma gondii* infection. *Journal of the American Association of Nurse Praciticioners*.

Hutchison, W. M., Aitken, P. P., & Wells, B. W. P. (1980). Chronic *Toxoplasma* infections and familiarity-novelty discrimination in the mouse. *Annals of Tropical Medicine and Parasitology*, *74*, 145–150.

Hutchison, W. M., Bradley, M., Cheyne, W. M., Wells, B. W. P., & Hay, J. (1980). Behavioural abnormalities in *Toxoplasma*-infected mice. *Annals of Tropical Medicine and Parasitology*, *74*, 507–510.

Hutchison, W. M., Dunachie, J. F., Siim, J., & Work, K. (1969). The life cycle of *Toxoplasma gondii*. *British Medical Journal*, 806–812.

Johnson, J., Suzuki, Y., & Mack, D. (2002). Genetic analysis of influences on survival following *Toxoplasma gondii* infection. *International Journal for Parasitology*, *32*, 179–185.

Jones-Brando, L., Torrey, F., & Yolken, R. (2003). Drugs used in the treatment of schizophrenia and bipolar disorder inhibit the replication of *Toxoplasma gondii*. *Schizophrenia Research*, *62*, 237–244.

Kannan, G., Moldovan, K., Xiao, J.-C., Yolken, R. H., Jones-Brando, L., & Pletnikov, M. V. (2010). Parasite strain-dependent effects of *Toxoplasma gondii* on mouse behaviour. *Folia Parasitologica*, *57*, 151–155.

Karlsson, H., Bachmann, S., Schröder, J., McArthur, J., Torrey, E. F., & Yolken, R. H. (2001). Retroviral RNA identified in the cerebrospinal fluids and brains of individuals with schizophrenia. *Proceedings of the National Academy of Sciences of the United States of America*, *98*, 4634–4639.

Kaushik, M., Knowles, S. C. L., & Webster, J. P. (2014). What makes a feline fatal in *Toxoplasma gondii*'s fatal feline attraction? Infected rats choose wild cats. *Integrative and Comparative Biology*.

Kaushik, M., Lamberton, P. H. L., & Webster, J. P. (2012). The role of parasites and pathogens in influencing generalized anxiety and predation-related fear in the mammalian central nervous system. *Hormones and Behavior*.

Kaushik, R. M., Mahajan, S. K., Sharma, A., Kaushik, R., & Kukreti, R. (2005). Toxoplasmic meningoencephalitis in an immunocompetent host. *Transactions of the Royal Society of Tropical Medicine and Hygiene*, *99*, 874–878.

Kenny, E. M., Cormican, P., Furlong, S., Heron, E., Kenny, G., Fahey, C., et al. (2014). Excess of rare novel loss-of-function variants in synaptic genes in schizophrenia and autism spectrum disorders. *Molecular Psychiatry*, *19*, 872–879.

Khademvatan, S., Khajeddin, N., Izadi, S., & Yousefi, E. (2014). Investigation of anti-*Toxocara* and anti-*Toxoplasma* antibodies in patients with schizophrenia disorder. *Schizophrenia Research and Treatment*, e230349.

Khan, A., Dubey, J. P., Su, C., Ajioka, J. W., Rosenthal, B. M., & Sibley, L. D. (2011). Genetic analyses of atypical *Toxoplasma gondii* strains reveal a fourth clonal lineage in North America. *International Journal for Parasitology*, *41*, 645–655.

Kirby, B. P., Waddington, J. L., & O'Tuathaigh, C. M. P. (2010). Advancing a functional genomics for schizophrenia: psychopathological and cognitive phenotypes in mutants with gene disruption. *Brain Research Bulletin*, *83*, 162–176.

Kocazeybeka, B., Onerb, Y. A., Turksoyc, R., Baburd, C., Cakane, H., Sahipb, N., et al. (2009). Higher prevalence of toxoplasmosis in victims of traffic accidents suggest increased risk of traffic accident in *Toxoplasma*-infected inhabitants of Istanbul and its suburbs. *Forensic Science International*, *187*, 103–108.

Kramer, W. (1966). Frontiers of neurological diagnosis in acquired toxoplasmosis. *Psychiatria, Neurologia, Neurochirurgia*, *69*, 43–64.

Kusbeci, O. Y., Miman, O., Yaman, M., Aktepe, O. C., & Yazar, S. (2011). Could *Toxoplasma gondii* have any role in Alzheimer disease? *Alzheimer Disease and Associated Disorders*, *25*, 1–3.

Lamberton, P. H. L., Donnelly, C. A., & Webster, J. P. (2008). Specificity of the *Toxoplasma gondii*-altered behaviour to definitive versus non-definitive host predation risk. *Parasitology*, *135*, 1143–1150.

Leweke, F. M., Gerth, C. W., Koethe, D., Klosterkötter, J., Ruslanova, I., Krivogorsky, B., et al. (2004). Antibodies to infectious agents in individuals with recent onset schizophrenia. *European Archives of Psychiatry and Clinical Neurosciences*, *254*, 4–8.

Ling, V. J., Lester, D., Mortensen, P. B., Langenberg, P. W., & Postolache, T. T. (2011). *Toxoplasma gondii* seropositivity and suicide rates in women. *Journal of Nervous and Mental Disorders*, *199*, 440–444.

Matheson, S. L., Shepherd, A. M., & Carr, V. J. (2014). How much do we know about schizophrenia and how well do we know it? Evidence from the schizophrenia library. *Psychological Medicine*, 1–19.

McConkey, G. A., Gaskell, E., Bristow, G. C., & Webster, J. P. (2013). *Toxoplasma gondii* brain infection and behaviour: location, location, location? *Journal of Experimental Biology*, *216*, 113–119.

Miller, M. A., Grigg, M. E., Kreuder, C., James, E. R., Melli, A. C., Crosbie, P. R., et al. (2004). An unusual genotype of *Toxoplasma gondii* is common in California sea otters (*Enhydra lutris nereis*) and is a cause of mortality. *International Journal for Parasitology, 34,* 275–284.

Miman, O., Kusbeci, O. Y., Aktepe, O. C., & Cetinkaya, Z. (2010). The probable relation between *Toxoplasma gondii* and Parkinson's disease. *Neuroscience Letters, 475,* 129–131.

Mortensen, P. B., Nørgaard-Pedersen, B., Waltoft, B. L., Sørensen, T. L., Hougaard, D., Torrey, E. F., et al. (2007). *Toxoplasma gondii* as a risk factor for early-onset schizophrenia: analysis of filter paper blood samples obtained at birth. *Biological Psychiatry, 61,* 688–693.

Niebuhr, D. W., Millikan, A. M., Cowan, D. N., et al. (2008). Selected infectious agents and risk of schizophrenia among US military personnel. *American Journal of Psychiatry, 164,* 99–106.

Nishikawa, Y., Ogiso, A., Kameyama, K., Nishimura, M., Xuan, X., & Ikehara, Y. (2013). α2-3 Sialic acid glycoconjugate loss and its effect on infection with *Toxoplasma* parasites. *Experimental Parasitology,* 479–485.

Niwa, M., Jaaro-Peled, H., Tankou, S., Seshadri, S., Hikida, T., Matsumoto, Y., et al. (2013). Adolescent stress-induced epigenetic control of dopaminergic neurons via glucocorticoids. *Science, 339,* 335–339.

Notarangelo, F. M., Wilson, E. H., Horning, K. J., Thomas, M. A., Harris, T. H., et al. (2014). Evaluation of kynurenine pathway metabolism in *Toxoplasma gondii*-infected mice: implications for schizophrenia. *Schizophrenia Research, 152,* 261–267.

Papaleo, F., Burdick, M. C., Callicott, J. H., & Weinberger, D. R. (2014). Epistatic interaction between COMT and DTNBP1 modulates prefrontal function in mice and in humans. *Molecular Psychiatry, 19,* 311–316.

Papaleo, F., Lipska, B. K., & Weinberger, D. R. (2012). Mouse models of genetic effects on cognition: relevance to schizophrenia. *Neuropharmacology, 62,* 12041220.

Pearce, B. D., Kruszon-Moran, D., & Jones, J. L. (2012). The relationship between *Toxoplasma gondii* infection and mood disorders in the third National Health and Nutrition Survey. *Biological Psychiatry, 72,* 290–295.

Pedersen, M. G., Mortensen, P. B., Norgaard-Pedersen, B., et al. (2012). *Toxoplasma gondii* infection and self-directed violence in mothers. *Archives of General Psychiatry, 69,* 1123–1130.

Peyron, F., Lobry, J. R., Musset, K., Ferrandiz, J., Gomez-Marin, J. E., Petersen, E., et al. (2006). Serotyping of *Toxoplasma gondii* in chronically infected pregnant women: predominance of type II in Europe and types I and III in Colombia (South America). *Microbes and Infection, 9,* 2333–2340.

Phillis, J. W., Horrocks, L. A., & Farooqui, A. A. (2006). Cyclooxygenases, lipoxygenases, and epoxygenases in CNS: their role and involvement in neurological disorders. *Brain Research Reviews, 52,* 201–243.

Piekarski, G., Zippelius, H. M., & Witting, P. A. (1978). Auswirkungen einer latenten *Toxoplasma*-infektion auf das Lernvermogen von weiben Laboratoriumsratten und mausen. *Zeitschrift für Parasitenkunde, 57,* 1–15.

Prandota, J. (2014). Possible link between *Toxoplasma gondii* and the anosmia associated with neurodegenerative diseases. *American Journal of Alzheimer's Diseases and Other Dementias, 29,* 205–214.

Prandovszky, E., Gaskell, E., Dubey, J. P., Webster, J. P., & McConkey, G. A. (2011). The neurotropic parasite *Toxoplasma gondii* increases dopamine metabolism. *PLoS One, 6,* e23866.

Purcell, S., Wray, N., Stone, J., Visscher, P., O'Donovan, M., Sullivan, P., & International Schizophrenia Consortium, et al. (2009). Common polygenic variation contributes to risk of schizophrenia and bipolar disorder. *Nature, 460,* 748–752.

Putnam, D. K., Sun, J., & Zhao, Z. (2011). Exploring schizophrenia drug-gene interactions through molecular network and pathway modeling. *AMIA Annual Symposium Proceedings Archive,* 1127–1133.

Ranganath, C., Minzenberg, M. J., & Ragland, J. D. (2008). The cognitive neuroscience of memory function and dysfunction in schizophrenia. *Biological Psychiatry, 64,* 18–25.

Reichelt, A. C., Rodgers, R. J., & Clapcote, S. J. (2012). The role of neurexins in schizophrenia and autistic spectrum disorder. *Neuropharmacology, 62,* 1519–1526.

Roy, A., Karoum, F., & Pollack, S. (1992). Marked reduction in indexes of dopamine metabolism among patients with depression who attempt suicide. *Archives of General Psychiatry, 49,* 447–450.

Saeij, J. P. J., Boyle, J. P., Grigg, M. E., Arrizabalaga, G., & Boothroyd, J. C. (2005). Bioluminescence imaging of *Toxoplasma gondii* infection in living mice reveals dramatic differences between strains. *Infection and Immunity, 73,* 695–702.

Sarnyai, Z., Jashar, C., & Olivier, B. (2015). Modeling combined schizophrenia-related behavioral and metabolic phenotypes in rodents. *Behavioural Brain Research, 276.*

Seeman, P. (1987). Dopamine receptors and the dopamine hypothesis of schizophrenia. *Synapse, 1,* 133–152.

Seeman, P., Lee, T., Chau-Wong, M., & Wong, K. (1976). Antipsychotic drug doses and neuroleptic/dopamine receptors. *Nature, 261,* 717–719.

Severance, E. G., Yolken, R. H., & Eaton, E. E. (2014). Autoimmune diseases, gastrointestinal disorders and the microbiome in schizophrenia: more than a gut feeling. *Schizophrenia Bulletin,* SO920-9964 (14) 00319-3. http://dx.doi.org/10.1016/j.schres.2014.06.027.

Sheiner, L., Demerly, J. L., Poulsen, N., Beatty, W. L., Lucas, O., Behnke, M. S., et al. (2011). A systematic screen to discover and analyze apicoplast proteins identifies a conserved and essential protein import factor. *PLoS Pathogens, 7,* e1002392.

Sibley, L. D., & Boothroyd, J. C. (1992). Virulent strains of *Toxoplasma gondii* comprise a single clonal lineage. *Nature, 359,* 82–85.

Sibley, L. D., Mordue, D. G., Su, C., Robben, P. M., & Howe, D. K. (2002). Genetic approaches to studying virulence and pathogenesis in *Toxoplasma gondii*. *Philosophical Transactions of the Royal Society London Series B: Biological Sciences, 357,* 81–88.

Simpson, E. H., Waltz, J. A., Kellendonk, C., & Balsam, P. D. (2012). Schizophrenia in translation: dissecting motivation in schizophrenia and rodents. *Schizophrenia Bulletin, 38,* 1111–1117.

Skallova, A., Kodym, P., Frynta, D., & Flegr, J. (2006). The role of dopamine in *Toxoplasma*-induced behavioural alterations in mice: an ethological and ethopharmacological study. *Parasitology,* 1–11.

Smith, G. (2014). Estimating the population attributable fraction for schizophrenia when *Toxoplasma gondii* is assumed absent in human populations. *Preventive Veterinary Medicine, 117,* 425–435.

Sorge, R. E., Martin, L. J., Isbester, K. A., Sotocinal, S. G., Rosen, S., et al. (2014). Olfactory exposure to males, including men, causes stress and related analgesia in rodents. *Nature Methods, 11,* 629–632.

Stibbs, H. H. (1985). Changes in brain concentrations of catecholamines and indoleamines in *Toxoplasma gondii* infected mice. *Annals of Tropical Medicine and Parasitology, 79,* 153–157.

Stilling, R. M., Dinan, T. G., & Cryan, J. F. (2013). Microbial genes, brain & behaviour – epigenetic regulation of the gut-brain axis. *Genes, Brain and Behavior, 11.*

Strekalova, T., Spanagel, R., Bartsch, D., Henn, F. A., & Gass, P. (2004). Stress-induced anhedonia in mice is associated with deficits in forced swimming and exploration. *Neuropsychopharmacology, 29,* 2007–2017.

Tanaka, K., Suzuki, M., Sumiyoshi, T., Murata, M., Tsunoda, M., & Kurachi, M. (2003). Subchronic phencyclidine administration alters central vasopressin receptor binding and social interaction in the rat. *Journal of Neuroscience, 992,* 239–245.

Thomas, F., Lafferty, K. D., Brodeur, J., Elguero, E., Gauthier-Clerc, M., & Misse, D. (2011). Incidence of adult brain cancers is higher in countries where the protozoan parasite *Toxoplasma gondii* is common. *Biology Letters.*

Torrey, E. F., Bartko, J. J., Lun, Z. R., & Yolken, R. H. (2007). Antibodies to *Toxoplasma gondii* in patients with schizophrenia: a meta-analysis. *Schizophrenia Bulletin, 33,* 729–736.

Torrey, E. F., Bartko, J. J., & Yolken, R. H. (2012). *Toxoplasma gondii* and other risk factors for schizophrenia: an update. *Schizophrenia Bulletin* Early online (March 4th).

Torrey, E. F., Rawlings, R., & Yolken, R. H. (2000). The antecedents of psychoses: a case-control study of selected risk factors. *Schizophrenia Research, 46,* 17–23.

Torrey, E. F., & Yolken, R. H. (1995). Could schizophrenia be a viral zoonosis transmitted from house cats? *Schizophrenia Bulletin, 21,* 167–171.

Torrey, E. F., & Yolken, R. H. (2003). *Toxoplasma gondii* and schizophrenia. *Emerging Infectious Diseases, 9,* 1375–1380.

Torrey, E. F., & Yolken, R. H. (2014). The urban risk and migration risk factors for schizophrenia: are cats the answer? *Schizophrenia Research, 159*(2-3), 299–302. http://dx.doi.org/10.1016/j.schres.2014.09.027. Epub 2014 Oct 11.

Vuillermot, S., Joodmardi, E., Perlmann, T., Ögren, S., Feldon, J., & Meyer, U. (2012). Prenatal immune activation interacts with genetic Nurr1 deficiency in the development of attentional impairments. *Journal of Neuroscience, 32,* 436–451.

Vyas, A., Kim, S. K., & Sapolsky, R. M. (2007). The effects of *Toxoplasma* infection on rodent behavior are dependent on dose of the stimulus. *Neuroscience, 148,* 342–348.

Vyas, A., Seon-Kyeong, K., Giacomini, N., Boothroyd, J. C., & Sapolsky, R. M. (2007). Behavioural changes induced by *Toxoplasma* infection of rodents are highly specific to aversion of cat odours. *Proceedings of the National Academy of Sciences of the United States of America, 104,* 6442–6447.

Wang, T., Tang, Z.-H., Li, J.-F., Li, X.-N., Wanga, X., & Zhao, Z.-J. (2013). A potential association between *Toxoplasma gondii* infection and schizophrenia in mouse models. *Experimental Parasitology, 135,* 497–502.

Webster, J. P. (1994). The effect of *Toxoplasma gondii* and other parasites on activity levels in wild and hybrid *Rattus norvegicus. Parasitology, 109,* 583–589.

Webster, J. P. (2001). Rats, cats, people and parasites: the impact of latent toxoplasmosis on behaviour. *Microbes and Infection, 3,* 1037–1045.

Webster, J. P. (2007). The impact of *Toxoplasma gondii* on animal behaviour: playing cat and mouse. *Schizophrenia Bulletin, 33,* 752–756.

Webster, J. P., Brunton, C. F. A., & Macdonald, D. W. (1994). Effect of *Toxoplasma gondii* on neophobic behaviour in wild brown rats, *Rattus norvegicus. Parasitology, 109,* 37–43.

Webster, J. P., Kaushik, M., Bristow, G. C., & McConkey, G. A. (2013). *Toxoplasma gondii* infection, from predation to schizophrenia: can animal behaviour help us understand human behaviour? *Journal of Experimental Biology, 216,* 99–112.

Webster, J. P., Lamberton, P. H. L., Donnelly, C. A., & Torrey, E. F. (2006). Parasites as causative agents of human affective disorders?: The impact of anti-psychotic and anti-protozoan medication on *Toxoplasma gondii*'s ability to alter host behaviour. *Proceedings of the Royal Society (London) Series B, 273,* 1023–1030.

Webster, J. P., & McConkey, G. A. (2010). *Toxoplasma gondii*-altered host behaviour: clues as to mechanism of action. *Folia Parasitologica, 57,* 95–104.

Witola, W. H., Liu, S., Montpetit, A., Welti, R., Hypolite, M., Roth, M., et al. (2014). ALOX12 in human toxoplasmosis. *Infection and Immunity, 82,* 2670–2679.

Witting, P. A. (1979). Learning capacity and memory of normal and *Toxoplasma*-infected laboratory rats and mice. *Zentralblatt fur Parasitologica, 61,* 29–51.

Wu, E. Q., Shi, L., Birnbaum, H., Hudson, T., & Kessler, R. (2006). Annual prevalence of diagnosed schizophrenia in the USA: a claims data analysis approach. *Pychological Medicine, 36,* 1535–1540.

Xiao, J., Kannan, G., Jones-Brando, L., Brannock, C., Krasnova, I. N., Cadet, J. L., et al. (2012). Sex-specific changes in gene expression and behavior induced by chronic *Toxoplasma* infection in mice. *Neuroscience* [Epub 2012 January 3].

Xiao, J., Li, Y., Jones-Brando, L., & Yolken, R. H. (2013). Abnormalities of neurotransmitter and neuropeptide systems in human neuroepithelioma cells infected by three *Toxoplasma* strains. *Journal of Neural Transmission, 120,* 1631–1639.

Yereli, K., Balcioğlu, I., & Ozbilgin, A. (2006). Is *Toxoplasma gondii* a potential risk for traffic accidents in Turkey? *Forensic Science International, 163,* 34–37.

Yolken, R. H., Bachmann, S., Rouslanova, I., Lillehoj, E., Ford, G., Torrey, E. F., et al. (2001). Antibodies to *Toxoplasma gondii* in individuals with first-episode schizophrenia. *Clinical Infectious Diseases, 32,* 842–844.

Yolken, R. H., Dickerson, F. B., & Torrey, E. F. (2009). Toxoplasma and schizophrenia. *Parasite Immunology, 31,* 706–715.

Yolken, R. H., & Torrey, E. F. (2008). Are some cases of psychosis caused by microbial agents? A review of the evidence. *Molecular Psychiatry, 13,* 470–479.

Yu, Z., Fang, Q., Xiao, X., Wang, Y.-Z., Cai, Y.-Q., et al. (2013). GABA Transporter-1 deficiency confers schizophrenia-like behavioral phenotypes. *PLoS One, 8,* e69883.

15

Maternal Nutritional Deficiencies and Schizophrenia: Lessons from Animal Models with a Focus on Developmental Vitamin D Deficiency

Darryl W. Eyles[*,§], *Angela J. Dean*[*,¶]

[*]Queensland Brain Institute, University of Queensland, Brisbane, QLD, Australia; [§]Queensland Centre for Mental Health Research, Wacol, QLD, Australia; [¶]Institute for Social Science Research, University of Queensland, Brisbane, QLD, Australia

MATERNAL NUTRITION AND SCHIZOPHRENIA: ECOLOGICAL DATA

There has been a long-standing interest in the connection between nutritional deficits and psychotic disorders. Historically, it was known that deficiency in nicotinic acid (vitamin B3, or niacin) led to *pellagra*, a syndrome that may involve psychotic symptoms (Ban, 2001; Hoffer, 2008). This, in part, led to the use of nicotinic acid as an early treatment for schizophrenia (Pauling, 1968). In the North American arctic, a syndrome of psychosis-like hysteria—*piblokto*—has been associated with the deficiency of vitamin D, calcium, or vitamin C, although the actual cause has not been established (Carney, 1995; Katz & Foulks, 2010). Research in the mid-twentieth century continued to report associations between vitamin deficiencies and disorders such as depression and schizophrenia. In his seminal article titled "Orthomolecular Psychiatry," Pauling synthesized the science linking brain functioning with brain concentrations of diverse vitamins and nutrients (Pauling, 1968). Importantly, this paper identified potential mechanisms linking nutrition and disease. Pauling's work provided a robust framework that paved the way for ongoing research examining the effects of nutrition on pathogenesis of schizophrenia and other psychiatric disorders (Hoffer, 2008).

Another pivotal shift in our understanding of the relationship between nutrition and schizophrenia emerged after a series of world events, which generated population data linking *maternal* malnutrition during gestation with the risk of schizophrenia in adulthood. The first of these studies examined the Dutch Hunger Winter (1944–1945). This period was associated with severe food shortages, for which there was excellent documentation of individual food rations (Susser, St Clair, & He, 2008). When compared with individuals conceived immediately before or after this famine, those conceived during the height of the famine exhibited a twofold increase in the risk of developing schizophrenia during adulthood (Susser et al., 1996). This finding was replicated in two studies examining health outcomes of those living during the 1959–1961 Chinese famine. Comprehensive demographic and clinical records in China allowed researchers to identify that individuals conceived or born during the peak period of the famine also exhibited a twofold increase in the risk of schizophrenia (St Clair et al., 2005; Xu et al., 2009). This risk was found to be higher in rural areas, where the severity of famine was greater (Xu et al., 2009).

These naturalistic studies not only reinforce the association between nutrition and schizophrenia risk, they establish a link between *maternal* nutrition and the risk of schizophrenia in offspring. This is consistent with the bulk of the risk-factor epidemiology for this disease, which indicates that exposure to certain risk factors during pre- or perinatal stages increases the risk of schizophrenia later in life. This epidemiology is largely responsible for the now long-held belief that schizophrenia has its origins in early brain development (Weinberger, 1987). Findings from a number of animal models, constructed to understand the neurobiology behind such nutritional factors, continue to highlight how maternal nutritional deficiencies adversely affect brain development.

WHICH MICRONUTRIENT DEFICIENCIES ARE MOST RELEVANT TO SCHIZOPHRENIA?

The famine studies described previously were not able to identify whether schizophrenia risk was mediated by deficiency of a specific nutrient, or via general effects of malnutrition. In recent decades, numerous epidemiological studies and intervention trials have attempted to elucidate the role of individual nutritional candidates in the hope of identifying preventive or treatment interventions. The types of candidates examined are diverse. Some, most noticeably polyunsaturated fatty acids (PUFAs), folate, iron, and vitamin D, have generated an important body of epidemiological or clinical research. This research indicates that deficiencies in such factors during early periods of brain development increase the risk of either schizophrenia or neurodevelopmental problems in later life. In turn, the animal models that simulate these deficiencies continue to inform us about epidemiologically plausible neurobiological pathways connecting maternal nutritional deficiencies with psychiatric disease.

Factors such as PUFAs, folate, iron, and vitamin D all have strong neurobiological plausibility because risk-modifying factors for schizophrenia as they all have well-described roles in fetal brain development, especially during early phases of gestation. Folate signaling is essential for many early neurodevelopmental processes, including development and closure of the neural tube (Lucock & Daskalakis, 2000), and its disruption has been implicated in the etiology of neural tube defects and schizophrenia (van der Linden, Afman, Heil, & Blom, 2006; Susser, Brown, Klonowski, Allen, & Lindenbaum, 1998). Vitamins A and D have key roles in early morphogenesis of the fetal central nervous system (CNS) via their actions as nuclear steroids in stimulating gene expression, promoting cell differentiation, and proliferation (Maden, 2001).

Adequate levels of iron and PUFAs are also essential for normal brain development (Georgieff & Innis, 2005). Research on PUFAs has usually focused on omega-3 fatty acids, and docosahexaenoic acid (DHA) and eicosapentaenoic acid (EPA) in particular. These fatty acids have a number of essential roles, including maintaining the structural integrity of neuronal membranes (Hibbeln, Ferguson, & Blasbalg, 2006). They may influence a range of other neural pathways, including those related to catecholamine neurotransmission (Hamazaki et al., 2005; Hibbeln et al., 1998), endogenous cannabinoid signaling (Lafourcade et al., 2011), or oxidative stress (Mahadik, Evans, & Lal, 2001). Finally, iron deficiencies are encountered during periods of anemia and are known to affect placental function (Gambling, Kennedy, & McArdle, 2011). Iron deficiencies appear to selectively affect developing dopaminergic structures (Beard et al., 2006) and myelination (Davis et al., 2003).

EPIDEMIOLOGY OF MATERNAL NUTRITIONAL RISK FACTORS FOR SCHIZOPHRENIA

Numerous epidemiological studies have attempted to unravel the relationship between diverse nutritional candidates and risk of schizophrenia. These studies generally fall into two groups: (1) cross-sectional studies comparing nutritional measures in adult schizophrenic patients with matched controls or (2) longitudinal studies which assess the impact of prenatal or early life nutritional deficiencies on the risk of developing schizophrenia in later life.

PUFAs

A recent meta-analysis reviewed 18 cross-sectional studies that compared red blood cell fatty acids in individuals with schizophrenia with matched controls (Hoen et al., 2013). Patients exhibited lower concentrations of two fatty acids—DHA and docosapentaenoic acid—compared with controls and this was independent of treatment with antipsychotic drugs. Unfortunately, this meta-analysis did not assess EPA, another omega-3 fatty acid of relevance to schizophrenia. Some studies use postmortem tissue to examine fatty acid concentrations in specific brain regions. For example, Hamazaki, Hamazaki, and Inadera (2013) reported that the entorhinal cortex of patients with schizophrenia contained lower concentrations of omega-6 docosatetraenoic acid and DHA (trend only) compared with matched controls. Nonanalytical epidemiological studies indicate that higher consumption of omega-6 and omega-3 fatty acids is associated with a lower risk of schizophrenia or psychotic-like experiences (Hedelin et al., 2010). Some research suggests that fatty acids are important in dealing with oxidative stress. One study examined lipid peroxidation in a case–control study, examining untreated inpatients with first-episode psychosis. No differences were observed in lipid peroxidation, but those with schizophrenia had lower vitamin E concentrations than controls. The authors attributed this to the poorer diet of those with schizophrenia (McCreadie et al., 2000).

No studies were identified that examined maternal exposure to fatty acids and the later development of schizophrenia in offspring. This makes it difficult to draw conclusions about how low fatty acid concentrations are related to schizophrenia. However, one study suggests that maternal PUFA levels may be important for healthy brain development (Helland, Smith, Saarem, Saugstad, & Drevon, 2003).

Homocysteine, Folate, and B Group Vitamins

Several adult case–control studies report elevated homocysteine levels and lower vitamin B12 levels in inpatients with schizophrenia compared with controls (Adler Nevo et al., 2006; Bouaziz et al., 2010; Kale et al., 2010; Petronijevic et al., 2008). To date, one study has examined the role of maternal homocysteine levels using a large birth cohort; the Child Health and Development Study. From this cohort, 63 cases with schizophrenia or related disorders diagnosed in adulthood were identified and compared with 122 matched controls. Elevated levels of maternal homocysteine during the third trimester were associated with a more than twofold increase in the risk of schizophrenia in adulthood (Brown et al., 2007).

Iron

Two studies report that maternal anemia may contribute to increased schizophrenia risk in offspring. Using the Child Health and Development Study cohort, Insel, Schaefer, McKeague, Susser, and Brown (2008) report that individuals whose mother had hemoglobin concentrations <100 g/L had a nearly fourfold increase in the risk of developing schizophrenia spectrum disorders (Insel et al., 2008). Using a Danish birth cohort, Sorensen, Nielsen, Pedersen, and Mortensen (2011) reported that individuals whose mother had a diagnosis of anemia (hemoglobin <110 g/L) at any time during pregnancy had a 1.6-fold increase in the risk of developing schizophrenia.

Vitamin D

Several case-control studies in adults have now been published, indicating that patients with schizophrenia have lower vitamin D concentrations than matched controls (Berg et al., 2010; Crews et al., 2013; Jamilian, Bagherzadeh, Nazeri, & Hassanijirdehi, 2013). In a study of adolescents presenting to mental health services, it was reported that patients with vitamin D insufficiency (<50 nM 25-OHD3) were more likely to exhibit psychotic symptoms than those with normal vitamin D levels (Gracious, Finucane, Friedman-Campbell, Messing, & Parkhurst, 2012). In a longitudinal study of children, lower concentrations of vitamin D at 9.8 years (range, 7.6–11.8) were associated with an elevated risk of psychotic experiences at 12.8 years (Tolppanen et al., 2012). Similarly, an increased dietary intake of vitamin D has been associated with lower rates of self-reported psychotic-like experiences (Hedelin et al., 2010).

Importantly, several studies also suggest a relationship between maternal vitamin D concentrations and subsequent risk of schizophrenia in offspring. A large study used a Danish birth cohort to examine neonatal vitamin D concentrations in 424 individuals with schizophrenia and 424 matched controls (McGrath et al., 2010). Those with lower vitamin D concentrations had a twofold increased risk of schizophrenia when compared with control individuals in the fourth quintile (25 hydroxy vitamin D3 (25OHD3) concentrations between 40.5 and 50.9 nmol/L). These findings were nonlinear; those with the highest concentrations of vitamin D (5th quintile) also exhibiting a slightly elevated risk of schizophrenia (McGrath et al., 2010). A study using a Finnish birth cohort reported that vitamin D supplementation in early life reduced the risk of schizophrenia in later life, in males only (McGrath et al., 2004). However, this finding has not been consistently replicated: a recent study using an English cohort reported no association between maternal vitamin D concentrations and psychotic experiences at 18 years (Sullivan, Wills, Lawlor, McGrath, & Zammit, 2013). However, this study was not powered to examine medium to small effect sizes, a fact readily acknowledged by these authors.

Retinol

One study has identified a potential effect of maternal retinol (vitamin A) levels on the risk of schizophrenia in offspring, again using the Child Health and Development Study cohort (Bao et al., 2012). From this cohort, 55 adults were identified as having schizophrenia or a related disorder as well as at least one available prenatal serum sample. Two matched controls were selected for each case. Low levels of maternal vitamin A during the second trimester were associated with a threefold increase in the risk of schizophrenia and related disorders in adulthood (Bao et al., 2012). No effect of third-trimester levels of vitamin A was observed. This study has not yet been replicated. Vitamin A is a major factor in neuron differentiation (Tafti & Ghyselinck, 2007). When administered to neonates, vitamins A and D have been shown to have long-term effects on catecholamine expression in adult brains (Tekes, Gyenge, Folyovich, & Csaba, 2009; Tekes, Gyenge, Hantos, & Csaba, 2009). Maternal vitamin A deficiencies have also been shown to induce cognitive deficits in offspring (Jiang et al., 2012; Mao et al., 2006). Despite these data, no animal model of maternal vitamin A deficiency/insufficiency that we are aware of has examined brain structural or behavioral phenotypes of relevance to schizophrenia. Table 1 summarizes *maternal* risk-factor epidemiology for schizophrenia.

TABLE 1   Epidemiological Studies That Have Examined Developmental Nutrient Deficiencies and Later Risk of Schizophrenia

Citations	Key Nutritional Marker	Cohort	Sample Size	Timing of Nutritional Exposure	Outcome Assessed in Offspring	Key Finding
McGrath, Eyles, Mowry, Yolken, Buka (2003)	Vitamin D (25OHD3)	National Collaborative Perinatal Project (US)	26 Cases 51 matched controls	Third trimester	Diagnosis of schizophrenia or schizoaffective disorder in adulthood	No association between maternal vitamin D and schizophrenia
McGrath et al. (2004)	Vitamin D (25OHD) (supplementation)	Northern Finland 1966 birth cohort	Total n=9144 (including 79 cases)	First year of life	Diagnosis of schizophrenia by age of 31 years	Use of vitamin D supplements (regular or irregular) was associated with reduced risk of schizophrenia, in males only. No association observed in females.
McGrath et al. (2010)	Vitamin D (25OHD)	Danish population (record linkage between Danish Psychiatric Central Register, the Danish Civil Registration System, and Newborn Screening Biobank)	424 Cases 424 matched controls	At birth	Diagnosis of schizophrenia	Low levels of vitamin D (lower 3 quintiles) were associated with a two fold increase in the risk of schizophrenia (compared with the 4th quintile reference group) Those with high levels of vitamin D (highest quintile) also had increased risk of schizophrenia
Sullivan et al. (2013)	Vitamin D (25OHD)	Avon Longitudinal Study of Parents and Children (UK)	Total n=2047 (including 177 cases)	Any time during pregnancy (52% sampled during third trimester)	Psychotic experiences at 18 years	No association between maternal vitamin D and psychotic experiences
Brown et al. (2007)	Homocysteine	Prenatal Determinants of Schizophrenia cohort, derived from Child Health and Development Study (US)	63 Cases 122 matched controls	Third trimester	Diagnosis of schizophrenia and schizophrenia spectrum disorders	Elevated homocysteine levels were associated with a twofold increase in risk of schizophrenia
Glaser et al. (2010)	Folate (supplementation)	Avon Longitudinal Study of Parents and Children (UK)	Total n=5344 (including 592 cases)	Any time during pregnancy	Psychotic-like symptoms at age 12	No association between markers of folate status and psychotic symptoms after correcting for multiple comparisons
Sorensen et al. (2011)	Iron (anemia)	Danish population (record linkage between Danish Psychiatric Central Register, the Danish Civil Registration System, and Newborn Screening Biobank)	Total n=1,115,752 (including 3422 cases)	Any time during pregnancy	Diagnosis of schizophrenia	Maternal anemia was associated with a 1.6-fold increase in the risk of schizophrenia

TABLE 1 Epidemiological Studies That Have Examined Developmental Nutrient Deficiencies and Later Risk of Schizophrenia—cont'd

Citations	Key Nutritional Marker	Cohort	Sample Size	Timing of Nutritional Exposure	Outcome Assessed in Offspring	Key Finding
Insel et al. (2008)	Iron (anemia)	Prenatal Determinants of Schizophrenia cohort, derived from Child Health and Development Study (US)	Total n=6872 (including 57 cases)	Any time during pregnancy	Diagnosis of schizophrenia spectrum disorders	Maternal anemia was associated with 4-fold increase in risk of schizophrenia spectrum disorders
Bao et al. (2012)	Retinol	Prenatal Determinants of Schizophrenia cohort, derived from Child Health and Development Study (US)	55 Cases 106 matched controls	Second and third trimesters	Diagnosis of schizophrenia and schizophrenia spectrum disorders	Low maternal vitamin A in the second trimester was associated with more than threefold increased risk of schizophrenia disorders
						No effect observed for maternal vitamin A in the third trimester

CONTROLLED TRIALS OF NUTRITIONAL SUPPLEMENTS FOR TREATMENT OF SCHIZOPHRENIA

If depletion of a specific nutrient increases the risk of schizophrenia, can restoration of normal nutrient levels (e.g., via supplementation) prevent schizophrenia or treat core symptoms of the disease? There are many clinical studies addressing this question. Most are focused on treatment, rather than prevention of schizophrenia. In addition, many are assessing the effects of supplementation as an adjunct to antipsychotic treatment in those with an established diagnosis. A small number of trials examine broad nutritional interventions. For example, one trial reported no effects of individualized megavitamin treatment on schizophrenia symptoms compared to placebo (Vaughan & McConaghy, 1999). Another trial currently in process (ClinicalTrials.gov:NCT01927276) is examining the impact of a gluten-free diet on mental health symptoms in gliadin-positive adults with schizophrenia. These broad studies are rare; most published trials focus on specific nutritional candidates.

PUFAs

Several published studies have examined PUFAs as an adjunct *treatment* for schizophrenia. Interestingly, unlike the epidemiological studies where the fatty acid most often discussed is DHA, the clinical trials typically focus on EPA. Although a range of open-label studies suggest the potential efficacy of fatty acid treatment (Reddy et al., 2011), most controlled studies do not indicate beneficial effects. The Cochrane review incorporates

8 studies, comprising 517 participants. Most studies were small and assessed the effects of PUFA supplementation over 6–16 weeks. Although some studies reported small benefits in functioning or mental state, overall evidence supporting a role for fatty acids in improving core symptoms in schizophrenia is limited (Joy, Mumby-Croft, & Joy, 2006). A recent meta-analysis reviewed seven trials of EPA supplementation, totaling 335 participants, and reported no significant beneficial effects on psychotic symptoms (Fusar-Poli & Berger, 2012).

Interestingly, a recent study reported that adding 2g of EPA to existing antipsychotic treatment in inpatients actually made psychotic symptoms worse (Bentsen, Osnes, Refsum, Solberg, & Bohmer, 2013). Adding EPA in combination with vitamins E and C ameliorated this negative effect, but did not generate any clinical benefits compared with placebo. This finding reinforces the importance of not assuming the safety of nutritional supplements, and of ensuring that trials examine both efficacy *and* safety. Numerous other trials are currently examining fatty acids in schizophrenia (Table 2).

Despite the lack of beneficial effects reported in trials of adults with established schizophrenia, one notable trial suggests a potential benefit of fatty acids in *preventing* transition to psychosis in high-risk groups (Amminger et al., 2010). Adolescents and young adults at ultra-high risk of transition to psychotic disorder were randomized to 12 weeks of treatment with omega-3 fatty acids (1.2 g daily) or placebo. After being monitored for 1 year, those receiving omega-3 fatty acids had significantly lower rates of conversion to psychosis (4.9%), compared with placebo (27.5%) (number needed to treat=6). Treatment with fatty acids also generated improvements in

TABLE 2   Examples of Currently Open Trials Listed in Clinical Trials Registries That Investigate Nutritional Interventions for Symptoms of Schizophrenia

Intervention	Scientific Title	Status	Identifier
Vitamin D	Vitamin D Supplementation as Adjunct to Clozapine-treated Chronic Schizophrenia Patients	Currently recruiting	NCT01759485
Vitamin D	A Pilot Study of Vitamin D Supplementation in Bronx Psychiatric Patients	Currently recruiting	NCT01169142
Vitamin D	The effect of vitamin D addition on treatment response in patients with schizophrenia in Zare Hospital	Current status is recruitment complete	IRCT201210163014N6
PUFAs	Omega-3 Fatty Acids Efficacy in Reducing the Risk of Relapse in Schizophrenia: A Double-Blind, Placebo-Controlled, Randomized Clinical Trial	Ongoing, but not currently recruiting	NCT02210962
PUFAs	Detecting Which Patients With Schizophrenia Will Improve With Omega-3 Treatment	Currently recruiting	NCT01786239
PUFAs	Randomized Double-Blind Trial of Omega 3 Fatty Acid Versus Placebo in Individuals at Risk for Psychosis	Ongoing, but not currently recruiting	NCT01429454
PUFAs	Efficacy of Omega-3 in the treatment of Schizophrenia	Recruitment complete	IRCT201202117373N2
Folate and B12	A Placebo-Controlled Trial of Folate with B12 in Patients with Schizophrenia with Residual Symptoms in Ethiopia	Currently recruiting	NCT01724476
Folate	A Placebo-Controlled Study of Physiologic Effects of L-methylfolate in Schizophrenia Patients	Study has been completed	NCT01091506
Magnesium Threonate	Effect of Magnesium Threonate (MgT) on Cognitive Enhancement in Schizophrenia	Currently recruiting	NCT02237235
Sodium Benzoate	An Adaptive, Phase IIb/III, Double-Blind, Randomized, Placebo-Controlled, Multi-Center Study of the Safety and Efficacy of NaBen® (Sodium Benzoate), A D-Amino acid Oxidase inhibitor, as an Add-on Treatment for Schizophrenia in Adolescents	Currently recruiting	NCT01908192
Sarcosine (N-Methylglycine)	Effect of Sarcosine on Symptomatology, Quality of Life, Oxidative Stress and Glutamatergic Parameters in Schizophrenia	Recruitment status unknown	NCT01503359
Gluten free diet	Randomized Controlled Trial of a Gluten Free Diet in Patients with Schizophrenia Who Are Gliadin-Positive	Currently recruiting	NCT01927276

ratings of positive and negative symptoms compared with placebo. Although this study requires replication, it highlights the potential role for nutritional candidates in *preventing* the onset of schizophrenia, rather than *treating* the symptoms of an established disorder.

Folate and B Group Vitamins

Two trials have examined the impact of folate supplementation. One small study reported that methyl folate (6 mg daily) generated improvements in global clinical ratings compared with placebo, in adults with schizophrenia who had low red-cell folate concentrations (<200 pg/L) (Godfrey et al., 1990). In contrast, a more recent study in adults with stable schizophrenia reported no effect of folate supplementation (2 mg daily) on negative symptoms, compared with placebo

(Hill et al., 2011). There has also been long-standing interest in B group vitamins as potential treatments for schizophrenia, especially vitamin B3 (nicotinic acid) (Petrie & Ban, 1985). However, early positive findings were not replicated in controlled trials (Petrie & Ban, 1985), and more recent studies examining B group vitamins have used them in conjunction with folate. One of the largest and most recent of these studies investigated the effects of folate (2 mg daily) and vitamin B12 (400 µg daily) on adults with stable but persistent symptoms of schizophrenia (Roffman et al., 2013). Fourteen weeks of supplementation led to a significant reduction in negative symptoms compared with placebo, but only when the analysis accounted for genetic variants in enzymes that regulate folate activity (Roffman et al., 2013). Another study focused on adults with schizophrenia and elevated homocysteine levels (>15 µmol/L). Compared with placebo, 12 weeks of treatment with folic acid (2 mg daily), vitamin B6 (25 mg daily), and vitamin B12 (400 µg daily) led to improvements in total Positive and Negative Syndrome Scale scores (but not separate positive and negative symptom scores) (Levine et al., 2006).

These collective findings suggest potential benefits of folate and B group supplementation in patients with pre-existing low folate function. It is unclear whether these putative benefits are limited to only this patient group or whether they may be demonstrated in a broader range of schizophrenia subtypes. Ongoing trials (Table 2) will hopefully inform future approaches to treatment.

Vitamin D

Although many epidemiological studies exist that link vitamin D deficiencies with schizophrenia, no published clinical trials have examined the potential for vitamin D to prevent or treat core symptoms of schizophrenia. One trial in healthy volunteers reported that vitamin D supplementation had no effect on psychotic-like experiences (Dean et al., 2011). Other studies have examined the role of vitamin D on treating side effects of antipsychotic treatment, such as metabolic syndrome (Thakurathi et al., 2013). Clinical trial registries list three current trials examining the effects of vitamin D supplementation on core symptoms of schizophrenia (Table 2). Other trials are examining the role of vitamin D on other neurodevelopmental disorders, such as autism. One study is investigating whether vitamin D supplementation in mothers who already have a child with autism can reduce the risk of autism in a new sibling (ClinicalTrials.gov: NCT01366885). This is a fertile field of research in which the evidence base is likely to grow.

Summary Thus Far

As presented here, there are many active trials recruiting to investigate the possibility of nutritional supplementation as a treatment for core symptoms of schizophrenia. There are also trials of other micronutrients including the use of choline (Ross et al., 2013), glycine (Heresco-Levy & Javitt, 2004; Woods et al., 2013), and vitamin C (Dakhale, Khanzode, Khanzode, & Saoji, 2005), but the neurobiological basis for these trials is less established. In addition, many nutritional studies are targeting related issues such as adverse metabolic effects arising from the use of atypical antipsychotics. Although such trials are of critical interest to patients and caregivers, and we anxiously await their outcome, the suggestion that psychiatric disease progression could be ameliorated, or even prevented, in early symptomatic individuals is revolutionary. Such a proposition would have been considered implausible 20 years ago.

However, the weight of both clinical and basic experimental data provides hope that nutritional supplementation may prove therapeutic for this disease.

There is one obvious limitation shared by all such interventions (including new antipsychotics) in the adult patient. They all are directed at mitigating psychiatric symptoms in either adult patients after disease onset, or in ultra-high-risk individuals (those who have not been formally diagnosed, but show symptomatic vulnerability). A primary challenge of studying early intervention therapies is the lengthy delay between exposure to nutrient depletion in utero and the development of schizophrenia in early adult life. This makes it difficult to design feasible clinical trials to assess the ability of supplementation to prevent disease onset. Current trials of maternal and early-life vitamin D supplementation may provide such evidence in the future. There are numerous trials underway examining the role of maternal vitamin D supplementation in a range of maternal and child health outcomes (Dawodu et al., 2013; Harvey et al., 2012; Litonjua et al., 2014; Oberhelman et al., 2013; Roth et al., 2013). These studies will prove a crucial resource in assessing long-term effects of gestational vitamin D supplementation on mental health outcomes in adulthood.

Epidemiological and clinical research has highlighted a number of potential nutritional candidates that influence schizophrenia risk and progression. However, these studies are not able to tell us *why* a particular nutritional deficiency adversely affects the developing brain. Nor can they tell us how this leads to serious psychiatric conditions. To understand the neurobiology behind early nutrient deficiencies and the effects on brain development, we turn to animal models. By manipulating nutrient depletion early in life, we can conduct longitudinal studies that explore the transition from early development to adult disorders and identify targets for possible intervention.

MATERNAL NUTRITIONAL DEFICIENCIES AND SCHIZOPHRENIA-RELEVANT PHENOTYPES IN ANIMAL MODELS

To understand the neurobiological link between nutritional deficiencies and schizophrenia risk, we need to model these specific nutritional factors in experimental animals. Although there are data on brain function for all of the aforementioned nutritional deficiencies in adult animals, in this section we will concentrate on studies that have modeled these nutritional deficiencies primarily in the maternal or early postweaning diet. We will omit our work on modeling developmental vitamin

D (DVD) deficiency here and deal with this in a subsequent section.

Animal Models of Maternal Protein Restriction

Maternal protein restriction has long been associated with adverse fetal outcomes. It is only more recently that this has been associated with an increased risk for psychiatric conditions like schizophrenia. There is an extensive array of animal studies in which rats undergo a variety of reduced dietary protein exposures. These studies consistently show that prenatal protein deficiency has adverse effects on adult brain morphogenesis in offspring, most noticeably in the hippocampus (Cintra et al., 1997; Cintra, Diaz-Cintra, Galvan, Kemper, & Morgane, 1990; Debassio, Kemper, Galler, & Tonkiss, 1994; Debassio, Kemper, Tonkiss, & Galler, 1996; Diaz-Cintra et al., 1991; Diaz-Cintra, Garcia-Ruiz, Corkidi, & Cintra, 1994; Lister et al., 2005; Morgane, Mokler, & Galler, 2002). Given the sheer number of studies in agreement, this is a compelling finding. It is also of no surprise that these structural changes are associated with changes in brain neurophysiology, such as altered long-term potentiation (Bronzino, Austin-LaFrance, Mokler, & Morgane, 1997).

Researchers have also begun to examine how maternal protein deficiency could affect adult behaviors in offspring. Most studies examine the effects of providing approximately only 25% of the normal maternal protein intake throughout gestation. Female offspring from such a condition were shown to have prepulse inhibition (PPI) deficits in adulthood (Palmer, Printz, Butler, Dulawa, & Printz, 2004). PPI is a measure of sensory motor gating function that is frequently altered in patients with schizophrenia. PPI has been widely proposed as a useful endophenotype for this disease. There was also increased N-methyl-D-aspartic acid (NMDA) receptor density in the striatum of these animals (Palmer et al., 2004). In a later study from the same group, these authors again showed female-specific adult-onset phenotypes of relevance to schizophrenia. In adulthood, females deprived of protein prenatally exhibited heightened sensitivity to dopamine (DA) agonists such as apomorphine (increased stereotypies) or the DA-releasing agent amphetamine (increased locomotion) compared with controls. They did not show any hyperlocomotor response to an NMDA antagonist, even though the finding of increased striatal NMDA receptor density in female offspring was replicated. Alterations in pre- and postsynaptic dopaminergic elements were also recorded in striatum from these females. No such changes were shown in prenatally protein-deficient males (Palmer et al., 2008). Prenatally protein-deprived animals also exhibited alterations in basal and stress-induced DA and serotonin release in the prefrontal and hippocampal areas (Chen, Turiak, Galler, & Volicer, 1995; Mokler, Torres, Galler, & Morgane, 2007).

Other studies have shown that prenatal protein deprivation leads to enhanced sensitization to indirect DA agonists such as cocaine (Shultz, Galler, & Tonkiss, 1999) and NMDA receptor antagonists (Tonkiss, Almeida, & Galler, 1998), although this was again sex selective for females.

Maternal protein restriction experiments (50% restriction) have also been conducted in mice. These animals were shown to have large increases in DA-related gene expression. This was most notable for tyrosine hydroxylase (TH), the rate-limiting enzyme in DA synthesis. Importantly, this correlated with a large reduction in TH promoter methylation in brain stem dopaminergic cell bodies in the ventral tegmental area, consistent with the increased expression of the TH gene. Not surprisingly, these animals also had increased locomotor responses to DA-elevating agents, and altered reward processing (Vucetic et al., 2010). Such studies in mice also clearly indicate working and reference memory impairments (Ranade et al., 2008). Proteomic analysis of maternally protein-restricted adult rats has now also identified alterations in glutamatergic pathways in the frontal cortex, and cytoskeletal proteins involved in hormonal secretion and synaptic remodeling in the hypothalamus (Guest et al., 2012).

Animal Models of Maternal Iron Deficiency

It is well-established that when substantial gestational iron deficiency occurs (when brain iron concentrations are reduced by more than 50%), severe neurological outcomes are observed both in humans (Connor & Menzies, 1996; Hare, Ayton, Bush, & Lei, 2013; Insel et al., 2008; Lozoff et al., 2006; Sorensen et al., 2011) and in experimental animal models (Gambling et al., 2002; Gambling et al., 2003; Morath & Mayer-Proschel, 2002). Less severe deficiency models have now been developed that mimic the levels of iron deficiency commonly observed in human gestational anemia. For instance, when iron levels in the brain are reduced by no more than 10–20%, a more subtle phenotype is produced (Beard et al., 2006). Using such a model, postnatal brain concentrations of bioactive amines such as serotonin and DA were significantly elevated, alongside elevations in their respective transporters and DA2 receptors. This is also correlated with early motor abnormalities. Maternal iron deficiency in mice also reduces hippocampal volume and increases errors in working and reference memory in offspring (Ranade et al., 2008).

More recently, studies have modeled the effect of maternal iron levels on the neurobiological response to other toxic events (such as maternal infection) during pregnancy. In the first of such studies, when the bacterial toxin lipopolysaccharide (LPS) was administered to pregnant rats, those that were also deficient in iron had increased inflammatory cytokine responses; however, the effects on pup behaviors were not additive (Harvey & Boksa, 2013). In a later and more thorough behavioral study of these dual exposures, the combined effect of maternal iron deficiency with the bacterial endotoxin treatment was not shown to be additive for the behaviors tested; however, PPI deficits were reported for the first time in the iron-deficient group (Harvey & Boksa, 2014).

Maternal or Early-Life Folate Deficiencies

Early studies investigating mice with gestational folate deficiency revealed that these offspring had increased anxiety-related behaviors in the elevated plus maze, but few other schizophrenia-related phenotypes (Ferguson et al., 2005). Later studies examined the reduction during the development of an enzyme responsible for processing folate. This reduction resulted in mild spontaneous hyperlocomotion in adult males and impairments in novel-object recognition in both sexes (Levav-Rabkin, Blumkin, Galron, & Golan, 2011). Folate is an essential cofactor in the methylation of homocysteine. When hyperhomocysteinemia is induced in rats in the early postnatal period, this is sufficient to induce spatial working memory deficits in these animals as adults. Concurrent treatment with folate at this early developmental stage restores spatial working memory when adult animals were tested in a Morris water maze (Matte et al., 2007).

The effect of *paternal* folate deficiency on epigenetic reprogramming in sperm has been of particular interest recently. Male mice fed a folate-deficient diet throughout life had altered rates of sperm methylation in genes important in development and in chronic disease, including schizophrenia. These mice also produced offspring with craniofacial and musculoskeletal malformations (Lambrot et al., 2013).

Omega-3 Fatty Acids Prevent Schizophrenia-Like Phenotypes in Animal Models

Subchronic exposure to the psychomimetic agent ketamine in adolescent rats results in increased spontaneous locomotion, decreased social interaction, and working memory deficits in adult animals. This exposure therefore reproduces the positive, negative, and cognitive symptom phenotypes seen in patients with schizophrenia. When omega-3 fatty acids were administered to weanling rats for 15 days before subchronic ketamine treatment, all such behaviors were ameliorated. This suggests that omega-3 can act through a protective mechanism (Gama et al., 2012). The same group later investigated whether PPI deficits induced by the same subchronic ketamine regime could also be corrected by

omega-3 supplementation in postweanling rats. The authors show that prior treatment with omega-3 fatty acids was protective not only against ketamine-induced PPI deficits, but also against ketamine-induced oxidative damage in the brains of these animals (Zugno et al., 2014). Omega-3 fatty acid dietary depletion has also been shown to lead to disturbed synaptic function, neuritogenesis, and mitochondrial function in adult animals (English et al., 2013). This has not yet been assessed in developing brains.

Most recently, an interesting study has attempted to model the reduction in dietary exposure to omega-3s reported in humans during the past 40–50 years. This group investigated the effects of dietary omega-3 deficiencies across two generations of rat breeding (Bondi et al., 2014). The study showed that dietary omega-3 deficiency across consecutive generations of rats produces anxiety-like phenotypes and learning deficits in a number of paradigms. In most cases, these behavioral differences were only significant (or were more pronounced) in the second generation of deficient adolescents. This indicates again that omega-3 fatty acids are protective against the development of schizophrenia-related phenotypes, but also suggests that there is a developmental component to this risk. Importantly, this dietary deficiency elevated levels of the TH enzyme in the dorsal striatum of adolescent, but not adult, animals. Increases in the synthesis and uptake of DA in the caudate nucleus (the equivalent region in humans) in young individuals at risk of developing schizophrenia may represent an early abnormality and a possible biomarker for the disorder (Howes, Bose, Turkheimer, Valli, Egerton, & Stahl, 2011; Howes, Bose, Turkheimer, Valli, Egerton, & Valmaggia, 2011).

Abnormalities in dopaminergic elements and alterations in behaviors mediated by DA are a remarkably consistent feature observed in the adult offspring of these maternal nutritional deficiency models. In the next section we will concentrate on what we have learned during the past 12 years from the DVD-deficiency model. In particular, we will outline the resultant molecular and behavioral phenotypes. These clearly show that this particular nutritional deficiency induces early developmental changes in DA neurons, corresponding to abnormal dopaminergic function in the adult brain.

THE DVD-DEFICIENCY ANIMAL MODEL OF SCHIZOPHRENIA

The effect of vitamin D on the developing brain has been examined in rats, largely via manipulation of the maternal diet. This effect in mice has largely been examined by genetically ablating the vitamin D receptor (VDR) or altering enzymes involved in vitamin D synthesis. Studies using these mutant mice do produce some phenotypes of interest to schizophrenia (Burne, McGrath, Eyles, & Mackay-Sim, 2005; Kalueff, Lou, Laaksi, & Tuohimaa, 2004). However, they also produce nontarget general health impairments such as increased fluid intake (Li et al., 2002), cardiac hypertrophy (Xiang et al., 2005), altered heart function (Tishkoff, Nibbelink, Holmberg, Dandu, & Simpson, 2008), impaired energy metabolism (Wong et al., 2009), and musculoskeletal changes (Ceglia, 2008). The use of inducible constructs for the VDR or vitamin D metabolic enzymes may be more useful. This would allow the expression of a more benign phenotype, while still allowing the investigator to study the effect of impaired vitamin D signaling during critical developmental windows. However, there have been no reported studies to date that examine schizophrenia-like phenotypes using such mouse mutants. DVD deficiency has also been produced in wild-type mice of various backgrounds (de Abreu et al., 2010; Harms, Eyles, McGrath, Mackay-Sim, & Burne, 2008). Although the phenotypes in adult offspring from these models may be of relevance to psychiatric disease, they suffer from being less studied than the rat models. The findings are also heavily strain dependent. The phenotypes produced are also less relevant to schizophrenia than those shown in the DVD-deficient rat.

Creating a DVD-Deficient Rat

There is no fetal synthesis of vitamin D, so the developing embryo is totally reliant on maternal vitamin D stores. Therefore a maternal deficiency of this vitamin will be mirrored in the developing fetus. To create a DVD-deficient rat we manipulate both the lighting and diet in female rats before breeding to ensure that the breeding female has very low circulating levels of 25OHD3 (between 0 and 4.5 nM) (Eyles, Burne, Alexander, Cui, & McGrath, 2011). In the current version of this model, the dam is returned to normal vitamin D levels within 12 h of the birth of her pups. This results in offspring with normalizing 25OHD3 levels by 14 days postpartum. This treatment has no other significant effect on other aspects of dam health, including weight gain, offspring weight, fecundity, ability to conceive, or any effect on calcium or phosphate levels. A description of how to reproduce this model in rats with a detailed troubleshooting section has now been published in detail (Eyles et al., 2011).

What Does DVD Deficiency Do to the Developing Brain?

Like other nuclear steroids, vitamin D is a potent differentiation agent in a variety of developing tissues (Darwish & DeLuca, 1993). However, until recently, its actions in the developing brain had never been studied.

Vitamin D is part of a large family of ligands—including testosterone, estrogen, corticosteroids, thyroid hormones, and vitamin A—that signal via nuclear receptors. Given the well-known effects of other nuclear steroids on the developing brain, it is likely that vitamin D may be similarly active. We have shown vitamin D to be a powerful differentiation agent in neurons (Brown, Bianco, McGrath, & Eyles, 2003; Cui, McGrath, Burne, Mackay-Sim, & Eyles, 2007). Given the pro-differentiation and antiapoptotic properties of vitamin D, it is of no surprise that DVD deficiency is associated with unimpeded proliferation across numerous regions of the embryonic rat brain (Eyles, Brown, Mackay-Sim, McGrath, & Feron, 2003; Ko, Burkert, McGrath, & Eyles, 2004). Accordingly, the onset of apoptosis in the developing brains of DVD-deficient rats is delayed (Ko et al., 2004). These findings were uniform across the cortical, allocortical, and subcortical regions of the developing brain. We also confirmed the corresponding changes in cell cycle and apoptotic gene expression in the same brain regions (Ko et al., 2004). When the anatomy of DVD-deficient embryonic brains was examined, it was found that the newborn offspring of DVD-deficient rats had larger brains, consistent with the increased cell proliferation and decreased cellular elimination observed (Eyles et al., 2003). When corrected for total brain volume, the neocortex was proportionally thinner and the lateral ventricle volume larger.

Alterations in cell proliferation in brain tissue can also be assayed using neurosphere cultures. Culturing embryonic brain tissue under the correct conditions in vitro can lead to the formation of small spheres of proliferating cells. Each sphere is indicative of a proliferating precursor cell. Neurosphere number is therefore an indicator of proliferation status in brain tissue (Reynolds & Rietze, 2005). When neurosphere cultures were prepared from the subventricular zone of DVD-deficient neonatal brains, the number of neurospheres was shown to be increased (Cui et al., 2007), confirming that cell division is elevated in these brains at birth. The same study also revealed that adding 100 µM of 1,25-dihydroxy-vitamin D3, the active form of vitamin D) predictably decreased the neurosphere number in tissue from control animals.

Is DVD Deficiency a Useful Animal Model of Schizophrenia?

Early studies examined the behavioral phenotypes of adult animals that had been both conceived and reared under vitamin D–deficient conditions. These animals displayed motor, perception, memory, and sensory motor gating abnormalities (Altemus, Finger, Wolf, & Birge, 1987; Burne, Feron, et al., 2004). However, musculoskeletal problems associated with hypocalcemia probably confounded these results; when calcium levels were returned to normal in a model of life-long vitamin

D deficiency, sensory motor gating deficits were normalized (Burne, Becker, et al., 2004). This confound of hypocalcemia only appears to be a problem in animals deficient in vitamin D for their whole life. Animals reared under vitamin D–deficient conditions until weaning still have normal calcium and vitamin D levels when tested as adults (Burne, Becker, et al., 2004).

The behavioral phenotype of adult DVD-deficient rats has been largely established by the efforts of two collaborating laboratories using Sprague–Dawley rats in Brisbane, Australia (Burne, Becker, et al., 2004), and Magdeburg, Germany (Becker, Eyles, McGrath, & Grecksch, 2005). Although there are several differences between laboratories regarding animal husbandry, the major difference is that in the Magdeburg protocol, dams receive 2 mM calcium in the drinking water. As previously noted, this is unnecessary in the Brisbane protocol because sera calcium levels are normal in vitamin D deficient dams, neonates and adult offspring (Burne, McGrath, Mackay-Sim, & Eyles, 2006; O'Loan et al., 2007).

Phenotypes of Relevance to Positive Symptoms

Adult DVD-deficient rats show enhanced novelty-induced locomotion for a range of tasks including the hole board and elevated plus maze (Burne, Becker, et al., 2004; Kesby, Burne, McGrath, & Eyles, 2006). Increased novelty-induced behaviors strongly indicate enhanced subcortical DA activity (Hooks & Kalivas, 1995). Both novelty and stress (e.g., handling) resulted in an increased DA release in the prefrontal cortex (Feenstra, Botterblom, & van Uum, 1995). However, this novelty-induced hyperlocomotion in DVD-deficient adults is abolished if the animal is briefly physically restrained (with or without injection) (Burne, O'Loan, McGrath, & Eyles, 2006; Kesby et al., 2006). Hypothalamic pituitary adrenal axis-mediated stress responses are also normal in these animals (Eyles et al., 2006). Therefore, stress-mediated factors are likely to be less important in DVD-deficient adults.

Agents such as amphetamine have been shown to induce psychosis-like phenotypes in nonpsychotic individuals; schizophrenia patients show enhanced DA release and increased positive symptoms after exposure to low doses (Janowsky, El-Yousel, Davis, & Sekerke, 1973; Laruelle, Abi-Dargham, Gil, Kegeles, & Innis, 1999; Lieberman, Kane, & Alvir, 1987). Amphetamine-induced behaviors in rodents are therefore considered to viably model the psychotic symptoms seen in human patients. Amphetamine induces DA release in the brain primarily because of its actions at the DA transporter (DAT) (Jones, Gainetdinov, Wightman, & Caron, 1998; Sulzer, Maidment, & Rayport, 1993; Wieczorek & Kruk, 1994). Enhanced responsiveness to novelty is also associated with an increased response to psychomimetics (Chefer, Zakharova, & Shippenberg, 2003). Locomotion in the response to psychomimetic agents has been extensively assessed in DVD-deficient rats. Female DVD-deficient rats show an increased sensitivity to amphetamine-induced locomotion as adults but not as juveniles (Kesby et al., 2010). Male DVD-deficient rats do not show an enhanced response relative to controls after an acute dose of amphetamine; enhanced sensitivity to amphetamine appears to emerge only after repeated dosing (Kesby et al., 2010). Adult female DVD-deficient rats also have increased levels of DAT in the caudate putamen and an increased affinity for DAT ligands in the nucleus accumbens (Kesby et al., 2010). This suggests that alterations in DAT function may mediate the enhanced response to amphetamine at least in female DVD-deficient offspring.

DVD-deficient rats are also selectively sensitive to postsynaptic DA blockade. One group has shown habituation deficits in DVD-deficient animals (Becker & Grecksch, 2006). When these DVD-deficient rats were treated with haloperidol, a widely used DA2 receptor blocker (and common antipsychotic), these habituation deficits were normalized. The effect of haloperidol in retarding locomotion was also shown to be greater in DVD-deficient animals. This became apparent once hyperlocomotion had first been induced using the NMDA antagonist MK-801 (Kesby et al., 2006). However, DA2 receptors do not appear to be altered in DVD-deficient rats (Kesby et al., 2010). Therefore these behavioral responses are not due to a simple alteration in postsynaptic DA receptors.

In healthy people, the symptoms induced by NMDA antagonists, such as phencyclidine, ketamine, and MK-801, are considered to mimic schizophrenia symptoms more closely than the symptoms induced by amphetamine (Krystal et al., 1994; Lahti, Weiler, Tamara Michaelidis, Parwani, & Tamminga, 2001). As a result, models of schizophrenia proposing endogenous NMDA receptor hypofunction have been proposed (Olney & Farber, 1995). Consequently, NMDA antagonists have also become widely employed in animal models of this disease. DVD-deficient rats have been repeatedly shown to have an enhanced locomotor response to MK-801 compared with controls (Kesby et al., 2006; Kesby, Eyles, Burne, & McGrath, 2011; O'Loan et al., 2007). We have also shown that the later period of gestation appears to be critical for this hyperlocomotion response. Rats exposed to DVD deficiency during late gestation showed this behavior, whereas if the period of DVD deficiency was restricted to early gestation, the effect was not apparent (O'Loan et al., 2007).

Phenotypes of Relevance to Impaired Cognition

DVD-deficient rats have also displayed learning and memory deficits. Latent inhibition refers to a normal learning phenomenon in which it takes longer to establish salience to a previous familiar stimulus compared with a novel stimulus. Acutely psychotic patients have impairments in latent inhibition (Gray, Feldon, Rawlins, Hemsley, & Smith, 1991; Lubow & Gewirtz, 1995) and DA agonists have been shown to decrease latent inhibition in healthy adult males (Swerdlow et al., 2003). DVD-deficient animals have disrupted latent inhibition (Becker et al., 2005), suggesting that these animals have an impaired ability to attend to relevant stimuli.

DVD-deficient rats show increased impulsivity and a lack of inhibitory control when assessed on the five-choice continuous performance task (Turner, Young, McGrath, Eyles, & Burne, 2013). The increased impulsivity in DVD-deficient rats can be attenuated with the atypical antipsychotic, clozapine. Impulsivity in healthy humans has been associated with the availability of the DAT (Costa et al., 2013) and in rats, DA receptors in the medial prefrontal cortex also appear to be critical (Pardey, Kumar, Goodchild, & Cornish, 2013). Thus, multiple dopaminergic elements could contribute to the cognitive deficits demonstrated by adult DVD-deficient rats.

Long-term potentiation (LTP) is a cellular correlate of learning and memory (Bliss & Gardner-Medwin, 1973). Vitamin D deficiency during adulthood reduces LTP in anaesthetized rats after tetanization, despite normal baseline hippocampal LTP (Salami, Talaei, Davari, & Taghizadeh, 2011). Using electrophysiological recordings from the hippocampus of freely moving rats, a subsequent study investigated LTP in DVD-deficient rats (Grecksch, Ruthrich, Hollt, & Becker, 2009). Paradoxically, DVD-deficient rats have *enhanced* baseline LTP. However, the LTP response to low doses of antipsychotics was abnormal in these animals. When low doses of haloperidol and risperidone were given to control animals, enhanced hippocampal LTP was seen. In DVD-deficient animals, this effect was reversed. We conclude that vitamin D must regulate different neurophysiological targets throughout normal hippocampal development.

Brain Structural Phenotypes and Gene/Protein Expression of Relevance to Schizophrenia

One of the most robust findings in schizophrenia research is mildly enlarged lateral ventricles, as detected postmortem or by neuroimaging (Harrison & Weinberger, 2005; Shenton, Dickey, Frumin, & McCarley, 2001). The enlargement in lateral ventricles seen in the DVD-deficient neonate brains (Eyles et al., 2003) persisted into adulthood. However, the timing of the reintroduction of vitamin D appears to be important. Lateral ventricles were enlarged in adult animals that had experienced a more prolonged vitamin D deficiency (i.e., until weaning). If vitamin D was reintroduced into the

maternal diet from birth, this partially ameliorated the anatomical change (Feron et al., 2005).

Gene array and proteomics analysis have been conducted in the prefrontal cortex and hippocampus of adult DVD-deficient rats. DVD deficiency was shown to significantly alter the expression of 74 genes and 36 proteins, with such diverse functions as cytoskeleton maintenance, calcium homeostasis, synaptic plasticity and neurotransmission, oxidative phosphorylation, redox balance, protein transport, chaperoning, cell-cycle control, and posttranslational modifications (Almeras et al., 2007; Eyles et al., 2007). A later study of protein expression in the nucleus accumbens of DVD-deficient rats showed that, although the degree of gene dysregulation was mild, there were significant alterations in several proteins involved in either calcium binding (calbindin, calretinin, and hippocalcin), or mitochondrial function (McGrath et al., 2008).

DVD Deficiency and Developing DA Systems

The VDR and the enzyme responsible for synthesizing the active form of the hormone, *CYP27B1*, are ubiquitous in the DA-rich substantia nigra of the human brain (Eyles, Smith, Kinobe, Hewison, & McGrath, 2005). Additionally, 1,25-dihydroxy-vitamin D3 has been consistently associated with the production of TH in various pathological scenarios (Chen, Lin, & Chiu, 2003; Sanchez, Relova, Gallego, Ben-Batalla, & Perez-Fernandez, 2009; Wang et al., 2001). Given the behavioral sensitivity of DVD-deficient adults to both DA agonists and antagonists, we have concentrated on how developing DA systems may have been altered by the absence of this steroid.

The VDR first appears in the developing midbrain of the rat on E12 (Veenstra et al., 1998). This represents the age when most DA neurons are being born (Gates, Torres, White, Fricker-Gates, & Dunnett, 2006). We have recently mapped the ontogeny of the VDR in the developing rat mesencephalon. We show a clear increase in the nuclear expression of this receptor in TH-positive neurons in the mesencephalon with increasing developmental age, and have also established this at the messenger RNA and protein level (Cui et al., 2013). In addition, we measured DA levels in DVD-deficient neonatal forebrains and showed that, although DA levels were normal, DA metabolism was altered. We found an increased ratio of 3,4-dihydroxyphenylacetic acid/ homovanillic acid, the two major DA metabolites (Kesby et al., 2009). This was accompanied by a reduction in catechol-*o*-methyl transferase (COMT), the enzyme that converts 3,4-dihydroxyphenylacetic acid to homovanillic acid (Kesby et al., 2009).

Given our previous data indicating that DVD deficiency delays brain maturational processes, we next examined whether DVD deficiency may specifically delay the differentiation of DA systems. We harvested mesencephalon from vitamin D–deficient embryos at both the peak period for DA neuron cell birth, E12, and a relatively postmitotic stage, E15. We examined the expression of a limited number of key postmitotic specification factors crucial for the formation and maturation of dopaminergic neurons (Smidt & Burbach, 2007). When compared with controls, DVD-deficient embryonic brains had a reduction in two of these factors: Nurr 1 and p57kip2a (Cui, Pelekanos, Burne, McGrath, & Eyles, 2010). When either of these specification factors is abolished or reduced in mice via genetic manipulation, reductions in DA neuron number and abnormal DA neuron positioning are seen (Joseph et al., 2003; Kadkhodaei et al., 2009; Wallen et al., 2001). This remains an active research interest in our laboratory.

These findings provide strong evidence that DVD deficiency affects the early ontogeny of DA systems. Along with others, we are now engaged in trying to understand how such early changes in the formation of dopaminergic systems could lead to the behavioral phenotypes reported in developmental animal models of schizophrenia (Eyles, Feldon, & Meyer, 2012).

MATERNAL NUTRITIONAL DEFICIENCIES PRODUCE A CONVERGENT PHENOTYPE IN ADULT OFFSPRING

We have presented a summary of the epidemiological studies indicating that a diverse range of maternal nutritional deficiencies during prenatal and/or perinatal stages of life can significantly increase the risk of schizophrenia and related disorders in offspring. Moreover, we have summarized findings from the animal models developed to understand the neurobiology behind these maternal nutritional deficiencies. This complements the broader epidemiological literature implicating nonnutritional risk-factors during pregnancy—such as obstetric complications, maternal infection/inflammation, or maternal stress—in increasing the risk of later onset of schizophrenia in adult offspring (Brown, 2011). Animal models of maternal hypoxia, maternal immune activation (using either bacterial or viral components), and maternal restraint have been used to examine these nonnutritional developmental epidemiological risk factors, respectively (Koenig, 2009). These models produce a constellation of outcomes that reflect phenotypes of both the positive symptoms and cognitive deficits observed in schizophrenia. Studying the negative symptoms of schizophrenia in animal models has proved more challenging.

Each developmental risk factor is likely to operate via a specific and independent series of physiological and cellular pathways in the fetal brain. However, each risk factor results in the same suite of phenotypes in the adult offspring that are relevant to schizophrenia. Therefore an obvious question is: "Via what mechanism could such diverse exposures during brain development, converge to produce these common phenotypes in the adult offspring?"

This conundrum has not escaped important figures in the field. It has been proposed that abnormalities in either maternal nutrition or maternal stress/infection/hypoxia may all operate via downstream changes in inflammatory cytokine/stress hormone signaling (Meyer & Feldon, 2010). This remains an attractive hypothesis and is worth testing. For instance, one can conceive of studies in which some combination of antiinflammatory factors and/or glucocorticoid antagonists could be used with the described maternal nutritional models to test this hypothesis. Or conversely, perhaps these candidate signaling pathways could be reexamined using genetic techniques. If certain schizophrenia-relevant phenotypes of the aforementioned maternal nutritional models were abolished by genetically altering inflammatory cytokine or corticosterone signaling, this would indicate a direct convergent link. This could be a particularly attractive approach if these studies used the techniques that alter genetic signaling during specific temporal stages of development. One caveat to this approach is that such genetic techniques are well-established in mice, whereas most maternal nutritional models have been generated in rats.

We can imagine future studies in which epidemiologically supported nutritional supplementation is used in some of the previously mentioned developmental animal models of schizophrenia. Unfortunately, there is currently a lack of such "intervention" studies. This may change, given the recent clinical interest in the use of certain amino acids (which act as coagonists at the NMDA receptor) as adjuncts to existing antipsychotic therapies (Heresco-Levy, Ermilov, Lichtenberg, Bar, & Javitt, 2004; Woods et al., 2013). However, there are some supportive data using maternal inflammation models. The bacterial membrane LPS induces a robust inflammatory response in its host via the Toll-4 receptor. When preadministered to pregnant rodents given LPS, the anti-inflammatory cytokine interleukin-10 prevents white matter loss in offspring (Pang, Rodts-Palenik, Cai, Bennett, & Rhodes, 2005; Robertson, Care, & Skinner, 2007; Robertson, Skinner, & Care, 2006). Similarly, when maternal rats are exposed to LPS, a prior administration of the antiinflammatory and antioxidant agent N-acetyl cysteine to the dams prevents hippocampal damage and learning deficits in offspring (Lante et al., 2008).

ARE ALTERATIONS IN THE ONTOGENY OF DEVELOPING DA SYSTEMS A CONVERGENT EARLY MECHANISM IN MODELS OF MATERNAL NUTRITIONAL DEFICIENCY?

A remarkably consistent and critically important feature of all animal models that reflect pre- and perinatal risk-factors for schizophrenia (both nutritional and nonnutritional) is that they all appear to produce adult offspring with a heightened behavioral sensitivity to psychomimetics such as amphetamine or cocaine. Amphetamine acts primarily through enhancing DA release, and cocaine acts by blocking DA reuptake. It is therefore likely that the diverse array of early life risk factors affects the developing DA system and the presynaptic dopaminergic system in particular.

Prominent figures within schizophrenia research have recently suggested that we refocus our efforts onto changes in presynaptic DA activity (Simpson, Kellendonk, & Kandel, 2010). There is substantial clinical support, based primarily on positron emission tomography (PET) studies in patients, which clearly indicates that there is enhanced uptake of C11-labeled DOPA (and presumably synthesis of DA) in the striatum of patients with schizophrenia. This literature appears to be highly robust with more than 10 separate studies conducted to date and two meta-analyses showing a consistent elevation in DOPA uptake in patients (Fusar-Poli & Meyer-Lindenberg, 2013; Howes et al., 2012).

Even more relevant to this discussion are recent PET studies in individuals at high risk of developing schizophrenia. An emerging research effort is now being directed towards identifying asymptomatic individuals who are at "high risk" of progressing to the clinical disorder. Such assessments are largely based on groupings of behavioral symptoms that allow the research clinician to enrich the population of people likely to progress to the eventual clinical disorder (Yung & Nelson, 2011; Yung et al., 1998). To date, two PET studies have been conducted using these cohorts. Because these studies are difficult to conduct in such a labile population and are still in their in early stages, sample sizes remain small. However, the findings appear to indicate that baseline C11 DOPA uptake not only predicts the later onset of schizophrenia (Howes, Bose, Turkheimer, Valli, Egerton, & Valmaggia, 2011; Howes et al., 2009), but that in patients who do transition to the clinical condition, C11 DOPA uptake progressively increases (Howes, Bose, Turkheimer, Valli, Egerton, & Stahl, 2011). This suggests that DA uptake may represent a potential biomarker before clinical diagnosis. Given the correlation between the progression of the disease and the progressive increase in DA uptake, this may also represent a promising therapeutic target. One obvious and parsimonious candidate for any alteration in presynaptic DA signaling would be an alteration in the expression or function of DAT, however a recent meta-analysis of DAT in schizophrenia firmly rules out any alteration in DAT expression (Howes et al., 2012).

These findings have galvanized both the basic and clinical schizophrenia research communities. The possibility of altering the course of this disease was unthinkable as little as 10 years ago. Unfortunately, PET studies are not suitable for use in routine screening tool in these populations, and a more practical biomarker needs to be found. However, with regards to the basic neurobiology of schizophrenia, these clinical findings strongly suggest that presynaptic DA systems are altered well before diagnosable symptoms appear.

This clinical data aligns well with our work in both the DVD-deficiency model, and research from the laboratory of Meyer and Feldon using the gestational day 9 Maternal Immune Activation model with the polyinosine-polycytidylic RNA viral construct. Both models produce adult animals that display behavioral sensitivity to DA agonists, and both demonstrate changes in various aspects of DA transport or synthesis (Kesby et al., 2010; Meyer & Feldon, 2009). More importantly, both models show early alterations in factors involved in the differentiation of DA neurons. Nurr1 is a nuclear transcription factor essential for the specification of DA neurons (Wallen et al., 2001). When Nurr1 is genetically ablated, DA neurons are not made and the foetus is nonviable (Zetterstrom et al., 1997). In both DVD-deficiency and Maternal Immune Activation embryos, there are early initial reductions in the expression of Nurr1 at precisely the time when most DA neurons are born in the developing rat and mouse CNS (Cui et al., 2010). This normalizes somewhat in both models by birth; however, persistent alterations remain in the expression of TH and levels of DA (Kesby et al., 2009; Meyer, Engler, Weber, Schedlowski, & Feldon, 2008). Close consideration of the overlapping findings from these two diverse models has led us to suggest that alterations in the ontogeny of developing DA systems may represent an early convergent path in the development of schizophrenia (Eyles et al., 2012).

There are a limited number of studies that have explored changes in the developing DA system occurring in maternal nutritional deficiency models relevant to schizophrenia. This is despite findings indicating that DA systems are universally altered in adult offspring from such models. A reexamination of the scant literature available indicates that nutritional deficiencies may also perturb the early ontogeny of developing DA systems.

When rat pups (postnatal day 14 (P14)) from a model of maternal undernutrition (50% food restriction during the last week of pregnancy only) were examined, they were shown to have reduced DA1 receptor density across the hypothalamus and increased DA2 receptor density in the arcuate nucleus. Unfortunately, pups were not studied at any earlier developmental ages, and nor was any other brain region examined. By adulthood, DA2 receptor abnormalities had normalized but DA1 receptor densities had reversed, potentially indicating some persistent over-compensation from this early exposure (Manuel-Apolinar, Rocha, Damasio, Tesoro-Cruz, & Zarate, 2014). In a previously cited model of maternal protein deficiency, early changes in potassium-evoked DA release from hippocampal slices was shown in P15 rat pups. Again, pups were not studied at any earlier developmental age and no other brain region was examined. This early functional abnormality in presynaptic DA function persisted into adulthood (Chen et al., 1995).

There have also been reports of early abnormal pup behavior in models of maternal iron deficiency (Felt & Lozoff, 1996). However, we are aware of only one study to date that has examined early changes in DA components in such models. DA content was dramatically increased in the brains of P10 rat pups from dams with moderate anemia (10–20% iron deficiency) (Beard et al., 2006). This increase persisted into weaning but became less dramatic. There were also increases in DAT expression, and regional changes in DA2 receptors in the P10 rat pups. These findings had normalized by weaning. These alterations correlated with very early sensorimotor defects. At the first postnatal time point assessed (P6), pups from maternally iron-deficient dams had reductions in bar gripping and forelimb placement. These deficiencies persisted into weaning. The authors chose these behaviors specifically to examine the effect of maternal iron deficiency on basal ganglia dopaminergic circuitry in offspring.

Several early studies have shown that dietary omega-3 fatty acid deficiencies produce alterations in both brain DA content and DA receptor expression in adult animals, (Delion, Chalon, Guilloteau, Besnard, & Durand, 1996; Delion et al., 1994). To the best of our knowledge, the effect of dietary omega-3 deficiency on the developing DA system has not been examined. However, one study has shown that varying the fatty acid content of the maternal diet with different sources of oil supplements does affect levels of DA and 3,4-dihydroxyphenylacetic acid (a major DA metabolite) in the newborn brain (Innis & de La Presa Owens, 2001). This may be important in explaining the previously discussed elevation in TH enzyme expression in the dorsal striatum of adolescent animals bred from omega-3 deficient dams (Bondi et al., 2014) (see Controlled Trials of Nutritional Supplements for Treatment of Schizophrenia Section). These ideas are summarized in Figure 1.

Finally the work of Boksa and colleagues is illuminating. Rather than investigating nutritional deficiency, this group examines animal models of maternal hypoxia. Their findings reveal that there are early developmental periods where intervention can prevent permanent abnormalities in DA signaling in adult offspring. This group investigated the role of early administration of adrenaline in a model of mild perinatal hypoxia. As previously mentioned, this model produces dopaminergic abnormalities in adult offspring. In particular, if the adult offspring are subjected to repeated mild isolation stress, then TH activity and DAT binding are enhanced, and locomotor sensitivity to amphetamine emerges. These phenotypes are not present in the absence of stress. A single perinatal injection of epinephrine to newborns subjected to perinatal hypoxia successfully prevented the onset of these phenotypes in adults (Boksa & Zhang, 2008). These results confirm that abnormal levels of catecholamines in neonates can induce subtle long-term changes in CNS function.

CONCLUSIONS

Animal models of complex disorders, such as schizophrenia, were traditionally created to clarify causal agents or pathways relevant to a specific risk relationship. For instance, this could be to clarify the actions of a particular gene or pathway in the developing brain. More recently, this genetic approach has been refined to assess the function of selective human-specific mutations in genes linked with schizophrenia. This allows researchers to examine the action of a defective gene product on brain development or function. The recent work with the well-described BDNF (Val66Met) polymorphisms best illustrates this approach (Chen et al., 2006). Historically, animal models based on disease-risk epidemiology were created to understand neurobiological plausibility. One purpose of this article has been to alert the reader to the possibility that such models may also provide promising experimental leads into potential shared pathways *between* risk factors. These models also provide a preclinical environment in which preventative therapies can be trialed. Studies of potential convergent pathways may suggest even more robust targets for preventive therapies.

What have we learned from studying one particular maternal nutritional risk factor, DVD deficiency, in animals over the past 10–12 years? This model was created more than a decade ago to establishing the "neurobiological plausibility" of this risk factor. At that time, there was an abundance of circumstantial evidence from naturalistic epidemiological studies implicating vitamin D deficiency as a risk factor for schizophrenia, but there was still no direct evidence. Since then, we have not only solidified this risk epidemiology, but have learnt a great deal more about how the absence of this vitamin adversely affects the developing brain (Eyles et al., 2013). Most importantly, we have shown that the absence

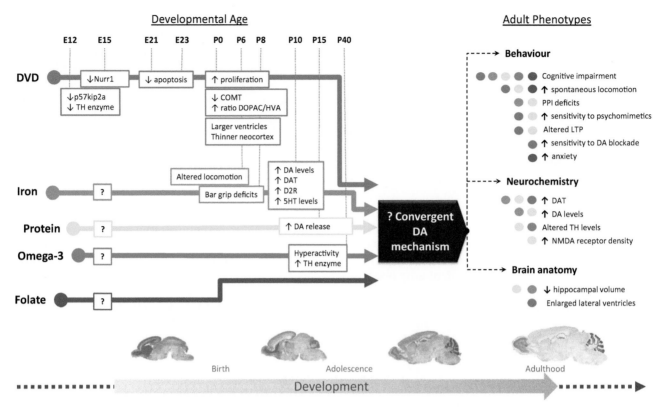

FIGURE 1   **Animal models of maternal nutrient deficiency produce phenotypes of relevance to schizophrenia: Impairments in dopamine ontogeny be a convergent early mechanism.** The five maternal nutrient deficiencies that have been most-studied in animals are: vitamin D, iron, protein, omega-3, and folate. On the left, the dopamine-related behavioral and neurochemical abnormalities in embryonic and early postnatal animals from these models are shown. These dopaminergic factors were measured during development, at ages ranging from embryonic day 12 to P40 (postnatal day 40). For the iron, protein, omega-3, and folate animal models, no information about embryonic brain dopaminergic function is available. At the bottom of the figure are sagittal sections representing the various stages of rodent brain development. On the right are adult phenotypes relevant to schizophrenia produced by these maternal nutrient deficiencies. These are grouped into behavioral phenotypes, changes in neurochemistry, and changes in brain anatomy. Many phenotypes are shared by offspring from diverse maternal nutrition deficits. We propose that deficiencies in each maternal nutrient may converge via some as yet unknown dopaminergic mechanism in adolescent/early adult offspring to produce schizophrenia-relevant phenotypes in the adult animals. COMT, catechol-o-methyl transferase; DOPAC, dihydroxyphenylacetic acid; HVA, homovanillic acid; serotonin; DA, dopamine; TH, tyrosine hydroxylase; developmental vitamin D = O; iron = O; protein = O; omega-3 = O; folate = O.

of vitamin D produces very early changes in the ontogeny of dopaminergic systems. It was a case of Pasteur's famous idiom of "chance favouring the prepared mind" when we recognized that very similar changes in the ontogeny of DA systems were occurring in the maternal immune activation model of Meyer and Feldon. This led us to hypothesize that perhaps other developmental risk factors for schizophrenia may also adversely affect the early ontogeny of DA neurons. We further hypothesized that such changes could represent a convergent pathway for the diverse developmental risk factors associated with schizophrenia (Eyles et al., 2012).

Despite a wealth of findings from animal models over the past decade implicating dopaminergic dysfunction in the adult offspring from maternal nutritional deficiency, very little research has been focused on the effects on DA systems more proximal to the actual exposure. In the last section, we outlined the initial encouraging data supporting the hypothesis that alterations in the

early ontogeny of DA systems may represent an early point of convergence in the study of schizophrenia etiology. Obviously, far more work remains to be done. However, we consider that the rewards of this research could be substantial. Pharmaceutical companies have voted with their feet and have abandoned investment in new antipsychotic medications (Abbott, 2010). This is largely because of issues regarding the substantial heterogeneity in the presentation and course of illness.

That developing DA systems appear to be particularly vulnerable to a wide range of nutritional and nonnutritional risk factors is critically important. We contend that it is vital for experimental research to explore the mechanism by which such diverse nutritional deficiencies could alter early brain ontogeny. This research should also investigate how this mechanism results in the observed clinical presymptomatic alterations in DA uptake and synthesis before disease onset. Ultimately, this may represent a truly novel and revolutionary approach to developing therapeutic interventions. This proposal is made more clinically attractive in the light of the recent PET evidence, indicating that dopaminergic abnormalities are present before disease onset in at high-risk individuals (Howes, Bose, Turkheimer, Valli, Egerton, & Valmaggia, 2011; Howes et al., 2009).

Dietary interventions represent low-risk, cost-effective prophylactic interventions that are easy to initiate. Moreover, understanding the molecular and cellular mechanisms of pathological insults during periods of vulnerability (such as during early brain development or adolescence) could prompt targeted interventions in at-risk populations. Health care policies in many countries are trending toward the importance of preventative interventions. Developing evidence-based approaches to augmentation of diets using vitamins, PUFAs, micronutrients, and increasing general adequate nutrition could lead to reduced rates of mental illness. Such an approach may contribute to diminishing the crippling burden that diseases such as schizophrenia place upon patients, their carers, and society.

Acknowledgments

Funding for this study was provided by the National Health and Medical Research Council of Australia and the Queensland Dept. of Health. We would like to thank Alice Petty for editorial assistance.

References

Abbott, A. (2010). Schizophrenia: the drug deadlock. *Nature, 468*(7321), 158–159.

de Abreu, D. A., Nivet, E., Baril, N., Khrestchatisky, M., Roman, F., & Feron, F. (2010). Developmental vitamin D deficiency alters learning in C57Bl/6J mice. *Behavioural Brain Research, 208*(2), 603–608.

Adler Nevo, G., Meged, S., Sela, B. A., Hanoch-Levi, A., Hershko, R., & Weizman, A. (2006). Homocysteine levels in adolescent schizophrenia patients. *European Neuropsychopharmacology, 16*(8), 588–591.

Almeras, L., Eyles, D., Benech, P., Laffite, D., Villard, C., Patatian, A., et al. (2007). Developmental vitamin D deficiency alters brain protein expression in the adult rat: implications for neuropsychiatric disorders. *Proteomics, 7*(5), 769–780.

Altemus, K. L., Finger, S., Wolf, C., & Birge, S. J. (1987). Behavioral correlates of vitamin D deficiency. *Physiology & Behavior, 39*(4), 435–440.

Amminger, G. P., Schafer, M. R., Papageorgiou, K., Klier, C. M., Cotton, S. M., Harrigan, S. M., et al. (2010). Long-chain omega-3 fatty acids for indicated prevention of psychotic disorders: a randomized, placebo-controlled trial. *Archives of General Psychiatry, 67*(2), 146–154.

Ban, T. A. (2001). Pharmacotherapy of mental illness–a historical analysis. *Progress in Neuro-Psychopharmacology and Biological Psychiatry, 25*(4), 709–727.

Bao, Y., Ibram, G., Blaner, W. S., Quesenberry, C. P., Shen, L., McKeague, I. W., et al. (2012). Low maternal retinol as a risk factor for schizophrenia in adult offspring. *Schizophrenia Research, 137*(1–3), 159–165.

Beard, J. L., Felt, B., Schallert, T., Burhans, M., Connor, J. R., & Georgieff, M. K. (2006). Moderate iron deficiency in infancy: biology and behavior in young rats. *Behavioural Brain Research, 170*(2), 224–232.

Becker, A., Eyles, D. W., McGrath, J. J., & Grecksch, G. (2005). Transient prenatal vitamin D deficiency is associated with subtle alterations in learning and memory functions in adult rats. *Behavioural Brain Research, 161*(2), 306–312.

Becker, A., & Grecksch, G. (2006). Pharmacological treatment to augment hole board habituation in prenatal vitamin D-deficient rats. *Behavioural Brain Research, 166*(1), 177–183.

Bentsen, H., Osnes, K., Refsum, H., Solberg, D. K., & Bohmer, T. (2013). A randomized placebo-controlled trial of an omega-3 fatty acid and vitamins E+C in schizophrenia. *Translational Psychiatry, 3*, e335.

Berg, A. O., Melle, I., Torjesen, P. A., Lien, L., Hauff, E., & Andreassen, O. A. (2010). A cross-sectional study of vitamin D deficiency among immigrants and Norwegians with psychosis compared to the general population. *Journal of Clinical Psychiatry*.

Bliss, T. V., & Gardner-Medwin, A. R. (1973). Long-lasting potentiation of synaptic transmission in the dentate area of the unanaestetized rabbit following stimulation of the perforant path. *Journal of Physiology, 232*(2), 357–374.

Boksa, P., & Zhang, Y. (2008). Epinephrine administration at birth prevents long-term changes in dopaminergic parameters caused by Cesarean section birth in the rat. *Psychopharmacology (Berl) 200*(3), 381–391.

Bondi, C. O., Taha, A. Y., Tock, J. L., Totah, N. K., Cheon, Y., Torres, G. E., et al. (2014). Adolescent behavior and dopamine availability are uniquely sensitive to dietary omega-3 fatty acid deficiency. *Biological Psychiatry, 75*(1), 38–46.

Bouaziz, N., Ayedi, I., Sidhom, O., Kallel, A., Rafrafi, R., Jomaa, R., et al. (2010). Plasma homocysteine in schizophrenia: determinants and clinical correlations in Tunisian patients free from antipsychotics. *Psychiatry Research, 179*(1), 24–29.

Bronzino, J. D., Austin-LaFrance, R. J., Mokler, D., & Morgane, P. J. (1997). Effects of prenatal protein malnutrition on hippocampal long-term potentiation in freely moving rats. *Experimental Neurology, 148*(1), 317–323.

Brown, A. S. (2011). The environment and susceptibility to schizophrenia. *Progress in Neurobiology, 93*(1), 23–58.

Brown, A. S., Bottiglieri, T., Schaefer, C. A., Quesenberry, C. P., Jr., Liu, L., Bresnahan, M., et al. (2007). Elevated prenatal homocysteine levels as a risk factor for schizophrenia. *Archives of General Psychiatry, 64*(1), 31–39.

Brown, J., Bianco, J. I., McGrath, J. J., & Eyles, D. W. (2003). 1,25-Dihydroxyvitamin D3 induces nerve growth factor, promotes neurite outgrowth and inhibits mitosis in embryonic rat hippocampal neurons. *Neuroscience Letters, 343*(2), 139–143.

Burne, T. H., Becker, A., Brown, J., Eyles, D. W., Mackay-Sim, A., & McGrath, J. J. (2004). Transient prenatal vitamin D deficiency is associated with hyperlocomotion in adult rats. *Behavioural Brain Research, 154*(2), 549–555.

Burne, T. H., Feron, F., Brown, J., Eyles, D. W., McGrath, J. J., & Mackay-Sim, A. (2004). Combined prenatal and chronic postnatal vitamin D deficiency in rats impairs prepulse inhibition of acoustic startle. *Physiology & Behavior, 81*(4), 651–655.

Burne, T. H., McGrath, J. J., Eyles, D. W., & Mackay-Sim, A. (2005). Behavioural characterization of vitamin D receptor knockout mice. *Behavioural Brain Research, 157*(2), 299–308.

Burne, T. H., O'Loan, J., McGrath, J. J., & Eyles, D. W. (2006). Hyperlocomotion associated with transient prenatal vitamin D deficiency is ameliorated by acute restraint. *Behavioural Brain Research, 174*(1), 119–124.

Burne, T. H. J., McGrath, J. J., Mackay-Sim, A., & Eyles, D. W. (2006). Prenatal vitamin D deficiency and brain development. In V. D. Stoltz (Ed.), *Vitamin D: New research* (vol. 1) (pp. 153–172). New York: Nova Science Publishers.

Carney, M. (1995). Neuropsychiatric disorders associated with nutritional deficiencies: incidence and therapeutic implications. *Pharmacology and Pathophysiology, 3*(4), 279–290.

Ceglia, L. (2008). Vitamin D and skeletal muscle tissue and function. *Molecular Aspects of Medicine, 29*(6), 407–414.

Chefer, V. I., Zakharova, I., & Shippenberg, T. S. (2003). Enhanced responsiveness to novelty and cocaine is associated with decreased basal dopamine uptake and release in the nucleus accumbens: quantitative microdialysis in rats under transient conditions. *Journal of Neuroscience, 23*(7), 3076–3084.

Chen, J. C., Turiak, G., Galler, J., & Volicer, L. (1995). Effect of prenatal malnutrition on release of monoamines from hippocampal slices. *Life Sciences, 57*(16), 1467–1475.

Chen, K. B., Lin, A. M., & Chiu, T. H. (2003). Systemic vitamin D3 attenuated oxidative injuries in the locus coeruleus of rat brain. *Annals of the New York Academy of Sciences, 993*, 313–324 discussion 345–319.

Chen, Z. Y., Jing, D., Bath, K. G., Ieraci, A., Khan, T., Siao, C. J., et al. (2006). Genetic variant BDNF (Val66Met) polymorphism alters anxiety-related behavior. *Science, 314*(5796), 140–143.

Cintra, L., Aguilar, A., Granados, L., Galvan, A., Kemper, T., DeBassio, W., et al. (1997). Effects of prenatal protein malnutrition on hippocampal CA1 pyramidal cells in rats of four age groups. *Hippocampus, 7*(2), 192–203.

Cintra, L., Diaz-Cintra, S., Galvan, A., Kemper, T., & Morgane, P. J. (1990). Effects of protein undernutrition on the dentate gyrus in rats of three age groups. *Brain Research, 532*(1–2), 271–277.

Connor, J. R., & Menzies, S. L. (1996). Relationship of iron to oligondendrocytes and myelination. *Glia, 17*(2), 83–93.

Costa, A., la Fougere, C., Pogarell, O., Moller, H. J., Riedel, M., & Ettinger, U. (2013). Impulsivity is related to striatal dopamine transporter availability in healthy males. *Psychiatry Research, 211*(3), 251–256.

Crews, M., Lally, J., Gardner-Sood, P., Howes, O., Bonaccorso, S., Smith, S., et al. (2013). Vitamin D deficiency in first episode psychosis: a case-control study. *Schizophrenia Research, 150*(2–3), 533–537.

Cui, X., McGrath, J. J., Burne, T. H., Mackay-Sim, A., & Eyles, D. W. (2007). Maternal vitamin D depletion alters neurogenesis in the developing rat brain. *International Journal of Developmental Neuroscience, 25*(4), 227–232.

Cui, X., Pelekanos, M., Burne, T. H., McGrath, J. J., & Eyles, D. W. (2010). Maternal vitamin D deficiency alters the expression of genes involved in dopamine specification in the developing rat mesencephalon. *Neuroscience Letters, 486*(3), 220–223.

Cui, X., Pelekanos, M., Liu, P. Y., Burne, T. H., McGrath, J. J., & Eyles, D. W. (2013). The vitamin D receptor in dopamine neurons; its presence in human substantia nigra and its ontogenesis in rat midbrain. *Neuroscience*.

Dakhale, G. N., Khanzode, S. D., Khanzode, S. S., & Saoji, A. (2005). Supplementation of vitamin C with atypical antipsychotics reduces oxidative stress and improves the outcome of schizophrenia. *Psychopharmacology (Berl), 182*(4), 494–498.

Darwish, H., & DeLuca, H. F. (1993). Vitamin D-regulated gene expression. *Critical Reviews in Eukaryotic Gene Expression, 3*(2), 89–116.

Davis, K. L., Stewart, D. G., Friedman, J. I., Buchsbaum, M., Harvey, P. D., Hof, P. R., et al. (2003). White matter changes in schizophrenia: evidence for myelin-related dysfunction. *Archives of General Psychiatry, 60*(5), 443–456.

Dawodu, A., Saadi, H. F., Bekdache, G., Javed, Y., Altaye, M., & Hollis, B. W. (2013). Randomized controlled trial (RCT) of vitamin D supplementation in pregnancy in a population with endemic vitamin D deficiency. *Journal of Clinical Endocrinology & Metabolism, 98*(6), 2337–2346.

Dean, A. J., Bellgrove, M. A., Hall, T., Phan, W. M., Eyles, D. W., Kvaskoff, D., et al. (2011). Effects of vitamin D supplementation on cognitive and emotional functioning in young adults–a randomised controlled trial. *PLoS One, 6*(11), e25966.

Debassio, W. A., Kemper, T. L., Galler, J. R., & Tonkiss, J. (1994). Prenatal malnutrition effect on pyramidal and granule cell generation in the hippocampal formation. *Brain Research Bulletin, 35*(1), 57–61.

Debassio, W. A., Kemper, T. L., Tonkiss, J., & Galler, J. R. (1996). Effect of prenatal protein deprivation on postnatal granule cell generation in the hippocampal dentate gyrus. *Brain Research Bulletin, 41*(6), 379–383.

Delion, S., Chalon, S., Guilloteau, D., Besnard, J. C., & Durand, G. (1996). alpha-Linolenic acid dietary deficiency alters age-related changes of dopaminergic and serotoninergic neurotransmission in the rat frontal cortex. *Journal of Neurochemistry, 66*(4), 1582–1591.

Delion, S., Chalon, S., Herault, J., Guilloteau, D., Besnard, J. C., & Durand, G. (1994). Chronic dietary alpha-linolenic acid deficiency alters dopaminergic and serotoninergic neurotransmission in rats. *Journal of Nutrition, 124*(12), 2466–2476.

Diaz-Cintra, S., Cintra, L., Galvan, A., Aguilar, A., Kemper, T., & Morgane, P. J. (1991). Effects of prenatal protein deprivation on postnatal development of granule cells in the fascia dentata. *Journal of Comparative Neurology, 310*(3), 356–364.

Diaz-Cintra, S., Garcia-Ruiz, M., Corkidi, G., & Cintra, L. (1994). Effects of prenatal malnutrition and postnatal nutritional rehabilitation on CA3 hippocampal pyramidal cells in rats of four ages. *Brain Research, 662*(1–2), 117–126.

English, J. A., Harauma, A., Focking, M., Wynne, K., Scaife, C., Cagney, G., et al. (2013). Omega-3 fatty acid deficiency disrupts endocytosis, neuritogenesis, and mitochondrial protein pathways in the mouse hippocampus. *Frontiers in Genetics, 4*, 208.

Eyles, D., Almeras, L., Benech, P., Patatian, A., Mackay-Sim, A., McGrath, J., et al. (2007). Developmental vitamin D deficiency alters the expression of genes encoding mitochondrial, cytoskeletal and synaptic proteins in the adult rat brain. *Journal of Steroid Biochemistry and Molecular Biology, 103*(3–5), 538–545.

Eyles, D., Brown, J., Mackay-Sim, A., McGrath, J., & Feron, F. (2003). Vitamin D3 and brain development. *Neuroscience, 118*(3), 641–653.

Eyles, D., Burne, T. H., & McGrath, J. J. (2013). Vitamin D, effects on brain development, adult brain function and the links between low levels of vitamin D and neuropsychiatric disease. *Frontiers in Neuroendocrinology, 34*(1), 47–64.

Eyles, D., Burne, T. H. J., Alexander, S., Cui, X., & McGrath, J. J. (2011). The developmental vitamin D (DVD) model of schizophrenia. In P. O'Donnell (Ed.), *Animal models of schizophrenia and related disorders* (pp. 113–126). New York: Springer Science+Business Media.

Eyles, D., Feldon, J., & Meyer, U. (2012). Schizophrenia: do all roads lead to dopamine or is this where they start? Evidence from two epidemiologically informed developmental rodent models. *Translational Psychiatry, 2*, e81.

Eyles, D., Rogers, F., Buller, K., McGrath, J. J., Ko, P., French, K., et al. (2006). Developmental vitamin D (DVD) deficiency in the rat alters adult behaviour independently of HPA function. *Psychoneuroendocrinology, 31*(8), 958–964.

Eyles, D., Smith, S., Kinobe, R., Hewison, M., & McGrath, J. J. (2005). Distribution of the vitamin D receptor and 1 alpha-hydroxylase in human brain. *Journal of Chemical Neuroanatomy, 29*(1), 21–30.

Feenstra, M. G., Botterblom, M. H., & van Uum, J. F. (1995). Novelty-induced increase in dopamine release in the rat prefrontal cortex in vivo: inhibition by diazepam. *Neuroscience Letters, 189*(2), 81–84.

Felt, B. T., & Lozoff, B. (1996). Brain iron and behavior of rats are not normalized by treatment of iron deficiency anemia during early development. *Journal of Nutrition, 126*(3), 693–701.

Ferguson, S. A., Berry, K. J., Hansen, D. K., Wall, K. S., White, G., & Antony, A. C. (2005). Behavioral effects of prenatal folate deficiency in mice. *Birth Defects Research Part A: Clinical and Molecular Teratology, 73*(4), 249–252.

Feron, F., Burne, T. H., Brown, J., Smith, E., McGrath, J. J., Mackay-Sim, A., et al. (2005). Developmental vitamin D3 deficiency alters the adult rat brain. *Brain Research Bulletin, 65*(2), 141–148.

Fusar-Poli, P., & Berger, G. (2012). Eicosapentaenoic acid interventions in schizophrenia: meta-analysis of randomized, placebo-controlled studies. *Journal of Clinical Psychopharmacology, 32*(2), 179–185.

Fusar-Poli, P., & Meyer-Lindenberg, A. (2013). Striatal presynaptic dopamine in schizophrenia, part II: meta-analysis of [(18)F/(11)C]-DOPA PET studies. *Schizophrenia Bulletin, 39*(1), 33–42.

Gama, C. S., Canever, L., Panizzutti, B., Gubert, C., Stertz, L., Massuda, R., et al. (2012). Effects of omega-3 dietary supplement in prevention of positive, negative and cognitive symptoms: a study in adolescent rats with ketamine-induced model of schizophrenia. *Schizophrenia Research, 141*(2–3), 162–167.

Gambling, L., Charania, Z., Hannah, L., Antipatis, C., Lea, R. G., & McArdle, H. J. (2002). Effect of iron deficiency on placental cytokine expression and fetal growth in the pregnant rat. *Biology of Reproduction*, 66(2), 516–523.

Gambling, L., Dunford, S., Wallace, D. I., Zuur, G., Solanky, N., Srai, S. K., et al. (2003). Iron deficiency during pregnancy affects postnatal blood pressure in the rat. *Journal of Physiology*, 552(Pt 2), 603–610.

Gambling, L., Kennedy, C., & McArdle, H. J. (2011). Iron and copper in fetal development. *Seminars in Cell & Developmental Biology*, 22(6), 637–644.

Gates, M. A., Torres, E. M., White, A., Fricker-Gates, R. A., & Dunnett, S. B. (2006). Re-examining the ontogeny of substantia nigra dopamine neurons. *European Journal of Neuroscience*, 23(5), 1384–1390.

Georgieff, M. K., & Innis, S. M. (2005). Controversial nutrients that potentially affect preterm neurodevelopment: essential fatty acids and iron. *Pediatric Research*, 57(5 Pt 2), 99r–103r.

Godfrey, P. S., Toone, B. K., Carney, M. W., Flynn, T. G., Bottiglieri, T., Laundy, M., et al. (1990). Enhancement of recovery from psychiatric illness by methylfolate. *Lancet*, 336(8712), 392–395.

Glaser, B., Ades, A. E., Lewis, S., Emmet, P., Lewis, G., Smith, G. D., Zammit, S. (2010). Perinatal folate-related exposures and risk of psychotic symptoms in the ALSPAC birth cohort. *Schizophrenia Research*, 120(1–3), 177–183.

Gracious, B. L., Finucane, T. L., Friedman-Campbell, M., Messing, S., & Parkhurst, M. N. (2012). Vitamin D deficiency and psychotic features in mentally ill adolescents: a cross-sectional study. *BMC Psychiatry*, 12, 38.

Gray, J. A., Feldon, J., Rawlins, J. N. P., Hemsley, D. R., & Smith, A. D. (1991). The neuropsychology of schizophrenia. *Behavioral Brain Sciences*, 14(01), 1–20.

Grecksch, G., Ruthrich, H., Hollt, V., & Becker, A. (2009). Transient prenatal vitamin D deficiency is associated with changes of synaptic plasticity in the dentate gyrus in adult rats. *Psychoneuroendocrinology*, 34(Suppl. 1), S258–S264.

Guest, P. C., Urday, S., Ma, D., Stelzhammer, V., Harris, L. W., Amess, B., et al. (2012). Proteomic analysis of the maternal protein restriction rat model for schizophrenia: identification of translational changes in hormonal signaling pathways and glutamate neurotransmission. *Proteomics*, 12(23–24), 3580–3589.

Hamazaki, K., Hamazaki, T., & Inadera, H. (2013). Abnormalities in the fatty acid composition of the postmortem entorhinal cortex of patients with schizophrenia, bipolar disorder, and major depressive disorder. *Psychiatry Research*, 210(1), 346–350.

Hamazaki, K., Itomura, M., Huan, M., Nishizawa, H., Sawazaki, S., Tanouchi, M., et al. (2005). Effect of omega-3 fatty acid-containing phospholipids on blood catecholamine concentrations in healthy volunteers: a randomized, placebo-controlled, double-blind trial. *Nutrition*, 21(6), 705–710.

Hare, D., Ayton, S., Bush, A., & Lei, P. (2013). A delicate balance: Iron metabolism and diseases of the brain. *Frontiers in Aging Neuroscience*, 5, 34.

Harms, L. R., Eyles, D. W., McGrath, J. J., Mackay-Sim, A., & Burne, T. H. (2008). Developmental vitamin D deficiency alters adult behaviour in 129/SvJ and C57BL/6J mice. *Behavioural Brain Research*, 187(2), 343–350.

Harrison, P. J., & Weinberger, D. R. (2005). Schizophrenia genes, gene expression, and neuropathology: on the matter of their convergence. *Molecular Psychiatry*, 10(1), 40–68 image 45.

Harvey, L., & Boksa, P. (2013). Do prenatal immune activation and maternal iron deficiency interact to affect neurodevelopment and early behavior in rat offspring? *Brain, Behavior, and Immunity*.

Harvey, L., & Boksa, P. (2014). Additive effects of maternal iron deficiency and prenatal immune activation on adult behaviors in rat offspring. *Brain, Behavior, and Immunity*, 40, 27–37.

Harvey, N. C., Javaid, K., Bishop, N., Kennedy, S., Papageorghiou, A. T., Fraser, R., et al. (2012). MAVIDOS Maternal Vitamin D Osteoporosis Study: study protocol for a randomized controlled trial. The MAVIDOS Study Group. *Trials*, 13, 13.

Hedelin, M., Lof, M., Olsson, M., Lewander, T., Nilsson, B., Hultman, C. M., et al. (2010). Dietary intake of fish, omega-3, omega-6 polyunsaturated fatty acids and vitamin D and the prevalence of psychotic-like symptoms in a cohort of 33,000 women from the general population. *BMC Psychiatry*, 10(1), 38.

Helland, I. B., Smith, L., Saarem, K., Saugstad, O. D., & Drevon, C. A. (2003). Maternal supplementation with very-long-chain n-3 fatty acids during pregnancy and lactation augments children's IQ at 4 years of age. *Pediatrics*, 111(1), e39–e44.

Heresco-Levy, U., Ermilov, M., Lichtenberg, P., Bar, G., & Javitt, D. C. (2004). High-dose glycine added to olanzapine and risperidone for the treatment of schizophrenia. *Biological Psychiatry*, 55(2), 165–171.

Heresco-Levy, U., & Javitt, D. C. (2004). Comparative effects of glycine and D-cycloserine on persistent negative symptoms in schizophrenia: a retrospective analysis. *Schizophrenia Research*, 66(2–3), 89–96.

Hibbeln, J. R., Ferguson, T. A., & Blasbalg, T. L. (2006). Omega-3 fatty acid deficiencies in neurodevelopment, aggression and autonomic dysregulation: opportunities for intervention. *International Review of Psychiatry*, 18(2), 107–118.

Hibbeln, J. R., Linnoila, M., Umhau, J. C., Rawlings, R., George, D. T., & Salem, N., Jr. (1998). Essential fatty acids predict metabolites of serotonin and dopamine in cerebrospinal fluid among healthy control subjects, and early- and late-onset alcoholics. *Biological Psychiatry*, 44(4), 235–242.

Hill, M., Shannahan, K., Jasinski, S., Macklin, E. A., Raeke, L., Roffman, J. L., et al. (2011). Folate supplementation in schizophrenia: a possible role for MTHFR genotype. *Schizophrenia Research*, 127(1–3), 41–45.

Hoen, W. P., Lijmer, J. G., Duran, M., Wanders, R. J., van Beveren, N. J., & de Haan, L. (2013). Red blood cell polyunsaturated fatty acids measured in red blood cells and schizophrenia: a meta-analysis. *Psychiatry Research*, 207(1–2), 1–12.

Hoffer, L. J. (2008). Vitamin therapy in schizophrenia. *Israel Journal of Psychiatry and Related Sciences*, 45(1), 3–10.

Hooks, M. S., & Kalivas, P. W. (1995). The role of mesoaccumbens–pallidal circuitry in novelty-induced behavioral activation. *Neuroscience*, 64(3), 587–597.

Howes, O. D., Bose, S., Turkheimer, F., Valli, I., Egerton, A., Stahl, D., et al. (2011). Progressive increase in striatal dopamine synthesis capacity as patients develop psychosis: a PET study. *Molecular Psychiatry*, 16(9), 885–886.

Howes, O. D., Bose, S. K., Turkheimer, F., Valli, I., Egerton, A., Valmaggia, L. R., et al. (2011). Dopamine synthesis capacity before onset of psychosis: a prospective [18F]-DOPA PET imaging study. *American Journal of Psychiatry*, 168(12), 1311–1317.

Howes, O. D., Kambeitz, J., Kim, E., Stahl, D., Slifstein, M., Abi-Dargham, A., et al. (2012). The nature of dopamine dysfunction in schizophrenia and what this means for treatment. *Archives of General Psychiatry*, 69(8), 776–786.

Howes, O. D., Montgomery, A. J., Asselin, M. C., Murray, R. M., Valli, I., Tabraham, P., et al. (2009). Elevated striatal dopamine function linked to prodromal signs of schizophrenia. *Archives of General Psychiatry*, 66(1), 13–20.

Innis, S. M., & de La Presa Owens, S. (2001). Dietary fatty acid composition in pregnancy alters neurite membrane fatty acids and dopamine in newborn rat brain. *Journal of Nutrition*, 131(1), 118–122.

Insel, B. J., Schaefer, C. A., McKeague, I. W., Susser, E. S., & Brown, A. S. (2008). Maternal iron deficiency and the risk of schizophrenia in offspring. *Archives of General Psychiatry*, 65(10), 1136–1144.

Jamilian, H., Bagherzadeh, K., Nazeri, Z., & Hassanijirdehi, M. (2013). Vitamin D, parathyroid hormone, serum calcium and phosphorus in patients with schizophrenia and major depression. *International Journal of Psychiatry in Clinical Practice*, 17(1), 30–34.

Janowsky, D. S., El-Yousel, M. K., Davis, J. M., & Sekerke, H. J. (1973). Provocation of schizophrenic symptoms by intravenous administration of methylphenidate. *Archives of General Psychiatry, 28*(2), 185–191.

Jiang, W., Yu, Q., Gong, M., Chen, L., Wen, E. Y., Bi, Y., et al. (2012). Vitamin A deficiency impairs postnatal cognitive function via inhibition of neuronal calcium excitability in hippocampus. *Journal of Neurochemistry, 121*(6), 932–943.

Jones, S. R., Gainetdinov, R. R., Wightman, R. M., & Caron, M. G. (1998). Mechanisms of amphetamine action revealed in mice lacking the dopamine transporter. *Journal of Neuroscience, 18*(6), 1979–1986.

Joseph, B., Wallen-Mackenzie, A., Benoit, G., Murata, T., Joodmardi, E., Okret, S., et al. (2003). p57(Kip2) cooperates with Nurr1 in developing dopamine cells. *Proceedings of the National Academy of Sciences of the United States of America, 100*(26), 15619–15624.

Joy, C. B., Mumby-Croft, R., & Joy, L. A. (2006). Polyunsaturated fatty acid supplementation for schizophrenia. *Cochrane Database of Systematic Reviews, 3*, Cd001257.

Kadkhodaei, B., Ito, T., Joodmardi, E., Mattsson, B., Rouillard, C., Carta, M., et al. (2009). Nurr1 is required for maintenance of maturing and adult midbrain dopamine neurons. *Journal of Neuroscience, 29*(50), 15923–15932.

Kale, A., Naphade, N., Sapkale, S., Kamaraju, M., Pillai, A., Joshi, S., et al. (2010). Reduced folic acid, vitamin B12 and docosahexaenoic acid and increased homocysteine and cortisol in never-medicated schizophrenia patients: implications for altered one-carbon metabolism. *Psychiatry Research, 175*(1–2), 47–53.

Kalueff, A. V., Lou, Y. R., Laaksi, I., & Tuohimaa, P. (2004). Increased anxiety in mice lacking vitamin D receptor gene. *NeuroReport, 15*(8), 1271–1274.

Katz, S. H., & Foulks, E. F. (2010). Mineral metabolism and behavior: abnormalities of calcium homeostasis. In Y. A. Cohen (Ed.), *Human adaptation: The biosocial background*. New Brunswish: Transaction Publishers.

Kesby, J. P., Burne, T. H., McGrath, J. J., & Eyles, D. W. (2006). Developmental vitamin D deficiency alters MK 801-induced hyperlocomotion in the adult rat: an animal model of schizophrenia. *Biological Psychiatry, 60*(6), 591–596.

Kesby, J. P., Cui, X., Ko, P., McGrath, J. J., Burne, T. H., & Eyles, D. W. (2009). Developmental vitamin D deficiency alters dopamine turnover in neonatal rat forebrain. *Neuroscience Letters, 461*(2), 155–158.

Kesby, J. P., Cui, X., O'Loan, J., McGrath, J. J., Burne, T. H., & Eyles, D. W. (2010). Developmental vitamin D deficiency alters dopamine-mediated behaviors and dopamine transporter function in adult female rats. *Psychopharmacology (Berl), 208*(1), 159–168.

Kesby, J. P., Eyles, D. W., Burne, T. H., & McGrath, J. J. (2011). The effects of vitamin D on brain development and adult brain function. *Molecular and Cellular Endocrinology, 347*(1–2), 121–127.

Ko, P., Burkert, R., McGrath, J., & Eyles, D. (2004). Maternal vitamin D3 deprivation and the regulation of apoptosis and cell cycle during rat brain development. *Brain Research. Developmental Brain Research, 153*(1), 61–68.

Koenig, J. (2009). Animal models for schizophrenia research*Schizophrenia research forum: A catalyst for creative thinking* . Retrieved October 14, 2014, from http://www.schizophreniaforum.org/res/animal/animal_tables.asp.

Krystal, J. H., Karper, L. P., Seibyl, J. P., Freeman, G. K., Delaney, R., Bremner, J. D., et al. (1994). Subanesthetic effects of the noncompetitive NMDA antagonist, ketamine, in humans. Psychotomimetic, perceptual, cognitive, and neuroendocrine responses. *Archives of General Psychiatry, 51*(3), 199–214.

Lafourcade, M., Larrieu, T., Mato, S., Duffaud, A., Sepers, M., Matias, I., et al. (2011). Nutritional omega-3 deficiency abolishes endocannabinoid-mediated neuronal functions. *Nature Neuroscience, 14*(3), 345–350.

Lahti, A. C., Weiler, M. A., Tamara Michaelidis, B. A., Parwani, A., & Tamminga, C. A. (2001). Effects of ketamine in normal and schizophrenic volunteers. *Neuropsychopharmacology, 25*(4), 455–467.

Lambrot, R., Xu, C., Saint-Phar, S., Chountalos, G., Cohen, T., Paquet, M., et al. (2013). Low paternal dietary folate alters the mouse sperm epigenome and is associated with negative pregnancy outcomes. *Nature Communications, 4*, 2889.

Lante, F., Meunier, J., Guiramand, J., De Jesus Ferreira, M. C., Cambonie, G., Aimar, R., et al. (2008). Late N-acetylcysteine treatment prevents the deficits induced in the offspring of dams exposed to an immune stress during gestation. *Hippocampus, 18*(6), 602–609.

Laruelle, M., Abi-Dargham, A., Gil, R., Kegeles, L., & Innis, R. (1999). Increased dopamine transmission in schizophrenia: relationship to illness phases. *Biological Psychiatry, 46*(1), 56–72.

Levav-Rabkin, T., Blumkin, E., Galron, D., & Golan, H. M. (2011). Sex-dependent behavioral effects of Mthfr deficiency and neonatal GABA potentiation in mice. *Behavioural Brain Research, 216*(2), 505–513.

Levine, J., Stahl, Z., Sela, B. A., Ruderman, V., Shumaico, O., Babushkin, I., et al. (2006). Homocysteine-reducing strategies improve symptoms in chronic schizophrenic patients with hyperhomocysteinemia. *Biological Psychiatry, 60*(3), 265–269.

Li, Y. C., Kong, J., Wei, M., Chen, Z. F., Liu, S. Q., & Cao, L. P. (2002). 1,25-Dihydroxyvitamin D(3) is a negative endocrine regulator of the renin-angiotensin system. *Journal of Clinical Investigation, 110*(2), 229–238.

Lieberman, J. A., Kane, J. M., & Alvir, J. (1987). Provocative tests with psychostimulant drugs in schizophrenia. *Psychopharmacology (Berl), 91*(4), 415–433.

van der Linden, I. J., Afman, L. A., Heil, S. G., & Blom, H. J. (2006). Genetic variation in genes of folate metabolism and neural-tube defect risk. *Proceedings of the Nutrition Society, 65*(2), 204–215.

Lister, J. P., Blatt, G. J., DeBassio, W. A., Kemper, T. L., Tonkiss, J., Galler, J. R., et al. (2005). Effect of prenatal protein malnutrition on numbers of neurons in the principal cell layers of the adult rat hippocampal formation. *Hippocampus, 15*(3), 393–403.

Litonjua, A. A., Lange, N. E., Carey, V. J., Brown, S., Laranjo, N., Harshfield, B. J., et al. (2014). The Vitamin D Antenatal Asthma Reduction Trial (VDAART): rationale, design, and methods of a randomized, controlled trial of vitamin D supplementation in pregnancy for the primary prevention of asthma and allergies in children. *Contemporary Clinical Trials, 38*(1), 37–50.

Lozoff, B., Beard, J., Connor, J., Barbara, F., Georgieff, M., & Schallert, T. (2006). Long-lasting neural and behavioral effects of iron deficiency in infancy. *Nutrition Reviews, 64*(5 Pt 2), S34–S43 discussion S72–91.

Lubow, R. E., & Gewirtz, J. C. (1995). Latent inhibition in humans: data, theory, and implications for schizophrenia. *Psychological Bulletin, 117*(1), 87–103.

Lucock, M., & Daskalakis, I. (2000). New perspectives on folate status: a differential role for the vitamin in cardiovascular disease, birth defects and other conditions. *British Journal of Biomedical Science, 57*(3), 254–260.

Maden, M. (2001). Role and distribution of retinoic acid during CNS development. *International Review of Cytology, 209*, 1–77.

Mahadik, S. P., Evans, D., & Lal, H. (2001). Oxidative stress and role of antioxidant and omega-3 essential fatty acid supplementation in schizophrenia. *Progress in Neuro-Psychopharmacology and Biological Psychiatry, 25*(3), 463–493.

Manuel-Apolinar, L., Rocha, L., Damasio, L., Tesoro-Cruz, E., & Zarate, A. (2014). Role of prenatal undernutrition in the expression of serotonin, dopamine and leptin receptors in adult mice: implications of food intake. *Molecular Medicine Reports, 9*(2), 407–412.

Mao, C. T., Li, T. Y., Qu, P., Zhao, Y., Wang, R., & Liu, Y. X. (2006). Effects of early intervention on learning and memory in young rats of marginal vitamin A deficiency and it's mechanism. *Zhonghua Er Ke Za Zhi, 44*(1), 15–20.

Matte, C., Scherer, E. B., Stefanello, F. M., Barschak, A. G., Vargas, C. R., Netto, C. A., et al. (2007). Concurrent folate treatment prevents Na+, K+-ATPase activity inhibition and memory impairments caused by chronic hyperhomocysteinemia during rat development. *International Journal of Developmental Neuroscience, 25*(8), 545–552.

McCreadie, R. G., Paterson, J. R., Blacklock, C., Wiles, D., Hall, D. J., Graham, J., et al. (2000). Smoking habits and plasma lipid peroxide and vitamin E levels in never-treated first-episode patients with schizophrenia. *British Journal of Psychiatry, 176,* 290–293.

McGrath, J., Eyles, D. W., Pedersen, C. B., Anderson, C., Ko, P., Burne, T. H., et al. (2010). Neonatal vitamin D status and risk of schizophrenia: a population-based case-control study. *Archives of General Psychiatry, 67*(9), 889–894.

McGrath, J., Iwazaki, T., Eyles, D., Burne, T., Cui, X., Ko, P., et al. (2008). Protein expression in the nucleus accumbens of rats exposed to developmental vitamin D deficiency. *PLoS One.*

McGrath, J., Saari, K., Hakko, H., Jokelainen, J., Jones, P., Jarvelin, M. R., et al. (2004). Vitamin D supplementation during the first year of life and risk of schizophrenia: a Finnish birth cohort study. *Schizophrenia Research, 67*(2–3), 237–245.

McGrath, J., Eyles, D., Mowry, B., Yolken, R., Buka, S. (2003). Low maternal vitamin D as a risk factor for schizophrenia: a pilot study using banked sera. *Schizophrenia Research, 63,* 73–78.

Meyer, U., Engler, A., Weber, L., Schedlowski, M., & Feldon, J. (2008). Preliminary evidence for a modulation of fetal dopaminergic development by maternal immune activation during pregnancy. *Neuroscience, 154*(2), 701–709.

Meyer, U., & Feldon, J. (2009). Prenatal exposure to infection: a primary mechanism for abnormal dopaminergic development in schizophrenia. *Psychopharmacology (Berl), 206*(4), 587–602.

Meyer, U., & Feldon, J. (2010). Epidemiology-driven neurodevelopmental animal models of schizophrenia. *Progress in Neurobiology, 90*(3), 285–326.

Mokler, D. J., Torres, O. I., Galler, J. R., & Morgane, P. J. (2007). Stress-induced changes in extracellular dopamine and serotonin in the medial prefrontal cortex and dorsal hippocampus of prenatally malnourished rats. *Brain Research, 1148,* 226–233.

Morath, D. J., & Mayer-Proschel, M. (2002). Iron deficiency during embryogenesis and consequences for oligodendrocyte generation in vivo. *Developmental Neuroscience, 24*(2–3), 197–207.

Morgane, P. J., Mokler, D. J., & Galler, J. R. (2002). Effects of prenatal protein malnutrition on the hippocampal formation. *Neuroscience & Biobehavioral Reviews, 26*(4), 471–483.

Oberhelman, S. S., Meekins, M. E., Fischer, P. R., Lee, B. R., Singh, R. J., Cha, S. S., et al. (2013). Maternal vitamin D supplementation to improve the vitamin D status of breast-fed infants: a randomized controlled trial. *Mayo Clinic Proceedings, 88*(12), 1378–1387.

Olney, J. W., & Farber, N. B. (1995). Glutamate receptor dysfunction and schizophrenia. *Archives of General Psychiatry, 52*(12), 998–1007.

O'Loan, J., Eyles, D. W., Kesby, J., Ko, P., McGrath, J. J., & Burne, T. H. (2007). Vitamin D deficiency during various stages of pregnancy in the rat; its impact on development and behaviour in adult offspring. *Psychoneuroendocrinology, 32*(3), 227–234.

Palmer, A. A., Brown, A. S., Keegan, D., Siska, L. D., Susser, E., Rotrosen, J., et al. (2008). Prenatal protein deprivation alters dopamine-mediated behaviors and dopaminergic and glutamatergic receptor binding. *Brain Research, 1237,* 62–74.

Palmer, A. A., Printz, D. J., Butler, P. D., Dulawa, S. C., & Printz, M. P. (2004). Prenatal protein deprivation in rats induces changes in prepulse inhibition and NMDA receptor binding. *Brain Research, 996*(2), 193–201.

Pang, Y., Rodts-Palenik, S., Cai, Z., Bennett, W. A., & Rhodes, P. G. (2005). Suppression of glial activation is involved in the protection of IL-10 on maternal *E. coli* induced neonatal white matter injury. *Developmental Brain Research, 157*(2), 141–149.

Pardey, M. C., Kumar, N. N., Goodchild, A. K., & Cornish, J. L. (2013). Catecholamine receptors differentially mediate impulsive choice in the medial prefrontal and orbitofrontal cortex. *Journal of Psychopharmacology, 27*(2), 203–212.

Pauling, L. (1968). Orthomolecular psychiatry: varying the concentrations of substances normally present in the human body may control mental disease. *Science, 160*(3825), 265–271.

Petrie, W. M., & Ban, T. A. (1985). Vitamins in psychiatry. Do they have a role? *Drugs, 30*(1), 58–65.

Petronijevic, N. D., Radonjic, N. V., Ivkovic, M. D., Marinkovic, D., Piperski, V. D., Duricic, B. M., et al. (2008). Plasma homocysteine levels in young male patients in the exacerbation and remission phase of schizophrenia. *Progress in Neuro-Psychopharmacology and Biological Psychiatry, 32*(8), 1921–1926.

Ranade, S. C., Rose, A., Rao, M., Gallego, J., Gressens, P., & Mani, S. (2008). Different types of nutritional deficiencies affect different domains of spatial memory function checked in a radial arm maze. *Neuroscience, 152*(4), 859–866.

Reddy, R., Fleet-Michaliszyn, S., Condray, R., Yao, J. K., Keshavan, M. S., & Reddy, R. (2011). Reduction in perseverative errors with adjunctive ethyl-eicosapentaenoic acid in patients with schizophrenia: preliminary study. *Prostaglandins, Leukotrienes, and Essential Fatty Acids, 84*(3–4), 79–83.

Reynolds, B. A., & Rietze, R. L. (2005). Neural stem cells and neurospheres–re-evaluating the relationship. *Nature Methods, 2*(5), 333–336.

Robertson, S. A., Care, A. S., & Skinner, R. J. (2007). Interleukin 10 regulates inflammatory cytokine synthesis to protect against lipopolysaccharide-induced abortion and fetal growth restriction in mice. *Biology of Reproduction, 76*(5), 738–748.

Robertson, S. A., Skinner, R. J., & Care, A. S. (2006). Essential role for IL-10 in resistance to lipopolysaccharide-induced preterm labor in mice. *Journal of Immunology, 177*(7), 4888–4896.

Roffman, J. L., Lamberti, J. S., Achtyes, E., Macklin, E. A., Galendez, G. C., Raeke, L. H., et al. (2013). Randomized multicenter investigation of folate plus vitamin B12 supplementation in schizophrenia. *JAMA Psychiatry, 70*(5), 481–489.

Ross, R. G., Hunter, S. K., McCarthy, L., Beuler, J., Hutchison, A. K., Wagner, B. D., et al. (2013). Perinatal choline effects on neonatal pathophysiology related to later schizophrenia risk. *American Journal of Psychiatry, 170*(3), 290–298.

Roth, D. E., Al Mahmud, A., Raqib, R., Akhtar, E., Perumal, N., Pezzack, B., et al. (2013). Randomized placebo-controlled trial of high-dose prenatal third-trimester vitamin D3 supplementation in Bangladesh: the AViDD trial. *Nutrition Journal, 12*(1), 47.

Salami, M., Talaei, S. A., Davari, S., & Taghizadeh, M. (2011). Hippocampal long term potentiation in rats under different regimens of vitamin D: an in vivo study. *Neuroscience Letters.*

Sanchez, B., Relova, J. L., Gallego, R., Ben-Batalla, I., & Perez-Fernandez, R. (2009). 1,25-Dihydroxyvitamin D3 administration to 6-hydroxydopamine-lesioned rats increases glial cell line-derived neurotrophic factor and partially restores tyrosine hydroxylase expression in substantia nigra and striatum. *Journal of Neuroscience Research, 87*(3), 723–732.

Shenton, M. E., Dickey, C. C., Frumin, M., & McCarley, R. W. (2001). A review of MRI findings in schizophrenia. *Schizophrenia Research, 49*(1–2), 1–52.

Shultz, P. L., Galler, J. R., & Tonkiss, J. (1999). Prenatal protein restriction increases sensitization to cocaine-induced stereotypy. *Behavioural Pharmacology, 10*(4), 379–387.

Simpson, E. H., Kellendonk, C., & Kandel, E. (2010). A possible role for the striatum in the pathogenesis of the cognitive symptoms of schizophrenia. *Neuron, 65*(5), 585–596.

Smidt, M. P., & Burbach, J. P. (2007). How to make a mesodiencephalic dopaminergic neuron. *Nature Reviews Neuroscience, 8*(1), 21–32.

Sorensen, H. J., Nielsen, P. R., Pedersen, C. B., & Mortensen, P. B. (2011). Association between prepartum maternal iron deficiency and off-spring risk of schizophrenia: population-based cohort study with linkage of Danish national registers. *Schizophrenia Bulletin, 37*(5), 982–987.

St Clair, D., Xu, M., Wang, P., Yu, Y., Fang, Y., Zhang, F., et al. (2005). Rates of adult schizophrenia following prenatal exposure to the Chinese famine of 1959–1961. *JAMA, 294*(5), 557–562.

Sullivan, S., Wills, A., Lawlor, D., McGrath, J., & Zammit, S. (2013). Prenatal vitamin D status and risk of psychotic experiences at age 18 years-a longitudinal birth cohort. *Schizophrenia Research, 148*(1–3), 87–92.

Sulzer, D., Maidment, N. T., & Rayport, S. (1993). Amphetamine and other weak bases act to promote reverse transport of dopamine in ventral midbrain neurons. *Journal of Neurochemistry, 60*(2), 527–535.

Susser, E., Brown, A. S., Klonowski, E., Allen, R. H., & Lindenbaum, J. (1998). Schizophrenia and impaired homocysteine metabolism: a possible association. *Biological Psychiatry, 44*(2), 141–143.

Susser, E., Neugebauer, R., Hoek, H. W., Brown, A. S., Lin, S., Labovitz, D., et al. (1996). Schizophrenia after prenatal famine. Further evidence. *Archives of General Psychiatry, 53*(1), 25–31.

Susser, E., St Clair, D., & He, L. (2008). Latent effects of prenatal malnutrition on adult health: the example of schizophrenia. *Annals of the New York Academy of Sciences, 1136,* 185–192.

Swerdlow, N. R., Stephany, N., Wasserman, L. C., Talledo, J., Sharp, R., & Auerbach, P. P. (2003). Dopamine agonists disrupt visual latent inhibition in normal males using a within-subject paradigm. *Psychopharmacology (Berl), 169*(3–4), 314–320.

Tafti, M., & Ghyselinck, N. B. (2007). Functional implication of the vitamin A signaling pathway in the brain. *Archives of Neurology, 64*(12), 1706–1711.

Tekes, K., Gyenge, M., Folyovich, A., & Csaba, G. (2009). Influence of neonatal vitamin A or vitamin D treatment on the concentration of biogenic amines and their metabolites in the adult rat brain. *Hormone and Metabolic Research, 41*(4), 277–280.

Tekes, K., Gyenge, M., Hantos, M., & Csaba, G. (2009). Transgenerational hormonal imprinting caused by vitamin A and vitamin D treatment of newborn rats. Alterations in the biogenic amine contents of the adult brain. *Brain & Development, 31*(9), 666–670.

Thakurathi, N., Stock, S., Oppenheim, C. E., Borba, C. P., Vincenzi, B., Seidman, L. J., et al. (2013). Open-label pilot study on vitamin D(3) supplementation for antipsychotic-associated metabolic anomalies. *International Clinical Psychopharmacology, 28*(5), 275–282.

Tishkoff, D. X., Nibbelink, K. A., Holmberg, K. H., Dandu, L., & Simpson, R. U. (2008). Functional vitamin D receptor (VDR) in the t-tubules of cardiac myocytes: VDR knockout cardiomyocyte contractility. *Endocrinology, 149*(2), 558–564.

Tolppanen, A. M., Sayers, A., Fraser, W. D., Lewis, G., Zammit, S., McGrath, J., et al. (2012). Serum 25-hydroxyvitamin D3 and D2 and non-clinical psychotic experiences in childhood. *PLoS One, 7*(7), e41575.

Tonkiss, J., Almeida, S. S., & Galler, J. R. (1998). Prenatally malnourished female but not male rats show increased sensitivity to MK-801 in a differential reinforcement of low rates task. *Behavioural Pharmacology, 9*(1), 49–60.

Turner, K. M., Young, J. W., McGrath, J. J., Eyles, D. W., & Burne, T. H. (2013). Cognitive performance and response inhibition in developmentally vitamin D (DVD)-deficient rats. *Behavioural Brain Research, 242,* 47–53.

Vaughan, K., & McConaghy, N. (1999). Megavitamin and dietary treatment in schizophrenia: a randomised, controlled trial. *Australian & New Zealand Journal of Psychiatry, 33*(1), 84–88.

Veenstra, T. D., Prufer, K., Koenigsberger, C., Brimijoin, S. W., Grande, J. P., & Kumar, R. (1998). 1,25-Dihydroxyvitamin D3 receptors in the central nervous system of the rat embryo. *Brain Research, 804*(2), 193–205.

Vucetic, Z., Totoki, K., Schoch, H., Whitaker, K. W., Hill-Smith, T., Lucki, I., et al. (2010). Early life protein restriction alters dopamine circuitry. *Neuroscience, 168*(2), 359–370.

Wallen, A. A., Castro, D. S., Zetterstrom, R. H., Karlen, M., Olson, L., Ericson, J., et al. (2001). Orphan nuclear receptor Nurr1 is essential for Ret expression in midbrain dopamine neurons and in the brain stem. *Molecular and Cellular Neuroscience, 18*(6), 649–663.

Wang, J. Y., Wu, J. N., Cherng, T. L., Hoffer, B. J., Chen, H. H., Borlongan, C. V., et al. (2001). Vitamin D-3 attenuates 6-hydroxy-dopamine-induced neurotoxicity in rats. *Brain Research, 904*(1), 67–75.

Weinberger, D. R. (1987). Implications of normal brain development for the pathogenesis of schizophrenia. *Archives of General Psychiatry, 44*(7), 660–669.

Wieczorek, W. J., & Kruk, Z. L. (1994). Differential action of (+)-amphetamine on electrically evoked dopamine overflow in rat brain slices containing corpus striatum and nucleus accumbens. *British Journal of Pharmacology, 111*(3), 829–836.

Wong, K. E., Szeto, F. L., Zhang, W., Ye, H., Kong, J., Zhang, Z., et al. (2009). Involvement of the vitamin D receptor in energy metabolism: regulation of uncoupling proteins. *American Journal of Physiology. Endocrinology and Metabolism, 296*(4), E820–E828.

Woods, S. W., Walsh, B. C., Hawkins, K. A., Miller, T. J., Saksa, J. R., D'Souza, D. C., et al. (2013). Glycine treatment of the risk syndrome for psychosis: report of two pilot studies. *European Neuropsychopharmacology, 23*(8), 931–940.

Xiang, W., Kong, J., Chen, S., Cao, L. P., Qiao, G., Zheng, W., et al. (2005). Cardiac hypertrophy in vitamin D receptor knockout mice: role of the systemic and cardiac renin-angiotensin systems. *American Journal of Physiology. Endocrinology and Metabolism, 288*(1), E125–E132.

Xu, M. Q., Sun, W. S., Liu, B. X., Feng, G. Y., Yu, L., Yang, L., et al. (2009). Prenatal malnutrition and adult schizophrenia: further evidence from the 1959–1961 Chinese famine. *Schizophrenia Bulletin, 35*(3), 568–576.

Yung, A. R., & Nelson, B. (2011). Young people at ultra high risk for psychosis: a research update. *Early Intervention in Psychiatry, 1*(5 Suppl.), 52–57.

Yung, A. R., Phillips, L. J., McGorry, P. D., McFarlane, C. A., Francey, S., Harrigan, S., et al. (1998). Prediction of psychosis. A step towards indicated prevention of schizophrenia. *British Journal of Psychiatry. Supplement, 172*(33), 14–20.

Zetterstrom, R. H., Solomin, L., Jansson, L., Hoffer, B. J., Olson, L., & Perlmann, T. (1997). Dopamine neuron agenesis in Nurr1-deficient mice. *Science, 276*(5310), 248–250.

Zugno, A. I., Chipindo, H. L., Volpato, A. M., Budni, J., Steckert, A. V., de Oliveira, et al. (2014). Omega-3 prevents behavior response and brain oxidative damage in the ketamine model of schizophrenia. *Neuroscience, 259,* 223–231.

Genetic Models

16

Mouse Models of Schizophrenia: Risk Genes

Lieve Desbonnet

School of Life Sciences, University of Glasgow, Glasgow, UK

INTRODUCTION

Genetics play a major role in the etiology of schizophrenia and, although this disorder is associated with more than 80% heritability (Sullivan, Kendler, & Neale, 2003), it is not inherited in a classical Mendelian fashion whereby dominant recessive or gender-linked inheritance patterns preside. As a result, two hypotheses exist to account for genetic contribution to etiology of schizophrenia, the first considers a number of interacting susceptibility genes of small effect that increase disease risk ("common disease, common variant" hypothesis), whereas the second proposes that single rare gene mutations of large effect accounts for pathophysiology in the majority of schizophrenia cases ("common disease, multiple variant" hypothesis), which is supported by the recent discovery of a relatively rare class of variants known as copy number variants that confer a high risk for schizophrenia (Doherty, O'Donovan, & Owen, 2012; Owen, Williams, & O'Donovan, 2009). It is proposed that the cumulative effects of multiple schizophrenia-associated gene loci abnormalities, whether they are inherited or occur as a result of spontaneous mutations, can, in the context of epigenetic or environmental factors, exceed a threshold where post-symptoms of the disorder become manifest (Escudero & Johnstone, 2014).

Advancements in molecular genetic technologies have uncovered convincing evidence to support the proposition that genetic heterogeneity plays a major part in the variability observed in clinical presentations of the disorder. Linkage analyses, which identify regions of the genome cotransmitted with schizophrenia in families with multiple affected members, have exposed a number of chromosomal regions that contain schizophrenia-risk alleles, including the 8p21–22 and 22q11–12 chromosomes (Owen, Williams, O'Donovan, 2004). Unfortunately, this approach is limited by the size and genetic architecture of the sample and is more suited to detecting candidate genes of large effect, which are less likely to be linked to the etiopathology of the disorder in the greater population than multiple genes of small effect. Genetic association approaches and the more recent contributions from genome-wide association studies (GWAS) have highlighted a number of disease-related genes of relatively small effect that may have relevance in the pathophysiology of schizophrenia (Ripke et al., 2013; Schizophrenia Working Group of the Psychiatric Genomics Consortium, 2014). Further examination of the putative roles of candidate genes is necessary to understand the specific involvement of genes identified by linkage and association studies in the pathogenesis of schizophrenia before any cumulative effects of gene–gene or gene–environment interaction are considered. The generation and phenotypic assessment of mutant mouse models of identified risk genes allows direct associations to be made between these genes, specific pathological processes, and behavioral phenotypes and hence sheds light on genetic contributions to the pathophysiology of schizophrenia. This "top-down" approach has significantly contributed to the steadily increasing pool of knowledge regarding the genetic etiology of schizophrenia (Desbonnet, O'Tuathaigh, & Waddington, 2012; O'Tuathaigh, Kirby, Moran, & Waddington, 2010). In turn, the ability to perform detailed analyses of genes involved in the regulation of related and intersecting neuropathological endophenotypes of schizophrenia in mutant animal models has also uncovered novel candidate genes for the genetic study in humans (bottom-up approach). At present, several promising mutant mouse models are being used in the field of neuroscience. Many of these genetic models have been engineered as a result of initial findings in human linkage and association analyses (e.g., neuregulin1, disrupted-in-schizophrenia1, dysbindin genes). Others are based on the putative involvement of specific genes in pathophysiological processes in schizophrenia (e.g., COMT, dopamine receptors, glutamate receptors).

ENDOPHENOTYPES

The heterogeneity of disease onset, course, and symptoms and the lack of consistent and quantifiable disease features in schizophrenia make it difficult to deconstruct the disorder into simpler forms that are reproducible in mouse models. Refining schizophrenia symptoms into separate, discernible subcategories that relate more closely to the underlying cause than the overt clinical features facilitates investigations into the etiopathology of the illness (Waddington et al., 2007). Endophenotypes are defined as measurable intermediate disease features that bridge the gap between the overt manifestations of schizophrenia and the underlying susceptibility genes (Gould & Gottesman, 2006). These variables are not always obvious to the naked eye and can be neurophysiological, biochemical, endocrinological, neuroanatomical, cognitive, or neuropsychological in nature (Allen, Griss, Folley, Hawkins, & Pearlson, 2009). The use of endophenotypes has been particularly advantageous for the development of animal models of schizophrenia, being relatively closer to the genetic source of the illness, and therefore considerably less complex to model. It is assumed that although a single gene can affect multiple behavioral endpoints, the intermediate biological endophenotypes are subject to fewer confounding influences, and as a result are "simpler" and more amenable to the scientific study.

CONSTITUTIVE, CONDITIONAL KNOCKOUTS, AND TRANSGENIC MODELS

Technological advances now allow for the construction of mutant mice with gene disruption, either by deletion (i.e., knockout) or insertion/overexpression (i.e., transgenic/knock-in); phenotypic assessment of these mice has greatly contributed to our understanding of the role of candidate risk genes in normal biological functions and in disease pathogenesis (O'Sullivan et al., 2006). However, each technique presents its own profile of advantages and disadvantage. Pleiotropy, which occurs when a single gene influences multiple phenotypic traits thereby potentially masking specific phenotypic effects associated with its deletion, often complicates the interpretation of results in studies using conventional models. The development of transgenic approaches, which permits the insertion of specific genetic sequences in mice, presented novel opportunities to investigate the phenotypic consequences of gene overexpression and the insertion of human mutated genes in vivo (Bockamp et al., 2002). As well as informing on the potential involvement of enhanced expression of certain risk genes in the pathogenesis of schizophrenia, transgenic models have also successfully been used to reverse phenotypes in isolated conventional mouse knockouts. The development of spatially and temporally controlled gene deletions, generally known as conditional knockouts, has made a significant contribution to the validity of genetic knockout models for schizophrenia by minimizing some of the possible drawbacks including compensatory and redundancy mechanisms, embryonic lethality, pleiotropic factors, and the lack of clarity that comes from deletion of a gene that is expressed ubiquitously (Beglopoulos & Shen, 2004). Temporal control of gene expression requires the use of inducible Cre lines, involving Cre promoters that are responsive to specific compounds, so that the administration of these compounds at any point during development will trigger the inactivation of the target gene (O'Neal & Agah, 2007). Applying spatial and temporal restrictions to risk-gene expression in a single genetic model has provided unique opportunities to answers increasingly complex biological questions in this disorder.

NEUREGULIN 1

The neuregulins are a family of growth factors encoded by four genes (NRG 1–4). Since its initial identification in an Icelandic patient sample more than a decade ago (Stefansson et al., 2002), NRG1 remains one of the best characterized schizophrenia risk genes, not only because of extensive studies conducted in human postmortem brain tissue (Hashimoto et al., 2004; Law et al., 2006; Parlapani et al., 2010; Weickert, Tiwari, Schofield, Mowry, & Fullerton, 2012), cell lines (Brennand & Gage, 2012), and GWAS (Agim et al., 2013; Athanasiu et al., 2010; Shi et al., 2009; Sullivan et al., 2008), but also mutant mouse models have proven to be a valuable source of evidence linking NRG1 gene disruption and the pathobiology of schizophrenia (Allen et al., 2008; Bertram, 2008; Gogos, 2007; Harrison & Law, 2006; Mei & Nave, 2014; Mei & Xiong, 2008; O'Tuathaigh, Desbonnet, & Waddington, 2009; Waddington et al., 2007). In the brain, interactions between NRG1 and membrane-associated tyrosine kinases (ErbBs) initiate an array of intracellular signaling pathways that play important roles in neurodevelopment processes relevant to schizophrenia including neuronal migration, myelination, neuronal survival, and plasticity that affect various populations of neurons and a number of neurotransmitters in the brain such as GABA, dopamine, acetylcholine, and glutamate (Andersson et al., 2012; Buonanno, 2010; Harrison & Law, 2006;

Lundgaard et al., 2013; Mei & Xiong, 2008; O'Tuathaigh et al., 2009). These effects of NRG1 signaling are particularly evident in the frontal cortex and hippocampus, brain areas that are associated with negative and cognitive symptoms in schizophrenia (Buonanno, 2010; Hashimoto et al., 2004; Mei & Xiong, 2008; Petryshen et al., 2005). Despite its obvious importance in the regulation of neurotransmission and neuronal development, there is some ambiguity relating to whether pathology can be attributed to loss of function or selective gain of function of the NRG1 gene. For the most part, increases in the expression of NRG1 and its receptor ErbB4 have been demonstrated in postmortem analysis of brain tissue of affected individuals (Hashimoto et al., 2004; Joshi, Fullerton, & Weickert, 2014; Law et al., 2006; Parlapani et al., 2010; Weickert et al., 2012), yet both mouse models with deficient expression of NRG1 (Boucher et al., 2007; Moy et al., 2009; O'Tuathaigh et al., 2006; Stefansson et al., 2002) and overexpression (Deakin et al., 2009, 2012; Luo, He, Hu, & Yan, 2014; Nawa, Sotoyama, Iwakura, Takei, & Namba, 2014; Yin et al., 2013), particularly in early postnatal life (Kato et al., 2011; Nawa et al., 2014), induce similar pathobiology and behavioral impairments in these mice, suggesting a complex molecular basis for NRG1 involvement in the pathogenesis of schizophrenia.

To add further complexity to the task of modeling NRG1-associated pathophysiology in rodents, at least 30 different known isoforms of NRG1 have been identified in humans, which in turn belong to six distinct families (types I–VI). Targeted mutations of these various isoforms have elucidated some of their specific functions.

NRG1 Transmembrane Domain Mutant

Because NRG1 is crucial to normal development of vital organs such as the heart and lungs, mutants with homozygous deletions die in mid-embryogenesis or shortly after birth. As a result, the vast majority of studies are conducted using heterozygous mutant animals. Most NRG1 proteins are synthesized with a transmembrane (TM) domain. Mice with a heterozygous deletion of the TM domain (generated from a C57BL/6 background strain) exhibit hyperactivity in anxiety- and exploration-related tasks (Boucher et al., 2007; van den Buuse et al., 2009; Karl et al., 2007; O'Tuathaigh et al., 2006, 2008; Stefansson et al., 2002), an effect that is ameliorated with antipsychotic treatment (Stefansson et al., 2002), deficits in prepulse inhibition (PPI) (Stefansson et al., 2002), a selective impairment in response to social novelty (O'Tuathaigh et al., 2007) and altered patterns of social interaction in dyadic encounters (O'Tuathaigh et al., 2007, 2008). Detailed, ethologically based assessment reveals sex-specific effects on individual topographies of exploratory behavior and their subsequent

habituation to the environment (O'Tuathaigh et al., 2006). Investigations into the potential neurological underpinnings of behavioral abnormalities have revealed deficits in N-methyl-D-aspartate (NMDA) receptor channel modulation (Bjarnadottir et al., 2007), elevated levels of the serotonin 2A receptor and serotonin transporter (Dean et al., 2008), and an increase in c-Fos (a marker of neuronal activation) following exposure to the stress of behavioral testing (Boucher et al., 2007a) in schizophrenia-related brain regions of mutants when compared with wild-type mice. Interactions between this mutation and environmental impact have also been examined in recent years with interesting findings relating to effects of prenatal infection, adolescent psychosocial stress, acute restraint stress, and Δ^9-tetrahydrocannabinol (the main psychoactive constituent of cannabis) on adult behavioral and neurochemical phenotypes (Boucher et al., 2007a, 2007; Chesworth et al., 2012; Chohan, Boucher, et al., 2014; Chohan, Nguyen, et al., 2014; Desbonnet et al., 2012; Long et al., 2013; O'Leary et al., 2014) and have contributed to the growing appreciation for the importance of gene × environment models among preclinical researchers.

NRG1 Isoform-Specific Mutant

As the heterozygous deletion of the NRG1 TM domain is likely to affect multiple isoforms containing this domain, it is not surprising that some overlap exists with regard to the phenotypic expression of this particular mutant and the more isoform-specific mutant mice. Phenotypic discrepancies between various NRG1 isoform knockouts can be particularly informative with respect to the specific contributions of these gene products to schizophrenia endophenotyes. For example, the type III NRG1$^{+/-}$ knockout mice display more pronounced deficits in PPI than those exhibited by TM-NRG1$^{+/-}$ mice, but also demonstrate impairments in working memory performance that were not identified in TM-NRG1$^{+/-}$ mutants, and are likely to be associated with the reduced dendritic spine density, enlarged lateral ventricles, and hypofunctionality of the medial prefrontal cortex and CA1 region of the hippocampus observed in these mice (Chen et al., 2008a). Type III NRG1$^{+/-}$ mutants do not exhibit any signs of increased aggression as was described in TM-NRG1$^{+/-}$ mice, which suggests that TM-containing NRG1 isoforms other than type III are involved in the expression of this endophenotype. In addition, NRG1 type III has been implicated in the regulation of α7 nAChR expression on the surface of axons (Hancock, Canetta, Role, & Talmage, 2008), which is interesting considering that the administration of nicotine attenuates some working memory and sensorimotor deficits (George et al., 2006; Postma et al., 2006), and that it is not uncommon for schizophrenia patients to self-medicate with nicotine (Kumari & Postma, 2005). What is intriguing is that in the type III NRG1$^{+/-}$ mutants (Chen et al., 2008), targeted disruption of type I/type II NRG1 (NRG1 isoforms containing an immunoglobulin-like domain) in mice (Rimer, Barrett, Maldonado, Vock, & Gonzalez-Lima, 2005), and NRG1 type II transgenic rats (Taylor, Markham, Taylor, Kanaskie, & Koenig, 2011) all fail to exhibit the hyperactivity, which is the characteristic of the TM-NRG1$^{+/-}$ knockouts. Immunoglobulin -NRG1$^{+/-}$ mutant mice and male NRG1 type II transgenic rats also perform normally in the PPI test and motor function tasks when tested in adulthood (Rimer et al., 2005; Taylor, Markham, et al., 2011). Whereas the mutant mice show signs of impaired latent inhibition (Rimer et al., 2005), the transgenic rats exhibit deficits in visuospatial learning and memory (Taylor, Taylor, & Koenig, 2012). Overall, a detailed analysis of the genotype–phenotype relationships of the various isoform-specific mutant models is complicated by the diversity of behavioral tests adopted and the different species of animals used. A more comprehensive and consistent approach to phenotypic assessment is required to provide some much-needed insight into the relative importance of specific isoforms to the pathogenesis of schizophrenia.

NRG1-Overexpressing Transgenic Mutants

As mentioned previously, mice overexpressing NRG1 also exhibit a schizophrenia-like phenotype. A transgenic mouse line selectively overexpressing NRG1 type 1, an isoform that is reported to be increased in postmortem schizophrenia tissue, was generated with the intention of investigating the role of this isoform in a genetic model with greater construct validity (Deakin et al., 2009, 2012). These mice exhibit impaired working memory, reduced PPI, and altered frequency of gamma oscillations in the hippocampus, but certain phenotypes present in NRG1 hypomorphs such as hyperactivity and decreased long-term potentiation (LTP) were not observed in the type 1 isoform overexpressing mice (Deakin et al., 2009, 2012). Separate lines of transgenic mice that express similar increases in the type 1 isoform were reported to have opposing effects on locomotor activity; increases in the full-length NRG1 isoform reducing locomotor activity (Kato et al., 2010), whereas overexpression of the B-site APP-cleaving enzyme 1 (BACE-1)–cleaved secreted form to NRG1 induced hyperactivity (Luo et al., 2014), the latter being consistent with observations in NRG1 hypomorphs. Surprisingly, this overlap of the phenotypic outcome in NRG1 overexpressing mice and NRG1 hypomorphs also extends to effects on social and cognitive behaviors (Kato et al., 2010; Luo et al., 2014). Forebrain-specific NRG1 type 1 overexpression induces schizophrenia-like impairments in PPI, social behavior, spatial

working memory, and reference memory in addition to hyperactivity and hypofunction of glutamate and GABA pathways in adult transgenic mice which are conducive with reports in NRG1-deficient mice (Yin et al., 2013). Interestingly, all of these effects on the phenotype were normalized when expression of the NRG1 transgene was switched off in adulthood, confirming that continuous NRG1 abnormality is required for the behavioral and neurochemical deficits to endure (Yin et al., 2013). It is not clear why reduced and elevated expression of the same gene induces similar deficits in mice. A possible explanation is that a U-shaped relationship exists between NRG1 expression and pathophysiology in the brain during development, whereby normal function requires an intermediate level of NRG1 expression but abnormally low or high levels of NRG1 signaling trigger pathological mechanisms with overlapping effects on the adult phenotype.

ErbB and BACE1 Mutants

There are a number of proteins that influence NRG1 signaling in the brain. These include the various ErbB receptors that bind NRG1, but also BACE-1, which is involved in proteolytic cleavage of NRG1 allowing binding of the N-terminal domain to ErbB receptors. Mutant mouse models of the genes encoding these proteins have provided valuable information about their respective roles in NRG1-mediated pathophysiology, and as a consequence also contribute to our knowledge of NRG1 involvement in schizophrenia. Mutants with heterozygous deletion of the ErbB4 receptor, but not ErbB2 or ErbB3, show hyperactivity in the open field environment (Gerlai, Pisacane, & Erickson, 2000), PPI deficits (Shamir et al., 2012) and reduced dendritic spine density in the prefrontal cortex (Cooper & Koleske, 2014). Conditional ErbB4 knockout mice with selective loss of ErbB4 in fast-spiking interneurons exhibit similar hyperactivity in novel environments, but also display abnormal emotional responses and impaired social and cognitive behaviors, implicating ErbB4 function in interneurons in NRG1-associated pathogenesis in schizophrenia (Del Pino et al., 2013). In contrast, a hypoactive phenotype has been described in mutants with loss of ErbB signaling in oligodendrocytes (Roy et al., 2007). Mutants with knockout of BACE1 demonstrate hyperactivity with disruption to PPI and heightened responsivity to MK-801 (Savonenko et al., 2008). Conversely, transgenic mice overexpressing BACE1 and consequently possessing increased NRG1 N-terminal fragments also exhibit a similar schizophrenia-like behavioral phenotype which is associated with decreased NMDA receptors (Luo et al., 2014). Similar to the overexpressing NRG1 transgenic mice, the latter study provides further evidence to suggest that the role of NRG1 signaling in the pathophysiology of schizophrenia is not as clear as originally assumed.

DISRUPTED IN SCHIZOPHRENIA 1

The disrupted-in-schizophrenia 1 (DISC1) gene, located at the breakpoint of a balanced t(1;11) chromosomal translocation, was first discovered when a genetic linkage study conducted in a Scottish sample found this gene to segregate in a statistically significant manner with mental illnesses, including schizophrenia (Bradshaw & Porteous, 2012; Chubb, Bradshaw, Soares, Porteous, & Millar, 2008). This finding has subsequently been replicated in a variety of ethnic groups worldwide (Hennah & Porteous, 2009; Hodgkinson et al., 2004; Porteous, Millar, Brandon, & Sawa, 2011; Qu et al., 2007). Although the precise functions of the DISC1 gene remain unclear, it is reported to be maximally expressed in the brain, particularly during fetal development, but is also expressed in the adult hippocampus. DISC1 is a scaffold protein and its main feature is its ability to interact with multiple cytoskeletal proteins, including phosphodiesterase 4B (Millar et al., 2005), which is a direct target for rolipram, a nonselective PDE4 inhibitor that possesses antipsychotic and antidepressant properties (Menniti, Chappie, Humphrey, & Schmidt, 2007). Hence, DISC1 is involved in numerous divergent pathways that regulate neurodevelopmental processes including neurite outgrowth, cell migration, synapse formation, and cell signaling (Mackie, Millar, & Porteous, 2007). Clinical investigations have also shown that DISC1 is associated with neurocognitive deficits; specifically, spatial and working memory impairments and neuroimaging analyses have uncovered region-specific morphological alterations in schizophrenia-relevant brain areas such as the hippocampus and prefrontal cortex (Burdick et al., 2005; Callicott et al., 2005; Cannon et al., 2005; Hennah et al., 2007). Similar neurocognitive deficits have been reported in DISC1 mutant mice.

DISC1 Mutants

Several DISC1 transgenic mice currently exist with varying spatial expression of truncated DISC1 throughout the whole mouse brain (Shen et al., 2008), and in the forebrain only (Hikida et al., 2007; Li et al., 2007; Pletnikov et al., 2008), but also with specific temporal expression during pre- and postnatal development (Ayhan et al., 2011; Li et al., 2007). In terms of morphology, mice carrying a mutation of the endogenous DISC1 gene demonstrate alterations to the organization of newly formed and mature neurons in the hippocampus, dilated lateral ventricles, and deficits in short-term plasticity, which likely contribute to the working memory impairments

reported in these mice (Koike et al., 2006; Kvajo et al., 2008; Shen et al., 2008). Other neuroanatomical features exhibited by DISC1 transgenic mice include thinning of the cortical layers II/III, selective decrease of neural proliferation in the developing cortex, partial agenesis of the corpus callosum, reduced parvalbumin neurons in the hippocampus, and displaced parvalbumin cells within the frontal cortex (Shen et al., 2008). Behaviorally, DISC1 seems to have a significant effect on sensorimotor gating and attentional processes (Clapcote et al., 2007; Lipina, Zai, Hlousek, Roder, & Wong, 2013), specifically chemical mutagenesis of exon 2 of the DISC1 gene in the mouse results in reduced PPI and latent inhibition and an enhanced locomotor response to novelty, which are reversed with antipsychotic treatment (Clapcote et al., 2007; Shen et al., 2008). Transgenic mice expressing the dominant-negative form of DISC1 under the CaMKII promoter exhibited a similar hyperactivity to novelty exposure and also had enlarged lateral ventricles at 6 weeks of age (Hikida et al., 2007). Interestingly, enlargement of the lateral ventricles was observed following both prenatal and separate postnatal alteration to DISC1 expression, whereas the emergence of additional behavioral phenotypes such as behavioral despair and social impairments only occurred following postnatal manipulation of the gene, suggesting temporal specificity of DISC1 effects on neurodevelopment and behavior (Ayhan et al., 2011). Social deficits, cognitive impairments, depressive-like behaviors, and lateral ventricle enlargement seem to be among the more consistent phenotypic observations in DISC1 mutants (Clapcote et al., 2007; Hikida et al., 2007; Li et al., 2007; Shen et al., 2008), which is not surprising considering that these endophenotypes are common to a number of DISC1-associated psychiatric conditions, including schizophrenia and major depression (Chubb et al., 2008).

The effects of DISC1 gene mutation may also be sex-dependent. Pletnikov et al. (2008), using an inducible transgenic mouse model restricted to forebrain expression of mutant DISC1, demonstrated that abnormalities of DISC1 gene expression in the forebrain induce hyperactivity in the open field and a reduced propensity for social investigation, which was only evident in male mutant mice. In this study, female mutants exhibited impaired spatial memory but displayed no other schizophrenia-associated phenotypic alterations (Pletnikov et al., 2008). Given the significant gender differences reported in schizophrenia with respect to the age of onset, response to treatment, and schizophrenia subtypes, further exploration of the influence of gender on the phenotypic expression of susceptibility genes such as DISC1 is warranted.

Multiple transgenic mouse models of DISC1 are now available and have proven to be informative, not only in relation to DISC1 protein interactions and the potential involvement of their downstream signaling pathways in the pathogenesis of schizophrenia, but also conditional mutant models allowing spatial and temporal control of DISC1 gene abnormalities have highlighted the importance of forebrain expression and the early postnatal period in DISC1-associated pathophysiology.

DYSBINDIN 1

Dystrobrevin-binding protein 1 (DTNBP1), also known as dysbindin, was identified as a gene associated with schizophrenia risk through linkage to chromosome 6p (Straub et al., 2002). It is located in synapses of brain areas commonly affected in schizophrenia, including the prefrontal cortex, striatum, and hippocampus (Talbot et al., 2004; Weickert, Rothmond, Hyde, Kleinman, & Straub, 2008; Weickert et al., 2004). Analyses of postmortem brain tissue of those diagnosed with schizophrenia indicate a decreased expression of DTNBP1 in the hippocampus (Talbot et al., 2004; Weickert et al., 2008) and dorsolateral prefrontal cortex (Talbot et al., 2004; Weickert et al., 2004). Three DTNBP1 isoforms have been described and expression is primarily confined to neuronal synapses; dysbindin-1A is associated almost exclusively with postsynaptic densities, dysbindin-1B is associated with synaptic vesicles, and dysbindin-1C is partially found in synaptic vesicles but is mainly associated with postsynaptic densities. The latter isoform, in particular, is reported to be reduced in the prefrontal cortex in schizophrenia sufferers, whereas there was no change in levels of the former two DTNBP1 isoforms (Tang, LeGros, et al., 2009). Consistent with its location at the synapse, DTNBP1 regulates synaptic release and neurotransmission of important neurotransmitters such as glutamate (Jentsch et al., 2009; Tang, Yang, et al., 2009). The modulatory role of dysbindin in glutamate neurotransmission is evident from primary cortical neuronal cultures where it was reported that reduced dysbindin can lower basal and stimulus-induced glutamate release, whereas overexpression of dysbindin elevates glutamate release (Numakawa et al., 2004).

Dysbindin "Sandy" Mouse

The "sandy" (sdy) mouse, a spontaneous mutation that arose in the DBA/2J strain, carries a spontaneously occurring deletion in the DTNBP1 (dysbindin) gene leading to reductions in the two major dysbindin-1 isoforms expressed in mice (i.e., dysbindin-1A and dysbindin-1C). In agreement with data implicating glutamate in DTNBP1-mediated pathophysiology, sdy mice display decreased excitability of glutamatergic neurons in the prefrontal cortex and decreased release of glutamate, increased the NR2-mediated synaptic currents

and enhanced LTP in the hippocampus (Chen et al., 2008; Jentsch et al., 2009; Tang, Yang, et al., 2009), providing a link between these two proteins implicated in schizophrenia. Behavioral phenotyping of these mutants produced inconsistent findings with reports indicating no changes (Bhardwaj et al., 2009; Feng et al., 2008), decreased (Takao et al., 2008) or increased (Hattori et al., 2008) spontaneous exploratory activity in an open field environment while also displaying abnormal locomotor habituation and enhanced locomotor sensitization to amphetamine (Bhardwaj et al., 2009). Because of the specific localization of DTNBP1 in prefrontal cortex and hippocampus, brain regions associated with cognition in humans and rodents, it is not surprising that cognitive behaviors are among the more consistently affected phenotypes in DTNBP1 mutant mice (Bhardwaj et al., 2009; Papaleo et al., 2012). For example, these mice exhibit impaired working memory in an operant delayed nonmatch-to-position task (Jentsch et al., 2009). However, varying reports on locomotor activity in this mutant has also complicated interpretation of findings from cognitive tests that firmly rely on motor activity. Moreover, because of the presence of other abnormal behavioral phenotypes in DBA/2J mice, including coordination deficits along with significant memory, genetic, and dopaminergic alterations, any effects of DTNBP1 mutation were confounded when studied on the DBA/2J genetic background (Talbot, 2009). To remove these effects, the dysbindin mutation was transferred to a more amenable background strain, the C57BL/6J genetic background.

Dysbindin Mutant

In behavioral tasks, dysbindin mutant mice on a C57BL/6J genetic background (dys$^{-/-}$) mice display hyperactivity in an open field (Cox et al., 2009; Papaleo et al., 2012), spatial memory deficits in the Morris water maze (Cox et al., 2009), working memory impairments in a discrete paired-trial T-maze task (Papaleo et al., 2012), and in a delayed nonmatch-to-position operant task (Karlsgodt et al., 2011) and increased compulsive and impulsive behaviors (Carr, Jenkins, Weinberger, & Papaleo, 2013). It is likely that many of the observed cognitive impairments are attributable to changes in dopamine and glutamate neurotransmission in these mutant mice (Papaleo & Weinberger, 2011; Papaleo et al., 2012). Cultured neurons from dys$^{-/-}$ mice express increased dopamine D2 receptors on their cell surface (Ji et al., 2009), and despite increased baseline activity of layer II/III pyramidal neurons from the prefrontal cortex, D2 stimulation in these mutants reduces pyramidal neuron activity compared with wild-type mice, suggesting that D2-mediated alterations in the excitability of fast-spiking GABAergic interneurons is affected (Ji et al., 2009; Papaleo et al., 2012). In accordance with cell culture experiments and findings in sdy mice linking altered glutamate neurotransmission with DTNBP1 mutation (Chen et al., 2008; Jentsch et al., 2009; Numakawa et al., 2004), dys$^{-/-}$ mice exhibit reduced NMDA-evoked currents and reduced NMDA receptor 1 (NR1) messenger RNA expression in the prefrontal cortex (Karlsgodt et al., 2011).

Dysbindin-Overexpressing Transgenic Mutant

Similar to NRG1, DTNBP1 gain-of-function studies have also been conducted with the development of transgenic mice that express the human DTNBP1 gene. To gain further insight into the role of DTNBP1 in schizophrenia, these transgenic mice were extensively screened for behavioral aberrations and sensitivity to psychotomimetic drugs (Shintani et al., 2014). Behavioral screening revealed only a marginal change in limb grasping and no effect of the mutation on sensorimotor gating performance, nonspatial memory, or locomotor activity. Locomotor responses to acutely administered methamphetamine were slightly enhanced, suggesting that overexpression of the gene may increase vulnerability to psychostimulants. These initial data indicate that overexpression of DTNBP1 has very subtle effects on the mouse phenotype. A more comprehensive behavioral assessment, with the inclusion of tests to evaluate effects on multidimensional cognitive function, is required to judge the heuristic value of this particular transgenic mouse and its validity as a model DTNBP dysfunction in schizophrenia.

Taken together, findings from the various DTNBP1 mutant models largely implicate reduced DTNBP1 function in behavioral and neurobiological effects associated with the development of cognitive abnormalities found in schizophrenia. Data from these studies indicate that this gene is an important modulator of glutamate and dopamine neurotransmission, particularly in prefrontal cortex and hippocampus, brain areas that are crucial to control cognitive functions. In general, studies suggest that DTNBP1 mutant models represent a valuable and useful means of examining the pathophysiology of cognitive endophenotypes, a symptom domain that as yet remains refractory to current treatment strategies in this disorder.

22q11.2 CHROMOSOME MICRODELETION

Misalignment of low-copy variants that flank the 22q11.2 region resulting in nonallelic homologous recombination gives rise to microdeletions of this chromosomal region, which harbors approximately 45 genes including proline dehydrogenase (PRODH), zinc finger, DHHC-type containing 8 (ZDHHC8), and

Catechol-*O*-methyltransferase (COMT). Schizophrenia develops in 20–25% of individuals with this genetic microdeletion and is thus considered to be one of the main schizophrenia susceptibility loci in humans (Philip & Bassett, 2011). The phenotypic expression of 22q11.2 deletion can be quite variable and include specific congenital heart defects, thymic hypoplasia, hypocalcemia, velopharyngeal defects, neurodevelopmental delays, cognitive deficits, and/or behavioral abnormalities, coupled with facial dysmorphologies (Karayiorgou & Gogos, 2004). These symptoms are also commonly known as DiGeorge syndrome and velocardiofacial syndrome (Scambler, 2000). Of those with the 22q11.2 microdeletion that are subsequently diagnosed with schizophrenia, profound neurodevelopmental, cognitive, and psychiatric symptoms are more prevalent and are often accompanied by the hallmark neuroanatomical features of classical schizophrenia (Chow, Zipursky, Mikulis, & Bassett, 2002; Drew et al., 2011).

Many of the genes affected in this deletion syndrome are expressed in humans and mice; hence mutant mouse models of 22q11.2 microdeletion have been, and continue to be, informative tools for investigation of potential molecular links between affected genes and phenotypic features (Paylor & Lindsay, 2006). Knock-out mice of the individual genes involved in this syndrome as well as mutants with complete long-range genetic deletions involving multiple genes have been engineered; the latter mouse lines, capturing more complex gene–gene interaction factors and redundancy mechanisms, and consequently, more accurately model the syndrome itself rather than simply informing on associations between single risk genes and pathology. Mouse models carrying chromosomal deficiencies spanning a segment syntenic to the 22q11.2 deletion syndrome include the Df(16)A$^{+/-}$ model (Stark et al., 2008) and the LgDel/+ model (Merscher et al., 2001). Phenotypic assessment of these mutant mice has revealed increased anxiety, deficits in PPI, and impaired working memory when compared with wild-types (Long et al., 2006; Sigurdsson, Stark, Karayiorgou, Gogos, & Gordon, 2010; Stark et al., 2008), which have been attributed to impaired functional connectivity between the hippocampus and prefrontal cortex (Sigurdsson et al., 2010) and altered neuronal morphology in the hippocampus (Mukai et al., 2008). High-resolution magnetic resonance imaging analysis of Df(16)A(+/−) mice indicates that this mouse model also recapitulates most of the hallmark neuroanatomical changes observed in human 22q11.2 deletion carriers (Ellegood et al., 2014).

Df1/+ transgenic mice are characterized by hemizygous deletion of 18 genes in the 22q11-related region and have specific deficits in learning, memory, and sensorimotor gating processes, and display enhanced locomotor responses to psychostimulants that resemble key features of 22q11 syndrome and schizophrenia (Kimoto et al., 2012; Paylor et al., 2001). Whether the behavioral phenotype in patients is caused by heterozygous loss of a single gene or multiple genes is unclear. Mice with single mutations of genes within the 22q11 region provide vital clues as to the extent and nature of the contributions of each gene to the overall phenotype. For example, similar sensorimotor gating deficits have been reported in *PRODH* (Gogos et al., 1999) and to a lesser extent in *ZDHHC8* null mutants (Mukai et al., 2004), but not in heterozygotes, whereas *Tbx1* and *Gnb1l* are the only ones that cause PPI impairments in the heterozygous state (Long et al., 2006; Paylor et al., 2006), suggesting that the latter two genes are major contributors to the psychiatric phenotype of patients with 22q11 deletion syndrome.

Interestingly, selective overexpression of COMT in the prefrontal cortex of Df1$^{-/+}$ and associated increases in GABA release in the prefrontal cortex rescue the observed schizophrenia-like phenotypes in these mice (Kimoto et al., 2012), suggesting that COMT might be involved in the behavioral pathogenesis and consequently may also have a role to play in future treatments for psychiatric symptoms of 22q11 deletion syndrome.

GENETIC MUTANT MODELS RELATED TO PUTATIVE PATHOPHYSIOLOGY

The Dopamine Hypothesis

The dopamine hypothesis of schizophrenia postulates that hyperactivity of dopamine D2 receptor neurotransmission in subcortical and limbic brain regions contributes to positive symptoms of schizophrenia, whereas negative and cognitive symptoms of the disorder can be attributed to hypofunctionality of dopamine D1 receptor neurotransmission in the prefrontal cortex (Toda & Abi-Dargham, 2007). In support of this, studies have shown an increased density of the dopamine D2 receptor in postmortem brain tissue of schizophrenia sufferers (Seeman et al., 2000). It is also reported that upregulation of D2 receptors in the caudate nucleus of patients with schizophrenia directly correlates with poorer performance in cognitive tasks involving corticostriatal pathways (Hirvonen et al., 2004). That dopamine-releasing drugs, such as amphetamine, possess psychotomimetic properties in addition to the D2-antagonist property common to many of the currently prescribed antipsychotic treatments, giving credence to the dopamine hypothesis of schizophrenia.

Catechol-O-Methyltransferase Mutants

COMT is an enzyme that facilitates the degradation of active dopamine in the synapse and is expressed in the pyramidal neurons of the prefrontal cortex and hippocampus (Papaleo et al., 2008). Deletion of chromosome 22q11, which contains the COMT gene, has been linked with elevated psychosis and schizophrenia-like neurocognitive and behavioral symptoms (Bearden et al., 2004). Reintroduction of COMT with consequent overexpression of the enzyme in the prefrontal cortex of mice with 22q11.2 deletion syndrome, involving hemizygous deletion of 18 genes in the 22q11-related region (Df1/+ mice), rescues the schizophrenia-like phenotype in this model; specifically, it normalized the enhanced sensitivity of Df1/+ mice to MK801 but also attenuated the abnormal response to GABAA receptor agonists, suggesting that the effects of COMT overexpression might be through the regulation of GABAergic system (Kimoto et al., 2012).

A functional polymorphism of the COMT gene, involving the allelic substitution of valine (Val) for methionine (Met), results in a fourfold reduction of COMT enzymatic activity; the enzymatic activity of the Val allele is ~40% higher than that of the Met allele in postmortem human prefrontal cortex tissue (Chen et al., 2004). Family-based genetic association studies in schizophrenic patients and investigations in transgenic mice expressing varying degrees of the Val/Met polymorphism (Val/Val homozygotes, Val/Met heterozygotes, Met/Met homozygotes) have produced sufficient data to indicate that there is a direct relationship between the level of expression of the Val genotype and deficits in executive function and cognitive performance, with the homozygous Val/Val genotype exhibiting the most severe impairments (Egan et al., 2001; Papaleo et al., 2008; Tunbridge et al., 2006). Studies using mutant mice that express either upregulation or downregulation of COMT enzyme have revealed a number of schizophrenia-relevant effects as a result of altered COMT expression. Mice overexpressing a human COMT-Val polymorphism (characterized by an increase in COMT activity), exhibited significant deficits in attention behavior, an attenuated sensitivity to stress and pain, and impaired working and recognition memory, the latter of which was ameliorated following amphetamine treatment, confirming the involvement of dopamine in cognition (Papaleo et al., 2008). On the other hand, COMT knockouts display an improvement in spatial and working memory (Babovic et al., 2008; Papaleo et al., 2008), a finding that is consistent with clinical studies showing an association between the Met allele (characterized by reduced COMT-mediated degradation of dopamine) and enhanced prefrontal cortex-mediated cognition. However, COMT inactivation, using both genetic and pharmacological methods, confers greater vulnerability to the effects of adolescent cannabinoid exposure on PPI in mice (O'Tuathaigh et al., 2012), extending previous reports of similar gene × environment effects in COMT knockouts on neurotransmitter function in the brain (Behan et al., 2012). Distinct behavioral differences between heterozygous and homozygous COMT knockouts have also been reported in which exploratory behavior and habituation to novelty were altered in the heterozygous group specifically with no effect on homozygous mutants (Babovic et al., 2007). Sex differences were also observed; spatial and working memory performances were enhanced in male COMT knockouts despite the absence of any effect on cognition in females (Babovic et al., 2008). Overall, these mutant data demonstrate that chronic increase or decrease in COMT enzymatic activity markedly impacts cognition, particularly working memory and attentional performance.

D2 Receptor Mutant Model

In light of the fact that many of the known antipsychotic drugs target the D2 receptor, it follows that mutant mouse models with altered expression of these receptors provide insight into the putative involvement of D2-signaling in psychotic illness.

To test a possible causal relationship between increased striatal D2 receptor density and cognitive endophenotypes, Kellendonk et al. (2006) developed conditional transgenic mice that overexpressed the D2 receptor in the striatum in a location-specific and temporally controlled manner. They reported an impaired prefrontal cortex-mediated working memory and a reduced behavioral flexibility in the T-maze that persisted after the transgene was switched off, indicating that these phenotypic changes occur as a result of secondary compensatory mechanisms and are not solely due to the direct effects of D2 receptor overexpression. Interestingly, D2 overexpression also induced an altered dopamine turnover and D1 receptor activation in the prefrontal cortex, which may account for the observed cognitive deficits in these transgenic mice. D2 receptor knockout mice also provide a means of assessing the importance of D2 receptor in antipsychotic treatments. For example, they have been used to show that D2 receptors are not essential to the mechanism by which antipsychotic drugs attenuate amphetamine disruption of learning in the latent inhibition test (Bay-Richter et al., 2013).

GLUTAMATE HYPOTHESIS OF SCHIZOPHRENIA

It has been proposed that the dopamine endophenotype emerges as a result of a general synaptic disconnectivity between cortical and subcortical brain areas involving abnormalities of glutamatergic function (Laruelle et al., 2003). There is a substantive body of evidence for hypoglutamatergic function in schizophrenia. For example, NMDA receptor antagonists have been shown to possess psychotomimetic properties in healthy subjects (Adler et al., 1999; Coyle, 2006; Kegeles et al., 2000), while also exacerbating psychotic symptoms in patients with schizophrenia (Malhotra et al., 1997). NMDA receptor deficits have been reported in postmortem brains of schizophrenia sufferers (Stone et al., 2008) and brains of living patients as measured using single-photon emission computed tomography (Pilowsky et al., 2006). Magnetic resonance spectroscopy also demonstrated reduced in vivo levels of glutamate in the medial frontal region of patients with schizophrenia as compared with healthy individuals (Marsman et al., 2013).

Metabotropic Glutamate Receptor 2/3

The finding that the metabotropic glutamate receptor 2/3 (mGlu2/3) metabotropic glutamate receptor agonist, LY404039, improves clinical symptoms in schizophrenia (Patil et al., 2007) has stimulated a greater interest in the putative interactions between mGlu2/3 receptors and dopamine D2 receptors. A study using mGlu2 and mGlu3 receptor knockout mice has demonstrated that the proportion of D2 receptors in the striata is elevated by 220% and that there is a 67-fold and 17-fold increase in the sensitivity to a D2 agonist, respectively, in these mutants (Seeman, Battaglia, Corti, Corsi, & Bruno, 2009), supporting the proposition that an interaction exists between these neurotransmitter systems in the brain. Behavioral phenotyping of mGluR2$^{-/-}$ knockout mice revealed hyperactivity in a novel environment and an increase in locomotor sensitization and a conditioned place preference in association with repeated cocaine administration (Morishima et al., 2005). This was paralleled by increased in vivo levels of dopamine and an altered pattern of glutamate release in the nucleus accumbens, indicating that mGluR2 contributes to behavioral and neurochemical responses underpinning addiction to cocaine in mice (Morishima et al., 2005). mGluR3$^{-/-}$ mice demonstrated similar hyperactivity in a novel environment but also cognitive deficits in the T-maze and contextual fear conditioning test (Fujioka et al., 2014), which were accompanied by enhanced sensitivity to MK-801 in the Y-maze test (Lainiola, Procaccini, & Linden, 2014). Double knockout mice lacking both mGlu2 and mGlu3 (mGlu2/3$^{-/-}$) have also been generated. These mice exhibit a subtle behavioral phenotype, being hypoactive under basal conditions and in response to amphetamine, present with a spatial memory deficit that depends on the arousal properties of the task (Lyon et al., 2011), but demonstrate significant decreases in dopamine in the striatum and nucleus accumbens (Lane et al., 2013), providing further evidence that group II metabotropic glutamate receptors influence dopamine neurotransmission.

Metabotropic Glutamate Receptor 5

The group 1 metabotropic glutamate receptor 5 (mGluR5) has been implicated in the neuropathology of various disorders including autism, Fragile X syndrome, attention deficit/hyperactive disorder, and schizophrenia. mGluR5 is expressed in the olfactory bulb, cortex, striatum, and hippocampus in the rodent brain where it is present in glutamatergic neurons, GABAergic inhibitory neurons, and glia (Shigemoto et al., 1993). Mice lacking the mGluR5 receptor are hyperactive in novel environments (Bird et al., 2010; Gray et al., 2009), defective in the PPI test (Gray et al., 2009; Kinney et al., 2003), and exhibit decreased anxiety (Olsen, Childs, Stanwood, & Winder, 2010) and impaired learning (Lu et al., 1997). mGluR5 knockouts also have enhanced sensitivity to the effects of the NMDA antagonist MK-801, which are reversed by chronic administration of clozapine (Gray et al., 2009) and a diminished sensitivity to the locomotor activating effects of cocaine, despite showing similar cocaine-induced increases in nucleus accumbens dopamine levels (Chiamulera et al., 2001). However, specific ablation of mGluR5 in cortical glutamatergic neurons increased novelty induced locomotor activity but had no effect on sensorimotor gating, anxiety, motor coordination/learning, social interactions, or fear conditioning behaviors (Jew et al., 2013); these data suggest that mGluR5 signaling in glutamatergic neurons of the cortex modulates locomotor activity, whereas altered subcortical expression may be implicated in the emergence of other behavioral endophenotypes.

NMDA Receptor 1 Mutant Model

Support for the involvement of glutamatergic-NMDA neurotransmission in schizophrenia is provided by the finding that a 90% reduction in NR1 expression in mice induces behavioral abnormalities in adulthood, including increased motor activity, stereotypy, and deficits in social and sexual interactions that match those reported in pharmacologically induced animal models of schizophrenia (Mohn, Gainetdinov, Caron, & Koller, 1999). Interestingly, each of these behavioral abnormalities has been shown to have a unique developmental trajectory which also differs between NR1-deficient males and females (Milenkovic, Mielnik, & Ramsey, 2014); specifically, deficits in working memory and social behavior emerged earlier in development and with greater severity in males than in females, whereas in both sexes executive function was most affected in periadolescent mice while the capacity for problem solving in the puzzle box deteriorated as the mutant mice approached adulthood. Behavioral deficits in NR1-deficient mice were ameliorated by treatment with antipsychotics haloperidol and clozapine, treatments that directly target dopaminergic neuronal transmission and not glutamate, indicating that these neurotransmitter systems interact at some level while contributing to the schizophrenia-like phenotype in these mutants (Mohn et al., 1999). Recent studies have also identified aspects of the NR1-deficient mouse phenotype that resemble core symptoms of autism spectrum disorders including decreased social interactions, altered ultrasonic vocalizations, and increased repetitive behaviors (Gandal et al., 2012). Selective reduction in the NMDA R1 subunit in paravalbumin-positive interneurons resulted in an autism-like phenotype (Saunders et al., 2013), highlighting the potential importance of NMDA receptor activation of GABAergic interneurons in endophenotypes common to schizophrenia and autism such as social impairments.

D-Amino Acid Oxidase

The NMDA endogenous coagonist D-serine is metabolized by D-amino acid oxidase (DAO), an enzyme that is widely distributed in the central nervous system of humans and mice (Sasabe, Suzuki, Imanishi, & Aiso, 2014) but is most abundant in the hindbrain (Yamanaka et al., 2012). Recent meta-analyses have confirmed the association between DAO and schizophrenia (Allen et al., 2008; Shi, Gershon, & Liu, 2008). Single-nucleotide polymorphisms within the G72 (also known as D-amino acid oxidase activator) and DAO locus have been associated with schizophrenia susceptibility (Chumakov et al., 2002; Labrie, Wong, & Roder, 2012). Consistent with the NMDA receptor hypofunction hypothesis in schizophrenia, an increase in DAO enzyme activity and gene expression has been reported in postmortem brain tissue of patients with schizophrenia (Bendikov et al., 2007).

Mice lacking DAO (DAO$^{-/-}$) exhibit increased occupancy of the NMDA receptor–associated glycine site, with a consequent increase in NMDA receptor signaling but also display a reduced behavioral sensitivity to acute administration of the NMDA antagonists MK-801 (Hashimoto, Yoshikawa, Niwa, & Konno, 2005) and phencyclidine (Almond et al., 2006). Behavioral analyses of these mutant mice revealed reduced exploration in a novel environment relative to their wild-type counterparts (Almond et al., 2006; Zhang et al., 2011), altered anxiety (Labrie, Clapcote, & Roder, 2009; Zhang et al., 2011), enhanced extinction of contextual fear memory and reversal learning abilities (Labrie, Duffy, et al., 2009), and both enhanced PPI responses (Zhang et al., 2011) and no effects in this test (Almond et al., 2006). However, DAO$^{-/-}$ mice displayed enhanced sensitivity to the PPI-disruptive effect induced by the competitive NMDA antagonist, SDZ 220-581 (Zhang et al., 2011), and a significant attenuation of the cumulative stereotypy score induced by MK-801 compared to DAO$^{+/+}$ mice (Hashimoto et al., 2005). Increased burst-firing of ventral tegmental area dopaminergic neurons in vivo has been reported in DAO$^{-/-}$ mice (Schweimer et al., 2014), which could be attributed to enhanced NMDA activity on dopaminergic neurons, or alternatively, reduced firing of nearby GABAergic neurons because GABAergic neurons in the VTA receive glutamatergic inputs that express NMDA receptors. Interestingly, sodium benzoate, the prototypical DAO inhibitor, has proven to be effective in ameliorating neurocognitive symptoms in a randomized clinical trial (Lane et al., 2013) and has led to greater interest in the development of DAO inhibitors for the treatment of schizophrenia (Sacchi, Rosini, Pollegioni, & Molla, 2013).

METHODOLOGICAL CHALLENGES AND LIMITATIONS OF GENETIC MOUSE MODELS

The use of rodents as models of human psychiatric disorders will inevitably prompt vigorous debate concerning the validity and translational value of these models. Whether gene function, neuronal circuitry, and the neurochemical underpinnings of disease features are conserved across the species is an important consideration in the development of any animal model. The assumption that genotype–phenotype relationships are shared in rodents and humans requires that the implicated gene affects analogous phenotypes in both species. Certain aspects of behavior and disease, particularly those that have their foundations in more primitive functions, can always be applied to animal constructs with greater ease than symptoms associated more complex processes involving brain areas that have evolved in humans but not to the same extent in rodents. From an evolutionary perspective, behaviors such as exploration, sociability, cognition, and aggression as well as biological processes involved in adaptation to variable and unpredictable environments, are features that are equally essential to survival and reproduction in rodents and humans, hence the genetic determinants of these traits are also likely to be conserved across the species.

Many of these behavioral domains are relevant to behavioral endophenotypes in schizophrenia (reviewed by Arguello & Gogos, 2006). Finding suitable phenotypic correlates of the positive symptoms of schizophrenia in genetic rodent models has been challenging (Kirby, Waddington, & O'Tuathaigh, 2010; O'Tuathaigh, Desbonnet, Moran, Kirby, & Waddington, 2011). Schizophrenia is a uniquely human disease and the identification of appropriate behavioral equivalents for paranoid delusions and auditory and visual hallucinations in mice is difficult, but some parameters such as hyperactivity in response to novelty and hypersensitivity to psychostimulants have been accepted as suitable counterparts in these models (Featherstone, Kapur, &

Fletcher, 2007). An aspect of the conceptual framework of genetic models that is often neglected in animal studies is the consideration of a rodents' natural environment and the appropriate use of ethological testing methods and interventions. Assessment of a particular aspect of behavior in a "naturalistic" setting (taking into consideration feeding habits, social structure, and hazards associated with the animal's natural habitat) provides a more accurate means of identifying links between gene mutations and behavioral phenotypes in mice, and is more likely to expose deficits that would not necessarily be apparent using more traditional behavioral testing methods (Gerlai & Clayton, 1999; Tecott & Nestler, 2004; Wimer & Wimer, 1985).

It is now evident that a variety of genetic, epigenetic, and methodological factors complicate both the expression and assessment of mutant phenotypes; these include embryonic lethality, mouse genetic background, compensatory and redundancy processes, pleiotropy, and the potential epigenetic effects of environmental variables. For a number of schizophrenia risk genes, notably those implicated in early development of the brain and heart such as NRG1, embryonic lethality can occur making it impossible to study the adult phenotype in homozygous knockouts. In these cases, phenotypic assessment of heterozygotes has been invaluable, and perhaps in some scenarios more accurately reflects the genetic abnormality in clinical situations that rarely involve complete deletions of the risk gene in question. Genetic and phenotypic variations between inbred mouse strains are also important factors to consider in the construction of genetic models of disease. Phenotypic differences between and within mouse strains are well-characterized (Gerlai et al., 1999; Waddington et al., 2005) and may confound interpretations of any phenotype derived from a mutant mice on different genetic backgrounds (Crusio, 2004; Gerlai, 1999; Phillips, Hen, & Crabbe, 1999), as has been reported for the sandy mouse where confounding variables presented by mutations in DBA/2J mice affecting brain function resulted in the transfer of the DTNBP1 mutation onto a C57BL/6J genetic background (Talbot, 2009). In contrast to current efforts exploiting the mouse as a model organism based on isolated and transient crosses, recent efforts to develop the Collaborative Cross experimental model provide a large, common set of genetically defined mice that more accurately reflects the genetic structure of human populations and therefore may represent a better genetic framework to model human disease processes and study genetic disorders in mice (Churchill et al., 2004).

Because genetic mutations occur upstream from neurophysiological phenomena in schizophrenia, they are inevitably subject to environmental influences (Caspi et al., 2005; van Os et al., 2014) and compensatory/adaptive genetic effects (Zhang, 2012) initiated by homeostatic processes during development. This genetic buffering effect, a phenomenon known as epistasis, usually involves alterations in the expression of other genes and hence introduces confounding factors that obscure any attempt to demarcate precise contributions made by a single gene to schizophrenia endophenotypes. Despite the unwanted complexity presented by epistatic processes in mutant models, they also add another dimension to these models with the potential to inform on relevant pathological processes involving gene–gene interactions in schizophrenia. Variable penetrance of susceptibility genes, both within and across populations, may be modeled and better understood by studying gene–gene interactions in knockout mice. Furthermore, because most schizophrenia risk genes are implicated in neurodevelopmental processes, it is likely that the mutation is present throughout the development and therefore analogous compensatory and redundancy processes present in the knockout mouse are also present in humans.

CONCLUSIONS

The use of transgenic lines that are both spatially localized and inducible at different stages across the lifespan of the mouse has circumvented many of the limitations of genetic models in schizophrenia. However, despite the merits of conventional and conditional genetic models, the fact remains that none of the candidate risk genes can account for a large proportion of disease cases. Hence, it is unlikely that examination of mouse models with single-gene mutations will lead to major breakthroughs in our understanding of the pathogenesis of schizophrenia and as yet no effective therapeutic strategy has emerged from these preclinical genetic studies. However, these challenges and limitations should not negate the value of genetic mouse models in schizophrenia research. Replicating gene mutations of identified human susceptibility genes of schizophrenia in rodents, despite obvious limitations, provides a useful means of examining genotype–phenotype relationships to disentangle the neurobiology of this complex disease, and consequently, will always have a place as an investigative tool to study specific genetic, and gene-environment contributions to the pathophysiology of schizophrenia.

References

Adler, C. M., Malhotra, A. K., Elman, I., Goldberg, T., Egan, M., Pickar, D., & Breier, A. (1999). Comparison of ketamine-induced thought disorder in healthy volunteers and thought disorder in schizophrenia. *The American Journal of Psychiatry, 156*(10), 1646–1649.

Agim, Z. S., Esendal, M., Briollais, L., Uyan, O., Meschian, M., Martinez, L. A., et al. (2013). Discovery, validation and characterization of Erbb4 and Nrg1 haplotypes using data from three genome-wide association studies of schizophrenia. *PLoS One, 8*(1), e53042.

Allen, A. J., Griss, M. E., Folley, B. S., Hawkins, K. A., & Pearlson, G. D. (2009). Endophenotypes in schizophrenia: a selective review. *Schizophrenia Research, 109*(1–3), 24–37.

Allen, N. C., Bagade, S., McQueen, M. B., Ioannidis, J. P., Kavvoura, F. K., Khoury, M. J., et al. (2008). Systematic meta-analyses and field synopsis of genetic association studies in schizophrenia: the SzGene database. *Nature Genetics, 40*(7), 827–834.

Almond, S. L., Fradley, R. L., Armstrong, E. J., Heavens, R. B., Rutter, A. R., Newman, R. J., et al. (2006). Behavioral and biochemical characterization of a mutant mouse strain lacking D-amino acid oxidase activity and its implications for schizophrenia. *Molecular and Cellular Neuroscience, 32*(4), 324–334.

Andersson, R. H., Johnston, A., Herman, P. A., Winzer-Serhan, U. H., Karavanova, I., Vullhorst, D., et al. (2012). Neuregulin and dopamine modulation of hippocampal gamma oscillations is dependent on dopamine D4 receptors. *Proceedings of the National Academy of Sciences of the United States of America, 109*(32), 13118–13123.

Arguello, P. A., & Gogos, J. A. (2006). Modeling madness in mice: one piece at a time. *Neuron, 52*(1), 179–196.

Athanasiu, L., Mattingsdal, M., Kähler, A. K., Brown, A., Gustafsson, O., Agartz, I., et al. (2010). Gene variants associated with schizophrenia in a Norwegian genome-wide study are replicated in a large European cohort. *Journal of Psychiatric Research, 44*(12), 748–753.

Ayhan, Y., Abazyan, B., Nomura, J., Kim, R., Ladenheim, B., Krasnova, I. N., et al. (2011). Differential effects of prenatal and postnatal expressions of mutant human DISC1 on neurobehavioral phenotypes in transgenic mice: evidence for neurodevelopmental origin of major psychiatric disorders. *Molecular Psychiatry, 16*(3), 293–306.

Babovic, D., O'Tuathaigh, C. M., O'Sullivan, G. J., Clifford, J. J., Tighe, O., Croke, D. T., Karayiorgou, M., Gogos, J. A., Cotter, D., & Waddington, J. L. (2007). Exploratory and habituation phenotype of heterozygous and homozygous COMT knockout mice. *Behavioural Brain Research, 183*(2), 236–239.

Babovic, D., O'Tuathaigh, C. M., O'Connor, A. M., O'Sullivan, G. J., Tighe, O., Croke, D. T., Karayiorgou, M., Gogos, J. A., Cotter, D., & Waddington, J. L. (2008). Phenotypic characterization of cognition and social behavior in mice with heterozygous versus homozygous deletion of catechol-O-methyltransferase. *Neuroscience, 155*(4), 1021–1029.

Bay-Richter, C. 1, O'Callaghan, M. J., Mathur, N., O'Tuathaigh, C. M., Heery, D. M., Fone, K. C., Waddington, J. L., & Moran, P. M. (2013). D-amphetamine and antipsychotic drug effects on latent inhibition in mice lacking dopamine D2. *Neuropsychopharmacology, 38*(8), 1512–1520.

Bearden, C. E., Jawad, A. F., Lynch, D. R., Sokol, S., Kanes, S. J., McDonald-McGinn, D. M., Saitta, S. C., Harris, S. E., Moss, E., Wang, P. P., Zackai, E., Emanuel, B. S., & Simon, T. J. (2004). Effects of a functional COMT polymorphism on prefrontal cognitive function in patients with 22q11.2 deletion syndrome. *The American Journal of Psychiatry, 161*(9), 1700–1702.

Beglopoulos, V., & Shen, J. (2004). Gene-targeting technologies for the study of neurological disorders. *NeuroMolecular Medicine, 6*(1), 13–30.

Bendikov, I., Nadri, C., Amar, S., Panizzutti, R., De Miranda, J., Wolosker, H., et al. (2007). A CSF and postmortem brain study of D-serine metabolic parameters in schizophrenia. *Schizophrenia Research, 90*(1–3), 41–51.

Behan, A. T., Hryniewiecka, M., O'Tuathaigh, C. M., Kinsella, A., Cannon, M., Karayiorgou, M., Gogos, J. A., Waddington, J. L., & Cotter, D. R. (2012). Chronic adolescent exposure to delta-9-tetrahydrocannabinol in COMT mutant mice: impact on indices of dopaminergic, endocannabinoid and GABAergic pathways. *Neuropsychopharmacology, 37*(7), 1773–1783.

Bertram, L. (2008). Genetic research in schizophrenia: new tools and future perspectives. *Schizophrenia Bulletin, 34*(5), 806–812.

Bhardwaj, S. K., Baharnoori, M., Sharif-Askari, B., Kamath, A., Williams, S., & Srivastava, L. K. (2009). Behavioral characterization of dysbindin-1 deficient sandy mice. *Behavioural Brain Research, 197*(2), 435–441.

Bird, M. K., Reid, C. A., Chen, F., Tan, H. O., Petrou, S., & Lawrence, A. J. (2010). Int J Cocaine-mediated synaptic potentiation is absent in VTA neurons from mGlu5-deficient mice. *Neuropsychopharmacology*, 13(2), 133–141.

Bjarnadottir, M., Misner, D. L., Haverfield-Gross, S., Bruun, S., Helgason, V. G., Stefansson, H., Sigmundsson, A., Firth, D. R., Nielsen, B., Stefansdottir, R., Novak, T. J., Stefansson, K., Gurney, M. E., & Andresson, T. (2007). Neuregulin1 (NRG1) signaling through Fyn modulates NMDA receptor phosphorylation: differential synaptic function in NRG1+/- knock-outs compared with wild-type mice. *Journal of Neuroscience*, 27(17), 4519–4529.

Bockamp, E., Maringer, M., Spangenberg, C., Fees, S., Fraser, S., Eshkind, L., et al. (2002). Of mice and models: improved animal models for biomedical research. *Physiological Genomics*, 11(3), 115–132.

Boucher, A. A., Arnold, J. C., Duffy, L., Schofield, P. R., Micheau, J., & Karl, T. (2007). Heterozygous neuregulin 1 mice are more sensitive to the behavioural effects of Δ^9-tetrahydrocannabinol. *Psychopharmacology (Berl)*, 192(3), 325–336.

Boucher, A. A., Hunt, G. E., Karl, T., Micheau, J., McGregor, I. S., & Arnold, J. C. (2007a). Heterozygous neuregulin 1 mice display greater baseline and Delta(9)-tetrahydrocannabinol-induced c-Fos expression. *Neuroscience*, 149(4), 861–870.

Bradshaw, N. J., & Porteous, D. J. (2012). DISC1-binding proteins in neural development, signalling and schizophrenia. *Neuropharmacology*, 62(3), 1230–1241.

Brennand, K. J., & Gage, F. H. (2012). Modeling psychiatric disorders through reprogramming. *Disease Models & Mechanisms*, 5(1), 26–32.

Buonanno, A. (2010). The neuregulin signaling pathway and schizophrenia: from genes to synapses and neural circuits. *Brain Research Bulletin*, 83(3–4), 122–131.

Burdick, K. E., Hodgkinson, C. A., Szeszko, P. R., Lencz, T., Ekholm, J. M., Kane, J. M., et al. (2005). DISC1 and neurocognitive function in schizophrenia. *Neuroreport*, 16(12), 1399–1402.

Callicott, J. H., Straub, R. E., Pezawas, L., Egan, M. F., Mattay, V. S., Hariri, A. R., et al. (2005). Variation in DISC1 affects hippocampal structure and function and increases risk for schizophrenia. *Proceedings of the National Academy of Sciences of the United States of America*, 102(24), 8627–8632.

Cannon, T. D., Hennah, W., van Erp, T. G., Thompson, P. M., Lonnqvist, J., Huttunen, M., et al. (2005). Association of DISC1/TRAX haplotypes with schizophrenia, reduced prefrontal gray matter, and impaired short- and long-term memory. *Archives of General Psychiatry*, 62(11), 1205–1213.

Carr, G. V., Jenkins, K. A., Weinberger, D. R., & Papaleo, F. (2013). Loss of dysbindin-1 in mice impairs reward-based operant learning by increasing impulsive and compulsive behavior. *Behavioural Brain Research*, 241, 173–184.

Caspi, A., Moffitt, T. E., Cannon, M., McClay, J., Murray, R., Harrington, H., et al. (2005). Moderation of the effect of adolescent-onset cannabis use on adult psychosis by a functional polymorphism in the catechol-*O*-methyltransferase gene: longitudinal evidence of a gene X environment interaction. *Biological Psychiatry*, 57(10), 1117–1127.

Chen, J., Lipska, B. K., Halim, N., Ma, Q. D., Matsumoto, M., Melhem, S., Kolachana, B. S., Hyde, T. M., Herman, M. M., Apud, J., Egan, M. F., Kleinman, J. E., & Weinberger, D. R. (2004). Functional analysis of genetic variation in catechol-O-methyltransferase (COMT): effects on mRNA, protein, and enzyme activity in postmortem human brain. *American Journal of Human Genetics*, 75(5), 807–821.

Chen, X. W., Feng, Y. Q., Hao, C. J., Guo, X. L., He, X., Zhou, Z. Y., et al. (2008a). DTNBP1, a schizophrenia susceptibility gene, affects kinetics of transmitter release. *Journal of Cell Biology*, 181(5), 791–801.

Chen, Y. J., Zhang, M., Wang, P., Zhu, X. H., & Gao, T. M. (2008). Neuregulin-1 temperature-dependently inhibits the long-term potentiation in the CA1 region in mouse hippocampal slices. *Nanfang Yike Daxue Xuebao*, 28(10), 1771–1774.

Chesworth, R., Yulyaningsih, E., Cappas, E., Arnold, J., Sainsbury, A., & Karl, T. (2012). The response of neuregulin 1 mutant mice to acute restraint stress. *Neuroscience Letters*, 515(1), 82–86.

Chiamulera, C., Epping-Jordan, M. P., Zocchi, A., Marcon, C., & Cottiny, C., Tacconi, S., Corsi, M., Orzi, F., Conquet, F. (2001). Reinforcing and locomotor stimulant effects of cocaine are absent in mGluR5 null mutant mice. *Nature Neuroscience*, 4(9), 873–874.

Chohan, T. W., Boucher, A. A., Spencer, J. R., Kassem, M. S., Hamdi, A. A., Karl, T., et al. (2014). Partial genetic deletion of neuregulin 1 modulates the effects of stress on sensorimotor gating, dendritic morphology, and HPA axis activity in adolescent mice. *Schizophrenia Bulletin*, 40(6), 1272–1284.

Chohan, T. W., Nguyen, A., Todd, S. M., Bennett, M. R., Callaghan, P., & Arnold, J. C. (2014). Partial genetic deletion of neuregulin 1 and adolescent stress interact to alter NMDA receptor binding in the medial prefrontal cortex. *Frontiers in Behavioral Neuroscience*, 8, 298.

Chow, E. W., Zipursky, R. B., Mikulis, D. J., & Bassett, A. S. (2002). Structural brain abnormalities in patients with schizophrenia and 22q11 deletion syndrome. *Biological Psychiatry*, 51(3), 208–215.

Chubb, J. E., Bradshaw, N. J., Soares, D. C., Porteous, D. J., & Millar, J. K. (2008). The DISC locus in psychiatric illness. *Molecular Psychiatry*, 13(1), 36–64.

Chumakov, I., Blumenfeld, M., Guerassimenko, O., Cavarec, L., Palicio, M., Abderrahim, H., et al. (2002). Genetic and physiological data implicating the new human gene G72 and the gene for D-amino acid oxidase in schizophrenia. *Proceedings of the National Academy of Sciences of the United States of America*, 99(21), 13675–13680.

Churchill, G. A., Airey, D. C., Allayee, H., Angel, J. M., Attie, A. D., Beatty, J., et al. (2004). The Collaborative Cross, a community resource for the genetic analysis of complex traits. *Nature Genetics*, 36(11), 1133–1137.

Clapcote, S. J., Lipina, T. V., Millar, J. K., Mackie, S., Christie, S., Ogawa, F., et al. (2007). Behavioral phenotypes of Disc1 missense mutations in mice. *Neuron*, 54(3), 387–402.

Cooper, M. A., & Koleske, A. J. (2014). Ablation of ErbB4 from excitatory neurons leads to reduced dendritic spine density in mouse prefrontal cortex. *Journal of Comparative Neurology*, 522(14), 3351–3362.

Cox, M. M., Tucker, A. M., Tang, J., Talbot, K., Richer, D. C., Yeh, L., et al. (2009). Neurobehavioral abnormalities in the dysbindin-1 mutant, sandy, on a C57BL/6J genetic background. *Genes, Brain and Behavior*, 8(4), 390–397.

Coyle, J. T. (2006). Substance use disorders and Schizophrenia: a question of shared glutamatergic mechanisms. *Neurotoxicity Research*, 10(3-4), 221–233.

Crusio, W. E. (2004). Flanking gene and genetic background problems in genetically manipulated mice. *Biological Psychiatry*, 56(6), 381–385.

Deakin, I. H., Law, A. J., Oliver, P. L., Schwab, M. H., Nave, K. A., Harrison, P. J., et al. (2009). Behavioural characterization of neuregulin 1 type I overexpressing transgenic mice. *Neuroreport*, 20(17), 1523–1528.

Deakin, I. H., Nissen, W., Law, A. J., Lane, T., Kanso, R., Schwab, M. H., et al. (2012). Transgenic overexpression of the type I isoform of neuregulin 1 affects working memory and hippocampal oscillations but not long-term potentiation. *Cerebral Cortex*, 22(7), 1520–1529.

Dean, B., Karl, T., Pavey, G., Boer, S., Duffy, L., & Scarr, E. (2008). Increased levels of serotonin 2A receptors and serotonin transporter in the CNS of neuregulin 1 hypomorphic/mutant mice. *Schizophrenia Research*, 99(1-3), 341–349.

Del Pino, I., García-Frigola, C., Dehorter, N., Brotons-Mas, J. R., Alvarez-Salvado, E., Martínez de Lagrán, M., et al. (2013). Erbb4 deletion from fast-spiking interneurons causes schizophrenia-like phenotypes. *Neuron*, 79(6), 1152–1168.

Desbonnet, L., O'Tuathaigh, C. M., & Waddington, J. L. (2012). Modeling schizophrenia: uncovering novel therapeutic targets. *Expert Review of Clinical Pharmacology*, 5(6), 667–676.

Doherty, J. L., O'Donovan, M. C., & Owen, M. J. (2012). Recent genomic advances in schizophrenia. *Clinical Genetics, 81*(2), 103–109.

Drew, L. J., Stark, K. L., Fénelon, K., Karayiorgou, M., Macdermott, A. B., & Gogos, J. A. (2011). Evidence for altered hippocampal function in a mouse model of the human 22q11.2 microdeletion. *Molecular and Cellular Neuroscience, 47*(4), 293–305.

Egan, M. F., Goldberg, T. E., Kolachana, B. S., Callicott, J. H., Mazzanti, C. M., Straub, R. E., Goldman, D., & Weinberger, D. R. (2001). Effect of COMT Val108/158 Met genotype on frontal lobe function and risk for schizophrenia. *Proceedings of the National Academy of Sciences of the United States of America, 98*(12), 6917–6922.

Ellegood, J., Markx, S., Lerch, J. P., Steadman, P. E., Genç, C., Provenzano, F., et al. (2014). Neuroanatomical phenotypes in a mouse model of the 22q11.2 microdeletion. *Molecular Psychiatry, 19*(1), 99–107.

Escudero, I., & Johnstone, M. (2014). Genetics of schizophrenia. *Current Psychiatry Reports, 16*(11), 502.

Featherstone, R. E., Kapur, S., & Fletcher, P. J. (2007). The amphetamine-induced sensitized state as a model of schizophrenia. *Progress in Neuro-Psychopharmacology & Biological Psychiatry, 31*(8), 1556–1571.

Feng, Y. Q., Zhou, Z. Y., He, X., Wang, H., Guo, X. L., Hao, C. J., et al. (2008). Dysbindin deficiency in sandy mice causes reduction of snapin and displays behaviors related to schizophrenia. *Schizophrenia Research, 106*(2–3), 218–228.

Fujioka, R., Nii, T., Iwaki, A., Shibata, A., Ito, I., Kitaichi, K., et al. (2014). Comprehensive behavioral study of mGluR3 knockout mice: implication in schizophrenia related endophenotypes. *Molecular Brain, 7*, 31.

Gandal, M. J., Anderson, R. L., Billingslea, E. N., Carlson, G. C., Roberts, T. P., & Siegel, S. J. (2012). Mice with reduced NMDA receptor expression: more consistent with autism than schizophrenia? *Genes, Brain and Behavior, 11*(6), 740–750.

George, T. P., Termine, A., Sacco, K. A., Allen, T. M., Reutenauer, E., Vessicchio, J. C., et al. (2006). A preliminary study of the effects of cigarette smoking on prepulse inhibition in schizophrenia: involvement of nicotinic receptor mechanisms. *Schizophrenia Research, 87*(1–3), 307–315.

Gerlai, R., & Clayton, N. S. (1999). Analysing hippocampal function in transgenic mice: an ethological perspective. *Trends in Neurosciences, 22*(2), 47–51.

Gerlai, R., Pisacane, P., & Erickson, S. (2000). Heregulin, but not ErbB2 or ErbB3, heterozygous mutant mice exhibit hyperactivity in multiple behavioral tasks. *Behavioural Brain Research, 109*(2), 219–227.

Gogos, J. A. (2007). Schizophrenia susceptibility genes: in search of a molecular logic and novel drug targets for a devastating disorder. *International Review of Neurobiology, 78*, 397–422.

Gogos, J. A., Santha, M., Takacs, Z., Beck, K. D., Luine, V., Lucas, L. R., Nadler, J. V., & Karayiorgou, M. (1999). The gene encoding proline dehydrogenase modulates sensorimotor gating in mice. *Nature Genetics, 21*(4), 434–439.

Gould, T. D., & Gottesman, I. I. (2006). Psychiatric endophenotypes and the development of valid animal models. *Genes, Brain and Behavior, 5*, 113–119.

Gray, L., van den Buuse, M., Scarr, E., Dean, B., & Hannan, A. J. (2009). Clozapine reverses schizophrenia-related behaviours in the metabotropic glutamate receptor 5 knockout mouse: association with N-methyl-D-aspartic acid receptor up-regulation. *The International Journal of Neuropsychopharmacology, 12*(1), 45–60.

Hancock, M. L., Canetta, S. E., Role, L. W., & Talmage, D. A. (2008). Presynaptic type III neuregulin1-ErbB signaling targets {alpha}7 nicotinic acetylcholine receptors to axons. *Journal of Cell Biology, 181*(3), 511–521.

Harrison, P. J., & Law, A. J. (2006). Neuregulin 1 and schizophrenia: genetics, gene expression, and neurobiology. *Biological Psychiatry, 60*(2), 132–140.

Hashimoto, A., Yoshikawa, M., Niwa, A., & Konno, R. (2005). Mice lacking D-amino acid oxidase activity display marked attenuation of stereotypy and ataxia induced by MK-801. *Brain Research, 1033*(2), 210–215.

Hashimoto, R., Straub, R. E., Weickert, C. S., Hyde, T. M., Kleinman, J. E., & Weinberger, D. R. (2004). Expression analysis of neuregulin-1 in the dorsolateral prefrontal cortex in schizophrenia. *Molecular Psychiatry, 9*(3), 299–307.

Hattori, S., Murotani, T., Matsuzaki, S., Ishizuka, T., Kumamoto, N., Takeda, M., et al. (2008). Behavioral abnormalities and dopamine reductions in sdy mutant mice with a deletion in Dtnbp1, a susceptibility gene for schizophrenia. *Biochemical and Biophysical Research, 373*(2), 298–302.

Hennah, W., & Porteous, D. (2009). The DISC1 pathway modulates expression of neurodevelopmental, synaptogenic and sensory perception genes. *PLoS One, 4*(3), e4906.

Hennah, W., Tomppo, L., Hiekkalinna, T., Palo, O. M., Kilpinen, H., Ekelund, J., Tuulio-Henriksson, A., Silander, K., Partonen, T., Paunio, T., Terwilliger, J. D., Lönnqvist, J., & Peltonen, L. (2007). Families with the risk allele of DISC1 reveal a link between schizophrenia and another component of the same molecular pathway, NDE1. *Human Molecular Genetics, 16*(5), 453–462.

Hikida, T., Jaaro-Peled, H., Seshadri, S., Oishi, K., Hookway, C., Kong, S., et al. (2007). Dominant-negative DISC1 transgenic mice display schizophrenia-associated phenotypes detected by measures translatable to humans. *Proceedings of the National Academy of Sciences of the United States of America, 104*(36), 14501–14506.

Hirvonen, M., Laakso, A., Någren, K., Rinne, J. O., Pohjalainen, T., & Hietala, J. (2004). C957T polymorphism of the dopamine D2 receptor (DRD2) gene affects striatal DRD2 availability in vivo. *Molecular Psychiatry, 9*(12), 1060–1061.

Hodgkinson, C. A., Goldman, D., Jaeger, J., Persaud, S., Kane, J. M., Lipsky, R. H., et al. (2004). Disrupted in schizophrenia 1 (DISC1): association with schizophrenia, schizoaffective disorder, and bipolar disorder. *American Journal of Human Genetics, 75*(5), 862–872.

Jentsch, J. D., Trantham-Davidson, H., Jairl, C., Tinsley, M., Cannon, T. D., & Lavin, A. (2009). Dysbindin modulates prefrontal cortical glutamatergic circuits and working memory function in mice. *Neuropsychopharmacology, 34*(12), 2601–2608.

Jew, C. P., Wu, C. S., Sun, H., Zhu, J., Huang, J. Y., Yu, D., et al. (2013). mGluR5 ablation in cortical glutamatergic neurons increases novelty-induced locomotion. *PLoS One, 8*(8), e70415.

Ji, Y., Yang, F., Papaleo, F., Wang, H. X., Gao, W. J., Weinberger, D. R., et al. (2009). Role of dysbindin in dopamine receptor trafficking and cortical GABA function. *Proceedings of the National Academy of Sciences of the United States of America, 106*(46), 19593–19598.

Joshi, D., Fullerton, J. M., & Weickert, C. S. (2014). Elevated ErbB4 mRNA is related to interneuron deficit in prefrontal cortex in schizophrenia. *Journal of Psychiatric Research, 53*, 125–132.

Karayiorgou, M., & Gogos, J. A. (2004). The molecular genetics of the 22q11-associated schizophrenia. *Brain Research Molecular Brain Research, 132*(2), 95–104.

Karl, T., Duffy, L., Scimone, A., Harvey, R. P., & Schofield, P. R. (2007). Altered motor activity, exploration and anxiety in heterozygous neuregulin 1 mutant mice: implications for understanding schizophrenia. *Genes, Brain, and Behavior, 6*(7), 677–687.

Karlsgodt, K. H., Robleto, K., Trantham-Davidson, H., Jairl, C., Cannon, T. D., Lavin, A., et al. (2011). Reduced dysbindin expression mediates N-methyl-D-aspartate receptor hypofunction and impaired working memory performance. *Biological Psychiatry, 69*(1), 28–34.

Kato, T., Abe, Y., Sotoyama, H., Kakita, A., Kominami, R., Hirokawa, S., et al. (2011). Transient exposure of neonatal mice to neuregulin-1 results in hyperdopaminergic states in adulthood: implication in neurodevelopmental hypothesis for schizophrenia. *Molecular Psychiatry, 16*(3), 307–320.

Kato, T., Kasai, A., Mizuno, M., Fengyi, L., Shintani, N., Maeda, S., et al. (2010). Phenotypic characterization of transgenic mice overexpressing neuregulin-1. *PLoS One, 5*(12), e14185.

Kegeles, L. S., Abi-Dargham, A., Zea-Ponce, Y., Rodenhiser-Hill, J., Mann, J. J., Van Heertum, R. L., Cooper, T. B., Carlsson, A., & Laruelle, M. (2000). Modulation of amphetamine-induced striatal dopamine release by ketamine in humans: implications for schizophrenia. *Biological Psychiatry, 48*(7), 627–640.

Kellendonk, C., Simpson, E. H., Polan, H. J., Malleret, G., Vronskaya, S., Winiger, V., Moore, H., & Kandel, E. R. (2006). Transient and selective overexpression of dopamine D2 receptors in the striatum causes persistent abnormalities in prefrontal cortex functioning. *Neuron, 49*(4), 603–615.

Kimoto, S. 1., Muraki, K., Toritsuka, M., Mugikura, S., Kajiwara, K., Kishimoto, T., Illingworth, E., & Tanigaki, K. (2012). Selective overexpression of Comt in prefrontal cortex rescues schizophrenia-like phenotypes in a mouse model of 22q11 deletion syndrome. *Translational Psychiatry, 2*, e146.

Kinney, G. G., Burno, M., Campbell, U. C., Hernandez, L. M., Rodriguez, D., Bristow, L. J., et al. (2003). Metabotropic glutamate subtype 5 receptors modulate locomotor activity and sensorimotor gating in rodents. *Journal of Pharmacology and Experimental Therapeutics, 306*(1), 116–123.

Kirby, B. P., Waddington, J. L., & O'Tuathaigh, C. M. (2010). Advancing a functional genomics for schizophrenia: psychopathological and cognitive phenotypes in mutants with gene disruption. *Brain Research Bulletin, 83*(3–4), 162–176.

Koike, H., Arguello, P. A., Kvajo, M., Karayiorgou, M., & Gogos, J. A. (2006). Disc1 is mutated in the 129S6/SvEv strain and modulates working memory in mice. *Proceedings of the National Academy of Sciences of the United States of America, 103*(10), 3693–3697.

Kumari, V., & Postma, P. (2005). Nicotine use in schizophrenia: the self medication hypotheses. *Neuroscience & Biobehavioral Reviews, 29*(6), 1021–1034.

Kvajo, M., McKellar, H., Arguello, P. A., Drew, L. J., Moore, H., MacDermott, A. B., et al. (2008). A mutation in mouse Disc1 that models a schizophrenia risk allele leads to specific alterations in neuronal architecture and cognition. *Proceedings of the National Academy of Sciences of the United States of America, 105*(19), 7076–7081.

Labrie, V., Clapcote, S. J., & Roder, J. C. (2009). Mutant mice with reduced NMDA-NR1 glycine affinity or lack of D-amino acid oxidase function exhibit altered anxiety-like behaviors. *Pharmacology Biochemistry and Behavior, 91*(4), 610–620.

Labrie, V., Duffy, S., Wang, W., Barger, S. W., Baker, G. B., & Roder, J. C. (2009). Genetic inactivation of D-amino acid oxidase enhances extinction and reversal learning in mice. *Learning & Memory, 16*(1), 28–37.

Labrie, V., Wong, A. H., & Roder, J. C. (2012). Contributions of the D-serine pathway to schizophrenia. *Neuropharmacology, 62*(3), 1484–1503.

Lainiola, M., Procaccini, C., & Linden, A. M. (2014). mGluR3 knockout mice show a working memory defect and an enhanced response to MK-801 in the T- and Y-maze cognitive tests. *Behavioural Brain Research, 266*, 94–103.

Lane, H. Y., Lin, C. H., Green, M. F., Hellemann, G., Huang, C. C., Chen, P. W., et al. (2013). Add-on treatment of benzoate for schizophrenia: a randomized, double-blind, placebo-controlled trial of D-amino acid oxidase inhibitor. *JAMA Psychiatry, 70*(12), 1267–1275.

Laruelle, M., Kegeles, L. S., & Abi-Dargham (2003). Glutamate, dopamine, and schizophrenia: from pathophysiology to treatment. *Annals of the New York Academy of Sciences, 1003*, 138–1358.

Law, A. J., Lipska, B. K., Weickert, C. S., Hyde, T. M., Straub, R. E., Hashimoto, R., et al. (2006). Neuregulin 1 transcripts are differentially expressed in schizophrenia and regulated by 5' SNPs associated with the disease. *Proceedings of the National Academy of Sciences of the United States of America, 103*(17), 6747–6752.

Li, W., Zhou, Y., Jentsch, J. D., Brown, R. A., Tian, X., Ehninger, D., et al. (2007). Specific developmental disruption of disrupted-in-schizophrenia-1 function results in schizophrenia-related phenotypes in mice. *Proceedings of the National Academy of Sciences of the United States of America, 104*(46), 18280–18285.

Lipina, T. V., Zai, C., Hlousek, D., Roder, J. C., & Wong, A. H. (2013). Maternal immune activation during gestation interacts with Disc1 point mutation to exacerbate schizophrenia-related behaviors in mice. *Journal of Neuroscience, 33*(18), 7654–7666.

Long, J. M., LaPorte, P., Merscher, S., Funke, B., Saint-Jore, B., Puech, A., et al. (2006). Behavior of mice with mutations in the conserved region deleted in velocardiofacial/DiGeorge syndrome. *Neurogenetics, 7*(4), 247–257.

Long, L. E., Chesworth, R., Huang, X. F., McGregor, I. S., Arnold, J. C., & Karl, T. (2013). Transmembrane domain Nrg1 mutant mice show altered susceptibility to the neurobehavioural actions of repeated THC exposure in adolescence. *International Journal of Neuropsychopharmacology, 16*(1), 163–175.

Lu, Y. M., Jia, Z., Janus, C., Henderson, J. T., Gerlai, R., Wojtowicz, J. M., et al. (1997). Mice lacking metabotropic glutamate receptor 5 show impaired learning and reduced CA1 long-term potentiation (LTP) but normal CA3 LTP. *Journal of Neuroscience, 17*(13), 5196–5205.

Lundgaard, I., Luzhynskaya, A., Stockley, J. H., Wang, Z., Evans, K. A., Swire, M., et al. (2013). Neuregulin and BDNF induce a switch to NMDA receptor-dependent myelination by oligodendrocytes. *PLoS Biology, 11*(12), e1001743.

Luo, X., He, W., Hu, X., & Yan, R. (2014). Reversible overexpression of bace1-cleaved neuregulin-1 N-terminal fragment induces schizophrenia-like phenotypes in mice. *Biological Psychiatry, 76*(2), 120–127.

Lyon, L., Burnet, P. W., Kew, J. N., Corti, C., Rawlins, J. N., Lane, T., et al. (2011). Fractionation of spatial memory in GRM2/3 (mGlu2/mGlu3) double knockout mice reveals a role for group II metabotropic glutamate receptors at the interface between arousal and cognition. *Neuropsychopharmacology, 36*(13), 2616–2628.

Mackie, S., Millar, J. K., & Porteous, D. J. (2007). Role of DISC1 in neural development and schizophrenia. *Current Opinion in Neurobiology, 17*(1), 95–102.

Marsman, A., van den Heuvel, M. P., Klomp, D. W., Kahn, R. S., Luijten, P. R., & Hulshoff Pol, H. E. (2013). Glutamate in schizophrenia: a focused review and meta-analysis of ¹H-MRS studies. *Schizophrenia Bulletin, 39*(1), 120–129.

Malhotra, A. K., Pinals, D. A., Adler, C. M., Elman, I., Clifton, A., Pickar, D., & Breier, A. (1997). Ketamine-induced exacerbation of psychotic symptoms and cognitive impairment in neuroleptic-free schizophrenics. *Neuropsychopharmacology, 17*(3), 141–150.

Mei, L., & Nave, K. A. (2014). Neuregulin-ERBB signaling in the nervous system and neuropsychiatric diseases. *Neuron, 83*(1), 27–49.

Mei, L., & Xiong, W. C. (2008). Neuregulin 1 in neural development, synaptic plasticity and schizophrenia. *Nature Reviews Neuroscience, 9*(6), 437–452.

Menniti, F. S., Chappie, T. A., Humphrey, J. M., & Schmidt, C. J. (2007). Phosphodiesterase 10A inhibitors: a novel approach to the treatment of the symptoms of schizophrenia. *Current Opinion in Investigational Drugs, 8*(1), 54–59.

Merscher, S., Funke, B., Epstein, J. A., Heyer, J., Puech, A., Lu, M. M., et al. (2001). TBX1 is responsible for cardiovascular defects in velo-cardio-facial/DiGeorge syndrome. *Cell, 104*(4), 619–629.

Milenkovic, M., Mielnik, C. A., & Ramsey, A. J. (2014). NMDA receptor deficient mice display sexual dimorphism in the onset and severity of behavioural abnormalities. *Genes, Brain and Behavior, 13*(8), 850–862.

Millar, J. K., Pickard, B. S., Mackie, S., James, R., Christie, S., Buchanan, S. R., et al. (2005). DISC1 and PDE4B are interacting genetic factors in schizophrenia that regulate cAMP signaling. *Science, 310*(5751), 1187–1191.

Mohn, A. R., Gainetdinov, R. R., Caron, M. G., & Koller, B. H. (1999). Mice with reduced NMDA receptor expression display behaviors related to schizophrenia. *Cell, 98*(4), 427–436.

Morishima, Y., Miyakawa, T., Furuyashiki, T., Tanaka, Y., Mizuma, H., & Nakanishi, S. (2005). Enhanced cocaine responsiveness and impaired motor coordination in metabotropic glutamate receptor subtype 2 knockout mice. *Proceedings of the National Academy of Sciences of the United States of America, 102*(11), 4170–4175.

Moy, S. S., Ghashghaei, H. T., Nonneman, R. J., Weimer, J. M., Yokota, Y., Lee, D., et al. (2009). Deficient NRG1-ERBB signaling alters social approach: relevance to genetic mouse models of schizophrenia. *Journal of Neurodevelopmental Disorders*, 1(4), 302–312.

Mukai, J., Liu, H., Burt, R. A., Swor, D. E., Lai, W. S., Karayiorgou, M., et al. (2004). Evidence that the gene encoding ZDHHC8 contributes to the risk of schizophrenia. *Nature Genetics*, 36(7), 725–731.

Mukai, J., Dhilla, A., Drew, L. J., Stark, K. L., Cao, L., MacDermott, A. B., Karayiorgou, M., & Gogos, J. A. (2008). Palmitoylation-dependent neurodevelopmental deficits in a mouse model of 22q11 microdeletion. *Nature Neuroscience*, 11(11), 1302–1310.

Nawa, H., Sotoyama, H., Iwakura, Y., Takei, N., & Namba, H. (2014). Neuropathologic implication of peripheral neuregulin-1 and EGF signals in dopaminergic dysfunction and behavioral deficits relevant to schizophrenia: their target cells and time window. *Biomed Research International*, 2014, 697935.

Numakawa, T., Yagasaki, Y., Ishimoto, T., Okada, T., Suzuki, T., Iwata, N., et al. (2004). Evidence of novel neuronal functions of dysbindin, a susceptibility gene for schizophrenia. *Human Molecular Genetics*, 13(21), 2699–2708.

O'Leary, C., Desbonnet, L., Clarke, N., Petit, E., Tighe, O., Lai, D., et al. (2014). Phenotypic effects of maternal immune activation and early postnatal milieu in mice mutant for the schizophrenia risk gene neuregulin-1. *Neuroscience*, 277, 294–305.

O'Neal, K. R., & Agah, R. (2007). Conditional targeting: inducible deletion by Cre recombinase. *Methods in Molecular Biology*, 366, 309–320.

O'Sullivan, G. J., O'Tuathaigh, C. M., Clifford, J. J., O'Meara, G. F., Croke, D. T., & Waddington, J. L. (2006). Potential and limitations of genetic manipulation in animals. *Drug Discovery Today: Technologies*, 3(2), 173–180.

O'Tuathaigh, C. M., Desbonnet, L., Moran, P. M., Kirby, B. P., & Waddington, J. L. (2011). Molecular genetic models related to schizophrenia and psychotic illness: heuristics and challenges. *Current Topics in Behavioral Neurosciences*, 7, 87–119.

O'Tuathaigh, C. M., Desbonnet, L., & Waddington, J. L. (2009). Neuregulin-1 signaling in schizophrenia: 'Jack of all trades' or master of some? *Expert Review of Neurotherapeutics*, 9(1), 1–3.

O'Tuathaigh, C. M., Clarke, G., Walsh, J., Desbonnet, L., Petit, E., O'Leary, C., Tighe, O., Clarke, N., Karayiorgou, M., Gogos, J. A., Dinan, T. G., Cryan, J. F., & Waddington, J. L. (2012). Genetic vs. pharmacological inactivation of COMT influences cannabinoid-induced expression of schizophrenia-related phenotypes. *The International Journal of Neuropsychopharmacology*, 15(9), 1331–1342.

O'Tuathaigh, C. M., Kirby, B. P., Moran, P. M., & Waddington, J. L. (2010). Mutant mouse models: genotype-phenotype relationships to negative symptoms in schizophrenia. *Schizophrenia Bulletin*, 36(2), 271–288.

O'Tuathaigh, C. M., O'Connor, A. M., O'Sullivan, G. J., Lai, D., Harvey, R., Croke, D. T., & Waddington, J. L. (2008). Disruption to social dyadic interactions but not emotional/anxiety-related behaviour in mice with heterozygous 'knockout' of the schizophrenia risk gene neuregulin-1. *Progress in Neuro-psychopharmacology & Biological Psychiatry*, 32(2), 462–466.

O'Tuathaigh, C. M., Babovic, D., O'Sullivan, G. J., Clifford, J. J., Tighe, O., Croke, D. T., Harvey, R., & Waddington, J. L. (2007). Phenotypic characterization of spatial cognition and social behavior in mice with 'knockout' of the schizophrenia risk gene neuregulin 1. *Neuroscience*, 147(1), 18–27.

O'Tuathaigh, C. M., O'Sullivan, G. J., Kinsella, A., Harvey, R. P., Tighe, O., Croke, D. T., et al. (2006). Sexually dimorphic changes in the exploratory and habituation profiles of heterozygous neuregulin-1 knockout mice. *Neuroreport*, 17(1), 79–83.

Olsen, C. M., Childs, D. S., Stanwood, G. D., & Winder, D. G. (2010). Operant sensation seeking requires metabotropic glutamate receptor 5 (mGluR5). *PLoS One*, 5(11), e15085.

van Os, J., Rutten, B. P., Myin-Germeys, I., Delespaul, P., Viechtbauer, W., van Zelst, C., et al. (2014). Identifying gene-environment interactions in schizophrenia: contemporary challenges for integrated, large-scale investigations. *Schizophrenia Bulletin*, 40(4), 729–736.

Owen, M. J., Williams, H. J., & O'Donovan, M. C. (2009). Schizophrenia genetics: advancing on two fronts. *Current Opinion in Genetics & Development*, 19(3), 266–270.

Owen, M. J., Williams, N. M., & O'Donovan, M. C. (2004). The molecular genetics of schizophrenia: new findings promise new insights. *Molecular Psychiatry*, 9(1), 14–27.

Papaleo, F., Crawley, J. N., Song, J., Lipska, B. K., Pickel, J., Weinberger, D. R., & Chen, J. (2008). Genetic dissection of the role of catechol-O-methyltransferase in cognition and stress reactivity in mice. *The Journal of Neuroscience*, 28(35), 8709–8723.

Papaleo, F., & Weinberger, D. R. (2011). Dysbindin and schizophrenia: it's dopamine and glutamate all over again. *Biological Psychiatry*, 69(1), 2–4.

Papaleo, F., Yang, F., Garcia, S., Chen, J., Lu, B., Crawley, J. N., et al. (2012). Dysbindin-1 modulates prefrontal cortical activity and schizophrenia-like behaviors via dopamine/D2 pathways. *Molecular Psychiatry*, 17(1), 85–98.

Parlapani, E., Schmitt, A., Wirths, O., Bauer, M., Sommer, C., Rueb, U., et al. (2010). Gene expression of neuregulin-1 isoforms in different brain regions of elderly schizophrenia patients. *World Journal of Biological Psychiatry*, 11(2 Pt 2), 243–250.

Patil, S. T., Zhang, L., Martenyi, F., Lowe, S. L., Jackson, K. A., Andreev, B. V., Avedisova, A. S., Bardenstein, L. M., Gurovich, I. Y., Morozova, M. A., Mosolov, S. N., Neznanov, N. G., Reznik, A. M., Smulevich, A. B., Tochilov, V. A., Johnson, B. G., Monn, J. A., & Schoepp, D. D. (2007). Activation of mGlu2/3 receptors as a new approach to treat schizophrenia: a randomized Phase 2 clinical trial. *Nature Medicine*, 13(9), 1102–1107.

Paylor, R., Glaser, B., Mupo, A., Ataliotis, P., Spencer, C., Sobotka, A., et al. (2006). Tbx1 haploinsufficiency is linked to behavioral disorders in mice and humans: implications for 22q11 deletion syndrome. *Proceedings of the National Academy of Sciences of the United States of America*, 103(20), 7729–7734.

Paylor, R., & Lindsay, E. (2006). Mouse models of 22q11 deletion syndrome. *Biological Psychiatry*, 59(12), 1172–1179.

Paylor, R., McIlwain, K. L., McAninch, R., Nellis, A., Yuva-Paylor, L. A., Baldini, A., et al. (2001). Mice deleted for the DiGeorge/velo-cardiofacial syndrome region show abnormal sensorimotor gating and learning and memory impairments. *Human Molecular Genetics*, 10(23), 2645–2650.

Petryshen, T. L., Middleton, F. A., Kirby, A., Aldinger, K. A., Purcell, S., Tahl, A. R., et al. (2005). Support for involvement of neuregulin 1 in schizophrenia pathophysiology. *Molecular Psychiatry*, 10(4), 366–374, 328.

Philip, N., & Bassett, A. (2011). Cognitive, behavioural and psychiatric phenotype in 22q11.2 deletion syndrome. *Behavior Genetics*, 41(3), 403–412.

Phillips, T. J., Hen, R., & Crabbe, J. C. (1999). Complications associated with genetic background effects in research using knockout mice. *Psychopharmacology (Berl)*, 147(1), 5–7.

Pilowsky, L. S., Bressan, R. A., Stone, J. M., Erlandsson, K., Mulligan, R. S., Krystal, J. H., & Ell, P. J. (2006). First in vivo evidence of an NMDA receptor deficit in medication-free schizophrenic patients. *Molecular Psychiatry*, 11(2), 118–119.

Pletnikov, M. V., Ayhan, Y., Nikolskaia, O., Xu, Y., Ovanesov, M. V., Huang, H., et al. (2008). Inducible expression of mutant human DISC1 in mice is associated with brain and behavioral abnormalities reminiscent of schizophrenia. *Molecular Psychiatry*, 13(2), 173–186, 115.

Porteous, D. J., Millar, J. K., Brandon, N. J., & Sawa, A. (2011). DISC1 at 10: connecting psychiatric genetics and neuroscience. *Trends in Molecular Medicine*, 17(12), 699–706.

Postma, P., Gray, J. A., Sharma, T., Geyer, M., Mehrotra, R., Das, M., et al. (2006). A behavioural and functional neuroimaging investigation into the effects of nicotine on sensorimotor gating in healthy subjects and persons with schizophrenia. *Psychopharmacology (Berl)*, *184*(3–4), 589–599.

Qu, M., Tang, F., Yue, W., Ruan, Y., Lu, T., Liu, Z., et al. (2007). Positive association of the Disrupted-in-Schizophrenia-1 gene (DISC1) with schizophrenia in the Chinese Han population. *American Journal of Medical Genetics Part B: Neuropsychiatric Genetics*, *144B*(3), 266–270.

Rimer, M., Barrett, D. W., Maldonado, M. A., Vock, V. M., & Gonzalez-Lima, F. (2005). Neuregulin-1 immunoglobulin-like domain mutant mice: clozapine sensitivity and impaired latent inhibition. *Neuroreport*, *16*(3), 271–275.

Ripke, S., O'Dushlaine, C., Chambert, K., Moran, J. L., Kahler, A. K., Akterin, S., et al. (2013). Genome-wide association analysis identifies 13 new risk loci for schizophrenia. *Nature Genetics*, *45*(10), 1150–1159.

Roy, K., Murtie, J. C., El-Khodor, B. F., Edgar, N., Sardi, S. P., Hooks, B. M., et al. (2007). Loss of erbB signaling in oligodendrocytes alters myelin and dopaminergic function, a potential mechanism for neuropsychiatric disorders. *Proceedings of the National Academy of Sciences of the United States of America*, *104*(19), 8131–8136.

Sacchi, S., Rosini, E., Pollegioni, L., & Molla, G. (2013). D-amino acid oxidase inhibitors as a novel class of drugs for schizophrenia therapy. *Current Pharmaceutical Design*, *19*(14), 2499–2511.

Sasabe, J., Suzuki, M., Imanishi, N., & Aiso, S. (2014). Activity of D-amino acid oxidase is widespread in the human central nervous system. *Frontiers in Synaptic Neuroscience*, *6*, 14.

Saunders, J. A., Tatard-Leitman, V. M., Suh, J., Billingslea, E. N., Roberts, T. P., & Siegel, S. J. (2013). Knockout of NMDA receptors in parvalbumin interneurons recreates autism-like phenotypes. *Autism Research*, *6*(2), 69–77.

Savonenko, A. V., Melnikova, T., Laird, F. M., Stewart, K. A., Price, D. L., & Wong, P. C. (2008). Alteration of BACE1-dependent NRG1/ErbB4 signaling and schizophrenia-like phenotypes in BACE1-null mice. *Proceedings of the National Academy of Sciences of the United States of America*, *105*(14), 5585–5590.

Scambler, P. J. (2000). The 22q11 deletion syndromes. *Human Molecular Genetics*, *9*(16), 2421–2426.

Schizophrenia Working Group of the Psychiatric Genomics Consortium. (2014). Biological insights from 108 schizophrenia-associated genetic loci. *Nature*, *511*(7510), 421–427.

Schweimer, J. V., Coullon, G. S., Betts, J. F., Burnet, P. W., Engle, S. J., Brandon, N. J., Harrison, P. J., & Sharp, T. (2014). Increased burst-firing of ventral tegmental area dopaminergic neurons in D-amino acid oxidase knockout mice in vivo. *The European Journal of Neuroscience*, *40*(7), 2999–3009.

Seeman, P., & Kapur, S. (2000). Schizophrenia: more dopamine, more D2 receptors. *Proceedings of the National Academy of Sciences of the United States of America*, *97*(14), 7673–7675.

Seeman, P., Battaglia, G., Corti, C., Corsi, M., & Bruno, V. (2009). Glutamate receptor mGlu2 and mGlu3 knockout striata are dopamine supersensitive, with elevated D2(High) receptors and marked supersensitivity to the dopamine agonist (+)PHNO. *Synapse*, *63*(3), 247–251.

Shamir, A., Kwon, O. B., Karavanova, I., Vullhorst, D., Leiva-Salcedo, E., Janssen, M. J., et al. (2012). The importance of the NRG-1/ErbB4 pathway for synaptic plasticity and behaviors associated with psychiatric disorders. *Journal of Neuroscience*, *32*(9), 2988–2997.

Shen, S., Lang, B., Nakamoto, C., Zhang, F., Pu, J., Kuan, S. L., et al. (2008). Schizophrenia-related neural and behavioral phenotypes in transgenic mice expressing truncated Disc1. *Journal of Neuroscience*, *28*(43), 10893–10904.

Shi, J., Gershon, E. S., & Liu, C. (2008). Genetic associations with schizophrenia: meta-analyses of 12 candidate genes. *Schizophrenia Research*, *104*(1–3), 96–107.

Shi, J., Levinson, D. F., Duan, J., Sanders, A. R., Zheng, Y., Pe'er, I., et al. (2009). Common variants on chromosome 6p22.1 are associated with schizophrenia. *Nature*, *460*(7256), 753–757.

Shigemoto, R. 1., Nomura, S., Ohishi, H., Sugihara, H., Nakanishi, S., & Mizuno, N. (1993). Immunohistochemical localization of a metabotropic glutamate receptor, mGluR5, in the rat brain. *Neuroscience Letters*, *163*(1), 53–57.

Shintani, N., Onaka, Y., Hashimoto, R., Takamura, H., Nagata, T., Umeda-Yano, S., et al. (2014). Behavioral characterization of mice overexpressing human dysbindin-1. *Molecular Brain*, *7*(1), 74.

Sigurdsson, T., Stark, K. L., Karayiorgou, M., Gogos, J. A., & Gordon, J. A. (2010). Impaired hippocampal-prefrontal synchrony in a genetic mouse model of schizophrenia. *Nature*, *464*(7289), 763–767.

Stark, K. L., Xu, B., Bagchi, A., Lai, W. S., Liu, H., Hsu, R., et al. (2008). Altered brain microRNA biogenesis contributes to phenotypic deficits in a 22q11-deletion mouse model. *Nature Genetics*, *40*(6), 751–760.

Stefansson, H., Sigurdsson, E., Steinthorsdottir, V., Bjornsdottir, S., Sigmundsson, T., Ghosh, S., et al. (2002). Neuregulin 1 and susceptibility to schizophrenia. *American Journal of Human Genetics*, *71*(4), 877–892.

Stone, J. M., Erlandsson, K., Arstad, E., Squassante, L., Teneggi, V., Bressan, R. A., Krystal, J. H., Ell, P. J., & Pilowsky, L. S. (2008). Relationship between ketamine-induced psychotic symptoms and NMDA receptor occupancy: a [(123)I]CNS-1261 SPET study. *Psychopharmacology (Berl)*, *197*(3), 401–408.

Straub, R. E., Jiang, Y., MacLean, C. J., Ma, Y., Webb, B. T., Myakishev, M. V., et al. (2002). Genetic variation in the 6p22.3 gene DTNBP1, the human ortholog of the mouse dysbindin gene, is associated with schizophrenia. *American Journal of Human Genetics*, *71*(2), 337–348.

Sullivan, P. F., Kendler, K. S., & Neale, M. C. (2003). Schizophrenia as a complex trait: evidence from a meta-analysis of twin studies. *Archives of General Psychiatry*, *60*(12), 1187–1192.

Sullivan, P. F., Lin, D., Tzeng, J. Y., van den Oord, E., Perkins, D., Stroup, T. S., et al. (2008). Genomewide association for schizophrenia in the CATIE study: results of stage 1. *Molecular Psychiatry*, *13*(6), 570–584.

Takao, K., Toyama, K., Nakanishi, K., Hattori, S., Takamura, H., Takeda, M., et al. (2008). Impaired long-term memory retention and working memory in sdy mutant mice with a deletion in Dtnbp1, a susceptibility gene for schizophrenia. *Molecular Brain*, *1*, 11.

Talbot, K., Eidem, W. L., Tinsley, C. L., Benson, M. A., Thompson, E. W., Smith, R. J., et al. (2004). Dysbindin-1 is reduced in intrinsic, glutamatergic terminals of the hippocampal formation in schizophrenia. *Journal of Clinical Investigation*, *113*(9), 1353–1363.

Talbot, K. (2009). The sandy (sdy) mouse: a dysbindin-1 mutant relevant to schizophrenia research. *Progress in Brain Research*, *179*, 87–94.

Tang, J., LeGros, R. P., Louneva, N., Yeh, L., Cohen, J. W., Hahn, C. G., et al. (2009). Dysbindin-1 in dorsolateral prefrontal cortex of schizophrenia cases is reduced in an isoform-specific manner unrelated to dysbindin-1 mRNA expression. *Human Molecular Genetics*, *18*(20), 3851–3863.

Tang, T. T., Yang, F., Chen, B. S., Lu, Y., Ji, Y., Roche, K. W., et al. (2009). Dysbindin regulates hippocampal LTP by controlling NMDA receptor surface expression. *Proceedings of the National Academy of Sciences of the United States of America*, *106*(50), 21395–21400.

Taylor, A. R., Taylor, S. B., & Koenig, J. I. (2012). The involvement of Type II Neuregulin-1 in rat visuospatial learning and memory. *Neuroscience Letters*, *531*(2), 131–135.

Taylor, S. B., Markham, J. A., Taylor, A. R., Kanaskie, B. Z., & Koenig, J. I. (2011). Sex-specific neuroendocrine and behavioral phenotypes in hypomorphic Type II Neuregulin 1 rats. *Behavioural Brain Research*, *224*(2), 223–232.

Tecott, L. H., & Nestler, E. J. (2004). Neurobehavioral assessment in the information age. *Nature Neuroscience*, *7*(5), 462–466.

Toda, M., & Abi-Dargham, A. (2007). Dopamine hypothesis of schizophrenia: making sense of it all. *Current Psychiatry Reports*, *9*(4), 329–336.

Tunbridge, E. M., Harrison, P. J., & Weinberger, D. R. (2006). Catechol-o-methyltransferase, cognition, and psychosis: Val158Met and beyond. *Biological Psychiatry*, 60(2), 141–151.

van den Buuse, M., Wischhof, L., Lee, R. X., Martin, S., & Karl, T. (2009). Neuregulin 1 hypomorphic mutant mice: enhanced baseline locomotor activity but normal psychotropic drug-induced hyperlocomotion and prepulse inhibition regulation. *The International Journal of Neuropsychopharmacology*, 12(10), 1383–1393.

Waddington, J. L., Corvin, A. P., Donohoe, G., O'Tuathaigh, C. M., Mitchell, K. J., & Gill, M. (2007). Functional genomics and schizophrenia: endophenotypes and mutant models. *Psychiatric Clinics of North America*, 30(3), 365–399.

Waddington, J. L., O'Tuathaigh, C., O'Sullivan, G., Tomiyama, K., Koshikawa, N., & Croke, D. T. (2005). Phenotypic studies on dopamine receptor subtype and associated signal transduction mutants: insights and challenges from 10 years at the psychopharmacology-molecular biology interface. *Psychopharmacology (Berl).*, 181(4), 611–638.

Weickert, C. S., Rothmond, D. A., Hyde, T. M., Kleinman, J. E., & Straub, R. E. (2008). Reduced DTNBP1 (dysbindin-1) mRNA in the hippocampal formation of schizophrenia patients. *Schizophrenia Research*, 98(1–3), 105–110.

Weickert, C. S., Straub, R. E., McClintock, B. W., Matsumoto, M., Hashimoto, R., Hyde, T. M., et al. (2004). Human dysbindin (DTNBP1) gene expression in normal brain and in schizophrenic prefrontal cortex and midbrain. *Archives of General Psychiatry*, 61(6), 544–555.

Weickert, C. S., Tiwari, Y., Schofield, P. R., Mowry, B. J., & Fullerton, J. M. (2012). Schizophrenia-associated HapICE haplotype is associated with increased NRG1 type III expression and high nucleotide diversity. *Translational Psychiatry*, 2, e104.

Wimer, R. E., & Wimer, C. C. (1985). Animal behavior genetics: a search for the biological foundations of behavior. *Annual Review of Psychology*, 36, 171–218.

Yamanaka, M. 1., Miyoshi, Y., Ohide, H., Hamase, K., & Konno, R. (2012). D-Amino acids in the brain and mutant rodents lacking D-amino-acid oxidase activity. *Amino Acids*, 43(5), 1811–1821.

Yin, D. M., Chen, Y. J., Lu, Y. S., Bean, J. C., Sathyamurthy, A., Shen, C., et al. (2013). Reversal of behavioral deficits and synaptic dysfunction in mice overexpressing neuregulin 1. *Neuron*, 78(4), 644–657.

Zhang, J. (2012). Genetic redundancies and their evolutionary maintenance. *Advances in Experimental Medicine and Biology*, 751, 279–300.

Zhang, M., Ballard, M. E., Basso, A. M., Bratcher, N., Browman, K. E., Curzon, P., et al. (2011). Behavioral characterization of a mutant mouse strain lacking D-amino acid oxidase activity. *Behavioural Brain Research*, 217(1), 81–87.

17

Dimensional Deconstruction and Reconstruction of CNV-Associated Neuropsychiatric Disorders

Noboru Hiroi*,§,¶, Akira Nishi*,‖‖

*Department of Psychiatry and Behavioral Sciences, Albert Einstein College of Medicine, Bronx, NY, USA;
§Department of Genetics, Albert Einstein College of Medicine, Bronx, NY, USA; ¶Dominick P. Purpura Department of
Neuroscience, Albert Einstein College of Medicine, Bronx, NY, USA; ‖‖Department of Psychiatry, Course of Integrated
Brain Sciences, Medical Informatics, Institute of Health Biosciences, University of Tokushima Graduate School,
Tokushima, Japan

Many rodent models of schizophrenia have been developed. Some models were developed on the premise that drugs that induce or ameliorate schizophrenic symptoms should provide mechanistic insights of the disorder (i.e., predictive validity). Indeed, these models were useful for probing potential mechanisms of the disorder and screening of potential antipsychotic drugs.

Rodent models are of renewed and increased interest, as robust, reliable genetic factors are identified. Some genetic variants confer extraordinary high levels of risk for schizophrenia and many other neuropsychiatric disorders. These genetic factors are being exploited to develop mouse models with construct validity.

In this chapter, we describe these genetic variants and how this knowledge is capitalized on to improve our understanding of neuropsychiatric disorders. Knowledge gained from these mouse studies, to date, has already forced us to rethink categorization of mental disorders. With genetic mouse models, we deconstruct mental disorders into genetically tractable elements and, hopefully, will then be able to reconstruct disorders from a mechanistic perspective.

COMMON AND RARE GENETIC VARIANTS

In recent years, there has been a concerted large-scale effort to identify genetic correlates of neuropsychiatric disorders. Many genetic variants have been identified, each of which is seen in a large percentage of individuals with schizophrenia (Ripke et al., 2013; Schizophrenia Working Group of the Psychiatric Genomics Consortium, 2014; Stefansson et al., 2009) and autism spectrum disorders (ASD) cases (Anney et al., 2010, 2012; Klei et al., 2012; Wang et al., 2009; Weiss, Arking, Daly, & Chakravarti, 2009). These "common variants" are thought to collectively confer considerable risk for mental diseases (Klei et al., 2012). However, the impact of each common variant on diseases is weak and may differ among individuals.

"Rare" genetic variants, each representing less than 1% of disease cases, have also been identified. Copy number variants (CNVs) belong to this category and are characterized by deletions or duplications of kilo- to mega-base chromosomal segments. Deletion at human chromosome 22q11.2 is one of the most extensively studied rare CNVs since its association with schizophrenia was established in 1992 (Driscoll, Budarf, & Emanuel, 1992; Driscoll, Spinner, et al., 1992; Scambler et al., 1992; Shprintzen, Goldberg, Golding-Kushner, & Marion, 1992). Up to 30% and 27% of 22q11.2 deletion carriers are diagnosed with schizophrenia and ASDs, respectively; this CNV is also associated with high rates of attention deficit hyperactivity disorder (ADHD) (up to 37%), anxiety disorders (up to 36%), and major depressive disorder (up to 16%) (Schneider et al., 2014). About half of 22q11.2 deletion carriers have intelligence quotients (IQs) lower than 70 and are diagnosed with mild to borderline intellectual disability(ID) (Butcher et al., 2012; De Smedt et al., 2007; Niklasson, Rasmussen, Oskarsdottir, & Gillberg, 2009). Further, 22q11.2 duplication is consistently associated with developmental delays in cognitive, socioemotional, and motor function, and carriers are often diagnosed, at high rates, with ASDs, mild to borderline ID and ADHD (Alberti et al., 2007; Brunet et al., 2006; van Campenhout et al., 2012; Courtens, Schramme, & Laridon, 2008; Descartes et al., 2008; Edelmann et al., 1999; Ensenauer et al., 2003; Hassed, Hopcus-Niccum, Zhang, Li, & Mulvihill, 2004; Hiroi et al., 2013; de La Rochebrochard et al., 2006; Lo-Castro et al., 2009; Mukaddes & Herguner, 2007; Ou et al., 2008; Portnoi, 2009; Portnoi et al., 2005; Ramelli et al., 2008; Wentzel, Fernstrom, Ohrner, Anneren, & Thuresson, 2008). Although some groups previously suggested caution about the diagnosis of ASDs in individuals with 22q11.2 hemizygosity, overwhelming evidence now indicates that deletion of the 22q11.2 locus is a robust risk factor for ASDs as well as schizophrenia (Hiroi, Hiramoto, Harper, Suzuki, & Boku, 2012; Hiroi et al., 2013).

A recent estimate based on the study of 19,084 schizophrenic patients conclusively established the rate of 22q11.2 deletion in this population between 0.2% and 0.3% (Rees, Walters, et al., 2014). Duplications at 22q11.2 have also been identified as a rare variant among individuals with ASDs, intellectual disability, and developmental delay (Bucan et al., 2009; Cai et al., 2008; Christian et al., 2008; Guilmatre et al., 2009; Itsara et al., 2010; Malhotra & Sebat, 2012; Marshall et al., 2008; Pinto et al., 2010; Sanders et al., 2011; Sebat et al., 2007; Szatmari et al., 2007).

Since 2007, many other rare CNVs have been discovered and found to be robustly and reproducibly associated with not only schizophrenia and ASDs but also ID, developmental delay, congenital malformations, bipolar disorder, and recurrent depression (Malhotra & Sebat, 2012), with some odds ratios estimated to be higher than 10. However, these odds ratios (ORs) are probably inflated because individuals with any neuropsychiatric disorder are excluded from controls (Kirov et al., 2013) and most CNV carriers have some neuropsychiatric disorders (Malhotra & Sebat, 2012). In fact, the penetrance of any mental disorder, including schizophrenia, ID, ASDs, and developmental delay, is close to complete in most CNVs (Kirov et al., 2013). Accordingly, no 22q11.2 CNV, for example, is included in the so-defined control, which in turn makes the OR of this CNV for schizophrenia infinite.

Kirov and colleagues corrected this bias and provided a more realistic risk estimate of various CNVs for schizophrenia and developmental delay (DD)/congenital malformations (CM)/ASDs (see Figure 1). Among them, 3q29

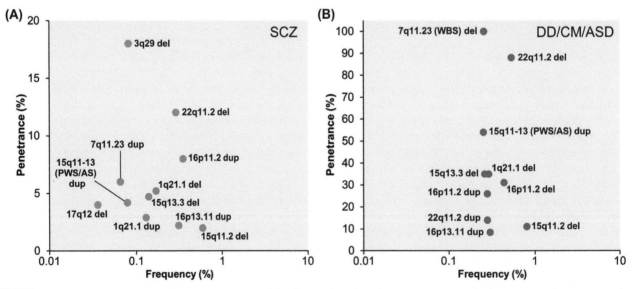

FIGURE 1   Risk for copy number variant (CNV) carriers of developing disorders. Some representative high-risk cases of rare variants (<1%) are shown. For developmental delay (DD)/congenital malformation (CM)/autism spectrum disorders (ASDs), only those cases with frequencies at 0.25% or higher are shown. Penetrance estimates for schizophrenia (SCZ) (A) and DD/CM/ASDs (B) are based on a modified formula (Kirov et al., 2013). Frequency indicates an estimated frequency of each CNV in a disease population.

deletion and 22q11.2 deletion confer extraordinarily high penetrance rates for schizophrenia; others confer considerable risk, including 16p11.2 duplication, 7q11.23 duplication, 1q21.1 deletion, and 15q13.3 deletion. CNVs with high penetrance rates for DD/CM/ASDs include 22q11.2 deletion, 15q11-13 duplication, 15q13.3 deletion, 1q21.1 deletion, 16p11.2 deletion, 16p11.2 duplication, 22q11.2 duplication, 15q11.2 deletion, and 16p13.11 duplication (Kirov et al., 2013; Malhotra & Sebat, 2012; Rees et al., 2013; Szatkiewicz et al., 2014). Although 7q11.23 deletion is listed as having high penetrance, it is associated with developmental delays, but not ASDs (Malhotra & Sebat, 2012).

Interestingly, some rare CNVs are not disease specific even among carriers of the same CNV size. For instance, both schizophrenia and ASDs occur at high rates among carriers of 22q11.2 deletion, 16p11.2 duplication, 1q21.1 deletion, 15q11-13 duplication, 15q13.3 deletion, 16p13.11 duplication, and 15q11.2 deletion; others are specific to either disorder (e.g., 7q11.23 deletion, 3q29 deletion, 1q21.1 duplication, 17q12 deletion, 22q11.2 duplication). The nonspecific impact of genetic variants for disorders might not be unique to rare CNVs. Some common variants contribute to susceptibility to multiple psychiatric disorders (Cross-Disorder Group of the Psychiatric Genomics Consortium, 2013; Ruderfer et al., 2014; Steinberg et al., 2014). Emerging evidence does not support the assumption that there are genetic variants that contribute so selectively to any single neuropsychiatric disorder. The remaining question is why a CNV generates so many diverse clinical diagnoses and why clinical diagnoses nevertheless differ among individual CNV carriers.

NEED FOR DIMENSIONAL SCALES OF NEUROPSYCHIATRIC DISORDERS

Neuropsychiatric disorders are defined by clinical diagnostic scales and diagnosis is done when symptoms thought to represent the essential, core feature(s) of a given psychiatric disorder are concurrently present. For example, the Diagnostic and Statistical Manual of Mental Disorders (DSM) successfully established diagnostic reliability using standardized criteria.

Schizophrenia is a clinically defined disorder by a set of specific diagnostic criteria. Psychopathological features of this diagnosis include positive symptoms, negative symptoms, and lowered levels of social functioning and self-care. The positive symptoms include delusions and hallucinations, and the negative symptoms include dimensions of drive and volition, manifesting as lack of motivation, reduction in spontaneous speech, and social withdrawal. The impaired neurocognitive functioning is characterized by lower scores than healthy subjects in attention, speed of processing, working and long-term memory, executive function, and social cognition (Fioravanti, Carlone, Vitale, Cinti, & Clare, 2005).

This constellation of disease-associated features is used to provide a categorical classification of schizophrenia. However, none of the symptomatic features is specific to schizophrenia. The cardinal symptoms of this disorder are delusions and hallucinations, but these are also seen in patients with bipolar disorder. Mild forms of delusions and hallucinations transiently appear in as much as 8% of healthy people (Van Os, Linscott, Myin-Germeys, Delespaul, & Krabbendam, 2009). The neurocognitive symptoms only quantitatively deviate from the norm, and are not an all-or-none feature or specific to schizophrenia; defective social cognition is seen in patients with ASDs, ADHD, and developmental language disorders (Korkmaz, 2011) as well as those with schizophrenia (Sprong, Schothorst, Vos, Hox, & van Engeland, 2007). Defective cognition, such as working memory, is seen in patients with schizophrenia (Piskulic, Olver, Norman, & Maruff, 2007). However, adolescents and adults with ASDs also perform poorly on working memory tasks, compared with age and IQ-matched controls, although negative results exist among children with ASDs in specific working memory tasks that do not include high memory load and temporal span (Bennett & Heaton, 2012; Luna, Doll, Hegedus, Minshew, & Sweeney, 2007; O'Hearn, Asato, Ordaz, & Luna, 2008; Pennington & Ozonoff, 1996; Russo et al., 2007). Working memory deficits are also associated with ADHD (Martinussen, Hayden, Hogg-Johnson, & Tannock, 2005). There is little evidence that these symptomatic elements are mechanistically related as a unit in the way they are perceived as construct elements of a disorder by clinical diagnosis. Therefore, a realistic and practical approach at this point is to separately identify mechanisms underlying each of the symptomatic elements or symptom dimensions.

In addition to inclusion criteria, an exclusion criterion of the DSM-V is inconsistent with CNV-associated psychiatric disorders. According to the DSM-V, schizophrenia-like symptoms are excluded from the diagnosis of schizophrenia if there is evidence from the history, physical examination, or laboratory findings that the disturbance is the direct physiological consequence of a general medical condition. For example, if a CNV or any resulting physical abnormalities are defined as "medical conditions," then by definition, any schizophrenic symptoms in these patients cannot be diagnosed as schizophrenia. However, it is difficult to prove that psychosis is the direct physiological consequence of physical abnormalities or associated stress. Almost all CNVs listed previously (see Figure 1) are associated with poor growth, craniofacial anomalies, cardiovascular abnormalities, or weak muscle tone (Girirajan et al., 2012). It is questionable to assume that diagnosis of schizophrenia should be limited to 'pure' schizophrenia without medical conditions.

It does not necessarily follow that a classification has a mechanistic basis simply because categorical classification is useful for clinical diagnosis and guidance for treatment of mental disorders. Clearly dimensional measures more akin to symptomatic elements should be focused.

DIMENSIONAL BEHAVIORAL MEASURES IN MICE

Many behavioral measures currently in use for assessment of mouse models of neuropsychiatric disorders were developed by psychologists and behavioral neuroscientists who were interested in specific psychological and behavioral properties in rodents. These tasks are dimensional and quantitative in nature. Various behavioral tasks are available to evaluate perception, cognitive, social, affective, emotional, and motor processes.

Prepulse Inhibition

Prepulse inhibition (PPI) is a phenomenon in which a weak acoustic auditory stimulus inhibits a startle response induced by the subsequent presentation of a loud sound. This is consistently seen in both humans and rodents. Defective PPI is seen not only in schizophrenic patients but also in individuals with schizotypal personality disorder, obsessive compulsive disorder, Tourette syndrome, Huntington disorder, bipolar disorder, seizures, Lewy body dementia, and ADHD (Geyer, 2006). PPI deficits are not consistently seen in individuals with ASDs but a subtle deficit appears only at a high PPI under a specific parameter (Belmonte et al., 2004; McAlonan et al., 2002; Ornitz, Lane, Sugiyama, & deTraversay, 1993; Perry, Minassian, Lopez, Maron, & Lincoln, 2007; Yuhas et al., 2010). Although often equated with a schizophrenia model, PPI deficits have no specificity.

Reciprocal Social Interaction

Defective social motivation and cognition are seen in patients with schizophrenia and ASDs (Penn, Corrigan, Bentall, Racenstein, & Newman, 1997; Sigman, 1998). Children with ADHD also have difficulties in social interaction for a different reason; their impulsive, self-centered nature often has a negative impact on their social interaction (Walcott & Landau, 2004). Such nuanced differences in the nature of social interaction deficits in humans cannot be clearly parceled out in rodent tasks.

There are two widely used methods to evaluate social behaviors in rodents. The naturalistic cage setup provides the most detailed insights into reciprocal social interactions (Silverman, Yang, Lord, & Crawley, 2010). This test evaluates the reciprocal nature of social interaction and allows evaluation of ethological details. In this task, two mice are placed into a home cage setting. Neither mouse has previously resided in the cage, so there is no "resident" mouse and aggressive behavior is minimized.

The other technique, known as the three-chamber "sociability" test, is also widely used because of its automated nature. In this task, a stimulus mouse is confined in a small cage or a compartment placed in one of the three chambers, and a test mouse's approach to the cage or compartment is measured. Several technical issues have arisen. First, the actual time spent near the caged stimulus mouse is highly variable across cohorts meaning that such quantitative measures cannot be compared (Crawley, 2014). Second, scores of sociability tests in the three-chamber apparatus do not correlate well with those of genuine reciprocal social interaction seen in the naturalistic test setup (Fairless et al., 2013; Spencer et al., 2011, Spencer, Alekseyenko, Serysheva, Yuva-Paylor, & Paylor, 2005). Thus, the naturalistic cage setup is desirable for evaluation of genuine reciprocal nature of social interaction.

Working Memory, Executive Functions, and Flexibility

Working memory is the cognitive capacity to temporarily hold incoming information to decide the next course of action based on that memory. This memory capacity is impaired in patients with schizophrenia (Piskulic et al., 2007) and ADHD (Martinussen et al., 2005; Westerberg, Hirvikoski, Forssberg, & Klingberg, 2004), and in adolescents and adults with ASDs (Bennett & Heaton, 2012; Pennington & Ozonoff, 1996; Russo et al., 2007).

Spontaneous alternation in the T- or Y-maze is a widely used task to measure working memory and memory-based repetitive behavioral tendencies (Lalonde, 2002). This task uses a mouse's natural behavioral tendency to alternate behavior based on memory. To alternate behavior, animals need to remember which of the two goal arms they just visited at a previous trial and alternate their visit at the next trial. One advantage of this task is that it does not need prior training that includes processes other than working memory. One interpretative caveat of this task is that repeated visits to the same arm could reflect a working memory deficit, repetitive behavioral tendency, or both; these elements cannot be easily dissociated.

Rewarded alternation and attentional set-shifting are also used to evaluate working memory and an overall executive function, respectively. Cognitive inflexibility is noted in patients with schizophrenia and ASDs.

Reversal learning has been used to evaluate the degree of cognitive flexibility in various memory tasks, including attentional set shifting, Morris water maze, T-maze, and discriminative operant learning (Brigman, Graybeal, & Holmes, 2010). If a previously acquired behavior cannot be easily modified upon a change in contingency, this is taken as lack of flexibility.

One technical issue with these tasks is that they require prior training that does not require working memory, executive function, or reversal. If a mutant mouse is altered in its motivation for food or general learning, subsequent performance in the target function would be indirectly affected and the phenotype cannot be attributed to deficits in the target function alone. Another interpretative caution for working memory is that mice might show deficits only when a delay between trials is imposed to increase working memory load. Unless delays are imposed, lack of a phenotype in this task should not been taken to suggest that working memory is not affected.

There are other rodent memory tasks, but their relevance to neuropsychiatric disorders is less clear. Executive function and working memory are far more affected in ASDs; individuals with ASDs are not impaired in cued recall, recognition, and new learning ability (Bennetto, Pennington, & Rogers, 1996). Schizophrenic patients also show varying degrees of impairments in different memory tasks (Heinrichs & Zakzanis, 1998); these individuals are more impaired in recall than recognition (Aleman, Hijman, de Haan, & Kahn, 1999). Working memory and executive functions are consistently lower in schizophrenic patients (Schaefer, Giangrande, Weinberger, & Dickinson, 2013; Wilk et al., 2005), but other memory forms (e.g., reference memory) might not genuinely be affected (Doughty & Done, 2009).

Anxiety-Like Behaviors

Anxiety is a highly prevalent comorbidity of schizophrenia. Although anxiety itself is not a symptomatic element of ASDs, it is also a highly comorbid trait of ASDs (van Steensel, Bogels, & de Bruin, 2013; van Steensel, Bogels, & Perrin, 2011). The elevated plus maze is a widely used standard task to evaluate anxiety-like behavior. Thigmotaxis in an inescapable open field is also a well-accepted measure of anxiety-related behavior.

Although the elevated plus maze and thigmotaxis both measure the level of anxiety, stress levels are considered much lower when mice have a choice to escape from an open arm to a closed arm in the elevated plus maze than when they do not in the inescapable open field (Misslin, Herzog, Koch, & Ropartz, 1982; Zhu, Lee, Agatsuma, & Hiroi, 2007). There are many other mouse tasks that rely on ethologically different aspects of anxiety-related behavior and involve varying degrees of stress. They include marble burying (Nicolas, Kolb, & Prinssen, 2006; Njung'e & Handley, 1991) and novelty-suppressed feeding (Dulawa & Hen, 2005).

When more than one anxiety task is used, a lack of consistent phenotypes in different anxiety tasks should not be taken to indicate weak effects or lack of corroboration. Stress levels differ in anxiety tasks with varying degrees of choices (Misslin et al., 1982). As each task includes a nonidentical mixture of behavioral elements, inconsistent phenotypes across those tasks could reveal the more nuanced nature of anxiety phenotypes. Evidence indicates that anxiety-like behaviors seen in different anxiety tasks have distinct genetic underpinnings (Takahashi, Nishi, Ishii, Shiroishi, & Koide, 2008). Phenotypic inconsistency among the various anxiety tasks could be exploited to explore the contribution of specific gene mutations to a select element of anxiety.

A phenotype often appears as a shift on a dimension; a behavioral phenotype is not a categorical inability of a given capacity (see Figure 2) (Hiroi et al., 2013). The way the average shifts also differs among behavioral phenotypes. In most cases, the data distribution shifts with varying degrees of overlap with control mice (see PPI and vocalization data). In other cases (see reciprocal social interaction), mutant data are distributed lower

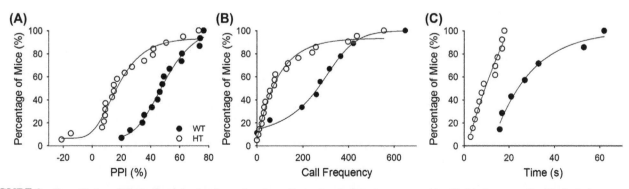

FIGURE 2 Quantitative shifts in the data structure of various dimensional phenotypes caused by *Tbx1* heterozygosity. Black circles represent wild-type mice and open circles represent heterozygous mice. (A) Prepulse inhibition, (B) ultrasonic neonatal vocal calls, and (C) reciprocal social interaction. *Adapted from our previous publication (Hiroi et al., 2013).*

than the lowest wild-type data. This again emphasizes the importance of a quantitative analysis of dimensional phenotypes.

VALIDITY OF MOUSE MODELS

Three criteria have been used to evaluate the validity of a rodent model. One is face validity, that is, what is modeled in rodents should look similar to what is seen in humans. Deficits in PPI are certainly similar in humans and mice. However, phenomenological similarities do not guarantee a shared mechanistic basis. Rodents and humans tend to use ethologically dominant sensory organs to achieve the same functions. For example, olfactory cues are dominant in social interaction in rodents, but visual and auditory cues are dominant in humans. Similarity should be evaluated considering this interpretative constraint.

A second criterion is predictive validity in that the effects of a drug on a rodent model should predict the effects of that drug on humans. Models that satisfy this criterion have been used to explore mechanistic bases of psychiatric disorders. For example, rodent studies have used drugs that induce symptoms of a neuropsychiatric disorder or drugs that attenuate disease symptoms in humans. This criterion also has interpretative caveats. First, drugs have many side effects that are not relevant to the symptoms of a disorder. For example, although antipsychotic drugs suppress positive symptoms (e.g., hallucination), they also induce motor side effects. Second, in most cases, drugs do not achieve specificity and thus do not reveal a disease-specific process. Antipsychotic drugs have been used to test the relevance of rodent behavior to schizophrenia. Clozapine, olanzapine, and risperidone reduce symptomatic severity of schizophrenia and have been tested to see if they attenuate a certain behavioral phenotype in rodent models. Many of these antipsychotic drugs are also used to suppress some symptomatic elements of ASDs (McDougle, Stigler, Erickson, & Posey, 2008), obsessive compulsive disorders, and bipolar disorder. Ketamine and phencyclidine, which induce both positive and negative symptoms of schizophrenia in humans, have been used to evaluate if a behavioral phenotype is exacerbated by these drugs in rodents. However, because ketamine has a rapid antidepressant effect as well (Abdallah, Sanacora, Duman, & Krystal, 2014), it is not clear if any behavior induced by ketamine is relevant to positive symptoms of schizophrenia or antidepressant effects. Nevertheless, rodent models that satisfy this criterion are likely to reveal mechanistic substrates of symptomatic elements that cut across disease classification.

The last criterion is construct validity, that is, a share etiology. Many CNVs can be reliably modeled in

mice, because genes encoded in CNVs are often well-conserved in the murine chromosomes. Mouse models of CNVs satisfy construct validity in that the human copy number variation can be faithfully recapitulated.

GENETIC MOUSE MODELS OF CNVs

There are published mouse models of several CNVs. They include paternal and maternal 15q11-13 duplication, 15q13.3 deletion, 16p11.2 deletion and duplication, and 22q11.2 duplication and deletion (see Table 1). Some of these CNV models recapitulate dimensional features of human CNVs. A mouse model of paternal 15q11-13 duplication exhibits low levels of sociability and flexibility and a heightened anxiety-like trait (Nakatani et al., 2009; Tamada et al., 2010). Mouse models of 15q13.3 hemizygous deletion show increased aggression and poor spatial memory performance (Fejgin et al., 2013). Mouse models of 22q11.2 hemizygosity exhibits lower levels of PPI, working memory and reversal learning, and a high level of anxiety (see Table 1).

Segmental overexpression and deletion in genetic mouse models is a highly effective approach for identification of small segments that are critical for behavioral dimensions. Using this approach, we identified specific small segments critical for distinct behavioral phenotypes. Overexpression of a 200-kb segment, termed a 200-kb critical region, of human 22q11.2, which includes TBX1, GP1BB, SEPT5, and GNB1L (Figure 3, see 200-kb Tg model; see also Table 1) caused social behavioral deficits and spontaneous exacerbation of repetitive hyperactivity, the latter of which was attenuated by chronic treatment with the antipsychotic drug clozapine (Hiroi et al., 2005).

Overexpression of an adjacent 190-kb region (TXNRD2, COMT, and ARVCF) selectively prevents developmental maturation of working memory capacity from 1 to 2 months of age (Figure 3, see 190-kb Tg model; see also Table 1); this copy number variant had no effect on PPI, social interactions, or anxiety-like behaviors (Suzuki, Harper, Hiramoto, Funke, et al., 2009). Complementing our observations, Stark and colleagues demonstrated that overexpression of segments outside these two segments had no effect on PPI (see Figure 3, Tg-2, and Table 1) or paradoxically increased PPI (see Figure 3, Tg-1, and Table 1) (Stark et al., 2009).

Paylor and colleagues compared the impact of various, partially overlapping hemizygous deletions of murine chromosome 16, the ortholog of human 22q11.2 (see Figure 3, Df(16)1/+ to Df(16)5/+) (Paylor et al., 2006). Their data showed that PPI was reduced in mice with large, partially overlapping deletions as long as the deletion included the 200-kb critical region (see blue frame, Df(16)1/+, Df(16)3/+, Df(16)4/+); hemizygous

TABLE 1 Phenotypes of CNV Mouse Models

CNV	Designation	ES or Zygote Cell Background	Additional Background	PPI	WM	RL	SI	Ax	LA	References
15q11-13 dup	patDp/+	129S7/SvEvBrd-Hprt<b-m2>	129S6/SvEvTac or C57BL/6J	–	–	↓	↓	↑	–	Nakatani et al. (2009)
	matDp/+			–	–	–	–	–	–	
15q11-13 dup	patDp/+	129S7/SvEvBrd-Hprt<b-m2>	C57BL/6J, congenic > 10 backcrosses	–	–		–	↑	↑	Tamada et al. (2010)
15q13.3 del	Df(h15q13)/+	C57BL/6NTac	C57BL/6NTac, co-isogenic	–	–			–	↑	Fejgin et al. (2013)
16p11.2 del	df/+	129S7/SvEvBrd-Hprt<b-m2>	F2 C57BL/6N				–	–	↑	Horev et al. (2011)
16p11.2 dup	df/+	129S7/SvEvBrd-Hprt<b-m2>						–	↑	
16p11.2 del	16p11+/-	129/Ola, 129S1/SvImJ	CD1; C57BL/6N, at least 5–7 backcrosses		–	–	–	–	↑	Portmann et al. (2014)
22q11.2 dup	200-kb Tg High copy	FVB	FVB, co-isogenic				↓		↑	Hiroi et al. (2005)
	Low copy	FVB	C57BL/6J; N4 FVB				↓		↑	
22q11.2 dup	190 kb Tg	FVB	C57BL/6J, congenic 10 backcrosses	–	↑		–	–	↑	Suzuki, Harper, Hiramoto, Funke, et al. (2009)
22q11.2 dup	Tg-1	FVB/N	FVB/N × SW × C57BL/6J, N2 backcross	↑			–	–	–	Stark et al. (2009)
	Tg-2			–			–	–	↑	
	Tg-3									
22q11.2 del		129S6/SvEvTac	129S6/SvEvTac co-isogenic or NIH Black Swiss	↑				–	–	Kimber et al. (1999)
22q11.2 del	Df(16)1/+	129S7/SvEvBrd-Hprt<b-m2>	129S5/SvEvBrd; C57BL/6c-/c-, 4–5 backcrosses	↑				–	–	Paylor et al. (2001)
22q11.2 del	Df(16)1/+	129S7/SvEvBrd-Hprt<b-m2>	129S5/SvEvBrd; C57BL/6c-/c-, 5–6 backcrosses	↑						Paylor et al. (2006)
	Df(16)2/+			–						
	Df(16)3/+			↑						
	Df(16)4/+			↑						
	Df(16)5/+			–						
22q11.2 del	Lgdel/+	129/Sv, C57BL/6J, SJL; 129S6/SvEvTac; FVB/N	C57BL/6; 129Sv; CD1; C57BL/6J, >5 backcrosses	↑				–	–	Long et al. (2006)
22q11.2 del	Df(16)A+/-	129S7/SvEvBrd-Hprt<b-m2>	C57BL/6J, 3 backcrosses	↑	↑			↑	↑	Stark et al. (2008)
22q11.2 del	Df(16)A+/-	129S7/SvEvBrd-Hprt<b-m2>	C57BL/6J, congenic		–					Sigurdsson et al. (2010)
22q11.2 del	Lgdel/+	129/Sv, C57BL/6J, SJL; 129S6/SvEvTac; FVB/N	C57BL/6; 129Sv; CD1; C57BL/6J, >25 backcrosses			↓				Meechan et al. (2013)

Del, deletion; dup, duplication; F#, generation of intercrossed line; N#, generation of backcrossed line; red arrow, effects consistent with human phenotypes; black arrow, effects inconsistent with phenotypes or not reported in humans; black bar, nonsignificant genetic effects on phenotypes.

II. NEUROBIOLOGY OF PSYCHOTIC DISORDERS

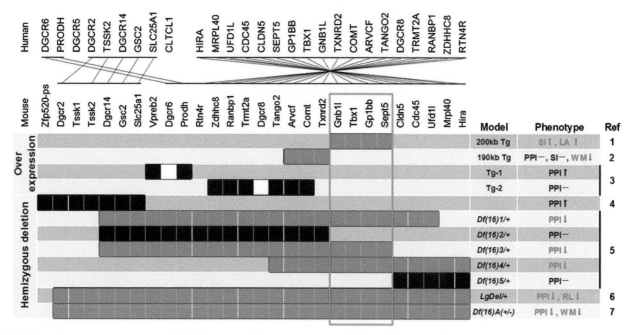

FIGURE 3   Mouse models of 22q11.2 CNVs. Regions of which copy number variants induce behavioral phenotypes consistent (red) and inconsistent (black) with human variant carriers are indicated. Blue frame shows a 200-kb critical region of which overexpression induces defective social behaviors and clozapine-responsive compulsive hyperactivity and outside of which hemizygous deletions do not induce prepulse inhibition deficits. 1, Hiroi et al. (2005); 2, Suzuki, Harper, Hiramoto, Funke, et al. (2009); 3, Stark, Burt, Gogos, and Karayiorgou (2009); 4, Kimber et al. (1999); 5, Paylor et al. (2001) and Paylor et al. (2006); 6, Long et al. (2006); 7, Stark et al. (2008). *Adapted and updated from Hiroi et al. (2013).*

deletions placed outside the 200-kb region had no effect on PPI (Figure 3; see Df(16)2/+ and Df(16)5/+). Further, Kimber and colleagues showed that hemizygous deletion from Zfp520-ps to Slc25a1 increases PPI, a trend opposite to what is seen in 22q11.2 hemizygous deletion patients (Sobin, Kiley-Brabeck, & Karayiorgou, 2005).

Taken together, these studies identified the 200-kb critical region and the adjacent190-kb region as causative for distinct sets of nonidentical behavioral phenotypes relevant to developmental neuropsychiatric disorders.

A similar approach was taken to narrow down specific genes responsible for intellectual disability and developmental delays associated with 7q11.23 hemizygous deletion. Deletion of the entire mouse ortholog of 7q11.23 from *Gtf2i* to *Fkbp6* impairs motor coordination and spatial memory and increases startle to an acoustic stimulus and social behavior, reminiscent of hypersociality in 7q11.23 deletion patients (Segura-Puimedon et al., 2014). Li and colleagues separately deleted the proximal (from *Gtf2i* to *Link1*) and distal (from *Link1* to *Trim50*) segments of murine 7q11.23 ortholog and demonstrated that the proximal deletion selectively induced increased reciprocal social interaction, acoustic startle response to pain and impaired PPI (Li et al., 2009). In contrast, mice with the distal deletion exhibited deficits in contextual and cued fear conditioning. Anxiety-related behaviors were affected by both proximal and distal deletions. The unequal effects of segmental deletions suggest that individual 7q11.23 genes have distinct

phenotypic targets, much in the same manner of 22q11.2 genes (Hiroi et al., 2013).

TECHNICAL ISSUES IN THE USE OF GENETIC MOUSE MODELS

Many technical issues have arisen in characterizing behavioral phenotypes of mouse models of CNVs or single gene knock-out or transgenic mice.

Indirect Effects

Note that behavioral deficits could result from secondary effects. Fuchs and colleagues recently reported that mice with a large hemizygous deletion of the murine 22q11.2 ortholog (i.e., Df(16)1/+) have a hearing impairment and suggested that PPI deficits seen in this mouse might reflect inability to reliably detect the subtle sound of a prepulse stimulus (Fuchs et al., 2013). Approximately 41% of 22q11.2 deletion patients (Dyce et al., 2002; Persson, Friman, Oskarsdottir, & Jonsson, 2012) have hearing impairment. Deletion of *Tbx1* alone, which is included in all large 22q11.2 hemizygous mouse models with PPI deficits and the 200-kb 22q11.2 Tg mouse, results in a hearing impairment (Liao et al., 2004). On the other hand, the absence of PPI deficits in small hemizygous mouse models (Df(16)2/+ and Df(16)5/+) and the 190-kb duplication mouse model still reliably rules out the functional contribution of genes encoded in these segments to PPI deficits and by exclusion still suggests the potential importance of the 200-kb critical region for PPI and other behavioral phenotypes (see Figure 3). In this regard, lack of phenotypic effect is as important as the presence of a phenotype in narrowing down a critical segment.

Genetic Background

A phenotype might be induced by unequal genetic backgrounds between mutant and wild-type littermates, in addition to or instead of the mutation. This interpretative issue is not unique to CNV models; it also affects single gene mutant mice. This issue arises when gene manipulation and breeding are performed in two different inbred mouse lines. Genetic manipulation is introduced into embryonic stem (ES) cells, and most widely used ES cells have their origin in various 129 inbred substrains. In this case, the genome of ES cells carries alleles specific to 129 inbred mouse lines. This mouse is then crossed to good breeders such as C57BL/6J or C57BL/6N inbred lines. When such breeding is performed, alleles in the genetic background of 129 substrains and C57BL/6 lines are mixed through recombination at F2 and onward, but they are not mixed evenly between wild-type mice and mutant mice. Alleles present near the targeted segment (or gene) do not easily go through recombination because of their very proximity and remain together on the chromosomal copy; the same chromosomal region of a wild-type copy is largely composed of alleles of a breeder mouse. Thus, whereas a hemizygous mouse carries one chromosomal copy with more 129-derived alleles and one wild-type copy with mostly breeder alleles (e.g., C57BL/6J), a wild-type littermate carries two chromosomal copies with mostly breeder alleles (e.g., C57BL/6J). In other words, mutant mice differ from their wild-type littermates not only in the targeted chromosomal segment or gene but also in the alleles linked to that region. Because different inbred mouse lines widely differ in behavior (Crusio, 2004; Gerlai, 2001; Marshall et al., 2013; Wolfer, Crusio, & Lipp, 2002), electrophysiological properties of neurons (Nguyen, Abel, Kandel, & Bourtchouladze, 2000; Nguyen, Duffy, & Young, 2000), and anatomical and neuronal development (Cominski, Turchin, Hsu, Ansonoff, & Pintar, 2012; Marshall et al., 2013; Rosen & Williams, 2001; Wahlsten, Metten, & Crabbe, 2003; Yoo et al., 2010), any phenotypic difference between wild-type and mutant (e.g., CNV, knock-out) mice could potentially reflect the impact of the allelic difference—as well as or instead of a CNV or the targeted gene. When initial behavioral characterization is conducted in mice with a mixed genetic background, this interpretative limitation should be taken into consideration (see Table 1).

One solution to this problem is to backcross such a mutant mouse to a breeder mouse (e.g., C57BL/6J or N) for 10 or more generations to achieve a higher degree of homogeneity (i.e., certified congenic mouse) in the genetic background between wild-type and mutant mice (Silver, 1995). The number of 129-Sv alleles from ES cells decreases at each backcrossing generation and is replaced by alleles of the breeder. On average, the amount of alleles from ES cells estimated to be retained is 321, 20 and 5 Mb at four, eight, and 10 generations of backcrossing, respectively (Bolivar, Cook, & Flaherty, 2001; Flaherty & Bolivar, 2007). However, this estimate is largely driven by genomic regions unlinked to the deleted gene. Alleles of genes located in the proximity of the targeted gene (i.e., linked genes) are not readily replaced by those of the breeder, and 82-, 46.7-, and 37.5-Mb alleles are estimated to be derived from ES cells at four, eight, and 10 generations of backcrossing, respectively (Bolivar et al., 2001; Crusio, 2004; Flaherty & Bolivar, 2007; Wolfer et al., 2002). Phenotypic data of noncongenic mice suffer from interpretative ambiguity.

Another solution is to generate a CNV copy using ES cells derived from C57BL/6N mice or FVB mice and breed with the same inbred mouse line to generate a co-isogenic mouse (Fejgin et al., 2013; Hiroi et al., 2005). This is the best currently available approach to rule out the impact of unequal genetic backgrounds between mutant and wild-type littermates.

Apparent Absence of Phenotypes

Available noncongenic mouse models of 16p11.2 hemizygous deletion and duplication show no detectable phenotypic features of working memory, "sociability," or anxiety (Horev et al., 2011; Portmann et al., 2014) (see Table 1). Even in congenic or co-isogenic mouse models, there are notable cases of apparent lack of phenotypes (Table 1). A congenic mouse model of large 22q11.2 deletion (Df(16)A/+) is not impaired in spatial working memory (Sigurdsson, Stark, Karayiorgou, Gogos, & Gordon, 2010). A co-isogenic mouse model of 15q13.3 deletion is apparently normal in PPI, working memory, or anxiety-like behaviors (Fejgin et al., 2013). Further, a congenic mouse model of paternal 15q11-13 duplication is indistinguishable from wild-type mice in PPI and working memory (Tamada et al., 2010).

There are many possible factors that contribute to the weak or absent phenotypes. First, it remains unclear if hemizygosity is a biologically equivalent event in humans and mice. We reported that *Sept5*, which is hemizygous in 22q11.2 hemizygous CNV cases, induce social interaction deficits when both copies were deleted (i.e., homozygosity) but not when one copy was deleted (i.e., heterozygosity) in mice (Suzuki, Harper, Hiramoto, Sawamura, et al., 2009). A gene dose alteration might be better tolerated in mice than in humans because of robustness of biological systems in mice. Accordingly, it would be predicted that homozygous deletion of a chromosomal segment would more readily induce phenotypes.

Another possibility is that some alleles in genetic background might modify phenotypic expression. We demonstrated that a 22q11.2 gene deletion causes varying degrees of social interaction deficits under different genetic backgrounds (Hiroi et al., 2012, 2013; Suzuki, Harper, Hiramoto, Sawamura,et al., 2009). Similarly, mouse models of fragile X syndrome (Spencer et al., 2011), *Nlgn3* mutants (Jaramillo, Liu, Pettersen, Birnbaum, & Powell, 2014), and *Shank3* mutation (Drapeau, Dorr, Elder, & Buxbaum, 2014) result in varying degrees of ASD-related behavioral phenotypes on different genetic backgrounds.

Behavioral tasks could also be a factor for apparent lack of phenotypes. Some rodent behavioral tasks might not sufficiently tax a given capacity. For example, over-expression of a 22q11.2 segment, including *TXNRD2, COMT,* and *ARVCF,* induces working memory deficit only when long delay is imposed between a probe trial and a test trial to tax working memory in rewarded alternation (Suzuki, Harper, Hiramoto, Funke, et al., 2009). To evaluate working memory capacity, the task needs to be maximally taxed. Moreover, some tasks might not measure an intended behavioral trait. The sociability test in a three chamber does not measure genuine reciprocal social interaction. In fact, phenotypes seen in the sociability test and in a naturalistic test for reciprocal social interaction are often inconsistent (Spencer et al., 2011; Fairless et al., 2012).

The nature of data distribution is another possibility. Not all CNV carriers exhibit any given neuropsychiatric disorder in humans (see Figure 1); incomplete penetrance and variable expressivity are noted. We previously pointed out that a behavioral phenotype in mutant mice often does not appear as a categorical phenotype and instead appears as an average shift by one to two standard deviations in mutant compared with wild-type littermates (see Figure 2) (Hiroi et al., 2013). Moreover, only a subpopulation of CNV-carrying mice might exhibit a detectable phenotype, and a statistically detectable group effect is difficult to achieve. A detailed distribution of raw data and the degree of variance should be examined. This point underlines the necessity of quantitative, rather than categorical, classification of mouse phenotypes and human diagnosis.

Finally, a laboratory environment might have a unique impact on phenotypes. Even when the same mutant mouse line is tested under conditions where many environmental variables are rigorously equated, behavioral phenotypes could still differ across laboratories (Crabbe, Wahlsten, & Dudek, 1999). Extraneous variables include

housing and breeding conditions and how often mice are disturbed per day by how many animal caretakers and laboratory personnel.

DECONSTRUCTING CNV MOUSE MODELS OF NEUROPSYCHIATRIC DISORDERS

To understand the precise genotype–phenotype relationship of a CNV, individual genes that are genuinely responsible for behavioral dimensions relevant to neuropsychiatric disorders must be identified. One approach is to identify deletion and duplication cases smaller than commonly found ones and use their phenotypes to identify critical segments within a CNV. For example, although most 22q11.2 deletions are 3.0 Mb in size and there are nested 1.5 deletion cases, there are also much smaller deletions and duplications. However, there are not many such cases and they are also found in control samples (http://projects.tcag.ca/variation/?source=hg18). Thus far, this approach has not been successful in definitively identifying critical specific genes.

Private mutations of single CNV-encoded genes can provide valuable information. For example, within 22q11.2, there are several individual cases of *TBX1* mutations that are associated with ASDs: an insertional mutation in exon 9 of *TBX1* (Gong et al., 2001); a frameshift mutation in *TBX1* (Paylor et al., 2006); and another frameshift mutation in exon 9 (Ogata et al., 2014). Moreover, homozygous deletion that affects SEPT5 and GP1BB has been identified in one child. This child showed developmental problems in motor coordination, language and speech development with severe attentional, perceptional, and socioemotional deficits (Bartsch et al., 2011). As mutations of GP1BB are associated with prolonged bleeding (i.e., Bernard–Soulier syndrome) with no psychiatric diagnosis, SEPT5 remains a possible contributory gene for the behavioral phenotypes in this individual. However, each of these ASD-associated mutations often represents a single subject case and variants of other genes are also present in these individuals (Ogata et al., 2014). Thus definitive identification of causative genes is difficult.

Another approach is to associate single-nucleotide polymorphisms in specific CNV-encoded genes in individuals with neuropsychiatric disorders but without CNVs. Although weak association is reported with multiple 22q11.2 genes, recent large-scale genome-wide association studies do not replicate any of the single-nucleotide polymorphisms in schizophrenia (Schizophrenia Working Group of the Psychiatric Genomics Consortium, 2014; Shi et al., 2011; Stefansson et al., 2009) or ASD samples (Anney et al., 2012; Wang et al., 2009; Weiss et al., 2009). This might be partly due to weak impacts of single-nucleotide polymorphisms on gene functions. Such impacts might not be sufficient to mimic the impact of half-copy of hemizygous cases.

Although choosing target genes based on their conceivable biological relevance and creating a single gene deletion mouse have been a common practice, there is no biological process known to be irrelevant to psychiatric disorders. Moreover, the brain functions of many CNV-encoded genes are so poorly understood that choosing a target gene based on presumed biological relevance could hinder the real progress in discovering the genuinely contributory genes. Thus, this is a less efficient initial strategy in CNV cases in which many genes are encoded. Once a small chromosomal segment is identified within a CNV using segmental deletion and overexpression mice, or if a CNV includes less than 10 genes, the strategy becomes highly effective in identifying the contribution of specific encoded genes to phenotypes.

The impacts of many single 22q11.2 gene deletions on various behavioral phenotypes have been examined (see Figure 4). Heterozygosity of *Tbx1* or *Gnb1l*, both of which are encoded in the 200-kb region, results in profoundly reduced PPI. Consistent with data from partially overlapping hemizygous mice (see Figure 3), single genes located in a segment with no PPI deficit (i.e., Df(16)2/+, Tg-1, and Tg-2; see Table 1) have no effect (e.g., *Gsc2*, *Rtn4r*, *Comt*) or very weak effects on PPI at only one or two prepulse levels (e.g., *Zdhhc8*, *Dgcr8*). Working memory is affected in *Dgcr8* and *Tbx1*. Social interaction is defective in *Tbx1* heterozygous mice and *Sept5* homozygous mice, but not in *Comt* heterozygous and homozygous mice. Anxiety-like

traits are potentiated in mice with gene dose reduction of *Zdhhc8*, *Comt*, and *Tbx1*, but not by *Gsc2*, *Prodh*, *Rtn4r*, or *Dgcr8*.

In light of extensive studies conducted for single 22q11.2 genes by many groups including ours, we previously proposed several hypothetical gene-phenotype mechanisms based on this CNV (Hiroi et al., 2013). Here we reevaluate whether these mechanisms are applicable to other CNVs.

Noncontiguous Gene Effect

We hypothesized that whereas the contiguous segment of a chromosome is deleted or duplicated in CNVs, encoded genes critical for a phenotype are noncontiguously distributed (Hiroi et al., 2013). Some large hemizygous 22q11.2 deletions do not impair PPI (see Figure 3; Df(16)2/+ and Df(16)5/+) (Paylor et al., 2006) and overexpression of a segment of 22q11.2 duplication, including *Zdhhc8*, *Ranbp1*, *Trmt2a*, *Tango2*, *Arvcf*. *Comt*, and *Txnrd2* has no impact on PPI (Stark et al., 2009; Suzuki, Harper, Hiramoto, Funke, et al., 2009). Single 22q11.2 deletion models also support this hypothesis. Contributory genes are noncontiguously distributed within 22q11.2 CNV.

Similarly, deletion of different segments within 7q11.23 results in nonidentical behavioral phenotypes. Among genes encoded in 7q11.23, homozygous *Gtf2ird1* deletion results in increased anxiety-like behaviors (Schneider et al., 2012) but homozygous *eif4h* deletion does not (Capossela et al., 2012).

If behavioral symptoms are collectively viewed as a whole, each of all encoded genes might have some contribution to some behavioral phenotypes. However, a mutation of some genes (e.g., GP1BB) alone located at 22q11.2 results in no apparent psychiatric diagnosis in Bernard–Soulier syndrome. From a dimensional standpoint, it is difficult to understand the available data of CNVs in terms of a contiguous gene effect.

Mass Action

We hypothesized that the dose of each gene has an optimal range on a linear or nonlinear function for a given phenotype and the ultimate phenotype of a CNV is the net result of mass action of these genes (Hiroi et al., 2013).

Each CNV is associated with similar or different sets of diagnoses. In some cases, duplication and deletion induce similar, but nonidentical effects. Whereas 22q11.2 hemizygous deletion is associated with high rates of schizophrenia, ASDs, ADHD, and ID, duplication is associated with ASDs and ID, but not with schizophrenia (Hiroi et al., 2013; Malhotra & Sebat, 2012; Rees, Kirov, et al., 2014). CNVs linearly alter a certain phenotype; duplication of 7q11.23 is associated with hyposociability

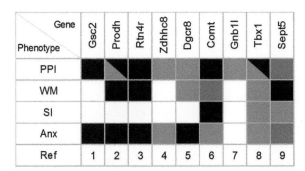

FIGURE 4 Effects of single 22q11.2 gene deletions on various behavioral phenotypes. Phenotypes consistent with (red) and opposite to (gray) 22q11.2 deletion and absent (black) are shown. Blank squares indicate phenotypes not tested or reported. Anx, anxiety-like behaviors; PPI, prepulse inhibition; SI, social behaviors; WM, working memory. 1, Long et al. (2006); 2, Gogos et al. (1999) and Paterlini et al. (2005); 3, Gogos et al. (1999) and Paterlini et al. (2005); 4, Mukai et al. (2004); 5, Stark et al. (2008), Ouchi et al. (2013), and Chun et al. (2014); 6, Gogos et al. (1998), Papaleo et al. (2008), Babovic et al. (2008), O'Tuathaigh et al. (2010), Brennand et al. (2015, 2011), and O'Tuathaigh et al. (2012); 7, Paylor et al. (2006); 8, Long et al. (2006), Paylor et al. (2006), and Hiramoto et al. (2011); 9, Paylor et al. (2006), Suzuki, Harper, Hiramoto, Sawamura, et al. (2009), and Harper et al. (2012). *Adapted and updated from Hiroi et al. (2013).*

and ASDs, but its deletion is associated with hypersociability (Jarvinen-Pasley et al., 2008; Malhotra & Sebat, 2012). On the other hand, there are cases in which deletion and duplication are associated with the same sets of disorders (Malhotra & Sebat, 2012).

These effects of CNVs are likely to reflect the mass action of many encoded single genes. When genotype–phenotype relation is viewed from the standpoint of behavioral phenotypes, many genes contribute to each phenotype, but their effects are not linear. Although 22q11.2 hemizygous patients have reduced PPI and working memory deficits, homozygous deletion of *Sept5* potentiates PPI (Suzuki, Harper, Hiramoto, Sawamura, et al., 2009) and *Comt* deletion improves working memory (Papaleo et al., 2008). In other words, some genes encoded in a CNV have an effect on a phenotype opposite to that of the CNV.

Pleiotropy

We hypothesized that many CNV-encoded genes have pleiotropic actions: each of the contributory genes has more than one phenotypic target (Hiroi et al., 2013). Single genes could have many phenotypic targets, as in the case with *Tbx1*, *Dgcr8*, and *Zdhhc8* of 22q11.2 CNV (see Figure 4). Heterozygous *Gtf2i* of 7q11.23 CNV results in impaired social interaction and response to novelty, but not working memory or anxiety (Sakurai et al., 2011). Among deleted genes encoded in 15q13.3 CNV, mice deficient for cholinergic receptor neuronal alpha 7 subunit (*Chrna7*) have been extensively examined. *Chrna7* homozygous mice are impaired in attentional processing (Hoyle, Genn, Fernandes, & Stolerman, 2006; Young et al., 2004, 2007), working memory (Young et al., 2007), impulsivity (Keller, Keller, Bowers, & Wehner, 2005), choice accuracy in spatial discrimination learning (Levin et al., 2009), and show decreased anxiety-like thigmotaxis; they are normal in contextual and cue fear conditioning, spatial learning in the Morris water maze, PPI, anxiety, locomotor activity, and motor coordination, and startle response to a noxious stimulus (Paylor et al., 1998).

Although there are no mouse models with overdose of individual genes encoded in the paternal 15q11-13 duplication, some encoded genes have been deleted and their behavioral phenotypes are characterized. Homozygosity of *GABRβ3* induces hyperactivity and repetitive, stereotypical behavior as well as impaired learning in passive avoidance, contextual fear conditioning, and motor coordination (DeLorey et al., 1998; Homanics et al., 1997). Deletion of small nucleolar RNA heightens anxiety and impairs motor learning but has no effect on working memory (Ding et al., 2008). *GABRβ3* heterozygous mice are hypersensitive to pain and tactile stimuli,

but exhibited an increase in PPI and decreased repetitive behavior, compared to wild-type mice (DeLorey et al., 2011).

Taken together, we submit that existing data are consistent with a series of hypothetical mechanisms of CNV-associated behavioral dimensions (Hiroi et al., 2013).

BRIDGING BEHAVIORAL DIMENSIONS TO NEUROBIOLOGICAL PHENOTYPES

The ultimate goal of mouse model studies is to gain insights into the molecular and neuronal mechanisms of neuropsychiatric disorders. A corollary of the noncontiguous gene effect hypothesis is that even if certain neuronal phenotypes are seen in the brain of CNV mouse models with behavioral phenotypes, it is not clear if such a neuronal phenotype represents the genuine mechanism of specific behavioral phenotypes. Some genes encoded in a CNV could have no functional role in a given behavioral phenotype, but nevertheless induce a certain neuronal phenotype. Thanks to extensive phenotypic characterization, this point is best illustrated with mouse models of 22q11.2 CNVs. For example, mice with deletion for a small nested 22q11.2 ortholog region from *Dgcr14* to *Txnrd2* (Df(16)2/+; see Figure 3) exhibit enhanced long-term potentiation at excitatory hippocampal synapses but are normal in hippocampal-dependent spatial memory (Earls et al., 2012) and PPI (Paylor et al., 2006).

At the single-gene level, there are many cases of dissociation between behavioral and neuronal phenotypes. *Rtn4r* is implicated in axonal growth and plasticity (Shao et al., 2005; Stephany et al., 2014), but its deletion has no detectable effect on PPI, working memory, or anxiety (Hsu et al., 2007). Proline degradation (*Prodh*) is critical for dopaminergic neurotransmission and synaptic plasticity, but its deficiency in a congenic mouse does not impair PPI or working memory (Paterlini et al., 2005). Deficiency of *Comt*, which degrades catecholamines, has no detectable effect on PPI or social interaction and, inconsistent with 22q11.2 hemizygous patients, *increases* working memory (Babovic et al., 2008; Brennand et al., 2015, 2011; Gogos et al., 1998; Papaleo et al., 2008; O'Tuathaigh et al., 2010, 2012).

These dissociation cases elegantly demonstrate that a neuronal phenotype seen in a CNV mouse model does not necessarily underlie the neuronal mechanism of a specific behavioral phenotype. Even if a certain neuronal phenotype is not correlated with one behavioral phenotype, other behavioral phenotypes might be. Because the phenotypic targets of genes differ, an extensive phenotypic characterization is needed to identify a behavioral correlate of a neuronal phenotype.

RECONSTRUCTING DIMENSIONAL PHENOTYPES OF CNVs

Analyses of single gene mouse models depict how each behavioral dimension changes in response to a gene dose alteration. One such case is illustrated with a *Tbx1* heterozygous mouse model of 22q11.2 deletion (see Figure 5). An emerging quantitative profile is that some dimensions deviate from the one standard deviation range from the average of wild-type mice and others remain within this range. Each of the genes encoded in 22q11.2 CNV or any other CNV is likely to have its own quantitative profile. Each profile does not necessarily mimic all or even most symptomatic elements of any disorder. Even if a single gene alteration affects only one particular behavioral dimension, this gene still contributes to the final phenotype of a CNV. For example, *Sept5* deletion and *Comt* overexpression selectively contribute to dimensional alteration in social interaction and working memory, respectively, but have no detectable effect on other behavioral phenotypes (Harper et al., 2012; Papaleo et al., 2008; Suzuki, Harper, Hiramoto, Funke, et al., 2009; Suzuki, Harper, Hiramoto, Sawamura, et al., 2009). Although they cannot be claimed to model ASDs or schizophrenia, these two genes nevertheless are contributory to symptomatic elements of ASDs and schizophrenia.

The ultimate behavioral phenotype of a CNV is likely to reflect the net sum of (1) additive, synergetic, even opposing forces of each CNV-encoded gene; (2) modulatory impacts of alleles in the genetic background; and (3) nongenetic factors such prenatal insults and postnatal environments (Hiroi et al., 2013). Instead of attempting to interpret a mouse model as ASD-like, schizophrenia-like or any disorder-like, it might be a better strategy to accept the profile of behavioral phenotypes as a quantitative dimensional pattern. This seems to be the best, currently achievable reconstruction of CNV-associated or even idiopathic neuropsychiatric disorders. Treatments are likely to change some dimensions, not necessarily the whole constellation of dimensional elements. Detailed analyses of many CNV mouse models will improve our understanding of neuronal and molecular mechanisms of behavioral profiles.

In summary, there is a tendency to impose a categorical label on seemingly random objects or events. Stellar constellations are a case in point. Stellar constellations do not exist in reality; they exist in our mind. They were invented simply as a means to easily memorize and recognize a set of stars to navigate at night. These categorical labels make it easier to grasp seemingly chaotic reality. Clinical diagnostic categories provide diagnostic reliability and serve to guide clinicians in decisions regarding treatment options. With a little more help from mouse studies, we hope to develop dimensional measures of new, mechanism-based clinical diagnoses.

Acknowledgments

This work was supported by the National Institutes of Health (R21HD05311 and R01MH099660), NARSAD Independent Investigator Award, and the Maltz Foundation to N.H. We thank Professor George Kirov of Cardiff University, England; Professor Toshihide Kuroki of Kyushu University; and Dr Ryota Hashimoto of Osaka University for their insightful comments.

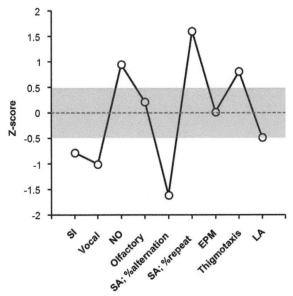

FIGURE 5 Z scores of various behavioral dimensions of a congenic *Tbx1* heterozygous mice (Hiramoto et al., 2011). Z scores were calculated based on the average scores of wild-type littermates. EPM, elevated plus maze; LA, motor activity in an inescapable open field; NO, novel object approach; olfactory, approach behavior toward olfactory cues; SA, % alternation, spontaneous alternation in a T-maze; SA, % repeat, repeated visits to the same arm; SI, social interaction; Thigmotaxis, thigmotaxis in an inescapable open field; vocal, neonatal ultrasonic vocalization during maternal separation. The blue zone represents a 1 standard deviation area around the average.

References

Abdallah, C. G., Sanacora, G., Duman, R. S., & Krystal, J. H. (2014). Ketamine and rapid-acting antidepressants: a window into a new neurobiology for mood disorder therapeutics. *Annual Review of Medicine.*

Alberti, A., Romano, C., Falco, M., Cali, F., Schinocca, P., Galesi, O., et al. (2007). 1.5 Mb de novo 22q11.21 microduplication in a patient with cognitive deficits and dysmorphic facial features. *Clinical Genetics, 71,* 177–182.

Aleman, A., Hijman, R., de Haan, E. H., & Kahn, R. S. (1999). Memory impairment in schizophrenia: a meta-analysis. *American Journal of Psychiatry, 156,* 1358–1366.

Anney, R., Klei, L., Pinto, D., Almeida, J., Bacchelli, E., Baird, G., et al. (2012). Individual common variants exert weak effects on the risk for autism spectrum disorders. *Human Molecular Genetics, 21,* 4781–4792.

Anney, R., Klei, L., Pinto, D., Regan, R., Conroy, J., Magalhaes, T. R., et al. (2010). A genome-wide scan for common alleles affecting risk for autism. *Human Molecular Genetics, 19,* 4072–4082.

Babovic, D., O'Tuathaigh, C. M., O'Connor, A. M., O'Sullivan, G. J., Tighe, O., Croke, D. T., et al. (2008). Phenotypic characterization of cognition and social behavior in mice with heterozygous versus homozygous deletion of catechol-O-methyltransferase. *Neuroscience, 155,* 1021–1029.

Bartsch, I., Sandrock, K., Lanza, F., Nurden, P., Hainmann, I., Pavlova, A., et al. (2011). Deletion of human GP1BB and SEPT5 is associated with Bernard–Soulier syndrome, platelet secretion defect, polymicrogyria, and developmental delay. *Thrombosis and Haemostasis, 106,* 475–483.

Belmonte, M. K., Cook, E. H., Jr., Anderson, G. M., Rubenstein, J. L., Greenough, W. T., Beckel-Mitchener, A., et al. (2004). Autism as a disorder of neural information processing: directions for research and targets for therapy. *Molecular Psychiatry, 9,* 646–663.

Bennett, E., & Heaton, P. (2012). Is talent in autism spectrum disorders associated with a specific cognitive and behavioural phenotype? *Journal of Autism and Developmental Disorders, 42,* 2739–2753.

Bennetto, L., Pennington, B. F., & Rogers, S. J. (1996). Intact and impaired memory functions in autism. *Child Development, 67,* 1816–1835.

Bolivar, V. J., Cook, M. N., & Flaherty, L. (2001). Mapping of quantitative trait loci with knockout/congenic strains. *Genome Research, 11,* 1549–1552.

Brennand, K., Savas, J. N., Kim, Y., Tran, N., Simone, A., Hashimoto-Torii, K., et al. (2015). Phenotypic differences in hiPSC NPCs derived from patients with schizophrenia. *Molecular Psychiatry, 20,* 361–368.

Brennand, K. J., Simone, A., Jou, J., Gelboin-Burkhart, C., Tran, N., Sangar, S., et al. (2011). Modelling schizophrenia using human induced pluripotent stem cells. *Nature, 473,* 221–225.

Brigman, J. L., Graybeal, C., & Holmes, A. (2010). Predictably irrational: assaying cognitive inflexibility in mouse models of schizophrenia. *Frontiers in Neuroscience, 4.*

Brunet, A., Gabau, E., Perich, R. M., Valdesoiro, L., Brun, C., Caballin, M. R., et al. (2006). Microdeletion and microduplication 22q11.2 screening in 295 patients with clinical features of DiGeorge/Velocardiofacial syndrome. *American Journal of Medical Genetics Part A, 140,* 2426–2432.

Bucan, M., Abrahams, B. S., Wang, K., Glessner, J. T., Herman, E. I., Sonnenblick, L. I., et al. (2009). Genome-wide analyses of exonic copy number variants in a family-based study point to novel autism susceptibility genes. *PLoS Genetics, 5,* e1000536.

Butcher, N. J., Chow, E. W., Costain, G., Karas, D., Ho, A., & Bassett, A. S. (2012). Functional outcomes of adults with 22q11.2 deletion syndrome. *Genetics in Medicine, 14,* 836–843.

Cai, G., Edelmann, L., Goldsmith, J. E., Cohen, N., Nakamine, A., Reichert, J. G., et al. (2008). Multiplex ligation-dependent probe amplification for genetic screening in autism spectrum disorders: efficient identification of known microduplications and identification of a novel microduplication in ASMT. *BMC Medical Genomics, 1,* 50.

van Campenhout, S., Devriendt, K., Breckpot, J., Frijns, J.-P., Peters, H., van Buggenhout, G., et al. (2012). Microduplication 22q11.2: a description of the clinical, developmental and behavioral characteristics during childhood. *Genetic Counseling, 23,* 135–147.

Capossela, S., Muzio, L., Bertolo, A., Bianchi, V., Dati, G., Chaabane, L., et al. (2012). Growth defects and impaired cognitive-behavioral abilities in mice with knockout for Eif4h, a gene located in the mouse homolog of the Williams-Beuren syndrome critical region. *American Journal of Pathology, 180,* 1121–1135.

Christian, S. L., Brune, C. W., Sudi, J., Kumar, R. A., Liu, S., Karamohamed, S., et al. (2008). Novel submicroscopic chromosomal abnormalities detected in autism spectrum disorder. *Biological Psychiatry, 63,* 1111–1117.

Chun, S., Westmoreland, J. J., Bayazitov, I. T., Eddins, D., Pani, A. K., Smeyne, R. J., et al. (2014). Specific disruption of thalamic inputs to the auditory cortex in schizophrenia models. *Science, 344,* 1178–1182.

Cominski, T. P., Turchin, C. E., Hsu, M. S., Ansonoff, M. A., & Pintar, J. E. (2012). Loss of the mu opioid receptor on different genetic backgrounds leads to increased bromodeoxyuridine labeling in the dentate gyrus only after repeated injection. *Neuroscience, 206,* 49–59.

Courtens, W., Schramme, I., & Laridon, A. (2008). Microduplication 22q11.2: a benign polymorphism or a syndrome with a very large clinical variability and reduced penetrance? Report of two families. *American Journal of Medical Genetics Part A, 146A,* 758–763.

Crabbe, J. C., Wahlsten, D., & Dudek, B. C. (1999). Genetics of mouse behavior: interactions with laboratory environment. *Science, 284,* 1670–1672.

Crawley, J. (September 23, 2014). *Optimizing behavioral assays for mouse models of autism.* SFARI News and Opinion. Ref Type: Internet Communication.

Cross-Disorder Group of the Psychiatric Genomics Consortium. (2013). Identification of risk loci with shared effects on five major psychiatric disorders: a genome-wide analysis. *Lancet, 381,* 1371–1379.

Crusio, W. E. (2004). Flanking gene and genetic background problems in genetically manipulated mice. *Biological Psychiatry, 56,* 381–385.

De Smedt, B., Devriendt, K., Fryns, J. P., Vogels, A., Gewillig, M., & Swillen, A. (2007). Intellectual abilities in a large sample of children with velo-cardio-facial syndrome: an update. *Journal of Intellectual Disability Research, 51,* 666–670.

DeLorey, T. M., Handforth, A., Anagnostaras, S. G., Homanics, G. E., Minassian, B. A., Asatourian, A., et al. (1998). Mice lacking the beta3 subunit of the GABAA receptor have the epilepsy phenotype and many of the behavioral characteristics of Angelman syndrome. *Journal of Neuroscience, 18,* 8505–8514.

DeLorey, T. M., Sahbaie, P., Hashemi, E., Li, W. W., Salehi, A., & Clark, D. J. (2011). Somatosensory and sensorimotor consequences associated with the heterozygous disruption of the autism candidate gene, Gabrb3. *Behavioural Brain Research, 216,* 36–45.

Descartes, M., Franklin, J., de Stahl, T. D., Piotrowski, A., Bruder, C. E., Dumanski, J. P., et al. (2008). Distal 22q11.2 microduplication encompassing the BCR gene. *American Journal of Medical Genetics Part A, 146A,* 3075–3081.

Ding, F., Li, H. H., Zhang, S., Solomon, N. M., Camper, S. A., Cohen, P., et al. (2008). SnoRNA Snord116 (Pwcr1/MBII-85) deletion causes growth deficiency and hyperphagia in mice. *PLoS One, 3,* e1709.

Doughty, O. J., & Done, D. J. (2009). Is semantic memory impaired in schizophrenia? A systematic review and meta-analysis of 91 studies. *Cognitive Neuropsychiatry, 14,* 473–509.

Drapeau, E., Dorr, N. P., Elder, G. A., & Buxbaum, J. D. (2014). Absence of strong strain effects in behavioral analyses of Shank3-deficient mice. *Disease Models & Mechanisms, 7,* 667–681.

Driscoll, D. A., Budarf, M. L., & Emanuel, B. S. (1992). A genetic etiology for DiGeorge syndrome: consistent deletions and microdeletions of 22q11. *American Journal of Human Genetics, 50,* 924–933.

Driscoll, D. A., Spinner, N. B., Budarf, M. L., Donald-McGinn, D. M., Zackai, E. H., Goldberg, R. B., et al. (1992). Deletions and microdeletions of 22q11.2 in velo-cardio-facial syndrome. *American Journal of Medical Genetics, 44,* 261–268.

Dulawa, S. C., & Hen, R. (2005). Recent advances in animal models of chronic antidepressant effects: the novelty-induced hypophagia test. *Neuroscience & Biobehavioral Reviews, 29,* 771–783.

Dyce, O., Donald-McGinn, D., Kirschner, R. E., Zackai, E., Young, K., & Jacobs, I. N. (2002). Otolaryngologic manifestations of the 22q11.2 deletion syndrome. *Archives of Otolaryngology Head and Neck Surgery, 128,* 1408–1412.

Earls, L. R., Fricke, R. G., Yu, J., Berry, R. B., Baldwin, L. T., & Zakharenko, S. S. (2012). Age-dependent microRNA control of synaptic plasticity in 22q11 deletion syndrome and schizophrenia. *Journal of Neuroscience, 32,* 14132–14144.

Edelmann, L., Pandita, R. K., Spiteri, E., Funke, B., Goldberg, R., Palanisamy, N., et al. (1999). A common molecular basis for rearrangement disorders on chromosome 22q11. *Human Molecular Genetics, 8*, 1157–1167.

Ensenauer, R. E., Adeyinka, A., Flynn, H. C., Michels, V. V., Lindor, N. M., Dawson, D. B., et al. (2003). Microduplication 22q11.2, an emerging syndrome: clinical, cytogenetic, and molecular analysis of thirteen patients. *American Journal of Human Genetics, 73*, 1027–1040.

Fairless, A. H., Dow, H. C., Kreibich, A. S., Torre, M., Kuruvilla, M., Gordon, E., et al. (2012). Sociability and brain development in BALB/cJ and C57BL/6J mice. *Behavioural Brain Research, 228*, 299–310.

Fairless, A. H., Katz, J. M., Vijayvargiya, N., Dow, H. C., Kreibich, A. S., Berrettini, W. H., et al. (2013). Development of home cage social behaviors in BALB/cJ vs. C57BL/6J mice. *Behavioural Brain Research, 237*, 338–347.

Fejgin, K., Nielsen, J., Birknow, M. R., Bastlund, J. F., Nielsen, V., Lauridsen, J. B., et al. (2013). A mouse model that recapitulates cardinal features of the 15q13.3 microdeletion syndrome including schizophrenia- and epilepsy-related alterations. *Biological Psychiatry, 76*, 128–137.

Fioravanti, M., Carlone, O., Vitale, B., Cinti, M. E., & Clare, L. (2005). A meta-analysis of cognitive deficits in adults with a diagnosis of schizophrenia. *Neuropsychology Review, 15*, 73–95.

Flaherty, L., & Bolivar, V. (2007). Congenic and consomic strains. In B. C. Jones, & P. Mormede (Eds.), *Neurobehavioral genetics* (2nd ed.) (pp. 115–127). New York: Taylor & Francis.

Fuchs, J. C., Zinnamon, F. A., Taylor, R. R., Ivins, S., Scambler, P. J., Forge, A., et al. (2013). Hearing loss in a mouse model of 22q11.2 deletion syndrome. *PLoS One, 8*, e80104.

Gerlai, R. (2001). Gene targeting: technical confounds and potential solutions in behavioral brain research. *Behavioural Brain Research, 125*, 13–21.

Geyer, M. A. (2006). The family of sensorimotor gating disorders: comorbidities or diagnostic overlaps? *Neurotoxicity Research, 10*, 211–220.

Girirajan, S., Rosenfeld, J. A., Coe, B. P., Parikh, S., Friedman, N., Goldstein, A., et al. (2012). Phenotypic heterogeneity of genomic disorders and rare copy-number variants. *New England Journal of Medicine, 367*, 1321–1331.

Gogos, J. A., Morgan, M., Luine, V., Santha, M., Ogawa, S., Pfaff, D., et al. (1998). Catechol-*O*-methyltransferase-deficient mice exhibit sexually dimorphic changes in catecholamine levels and behavior. *Proceedings of the National Academy of Sciences of the United States of America, 95*, 9991–9996.

Gogos, J. A., Santha, M., Takacs, Z., Beck, K. D., Luine, V., Lucas, L. R., et al. (1999). The gene encoding proline dehydrogenase modulates sensorimotor gating in mice. *Nature Genetics, 21*, 434–439.

Gong, W., Gottlieb, S., Collins, J., Blescia, A., Dietz, H., Goldmuntz, E., et al. (2001). Mutation analysis of TBX1 in non-deleted patients with features of DGS/VCFS or isolated cardiovascular defects. *Journal of Medical Genetics, 38*, E45.

Guilmatre, A., Dubourg, C., Mosca, A. L., Legallic, S., Goldenberg, A., Drouin-Garraud, V., et al. (2009). Recurrent rearrangements in synaptic and neurodevelopmental genes and shared biologic pathways in schizophrenia, autism, and mental retardation. *Archives of General Psychiatry, 66*, 947–956.

Harper, K. M., Hiramoto, T., Tanigaki, K., Kang, G., Suzuki, G., Trimble, W., et al. (2012). Alterations of social interaction through genetic and environmental manipulation of the 22q11.2 gene *Sept5* in the mouse brain. *Human Molecular Genetics, 21*, 3489–3499.

Hassed, S. J., Hopcus-Niccum, D., Zhang, L., Li, S., & Mulvihill, J. J. (2004). A new genomic duplication syndrome complementary to the velocardiofacial (22q11 deletion) syndrome. *Clinical Genetics, 65*, 400–404.

Heinrichs, R. W., & Zakzanis, K. K. (1998). Neurocognitive deficit in schizophrenia: a quantitative review of the evidence. *Neuropsychology, 12*, 426–445.

Hiramoto, T., Kang, G., Suzuki, G., Satoh, Y., Kucherlapati, R., Watanabe, Y., et al. (2011). Tbx1: identification of a 22q11.2 gene as a risk factor for autism spectrum disorder in a mouse model. *Human Molecular Genetics, 20*, 4775–4785.

Hiroi, N., Hiramoto, T., Harper, K. M., Suzuki, G., & Boku, S. (2012). Mouse models of 22q11.2-associated autism spectrum disorder. *Autism, S1*, 1–9.

Hiroi, N., Takahashi, T., Hishimoto, A., Izumi, T., Boku, S., & Hiramoto, T. (2013). Copy number variation at 22q11.2: from rare variants to common mechanisms of developmental neuropsychiatric disorders. *Molecular Psychiatry, 18*, 1153–1165.

Hiroi, N., Zhu, H., Lee, M., Funke, B., Arai, M., Itokawa, M., et al. (2005). A 200-kb region of human chromosome 22q11.2 confers antipsychotic-responsive behavioral abnormalities in mice. *Proceedings of the National Academy of Sciences of the United States of America, 102*, 19132–19137.

Homanics, G. E., DeLorey, T. M., Firestone, L. L., Quinlan, J. J., Handforth, A., Harrison, N. L., et al. (1997). Mice devoid of gamma-aminobutyrate type A receptor beta3 subunit have epilepsy, cleft palate, and hypersensitive behavior. *Proceedings of the National Academy of Sciences of the United States of America, 94*, 4143–4148.

Horev, G., Ellegood, J., Lerch, J. P., Son, Y. E., Muthuswamy, L., Vogel, H., et al. (2011). Dosage-dependent phenotypes in models of 16p11.2 lesions found in autism. *Proceedings of the National Academy of Sciences of the United States of America, 108*, 17076–17081.

Hoyle, E., Genn, R. F., Fernandes, C., & Stolerman, I. P. (2006). Impaired performance of alpha7 nicotinic receptor knockout mice in the five-choice serial reaction time task. *Psychopharmacology (Berl), 189*, 211–223.

Hsu, R., Woodroffe, A., Lai, W. S., Cook, M. N., Mukai, J., Dunning, J. P., et al. (2007). Nogo Receptor 1 (RTN4R) as a candidate gene for schizophrenia: analysis using human and mouse genetic approaches. *PLoS One, 2*, e1234.

Itsara, A., Wu, H., Smith, J. D., Nickerson, D. A., Romieu, I., London, S. J., et al. (2010). De novo rates and selection of large copy number variation. *Genome Research, 20*, 1469–1481.

Jaramillo, T. C., Liu, S., Pettersen, A., Birnbaum, S. G., & Powell, C. M. (2014). Autism-related neuroligin-3 mutation alters social behavior and spatial learning. *Autism Research*.

Jarvinen-Pasley, A., Bellugi, U., Reilly, J., Mills, D. L., Galaburda, A., Reiss, A. L., et al. (2008). Defining the social phenotype in Williams syndrome: a model for linking gene, the brain, and behavior. *Development and Psychopathology, 20*, 1–35.

Keller, J. J., Keller, A. B., Bowers, B. J., & Wehner, J. M. (2005). Performance of α7 nicotinic receptor null mutants is impaired in appetitive learning measured in a signaled nose poke task. *Behavioural Brain Research, 162*, 143–152.

Kimber, W. L., Hsieh, P., Hirotsune, S., Yuva-Paylor, L., Sutherland, H. F., Chen, A., et al. (1999). Deletion of 150 kb in the minimal DiGeorge/velocardiofacial syndrome critical region in mouse. *Human Molecular Genetics, 8*, 2229–2237.

Kirov, G., Rees, E., Walters, J. T., Escott-Price, V., Georgieva, L., Richards, A. L., et al. (2013). The penetrance of copy number variations for schizophrenia and developmental delay. *Biological Psychiatry, 75*, 378–385.

Klei, L., Sanders, S. J., Murtha, M. T., Hus, V., Lowe, J. K., Willsey, A. J., et al. (2012). Common genetic variants, acting additively, are a major source of risk for autism. *Molecular Autism, 3*, 9.

Korkmaz, B. (2011). Theory of mind and neurodevelopmental disorders of childhood. *Pediatric Research, 69*, 101R–108R.

de La Rochebrochard, C., Joly-Helas, G., Goldenberg, A., Durand, I., Laquerriere, A., Ickowicz, V., et al. (2006). The intrafamilial variability of the 22q11.2 microduplication encompasses a spectrum from minor cognitive deficits to severe congenital anomalies. *American Journal of Medical Genetics Part A, 140*, 1608–1613.

Lalonde, R. (2002). The neurobiological basis of spontaneous alternation. *Neuroscience & Biobehavioral Reviews, 26*, 91–104.

Levin, E. D., Petro, A., Rezvani, A. H., Pollard, N., Christopher, N. C., Strauss, M., et al. (2009). Nicotinic α7- or β2-containing receptor knockout: effects on radial-arm maze learning and long-term nicotine consumption in mice. *Behavioural Brain Research, 196*, 207–213.

Liao, J., Kochilas, L., Nowotschin, S., Arnold, J. S., Aggarwal, V. S., Epstein, J. A., et al. (2004). Full spectrum of malformations in velo-cardio-facial syndrome/DiGeorge syndrome mouse models by altering Tbx1 dosage. *Human Molecular Genetics, 13*, 1577–1585.

Li, H. H., Roy, M., Kuscuoglu, U., Spencer, C. M., Halm, B., Harrison, K. C., et al. (2009). Induced chromosome deletions cause hyposociability and other features of Williams-Beuren syndrome in mice. *EMBO Molecular Medicine, 1*, 50–65.

Lo-Castro, A., Galasso, C., Cerminara, C., El-Malhany, N., Benedetti, S., Nardone, A. M., et al. (2009). Association of syndromic mental retardation and autism with 22q11.2 duplication. *Neuropediatrics, 40*, 137–140.

Long, J. M., Laporte, P., Merscher, S., Funke, B., Saint-Jore, B., Puech, A., et al. (2006). Behavior of mice with mutations in the conserved region deleted in velocardiofacial/DiGeorge syndrome. *Neurogenetics, 7*, 247–257.

Luna, B., Doll, S. K., Hegedus, S. J., Minshew, N. J., & Sweeney, J. A. (2007). Maturation of executive function in autism. *Biological Psychiatry, 61*, 474–481.

Malhotra, D., & Sebat, J. (2012). CNVs: harbingers of a rare variant revolution in psychiatric genetics. *Cell, 148*, 1223–1241.

Marshall, C. R., Noor, A., Vincent, J. B., Lionel, A. C., Feuk, L., Skaug, J., et al. (2008). Structural variation of chromosomes in autism spectrum disorder. *American Journal of Human Genetics, 82*, 477–488.

Marshall, A. G., Watson, J. A., Hallengren, J. J., Walters, B. J., Dobrunz, L. E., Francillon, L., et al. (2013). Genetic background alters the severity and onset of neuromuscular disease caused by the loss of ubiquitin-specific protease 14 (usp14). *PLoS One, 8*, e84042.

Martinussen, R., Hayden, J., Hogg-Johnson, S., & Tannock, R. (2005). A meta-analysis of working memory impairments in children with attention-deficit/hyperactivity disorder. *Journal of the American Academy of Child and Adolescent Psychiatry, 44*, 377–384.

McAlonan, G. M., Daly, E., Kumari, V., Critchley, H. D., van, A. T., Suckling, J., et al. (2002). Brain anatomy and sensorimotor gating in Asperger's syndrome. *Brain, 125*, 1594–1606.

McDougle, C. J., Stigler, K. A., Erickson, C. A., & Posey, D. J. (2008). Atypical antipsychotics in children and adolescents with autistic and other pervasive developmental disorders. *Journal of Clinical Psychiatry, 69*(Suppl. 4), 15–20.

Meechan, D. W., et al. (2013). *Cerebral Cortex* (Epub ahead of print).

Misslin, R., Herzog, F., Koch, B., & Ropartz, P. (1982). Effects of isolation, handling and novelty on the pituitary–adrenal response in the mouse. *Psychoneuroendocrinology, 7*, 217–221.

Mukaddes, N. M., & Herguner, S. (2007). Autistic disorder and 22q11.2 duplication. *World Journal of Biological Psychiatry, 8*, 127–130.

Mukai, J., Liu, H., Burt, R. A., Swor, D. E., Lai, W. S., Karayiorgou, M., et al. (2004). Evidence that the gene encoding ZDHHC8 contributes to the risk of schizophrenia. *Nature Genetics, 36*, 725–731.

Nakatani, J., Tamada, K., Hatanaka, F., Ise, S., Ohta, H., Inoue, K., et al. (2009). Abnormal behavior in a chromosome-engineered mouse model for human 15q11-13 duplication seen in autism. *Cell, 137*, 1235–1246.

Nguyen, P. V., Abel, T., Kandel, E. R., & Bourtchouladze, R. (2000). Strain-dependent differences in LTP and hippocampus-dependent memory in inbred mice. *Learning & Memory, 7*, 170–179.

Nguyen, P. V., Duffy, S. N., & Young, J. Z. (2000). Differential maintenance and frequency-dependent tuning of LTP at hippocampal synapses of specific strains of inbred mice. *Journal of Neurophysiology, 84*, 2484–2493.

Nicolas, L. B., Kolb, Y., & Prinssen, E. P. (2006). A combined marble burying-locomotor activity test in mice: a practical screening test with sensitivity to different classes of anxiolytics and antidepressants. *European Journal of Pharmacology, 547*, 106–115.

Niklasson, L., Rasmussen, P., Oskarsdottir, S., & Gillberg, C. (2009). Autism, ADHD, mental retardation and behavior problems in 100 individuals with 22q11 deletion syndrome. *Research in Developmental Disabilities, 30*, 763–773.

Njung'e, K., & Handley, S. L. (1991). Evaluation of marble-burying behavior as a model of anxiety. *Pharmacology Biochemistry and Behavior, 38*, 63–67.

O'Hearn, K., Asato, M., Ordaz, S., & Luna, B. (2008). Neurodevelopment and executive function in autism. *Development and Psychopathology, 20*, 1103–1132.

O'Tuathaigh, C. M., Clarke, G., Walsh, J., Desbonnet, L., Petit, E., O'Leary, C., et al. (2012). Genetic vs. pharmacological inactivation of COMT influences cannabinoid-induced expression of schizophrenia-related phenotypes. *International Journal of Neuropsychopharmacology, 15*, 1331–1342.

O'Tuathaigh, C. M., Hryniewiecka, M., Behan, A., Tighe, O., Coughlan, C., Desbonnet, L., et al. (2010). Chronic adolescent exposure to Δ-9-tetrahydrocannabinol in COMT mutant mice: impact on psychosis-related and other phenotypes. *Neuropsychopharmacology, 35*, 2262–2273.

Ogata, T., Niihori, T., Tanaka, N., Kawai, M., Nagashima, T., Funayama, R., et al. (2014). TBX1 mutation identified by exome sequencing in a Japanese family with 22q11.2 deletion syndrome-like craniofacial features and hypocalcemia. *PLoS One, 9*, e91598.

Ornitz, E. M., Lane, S. J., Sugiyama, T., & deTraversay, J. (1993). Startle modulation studies in autism. *Journal of Autism and Developmental Disorders, 23*, 619–637.

Ou, Z., Berg, J. S., Yonath, H., Enciso, V. B., Miller, D. T., Picker, J., et al. (2008). Microduplications of 22q11.2 are frequently inherited and are associated with variable phenotypes. *Genetics in Medicine, 10*, 267–277.

Ouchi, Y., Banno, Y., Shimizu, Y., Ando, S., Hasegawa, H., Adachi, K., et al. (2013). Reduced adult hippocampal neurogenesis and working memory deficits in the Dgcr8-deficient mouse model of 22q11.2 deletion-associated schizophrenia can be rescued by IGF2. *Journal of Neuroscience, 33*, 9408–9419.

Papaleo, F., Crawley, J. N., Song, J., Lipska, B. K., Pickel, J., Weinberger, D. R., et al. (2008). Genetic dissection of the role of catechol-*O*-methyltransferase in cognition and stress reactivity in mice. *Journal of Neuroscience, 28*, 8709–8723.

Paterlini, M., Zakharenko, S. S., Lai, W. S., Qin, J., Zhang, H., Mukai, J., et al. (2005). Transcriptional and behavioral interaction between 22q11.2 orthologs modulates schizophrenia-related phenotypes in mice. *Nature Neuroscience, 8*, 1586–1594.

Paylor, R., Glaser, B., Mupo, A., Ataliotis, P., Spencer, C., Sobotka, A., et al. (2006). Tbx1 haploinsufficiency is linked to behavioral disorders in mice and humans: implications for 22q11 deletion syndrome. *Proceedings of the National Academy of Sciences of the United States of America, 103*, 7729–7734.

Paylor, R., McIlwain, K. L., McAninch, R., Nellis, A., Yuva-Paylor, L. A., Baldini, A., et al. (2001). Mice deleted for the DiGeorge/velocardiofacial syndrome region show abnormal sensorimotor gating and learning and memory impairments. *Human Molecular Genetics, 10*, 2645–2650.

Paylor, R., Nguyen, M., Crawley, J. N., Patrick, J., Beaudet, A., & Orr-Urtreger, A. (1998). α7 nicotinic receptor subunits are not necessary for hippocampal-dependent learning or sensorimotor gating: a behavioral characterization of Acra7-deficient mice. *Learning & Memory, 5*, 302–316.

Penn, D. L., Corrigan, P. W., Bentall, R. P., Racenstein, J. M., & Newman, L. (1997). Social cognition in schizophrenia. *Psychological Bulletin, 121*, 114–132.

Pennington, B. F., & Ozonoff, S. (1996). Executive functions and developmental psychopathology. *Journal of Child Psychology and Psychiatry, 37,* 51–87.

Perry, W., Minassian, A., Lopez, B., Maron, L., & Lincoln, A. (2007). Sensorimotor gating deficits in adults with autism. *Biological Psychiatry, 61,* 482–486.

Persson, C., Friman, V., Oskarsdottir, S., & Jonsson, R. (2012). Speech and hearing in adults with 22q11.2 deletion syndrome. *American Journal of Medical Genetics Part A, 158A,* 3071–3079.

Pinto, D., Pagnamenta, A. T., Klei, L., Anney, R., Merico, D., Regan, R., et al. (2010). Functional impact of global rare copy number variation in autism spectrum disorders. *Nature, 466,* 368–372.

Piskulic, D., Olver, J. S., Norman, T. R., & Maruff, P. (2007). Behavioural studies of spatial working memory dysfunction in schizophrenia: a quantitative literature review. *Psychiatry Research, 150,* 111–121.

Portmann, T., Yang, M., Mao, R., Panagiotakos, G., Ellegood, J., Dolen, G., et al. (2014). Behavioral abnormalities and circuit defects in the basal ganglia of a mouse model of 16p11.2 deletion syndrome. *Cell Reports, 7,* 1077–1092.

Portnoi, M. F. (2009). Microduplication 22q11.2: a new chromosomal syndrome. *European Journal of Medical Genetics, 52,* 88–93.

Portnoi, M. F., Lebas, F., Gruchy, N., Ardalan, A., Biran-Mucignat, V., Malan, V., et al. (2005). 22q11.2 duplication syndrome: two new familial cases with some overlapping features with DiGeorge/velocardiofacial syndromes. *American Journal of Medical Genetics A, 137,* 47–51.

Ramelli, G. P., Silacci, C., Ferrarini, A., Cattaneo, C., Visconti, P., & Pescia, G. (2008). Microduplication 22q11.2 in a child with autism spectrum disorder: clinical and genetic study. *Developmental Medicine and Child Neurology, 50,* 953–955.

Rees, E., Kirov, G., Sanders, A., Walters, J. T., Chambert, K. D., Shi, J., et al. (2014). Evidence that duplications of 22q11.2 protect against schizophrenia. *Molecular Psychiatry, 19,* 37–40.

Rees, E., Walters, J. T., Chambert, K. D., O'Dushlaine, C., Szatkiewicz, J., Richards, A. L., et al. (2013). CNV analysis in a large schizophrenia sample implicates deletions at 16p12.1 and SLC1A1 and duplications at 1p36.33 and CGNL1. *Human Molecular Genetics.*

Rees, E., Walters, J. T., Georgieva, L., Isles, A. R., Chambert, K. D., Richards, A. L., et al. (2014). Analysis of copy number variations at 15 schizophrenia-associated loci. *British Journal of Psychiatry, 204,* 108–114.

Ripke, S., O'Dushlaine, C., Chambert, K., Moran, J. L., Kahler, A. K., Akterin, S., et al. (2013). Genome-wide association analysis identifies 13 new risk loci for schizophrenia. *Nature Genetics, 45,* 1150–1159.

Rosen, G. D., & Williams, R. W. (2001). Complex trait analysis of the mouse striatum: independent QTLs modulate volume and neuron number. *BMC Neuroscience, 2,* 5.

Ruderfer, D. M., Fanous, A. H., Ripke, S., McQuillin, A., Amdur, R. L., Gejman, P. V., et al. (2014). Polygenic dissection of diagnosis and clinical dimensions of bipolar disorder and schizophrenia. *Molecular Psychiatry, 19,* 1017–1024.

Russo, N., Flanagan, T., Iarocci, G., Berringer, D., Zelazo, P. D., & Burack, J. A. (2007). Deconstructing executive deficits among persons with autism: implications for cognitive neuroscience. *Brain and Cognition, 65,* 77–86.

Sakurai, T., Dorr, N. P., Takahashi, N., McInnes, L. A., Elder, G. A., & Buxbaum, J. D. (2011). Haploinsufficiency of Gtf2i, a gene deleted in Williams Syndrome, leads to increases in social interactions. *Autism Research, 4,* 28–39.

Sanders, S. J., Ercan-Sencicek, A. G., Hus, V., Luo, R., Murtha, M. T., Moreno-De-Luca, D., et al. (2011). Multiple recurrent de novo CNVs, including duplications of the 7q11.23 Williams syndrome region, are strongly associated with autism. *Neuron, 70,* 863–885.

Scambler, P. J., Kelly, D., Lindsay, E., Williamson, R., Goldberg, R., Shprintzen, R., et al. (1992). Velo-cardio-facial syndrome associated with chromosome 22 deletions encompassing the DiGeorge locus. *Lancet, 339,* 1138–1139.

Schaefer, J., Giangrande, E., Weinberger, D. R., & Dickinson, D. (2013). The global cognitive impairment in schizophrenia: consistent over decades and around the world. *Schizophrenia Research, 150,* 42–50.

Schizophrenia Working Group of the Psychiatric Genomics Consortium. (2014). Biological insights from 108 schizophrenia-associated genetic loci. *Nature, 511,* 421–427.

Schneider, M., Debbane, M., Bassett, A. S., Chow, E. W., Fung, W. L., van den Bree, M. B., et al. (2014). Psychiatric disorders from childhood to adulthood in 22q11.2 deletion syndrome: results from the International Consortium on Brain and Behavior in 22q11.2 Deletion Syndrome. *American Journal of Psychiatry, 171,* 627–639.

Schneider, T., Skitt, Z., Liu, Y., Deacon, R. M., Flint, J., Karmiloff-Smith, A., et al. (2012). Anxious, hypoactive phenotype combined with motor deficits in Gtf2ird1 null mouse model relevant to Williams syndrome. *Behavioural Brain Research, 233,* 458–473.

Sebat, J., Lakshmi, B., Malhotra, D., Troge, J., Lese-Martin, C., Walsh, T., et al. (2007). Strong association of de novo copy number mutations with autism. *Science, 316,* 445–449.

Segura-Puimedon, M., Sahun, I., Velot, E., Dubus, P., Borralleras, C., Rodrigues, A. J., et al. (2014). Heterozygous deletion of the Williams-Beuren syndrome critical interval in mice recapitulates most features of the human disorder. *Human Molecular Genetics.*

Shao, Z., Browning, J. L., Lee, X., Scott, M. L., Shulga-Morskaya, S., Allaire, N., et al. (2005). TAJ/TROY, an orphan TNF receptor family member, binds Nogo-66 receptor 1 and regulates axonal regeneration. *Neuron, 45,* 353–359.

Shi, Y., Li, Z., Xu, Q., Wang, T., Li, T., Shen, J., et al. (2011). Common variants on 8p12 and 1q24.2 confer risk of schizophrenia. *Nature Genetics, 43,* 1224–1227.

Shprintzen, R. J., Goldberg, R., Golding-Kushner, K. J., & Marion, R. W. (1992). Late-onset psychosis in the velo-cardio-facial syndrome. *American Journal of Medical Genetics, 42,* 141–142.

Sigman, M. (1998). The Emanuel Miller Memorial Lecture 1997. Change and continuity in the development of children with autism. *Journal of Child Psychology and Psychiatry, 39,* 817–827.

Sigurdsson, T., Stark, K. L., Karayiorgou, M., Gogos, J. A., & Gordon, J. A. (2010). Impaired hippocampal-prefrontal synchrony in a genetic mouse model of schizophrenia. *Nature, 464,* 763–767.

Silver, L. M. (1995). *Mouse genetics: Concepts and applications.* New York: Oxford University Press.

Silverman, J. L., Yang, M., Lord, C., & Crawley, J. N. (2010). Behavioural phenotyping assays for mouse models of autism. *Nature Reviews Neuroscience, 11,* 490–502.

Sobin, C., Kiley-Brabeck, K., & Karayiorgou, M. (2005). Associations between prepulse inhibition and executive visual attention in children with the 22q11 deletion syndrome. *Molecular Psychiatry, 10,* 553–562.

Spencer, C. M., Alekseyenko, O., Hamilton, S. M., Thomas, A. M., Serysheva, E., Yuva-Paylor, L. A., et al. (2011). Modifying behavioral phenotypes in Fmr1KO mice: genetic background differences reveal autistic-like responses. *Autism Research, 4,* 40–56.

Spencer, C. M., Alekseyenko, O., Serysheva, E., Yuva-Paylor, L. A., & Paylor, R. (2005). Altered anxiety-related and social behaviors in the Fmr1 knockout mouse model of fragile X syndrome. *Genes, Brain and Behavior, 4,* 420–430.

Sprong, M., Schothorst, P., Vos, E., Hox, J., & van Engeland, H. (2007). Theory of mind in schizophrenia: meta-analysis. *British Journal of Psychiatry, 191,* 5–13.

Stark, K. L., Burt, R. A., Gogos, J. A., & Karayiorgou, M. (2009). Analysis of prepulse inhibition in mouse lines overexpressing 22q11.2 orthologues. *International Journal of Neuropsychopharmacology, 12,* 983–989.

Stark, K. L., Xu, B., Bagchi, A., Lai, W. S., Liu, H., Hsu, R., et al. (2008). Altered brain microRNA biogenesis contributes to phenotypic deficits in a 22q11-deletion mouse model. *Nature Genetics, 40,* 751–760.

van Steensel, F. J., Bogels, S. M., & de Bruin, E. I. (2013). Psychiatric comorbidity in children with autism spectrum disorders: a comparison with children with ADHD. *Journal of Child and Family Studies, 22*, 368–376.

van Steensel, F. J., Bogels, S. M., & Perrin, S. (2011). Anxiety disorders in children and adolescents with autistic spectrum disorders: a meta-analysis. *Clinical Child and Family Psychology Review, 14*, 302–317.

Stefansson, H., Ophoff, R. A., Steinberg, S., Andreassen, O. A., Cichon, S., Rujescu, D., et al. (2009). Common variants conferring risk of schizophrenia. *Nature, 460*, 744–747.

Steinberg, S., de, J. S., Mattheisen, M., Costas, J., Demontis, D., Jamain, S., et al. (2014). Common variant at 16p11.2 conferring risk of psychosis. *Molecular Psychiatry, 19*, 108–114.

Stephany, C. E., Chan, L. L., Parivash, S. N., Dorton, H. M., Piechowicz, M., Qiu, S., et al. (2014). Plasticity of binocularity and visual acuity are differentially limited by nogo receptor. *Journal of Neuroscience, 34*, 11631–11640.

Suzuki, G., Harper, K. M., Hiramoto, T., Funke, B., Lee, M., Kang, G., et al. (2009). Over-expression of a human chromosome 22q11.2 segment including TXNRD2, COMT, and ARVCF developmentally affects incentive learning and working memory in mice. *Human Molecular Genetics, 18*, 3914–3925.

Suzuki, G., Harper, K. M., Hiramoto, T., Sawamura, T., Lee, M., Kang, G., et al. (2009). Sept5 deficiency exerts pleiotropic influence on affective behaviors and cognitive functions in mice. *Human Molecular Genetics, 18*, 1652–1660.

Szatkiewicz, J. P., O'Dushlaine, C., Chen, G., Chambert, K., Moran, J. L., Neale, B. M., et al. (2014). Copy number variation in schizophrenia in Sweden. *Molecular Psychiatry, 19*, 762–773.

Szatmari, P., Paterson, A. D., Zwaigenbaum, L., Roberts, W., Brian, J., Liu, X. Q., et al. (2007). Mapping autism risk loci using genetic linkage and chromosomal rearrangements. *Nature Genetics, 39*, 319–328.

Takahashi, A., Nishi, A., Ishii, A., Shiroishi, T., & Koide, T. (2008). Systematic analysis of emotionality in consomic mouse strains established from C57BL/6J and wild-derived MSM/Ms. *Genes, Brain and Behavior, 7*, 849–858.

Tamada, K., Tomonaga, S., Hatanaka, F., Nakai, N., Takao, K., Miyakawa, T., et al. (2010). Decreased exploratory activity in a mouse model of 15q duplication syndrome; implications for disturbance of serotonin signaling. *PLoS One, 5*, e15126.

Van Os, J., Linscott, R. J., Myin-Germeys, I., Delespaul, P., & Krabbendam, L. (2009). A systematic review and meta-analysis of the psychosis continuum: evidence for a psychosis proneness-persistence-impairment model of psychotic disorder. *Psychological Medicine, 39*, 179–195.

Wahlsten, D., Metten, P., & Crabbe, J. C. (2003). Survey of 21 inbred mouse strains in two laboratories reveals that BTBR T/+ tf/tf has severely reduced hippocampal commissure and absent corpus callosum. *Brain Research, 971*, 47–54.

Walcott, C. M., & Landau, S. (2004). The relation between disinhibition and emotion regulation in boys with attention deficit hyperactivity disorder. *Journal of Clinical Child and Adolescent Psychology, 33*, 772–782.

Wang, K., Zhang, H., Ma, D., Bucan, M., Glessner, J. T., Abrahams, B. S., et al. (2009). Common genetic variants on 5p14.1 associate with autism spectrum disorders. *Nature, 459*, 528–533.

Weiss, L. A., Arking, D. E., Daly, M. J., & Chakravarti, A. (2009). A genome-wide linkage and association scan reveals novel loci for autism. *Nature, 461*, 802–808.

Wentzel, C., Fernstrom, M., Ohrner, Y., Anneren, G., & Thuresson, A. C. (2008). Clinical variability of the 22q11.2 duplication syndrome. *European Journal of Medical Genetics, 51*, 501–510.

Westerberg, H., Hirvikoski, T., Forssberg, H., & Klingberg, T. (2004). Visuo-spatial working memory span: a sensitive measure of cognitive deficits in children with ADHD. *Child Neuropsychology, 10*, 155–161.

Wilk, C. M., Gold, J. M., McMahon, R. P., Humber, K., Iannone, V. N., & Buchanan, R. W. (2005). No, it is not possible to be schizophrenic yet neuropsychologically normal. *Neuropsychology, 19*, 778–786.

Wolfer, D. P., Crusio, W. E., & Lipp, H. P. (2002). Knockout mice: simple solutions to the problems of genetic background and flanking genes. *Trends in Neurosciences, 25*, 336–340.

Yoo, J. H., Bailey, A., Ansonoff, M., Pintar, J. E., Matifas, A., Kieffer, B. L., et al. (2010). Lack of genotype effect on D1, D2 receptors and dopamine transporter binding in triple MOP-, DOP-, and KOP-opioid receptor knockout mice of three different genetic backgrounds. *Synapse, 64*, 520–527.

Young, J. W., Crawford, N., Kelly, J. S., Kerr, L. E., Marston, H. M., Spratt, C., et al. (2007). Impaired attention is central to the cognitive deficits observed in alpha 7 deficient mice. *European Neuropsychopharmacology, 17*, 145–155.

Young, J. W., Finlayson, K., Spratt, C., Marston, H. M., Crawford, N., Kelly, J. S., et al. (2004). Nicotine improves sustained attention in mice: evidence for involvement of the alpha7 nicotinic acetylcholine receptor. *Neuropsychopharmacology, 29*, 891–900.

Yuhas, J., Cordeiro, L., Tassone, F., Ballinger, E., Schneider, A., Long, J. M., et al. (2010). Brief report: sensorimotor gating in idiopathic autism and autism associated with fragile X syndrome. *Journal of Autism and Developmental Disorders, 41*, 248–253.

Zhu, H., Lee, M., Agatsuma, S., & Hiroi, N. (2007). Pleiotropic impact of constitutive fosB inactivation on nicotine-induced behavioral alterations and stress-related traits in mice. *Human Molecular Genetics, 16*, 820–836.

18

Genetic Rat Models for Schizophrenia

Bart A. Ellenbroek*, Tim Karl[§,¶,||]

*Victoria University of Wellington, Wellington, New Zealand; [§]Neuroscience Research Australia, Randwick, NSW, Australia; [¶]School of Medical Sciences, University of New South Wales, Sydney, NSW, Australia; [||]Schizophrenia Research Institute, Darlinghurst, NSW, Australia

INTRODUCTION

Schizophrenia is a pervasive psychiatric disorder with a usual onset of between 18 and 30 years of age. However, it is now generally regarded to have a strong neurodevelopmental component (see Chapters 1 and 2) and premorbid symptoms can be identified (at least at a group level) from very early on in development (Jones, Rodgers, Murray, & Marmot, 1994; Walker & Lewine, 1990). Schizophrenia occurs in roughly 1% of the population and patients can suffer from a large variety of symptoms. Traditionally, these symptoms were subdivided into two sets of symptoms: (1) *positive symptoms*, representing features that were not present in the healthy population, but were present in schizophrenia patients; and (2) *negative symptoms*, representing features normally present in healthy volunteers, but significantly reduced or absent in patients with schizophrenia. Hallucinations and delusions are the prototypical positive symptoms, whereas apathy, social withdrawal, and anhedonia are among the most prominent negative symptoms (Andreasen, Flaum, Swayze, Tyrrell, & Arndt, 1990; Andreasen & Olsen, 1982). Although several scales were developed to assess (changes in) these symptoms, the one most widely used now is the Positive and Negative Syndrome Symptoms Scale. This scale, developed in 1987, consists of 30 items (Kay, Fiszbein, & Opler, 1987), originally thought to reflect positive (7 items) and negative (7 items), symptoms as well as general psychopathology (14 items). Subsequently, a more detailed evaluation of the items within the Positive and Negative Syndrome Symptoms Scale has suggested that a more homogeneous subdivision can be achieved with five different symptom categories (Kawasaki et al., 1994; Van der Gaag, Cuijpers, et al., 2006; Van der Gaag,

Hoffman, et al., 2006; Wallwork, Fortgang, Hashimoto, Weinberger, & Dickinson, 2012). A recent reanalysis using confirmatory factor analysis on samples from the United States, Brazil, and China supported this five factor model while at the same time reducing the total items to 20. These five factors are labeled as: (1) positive; (2) negative; (3) disorganized; (4) excited; and (5) depressed (Stefanovics, Elkis, Liu, Zhang, & Rosenheck, 2014).

In addition to these five symptoms, patients with schizophrenia suffer from cognitive deficits. Although cognitive symptoms are not part of the diagnosis of schizophrenia, they are nonetheless prominently present in virtually all patients with schizophrenia (Marder & Fenton, 2004; Marder, Fenton, Youens, & Tamminga, 2004; Nuechterlein et al., 2004). Patients with schizophrenia seem to have a global deficit in cognition, scoring below average in virtually all cognitive domains, and appear particularly deficient in executive functioning, attention, and verbal and working memory (Heinrichs & Zakzanis, 1998; Mesholam-Gately, Giuliano, Goff, Faraone, & Seidman, 2009). Moreover, cognitive deficits are found in drug-naive patients (Fatouros-Bergman, Cervenka, Flyckt, Edman, & Farde, 2014). Interestingly, cognitive deficits did not change substantially over a 10-year period in a recent longitudinal study (Dickerson et al., 2014). It is, however, important to note that this study investigated middle-aged patients with a mean duration of illness of 22 years. It might well be that cognitive functioning declines within the first years after disease onset.

Antipsychotic drugs are the first choice for the treatment of schizophrenia, although nonpharmacological treatment options (such as cognitive behavioral therapy) are also available and have been found effective in pharmacotherapy resistant patients (Burns, Erickson, & Brenner, 2014).

Handbook of Behavioral Neuroscience
http://dx.doi.org/10.1016/B978-0-12-800981-9.00018-3

The effectiveness of antipsychotic drugs has been the subject of many meta-analyses and review papers and will not be discussed here in great detail (for details see, e.g., Ellenbroek, 2012; Ellenbroek & Cesura, 2015). Antipsychotics are routinely classified as classical and atypical antipsychotics, or, alternatively, first- and second-generation antipsychotics. Classical and atypical antipsychotics refer to the presence or (virtual) absence of extrapyramidal side effects (e.g., tremor, dystonia, dyskinesia). Although this distinction has been used extensively in the past, more recent studies have suggested that the extent to which antipsychotics induce extrapyramidal side effects is strongly dependent on the dose (Nord & Farde, 2011) and represents a more quantitative than qualitative difference (with the possible exception of clozapine). For that reason, most researchers now prefer the term first- and second-generation antipsychotics, with all the drugs introduced after 1989 (when clozapine was reintroduced) commonly referred to as second generation. Some authors have suggested that aripiprazole, as a partial agonist, may represent a third generation of antipsychotics (Mailman & Murthy, 2010). However, so far no other partial agonists have been registered and several others such as bifeprunox and SDZ-MAR-327 failed in clinical trials. We therefore feel it is too early to place aripiprazole in a category of its own, also because the therapeutic properties do not seem to differ substantially from other second-generation drugs.

Although the large multicenter studies on schizophrenia treatment options that have been published have different primary and secondary outcome parameters, differ in patient population, and include different antipsychotic treatment options (Agius, Davis, Gilhooley, Chapman, & Zaman, 2010), the overall conclusions of these studies are remarkably similar (Jones et al., 2006; Kahn et al., 2008; Lieberman et al., 2005; McEvoy et al., 2007):

1. There are no major clinical differences between different antipsychotics. Although subtle differences between individual antipsychotics definitely exist (Samara, Cao, Helfer, Davis, & Leucht, 2014), the similarities are much more prominent. In line with this, a recent reevaluation of several large studies using structured equation modeling showed that all antipsychotics worked via one common factor (Marques et al., 2014), most likely blockade of the dopamine D2 receptor.

2. Antipsychotics effectively reduce positive, but not negative or cognitive deficits. For instance, in the Clinical Antipsychotic Trials of Intervention Effectiveness study, antipsychotics reduced positive symptoms by about 35% in a 12-month treatment period, whereas the improvement in negative and cognitive symptoms was less than 15% (Keefe et al., 2007; Lieberman et al., 2005; McEvoy et al., 2006).

This, again, is in general agreement with most meta-analyses that show that the effects of antipsychotics on negative and cognitive symptoms are much more modest than on the positive symptoms.

3. Therapy compliance is very low, with 65–75% of the patients refusing medication within the first 12 months of treatment. This lack of therapy compliance is particularly troublesome because this will almost inevitably lead to psychotic relapse. For example, in a recent study, it was shown that only 10% of patients on long-acting risperidone relapsed within 2 years (Emsley et al., 2008). However, after patients stopped taking the medication 79% relapsed within 12 months and 94% within 24 months (Emsley, Oosthuizen, Koen, Niehaus, & Martinez, 2012). Although the reasons for discontinuing medication were not always clear in these multicenter trials, a combination of lack of effect, and severity of side effects were certainly prominent factors.

These data clearly indicate that improved therapeutic options for the treatment of schizophrenia are urgently needed. However, so far the development of drugs for mental disorders including schizophrenia has not met with great success. Indeed, together with drugs for oncological conditions, drugs for treating brain disorders have the lowest chance of achieving market approval (Kola & Landis, 2004), mainly because of their failure in clinical phases II and III (Arrowsmith & Miller, 2013). Good (or bad) examples are the recent failures of drugs working on the glutamatergic system, including the mGlu2-positive allosteric modulator AZD8529 (Cook et al., 2014) and the inhibitor of the glycine 1 transporter bitopertin (Bugarski-Kirola, Wang, Abi-Saab, & Blattler, 2014; Kingwell, 2014). As emphasized by Cook and his colleagues, AZD8529 was found active in seven preclinical models that are currently used for detecting antipsychotic activity but was ineffective in clinical trials (Cook et al., 2014), highlighting the fundamental problem of translatability from animal research to clinical practice.

ANIMAL MODELS FOR SCHIZOPHRENIA

As mentioned previously, the poor success rate of drug development in general and for mental disorders in particular occurs predominantly in phases II and III (Pammolli, Magazzini, & Riccaboni, 2011). A detailed analysis of this failure (as far as this has been published) shows that, whereas in the past especially pharmacokinetic factors were the cause of failure, this has now shifted to problems with efficacy (Kola & Landis, 2004). In line with this, a recent analysis of phases II and III failures in 2011 and 2012 found lack of efficacy to be the cause of 56% of all the failed trials (Arrowsmith & Miller, 2013). Given that predictions of efficacy are generally made on the basis of efficacy in animal models, this clearly indicates that the current generation of animal models is far from optimal. It would be beyond the scope of this review to evaluate the current generation of animal models, and made of the novel ones are discussed throughout this volume. Suffice it to say, that the classical models often fall into the class of the traditional screening models, or models with predictive validity (Matthysse, 1986; Willner, 1984).

Predictive validity in this respect refers to the accuracy with which therapeutic effects in humans can be predicted on the basis of the results in animals. In other words, can antipsychotic drugs reverse schizophrenia-relevant symptoms or endophenotypes (the latter is generally defined as biological, behavioral, or cognitive markers that are found in individuals with schizophrenia, mostly with a clear genetic basis) in animal models for the disorder (Takao, Yamasaki, & Miyakawa, 2007). As discussed at length elsewhere (Ellenbroek, 2010; Ellenbroek & Cools, 1990), such models are generally based on comparison of new drugs with known therapeutic agents (so-called gold standards). Therefore, such models tend to produce more of the same rather than leading to actual breakthroughs (Ellenbroek, 1993, 2010).

Fortunately, in the past two decades, a flurry of novel animal models aspiring construct validity have been proposed. Construct validity refers to how well the model mimics the etiology of the underlying disease. In addition to predictive and construct validity, animal models are usually also evaluated for face validity, referring to how accurate signs and symptoms (in the broadest sense, thus also including biomarkers and/or endophenotypes) are being displayed in the animal (i.e., phenomenological similarities between disorder in question and the animal model, Takao et al., 2007). These novel models are often based on genetic and or environmental risk factors, with a strong focus on the neurodevelopmental aspects of schizophrenia (Burrows, McOmish, & Hannan, 2011; Hida, Mouri, & Noda, 2013; Jones, Watson, & Fone, 2011; Yee & Singer, 2013). In this respect, it is important to realize that such models are generally based on hypothesized etiologies of schizophrenia, because schizophrenia still remains largely an enigma. Moreover, although sets of criteria for the various validities have been developed in the past (Ellenbroek, 1993; Matthysse, 1981, 1986; Powell & Miyakawa, 2006; Willner, 1984), most of the novel animal models for schizophrenia have yet to be fully evaluated against these.

In the remainder of this chapter, we will specifically focus on genetic rat models. In contrast to the abundance of genetic mice models, relatively few genetic rat models are currently available. This is primarily because of the (at least until recently) limited genetic toolbox available for rats. Especially, the absence of pluripotent or omnipotent stem cells (readily available in some strains of mice such as the S129V since the early 1990s) has

prevented the development of transgenic rats based on homologous recombination. However, the situation has dramatically changed in the past decade and several novel techniques are now available for genetic manipulation of rats (Blair, Wray, & Smith, 2011; Cui et al., 2011; Jacob, Lazar, Dwinell, Moreno, & Geurts, 2010; Kitada et al., 2007; Smits et al., 2006). Therefore, before discussing selected genetic schizophrenia rat models in more detail, we will first describe several of the techniques now available for developing genetic rat models.

GENETIC MODELING IN RATS

The production of genetically engineered rat models has only recently evolved. The first engineered mutant rat models were described in 2003 (von Horsten et al., 2003; Zan et al., 2003), more than a decade after the first genetically engineered mouse models had been established (Capecchi, 2001; Koller et al., 1989; Thomas & Capecchi, 1987, 1990; Thompson, Clarke, Pow, Hooper, & Melton, 1989; Zijlstra, Li, Sajjadi, Subramani, & Jaenisch, 1989). Before this milestone development, genetic rat models were based on selective breeding (e.g., Bignami, 1965; Brush, Froehlich, & Sakellaris, 1979; Cools, Brachten, Heeren, Willemen, & Ellenbroek, 1990; Liebsch, Montkowski, Holsboer, & Landgraf, 1998; Schaefer, Brackett, Gunn, & Wilson, 1978; Schaefer, Brackett, Wilson, & Gunn, 1978) and "spontaneous sequence alterations" (i.e., genetic drifting) only (e.g., Swerdlow et al., 2001; Thompson et al., 1991; Watanabe, Kojima, & Fujimoto, 1987). This was partially because of our limited understanding of rat reproductive physiology and the sensitivity and fragility of fertilized rat eggs in vitro. These factors delayed the development of reliable and reproducible techniques for the development of transgenic rats.

Another major hurdle in establishing genetic engineering techniques for rats was the lack of germline competent embryonic stem (ES) cells. Scientists have overcome this hurdle only in the recent past by capturing authentic ES cells from rat blastocysts (Buehr et al., 2008; Kanatsu-Shinohara et al., 2011; Li et al., 2008). Embryoid body and monolayer differentiation confirmed that these cells retained their differentiation potential post targeting and selection (Meek et al., 2010). Rat ES cells can now be used for the state-of-the-art genetic engineering of conditional gene replacement knock-in as well as loss of function mutation (i.e., knock-out) rat models for an ever increasing number of genetic loci, for which targeting vectors have been designed. The completion of the genome sequence of the Brown Norway rat in 2004 (Gibbs et al., 2004) is highly relevant to this technological breakthrough. Importantly, ES cells also allow the functional evaluation of pluripotent ES cell-derived tissue repair and generation.

FORWARD GENETIC RAT MODELS

The traditional genetic rat models are based on the principle of forward genetics, that is, they start with a specific phenotype (usually but not always a behavior) and then move forward to identify the gene or genes involved in this specific phenotype (see Figure 1). Using the forward genetics principle, several approaches have been described in the literature.

Selective Breeding

Selective breeding (or artificial selection) is a process in which rats are bred for a particular trait or phenotype. This technique has long been established in experimental medical research with first reports of selective breeding lines published early in the last century (Tryon, 1930). Based on the knowledge, that strong heritable variations in behaviors exist not only across rat strains (e.g., regarding pharmacologically induced sensorimotor gating deficits (Swerdlow, Platten, et al., 2003; Swerdlow et al., 2004; Swerdlow, Shoemaker, et al., 2003; Swerdlow, Varty, & Geyer, 1998)), but can also be found among individuals within one strain, researchers have carried out breeding regimes to develop rats for the occurrence/absence of particular behaviors such as avoidance behavior (Roman high/low avoidance rats (Bignami, 1965; Brush et al., 1979)), hypertension (spontaneously hypertensive rats (Schaefer, Brackett, Gunn, & Wilson, 1978; Schaefer, Brackett, Wilson, &

Gunn, 1978)), anxiety (Liebsch et al., 1998), and emotionality (as measured by defecation in the open field: Maudsley reactive/nonreactive (Blizard & Adams, 2002)). Furthermore, breeding regimes have been used to select for pharmacological sensitivity to, for example, cholinergic agonists (Flinders Sensitive Line: reviewed in Overstreet & Wegener, 2013) or apomorphine (apomorphine susceptible/unsusceptible rats (Cools et al., 1990; Cools et al., 1993; Ellenbroek, Geyer, & Cools, 1995)).

To give an example, Bignami and coworkers defined selection criteria for low/high rates of conditioned avoidance response acquisition in Wistar rats and selected breeding animals out of those two test groups for five generations. Inbreeding was avoided whenever possible to maintain heterozygosity. Analysis at the end of the breeding regime confirmed that rats from the high avoidance group were consistently better in acquiring conditioned avoidance responses than animals from both the low avoidance group as well as an unselected control rat group. Cross-fostering experiments confirmed the robustness of the effect because the differences between the two strains were maintained (Bignami, 1965). Since this first publication, other groups have generated similar avoidance models using other rat strains (e.g., Long-Evans rats) and selectively bred these animals for more than 20 generations (Brush et al., 1979).

In relation to schizophrenia, it is important to note that these strains are usually bred for one specific characteristic, while schizophrenia (as discussed previously) is a highly complex disorder with many different symptoms, none of which is pathognomonic for the disorders. Although this suggests that selection strategies as outlined previously may not be useful for complex disorders, there is evidence for the contrary. For instance the Finders Sensitive and Resistance rats were originally bred for their difference in the sensitivity to acetylcholinesterase inhibitors. However, they are now most well-known as an animal model for depression, recapturing a wide range of symptoms and biomarkers (Overstreet & Wegener, 2013). Likewise, spontaneous hypertensive rats (originally selected for their high blood pressure) were shown to show a large number of characteristics also seen in patients with attention deficit hyperactive disorder (Sagvolden et al., 1992).

In an alternative approach, different strains are compared to identify meaningful differences in behavior. For example, Glowa and colleagues studied acoustic basal startle responses in a large number of different rat strains (Glowa, Geyer, Gold, & Sternberg, 1992; Glowa & Hansen, 1994). Likewise, we investigated the stereotyped gnawing response to the dopamine receptor agonist apomorphine in several different strains (Ellenbroek & Cools, 2002). Again, as with the within-strain approach, strain differences in a single behavioral parameter may

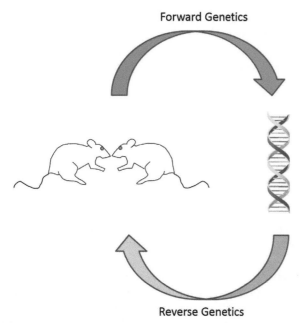

Forward Genetics

Reverse Genetics

FIGURE 1 **The two genetic approaches in animal research.** Forward genetics starts at the level of the behaviour and moves forward to the underlying genes. Reverse genetics starts with the genes and move backward to behaviour.

not be very useful for a complex disorder such as schizophrenia. However, if in addition, these strains show similar differences in other parameters relevant for the same disorder, the model becomes much more interesting and may produce insights into the genetic loci involved in those abnormalities.

Spontaneous Sequence Alteration ("Genetic Drifting")

The constant tendency of genes to evolve even in the absence of selective forces is called "genetic drifting." Spontaneous neutral mutations that disappear or become fixed in a population at random are a driving force behind this phenomenon. Other reasons can lie in copy number variations, residual heterozygosity in, or incomplete breeding of a mouse colony before it is separated from its progenitors, and separation of a subcolony from its parent colony for more than 20 generations.

One of the first examples for a spontaneous sequence alteration model (i.e., spontaneous mutation) was discovered in 1991. Fischer 344 (F344) rat substrains commercially available from Charles River Laboratories breeding colonies in Japan and Germany exhibited an extreme reduction in the endogenous activity of dipeptidyl-peptidase IV activity compared with F344 substrains from breeding colonies in the United States (Thompson et al., 1991). This discovery led to some of the first studies using a gene sequence alteration rat model. This rat model was used to investigate the functionality of the *Dppiv* gene product in a variety of domains including assimilation of prolyl peptides (Tiruppathi, Miyamoto, Ganapathy, & Leibach, 1993), natural killer cell function (Karl, Chwalisz, et al., 2003), and behavior (Karl, Hoffmann, Pabst, & von Horsten, 2003b) and established a role for *Dppiv* in the degradation and behavioral effects of the abundantly expressed neurotransmitter neuropeptide Y (Karl, Hoffmann, Pabst, & von Horsten, 2003a). These early studies gave evidence to the power of genetically modified (although not engineered) rat models for medical research and behavioral neuroscience in particular.

Chromosome Substitution

A chromosome substitution strain (CSS) or consomic strain is an inbred strain in which a single chromosome from a donor strain replaces the corresponding chromosome in the host/parental strain on a defined and uniform genetic background. In the rat, a CSS panel consists of 23 strains, corresponding to 21 autosomes, and 2 sex chromosomes (mouse: 19 autosomes and 2 sex chromosomes) (Nadeau, Singer, Matin, & Lander, 2000), which is generated by constructing those 23 strains through a "marker-assisted" breeding program. Donor and host strains are crossed and the F1 progeny is backcrossed to the host strain. Backcrossing is carried out using an offspring of each generation, which carries the nonrecombinant chromosome of interest from the donor strain. Genotyping the offspring for genetic markers (more than 5500 markers available for rats (Steen et al., 1999)), which cover the length of this chromosome, will reveal those animals that are heterozygous across the entire chromosome. In the tenth backcross generation, males and females carrying the nonrecombinant chromosome of the donor strain are intercrossed. Offspring of this intercross which are homozygous for the target chromosome (around 25%) are then used to breed the homozygous CSS strain, which carries an intact chromosome substitute from the donor strain (Nadeau et al., 2000). These rats can be inbred thereby providing a renewable resource. The breeding regime outlined can be improved by applying "speed congenics" (for details see Markel et al., 1997; Wakeland, Morel, Achey, Yui, & Longmate, 1997). CSS rats are essentially genetic "twins" and multiple crosses between two strains can be setup without the risk of introducing modifier genes (Cowley, Roman, & Jacob, 2004).

To give an example, two CCS panels have been developed where chromosomes from the normotensive Brown Norway rat were substituted into SS/JrHsdMcwi Dahl salt-sensitive and Fawn Hooded Hypertensive/EurMcwi Fawn Hooded Hypertensive rats. The Dahl salt-sensitive strain has been used for research into, for example, insulin resistance and vascular injury, whereas the Fawn Hooded Hypertensive strain has been used for investigations into renal disease and alcoholism (for more details, see Cowley et al., 2004). The CCS panel using Dahl salt-sensitive rats provided evidence that chromosomes 13 and 18 are important to determine whether a high-salt diet will lead to hypertension and renal disease (Cowley et al., 2004). In another example, CSS technology identified quantitative trait loci (QTL) on chromosome 14 and 17 as being responsible for strain-specificity of rat placentation (Konno et al., 2011).

Thus, CSS panels allow researchers to associate a phenotype with a particular chromosome for which the donor and host differ (i.e., partitioning of the genome). It also provides a powerful and fast way to identify QTL (i.e., QTL mapping), as at least one QTL must be located on the substituted chromosome if donor strain and host strain differ for a phenotype of interest. Fine-structure mapping after two-generation crosses and intercrossing to generate a homozygous chromosome segment of the region can then be used to study individual loci. Alternatively, CSS can be used to quickly produce a series of congenic strains (i.e., by backcrossing the appropriate CSS strain to the host strain; for details, see Cowley et al., 2004), which subdivide the chromosome into segments and thus refine the position of the QTL

(Nadeau et al., 2000). There are further advantages of the CSS technique. The phenotype of a homozygous CSS can be compared with heterozygous animals of the F1, allowing a direct "test of dominance." Furthermore, QTLs of relatively weak effect can be detected because comparing a CSS with its host strain avoids any of the "phenotypic noise" commonly seen by segregation of unlinked QTLs in linkage crosses, thereby providing considerably more statistical power (and fewer animals are needed) (Cowley et al., 2004; Nadeau et al., 2000). Finally, CCS can be used to develop several chromosome substitution models for investigations into gene–gene interactions of complex traits or diseases (Cowley et al., 2004). However, there are two limitations to CCS panels: (1) QTLs are assigned to an entire chromosome rather than a chromosomal region and (2) discrimination between single and multiple QTLs is not possible. Nonetheless, the ability to proceed directly to fine-structure mapping (as outlined previously) offsets these limitations. Thus, CSSs are a powerful tool for studying multigenetic traits and allow unique experimental designs (Cowley et al., 2004; Hill, Lander, & Nadeau, 2006).

REVERSE GENETIC RAT MODELS

Although the forward genetic models have dominated in the field of genetic rat modeling, recent advances in our understanding of the rat genome, coupled with an increased toolbox, have led to a flurry of novel rat models, based on reverse genetic principles. These models start off by changing the genome and then moving backwards to the behavior (see Figure 1). In this respect, we often distinguish between random techniques and techniques in which a specific gene is targeted. These latter techniques are often subdivided into two different categories: indirect and direct. In the indirect technique (most popular in mice) ES cells are first removed from pregnant mothers, and genetically altered in vitro, before being placed back into a host mother. In the direct technique, on the other hand, the mutagenesis takes place by microinjections directly into the embryo (see the following section).

Random Gene Targeting

N-Ethyl-N-Nitrosourea Mutagenesis

N-ethyl-N-nitrosourea (ENU: chemical formula is $C_3H_7N_3O_2$) is a highly potent mutagen that can transfer its ethyl group to oxygen or nitrogen radicals of DNA, thereby inducing mispairings and base-pair substitutions if the DNA does not get repaired (Hitotsumachi, Carpenter, & Russell, 1985; Russell et al., 1979). ENU predominantly modifies A/T base pairs in

spermatogonial stem cells, with 44% A/T->T/A transversions, 38% A/T->G/C transitions, 8% G/C->A/T transitions, 3% G/C->C/G transversions, 5% A/T->C/G transitions, and 2% G/C->T/A transitions. When translated into a protein product, these changes result in 64% missense mutations, 10% nonsense mutations, and 26% splicing errors (these rates have been established in mice (Justice, Noveroske, Weber, Zheng, & Bradley, 1999)). This process makes ENU a powerful tool for generating isolated mutations in genes, thereby generating loss-of-function mutations, gain-of-function mutations, viable hypomorphs of lethal complementation groups, and antimorphs. ENU can induce new point mutations at approximately 1–2 Mb intervals occurring in approximately 1 per 700 gametes.

Genetic screens are used to identify ENU-induced mutations using phenotype information as molecular markers are not available. More specifically, mutations are mapped in meiotic backcrosses segregating the phenotype relative to multiple molecular polymorphisms. For a resolution of 10 cM, analysis of 100 meioses is necessary (i.e., for one mutation, 100 mice must be screened). Thus, mapping represents the bottleneck of this technique and simpler mapping technologies such as DNA pooling have been applied in the recent past (Taylor, Navin, & Phillips, 1994). Importantly, the mutant phenotype must vary significantly from the background phenotype to be clearly identified. Further limitations of ENU technology include the high maintenance costs and the labor-intensive screening of large numbers of animals.

In 2003, genome-wide mutagenesis protocols using ENU were established for the rat inbred strains Wistar-Furth and F344 and for the rat outbred strain Sprague–Dawley (SD) (Zan et al., 2003). The effect of ENU on fertility was strain and dose-dependent (for more details on fertility and litter size effects as well as ENU toxicity, see Zan et al., 2003). Mutagenized male rats were used to generate F1 offspring and phenotypic abnormalities were identified (e.g., regarding growth and eye development). Approximately 50% of those phenotypic mutants, which produced viable litters, showed heritability of the trait/phenotype. In the following, SD rats were used for the mutation-screening studies. ENU was administered twice at a dose of 60 mg/kg to mutagenize male rats, which were then bred to wild-type-like female SD rats. F1 animals were screened for mutant alleles of the breast cancer suppressor genes Brca1 and Brca2. Yeast gap-repair, ADE2-reporter truncation assays were developed to identify functional mutations in those genes (for details and differences between screening assays, see Zan et al., 2003). The following procedures are outlined for Brca2 only. One of 296 F1 offspring carried a functional mutation in Brca2. The Brca2 knockout founder male rat was then bred to SD control females to generate N2 offspring, which included 35 heterozygous knock-out rats out of a total of 64 pubs suggesting Mendelian inheritance of the *Brca2* mutation. *Brca2* heterozygous N2 male and female rats were then used to generate homozygous knock-out pubs (ratio of 1:2:1). An important outcome of this study was that *Brca2* knock-out mice, carrying similar mutations in exon 11 as the newly generated rat model, develop a very different phenotype compared with *Brca2* mutant rats (mice show either embryonic lethality or premature death). This suggests that homogeneity of genetic modulations across species (i.e., mouse and rat) cannot be assumed.

Since 2003, the technology to generate ENU-induced mutations in rats has been adapted, optimized, and developed further and additional strains can now be used (e.g., Lewis and Brown Norway rats). For example, Targeting Induced Local Lesions in Genomes or resequencing-based screening technology allows the retrieval of not only stop mutations but also loss-of-function mutations as a result of missense mutations. It also allows the screening of large number of animals and can be fully automated for higher throughput screening (Smits, Mudde, Plasterk, & Cuppen, 2004; Smits et al., 2006). Other techniques include Mu Transposition Pooling Method With Sequencer and Institute for Clinical Systems Improvement technology (Mashimo et al., 2008).

To give an example, using ENU mutagenesis, several years ago, we developed a series of genetically altered rats including the serotonin transporter knock-out rat (see the following section) and a rat with a premature stop codon in exon 1 (K50X) of the melanin concentrating hormone precursor gene *PMCH* (Smits et al., 2006). This gene gives rise to melanin concentration hormone, but also to two other, less well-studied peptides labeled neuropeptide glycine–glutamic acid and neuropeptide glutamic acid–isoleucine. Thus, the homozygous Pmch knockout is devoid of all three peptides. *Pmch* knockout rats show decreased body weight and food intake on three different diets (Mul et al., 2010). Subsequent studies showed that these rats also show reduced motivation to lever press for food (Mul et al., 2011). Although these data are in line with melanin concentration hormone's role in food intake and satiety, it should be noted that the relative contribution of neuropeptide glycine–glutamic acid and neuropeptide glutamic acid–isoleucine in these rats is not entirely clear.

Transposable Elements (Transposon)

The discovery of transposable elements or so-called "jumping genes" or mobile genetic units in maize by the Nobel laureate Barbara McClintock mid-last century (McClintock, 1950) paved the way for the development of transposon technology. Transposable elements (i.e., transposon) are DNA sequences that can change their location within the genome. They can create mutations and are therefore a very useful tool for altering DNA of living organisms.

Initially, transposons were routinely used as a genetic tool to generate transgenic animals or insertional mutagenesis in lower organisms, but not rodents or other vertebrates because no efficient transposition systems were available. Several research teams then established efficient transposon technology for mice using systems such as *piggyBack* (a DNA transposon from the cabbage looper moth *Trichoplusia ni*: Ding et al., 2005) and *Sleeping Beauty* (a Tc1/mariner-like transposable element reconstructed from fish in vitro: Fischer, Wienholds, & Plasterk, 2001; Horie et al., 2001; Luo, Ivics, Izsvak, & Bradley, 1998) transposon systems. More recently, the *Sleeping beauty* (*SB*) transposon system has been applied to generate rat mutants (Kitada et al., 2007; Lu et al., 2007). The system uses a cut-and-paste mechanism where the transposase catalyzes the excision of the transposon from its original location and promotes its reintegration elsewhere in the genome (for details on the generation of transposon vectors, see Lu et al., 2007). Lu and coworkers also incorporated a tyrosinase minigene into the system so that successful transposition could be detected via changes in coat color (albino Fischer F344 inbred rats were used). Another advantage of this incorporation was that it allowed the distinction of homozygous and heterozygous rats via coat color intensity without polymerase chain reaction (PCR) analysis. Finally, splice acceptor gene-trapping elements were included for increased efficiency of mutagenesis.

In more detail, the transposon vector was delivered using pronuclear injections into fertilized eggs of F344 rats to generate pigmented founders. Transgenic rats were bred to homozygosity and had multiple copies of the transposon integrated in the genome. Transposon-carrying transgenic rats were then mated with transgenic transposase rats (expressing *SB* transposase) and bigenic offspring identified by coat color (i.e., for transposon) and tail DNA PCR (i.e., for transposase). Bigenic male offspring termed "seed rats" were mated with wild-type-like F344 females and checked for pigmented offspring. PCR amplification confirmed that all rats with new coat color had transposition events. PCRs were used to clone transposon insertion sites. It was found that many rats carried more than one transposition event (e.g., one rat exhibited five independent transposition events). In total, 12 different genes were targeted by transposition events in a total of 57 rats. Importantly, gene size and vicinity to the integration site of the original transposon concatemer impacted on the transposition target rate (i.e., majority of transpositions were "local hops" on the same chromosome). Southern blotting revealed 1.2–1.3 transposition events per gamete, similar to what had been described for mouse technology. It was estimated that in every litter of a double-transgenic male,

1–2 gene knockouts will be evident (Lu et al., 2007). Lu and coworkers predicted that about 1 in 10 transpositions will generate a new rat mutant, which is unrelated to other transposon-induced mutations (see also Kitada et al., 2007).

In summary, the transposition efficiency in the rat germline was similar to what has been observed in mice and a significant percentage of transposon integration sites was located within known or predicted genes confirming that the *SB* system can be a powerful and efficient method for creating rat mutants on a larger scale than previously possible. The inclusion of bidirectional splice acceptor gene trap elements enhanced the mutagenic potential of the transposon and allowed the quick localization of the integrated transposon via PCR, which is not possible when using ENU mutagenesis because ENU requires positional cloning or large-scale sequencing. Another advantage of the *SB* system over chemical mutagenesis is that unknown mutations can exist outside of the gene of interest using ENU, whereas mutations created by transposon systems can be located using transposon sequence as a tag (Kitada et al., 2007). Finally, the *SB* transposon system has potential for chromosome engineering because inclusion of LoxP sites in the transposon allows deletions and inversions by Cre recombinase expression. This enables the creation of rat models resembling human genetic deficiencies (see also Zheng, Mills, & Bradley, 2001).

Importantly, the transposon technique outlined above does not allow the preselection of transposition events that disrupt gene expression in the germline before producing mutant progeny. Thus, more recent studies have focused on selecting transposition events that disrupt gene expression using clonally selected germline stem cells from culture before production of transgenic rats (for details, see Ivics, Izsvak, Chapman, & Hamra, 2011; Izsvak et al., 2010). In addition, stem cells from different epigenetic states (i.e., spermatogonia and ES cells) can now be used to broaden the spectrum of functional genomic elements that can be disrupted during mutagenesis screens (see the following sections and Buehr et al., 2008; Li et al., 2008).

To give an example for the Transposon technique, Rasmus and coworkers developed a rat model for the canonical transient receptor potential (TRPC) family of Ca (2+) permeable, nonselective cation channels (Rasmus, O'Neill, Bachtell, & Cooper, 2013). These channels are abundantly expressed throughout the brain and play a significant role in cellular excitability. The TRPC4 channel subtype is predominantly expressed in structures that receive dopaminergic innervations. This suggests an involvement of TRPC4 in motivation- and reward-related behaviors. Indeed, TRPC4 knock-out rats exhibited reduced cocaine-seeking behavior in a self-administration experiment.

Indirect Gene Targeting (Homologous Recombination)

Homologous recombination can be used to modify genes in ES cells. Once ES rat cells had been established (Buehr et al., 2008; Kanatsu-Shinohara et al., 2011; Li et al., 2008), the genetic locus of interest could be disrupted via homologous recombination. This is a process where genetic recombination is based on an exchange between two similar or identical DNA molecules (e.g., during meiosis). The technique had initially been developed in mice by Capecchi, Evans and Smithies, for which they were awarded the Nobel Prize in 2007 (Capecchi, 1980, 2001; Evans & Kaufman, 1981; Folger, Wong, Wahl, & Capecchi, 1982; Koller et al., 1989; Thomas & Capecchi, 1987). In brief, the specifically designed targeting vector is introduced into drug-resistant (e.g., puromycin-resistant) ES cells using electroporation. Drug-resistant cell colonies are then selected to guarantee the proliferation/expansion of correctly targeted cells. Successful targeting (i.e., homologous recombination) is confirmed using PCR, sequencing, and Southern blot analysis. In case the targeting vector has indeed replaced the endogenous gene, locus ES cell rat chimeras are produced by microinjecting the genetically modified cells into rat donor blastocysts (timing: embryonic day 4.5). These microinjected blastocysts are then transferred into pseudo-pregnant female recipient rats. Adult chimeric offspring are then mated with control rats to evaluate successful germline transmission of the target allele (producing heterozygous rat mutants). After it has been established that the ES cells indeed contribute to the germline (chromosomal abnormalities in ES cells can prevent this), homozygous mutant rats can be generated by cross-breeding. Major differences between the genetic engineering of mouse and rat models by homologous recombination include ES cell culture methods, drug selection schemes, colony picking, and screening strategies (for more details, see Tong, Huang, Ashton, Li, & Ying, 2011). Importantly, the use of Cre/loxP and inducible gene expression systems allows temporal control and tissue specific changes in rat genes, similar to what has been described for mouse models (Feil, 2007; Kuhn & Torres, 2002; Witten et al., 2011). Efficient gene targeting using homologous recombination has now been reported for a variety of rat strains including dark agouti, S), Long-Evans, and F344 rats. However, the method of generating knockout rats via "conventional" gene-targeting methodology in rat ES cells is time consuming and a laborious process. Thus, more efficient and direct tools have been developed in the recent past (see the following section) (Tong et al., 2012).

One of the first mutant rat models generated using homologous recombination was the *p53* gene knockout rat (Tong, Li, Wu, Yan, & Ying, 2010). Tong and coworkers used ES cell-based gene targeting technology: the team designed a targeting vector to disrupt the tumor suppressor gene p53 in rat ES cells by means of homologous recombination. The mutation in the ES cells was transmitted by microinjecting subclones of these cells into blastocysts from F344 rats. Two chimeras were produced, one of those a germline chimera, which generated six mutant germline pubs. Genotyping and Southern blot analysis further confirmed that three of these pubs were p53 heterozygous knockout rats. Follow-up research revealed that p53 homozygous knockout rats develop sarcomas with a high occurrence of pulmonary metastases at around 4 months of age, whereas p53 heterozygous rats show the same phenotype not before 8 months of age (van Boxtel et al., 2011). These unique features make this rat highly complementary to other genetic rodent models of p53.

Direct Gene Targeting

Zinc-Finger Nucleases

Zinc-finger nucleases (ZFNs) technology allows the rapid and targeted modification of the rat genome. ZFNs are artificial restriction enzymes, which are generated by fusing zinc finger DNA-binding domain to a DNA-cleavage domain. ZFNs can be developed to target a particular DNA sequence and thereby disrupt genes of interest (by sequence-specific DNA double-strand breaks) in cultured rat cells and in embryos from inbred as well as outbred rat strains. ZFN-induced double-strand breaks can be repaired by error-prone nonhomologous end joining to produce small alterations at the targeted genomic loci (i.e., targeted mutation). The process can lead to the development of genetically modified rats (Gaj, Guo, Kato, Sirk, & Barbas, 2012; Geurts et al., 2010).

Geurts and colleagues published one of the first reports using embryo microinjection of ZFNs to generate knock-out rats (Geurts et al., 2009). The group designed ZFN reagents for the *green fluorescent protein* (*GFP*) gene, and the genes for *immunoglobulin M* (*IgM*) and *Rab38* for which they modified genetic technology, which had been established in Zebra fish (Doyon et al., 2008). In brief, ZFNs were assembled using PCR-based procedures and cloned into yeast expression vectors. Candidate ZFN pairs were subcloned into a cytomegalovirus expression plasmid for testing in cultured rat cells. ZFNs were screened for gene disruption activity (see supplementary materials of Geurts et al., 2009). Following this, five- and six-finger ZFNs were delivered to inbred and outbred rat embryos via pronuclear or intracytoplasmic injections of different concentrations of ZFN-encoding DNA or messenger RNA (mRNA). Twelve percent of founder rats actually carried the targeted mutation at various levels, including one animal with biallelic mutations in *IgM* (Geurts et al., 2009). Importantly, no

ZFN-induced mutations were detected in off-target sites (those could have been segregated away by backcrossing to the parental strain). Mutant rats were bred to wild-type-like control rats: one *GFP* and three *IgM* mutations were transmitted through the germline. The study demonstrated that ZFNs are active in early rat embryos from inbred (i.e., Dahl S and Fawn-hooded hypertensive) as well as outbred strains (i.e., SD) and that they can lead to both mono- and biallelic gene disruption. Importantly, the genetic engineering of rat mutants was achieved within a 4-month time frame.

Another example for ZFN-based development of a rat model for medical research is the Rag1 mutant rat. The *Rag1* gene is essential for immunoglobulin production process and for the differentiation of mature B and T lymphocytes. The immunodeficient rat model was developed by Zschemisch and coworkers microinjecting *Rag1*-specific ZFN mRNAs into zygotes of inbred LEW/Ztm rats (Zschemisch et al., 2012). A 4-base-pair deletion in one of the offspring caused a frame shift mutation, which led to a premature stop codon and a subsequently truncated Rag1 protein. This caused a complete depletion of mature B cells and a reduced development of T cells, which was associated with a hypoplastic thymus. Furthermore, there was a near complete absence of lymphocytes in spleen and lymph nodes in these immunodeficient *Rag1* mutant rats.

In conclusion, ZFNs can be developed for a multitude of sequences thereby providing a new, gene-specific and time-efficient tool to generate rat models of human diseases. Furthermore, they have facilitated the progress of targeted gene therapy in humans (e.g., HIV therapy: Holt et al., 2010; Perez et al., 2008). Importantly, in the past few years, the technology developed by Geurts and coworkers has been improved and researchers have started optimizing the delivery method for ZFNs (Doyon et al., 2010, 2011; Guo, Gaj, & Barbas, 2010; Sander et al., 2011). Viral vector delivery is problematic as it can be associated with side effects (e.g., insertional mutagenesis) and the vector production is time consuming. The delivery via nonviral DNA and mRNA as outlined by Geurts in 2009 can be toxic, nonefficient, and is restricted to specific cell types. Thus, researchers have developed a method to directly deliver purified ZFN proteins to cells and confirmed that this new technology can be used to disrupt gene expression in a variety of mammalian cells (Gaj et al., 2012). This technology might also be applicable to user designer nucleases including transcription activator-like effector nucleases (TALENs), which are described in the following section.

Transcription Activator-Like Effector Nucleases

TALENs can be used for in vivo genetic engineering of mutant rat models. TALENs are artificial restriction enzymes and can cut DNA strands at any desired sequence, which makes them an attractive tool for genetic engineering. TALENs are generated by fusing DNA binding domains of transcription activator-like (TAL) effectors to DNA cleavage domains. TAL effectors are secreted by *Xanthomonas* bacteria and can bind DNA sequences (via repetitive amino acid residues in the central domain) and activate gene expression. The simple relationship between amino acids in the TAL effector and the DNA bases in its target provides the possibility of engineering TAL effector proteins with an affinity for a predetermined DNA sequence (Tong et al., 2012). Several researchers have fused the FokI nuclease domain to TAL effector proteins to create TALENs (e.g., Miller et al., 2011). When TALENs are introduced into cells they can be used for genome editing in situ. For example, TALENs were used to disrupt the *IgM* locus in the rat and to create a heritable mutation that eliminates *IgM* function. For this, titrations of specifically designed TALENs were microinjected either as DNA or mRNA into one-cell rat embryos (similar to what has been described for ZFN technology), of which a proportion (DNA, 9.5%; mRNA, 58%) showed subsequent alterations to the *IgM* locus. IgM mutation frequency was a function of TALEN dose as was the rate of biallelically modified rats, which were generated by mRNA (but not DNA) injections only. Genetically modified rats were then bred with wild-type-like control rats and the resulting F1 generation was checked for mutant alleles using PCRs. This procedure established TALEN technology as a valid tool for the generation of in vivo gene knockouts in rats (Tesson et al., 2011).

However, the technique to generate TALEN-mediated DNA double-strand breaks described previously can be technically challenging using the regular cloning methods and is relatively expensive. Tong and coworkers recently developed TALEN-targeting vectors using Golden Gate cloning technique thereby providing a more time-efficient tool to generate gene-targeted rat ES cells (i.e., construction of a pair of TALENs targeting any sequence of interest can be completed in just 5 days) (Tong et al., 2012). Furthermore, TALEN-mediated homologous recombination has been utilized to generate a knock-in rat model using oocyte microinjections of TALENs mRNA with a linear donor (instead of a supercoiled donor, which was ineffective in producing knock-in rats) (Ponce de Leon, Merillat, Tesson, Anegon, & Hummler, 2014).

In conclusion, efficient gene targeting in rat ES cells can be achieved quickly using either TALEN-mediated DNA double-strand breaks (Tong et al., 2012) or integration of TALENs by homologous recombination (Ponce de Leon et al., 2014). Thus, TALENs are an affordable and highly efficient option for the generation of targeted and specific mutagenesis of the rat and will reduce significantly time expenditure.

To give an example, Ferguson and coworkers selected the gene for the toll-like receptor 4 (*TLR4*) for TALEN-mediated gene inactivation (Ferguson, McKay, Harris, & Homanics, 2013). The team developed a pair of TALEN constructs that specifically target exon 1 immediately downstream of the start of translation. TALEN mRNAs were microinjected into the cytoplasm of one-cell Wistar rat embryos and heterozygous F1 offspring were interbred to produce homozygous F2 animals. The homozygous knockout rats had a markedly attenuated increase in plasma tumor necrosis factor alpha in response to a lipopolysaccharide challenge compared to control rats. TLR4 knockout rats will also be valuable for studies of ethanol action and of inflammatory conditions including septic shock, as *TLR4* appears to play a role in ethanol-induced neuroinflammation and neurodegeneration.

GENETIC RAT MODELS FOR SCHIZOPHRENIA: SOME EXAMPLES

Although genetic modeling in rat, especially those based on reverse genetics, is still in its infancy, the field is rapidly increasing. This is part fueled by several companies that now offer standard genetic rat models and/or custom make genetic models. Rather than giving an extensive overview of all the different models currently available, we will discuss a few models in some detail and summarize the remaining models in Table 1.

Apomorphine Susceptible/Unsusceptible Rats

The apomorphine susceptible/unsusceptible (APO-SUS/UNSUS) breeding program started in the early 1980s and resulted from the finding that there was a large interindividual difference in the stereotyped gnawing response within a Wistar rat population. A detailed analysis showed that there was actually a bimodal distribution with about 40% of the animals showing a very strong (>500 gnaws per 45 min) and 40% showing a very weak (<10 gnaws per 45 min) stereotypy response (Cools et al., 1990; Ellenbroek & Cools, 2002). Males and females from the highest and lowest scoring litters were subsequently mated and their apomorphine response was evaluated for the next 25 generations. In addition, we replicated the same procedure in a completely independent population of Wistar rats about a decade after the original selection started and basically found very similar results in these replication lines.

Dopamine plays a crucial role in schizophrenia, and challenge studies have shown that patients with schizophrenia are more sensitive to apomorphine (Muller Spahn, Modell, Ackenheil, Brachner, & Kurtz, 1998), suggesting that APO-SUS rats are a valid animal model for schizophrenia. Indeed, several similarities were

TABLE 1   Characteristics of Genetic Rat Models for Schizophrenia

Model	Phenotype
SELECTIVE BREEDING	
APO-SUS rat	See text body (Apomorphine Susceptible/Unsusceptible Rats Section) and Table 2
Brattleboro rat	See text body (The Brattleboro Rat Section)
SHR	Increased behavioral activity and emotionality of SHR rats (Schaefer, Brackett, Gunn, & Wilson, 1978) Hyperlocomotion and deficits in social interaction, contextual fear conditioning, and prepulse inhibition (all reversible by APDs) (Calzavara, Levin, et al., 2011; Calzavara et al., 2009; Calzavara, Medrano, et al., 2011; Levin et al., 2011) Deficit in latent inhibition (Calzavara et al., 2009) Improved spatial memory and unaltered anxiety-like plus maze behavior of SHR rats (Ferguson & Cada, 2004) Behaviors (e.g., PPI) differentially affected by cannabinoid and vanilloid drugs (Almeida et al., 2014; Levin et al., 2014)
RHA/RLA rats	RHA rats display a robust sensation/novelty seeking profile (reviewed in Giorgi, Piras, & Corda, 2007) and lower levels of conditioned fear response (Lopez-Aumatell et al., 2009) RHA but not RLA rats develop a behavioral sensitization to amphetamine (Corda et al., 2005) RHA rats exhibit stronger response to novelty and motility patterns induced by various doses of apomorphine are different between RHA and RLA (Gimenez-Llort, Canete, Guitart-Masip, Fernandez-Teruel, & Tobena, 2005) Strain-dependent differences in anxiety-induced cortical dark agouti output (Giorgi, Lecca, Piras, Driscoll, & Corda, 2003) RHA rats exhibit a marked preference and intake of rewards, and a more pronounced behavioral and neurochemical response to acute morphine and psychotropic drugs (reviewed in Giorgi et al., 2007) Acute morphine and cocaine cause a larger increment in dopamine output in the core and an attenuated dopaminergic response in the shell of the nucleus accumbens in sensitized RHA rats (reviewed in Giorgi et al., 2007) Social stress during adolescence disturbed normal behavioral development predominantly in RHA rats (Coppens, de Boer, Steimer, & Koolhaas, 2012) 5-HT_{2A}, 5-HT_{1A} and SERT binding is increased in the frontal cortex of RHA rats, whereas $\text{mGlu}_{2/3}$ receptor binding was decreased compared to RLA rats (Klein et al., 2014)
Rats selectively bred for deficient sensorimotor gating	PPI deficits (reversible by APDs) (Hadamitzky, Harich, Koch, & Schwabe, 2007; Schwabe, Freudenberg, & Koch, 2007) Deteriorated social behavior toward adolescent rats and reduced motivation for food rewards in low PPI rats (Dieckmann, Freudenberg, Klein, Koch, & Schwabe, 2007) Enhanced perseveration in radial arm maze (i.e., during switching between an egocentric and allocentric version of the task) and in an operant behavioral task (Freudenberg, Dieckmann, Winter, Koch, & Schwabe, 2007)
ENU MUTAGENESIS	
SERT knock-out rat	See text body (The SERT Knock-Out Rat Section)
TRANSPOSON	
Type II *Nrg1* transgenic rat	See text body (Neuregulin 1 Hypomorphic Rat Section)
HOMOLOGOUS RECOMBINATION	
Nogo-A transgenic rat	Reduced social interaction, deficient PPI, and impaired object recognition and spatial reversal memory (Tews et al., 2013) Decreased cognitive functions and behavioral flexibility in a spatial active avoidance task, reduced anxiety, and altered circadian activity patterns (Petrasek, Prokopova, Bahnik, et al., 2014; Petrasek, Prokopova, Sladek, et al., 2014)
NR2B transgenic rat	Transgenic rats exhibit enhanced hippocampal long-term potentiation as well as improved object recognition memory, spatial memory, and delayed-to-nonmatch working memory; NR2B rats also showed more NR2B-containing NMDARs (Wang et al., 2009)

APDs, Antipsychotic Drugs; PPI, prepulse inhibition; RHA, Roman high avoidance; RLA, Roman low avoidance; APO-SUS, apomorphine susceptible; SHR, spontaneously hypertensive rat.
See also Del Rio et al. (2014).

found between the APO-SUS model and schizophrenia, including behavioral, neurochemical, immunological, and developmental similarities (Table 2). Given that the animals were originally only selected for their sensitivity to a dopaminergic agonist, it was quite surprising that the animals differed in so many physiological domains. However, it clearly gives the model interesting face validity (Jones et al., 2011; Lipska & Weinberger, 2000).

Because the original selection of the APO-SUS/UNSUS rats was based on behavior, it is a classic example of a forward genetic model and subsequent research has focused on trying to identify the underlying genetic factor(s). This has led to the identification of a copy number variation between the two lines in the *aph-1b* gene: whereas APO-UNSUS, just like normal Wistar rats contain three copies of the *aph-1b* gene, APO-SUS rats only had one or two. APH-1B is a key element of the γ-secretase complex, known to play an important role in development (Coolen et al., 2005). Subsequent detailed analysis identified several other genetic differences between APO-SUS and APO–UNSUS (van Loo & Martens, 2007). It, however, remains to be determined whether these genetic differences are causally related to some or all of the phenotypical differences between the two rat lines.

Although the APO-SUS/UNSUS model has several interesting and unique characteristics, the model also has several limitations. First of all, although the model has been quite extensively characterized, two areas of schizophrenia have received little or no attention: the negative and cognitive symptoms. So far, the APO-SUS/UNSUS model has not been evaluated in relation to changes in social behavior and/or communication or aspects of anhedonia. Likewise, apart from deficits in latent inhibition, the model has not been evaluated with respect to other areas of cognition, such as cognitive rigidity, executive functioning, or working memory, domains that are deficient in patients with schizophrenia. In addition to this, the APO-SUS/UNSUS model has not been evaluated with respect to predictive validity. For instance, although the APO-SUS rats show a deficit in prepulse inhibition and latent inhibition, it is unclear whether these deficits are reversible by first- and/or second-generation antipsychotics. To enhance the validity of the model, these aspects will need to be addressed.

The Brattleboro Rat

The Brattleboro rat is a strain originally derived from a single litter of Long Evans rats born in 1961 at Dartmouth Medical School. Close inspection of the litter showed that several pups showed severe polydipsia and polyuria. Subsequent breeding showed that this behavior could be attributed to a lack of circulation vasopressin due to a frame shift mutation in a single gene resulting in a deficient release of vasopressin. As such, the Brattleboro rat is one of the very few "naturally" occurring genetic knockouts and an important model for *diabetes insipidus* (Bouby, Hassler, & Bankir, 1999; Valtin & Schroeder, 1964).

However, in addition to its role in the kidney (via the V2 receptor), vasopressin also plays a crucial

TABLE 2   The Major Schizophrenia-Like Characteristics of APO-SUS Rats

Characteristic	Effect	APO-SUS	Schizophrenia
Prepulse inhibition	Decreased	Ellenbroek et al. (1995)	Braff et al. (1978)
Latent inhibition	Decreased	Ellenbroek et al. (1995)	Baruch, Hemsley, and Gray (1988)
Cocaine self-administration	Enhanced	van der Kam, Ellenbroek, and Cools (2005)	Miller and Fine (1993)
Tyrosine hydroxylase messenger RNA	Enhanced	Rots, Cools, Berod, et al. (1996)	Nagatsu (1995)
Dopamine release	Enhanced	van der Elst et al. (2005)	Howes et al. (2012)
Dopamine D2 receptor density	Enhanced	Rots, Cools, Berod, et al. (1996)	Seeman (2013)
Developmental milestones	Delayed	Degen, Ellenbroek, Wiegant, and Cools (2005)	Walker and Lewine (1990)
Hypothalamic pituitary adrenal axis	Hyper-reactive	Rots, Cools, Oitzl, et al. (1996)	Lammers et al. (1995)
Th1–Th2 balance	Th2 > Th1	Kavelaars, Heijnen, Ellenbroek, van Loveren, and Cools (1997)	Muller, Riedel, Ackenheil, and Schwarz (1999)
Sensitivity for rheumatoid arthritis	Reduced	van de Langerijt et al. (1994)	Vinogradov, Gottesman, Moises, and Nichol (1991)
Lung cancer metastasis	Reduced	Teunis et al. (2002)	Mortensen (1994)
Periodontitis	Enhanced	Breivik, Sluyter, Hof, and Cools (2000)	Eltas, Kartalci, Eltas, Dundar, and Uslu (2013)

APO-SUS, apomorphine susceptible.

neurotransmitter role in the brain, via the interaction with the V1a and V1b receptor. Moreover, vasopressin has appreciable affinity for the oxytocin receptor. Both neuropeptides are known to play a complex role in the brain, being involved in emotion (especially anxiety), reward, social behavior, and cognition (Griebel & Holsboer, 2012; Meyer-Lindenberg, Domes, Kirsch, & Heinrichs, 2011). It is therefore not surprising that the Brattleboro rat shows a wide range of behavioral abnormalities (for a recent review, see Feifel & Shilling, 2013).

With respect to schizophrenia, David Feifel and his colleagues have extensively studied the Brattleboro rat and shown that, like patients with schizophrenia, these rats show deficits in prepulse inhibition, latent inhibition, and startle habituation (Feifel & Priebe, 2001; Feifel & Shilling, 2013). In addition, they show an increased hyperactivity in a novel open field (Cilia et al., 2010). Moreover, there is some evidence for dopaminergic changes in the Brattleboro rat, including increased striatal D2 receptor binding (Shilling et al., 2006) and dopamine levels (Dawson, Wallace, & King, 1990; Feenstra, Snijdewint, Van Galen, & Boer, 1990). However, a recent study did not find any changes in dopamine levels or utilization, except for a significant decrease in frontal cortex dopamine (Cilia et al., 2010).

In contrast to the APO-SUS rats, the validity of the Brattleboro rat as a model for schizophrenia has been studied more extensively, mostly in relation to the deficit in prepulse inhibition. However, several striking features have been found, which casts some doubt on the predictive validity of this rat model. First of all, the deficit in prepulse inhibition in the Brattleboro rat is already seen before puberty (Feifel & Shilling, 2013). As schizophrenia generally has an onset after puberty, most authors suggest that the symptoms in an animal model for schizophrenia should also not occur until adulthood (Ellenbroek, 2010; Lipska & Weinberger, 2000). On the other hand, it is important to realize that the diagnosis of schizophrenia is usually based on the presence of positive symptoms (hallucinations and/or delusions) and it is well-known that others symptoms occur during the prodromal phase. So far to our knowledge, no study has looked at the presence or absence of prepulse inhibition deficits before the onset of florid positive symptoms. Another, perhaps more serious, difference between patients and animals relates to the interstimulus interval. Thus, whereas the deficit in patients is seen with short (60–120 ms) but not long (250–500 ms) intervals between the prepulse and startle stimulus (Braff et al., 1978), the reverse is true for the Brattleboro rat, that is, the largest deficits in prepulse inhibition as seen with intervals of 300 and 600 ms (Cilia et al., 2010). With respect to the predictive validity, it seems that both first- (chlorpromazine, haloperidol) and second- (risperidone, clozapine, olanzapine) generation antipsychotics

reverse the prepulse inhibition deficits in the Brattleboro rats (Cilia et al., 2010; Feifel, Melendez, & Shilling, 2004; Feifel, Shilling, & Melendez, 2005; Feifel & Shilling, 2013), although the effects of haloperidol are somewhat contentious because at least one report showed no effect (Feifel et al., 2004). Nonetheless, the reversal of the prepulse inhibition deficit by acute administration of an antipsychotic drug seems to be in contrast with clinical observations, and the effects of second-generation antipsychotics on prepulse inhibition are questionable. In fact, whether antipsychotics improve prepulse inhibition deficits in schizophrenia patients is still actively being discussed. Several longitudinal studies found no improvement of prepulse inhibition after antipsychotic treatment, even in patients that showed a reduction in other symptoms (During, Glenthoj, Andersen, & Oranje, 2014; Mackeprang, Kristiansen, & Glenthoj, 2002). Other studies found a significant improvement (Aggernaes et al., 2010; Meincke et al., 2004; Quednow et al., 2006), but usually only after 4 or more weeks of treatment.

An interesting recent development in the Brattleboro model is the finding that rats heterozygous for the vasopressin genetic mutation also show deficits in prepulse inhibition. Interestingly, these animals do not show polyuria and polydipsia, but do show deficits in spatial working memory (Feifel & Shilling, 2013). This is an important development as it shows that polydipsia/polyuria (and the many physiological changes that accompany it) can be separated from schizophrenia-like symptoms.

The SERT Knock-Out Rat

The serotonin transporter is the most important regulator of extracellular 5-HT levels, and in humans a large number of genetic polymorphisms have been identified (Murphy et al., 2008). However, the most studied polymorphism is a 44-base-pair deletion/insertion within the promoter region, generally referred to as the 5-hydroxytryptamine transporter linked promoter region (5-HTTLPR), where the short (s-)allele leads to a 50% reduction in SERT activity (Karg, Burmeister, Shedden, & Sen, 2011; Lesch et al., 1996). Interestingly, this s-allele is a very common polymorphism, especially in Asians (Chiao & Blizinsky, 2010). Although the s-allele has been linked to an increased vulnerability for several psychiatric disorders including major depression, anxiety disorders, bipolar disorder, autism, and drug and alcohol addiction (Cao, Hudziak, & Li, 2013; Kenna et al., 2012), its relation to schizophrenia is less clear. Although there is clear evidence of abnormal 5-HT neurotransmission in schizophrenia (Selvaraj, Arnone, Cappai, & Howes, 2014), most studies did not find a relation between the s-allele and schizophrenia (Golimbet, Korovaitseva, Faktor, Ganisheva, & Dmitriev, 2010; Pae et al., 2006;

Serretti, Catalano, & Smeraldi, 1999; Tsai et al., 2000). However, this does not necessarily preclude a role for the SERT in schizophrenia. Indeed, another polymorphism (the s-called STin2 VNTR) was found to be related to schizophrenia (Gatt, Burton, Williams, & Schofield, 2014), and a recent study also found DNA hypermethylation of the SERT in drug-naive patients with schizophrenia (Abdolmaleky et al., 2014). One possible explanation for these discrepancies is that genetic alterations in SERT activity may be more related to specific endophenotypes of schizophrenia rather than the disorder itself (e.g., negative symptoms: (Golimbet et al., 2004; Pae et al., 2003), impaired facial recognition (Alfimova et al., 2014), and/or impaired decision making (Gu et al., 2013)).

Several years ago, using the ENU mutagenesis technique we created a SERT knockout rat, resulting from a premature stop codon in amino acid position 209 (Smits et al., 2006). Since then, we have extensively characterized these animals and have found that they show increased anxiety and depression-like symptoms (Olivier et al., 2008). As mentioned previously, these symptoms often occur in schizophrenia and form one of the symptoms clusters of the PANNS. SERT KO rats show an increase in locomotor activity in a novel open field (Ellenbroek & Hulst, unpublished data), which is often regarded as a biomarker for positive symptoms as it can be a behavioral effect of a hyperdopaminergic tone in the brain. In addition, these rats are also more sensitive to the reinforcing effects of dopamine agonists such as cocaine and 3,4-methylenedioxy-methamphetamine (MDMA) (Homberg et al., 2008; Oakly, Brox, Schenk, & Ellenbroek, 2014). This is reminiscent of the high comorbidity of drug addiction and schizophrenia. In this respect, it is interesting to see that with respect to MDMA also the heterozygous SERT knockouts show enhanced self-administration (Brox & Ellenbroek, unpublished results). This is important as heterozygous SERT knockout rats have about a 50% reduction in SERT activity (Homberg, Olivier, et al., 2007) similar to that seen in humans with the s-allele. Moreover, the results on MDMA are in sharp contrast to findings in SERT knockout mice, which actually show reduced self-administration (Trigo et al., 2007), emphasizing the importance of genetic modeling in different species.

SERT knockout rats also exhibit deficits in social behavior (Homberg, Pattij, et al., 2007; Homberg, Schiepers, Schoffelmeer, Cuppen, & Vanderschuren, 2007) and cognitive performance including object recognition (Olivier et al., 2009) and latent inhibition (Nonkes et al., 2012). So far, no studies have been published on prepulse inhibition and/or startle habituation in SERT knockout rats. However, preliminary data from our own laboratory suggest that both prepulse inhibition and startle habituation are not different between wild-type-like and homozygous knockout rats (Oakly & Ellenbroek,

unpublished data). This is in line with a recent paper showing no effects of (spontaneous) polymorphism in the rat SERT (rs8154473, C3598T) on prepulse inhibition (Belay et al., 2011). Unfortunately, the effects of antipsychotic drugs have not been tested in SERT knockout rats so far, thus it is at present difficult to assess the predictive validity of the model for schizophrenia.

Neuregulin 1 Hypomorphic Rat

This rat model is another example of a reverse genetic model, created using the BART3 gen-trap transposon vector technique (see the previous section). So far only few studies have evaluated the behavior of this rat model, but studies on open-field behavior showed that habituation is diminished in the male neuregulin 1 hypomorphic (Nrg1^{Tn}) rat (Taylor, Taylor, et al., 2011), although there seems to be no difference in the initial locomotor response to novelty. Likewise, although the Nrg1^{Tn} rats had higher basal levels of serum cortisol, there were no differences in stress sensitivity, although glucocorticoid receptors were altered in several brain regions including the paraventricular nucleus of the hypothalamus and the hippocampus and pituitary gland (Taylor, Taylor, et al., 2011). Interestingly, in female Nrg1^{Tn} rat, the opposite was found, that is, an increased habituation to the open field. On the other hand, female Nrg1^{Tn} rats showed a reduction in prepulse inhibition, which was not observed in male Nrg1^{Tn} rats (Taylor, Markham, Taylor, Kanaskie, & Koenig, 2011). Sex differences were also observed in relation to anxiety, with female Nrg1^{Tn} rats showing a reduced anxiety and males a strong tendency for an increased anxiety as evaluated in the elevated plus maze (Taylor, Taylor, & Koenig, 2013). As with most of the other models, the predictive validity has so far not been studied in any detail in the Nrg1^{Tn} model.

CONCLUSIONS AND THE ROAD AHEAD

In the present chapter, we have discussed the current state of genetic modeling in rats in general and for schizophrenia in particular. The establishment of gene targeting technology in rat ES cells, in combination with advances in genomics and the vast amount of research data on physiology and pharmacology in this species, now provides a powerful new platform for the study of human disease. The rat offers a complementary model choice to the mouse because rat models have been shown to more closely mimic human disease than mouse models in several areas such as neurodegenerative diseases, hypertension, and Huntington's disease (reviewed in Lu et al., 2007). For example, there are clear differences between the SERT knockout rat and the SERT knockout mouse (see the previous section). Likewise, we have recently found clear differences between the BAC-HD rat and mouse models for Huntington's disease (Abada, Nguyen, Schreiber, & Ellenbroek, 2013; Abada, Schreiber, & Ellenbroek, 2013).

The rat is the model of choice in diverse areas of biomedical research such as cardiovascular diseases, pharmacology, behavioral/addiction studies, and neurobiology (Gibbs et al., 2004; Tesson et al., 2005). Moreover, rats are approximately 10 times larger than mice, allowing investigators to perform procedures such as nerve recordings, collection of tissue from small structures, and serial blood sampling more easily. Finally, their cognitive and social performance is much closer related to the human condition than mice (Abbott, 2004).

In relation to complex disorder such as schizophrenia, we do, however, need to realize the limitations of genetic modeling. Although the technology is now available to selectively alter any gene in the genome, it is well accepted that schizophrenia is not caused by a single gene defect. Indeed, the 2009 release of the schizophrenia gene resource database listed 7855 genes that were somehow involved in the etiology of schizophrenia (Sun, Kuo, Riley, Kendler, & Zhao, 2008), most of which led to only a small increase in risk (Purcell et al., 2014). This suggests that reverse genetic models based on a single genetic alteration (i.e., the SERT knockout, the BDNF knockout, or the $Nrg1^{Tn}$ rat) may have less construct validity than forward genetic models (such as the APO-SUS or the Brattleboro rat).

Related to this, it is becoming increasingly clear that schizophrenia is not a homogeneous disease, but rather a collection of different disorders with multiple pathologies and etiologies (Arnedo et al., 2014; Zhang, Koutsouleris, Meisenzahl, & Davatzikos, 2015). If this is confirmed, it will have important implications for animal modeling. Thus, rather than attempting to model schizophrenia as a single disease, it would be more fruitful to develop models for specific subgroups of schizophrenia. However, at present we cannot clearly distinguish these subgroups in terms of symptoms or responsiveness to antipsychotic drugs, and modeling is therefore not yet possible. One solution to this problem is modeling endophenotypes rather than attempting to model the full spectrum of the disorder.

Finally, it is important to note that although genetic alterations are a significant risk factor for schizophrenia, they by no means cause schizophrenia. Family studies have clearly shown that the concordance rates in monozygotic twins are around 50%, indicating that additional, environmental risk factors also play an important role. Thus, it is the combined action of multiple genes of small effect size (Owen, Craddock, & O'Donovan, 2005) and several environmental risk factors such as cannabis abuse or early life stress (McGrath et al., 2004), which causes the development of this mental disorder (Mackay-Sim, Feron, Eyles, Burne, & McGrath, 2004). For example, it has been shown that one such environmental challenge is adolescent cannabis use, which has been shown to enhance the risk of schizophrenia especially in interaction with genetic risk factors such as the catechol-O-methyltransferase polymorphism (Caspi et al., 2005), the Akt (rs2494732) polymorphism (Di Forti et al., 2012), or mutant *neuregulin 1* (Karl, 2013). This is summarized in the "two-hit hypothesis" of schizophrenia, which predicts that genetic and environmental risk factors interactively trigger the development of the disorder (Bayer, Falkai, & Maier, 1999; Caspi & Moffitt, 2006; Ellenbroek, 2003).

Thus, although the genetic rat models can help us understand how changes at the level of the DNA can alter the development of brain and behavior, the incorporation of early and/or later environmental factors will improve the construct validity of such models. So far, only few attempts have been made, and even fewer have investigated the predictive validity of such models. However, the enhanced understanding of the clinical picture of schizophrenia (including the etiological role of genetic and environmental risk factors) coupled with the enhanced genetic toolbox for rats offer great promise for the future.

References

Abada, Y. S., Nguyen, H. P., Schreiber, R., & Ellenbroek, B. (2013). Assessment of motor function, sensory motor gating and recognition memory in a novel BACHD transgenic rat model for Huntington's disease. *PLoS One, 8*, e68584.

Abada, Y. S., Schreiber, R., & Ellenbroek, B. (2013). Motor, emotional and cognitive deficits in adult BACHD mice: a model for Huntington's disease. *Behavioural Brain Research, 238*, 243–251.

Abbott, A. (2004). Laboratory animals: the Renaissance rat. *Nature, 428*, 464–466.

Abdolmaleky, H. M., Nohesara, S., Ghadirivasfi, M., Lambert, A. W., Ahmadkhaniha, H., Ozturk, S., et al. (2014). DNA hypermethylation of serotonin transporter gene promoter in drug naive patients with schizophrenia. *Schizophrenia Research, 152*, 373–380.

Aggernaes, B., Glenthoj, B. Y., Ebdrup, B. H., Rasmussen, H., Lublin, H., & Oranje, B. (2010). Sensorimotor gating and habituation in antipsychotic-naive, first-episode schizophrenia patients before and after 6 months' treatment with quetiapine. *International Journal of Neuropsychopharmacology, 13*, 1383–1395.

Agius, M., Davis, A., Gilhooley, M., Chapman, S., & Zaman, R. (2010). What do large scale studies of medication in schizophrenia add to our management strategies? *Psychiatria Danubina, 22*, 323–328.

Alfimova, M. V., Golimbet, V. E., Korovaitseva, G. I., Lezheiko, T. V., Abramova, L. I., Aksenova, E. V., et al. (2014). [The effect of the serotonin transporter 5-HTTLPR polymorphism on the recognition of facial emotions in schizophrenia]. *Zhurnal nevrologii i psikhiatrii imeni SS Korsakova/Ministerstvo zdravookhraneniia i meditsinskoi promyshlennosti Rossiiskoi Federatsii. Vserossiiskoe obshchestvo nevrologov [i] Vserossiiskoe obshchestvo psikhiat, 114*, 42–48.

Almeida, V., Peres, F. F., Levin, R., Suiama, M. A., Calzavara, M. B., Zuardi, A. W., et al. (2014). Effects of cannabinoid and vanilloid drugs on positive and negative-like symptoms on an animal model of schizophrenia: the SHR strain. *Schizophrenia Research, 153*, 150–159.

Andreasen, N. C., Flaum, M., Swayze, V. W., Tyrrell, G., & Arndt, S. (1990). Positive and negative symptoms in schizophrenia. A critical reappraisal. *Archives of General Psychiatry, 47*, 615–621.

Andreasen, N. C., & Olsen, S. A. (1982). Negative vs. positive schizophrenia. Definition and validation. *Archives of General Psychiatry, 39*, 789–794.

Arnedo, J., Svrakic, D. M., Del Val, C., Romero-Zaliz, R., Hernandez-Cuervo, H., Fanous, A. H., Molecular Genetics of Schizophrenia Consortium, et al. (2014). Uncovering the hidden risk architecture of the schizophrenias: confirmation in three independent genome-wide association studies. *American Journal of Psychiatry.*

Arrowsmith, J., & Miller, P. (2013). Trial watch: phase II and phase III attrition rates 2011–2012. *Nature Reviews Drug Discovery, 12*, 569.

Baruch, I., Hemsley, D. R., & Gray, J. A. (1988). Differential performance of acute and chronic schizophrenics in a latent inhibition task. *Journal of Nervous and Mental Disease, 176*, 598–606.

Bayer, T. A., Falkai, P., & Maier, W. (1999). Genetic and non-genetic vulnerability factors in schizophrenia: the basis of the "two hit hypothesis". *Journal of Psychiatric Research, 33*, 543–548.

Belay, H., Burton, C. L., Lovic, V., Meaney, M. J., Sokolowski, M., & Fleming, A. S. (2011). Early adversity and serotonin transporter genotype interact with hippocampal glucocorticoid receptor mRNA expression, corticosterone, and behavior in adult male rats. *Behavioral Neuroscience, 125*, 150–160.

Bignami, G. (1965). Selection for high rates and low rates of avoidance conditioning in the rat. *Animal Behaviour, 13*, 221–227.

Blair, K., Wray, J., & Smith, A. (2011). The liberation of embryonic stem cells. *PLoS Genetics, 7*, e1002019.

Blizard, D. A., & Adams, N. (2002). The Maudsley Reactive and Nonreactive strains: a new perspective. *Behavior Genetics, 32*, 277–299.

Bouby, N., Hassler, C., & Bankir, L. (1999). Contribution of vasopressin to progression of chronic renal failure: study in Brattleboro rats. *Life Sciences, 65*, 991–1004.

van Boxtel, R., Kuiper, R. V., Toonen, P. W., van Heesch, S., Hermsen, R., de Bruin, A., et al. (2011). Homozygous and heterozygous p53 knockout rats develop metastasizing sarcomas with high frequency. *American Journal of Pathology, 179*, 1616–1622.

Braff, D., Stone, C., Callaway, E., Geyer, M. A., Glick, I. D., & Bali, L. (1978). Prestimulus effects of human startle reflex in normals and schizophrenics. *Psychophysiology, 15*, 339–343.

Breivik, T., Sluyter, F., Hof, M., & Cools, A. R. (2000). Differential susceptibility to periodontitis in genetically selected Wistar rat lines that differ in their behavioral and endocrinological response to stressors. *Behavioural Genetics, 30*, 123–130.

Brush, F. R., Froehlich, J. C., & Sakellaris, P. C. (1979). Genetic selection for avoidance behavior in the rat. *Behavioural Genetics, 9*, 309–316.

Buehr, M., Meek, S., Blair, K., Yang, J., Ure, J., Silva, J., et al. (2008). Capture of authentic embryonic stem cells from rat blastocysts. *Cell, 135*, 1287–1298.

Bugarski-Kirola, D., Wang, A., Abi-Saab, D., & Blattler, T. (2014). A phase II/III trial of bitopertin monotherapy compared with placebo in patients with an acute exacerbation of schizophrenia – results from the CandleLyte study. *European Neuropsychopharmacology, 24*, 1024–1036.

Burns, A. M. N., Erickson, D. H., & Brenner, C. A. (2014). Cognitive-behavioral therapy for medication-resistant psychosis: a meta-analytic review. *Psychiatric Services, 65*, 874–880.

Burrows, E. L., McOmish, C. E., & Hannan, A. J. (2011). Gene-environment interactions and construct validity in preclinical models of psychiatric disorders. *Progress in Neuro-Psychopharmacology & Biological Psychiatry, 35*, 1376–1382.

Calzavara, M. B., Levin, R., Medrano, W. A., Almeida, V., Sampaio, A. P., Barone, L. C., et al. (2011). Effects of antipsychotics and amphetamine on social behaviors in spontaneously hypertensive rats. *Behavioural Brain Research, 225*, 15–22.

Calzavara, M. B., Medrano, W. A., Levin, R., Kameda, S. R., Andersen, M. L., Tufik, S., et al. (2009). Neuroleptic drugs revert the contextual fear conditioning deficit presented by spontaneously hypertensive rats: a potential animal model of emotional context processing in schizophrenia? *Schizophrenia Bulletin, 35*, 748–759.

Calzavara, M. B., Medrano, W. A., Levin, R., Libanio, T. C., de Alencar Ribeiro, R., & Abilio, V. C. (2011). The contextual fear conditioning deficit presented by spontaneously hypertensive rats (SHR) is not improved by mood stabilizers. *Progress in Neuro-Psychopharmacology & Biological Psychiatry, 35*, 1607–1611.

Cao, J., Hudziak, J. J., & Li, D. (2013). Multi-cultural association of the serotonin transporter gene (SLC6A4) with substance use disorder. *Neuropsychopharmacology, 38*, 1737–1747.

Capecchi, M. R. (1980). High efficiency transformation by direct microinjection of DNA into cultured mammalian cells. *Cell, 22*, 479–488.

Capecchi, M. R. (2001). Generating mice with targeted mutations. *Nature Medicine, 7*, 1086–1090.

Caspi, A., & Moffitt, T. E. (2006). Opinion – gene-environment interactions in psychiatry: joining forces with neuroscience. *Nature Reviews Neuroscience, 7*, 583–590.

Caspi, A., Moffitt, T. E., Cannon, M., McClay, J., Murray, R., Harrington, H., et al. (2005). Moderation of the effect of adolescent-onset cannabis use on adult psychosis by a functional polymorphism in the catechol-*O*-methyltransferase gene: longitudinal evidence of a gene X environment interaction. *Biological Psychiatry, 57*, 1117–1127.

Chiao, J. Y., & Blizinsky, K. D. (2010). Culture-gene coevolution of individualism-collectivism and the serotonin transporter gene. *Proceedings of the Royal Society B-Biological Sciences, 277*, 529–537.

Cilia, J., Gartlon, J. E., Shilliam, C., Dawson, L. A., Moore, S. H., & Jones, D. N. (2010). Further neurochemical and behavioural investigation of Brattleboro rats as a putative model of schizophrenia. *Journal of Psychopharmacology, 24*, 407–419.

Cook, D., Brown, D., Alexander, R., March, R., Morgan, P., Satterthwaite, G., et al. (2014). Lessons learned from the fate of AstraZeneca's drug pipeline: a five-dimensional framework. *Nature Reviews Drug Discovery, 13*, 419–431.

Coolen, M. W., van Loo, K. M. J., van Bakel, N. N. H. M., Pulford, D. J., Serneels, L., De Strooper, B., et al. (2005). Gene dosage effect on γ-secretase component Aph-1b in a rat model for neurodevelopmental disorders. *Neuron, 45*, 497–503.

Cools, A. R., Brachten, R., Heeren, D., Willemen, A., & Ellenbroek, B. (1990). Search after neurobiological profile of individual-specific features of Wistar rats. *Brain Research Bulletin, 24*, 49–69.

Cools, A. R., Dierx, J., Coenders, C., Heeren, D., Ried, S., Jenks, B. G., et al. (1993). Apomorphine-susceptible and apomorphine-unsusceptible Wistar rats differ in novelty-induced changes in hippocampal dynorphin B expression and two-way active avoidance: a new key in the search for the role of the hippocampal-accumbens axis. *Behavioural Brain Research, 55*, 213–221.

Coppens, C. M., de Boer, S. F., Steimer, T., & Koolhaas, J. M. (2012). Impulsivity and aggressive behavior in Roman high and low avoidance rats: baseline differences and adolescent social stress induced changes. *Physiology & Behavior, 105*, 1156–1160.

Corda, M. G., Piras, G., Lecca, D., Fernandez-Teruel, A., Driscoll, P., & Giorgi, O. (2005). The psychogenetically selected Roman rat lines differ in the susceptibility to develop amphetamine sensitization. *Behavioural Brain Research, 157*, 147–156.

Cowley, A. W., Jr., Roman, R. J., & Jacob, H. J. (2004). Application of chromosomal substitution techniques in gene-function discovery. *Journal of Physiology, 554*, 46–55.

Cui, X., Ji, D., Fisher, D. A., Wu, Y., Briner, D. M., & Weinstein, E. J. (2011). Targeted integration in rat and mouse embryos with zinc-finger nucleases. *Nature Biotechnology, 29*, 64–67.

Dawson, R., Jr., Wallace, D. R., & King, M. J. (1990). Monoamine and amino acid content in brain regions of Brattleboro rats. *Neurochemical Research, 15*, 755–761.

Degen, S. B., Ellenbroek, B. A., Wiegant, V. M., & Cools, A. R. (2005). The development of various somatic markers is retarded in an animal model for schizophrenia, namely apomorphine-susceptible rats. *Behavioural Brain Research, 157*, 369–377.

Del Rio, C., Oliveras, I., Canete, T., Blazquez, G., Tobena, A., & Fernandez-Teruel, A. (2014). Genetic rat models of schizophrenia-relevant symptoms. *World Journal of Neuroscience, 4*, 261–278.

Di Forti, M., Iyegbe, C., Sallis, H., Kolliakou, A., Falcone, M. A., Paparelli, A., et al. (2012). Confirmation that the AKT1 (rs2494732) genotype influences the risk of psychosis in cannabis users. *Biological Psychiatry, 72*, 811–816.

Dickerson, F., Schroeder, J., Stallings, C., Origoni, A., Katsafanas, E., Schwienfurth, L. A. B., et al. (2014). A longitudinal study of cognitive functioning in schizophrenia: clinical and biological predictors. *Schizophrenia Research, 156*, 248–253.

Dieckmann, M., Freudenberg, F., Klein, S., Koch, M., & Schwabe, K. (2007). Disturbed social behavior and motivation in rats selectively bred for deficient sensorimotor gating. *Schizophrenia Research, 97*, 250–253.

Ding, S., Wu, X., Li, G., Han, M., Zhuang, Y., & Xu, T. (2005). Efficient transposition of the piggyBac (PB) transposon in mammalian cells and mice. *Cell, 122*, 473–483.

Doyon, Y., Choi, V. M., Xia, D. F., Vo, T. D., Gregory, P. D., & Holmes, M. C. (2010). Transient cold shock enhances zinc-finger nuclease-mediated gene disruption. *Nature Methods, 7*, 459–460.

Doyon, Y., McCammon, J. M., Miller, J. C., Faraji, F., Ngo, C., Katibah, G. E., et al. (2008). Heritable targeted gene disruption in zebrafish using designed zinc-finger nucleases. *Nature Biotechnology, 26*, 702–708.

Doyon, Y., Vo, T. D., Mendel, M. C., Greenberg, S. G., Wang, J., Xia, D. F., et al. (2011). Enhancing zinc-finger-nuclease activity with improved obligate heterodimeric architectures. *Nature Methods, 8*, 74–79.

During, S., Glenthoj, B. Y., Andersen, G. S., & Oranje, B. (2014). Effects of dopamine d2/d3 blockade on human sensory and sensorimotor gating in initially antipsychotic-naive, first-episode schizophrenia patients. *Neuropsychopharmacology, 39*, 3000–3008.

Ellenbroek, B. A. (1993). Treatment of schizophrenia: a clinical and preclinical evaluation of neuroleptic drugs. *Pharmacology & Therapeutics, 57*, 1–78.

Ellenbroek, B. A. (2003). Animal models in the genomic era: possibilities and limitations with special emphasis on schizophrenia. *Behavioural Pharmacology, 14*, 409–417.

Ellenbroek, B. A. (2010). Schizophrenia: animal models. In *Encyclopedia of Psychopharmacology* (pp. 1181–1186). Heidelberg: Springer.

Ellenbroek, B. A. (2012). Psychopharmacological treatment of schizophrenia: what do we have and what could we get? *Neuropharmacology, 62*, 1371–1380.

Ellenbroek, B. A., & Cesura, A. M. (2015). Antipsychotics and the dopamine - serotonin connection. In S. Celanire, & S. Poli (Eds.), *Topics in Medicinal Chemistry* (pp. 1–50). Heidelberg: Springer.

Ellenbroek, B. A., & Cools, A. R. (1990). Animal models with construct validity for schizophrenia. *Behavioural Pharmacology, 1*, 469–490.

Ellenbroek, B. A., & Cools, A. R. (2002). Apomorphine susceptibility and animal models for psychopathology: genes and environment. *Behavior Genetics, 32*, 349–361.

Ellenbroek, B. A., Geyer, M. A., & Cools, A. R. (1995). The behavior of APO-SUS rats in animal models with construct validity for schizophrenia. *Journal of Neuroscience, 15*, 7604–7611.

van der Elst, M. C. J., Verheij, M. M. M., Roubos, E. W., Ellenbroek, B. A., Veening, J. G., & Cools, A. R. (2005). A single exposure to novelty increases the tyrosine hydroxylase-immunoreactive network and the dopamine release in the nucleus accumbens in apomorphine-susceptible rats. *Life Sciences, 76*, 1391–1406.

Eltas, A., Kartalci, S., Eltas, S. D., Dundar, S., & Uslu, M. O. (2013). An assessment of periodontal health in patients with schizophrenia and taking antipsychotic medication. *International Journal of Dental Hygiene, 11*, 78–83.

Emsley, R., Oosthuizen, P., Koen, L., Niehaus, D. J., Medori, R., & Rabinowitz, J. (2008). Remission in patients with first-episode schizophrenia receiving assured antipsychotic medication: a study with risperidone long-acting injection. *International Clinical Psychopharmacology, 23*, 325–331.

Emsley, R., Oosthuizen, P. P., Koen, L., Niehaus, D. J., & Martinez, G. (2012). Symptom recurrence following intermittent treatment in first-episode schizophrenia successfully treated for 2 years: a 3-year open-label clinical study. *Journal of Clinical Psychiatry, 73*, e541–547.

Evans, M. J., & Kaufman, M. H. (1981). Establishment in culture of pluripotential cells from mouse embryos. *Nature, 292*, 154–156.

Fatouros-Bergman, H., Cervenka, S., Flyckt, L., Edman, G., & Farde, L. (2014). Meta-analysis of cognitive performance in drug-naive patients with schizophrenia. *Schizophrenia Research, 158*, 156–162.

Feenstra, M. G., Snijdewint, F. G., Van Galen, H., & Boer, G. J. (1990). Widespread alterations in central noradrenaline, dopamine, and serotonin systems in the Brattleboro rat not related to the local absence of vasopressin. *Neurochemical Research, 15*, 283–288.

Feifel, D., Melendez, G., & Shilling, P. D. (2004). Reversal of sensorimotor gating deficits in Brattleboro rats by acute administration of clozapine and a neurotensin agonist, but not haloperidol: a potential predictive model for novel antipsychotic effects. *Neuropsychopharmacology, 29*, 731–738.

Feifel, D., & Priebe, K. (2001). Vasopressin-deficient rats exhibit sensorimotor gating deficits that are reversed by subchronic haloperidol. *Biological Psychiatry, 50*, 425–433.

Feifel, D., Shilling, P., & Melendez, G. (2005). Natural prepulse inhibition deficits in Brattleboro rats respond to valproic acid augmentation of clozapine: further support for the predictive validity of this animal model. *Neuropsychopharmacology, 30*, S125.

Feifel, D., & Shilling, P. D. (2013). Modelling schizophrenia in animals. In P. M. Conn (Ed.), *Animal models for the study of human disease* (pp. 727–755). Amsterdam: Elsevier.

Feil, R. (2007). Conditional somatic mutagenesis in the mouse using site-specific recombinases. *Handbook of Experimental Pharmacology, 178*, 3–28.

Ferguson, C., McKay, M., Harris, R. A., & Homanics, G. E. (2013). Toll-like receptor 4 (Tlr4) knockout rats produced by transcriptional activator-like effector nuclease (TALEN)-mediated gene inactivation. *Alcohol, 47*, 595–599.

Ferguson, S. A., & Cada, A. M. (2004). Spatial learning/memory and social and nonsocial behaviors in the spontaneously hypertensive, Wistar-Kyoto and Sprague-Dawley rat strains. *Pharmacology, Biochemistry, and Behavior, 77*, 583–594.

Fischer, S. E., Wienholds, E., & Plasterk, R. H. (2001). Regulated transposition of a fish transposon in the mouse germ line. *Proceedings of the National Academy of Sciences of the United States of America, 98*, 6759–6764.

Folger, K. R., Wong, E. A., Wahl, G., & Capecchi, M. R. (1982). Patterns of integration of DNA microinjected into cultured mammalian cells: evidence for homologous recombination between injected plasmid DNA molecules. *Molecular and Cellular Biology, 2*, 1372–1387.

Freudenberg, F., Dieckmann, M., Winter, S., Koch, M., & Schwabe, K. (2007). Selective breeding for deficient sensorimotor gating is accompanied by increased perseveration in rats. *Neuroscience, 148*, 612–622.

Gaj, T., Guo, J., Kato, Y., Sirk, S. J., & Barbas, C. F., 3rd (2012). Targeted gene knockout by direct delivery of zinc-finger nuclease proteins. *Nature Methods, 9*, 805–807.

Gatt, J. M., Burton, K. L., Williams, L. M., & Schofield, P. R. (2014). Specific and common genes implicated across major mental disorders: a review of meta-analysis studies. *Journal of Psychiatric Research, 60*, 1–13.

Geurts, A. M., Cost, G. J., Freyvert, Y., Zeitler, B., Miller, J. C., Choi, V. M., et al. (2009). Knockout rats via embryo microinjection of zinc-finger nucleases. *Science, 325*, 433.

Geurts, A. M., Cost, G. J., Remy, S., Cui, X., Tesson, L., Usal, C., et al. (2010). Generation of gene-specific mutated rats using zinc-finger nucleases. *Methods in Molecular Biology (Clifton, NJ), 597,* 211–225.

Gibbs, R. A., Weinstock, G. M., Metzker, M. L., Muzny, D. M., Sodergren, E. J., Scherer, S., et al. (2004). Genome sequence of the Brown Norway rat yields insights into mammalian evolution. *Nature, 428,* 493–521.

Gimenez-Llort, L., Canete, T., Guitart-Masip, M., Fernandez-Teruel, A., & Tobena, A. (2005). Two distinctive apomorphine-induced phenotypes in the Roman high- and low-avoidance rats. *Physiology & Behavior, 86,* 458–466.

Giorgi, O., Lecca, D., Piras, G., Driscoll, P., & Corda, M. G. (2003). Dissociation between mesocortical dopamine release and fear-related behaviours in two psychogenetically selected lines of rats that differ in coping strategies to aversive conditions. *European Journal of Neuroscience, 17,* 2716–2726.

Giorgi, O., Piras, G., & Corda, M. G. (2007). The psychogenetically selected Roman high- and low-avoidance rat lines: a model to study the individual vulnerability to drug addiction. *Neuroscience and Biobehavioral Reviews, 31,* 148–163.

Glowa, J. R., Geyer, M. A., Gold, P. W., & Sternberg, E. M. (1992). Differential startle amplitude and corticosterone response in rats. *Neuroendocrinology, 56,* 719–723.

Glowa, J. R., & Hansen, C. T. (1994). Differences in response to an acoustic startle stimulus among forty-six rat strains. *Behavior Genetics, 24,* 79–84.

Golimbet, V. E., Alfimova, M. V., Shchebatykh, T. V., Abramova, L. I., Kaleda, V. G., & Rogaev, E. I. (2004). Serotonin transporter polymorphism and depressive-related symptoms in schizophrenia. *American Journal of Medical Genetics Part B Neuropsychiatric Genetics, 126B,* 1–7.

Golimbet, V. E., Korovaitseva, G. I., Faktor, M. I., Ganisheva, T. K., & Dmitriev, D. A. (2010). Functional state of serotoninergic system and the 5-HTTLPR polymorphism of the serotonin transporter gene in patients with schizophrenia. *Molekuliarnaia Biologiia, 44,* 251–256.

Griebel, G., & Holsboer, F. (2012). Neuropeptide receptor ligands as drugs for psychiatric diseases: the end of the beginning? *Nature Reviews Drug Discovery, 11,* 462–478.

Gu, H., Liu, C., Chen, M., Zhang, Q., Zhai, J., Wang, K., et al. (2013). The combined effects of the 5-HTTLPR and HTR1A rs6295 polymorphisms modulate decision making in schizophrenia patients. *Genes, Brain, and Behavior, 12,* 133–139.

Guo, J., Gaj, T., & Barbas, C. F., 3rd (2010). Directed evolution of an enhanced and highly efficient FokI cleavage domain for zinc finger nucleases. *Journal of Molecular Biology, 400,* 96–107.

Hadamitzky, M., Harich, S., Koch, M., & Schwabe, K. (2007). Deficient prepulse inhibition induced by selective breeding of rats can be restored by the dopamine D2 antagonist haloperidol. *Behavioural Brain Research, 177,* 364–367.

Heinrichs, R. W., & Zakzanis, K. K. (1998). Neurocognitive deficit in schizophrenia: a quantitative review of the evidence. *Neuropsychology, 12,* 426–445.

Hida, H., Mouri, A., & Noda, Y. (2013). Behavioral phenotypes in schizophrenic animal models with multiple combinations of genetic and environmental factors. *Journal of Pharmacological Sciences, 121,* 185–191.

Hill, A. E., Lander, E. S., & Nadeau, J. H. (2006). Chromosome substitution strains: a new way to study genetically complex traits. *Methods in Molecular Medicine, 128,* 153–172.

Hitotsumachi, S., Carpenter, D. A., & Russell, W. L. (1985). Dose-repetition increases the mutagenic effectiveness of N-ethyl-N-nitrosourea in mouse spermatogonia. *Proceedings of the National Academy of Sciences of the United States of America, 82,* 6619–6621.

Holt, N., Wang, J., Kim, K., Friedman, G., Wang, X., Taupin, V., et al. (2010). Human hematopoietic stem/progenitor cells modified by zinc-finger nucleases targeted to CCR5 control HIV-1 in vivo. *Nature Biotechnology, 28,* 839–847.

Homberg, J. R., De Boer, S. F., Raaso, H. S., Olivier, J. D. A., Verheul, M., Ronken, E., et al. (2008). Adaptations in pre- and postsynaptic 5-HT1A receptor function and cocaine supersensitivity in serotonin transporter knockout rats. *Psychopharmacology, 200,* 367–380.

Homberg, J. R., Olivier, J. D. A., Smits, B. M. G., Mul, J. D., Mudde, J., Verheul, M., et al. (2007). Characterization of the serotonin transporter knockout rat: a selective change in the functioning of the serotonergic system. *Neuroscience, 146,* 1662–1676.

Homberg, J. R., Pattij, T., Janssen, M. C. W., Ronken, E., De Boer, S. F., Schoffelmeer, A. N. M., et al. (2007). Serotonin transporter deficiency in rats improves inhibitory control but not behavioural flexibility. *European Journal of Neuroscience, 26,* 2066–2073.

Homberg, J. R., Schiepers, O. J., Schoffelmeer, A. N., Cuppen, E., & Vanderschuren, L. J. (2007). Acute and constitutive increases in central serotonin levels reduce social play behaviour in peri-adolescent rats. *Psychopharmacology (Berl), 195,* 175–182.

Horie, K., Kuroiwa, A., Ikawa, M., Okabe, M., Kondoh, G., Matsuda, Y., et al. (2001). Efficient chromosomal transposition of a Tc1/mariner-like transposon Sleeping Beauty in mice. *Proceedings of the National Academy of Sciences of the United States of America, 98,* 9191–9196.

von Horsten, S., Schmitt, I., Nguyen, H. P., Holzmann, C., Schmidt, T., Walther, T., et al. (2003). Transgenic rat model of Huntington's disease. *Human Molecular Genetics, 12,* 617–624.

Howes, O. D., Kambeitz, J., Kim, E., Stahl, D., Slifstein, M., Abi-Dargham, A., et al. (2012). The nature of dopamine dysfunction in schizophrenia and what this means for treatment. *Archives of General Psychiatry, 69,* 776–786.

Ivics, Z., Izsvak, Z., Chapman, K. M., & Hamra, F. K. (2011). Sleeping Beauty transposon mutagenesis of the rat genome in spermatogonial stem cells. *Methods (San Diego, Calif.), 53,* 356–365.

Izsvak, Z., Frohlich, J., Grabundzija, I., Shirley, J. R., Powell, H. M., Chapman, K. M., et al. (2010). Generating knockout rats by transposon mutagenesis in spermatogonial stem cells. *Nature Methods, 7,* 443–445.

Jacob, H. J., Lazar, J., Dwinell, M. R., Moreno, C., & Geurts, A. M. (2010). Gene targeting in the rat: advances and opportunities. *Trends in Genetics, 26,* 510–518.

Jones, C. A., Watson, D. J. G., & Fone, K. C. F. (2011). Animal models of schizophrenia. *British Journal of Pharmacology, 164,* 1162–1194.

Jones, P., Rodgers, B., Murray, R., & Marmot, M. (1994). Child development risk factors for adult schizophrenia in the British 1946 birth cohort. *Lancet, 344,* 1398–1402.

Jones, P. B., Barnes, T. R. E., Davies, L., Dunn, G., Lloyd, H., Hayhurst, K. P., et al. (2006). Randomized controlled trial of the effect on quality of life of second- vs first-generation antipsychotic drugs in schizophrenia: cost Utility of the Latest Antipsychotic Drugs in Schizophrenia Study (CUtLASS 1). *Archives of General Psychiatry, 63,* 1079–1087.

Justice, M. J., Noveroske, J. K., Weber, J. S., Zheng, B., & Bradley, A. (1999). Mouse ENU mutagenesis. *Human Molecular Genetics, 8,* 1955–1963.

Kahn, R. S., Fleischhacker, W. W., Boter, H., Davidson, M., Vergouwe, Y., Keet, I. P., et al. (2008). Effectiveness of antipsychotic drugs in first-episode schizophrenia and schizophreniform disorder: an open randomised clinical trial. *Lancet, 371,* 1085–1097.

van der Kam, E. L., Ellenbroek, B. A., & Cools, A. R. (2005). Gene-environment interactions determine the individual variability in cocaine self-administration. *Neuropharmacology, 48,* 685–695.

Kanatsu-Shinohara, M., Kato-Itoh, M., Ikawa, M., Takehashi, M., Sanbo, M., Morioka, Y., et al. (2011). Homologous recombination in rat germline stem cells. *Biology of Reproduction, 85,* 208–217.

Karg, K., Burmeister, M., Shedden, K., & Sen, S. (2011). The serotonin transporter promoter variant (5-HTTLPR), stress, and depression meta-analysis revisited: evidence of genetic moderation. *Archives of General Psychiatry, 68,* 444–454.

Karl, T. (2013). Neuregulin 1: a prime candidate for research into gene-environment interactions in schizophrenia? Insights from genetic rodent models. *Frontiers in Behavioral Neuroscience, 7*, 106.

Karl, T., Chwalisz, W. T., Wedekind, D., Hedrich, H. J., Hoffmann, T., Jacobs, R., et al. (2003). Localization, transmission, spontaneous mutations, and variation of function of the Dpp4 (Dipeptidyl-peptidase IV; CD26) gene in rats. *Regulatory Peptides, 115*, 81–90.

Karl, T., Hoffmann, T., Pabst, R., & von Horsten, S. (2003a). Behavioral effects of neuropeptide Y in F344 rat substrains with a reduced dipeptidyl-peptidase IV activity. *Pharmacology, Biochemistry, and Behavior, 75*, 869–879.

Karl, T., Hoffmann, T., Pabst, R., & von Horsten, S. (2003b). Extreme reduction of dipeptidyl peptidase IV activity in F344 rat substrains is associated with various behavioral differences. *Physiology & Behavior, 80*, 123–134.

Kavelaars, A., Heijnen, C. J., Ellenbroek, B., van Loveren, H., & Cools, A. (1997). Apomorphine-susceptible and apomorphine-unsusceptible Wistar rats differ in their susceptibility to inflammatory and infectious diseases: a study on rats with group-specific differences in structure and reactivity of hypothalamic-pituitary-adrenal axis. *Journal of Neuroscience, 17*, 2580–2584.

Kawasaki, Y., Maeda, Y., Sakai, N., Higashima, M., Urata, K., Yamaguchi, N., et al. (1994). Evaluation and interpretation of symptom structures in patients with schizophrenia. *Acta Psychiatrica Scandinavica, 89*, 399–404.

Kay, S. R., Fiszbein, A., & Opler, L. A. (1987). The positive and negative syndrome scale (PANSS) for schizophrenia. *Schizophrenia Bulletin, 13*, 261–276.

Keefe, R. S. E., Bilder, R. M., Davis, S. M., Harvey, P. D., Palmer, B. W., Gold, J. M., et al. (2007). Neurocognitive effects of antipsychotic medications in patients with chronic schizophrenia in the CATIE trial. *Archives of General Psychiatry, 64*, 633–647.

Kenna, G. A., Roder-Hanna, N., Leggio, L., Zywiak, W. H., Clifford, J., Edwards, S., et al. (2012). Association of the 5-HTT gene-linked promoter region (5-HTTLPR) polymorphism with psychiatric disorders: review of psychopathology and pharmacotherapy. *Pharmacogenomics and Personalized Medicine, 5*, 19–35.

Kingwell, K. (2014). Schizophrenia drug gets negative results for negative symptoms. *Nature Reviews Drug Discovery, 13*, 244–245.

Kitada, K., Ishishita, S., Tosaka, K., Takahashi, R., Ueda, M., Keng, V. W., et al. (2007). Transposon-tagged mutagenesis in the rat. *Nature Methods, 4*, 131–133.

Klein, A. B., Ultved, L., Adamsen, D., Santini, M. A., Tobena, A., Fernandez-Teruel, A., et al. (2014). 5-HT(2A) and mGlu2 receptor binding levels are related to differences in impulsive behavior in the Roman Low- (RLA) and High- (RHA) avoidance rat strains. *Neuroscience, 263*, 36–45.

Kola, I., & Landis, J. (2004). Can the pharmaceutical industry reduce attrition rates? *Nature Reviews Drug Discovery, 3*, 711–715.

Koller, B. H., Hagemann, L. J., Doetschman, T., Hagaman, J. R., Huang, S., Williams, P. J., et al. (1989). Germ-line transmission of a planned alteration made in a hypoxanthine phosphoribosyltransferase gene by homologous recombination in embryonic stem cells. *Proceedings of the National Academy of Sciences of the United States of America, 86*, 8927–8931.

Konno, T., Rempel, L. A., Rumi, M. A., Graham, A. R., Asanoma, K., Renaud, S. J., et al. (2011). Chromosome-substituted rat strains provide insights into the genetics of placentation. *Physiological Genomics, 43*, 930–941.

Kuhn, R., & Torres, R. M. (2002). Cre/loxP recombination system and gene targeting. *Methods in Molecular Biology (Clifton, NJ), 180*, 175–204.

Lammers, C. H., Garcia-Borreguero, D., Schmider, J., Gotthardt, U., Dettling, M., Holsboer, F., et al. (1995). Combined dexamethasone/corticotropin-releasing hormone test in patients with schizophrenia and in normal controls II. *Biological Psychiatry, 38*, 803–807.

van de Langerijt, A. G., van Lent, P. L., Hermus, A. R., Sweep, C. G., Cools, A. R., & van den Berg, W. B. (1994). Susceptibility to adjuvant arthritis: relative importance of adrenal activity and bacterial flora. *Clinical & Experimental Immunology, 97*, 33–38.

Lesch, K. P., Bengel, D., Heils, A., Sabol, S. Z., Greenberg, B. D., Petri, S., et al. (1996). Association of anxiety-related traits with a polymorphism in the serotonin transporter gene regulatory region. *Science, 274*, 1527–1531.

Levin, R., Calzavara, M. B., Santos, C. M., Medrano, W. A., Niigaki, S. T., & Abilio, V. C. (2011). Spontaneously Hypertensive Rats (SHR) present deficits in prepulse inhibition of startle specifically reverted by clozapine. *Progress in Neuro-Psychopharmacology & Biological Psychiatry, 35*, 1748–1752.

Levin, R., Peres, F. F., Almeida, V., Calzavara, M. B., Zuardi, A. W., Hallak, J. E., et al. (2014). Effects of cannabinoid drugs on the deficit of prepulse inhibition of startle in an animal model of schizophrenia: the SHR strain. *Frontiers in Pharmacology, 5*, 10.

Li, P., Tong, C., Mehrian-Shai, R., Jia, L., Wu, N., Yan, Y., et al. (2008). Germline competent embryonic stem cells derived from rat blastocysts. *Cell, 135*, 1299–1310.

Lieberman, J. A., Scott Stroup, T., McEvoy, J. P., Swartz, M. S., Rosenheck, R. A., Perkins, D. O., et al. (2005). Effectiveness of antipsychotic drugs in patients with chronic schizophrenia. *New England Journal of Medicine, 353*, 1209–1223.

Liebsch, G., Montkowski, A., Holsboer, F., & Landgraf, R. (1998). Behavioural profiles of two Wistar rat lines selectively bred for high or low anxiety-related behaviour. *Behavioural Brain Research, 94*, 301–310.

Lipska, B. K., & Weinberger, D. R. (2000). To model a psychiatric disorder in animals: schizophrenia as a reality test. *Neuropsychopharmacology, 23*, 223–239.

van Loo, K. M., & Martens, G. J. (2007). Identification of genetic and epigenetic variations in a rat model for neurodevelopmental disorders. *Behavior Genetics, 37*, 697–705.

Lopez-Aumatell, R., Blazquez, G., Gil, L., Aguilar, R., Canete, T., Gimenez-Llort, L., et al. (2009). The Roman High- and Low-Avoidance rat strains differ in fear-potentiated startle and classical aversive conditioning. *Psicothema, 21*, 27–32.

Lu, B., Geurts, A. M., Poirier, C., Petit, D. C., Harrison, W., Overbeek, P. A., et al. (2007). Generation of rat mutants using a coat color-tagged Sleeping Beauty transposon system. *Mammalian Genome: Official Journal of the International Mammalian Genome Society, 18*, 338–346.

Luo, G., Ivics, Z., Izsvak, Z., & Bradley, A. (1998). Chromosomal transposition of a Tc1/mariner-like element in mouse embryonic stem cells. *Proceedings of the National Academy of Sciences of the United States of America, 95*, 10769–10773.

Mackay-Sim, A., Feron, F., Eyles, D., Burne, T., & McGrath, J. (2004). Schizophrenia, vitamin D, and brain development. *International Review of Neurobiology, 59*, 351–380.

Mackeprang, T., Kristiansen, K. T., & Glenthoj, B. Y. (2002). Effects of antipsychotics on prepulse inhibition of the startle response in drug-naive schizophrenic patients. *Biological Psychiatry, 52*, 863–873.

Mailman, R. B., & Murthy, V. (2010). Third generation antipsychotic drugs: partial agonism or receptor functional selectivity? *Current Pharmaceutical Design, 16*, 488–501.

Marder, S. R., & Fenton, W. (2004). Measurement and Treatment Research to Improve Cognition in Schizophrenia: NIMH MATRICS initiative to support the development of agents for improving cognition in schizophrenia. *Schizophrenia Research, 72*, 5–9.

Marder, S. R., Fenton, W., Youens, K., & Tamminga, C. A. (2004). Schizophrenia, IX – cognition in schizophrenia – the MATRICS initiative. *American Journal of Psychiatry, 161*, 25.

Markel, P., Shu, P., Ebeling, C., Carlson, G. A., Nagle, D. L., Smutko, J. S., et al. (1997). Theoretical and empirical issues for marker-assisted breeding of congenic mouse strains. *Nature Genetics, 17*, 280–284.

Marques, T. R., Levine, S. Z., Reichenberg, A., Kahn, R., Derks, E. M., Fleischhacker, W. W., et al. (2014). How antipsychotics impact the different dimensions of schizophrenia: a test of competing hypotheses. *European Neuropsychopharmacology: The Journal of the European College of Neuropsychopharmacology, 24*, 1279–1288.

Mashimo, T., Yanagihara, K., Tokuda, S., Voigt, B., Takizawa, A., Nakajima, R., et al. (2008). An ENU-induced mutant archive for gene targeting in rats. *Nature Genetics, 40*, 514–515.

Matthysse, S. (1981). Nucleus accumbens and schizophrenia. In R. Chronister, & J. DeFrance (Eds.), *The neurobiology of the nucleus accumbens* (pp. 351–359). Maine: Haer Inst. for Electrophysiol. Res.

Matthysse, S. (1986). Animal models in psychiatric research. *Progress in Brain Research, 65*, 259–270.

McClintock, B. (1950). The origin and behavior of mutable loci in maize. *Proceedings of the National Academy of Sciences of the United States of America, 36*, 344–355.

McEvoy, J. P., Lieberman, J. A., Perkins, D. O., Hamer, R. M., Gu, H., Lazarus, A., et al. (2007). Efficacy and tolerability of olanzapine, quetiapine, and risperidone in the treatment of early psychosis: a randomized, double-blind 52-week comparison. *American Journal of Psychiatry, 164*, 1050–1060.

McEvoy, J. P., Lieberman, J. A., Stroup, T. S., Davis, S. M., Meltzer, H. Y., Rosenheck, R. A., et al. (2006). Effectiveness of clozapine versus olanzapine, quetiapine, and risperidone in patients with chronic schizophrenia who did not respond to prior atypical antipsychotic treatment. *American Journal of Psychiatry, 163*, 600–610.

McGrath, J., Saha, S., Welham, J., El Saadi, O., MacCauley, C., & Chant, D. (2004). A systematic review of the incidence of schizophrenia: the distribution of rates and the influence of sex, urbanicity, migrant status and methodology. *BMC Medicine, 2*, 13.

Meek, S., Buehr, M., Sutherland, L., Thomson, A., Mullins, J. J., Smith, A. J., et al. (2010). Efficient gene targeting by homologous recombination in rat embryonic stem cells. *PLoS One, 5*, e14225.

Meincke, U., Morth, D., Voss, T., Thelen, B., Geyer, M. A., & Gouzoulis-Mayfrank, E. (2004). Prepulse inhibition of the acoustically evoked startle reflex in patients with an acute schizophrenic psychosis - a longitudinal study. *European Archives of Psychiatry and Clinical Neuroscience, 254*, 415–421.

Mesholam-Gately, R. I., Giuliano, A. J., Goff, K. P., Faraone, S. V., & Seidman, L. J. (2009). Neurocognition in first-episode schizophrenia: a meta-analytic review. *Neuropsychology, 23*, 315–336.

Meyer-Lindenberg, A., Domes, G., Kirsch, P., & Heinrichs, M. (2011). Oxytocin and vasopressin in the human brain: social neuropeptides for translational medicine. *Nature Reviews Neuroscience, 12*, 524–538.

Miller, J. C., Tan, S., Qiao, G., Barlow, K. A., Wang, J., Xia, D. F., et al. (2011). A TALE nuclease architecture for efficient genome editing. *Nature Biotechnology, 29*, 143–148.

Miller, N. S., & Fine, J. (1993). Current epidemiology of comorbidity of psychiatric and addictive disorders. *The Psychiatric Clinics of North America, 16*, 1–10.

Mortensen, P. B. (1994). The occurrence of cancer in first admitted schizophrenic patients. *Schizophrenia Research, 12*, 185–194.

Mul, J. D., la Fleur, S. E., Toonen, P. W., Afrasiab-Middelman, A., Binnekade, R., Schetters, D., et al. (2011). Chronic loss of melanin-concentrating hormone affects motivational aspects of feeding in the rat. *PLoS One, 6*, e19600.

Mul, J. D., Yi, C. X., van den Berg, S. A., Ruiter, M., Toonen, P. W., van der Elst, M. C., et al. (2010). Pmch expression during early development is critical for normal energy homeostasis. *American Journal of Physiology Endocrinology and Metabolism, 298*, E477–E488.

Muller, N., Riedel, M., Ackenheil, M., & Schwarz, M. J. (1999). The role of immune function in schizophrenia: an overview. *European Archives of Psychiatry and Clinical Neuroscience, 249*(Suppl. 4), 62–68.

Muller Spahn, F., Modell, S., Ackenheil, M., Brachner, A., & Kurtz, G. (1998). Elevated response of growth hormone to graded doses of apomorphine in schizophrenic patients. *Journal of Psychiatric Research, 32*, 265–271.

Murphy, D. L., Fox, M. A., Timpano, K. R., Moya, P. R., Ren-Patterson, R., Andrews, A. M., et al. (2008). How the serotonin story is being rewritten by new gene-based discoveries principally related to SLC6A4, the serotonin transporter gene, which functions to influence all cellular serotonin systems. *Neuropharmacology, 55*, 932–960.

Nadeau, J. H., Singer, J. B., Matin, A., & Lander, E. S. (2000). Analysing complex genetic traits with chromosome substitution strains. *Nature Genetics, 24*, 221–225.

Nagatsu, T. (1995). Tyrosine hydroxylase: human isoforms, structure and regulation in physiology and pathology. *Essays in Biochemistry, 30*, 15–35.

Nonkes, L. J., van de, V., II, de Leeuw, M. J., Wijlaars, L. P., Maes, J. H., & Homberg, J. R. (2012). Serotonin transporter knockout rats show improved strategy set-shifting and reduced latent inhibition. *Learning & Memory, 19*, 190–193.

Nord, M., & Farde, L. (2011). Antipsychotic occupancy of dopamine receptors in schizophrenia. *CNS Neuroscience & Therapeutics, 17*, 97–103.

Nuechterlein, K. H., Barch, D. M., Gold, J. M., Goldberg, T. E., Green, M. F., & Heaton, R. K. (2004). Identification of separable cognitive factors in schizophrenia. *Schizophrenia Research, 72*, 29–39.

Oakly, A. C., Brox, B. W., Schenk, S., & Ellenbroek, B. A. (2014). A genetic deletion of the serotonin transporter greatly enhances the reinforcing properties of MDMA in rats. *Molecular Psychiatry, 19*, 534–535.

Olivier, J. D. A., Jans, L. A. W., Blokland, A., Broers, N. J., Homberg, J. R., Ellenbroek, B. A., et al. (2009). Serotonin transporter deficiency in rats contributes to impaired object memory. *Genes, Brain, and Behavior, 8*, 829–834.

Olivier, J. D. A., Van Der Hart, M. G. C., Van Swelm, R. P. L., Dederen, P. J., Homberg, J. R., Cremers, T., et al. (2008). A study in male and female 5-HT transporter knockout rats: an animal model for anxiety and depression disorders. *Neuroscience, 152*, 573–584.

Overstreet, D. H., & Wegener, G. (2013). The flinders sensitive line rat model of depression–25 years and still producing. *Pharmacological Reviews, 65*, 143–155.

Owen, M. J., Craddock, N., & O'Donovan, M. C. (2005). Schizophrenia: genes at last? *Trends in Genetics, 21*, 518–525.

Pae, C. U., Kim, J. J., Lee, S. J., Lee, C. U., Lee, C., Paik, I. H., et al. (2003). Polymorphism of the serotonin transporter gene and symptomatic dimensions of schizophrenia in the Korean population. *Neuropsychobiology, 47*, 182–186.

Pae, C. U., Serretti, A., Artioli, P., Kim, T. S., Kim, J. J., Lee, C. U., et al. (2006). Interaction analysis between 5-HTTLPR and TNFA-238/-308 polymorphisms in schizophrenia. *Journal of Neural Transmission, 113*, 887–897.

Pammolli, F., Magazzini, L., & Riccaboni, M. (2011). The productivity crisis in pharmaceutical R&D. *Nature Reviews Drug Discovery, 10*, 428–438.

Perez, E. E., Wang, J., Miller, J. C., Jouvenot, Y., Kim, K. A., Liu, O., et al. (2008). Establishment of HIV-1 resistance in CD4+ T cells by genome editing using zinc-finger nucleases. *Nature Biotechnology, 26*, 808–816.

Petrasek, T., Prokopova, I., Bahnik, S., Schonig, K., Berger, S., Vales, K., et al. (2014). Nogo-A downregulation impairs place avoidance in the Carousel maze but not spatial memory in the Morris water maze. *Neurobiology of Learning and Memory, 107*, 42–49.

Petrasek, T., Prokopova, I., Sladek, M., Weissova, K., Vojtechova, I., Bahnik, S., et al. (2014). Nogo-A-deficient transgenic rats show deficits in higher cognitive functions, decreased anxiety, and altered circadian activity patterns. *Frontiers in Behavioral Neuroscience, 8*, 90.

Ponce de Leon, V., Merillat, A. M., Tesson, L., Anegon, I., & Hummler, E. (2014). Generation of TALEN-mediated GRdim knock-in rats by homologous recombination. *PLoS One, 9*, e88146.

Powell, C. M., & Miyakawa, T. (2006). Schizophrenia-relevant behavioral testing in rodent models: a uniquely human disorder? *Biological Psychiatry, 59*, 1198–1207.

Purcell, S. M., Moran, J. L., Fromer, M., Ruderfer, D., Solovieff, N., Roussos, P., et al. (2014). A polygenic burden of rare disruptive mutations in schizophrenia. *Nature, 506,* 185–190.

Quednow, B. B., Wagner, M., Westheide, J., Beckmann, K., Bliesener, N., Maier, W., et al. (2006). Sensorimotor gating and habituation of the startle response in schizophrenic patients randomly treated with amisulpride or olanzapine. *Biological Psychiatry, 59,* 536–545.

Rasmus, K. C., O'Neill, C. E., Bachtell, R. K., & Cooper, D. C. (2013). Cocaine self-administration in rats lacking a functional trpc4 gene. *F1000Research, 2,* 110.

Rots, N. Y., Cools, A. R., Berod, A., Voorn, P., Rostene, W., & de Kloet, E. R. (1996). Rats bred for enhanced apomorphine susceptibility have elevated tyrosine hydroxylase mRNA and dopamine D2-receptor binding sites in nigrostriatal and tuberoinfundibular dopamine systems. *Brain Research, 710,* 189–196.

Rots, N. Y., Cools, A. R., Oitzl, M. S., de Jong, J., Sutanto, W., & de Kloet, E. R. (1996). Divergent prolactin and pituitary-adrenal activity in rats selectively bred for different dopamine responsiveness. *Endocrinology, 137,* 1678–1686.

Russell, W. L., Kelly, E. M., Hunsicker, P. R., Bangham, J. W., Maddux, S. C., & Phipps, E. L. (1979). Specific-locus test shows ethylnitrosourea to be the most potent mutagen in the mouse. *Proceedings of the National Academy of Sciences of the United States of America, 76,* 5818–5819.

Sagvolden, T., Metzger, M. A., Schiorbeck, H. K., Rugland, A. L., Spinnangr, I., & Sagvolden, G. (1992). The spontaneously hypertensive rats (SHR) as an animal model of childhood hyperactivity (ADHD): changed reactivity to reinforcers and to psychomotor stimulation. *Behavioral and Neural Biology, 58,* 103–112.

Samara, M. T., Cao, H. Y., Helfer, B., Davis, J. M., & Leucht, S. (2014). Chlorpromazine versus every other antipsychotic for schizophrenia: a systematic review and meta-analysis challenging the dogma of equal efficacy of antipsychotic drugs. *European Neuropsychopharmacology, 24,* 1046–1055.

Sander, J. D., Dahlborg, E. J., Goodwin, M. J., Cade, L., Zhang, F., Cifuentes, D., et al. (2011). Selection-free zinc-finger-nuclease engineering by context-dependent assembly (CoDA). *Nature Methods, 8,* 67–69.

Schaefer, C. F., Brackett, D. J., Gunn, C. G., & Wilson, M. F. (1978). Behavioral hyperreactivity in the spontaneously hypertensive rat compared to its normotensive progenitor. *Pavlovian Journal of Biological Science, 13,* 211–216.

Schaefer, C. F., Brackett, D. J., Wilson, M. F., & Gunn, C. G. (1978). Lifelong hyperarousal in the spontaneously hypertensive rat indicated by operant behavior. *Pavlovian Journal of Biological Science, 13,* 217–225.

Schwabe, K., Freudenberg, F., & Koch, M. (2007). Selective breeding of reduced sensorimotor gating in Wistar rats. *Behavior Genetics, 37,* 706–712.

Seeman, P. (2013). Schizophrenia and dopamine receptors. *European Neuropsychopharmacology: The Journal of the European College of Neuropsychopharmacology, 23,* 999–1009.

Selvaraj, S., Arnone, D., Cappai, A., & Howes, O. (2014). Alterations in the serotonin system in schizophrenia: a systematic review and meta-analysis of postmortem and molecular imaging studies. *Neuroscience and Biobehavioral Reviews, 45,* 233–245.

Serretti, A., Catalano, M., & Smeraldi, E. (1999). Serotonin transporter gene is not associated with symptomatology of schizophrenia. *Schizophrenia Research, 35,* 33–39.

Shilling, P. D., Kinkead, B., Murray, T., Melendez, G., Nemeroff, C. B., & Feifel, D. (2006). Upregulation of striatal dopamine-2 receptors in Brattleboro rats with prepulse inhibition deficits. *Biological Psychiatry, 60,* 1278–1281.

Smits, B. M., Mudde, J., Plasterk, R. H., & Cuppen, E. (2004). Target-selected mutagenesis of the rat. *Genomics, 83,* 332–334.

Smits, B. M., Mudde, J. B., van de Belt, J., Verheul, M., Olivier, J., Homberg, J., et al. (2006). Generation of gene knockouts and mutant models in the laboratory rat by ENU-driven target-selected mutagenesis. *Pharmacogenetics and Genomics, 16,* 159–169.

Steen, R. G., Kwitek-Black, A. E., Glenn, C., Gullings-Handley, J., Van Etten, W., Atkinson, O. S., et al. (1999). A high-density integrated genetic linkage and radiation hybrid map of the laboratory rat. *Genome Research, 9,* AP1–AP8.

Stefanovics, E. A., Elkis, H., Liu, Z. N., Zhang, X. Y., & Rosenheck, R. A. (2014). A cross-national factor analytic comparison of three models of PANSS symptoms in schizophrenia. *Psychiatry Research, 219,* 283–289.

Sun, J., Kuo, P. H., Riley, B. P., Kendler, K. S., & Zhao, Z. (2008). Candidate genes for schizophrenia: a survey of association studies and gene ranking. *American Journal of Medical Genetics Part B Neuropsychiatric Genetics, 147B,* 1173–1181.

Swerdlow, N. R., Platten, A., Hanlon, F. M., Martinez, Z. A., Printz, M. P., & Auerbach, P. (2003). Sensitivity to sensorimotor gating-disruptive effects of apomorphine in two outbred parental rat strains and their F1 and N2 progeny. *Neuropsychopharmacology, 28,* 226–234.

Swerdlow, N. R., Platten, A., Kim, Y. K., Gaudet, I., Shoemaker, J., Pitcher, L., et al. (2001). Sensitivity to the dopaminergic regulation of prepulse inhibition in rats: evidence for genetic, but not environmental determinants. *Pharmacology, Biochemistry, and Behavior, 70,* 219–226.

Swerdlow, N. R., Shoemaker, J. M., Platten, A., Pitcher, L., Goins, J., & Auerbach, P. P. (2004). Heritable differences in the dopaminergic regulation of sensorimotor gating. I. Apomorphine effects on startle gating in albino and hooded outbred rat strains and their F1 and N2 progeny. *Psychopharmacology, 174,* 441–451.

Swerdlow, N. R., Shoemaker, J. M., Platten, A., Pitcher, L., Goins, J., & Crain, S. (2003). Heritable differences in the effects of amphetamine but not DOI on startle gating in albino and hooded outbred rat strains. *Pharmacology, Biochemistry, and Behavior, 75,* 191–197.

Swerdlow, N. R., Varty, G. B., & Geyer, M. A. (1998). Discrepant findings of clozapine effects on prepulse inhibition of startle: is it the route or the rat? *Neuropsychopharmacology, 18,* 50–56.

Takao, K., Yamasaki, N., & Miyakawa, T. (2007). Impact of brain-behavior phenotyping of genetically-engineered mice on research of neuropsychiatric disorders. *Neuroscience Research, 58,* 124–132.

Taylor, B. A., Navin, A., & Phillips, S. J. (1994). PCR-amplification of simple sequence repeat variants from pooled DNA samples for rapidly mapping new mutations of the mouse. *Genomics, 21,* 626–632.

Taylor, S. B., Markham, J. A., Taylor, A. R., Kanaskie, B. Z., & Koenig, J. I. (2011). Sex-specific neuroendocrine and behavioral phenotypes in hypomorphic Type II Neuregulin 1 rats. *Behavioural Brain Research, 224,* 223–232.

Taylor, S. B., Taylor, A. R., & Koenig, J. I. (2013). The interaction of disrupted type II neuregulin 1 and chronic adolescent stress on adult anxiety- and fear-related behaviors. *Neuroscience, 249,* 31–42.

Taylor, S. B., Taylor, A. R., Markham, J. A., Geurts, A. M., Kanaskie, B. Z., & Koenig, J. I. (2011). Disruption of the neuregulin 1 gene in the rat alters HPA axis activity and behavioral responses to environmental stimuli. *Physiology & Behavior, 104,* 205–214.

Tesson, L., Cozzi, J., Menoret, S., Remy, S., Usal, C., Fraichard, A., et al. (2005). Transgenic modifications of the rat genome. *Transgenic Research, 14,* 531–546.

Tesson, L., Usal, C., Menoret, S., Leung, E., Niles, B. J., Remy, S., et al. (2011). Knockout rats generated by embryo microinjection of TALENs. *Nature Biotechnology, 29,* 695–696.

Teunis, M. A. T., Kavelaars, A., Voest, E., Bakker, J. M., Ellenbroek, B. A., Cools, A. R., et al. (2002). Reduced tumor growth, experimental metastasis formation, and angiogenesis in rats with a hyperreactive dopaminergic system. *FASEB Journal, 16,* 1465–1467.

Tews, B., Schonig, K., Arzt, M. E., Clementi, S., Rioult-Pedotti, M. S., Zemmar, A., et al. (2013). Synthetic microRNA-mediated downregulation of Nogo-A in transgenic rats reveals its role as regulator of synaptic plasticity and cognitive function. *Proceedings of the National Academy of Sciences of the United States of America, 110,* 6583–6588.

Thomas, K. R., & Capecchi, M. R. (1987). Site-directed mutagenesis by gene targeting in mouse embryo-derived stem cells. *Cell, 51,* 503–512.

Thomas, K. R., & Capecchi, M. R. (1990). Targeted disruption of the murine int-1 proto-oncogene resulting in severe abnormalities in midbrain and cerebellar development. *Nature, 346,* 847–850.

Thompson, N. L., Hixson, D. C., Callanan, H., Panzica, M., Flanagan, D., Faris, R. A., et al. (1991). A Fischer rat substrain deficient in dipeptidyl peptidase IV activity makes normal steady-state RNA levels and an altered protein. Use as a liver-cell transplantation model. *Biochemical Journal, 273*(Pt 3), 497–502.

Thompson, S., Clarke, A. R., Pow, A. M., Hooper, M. L., & Melton, D. W. (1989). Germ line transmission and expression of a corrected HPRT gene produced by gene targeting in embryonic stem cells. *Cell, 56,* 313–321.

Tiruppathi, C., Miyamoto, Y., Ganapathy, V., & Leibach, F. H. (1993). Genetic evidence for role of DPP IV in intestinal hydrolysis and assimilation of prolyl peptides. *American Journal of Physiology, 265,* G81–G89.

Tong, C., Huang, G., Ashton, C., Li, P., & Ying, Q. L. (2011). Generating gene knockout rats by homologous recombination in embryonic stem cells. *Nature Protocols, 6,* 827–844.

Tong, C., Huang, G., Ashton, C., Wu, H., Yan, H., & Ying, Q. L. (2012). Rapid and cost-effective gene targeting in rat embryonic stem cells by TALENs. *Journal of Genetics and Genomics = Yi chuan xue bao, 39,* 275–280.

Tong, C., Li, P., Wu, N. L., Yan, Y., & Ying, Q. L. (2010). Production of p53 gene knockout rats by homologous recombination in embryonic stem cells. *Nature, 467,* 211–213.

Trigo, J. M., Renoir, T., Lanfumey, L., Hamon, M., Lesch, K. P., Robledo, P., et al. (2007). 3,4-Methylenedioxymethamphetamine self-administration is abolished in serotonin transporter knockout mice. *Biological Psychiatry, 62,* 669–679.

Tryon, R. C. (1930). Studies in individual differences in maze ability. I. The measurement of the reliability of individual differences. *Journal of Comparative Psychology, 11,* 145–170.

Tsai, S. J., Hong, C. J., Yu, Y. Y., Lin, C. H., Song, H. L., Lai, H. C., et al. (2000). Association study of a functional serotonin transporter gene polymorphism with schizophrenia, psychopathology and clozapine response. *Schizophrenia Research, 44,* 177–181.

Valtin, H., & Schroeder, H. A. (1964). Familial hypothalamic diabetes insipidus in rats (Brattleboro strain). *American Journal of Physiology, 206,* 425–430.

Van der Gaag, M., Cuijpers, A., Hoffman, T., Remijsen, M., Hijman, R., de Haan, L., et al. (2006). The five-factor model of the Positive and Negative Syndrome Scale – I: confirmatory factor analysis fails to confirm 25 published five-factor solutions. *Schizophrenia Research, 85,* 273–279.

Van der Gaag, M., Hoffman, T., Remijsen, M., Hijman, R., de Haan, L., van Meijel, B., et al. (2006). The five-factor model of the Positive and Negative Syndrome Scale – II: a ten-fold cross-validation of a revised model. *Schizophrenia Research, 85,* 280–287.

Vinogradov, S., Gottesman, I. I., Moises, H. W., & Nichol, S. (1991). Negative association between schizophrenia and rheumatoid arthritis. *Schizophrenia Bulletin, 17,* 669–678.

Wakeland, E., Morel, L., Achey, K., Yui, M., & Longmate, J. (1997). Speed congenics: a classic technique in the fast lane (relatively speaking). *Immunology Today, 18,* 472–477.

Walker, E. F., & Lewine, R. J. (1990). Prediction of adult-onset schizophrenia from childhood home movies of the patients. *American Journal of Psychiatry, 147,* 1052–1056.

Wallwork, R. S., Fortgang, R., Hashimoto, R., Weinberger, D. R., & Dickinson, D. (2012). Searching for a consensus five-factor model of the Positive and Negative Syndrome Scale for schizophrenia. *Schizophrenia Research, 137,* 246–250.

Wang, D., Cui, Z., Zeng, Q., Kuang, H., Wang, L. P., Tsien, J. Z., et al. (2009). Genetic enhancement of memory and long-term potentiation but not CA1 long-term depression in NR2B transgenic rats. *PLoS One, 4,* e7486.

Watanabe, Y., Kojima, T., & Fujimoto, Y. (1987). Deficiency of membrane-bound dipeptidyl aminopeptidase IV in a certain rat strain. *Experientia, 43,* 400–401.

Willner, P. (1984). The validity of animals models of depression. *Psychopharmacology, 83,* 1–16.

Witten, I. B., Steinberg, E. E., Lee, S. Y., Davidson, T. J., Zalocusky, K. A., Brodsky, M., et al. (2011). Recombinase-driver rat lines: tools, techniques, and optogenetic application to dopamine-mediated reinforcement. *Neuron, 72,* 721–733.

Yee, B. K., & Singer, P. (2013). A conceptual and practical guide to the behavioural evaluation of animal models of the symptomatology and therapy of schizophrenia. *Cell and Tissue Research, 354,* 221–246.

Zan, Y., Haag, J. D., Chen, K. S., Shepel, L. A., Wigington, D., Wang, Y. R., et al. (2003). Production of knockout rats using ENU mutagenesis and a yeast-based screening assay. *Nature Biotechnology, 21,* 645–651.

Zhang, T., Koutsouleris, N., Meisenzahl, E., & Davatzikos, C. (2015). Heterogeneity of structural brain changes in subtypes of schizophrenia revealed using magnetic resonance imaging pattern analysis. *Schizophrenia Bulletin, 41,* 74–84.

Zheng, B., Mills, A. A., & Bradley, A. (2001). Introducing defined chromosomal rearrangements into the mouse genome. *Methods (San Diego, California), 24,* 81–94.

Zijlstra, M., Li, E., Sajjadi, F., Subramani, S., & Jaenisch, R. (1989). Germ-line transmission of a disrupted beta 2-microglobulin gene produced by homologous recombination in embryonic stem cells. *Nature, 342,* 435–438.

Zschemisch, N. H., Glage, S., Wedekind, D., Weinstein, E. J., Cui, X., Dorsch, M., et al. (2012). Zinc-finger nuclease mediated disruption of Rag1 in the LEW/Ztm rat. *BMC Immunology, 13,* 60.

Gene–Gene and Gene–Environment Models

CHAPTER

19

Modeling Gene–Gene Interactions in Schizophrenia

E. Von Cheong, Colm M.P. O'Tuathaigh

School of Medicine, Brookfield Health Sciences Complex, University College Cork, Cork, Ireland

INTRODUCTION

Schizophrenia is a highly heritable neurodevelopmental disorder, characterized by heterogeneous display of psychotic ("positive") and negative symptoms as well as cognitive deficits (Harvey, Wingo, Burdick, & Baldessarini, 2010; van Os & Kapur, 2009; Waddington et al., 2007). The emergence of psychotic symptoms is conceptualized as representing the end product of a pathobiological cascade which originates in early brain development (Rapoport, Giedd, & Gogtay, 2012; Waddington, Hennessy, O'Tuathaigh, Owoeye, & Russell, 2012). Our understanding of schizophrenia is challenged by its complex life course and multifactorial origins that involve contributions from diverse genetic, epigenetic, and environmental factors (Brown, 2011; Hall, Trent, Thomas, O'Donovan, & Owen, 2014; van Os & Kapur, 2009). The challenge is heightened by the absence of diagnostic pathobiology and causative genetic mutations (Del Pino et al., 2013). Although recent research has advanced our understanding of the genetic basis of the disorder, identifying risk loci, and suggesting mechanisms by which genetic risk is conferred (Gratten, Wray, Keller, & Visscher, 2014), much is still unknown, and the challenge also remains as to how these advances might be translated into therapeutically significant advances (Harrison, 2015). Several factors, including genetic and phenotypic heterogeneity, epistatic gene interactions, and the role that the environment plays in the development/expression of psychiatric illness, amplify the difficulties associated with solving the schizophrenia genetics puzzle (Burmeister, 1999; Burmeister, McInnis, & Zollner, 2008). As a result, although investigations on

the genetics of schizophrenia and related psychotic disorders continue to progress in an incremental fashion, they have yet to lead to major advances in the development of novel antipsychotic drugs.

GENETICS OF SCHIZOPHRENIA

The risk of developing schizophrenia increases with the degree of biological relatedness to the patient (Gottesman, 1991). Meta-analyses of twin and adoption studies have shown that heritability accounts for ~70% of disease risk in schizophrenia (Sullivan, Kendler, & Neale, 2003). Clinical genetic studies would suggest that the magnitude of risk conferred varies widely, from relatively modest odds for common genetic variants to substantial risks due to relatively rare variants. The common-disease/common-variant approach suggests that schizophrenia is a polygenic disorder, in which many common variants of small to moderate effect account for genetic liability (Ripke et al., 2013). In contrast, the common-disease/rare variant position posits that not only common genes of small effect, but also rare variants of large effect, contribute to disease susceptibility (Owen, 2012). It has been repeatedly demonstrated that rare chromosomal deletions and duplications, known as copy number variants (CNVs), can increase risk for the disorder, with the magnitude of the increase in risk substantially greater than that observed for common variants (International Schizophrenia Consortium, 2008; Kirov et al., 2009; Stefansson et al., 2008).

Partitioning the genetic contribution to the development of schizophrenia has proven challenging, with

Handbook of Behavioral Neuroscience
http://dx.doi.org/10.1016/B978-0-12-800981-9.00019-5

recent progress largely from technological advances and large-scale collaborative efforts (Hall et al., 2014). Recent advances in understanding the role of common risk variants to schizophrenia have been largely attributable to whole genome, array-based association studies. To date, genome-wide association study (GWAS) data have largely failed to provide supportive evidence for hitherto prominent susceptibility targets (e.g., disrupted-in-schizophrenia-1 (DISC1), NRG1), while also identifying previously unknown targets (e.g., the major histocompatibility complex (MHC) region, TCF4, neurogranin, Mir-137; Gejman, Sanders, & Kendler, 2011). The earliest GWAS identified an MHC region as a risk factor (International Schizophrenia Consortium, 2009). Subsequent studies identified several loci as conferring increased risk for schizophrenia, including 1p21.2 (Mir-137), 2q32.3 (PCGEM1), 8p23.2 (CSMD1), 8q21.3 (MMP16), and 10q24.32-33 (Schizophrenia Psychiatric Genome-Wide Association Study Consortium, 2011). A more recent study identified an additional 13 loci, including genomic regions where genes implicated in calcium signaling (including *CACNA1C and CACNB2*) are based (Ripke et al., 2013). The most recent analysis has identified 108 agreed-on loci that contribute to risk for schizophrenia, identifying 83 novel risk markers and replicating 25 existing markers (Schizophrenia Working Group of the Psychiatric Genomics Consortium, 2014). Among the loci found are markers in or near genes involved in glutamatergic (GRM3, GRIA1 GRIN2A, SRR) and dopaminergic (DA-ergic; DRD2) function, calcium signaling (CACNA1, NRGN), synaptic function and plasticity (NLGN-4X), and other neurodevelopmental processes (e.g., MHC genes, Mir-137). Importantly, after considerable debate in the field about the failure of initial GWAS studies to replicate several of the pre-GWAS risk genes, the Schizophrenia Working Group of the Psychiatric Genomics Consortium (2014) analysis has implicated several candidate genes with a strong link to the pathophysiology of the disorder (Harrison, 2015).

However, it has been highlighted that the GWAS-identified loci account only for a small proportion of overall genetic risk, and that only large-scale sequencing efforts have the potential to reveal rare small variants implicated in schizophrenia (Hall et al., 2014; Veltman & Brunner, 2012). CNV analyses that detect structural variants in the form of submicroscopic deletions and duplications of DNA have identified rare de novo and inherited variants that confer high risk for schizophrenia (odds ratio 3–20) (Winchester, Pratt, & Morris, 2014). Most of these variants are, however, private mutations and occur in only a small number of cases (<3%) (Winchester et al., 2014). The large size of the associated CNVs gives us an inkling of the multiple genes that may be harbored in these variants. These genes may in turn, affect the dosage of multiple genes and the disruption of several genes at chromosomal breakpoints (Winchester et al., 2014). CNV studies in schizophrenia have employed a systems-based statistical approach to identify biological pathways enriched for genes within CNV loci. Kirov et al. (2009) and others have identified genes encoding components of the N-methyl-D-aspartate (NMDA) receptor signaling complex, synaptic protein interactors of the activity-regulated cytoskeleton-associated protein, and CYFIP1, a recently characterized protein-binding partner of the fragile X mental retardation protein (Fromer et al., 2014; Kirov et al., 2012). In a recent large-scale, case–control, exome-sequencing study involving 2536 schizophrenia cases and 2543 controls, Purcell et al. (2014) demonstrated a polygenic burden primarily arising from rare (<1 in 10,000), disruptive mutations distributed across many genes. They were able to detect several small and highly enriched sets, notably of genes related to NMDA receptor-associated PSD-95 protein complexes, MHC–interacting proteins, and FMRP targets. It has been noted that such rare variant studies do not implicate conclusively any specific gene but instead reveal an overall excess of such variants in schizophrenia, with clustering to functionally defined gene networks (Harrison, 2015; MacArthur et al., 2014). In a recent review of common-disease/rare variant data, some authors have noted the convergence of CNV data onto a set of biological processes involved in regulation of neuronal plasticity, especially at glutamatergic synapses (Hall et al., 2014).

Importantly, some of the genetic factors linked with increased risk for schizophrenia also display association to broader phenotypes including bipolar disorder as well as major depression, attention deficit hyperactivity disorder, and autism (Cross Disorder Group of the Psychiatric Genomics Consortium, 2013), suggesting that clinical overlap between these disorders may in part reflect a shared genetic basis. On the basis of these findings, it is clear that there is much greater overlap in terms of etiological factors than is accounted for in current classification systems (Hall et al., 2014; Owen, 2012). In a joint GWAS analysis between schizophrenia and bipolar disorder, the following three genes reached genome-wide significance: CACNA1C, ANK3, and ITIH3-ITIH4 (Schizophrenia Psychiatric Genome-Wide Association Study Consortium, 2011). CACNA1C was further implicated in a combined analysis of five psychiatric disorders (schizophrenia, bipolar disorder, autistic spectrum disorder, major depressive disorder, attention deficit hyperactivity disorder), along with ITIH3, AS34MT, and CACNB2 (Cross-Disorder Group of the Psychiatric Genomics Consortium, 2013). In the most recent combined GWAS of 19,779 bipolar disorder and schizophrenia cases versus 19,423 controls, in addition to a direct comparison GWAS of 7129 schizophrenia cases versus 9252 bipolar disorder cases, the authors identify five previously identified regions reaching genome-wide significance (CACNA1C, IFI44L, MHC, TRANK1, and MAD1L1) and a novel locus near PIK3C2A (Ruderfer et al., 2014). Interestingly, they demonstrated a significant correlation between a bipolar disorder polygenic risk score and the clinical dimension of mania in patients with schizophrenia. It has been proposed that overlapping disease pathways may partially explain shared symptoms across diagnoses, multiple diagnoses within patients, and patients receiving different diagnosis across the life span (McCarroll, Feng, & Hyman, 2014).

In summary, although the precise nature of the genetic component of schizophrenia remains elusive, recent GWAS and rare mutation studies have provided new insights into the etiology of this and related disorders and hold out the prospect (as yet unrealized) of new directions for antipsychotic drug discovery (Pratt, Winchester, Dawson, & Morris, 2012; Schizophrenia Working Group of the Psychiatric Genomics Consortium, 2014; Winchester et al., 2014). However, it must be emphasized that the existing findings only account for a minority of the heritability of schizophrenia (Lee, Kaidanovich-Beilin, Roder, Woodgett, & Wong, 2011). It is likely that some, and possibly a great deal, of the genetic risk reflects gene–gene interactions rather than simply the cumulative effect of multiple independent genes (Harrison, 2015).

GENE–GENE INTERACTIONS: CLOSING THE "MISSING HERITABILITY" GAP

Despite the distinct contributions of common-disease/common-variant and common-disease/rare variant approaches to our understanding of the genetic basis of schizophrenia, the collective findings highlight some common themes as: (1) "missing heritability:" The lack of robust findings from genetic studies does not concur with the high heritability estimates of schizophrenia. This fuels the important question of where the "missing heritability" of this complex disorder might be found. (2) Polygenic inheritance: The large number of contributing loci and susceptibility alleles and their incomplete penetrance suggest a polygenic model where multiple risk genes of small effect sizes act additively or multiplicatively to cause a substantial increase in disease risk. Given that no single gene has been shown to consistently confer a significant increase in disease risk across independent studies, simple major gene effects are unlikely. Additionally, we may assume that the development of complex traits, such as psychosis, is likely to involve the combination of a large number of independent and/or interacting genetic variants (Lvovs, Favorova, & Favorov, 2012; Shao et al., 2008). (3) Epistasis: gene–gene interactions add additional layers of complexity to the

relationship between genotype and disease risk manifestation. This complexity may hinder the detection of association when genes/single nucleotide proteins (SNPs) are tested one at a time. Such interactions would most likely depend on multiple genetic variations, making it impossible to explain disease risk by the addition of independent genetic effects.

The term "epistasis" was first coined by William Bateson in 1908 to describe a masking effect in which a specific variant or allele at one locus is prevented from manifesting its effects by a variant from another locus (Bateson, 1909). Epistasis, also frequently used to refer generally to the interaction between different genes, has become a crucial element in molecular genetics studies of psychiatric disorders in recent years (Gelernter, 2015). As a possible underlying disease mechanism in schizophrenia, epistasis is of particular significance because, if the effect of one locus is altered or masked by effects at another locus, power to detect the first locus is likely to be reduced (Cordell, 2002). Additionally, interrogation of the combined effects of these two loci will therefore be hindered by this interaction. If more than two loci are involved, this adds another layer of complexity in the relationship between genotype and disease risk because of the possibility of multiway interactions among some or all of the contributing loci (Cordell, 2002). In essence, epistasis illustrates the interdependence of the effects of different genetic loci in manifestation of disease risk.

In a typical GWAS analysis, the effect of each variant on the disease trait of interest is examined one at a time. The effects of all variants are then summed to deduce the total amount of genetic variation explained by DNA polymorphisms that affect the trait. The additive model of inheritance assumes that the effects of individual variants are independent of the effects of other contributing loci. Epistasis occurs if the effect of one variant affecting a complex trait depends on the genotype of a second variant affecting the trait. It has been proposed that quantitative variation in risk for the disorder or the expression of disease-related endophenotypes must reflect in part a disturbance of highly dynamic, interconnected, and nonlinear networks (e.g., developmental and biochemical networks) by multiple genetic variants and thus gene–gene interactions are likely (Mackay & Moore, 2014).

The challenge for detecting epistasis in human populations is threefold (Mackay, 2014). The first is statistical, in which a parametric modeling approach for epistasis requires much larger sample sizes than for tests of the effects of single loci. Proving the interactions statistically using an agnostic approach is dogged by the potential for false-positive and false-negative errors. As the number of risk factors increase, the potential interactions also increase exponentially, posing challenges for detection (Prasad et al., 2010). Additionally, complex interactions with nonadditive effects can be difficult to statistically understand and may be difficult to explain and/or empirically test in relation to underlying biological mechanisms. Another problem is computational, based on the large number of tests that must be evaluated. Novel methods such as multifactor dimensionality reduction (Ritchie et al., 2001) and machine-learning methods such as random forests (Breiman, 2001) are capable of modeling nonadditive interactions.

Therefore, "missing heritability" may reflect our limited understanding of gene–gene interactions that might influence the development of schizophrenia (Hemani, Knott, & Haley, 2013; Zuk, Hechter, Sunyaev, & Lander, 2012), in particular idiopathic disruption of different networks of interacting genes (Wu et al., 2010, 2011). To date, schizophrenia GWAS results have highlighted the degree of polygenicity, consistent with thousands of genes and noncoding loci containing risk alleles (Purcell et al., 2009). Progress has been made in implicating biological systems and quantifying shared genetics among related psychiatric disorders. A recent large-scale analysis of the relationship between genotypic networks and distinct clinical phenotypes in the Molecular Genetics of Schizophrenia GWAS dataset has identified 17 genotypic networks that were associated with distinct gene products and clinical syndromes (Arnedo et al., 2015). These analyses would suggest that a hidden heritability component is encoded in a complex distribution of gene–gene and gene–phenotype relationships. Additionally, this analysis revealed that these networks belong to signaling pathways already implicated in schizophrenia, including neural development, neurotrophin function, neurotransmission, and neuronal function and neurodegenerative disorders (Arnedo et al., 2015).

GENE–GENE INTERACTIONS AND SCHIZOPHRENIA: EVIDENCE FROM CLINICAL AND NEUROIMAGING STUDIES

Epistasis is one of several nonmutually exclusive explanations for small effects, missing heritability and lack of replication of top trait-associated variants in different populations in GWASs. Therefore, determining epistasis in the context of risk for schizophrenia might be expected to improve our understanding of the biological underpinnings of variation in schizophrenia risk as well as increase the accuracy of individual risk prediction (Mackay, 2014).

The wealth of genetic and imaging data related to symptoms of psychiatric disorders would support the notion of psychiatric disorders as heterogeneous spectra that deviate quantitatively but not qualitatively from health (McArthur et al., 2014). This has led some authors to suggest that rather than seeking to examine the relationship between genetic variation and presence of clinical symptoms, the concept of the endophenotype should be adopted (Flint & Munafò, 2014; van Os, Kenis, & Rutten, 2010). Endophenotypes are quantifiable, intermediate disease features that bridge the gap between the symptoms of schizophrenia and underlying risk genes (Braff, Schork, & Gottesman, 2007; Gottesman & Gould, 2003). This places considerable emphasis on dissection of the schizophrenia phenotype into distinct and accessible endophenotypes that may relate more closely to underlying pathobiology.

Evidence for epistasis in schizophrenia or in the expression of schizophrenia-related cognitive endophenotypes in patients or healthy controls is described in the following section for candidate genes either directly associated with increased risk for schizophrenia or those associated with the pathophysiology of schizophrenia.

Dopamine

These prevailing DA theory of schizophrenia is predicated on enduring evidence for DA-ergic hyperfunction as a substrate for psychosis, and for DA receptor antagonism (particularly at the DA D_2 receptor, DRD2) as the only mechanism common to all clinically used antipsychotic drugs (Tost, Alam, & Meyer-Lindenberg, 2010). The DA transporter (DAT) regulates DA availability in the DA-ergic synapse via reuptake of DA from the synaptic cleft (Mason et al., 2005); it is abundantly expressed in the striatum, substantia nigra, and ventral tegmental area as well as the posterior cingulated, motor, and insular cortices (Lewis et al., 2001). In contrast, the catechol-o-methyltransferase (COMT) enzyme, which is highly expressed in the prefrontal cortex (PFC), anterior cingulate, and occipital cortices, plays a greater role than DAT in DA degradation in these areas (Lewis et al., 2001). The evidence does not support a role for DAT or COMT as susceptibility genes which confer increased risk for schizophrenia (Gamma, Faraone, Glatt, Yeh, & Tsuang, 2005; Williams, Owen, & O'Donovan, 2007). However, the data suggest that variation in both genes moderates degree of impairment across cognitive endophenotypes linked with the disorder. The DAT gene displays a polymorphic 40-base-pair variable number of tandem repeats in the 3′ untranslated region (DAT 3′UTR VNTR), which yields common, 9- and 10-repeat alleles (Vandenbergh et al., 1992). The 9-repeat has been associated with overactivation in the frontal cortex during working memory and reward-related processing tasks in schizophrenia (Bertolino et al., 2006; Dreher, Kohn, Kolachana, Weinberger, & Berman, 2009), and in the caudate nucleus and ventromedial striatum during a reward task in a nonclinical population (Aarts et al., 2010; Dreher et al., 2009). Studies have shown epistatic interactions between COMT and DAT during cognitive tasks in healthy controls (Bertolino et al., 2008; Caldu et al., 2007; Prata et al., 2009). In a study by Prata et al. (2009), the authors examined the possibility of a nonadditive interaction between two DA-associated genes, DAT and COMT, on brain activation during a verbal fluency task, and the extent to which this effect is modified in schizophrenia. Specifically, they examined evidence for epistasis between the DAT 3' UTR VNTR and COMT rs4680 (Val158Met) polymorphisms. They observed a significant COMT×DAT nonadditive interaction effect on activation in the left supramarginal gyrus in both patients and controls; increased activation in this area was detected only when COMT rs4680 Met/Met (low-activity) subjects also carried the 9-repeat DAT allele, or when, reversely, Val/Val (high-activity) subjects carried the 10/10-repeat genotype. They also observed a diagnosis×COMT×DAT nonadditive interaction in the right orbital gyrus where, only within patients, greater activation was only associated with 9-repeat allele and Val/Val, and with a 10-repeat and Met/Met, conjunction.

AKT1 is a serine/threonine kinase of the AKT family, where AKT is downstream of DRD2 receptor activation, interacting with the β-arrestin 2/PP2A signaling complex in the regulation of DA signaling cascades and the expression of striatal DA-mediated behaviors (Beaulieu, Gainetdinov, & Caron, 2007; Beaulieu et al., 2005). Specifically, DRD2 receptors engage the AKT/Glycogen Synthase Kinase 3 (GSK-3) signaling pathway by a G protein–independent mechanism that involves a signaling complex comprised of β-arrestin 2, AKT, and the multimeric protein phosphatase PP2A (Beaulieu et al., 2007, 2005). Several lines of evidence indicate that AKT/GSK-3 signaling also plays an important role in the development of DA-related neuropsychiatric diseases including schizophrenia (Beaulieu, Del'guidice, Sotnikova, Lemasson, & Gainetdinov, 2011). Relative to control patients, patients with schizophrenia demonstrate significant cortical and hippocampal reduction in AKT expression and activity (Balu et al., 2012; Emamian, Hall, Birnbaum, Karayiorgou, & Gogos, 2004; Zhao, Ksiezak-Reding, Riggio, Haroutunian, & Pasinetti, 2006) as well as decreased activity of downstream GSK-3 (Kozlovsky, Belmaker, & Agam, 2001). Additionally, downstream effectors of AKT including GSK-3β, β-catenin, and CREB have all been implicated in the pathophysiology of schizophrenia based on protein, messenger RNA, and enzyme activity changes (Lang, Puls, Muller, Strutz-Seebohm, & Gallinat, 2007). Blasi et al. (2011) investigated the relative impact of DRD2 rs1076560 and AKT1 rs1130233 across several endophenotypic measures and molecular markers in healthy participants and patients with schizophrenia. In healthy individuals, they found that the interaction between the T allele of DRD2 rs1076560 and the A allele of AKT1 rs1130233 was associated with reduced AKT1 protein levels, reduced

phosphorylation of GSK-3β, in addition to altered cingulate response and reduced behavioral accuracy during a task that measured attentional function. Interestingly, interaction of these two alleles was associated with greater improvement of Positive and Negative Syndrome Scale scores in patients with schizophrenia after treatment with the antipsychotic drug olanzapine.

Tan et al. (2008) examined interactional effects of SNPs at AKT1 and COMT polymorphisms on PFC function in schizophrenia. They reported a main effect of AKT1 rs1130233 on a range of cognitive functions (tasks engaging IQ, processing speed, and executive cognitive control processes) and frontostriatal gray matter volume. An epistatic interaction of AKT1 with a COMT SNP (rs4680; Val/Met polymorphism) was observed on PFC gray matter volume. An epistatic interaction between allele A of rs1130233 and the Val allele of COMT rs4680 was also observed in relation to inefficient PFC activation.

Glutamate

D-amino acid oxidase (DAAO) is an enzyme involved in metabolism of the NMDA receptor activator, D-serine. An increase in DAAO enzyme activity and gene expression has been reported in postmortem cerebellar tissue of patients with schizophrenia (Verrall et al., 2007), which is consistent with the NMDA receptor hypofunction hypothesis of schizophrenia. G72 regulates transmission, by activating DAAO, which modulates metabolism of D-amino acids like D-serine, a coagonist for the NMDA glutamate receptor (Boks et al., 2007). A review of clinical genetic data has supported the association between G72/DAOA and risk for schizophrenia (Boks et al., 2007; Li & He, 2007). An epistatic interaction was observed between SNPs at the schizophrenia susceptibility gene G72 (also known as D-amino acid oxidase activator (DAOA); rs3916965) and DAO (DAO-M5, rs3918346) for schizophrenia risk (Corvin et al., 2007). This interaction was further supported by a neuroimaging study which examined the impact of G72 rs746187 and DAAO rs2111902 genotypes on brain function during a verbal fluency task in patients with schizophrenia, bipolar disorder as well as healthy volunteers. A significant interaction was observed between G72, DAAO SNPs, and schizophrenia diagnosis in relation to right middle temporal gyrus activation, which points toward of a nonadditive interaction between gene variants implicated in glutamate regulation that affects cortical function.

Dopamine-Glutamate

Psychosis may involve changes in both DA-ergic and glutamatergic function and contemporary models propose that it results from an interaction between these two systems (Carlsson & Carlsson, 1990; Lisman et al., 2008). Pauli et al. (2013) investigated the possibility of epistasis between DAT (3′UTR VNT) and G72 (rs746187) on brain function, on the basis that striatal DA activity modulates and is modulated by cortical and medial temporal glutamatergic activity (which G72 regulates). In a verbal fluency task, a significant task load-dependent nonadditive interaction was observed between G72 and DAT genotype on activation in the putamen and parahippocampal gyri bilaterally as well as in the supramarginal/angular gyri bilaterally, and in the right insula, the left posterior cingulated/retrosplenial gyri and the right pre-/postcentral gyri. This epistatic effect on activation was not reflected in any changes to task performance.

Nicodemus et al. (2007) reported an epistatic interaction between the G72 M24 (T allele) and a functionally inefficient three-marker COMT haplotype on risk for schizophrenia. The same group also reported epistatic interactions of specific COMT SNPs including rs4680, rs2097603, and rs165599 with SNPs at RGS4, GRM3, and DISC1 on PFC efficiency (Nicodemus et al., 2007). Nixon et al. (2011) further investigated this G72-COMT gene–gene interaction by examining their relative impact on performance in a working memory task (where patients with schizophrenia typically show impairment) in healthy individuals. Their study results supported their hypothesis that individuals possessing both risk genotypes for DAOA M24 (T/T) and COMT rs4860 (Val/Val) would exhibit inefficient activation of the DLPFC while completing a PFC-dependent working memory task. The observed epistasis captured the multiplicative influence of DAOA (T/T) and COMT (Val/Val) risk genes on PFC physiology.

Genetic variation in GRM3 (which encodes group II metabotropic glutamate receptor 3) has been associated with altered glutamatergic transmission, poorer cognitive performance, and disrupted mismatch negativity (Kawakubo et al., 2011; Marenco et al., 2006) as well as changes in working memory in patients with schizophrenia following antipsychotic treatment (Bishop et al., 2014). Functional magnetic resonance imaging (MRI) studies have investigated the separate and combined effects of variants in COMT and GRM3 on regulation of PFC activation and related cognitive task performance (Tan et al., 2007). Pronounced combined effects of COMT and GRM3 variation were pronounced on PFC-dependent working memory processing. Specifically, the GRM3 genotype (allele A of rs6465084), previously associated with suboptimal glutamatergic signaling, was associated with inefficient PFC engagement and altered PFC-parietal coupling against the background of COMT rs4680 (Val/Val). In contrast, the COMT rs4860 Met/Met background appeared to ameliorate the disruptive effects of GRM3 genotype on PFC processing (Tan et al., 2007).

The PRODH gene codes for proline dehydrogenase; PRODH has been implicated in schizophrenia, in part, through its role in the regulation of glutamatergic signaling (Kempf et al., 2008). COMT and PRODH SNPs were examined for their associations with MRI morphometric measures in young patients with schizophrenia or schizoaffective disorder (Zinkstok et al., 2008). Although main effects for COMT and PRODH SNPs were observed, an epistatic interaction were also observed on the inferior frontal lobe white matter when COMT rs4860 Val allele was indexed with PRODH (rs20086720) alleles (GT or TT) and compared with the rest of patients (Zinkstok et al., 2008).

Schizophrenia Susceptibility Genes

The significance of epistasis in relation to understanding the contribution of candidate susceptibility genes to the development of schizophrenia was highlighted in a paper by Nancy Andreasen and colleagues in 2012. Using machine-learning algorithms, their study sought to identify genes/SNPs that interacted with one another to predict the emergence of a schizophrenia-related anatomical endophenotype, specifically changes in brain structure occurring after the onset of the disorder. These authors identified 11 interactions involving 5 genes and 17 SNPs (five of which had been previously identified as schizophrenia vulnerability markers or implicate cognitive deficits in schizophrenia) that had a significant relationship with biologically plausible tissue change in at least two brain regions. These interactions included interactions between the following genes: Erbb4 and DISC1, PDE4B, RELN; NRG1 and RELN; DISC1 and PDE4B, Erbb4, and RELN.

The neuregulins are a family of signaling proteins that are encoded by four genes (NRG 1–4) and share a common epidermal growth factor–like domain; interaction of these extracellular epidermal growth factor–like domains with membrane-associated tyrosine kinases (Erbb receptors) activate intracellular signaling pathways that are known to play an important role in various developmental processes implicated in schizophrenia (Harrison & Law, 2006; Mei & Xiong, 2008). NRG1 was identified as a putative risk gene for schizophrenia initially in an Icelandic sample (Stefannsson et al., 2002). In meta-analysis, the association between the NRG1 schizophrenia-associated risk haplotype (HapICE) and schizophrenia has proved replicable, although GWAS findings have largely failed to support NRG1 as a risk gene (Bertram, 2008). Few studies of NRG1 epistasis have been conducted to date. There have been reports of interaction between the original NRG1 schizophrenia-risk haplotype (HapICE) and its receptor Erbb4 in modulating risk for schizophrenia (Norton et al., 2006; Shiota et al., 2008).

In a study by Nicodemus and colleagues (Nicodemus, Law, et al., 2010), they investigated epistasis between NRG1 and selected NMDA–glutamate pathway partners implicated in its effects, including Erbb4, AKT1, DLG4, NOS1, and nNOS1-neuronal nitric oxide synthase. NRG1 pathway partners implicated in NMDA signaling were selected because they either directly interacted with NRG1 (Erbb4 and PSD-95) or they interacted directly with genes in the extended Erbb4-NMDA signaling pathway (PSD-95-nNOS1, nNOS1-neuronal nitric oxide synthase, and AKT1). A three-way interaction between a nonsynonymous SNP in NRG1 and SNPs in Erbb4 and AKT1 was associated with substantial increased risk for schizophrenia and inefficient physiological processing of working memory in healthy participants. Epistatic interactions were stronger than SNP effects and in some cases occurred in the absence main effects for the SNPs implicated, providing strong evidence for genuine epistasis. In the case–control comparison, the following interactions were observed between SNPs and schizophrenia: NRG1 5′ and 3′ SNPs rs4560751 and rs3802160; NRG1 (rs10503929; Thr286/289/294Met) and its receptor Erbb4 (rs1026882); a three-way interaction with the latter two SNPs and AKT1 was also observed. For all forms of schizophrenia-associated genetic variation, there is increasing evidence that the implicated genes converge upon biochemical pathways and networks. One of the clearer examples of convergence of multiple genetic hits within a well-established biochemical pathway is the NRG1-Erbb4-PI3K-AKT1 pathway. Although it should be noted that none of these genes is significant in the large GWAS studies, there is evidence for association of all four genes with schizophrenia, and for epistasis between them (Harrison, 2015; Law et al., 2012; Nicodemus, Law, et al., 2010).

Lateral ventricle enlargement represents one of the most consistent findings in first-episode schizophrenia studies (Vita, De Peri, Silenzi, & Dieci, 2006) and has been postulated as a potential endophenotype for schizophrenia (Andreasen et al., 2011; McDonald et al., 2006). Three SNPs within the DISC1 gene rs6675281, rs821616, and rs2793092 were examined for an interaction with SNP8NRG243177 of the NRG1 gene, which had previously been shown to independently predict lateral ventricle volume in a schizophrenia patient sample (Mata et al., 2010). The first finding was a significant association between lateral ventricle volume and the rs2793092 SNP in the DISC1 gene, whereby those patients who were T/T homozygotes presented substantially enlarged lateral ventricles. In a previous study (Mata et al., 2009), they reported similar results with SNP8NRG243177 within the NRG1 gene; those patients carrying T allele presented substantially enlarged lateral ventricles. They also reported an additive effect of SNP8NRG243177 in the NRG1 gene and rs2793092 in the DISC1 gene on lateral ventricle enlargement.

A study in a Scottish pedigree demonstrated that a familial mutation in the DISC1 gene resulting from a balanced chromosomal translocation at 1q42.1-1q42.3, segregated with several psychiatric disorders, including schizophrenia; this association between DISC1 and schizophrenia has been replicated across diverse populations (Chubb, Bradshaw, & Soares, 2008; Hennah et al., 2009; Schumacher et al., 2009). During embryonic development, DISC1 appears to play an important role in neurodevelopment and neuronal plasticity via interaction with several proteins, including phosphodiesterase-4B, Fez1, NudEL, and LIS1; these functions likely alternate, depending upon the stage of development (Chubb et al., 2008). Several studies have examined whether variation within the putative DISC1 protein pathway influences risk for schizophrenia or the expression of schizophrenia-associated cognitive endophenotypes. NDE1 and NDEL1 have been shown to interact with DISC1 to increase risk for schizophrenia. A study conducted by Burdick and colleagues tested for association and interaction between the functional SNP Ser704Cys in DISC1 and NDEL1 and risk for schizophrenia (Burdick et al., 2008). They observed a significant interaction between the rs1391768 SNP in NDEL1 and DISC1 Ser704Cys, with the effect of NDEL1 on risk of schizophrenia evident only against the background of DISC1 Ser704 homozygosity (Burdick et al., 2008). Nicodemus, Callicott, et al. (2010) also reported evidence that SNPs in three genes in the putative DISC1 pathway, DISC1, CIT, and NDEL1, act in epistasis to influence risk for schizophrenia in a sample of patients with schizophrenia. In a complementary neuroimaging analysis, three of the four interactions were validated via neuroimaging in healthy controls; carriers of the combinations of schizophrenia risk-associated genotypes showed less efficient cognitive processing, similar to schizophrenia patients, than those carrying no risk-associated genotypes during a test of working memory.

Kim et al. (2012) reported a significant interaction at both the molecular and clinical level between DISC1 and SLC12A2 (which encodes NKCC1, a cortical chloride transporter). Research has demonstrated that functional variation in the SLC12A2 gene was associated with a modest increase in schizophrenia risk, together with working memory performance variation, global cognition, and inefficient prefrontal cortical activation in healthy participants (Morita et al., 2014). During adult and early postnatal hippocampal neurogenesis in the mouse, they also showed that DISC1 knockdown-induced dendritic overgrowth of newborn neurons required GABA-induced depolarization, which is crucially dependent upon abundant expression of SLC12A2 (Kim et al., 2012). A significant interaction between SNPs in DISC1 and SLC12A2 (rs10089) and risk for schizophrenia was also demonstrated in a combined analysis of three independent case–control samples (Kim et al., 2012). Using functional MRI, Callicott et al. (2013) reported that healthy participants carrying minor alleles in the same two SNPs show a significant decrease in hippocampal region activation and hippocampal connectivity with PFC during a recognition memory task, confirming a biological interaction between these genes on risk for schizophrenia and the expression of schizophrenia-related cognitive endophenotypes.

Meta-analyses have shown that the association between the dysbindin gene DTNBP1 (which encodes a neuronal protein that is part of the dystrophin protein complex) and schizophrenia have proven replicable across numerous independent samples (Allen et al., 2008); however, no functional variant has been identified and there is inconsistency as to the reported alleles/haplotypes between studies. DTNBP1 functions as a component of a protein complex, termed the biogenesis of lysosome-related organelles complex 1 (BLOC-1; Li et al., 2003). The BLOC-1 is a 200-kDa ubiquitously expressed soluble oligomeric protein complex known to consist of proteins encoded by at least eight genes: DTNBP1, MUTED, PLDN, CNO, SNAPAP, BLOC1S1, BLOC1S2, and BLOC1S3 (Ciciotte et al., 2003). Using canonical correlation analysis to perform gene-based tests of epistasis in schizophrenia, Morris et al. (2008) examined the interaction between DTNBP1 and other BLOC1 genes (MUTED, PLDN, CNO, SNAPAP, BLOC1S1, BLOC1S2, BLOC1S3) and risk for schizophrenia. They reported epistatic interactions between DTNBP1 and MUTED, although a main effect was not reported for the latter gene. Another study looked at the interaction between DTNBP1, the candidate susceptibility gene RGS4, and IL3 (Edwards et al., 2008). In the family-based sample, a three-locus interaction between IL3 SNP rs2069803, DTNBP1 SNP rs2619539, and RGS4 SNP rs2661319 was observed (Edwards et al., 2008). In the case–control sample, a two-locus interaction was observed between IL3 SNP rs31400 and DTNBP1 SNP rs760761 and risk for schizophrenia.

Nicodemus et al. (2014) recently investigated the relative explanatory power of polygenic scores versus epistatic analyses in accounting for the variation in working memory performance. Impaired working memory, one of the cognitive deficits of schizophrenia, was used as the outcome measure while epistatic analyses were measured in the context of interactions between SNPs in the psychosis susceptibility gene ZNF804A pathway. It was shown that the removal of SNPs within ZNF804A reduced the R^2 values only slightly, suggesting that the joint contribution of genes within the pathways is more significant than the independent effects of single SNPs. It was also shown that when epistasis was included in the interaction term in addition to polygenic scores, the amount of variation explained in two independent test sets of cases increased threefold. Furthermore, they showed that the combined effects of schizophrenia risk alleles led to worse performance of patients with schizophrenia in measures of working memory and social cognition.

Several studies have supported a link between increased susceptibility for schizophrenia and microdeletions affecting the gene neurexin 1 (NRXN1; Kirov et al., 2009; Levinson et al., 2012). Neurexins are presynaptic proteins that act as synaptic recognition molecules and may contribute to various aspects of synaptic function via binding to neuroligins (Ichtchenko et al., 1995). Mozhui et al. (2011) demonstrated that markers in NRXN1 and GSK-3β show epistatic interactions in modulating risk for schizophrenia. They reported a significant two-loci interaction between rs4563262 (NRXN1) and rs4340737 (GSK-3β) with risk, and using a three-loci model, there was a significant interaction between rs6736816 and rs9309200 in NRXN1 and rs9826659 in GSK-3β. This neurobiological interaction may focus on cellular interaction between both proteins at the presynaptic region.

TRANSLATIONAL GENETIC APPROACHES FOR STUDYING SCHIZOPHRENIA

A survey of the literature reveals that preclinical genetic models of neurodevelopmental or neuropsychiatric disease have primarily involved use of mice with targeted mutation of a single risk-associated gene via knockout or transgenesis (e.g., gain-of-function and dominant negative mutants). Oft-cited limitations associated with constitutive single-gene knockout models include the potential for embryonic or perinatal lethality, especially pertinent when one consists that many of the most prominent schizophrenia risk genes play a role in central nervous system and non–central nervous system developmental processes (Desbonnet, Waddington, & Tuathaigh, 2009; O'Tuathaigh & Waddington, 2015). Additionally, interpretation of mutant phenotype is complicated by the potential influence of compensatory mechanisms, and the potential for redundancy. The strength of the constitutive approach includes the ability to vary gene dosage as well as the ability to achieve a level of molecular specificity that may not be available if the researcher is reliant on existing pharmacological tools.

Taking into account the evidence for complex interactions between many genes and environmental factors in modulating risk for schizophrenia, several issues with implications for preclinical modelling have been summarized in reviews of the field: (1) the notable absence of clinically implicated functional variants for the majority of the genes associated with the disorder, thereby limiting validity of mutant models for the risk allele in question; (2) the absence of null mutations in this disorder, which has led some authors to question the scientific value of constructing single-gene knockout models for schizophrenia (Harrison et al., 2012); (3) poor evolutionary conservation of disease-associated noncoding DNA sequences and species differences in neural circuits and/or molecular networks that might link the risk gene to aberrant circuitry, thereby potentially limiting the value of a model species like the mouse (McCarroll et al., 2014); (4) where a gene has been shown to be downregulated in schizophrenia, a heterozygous knockout model may represent a valid modeling approach (Meck et al., 2012); and (5) where the expression of some genes is upregulated in schizophrenia, transgenic overexpression is a frequently used approach; the caveat should be added that the magnitude of overexpression in a mouse model can be dramatically different from the clinical situation (Harrison et al., 2012). In summary, studies employing constitutive gene knockout models might be better conceptualized as phenotypic examinations of the functional roles of genes associated with risk for psychosis as opposed to isomorphic models of psychotic illness itself.

It has been proposed that new approaches to preclinical modeling require incorporating emerging knowledge regarding the polygenic architecture of schizophrenia (McCarroll et al., 2014). Double- and triple-knockout or transgenic models constitute one step toward addressing this challenge, but practical concerns restrict the viability of such approaches (Lyon, Kew, Corti, Harrison, & Burnet, 2008). Additionally, careful consideration must be taken when selecting which gene combinations to manipulate; promising candidates should include genes with a known biochemical pathway or genes within a candidate genomic locus (Arguello, Markx, Gogos, & Karayiorgou, 2010; Harrison et al., 2012).

MEASURING SCHIZOPHRENIA IN MICE

Modeling a disorder characterized by symptomatic and likely etiological heterogeneity is best addressed from a pragmatic standpoint by focusing on specific components of the disease phenotype rather than disease phenotype in its entirety (O'Tuathaigh, Desbonnet, & Waddington, 2014). It has been often stated that the psychotic symptoms (e.g., hallucinations, delusions, thought disorders) as well as negative symptoms (e.g., blunted affect) may not be measurable in small rodents, thereby restricting model validation efforts to assessment of face and (in some cases) predictive validity (Moran, O'Tuathaigh, Papaleo, & Waddington, 2014). Phenotypic modeling of negative symptoms has focused primarily on a small number of cross-species behavioral features that are quantifiable in both humans and animals (e.g., deficits in social interaction and motivation) (O'Tuathaigh &

Waddington, 2015). DA-associated motor-based measures (e.g., novelty- or stimulant-induced hyperactivity), and/or preattentional and attentional phenomena such as prepulse inhibition (PPI) or latent inhibition (LI) have been employed a proxy measures of psychotic symptoms in mice. PPI and LI disruption in animal models of schizophrenia are considered analogous to the basic information processing deficits observed in schizophrenia (van den Buuse, 2010; Moran et al., 2014). Maze- and operant-based tasks have been used to measure cognitive processes analogous to those observed in patients with schizophrenia (Desbonnet et al., 2009).

GENE–GENE INTERACTIONS AND SCHIZOPHRENIA: EVIDENCE FROM MUTANT MOUSE MODELS

Assuming a polygenic basis for schizophrenia, neither partial nor complete loss of function or overexpression of any single gene in a mouse model will result in generation of a valid mouse model for the disease. It has been suggested that simultaneous dysregulation of multiple risk genes will more closely reflect the genetic risk component of the disorder (O'Tuathaigh & Waddington, 2015). In this context, mice containing partial loss- or gain-of-function for multiple candidate genes could perhaps mimic more precisely the etiopathologic mechanisms as well as the pathophysiological features of schizophrenia. Evidence from cellular and molecular studies conducted to date suggests that multiple common alleles and/or rare variants converge on a specific number of biochemical pathways that may reflect the etiopathobiology of schizophrenia (Harrison, 2015; O'Tuathaigh & Waddington, 2015). For example, NRG1, AKT, and DISC1 dysfunction have been characterized as elements in a common pathway that may regulate neurodevelopment and contribute to susceptibility to schizophrenia (Desbonnet et al., 2009).

Characterization of mice with simultaneous dysregulation of several risk genes has the potential to provide insight into resultant additive and multiplicative effects that contribute to the expression of schizophrenia-related endophenotypes. Evidence for epistasis in schizophrenia or in the expression of schizophrenia-related endophenotypes from studies employing mutant model are described later for candidate susceptibility genes either directly implicated in clinical genetic analyses, or those which have been implicated in pathophysiological processes associated with schizophrenia.

Dopamine

As stated previously (Section 4.1), COMT is expressed in the pyramidal neurons of the PFC and hippocampus and plays a specific role in the catabolism of cortical dopamine but not noradrenaline (Papaleo et al., 2008). Several studies suggest that functional polymorphisms of the COMT gene are associated with performance on PFC-dependent cognitive tasks which are disrupted in schizophrenia (Desbonnet et al., 2009). Studies in COMT knockout mice have investigated motor activity, anxiety, aggression, and sensorimotor gating, and have reported only minor effects on aggression and anxiety (Gogos et al., 1998; Haasio, Huotari, Nissinen, & Männistö, 2003). COMT knockout mice also display a mild improvement in cognitive tasks that are dependent upon PFC DA availability (Papaleo et al., 2008).

Meta-analyses have indicated DTNBP1 to be a replicable risk gene for schizophrenia (Section Schizophrenia Susceptibility Genes). In vitro work indicates that reduction in dysbindin can lower glutamate release, whereas overexpression of dysbindin elevates glutamate release, suggesting a modulatory role for dysbindin in glutamate neurotransmission is indicated in cortical neuronal cultures (Numakawa et al., 2004). The "sandy" (Sdy) mouse, a spontaneous mutation identified in the DBA/2J strain, carries a naturally occurring deletion that includes the DTNBP1 gene. Jentsch et al. (2009) reported a disruption in working memory in the Sdy mutant using the choice accuracy measure in delayed-nonmatch-to-position task; this deficit was accompanied by disruption of excitatory neurotransmission in the PFC, as indexed by both a reduction in the amplitude of action potential-evoked excitatory postsynaptic currents and the frequency of miniature excitatory postsynaptic currents as well as the abolition of paired-pulse facilitation. DTNBP1 knockout also caused deficits in working memory as measured by the delayed-nonmatch-to-position task; this deficit was accompanied by a decrease in cortical NR1 messenger RNA expression, which was found to be significantly correlated with working memory performance (Karlsgodt et al., 2011). In a separate study, modified T-maze working memory task, Sdy mice displayed enhanced learning of the in the acquisition phase of a modified T-maze working memory task; with the introduction of delay intervals, DTNBP1 mutants displayed overall worse performance relative to wild-type controls (Papaleo et al., 2012). Cellular studies including data reported in the same study suggested that the interaction between CaMKII and enhanced signaling at cortical DRD2 may at least partially contribute to the working memory phenotypes reported for DTNBP1 knockout mice in these studies (Ji et al., 2009; Papaleo et al., 2012).

Based on these data implicating a role for DTNBP1 and COMT on cortical DA-ergic signaling (Moran et al., 2014), epistasis between both genes in relation to the development of schizophrenia-like phenotypes was investigated by intercrossing the COMT knockout and Sdy mutant strains (Papaleo, Burdick, Callicott, &

Weinberger, 2014). In contrast to effects produced by DTNBP1 or COMT single-gene knockout, the combined reduction of both genes in the same mouse produced a marked deficit in working memory function (Papaleo et al., 2014). Importantly, this same epistatic effect was found in healthy humans performing an n-back working memory test in conjunction with functional MRI: individuals homozygous for COMT rs4680 Met alleles (i.e., with relative reduction in COMT) and displaying no reduction in dysbindin activity (i.e., not carrying a specific functional variant for DTNBP1) performed better than other COMT genotypes; in contrast, individuals with COMT rs4680 Met/Met genotypes and who were also homozygous for the low dysbindin expression-associated haplotype were the poorest performing compared with other COMT genotypes (Papaleo et al., 2014). These results are consistent with an inverted U function showing nonlinear effects of increasing DRD2 signaling in PFC-dependent cognitive functions. These findings once again highlight an important point with respect to epistasis underlying the genetic basis of behavior: that such processes are often nonlinear, and that their genetic origins might be epistatic and bidirectional.

DARPP32 (dopamine and cyclic-adenosine 50-phosphate–regulated phosphoprotein, Mr 32 kDa) is a shared downstream component of both DA-ergic and serotonergic pathways (Fienberg et al., 1998; Svenningsson et al., 2000). The data suggest that PDE1B may participate in the same pathways (Ehrman et al., 2006). Targeted deletion of DARPP32 produces a reduction in the locomotor response to psychostimulants such as cocaine or amphetamine at moderate doses (Svenningsson et al., 2003). Mice deficient for both PDE1B and DARPP32 demonstrated a normalization of changes to locomotor activity response to methamphetamine compared with PDE1B knockout mice (Ehrman et al., 2006). In a test of anxiety behavior, the elevated zero-maze, DARPP32 knockout mice spent more time in the open, indicative of less anxiety, but PDE1B deletion normalized the anxiety state in these mice relative to DARPP32 mutant mice. Using the Morris water maze as a test for spatial learning and memory, genetic inactivation of both DARPP32 and PDE1B caused spatial navigation deficits, manifested in delayed acquisition and reversal learning.

Glutamate

Allelic variation in GRM3 has been associated with risk to develop schizophrenia, and mGlu2/3 agonists have shown efficacy in experimental models of schizophrenia (Patil et al., 2007; however, see Kinon et al., 2011). In mice with simultaneous knockout of GRM2 and GRM3 or GRM2 alone, the ameliorative effects of the mGlu2/3 receptor agonist LY404039 on phencyclidine- and amphetamine-evoked hyperactivity were absent;

the same profile was not present in GRM3 knockout mice, indicating that activation of mGlu2 and not mGlu3 receptors may be responsible for the antipsychotic-like effects of LY404039 (Fell, Svensson, Johnson, & Schoepp, 2008).

A recent comparative characterization of behavioral phenotypes across GRM2, GRM3, and GRM2/GRM3 knockout lines revealed no effects on anxiety across or cognition in the rewarded alternation test (De Filippis et al., 2014). Lane et al. (2013) reported a reduction in DA levels (accompanied by a reduction in the metabolites DOPAC and HVA) in the striatum (particularly the nucleus accumbens) of double GRM2/GRM3 mutant mice. In contrast, no differences in monoamines or their metabolites between genotypes were observed in single-gene GRM2 or GRM3 knockout mice.

In a series of elegant studies described by Lyon et al. (2011), mice with simultaneous disruption of GRM2 and GRM3 demonstrated a pattern of subtle deficits in hippocampus-dependent spatial memory. They were selectively impaired in an appetitively motivated spatial memory tasks but not in the aversively motivated open field water maze. These deficits were shown not to reflect reduced appetitive reward-related motivation; instead, the pattern of results suggested a change in the arousal–cognition function in GRM2/GRM3 knockout mice. Consistent with this altered arousal phenotype in double-mutant mice, they displayed locomotor hypoactivity relative to wild-type controls in both the absence and presence of amphetamine (Lyon et al., 2011).

Schizophrenia Susceptibility Genes

AKT1 (see Section 4.1) is one of the downstream kinases of the NRG1 signaling pathway (Huang et al., 2015), and in vitro studies have demonstrated that NRG1 signaling is associated with schizophrenia via the PI3K/AKT-dependent pathway (Kanakry, Li, Nakai, Sei, & Weinberger, 2007). Additionally, diminution of sensory gating function and decreased NRG1-stimulated AKT phosphorylation was reported in nontreated, first-episode schizophrenic patients (Kéri, Beniczky, & Kelemen, 2010). NRG1-AKT1 epistasis was further examined via generation of double heterozygous AKT1 × NRG1 mutant mice by intercrossing heterozygous AKT1 knockout and NRG1 TM-domain knockout mice. Both AKT1-deficient and double heterozygous mice had less striatal glucose uptake, as measured in a fluorine-18-fluorodeoxyglucose positron emission tomography scan, compared with wild-type controls, which is indicative of less brain activity in the striatum (but not the medial PFC). No significant effect of either genotype or both was observed in relation to PPI performance or novelty-induced locomotion. In the "what-when-where" episodic memory object recognition task, the only genotypic effect observed was

that on "where" memory, where NRG1 heterozygotes and double-mutant mice showed significantly lower ability to discriminate the spatial trace compared with AKT1 heterozygotes and wild-type mice. In the sociability test, a marginal disruption of social approach behavior, and reduced social sniffing toward a novel male conspecific, was observed in double mutants. In the social novelty preference task, both single-gene mutants and the double-mutant group showed disruption of preference for the socially novel stimulus. No effect of genotype was observed in a measure of spatial working memory, the delayed nonmatch to sample test, employing several delay periods (5, 15, and 30 s).

GSK-3 is a highly conserved serine/threonine protein kinase that is expressed as two coenzymes: GSK-3α and GSK-3β (Woodgett, 1990). It is ubiquitously expressed in the brain and has been implicated in basic neuronal functions such as neurodevelopment (Kim et al., 2009), neurotransmitter function (Beaulieu et al., 2007, 2005), and synaptic plasticity (Peineau et al., 2007). In one of two DISC1 gene mutant models, the L100P line, generated via ENU mutagenesis in exon 2 of DISC1, demonstrate impairment across several behavioral models related to schizophrenia, including PPI and LI (both reversible by antipsychotic treatment), working memory as well as novelty-induced hyperactivity (Clapcote et al., 2007). Both the phosphodiesterase 4 inhibitor rolipram and the GSK-3 inhibitor TDZD-8 synergized to reverse PPI deficits and hyperactivity in the L100P DISC1 mutant (Lipina et al., 2011).

Lentiviral silencing of DISC1 expression in the adult mouse dentate gyrus was accompanied by an increase in novelty-induced hyperlocomotion; this behavioral effect was reversed following treatment with the GSK-3β inhibitor SB-216,763, suggesting that increased GSK-3β activity secondary to DISC1 loss of function might be associated with schizophrenia-like behaviors (Mao et al., 2009). Further support for molecular interactions between DISC1 and GSK-3 in schizophrenia has come from reports that pharmacological or genetic inactivation of GSK-3 in the ENU-generated DISC1 mutant (L100P) reversed phenotypic deficits in PPI and LI, and normalized their hyperactivity profile (Lipina, Wang, Liu, & Roder, 2012). In summary, it was shown that genetic deletion of GSK-3α was equally as effective in reversing the behavioral deficits in the DISC1-L100P mouse model as acute administration of the GSK-3 antagonist TDZD-8. GSK-3α heterozygotes were intercrossed with DISC1-100P homozygous, heterozygous, or wild-type mice. Introduction of the GSK-3α mutation reversed hyperactivity observed in DISC1-L100P homozygotes (to the level observed in wild-type mice). Similarly, both DISC1-L100P heterozygous and homozygous mutants displayed deficits in PPI; these deficits were abolished in mice also lacking a GSK-3α allele. In the test of LI, both

DISC1-L100P heterozygous and homozygous mutants evidenced LI deficits in the conditioned lick suppression task, which could not be attributed to a nonspecific effect on learning or reward. Once again, partial deletion of GSK-3α in DISC1-L100P heterozygotes and homozygotes normalized LI deficits in these mice. In a similar manner, administration of the selective GSK-3 inhibitor, TDZD-8, reversed PPI and LI deficits, and normalized hyperactivity of DISC1-L100P mutant mice.

They also explored molecular interactions and the consequence of the L100P mutation on GSK-3 function. They reported that the DISC1 L100P mutation did not affect tyrosine phosphorylation of both GSK-3 isoforms, but that the interaction between DISC1 and GSK-3 was significantly reduced within the striatum of the DISC1-L100P (Lipina et al., 2012). DISC1-L100P mutants also display abnormalities of frontal cortical pyramidal neurons, including reduced dendritic length, dendrite surface area, and spine density (Lee et al., 2011). They reported the morphological deficits previously reported in DISC1-L100P mutants, and a similar pattern of abnormalities in GSK-3α mutant mice. However, in double DISC1-L100P × GSK-3α mutant mice, genetic inactivation of GSK-3α significantly rescued spine density but had no effect on dendritic length, surface area, arborization (Lee et al., 2011). These findings further implicate impaired DISC1- GSK-3 interplay in the emergence of schizophrenia-relevant endophenotypes.

Another recent study described the phenotypic consequences of intercrossing the heterozygous TM-domain NRG1 knockout model and the DISC1 L100P mutant (O'Tuathaigh et al., 2012). It was shown that mice with partial or complete codisruption of DISC1 and NRG1 demonstrated pronounced impairments across various domains of social behavior implicated in schizophrenia. This negative symptom-like profile in simultaneous NRG1/DISC1 mutant mice, largely restricted to males, was reflected in disruption across various measures of social interaction and cognition as well as alteration of hypothalamic expression of the oxytocin and/or vasopressin genes relative to control mice. They also observed postpubertal induction of PPI deficits and novelty-induced hyperactivity in mice with heterozygous deletion of NRG1; these deficits were reversed by the antipsychotic drug clozapine.

CONCLUSIONS

Clinical studies highlight the challenges associated with modeling epistasis in schizophrenia, where such interactions require enormous statistical power and place vast demands on sample size. However, various hypothesis-based studies have demonstrated evidence for epistatic interactions between two or more individual risk genes in mediating risk for schizophrenia and variation across schizophrenia-associated cognitive endophenotypic measures in healthy participants. Against the backdrop of a relative lack of clinical studies, preclinical modeling of epistatic interactions offers the possibility of multitiered investigation of convergence of multiple risk genes on selected molecular or biochemical pathways. These types of insights represent an important step toward the development of novel therapeutics that might involve targeted modulation of specific components on such disease-associated pathways.

References

Aarts, E., Roelofs, A., Franke, B., Rijpkema, M., Fernández, G., Helmich, R. C., et al. (2010). Striatal dopamine mediates the interface between motivational and cognitive control in humans: evidence from genetic imaging. *Neuropsychopharmacology, 35,* 1943–1951.

Allen, N. C., Bagade, S., McQueen, M. B., Ioannidis, J. P., Kavvoura, F. K., Khoury, M. J., et al. (2008). Systematic meta-analyses and field synopsis of genetic association studies in schizophrenia: the SzGene database. *Nature Genetics, 40,* 827–834.

Andreasen, N. C., Nopoulos, P., Magnotta, V., Pierson, R., Ziebell, S., & Ho, B. C. (2011). Progressive brain change in schizophrenia: a prospective longitudinal study of first-episode schizophrenia. *Biological Psychiatry, 70,* 672–679.

Andreasen, N. C., Wilcox, M. A., Ho, B. C., Epping, E., Ziebell, S., Zeien, E., et al. (2012). Statistical epistasis and progressive brain change in schizophrenia: an approach for examining the relationships between multiple genes. *Molecular Psychiatry, 17,* 1093–1102.

Arguello, P. A., Markx, S., Gogos, J. A., & Karayiorgou, M. (2010). Development of animal models for schizophrenia. *Disease Models and Mechanisms, 3,* 22–26.

Arnedo, J., Svrakic, D. M., Del Val, C., Romero-Zaliz, R., Hernández-Cuervo, H., Molecular Genetics of Schizophrenia Consortium, Fanous, A. H., et al. (2015). Uncovering the hidden risk architecture of the schizophrenias: confirmation in three independent genome-wide association studies. *American Journal of Psychiatry, 172,* 139–153.

Balu, D. T., Carlson, G. C., Talbot, K., Kazi, H., Hill-Smith, T. E., Easton, R. M., et al. (2012). Akt1 deficiency in schizophrenia and impairment of hippocampal plasticity and function. *Hippocampus, 22,* 230–240.

Bateson, W. (1909). *Mendel's principles of heredity.* Cambridge: Cambridge University Press.

Beaulieu, J. M., Del'guidice, T., Sotnikova, T. D., Lemasson, M., & Gainetdinov, R. R. (2011). Beyond cAMP: the regulation of Akt and GSK3 by dopamine receptors. *Frontiers in Molecular Neuroscience, 4,* 38.

Beaulieu, J. M., Gainetdinov, R. R., & Caron, M. G. (2007). The Akt-GSK-3 signaling cascade in the actions of dopamine. *Trends in Pharmacological Sciences, 28,* 166–172.

Beaulieu, J. M., Sotnikova, T. D., Marion, S., Lefkowitz, R. J., Gainetdinov, R. R., & Caron, M. G. (2005). An Akt/β-arrestin 2/PP2A signaling complex mediates dopaminergic neurotransmission and behavior. *Cell, 122,* 261–273.

Bertolino, A., Blasi, G., Latorre, V., Rubino, V., Rampino, A., Sinibaldi, L., et al. (2006). Additive effects of genetic variation in dopamine regulating genes on working memory cortical activity in human brain. *Journal of Neuroscience, 26,* 3918–3922.

Bertolino, A., Di Giorgio, A., Blasi, G., Sambataro, F., Caforio, G., Sinibaldi, L., et al. (2008). Epistasis between dopamine regulating genes identifies a nonlinear response of the human hippocampus during memory tasks. *Biological Psychiatry, 64,* 226–234.

Bertram, L. (2008). Genetic research in schizophrenia: new tools and future perspectives. *Schizophrenia Bulletin, 34,* 806–812.

Bishop, J. R., Reilly, J. L., Harris, M. S., Patel, S. R., Kittles, R., Badner, J. A., et al. (2014). Pharmacogenetic associations of the type-3 metabotropic glutamate receptor (GRM3) gene with working memory and clinical symptom response to antipsychotics in first-episode schizophrenia. *Psychopharmacology, 232,* 145–154.

Blasi, G., Napolitano, F., Ursini, G., Taurisano, P., Romano, R., Caforio, G., et al. (2011). DRD2/AKT1 interaction on D2 c-AMP independent signaling, attentional processing, and response to olanzapine treatment in schizophrenia. *Proceedings of the National Academy of Sciences of the United States of America, 108,* 1158–1163.

Boks, M. P., Rietkerk, T., van de Beek, M. H., Sommer, I. E., de Koning, T. J., & Kahn, R. S. (2007). Reviewing the role of the genes G72 and DAAO in glutamate neurotransmission in schizophrenia. *European Neuropsychopharmacology, 17,* 567–572.

Braff, D., Schork, N. J., & Gottesman, I. I. (2007). Endophenotyping schizophrenia. *American Journal of Psychiatry, 164,* 705–707.

Breiman, L. (2001). Random forests. *Machine Learning, 45,* 5–32.

Brown, A. S. (2011). Exposure to prenatal infection and schizophrenia. *Frontiers in Psychiatry, 2,* 63.

Burdick, K. E., Kamiya, A., Hodgkinson, C. A., Lencz, T., DeRosse, P., Ishizuka, K., et al. (2008). Elucidating the relationship between DISC1, NDEL1 and NDE1 and the risk for schizophrenia: evidence of epistasis and competitive binding. *Human Molecular Genetics, 17,* 2462–2473.

Burmeister, M. (1999). Basic concepts in the study of diseases with complex genetics. *Biological Psychiatry, 45,* 522–532.

Burmeister, M., McInnis, M. G., & Zollner, S. (2008). Psychiatric genetics: progress amid controversy. *Nature Reviews Genetics, 9,* 527–540.

van den Buuse, M. (2010). Modeling the positive symptoms of schizophrenia in genetically modified mice: pharmacology and methodology aspects. *Schizophrenia Bulletin, 36,* 246–270.

Caldú, X., Vendrell, P., Bartrés-Faz, D., Clemente, I., Bargalló, N., Jurado, M. A., et al. (2007). Impact of the COMT Val108/158 Met and DAT genotypes on prefrontal function in healthy subjects. *Neuroimage, 37,* 1437–1444.

Callicott, J. H., Feighery, E. L., Mattay, V. S., White, M. G., Chen, Q., Baranger, D. A., et al. (2013). DISC1 and SLC12A2 interaction affects human hippocampal function and connectivity. *Journal of Clinical Investigation, 123,* 2961–2964.

Carlsson, M., & Carlsson, A. (1990). Interactions between glutamatergic and monoaminergic systems within the basal ganglia–implications for schizophrenia and Parkinson's disease. *Trends in Neuroscience, 13,* 272–276.

Chubb, J. E., Bradshaw, N. J., & Soares, D. C. (2008). The DISC locus in psychiatric illness. *Molecular Psychiatry, 13,* 36–64.

Ciciotte, S. L., Gwynn, B., Moriyama, K., Huizing, M., Gahl, W. A., Bonifacino, J. S., et al. (2003). Cappuccino, a mouse model of Hermansky-Pudlak syndrome, encodes a novel protein that is part of the pallidin-muted complex (BLOC-1). *Blood, 101,* 4402–4407.

Clapcote, S. J., Lipina, T. V., Millar, J. K., Mackie, S., Christie, S., Ogawa, F., et al. (2007). Behavioral phenotypes of Disc1 missense mutations in mice. *Neuron, 54,* 387–402.

Cordell, H. J. (2002). Epistasis: what it means, what it doesn't mean, and statistical methods to detect it in humans. *Human Molecular Genetics, 11,* 2463–2468.

Corvin, A., McGhee, K. A., Murphy, K., Donohoe, G., Nangle, J. M., Schwaiger, S., et al. (2007). Evidence for association and epistasis at the DAOA/G30 and D-amino acid oxidase loci in an Irish schizophrenia sample. *American Journal of Medical Genetics B Neuropsychiatric Genetics, 144B,* 949–953.

Cross-Disorder Group of the Psychiatric Genomics Consortium. (2013). Genetic relationship between five psychiatric disorders estimated from genome-wide SNPs. *Nature Genetics, 45,* 984.

De Filippis, B., Lyon, L., Taylor, A., Lane, T., Burnet, P. W., Harrison, P. J., et al. (2014). The role of group II metabotropic glutamate receptors in cognition and anxiety: comparative studies in GRM2$^{-/-}$, GRM3$^{-/-}$ and GRM2/3$^{-/-}$ knockout mice. *Neuropharmacology, 89C,* 19–32.

Del Pino, I., García-Frigola, C., Dehorter, N., Brotons-Mas, J. R., Alvarez-Salvado, E., Martínez de Lagrán, M., et al. (2013). Erbb4 deletion from fast-spiking interneurons causes schizophrenia-like phenotypes. *Neuron, 79,* 1152–1168.

Desbonnet, L., Waddington, J. L., & Tuathaigh, C. M. (2009). Mice mutant for genes associated with schizophrenia: common phenotype or distinct endophenotypes? *Behavioural Brain Research, 204,* 258–273.

Dreher, J. C., Kohn, P., Kolachana, B., Weinberger, D. R., & Berman, K. F. (2009). Variation in dopamine genes influences responsivity of the human reward system. *Proceedings of the National Academy of Sciences of the United States of America, 106,* 617–622.

Edwards, T. L., Wang, X., Chen, Q., Wormly, B., Riley, B., O'Neill, F. A., et al. (2008). Interaction between interleukin 3 and dystrobrevin-binding protein 1 in schizophrenia. *Schizophrenia Research, 106,* 208–217.

Ehrman, L. A., Williams, M. T., Schaefer, T. L., Gudelsky, G. A., Reed, T. M., Fienberg, A. A., et al. (2006). Phosphodiesterase 1B differentially modulates the effects of methamphetamine on locomotor activity and spatial learning through DARPP32-dependent pathways: evidence from PDE1B-DARPP32 double-knockout mice. *Genes Brain and Behaviour, 5,* 540–551.

Emamian, E. S., Hall, D., Birnbaum, M. J., Karayiorgou, M., & Gogos, J. A. (2004). Convergent evidence for impaired AKT1-GSK3β signaling in schizophrenia. *Nature Genetics, 36,* 131–137.

Fell, M. J., Svensson, K. A., Johnson, B. G., & Schoepp, D. D. (2008). Evidence for the role of metabotropic glutamate (mGlu)2 not mGlu3 receptors in the preclinical antipsychotic pharmacology of the mGlu2/3 receptor agonist (-)-(1R,4S,5S,6S)-4-amino-2-sulfonylbicyclo[3.1.0]hexane-4,6-dicarboxylic acid (LY404039). *Journal of Pharmacology and Experimental Therapeutics, 326,* 209–217.

Fienberg, A. A., Hiroi, N., Mermelstein, P. G., Song, W., Snyder, G. L., Nishi, A., et al. (1998). DARPP-32: regulator of the efficacy of dopaminergic neurotransmission. *Science, 281,* 838–842.

Flint, J., & Munafò, M. R. (2014). Genetics: finding genes for schizophrenia. *Current Biology, 24,* R755–R757.

Fromer, M., Pocklington, A. J., Kavanagh, D. H., Williams, H. J., Dwyer, S., Gormley, P., et al. (2014). De novo mutations in schizophrenia implicate synaptic networks. *Nature, 506,* 179–184.

Gamma, F., Faraone, S. V., Glatt, S. J., Yeh, Y. C., & Tsuang, M. T. (2005). Meta-analysis shows schizophrenia is not associated with the 40-base-pair repeat polymorphism of the dopamine transporter gene. *Schizophrenia Research, 73,* 55–58.

Gejman, P. V., Sanders, A. R., & Kendler, K. S. (2011). Genetics of schizophrenia: new findings and challenges. *Annual Review of Genomics and Human Genetics, 12,* 121–144.

Gelernter, J. (2015). Genetics of complex traits in psychiatry. *Biological Psychiatry, 77,* 36–42.

Gogos, J. A., Morgan, M., Luine, V., Santha, M., Ogawa, S., Pfaff, D., et al. (1998). Catechol-O-methyltransferase-deficient mice exhibit sexually dimorphic changes in catecholamine levels and behavior. *Proceedings of the National Academy of Sciences of the United States of America, 95,* 9991–9996.

Gottesman, I. I., & Gould, T. D. (2003). The endophenotype concept in psychiatry: etymology and strategic intentions. *American Journal of Psychiatry, 160,* 636–645.

Gottesman, I. I. (1991). *Schizophrenia Genesis: The Origin of Madness..* New York: Freeman.

Gratten, J., Wray, N. R., Keller, M. C., & Visscher, P. M. (2014). Large-scale genomics unveils the genetic architecture of psychiatric disorders. *Nature Neuroscience, 17,* 782–790.

Haasio, K., Huotari, M., Nissinen, E., & Männistö, P. T. (2003). Tissue histopathology, clinical chemistry and behaviour of adult Comt-gene-disrupted mice. *Journal of Applied Toxicology, 23,* 213–219.

Hall, J., Trent, S., Thomas, K. L., O'Donovan, M. C., & Owen, M. J. (2014). Genetic risk for schizophrenia: convergence on synaptic pathways involved in plasticity. *Biological Psychiatry, 77*(1), 52–58. pii:S0006-3223(14) 00519-8.

Harrison, P. J. (2015). Recent genetic findings in schizophrenia and their therapeutic relevance. *Journal of Psychopharmacology, 29*, 85–96.

Harrison, P. J., & Law, A. J. (2006). Neuregulin 1 and schizophrenia: genetics, gene expression, and neurobiology. *Biological Psychiatry, 60*, 132–140.

Harrison, P. J., Pritchett, D., Stumpenhorst, K., Betts, J. F., Nissen, W., Schweimer, J., et al. (2012). Developing predictive animal models and establishing a preclinical trials network for assessing treatment effects on cognition in schizophrenia. *Neuropharmacology, 62*, 1164–1167.

Harvey, P. D., Wingo, A. P., Burdick, K. E., & Baldessarini, R. J. (2010). Cognition and disability in bipolar disorder: lessons from schizophrenia research. *Bipolar Disorder, 12*, 364–375.

Hemani, G., Knott, S., & Haley, C. (2013). An evolutionary perspective on epistasis and the missing heritability. *PLoS Genetics, 9*, e1003295.

Hennah, W., Thomson, P., McQuillin, A., Bass, N., Loukola, A., Anjorin, A., et al. (2009). DISC1 association, heterogeneity and interplay in schizophrenia and bipolar disorder. *Molecular Psychiatry, 14*, 865–873.

Huang, C. H., Pei, J. C., Luo, D. Z., Chen, C., Chen, Y. W., & Lai, W. S. (2015). Investigation of gene effects and epistatic interactions between Akt1 and neuregulin 1 in the regulation of behavioral phenotypes and social functions in genetic mouse models of schizophrenia. *Frontiers in Behavioural Neuroscience, 8*, 455.

Ichtchenko, K., Hata, Y., Nguyen, T., Ullrich, B., Missler, M., Moomaw, C., et al. (1995). Neuroligin 1: a splice site-specific ligand for beta-neurexins. *Cell, 81*, 435–443.

International Schizophrenia Consortium. (2008). Rare chromosomal deletions and duplications increase risk of schizophrenia. *Nature, 455*, 237–241.

International Schizophrenia Consortium. (2009). Common polygenic variation contributes to risk of schizophrenia and bipolar disorder. *Nature, 460*, 748–752.

Jentsch, J. D., Trantham-Davidson, H., Jairl, C., Tinsley, M., Cannon, T. D., & Lavin, A. (2009). Dysbindin modulates prefrontal cortical glutamatergic circuits and working memory function in mice. *Neuropsychopharmacology, 34*, 2601–2608.

Ji, Y., Yang, F., Papaleo, F., Wang, H. X., Gao, W. J., Weinberger, D. R., et al. (2009). Role of dysbindin in dopamine receptor trafficking and cortical GABA function. *Proceedings of the National Academy of Sciences U S A, 106*, 19593–19598.

Kanakry, C. G., Li, Z., Nakai, Y., Sei, Y., & Weinberger, D. R. (2007). Neuregulin-1 regulates cell adhesion via an ErbB2/phosphoinositide-3 kinase/Akt-dependent pathway: potential implications for schizophrenia and cancer. *PLoS One, 2*, e1369.

Karlsgodt, K. H., Robleto, K., Trantham-Davidson, H., Jairl, C., Cannon, T. D., Lavin, A., et al. (2011). Reduced dysbindin expression mediates N-methyl-D-aspartate receptor hypofunction and impaired working memory performance. *Biological Psychiatry, 69*, 28–34.

Kawakubo, Y., Suga, M., Tochigi, M., Yumoto, M., Itoh, K., Sasaki, T., et al. (2011). Effects of metabotropic glutamate receptor 3 genotype on phonetic mismatch negativity. *PLoS One, 6*, e24929.

Kempf, L., Nicodemus, K. K., Kolachana, B., Vakkalanka, R., Verchinski, B. A., Egan, M. F., et al. (2008). Functional polymorphisms in PRODH are associated with risk and protection for schizophrenia and fronto-striatal structure and function. *PLoS Genetics, 4*, e1000252.

Kéri, S., Beniczky, S., & Kelemen, O. (2010). Suppression of the P50 evoked response and neuregulin 1-induced AKT phosphorylation in first-episode schizophrenia. *American Journal of Psychiatry, 167*, 444–450.

Kim, J. Y., Duan, X., Liu, C. Y., Jang, M. H., Guo, J. U., Pow-anpongkul, N., Kang, E., Song, H., & Ming, G. L. (2009). DISC1 regulates new neuron development in the adult brain via modulation of AKT-mTOR signaling through KIAA1212. *Neuron, 63*, 761–773.

Kim, J. Y., Liu, C. Y., Zhang, F., Duan, X., Wen, Z., Song, J., et al. (2012). Interplay between DISC1 and GABA signaling regulates neurogenesis in mice and risk for schizophrenia. *Cell, 148*, 1051–1064.

Kinon, B. J., Zhang, L., Millen, B. A., Osuntokun, O. O., Williams, J. E., Kollack-Walker, S., & HBBI Study Group., et al. (2011). A multicenter, inpatient, phase 2, double-blind, placebo-controlled dose-ranging study of LY2140023 monohydrate in patients with DSM-IV schizophrenia. *Journal of Clinical Psychopharmacology, 31*, 349–355.

Kirov, G., Pocklington, A. J., Holmans, P., Ivanov, D., Ikeda, M., Ruderfer, D., et al. (2012). De novo CNV analysis implicates specific abnormalities of postsynaptic signalling complexes in the pathogenesis of schizophrenia. *Molecular Psychiatry, 17*, 142–153.

Kirov, G., Rujescu, D., Ingason, A., Collier, D. A., O'Donovan, M. C., & Owen, M. J. (2009). Neurexin 1 (NRXN1) deletions in schizophrenia. *Schizophrenia Bulletin, 35*, 851–854.

Kozlovsky, N., Belmaker, R. H., & Agam, G. (2001). Low GSK-3 activity in frontal cortex of schizophrenic patients. *Schizophrenia Research, 52*, 101–105.

Lane, T. A., Boerner, T., Bannerman, D. M., Kew, J. N., Tunbridge, E. M., Sharp, T., et al. (2013). Decreased striatal dopamine in group II metabotropic glutamate receptor (mGlu2/mGlu3) double knock-out mice. *BMC Neuroscience, 14*, 102.

Lang, U. E., Puls, I., Muller, D. J., Strutz-Seebohm, N., & Gallinat, J. (2007). Molecular mechanisms of schizophrenia. *Cellular and Physiological Biochemistry, 20*, 687–702.

Law, A. J., Wang, Y., Sei, Y., O'Donnell, P., Piantadosi, P., Papaleo, F., et al. (2012). Neuregulin 1-ErbB4-PI3K signaling in schizophrenia and phosphoinositide 3-kinase-p110δ inhibition as a potential therapeutic strategy. *Proceedings of the National Academy of Sciences of the United States of America, 109*, 12165–12170.

Lee, F. H., Kaidanovich-Beilin, O., Roder, J. C., Woodgett, J. R., & Wong, A. H. (2011). Genetic inactivation of GSK3α rescues spine deficits in Disc1-L100P mutant mice. *Schizophrenia Research, 129*, 74–79.

Levinson, D. F., Shi, J., Wang, K., Oh, S., Riley, B., Pulver, A. E., & Schizophrenia Psychiatric GWAS Consortium., et al. (2012). Genome-wide association study of multiplex schizophrenia pedigrees. *American Journal of Psychiatry, 169*, 963–973.

Lewis, D. A., Melchitzky, D. S., Sesack, S. R., Whitehead, R. E., Auh, S., & Sampson, A. (2001). Dopamine transporter immunoreactivity in monkey cerebral cortex: regional, laminar, and ultrastructural localization. *Journal of Comparative Neurology, 432*, 119–136.

Li, D., & He, L. (2007). G72/G30 genes and schizophrenia: a systematic meta-analysis of association studies. *Genetics, 175*, 917–922.

Lipina, T. V., Kaidanovich-Beilin, O., Patel, S., Wang, M., Clapcote, S. J., Liu, F., et al. (2011). Genetic and pharmacological evidence for schizophrenia-related Disc1 interaction with GSK-3. *Synapse, 65*, 234–248.

Lipina, T. V., Wang, M., Liu, F., & Roder, J. C. (2012). Synergistic interactions between PDE4B and GSK-3: DISC1 mutant mice. *Neuropharmacology, 62*, 1252–1262.

Lisman, J. E., Coyle, J. T., Green, R. W., Javitt, D. C., Benes, F. M., Heckers, S., et al. (2008). Circuit-based framework for understanding neurotransmitter and risk gene interactions in schizophrenia. *Trends in Neuroscience, 31*, 234–242.

Li, W., Zhang, Q., Oiso, N., Novak, E. K., Gautam, R., O'Brien, E. P., et al. (2003). Hermansky-Pudlak syndrome type 7 (HPS-7) results from mutant dysbindin, a member of the biogenesis of lysosome-related organelles complex 1 (BLOC-1). *Nature Genetics, 35*, 84–89.

Lvovs, D., Favorova, O. O., & Favorov, A. V. (2012). A polygenic approach to the study of polygenic diseases. *Acta Naturae, 4*, 59–71.

Lyon, L., Burnet, P. W., Kew, J. N., Corti, C., Rawlins, J. N., Lane, T., et al. (2011). Fractionation of spatial memory in GRM2/3 (mGlu2/mGlu3) double knockout mice reveals a role for group II metabotropic glutamate receptors at the interface between arousal and cognition. *Neuropsychopharmacology, 36*, 2616–2628.

Lyon, L., Kew, J. N., Corti, C., Harrison, P. J., & Burnet, P. W. (2008). Altered hippocampal expression of glutamate receptors and transporters in GRM2 and GRM3 knockout mice. *Synapse, 62*, 842–850.

MacArthur, D. G., Manolio, T. A., Dimmock, D. P., Rehm, H. L., Shendure, J., Abecasis, G. R., Adams, D. R., Altman, R. B., Antonarakis, S. E., Ashley, E. A., Barrett, J. C., Biesecker, L. G., Conrad, D. F., Cooper, G. M., Cox, N. J., Daly, M. J., Gerstein, M. B., Goldstein, D. B., Hirschhorn, J. N., Leal, S. M., Pennacchio, L. A., Stamatoyannopoulos, J. A., Sunyaev, S. R., Valle, D., Voight, B. F., Winckler, W., & Gunter, C. (2014). Guidelines for investigating causality of sequence variants in human disease. *Nature, 508*, 469–476.

Mackay, T. F. (2014). Epistasis and quantitative traits: using model organisms to study gene-gene interactions. *Nature Review Genetics, 15*, 22–33.

Mackay, T. F., & Moore, J. H. (2014). Why epistasis is important for tackling complex human disease genetics. *Genome Medicine, 6*, 42.

Mao, Y., Ge, X., Frank, C. L., Madison, J. M., Koehler, A. N., Doud, M. K., et al. (2009). Disrupted in schizophrenia 1 regulates neuronal progenitor proliferation via modulation of GSK3beta/beta-catenin signalling. *Cell, 136*, 1017–1031.

Marenco, S., Steele, S. U., Egan, M. F., Goldberg, T. E., Straub, R. E., Sharrief, A. Z., et al. (2006). Effect of metabotropic glutamate receptor 3 genotype on *N*-acetylaspartate measures in the dorsolateral prefrontal cortex. *American Journal of Psychiatry, 163*, 740–742.

Mason, J. N., Farmer, H., Tomlinson, I. D., Schwartz, J. W., Savchenko, V., DeFelice, L. J., et al. (2005). Novel fluorescence-based approaches for the study of biogenic amine transporter localization, activity, and regulation. *Journal of Neuroscience Methods, 143*, 3–25.

Mata, I., Perez-Iglesias, R., Roiz-Santiañez, R., Tordesillas-Gutierrez, D., Gonzalez-Mandly, A., Berja, A., et al. (2010). Additive effect of NRG1 and DISC1 genes on lateral ventricle enlargement in first episode schizophrenia. *Neuroimage, 53*, 1016–1022.

Mata, I., Perez-Iglesias, R., Roiz-Santianez, R., Tordesillas-Gutierrez, D., Gonzalez-Mandly, A., Vazquez-Barquero, J. L., et al. (2009). A neuregulin 1 variant, is associated with increased lateral ventricle volume in patients with first-episode, schizophrenia. *Biological Psychiatry, 65*, 535–540.

McCarroll, S. A., Feng, G., & Hyman, S. E. (2014). Genome-scale neurogenetics: methodology and meaning. *Nature Neuroscience, 17*, 756–763.

McDonald, C., Marshall, N., Sham, P. C., Bullmore, E. T., Schulze, K., Chapple, B., et al. (2006). Regional brain, morphometry in patients with schizophrenia or bipolar disorder and their, unaffected relatives. *American Journal of Psychiatry, 163*, 478–487.

Meck, M. H., Cheng, R. K., MacDonald, C. J., Gainetdinov, R. R., Caron, M. G., & Cevik, M. O. (2012). Gene-dose dependent effects of methamphetamine on interval timing in dopamine-transporter mice. *Neuropharmacology, 62*, 1221–1229.

Mei, L., & Xiong, W. C. (2008). Neuregulin 1 in neural development, synaptic plasticity and schizophrenia. *Nature Reviews Neuroscience, 9*, 437–452.

Moran, P. M., O'Tuathaigh, C. M., Papaleo, F., & Waddington, J. L. (2014). Dopaminergic function in relation to genes associated with risk for schizophrenia: translational mutant mouse models. *Progress in Brain Research, 211*, 79–112.

Morita, Y., Callicott, J. H., Testa, L. R., Mighdoll, M. I., Dickinson, D., Chen, Q., et al. (2014). Characteristics of the cation cotransporter NKCC1 in human brain: alternate transcripts, expression in development, and potential relationships to brain function and schizophrenia. *Journal of Neuroscience, 34*, 4929–4940.

Morris, D. W., Murphy, K., Kenny, N., Purcell, S. M., McGhee, K. A., Schwaiger, S., et al. (2008). Dysbindin (DTNBP1) and the biogenesis of lysosome-related organelles complex 1 (BLOC-1): main and epistatic gene effects are potential contributors to schizophrenia susceptibility. *Biological Psychiatry, 63*, 24–31.

Mozhui, K., Wang, X., Chen, J., Mulligan, M. K., Li, Z., Ingles, J., et al. (2011). Genetic regulation of Nrxn1 [corrected] expression: an integrative cross-species analysis of schizophrenia candidate genes. *Translational Psychiatry, 1*, e25.

Nicodemus, K. K., Callicott, J. H., Higier, R. G., Luna, A., Nixon, D. C., Lipska, B. K., et al. (2010). Evidence of statistical epistasis between DISC1, CIT and NDEL1 impacting risk for schizophrenia: biological validation with functional neuroimaging. *Human Genetics, 127*, 441–452.

Nicodemus, K. K., Hargreaves, A., Morris, D., Anney, R., Gill, M., Corvin, A., & Schizophrenia Psychiatric Genome-wide Association Study (GWAS) Consortium, & Wellcome Trust Case Control Consortium 2., et al. (2014). Variability in working memory performance explained by epistasis vs polygenic scores in the ZNF804A pathway. *JAMA Psychiatry, 71*, 778–785.

Nicodemus, K. K., Kolachana, B. S., Vakkalanka, R., Straub, R. E., Giegling, I., Egan, M. F., et al. (2007). Evidence for statistical epistasis between catechol-O-methyltransferase (COMT) and polymorphisms in RGS4, G72 (DAOA), GRM3, and DISC1: influence on risk of schizophrenia. *Human Genetics, 120*, 889–906.

Nicodemus, K. K., Law, A. J., Radulescu, E., Luna, A., Kolachana, B., Vakkalanka, R., et al. (2010). Biological validation of increased schizophrenia risk with NRG1, ERBB4, and AKT1 epistasis via functional neuroimaging in healthy controls. *Archives of General Psychiatry, 67*, 991–1001.

Nixon, D. C., Prust, M. J., Sambataro, F., Tan, H. Y., Mattay, V. S., Weinberger, D. R., et al. (2011). Interactive effects of DAOA (G72) and catechol-O-methyltransferase on neurophysiology in prefrontal cortex. *Biological Psychiatry, 69*, 1006–1008.

Norton, N., Moskvina, V., Morris, D. W., Bray, N. J., Zammit, S., Williams, N. M., et al. (2006). Evidence that interaction between neuregulin 1 and its receptor erbB4 increases susceptibility to schizophrenia. *American Journal of Medical Genetics B Neuropsychiatric Genetics, 141*, 96–101.

Numakawa, T., Yagasaki, Y., Ishimoto, T., Okada, T., Suzuki, T., Iwata, N., et al. (2004). Evidence of novel neuronal functions of dysbindin, a susceptibility gene for schizophrenia. *Human Molecular Genetics, 13*, 2699–2708.

O'Tuathaigh, C. M., Desbonnet, L., & Waddington, J. L. (2014). Genetically modified mice related to schizophrenia and other psychoses: seeking phenotypic insights into the pathobiology and treatment of negative symptoms. *European Neuropsychopharmacology, 24*, 800–821.

O'Tuathaigh, C. M., Desbonnet, L., Perez-Branguli, F., Petit, E., O'Leary, C., Clarke, N., et al. (2012). *Mice with simultaneous disruption of DISC1 and NRG1 genes exhibit phenotypes related to schizophrenia.* Program No. 663.19. 2012 Neuroscience Meeting Planner. New Orleans, LA: Society for Neuroscience. Online.

O'Tuathaigh, C. M., & Waddington, J. L. (January 20, 2015). Closing the translational gap between mutant mouse models and the clinical reality of psychotic illness. *Neuroscience and Biobehavioural Reviews.* pii:S0149-7634(15) 00018-4.

van Os, J., & Kapur, S. (2009). Schizophrenia. *Lancet, 374*, 635–645.

van Os, J., Kenis, G., & Rutten, B. P. (2010). The environment and schizophrenia. *Nature, 468*, 203–212.

Owen, M. J. (2012). Implications of genetic findings for understanding schizophrenia. *Schizophrenia Bulletin, 38*, 904–907.

Papaleo, F., Burdick, M. C., Callicott, J. H., & Weinberger, D. R. (2014). Epistatic interaction between COMT and DTNBP1 modulates prefrontal function in mice and in humans. *Molecular Psychiatry, 19*, 311–316.

Papaleo, F., Crawley, J. N., Song, J., Lipska, B. K., Pickel, J., Weinberger, D. R., et al. (2008). Genetic dissection of the role of catechol-O-methyltransferase in cognition and stress reactivity in mice. *Journal of Neuroscience, 28,* 8709–8723.

Papaleo, F., Yang, F., Garcia, S., Chen, J., Lu, B., Crawley, J. N., et al. (2012). Dysbindin-1 modulates prefrontal cortical activity and schizophrenia-like behaviors via dopamine/D2 pathways. *Molecular Psychiatry, 17,* 85–98.

Patil, S. T., Zhang, L., Martenyi, F., Lowe, S. L., Jackson, K. A., Andreev, B. V., et al. (2007). Activation of mGlu2/3 receptors as a new approach to treat schizophrenia: a randomized Phase 2 clinical trial. *Nature Medicine, 13,* 1102–1107.

Pauli, A., Prata, D. P., Mechelli, A., Picchioni, M., Fu, C. H., Chaddock, C. A., et al. (2013). Interaction between effects of genes coding for dopamine and glutamate transmission on striatal and parahippocampal function. *Human Brain Mapping, 34,* 2244–2258.

Peineau, S., Taghibiglou, C., Bradley, C., Wong, T. P., Liu, L., Lu, J., et al. (2007). LTP inhibits LTD in the hippocampus via regulation of GSK3β. *Neuron, 53,* 703–717.

Prasad, K. M., Talkowski, M. E., Chowdari, K. V., McClain, L., Yolken, R. H., & Nimgaonkar, V. L. (2010). Candidate genes and their interactions with other genetic/environmental risk factors in the etiology of schizophrenia. *Brain Research Bulletin, 83,* 86–92.

Prata, D. P., Mechelli, A., Fu, C. H., Picchioni, M., Toulopoulou, T., Bramon, E., et al. (2009). Epistasis between the DAT 3′ UTR VNTR and the COMT Val158Met SNP on cortical function in healthy subjects and patients with schizophrenia. *Proceedings of the National Academy of Sciences of the United States of America, 106,* 13600–13605.

Pratt, J., Winchester, C., Dawson, N., & Morris, B. (2012). Advancing schizophrenia drug discovery: optimizing rodent models to bridge the translational gap. *Nature Reviews Drug Discovery, 11,* 560–579.

Purcell, S. M., Moran, J. L., Fromer, M., Ruderfer, D., Solovieff, N., Roussos, P., O'Dushlaine, C., Chambert, K., Bergen, S. E., Kähler, A., Duncan, L., Stahl, E., Genovese, G., Fernández, E., Collins, M. O., Komiyama, N. H., Choudhary, J. S., Magnusson, P. K., Banks, E., Shakir, K., Garimella, K., Fennell, T., DePristo, M., Grant, S. G., Haggarty, S. J., Gabriel, S., Scolnick, E. M., Lander, E. S., Hultman, C. M., Sullivan, P. F., McCarroll, S. A., & Sklar, P. (2014). A polygenic burden of rare disruptive mutations in schizophrenia. *Nature, 506,* 185–190.

Purcell, S. M., Moran, J. L., Fromer, M., Ruderfer, D., Solovieff, N., Roussos, P., et al. (2009). A polygenic burden of rare disruptive mutations in schizophrenia. *Nature, 506,* 185–190.

Rapoport, J. L., Giedd, J. N., & Gogtay, N. (2012). Neurodevelopmental model of schizophrenia: update 2012. *Molecular Psychiatry, 17,* 1228–1238.

Ripke, S., O'Dushlaine, C., Chambert, K., Moran, J. L., Kähler, A. K., Akterin, S., & Multicenter Genetic Studies of Schizophrenia Consortium, & Psychosis Endophenotypes International Consortium, & Wellcome Trust Case Control Consortium 2., et al. (2013). Genome-wide association analysis identifies 13 new risk loci for schizophrenia. *Nature Genetics, 45,* 1150–1159.

Ritchie, M. D., Hahn, L. W., Roodi, N., Bailey, L. R., Dupont, W. D., Parl, F. F., et al. (2001). Multifactor-dimensionality reduction reveals high-order interactions among estrogen-metabolism genes in sporadic breast cancer. *American Journal of Human Genetics, 69,* 138–147.

Ruderfer, D. M., Fanous, A. H., Ripke, S., McQuillin, A., Amdur, R. L., Schizophrenia Working Group of Psychiatric Genomics Consortium, Bipolar Disorder Working Group of Psychiatric Genomics Consortium, Cross-Disorder Working Group of Psychiatric Genomics Consortium, Gejman, P. V., et al. (2014). Polygenic dissection of diagnosis and clinical dimensions of bipolar disorder and schizophrenia. *Molecular Psychiatry, 19,* 1017–1024.

Schizophrenia Psychiatric Genome-Wide Association Study (GWAS) Consortium. (2011). Genome-wide association study identifies five new schizophrenia loci. *Nature Genetics, 43,* 969–976.

Schizophrenia Working Group of the Psychiatric Genomics Consortium. (2014). Biological insights from 108 schizophrenia-associated genetic loci. *Nature, 511,* 421–427.

Schumacher, J., Laje, G., Abou Jamra, R., Becker, T., Mühleisen, T. W., Vasilescu, C., et al. (2009). The DISC locus and schizophrenia: evidence from an association study in a central European sample and from a meta-analysis across different European populations. *Human Molecular Genetics, 18,* 2719–2727.

Shao, H., Burrage, L. C., Sinasac, D. S., Hill, A. E., Ernest, S. R., O'Brien, W., Courtland, H. W., Jepsen, K. J., Kirby, A., Kulbokas, E. J., Daly, M. J., Broman, K. W., Lander, E. S., & Nadeau, J. H. (2008). Genetic architecture of complex traits: Large phenotypic effects and pervasive epistasis. *Proceedings of the National Academy of Sciences U S A, 105,* 19910–19914.

Shiota, S., Tochigi, M., Shimada, H., Ohashi, J., Kasai, K., Kato, N., et al. (2008). Association and interaction analyses of NRG1 and ERBB4 genes with schizophrenia in a Japanese population. *Journal of Human Genetics, 53,* 929–935.

Stefansson, H., Rujescu, D., Cichon, S., Pietiläinen, O. P., Ingason, A., Steinberg, S., et al. (2008). Large recurrent microdeletions associated with schizophrenia. *Nature, 455,* 232–236.

Stefansson, H., Sigurdsson, E., Steinthorsdottir, V., Bjornsdottir, S., Sigmundsson, T., Ghosh, S., et al. (2002). Neuregulin 1 and susceptibility to schizophrenia. *American Journal of Human Genetics, 71,* 877–892.

Sullivan, P. F., Kendler, K. S., & Neale, M. C. (2003). Schizophrenia as a complex trait: evidence from a meta-analysis of twin studies. *Archives of General Psychiatry, 60,* 1187–1192.

Svenningsson, P., Lindskog, M., Ledent, C., Parmentier, M., Greengard, P., Fredholm, B. B., et al. (2000). Regulation of the phosphorylation of the dopamine- and cAMP-regulated phosphoprotein of 32 kDa in vivo by dopamine D1, dopamine D2, and adenosine A2A receptors. *Proceedings of the National Academy of Sciences of the United States of America, 97,* 1856–1860.

Svenningsson, P., Tzavara, E. T., Carruthers, R., Rachleff, I., Wattler, S., Nehls, M., et al. (2003). Diverse psychotomimetics act through a common signaling pathway. *Science, 302,* 1412–1415.

Tan, H. Y., Chen, Q., Sust, S., Buckholtz, J. W., Meyers, J. D., Egan, M. F., et al. (2007). Epistasis between catechol-O-methyltransferase and type II metabotropic glutamate receptor 3 genes on working memory brain function. *Proceedings of the National Academy of Sciences of the United States of America, 104,* 12536–12541.

Tan, H. Y., Nicodemus, K. K., Chen, Q., Li, Z., Brooke, J. K., Honea, R., et al. (2008). Genetic variation in AKT1 is linked to dopamine-associated prefrontal cortical structure and function in humans. *Journal of Clinical Investigation, 118,* 2200–2208.

Tost, H., Alam, T., & Meyer-Lindenberg, A. (2010). Dopamine and psychosis: theory, pathomechanisms and intermediate phenotypes. *Neuroscience and Biobehavioural Reviews, 34,* 689–700.

Vandenbergh, D. J., Persico, A. M., Hawkins, A. L., Griffin, C. A., Li, X., Jabs, E. W., et al. (1992). Human dopamine transporter gene (DAT1) maps to chromosome 5p15.3 and displays a VNTR. *Genomics, 14,* 1104–1106.

Veltman, J. A., & Brunner, H. G. (2012). De novo mutations in human genetic disease. *Nature Reviews Genetics, 13,* 565–575.

Verrall, L., Walker, M., Rawlings, N., Benzel, I., Kew, J. N. C., Harrison, P. J., et al. (2007). D-amino acid oxidase and serine racemase in human brain: normal distribution and altered expression in schizophrenia. *European Journal of Neuroscience, 26,* 1657–1669.

Vita, A., De Peri, L., Silenzi, C., & Dieci, M. (2006). Brain morphology in first-episode, schizophrenia: a meta-analysis of quantitative magnetic resonance imaging, studies. *Schizophrenia Research, 82,* 75–88.

Waddington, J. L., Corvin, A. P., Donohoe, G., O'Tuathaigh, C. M. P., Mitchell, K. J., & Gill, M. (2007). Functional genomics and schizophrenia: endophenotypes and mutant models. *Psychiatric Clinics of North America, 30,* 365–399.

Waddington, J. L., Hennessy, R. J., O'Tuathaigh, C. M. P., Owoeye, O., & Russell, V. (2012). Schizophrenia and the lifetime trajectory of psychotic illness: developmental neuroscience and pathobiology, redux. In A. S. Brown, & P. H. Patterson (Eds.), *The origins of schizophrenia* (pp. 3–21). New York: Columbia University Press.

Williams, H. J., Owen, M. J., & O'Donovan, M. C. (2007). Is COMT a susceptibility gene for schizophrenia? *Schizophrenia Bulletin, 33,* 635–641.

Winchester, C. L., Pratt, J. A., & Morris, B. J. (2014). Risk genes for schizophrenia: translational opportunities for drug discovery. *Pharmacology and Therapeutics, 143,* 34–50.

Woodgett, J. R. (1990). Molecular cloning and expression of glycogen synthase kinase-3/factor A. *EMBO Journal, 9,* 2431–2438.

Wu, M. C., Kraft, P., Epstein, M. P., Taylor, D. M., Chanock, S. J., Hunter, D. J., et al. (2010). Powerful SNP-set analysis for case-control genome-wide association studies. *American Journal of Human Genetics, 86,* 929–942.

Wu, M. C., Lee, S., Cai, T., Li, Y., Boehnke, M., & Lin, X. (2011). Rare-variant association testing for sequencing data with the sequence kernel association test. *American Journal of Human Genetics, 89,* 82–93.

Zhao, Z., Ksiezak-Reding, H., Riggio, S., Haroutunian, V., & Pasinetti, G. M. (2006). Insulin receptor deficits in schizophrenia and in cellular and animal models of insulin receptor dysfunction. *Schizophrenia Research, 84,* 1–14.

Zinkstok, J., Schmitz, N., van Amelsvoort, T., Moeton, M., Baas, F., & Linszen, D. (2008). Genetic variation in COMT and PRODH is associated with brain anatomy in patients with schizophrenia. *Genes Brain and Behaviour, 7,* 61–69.

Zuk, O., Hechter, E., Sunyaev, S. R., & Lander, E. S. (2012). The mystery of missing heritability: genetic interactions create phantom heritability. *Proceedings of the National Academy of Sciences of the United States of America, 109,* 1193–1198.

20

Modeling Gene–Environment Interaction in Schizophrenia

Yan Jouroukhin*, Ross McFarland*,||, Yavuz Ayhan*,#,
Mikhail V. Pletnikov*,§,¶,||

*Department of Psychiatry and Behavioral Sciences, Johns Hopkins University School of Medicine, Baltimore, MD, USA; §Solomon H Snyder Department of Neuroscience, Johns Hopkins University School of Medicine, Baltimore, MD, USA; ¶Department of Molecular and Comparative Pathobiology, Johns Hopkins University School of Medicine, Baltimore, MD, USA; ||Department of Molecular Microbiology and Immunology, Johns Hopkins Bloomberg School of Public Health, Baltimore, MD, USA; #Department of Psychiatry, Faculty of Medicine, Hacettepe University, Sihhiye, Ankara, Turkey

INTRODUCTION

Awareness is increasing that the burden created by psychiatric disorders is enormous, as is the amount of research conducted on the causes of mental illnesses (Murray et al., 2012). With 0.5–0.7% of the human population affected by schizophrenia (Saha, Chant, Welham, & McGrath, 2005), it represents a major public health concern, having an overall disability burden exceeding that of many infectious diseases (Murray et al., 2012). Despite its enormous impact and the work being done to understand it, the disease is still defined by many variable symptoms without a single unifying definition of presentation. Put as simply as it is possible to, schizophrenia is a debilitating psychiatric disorder characterized by positive (e.g., hallucinations and delusion), negative (e.g., social withdrawal and flat affect), and cognitive impairment. These abnormalities usually lead to a lifelong disability, reduced socioeconomic status, and increased risk for suicide among patients (Goldberg et al., 2011).

Heterogeneous clinical manifestations and symptoms of schizophrenia overlap with those of other psychotic disorders (i.e., bipolar and substance-induced psychotic disorders). This continuity of presentation with other diseases, and also growing genetic evidence, has caused many researchers to question the very

concept of schizophrenia as a disorder (Berrios, Luque, & Villagran-Moreno, 2003). This uncertainty has also led to the development of diagnosis category-independent perspectives for psychotic disorders, including dimensional approach and research domain criteria matrix. van Os and Kapur (2009) propose to group symptoms of psychotic disorders into five dimensions, including psychosis ("the positive-symptom dimension"), avolition and social withdrawal ("the negative-symptom dimension"), cognitive impairments ("the cognitive-symptom dimension"), and affective disorders clustered into depressive and manic symptoms. Also reflecting this sea change in the view of schizophrenia disease, a review of schizophrenia by a group of prominent psychiatrists has led to the Fifth Edition of the *Diagnostic and Statistical Manual of Mental Disorders* now including dimensional assessments (Heckers et al., 2013).

Meta-analysis of twin studies has estimated the heritability for schizophrenia at approximately 80%, and the impact of environmental influences on risk to account for a value near 11% (Sullivan, Daly, & O'Donovan, 2012; Sullivan, Kendler, & Neale, 2003). The psychiatric research field is approaching consensus that gene–environment interaction (GEI) plays a considerable role in the pathogenesis of the disorder (van Os & Kapur, 2009; Uher, 2014). The chapter overviews existing animal models of GEI related to schizophrenia. In doing so, we

Handbook of Behavioral Neuroscience
http://dx.doi.org/10.1016/B978-0-12-800981-9.00020-1

suggest a modification in research approach. Given the complexity of human disease manifestation and etiology, the existing research highlights the need in focusing on modeling a specific disease as an etiologically and pathobiologically separate category (Nestler & Hyman, 2010). Instead, consistent with the main theme of the book (please, also see the chapter by John Waddington), we suggest that a dimensional approach will better facilitate mechanistic studies to understand GEI in schizophrenia and other psychotic disorders.

GENES AND ENVIRONMENT IN SCHIZOPHRENIA

The greatest progress in understanding the genetics of schizophrenia has comes from the large sample-sized genome-wide-association studies (GWAS). Psychiatric Genomics Consortium, established in 2007, is made up of more than 500 investigators from 25 countries (Sullivan, 2010). The latest Psychiatric Genomics Consortium paper describes the genotyping data of 36,989 cases and 113,075 controls. With this sample size, 108 loci contributing to risk of schizophrenia were identified including 25 replicating and 83 newly described risk markers. More than 70% of discovered loci were located in regions encoding proteins involved in dopaminergic and glutamatergic neurotransmission, calcium signaling, synaptic plasticity, potassium channels, and neurodevelopment (Schizophrenia Working Group of the Psychiatric Genomics Consortium, 2014). Single nucleotide polymorphisms in the extended major histocompatibility complex region on chromosome 6 were significantly associated with schizophrenia, suggesting etiological relevance of immune responses and inflammatory pathways (Shi et al., 2009; Sullivan et al., 2012). Genomic structural alterations also play an important role in etiology of schizophrenia (Walsh et al., 2008; the Chapter 15B by N. Hiroi). Various mutations affecting single genes were found in several families exhibiting large phenotypic abnormalities (Goate et al., 1991; Klein & Westenberger, 2012; Rogaev et al., 1995).

There are many environmental insults that have been found to be associated with schizophrenia. Among them are in utero exposure to infection, diet, perinatal complications, maternal malnutrition, stressful events during pregnancy, and early postnatal development as well as substance abuse (Brown, 2011; Meyer & Feldon, 2010). It is important to note, however, that the various environmental risk factors are suggested to lead to development of schizophrenia by engaging genetic liability for the disorder, which in itself is not enough to result in any clinical phenotype (van Os & Kapur, 2009; Rethelyi, Benkovits, & Bitter, 2013; Uher, 2014).

GENE–ENVIRONMENT INTERPLAY IN SCHIZOPHRENIA

Gene–environment interdependence encompasses the combined influence of genes and environment (Kendler & Eaves, 1986; Rutter, 2007; Rutter, Moffitt, & Caspi, 2006). Kendler and Eaves suggested two major models describing the combined effect of genes and environment on liability to psychiatric illness: gene–environment correlations (rGE) and GEI (Kendler & Eaves, 1986). rGEs are characterized by genetic differences in exposure to particular environments, whereas GEI is characterized by genetic differences in susceptibility to particular environments. The mechanistic explanations behind gene–environment interdependence can run the spectrum from highly complicated to intuitively simple. As an example of one of the simplest interplay mechanisms, we can consider the epigenetic modifications (Jaffe, Eaton, Straub, Marenco, & Weinberger, 2014). In this case, the environmental insult directly impacts the genetic background of the patient. Other interactions do not always offer such a direct linkage between genetics and environment.

rGE refer to genetically maintained predisposition toward certain environmental conditions (Plomin, DeFries, & Loehlin, 1977; Rutter, 2007). In other words, choice of environmental factors is driven by an individual's genetic predisposition to a particular milieu. rGE includes three main subtype: passive, active, and evocative. Passive correlation denotes effects of the environment in which child is raised and which is formed by genetic predisposition of his parents (or another external subject) to that environment. In other words, the genetically controlled parental behavior creates an environment that, in turn, influences the child's personality and behavior. Evocative correlation happens when an individual's genetically influenced behavior evokes an environmental response. A popular example of that rGE is maternal conflict, often occurring when one of the parents has a depressive disorder. Finally, active correlation is associated with an individual's inherited propensity toward active searching for a specific environment, and the results from exposure to that environment (Scarr & McCartney, 1983).

GEI includes a genetic control of responses to protective or adverse environment, and often a dependency of genetic effects on an environment (i.e., genetic effects can be stronger in one environment than in the other) (Rutter et al., 2006). In some cases, both GEI and rGE can be involved. As an example, polymorphisms of one of the genes for the alcohol dehydrogenase enzyme family, the ADH1B, contribute to fetal alcohol spectrum disorders (FASD). Whereas ADH1B*1 has been suggested to be a risk factor for FASD, ADH1B*2 and ADH1B*3 have been shown to reduce the risk for FASD. Because these gene variants have differential impacts on susceptibility to the effect of alcohol, they may refer to GEI. At the same time, the association between alcohol exposure in utero and FASD may refer to a passive rGE since mothers who carried the ADH1B*1 allele are identified to be at higher risk for greater alcohol consumption than mothers who carried the ADH1B*2 or 3. This example suggests that investigators who measure genes and environments should be observing for both rGE and GEI (Edenberg & Foroud, 2013).

Recent epidemiological studies have shed light on the underpinnings of GEI relevant to schizophrenia and related psychotic disorders (Modinos et al., 2013; van Winkel, van Beveren, Simons, & Genetic Risk and Outcome of Psychosis (GROUP) Investigators, 2011). Even if the available GEI results are limited, they have allowed for developing animal models to determine the molecular and neurobiological mechanisms, whereby environmental and genetic risk factors interact to lead to schizophrenia (Iyegbe, Campbell, Butler, Ajnakina, & Sham, 2014).

ANIMAL MODELS OF GEI RELEVANT TO SCHIZOPHRENIA

The main goal of animal models of GEI is to provide mechanistic insights into how genetic and environmental factors interact with each other to explain the heterogeneity of clinical manifestations and symptoms of schizophrenia (Ayhan et al., 2009; Hida et al., 2013; Kannan, Sawa, & Pletnikov, 2013; Rethelyi et al., 2013; van Winkel et al., 2011). The main environmental risk factors applied to GEI animal models can be largely separated into four groups: immune dysfunction, stress, substance abuse, and environmental toxins.

Models of Immune Activation

Several lines of evidence suggest that prenatal and early childhood infections increase the risk of schizophrenia. In particular, maternal infection and in utero exposure to influenza as well as toxoplasma have been shown to increase the risk of schizophrenia in offspring (Brown, 2011). One of the most popular approaches to simulate prenatal infection is maternal immune activation (MIA) using viral or bacterial-like immune activating agents (Meyer & Feldon, 2012; and Chapter 12A by Malkova et al.). This approach is widely used with mice carrying genetic variants of the candidate genes.

Interaction with DISC1

The first studies of GEI applying MIA to a genetic model were done using mice carrying human mutations of Disrupted-In-Schizophrenia (DISC1), a rare genetic factor associated with major psychiatric disorders (Porteous et al., 2011). DISC1 has been shown to regulate major neuronal functions, including neural proliferation, migration, dendritic arborization, spine formation, and the maintenance of synapses (Brandon & Sawa, 2011; Wen et al., 2014). Recently, the important role of DISC1 in regulation of mitochondrial functions, oligodendrocyte differentiation, and astrocyte functioning has also been demonstrated (Eykelenboom et al., 2012; Kim et al., 2012; Ma et al., 2013; Park et al., 2010; Wood, Bonath, Kumar, Ross, & Cunliffe, 2009). Our group generated a transgenic model of inducible expression of mutant human DISC1, a putative product of the translocation (Pletnikov et al., 2008). Expression of mutant DISC1 in forebrain neurons leads to increased spontaneous locomotor activity, decreased social interaction, and increased aggressive behavior in males and decreased spatial recognition memory in the Morris water maze in females.

To assess the interaction of DISC1 and MIA, mutant DISC1 mice were prenatally exposed to polyinosine-polycytidylic (poly I:C) treatment of pregnant dams (Abazyan et al., 2010). Injection of pregnant mice with poly I:C at gestational day (GD) 9 resulted in the altered pattern of secreted cytokines in the mutant DISC1 fetal brains. In addition, a prenatal exposure to poly I:C increased anxiety-like and depressive-like behaviors and decreased sociability in adult mice carrying DISC1 mutation. These findings have been correlated with the morphometric analysis of amygdala and periaqueductal gray matter, brain regions involved in the circuitries of fear and anxiety responses. The volumes of these regions were significantly decreased in mutant mice treated with poly I:C. In addition, MIA led to altered functioning of the hypothalamus-pituitary-adrenal axis by blunting the corticosterone response of DISC1 mice to restrain stress. Importantly, the expression of mutant DISC1 was necessary during the entire period of prenatal and postnatal development to induce neurobehavioral alterations following immune challenge (Abazyan et al., 2010).

Another group evaluated the effect of poly I:C exposure during early postnatal development using the mouse model constitutively expressing mutant DISC1 (Hikida et al., 2007). Poly I:C injection for 5 consecutive days from postnatal day (PND) 2 resulted in the impaired short-term memory in adulthood in both control and mutant mice. Yet, only in mutant DISC1 mice did it also produce impaired fear memory, increased locomotor activity, decreased social interaction, and increased aggressive behaviors. Moreover, immune response activated by poly I:C treatment in mutant DISC1 mice resulted in the decreased number of parvalbumin positive cells in the medial prefrontal cortex (PFC) and the increased number of BrdU-positive cells (an indicator of neurogenesis) in the granular cell layer of the dentate gyrus of the mouse hippocampus. This study has demonstrated that some schizophrenia-resembling abnormalities (e.g., reduced parvalbumin reactivity) can be precipitated by an early postnatal immune challenge in DISC1 mice (Ibi et al., 2010).

Interaction of poly I:C exposure with expression of mutant DISC1 genes were also investigated using *Disc1*-L100P and *Disc1*-Q31L mutant mice carrying Q31L and L100P point mutations in the second exon of the *Disc1* gene, respectively (Clapcote et al., 2007). Intact Q31L mutant mice demonstrate increased immobility in forced swim test (FST), decreased sociability and social novelty, and reduced sucrose consumption, consistent with depressive-like phenotypes. L100P mutant mice show the increased locomotor activity, decreased prepulse inhibition (PPI) of the acoustic startle and latent inhibition (LI) and a poor memory assessed in T-maze. Both Q31L and L100P heterozygous animals were challenged with poly I:C MIA at GD 9. MIA reduced sociability, worsened PPI deficit, and impaired novel object recognition in all tested animals. However, compared with wild-type (WT) animals and *Disc1*-Q31L, *Disc1*-L100P mutants were more sensitive to the effects of MIA, consistent with the concept of GEI. MIA also resulted in increased IL-6 expression in the fetal brains, with a strongest effect being observed in L100P mice. Notably, anti-interleukin-6 (IL-6) treatment reversed the poly I:C effects on PPI and LI in mutant mice, supporting the previous findings that IL-6 mediates adverse effects of MIA (Lipina, Zai, Hlousek, Roder, & Wong, 2013; Smith, Li, Garbett, Mirnics, & Patterson, 2007). Taken together, these studies of GEI in DISC1 mice exposed to MIA provide important data suggesting how an environmental factor could trigger pathological outcomes by interaction with risk gene factors.

Interaction with Nuclear Receptor Related-1 Protein

The nuclear receptor related-1 protein (Nurr1) is a transcription factor and orphan member of the steroid/thyroid nuclear receptor superfamily. The Nurr1 is expressed predominantly in mesencephalic dopaminergic neurons and regulates their differentiation during early development (Buervenich et al., 2000; Moore, Brown, Cade, & Eells, 2008; Xing, Zhang, Russell, & Post, 2006). Native heterozygous Nurr1 knockout (KO) mice, which are characterized by increased activity, display greater levels of activity following phencyclidine or amphetamine administration. This effect has been reversed by the typical antipsychotic drug, haloperidol (Rojas, Joodmardi, Hong, Perlmann, & Ogren, 2007). Altered dopamine (DA) and serotonin metabolism in the frontal cortex, striatum, and hippocampus of mutant animals (Rojas et al., 2007) has been accompanied with the increased immobility and impaired retention memory in males, suggesting a depression-like phenotype

of this mouse model. Interaction of MIA with mutant Nurr1 has been evaluated using poly I:C challenge at GD17. Treated mutants exhibited the increased locomotor activity, startle reactivity, PPI, and LI at PND 70–120. Immunohistochemical analysis revealed decreased tyrosine hydroxylase and increased catechol-*O*-methyltransferase (COMT) levels in nucleus accumbens and PFC staining. Curiously, poly I:C injection raised IL-6, IL-10, and tumor necrosis factor (TNF)-α production in WT animals but not in mutant mice which, in a naive state, had decreased levels of those factors (Vuillermot, Feldon, & Meyer, 2011; Vuillermot et al., 2012).

Interaction with Neuregulin-1

Neuregulin-1 (NRG1) is a protein that plays the important role in synaptic plasticity and neuroinflammation (Li, Woo, Mei, & Malinow, 2007). In addition, it has been shown that mutations in the NGB1 gene are associated with schizophrenia. NRG1 interacts with IL-1β and increases the activation of pro-inflammatory cytokines such as IL-6, IL-8, and TNF-α in patients with schizophrenia (Marballi et al., 2010). O'Leary et al. (2014) employed a complex design of cross-fostering to assess multiple effects of GEI, including dams' behaviors following an adverse environmental exposure during pregnancy. The study evaluated the schizophrenia-related interactions between MIA and NRG1. Several behavioral abnormalities were found depending on the combinations of NRG1, prenatal insult, and cross-fostering. The authors propose that numerous interactions of individual genes and different environmental factors are to be analyzed and recreated in future animal models.

Modeling of Stress

Multiple observations lead to an increasing appreciation that stress is a major environmental risk factor for psychiatric illness (Dvir, Denietolis, & Frazier, 2013; Fine, Zhang, & Stevens, 2014; van Winkel et al., 2008). To modulate stressful events in animals several different approaches can be used. The most popular ones are prenatal stress (Hillerer, Neumann, & Slattery, 2012; Markham & Koenig, 2011), maternal separation (Boccia et al., 2007), or social defeat paradigm (Willner et al., 1984; Nestler & Hyman, 2010). Several recent reviews have described the effects of the prenatal and postnatal stresses on the activity of the hypothalamus-pituitary-adrenal axis and resultant behavioral phenotypes, and readers are directed to these reviews (Koenig, 2006; Weinstock, 2005; also, please see the Chapter 12C by F. Cirulli).

Interaction with Reelin

Reelin is a large extracellular matrix glycoprotein involved in neuronal migration in the developing brain through control of cell–cell interactions

(Rogers & Weeber, 2008). The lack of reelin expression in mutant reeler mice leads to defects in neuronal position and dendrite development. Reelin messenger RNA (mRNA) and protein levels have been found to decrease in brain (Impagnatiello et al., 1998) and blood (Fatemi, Kroll, & Stary, 2001) of schizophrenia patients. The decreased neuronal levels of reelin were accompanied with increased activity of D-N-methyltransferase, suggesting that hypermethylation in the reelin promoter might be responsible for decreased reelin expression (Eastwood & Harrison, 2003; Grayson et al., 2005; Ruzicka et al., 2007). Yet, while a reduced reelin level has been confirmed by many studies (Fatemi, Earle, & McMenomy, 2000; Guidotti et al., 2000), some works failed to reproduce these results (Tochigi et al., 2008). Therefore, this suggests that additional factors can be implicated in the reelin-related pathophysiology of schizophrenia.

Early maternal separation was associated with reduced reelin, brain-derived neurotrophic factor (BDNF), and glia-derived neurotrophic factor levels over the developing period in WT mice (Ognibene et al., 2008; Zhang, Qin, & Zhao, 2013). Interactions between early maternal separation and reeler expression have been studied using a protocol of 5 h of daily maternal separation applied from PND 2–6 (Laviola, Adriani, Gaudino, Marino, & Keller, 2006). The social motivation was assessed by the homing test paradigm conducted on PND 9. During this test the locomotor activity directed by motivation to find the nest was measured. However, whereas maternal separation applied to WT mice significantly reduced social motivation, homozygous and heterozygous reeler mice were found unaffected (Ognibene, Adriani, Macri, & Laviola, 2007). Also, the decreased body weight found in WT mice after maternal separation was not detected in heterozygous reeler mice. Furthermore, maternal separation resulted in a smaller decline in expression of BDNF and glia-derived neurotrophic factor but enhanced stimulating effects of antipsychotic treatment on BDNF levels. Moreover, reelin level was up regulated in 3-month-old male mice as a result of maternal separation. These observations allowed the authors to hypothesize that the "beneficial" effects of maternal separation in reeler mice may result from a compensation of neural plasticity defects, most probably by the activation of hormonal steroid pathways.

Interaction with Nurr1

Another approach to recapitulate aspects of childhood trauma includes social isolation (SI) during adolescence. SI between PND 19–21 of heterozygous Nurr1 mice has been shown to result in impaired PPI when assessed 12 weeks after the cessation of isolation in adult mice and was accompanied by decreased levels of DA and dihydroxyphenylacetic acid in the PFC in mutants but not in WT animals (Eells, Misler, & Nikodem, 2006). However, corticosterone levels measured in mutants and controls before and after isolation did not reveal any group differences, suggesting that SI does not affect stress reactivity in mutant mice (Eells et al., 2006).

Interaction with SEPT5

The effects of SI were also studies in a mouse model of the SEPTIN5 (SEPT5) gene. The gene is located within 22q11 region, and therefore it has long been considered as a possible risk factor for schizophrenia (Harper et al., 2012). SEPT5 is expressed in the brain both during neurodevelopment and adulthood (Asada et al., 2010) and involved in vesicular exocytosis by binding to syntaxin in presynaptic soluble N-ethylmaleimide-sensitive factor attachment receptor complexes (Beites, Campbell, & Trimble, 2005). SEPT5 KO mice exhibit decreased social interaction, increased PPI, and spent more time in the open arms of the elevated plus maze. SEPT5 deletion was also associated with the longer latency to reach the goal in the L-maze. However, no differences were observed in spontaneous activity, T-maze, rewarded alternation, and tail suspension tests (Suzuki et al., 2009). Moreover, virally guided overexpression of SEPT5 in the hippocampus or amygdala enhanced social interaction in C57BL/6J mice. In addition, it has been shown that individually postweaning housing leads to the elevated SEPT5 level in the amygdala and increased active affiliated social interaction in comparison to group-housed animals. Compared with group-housed mutants, single-housed mice demonstrated less thigmotaxis in open field, spent more time in the open arms of the elevated plus maze, and spent more time in active social interaction compared with group housed mutants, consistent with reduced anxiety levels. This study is another example when seemingly adverse environmental effects may interact with a genetic mutation to ameliorate the negative effects of either one presented separately (Harper et al., 2012).

Interaction with Pituitary Adenylate Cyclase-Activating Polypeptide

Pituitary adenylate cyclase-activating polypeptide (PACAP) is a neuropeptide that displays structural similarity to vasoactive intestinal peptide and a member of the secretin/glucagon/vasoactive intestinal peptide family. PACAP is crucial for the regulation of circadian rhythms, axonal maturation, axonal integrity, and cellular stress responses (Waschek, 2013). PACAP is encoded by the ADYCAP1 gene located in locus associated with schizophrenia to 18p11.32 (Faraone et al., 2005; Mukherjee et al., 2006; Schwab et al., 1998). In addition, ADYCAP1 variants were associated with schizophrenia, deficits in verbal memory, and hippocampal volume (Hashimoto et al., 2007; Koga et al., 2010). Moreover, PACAP directly interacts with DISC1-Binding Zinc-finger protein resulting in increased DISC1 expression and reduction in neurite outgrowth, both of which are suggested as factors potentially relevant to schizophrenia (Hattori et al., 2007).

In a study addressing whether stress can modulate the phenotype of mice lacking the Adycap1 gene, animals have been subjected to two different rearing conditions, namely a short-term SI at PND 28 or environmental enrichment (EE) starting at PND 28 or 56. SI applied to Adcyap1$^{-/-}$ mice resulted in increased locomotor activity, decreased latency to attack, and increased attacking time in social interaction tests, suggesting elevated aggression. In addition, SI further led to decreased PPI in mutants. On the contrary, EE started from PND 28 but not from PND 56 decreased hyperactivity; increased time spent in social interaction tests and decreased duration of immobility in FST. Importantly, that this applied earlier EE worsened the results of PPI in Adcyap1$^{-/-}$ mice (Ishihama et al., 2010), suggesting that outcome of EE × PACAP is time-dependent and cannot be explain by "rescue" effects of positive environment.

Thus, ameliorative effects of cannot be generalized to all behavioral changes, with some, in fact, possibly being adverse (Burrows, McOmish, & Hannan, 2011; Takuma, Ago, & Matsuda, 2011). Still, exposing mutants to may shed some light on this "preventive" therapy and might point to treatments of the cognitive and negative symptoms that resistant to the current antipsychotics (Pratt, Winchester, Dawson, & Morris, 2012).

Interaction with DISC1

Recently, a dominant negative mouse model with expression of mutant DISC1 under the PrP promoter was used to study stress effect on animals expressing DISC1 mutation. Mutant and control were exposed to 3-week isolation from 5 to 8 weeks of age. It was found that only mutants exposed to SI displayed increased locomotor activity, deficient PPI, and increased immobility in FST, suggesting GxE effects. These effects were associated with decreased extracellular levels of DA and tyrosine hydroxylase expression, and increased D2R expression in the frontal cortex and increased DA levels in the nucleus accumbens, the main forebrain targets of DA projections of the ventral tegmental area. SI applied to these mice resulted in increased corticosterone level, hypomethylation of the tyrosine hydroxylase promoter, and selectively reduced tyrosine hydroxylase expression in the mesocortical pathway. Treatment with glucocorticoid receptor antagonist, mifepristone, rescued the SI-induced behavioral and biochemical abnormalities (Niwa et al., 2013).

The GEI effects of chronic social defeat (CSD) were evaluated in mice carrying Q31L or L100P *Disc1*

mutations. CSD applied at PND 50 for 20 days resulted in increased time spent in open arms of the elevated plus maze in Q31L mice. However, this time was significantly decreased in L100P mice after CSD. Also, CSD led to diminished PPI and enhanced sociability and social novelty in L100P mutants (Haque, Lipina, Roder, & Wong, 2012).

Interaction with Glutamic Acid Decarboxylase

Glutamic acid decarboxylase (GAD) is an enzyme responsible for conversion of glutamate to gamma-aminobutyric acid (GABA). Decreased expression of GAD, specifically the GAD67 isoform, has been found in Parvalbumin-positive interneurons in the PFC of schizophrenia patients (Akbarian et al., 1995; Beneyto, Morris, Rovensky, & Lewis, 2012; Curley et al., 2011; Hashimoto et al., 2003; Kimoto, Bazmi, & Lewis, 2014; Volk, Austin, Pierri, Sampson, & Lewis, 2000; Volk et al., 2012). Reduced GAD67 expression has also been accompanied with increased levels of DNA methyltransferases, which silence transcription by methylation of the promoter region (Veldic, Guidotti, Maloku, Davis, & Costa, 2005). Recent data suggest that methylation is a dynamic process that can be activated in response to stressful environmental factors and lead to abnormal development and functions of GABAergic neurons (Fine et al., 2014). Prenatal stress has been used in an animal model that was designed as knock-in mice expressing green fluorescence protein under GAD67 promoter to label GAD67-positive interneurons (Tamamaki et al., 2003). Therefore, heterozygous mice have reduced GAD67 expression and can be considered as a knock-down GAD67 model (Tamamaki et al., 2003). Restraint-and-light stress at GD17 increased maternal cortisol levels in both WT and knock-down GAD67 mothers, with mutant having a greater increase. Maternal stress resulted in decreased fetal body weight, which was much lower in the mutant fetuses. Moreover, fetal cortisol levels in mutants were much higher (Uchida, Oki, Yanagawa, & Fukuda, 2011). Restraint-light stress during GD15–17.5 was associated with the decreased number of parvalbumin-positive interneurons in the PFC, somatosensory cortex, and hippocampus of mutant offspring only (Uchida, Furukawa, Iwata, Yanagawa, & Fukuda, 2014).

Interaction with Synaptosomal-Associated Protein-25

Synaptosomal-associated protein-25 (SNAP25) is a presynaptic protein that takes part in vesicular exocytosis (Chen & Scheller, 2001), neurite outgrowth (Wu et al., 2011), and long-term potentiation (Jurado et al., 2013). Evaluation of synaptic proteins in the postmortem samples revealed decreased SNAP25 levels in the frontal and temporal lobes (Karson et al., 1999; Thompson, Sower, & Perrone-Bizzozero, 1998), and also in the entorhinal cortex (Young et al., 1998), hippocampus (Fatemi, Earle, Stary, Lee, & Sedgewick, 2001; Thompson, Egbufoama, & Vawter, 2003), and cerebellum (Mukaetova-Ladinska, Hurt, Honer, Harrington, & Wischik, 2002) of schizophrenia patients. Additional evidence for the role of SNAP25 came from relatively small-scale genetic epidemiologic studies, some of which reported positive association with SNAP25 variants and schizophrenia (Carroll, Kendall, O'Donovan, Owen, & Williams, 2009; Lochman, Balcar, Stastny, & Sery, 2013), but negative studies also exist (Dai et al., 2014; Kawashima et al., 2008). I67T point mutation in SNAP25 results in an increased binding affinity within the core SNARE complex, preventing the normal recycling of synaptic vesicles. Mice carrying this dominant mutation were named blind-drunk (Bdr) because of its distinctive ataxic gait (Jeans et al., 2007). Bdr mice displayed PPI impairment, reduced social interaction, and exploratory behavior (Jeans et al., 2007). Circadian rhythm impairment, namely phase advance in the sleep pattern, as well as altered blood corticosterone and arginine-vasopressin levels have been observed in these mice (Oliver et al., 2012). Stressful treatment of Bdr and control mice resulted in reduced PPI that could be improved with antipsychotics (Oliver & Davies, 2009). However, only Bdr mice subjected to prenatal stress showed decreased time spent with another mouse (as a sociability index) and decreased time spent with a novel stranger mouse (as a social novelty index).

Interaction with NRG1

NRG-1 mutations are associated with impairments in glutamatergic, dopaminergic, and GABAergic neurotransmission (Li et al., 2007; Newell, Karl, & Huang, 2013). Nrg1 is necessary for the establishment of excitatory synapses in GABAergic interneurons and for the development of a balanced excitatory/inhibitory tone in the brain (Ting et al., 2011). The association of NRG1 and schizophrenia was first suggested in a large Icelandic sample (Stefansson et al., 2002). Follow-up epidemiologic studies reported both positive and negative associations of different NRG1 variants and schizophrenia (Iwata et al., 2004; Li et al., 2004; Stefansson et al., 2003; Thiselton et al., 2004; Williams et al., 2003). Several postmortem studies indicated increased NRG1 signaling in schizophrenic patients (Chong et al., 2008; Hahn et al., 2006; Hashimoto et al., 2004). Upregulation of NRG1 signaling leads to increased GABAergic inhibition of glutamatergic pyramidal neurons, resulting in a hypoglutamatergic state (Deng, Pan, Engel, & Huang, 2013; Mei & Nave, 2014; Mei & Xiong, 2008). Also, NRG1 polymorphism interacts with the psychosocial stress modifying reactivity to expressed emotions in schizophrenia patients (Kéri et al., 2009). Therefore, several research teams have investigated the response of Nrg1 rodent models to stress. A NRG1 knock-down model carrying

mutation in the transmembrane domain has demonstrated increased spontaneous activity, an anxiolytic-like phenotype, and PPI deficiency (Golub, Germann, & Lloyd, 2004). CSD was applied to these mutants starting on PND35. When evaluated at adulthood, CSD in Nrg1 mutant mice decreased locomotor activity, numbers of alternation in Y-maze, decreased the proportion of time spent with a novel subject in a social interaction test, and increased the number of walkovers in social investigation. Analyses of selected immunological variables were carried out and revealed that CSD in mutants differentially increased the levels of basal cytokines and caused variable changes in IL-1β and TNF-α levels in different brain regions (Desbonnet et al., 2012).

Modeling Substance Abuse

Cannabis

Long-term and high-dose cannabis use during adolescence significantly increase the risk for schizophrenia development in adulthood (Andreasson, Allebeck, Engstrom, & Rydberg, 1987; Arseneault et al., 2002; Fergusson, Horwood, & Ridder, 2005; van Os et al., 2002). Also, epidemiologic studies indicate that early use of cannabis is associated with an earlier onset of schizophrenic symptoms (Barnes, Mutsatsa, Hutton, Watt, & Joyce, 2006). Still, the role of cannabis use in schizophrenia remains poorly understood. One suggestion is that heavy cannabis usage during adolescence may have particularly harmful effects on cognition and the development of psychoses in genetically vulnerable individuals (Murray et al., 2012). Clinical and preclinical studies have suggested that genes encoding to proteins involved in DA signaling can contribute to the cannabis–psychosis association (O'Tuathaigh et al., 2012).

Interaction with COMT

COMT is an enzyme involved in degradation of DA, the role of which has been extensively evaluated as it relates to the pathogenesis of schizophrenia. Also, increased risk of psychosis was associated with deletion of 22q11, where COMT gene is located (Gothelf et al., 2014; Karayiorgou et al., 1998; Murphy, Jones, & Owen, 1999; Paterlini et al., 2005). In addition, the COMT Val-158Met polymorphism was demonstrated to moderate the effects of cannabis use on adult psychosis (Heim, Coyne, Kamboh, Ryan, & Jennings, 2013; Mueller, Makeig, Stemmler, Hennig, & Wacker, 2011; Nixon et al., 2011; Ucok, Ozturk, Duman, & Saruhan-Direskeneli, 2010; Wirgenes et al., 2010).

COMT-deficient mice have been available for close to two decades, allowing for several interesting lines of inquiry with this model (Gogos et al., 1998). Homozygous mice have no COMT activity, accompanied with increased levels of dihydroxyphenylacetic acid and homovanillic acid, but no changes in striatal, cortical, or hypothalamic content of DA or noradrenaline (Huotari et al., 2002). Heterozygous mutants displayed increased sifting and chewing, and reduced "free" rearing (Babovic et al., 2007). To evaluate possible effects of GEI between cannabis and COMT variants, COMT-deficient mice were exposed to chronic adolescent tetrahydrocannabinol (THC) treatment, an active ingredient of cannabis, at PND 32–52. Adolescent THC treatment led to increased exploration, impairment in spatial working memory, and a stronger antianxiety effect in COMT KO mice compared with WT. The study demonstrated interaction between genes and adverse environmental exposures over adolescence a particular stage of development in the expression of the psychosis phenotype (O'Tuathaigh et al., 2010). A follow-up study also showed that adolescent THC exposure resulted in decreased density and soma size of dopaminergic neurons in the ventral tegmental area (Behan et al., 2012). A related work from the same group assessed the effects of treatment with the cannabinoid receptor agonist, WIN 55212, of COMT mutants at PND 32–52. This treatment, assessed 21 days later, led to increase of the startle response, decrease of PPI, and increase of the time spent in light area in light/dark test in mutant mice. Notably, the COMT inhibitor, tolcapone, reversed all these effects, suggesting that at least some of the behavioral effects in COMT-deficient mice are mediated by disturbances of DA metabolism (O'Tuathaigh et al., 2012).

Interaction with NRG1

The clinical importance of NRG1 cannabis interaction has recently been shown by a genetic study in African-Americans, which found that NRG1 is major candidate for the development of cannabis dependence (Han et al., 2012). This observation is in line with an early experimental study demonstrating that NRG1-deficient mice exposed to THC displayed no differences in the appearance but exhibit increased spontaneous activity and deficient PPI (Golub et al., 2004).

Analyses of Nrg1 × cannabis interactions in transmembrane domain Nrg1-mutant mice (NRG1 KD model) suggest that Nrg1 increases the susceptibility to the neurobehavioral effects of cannabis (Boucher et al., 2007). In this study, 6–7 month-old WT, Nrg1 KO, and KD animals were tested for acute THC treatment effect. Native Nrg1 KD mice spent more time in the light compartment in light–dark and in open arms in elevated-plus maze tests and displayed hyperactivity. Only in these mice but not in controls, THC treatment led to reduced locomotor activity, decreased time spent in open arms, and decreased time spent in light area and changed PPI. Similar results were received when Nrg1 mice were treated with THC from PND 21–32 and a comprehensive

evaluation was carried out at adulthood. THC administration resulted in a decreased hyperactive phenotype in mutant mice. Furthermore, THC chronic treatment led to sniffing reduction (an index of social interaction). The effects of chronic THC administration can be at least in part explained by increased CBR1 binding and affected 5HT2A and NMDA receptor binding in Nrg1 mutants (Long et al., 2013).

Methamphetamine

Besides cannabis, methamphetamine (METH) was also implicated in the pathophysiology of schizophrenia in some populations. Chronic METH abuse commonly leads to psychoses similar to those of schizophrenia (Bramness et al., 2012; Callaghan et al., 2012; Hsieh et al., 2014; Li et al., 2014). The first evidence of METH-induced psychosis came from Japan after the 1950s epidemic of METH use and was described as a long-lasting psychotic syndrome following METH-associated brain damage (Sato, 1992). The second and third epidemic in Japan followed at 1980s and 1990s, respectively, and the characteristics of the syndrome was defined as progressive impairment in mental and cognitive status with repeated use, vulnerability to relapse of psychotic symptoms, and a long duration for this vulnerability (Ujike & Sato, 2004). Similar to cannabis use, GEI may play a role in the genesis of METH-associated psychosis. A recent study has revealed that the risk alleles for METH-induced psychosis were enriched in schizophrenia GWAS dataset (Ikeda et al., 2013).

Interaction with DISC1

Our laboratory has evaluated putative effects of chronic METH administration in mutant DISC1 mice. To mimic a pattern of human METH abuse, a nontoxic, gradually escalating dose regimen was used. Specifically, METH doses were gradually increased over a 2-week period. Mutant DISC1 mice exhibited reduced METH-induced locomotor sensitization and attenuated conditioned place preference in female mice. We also found decreased DA D2 receptor binding and altered AKT/GSK3 signaling in the ventral striatum in female mutant DISC1 mice. These findings suggest that DISC1 signaling may be involved in the neurobehavioral changes induced by psychostimulants to moderate their contribution to schizophrenia (Pogorelov et al., 2012).

Environmental Toxins Models

Organophosphates

Although the putative role of environmental toxins in schizophrenia is only now becoming a focus of epidemiological and basic research, the detrimental effects of neurotoxins on brain and behavior have been convincingly demonstrated. For example, organophosphates were used to model abnormal neurodevelopment as prenatal organophosphates exposure was linked to neurocognitive impairment (Whyatt & Barr, 2001.)

Previously it was shown that chlorpyrifos (CPF), an organophosphate pesticide, might induce behavioral disturbances after intrauterine exposure, consistent with epidemiological (Whyatt & Barr, 2001) and animal data (Levin et al., 2002). It was hypothesized that a deficiency in reelin may ameliorate the abnormal behavioral rose by CPF insults. Pregnant heterozygous reelin females were exposed to CPF to assess the effects prenatal treatment on neurobehavioral development of the offspring. Decreased ultrasonic vocalization as a measure of communication in mice was tested at PND 7 and found increased in reeler mice up to WT levels after CPF treatment (Scattoni, Crawley, & Ricceri, 2009). Similar modulatory effects of CPF exposure were found with regard to amphetamine-induced hyperactivity and increased stereotypy (Laviola et al., 2006). The behavioral effects of CPF were associated with the brain changes in the olfactory bulb and the cerebellum in reeler mice (Mullen, Khialeeva, Hoffman, Ghiani, & Carpenter, 2013). These findings may be relevant to cholinergic abnormalities in autism and schizophrenia and demonstrate how adverse effects of environmental toxins could become paradoxical when combined with genetic variants.

Lead

Exposure to lead (Pb^{2+}) during prenatal and early postnatal development was recently also suggested as potential environmental risk of schizophrenia (citations). Although the epidemiological evidence for this association is relatively weak, there is the strong biological plausibility for the putative link as both schizophrenia and developmental Pb^{2+} exposure are characterized by hypoactivity of the NMDA receptors (Guilarte, 2009).

To experimentally test this hypothesis, we investigated the effects of prenatal exposure to Pb^{2+} in mutant DISC1 mice (Abazyan et al., 2014; Guilarte, 2009). The experimental groups of mice were fed with moderate levels of Pb^{2+} throughout their lifetime, whereas the control group received regular diet. Male mutant DISC1 mice exposed to Pb^{2+} displayed increased peripheral activity and decreased rearing. Pb^{2+} decreased the time spent in open arm in both mutants and controls consistent with increased anxiety-like behavior. In both female and male mice, Pb^{2+} exposure and mutant DISC1 additively increased locomotor activity induced by the NMDA receptors antagonist, MK-801. Because Pb^{2+} plays a role in vesicular exocytosis and high doses alters the structure and formation of NMDA-containing synapses (Neal, Stansfield, Worley, Thompson, & Guilarte, 2010; Neal,

Worley, & Guilarte, 2011), we tried to rescue the effects of Pb^{2+} by administering an NMDA receptor coagonist, D-serine. D-serine is an allosteric modulator of NMDA receptors and has been used in translational studies as well as in clinical trials (Kantrowitz et al., 2010; Labrie & Roder, 2010; Yang & Svensson, 2008). DISC1 binds serine racemase, the enzyme producing D-serine and mutant DISC1 decreases D-serine production by altering the binding properties of serine racemase (Ma et al., 2013). Administration of D-serine was able to rescue the effects of Pb^{2+} on PPI (Abazyan et al., 2014). The results seem to support the hypothesis that some environmental neurotoxins may be able to contribute to the pathogenesis of schizophrenia or related mental illnesses via interacting with genetic liability in susceptible individuals.

SUMMARY

Recent advances in genetics and epidemiology have provided the foundation for the development of GEI animal models relevant to schizophrenia. The existing animal preparations model the complex interactions between different factors implicated in the disorder as summarized in Table 1.

In reviewing the models published for the past 5–6 years, one can identify the main features common among many models. Although many investigators seem to expect detecting synergistic effects of a genetic mutation and an environmental adversity, there have been described different results of GEI as well. It is not uncommon to observe so-called "protective" effects in some GEI models or neurobehavioral changes that were not previously seen in any of experimental groups. These diverse outcomes of GEI are consistent with the notion of the shared etiology and underlying pathobiology of several psychiatric disorders (Hall, Trent, Thomas, O'Donovan, & Owen, 2015; Insel, 2010). This book is a first compilation of the chapters to argue that animal models should stop mimicking a disease as a category and instead focus on recapitulating and assessing dimensions and endophenotypes as a way of advancing the field of GEI (see the Chapter 3 by J. Waddington).

FUTURE PROSPECTS

Recent progress in psychiatric genetics and epidemiology has facilitated the development of animal models of GEI relevant to schizophrenia. Although these models have provided some important insights, many caveats of recent preparations need to be addressed in the future studies.

To overcome these roadblocks for the clinical and basic research, terms such as "endophenotype" and

TABLE 1   Animal Models of GEI in Schizophrenia

Gene	Environmental Insult	Effects	References
INFECTION AND IMMUNITY MODELS			
DISC1	Prenatal poly I:C	Synergistic increases in anxiety- and depressive-like behaviors	Abazyan et al. (2010)
DISC1	Early postnatal poly I:C	Synergistic impairment of short-term memory	Hikida et al. (2007) and Ibi et al. (2010)
DISC1	Prenatal poly I:C	Synergistic increase in IL-6, impaired novel object recognition and PPI	Smith et al. (2007) and Lipina et al. (2013)
Nurr1	Prenatal poly I:C	Synergistic impact on PPI, startle response, and latent inhibition	Vuillermot et al. (2011, 2012)
NRG1	Prenatal poly I:C	Several impacts: some additive, some with no combined effect	O'Leary et al. (2014)
STRESS MODELS			
Reelin	Maternal separation	Protective effect of mutation on social motivation	Laviola et al. (2009), Ognibene et al. (2007), and Ognibene et al. (2008)
Nurr1	Social isolation, restraint stress	Synergistic impairment of PPI	Eells et al. (2006)
SEPT5	Social isolation	Protective effect of mutation on anxiety like behaviors	Harper et al. (2012)
PACAP	Social isolation vs environmental enrichment	Synergistic elevation of aggression and impact on PPI	Ishihama et al. (2010)
DISC1	Social isolation	Synergistic increases in locomotion, immobility in FST, and PPI deficiencies	Niwa et al. (2013)
DISC1	Chronic social defeat	Opposite effects of social defeat stress on mutant vs WT in tests of anxiety, synergistic effect on PPI and social interaction	Haque et al. (2012)
GAD	Maternal stress	Synergistic effects on fetal cortisol and birth weight	Uchida et al. (2014, 2011)
SNAP25 (_bdr_)	Maternal stress	Synergistic effects on sociability and PPI	Oliver and Davies (2009)
NRG1	Social stress	Additive effects on locomotion, memory, sociability, and synergistic effect on brain cytokine levels	Desbonnet et al. (2012)
DRUG EXPOSURE MODELS			
COMT	Cannabis	Additive decreases in size and density of dopaminergic cells	Behan et al. (2012)
COMT	Cannabis	Additive increase in startle response, PPI deficit, and decreases in anxiety	O'Tuathaigh et al. (2010, 2012)
NRG1	Cannabis	Synergistic reduction of locomotor activity, increased anxiety, and impact on PPI	Boucher et al. (2007) and Long et al. (2013)
DISC1	Methamphetamine	Mutation blunted response to methamphetamine, synergistic attenuated response to conditioned place preference	Pogorelov et al. (2012)
TOXIN EXPOSURE MODELS			
Reelin	Prenatal chlorpyrifos	Protective impact of toxic exposure on ultrasonic vocalization and on stimulant response	Scattoni et al. (2009), Laviola et al. (2006), and Mullen et al. (2013)
DISC1	Prenatal lead	Synergistic increases in anxiety like behaviors and in response to MK-801 administration	Abazyan et al. (2014) and Guilarte (2009)

GEI, gene–environment interaction; poly I:C, polyinosine-polycytidylic; IL, interleukin; PPI, prepulse inhibition; FST, forced swim test; WT, wild-type.

"intermediate phenotype" have been introduced (Donaldson & Hen, 2014). How the endophenotype concept has been shaping GEI animal models has been recently reviewed (Kannan et al., 2013). Briefly, the next generation of animal models should expand use of physiological and neural circuitries intermediate phenotypes, genome-wide gene expression, and epigenetic modification profiling in specific cell types (e.g., neurons vs astrocytes). We believe that utilization of standard endophenotypic measures may not only help minimize variability in effects of GEI but also bring in new model organisms to study the molecular mechanisms of GEI across species (e.g., worms, fruit flies, and zebrafish).

We need to take our animal models beyond studying a single pathophysiological process involved in GEI even if we model an interaction with a single adverse event. For example, in addition to the hypothalamus-pituitary-adrenal axis, studies of stress exposure should include the immune response to stressful stimuli (Dantzer et al., 2008). Similarly, the role of innate and adaptive immune responses in mediating effects of illicit drugs will need to be addressed in future GEI models, including the immune responses taking place in the intestinal tract (Miller, Boulter, Ikin, & Smith, 2009).

Practically all basic (and human) GEI studies have been performed in candidate risk factors, the majority of which have not been confirmed by the recent GWAS (McCarroll, Feng, & Hyman, 2014; Nestler & Hyman, 2010). Although GEI studies based on rare highly penetrants mutations will likely remain the mainstream direction for years to come, there is an emergence of new models that incorporate polymorphisms identified by the Psychiatric Genomics Consortium (Quednow, Brzozka, & Rossner, 2014).

It is important to take developmental considerations into account when interpreting environmental effects that vary across different time points (Moffitt, Caspi, & Rutter, 2005; Rutter, 2008). In the past, addressing time-dependent interaction in GEI models has been achieved by changing the time when genetically modified animals are challenged with an environmental adversity. Future studies should also attempt to regulate timing of the effects of a specific mutation as exemplified by a recent study with inducible expression of mutant DISC1 in mice prenatally exposed to MIA (Abazyan et al., 2011).

Combining an environmental challenge with a genetic mutation can produce diverse effects. Appearance of new brain and behavioral phenotypes, particularly while using the genetic mutation implicated in various psychiatric conditions, could inform us about the role of environment in bringing about diverse clinical outcomes in patients with the same mutation. The Scottish pedigree with the disruption of DISC1 due to the chromosomal defect is a most prominent example of such a possibility (Blackwood et al., 2001).

The focus of most published GEI research has been on risk factors. However, the contribution of protective factors is also important and has so far been relatively neglected, although there are some exceptions. Identification of genes conferring resilience to schizophrenia-related abnormalities is a new emerging research to uncover unrecognized molecular targets (Mihali, Subramani, Kaunitz, Rayport, & Gaisler-Salomon, 2012). In this context, the role for environment enrichment in ameliorating/rescuing genetically produced abnormalities has been recently reviewed (Pratt et al., 2012; Takuma et al., 2011).

New models with mutations in regulatory elements in candidate genes with more subtle regional, cell type- and time-specific manipulations, or human genetic variants knock-in models will better reflect the complex genetic and molecular mechanisms of schizophrenia (Papaleo, Lipska, & Weinberger, 2012). Therefore, time-dependent or circuitry- or cell-specific manipulations to target mRNA and/or proteins should be used.

Most studies have focused on neuronal functions of susceptibility genes. However, these genes are also expressed by glial cells (Iijima et al., 2009; Prevot et al., 2003). Given growing interest in the role for glia cells in mediating the effects of stress and microbial pathogens, GEI models with cell-specific perturbation of candidate genes are also needed. A recent study has provided the first evidence for the potential role of DISC1 in astrocytes, connecting DISC1 and serine racemase in modulating NMDA receptor functions (Ma et al., 2013).

In conclusion, GEI animal models have already begun to provide new insights into the etiological complexity and heterogeneity of schizophrenia. We believe GEI animal models will continue to be a crucial tool to advance our knowledge about this debilitating disease and help searching for new treatment options.

Acknowledgments

We thank the following funding agencies for the support: MH-083728, MH-094268 Silvo O. Conte center and the Brain and Behavior Research Foundation, and Tabakman Trust Gift Grant (MVP).

References

Abazyan, B., et al. (2010). Prenatal interaction of mutant DISC1 and immune activation produces adult psychopathology. *Biological Psychiatry, 68*, 1172–1181.

Abazyan, B., et al. (2011). Prenatal interaction of mutant DISC1 and immune activation produces adult psychopathology. *Biological Psychiatry, 68*, 1172–1181.

Abazyan, B., et al. (2014). Chronic exposure of mutant DISC1 mice to lead produces sex-dependent abnormalities consistent with schizophrenia and related mental disorders: a gene-environment interaction study. *Schizophrenia Bulletin, 40*, 575–584.

Akbarian, S., et al. (1995). Gene expression for glutamic acid decarboxylase is reduced without loss of neurons in prefrontal cortex of schizophrenics. *Archives of General Psychiatry, 52*, 258–266.

Andreasson, S., Allebeck, P., Engstrom, A., & Rydberg, U. (1987). Cannabis and schizophrenia. A longitudinal study of Swedish conscripts. *Lancet, 2*, 1483–1486.

Arseneault, L., Cannon, M., Poulton, R., Murray, R., Caspi, A., & Moffitt, T. E. (2002). Cannabis use in adolescence and risk for adult psychosis: longitudinal prospective study. *BMJ, 325*, 1212–1213.

Asada, A., et al. (2010). Neuronal expression of two isoforms of mouse Septin 5. *Journal of Neuroscience Research, 88*, 1309–1316.

Ayhan, Y., Sawa, A., Ross, C. A., & Pletnikov, M. V. (2009). Animal model of gene-enviroment interaction in schizophrenia. *Behavioral Brain Research, 204*(2), 274–281.

Babovic, D., et al. (2007). Exploratory and habituation phenotype of heterozygous and homozygous COMT knockout mice. *Behavioural Brain Research, 183*, 236–239.

Barnes, T. R., Mutsatsa, S. H., Hutton, S. B., Watt, H. C., & Joyce, E. M. (2006). Comorbid substance use and age at onset of schizophrenia. *The British Journal of Psychiatry: The Journal of Mental Science, 188*, 237–242.

Behan, A. T., et al. (2012). Chronic adolescent exposure to delta-9-tetrahydrocannabinol in COMT mutant mice: impact on indices of dopaminergic, endocannabinoid and GABAergic pathways. *Neuropsychopharmacology: Official Publication of the American College of Neuropsychopharmacology, 37*, 1773–1783.

Beites, C. L., Campbell, K. A., & Trimble, W. S. (2005). The septin Sept5/CDCrel-1 competes with alpha-SNAP for binding to the SNARE complex. *The Biochemical Journal, 385*, 347–353.

Beneyto, M., Morris, H. M., Rovensky, K. C., & Lewis, D. A. (2012). Lamina- and cell-specific alterations in cortical somatostatin receptor 2 mRNA expression in schizophrenia. *Neuropharmacology, 62*, 1598–1605.

Berrios, G. E., Luque, R., & Villagran-Moreno, J. M. (2003). Schizophrenia: a conceptual history. *International Journal of Psychology and Psychological Therapy, 3*, 111–140.

Blackwood, D. H., Fordyce, A., Walker, M. T., St Clair, D. M., Porteous, D. J., & Muir, W. J. (2001). Schizophrenia and affective disorders–cosegregation with a translocation at chromosome 1q42 that directly disrupts brain-expressed genes: clinical and P300 findings in a family. *American Journal of Human Genetics, 69*, 428–433.

Boccia, M. L., et al. (2007). Repeated long separations from pups produce depression-like behavior in rat mothers. *Psychoneuroendocrinology, 32*, 65–71.

Boucher, A. A., Arnold, J. C., Duffy, L., Schofield, P. R., Micheau, J., & Karl, T. (2007). Heterozygous neuregulin 1 mice are more sensitive to the behavioural effects of Δ^9-tetrahydrocannabinol. *Psychopharmacology, 192*, 325–336.

Bramness, J. G., et al. (2012). Amphetamine-induced psychosis – a separate diagnostic entity or primary psychosis triggered in the vulnerable? *BMC Psychiatry, 12*, 221.

Brandon, N. J., & Sawa, A. (2011). Linking neurodevelopmental and synaptic theories of mental illness through DISC1. *Nature Reviews. Neuroscience, 12*, 707–722.

Brown, A. S. (2011). The environment and susceptibility to schizophrenia. *Progress in Neurobiology, 93*, 23–58.

Buervenich, S., et al. (2000). NURR1 mutations in cases of schizophrenia and manic-depressive disorder. *American Journal of Medical Genetics, 96*, 808–813.

Burrows, E. L., McOmish, C. E., & Hannan, A. J. (August 1, 2011). Gene-environment interactions and construct validity in preclinical models of psychiatric disorders. *Progress in Neuro-Psychopharmacology & Biological Psychiatry, 35*(6), 1376–1382.

Callaghan, R. C., et al. (2012). Methamphetamine use and schizophrenia: a population-based cohort study in California. *The American Journal of Psychiatry, 169*, 389–396.

Carroll, L. S., Kendall, K., O'Donovan, M. C., Owen, M. J., & Williams, N. M. (2009). Evidence that putative ADHD low risk alleles at SNAP25 may increase the risk of schizophrenia. *American Journal of Medical Genetics. Part B, Neuropsychiatric Genetics: The Official Publication of the International Society of Psychiatric Genetics, 150B*, 893–899.

Chen, Y. A., & Scheller, R. H. (2001). SNARE-mediated membrane fusion. *Nature Reviews Molecular Cell Biology, 2*, 98–106.

Chong, V. Z., Thompson, M., Beltaifa, S., Webster, M. J., Law, A. J., & Weickert, C. S. (2008). Elevated neuregulin-1 and ErbB4 protein in the prefrontal cortex of schizophrenic patients. *Schizophrenia Research, 100*, 270–280.

Clapcote, S. J., et al. (2007). Behavioral phenotypes of Disc1 missense mutations in mice. *Neuron, 54*, 387–402.

Curley, A. A., et al. (2011). Cortical deficits of glutamic acid decarboxylase 67 expression in schizophrenia: clinical, protein, and cell type-specific features. *The American Journal of Psychiatry, 168*, 921–929.

Dai, D., et al. (2014). Meta-analyses of 10 polymorphisms associated with the risk of schizophrenia. *Biomedical Reports, 2*, 729–736.

Dantzer, R., O'Connor, J. C., Freund, G. G., Johnson, R. W., & Kelley, K. W. (2008). From inflammation to sickness and depression: when the immune system subjugates the brain. *Nature Reviews Neuroscience, 9*(1), 46-56.

Deng, C., Pan, B., Engel, M., & Huang, X. F. (2013). Neuregulin-1 signalling and antipsychotic treatment: potential therapeutic targets in a schizophrenia candidate signalling pathway. *Psychopharmacology, 226*, 201–215.

Desbonnet, L., et al. (2012). Phenotypic effects of repeated psychosocial stress during adolescence in mice mutant for the schizophrenia risk gene neuregulin-1: a putative model of gene x environment interaction. *Brain, Behavior, and Immunity, 26*, 660–671.

Donaldson, Z. R., & Hen, R. (2014). From psychiatric disorders to animal models: a bidirectional and dimensional approach. *Biological Psychiatry*.

Dvir, Y., Denietolis, B., & Frazier, J. A. (2013). Childhood trauma and psychosis. *Child and Adolescent Psychiatric Clinics of North America, 22*, 629–641.

Eastwood, S. L., & Harrison, P. J. (2003). Interstitial white matter neurons express less reelin and are abnormally distributed in schizophrenia: towards an integration of molecular and morphologic aspects of the neurodevelopmental hypothesis. *Molecular Psychiatry, 8*(769), 821–831.

Edenberg, H. J., & Foroud, T. (August 2013). Genetics and alcoholism. *Nature Reviews Gastroenterology and Hepatology, 10*(8), 487–494.

Eells, J. B., Misler, J. A., & Nikodem, V. M. (2006). Early postnatal isolation reduces dopamine levels, elevates dopamine turnover and specifically disrupts prepulse inhibition in Nurr1-null heterozygous mice. *Neuroscience, 140*, 1117–1126.

Eykelenboom, J. E., et al. (2012). A t(1;11) translocation linked to schizophrenia and affective disorders gives rise to aberrant chimeric DISC1 transcripts that encode structurally altered, deleterious mitochondrial proteins. *Human Molecular Genetics, 21*, 3374–3386.

Faraone, S. V., et al. (2005). Genome scan of schizophrenia families in a large Veterans Affairs Cooperative Study sample: evidence for linkage to 18p11.32 and for racial heterogeneity on chromosomes 6 and 14. *American Journal of Medical Genetics. Part B, Neuropsychiatric Genetics: The Official Publication of the International Society of Psychiatric Genetics, 139B*, 91–100.

Fatemi, S. H., Earle, J. A., & McMenomy, T. (2000). Reduction in Reelin immunoreactivity in hippocampus of subjects with schizophrenia, bipolar disorder and major depression. *Molecular Psychiatry, 5*, 654–663 571.

Fatemi, S. H., Earle, J. A., Stary, J. M., Lee, S., & Sedgewick, J. (2001). Altered levels of the synaptosomal associated protein SNAP-25 in hippocampus of subjects with mood disorders and schizophrenia. *Neuroreport, 12*, 3257–3262.

Fatemi, S. H., Kroll, J. L., & Stary, J. M. (2001). Altered levels of Reelin and its isoforms in schizophrenia and mood disorders. *Neuroreport, 12*, 3209–3215.

Fergusson, D. M., Horwood, L. J., & Ridder, E. M. (2005). Tests of causal linkages between cannabis use and psychotic symptoms. *Addiction, 100*, 354–366.

Fine, R., Zhang, J., & Stevens, H. E. (2014). Prenatal stress and inhibitory neuron systems: implications for neuropsychiatric disorders. *Molecular Psychiatry, 19*, 641–651.

Goate, A., et al. (1991). Segregation of a missense mutation in the amyloid precursor protein gene with familial Alzheimer's disease. *Nature, 349*, 704–706.

Gogos, J. A., et al. (1998). Catechol-O-methyltransferase-deficient mice exhibit sexually dimorphic changes in catecholamine levels and behavior. *Proceedings of the National Academy of Sciences of the United States of America, 95*, 9991–9996.

Goldberg, S., Fruchter, E., Davidson, M., Reichenberg, A., Yoffe, R., & Weiser, M. (2011). The relationship between risk of hospitalization for schizophrenia, SES, and cognitive functioning. *Schizophrenia Bulletin, 37*, 664–670.

Golub, M. S., Germann, S. L., & Lloyd, K. C. (2004). Behavioral characteristics of a nervous system-specific erbB4 knock-out mouse. *Behavioural Brain Research, 153*, 159–170.

Gothelf, D., et al. (2014). Biological effects of COMT haplotypes and psychosis risk in 22q11.2 deletion syndrome. *Biological Psychiatry, 75*, 406–413.

Grayson, D. R., et al. (2005). Reelin promoter hypermethylation in schizophrenia. *Proceedings of the National Academy of Sciences of the United States of America, 102*, 9341–9346.

Guidotti, A., et al. (2000). Decrease in reelin and glutamic acid decarboxylase67 (GAD67) expression in schizophrenia and bipolar disorder: a postmortem brain study. *Archives of General Psychiatry, 57*, 1061–1069.

Guilarte, T. R. (2009). Prenatal lead exposure and schizophrenia: further evidence and more neurobiological connections. *Environmental Health Perspectives, 117*, A190–A191.

Hahn, C. G., et al. (2006). Altered neuregulin 1-erbB4 signaling contributes to NMDA receptor hypofunction in schizophrenia. *Nature Medicine, 12*, 824–828.

Hall, J., Trent, S., Thomas, K. L., O'Donovan, M. C., & Owen, M. J. (2015). Genetic risk for schizophrenia: convergence on synaptic pathways involved in plasticity. *Biological Psychiatry, 77*, 52–58.

Han, S., et al.(2012). Linkage analysis followed by association show NRG1 associated with cannabis dependence in African Americans. *Biological psychiatry, 72*(8), 637–644.

Haque, F. N., Lipina, T. V., Roder, J. C., & Wong, A. H. (2012). Social defeat interacts with Disc1 mutations in the mouse to affect behavior. *Behavioural Brain Research, 233*, 337–344.

Harper, K. M., et al. (2012). Alterations of social interaction through genetic and environmental manipulation of the 22q11.2 gene Sept5 in the mouse brain. *Human Molecular Genetics, 21*, 3489–3499.

Hashimoto, T., et al. (2003). Gene expression deficits in a subclass of GABA neurons in the prefrontal cortex of subjects with schizophrenia. *The Journal of Neuroscience: The Official Journal of the Society for Neuroscience, 23*, 6315–6326.

Hashimoto, R., et al. (2007). Pituitary adenylate cyclase-activating polypeptide is associated with schizophrenia. *Molecular Psychiatry, 12*, 1026–1032.

Hashimoto, R., Straub, R. E., Weickert, C. S., Hyde, T. M., Kleinman, J. E., & Weinberger, D. R. (2004). Expression analysis of neuregulin-1 in the dorsolateral prefrontal cortex in schizophrenia. *Molecular Psychiatry, 9*, 299–307.

Hattori, T., et al. (2007). A novel DISC1-interacting partner DISC1-Binding Zinc-finger protein: implication in the modulation of DISC1-dependent neurite outgrowth. *Molecular Psychiatry, 12*, 398–407.

Heckers, S., et al. (2013). Structure of the psychotic disorders classification in DSM-5. *Schizophrenia Research, 150*, 11–14.

Heim, A. F., Coyne, M. J., Kamboh, M. I., Ryan, C., & Jennings, J. R. (2013). The catechol-O-methyltransferase Val^{158} Met polymorphism modulates organization of regional cerebral blood flow response to working memory in adults. *International Journal of Psychophysiology: Official Journal of the International Organization of Psychophysiology, 90*, 149–156.

Hida, H., Mouri, A., & Noda, Y. (2013). Behavioral phenotypes in schizophrenic animal models with multiple combinations of genetic and environmental factors. *Journal of Pharmacological Sciences, 121*(3), 185–191.

Hikida, T., et al. (2007). Dominant-negative DISC1 transgenic mice display schizophrenia-associated phenotypes detected by measures translatable to humans. *Proceedings of the National Academy of Sciences of the United States of America, 104*, 14501–14506.

Hillerer, K. M., Neumann, I. D., & Slattery, D. A. (2012). From stress to postpartum mood and anxiety disorders: how chronic peripartum stress can impair maternal adaptations. *Neuroendocrinology, 95*, 22–38.

Hsieh, J. H., Stein, D. J., & Howells, F. M. (2014). The neurobiology of methamphetamine induced psychosis. *Frontiers in Human Neuroscience, 8*, 537.

Huotari, M., et al. (2002). Brain catecholamine metabolism in catechol-O-methyltransferase (COMT)-deficient mice. *The European Journal of Neuroscience, 15*, 246–256.

Ibi, D., et al. (2010). Combined effect of neonatal immune activation and mutant DISC1 on phenotypic changes in adulthood. *Behavioural Brain Research, 206*, 32–37.

Iijima, S., et al. (2009). Immunohistochemical detection of dysbindin at the astroglial endfeet around the capillaries of mouse brain. *Journal of Molecular Histology, 40*, 117–121.

Ikeda, M., et al. (2013). Evidence for shared genetic risk between methamphetamine-induced psychosis and schizophrenia. *Neuropsychopharmacology: official publication of the American College of Neuropsychopharmacology, 38*, 1864–1870.

Impagnatiello, F., et al. (1998). A decrease of reelin expression as a putative vulnerability factor in schizophrenia. *Proceedings of the National Academy of Sciences of the United States of America, 95*, 15718–15723.

Insel, T. R. (2010). Rethinking schizophrenia. *Nature, 468*, 187–193.

Ishihama, T., et al. (2010). Environmental factors during early developmental period influence psychobehavioral abnormalities in adult PACAP-deficient mice. *Behavioural Brain Research, 209*, 274–280.

Iwata, N., et al. (2004). No association with the neuregulin 1 haplotype to Japanese schizophrenia. *Molecular Psychiatry, 9*, 126–127.

Iyegbe, C., Campbell, D., Butler, A., Ajnakina, O., & Sham, P. (2014). The emerging molecular architecture of schizophrenia, polygenic risk scores and the clinical implications for GxE research. *Social Psychiatry and Psychiatric Epidemiology, 49*, 169–182.

Jaffe, A. E., Eaton, W. W., Straub, R. E., Marenco, S., & Weinberger, D. R. (2014). Paternal age, de novo mutations and schizophrenia. *Molecular Psychiatry, 19*, 274–275.

Jeans, A. F., et al. (2007). A dominant mutation in Snap25 causes impaired vesicle trafficking, sensorimotor gating, and ataxia in the blind-drunk mouse. *Proceedings of the National Academy of Sciences of the United States of America, 104*, 2431–2436.

Jurado, S., Goswami, D., Zhang, Y., Molina, A. J., Sudhof, T. C., & Malenka, R. C. (2013). LTP requires a unique postsynaptic SNARE fusion machinery. *Neuron, 77*, 542–558.

Kannan, G., Sawa, A., & Pletnikov, M. (2013). Mouse models of gene-environment interactions in schizophrenia. *Neurobiology of Disease, 57*, 5–11.

Kantrowitz, J. T., et al. (2010). High dose D-serine in the treatment of schizophrenia. *Schizophrenia Research, 121*, 125–130.

Karayiorgou, M., et al. (1998). Identification of sequence variants and analysis of the role of the catechol-O-methyl-transferase gene in schizophrenia susceptibility. *Biological Psychiatry, 43*, 425–431.

Karson, C. N., Mrak, R. E., Schluterman, K. O., Sturner, W. Q., Sheng, J. G., & Griffin, W. S. (1999). Alterations in synaptic proteins and their encoding mRNAs in prefrontal cortex in schizophrenia: a possible neurochemical basis for 'hypofrontality'. *Molecular Psychiatry, 4*, 39–45.

Kawashima, K., et al. (2008). No association between tagging SNPs of SNARE complex genes (STX1A, VAMP2 and SNAP25) and schizophrenia in a Japanese population. *American Journal of Medical Genetics. Part B, Neuropsychiatric Genetics: The Official Publication of the International Society of Psychiatric Genetics, 147B*, 1327–1331.

II. NEUROBIOLOGY OF PSYCHOTIC DISORDERS

Kendler, K. S., & Eaves, L. J. (1986). Models for the joint effect of genotype and environment on liability to psychiatric illness. *The American Journal of Psychiatry, 143*, 279–289.

Kéri, S., Kiss, I., Seres, I., & Kelemen, O. (2009). A polymorphism of the neuregulin 1 gene (SNP8NRG243177/rs6994992) affects reactivity to expressed emotion in schizophrenia. *Am J Med Genet B Neuropsychiatr Genet, 150B*(3), 418–420.

Kim, J. Y., et al. (2012). Interplay between DISC1 and GABA signaling regulates neurogenesis in mice and risk for schizophrenia. *Cell, 148*, 1051–1064.

Kimoto, S., Bazmi, H. H., & Lewis, D. A. (2014). Lower expression of glutamic acid decarboxylase 67 in the prefrontal cortex in schizophrenia: contribution of altered regulation by Zif268. *The American Journal of Psychiatry, 171*, 969–978.

Klein, C., & Westenberger, A. (2012). Genetics of Parkinson's disease. *Cold Spring Harbor Perspectives in Medicine, 2*, a008888.

Koenig, J. I. (2006). Schizophrenia: a unique translational opportunity in behavioral neuroendocrinologt. *Hormones and Behavior, 50*, 602–611.

Koga, M., et al. (2010). Replication study of association between ADCYAP1 gene polymorphisms and schizophrenia. *Psychiatric Genetics, 20*, 123–125.

Labrie, V., & Roder, J. C. (2010). The involvement of the NMDA receptor D-serine/glycine site in the pathophysiology and treatment of schizophrenia. *Neuroscience and Biobehavioral Reviews, 34*, 351–372.

Laviola, G., Adriani, W., Gaudino, C., Marino, R., & Keller, F. (2006). Paradoxical effects of prenatal acetylcholinesterase blockade on neuro-behavioral development and drug-induced stereotypies in reeler mutant mice. *Psychopharmacology, 187*, 331–344.

Laviola, G., Ognibene, E., Romano, E., Adriani, W., & Keller, F. (2009). Gene-environment interaction during early development in the heterozygous reeler mouse: clues for modelling of major neurobehavioral syndromes. *Neuroscience & Biobehavioral Reviews, 33*(4), 560–572.

Levin, E. D., et al. (2002). Prenatal chlorpyrifos exposure in rats causes persistent behavioral alterations. *Neurotoxicology and Teratology, 24*, 733–741.

Li, T., et al. (2004). Identification of a novel neuregulin 1 at-risk haplotype in Han schizophrenia Chinese patients, but no association with the Icelandic/Scottish risk haplotype. *Molecular Psychiatry, 9*, 698–704.

Li, H., Lu, Q., Xiao, E., Li, Q., He, Z., & Mei, X. (2014). Methamphetamine enhances the development of schizophrenia in first-degree relatives of patients with schizophrenia. *Canadian Journal of Psychiatry. Revue Canadienne de Psychiatrie, 59*, 107–113.

Lipina, T. V., Zai, C., Hlousek, D., Roder, J. C., & Wong, A. H. (2013). Maternal immune activation during gestation interacts with Disc1 point mutation to exacerbate schizophrenia-related behaviors in mice. *The Journal of Neuroscience: The Official Journal of the Society for Neuroscience, 33*, 7654–7666.

Li, B., Woo, R. S., Mei, L., & Malinow, R. (2007). The neuregulin-1 receptor erbB4 controls glutamatergic synapse maturation and plasticity. *Neuron, 54*, 583–597.

Lochman, J., Balcar, V. J., Stastny, F., & Sery, O. (2013). Preliminary evidence for association between schizophrenia and polymorphisms in the regulatory Regions of the ADRA2A, DRD3 and SNAP-25 Genes. *Psychiatry Research, 205*, 7–12.

Long, L. E., Chesworth, R., Huang, X. F., McGregor, I. S., Arnold, J. C., & Karl, T. (2013). Transmembrane domain Nrg1 mutant mice show altered susceptibility to the neurobehavioural actions of repeated THC exposure in adolescence. *The International Journal of Neuropsychopharmacology/Official Scientific Journal of the Collegium Internationale Neuropsychopharmacologicum, 16*, 163–175.

Ma, T. M., et al. (2013). Pathogenic disruption of DISC1-serine racemase binding elicits schizophrenia-like behavior via D-serine depletion. *Molecular Psychiatry, 18*, 557–567.

Marballi, K., et al. (2010). In vivo and in vitro genetic evidence of involvement of neuregulin 1 in immune system dysregulation. *Journal of Molecular Medicine (Berlin), 88*, 1133–1141.

Markham, J. A., & Koenig, J. I. (2011). Prenatal stress: role in psychotic and depressive diseases. *Psychopharmacology, 214*, 89–106.

McCarroll, S. A., Feng, G., & Hyman, S. (2014). Genome -scale neurogenetics: methodology and meaning. *Nature Neuroscience, 17*, 756–763.

Mei, L., & Nave, K. A. (2014). Neuregulin-ERBB signaling in the nervous system and neuropsychiatric diseases. *Neuron, 83*, 27–49.

Mei, L., & Xiong, W. C. (2008). Neuregulin 1 in neural development, synaptic plasticity and schizophrenia. *Nature Reviews. Neuroscience, 9*, 437–452.

Meyer, U., & Feldon, J. (2010). Epidemiology-driven neurodevelopmental animal models of schizophrenia. *Progress in Neurobiology, 90*, 285–326.

Meyer, U., & Feldon, J. (2012). To poly(I:C) or not to poly(I:C): advancing preclinical schizophrenia research through the use of prenatal immune activation models. *Neuropharmacology, 62*(3), 1308–1321.

Mihali, A., Subramani, S., Kaunitz, G., Rayport, S., & Gaisler-Salomon, I. (2012). Modeling resilience to schizophrenia in genetically modified mice: a novel approach to drug discovery. *Expert Review of Neurotherapeutics, 12*, 785–799.

Miller, C. M., Boulter, N. R., Ikin, R. J., & Smith, N. C. (2009). The immunobiology of the innate response to *Toxoplasma gondii*. *International Journal for Parisitology, 39*, 23–39.

Modinos, G., Iyegbe, C., Prata, D., Rivera, M., Kempton, M. J., Valmaggia, L. R., et al. (November 2013). Molecular genetic gene-environment studies using candidate genes in schizophrenia: a systematic review. *Schizophr Research, 150*(2–3), 356–365.

Moffitt, T. E., Caspi, A., & Rutter, M. (2005). Strategy for investigating interactions between measured genes and measured environments. *Archives of General Psychiatry, 62*, 473–481.

Moore, T. M., Brown, T., Cade, M., & Eells, J. B. (2008). Alterations in amphetamine-stimulated dopamine overflow due to the Nurr1-null heterozygous genotype and postweaning isolation. *Synapse, 62*, 764–774.

Mueller, E. M., Makeig, S., Stemmler, G., Hennig, J., & Wacker, J. (2011). Dopamine effects on human error processing depend on catechol-O-methyltransferase VAL158MET genotype. *The Journal of Neuroscience: The Official Journal of the Society for Neuroscience, 31*, 15818–15825.

Mukaetova-Ladinska, E., Hurt, J., Honer, W. G., Harrington, C. R., & Wischik, C. M. (2002). Loss of synaptic but not cytoskeletal proteins in the cerebellum of chronic schizophrenics. *Neuroscience Letters, 317*, 161–165.

Mukherjee, O., et al. (2006). Evidence of linkage and association on 18p11.2 for psychosis. *American Journal of Medical Genetics. Part B, Neuropsychiatric Genetics: The Official Publication of the International Society of Psychiatric Genetics, 141B*, 868–873.

Mullen, B. R., Khaleeva, E., Hoffman, D. B., Ghiani, C. A., & Carpenter, E. M. (2013). Decreased reelin expression and organophosphate pesticide exposure alters mouse behaviour and brain morphology. *ASN Neuro, 5*, e00106.

Murphy, K. C., Jones, L. A., & Owen, M. J. (1999). High rates of schizophrenia in adults with velo-cardio-facial syndrome. *Archives of General Psychiatry, 56*, 940–945.

Murray, C. J., et al. (2012). Disability-adjusted life years (DALYs) for 291 diseases and injuries in 21 regions, 1990–2010: a systematic analysis for the Global Burden of Disease Study 2010. *Lancet, 380*, 2197–2223.

Neal, A. P., Stansfield, K. H., Worley, P. F., Thompson, R. E., & Guilarte, T. R. (2010). Lead exposure during synaptogenesis alters vesicular proteins and impairs vesicular release: potential role of NMDA receptor-dependent BDNF signaling. *Toxicological Sciences: An Official Journal of the Society of Toxicology, 116*, 249–263.

Neal, A. P., Worley, P. F., & Guilarte, T. R. (2011). Lead exposure during synaptogenesis alters NMDA receptor targeting via NMDA receptor inhibition. *Neurotoxicology, 32*, 281–289.

Nestler, E. J., & Hyman, S. E. (2010). Animal models of neuropsychiatric disorders. *Nature Neuroscience, 13*, 1161–1169.

Newell, K. A., Karl, T., & Huang, X. F. (2013). A neuregulin 1 transmembrane domain mutation causes imbalanced glutamatergic and dopaminergic receptor expression in mice. *Neuroscience, 248*, 670–680.

Niwa, M., et al. (2013). Adolescent stress-induced epigenetic control of dopaminergic neurons via glucocorticoids. *Science, 339*, 335–339.

Nixon, D. C., et al. (2011). Interactive effects of *DAOA* (G72) and catechol-*O*-methyltransferase on neurophysiology in prefrontal cortex. *Biological Psychiatry, 69*, 1006–1008.

O'Leary, C., Desbonnet, L., Clarke, N., Petit, E., Tighe, O., Lai, D., et al. (2014). Phenotypic effects of maternal immune activation and early postnatal milieu in mice mutant for the schizophrenia risk gene neuregulin-1. *Neuroscience, 277*, 294–305.

O'Tuathaigh, C. M., et al. (2010). Chronic adolescent exposure to Delta-9-tetrahydrocannabinol in COMT mutant mice: impact on psychosis-related and other phenotypes. *Neuropsychopharmacology: Official Publication of the American College of Neuropsychopharmacology, 35*, 2262–2273.

O'Tuathaigh, C. M., et al. (2012). Genetic vs. pharmacological inactivation of COMT influences cannabinoid-induced expression of schizophrenia-related phenotypes. *The International Journal of Neuropsychopharmacology/Official Scientific Journal of the Collegium Internationale Neuropsychopharmacologicum, 15*, 1331–1342.

Ognibene, E., Adriani, W., Macri, S., & Laviola, G. (2007). Neurobehavioural disorders in the infant reeler mouse model: interaction of genetic vulnerability and consequences of maternal separation. *Behavioural Brain Research, 177*, 142–149.

Ognibene, E., et al. (2008). The effect of early maternal separation on brain derived neurotrophic factor and monoamine levels in adult heterozygous reeler mice. *Progress in Neuro-Psychopharmacology & Biological Psychiatry, 32*, 1269–1276.

Oliver, P. L., & Davies, K. E. (2009). Interaction between environmental and genetic factors modulates schizophrenic endophenotypes in the Snap-25 mouse mutant blind-drunk. *Human Molecular Genetics, 18*, 4576–4589.

Oliver, P. L., et al. (2012). Disrupted circadian rhythms in a mouse model of schizophrenia. *Current Biology, 22*, 314–319.

van Os, J., Bak, M., Hanssen, M., Bijl, R. V., de Graaf, R., & Verdoux, H. (2002). Cannabis use and psychosis: a longitudinal population-based study. *American Journal of Epidemiology, 156*, 319–327.

van Os, J., & Kapur, S. (2009). Schizophrenia. *Lancet, 374*, 635–645.

Papaleo, F., Lipska, B. K., & Weinberger, D. R. (2012). Mouse models of genetic effects on cognition: relevance to schizophrenia. *Neuropharmacology, 62*, 1204–1220.

Park, Y. U., et al. (2010). Disrupted-in-schizophrenia 1 (DISC1) plays essential roles in mitochondria in collaboration with Mitofilin. *Proceedings of the National Academy of Sciences of the United States of America, 107*, 17785–17790.

Paterlini, M., et al. (2005). Transcriptional and behavioral interaction between 22q11.2 orthologs modulates schizophrenia-related phenotypes in mice. *Nature Neuroscience, 8*, 1586–1594.

Pletnikov, M. V., et al. (2008). Inducible expression of mutant human DISC1 in mice is associated with brain and behavioral abnormalities reminiscent of schizophrenia. *Molecular Psychiatry, 13*, 173–186 115.

Plomin, R., DeFries, J. C., & Loehlin, J. C. (1977). Genotype-environment interaction and correlation in the analysis of human behavior. *Psychological Bulletin, 84*, 309–322.

Pogorelov, V. M., et al. (2012). Mutant DISC1 affects methamphetamine-induced sensitization and conditioned place preference: a comorbidity model. *Neuropharmacology, 62*, 1242–1251.

Porteous, D. J., Millar, J. K., Brandon, N. J., & Sawa, A. (2011). DISC1 at 10: connecting psychiatric genetics and neuroscience. *Trends in Molecular Medicine, 17*, 699–706.

Pratt, J., Winchester, C., Dawson, N., & Morris, B. (2012). Advancing schizophrenia drug discovery: optimizing rodent models to bridge the translational gap. *Nature Reviews Drug Discovery, 11*, 560–579.

Prevot, V., et al. (2003). Normal female sexual development requires neuregulin-erbB receptor signaling in hypothalamic astrocytes. *Journal of Neuroscience, 23*, 230–239.

Quednow, B. B., Brzozka, M. M., & Rossner, M. J. (2014). Transcription factor 4 (TCF4) and sczophrenia: integrating the animal and the human perspective. *Cellular and Molecular Life Sciences, 71*, 2815–2835.

Rethelyi, J. M., Benkovits, J., & Bitter, I. (2013). Genes and environments in schizophrenia: the different pieces of a manifold puzzle. *Neuroscience and Biobehavioral Reviews, 37*, 2424–2437.

Rogaev, E. I., et al. (1995). Familial Alzheimer's disease in kindreds with missense mutations in a gene on chromosome 1 related to the Alzheimer's disease type 3 gene. *Nature, 376*, 775–778.

Rogers, J. T., & Weeber, E. J. (2008). Reeling and apoE actions on signal transduction, synaptic function and memory formation. *Neuron Glia Biology, 4*, 259–270.

Rojas, P., Joodmardi, E., Hong, Y., Perlmann, T., & Ogren, S. O. (2007). Adult mice with reduced Nurr1 expression: an animal model for schizophrenia. *Molecular Psychiatry, 12*, 756–766.

Rutter, M. (2007). Gene-environment interdependence. *Developmental Science, 10*, 12–18.

Rutter, M. (2008). Biological implications of gene-environment interaction. *Journal of Abnormal Child Psychology, 36*, 969–975.

Rutter, M., Moffitt, T. E., & Caspi, A. (2006). Gene-environment interplay and psychopathology: multiple varieties but real effects. *Journal of Child Psychology and Psychiatry, 47*, 226–261.

Ruzicka, W. B., Zhubi, A., Veldic, M., Grayson, D. R., Costa, E., & Guidotti, A. (2007). Selective epigenetic alteration of layer I GABAergic neurons isolated from prefrontal cortex of schizophrenia patients using laser-assisted microdissection. *Molecular Psychiatry, 12*, 385–397.

Saha, S., Chant, D., Welham, J., & McGrath, J. (2005). A systematic review of the prevalence of schizophrenia. *PLoS Medicine, 2*, e141.

Sato, M. (1992). A lasting vulnerability to psychosis in patients with previous methamphetamine psychosis. *Annals of the New York Academy of Sciences, 654*, 160–170.

Scarr, S., & McCartney, K. (1983). How people make their own environments: a theory of genotype greater than environment effects. *Child Development, 54*, 424–435.

Scattoni, M. L., Crawley, J., & Ricceri, L. (2009). Ultrasonic vocalizations: a tool for behavioural phenotyping of mouse models of neurodevelopmental disorders. *Neuroscience and Biobehavioral Reviews, 33*, 508–515.

Schizophrenia Working Group of the Psychiatric Genomics Consortium. (2014). Biological insights from 108 schizophrenia-associated genetic loci. *Nature, 511*, 421–427.

Schwab, S. G., et al. (1998). Support for a chromosome 18p locus conferring susceptibility to functional psychoses in families with schizophrenia, by association and linkage analysis. *American Journal of Human Genetics, 63*, 1139–1152.

Shi, J., et al. (2009). Common variants on chromosome 6p22.1 are associated with schizophrenia. *Nature, 460*, 753–757.

Smith, S. E., Li, J., Garbett, K., Mirnics, K., & Patterson, P. H. (2007). Maternal immune activation alters fetal brain development through interleukin-6. *The Journal of Neuroscience: The Official Journal of the Society for Neuroscience, 27*, 10695–10702.

Stefansson, H., et al. (2002). Neuregulin 1 and susceptibility to schizophrenia. *American Journal of Human Genetics, 71*, 877–892.

Stefansson, H., et al. (2003). Association of neuregulin 1 with schizophrenia confirmed in a Scottish population. *American Journal of Human Genetics, 72*, 83–87.

Sullivan, P. F. (2010). The psychiatric GWAS consortium: big science comes to psychiatry. *Neuron, 68*, 182–186.

Sullivan, P. F., Daly, M. J., & O'Donovan, M. (2012). Genetic architectures of psychiatric disorders: the emerging picture and its implications. *Nature Reviews Genetics, 13*, 537–551.

Sullivan, P. F., Kendler, K. S., & Neale, M. C. (2003). Schizophrenia as a complex trait: evidence from a meta-analysis of twin studies. *Archives of General Psychiatry, 60,* 1187–1192.

Suzuki, G., et al. (2009). Sept5 deficiency exerts pleiotropic influence on affective behaviors and cognitive functions in mice. *Human Molecular Genetics, 18,* 1652–1660.

Takuma, K., Ago, Y., & Matsuda, T. (2011). Preventive effects of an enriched environment on rodent psychiatric disorder models. *Journal of Pharmacological Sciences, 117,* 71–76.

Tamamaki, N., Yanagawa, Y., Tomioka, R., Miyazaki, J., Obata, K., & Kaneko, T. (2003). Green fluorescent protein expression and colocalization with calretinin, parvalbumin, and somatostatin in the GAD67-GFP knock-in mouse. *The Journal of Comparative Neurology, 467,* 60–79.

Thiselton, D. L., et al. (2004). No evidence for linkage or association of neuregulin-1 (NRG1) with disease in the Irish study of high-density schizophrenia families (ISHDSF). *Molecular Psychiatry, 9,* 777–783 Image 729.

Thompson, P. M., Egbufoama, S., & Vawter, M. P. (2003). SNAP-25 reduction in the hippocampus of patients with schizophrenia. *Progress in Neuro-Psychopharmacology & Biological Psychiatry, 27,* 411–417.

Thompson, P. M., Sower, A. C., & Perrone-Bizzozero, N. I. (1998). Altered levels of the synaptosomal associated protein SNAP-25 in schizophrenia. *Biological Psychiatry, 43,* 239–243.

Ting, A. K., et al. (2011). Neuregulin 1 promotes excitatory synapse development and function in GABAergic interneurons. *The Journal of Neuroscience, 31*(1), 15–25.

Tochigi, M., et al. (2008). Methylation status of the reelin promoter region in the brain of schizophrenic patients. *Biological Psychiatry, 63,* 530–533.

Uchida, T., Furukawa, T., Iwata, S., Yanagawa, Y., & Fukuda, A. (2014). Selective loss of parvalbumin-positive GABAergic interneurons in the cerebral cortex of maternally stressed Gad1-heterozygous mouse offspring. *Translational Psychiatry, 4,* e371.

Uchida, T., Oki, Y., Yanagawa, Y., & Fukuda, A. (2011). A heterozygous deletion in the glutamate decarboxylase 67 gene enhances maternal and fetal stress vulnerability. *Neuroscience Research, 69,* 276–282.

Ucok, A., Ozturk, M., Duman, Z., & Saruhan-Direskeneli, G. (2010). COMT Val^{158} Met polymorphism is related with interpersonal problem solving in schizophrenia. *European Psychiatry: The Journal of the Association of European Psychiatrists, 25,* 320–322.

Uher, R. (2014). Gene-environment interactions in severe mental illness. *Frontiers in Psychiatry, 5,* 48.

Ujike, H., & Sato, M. (2004). Clinical features of sensitization to methamphetamine observed in patients with methamphetamine dependence and psychosis. *Annals of the New York Academy of Sciences, 1025,* 279–287.

Veldic, M., Guidotti, A., Maloku, E., Davis, J. M., & Costa, E. (2005). In psychosis, cortical interneurons overexpress DNA-methyltransferase 1. *Proceedings of the National Academy of Sciences of the United States of America, 102,* 2152–2157.

Volk, D. W., Austin, M. C., Pierri, J. N., Sampson, A. R., & Lewis, D. A. (2000). Decreased glutamic acid decarboxylase67 messenger RNA expression in a subset of prefrontal cortical gamma-aminobutyric acid neurons in subjects with schizophrenia. *Archives of General Psychiatry, 57,* 237–245.

Volk, D. W., et al. (2012). Deficits in transcriptional regulators of cortical parvalbumin neurons in schizophrenia. *The American Journal of Psychiatry, 169,* 1082–1091.

Vuillermot, S., Feldon, J., & Meyer, U. (2011). Nurr1 is not essential for the development of prepulse inhibition deficits induced by prenatal immune activation. *Brain, Behavior, and Immunity, 25,* 1316–1321.

Vuillermot, S., Joodmardi, E., Perlmann, T., Ogren, S. O., Feldon, J., & Meyer, U. (2012). Prenatal immune activation interacts with genetic Nurr1 deficiency in the development of attentional impairments. *The Journal of Neuroscience: The Official Journal of the Society for Neuroscience, 32,* 436–451.

Walsh, T., et al. (2008). Rare structural variants disrupt multiple genes in neurodevelopmental pathways in schizophrenia. *Science, 320,* 539–543.

Waschek, J. A. (2013). VIP and PACAP: neuropeptide modulators of CNS inflammation, injury, and repair. *British Journal of Pharmacology, 169,* 512–523.

Weinstock, M. (2005). The potential influence of maternal stress hormones on development and mental health of the offspring. *Brain, Behavior, and Immunity, 19,* 296–308.

Wen, Z., et al. (2014). Synaptic dysregulation in a human iPS cell model of mental disorders. *Nature, 515,* 414–418.

Whyatt, R. M., & Barr, D. B. (2001). Measurement of organophosphate metabolites in postpartum meconium as a potential biomarker of prenatal exposure: a validation study. *Environmental Health Perspectives, 109,* 417–420.

Williams, N. M., et al. (2003). Support for genetic variation in neuregulin 1 and susceptibility to schizophrenia. *Molecular Psychiatry, 8,* 485–487.

Willner, P. (1984). The validity of animal models of depression. *Psychopharmacology, 83*(1), 1–16.

van Winkel, R., et al. (2008). Evidence that the COMT(Val158Met) polymorphism moderates subclinical psychotic and affective symptoms in unaffected first-degree relatives of patients with schizophrenia. *European Psychiatry, 23,* 219–222.

van Winkel, R., van Beveren, N. J., Simons, C., & Genetic Risk and Outcome of Psychosis (GROUP) Investigators. (2011). AKT1 moderation of cannabis-induced cognitive alterations in psychotic disorder. *Neuropsychopharmacology: Official Publication of the American College of Neuropsychopharmacology, 36,* 2529–2537.

Wirgenes, K. V., et al. (2010). Catechol O-methyltransferase variants and cognitive performance in schizophrenia and bipolar disorder versus controls. *Schizophrenia Research, 122,* 31–37.

Wood, J. D., Bonath, F., Kumar, S., Ross, C. A., & Cunliffe, V. T. (2009). Disrupted-in-schizophrenia 1 and neuregulin 1 are required for the specification of oligodendrocytes and neurones in the zebrafish brain. *Human Molecular Genetics, 18,* 391–404.

Wu, C. S., et al. (2011). Type VI adenylyl cyclase regulates neurite extension by binding to Snapin and Snap25. *Molecular and Cellular Biology, 31,* 4874–4886.

Xing, G., Zhang, L., Russell, S., & Post, R. (2006). Reduction of dopamine-related transcription factors Nurr1 and NGFI-B in the prefrontal cortex in schizophrenia and bipolar disorders. *Schizophrenia Research, 84,* 36–56.

Yang, C. R., & Svensson, K. A. (2008). Allosteric modulation of NMDA receptor via elevation of brain glycine and D-serine: the therapeutic potentials for schizophrenia. *Pharmacology & Therapeutics, 120,* 317–332.

Young, C. E., et al. (1998). SNAP-25 deficit and hippocampal connectivity in schizophrenia. *Cerebral Cortex, 8,* 261–268.

Zhang, J., Qin, L., & Zhao, H. (2013). Early repeated maternal separation induces alterations of hippocampus reelin expression in rats. *Journal of Biosciences, 38,* 27–33.

Rodent Models of Multiple Environmental Exposures with Relevance to Schizophrenia

Urs Meyer

Physiology and Behavior Laboratory, ETH Zurich, Zurich, Switzerland

INTRODUCTION

The search for etiological mechanisms in schizophrenia has long been dominated by investigations exploring the genetic basis of the disease (Gejman, Sanders, & Kendler, 2011; Shields & Gottesman, 1972). The obvious reason for these efforts lies in the fact that schizophrenia is, to a considerable degree, a heritable brain disorder, in which polygenic etiological mechanisms seem pivotal (Gejman et al., 2011; Hall, Trent, Thomas, O'Donovan, & Owen, 2015; Purcell et al., 2014). Based on population genetics, it has been suggested that the heritability of schizophrenia may reflect a combination of relatively common alleles with small effect sizes and rare alleles with relatively large effect sizes (Doherty, O'Donovan, & Owen, 2012). Genome-wide association studies have identified several risk loci at the genome-wide level and have provided evidence for a substantial burden of common risk loci (Doherty et al., 2012). In addition, these studies point to an important etiological role of relatively uncommon chromosomal abnormalities such as copy number variations, which can confer high risk of schizophrenia and related neurodevelopmental brain disorders (Giaroli, Bass, Strydom, Rantell, & McQuillin, 2014; Grayton, Fernandes, Rujescu, & Collier, 2012; Hiroi et al., 2013). These novel insights into the genetic basis of schizophrenia readily support the conclusions derived from family, adoption, and twin studies, suggesting a major involvement of genetic predisposition in schizophrenia (Kendler, 2001; Shields & Gottesman, 1972). For example, the concordance rate of schizophrenia for monozygotic twins is estimated to be approximately 40–60%, whereas it is 5–25% for dizygotic twins (Cardno & Gottesman, 2000). Even though the former underscores a major genetic contribution to schizophrenia risk, it is similarly important to emphasize the 40–60% discordance rate

for schizophrenia cases who share identical genes. Hence, there seems to be considerable room for "nongenetic" factors in influencing the risk of developing schizophrenia, which is one of the main reasons why environmental factors are now being considered as crucial components in schizophrenia etiology.

In fact, the methodological advances in human epidemiological research suggest that exposures to adverse environmental factors may play a more important role in the etiopathogenesis of schizophrenia than previously assumed (Schwartz & Susser, 2006; Torrey, 1992), and the evidence for significant associations between schizophrenia and discrete environmental exposures is accumulating (Brown, 2011; van Os, Kenis, & Rutten, 2010). These environmental adversities typically operate at sensitive periods of early brain development and/or maturation and therefore may negatively affect a number of neurodevelopmental and maturational processes required for normal adult brain functions, including neuronal specification and migration, synaptogenesis and synaptic pruning, myelination, and neuronal plasticity (Figure 1). Among the most established prenatal or perinatal factors that increase the risk of schizophrenia are prenatal or neonatal infections, prenatal exposure to stress, obstetric complications, and macro- and/or micronutrient deficiencies such as nutritional protein deprivation or iron and vitamin D deficiencies (Brown, 2011; van Os et al., 2010). In addition to these early-life environmental factors, the risk of developing schizophrenia is significantly increased after exposure to environmental adversities taking place during juvenile and/or adolescent periods, including childhood infections, periadolescent exposures to traumatizing events, low socioeconomic status, and excessive intake of drugs of abuse such as cannabis (Brown, 2011; van Os et al., 2010). The etiological relevance of environmental

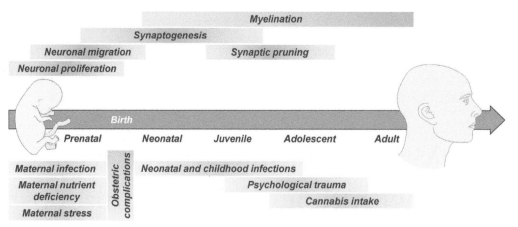

FIGURE 1   Graphical summary of main environmental risk factors of schizophrenia. The figure outlines individual risk factors in correspondence to main neurodevelopmental processes and stages of life.

exposures in schizophrenia has also received substantial support from diverse animal models, which demonstrate the development of schizophrenia-relevant brain and behavioral abnormalities following exposures to distinct environmental detriments (Meyer & Feldon, 2010; Powell, 2010). Some of these animal models are discussed in this book (see Chapters 9–13).

It is interesting to note that the relative effect size of some of these environmental risk factors can be quite substantial when compared with the effect sizes of individual genetic risk factors for schizophrenia. For example, serologically verified maternal exposure to influenza infection has been reported to increase the offspring's risk of schizophrenia by a factor of three- to sevenfold (Brown et al., 2004). This contrast with the relatively small effect sizes attributed to individual schizophrenia susceptibility genes such as neuregulin-1 (NRG1), disrupted in schizophrenia-1 (DISC1), or catechol-O-methyltransferase (COMT), which typically show odd ratios ranging between 0.7 and 1.5 when considered individually (Brown, 2011). Similarly to the small effect sizes reported for individual susceptibility genes, however, it seems that most environmental factors have modest effects on schizophrenia risk in large populations (Khashan et al., 2008; Nielsen, Benros, & Mortensen, 2014; Sørensen, Nielsen, Pedersen, & Mortensen, 2011). Against these backgrounds, it has been suggested that environmental exposures may unfold their etiopathological impact primarily in genetically predisposed subjects. According to this concept of gene–environment (G × E) interactions, the effect of a certain environmental factor on increasing schizophrenia risk would be more pronounced or only detectable in subjects with genetic vulnerability to the disorder compared with subjects without a genetic predisposition. As reviewed in numerous excellent articles elsewhere (European Network of National Networks studying Gene-Environment Interactions in Schizophrenia (EU-GEI), et al., 2014; Kannan,

Sawa, & Pletnikov, 2013; McGrath, Mortensen, Visscher, & Wray, 2013; Modinos et al., 2013; see also Chapter 17), such G × E interactions have been described for various environmental adversities, including prenatal infection (Clarke, Tanskanen, Huttunen, Whittaker, & Cannon, 2009; Demontis et al., 2011), periadolescent exposure to traumatizing events (Vinkers et al., 2013), and chronic cannabis intake (Power et al., 2014). Notably, the combination of genome-wide association studies with the epidemiological assessment of specific environmental risk factors can lead to the detection of novel schizophrenia susceptibility genes (Børglum et al., 2014). This would be the case when a specific environmental factor may unmask the (statistical and biological) significance of certain genetic variations, which would be left unnoticed when studied without inclusion of environmental exposures (Børglum et al., 2014).

In contrast to the wide appreciation of G × E interactions in schizophrenia, the possible etiological importance of multiple environmental exposures is somewhat less frequently acknowledged. Indeed, epidemiological evidence supporting a role for such environment–environment (E × E) interactions is still limited to a few epidemiological investigations, which have been conducted primarily in relation to the impact of adverse social contexts. For example, there is evidence suggesting that the effects of social deprivation on increasing the risk psychosis are significantly potentiated by environmental exposures at the individual level, including cannabis misuse (Heinz, Deserno, & Reininghaus, 2013). Whether and to what extent other established environmental risk factors can interact with each other to shape the risk of schizophrenia remains largely unanswered by current epidemiological research. Hence, direct epidemiological evidence is lacking for the cumulative impact of distinct prenatal and postnatal environmental challenges on the vulnerability to schizophrenia and related psychotic disorders.

Despite this apparent lack of knowledge, however, various new findings from environmental rodent models strongly support the biological plausibility for E × E interactions to facilitate abnormal brain development and/or maturation. In these models, the combined effects of exposures to multiple environmental insults are typically compared with those evoked by exposure to a single factor alone (Meyer, 2014). The common theoretical construct underlying these models is that exposure to an initial environmental insult can increase the subject's vulnerability to the detrimental effects of subsequent exposures to the same or other environmental adversities. Conceptually, these models thus incorporate environmental aspects of the "two-hit hypothesis" of schizophrenia (Bayer, Falkai, & Maier, 1999; Maynard, Sikich, Lieberman, & LaMantia, 2001). This hypothesis posits that early neurodevelopmental programs can be the targets for a "first hit" during early development, which in turn can predispose the affected neuronal networks to a more severe and/or enduring pathological response to a second hit occurring later in life. With respect to E × E interaction models of schizophrenia, this hypothesis further implies that the effect of a certain environmental factor on increasing disease risk would be more pronounced or only detectable in subjects with an early-life history of exposure to environmental adversities.

This chapter summarizes and integrates current attempts to model such E × E interactions in rodent models. A special emphasis is placed on their relevance to schizophrenia and related psychotic diseases. Whenever possible, these models are also discussed with respect to their relevance to other neuropsychiatric disorders, in which aberrant brain developmental processes seem critical.

PRENATAL INFECTION × POSTNATAL STRESS

Based on the findings provided by human epidemiological studies, a great deal of interest has been centered upon the establishment and use of etiological environmental animal models in which the basic experimental manipulation takes the form of prenatal exposure to infection and/or immune activation (Meyer, 2014; Meyer & Feldon, 2010, 2012; see also Chapter 11). This class of animal models has been driven, to a great extent, by the human epidemiological literature documenting elevated risk to develop schizophrenia following prenatal exposure to infection and/or inflammation (Brown & Derkits, 2010). Several different experimental approaches are commonly used in rodents, including maternal gestational exposure to human influenza virus, the bacterial endotoxin lipopolysaccharide (LPS),

the viral mimic polyinosine-polycytidylic acid—poly (I:C)—the locally acting inflammatory agent turpentine, or selected pro-inflammatory cytokines (Meyer, Feldon, & Fatemi, 2009). These models have been proven very helpful for the establishment of causal relationships and for the identification of cellular and molecular mechanisms affecting normal brain development in the event of early-life immune exposures. They also allow a multifaceted, longitudinal monitoring of the disease process as it unfolds during the course of neurodevelopment from prenatal to adult stages of life (Piontkewitz, Arad, & Weiner, 2011; Piontkewitz, Arad, & Weiner, 2012; Richetto, Calabrese, Riva, & Meyer, 2014; Vuillermot, Weber, Feldon, & Meyer, 2010).

An important recent refinement of these models is the incorporation of multiple etiologically relevant risk factors by combining prenatal immune challenges with specific genetic manipulations (see Chapter 17) or additional environmental adversities. One of the most widely used experimental approaches for these purposes is based on maternal gestational treatment with poly (I:C). Poly (I:C) is a commercially available synthetic analog of double-stranded RNA. Double-stranded RNA is generated during viral infection as a replication intermediate for single-stranded RNA or as a by-product of symmetrical transcription in DNA viruses (Takeuchi & Akira, 2007). It is recognized by the mammalian immune system through the transmembrane protein Toll-like receptor 3 (TLR3) (Alexopoulou, Holt, Medzhitov, & Flavell, 2001). TLRs are a class of pathogen recognition receptors that recognize invariant structures present on and/or associated with virulent pathogens. Upon binding to TLRs, double-stranded RNA or its synthetic analog poly (I:C) stimulates the production and release of many pro-inflammatory cytokines, including interleukin (IL)-1β, IL-6, and tumor necrosis factor-α (Cunningham, Campion, Teeling, Felton, & Perry, 2007; Meyer et al., 2006). In addition, poly (I:C) is a potent inducer of the type I interferons α and β (Cunningham et al., 2007; Meyer et al., 2006). Administration of poly (I:C) can therefore efficiently mimic the acute phase response to viral infection (Traynor, Majde, Bohnet, & Krueger, 2004).

As reviewed in detail elsewhere (Meyer & Feldon, 2012), there are several features of the maternal poly (I:C) administration model that make it highly suitable for the experimental investigation of E × E (or G × E) interactions with relevance to schizophrenia pathogenesis. Perhaps one of the most relevant aspects for the present discussion is that the poly (I:C) model can be modified in such a way that the intensity of the maternal inflammatory response can be adjusted by appropriate dosing (Meyer & Feldon, 2012). This allows researchers to study the impact of immune stimulus intensity in shaping the vulnerability to long-lasting brain disorders. Indeed, whereas prenatal exposure to high doses of poly (I:C) typically induce robust brain and behavioral changes in the offspring (Meyer, 2014; Meyer & Feldon, 2010, 2012), prenatal treatment with low doses of poly (I:C) only induces mild (or even latent) abnormalities in adult brain functions (Lipina, Zai, Hlousek, Roder, & Wong, 2013; Meyer, Feldon, Schedlowski, & Yee, 2005). Hence, the sensitivity of the poly (I:C) model to dosing effects yields to the identification of threshold effects in neurodevelopmental brain dysfunctions associated with prenatal exposure to infection/inflammation. Furthermore, this feature of the model strongly facilitates the identification of possible interactive effects between (mild) prenatal immune activation and other environmental (or genetic) risk factors implicated in schizophrenia.

Giovanoli et al. (2013) have recently taken advantage of this feature of the prenatal poly (I:C) model with the aim to explore possible interactions between mild (and physiologically relevant) prenatal immune activation and exposure to another environmental risk factor implicated in schizophrenia, namely experience of traumatizing events during adolescent development (Varese et al., 2012). In this two-hit mouse model, maternal treatment with a low (subthreshold) dose of poly (I:C) served as the first hit and exposure to subchronic stress in pubescence served as the second hit (Giovanoli et al., 2013). The authors found that mild prenatal immune activation and peripubertal stress caused synergistic effects in the development of specific behavioral abnormalities such as sensorimotor gating deficiency and enhanced sensitivity to psychotomimetic drugs, both of which are key pathological features of schizophrenia and related psychotic disorders (Giovanoli et al., 2013). Neither immune activation alone nor stress alone affected these behavioral functions in adulthood, so that abnormalities in these domains became evident only after combined exposure to the two environmental factors (Giovanoli et al., 2013). Interestingly, the emergence of multiple behavioral dysfunctions in offspring with combined exposure to prenatal immune activation and pubertal stress was clearly dependent on postpubertal maturational processes, which, in turn, is consistent with the clinical course of mental illnesses with delayed onsets, including schizophrenia (Paus, Keshavan, & Giedd, 2008). Moreover, interactive effects between prenatal immune activation and postnatal stress were not seen in this model when stress was applied in late adolescence (Giovanoli et al., 2013), suggesting that the precise timing of postnatal stress is critical for the interaction with the prenatal immune challenge. In a follow-up study, Giovanoli, Weber, and Meyer (2014) further found a significant reduction of parvalbumin-expressing interneurons in the ventral dentate gyrus of adult mice exposed to combined prenatal immune activation and pubertal stress. Single exposure to either environmental factor was insufficient to cause similar neuropathology. These findings thus added additional support for the hypothesis that prenatal immune activation and stress in puberty can interact with each other to cause cellular abnormalities commonly observed in schizophrenia (Giovanoli et al., 2014). Taken together, the combination of a subthreshold prenatal immune activation model with peripubertal stress exposure in mice illustrates that prenatal infection can act as a "disease primer" that increases the vulnerability of the offspring to the detrimental neuropathological effects of other environmental insults such as peripubertal stress.

A similar conclusion can be drawn on the basis of the findings reported by Deslauriers, Larouche, Sarret, and Grignon (2013), who combined poly (I:C)–induced prenatal immune activation with peripubertal stress exposure in the form of restraint stress in mice. The behavioral deficits caused by the combined exposure of immune activation and stress were accompanied by cellular abnormalities in the prefrontal and striatal γ-aminobutyric acid (GABA)ergic and dopaminergic systems. These neuropathological changes were characterized by reduced expression of the 67-kDa form of glutamic acid decarboxylase (GAD67), the main rate-limiting enzyme of GABA synthesis, and by increased dopamine D2 receptor expression. Similar abnormalities have been noted in the brain of patients with schizophrenia and other neurodevelopmental disorders, including bipolar disorder and autism (Deslauriers et al., 2013).

The potential of prenatal immune activation to interact with postnatal stressor does not seem to be limited to the priming by viral-like immune activation, but similar interactions can also occur following initial exposure to bacterial-like immune activation induced by maternal LPS treatment. LPS is recognized primarily by the pathogen recognition receptor TLR4 and induces a cytokine-associated innate immune response that is typically seen after infection with gram-negative bacteria (Triantafilou & Triantafilou, 2002). Using an LPS-based rat model of prenatal immune activation, Burt, Tse, Boksa, and Wong (2013) revealed significant interactions between this early prenatal insult and acute stress exposure in early adolescence, the latter of which was induced by acute restraint stress or by exogenous application of the stress hormone corticosterone. The authors found that maternal LPS treatment alone, that is, in the absence of additional stress exposure, was sufficient to abolish hippocampal long-term depression and other N-methyl-D-aspartate (NMDA) receptor-dependent electrophysiological parameters in the offspring. Interestingly, however, acute exposure to restraint stress or corticosterone treatment stress facilitated long-term depression in hippocampal slices from prenatal LPS rats but not prenatal control rats, indicating that the prenatal manipulation altered the responsiveness of the adolescent offspring to physiological and pharmacological stressors

(Burt et al., 2013). Indeed, these findings suggest a level of interaction where (supra-threshold) prenatal infection causes NMDA receptor hypofunction in resting conditions but heightened responsiveness of NMDA receptor–mediated synaptic functions to (acute) stress (Burt et al., 2013).

PRENATAL INFECTION × ADOLESCENT CANNABIS INTAKE

Prenatal immune activation models have also been used recently to explore possible interactive effects with another environmental risk factor of schizophrenia, namely adolescent cannabis intake. Chronic cannabis use during adolescence has been repeatedly found to increase the risk to develop psychotic disorders in early adulthood (Henquet, Murray, Linszen, & van Os, 2005; Moore et al., 2007). The endocannabinoid signaling system, which is targeted by the main psychoactive component of cannabis (Δ^9-tetrahydrocannabinol), plays an important role in processes of brain maturation and cognitive development (Trezza et al., 2012). Altering endocannabinoid neurotransmission by chronic consumption of cannabis during adolescence may thus negatively affect brain maturational sequences and facilitate the emergence of behavioral, emotional, and cognitive disturbances associated with psychotic disorders (Luzi, Morrison, Powell, di Forti, & Murray, 2008). It needs to be pointed out, however, that only a minority of cannabis users will eventually develop psychotic disorders. It has therefore been suggested that an interaction of cannabis with other genetic and/or environmental risk factors is required to induce psychosis (Pelayo-Terán, Suárez-Pinilla, Chadi, & Crespo-Facorro, 2012; Power et al., 2014).

Recent experimental research in rats has therefore sought evidence for the possibility that the negative effects of adolescent cannabis exposure could be potentiated by prenatal immune challenge. In this E × E interaction model, maternal gestational exposure to the viral mimic poly (I:C) served as the "first hit" and chronic adolescent administration of the synthetic cannabinoid HU210 as the second hit. In a first study, Dalton et al. (Schwartz & Susser, 2006) revealed synergistic interactions between these two environmental exposures on serotonin receptor binding in the hippocampus, which is one of the main brain areas derogated in schizophrenia (Harrison, 2004). More specifically, the authors found that although HU210 alone did not exert any noticeable effects, it significantly potentiated the increase in serotonin 1_A receptor binding induced by prenatal poly (I:C) treatment (Dalton, Verdurand, Walker, Hodgson, & Zavitsanou, 2012). These synergistic effects became apparent at late adolescence and persisted into adulthood, indicating the combined exposure to prenatal immune activation and adolescent cannabinoid exposure resulted in long-lasting

serotonergic changes in the hippocampus. Using the same E × E interaction model in rats, Hollins et al. (Hollins, Zavitsanou, Walker, & Cairns, 2014) recently compared the single and combined effects of prenatal poly (I:C)–induced immune activation and adolescent cannabinoid exposure on genome-wide microRNA (miRNA) expression in the entorhinal cortex, which represents another brain region strongly associated with schizophrenia (Benes & Berretta, 2000). MiRNAs are small noncoding RNA molecules that can regulate gene expression post-transcriptionally, thereby affecting the de novo synthesis of proteins (Ambros, 2004). Accumulating evidence suggests that numerous miRNAs are deregulated in peripheral and central tissues of patients with schizophrenia and other neurodevelopmental disorders (Geaghan & Cairns, in press). These aberrations may readily represent a molecular mechanism for altered gene translation in these brain disorders (Geaghan & Cairns, in press), but the underlying etiopathological processes leading to altered miRNA expression remain unclear. By revealing an altered miRNA expression signature following combined prenatal immune activation and cannabinoid exposure, the recent E × E interaction study by Hollins et al. (2014) thus provides an important contribution to our understanding of how environmental risk factors could cause long-term changes in miRNA expression with relevance to schizophrenia and related disorders. Interestingly, the miRNA expression profile induced by combined prenatal immune activation and cannabinoid exposure was largely characterized by altered expression of miRNAs residing within the imprinted DLK1-DIO3 locus on chromosome 6q32 (Hollins et al., 2014). The rat 6q32 locus corresponds to the 14q32 locus in humans, which similarly encodes a large proportion of miRNAs differentially expressed in peripheral blood lymphocytes from patients with schizophrenia (Ambros, 2004; Gardiner et al., 2012). Hence, the findings obtained from this novel E × E interaction model suggest that interaction of early (prenatal infection) and late (adolescent cannabinoid exposure) environmental insults may affect miRNA expression profile in a way that is relevant to schizophrenia.

PRENATAL INFECTION × PRENATAL IRON DEFICIENCY

Prenatal iron deficiency is another relatively well-documented environmental risk factor of schizophrenia (Ellman et al., 2012; Insel, Schaefer, McKeague, Susser, & Brown, 2008; Sørensen, Nielsen, Pedersen, & Mortensen, 2011). Depending on the population, maternal iron deficiency has been shown to increase the offspring's disease risk by a factor of 1.5- to 4-fold (Insel et al., 2008; Sørensen et al., 2011). It has been proposed recently that prenatal exposure to infection may interact with maternal iron deficiency to disrupt normal brain and behavioral development (Harvey & Boksa, in press). This potential link indeed appears plausible for several reasons. First, both environmental factors show a high global incidence (Gangopadhyay, Karoshi, & Keith, 2011; Silasi et al., 2015), so that these two insults may occur simultaneously during pregnancy. Second, activation of the immune system typically induces a transient state of hypoferremia (Kluger & Rothenburg, 1979). This process is mediated to a great extent by the pro-inflammatory cytokines IL-1β and IL-6 (Lee, Peng, Gelbart, Wang, & Beutler, 2005; Nemeth et al., 2004) and serves to reduce the availability of this essential micronutrient to the invading pathogens as part of the host's inherent defense system (Kluger & Rothenburg, 1979). Because iron is also pivotal for normal brain development (Kwik-Uribe, Golub, & Keen, 2000; Unger et al., 2007), infection-induced hypoferremia may readily contribute to neurodevelopmental abnormalities caused by prenatal immune challenges.

To test possible interactive effects between prenatal infection and iron deficiency on abnormal brain and behavioral development, Harvey and Boksa developed a model in which pregnant rats were placed on iron-sufficient or iron-deficient diets from early gestation until the early postpartum period and were treated with the bacterial endotoxin LPS or vehicle control solution during mid-/late gestation (Harvey & Boksa, in press). In a first series of investigations, the authors showed that LPS administration in iron-deficient rats induced more excessive pro-inflammatory cytokine responses compared with LPS exposure in iron-sufficient rats, suggesting that the maternal iron status is a critical determinant of inflammatory responses to bacterial-like immune challenge (Harvey & Boksa, in press). Despite these interactions at the level of maternal inflammatory responses, however, the two environmental exposures appeared to induce distinct neurodevelopmental changes and adult behavioral abnormalities in the offspring (Harvey & Boksa, 2014; Harvey & Boksa, in press). For example, adult offspring born to iron-deficient dams (in the absence of additional LPS exposure) displayed significant deficits in sensorimotor gating and emotional learning, whereas offspring from LPS-treated dams (under iron-sufficient diets) showed altered social behavior with unfamiliar rats and locomotor changes in a novel environment and during exploration in response to the psychotomimetic drug amphetamine (Harvey & Boksa, 2014). These findings suggest that the long-term effects of prenatal (bacterial-like) immune challenge and iron deficiency on adult behavioral functions are additive, such that offspring exposed to both insults develop quantitatively more adult behavioral abnormalities than offspring exposed to either factor alone (Harvey & Boksa, 2014). It is therefore likely that maternal infection and iron deficiency may disrupt brain and

behavioral development in the offspring through independent mechanisms of action, despite the existence of interactive effects at the level of the maternal immune response to infection (Harvey & Boksa, in press). This interpretation may seem surprising given that the severity of long-term brain abnormalities following prenatal immune challenge has previously been shown to correlate with the intensity of maternal immune reactions, both in experimental models (Meyer et al., 2005; Lipina et al., 2013; Shi, Fatemi, Sidwell, & Patterson, 2003) as well as in human settings (Ellman et al., 2010). The findings from Harvey and Boksa (2014, in press) may, in fact, be taken to support the idea that multiple (and yet unknown) mechanisms exist whereby maternal infection and/or inflammation during pregnancy can affect brain development in the offspring (Meyer & Feldon, 2010). Hence, the assumption that greater inflammatory reactions in the pregnant maternal host may lead to more severe neuropathological outcomes in the offspring may hold true for some cases (Ellman et al., 2010; Meyer et al., 2005; Shi et al., 2003; Smith, Li, Garbett, Mirnics, & Patterson, 2007), but not necessarily for others (Harvey & Boksa, 2014, in press). This consideration may be particularly relevant when the nature and/or severity of the maternal inflammatory responses are compared against different nutritional statuses (Harvey & Boksa, 2014, in press) or immune-pathogens (Harvey & Boksa, 2012).

CESAREAN SECTION × PERINATAL ANOXIA

Schizophrenia has frequently been associated with obstetric complications, with such perinatal complications reported in the medical histories of ~20% of schizophrenic patients (Cannon, Jones, & Murray, 2002; Lewis & Murray, 1987). Meta-analyses of population-based data identified three main categories of obstetric complications that are significantly associated with schizophrenia (Cannon et al., 2002): (1) complications of pregnancy (bleeding, preeclampsia, diabetes, and rhesus incompatibility), (2) abnormal fetal growth and development (low birth weight, congenital malformations, and small head circumference), and (3) complications of delivery (asphyxia, uterine atony, and emergency cesarean section). The pooled odds ratio of the effect of exposure to obstetric complications on the subsequent development of schizophrenia has been estimated to be approximately 2.0 (Geddes & Lawrie, 1995), indicating that individuals with a medical history of obstetric complication are twice as likely to develop schizophrenia.

The effects of obstetric complications, including diabetes during pregnancy, preeclampsia, intrauterine growth restriction, cesarean section, and perinatal hypoxia, have also been extensively studied in laboratory animals (Boksa, 2004). Some of these experimental studies (e.g., diabetes during pregnancy, preeclampsia, intrauterine growth restriction) have primarily focused on acute developmental effects in fetal or neonatal life, so that their possible long-term influences on schizophrenia-related phenotypes in adulthood remain largely unknown (Boksa, 2004). Some models of obstetric complications, however, have also documented the long-term consequences on brain and behavioral functions. As reviewed in detail elsewhere (Boksa, 2004), these include models of obstetric complication in the form of birth by cesarean section, perinatal/postnatal hypoxia, and placental insufficiency.

The existing evidence derived from animal models suggests that discrete obstetric complications can each induce a certain degree of brain and behavioral abnormalities, some of which are long-lasting and reminiscent of schizophrenia-related dysfunctions (Boksa, 2004). In support of possible E × E interactions, however, some of the negative effects on brain functions appear to be more extensive when several obstetric complications cooccur. For example, in comparison to rats born by rapid cesarean section alone, animals born by cesarean section with acute perinatal anoxia develop helpless-like behavior and show alterations in passive avoidance pretraining (Boksa, Wilson, & Rochford, 1998), indicating impaired coping with stressful situations upon combined exposure to these perinatal factors. Consistent with this interpretation, adult rats born by cesarean section with acute anoxia display enhanced locomotor activity in response to stress compared with animals born vaginally or by cesarean section alone (El-Khodor & Boksa, 2000). Combined exposure to cesarean section and perinatal anoxia further leads to differential dopaminergic responses to adult stress compared with animals exposed to either obstetric complication alone (El-Khodor & Boksa, 2001). Taken together, these findings suggest that obstetric complications can interact with stress in adulthood to alter behavior and dopaminergic functions, especially when several perinatal complications cooccur (Boksa & El-Khodor, 2003). Obstetric events are often interlinked, so that any complication during pregnancy is likely to increase the risk of further pregnancy complications and impact on the eventual labor and delivery (Clarke, Harley, & Cannon, 2006). Therefore, additional investigations towards a better understanding of the long-term effects of exposure to multiple obstetric events on brain and behavioral are clearly warranted.

NEONATAL × ADOLESCENT STRESS

In view of the apparent role of stress exposure in the etiology of schizophrenia (Corcoran et al., 2003; Holtzman et al., 2013; Varese et al., 2012), several animal models have been developed in order to unravel the neuroendocrine and neuronal processes underlying the disruption of adult brain functions following stress exposure at sensitive developmental and maturational periods (Goel & Bale, 2009; see also Chapters 9 and 11C). To model prenatal stress exposure in laboratory rodents, researchers typically subject pregnant dams to subchronic or chronic psychological stressors (e.g., restraint stress of electrical foot shock) or stress-hormone treatments (e.g., glucocorticoid administration). Depending on the severity and gestational timing, maternal stress exposure has been shown to induce a variety of brain and behavioral abnormalities in the offspring, some of which are reminiscent of schizophrenia-related dysfunctions (Goel & Bale, 2009; Koenig, 2006; Koenig et al., 2005; Meyer & Feldon, 2010). One commonly used experimental procedure to induce early neonatal stress is based on maternal deprivation, in which neonates are daily separated from the lactating dam for a certain amount of time (Franklin, Saab, & Mansuy, 2012). This can be coupled with additional social isolation of the neonates by separating pups individually from each other during the phase of maternal deprivation. Social isolation procedures are also used to induce postweaning stress; that is, after the animals have been weaned from their mothers (typically on postnatal day 21 in rats and mice) (see Chapter 9). In addition to social isolation, several other procedures are frequently used in rodents to induce stress during adolescent maturation, including chronic restraint stress, exogenous glucocorticoid treatment, and exposure to unpredictable, variable stress (Burke & Miczek, 2014; Green & McCormick, 2013).

Exposure to each of these pre- and postweaning stressors can induce long-term brain and behavioral deficits relevant to schizophrenia (Bouet, Lecrux, Tran, & Freret, 2011; Niwa, Matsumoto, Mouri, Ozaki, & Nabeshima, 2011; Van den Buuse, Garner, & Koch, 2003). Accumulating evidence suggests that specific stressors applied at different periods of neonatal or adolescent development can interact with each other to shape the vulnerability for adult brain dysfunctions. For example, the combination of early neonatal stress (induced by maternal deprivation) and adolescent stress (induced by corticosterone treatment) has been shown to decrease hippocampal levels of brain-derived neurotrophic factor in adulthood and to impair hippocampus-dependent learning and memory (Choy, de Visser, Nichols, & van den Buuse, 2008). Even though single exposure to either of these stressors was found to induce mild cognitive abnormalities, the severity of hippocampus-dependent learning and memory was markedly increased following combined exposure to neonatal and adolescent stress (Choy et al., 2008). Interestingly, these effects appear to be sex-specific in that cognitive deficits emerge in male rats only (Hill, Klug, et al., 2014). On the other hand, female rats exposed to the combination of early neonatal stress (maternal deprivation) and adolescent stress (corticosterone treatment) developed signs of anhedonia (as assessed using a sucrose preference test), which were absent in males (Hill, Klug, et al., 2014). Sex-specific effects of combined exposure to these stressors have also been noted with respect to hippocampal and prefrontal brain-derived neurotrophic factor levels (Hill, Kiss Von Soly, et al., 2014; Hill, Klug, et al., 2014) and dopamine receptor alterations in forebrain structures (Hill, Kiss Von Soly, et al., 2014). Together, these findings highlight that exposure to (multiple) stressors can induce a distinct pattern of long-term brain pathology in males and females, with cognitive and affective functions being more readily impaired in the male and female sex, respectively.

Long-term brain pathology can also be induced by combined developmental exposure to "pharmacological" stressors and psychological stressors. Based on the suggested involvement of altered glutamatergic development and functions in schizophrenia (Javitt, Zukin, Heresco-Levy, & Umbricht, 2012; Snyder & Gao, 2013), a great deal of interest has been placed on the effects of developmental exposure to noncompetitive NMDA blockers such as phencyclidine or dizocilpine (MK-801) in rodent models (Mouri, Noda, Enomoto, & Nabeshima, 2007; Seillier & Giuffrida, 2009). Recent investigations in rats show that combined neonatal MK-801 treatment and chronic adolescent stress exposure induced by postweaning isolation rearing have interactive effects on adult schizophrenia-related abnormalities: whereas neonatally MK-801–treated rats that had been reared in isolation displayed long-lasting deficits in sensorimotor gating, hyperlocomotion, and impaired object recognition memory, animals exposed to one of these manipulations alone exhibited less robust sensorimotor gating abnormalities and normal locomotor and cognitive functions (Lim, Taylor, & Malone, 2012). Similar findings were obtained when postweaning social isolation was combined with phencyclidine (Gaskin, Alexander, & Fone, 2014), suggesting that pharmacologically induced NMDA receptor blockade during early neonatal periods represents a robust priming event for subsequent stress-induced brain dysfunctions.

CONCLUDING REMARKS

Human epidemiological findings have been highly influential in shaping our current thinking on how to model schizophrenia-relevant etiological factors in animals. Indeed, they have encouraged the establishment of neurodevelopmental animal models that are based on exposure to specific environmental insults during prenatal, neonatal, and adolescent periods of life, including immune activation, obstetric complications, nutritional deficiencies, and psychological stressors. With the attempts to incorporate multiple environmental factors, we have seen an important refinement of these environmental models over the past several years. The findings from these models suggest that early-life exposure to an initial environmental insult can increase the vulnerability of the developing organism to the detrimental effects of subsequent adversities during postnatal maturation. Hence, models of multiple environmental exposures can be used to test key aspects of the "multiple-hit hypothesis" of schizophrenia (Bayer et al., 1999; Maynard et al., 2001).

Whereas the importance of G × E interactions has been widely appreciated in this hypothesis, the etiological relevance of E × E interactions has attracted somewhat less attention thus far. The findings from current E × E interaction models may therefore encourage epidemiologists and basic researchers to extend their research efforts toward a closer examination of such interactions. Such efforts would be highly desirable because environmental factors are more amenable to preventive interventions compared with genetic factors (Brown & Patterson, 2011; McGrath, Brown, & St Clair, 2011). Ongoing experimental research in rodent models is beginning to determine the specificity of brain and behavioral pathology following exposure to multiple environmental factors. The continuous use and further extension of E × E interaction models may provide important information to guide future epidemiological research and to establish preventive interventions that could reduce the risk of developing long-term brain abnormalities associated with environmental exposures.

References

Alexopoulou, L., Holt, A. C., Medzhitov, R., & Flavell, R. A. (2001). Recognition of double-stranded RNA and activation of NF-kappaB by Toll-like receptor 3. *Nature, 413*, 732–738.

Ambros, V. (2004). The functions of animal microRNAs. *Nature, 431*, 350–355.

Bayer, T. A., Falkai, P., & Maier, W. (1999). Genetic and non-genetic vulnerability factors in schizophrenia: the basis of the "two hit hypothesis". *Journal of Psychiatric Research, 33*, 543–548.

Benes, F. M., & Berretta, S. (2000). Amygdalo-entorhinal inputs to the hippocampal formation in relation to schizophrenia. *Annals of the New York of Academy of Sciences, 911*, 293–304.

Boksa, P. (2004). Animal models of obstetric complications in relation to schizophrenia. *Brain Research. Brain Research Reviews, 45*, 1–17.

Boksa, P., & El-Khodor, B. F. (2003). Birth insult interacts with stress at adulthood to alter dopaminergic function in animal models: possible implications for schizophrenia and other disorders. *Neuroscience & Biobehavioral Reviews, 27*, 91–101.

Boksa, P., Wilson, D., & Rochford, J. (1998). Responses to stress and novelty in adult rats born vaginally, by cesarean section or by cesarean section with acute anoxia. *Biology of the Neonate, 74*, 48–59.

Børglum, A. D., Demontis, D., Grove, J., Pallesen, J., Hollegaard, M. V., Pedersen, C. B., GROUP investigators10, et al. (2014). Genome-wide study of association and interaction with maternal cytomegalovirus infection suggests new schizophrenia loci. *Molecular Psychiatry, 19*, 325–333.

Bouet, V., Lecrux, B., Tran, G., & Freret, T. (2011). Effect of pre- versus post-weaning environmental disturbances on social behaviour in mice. *Neuroscience Letters, 488*, 221–224.

Brown, A. S. (2011). The environment and susceptibility to schizophrenia. *Progress in Neurobiology, 93*, 23–58.

Brown, A. S., Begg, M. D., Gravenstein, S., Schaefer, C. A., Wyatt, R. J., Bresnahan, M., et al. (2004). Serologic evidence of prenatal influenza in the etiology of schizophrenia. *Archives of General Psychiatry, 61*, 774–780.

Brown, A. S., & Derkits, E. J. (2010). Prenatal infection and schizophrenia: a review of epidemiologic and translational studies. *American Journal of Psychiatry, 167*, 261–280.

Brown, A. S., & Patterson, P. H. (2011). Maternal infection and schizophrenia: implications for prevention. *Schizophrenia Bulletin, 37*, 284–290.

Burke, A. R., & Miczek, K. A. (2014). Stress in adolescence and drugs of abuse in rodent models: role of dopamine, CRF, and HPA axis. *Psychopharmacology, 231*, 1557–1580.

Burt, M. A., Tse, Y. C., Boksa, P., & Wong, T. P. (2013). Prenatal immune activation interacts with stress and corticosterone exposure later in life to modulate N-methyl-D-aspartate receptor synaptic function and plasticity. *International Journal of Neuropsychopharmacology, 16*, 1835–1848.

Cannon, M., Jones, P. B., & Murray, R. M. (2002). Obstetric complications and schizophrenia: historical and meta-analytic review. *American Journal of Psychiatry, 159*, 1080–1092.

Cardno, A. G., & Gottesman, I. I. (2000). Twin studies of schizophrenia: from bow-and-arrow concordances to star wars Mx and functional genomics. *American Journal of Medical Genetics, 97*, 12–17.

Choy, K. H., de Visser, Y., Nichols, N. R., & van den Buuse, M. (2008). Combined neonatal stress and young-adult glucocorticoid stimulation in rats reduce BDNF expression in hippocampus: effects on learning and memory. *Hippocampus, 18*, 655–667.

Clarke, M. C., Harley, M., & Cannon, M. (2006). The role of obstetric events in schizophrenia. *Schizophrenia Bulletin, 32*, 3–8.

Clarke, M. C., Tanskanen, A., Huttunen, M., Whittaker, J. C., & Cannon, M. (2009). Evidence for an interaction between familial liability and prenatal exposure to infection in the causation of schizophrenia. *American Journal of Psychiatry, 166*(9), 1025–1030.

Corcoran, C., Walker, E., Huot, R., Mittal, V., Tessner, K., Kestler, L., et al. (2003). The stress cascade and schizophrenia: etiology and onset. *Schizophrenia Bulletin, 29*, 671–692.

Cunningham, C., Campion, S., Teeling, J., Felton, L., & Perry, V. H. (2007). The sickness behaviour and CNS inflammatory mediator profile induced by systemic challenge of mice with synthetic double-stranded RNA (poly I:C). *Brain, Behavior, and Immunity, 21*, 490–502.

Dalton, V. S., Verdurand, M., Walker, A., Hodgson, D. M., & Zavitsanou, K. (2012). Synergistic effect between maternal infection and adolescent cannabinoid exposure on serotonin 5HT1A receptor binding in the hippocampus: testing the "two hit" hypothesis for the development of schizophrenia. *ISRN Psychiatry, 2012*, 451865.

Demontis, D., Nyegaard, M., Buttenschøn, H. N., Hedemand, A., Pedersen, C. B., Grove, J., et al. (2011). Association of GRIN1 and GRIN2A-D with schizophrenia and genetic interaction with maternal herpes simplex virus-2 infection affecting disease risk. *American Journal of Medical Genetics Part B: Neuropsychiatric Genetics, 156B*, 913–922.

Deslauriers, J., Larouche, A., Sarret, P., & Grignon, S. (2013). Combination of prenatal immune challenge and restraint stress affects prepulse inhibition and dopaminergic/GABAergic markers. *Progress in Neuro-Psychopharmacology & Biological Psychiatry, 45*, 156–164.

Doherty, J. L., O'Donovan, M. C., & Owen, M. J. (2012). Recent genomic advances in schizophrenia. *Clinical Genetics, 81*, 103–109.

El-Khodor, B. F., & Boksa, P. (2000). Transient birth hypoxia increases behavioral responses to repeated stress in the adult rat. *Behavioural Brain Research, 107*, 171–175.

El-Khodor, B., & Boksa, P. (2001). Caesarean section birth produces long term changes in dopamine D1 receptors and in stress-induced regulation of D3 and D4 receptors in the rat brain. *Neuropsychopharmacology, 25*, 423–439.

Ellman, L. M., Deicken, R. F., Vinogradov, S., Kremen, W. S., Poole, J. H., Kern, D. M., et al. (2010). Structural brain alterations in schizophrenia following fetal exposure to the inflammatory cytokine interleukin-8. *Schizophrenia Research, 121*, 46–54.

Ellman, L. M., Vinogradov, S., Kremen, W. S., Poole, J. H., Kern, D. M., Deicken, R. F., et al. (2012). Low maternal hemoglobin during pregnancy and diminished neuromotor and neurocognitive performance in offspring with schizophrenia. *Schizophrenia Research, 138*, 81–87.

European Network of National Networks studying Gene-Environment Interactions in Schizophrenia (EU-GEI), van Os, J., Rutten, B. P., Myin-Germeys, I., Delespaul, P., Viechtbauer, W., van Zelst, C., et al. (2014). Identifying gene-environment interactions in schizophrenia: contemporary challenges for integrated, large-scale investigations. *Schizophrenia Bulletin, 40*, 729–736.

Franklin, T. B., Saab, B. J., & Mansuy, I. M. (2012). Neural mechanisms of stress resilience and vulnerability. *Neuron, 75*, 747–761.

Gangopadhyay, R., Karoshi, M., & Keith, L. (2011). Anemia and pregnancy: a link to maternal chronic diseases. *International Journal of Gynecology & Obstetrics, 115*(Suppl. 1), S11–S15.

Gardiner, E., Beveridge, N. J., Wu, J. Q., Carr, V., Scott, R. J., Tooney, P. A., et al. (2012). Imprinted DLK1-DIO3 region of 14q32 defines a schizophrenia-associated miRNA signature in peripheral blood mononuclear cells. *Molecular Psychiatry, 17*, 827–840.

Gaskin, P. L., Alexander, S. P., & Fone, K. C. (2014). Neonatal phencyclidine administration and post-weaning social isolation as a dual-hit model of 'schizophrenia-like' behaviour in the rat. *Psychopharmacology, 231*, 2533–2545.

Geaghan, M., Cairns M. J. MicroRNA and posttranscriptional dysregulation in psychiatry. *Biological Psychiatry*, in press (Epub ahead of print [PMID: 25636176]).

Geddes, J. R., & Lawrie, S. M. (1995). Obstetric complications and schizophrenia: a meta-analysis. *British Journal of Psychiatry, 167*, 786–793.

Gejman, P. V., Sanders, A. R., & Kendler, K. S. (2011). Genetics of schizophrenia: new findings and challenges. *Annual Review of Genomics and Human Genetics, 12*, 121–144.

Giaroli, G., Bass, N., Strydom, A., Rantell, K., & McQuillin, A. (2014). Does rare matter? Copy number variants at 16p11.2 and the risk of psychosis: a systematic review of literature and meta-analysis. *Schizophrenia Research, 159*, 340–346.

Giovanoli, S., Engler, H., Engler, A., Richetto, J., Voget, M., Willi, R., et al. (2013). Stress in puberty unmasks latent neuropathological consequences of prenatal immune activation in mice. *Science, 339*, 1095–1099.

Giovanoli, S., Weber, L., & Meyer, U. (2014). Single and combined effects of prenatal immune activation and peripubertal stress on parvalbumin and reelin expression in the hippocampal formation. *Brain, Behavior, and Immunity, 40*, 48–54.

Goel, N., & Bale, T. L. (2009). Examining the intersection of sex and stress in modelling neuropsychiatric disorders. *Journal of Neuroendocrinology, 21*, 415–420.

Grayton, H. M., Fernandes, C., Rujescu, D., & Collier, D. A. (2012). Copy number variations in neurodevelopmental disorders. *Progress in Neurobiology, 99*, 81–91.

Green, M. R., & McCormick, C. M. (2013). Effects of stressors in adolescence on learning and memory in rodent models. *Hormones and Behavior, 64*, 364–379.

Hall, J., Trent, S., Thomas, K. L., O'Donovan, M. C., & Owen, M. J. (2015). Genetic risk for schizophrenia: convergence on synaptic pathways involved in plasticity. *Biological Psychiatry, 77*, 52–58.

Harrison, P. J. (2004). The hippocampus in schizophrenia: a review of the neuropathological evidence and its pathophysiological implications. *Psychopharmacology, 174*, 151–162.

Harvey, L., & Boksa, P. (2012). A stereological comparison of GAD67 and reelin expression in the hippocampal stratum oriens of offspring from two mouse models of maternal inflammation during pregnancy. *Neuropharmacology, 62*, 1767–1776.

Harvey, L., & Boksa, P. (2014). Additive effects of maternal iron deficiency and prenatal immune activation on adult behaviors in rat offspring. *Brain, Behavior, and Immunity, 40*, 27–37.

Harvey, L., Boksa, P. Do prenatal immune activation and maternal iron deficiency interact to affect neurodevelopment and early behavior in rat offspring? *Brain, Behavior, and Immunity*, in press (Epub ahead of print [PMID: 24064370]).

Heinz, A., Deserno, L., & Reininghaus, U. (2013). Urbanicity, social adversity and psychosis. *World Psychiatry, 12*, 187–197.

Henquet, C., Murray, R., Linszen, D., & van Os, J. (2005). The environment and schizophrenia: the role of cannabis use. *Schizophrenia Bulletin, 31*, 608–612.

Hill, R. A., Kiss Von Soly, S., Ratnayake, U., Klug, M., Binder, M. D., Hannan, A. J., et al. (2014). Long-term effects of combined neonatal and adolescent stress on brain-derived neurotrophic factor and dopamine receptor expression in the rat forebrain. *Biochimica et Biophysica Acta, 1842*, 2126–2135.

Hill, R. A., Klug, M., Kiss Von Soly, S., Binder, M. D., Hannan, A. J., & van den Buuse, M. (2014). Sex-specific disruptions in spatial memory and anhedonia in a "two hit" rat model correspond with alterations in hippocampal brain-derived neurotrophic factor expression and signaling. *Hippocampus, 24*, 1197–1211.

Hiroi, N., Takahashi, T., Hishimoto, A., Izumi, T., Boku, S., & Hiramoto, T. (2013). Copy number variation at 22q11.2: from rare variants to common mechanisms of developmental neuropsychiatric disorders. *Molecular Psychiatry, 18*, 1153–1165.

Hollins, S. L., Zavitsanou, K., Walker, F. R., & Cairns, M. J. (2014). Alteration of imprinted Dlk1-Dio3 miRNA cluster expression in the entorhinal cortex induced by maternal immune activation and adolescent cannabinoid exposure. *Translational Psychiatry, 4*, e452.

Holtzman, C. W., Trotman, H. D., Goulding, S. M., Ryan, A. T., Macdonald, A. N., Shapiro, D. I., et al. (2013). Stress and neurodevelopmental processes in the emergence of psychosis. *Neuroscience, 249*, 172–191.

Insel, B. J., Schaefer, C. A., McKeague, I. W., Susser, E. S., & Brown, A. S. (2008). Maternal iron deficiency and the risk of schizophrenia in offspring. *Archives of General Psychiatry, 65*, 1136–1144.

Javitt, D. C., Zukin, S. R., Heresco-Levy, U., & Umbricht, D. (2012). Has an angel shown the way? Etiological and therapeutic implications of the PCP/NMDA model of schizophrenia. *Schizophrenia Bulletin, 38*, 958–966.

Kannan, G., Sawa, A., & Pletnikov, M. V. (2013). Mouse models of gene-environment interactions in schizophrenia. *Neurobiology of Disease, 57*, 5–11.

Kendler, K. S. (2001). Twin studies of psychiatric illness: an update. *Archives of General Psychiatry, 58*, 1005–1014.

Khashan, A. S., Abel, K. M., McNamee, R., Pedersen, M. G., Webb, R. T., Baker, P. N., et al. (2008). Higher risk of offspring schizophrenia following antenatal maternal exposure to severe adverse life events. *Archives of General Psychiatry, 65*, 146–152.

Kluger, M. J., & Rothenburg, B. A. (1979). Fever and reduced iron: their interaction as a host defense response to bacterial infection. *Science, 203*, 374–376.

Koenig, J. I. (2006). Schizophrenia: a unique translational opportunity in behavioral neuroendocrinology. *Hormones and Behavior, 50*, 602–611.

Koenig, J. I., Elmer, G. I., Shepard, P. D., Lee, P. R., Mayo, C., Joy, B., et al. (2005). Prenatal exposure to a repeated variable stress paradigm elicits behavioral and neuroendocrinological changes in the adult offspring: potential relevance to schizophrenia. *Behavioural Brain Research, 156*, 251–261.

Kwik-Uribe, C. L., Golub, M. S., & Keen, C. L. (2000). Chronic marginal iron intakes during early development in mice alter brain iron concentrations and behavior despite postnatal iron supplementation. *Journal of Nutrition, 130*, 2040–2048.

Lee, P., Peng, H., Gelbart, T., Wang, L., & Beutler, E. (2005). Regulation of hepcidin transcription by interleukin-1 and interleukin-6. *Proceedings of the National Academy of Science of the United States of America, 102*, 1906–1910.

Lewis, S. W., & Murray, R. M. (1987). Obstetric complications, neurodevelopmental deviance, and risk of schizophrenia. *Journal of Psychiatric Research, 21*, 413–421.

Lim, A. L., Taylor, D. A., & Malone, D. T. (2012). A two-hit model: behavioural investigation of the effect of combined neonatal MK-801 administration and isolation rearing in the rat. *Journal of Psychopharmacology, 26*, 1252–1264.

Lipina, T. V., Zai, C., Hlousek, D., Roder, J. C., & Wong, A. H. (2013). Maternal immune activation during gestation interacts with Disc1 point mutation to exacerbate schizophrenia-related behaviors in mice. *Journal of Neuroscience, 33*, 7654–7666.

Luzi, S., Morrison, P. D., Powell, J., di Forti, M., & Murray, R. M. (2008). What is the mechanism whereby cannabis use increases risk of psychosis? *Neurotoxicity Research, 14*, 105–112.

Maynard, T. M., Sikich, L., Lieberman, J. A., & LaMantia, A. S. (2001). Neural development, cell-cell signaling, and the "two-hit" hypothesis of schizophrenia. *Schizophrenia Bulletin, 27*, 457–476.

McGrath, J., Brown, A., & St Clair, D. (2011). Prevention and schizophrenia – the role of dietary factors. *Schizophrenia Bulletin, 37*, 272–283.

McGrath, J. J., Mortensen, P. B., Visscher, P. M., & Wray, N. R. (2013). Where GWAS and epidemiology meet: opportunities for the simultaneous study of genetic and environmental risk factors in schizophrenia. *Schizophrenia Bulletin, 39*, 955–959.

Meyer, U. (2014). Prenatal poly(I:C) exposure and other developmental immune activation models in rodent systems. *Biological Psychiatry, 75*, 307–315.

Meyer, U., & Feldon, J. (2010). Epidemiology-driven neurodevelopmental animal models of schizophrenia. *Progress in Neurobiology, 90*, 285–326.

Meyer, U., & Feldon, J. (2012). To poly(I:C) or not to poly(I:C): advancing preclinical schizophrenia research through the use of prenatal immune activation models. *Neuropharmacology, 62*, 1308–1321.

Meyer, U., Feldon, J., & Fatemi, S. H. (2009). In-vivo rodent models for the experimental investigation of prenatal immune activation effects in neurodevelopmental brain disorders. *Neuroscience & Biobehavioral Reviews, 33*, 1061–1079.

Meyer, U., Feldon, J., Schedlowski, M., & Yee, B. K. (2005). Towards an immuno-precipitated neurodevelopmental animal model of schizophrenia. *Neuroscience & Biobehavioral Reviews, 29*, 913–947.

Meyer, U., Nyffeler, M., Engler, A., Urwyler, A., Schedlowski, M., Knuesel, I., et al. (2006). The time of prenatal immune challenge determines the specificity of inflammation-mediated brain and behavioral pathology. *Journal of Neuroscience, 26*, 4752–4762.

Modinos, G., Iyegbe, C., Prata, D., Rivera, M., Kempton, M. J., Valmaggia, L. R., et al. (2013). Molecular genetic gene-environment studies using candidate genes in schizophrenia: a systematic review. *Schizophrenia Research, 150*, 356–365.

Moore, T. H., Zammit, S., Lingford-Hughes, A., Barnes, T. R., Jones, P. B., Burke, M., et al. (2007). Cannabis use and risk of psychotic or affective mental health outcomes: a systematic review. *Lancet, 370*, 319–328.

Mouri, A., Noda, Y., Enomoto, T., & Nabeshima, T. (2007). Phencyclidine animal models of schizophrenia: approaches from abnormality of glutamatergic neurotransmission and neurodevelopment. *Neurochemistry International, 51*, 173–184.

Nemeth, E., Rivera, S., Gabayan, V., Keller, C., Taudorf, S., Pedersen, B. K., et al. (2004). IL-6 mediates hypoferremia of inflammation by inducing the synthesis of the iron regulatory hormone hepcidin. *Journal of Clinical Investigation, 113*, 1271–1276.

Nielsen, P. R., Benros, M. E., & Mortensen, P. B. (2014). Hospital contacts with infection and risk of schizophrenia: a population-based cohort study with linkage of Danish national registers. *Schizophrenia Bulletin, 40*, 1526–1532.

Niwa, M., Matsumoto, Y., Mouri, A., Ozaki, N., & Nabeshima, T. (2011). Vulnerability in early life to changes in the rearing environment plays a crucial role in the aetiopathology of psychiatric disorders. *International Journal of Neuropsychopharmacology, 14,* 459–477.

van Os, J., Kenis, G., & Rutten, B. P. (2010). The environment and schizophrenia. *Nature, 468,* 203–212.

Paus, T., Keshavan, M., & Giedd, J. N. (2008). Why do many psychiatric disorders emerge during adolescence? *Nature Reviews Neuroscience, 9,* 947–957.

Pelayo-Terán, J. M., Suárez-Pinilla, P., Chadi, N., & Crespo-Facorro, B. (2012). Gene-environment interactions underlying the effect of cannabis in first episode psychosis. *Current Pharmaceutical Design, 18,* 5024–5035.

Piontkewitz, Y., Arad, M., & Weiner, I. (2011). Abnormal trajectories of neurodevelopment and behavior following in utero insult in the rat. *Biological Psychiatry, 70,* 842–851.

Piontkewitz, Y., Arad, M., & Weiner, I. (2012). Tracing the development of psychosis and its prevention: what can be learned from animal models. *Neuropharmacology, 62,* 1273–1289.

Powell, S. B. (2010). Models of neurodevelopmental abnormalities in schizophrenia. *Current Topics in Behavioral Neurosciences, 4,* 435–481.

Power, R. A., Verweij, K. J., Zuhair, M., Montgomery, G. W., Henders, A. K., Heath, A. C., et al. (2014). Genetic predisposition to schizophrenia associated with increased use of cannabis. *Molecular Psychiatry, 19,* 1201–1204.

Purcell, S. M., Moran, J. L., Fromer, M., Ruderfer, D., Solovieff, N., Roussos, P., et al. (2014). A polygenic burden of rare disruptive mutations in schizophrenia. *Nature, 506,* 185–190.

Richetto, J., Calabrese, F., Riva, M. A., & Meyer, U. (2014). Prenatal immune activation induces maturation-dependent alterations in the prefrontal GABAergic transcriptome. *Schizophrenia Bulletin, 40,* 351–361.

Schwartz, S., & Susser, E. (2006). Commentary: what can epidemiology accomplish? *International Journal of Epidemiology, 35,* 587–590.

Seillier, A., & Giuffrida, A. (2009). Evaluation of NMDA receptor models of schizophrenia: divergences in the behavioral effects of subchronic PCP and MK-801. *Behavioural Brain Research, 204,* 410–415.

Shi, L., Fatemi, S. H., Sidwell, R. W., & Patterson, P. H. (2003). Maternal influenza infection causes marked behavioral and pharmacological changes in the offspring. *Journal of Neuroscience, 23,* 297–302.

Shields, J., & Gottesman, I. I. (1972). Cross-national diagnosis of schizophrenia in twins. The heritability and specificity of schizophrenia. *Archives of General Psychiatry, 27,* 725–730.

Silasi, M., Cardenas, I., Kwon, J. Y., Racicot, K., Aldo, P., & Mor, G. (2015). Viral infections during pregnancy. *American Journal of Reproductive Immunology, 73,* 199–213.

Smith, S. E., Li, J., Garbett, K., Mirnics, K., & Patterson, P. H. (2007). Maternal immune activation alters fetal brain development through interleukin-6. *Journal of Neuroscience, 27,* 10695–10702.

Snyder, M. A., & Gao, W. J. (2013). NMDA hypofunction as a convergence point for progression and symptoms of schizophrenia. *Frontiers in Cellular Neuroscience, 7,* 31.

Sørensen, H. J., Nielsen, P. R., Pedersen, C. B., & Mortensen, P. B. (2011). Association between prepartum maternal iron deficiency and offspring risk of schizophrenia: population-based cohort study with linkage of Danish national registers. *Schizophrenia Bulletin, 37,* 982–987.

Takeuchi, O., & Akira, S. (2007). Recognition of viruses by innate immunity. *Immunological Reviews, 220,* 214–224.

Torrey, E. F. (1992). Are we overestimating the genetic contribution to schizophrenia? *Schizophrenia Bulletin, 18,* 159–170.

Traynor, T. R., Majde, J. A., Bohnet, S. G., & Krueger, J. M. (2004). Intratracheal double-stranded RNA plus interferon-gamma: a model for analysis of the acute phase response to respiratory viral infections. *Life Sciences, 74,* 2563–2576.

Trezza, V., Campolongo, P., Manduca, A., Morena, M., Palmery, M., Vanderschuren, L. J., et al. (2012). Altering endocannabinoid neurotransmission at critical developmental ages: impact on rodent emotionality and cognitive performance. *Frontiers in Behavioral Neuroscience, 6,* 2.

Triantafilou, M., & Triantafilou, K. (2002). Lipopolysaccharide recognition: CD14, TLRs and the LPS-activation cluster. *Trends in Immunology, 23,* 301–304.

Unger, E. L., Paul, T., Murray-Kolb, L. E., Felt, B., Jones, B. C., & Beard, J. L. (2007). Early iron deficiency alters sensorimotor development and brain monoamines in rats. *Journal of Nutrition, 137,* 118–124.

Van den Buuse, M., Garner, B., & Koch, M. (2003). Neurodevelopmental animal models of schizophrenia: effects on prepulse inhibition. *Current Molecular Medicine, 3,* 459–471.

Varese, F., Smeets, F., Drukker, M., Lieverse, R., Lataster, T., Viechtbauer, W., et al. (2012). Childhood adversities increase the risk of psychosis: a meta-analysis of patient-control, prospective- and cross-sectional cohort studies. *Schizophrenia Bulletin, 38,* 661–671.

Vinkers, C. H., Van Gastel, W. A., Schubart, C. D., Van Eijk, K. R., Luykx, J. J., Van Winkel, R., Genetic Risk and OUtcome of Psychosis (GROUP) Investigators, et al. (2013). The effect of childhood maltreatment and cannabis use on adult psychotic symptoms is modified by the COMT Val[158]Met polymorphism. *Schizophrenia Research, 150,* 303–311.

Vuillermot, S., Weber, L., Feldon, J., & Meyer, U. (2010). A longitudinal examination of the neurodevelopmental impact of prenatal immune activation in mice reveals primary defects in dopaminergic development relevant to schizophrenia. *Journal of Neuroscience, 30,* 1270–1287.

Cell Models

22

Synaptic Abnormalities and Neuroplasticity
Molecular Mechanisms of Cognitive Dysfunction in Genetic Mouse Models of Schizophrenia

Ruoqi Gao[*,§], *Theron A. Russell*[*,§], *Peter Penzes*[*,§]

[*]Department of Physiology, Northwestern University Feinberg School of Medicine, Chicago, IL, USA; [§]Department of Psychiatry and Behavioral Sciences, Northwestern University Feinberg School of Medicine, Chicago, IL, USA

INTRODUCTION

Schizophrenia is a behaviorally and pathophysiologically complex disorder that affects more than 1% of the world's population (Bromet & Fennig, 1999). The syndrome is characterized by three classes of symptoms: positive (delusions, hallucinations, and a disorganization of thought), negative (affective flattening, anhedonia, alogia, and social withdrawal), and cognitive (deficits in executive function, attention, and working memory). Decades of genetic and environmental studies show a heritability of 50–80%, suggesting the disease is a multifactorial neurodevelopmental disorder caused by a combination of genetic and environmental factors (Sullivan, Kendler, & Neale, 2003). Such complexity greatly exacerbates the challenge of developing effective clinical treatments.

The first drugs used for treating schizophrenia, called first-generation antipsychotics, have been used since the 1950s to treat the positive psychotic symptoms of the disease. Unfortunately, these drugs do little to ameliorate the negative and cognitive symptoms and can cause extrapyramidal side effects. The development of a second generation of antipsychotics, the atypical antipsychotics, reduced many of the unwanted side effects but still had little therapeutic advantage over the first generation (Lieberman et al., 2005). Thus, there is an ongoing need to identify more efficacious therapeutics for schizophrenia patients, particularly in regard to treating cognitive impairments. Cognitive deterioration often precedes the development of psychosis (Caspi et al., 2003; Jones,

Rodgers, Murray, & Marmot, 1994) and is the most accurate predictor of clinical outcome (Green, 1996). Cognitive symptoms are relatively stable over time (Albus et al., 2002), remain resistant to current treatments, and continue to be present even after psychosis remission (Keefe et al., 2007). However, for advances in the treatment of cognitive symptoms to occur, researchers must reach a clearer understanding of how affected molecular pathways shape these symptoms.

Mutant animal models are valuable tools with which to investigate the neurobiological basis of psychiatric disorders because they allow for rapid monitoring of disease progression, the chance to test novel therapeutics, and the opportunity to study the biological function of the genetic variants implicated in association studies. However, schizophrenia's heterogeneous symptoms are the result of a complex constellation of genetic and environmental stressors, making the development of reliable and predictable rodent models difficult. Moreover, several aspects of the disorder, such as hallucinations and delusions, are difficult to emulate or measure in nonprimate animals. Thus, rather than mimicking the entire syndrome, a more focused approach is taken. Schizophrenic endophenotypes—individual and objectively measured markers that each represents one single subclinical, genetically linked component of the disease—serve as compartmentalized substitutes of complicated behaviors and can be used as tools to establish a disease model's validity (Kellendonk, Simpson, & Kandel, 2009; Waddington et al., 2007), although these ideas have been contested (Walters & Owen, 2007).

Several schizophrenia endophenotypes have well-established homology in mice: for positive symptoms, these include indirect dopamine-linked measures, such as hyperactivity and stereotypy (O'Tuathaigh, Desbonnet, & Waddington, 2012), whereas models of negative symptoms focus primarily on a selected range of social behaviors such as social interaction deficits (O'Tuathaigh et al., 2008). On the other hand, the exact nature of the cognitive disturbance(s) present in schizophrenia and the accuracy of cognitive paradigms in animal models are ongoing sources of debate (Insel, 2010). These ambiguities, juxtaposed with the need for novel cognitive therapies, were the incentives for the US National Institute of Mental Health to spearhead the Measurement and Treatment Research to Improve Cognition in Schizophrenia (MATRICS)—an initiative to attempt to establish a reliable, valid, and consensus-derived method of assessing cognition in schizophrenia. The study has identified seven distinct cognitive domains in which schizophrenia patients show deficits: attention/vigilance; working memory; reasoning and problem-solving; processing speed; visual learning and memory; verbal learning and memory; and social cognition (Green et al., 2004). This attempt to operationalize cognition has been paralleled by the development of animal behavioral paradigms for these domains (Young, Powell, Risbrough, Marston, & Geyer, 2009). A comprehensive list of cognitive tasks that measure specific cognitive domain endophenotypes can be found elsewhere (Arguello & Gogos, 2010; Kellendonk et al., 2009; Young et al., 2009).

As expected of endophenotypes, genetic mouse models displaying particular cognitive deficits often show functional, anatomical, and ultrastructural changes in the brain regions necessary for performance of specific tasks, particularly the frontal cortices and the hippocampus (Arguello & Gogos, 2006; Papaleo, Lipska, & Weinberger, 2012). As a result, there might be a direct link between an individual gene and a specific endophenotype, paving the way for mechanistic studies linking the two. However, these underlying pathological mechanisms—particularly spine pathology, which has been consistently verified to be deficient schizophrenia—have been underexplored.

DENDRITIC SPINES INFLUENCE COGNITIVE FUNCTION

Dendritic spines are small bulbous structures protruding from the dendrites of pyramidal cells and serve as postsynaptic sites for the majority of excitatory synapses in the central nervous system (DeFelipe & Farinas, 1992). Each spine usually receives one glutamatergic axon bouton, and its synapse strength is influenced by the spine's morphological properties because spine geometry correlates with its glutamatergic receptor content (Rochefort & Konnerth, 2012). Thus, structural plasticity, via changes in spine density and shape, is a key indicator of the neuron's electrophysiological properties and neural firing patterns.

During postnatal development, many highly mobile filopodia appear on dendrites, initiate synaptic contacts with neighboring axons, and subsequently mature into more stable mushroom-shaped spines (Ziv & Smith, 1996). These spines are then maintained or eliminated during adolescence in response to a variety of physiological stimuli (Engert & Bonhoeffer, 1999; Zhou, Homma, & Poo, 2004). For example, during adolescence, spines can undergo experience-dependent changes: rapid spine enlargement and increases in spine density correspond with long-term potentiation (Matsuzaki, Honkura, Ellis-Davies, & Kasai, 2004), whereas spine shrinkage is associated with long-term depression (Zhou et al., 2004). Likewise, animal models that show deficits in cortical and hippocampal spine dynamics are associated with impairments in cognitive tasks (Cahill et al., 2009; Hains et al., 2009). Therefore, the formation, remodeling, and pruning of spiny synapses are intimately linked with cognition, and disruptions may serve as a common substrate for many cognitive symptoms in neuropsychiatric disorders.

DENDRITIC SPINES AND SCHIZOPHRENIA

One of the defining neuropathological features of schizophrenia is gray matter loss (Selemon & Goldman-Rakic, 1999; Thompson et al., 2001; Vita, De Peri, Deste, & Sacchetti, 2012). Several postmortem studies have shown brain regions—many of which have been associated with perturbed function in the disease—with the highest indices of gray matter loss also have noticeable reductions in spine density. For example, the dorsolateral prefrontal cortex is critical for working memory function, and schizophrenic individuals show reduced activity of this region during working memory tasks (Weinberger, Berman, & Zec, 1986). Spine loss in the dorsolateral prefrontal cortex has been reproducibly reported, particularly in layer 3 neurons (Glantz & Lewis, 2000). Reductions in hippocampal volume and reduced spine density on CA3 dendrites in schizophrenia (Kolomeets, Orlovskaya, Rachmanova, & Uranova, 2005; Steen, Mull, McClure, Hamer, & Lieberman, 2006) could be the physiological reason why patients have problems with memory and spatial learning. Finally, genetic linkage and genome-wide association studies have discovered a plethora of disease-associated genes encoding synaptic proteins involved in neuronal plasticity, neuronal transmission, and synaptogenesis (Fromer et al.,

2014). Taken together, these findings suggest that dysregulation of glutamatergic neurotransmission is a probable contributor to abnormal cognition apparent in patients with schizophrenia, likely as a result of a causal chain between abnormal expression, localization, and function of the products of synapse-specific susceptibility genes for schizophrenia, spine pathology, and the concomitant loss of gray matter in brain regions responsible for cognitive function.

GENETIC MOUSE MODELS OF SCHIZOPHRENIA

Twin studies have demonstrated that schizophrenia has a heritable genetic component that can be largely divided into two etiological categories: the result of a combination of many common, low penetrant alleles (e.g., single nucleotide polymorphisms (SNP)), or several rare but highly penetrant variants (e.g., copy number variants, functional point mutations). Common alleles usually have no obvious effect on protein structure or expression (Rebbeck, Spitz, & Wu, 2004) and in some cases serve as physical proxies for true risk variants residing nearby (Newton-Cheh & Hirschhorn, 2005). On the other hand, despite having a low frequency in the overall population, rare variants usually have strong detrimental effects on gene function and thus are more likely to be accurately reproduced by genetic knock outs.

Modeling high-risk susceptibility alleles in mice, therefore, holds tremendous promise for uncovering the function of a gene and its contribution to the pathophysiology of the associated disease or disease-related endophenotypes; with genetic models, researchers can ascertain the selective effects of particular disease-associated molecules on underlying molecular and cellular pathways, neural circuits and behaviors, and interactions with environmental factors in a gene-dosage manner (Arguello & Gogos, 2006). Conversely, caveats to this approach exist. Foremost, robust genetic findings are critical for the creation of reliable mouse models, but there have been few rare alleles that are consistently associated with schizophrenia in multiple studies. Next, many genetic models employ constitutive or conditional knockout strategies, which cannot be accurately used to examine the subtle variations in patient risk alleles. For example, there is considerable phenotypic difference between an autism-associated Arg451Cys knock-in and a knock out neuroligin-3 mouse (Radyushkin et al., 2009; Tabuchi et al., 2007). In addition, because many risk alleles are heterozygous, phenotypes of homozygous mice may be poor predictors of the disease pathophysiology. Finally, compensatory effects, particularly in constitutive models, can dampen the robustness of endophenotypic readouts (Kvajo, McKellar, & Gogos, 2012).

Taken together, this information suggests that etiological genetic mouse models, although useful in pinpointing the molecular roles of rare, highly penetrant variants in schizophrenia neurobiology, cannot be relied upon exclusively. Fortunately, other models of disease induction exist, including genetic pathophysiological (e.g., genetically modeling pathways rather than susceptibility alleles), developmental, pharmacological, and lesion-induced, all of which serve as standards of comparisons for model validity and as collective tools to uncover convergent signaling pathways (Jones, Watson, & Fone, 2011).

Our focus here, however, will be on summarizing spine and cognitive data of etiological genetic mouse models of experimentally proven schizophrenia risk factors (see Table 1 for a summary).

NRXN1

Neurexins (Nrxns) are a group of presynaptic cell adhesion proteins (Sudhof, 2008) which interact with postsynaptic neuroligins (NLs 1–4) to form transsynaptic adhesions (Chih, Gollan, & Scheiffele, 2006; Comoletti et al., 2006; Ichtchenko et al., 1995; Ichtchenko, Nguyen, & Sudhof, 1996). The three NRXN genes each encode an α protein and a β protein from independent promoters, each of which can be processed by alternative splicing, giving potentially thousands of distinct protein isoforms (Ullrich, Ushkaryov, & Sudhof, 1995). Knockout mice lacking all three α-Nrxns (or NLs 1–3) show little change in total number of synapses, but exhibit severe presynaptic transmission phenotypes (Missler et al., 2003; Varoqueaux et al., 2006), thereby implicating Nrxns in presynaptic maintenance, but not formation, in vivo (although some studies contest this idea (Kwon et al., 2012)).

Although NRXN1 mutations have been linked strongly to autism risk, recent studies uncovered rare NRXN1 copy number variations (CNVs) in patients with schizophrenia. Kirov et al. (2008) initially reported a deletion of NRXN1 (promoter and exon 1) in a female case, which was also present in her affected brother, but not in 372 controls, and further studies confirmed this preliminary finding (Kirov et al., 2009; Rujescu et al., 2009). Recent studies have shown large CNVs—particularly deletions (e.g., 1q21.1, 15q11.2, and 22q11.2)—confer significant risk for schizophrenia (Zhang, Gu, Hurles, & Lupski, 2009); however, because of the large number of genes within these CNVs, understanding the relationship between particular genes and endophenotypes has been challenging. On the other hand, the deletions found in NRXN1 are specific and thus represents a decisive step toward identification of a specific pathogenic pathway in schizophrenia.

TABLE 1 Concise Summary of Spine and Cognitive Findings for Genetic Mouse Models Discussed in This Review

Gene	Evidence for Schizophrenia Association	Cognitive Deficits	Spine Deficits	References for Cognitive Deficits	References for Spine Deficits
NRXN1	CNVs	PPI	Mildly reduced type II spine density in cortex	Etherton, Blaiss, Powell, and Sudhof (2009)	Dudanova, Tabuchi, Rohlmann, Sudhof, and Missler (2007)
22q11	CNVs	Spatial working memory, fear conditioning, PPI	Reduced spine density and size in hippocampal neurons	Paylor et al. (2006) and Stark et al. (2008)	Mukai et al. (2008)
MIR137	SNPs; other schizophrenia risk genes are miR137 targets	Not reported	Reduced spine density in hippocampus (miR-137 overexpression by retroviral injection)	NA	Smrt et al. (2010)
GRIN1	SNPs; mutations; expression changes; behavioral effects of NMDAR antagonists	Social interaction, PPI (global *GRIN1* ablation); spatial working memory (hippocampal-specific *GRIN1* ablation); working memory, habituation, and associative learning (PV-specific *GRIN1* ablation)	Reduced spine density, increased spine head size in cortical 2/3 layer (pyramidal-specific *GRIN1* ablation)	Carlen et al. (2012), Duncan et al. (2004), Mohn, Gainetdinov, Caron, and Koller (1999), and Niewoehner et al. (2007)	Ultanir et al. (2007)
RELN	Expression changes; hypermethylation of RELN promoter	PPI, executive function, fear conditioning (HRM)	Reduced spine density in hippocampal neurons (HRM)	Barr, Fish, Markou, and Honer (2008), Brigman, Padukiewicz, Sutherland, and Rothblat (2006), and Qiu et al. (2006)	Liu et al. (2001) and Niu, Yabut, and D'Arcangelo (2008)
DISC1	Translocations; mutations	Fear conditioning, working memory (Q31L/L100P); spatial memory (hDISC1); working memory (DISC1ᵗᵐᵏᵃʳᵃ)	Reduced spine density in hippocampus and cortex (Q31L/L100P and DISC1ᵗᵐᵏᵃʳᵃ)	Clapcote et al. (2007), Kvajo et al. (2008), and Pletnikov et al. (2008)	Lee et al. (2011) and Lepagnol-Bestel, Kvajo, Karayiorgou, Simonneau, and Gogos (2013)
NRG1/ ERBB	SNPs	Spatial working memory, reference memory (NRG1 hypermorph); novel object recognition, fear conditioning (NRG1 hypomorph)	Increased bifurcated-type spines in cortical layer V pyramidal neurons (NRG1 hypermorph); reduced spine density in hippocampus and cortex (*ERBB2* KO, *ERBB4* KO, *ERBB4* pyramidal cell-specific KO)	Duffy, Cappas, Lai, Boucher, and Karl (2010) and Yin, Chen, et al. (2013)	Agarwal et al. (2014), Barros et al. (2009), and Cooper and Koleske (2014)
KALRN	Mutations; altered expression	Fear conditioning (pan-kalirin KO and kalirin-7 KO); working memory (pan-kalirin KO)	Reduced cortical (pan-kalirin KO) and hippocampal spine density (kalirin-7 KO)	Cahill et al. (2009), Ma et al. (2008), Xie, Cahill, and Penzes (2010), and Xie et al. (2011)	Cahill et al. (2009), Xie, Cahill, and Penzes (2010), and Xie et al. (2011)
DTNBP1	SNPs, altered expression	Working memory, spatial learning, contextual fear conditioning, novel object recognition, PPI, social interaction	Reduced hippocampal spine density	Bhardwaj et al. (2009), Feng et al. (2008), Glen et al. (2014), Hattori et al. (2008), Karlsgodt et al. (2011), and Papaleo, Yang, et al. (2012)	Jia, Hu, Nordman, and Li (2014) and Jia, Zhao, Hu, Lindberg, and Li (2013)
PAK	Altered expression; mutations; splicing variants; CNVs	No data	Reduced cortical (*PAK1* DN) and hippocampal (*PAK1/3* KO) spine density; increased synapse size (*PAK1* DN and *PAK1/3* KO)	NA	Hayashi et al. (2004) and Huang et al. (2011)

CNV, copy number variation; HRM, heterozygous mice; KO, knockout; miR, microRNA; NA, not available; NMDAR, *N*-methyl-D-aspartate receptor; PPI, prepulse inhibition; PV, parvalbumin; SNP, single nucleotide polymorphism.

The α-NRXN1-knockout mouse has imbalanced excitatory and inhibitory neurotransmission in the hippocampus due to loss of presynaptic strength. These animals also exhibit decreased prepulse inhibition (PPI), but no changes in social behavior and normal spatial learning (Etherton et al., 2009). An α-NRXN double knockout model shows only slight reductions in total spine density in type II synapses, but no changes in the distribution of synaptic proteins (Dudanova et al., 2007). Overall, these data suggest the gene has only a limited contribution to spine formation and cognitive endophenotypes and is therefore not the most robust disease model. However, it may be useful for investigating particular cognitive deficits, such as sensorimotor gating.

22Q11

The 22q11 microdeletion syndrome, also known as velocardiofacial/DiGeorge syndrome, is caused by a microdeletion ranging from 1.5 to 3 Mb of the long arm of chromosome 22. This microdeletion results in a spectrum of physical and cognitive abnormalities for carriers, including increased risk for psychiatric disease, with 30% of 22q11 microdeletion syndrome patients developing schizophrenia. It is also the most common CNV associated with schizophrenia, accounting for up to 1–2% of total cases (Karayiorgou et al., 1995).

Mice engineered to carry a heterozygous deletion of the 1.3-Mb orthologous chromosomal region (*Df(16) A*$^{+/-}$) display cognitive deficits including deficits in spatial working memory, fear conditioning, and PPI (Stark et al., 2008). Primary hippocampal neurons cultured from these mice showed reduced spine density and size (Mukai et al., 2008), although another 22q11 mouse model was unable to reproduce these results, likely because of different engineering strategies (Earls et al., 2010). Interestingly, loss of either of two genes within this region, *ZDHHC8* and *DGCR8*, was sufficient to impair spine morphology. ZDHHC8 is a palmitoyl transferase which palmitoylates PSD-95; its loss results in reduced spine density and simpler dendrites, and its replacement into *Df(16)A*$^{+/-}$ neurons rescued spine deficiency (Mukai et al., 2008). DGCR8 is involved in microRNA (miRNA) processing, and its loss results in smaller spines and reduced short-term synaptic plasticity (Fenelon et al., 2011; Stark et al., 2008). Further investigation of *DGCR8*$^{+/-}$ mice revealed a dramatic downregulation of miR-185, which is located in the deletion region of 22q11. miR-185 is also reduced in the hippocampus and prefrontal cortex (PFC) of *Df(16)A*$^{+/-}$ mice (Xu, Hsu, Stark, Karayiorgou, & Gogos, 2013) and reduced in peripheral blood of 22q11 patients (de la Morena et al., 2013). *In vitro* culture experiments confirmed its role in spinogenesis (Xu et al., 2013), and several validated miR-185

targets have altered expression levels in schizophrenia (Liu et al., 2011). Hence, it is likely that microRNA regulation of synaptic plasticity may be a primary contributor to the 22q11.2-related cognitive impairments.

However, given the breadth of the 22q11 deletion, this may only be but one pathological aspect, and other deleted genes (e.g., *ZDHHC8*) within the region may contribute to the overall phenotype via different mechanisms (e.g., deficient palmitoylation). For example, haploinsufficiency of a 22q11 gene *TBX1* is sufficient to reduce PPI, implicating transcription as a possible disease pathway (Paylor et al., 2006). Moreover, PFC synaptic plasticity deficits are more widespread in Df(16)A$^{+/-}$ mice than in the *DGCR8*$^{+/-}$ model, but inclusive of the effects observed in the latter (Fenelon et al., 2013).

MIR137

miRNAs are small noncoding RNAs that modulate gene expression by either reducing translation efficiency or cleaving target messenger RNAs (mRNAs). Because of their short nucleotide length, miRNAs have the potential to posttranscriptionally influence thousands of genes and thus can have an enormous impact on many cellular mechanisms (Selbach et al., 2008). Dysregulation of a single miRNA can be sufficient to alter a cell's gene–expression profile and influence its developmental trajectory (Lim et al., 2005).

A large genome-wide association study with more than 50,000 subjects revealed a genome-wide significant association of an *MIR137* (the gene encoding miR-137) SNP with schizophrenia, whereas four other loci with statistical significance contained verified miR-137 targets (Schizophrenia Psychiatric Genome-Wide Association Study (GWAS) Consortium, 2011; Kwon, Wang, & Tsai, 2013; Ripke et al., 2013). Recent studies also verified the role of miR-137 on other functional schizophrenia endophenotypes (Cummings et al., 2013; Decoster et al., 2012; Green et al., 2013). Moreover, transcriptome analysis of miR-137 targets revealed genes responsible for synaptogenesis and neuronal transmission, whereas sequence analysis of miR-137 in the schizophrenic brain discovered two function variants that lead to lowered miR-137 expression in SH-SY5Y cell lines (Strazisar et al., 2014). miR-137 has also been linked to regulation of adult neurogenesis (Szulwach et al., 2010) and neuron maturation (Smrt et al., 2010), which is analogous to the phenotypes following knockdown of the schizophrenia-related gene DISC1 (Mao et al., 2009). This growing body of data suggest miR-137 may be a central modulator of multiple pathways involved with schizophrenia neurobiology, such as synaptic signaling and neuron maturation, and hence may be essential for the disease's pathology (see the section describing 22q11 for more information on miRNAs).

Because the association of miR-137 with schizophrenia is relatively novel, no mouse model has been developed yet. However, mouse models of miR-137 downstream targets, such as schizophrenia risk genes *CACNAC1* and *TCF4*, show schizophrenia-like behavior (Brzozka, Radyushkin, Wichert, Ehrenreich, & Rossner, 2010; Lee et al., 2012). Furthermore, in situ hybridization showed an enhanced expression of miR-137 within the adult hippocampus, a region of the brain with significant plasticity and continuous production of new neurons. Overexpression of miR-137 via retroviral injection in this region led to decreased dendritic branching and spine density in adult mice, implicating its importance in adult neurogenesis (Smrt et al., 2010). Because many miR-137 targets are involved with spinogenesis, miR-137 could have an active role in spine dynamics and signaling.

NR1

N-methyl-D-aspartate receptors (NMDARs) are ionotropic glutamate receptors essential for mediating ion flux and signaling. NMDARs exist as multiple subtypes, are spatially and developmentally regulated, and are differentially distributed across neuronal subtypes (Paoletti, Bellone, & Zhou, 2013). This complex diversity, coupled with a subtype-dependent permeability to calcium influx, make NMDARs the predominant molecular devices for controlling complex experience-dependent spine remodeling and long-lasting synaptic changes. Such enduring changes in synaptic strength are crucial for associative learning, working memory, behavioral flexibility, or attention (Lisman, Schulman, & Cline, 2002).

Several lines of evidence implicate hypofunctioning NMDARs either in the cause of schizophrenia or in the pathophysiological manifestations of the disease. For example, administration of NMDAR antagonists, such as phencyclidine, MK-801, and ketamine, to normal subjects produces metabolic, neurochemical, and cognitive deficits almost identical to those seen in schizophrenia patients (Morris, Cochran, & Pratt, 2005). Postmortem studies report abnormalities in NMDAR density and subunit composition in schizophrenia patients (Akbarian et al., 1996; Kristiansen, Beneyto, Haroutunian, & Meador-Woodruff, 2006). Genetic studies have reported several schizophrenia-specific polymorphisms in *GRIN1* (Begni et al., 2003; Greenwood et al., 2011; Zhao et al., 2006) and discovered several genes encoding for NMDAR-interacting proteins associated with the disease (Fromer et al., 2014; Kirov et al., 2012). These data have lent further support to the notion that

NMDAR signaling could be a point of convergence for various schizophrenia-associated pathways.

Global *GRIN1*-knockdown mice, which reduced NR1 levels to 10% of normal levels, have been generated as a model for NMDAR hypofunction. Cognitively, these mice exhibit reduced PPI and sociability, which can be normalized to some extent by administration of antipsychotic agents (Duncan et al., 2004; Mohn et al., 1999). Furthermore, selective disruption of *GRIN1* in the hippocampus leads to reduced spatial memory (Niewoehner et al., 2007; Tsien, Huerta, & Tonegawa, 1996), whereas specific disruption of *GRIN1* in parvalbumin (PV) interneurons leads to deficits in habituation, working memory, and associative learning, but normal social activity (Carlen et al., 2012; Korotkova, Fuchs, Ponomarenko, von Engelhardt, & Monyer, 2010).

Characterization of a pyramidal cell-specific *GRIN1*-knockdown mouse revealed decreased spine density, increased spine head size, and increased PSD size in layer 2/3 pyramidal neurons (Ultanir et al., 2007), suggesting NMDARs regulate spine development and function in the developing cortex. This finding is consistent with the discovery that dendritic protrusions can be triggered by NMDAR-dependent long-term potentiation stimuli (Engert & Bonhoeffer, 1999; Maletic-Savatic, Malinow, & Svoboda, 1999). Interestingly, pyramidal cells become hyperexcitable in a PV-specific *GRIN1* knockdown model (Belforte et al., 2010).

Taken together, this information suggests molecular and cognitive endophenotypes are affected by temporally and spatially diverse patterns of NMDAR signaling, making cell-autonomous and systemic influences of NMDAR dysfunction difficult to dissect.

RELN

Reelin, coded for by the *RELN* gene, is a secreted glycoprotein that acts as a modulator of neuronal migration in the developing brain (Caviness, 1982) through its interaction with receptors ApoER2/VLDLR and subsequent downstream signaling to the adaptor protein Dab1 (Niu, Renfro, Quattrocchi, Sheldon, & D'Arcangelo, 2004). Postnatally, reelin has been linked—via the same mechanisms—to dendritic and axonal growth (Hiesberger et al., 1999; Niu et al., 2004), spine plasticity (Chen et al., 2005; Rogers et al., 2011), and long-term potentiation (Weeber et al., 2002).

Given its importance in neurodevelopment, synaptogenesis, and plasticity, it is no surprise that several postmortem studies revealed decreased levels of reelin expression in regions of the schizophrenic brain involved in cognition, such as the hippocampus and frontal cortices (Impagnatiello et al., 1998). These findings may be partially explained by the finding that the *RELN* promoter is hypermethylated in the schizophrenic brain, which may lead to decreased reelin mRNA expression (Grayson et al., 2005), or by the fact that antipsychotic medications can alter the levels of reelin (Fatemi, Reutiman, & Folsom, 2009). Moreover, decreased very low-density lipoprotein receptor (VLDLR) mRNA expression was associated with severity of schizophrenia (Suzuki et al., 2008), also possibly underlining the role of reelin-ApoE2/VLDLR pathway in pathogenesis of the disorder.

Homozygous null reelin mice have a characteristic reeling gait as well as severe cellular disorganization in cortical structures in the brain, particularly cellular ectopia that leads to an inverted cortical development pattern and impaired dendrite development (Niu et al., 2004; Tissir & Goffinet, 2003). Heterozygous mice, which display a 50% reduction in reelin, appear grossly normal but exhibit schizophrenic-like neuroanatomical and behavioral characteristics. For instance, heterozygous mice have decreased cortical thickness and decreased GAD67 (Liu et al., 2001) as well as cognitive deficits in PPI, executive function, and contextual fear conditioning (Barr et al., 2008; Brigman et al., 2006; Qiu et al., 2006). Unfortunately, such behavioral studies have not been consistently replicated, thus warranting further study before its validity as a schizophrenia model can be ensured (Podhorna & Didriksen, 2004).

Reelin loss leads to decreases of dendritic spine density in hippocampal pyramidal neurons (Liu et al., 2001; Niu et al., 2008). This deficit can be rescued with recombinant reelin, suggesting a direct role of reelin in spinogenesis (Niu et al., 2008). Interesting, many gamma-aminobutyric acid–ergic cells synapsing onto dendritic spines (e.g., horizontal, bitufted, Martinotti cells) are reelin-immunopositive, whereas those that do not (e.g., basket and chandelier cells) are reelin-negative (Pesold, Liu, Guidotti, Costa, & Caruncho, 1999). Thus, it is likely reelin is secreted from dendritic spine synapsing interneurons, adheres to dendritic spines (Niu et al., 2008; Rodriguez et al., 2000) through ApoE2/VLDLR (Niu et al., 2008) or integrins (Rodriguez et al., 2000), and signals to downstream postsynaptic proteins.

DISC1

DISC1 was first identified as a risk factor for schizophrenia when it was shown that a chromosomal translocation in the DISC1 locus segregated with the disease in a Scottish pedigree (Millar et al., 2000). In addition to this variant, exon sequencing revealed that both rare and common missense variants in DISC1 elevate the risk for schizophrenia (Song et al., 2008).

DISC1 is a scaffolding protein found abundantly at the spines (Kirkpatrick et al., 2006), where it interacts with several proteins involved in intracellular signaling,

neurite outgrowth (e.g., PDE4, GSK3beta), and synaptic function (e.g., kalirin-7, TNIK) (Bradshaw & Porteous, 2012). Several DISC1 mutations have been introduced to mice, including truncations (Lepagnol-Bestel et al., 2013; Pletnikov et al., 2008), dominant-negative constructs (Hikida et al., 2007), and point mutations (Clapcote et al., 2007; Lee et al., 2011). The truncation designs are based on the assumption that the Scottish pedigree translocation produces a truncated DISC1 protein that interferes with the intact copy's function in a dominant-negative manner or results in a haplosufficiency, whereas the point mutations are thought to be rare variants with high penetrances. Although the exact mechanisms through which these manipulations impair neuronal function is unknown, mice carrying them display both behavioral and neuromorphological phenotypes similar to those seen in schizophrenia.

A carboxy-terminal truncated DISC1 construct was shown to act in a dominant negative fashion to stunt neurite outgrowth in cortical layer 2/3 pyramidal neurons when expressed via in utero electroporation; interestingly, the same phenotype occurs when a DISC1 short hairpin RNA construct was used (Kamiya et al., 2005). Similarly, primary cortical neurons from transgenic mice overexpressing a C-terminal truncated version of human DISC1 display reductions in neurite outgrowth as well as reduced levels of the presynaptic marker SNAP-25 (Pletnikov et al., 2008). Animals carrying human DISC1 mutations also display deficiencies in spatial memory, as assessed via the Morris water maze. Furthermore, a mouse model harboring two terminating codons near the Scottish translocation site in the DISC1 gene (DISC1^{Tm1Kara}) resulted in abolished expression of several major endogenous DISC1 isoforms and a decrease in PFC volume, which the authors hypothesized was due in part to an attenuation of apical dendrite length in layer 5 pyramidal neurons (Kvajo et al., 2008). DISC1^{Tm1Kara} animals also have working memory deficits (Kvajo et al., 2008) and primary hippocampal and cortical neurons derived from this model display reductions in dendritic complexity and dendritic spine density (Lepagnol-Bestel et al., 2013). Finally, mice carrying either of two ENU-induced point mutations (Q31L and L100P) known to cause schizophrenia-related behavioral phenotypes have been shown to have reduced spine density in cortical and hippocampal pyramidal neurons (Lee et al., 2011). These Q31L and L100P models also had similar, but not identical, cognitive deficiencies when subjected to tests of latent inhibition of fear conditioning and working memory via the T-maze (Clapcote et al., 2007). Taken together, these data suggest that although DISC1 mice have cognitive and physiological differences (possibly because of variable methodological approaches), their accurate recapitulation of several schizophrenia endophenotypes highlights the utility of studying DISC1 hypofunction.

NRG1/ERRB

Among the more well-characterized schizophrenia susceptibility alleles are those that code for neuregulin 1 (NRG1), and its receptor, the epidermal growth factor receptor ErbB4 (Law, Kleinman, Weinberger, & Weickert, 2007; Stefansson et al., 2002), although the directionality of the expression of these proteins in the schizophrenic brain is still debated (Geddes, Huang, & Newell, 2011; Mei & Xiong, 2008). There are several subtypes of NRG1 protein, generated by both alternative splicing and multiple promoters. Nevertheless, all are transmembrane proteins that are cleaved by extracellular peptidases, allowing for the extracellular epidermal growth factor–like motif to bind to either ErbB3 or ErbB4. Upon binding, these receptors form dimers with each other or with ErbB1/ErbB2; this dimerization elicits signaling through the mitogen-activated protein kinase and phosphatidylinositol 3-kinase pathways, resulting, among other things, in the regulation of functional NMDARs (Bjarnadottir et al., 2007; Hahn et al., 2006; Pitcher et al., 2011). Although it has been repeatedly established that ErbB4 signaling plays a pivotal role in the function of PV-expressing interneurons (Fazzari et al., 2010; Shamir & Buonanno, 2010; Yin, Sun, et al., 2013), there is also evidence for its localization and direct role in spines on pyramidal neurons (Garcia, Vasudevan, & Buonanno, 2000; Huang et al., 2000).

As homozygous deletion of *NRG1*, *ERBB2*, or *ERBB4* results in embryonic lethality in mice, several groups have examined the function of these genes in organotypic slices, heterozygous models, or conditional knockouts. RNA interference–mediated knockdown of ErbB4 expression has been shown to result in decreased spine area in both hippocampal slices and primary cortical neurons (Cahill et al., 2013; Li, Woo, Mei, & Malinow, 2007). Conversely, treatment of primary cortical neurons with recombinant NRG1 leads to an increase in dendritic spine area and density (Cahill et al., 2013), whereas a transgenic mouse overexpressing NRG1 leads to a three-fold increase in bifurcated spines on cortical layer V projection neurons (Agarwal et al., 2014). MK-801 binding studies of forebrain homogenates from *NRG1*[+/−] mice revealed significantly reduced levels of functional forebrain NMDARs (Stefansson et al., 2002), keeping with observations of NMDAR hypofunction in schizophrenia patients (Goff & Coyle, 2001). Similarly, mice lacking the full complement of *ERBB* alleles also display morphological deficits in pyramidal neurons. Knockingout *ERBB2* and *ERBB4* specifically in the central nervous system causes a reduction in spines both in the CA1 hippocampus and PFC by postnatal day 26 (Barros et al., 2009). Other mouse lines carrying either a brain-specific or a more restricted principal neuron-specific knockout of *ERBB4* exhibited reduced mushroom-shaped spine density in layer 5 dorsomedial PFC neurons at postnatal day 21 and persisted through postnatal day 63, despite being unchanged at postnatal day 16 (Cooper & Koleske, 2014). These data highlight the importance of the NRG1-ErbB4 signaling pathway for dendritic spine maintenance throughout forebrain development and into adulthood, possibly through non–cell-autonomous interactions with ErbB4-positive PV interneurons (Fazzari et al., 2010; Yin, Sun, et al., 2013).

Although behavioral abnormalities have been reported in mice with altered NRG/ErbB signaling, these models have not fully elucidated how increases or decreases in this pathway's activity might be related to cognitive symptoms in patients. Mice that conditionally overexpress type I NRG1β in forebrain glutamatergic neurons have deficits in the radial arm maze and the Morris water maze, indicating impaired spatial working memory and reference memory (Yin, Chen, et al., 2013). In contrast to mice with increased levels of NRG1, those carrying only a single copy of the gene have no deficits in these tasks, but are deficient in the novel object recognition task and in a fear conditioning paradigm (Duffy et al., 2010).

KALRN

The gene encoding the guanine nucleotide exchange factor kalirin, *KALRN*, has recently emerged as another factor contributing to several neuropsychiatric disorders, particularly schizophrenia (Penzes & Remmers, 2012). *KALRN* encodes a large number of isoforms, the most abundant being kalirin-7, -9, and -12. In postmortem studies, kalirin mRNA and kalirin-7 protein levels were reduced in the prefrontal cortex of schizophrenia patients (Hill, Hashimoto, & Lewis, 2006; Rubio, Haroutunian, & Meador-Woodruff, 2012). On the other hand, kalirin-9 was upregulated in the auditory cortex in schizophrenia (Deo et al., 2012). Several rare missense mutations in the human *KALRN* gene have been identified and were shown to be enriched in patients with schizophrenia (Kushima et al., 2012). Because of the presence of a PDZ interacting domain not found in other isoforms, kalirin-7 is highly abundant in spines, where it plays a key role in plasticity by activating Rac1 and its downstream effector, p21-activate kinase (PAK), and ultimately facilitating remodeling of the actin cytoskeleton (Penzes et al., 2003). In spines, kalirin-7 functions as a signaling hub receiving upstream signals from NMDARs, ephrinB/EphB, neuregulin1/ErbB, cadherins, and the 5-HT2A serotonin receptor (Penzes & Jones, 2008). It also binds DISC1 and the NR2B subunit of the NMDAR, further suggesting its importance in spine structure and function in both normal and pathological states (Hayashi-Takagi et al., 2010; Kiraly, Lemtiri-Chlieh, Levine, Mains, & Eipper, 2011).

While the kalirin-7 specific and pan-kalirin knockout mice both exhibit fear conditioning impairments, only the latter has working memory deficits (Cahill et al., 2009; Ma et al., 2008; Xie et al., 2011). Although more work is needed to reconcile the discrepancies between the cognitive endophenotypes of these mice, these findings indicate that the complete absence of kalirin versus the targeted deletion of kalirin-7 produce some nonoverlapping deficits.

In addition to displaying cognitive phenotypes related to schizophrenia, cortical neurons from pan-kalirin mice exhibit reduced spine density (Xie et al., 2010). These neurons also fail to undergo the usual increases in spine size and AMPA receptor content seen in wild-type neurons following chemically induced long-term potentiation. Additionally, pan-kalirin knockout mice display reduced dendritic spine density on cortical pyramidal neurons at 12 weeks of age, but not at 3 weeks of age (Cahill et al., 2009); this age-dependent spine loss resembles the time course of the progression of schizophrenia symptomatology. Neurons cultured from kalirin-7–specific knockouts show spine dysfunction as well, having diminished spine density in hippocampal CA1 pyramidal neurons (Ma et al., 2008).

DTNBP1

Dysbindin, encoded by the *DTNBP1* (dystrobrevin binding protein) gene, was first identified as a schizophrenia risk allele in a study of 270 Irish families in 2002 (Straub et al., 2002). Subsequent meta-analyses have confirmed a positive association between *DTNBP1* and schizophrenia (Allen et al., 2008), and several *DTNBP1* risk variants appear to correlate with the severity of cognitive symptoms in patients (Rethelyi et al., 2010). Postmortem studies of patients show a decrease of dysbindin protein levels in several brain regions, notably the dorsolateral prefrontal cortex, superior temporal gyrus, and hippocampus (Talbot, 2009), with specific isoforms showing decreased levels in postsynaptic densities of the superior temporal gyrus and hippocampus (Talbot et al., 2011).

The mouse model most commonly used in studies of dysbindin function was derived from animals carrying a spontaneous mutation affecting coat color—the so-called sandy (sdy) mice (Swank, Sweet, Davisson, Reddington, & Novak, 1991). Surprisingly, these mice were found to have two exon deletions in the *DTNBP1* gene that results in reduction and elimination of protein expression in heterozygotes and homozygotes, respectively, making it an accurate model for dysbindin-1 function (Li et al., 2003). Cognitively, homozygous sdy mice displayed clear deficits in spatial working memory, contextual fear conditioning, and novel object recognition (Bhardwaj et al., 2009; Glen et al., 2014; Karlsgodt

et al., 2011); additional tests revealed changes in PPI and social interaction (Feng et al., 2008; Hattori et al., 2008; Papaleo, Yang, et al., 2012). However, there are also some inconsistencies in the published results, likely because of strain-specific backgrounds differences (DBA/2J vs C57BL) (Talbot, 2009).

Primary hippocampal neurons prepared from the sdy mouse display reduced spine densities due to the decline of mushroom and thin spines, whereas filopodia appear at higher levels. This effect is mediated by hyperactivation of the D2 dopamine receptor (Jia et al., 2013) and hypoactivation of CaMKIIα (Jia et al., 2014). At the functional level, dysbindin plays a role in NMDAR function because sdy hippocampal neurons exhibit an upregulation of NR2A subunits and enhanced long-term potentiation (Tang et al., 2009). Dysbindin is a component of the multisubunit BLOC-1 (biogenesis of lysosome-related organelles complex 1) (Ghiani & Dell'Angelica, 2011), which through its interaction with the cytoskeletal WAVE complex, is capable of altering the degree of actin filament branching in the dendritic spines—a process necessary for the regulation of spine dynamics (Ito et al., 2010). Moreover, BLOC-1 is thought to regulate protein sorting from early endosomes to lysosome-related organelles; deficiency in dysbindin likely decreases trafficking from endosomes to lysomes. As a secondary effect, receptors that are preferentially recycled via the endosome–lysosome pathway, such as NR2A and D2 (Bartlett et al., 2005; Lavezzari, McCallum, Dewey, & Roche, 2004), may be diverted to the recycling endosome pathway, leading to an increase in the incorporation into the plasma membrane.

PAK

PAK is a downstream effector of kalirin-7 and Rac1 (Penzes et al., 2003) and a key regulator of actin remodeling. Missense and splicing variants in *PAK3* have been associated with intellectual disability as well as with schizophrenia with premorbid mental retardation (Gedeon, Nelson, Gecz, & Mulley, 2003; Morrow, Kane, Goff, & Walsh, 2008; Rejeb et al., 2008). Microdeletions that encompass *PAK2* (3q29) have also been found to have a strong association with schizophrenia (Mulle et al., 2010). In addition, PAK1 expression and phosphorylation are altered in the prefrontal cortex in schizophrenia patients (Rubio et al., 2012).

Although mouse models of PAK dysfunction have not been used for investigations of schizophrenia pathogenesis *per se*, they may hold potential for future studies. For instance, although no behavioral paradigms have been performed on *PAK* knockout mice, inhibition of PAK has been shown to rescue symptoms in other schizophrenia disease models such DISC1 (Hayashi-Takagi et al., 2014), hence implicating the PAK pathway as important in the etiology of cognitive endophenotypes.

Cortical neurons in forebrain-specific dominant negative *PAK1* transgenic mice show reduced spine density and larger individual synapses (Hayashi et al., 2004). In contrast to this model, fixed hippocampal sections of *PAK1* knockout mice show normal synapse and spine density and primary hippocampal cultures derived from these animals had significantly reduced levels of filamentous actin on spines, coinciding with higher levels of the active form of the actin depolymerization factor cofilin (Asrar et al., 2009). The authors account for the discrepancy between dominant negative and knock-out *PAK* models by highlighting that a dominant negative PAK1 protein may suppress the activity of other PAK isoforms, particularly PAK3. Indeed, expression of some, but not all, mental retardation–associated *PAK3* missense mutations leads to reductions in spine density in cultured hippocampal neurons, and an overabundance of immature filopodia-like spines (Kreis et al., 2007). Similarly, a double knockout *PAK1/3* model exhibited markedly reduced hippocampal synapse density and enlarged individual synapses (Huang et al., 2011). However, future studies are needed to directly elucidate the effect of these changes in spine function on cognition and behavior.

CONCLUSION

The ineffectiveness of current therapeutics in improving clinical outcomes in schizophrenia has been partially from focus on reversing positive symptoms, as opposed to ameliorating core cognitive deficits. However, the greatest impediments to therapeutic development in this area are the lack of understanding of the neurobiology of cognition and the unreliable predictive power of animal models for testing cognitive traits. On the other hand, the continuous development and research into genetic mouse models of schizophrenia, as well as the establishment of the standardized MATRICS program to compartmentalize cognition into measurable endophenotypic domains, have allowed for detailed illumination of how genetic insults can affect the relationship between spine dynamics and cognitive dysfunction in mental illness. Nevertheless, there are many inconsistencies, missing tests, and difficulties in interpretation that cloud the available literature, as is evident from the models discussed here. From laboratory to laboratory, animals are not typically subjected to standard batteries of behavioral tests, and spine pathologies in schizophrenia models are not always investigated in the same brain region or neuron type, if at all. These factors have severely limited researchers' abilities to interpret mechanisms of pathogenesis, and

make it difficult, if not impossible, to make valid generalizations and/or comparisons between one model and another. Moreover, the absence of a consensus cognitive battery has hampered standardized evaluation of new treatments targeting cognitive deficits in schizophrenia. The next step, therefore, lies in implementing uniform behavioral paradigms and organized molecular characterization of affected brain regions.

References

Agarwal, A., Zhang, M., Trembak-Duff, I., Unterbarnscheidt, T., Radyushkin, K., Dibaj, P., et al. (2014). Dysregulated expression of neuregulin-1 by cortical pyramidal neurons disrupts synaptic plasticity. *Cell Reports, 8*(4), 1130–1145. http://dx.doi.org/10.1016/j.celrep.2014.07.026.

Akbarian, S., Sucher, N. J., Bradley, D., Tafazzoli, A., Trinh, D., Hetrick, W. P., et al. (1996). Selective alterations in gene expression for NMDA receptor subunits in prefrontal cortex of schizophrenics. *Journal of Neuroscience, 16*(1), 19–30.

Albus, M., Hubmann, W., Scherer, J., Dreikorn, B., Hecht, S., Sobizack, N., et al. (2002). A prospective 2-year follow-up study of neurocognitive functioning in patients with first-episode schizophrenia. *European Archives of Psychiatry and Clinical Neuroscience, 252*(6), 262–267. http://dx.doi.org/10.1007/s00406-002-0391-4.

Allen, N. C., Bagade, S., McQueen, M. B., Ioannidis, J. P., Kavvoura, F. K., Khoury, M. J., et al. (2008). Systematic meta-analyses and field synopsis of genetic association studies in schizophrenia: the SzGene database. *Nature Genetics, 40*(7), 827–834. http://dx.doi.org/10.1038/ng.171.

Arguello, P. A., & Gogos, J. A. (2006). Modeling madness in mice: one piece at a time. *Neuron, 52*(1), 179–196. http://dx.doi.org/10.1016/j.neuron.2006.09.023.

Arguello, P. A., & Gogos, J. A. (2010). Cognition in mouse models of schizophrenia susceptibility genes. *Schizophrenia Bulletin, 36*(2), 289–300. http://dx.doi.org/10.1093/schbul/sbp153.

Asrar, S., Meng, Y., Zhou, Z., Todorovski, Z., Huang, W. W., & Jia, Z. (2009). Regulation of hippocampal long-term potentiation by p21-activated protein kinase 1 (PAK1). *Neuropharmacology, 56*(1), 73–80. http://dx.doi.org/10.1016/j.neuropharm.2008.06.055.

Barr, A. M., Fish, K. N., Markou, A., & Honer, W. G. (2008). Heterozygous reeler mice exhibit alterations in sensorimotor gating but not presynaptic proteins. *European Journal of Neuroscience, 27*(10), 2568–2574. http://dx.doi.org/10.1111/j.1460-9568.2008.06233.x.

Barros, C. S., Calabrese, B., Chamero, P., Roberts, A. J., Korzus, E., Lloyd, K., et al. (2009). Impaired maturation of dendritic spines without disorganization of cortical cell layers in mice lacking NRG1/ErbB signaling in the central nervous system. *Proceedings of the National Academy of Sciences of the United States of America, 106*(11), 4507–4512. http://dx.doi.org/10.1073/pnas.0900355106.

Bartlett, S. E., Enquist, J., Hopf, F. W., Lee, J. H., Gladher, F., Kharazia, V., et al. (2005). Dopamine responsiveness is regulated by targeted sorting of D2 receptors. *Proceedings of the National Academy of Sciences of the United States of America, 102*(32), 11521–11526. http://dx.doi.org/10.1073/pnas.0502418102.

Begni, S., Moraschi, S., Bignotti, S., Fumagalli, F., Rillosi, L., Perez, J., et al. (2003). Association between the G1001C polymorphism in the GRIN1 gene promoter region and schizophrenia. *Biological Psychiatry, 53*(7), 617–619. pii:S0006322302017833.

Belforte, J. E., Zsiros, V., Sklar, E. R., Jiang, Z., Yu, G., Li, Y., et al. (2010). Postnatal NMDA receptor ablation in corticolimbic interneurons confers schizophrenia-like phenotypes. *Nature Neuroscience, 13*(1), 76–83. http://dx.doi.org/10.1038/nn.2447.

Bhardwaj, S. K., Baharnoori, M., Sharif-Askari, B., Kamath, A., Williams, S., & Srivastava, L. K. (2009). Behavioral characterization of dysbindin-1 deficient sandy mice. *Behavioural Brain Research, 197*(2), 435–441. http://dx.doi.org/10.1016/j.bbr.2008.10.011.

Bjarnadottir, M., Misner, D. L., Haverfield-Gross, S., Bruun, S., Helgason, V. G., Stefansson, H., et al. (2007). Neuregulin1 (NRG1) signaling through Fyn modulates NMDA receptor phosphorylation: differential synaptic function in NRG1[+/−] knock-outs compared with wild-type mice. *Journal of Neuroscience, 27*(17), 4519–4529. http://dx.doi.org/10.1523/JNEUROSCI.4314-06.2007.

Bradshaw, N. J., & Porteous, D. J. (2012). DISC1-binding proteins in neural development, signalling and schizophrenia. *Neuropharmacology, 62*(3), 1230–1241. http://dx.doi.org/10.1016/j.neuropharm.2010.12.027.

Brigman, J. L., Padukiewicz, K. E., Sutherland, M. L., & Rothblat, L. A. (2006). Executive functions in the heterozygous reeler mouse model of schizophrenia. *Behavioral Neuroscience, 120*(4), 984–988. http://dx.doi.org/10.1037/0735-7044.120.4.984.

Bromet, E. J., & Fennig, S. (1999). Epidemiology and natural history of schizophrenia. *Biological Psychiatry, 46*(7), 871–881. pii:S0006-3223 (99)00153-5.

Brzozka, M. M., Radyushkin, K., Wichert, S. P., Ehrenreich, H., & Rossner, M. J. (2010). Cognitive and sensorimotor gating impairments in transgenic mice overexpressing the schizophrenia susceptibility gene Tcf4 in the brain. *Biological Psychiatry, 68*(1), 33–40. http://dx.doi.org/10.1016/j.biopsych.2010.03.015. pii:S0006-3223(10)00244-1.

Cahill, M. E., Remmers, C., Jones, K. A., Xie, Z., Sweet, R. A., & Penzes, P. (2013). Neuregulin1 signaling promotes dendritic spine growth through kalirin. *Journal of Neurochemistry, 126*(5), 625–635. http://dx.doi.org/10.1111/jnc.12330.

Cahill, M. E., Xie, Z., Day, M., Photowala, H., Barbolina, M. V., Miller, C. A., et al. (2009). Kalirin regulates cortical spine morphogenesis and disease-related behavioral phenotypes. *Proceedings of the National Academy of Sciences of the United States of America, 106*(31), 13058–13063. http://dx.doi.org/10.1073/pnas.0904636106.

Carlen, M., Meletis, K., Siegle, J. H., Cardin, J. A., Futai, K., Vierling-Claassen, D., et al. (2012). A critical role for NMDA receptors in parvalbumin interneurons for gamma rhythm induction and behavior. *Molecular Psychiatry, 17*(5), 537–548. http://dx.doi.org/10.1038/mp.2011.31.

Caspi, A., Reichenberg, A., Weiser, M., Rabinowitz, J., Kaplan, Z., Knobler, H., et al. (2003). Cognitive performance in schizophrenia patients assessed before and following the first psychotic episode. *Schizophrenia Research, 65*(2–3), 87–94. pii:S0920996403000562.

Caviness, V. S., Jr. (1982). Neocortical histogenesis in normal and reeler mice: a developmental study based upon [3H]thymidine autoradiography. *Brain Research, 256*(3), 293–302.

Chen, Y., Beffert, U., Ertunc, M., Tang, T. S., Kavalali, E. T., Bezprozvanny, I. , et al. (2005). Reelin modulates NMDA receptor activity in cortical neurons. *Journal of Neuroscience, 25*(36), 8209–8216. http://dx.doi.org/10.1523/JNEUROSCI.1951-05.2005.

Chih, B., Gollan, L., & Scheiffele, P. (2006). Alternative splicing controls selective trans-synaptic interactions of the neuroligin-neurexin complex. *Neuron, 51*(2), 171–178. http://dx.doi.org/10.1016/j.neuron.2006.06.005. pii:S0896-6273(06)00458-2.

Clapcote, S. J., Lipina, T. V., Millar, J. K., Mackie, S., Christie, S., Ogawa, F., et al. (2007). Behavioral phenotypes of Disc1 missense mutations in mice. *Neuron, 54*(3), 387–402. http://dx.doi.org/10.1016/j.neuron.2007.04.015.

Comoletti, D., Flynn, R. E., Boucard, A. A., Demeler, B., Schirf, V., Shi, J., et al. (2006). Gene selection, alternative splicing, and post-translational processing regulate neuroligin selectivity for beta-neurexins. *Biochemistry, 45*(42), 12816–12827. http://dx.doi.org/10.1021/bi0614131.

Cooper, M. A., & Koleske, A. J. (2014). Ablation of ErbB4 from excitatory neurons leads to reduced dendritic spine density in mouse prefrontal cortex. *Journal of Comparative Neurology, 522*(14), 3351–3362. http://dx.doi.org/10.1002/cne.23615.

Cummings, E., Donohoe, G., Hargreaves, A., Moore, S., Fahey, C., Dinan, T. G., et al. (2013). Mood congruent psychotic symptoms and specific cognitive deficits in carriers of the novel schizophrenia risk variant at MIR-137. *Neuroscience Letters, 532*, 33–38. http://dx.doi.org/10.1016/j.neulet.2012.08.065. pii:S0304-3940(12)01159-7.

Decoster, J., De Hert, M., Viechtbauer, W., Nagels, G., Myin-Germeys, I., Peuskens, J., et al. (2012). Genetic association study of the P300 endophenotype in schizophrenia. *Schizophrenia Research, 141*(1), 54–59. http://dx.doi.org/10.1016/j.schres.2012.07.018. pii:S0920-9964(12)00412-4.

DeFelipe, J., & Farinas, I. (1992). The pyramidal neuron of the cerebral cortex: morphological and chemical characteristics of the synaptic inputs. *Progress in Neurobiology, 39*(6), 563–607. http://dx.doi.org/10.1016/0301-0082(92)90015-7.

Deo, A. J., Cahill, M. E., Li, S., Goldszer, I., Henteleff, R., Vanleeuwen, J. E., et al. (2012). Increased expression of Kalirin-9 in the auditory cortex of schizophrenia subjects: its role in dendritic pathology. *Neurobiology of Disease, 45*(2), 796–803. http://dx.doi.org/10.1016/j.nbd.2011.11.003.

Dudanova, I., Tabuchi, K., Rohlmann, A., Sudhof, T. C., & Missler, M. (2007). Deletion of alpha-neurexins does not cause a major impairment of axonal pathfinding or synapse formation. *Journal of Comparative Neurology, 502*(2), 261–274. http://dx.doi.org/10.1002/cne.21305.

Duffy, L., Cappas, E., Lai, D., Boucher, A. A., & Karl, T. (2010). Cognition in transmembrane domain neuregulin 1 mutant mice. *Neuroscience, 170*(3), 800–807. http://dx.doi.org/10.1016/j.neuroscience.2010.07.042. pii:S0306-4522(10)01045-6.

Duncan, G. E., Moy, S. S., Perez, A., Eddy, D. M., Zinzow, W. M., Lieberman, J. A., et al. (2004). Deficits in sensorimotor gating and tests of social behavior in a genetic model of reduced NMDA receptor function. *Behavioural Brain Research, 153*(2), 507–519. http://dx.doi.org/10.1016/j.bbr.2004.01.008. pii:S0166432804000117.

Earls, L. R., Bayazitov, I. T., Fricke, R. G., Berry, R. B., Illingworth, E., Mittleman, G., et al. (2010). Dysregulation of presynaptic calcium and synaptic plasticity in a mouse model of 22q11 deletion syndrome. *Journal of Neuroscience, 30*(47), 15843–15855. http://dx.doi.org/10.1523/JNEUROSCI.1425-10.2010.

Engert, F., & Bonhoeffer, T. (1999). Dendritic spine changes associated with hippocampal long-term synaptic plasticity. *Nature, 399*(6731), 66–70. http://dx.doi.org/10.1038/19978.

Etherton, M. R., Blaiss, C. A., Powell, C. M., & Sudhof, T. C. (2009). Mouse neurexin-1alpha deletion causes correlated electrophysiological and behavioral changes consistent with cognitive impairments. *Proceedings of the National Academy of Sciences of the United States of America, 106*(42), 17998–18003. http://dx.doi.org/10.1073/pnas.0910297106.

Fatemi, S. H., Reutiman, T. J., & Folsom, T. D. (2009). Chronic psychotropic drug treatment causes differential expression of Reelin signaling system in frontal cortex of rats. *Schizophrenia Research, 111*(1–3), 138–152. http://dx.doi.org/10.1016/j.schres.2009.03.002.

Fazzari, P., Paternain, A. V., Valiente, M., Pla, R., Lujan, R., Lloyd, K., et al. (2010). Control of cortical GABA circuitry development by Nrg1 and ErbB4 signalling. *Nature, 464*(7293), 1376–1380. http://dx.doi.org/10.1038/nature08928.

Fenelon, K., Mukai, J., Xu, B., Hsu, P. K., Drew, L. J., Karayiorgou, M., et al. (2011). Deficiency of Dgcr8, a gene disrupted by the 22q11.2 microdeletion, results in altered short-term plasticity in the prefrontal cortex. *Proceedings of the National Academy of Sciences of the United States of America, 108*(11), 4447–4452. http://dx.doi.org/10.1073/pnas.1101219108.

Fenelon, K., Xu, B., Lai, C. S., Mukai, J., Markx, S., Stark, K. L., et al. (2013). The pattern of cortical dysfunction in a mouse model of a schizophrenia-related microdeletion. *Journal of Neuroscience, 33*(37), 14825–14839. http://dx.doi.org/10.1523/JNEUROSCI.1611-13.2013.

Feng, Y. Q., Zhou, Z. Y., He, X., Wang, H., Guo, X. L., Hao, C. J., et al. (2008). Dysbindin deficiency in sandy mice causes reduction of snapin and displays behaviors related to schizophrenia. *Schizophrenia Research*, 106(2–3), 218–228. http://dx.doi.org/10.1016/j.schres.2008.07.018.

Fromer, M., Pocklington, A. J., Kavanagh, D. H., Williams, H. J., Dwyer, S., Gormley, P., et al. (2014). De novo mutations in schizophrenia implicate synaptic networks. *Nature*, 506(7487), 179–184. http://dx.doi.org/10.1038/nature12929.

Garcia, R. A., Vasudevan, K., & Buonanno, A. (2000). The neuregulin receptor ErbB-4 interacts with PDZ-containing proteins at neuronal synapses. *Proceedings of the National Academy of Sciences of the United States of America*, 97(7), 3596–3601. http://dx.doi.org/10.1073/pnas.070042497.

Geddes, A. E., Huang, X. F., & Newell, K. A. (2011). Reciprocal signalling between NR2 subunits of the NMDA receptor and neuregulin1 and their role in schizophrenia. *Progress in Neuro-Psychopharmacology and Biological Psychiatry*, 35(4), 896–904. http://dx.doi.org/10.1016/j.pnpbp.2011.02.017.

Gedeon, A. K., Nelson, J., Gecz, J., & Mulley, J. C. (2003). X-linked mild non-syndromic mental retardation with neuropsychiatric problems and the missense mutation A365E in PAK3. *American Journal of Medical Genetics Part A*, 120A(4), 509–517. http://dx.doi.org/10.1002/ajmg.a.20131.

Ghiani, C. A., & Dell'Angelica, E. C. (2011). Dysbindin-containing complexes and their proposed functions in brain: from zero to (too) many in a decade. *ASN Neuro*, 3(2). http://dx.doi.org/10.1042/AN20110010.

Glantz, L. A., & Lewis, D. A. (2000). Decreased dendritic spine density on prefrontal cortical pyramidal neurons in schizophrenia. *Archives of General Psychiatry*, 57(1), 65–73.

Glen, W. B., Jr., Horowitz, B., Carlson, G. C., Cannon, T. D., Talbot, K., Jentsch, J. D., et al. (2014). Dysbindin-1 loss compromises NMDAR-dependent synaptic plasticity and contextual fear conditioning. *Hippocampus*, 24(2), 204–213. http://dx.doi.org/10.1002/hipo.22215.

Goff, D. C., & Coyle, J. T. (2001). The emerging role of glutamate in the pathophysiology and treatment of schizophrenia. *American Journal of Psychiatry*, 158(9), 1367–1377.

Grayson, D. R., Jia, X., Chen, Y., Sharma, R. P., Mitchell, C. P., Guidotti, A., et al. (2005). Reelin promoter hypermethylation in schizophrenia. *Proceedings of the National Academy of Sciences of the United States of America*, 102(26), 9341–9346. http://dx.doi.org/10.1073/pnas.0503736102.

Green, M. F. (1996). What are the functional consequences of neurocognitive deficits in schizophrenia? *American Journal of Psychiatry*, 153(3), 321–330. http://dx.doi.org/10.1176/ajp.153.3.321.

Green, M. J., Cairns, M. J., Wu, J., Dragovic, M., Jablensky, A., Tooney, P. A., et al. (2013). Genome-wide supported variant MIR137 and severe negative symptoms predict membership of an impaired cognitive subtype of schizophrenia. *Molecular Psychiatry*, 18(7), 774–780. http://dx.doi.org/10.1038/mp.2012.84.

Green, M. F., Nuechterlein, K. H., Gold, J. M., Barch, D. M., Cohen, J., Essock, S., et al. (2004). Approaching a consensus cognitive battery for clinical trials in schizophrenia: the NIMH-MATRICS conference to select cognitive domains and test criteria. *Biological Psychiatry*, 56(5), 301–307. http://dx.doi.org/10.1016/j.biopsych.2004.06.023.

Greenwood, T. A., Lazzeroni, L. C., Murray, S. S., Cadenhead, K. S., Calkins, M. E., Dobie, D. J., et al. (2011). Analysis of 94 candidate genes and 12 endophenotypes for schizophrenia from the Consortium on the Genetics of Schizophrenia. *American Journal of Psychiatry*, 168(9), 930–946. http://dx.doi.org/10.1176/appi.ajp.2011.10050723.

Hahn, C. G., Wang, H. Y., Cho, D. S., Talbot, K., Gur, R. E., Berrettini, W. H., et al. (2006). Altered neuregulin 1-erbB4 signaling contributes to NMDA receptor hypofunction in schizophrenia. *Nature Medicine*, 12(7), 824–828. http://dx.doi.org/10.1038/nm1418.

Hains, A. B., Vu, M. A., Maciejewski, P. K., van Dyck, C. H., Gottron, M., & Arnsten, A. F. (2009). Inhibition of protein kinase C signaling protects prefrontal cortex dendritic spines and cognition from the effects of chronic stress. *Proceedings of the National Academy of Sciences of the United States of America*, 106(42), 17957–17962. http://dx.doi.org/10.1073/pnas.0908563106.

Hattori, S., Murotani, T., Matsuzaki, S., Ishizuka, T., Kumamoto, N., Takeda, M., et al. (2008). Behavioral abnormalities and dopamine reductions in sdy mutant mice with a deletion in Dtnbp1, a susceptibility gene for schizophrenia. *Biochemical and Biophysical Research Communications*, 373(2), 298–302. http://dx.doi.org/10.1016/j.bbrc.2008.06.016.

Hayashi, M. L., Choi, S. Y., Rao, B. S., Jung, H. Y., Lee, H. K., Zhang, D., et al. (2004). Altered cortical synaptic morphology and impaired memory consolidation in forebrain-specific dominant-negative PAK transgenic mice. *Neuron*, 42(5), 773–787. http://dx.doi.org/10.1016/j.neuron.2004.05.003.

Hayashi-Takagi, A., Araki, Y., Nakamura, M., Vollrath, B., Duron, S. G., Yan, Z., et al. (2014). PAKs inhibitors ameliorate schizophrenia-associated dendritic spine deterioration in vitro and in vivo during late adolescence. *Proceedings of the National Academy of Sciences of the United States of America*, 111(17), 6461–6466. http://dx.doi.org/10.1073/pnas.1321109111.

Hayashi-Takagi, A., Takaki, M., Graziane, N., Seshadri, S., Murdoch, H., Dunlop, A. J., et al. (2010). Disrupted-in-Schizophrenia 1 (DISC1) regulates spines of the glutamate synapse via Rac1. *Nature Neuroscience*, 13(3), 327–332. http://dx.doi.org/10.1038/nn.2487.

Hiesberger, T., Trommsdorff, M., Howell, B. W., Goffinet, A., Mumby, M. C., Cooper, J. A., et al. (1999). Direct binding of Reelin to VLDL receptor and ApoE receptor 2 induces tyrosine phosphorylation of disabled-1 and modulates tau phosphorylation. *Neuron*, 24(2), 481–489. pii:S0896-6273(00)80861-2.

Hikida, T., Jaaro-Peled, H., Seshadri, S., Oishi, K., Hookway, C., Kong, S., et al. (2007). Dominant-negative DISC1 transgenic mice display schizophrenia-associated phenotypes detected by measures translatable to humans. *Proceedings of the National Academy of Sciences of the United States of America*, 104(36), 14501–14506. http://dx.doi.org/10.1073/pnas.0704774104.

Hill, J. J., Hashimoto, T., & Lewis, D. A. (2006). Molecular mechanisms contributing to dendritic spine alterations in the prefrontal cortex of subjects with schizophrenia. *Molecular Psychiatry*, 11(6), 557–566. http://dx.doi.org/10.1038/sj.mp.4001792.

Huang, Y. Z., Won, S., Ali, D. W., Wang, Q., Tanowitz, M., Du, Q. S., et al. (2000). Regulation of neuregulin signaling by PSD-95 interacting with ErbB4 at CNS synapses. *Neuron*, 26(2), 443–455.

Huang, W., Zhou, Z., Asrar, S., Henkelman, M., Xie, W., & Jia, Z. (2011). p21-Activated kinases 1 and 3 control brain size through coordinating neuronal complexity and synaptic properties. *Molecular and Cellular Biology*, 31(3), 388–403. http://dx.doi.org/10.1128/MCB.00969-10.

Ichtchenko, K., Hata, Y., Nguyen, T., Ullrich, B., Missler, M., Moomaw, C., et al. (1995). Neuroligin 1: a splice site-specific ligand for beta-neurexins. *Cell*, 81(3), 435–443. http://dx.doi.org/10.1016/0092-8674(95)90396-8.

Ichtchenko, K., Nguyen, T., & Sudhof, T. C. (1996). Structures, alternative splicing, and neurexin binding of multiple neuroligins. *Journal of Biological Chemistry*, 271(5), 2676–2682.

Impagnatiello, F., Guidotti, A. R., Pesold, C., Dwivedi, Y., Caruncho, H., Pisu, M. G., et al. (1998). A decrease of Reelin expression as a putative vulnerability factor in schizophrenia. *Proceedings of the National Academy of Sciences of the United States of America*, 95(26), 15718–15723.

Insel, T. R. (2010). Rethinking schizophrenia. *Nature*, 468(7321), 187–193. http://dx.doi.org/10.1038/nature09552.

Ito, H., Morishita, R., Shinoda, T., Iwamoto, I., Sudo, K., Okamoto, K., et al. (2010). Dysbindin-1, WAVE2 and Abi-1 form a complex that regulates dendritic spine formation. *Molecular Psychiatry*, 15(10), 976–986. http://dx.doi.org/10.1038/mp.2010.69.

Jia, J. M., Hu, Z., Nordman, J., & Li, Z. (2014). The schizophrenia susceptibility gene dysbindin regulates dendritic spine dynamics. *Journal of Neuroscience*, 34(41), 13725–13736. http://dx.doi.org/10.1523/JNEUROSCI.0184-14.2014.

Jia, J. M., Zhao, J., Hu, Z., Lindberg, D., & Li, Z. (2013). Age-dependent regulation of synaptic connections by dopamine D2 receptors. *Nature Neuroscience*, 16(11), 1627–1636. http://dx.doi.org/10.1038/nn.3542.

Jones, P., Rodgers, B., Murray, R., & Marmot, M. (1994). Child development risk factors for adult schizophrenia in the British 1946 birth cohort. *Lancet*, 344(8934), 1398–1402.

Jones, C. A., Watson, D. J., & Fone, K. C. (2011). Animal models of schizophrenia. *British Journal of Pharmacology*, 164(4), 1162–1194. http://dx.doi.org/10.1111/j.1476-5381.2011.01386.x.

Kamiya, A., Kubo, K., Tomoda, T., Takaki, M., Youn, R., Ozeki, Y., et al. (2005). A schizophrenia-associated mutation of DISC1 perturbs cerebral cortex development. *Nature Cell Biology*, 7(12), 1167–1178. http://dx.doi.org/10.1038/ncb1328.

Karayiorgou, M., Morris, M. A., Morrow, B., Shprintzen, R. J., Goldberg, R., Borrow, J., et al. (1995). Schizophrenia susceptibility associated with interstitial deletions of chromosome 22q11. *Proceedings of the National Academy of Sciences of the United States of America*, 92(17), 7612–7616.

Karlsgodt, K. H., Robleto, K., Trantham-Davidson, H., Jairl, C., Cannon, T. D., Lavin, A., et al. (2011). Reduced dysbindin expression mediates N-methyl-D-aspartate receptor hypofunction and impaired working memory performance. *Biological Psychiatry*, 69(1), 28–34. http://dx.doi.org/10.1016/j.biopsych.2010.09.012.

Keefe, R. S., Bilder, R. M., Davis, S. M., Harvey, P. D., Palmer, B. W., Gold, J. M., et al. (2007). Neurocognitive effects of antipsychotic medications in patients with chronic schizophrenia in the CATIE Trial. *Archives of General Psychiatry*, 64(6), 633–647. http://dx.doi.org/10.1001/archpsyc.64.6.633.

Kellendonk, C., Simpson, E. H., & Kandel, E. R. (2009). Modeling cognitive endophenotypes of schizophrenia in mice. *Trends in Neurosciences*, 32(6), 347–358. http://dx.doi.org/10.1016/j.tins.2009.02.003.

Kiraly, D. D., Lemtiri-Chlieh, F., Levine, E. S., Mains, R. E., & Eipper, B. A. (2011). Kalirin binds the NR2B subunit of the NMDA receptor, altering its synaptic localization and function. *Journal of Neuroscience*, 31(35), 12554–12565. http://dx.doi.org/10.1523/JNEUROSCI.3143-11.2011.

Kirkpatrick, B., Xu, L., Cascella, N., Ozeki, Y., Sawa, A., & Roberts, R. C. (2006). DISC1 immunoreactivity at the light and ultrastructural level in the human neocortex. *Journal of Comparative Neurology*, 497(3), 436–450. http://dx.doi.org/10.1002/cne.21007.

Kirov, G., Gumus, D., Chen, W., Norton, N., Georgieva, L., Sari, M., et al. (2008). Comparative genome hybridization suggests a role for NRXN1 and APBA2 in schizophrenia. *Human Molecular Genetics*, 17(3), 458–465. http://dx.doi.org/10.1093/hmg/ddm323.

Kirov, G., Pocklington, A. J., Holmans, P., Ivanov, D., Ikeda, M., Ruderfer, D., et al. (2012). De novo CNV analysis implicates specific abnormalities of postsynaptic signalling complexes in the pathogenesis of schizophrenia. *Molecular Psychiatry*, 17(2), 142–153. http://dx.doi.org/10.1038/mp.2011.154.

Kirov, G., Rujescu, D., Ingason, A., Collier, D. A., O'Donovan, M. C., & Owen, M. J. (2009). Neurexin 1 (NRXN1) deletions in schizophrenia. *Schizophrenia Bulletin*, 35(5), 851–854. http://dx.doi.org/10.1093/schbul/sbp079.

Kolomeets, N. S., Orlovskaya, D. D., Rachmanova, V. I., & Uranova, N. A. (2005). Ultrastructural alterations in hippocampal mossy fiber synapses in schizophrenia: a postmortem morphometric study. *Synapse*, 57(1), 47–55. http://dx.doi.org/10.1002/syn.20153.

Korotkova, T., Fuchs, E. C., Ponomarenko, A., von Engelhardt, J., & Monyer, H. (2010). NMDA receptor ablation on parvalbumin-positive interneurons impairs hippocampal synchrony, spatial representations, and working memory. *Neuron*, 68(3), 557–569. http://dx.doi.org/10.1016/j.neuron.2010.09.017. pii:S0896-6273(10)00759-2.

Kreis, P., Thevenot, E., Rousseau, V., Boda, B., Muller, D., & Barnier, J. V. (2007). The p21-activated kinase 3 implicated in mental retardation regulates spine morphogenesis through a Cdc42-dependent pathway. *Journal of Biological Chemistry*, 282(29), 21497–21506. http://dx.doi.org/10.1074/jbc.M703298200.

Kristiansen, L. V., Beneyto, M., Haroutunian, V., & Meador-Woodruff, J. H. (2006). Changes in NMDA receptor subunits and interacting PSD proteins in dorsolateral prefrontal and anterior cingulate cortex indicate abnormal regional expression in schizophrenia. *Molecular Psychiatry*, 11(8), 737–747, 705. http://dx.doi.org/10.1038/sj.mp.4001844.

Kushima, I., Nakamura, Y., Aleksic, B., Ikeda, M., Ito, Y., Shiino, T., et al. (2012). Resequencing and association analysis of the KALRN and EPHB1 genes and their contribution to schizophrenia susceptibility. *Schizophrenia Bulletin*, 38(3), 552–560. http://dx.doi.org/10.1093/schbul/sbq118.

Kvajo, M., McKellar, H., Arguello, P. A., Drew, L. J., Moore, H., MacDermott, A. B., et al. (2008). A mutation in mouse Disc1 that models a schizophrenia risk allele leads to specific alterations in neuronal architecture and cognition. *Proceedings of the National Academy of Sciences of the United States of America*, 105(19), 7076–7081. http://dx.doi.org/10.1073/pnas.0802615105.

Kvajo, M., McKellar, H., & Gogos, J. A. (2012). Avoiding mouse traps in schizophrenia genetics: lessons and promises from current and emerging mouse models. *Neuroscience*, 211, 136–164. http://dx.doi.org/10.1016/j.neuroscience.2011.07.051. pii:S0306-4522(11)00876-1.

Kwon, H. B., Kozorovitskiy, Y., Oh, W. J., Peixoto, R. T., Akhtar, N., Saulnier, J. L., et al. (2012). Neuroligin-1-dependent competition regulates cortical synaptogenesis and synapse number. *Nature Neuroscience*, 15(12), 1667–1674. http://dx.doi.org/10.1038/nn.3256.

Kwon, E., Wang, W., & Tsai, L. H. (2013). Validation of schizophrenia-associated genes CSMD1, C10orf26, CACNA1C and TCF4 as miR-137 targets. *Molecular Psychiatry*, 18(1), 11–12. http://dx.doi.org/10.1038/mp.2011.170.

Lavezzari, G., McCallum, J., Dewey, C. M., & Roche, K. W. (2004). Subunit-specific regulation of NMDA receptor endocytosis. *Journal of Neuroscience*, 24(28), 6383–6391. http://dx.doi.org/10.1523/JNEUROSCI.1890-04.2004.

Law, A. J., Kleinman, J. E., Weinberger, D. R., & Weickert, C. S. (2007). Disease-associated intronic variants in the ErbB4 gene are related to altered ErbB4 splice-variant expression in the brain in schizophrenia. *Human Molecular Genetics*, 16(2), 129–141. http://dx.doi.org/10.1093/hmg/ddl449.

Lee, F. H., Fadel, M. P., Preston-Maher, K., Cordes, S. P., Clapcote, S. J., Price, D. J., et al. (2011). Disc1 point mutations in mice affect development of the cerebral cortex. *Journal of Neuroscience*, 31(9), 3197–3206. http://dx.doi.org/10.1523/JNEUROSCI.4219-10.2011.

Lee, A. S., Ra, S., Rajadhyaksha, A. M., Britt, J. K., De Jesus-Cortes, H., Gonzales, K. L., et al. (2012). Forebrain elimination of cacna1c mediates anxiety-like behavior in mice. *Molecular Psychiatry*, 17(11), 1054–1055. http://dx.doi.org/10.1038/mp.2012.71.

Lepagnol-Bestel, A. M., Kvajo, M., Karayiorgou, M., Simonneau, M., & Gogos, J. A. (2013). A Disc1 mutation differentially affects neurites and spines in hippocampal and cortical neurons. *Molecular and Cellular Neuroscience*, 54, 84–92. http://dx.doi.org/10.1016/j.mcn.2013.01.006.

Li, B., Woo, R. S., Mei, L., & Malinow, R. (2007). The neuregulin-1 receptor erbB4 controls glutamatergic synapse maturation and plasticity. *Neuron*, 54(4), 583–597. http://dx.doi.org/10.1016/j.neuron.2007.03.028.

Li, W., Zhang, Q., Oiso, N., Novak, E. K., Gautam, R., O'Brien, E. P., et al. (2003). Hermansky-Pudlak syndrome type 7 (HPS-7) results from mutant dysbindin, a member of the biogenesis of lysosome-related organelles complex 1 (BLOC-1). *Nature Genetics*, 35(1), 84–89. http://dx.doi.org/10.1038/ng1229.

Lieberman, J. A., Stroup, T. S., McEvoy, J. P., Swartz, M. S., Rosenheck, R. A., Perkins, D. O., et al. (2005). Effectiveness of antipsychotic drugs in patients with chronic schizophrenia. *New England Journal of Medicine, 353*(12), 1209–1223. http://dx.doi.org/10.1056/NEJMoa051688.

Lim, L. P., Lau, N. C., Garrett-Engele, P., Grimson, A., Schelter, J. M., Castle, J., et al. (2005). Microarray analysis shows that some microRNAs downregulate large numbers of target mRNAs. *Nature, 433*(7027), 769–773. http://dx.doi.org/10.1038/nature03315.

Lisman, J., Schulman, H., & Cline, H. (2002). The molecular basis of CaM-KII function in synaptic and behavioural memory. *Nature Reviews Neuroscience, 3*(3), 175–190. http://dx.doi.org/10.1038/Nrn753.

Liu, M., Lang, N., Chen, X., Tang, Q., Liu, S., Huang, J., et al. (2011). miR-185 targets RhoA and Cdc42 expression and inhibits the proliferation potential of human colorectal cells. *Cancer Letters, 301*(2), 151–160. http://dx.doi.org/10.1016/j.canlet.2010.11.009.

Liu, W. S., Pesold, C., Rodriguez, M. A., Carboni, G., Auta, J., Lacor, P., et al. (2001). Down-regulation of dendritic spine and glutamic acid decarboxylase 67 expressions in the reelin haploinsufficient heterozygous reeler mouse. *Proceedings of the National Academy of Sciences of the United States of America, 98*(6), 3477–3482. http://dx.doi.org/10.1073/pnas.051614698.

Ma, X. M., Kiraly, D. D., Gaier, E. D., Wang, Y., Kim, E. J., Levine, E. S., et al. (2008). Kalirin-7 is required for synaptic structure and function. *Journal of Neuroscience, 28*(47), 12368–12382. http://dx.doi.org/10.1523/JNEUROSCI.4269-08.2008.

Maletic-Savatic, M., Malinow, R., & Svoboda, K. (1999). Rapid dendritic morphogenesis in CA1 hippocampal dendrites induced by synaptic activity. *Science, 283*(5409), 1923–1927.

Mao, Y., Ge, X., Frank, C. L., Madison, J. M., Koehler, A. N., Doud, M. K., et al. (2009). Disrupted in schizophrenia 1 regulates neuronal progenitor proliferation via modulation of GSK3beta/beta-catenin signaling. *Cell, 136*(6), 1017–1031. http://dx.doi.org/10.1016/j.cell.2008.12.044. pii:S0092-8674(09)00021-X.

Matsuzaki, M., Honkura, N., Ellis-Davies, G. C., & Kasai, H. (2004). Structural basis of long-term potentiation in single dendritic spines. *Nature, 429*(6993), 761–766. http://dx.doi.org/10.1038/nature02617.

Mei, L., & Xiong, W. C. (2008). Neuregulin 1 in neural development, synaptic plasticity and schizophrenia. *Nature Reviews Neuroscience, 9*(6), 437–452. http://dx.doi.org/10.1038/nrn2392.

Millar, J. K., Wilson-Annan, J. C., Anderson, S., Christie, S., Taylor, M. S., Semple, C. A., et al. (2000). Disruption of two novel genes by a translocation co-segregating with schizophrenia. *Human Molecular Genetics, 9*(9), 1415–1423.

Missler, M., Zhang, W., Rohlmann, A., Kattenstroth, G., Hammer, R. E., Gottmann, K., et al. (2003). Alpha-neurexins couple Ca²⁺ channels to synaptic vesicle exocytosis. *Nature, 423*(6943), 939–948. http://dx.doi.org/10.1038/nature01755.

Mohn, A. R., Gainetdinov, R. R., Caron, M. G., & Koller, B. H. (1999). Mice with reduced NMDA receptor expression display behaviors related to schizophrenia. *Cell, 98*(4), 427–436. pii:S0092-8674(00)81972-8.

de la Morena, M. T., Eitson, J. L., Dozmorov, I. M., Belkaya, S., Hoover, A. R., Anguiano, E., et al. (2013). Signature MicroRNA expression patterns identified in humans with 22q11.2 deletion/DiGeorge syndrome. *Clinical Immunology, 147*(1), 11–22. http://dx.doi.org/10.1016/j.clim.2013.01.011. pii:S1521-6616(13)00022-3.

Morris, B. J., Cochran, S. M., & Pratt, J. A. (2005). PCP: from pharmacology to modelling schizophrenia. *Current Opinion in Pharmacology, 5*(1), 101–106. http://dx.doi.org/10.1016/j.coph.2004.08.008. pii:S1471-4892(04)00195-X.

Morrow, E. M., Kane, A., Goff, D. C., & Walsh, C. A. (2008). Sequence analysis of P21-activated kinase 3 (PAK3) in chronic schizophrenia with cognitive impairment. *Schizophrenia Research, 106*(2–3), 265–267. http://dx.doi.org/10.1016/j.schres.2008.08.021.

Mukai, J., Dhilla, A., Drew, L. J., Stark, K. L., Cao, L., MacDermott, A. B., et al. (2008). Palmitoylation-dependent neurodevelopmental deficits in a mouse model of 22q11 microdeletion. *Nature Neuroscience, 11*(11), 1302–1310. http://dx.doi.org/10.1038/nn.2204.

Mulle, J. G., Dodd, A. F., McGrath, J. A., Wolyniec, P. S., Mitchell, A. A., Shetty, A. C., et al. (2010). Microdeletions of 3q29 confer high risk for schizophrenia. *American Journal of Human Genetics, 87*(2), 229–236. http://dx.doi.org/10.1016/j.ajhg.2010.07.013.

Newton-Cheh, C., & Hirschhorn, J. N. (2005). Genetic association studies of complex traits: design and analysis issues. *Mutation Research, 573*(1–2), 54–69. http://dx.doi.org/10.1016/j.mrfmmm.2005.01.006. pii:S0027-5107(05)00026-6.

Niewoehner, B., Single, F. N., Hvalby, O., Jensen, V., Meyer zum Alten Borgloh, S., Seeburg, P. H., et al. (2007). Impaired spatial working memory but spared spatial reference memory following functional loss of NMDA receptors in the dentate gyrus. *European Journal of Neuroscience, 25*(3), 837–846. http://dx.doi.org/10.1111/j.1460-9568.2007.05312.x.

Niu, S., Renfro, A., Quattrocchi, C. C., Sheldon, M., & D'Arcangelo, G. (2004). Reelin promotes hippocampal dendrite development through the VLDLR/ApoER2-Dab1 pathway. *Neuron, 41*(1), 71–84. pii:S0896627303008195.

Niu, S., Yabut, O., & D'Arcangelo, G. (2008). The Reelin signaling pathway promotes dendritic spine development in hippocampal neurons. *Journal of Neuroscience, 28*(41), 10339–10348. http://dx.doi.org/10.1523/JNEUROSCI.1917-08.2008.

O'Tuathaigh, C. M., Desbonnet, L., & Waddington, J. L. (2012). Mutant mouse models in evaluating novel approaches to antipsychotic treatment. *Handbook of Experimental Pharmacology, 213*, 113–145. http://dx.doi.org/10.1007/978-3-642-25758-2_5.

O'Tuathaigh, C. M., O'Connor, A. M., O'Sullivan, G. J., Lai, D., Harvey, R., Croke, D. T., et al. (2008). Disruption to social dyadic interactions but not emotional/anxiety-related behaviour in mice with heterozygous 'knockout' of the schizophrenia risk gene neuregulin-1. *Progress in Neuro-Psychopharmacology and Biological Psychiatry, 32*(2), 462–466. http://dx.doi.org/10.1016/j.pnpbp.2007.09.018.

Paoletti, P., Bellone, C., & Zhou, Q. (2013). NMDA receptor subunit diversity: impact on receptor properties, synaptic plasticity and disease. *Nature Reviews Neuroscience, 14*(6), 383–400. http://dx.doi.org/10.1038/nrn3504.

Papaleo, F., Lipska, B. K., & Weinberger, D. R. (2012). Mouse models of genetic effects on cognition: relevance to schizophrenia. *Neuropharmacology, 62*(3), 1204–1220. http://dx.doi.org/10.1016/j.neuropharm.2011.04.025.

Papaleo, F., Yang, F., Garcia, S., Chen, J., Lu, B., Crawley, J. N., et al. (2012). Dysbindin-1 modulates prefrontal cortical activity and schizophrenia-like behaviors via dopamine/D2 pathways. *Molecular Psychiatry, 17*(1), 85–98. http://dx.doi.org/10.1038/mp.2010.106.

Paylor, R., Glaser, B., Mupo, A., Ataliotis, P., Spencer, C., Sobotka, A., et al. (2006). Tbx1 haploinsufficiency is linked to behavioral disorders in mice and humans: implications for 22q11 deletion syndrome. *Proceedings of the National Academy of Sciences of the United States of America, 103*(20), 7729–7734. http://dx.doi.org/10.1073/pnas.0600206103.

Penzes, P., Beeser, A., Chernoff, J., Schiller, M. R., Eipper, B. A., Mains, R. E., et al. (2003). Rapid induction of dendritic spine morphogenesis by trans-synaptic ephrinB-EphB receptor activation of the Rho-GEF kalirin. *Neuron, 37*(2), 263–274.

Penzes, P., & Jones, K. A. (2008). Dendritic spine dynamics–a key role for kalirin-7. *Trends in Neurosciences, 31*(8), 419–427. http://dx.doi.org/10.1016/j.tins.2008.06.001. pii:S0166-2236(08)00146-X.

Penzes, P., & Remmers, C. (2012). Kalirin signaling: implications for synaptic pathology. *Molecular Neurobiology, 45*(1), 109–118. http://dx.doi.org/10.1007/s12035-011-8223-z.

Pesold, C., Liu, W. S., Guidotti, A., Costa, E., & Caruncho, H. J. (1999). Cortical bitufted, horizontal, and Martinotti cells preferentially express and secrete reelin into perineuronal nets, nonsynaptically modulating gene expression. *Proceedings of the National Academy of Sciences of the United States of America, 96*(6), 3217–3222.

Pitcher, G. M., Kalia, L. V., Ng, D., Goodfellow, N. M., Yee, K. T., Lambe, E. K., et al. (2011). Schizophrenia susceptibility pathway neuregulin 1-ErbB4 suppresses Src upregulation of NMDA receptors. *Nature Medicine, 17*(4), 470–478. http://dx.doi.org/10.1038/nm.2315.

Pletnikov, M. V., Ayhan, Y., Nikolskaia, O., Xu, Y., Ovanesov, M. V., Huang, H., et al. (2008). Inducible expression of mutant human DISC1 in mice is associated with brain and behavioral abnormalities reminiscent of schizophrenia. *Molecular Psychiatry, 13*(2), 173–186, 115. http://dx.doi.org/10.1038/sj.mp.4002079.

Podhorna, J., & Didriksen, M. (2004). The heterozygous reeler mouse: behavioural phenotype. *Behavioural Brain Research, 153*(1), 43–54. http://dx.doi.org/10.1016/j.bbr.2003.10.033. pii:S0166432803004169.

Qiu, S., Korwek, K. M., Pratt-Davis, A. R., Peters, M., Bergman, M. Y., & Weeber, E. J. (2006). Cognitive disruption and altered hippocampus synaptic function in Reelin haploinsufficient mice. *Neurobiology of Learning and Memory, 85*(3), 228–242. http://dx.doi.org/10.1016/j.nlm.2005.11.001.

Radyushkin, K., Hammerschmidt, K., Boretius, S., Varoqueaux, F., El-Kordi, A., Ronnenberg, A., et al. (2009). Neuroligin-3-deficient mice: model of a monogenic heritable form of autism with an olfactory deficit. *Genes, Brain and Behavior, 8*(4), 416–425. http://dx.doi.org/10.1111/j.1601-183X.2009.00487.x.

Rebbeck, T. R., Spitz, M., & Wu, X. (2004). Assessing the function of genetic variants in candidate gene association studies. *Nature Reviews Genetics, 5*(8), 589–597. http://dx.doi.org/10.1038/nrg1403.

Rejeb, I., Saillour, Y., Castelnau, L., Julien, C., Bienvenu, T., Taga, P., et al. (2008). A novel splice mutation in PAK3 gene underlying mental retardation with neuropsychiatric features. *European Journal of Human Genetics, 16*(11), 1358–1363. http://dx.doi.org/10.1038/ejhg.2008.103.

Rethelyi, J. M., Bakker, S. C., Polgar, P., Czobor, P., Strengman, E., Pasztor, P. I., et al. (2010). Association study of NRG1, DTNBP1, RGS4, G72/G30, and PIP5K2A with schizophrenia and symptom severity in a Hungarian sample. *American Journal of Medical Genetics Part B: Neuropsychiatric Genetics, 153B*(3), 792–801. http://dx.doi.org/10.1002/ajmg.b.31049.

Ripke, S., O'Dushlaine, C., Chambert, K., Moran, J. L., Kahler, A. K., Akterin, S., et al. (2013). Genome-wide association analysis identifies 13 new risk loci for schizophrenia. *Nature Genetics, 45*(10), 1150–1159. http://dx.doi.org/10.1038/ng.2742.

Rochefort, N. L., & Konnerth, A. (2012). Dendritic spines: from structure to in vivo function. *EMBO Reports, 13*(8), 699–708. http://dx.doi.org/10.1038/embor.2012.102.

Rodriguez, M. A., Pesold, C., Liu, W. S., Kriho, V., Guidotti, A., Pappas, G. D., et al. (2000). Colocalization of integrin receptors and reelin in dendritic spine postsynaptic densities of adult nonhuman primate cortex. *Proceedings of the National Academy of Sciences of the United States of America, 97*(7), 3550–3555. http://dx.doi.org/10.1073/pnas.050589797.

Rogers, J. T., Rusiana, I., Trotter, J., Zhao, L., Donaldson, E., Pak, D. T., et al. (2011). Reelin supplementation enhances cognitive ability, synaptic plasticity, and dendritic spine density. *Learning & Memory, 18*(9), 558–564. http://dx.doi.org/10.1101/lm.2153511.

Rubio, M. D., Haroutunian, V., & Meador-Woodruff, J. H. (2012). Abnormalities of the Duo/Ras-related C3 botulinum toxin substrate 1/p21-activated kinase 1 pathway drive myosin light chain phosphorylation in frontal cortex in schizophrenia. *Biological Psychiatry, 71*(10), 906–914. http://dx.doi.org/10.1016/j.biopsych.2012.02.006.

Rujescu, D., Ingason, A., Cichon, S., Pietilainen, O. P., Barnes, M. R., Toulopoulou, T., et al. (2009). Disruption of the neurexin 1 gene is associated with schizophrenia. *Human Molecular Genetics, 18*(5), 988–996. http://dx.doi.org/10.1093/hmg/ddn351.

Schizophrenia Psychiatric Genome-Wide Association Study (GWAS) Consortium. (2011). Genome-wide association study identifies five new schizophrenia loci. *Nature Genetics, 43*(10), 969–976. http://dx.doi.org/10.1038/ng.940.

Selbach, M., Schwanhausser, B., Thierfelder, N., Fang, Z., Khanin, R., & Rajewsky, N. (2008). Widespread changes in protein synthesis induced by microRNAs. *Nature, 455*(7209), 58–63. http://dx.doi.org/10.1038/nature07228.

Selemon, L. D., & Goldman-Rakic, P. S. (1999). The reduced neuropil hypothesis: a circuit based model of schizophrenia. *Biological Psychiatry, 45*(1), 17–25. pii:S0006-3223(98)00281-9.

Shamir, A., & Buonanno, A. (2010). Molecular and cellular characterization of Neuregulin-1 type IV isoforms. *Journal of Neurochemistry, 113*(5), 1163–1176. http://dx.doi.org/10.1111/j.1471-4159.2010.06677.x.

Smrt, R. D., Szulwach, K. E., Pfeiffer, R. L., Li, X., Guo, W., Pathania, M., et al. (2010). MicroRNA miR-137 regulates neuronal maturation by targeting ubiquitin ligase mind bomb-1. *Stem Cells, 28*(6), 1060–1070. http://dx.doi.org/10.1002/stem.431.

Song, W., Li, W., Feng, J., Heston, L. L., Scaringe, W. A., & Sommer, S. S. (2008). Identification of high risk DISC1 structural variants with a 2% attributable risk for schizophrenia. *Biochemical and Biophysical Research Communications, 367*(3), 700–706. http://dx.doi.org/10.1016/j.bbrc.2007.12.117.

Stark, K. L., Xu, B., Bagchi, A., Lai, W. S., Liu, H., Hsu, R., et al. (2008). Altered brain microRNA biogenesis contributes to phenotypic deficits in a 22q11-deletion mouse model. *Nature Genetics, 40*(6), 751–760. http://dx.doi.org/10.1038/ng.138.

Steen, R. G., Mull, C., McClure, R., Hamer, R. M., & Lieberman, J. A. (2006). Brain volume in first-episode schizophrenia: systematic review and meta-analysis of magnetic resonance imaging studies. *British Journal of Psychiatry, 188*, 510–518. http://dx.doi.org/10.1192/bjp.188.6.510.

Stefansson, H., Sigurdsson, E., Steinthorsdottir, V., Bjornsdottir, S., Sigmundsson, T., Ghosh, S., et al. (2002). Neuregulin 1 and susceptibility to schizophrenia. *American Journal of Human Genetics, 71*(4), 877–892. http://dx.doi.org/10.1086/342734.

Straub, R. E., Jiang, Y., MacLean, C. J., Ma, Y., Webb, B. T., Myakishev, M. V., et al. (2002). Genetic variation in the 6p22.3 gene DTNBP1, the human ortholog of the mouse dysbindin gene, is associated with schizophrenia. *American Journal of Human Genetics, 71*(2), 337–348. http://dx.doi.org/10.1086/341750.

Strazisar, M., Cammaerts, S., van der Ven, K., Forero, D. A., Lenaerts, A. S., Nordin, A., et al. (2014). MIR137 variants identified in psychiatric patients affect synaptogenesis and neuronal transmission gene sets. *Molecular Psychiatry, 20*, 472–481. http://dx.doi.org/10.1038/mp.2014.53.

Sudhof, T. C. (2008). Neuroligins and neurexins link synaptic function to cognitive disease. *Nature, 455*(7215), 903–911. http://dx.doi.org/10.1038/nature07456.

Sullivan, P. F., Kendler, K. S., & Neale, M. C. (2003). Schizophrenia as a complex trait: evidence from a meta-analysis of twin studies. *Archives of General Psychiatry, 60*(12), 1187–1192. http://dx.doi.org/10.1001/archpsyc.60.12.1187.

Suzuki, K., Nakamura, K., Iwata, Y., Sekine, Y., Kawai, M., Sugihara, G., et al. (2008). Decreased expression of reelin receptor VLDLR in peripheral lymphocytes of drug-naive schizophrenic patients. *Schizophrenia Research, 98*(1–3), 148–156. http://dx.doi.org/10.1016/j.schres.2007.09.029. pii:S0920-9964(07)00435-5.

Swank, R. T., Sweet, H. O., Davisson, M. T., Reddington, M., & Novak, E. K. (1991). Sandy: a new mouse model for platelet storage pool deficiency. *Genetics Research, 58*(1), 51–62.

Szulwach, K. E., Li, X., Smrt, R. D., Li, Y., Luo, Y., Lin, L., et al. (2010). Cross talk between microRNA and epigenetic regulation in adult neurogenesis. *Journal of Cell Biology, 189*(1), 127–141. http://dx.doi.org/10.1083/jcb.200908151.

Tabuchi, K., Blundell, J., Etherton, M. R., Hammer, R. E., Liu, X., Powell, C. M., et al. (2007). A neuroligin-3 mutation implicated in autism increases inhibitory synaptic transmission in mice. *Science*, *318*(5847), 71–76. http://dx.doi.org/10.1126/science.1146221.

Talbot, K. (2009). The sandy (sdy) mouse: a dysbindin-1 mutant relevant to schizophrenia research. *Progress in Brain Research*, *179*, 87–94. http://dx.doi.org/10.1016/S0079-6123(09)17910-4.

Talbot, K., Louneva, N., Cohen, J. W., Kazi, H., Blake, D. J., & Arnold, S. E. (2011). Synaptic dysbindin-1 reductions in schizophrenia occur in an isoform-specific manner indicating their subsynaptic location. *PLoS One*, *6*(3), e16886. http://dx.doi.org/10.1371/journal.pone.0016886.

Tang, T. T., Yang, F., Chen, B. S., Lu, Y., Ji, Y., Roche, K. W., et al. (2009). Dysbindin regulates hippocampal LTP by controlling NMDA receptor surface expression. *Proceedings of the National Academy of Sciences of the United States of America*, *106*(50), 21395–21400. http://dx.doi.org/10.1073/pnas.0910499106.

Thompson, P. M., Vidal, C., Giedd, J. N., Gochman, P., Blumenthal, J., Nicolson, R., et al. (2001). Mapping adolescent brain change reveals dynamic wave of accelerated gray matter loss in very early-onset schizophrenia. *Proceedings of the National Academy of Sciences of the United States of America*, *98*(20), 11650–11655. http://dx.doi.org/10.1073/pnas.201243998.

Tissir, F., & Goffinet, A. M. (2003). Reelin and brain development. *Nature Reviews Neuroscience*, *4*(6), 496–505. http://dx.doi.org/10.1038/nrn1113.

Tsien, J. Z., Huerta, P. T., & Tonegawa, S. (1996). The essential role of hippocampal CA1 NMDA receptor-dependent synaptic plasticity in spatial memory. *Cell*, *87*(7), 1327–1338.

Ullrich, B., Ushkaryov, Y. A., & Sudhof, T. C. (1995). Cartography of neurexins: more than 1000 isoforms generated by alternative splicing and expressed in distinct subsets of neurons. *Neuron*, *14*(3), 497–507. http://dx.doi.org/10.1016/0896-6273(95)90306-2.

Ultanir, S. K., Kim, J. E., Hall, B. J., Deerinck, T., Ellisman, M., & Ghosh, A. (2007). Regulation of spine morphology and spine density by NMDA receptor signaling in vivo. *Proceedings of the National Academy of Sciences of the United States of America*, *104*(49), 19553–19558. http://dx.doi.org/10.1073/pnas.0704031104.

Varoqueaux, F., Aramuni, G., Rawson, R. L., Mohrmann, R., Missler, M., Gottmann, K., et al. (2006). Neuroligins determine synapse maturation and function. *Neuron*, *51*(6), 741–754. http://dx.doi.org/10.1016/j.neuron.2006.09.003. pii:S0896-6273(06)00680-5.

Vita, A., De Peri, L., Deste, G., & Sacchetti, E. (2012). Progressive loss of cortical gray matter in schizophrenia: a meta-analysis and meta-regression of longitudinal MRI studies. *Translational Psychiatry*, *2*, e190. http://dx.doi.org/10.1038/tp.2012.116.

Waddington, J. L., Corvin, A. P., Donohoe, G., O'Tuathaigh, C. M., Mitchell, K. J., & Gill, M. (2007). Functional genomics and schizophrenia: endophenotypes and mutant models. *Psychiatric Clinics of North America*, *30*(3), 365–399. http://dx.doi.org/10.1016/j.psc.2007.04.011.

Walters, J. T., & Owen, M. J. (2007). Endophenotypes in psychiatric genetics. *Molecular Psychiatry*, *12*(10), 886–890. http://dx.doi.org/10.1038/sj.mp.4002068.

Weeber, E. J., Beffert, U., Jones, C., Christian, J. M., Forster, E., Sweatt, J. D., et al. (2002). Reelin and ApoE receptors cooperate to enhance hippocampal synaptic plasticity and learning. *Journal of Biological Chemistry*, *277*(42), 39944–39952. http://dx.doi.org/10.1074/jbc.M205147200.

Weinberger, D. R., Berman, K. F., & Zec, R. F. (1986). Physiologic dysfunction of dorsolateral prefrontal cortex in schizophrenia. I. Regional cerebral blood flow evidence. *Archives of General Psychiatry*, *43*(2), 114–124.

Xie, Z., Cahill, M. E., & Penzes, P. (2010). Kalirin loss results in cortical morphological alterations. *Molecular and Cellular Neuroscience*, *43*(1), 81–89. http://dx.doi.org/10.1016/j.mcn.2009.09.006.

Xie, Z., Cahill, M. E., Radulovic, J., Wang, J., Campbell, S. L., Miller, C. A., et al. (2011). Hippocampal phenotypes in kalirin-deficient mice. *Molecular and Cellular Neuroscience*, *46*(1), 45–54. http://dx.doi.org/10.1016/j.mcn.2010.08.005. pii:S1044-7431(10)00196-X.

Xu, B., Hsu, P. K., Stark, K. L., Karayiorgou, M., & Gogos, J. A. (2013). Derepression of a neuronal inhibitor due to miRNA dysregulation in a schizophrenia-related microdeletion. *Cell*, *152*(1–2), 262–275. http://dx.doi.org/10.1016/j.cell.2012.11.052. pii:S0092-8674(12)01440-7.

Yin, D. M., Chen, Y. J., Lu, Y. S., Bean, J. C., Sathyamurthy, A., Shen, C., et al. (2013). Reversal of behavioral deficits and synaptic dysfunction in mice overexpressing neuregulin 1. *Neuron*, *78*(4), 644–657. http://dx.doi.org/10.1016/j.neuron.2013.03.028.

Yin, D. M., Sun, X. D., Bean, J. C., Lin, T. W., Sathyamurthy, A., Xiong, W. C., et al. (2013). Regulation of spine formation by ErbB4 in PV-positive interneurons. *Journal of Neuroscience*, *33*(49), 19295–19303. http://dx.doi.org/10.1523/JNEUROSCI.2090-13.2013.

Young, J. W., Powell, S. B., Risbrough, V., Marston, H. M., & Geyer, M. A. (2009). Using the MATRICS to guide development of a preclinical cognitive test battery for research in schizophrenia. *Pharmacology & Therapeutics*, *122*(2), 150–202. http://dx.doi.org/10.1016/j.pharmthera.2009.02.004. pii:S0163-7258(09)00035-7.

Zhang, F., Gu, W., Hurles, M. E., & Lupski, J. R. (2009). Copy number variation in human health, disease, and evolution. *Annual Review of Genomics and Human Genetics*, *10*, 451–481. http://dx.doi.org/10.1146/annurev.genom.9.081307.164217.

Zhao, X., Li, H., Shi, Y., Tang, R., Chen, W., Liu, J., et al. (2006). Significant association between the genetic variations in the 5′ end of the N-methyl-D-aspartate receptor subunit gene GRIN1 and schizophrenia. *Biological Psychiatry*, *59*(8), 747–753. http://dx.doi.org/10.1016/j.biopsych.2005.10.023. pii:S0006-3223(05)01428-9.

Zhou, Q., Homma, K. J., & Poo, M. M. (2004). Shrinkage of dendritic spines associated with long-term depression of hippocampal synapses. *Neuron*, *44*(5), 749–757. http://dx.doi.org/10.1016/j.neuron.2004.11.011. pii:S0896627304007226.

Ziv, N. E., & Smith, S. J. (1996). Evidence for a role of dendritic filopodia in synaptogenesis and spine formation. *Neuron*, *17*(1), 91–102 pii:S0896-6273(00)80283-4.

23

hiPSC Models Relevant to Schizophrenia

Brigham J. Hartley[a], Yoav Hadas[a], Kristen J. Brennand

Department of Psychiatry, Icahn School of Medicine at Mount Sinai, New York, NY, USA

INTRODUCTION

One of the biggest obstacles in studying schizophrenia (SCZ) is the lack of live brain tissue from patients with which to study the cellular mechanism underlying the disorder. Postmortem material, when available, is confounded by variables such as patient treatment history, poverty, drug and alcohol abuse, and cause of death. Although postmortem studies can reveal a lot about the state of the brain at the end of a long illness, it teaches us very little about disease initiation or progression. Furthermore, the heterogenic genetic contribution to SCZ risk is inadequately captured in even the best mouse models, which tend to investigate the effect of single highly penetrant risk alleles (such as DISC1 or NRG1 (Brandon & Sawa, 2011; Jaaro-Peled et al., 2010; Mei & Xiong, 2008)) in isolation. Furthermore, these animal models recapitulate some symptoms (such as anxiety, depression, and some cognitive deficits), but not all of the most relevant characteristics (such as hallucinations, delusions) associated with this very human condition.

The use of human-induced pluripotent stem cells (hiPSCs) in scientific research and medicine immediately bypassed the ethical issues associated with using human embryonic stem cells (hESCs). Ultimately, there are two obvious applications for induced pluripotent stem cells (iPSCs) in human medicine. First, hiPSCs should be useful as a source of cells for transplantation in any medical condition that is characterized by the loss of specific population of cells, such as dopaminergic neurons in Parkinson's disease (Ganat et al., 2012; Kriks et al., 2011), motor neurons in amyotrophic lateral sclerosis (Kondo et al., 2014), retinal cells in retinitis pigmentosa (Lamba, Karl, Ware, & Reh, 2006; Zhong et al., 2014), and insulin-producing β cells in diabetes (Pagliuca et al., 2014). It is

hoped that the use of cells that are genetically identical to those of the patient will reduce the risk for tissue rejection (Kiskinis & Eggan, 2010); clinical trials for the treatment of retinitis pigmentosa, diabetes, and spinal cord injury have already begun. Second, hiPSCs can also be used as a source of patient-derived cells for developing in vitro disease models (reviewed by Han, Williams, & Eggan, 2011; Sandoe & Eggan, 2013). Because these hiPSC-based studies recapitulate all of the (known and unknown) genetic factors interacting to produce the disease state, they can be developed not only for simple Mendelian disorders, but also for complex genetic disorders such as SCZ. These hiPSC-based studies will be useful to elucidate the molecular and cellular factors contributing to disease initiation and progression, but may also serve as a platform one day for high-throughput drug screening to identify novel therapeutic compounds for the treatment of this common and debilitating disease (Egawa et al., 2012).

EXISTING CELL-BASED MODELS

Nonneural Cell-Based Models (Lymphocytes and Fibroblasts)

Early attempts to generate cell-based models of SCZ relied on nonneuronal cells obtained from patients, such as lymphocytes and fibroblasts. A primary objective of these studies was to elucidate biomarkers with which to either improve diagnosis or predict patient drug responsiveness. Although the first reports focused on single traits, such as elevated dopamine antagonist [^{3}H]-spiperone binding (Bondy, Ackenheil, Birzle, Elbers, & Frohler, 1984) and increased levels of D_3 dopamine

---

[a] These authors contributed equally to this work.

receptor messenger RNA (mRNA) in SCZ patient lymphocytes (Ilani et al., 2001), more recent studies have focused on developing multiplex assays. Though several serum-based analyte signatures, comprising primarily cytokines, chemokines, and neurotrophins, are capable of distinguishing SCZ from healthy control subjects with high sensitivity and specificity (Domenici et al., 2010; Schwarz et al., 2010), unfortunately, to date, these assays show little specificity of this signature for SCZ relative to other psychiatric conditions (Schwarz et al., 2012). Studies of SCZ patient-derived fibroblast cultures have identified aberrations in growth and morphology (Mahadik, Mukherjee, Laev, Reddy, & Schnur, 1991), decreased cellular adhesion (Mahadik et al., 1994), and altered apoptotic pathways (Catts et al., 2006), many of which were subsequently confirmed by transcriptomic and proteomic approaches (Wang et al., 2010). Although these nonneuronal strategies have revealed abnormalities in peripheral tissues of SCZ patients that may one day serve as diagnostic tools for clinicians, to understand the mechanism that underlays the abnormal mental state, one must have an access to central nervous system tissues, including neurons and glia cells.

Neural Cell-Based Models (Olfactory Neural Progenitor Cells)

Neural tissue is not accessible from living SCZ patients (or healthy controls, as a point of comparison) unless the patient requires a surgical procedure to remove brain tissue, as in the case of severe epilepsy (Nunes et al., 2003; Oliver-De La Cruz et al., 2014) or brain tumors (Pavon et al., 2014). Nonetheless, viable neural progenitor cells (NPCs) have been successfully obtained during autopsies, which have been shown capable of further differentiation into mature neurons and glia in vitro (Nunes et al., 2003; Palmer, Schwartz, Taupin, Kaspar, & Stein, 2001). A similar study of postmortem obtained NPCs revealed that Alzheimer's disease patients have significantly fewer viable precursor cells in the hippocampus relative to age-matched healthy controls, and that Alzheimer's disease NPCs reach senescence earlier than NPCs isolated from aged-matched healthy controls (Lovell, Geiger, Van Zant, Lynn, & Markesbery, 2006).

A more accessible source of patient NPCs is the olfactory epithelium of the nasal cavity, which can be biopsied under local anesthesia (Feron, Perry, Hirning, McGrath, & Mackay-Sim, 1999). The olfactory epithelium comprises sensory neurons and supporting cells, including a population of NPCs (Mackay-Sima & Chuahb, 2000). Olfactory neural progenitor cells (ONPs) can be cultured and subsequently differentiated into neurons (Murrell et al., 2005). Several molecular and cellular phenotypic differences in SCZ patient ONPs have now been well-characterized, although such studies need to be carefully controlled

for such confounding variables and patient age, medication, and, most notably, smoking habits. The first such study found that SCZ ONPs show reduced adhesion, elevated mitosis, and altered response to dopamine relative to healthy controls (Feron et al., 1999). A subsequent study across a larger cohort of SCZ and bipolar disorder (BD) patients confirmed increased mitosis in SCZ ONPs (and further demonstrated increased cellular death in BD ONPs), and also found altered expression of genes involved in cell-cycle and vesicle transport (McCurdy et al., 2006). Recent insights now better explain increased replication and reduced adhesion in SCZ ONPs: increased mitosis occurs as a result of a larger pool of proliferating progenitors replicating with a reduced cell-cycle period (Fan, Abrahamsen, McGrath, & Mackay-Sim, 2012), whereas reduced adhesion in SCZ ONPs occurs as a direct consequence of significantly dysregulated focal adhesion kinase signaling (Fan et al., 2013). Gene expression and protein levels in SCZ ONPs show dysregulation in neurodevelopmental cell signaling pathways that are not detected in patient-matched fibroblasts (Matigian et al., 2010), in conjunction with reduced overall variability in gene expression relative to healthy controls (Mar et al., 2011). Although ONPs can differentiate to neurons and astrocytes, demonstrated by immunostaining for the neuronal marker βIII-TUBULIN and the astrocyte marker GFAP, respectively (Murrell et al., 2005), no ONP study has yet reported functional differences in ONP-derived neurons from SCZ patient relative to those from healthy controls, which we expect will be a critical area of interest in the future.

REPROGRAMMING OVERVIEW

Based on the notion that fully differentiated cells can be reprogrammed to a fully pluripotent state and give rise to a viable animal (Campbell, McWhir, Ritchie, & Wilmut, 1996; Gurdon, Elsdale, & Fischberg, 1958; Wilmut, Schnieke, McWhir, Kind, & Campbell, 1997), Takahashi and Yamanaka screened for factors that can revert the differentiation status of somatic cells. They found that transient overexpression of just four factors—SOX2, OCT3/4, c-MYC, and KLF4—were sufficient to reprogram mouse or human fibroblasts into iPSCs (Figure 1) (Okita, Ichisaka, & Yamanaka, 2007; Takahashi et al., 2007; Takahashi & Yamanaka, 2006). Whether derived from mice or humans, iPSCs have markedly similar morphology, proliferation, propensity to differentiate to all three germ layers, and ability to contribute to germline transmission (tested in mice only), as ESCs. These pioneering studies led to a burst of investigations into the generation of iPSCs from different tissues using different delivery methods and under different conditions (reviewed by Gonzalez,

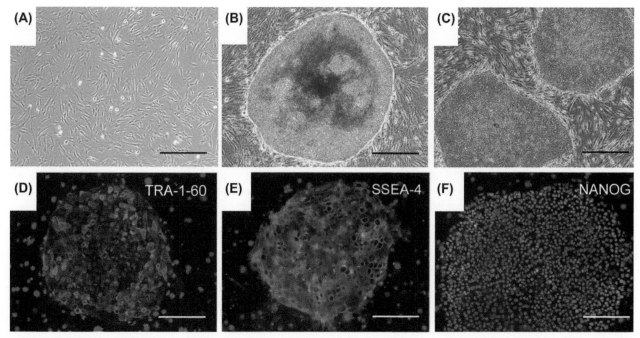

FIGURE 1 **Derivation of hiPSCs from human fibroblasts.** Typical morphology of (A) human fibroblasts and (B) hESC colony. (C) Morphology of an established hiPSC colony at passage number 6. Immunostaining of hiPSC colony demonstrating expression of pluripotency markers (D) TRA-1-60 (red), (E) SSEA-4 (green), and (F) NANOG (green), all counterstained with DAPI. hESC, human embryonic stem cell; hiPSC, human-induced pluripotent stem cell. *Adapted from Takahasi, K., Tanabe, K., Ohnuki, M., Narita, M., Ichisaka, T., Tomoda, K., et al. (2007). Induction of pluripotent stem cells from adult human fibroblasts by defined factors.* Cell, 131, 861–872.

Boue, & Izpisua Belmonte, 2011), all of which will be discussed at length in this section.

Source of Cells for hiPSCs

The somatic origin of the reprogrammed cells affects the efficiency of the reprogramming process, for review see (Li, Song, Pan, & Zhou, 2014), but may also influence the epigenetic status of the resultant iPSCs. The first hiPSCs were generated from fibroblasts, and this is still the preferred source of patient somatic cells in many laboratories because of both the ease of the expansion and cryostorage as primary cells. The reprogramming efficiency from fibroblasts varies, from 0.001% to 6.2% (Li et al., 2014), but is robust methodology, even from elderly patients' samples (Israel et al., 2012). Because skin biopsies, from which fibroblasts are obtained, require local anesthesia and have an associated risk of bleeding or infection (Villegas & McPhaul, 2005), methodologies have been developed to reprogram a variety of other primary cell types.

Many groups have robustly demonstrated that it is possible to generate hiPSCs from a variety of arguably more accessible tissues. One of the first such reports demonstrated that generation of hiPSCs from hair follicle keratinocytes can be 100-fold more efficient and twofold faster relative to fibroblasts (Aasen et al., 2008), although this methodology was never widely adopted. Other groups have shown that

hiPSCs can be generated from dental pulp, a strategy particularly amenable to the study of pediatric developmental disorders (Beltrao-Braga et al., 2011) and from human urine (Zhou et al., 2011). Though early reports of reprogramming from primary blood cells were exceedingly inefficient (Loh et al., 2009), this methodology has now been greatly improved and is widely used (Dowey, Huang, Chou, Ye, & Cheng, 2012). To date, few studies have compared the effect of the tissue of origin on the genetic mutation load and epigenetic status of the resultant hiPSCs.

Method of Reprogramming to Generate hiPSCs

Two critical aspects of the reprogramming process are the precise factors used and their method of delivery into the somatic cell. One of the major disadvantages of the original methodologies was that they relied on introducing the reprogramming factors using retroviral and lentiviral vectors, which results in stable integration of the exogenous factors into the genome (Takahashi et al., 2007; Yu et al., 2007). On average, every factor integrated into three to six different genomic loci; each site represented not just a novel mutation but additional loci with the potential to be reactivated during the differentiation process (Takahashi et al., 2007). In the context of transplantation studies, an additional concern was the potential to reactivate the oncogene c-MYC. Attempts centered on improving reprogramming efficiency in the absence of c-MYC demonstrated that it is possible to generate hiPSCs from fibroblasts using OCT3/4, SOX2, NANOG, and LIN28 without c-Myc (Yu et al., 2007). In addition, it was shown that hiPSCs can be generated using just OCT3/4, SOX2, and KLF4, although the reprogramming efficiency falls drastically to less than 0.001% (Nakagawa et al., 2008). The addition of valproic acid improves this process (to 1% efficiency) even permitting hiPSC generation with just OCT3/4 and SOX2 alone, though, again reducing efficiency below 0.001% (Huangfu et al., 2008). Given their endogenous SOX2 expression, human keratinocytes can be reprogrammed with just OCT4 and KLF4, if treated with a glycogen synthase kinase 3 beta inhibitor and an inhibitor of lysine specific demethylase 1 (Li et al., 2009).

The next advance was to permit tetracycline inducible expression of the reprogramming factors, either as multiple lentiviral vectors (Maherali et al., 2008) or as a single polycistronic vector encoding all four classic reprogramming factors (Carey et al., 2009). To completely eliminate the possibility of exogenous factor reactivation, floxed-reprogramming cassettes permitted transgene excision by Cre recombinase after the reprogramming procedure (Soldner et al., 2009; Sommer et al., 2009), though the loxP site was not excised from the genome. A similar strategy relied upon transposons carrying the polycistronic reprogramming cassette. The PiggyBac transposase can insert and remove DNA fragments flanked by defined terminal repeats without leaving a footprint (Ding et al., 2005) and can be used to generate hiPSCs free of exogenous reprogramming factors (Woltjen et al., 2009).

Ultimately, these strategies were abandoned in favor of integration free methods. Though it is possible to generate hiPSCs using plasmids (Okita et al., 2011), episomes (Yu, Chau, Vodyanik, Jiang, & Jiang, 2011), artificial chromosomes (Song, Chung, & Xu, 2010), and direct delivery of recombinant proteins (Kim et al., 2009), application of these methods has been constrained by their relatively low efficiencies. At this time, the two most commonly used reprogramming methods involve the use of modified mRNAs or sendai viruses (SeV) to transiently express the reprogramming factors. For mRNA-based reprogramming, the five factors (SOX2, OCT3/4, c-MYC KLF4, and LIN28) must be encoded by synthetic mRNAs designed to overcome the innate antiviral responses and repeatedly transfected into human fibroblasts (Warren et al., 2010). The addition of the microRNAs miR302/367 has further improved efficiencies (Anokye-Danso et al., 2011), and this platform has been successfully adopted to an automated high-throughput format (Paull et al., 2014). SeV-based reprogramming is highly efficient, owing to the ability of SeV to robustly infect most mammalian cells and mediate high levels of gene expression (Fusaki, Ban, Nishiyama, Saeki, & Hasegawa, 2009). SeV is a single-stranded RNA virus with an exclusively cytoplasmic replication cycle, making this virus incapable

of integrating its genetic information into the host cell genome (Faisca & Desmecht, 2007). SeV reprogramming typically relies on F-protein deficient, nontransmissible SeV (Fusaki et al., 2009), although complete removal of the SeV factors can be improved by using a temperature-sensitive SeV strain that can be deactivated by elevating the culture temperature (Ban et al., 2011). Both mRNA- and SeV-based reprogramming reagents are now commercially available and capable of reprogramming primary patient fibroblast or blood samples, allowing higher throughput hiPSC generation from larger patient cohorts than previously envisioned possible.

Genetic and Epigenetic Status of hiPSCs

It has been widely reported that spontaneous genomic mutations can and do occur during the reprogramming process. Although de novo genetic mutations could certainly confer increased risk in the context of cell replacement therapies, the negative implications of genomic stability in hiPSC-based disease models are less profound. Most hiPSCs lines appear to carry a handful of chromosomal aberrations (Mayshar et al., 2010), copy number variations (Hussein et al., 2011), and point mutations in coding regions (Gore et al., 2011). Although substantial subsets of reprogramming-associated mutations seem to preexist in fibroblasts at low frequencies (Gore et al., 2011), the rate of protein coding mutation is comparable regardless of the somatic cell source (Ruiz et al., 2013). Of those genetic lesions that occurred during or after the reprogramming process, there is a functional association between reorganization of DNA replication timing and the copy number variant copy number variant landscape that emerges during reprogramming (Lu et al., 2014). Passage number is a major contributor to genomic structural variations (Lu et al., 2014); significantly more copy number variants are present in early-passage hiPSCs than are found in either the source fibroblasts or intermediate passage hiPSCs (Hussein et al., 2011). Intriguingly, most novel copy number variants are a selective disadvantage and expansion of hiPSCs appears to drive the lines towards a less mutated state (Hussein et al., 2011).

The epigenetic status of hiPSCs relative to human ESCs remains unclear; hiPSCs show significant reprogramming variability, including somatic memory and aberrant reprogramming of DNA methylation. Investigators now recognize that there is some extent of residual DNA methylation signatures characteristic of the tissue of origin (Doi et al., 2009). Donor cell type (in this case, patient-matched cord blood cells and neonatal keratinocytes) results in distinct genome-wide DNA methylation and variable differentiation potential of the resultant hiPSCs (Kim, Zhao, et al., 2011). For example, pancreatic insulin-producing β cell–derived hiPSCs maintained open chromatin structure and unique DNA methylation signature at key β-cell genes, ultimately contributing to an increased ability to differentiate into insulin-producing β cells (Bar-Nur, Russ, Efrat, & Benvenisty, 2011). Because of this, hiPSC-based disease modeling experiments should be carefully designed to control for donor cell type.

The first evidence of incomplete epigenetic remodeling of (many, if not all) hiPSCs was that hiPSCs tend to undergo neuronal differentiation with significantly reduced efficiency and increased variability relative to hESCs (Hu et al., 2010). Epigenetic aberrations occur in hiPSCs regardless of the somatic cell type of origin, and aberrant methylation is maintained through hiPSC differentiation (Ruiz et al., 2012). hiPSCs show large (megabase-scale) differentially methylated regions, particularly close to centromeres and telomeres (Lister et al., 2011), and reprogramming efficiency inversely correlates with the percentage of epigenetic modifications observed after reprogramming (Ruiz et al., 2012). Furthermore, there is a loss of dosage compensation with passage in hiPSCs; although low-passage female hiPSCs retain the inactive X chromosome of the somatic cell they are derived from, over time in culture they undergo an "erosion" of X chromosome inactivation (Mekhoubad et al., 2012; Nazor et al., 2012). These epigenetic differences in hiPSCs may reflect errors in the reprogramming process: although both nuclear transfer–derived hESCs and hiPSCs derived from the same somatic cells contained comparable numbers of de novo CNVs, the DNA methylation and transcriptome profiles of nuclear transfer hESCs corresponded more closely to traditional hESCs (Ma et al., 2014).

Although it is important to be mindful of the genetic and epigenetic differences that may distinguish hiPSC lines from the same individual, the relative differences between hiPSCs and ESCs tend to be a distraction in the larger context of hiPSC-based disease modeling. Though both genetic and epigenetic mutations do occur, the frequency of these events is not believed to differ between patients and controls. With markedly improved reprogramming efficiencies by recent methodologies, hiPSC-based studies can now be designed from larger cohorts and include multiple hiPSCs from each individual. Although ideally each hiPSC line might one day be fully genotyped and epigenetically profiled, for now, including multiple hiPSC lines for each of multiple patients will allow careful comparisons of SCZ and control hiPSC-derived neurons to proceed.

OVERVIEW OF NEURONAL DIFFERENTIATION

The ability of human pluripotent stem cells (PSCs, both human ESCs and hiPSCs) to self-renew also differentiate into (theoretically) all of the somatic cell types present in the adult human make them an attractive cell source for both research and clinical applications. For the in vitro modeling of neuropsychiatric diseases, such as SCZ, the derivation of NPCs and neurons is required. Neuronal differentiation protocols attempt to mimic in vivo neurodevelopment, whereby extrinsic cytokines iteratively activate specific signaling pathways, first to induce neural commitment, and subsequently to specify neuronal phenotypes.

Over the years, many protocols have been established to direct PSCs toward neural lineages. Initial approaches used embryoid bodies (EBs), a three-dimensional structure resulting from the culture of PSCs in suspension (Bain, Kitchens, Yao, Huettner, & Gottlieb, 1995). In the EB protocol, neural induction results from the propensity of PSCs to default to a neural identity in the absence of specification cues, such as bone morphogenetic proteins; however, traditional EBs encompass multicellular multidifferentiated structures, of which neuronal derivatives are present only in limited amounts (Bain et al., 1995). To address this, a modified EB-based protocol was developed (Lee, Lumelsky, Studer, Auerbach, & McKay, 2000), in which neural precursors are preferentially selected from EBs using a chemically defined media. These precursors form organized structures known as neural rosettes, and express markers of the developing neural tube (Figure 2) (Elkabetz et al., 2008). Neural rosettes can be robustly expanded and differentiated into neurons (Elkabetz et al., 2008). The efficiency of neural rosette derivation can be increased by the addition of Noggin and/or fibroblast growth factor (FGF) 2, which act to antagonize bone morphogenetic protein signaling or inhibit nonneural differentiation (Tropepe et al., 2001; Ying, Nichols, Chambers, & Smith, 2003; Zhang, Wernig, Duncan, Brustle, & Thomson, 2001). Neural rosettes can be either manually or enzymatically harvested and propagated for numerous passages (Zhang et al., 2001). Although growth factor withdrawal results in the differentiation of NPCs into astrocytes and neurons (Zhang et al., 2001), investigators have little control over the ratio of particular phenotypes.

An alternative methodology is the coculture of PSCs with a monolayer of bone marrow stromal cells, such as PA6 or MS5 cells. When cultured at a low density, PSCs readily colonize and undergo efficient neural induction (Kawasaki et al., 2000). Moreover, specific neuronal phenotypes such as midbrain dopaminergic neurons are spontaneously differentiated. Because known midbrain dopaminergic neuron patterning factors, such as sonic hedgehog (SHH), FGF8, retinoic acid, or members of the wingless-type MMTV integration family (WNT) (Nefzger et al., 2012) are not added to cultures during differentiation, the inference has been made that stromal cells secrete/express their own patterning factors (Kawasaki et al., 2000; Perrier et al., 2004), an effect now known as stromal-derived inducing activity (Kawasaki

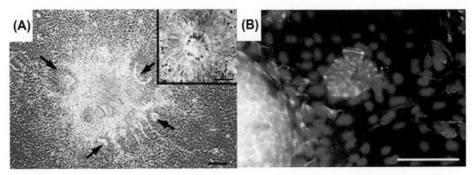

FIGURE 2   **Derivation of NPCs from human PS cells.** (A) Seven days postplating of EBs, rosettes appear (arrows). Inset: A rosette stained with toluidine blue, demonstrating columnar cells arranged in a tubular structure. (B) Immunostaining of a rosette. Cells are positive for the neural progenitor markers Nestin (green) and Musashi-1 (red). Counterstained with DAPI. NPC, neural progenitor cell; PS, pluripotent stem. *Adapted from Zhang, S. C., Wernig, M., Duncan, I. D., Brustle, O., & Thomson, J. A. (2001). In vitro differentiation of transplantable neural precursors from human embryonic stem cells.* Nature Biotechnology, 19, 1129–1133.

et al., 2000). Stromal coculture systems can also be used to derive other neurotransmitter subtypes. By altering the timing, concentration and type of morphogens added to an MS5 coculture of human PSCs, gamma-aminobutyric acid (GABA)ergic, serotoninergic, cholinergic, and motor neurons as well as astrocytes and oligodendrocytes, could be selectively generated (Barberi et al., 2003). Although this technique derives subtype specific neural cell types, the presence of undifferentiated PSCs, the difficulty separating PSC-derived cells from the stromal cell layer, and the undefined nature of stromal-derived inducing activity represent major drawbacks in the utilization of the stromal coculture method.

Consequently, Ying and Smith (2003) developed an adherent monolayer differentiation protocol using serum-free neural basal media together with a supportive extracellular matrix (Ying, Stavridis, Griffiths, Li, & Smith, 2003). A key feature of this protocol is that it allowed the observation, analysis, and manipulation of neural specification independent of multicellular aggregates, coculture, serum, uncharacterized media constituents, or cell selection methods (Ying, Stavridis, et al., 2003). Using this adherent monolayer protocol, mouse PSCs can be efficiently converted into neural precursors in the absence of any additional extrinsic factors and subsequently differentiated into neurons (Nefzger et al., 2012; Ying, Stavridis, et al., 2003).

Initially, differentiation of human PSCs was limited by the lack of viability after single cell dissociation (Watanabe et al., 2007), the heterogeneous nature of EB differentiation (Itskovitz-Eldor et al., 2000), and the low yield of neural phenotypes following selective survival strategies. The discovery of that Rho-associated protein kinase inhibition promoted the survival of human PSCs after single cell dissociation (Watanabe et al., 2007), together with the observation that neuralization of human PSCs via dual SMAD inhibition (bone morphogenetic proteins and activin/nodal signals inhibition) (Chambers et al., 2009), has resulted in improved protocols using monolayer differentiation that yield more efficient and synchronized neural progenitors cultures (Figure 3).

Using monolayer-based differentiation, it is now possible to derive specific regional and neurotransmitter phenotypes. Midbrain dopaminergic neurons, arguably the most well-studied cell type in the differentiation of hiPSCs into subtype specific neurons, can be efficiently generated by mimicking early signaling cues that arise in the developing floor plate of the prospective ventral midbrain, such as SHH and WNT (Fasano, Chambers, Lee, Tomishima, & Studer, 2010; Kriks et al., 2011; Miller et al., 2013) (Table 1). Through the inhibition of WNT signaling, either via protein (DKK1) or chemical (XAV939) antagonism, and timed exposure to SHH, forebrain GABAergic neurons, implicated in SCZ (Lewis, Hashimoto, & Volk, 2005) can be now be generated with high efficiency (Maroof et al., 2013; Nicholas et al., 2013) (Table 1). However, because of the paucity of information regarding GABAergic subtype specification, the selective derivation of parvalbumin, somatostatin, cholecystokinin, or vasoactive intestinal polypeptide positive cell subtypes remains unobtainable to date. For the major excitatory cell type of the mammalian brain, differentiation protocols that rely on default anterior patterning and/or the inhibition of SHH signaling via a smoothed receptor antagonist can yield glutamatergic neurons, though considerable variability exists in the ratios of the final subtype generated (Espuny-Camacho et al., 2013; Mariani et al., 2012; Shi, Kirwan, Smith, Robinson, & Livesey, 2012) (Table 1).

A more recent potential source of cells for experimental disease modeling, which negates the need to generate a pluripotent intermediate, is via the transdifferentiation directly from the source fibroblast population into the desired cell type. This method can yield neurons (induced neurons, iNs) via the forced expression of neural specific genes (Ambasudhan et al., 2011; Ladewig et al., 2012; Liu et al., 2012; Marro et al., 2011;

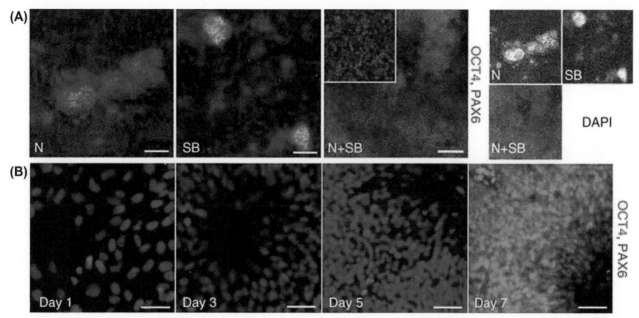

FIGURE 3 **Dual SMAD monolayer neural induction from human PS cells.** (A) Dual SMAD inhibition (N, Noggin, and SB, SB431542) improves neural induction as demonstrated by lack of OCT4 (red) and significant PAX6 expression (green), third panel. Low neural conversion is observed when either factor is used alone, first two panels. (B) Immunostaining for OCT4 (red) and PAX6 (green) indicates that rapid neural induction has occurred by day 7 of differentiation. All counterstained with DAPI. *Adapted from Chambers, S. M., Fasano, C. A., Papaetrou, E. P., Tomishima, M., Sadelain, M., & Studer, L. (2009) Highly efficient neural conversion of human ES and iPS cells by dual inhibition of SMAD signaling.* Nature Biotechnology, 27, 275–280.

TABLE 1   Summary of the Protocols Employed to Derive Neuronal Subtypes Relevant to the In Vitro Modeling of SCZ

Cell Source	Target Cell Type	Purity	Protocol	Characterization	References
hiPSCs	Cortical neurons	70% Glut/30% GABA	Dual SMAD, FGF2/cyclopamine/retinoids	Grafting, electrophysiology, protein and transcript expression	Espuny-Camacho et al. (2013), Mariani et al. (2012), and Shi et al. (2012)
hiPSCs	Midbrain dopaminergic neurons	~80%	Dual SMAD, SHH, WNT mimetic	Grafting, electrophysiology, protein and transcript expression	Chambers et al. (2009), Kriks et al. (2011), and Miller et al. (2013)
hiPSCs	Excitatory cortical neurons	100%	NGN2 overexpression	Grafting, electrophysiology, protein and transcript expression	Zhang et al. (2013)
hiPSCs	GABAergic interneurons	~80%	Dual SMAD, WNT antagonism, SHH	Grafting, electrophysiology, protein and transcript expression	Maroof et al. (2013) and Nicholas et al. (2013)
HEFs	Neurons	~70%	BRN2, ASCL1, MTYL1 and NEUROD1 overexpression	Electrophysiology, protein and transcript expression	Pang et al. (2011)
Hefs	Midbrain dopaminergic neurons	15–30%	BRN2, ASCL1, MTYL1, LMX1A, FOXA2/NURR1 overexpression	Grafting, electrophysiology, protein and transcript expression	Caiazzo et al. (2011) and Pfisterer et al. (2011)
HEFs*/MEFs	NPCs		Overexpression of different factors	Electrophysiology, protein and transcript expression	Han et al. (2012), Lujan et al. (2012), Ring et al. (2012), and Thier et al. (2012)

Abbreviations: HEFs, human embryonic fibroblasts; MEFs, mouse embryonic fibroblasts; Glut, glutamatergic. * Means associated study.

Meng et al., 2012; Pang et al., 2011; Pfisterer et al., 2011; Son et al., 2011; Vierbuchen et al., 2010; Xue et al., 2013) (Figure 4). Early reports demonstrated that the transdifferentiation approach was rapid, but highly inefficient, yielding functionally immature neurons with highly heterogeneous identities (Pang et al., 2011; Vierbuchen et al., 2010) (Table 1). This technique has now been refined, with reports of iN cells with functional synapses (Yoo et al., 2011) or the derivation of specific neuronal subtypes by the overexpression of particular

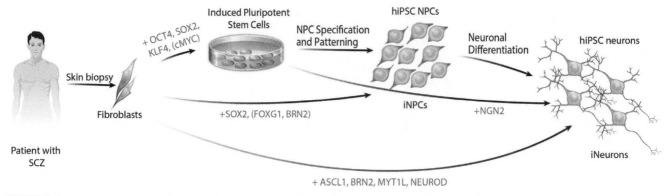

FIGURE 4   **Derivation of NPCs and neurons from human cells.** Fibroblast cells obtained from SCZ patients can be used to generate live human neurons. Fibroblasts can be reprogrammed to hiPSCs by transient expression of *OCT4*, *SOX2*, *KLF4*, and *c-MYC* and then subsequently differentiated into NPCs and mature neurons. Alternatively, fibroblasts can be directly converted to tri-potent neural progenitor cells (iNPCs) by transient expression of *SOX2* and then subsequently differentiated to neurons. Fibroblasts can be directly converted into a neuronal fate by transient expression of ASCL1, BRN2, MYT1L, and NEUROD. Alternatively, the use of NGN2 overexpression can drive the induction of neurons from PSCs. hiPSC, human-induced pluripotent stem cell; NPC, neural progenitor cell; SCZ, schizophrenia. *Adapted from Tran, N. N., Ladran, I. G., & Brennand, K. J. (2013) Modeling schizophrenia using induced pluripotent stem cell-derived and fibroblast-induced neurons.* Schizophrenia Bulletin, 39(1), 4–10.

lineage-specific transcription factors (Caiazzo et al., 2011; Pfisterer et al., 2011; Son et al., 2011) (Table 1). As advantageous as this strategy appears to be, the limited proliferation of the source fibroblasts, when combined with the nonproliferative nature of iN cells, leads to an inability to generate sufficient cell numbers for experimental applications. To this end, several groups have now shown that it is possible to transdifferentiate to self-renewing tri-potent neural progenitor cell populations, which can be expanded and differentiated into neurons, astrocytes, and oligodendrocytes (Han et al., 2012; Lujan, Chanda, Ahlenius, Sudhof, & Wernig, 2012; Ring et al., 2012; Thier et al., 2012) (Figure 4; Table 1).

Even the most robust differentiation protocols, whether based on growth factor addition or overexpression of lineage-specific transcription factors, yield cultures that comprise a myriad of neuronal subtypes as well as neural progenitors, astrocytes, oligodendrocytes, and nonneural cells. Additionally, the protracted differentiation timeline required to derive neuronal cultures with functional synapses severely impedes the use of PSC-derived neuronal cultures for disease modeling or cell replacement therapy. A recent paper has addressed such caveats by demonstrating that it is possible to induce neurons from renewable human PSC sources, rather than fibroblasts. Strikingly, the forced expression of only one lineage-specific transcription factor is required to derive neurons with robust synapses formation capabilities within 21 days (Zhang et al., 2001). Moreover, the inclusion of a puromycin selection results in cultures approaching 100% pure excitatory neurons with expression profiles similar to layer 2/3 neurons of the cortex (Zhang et al., 2013) (Figure 4; Table 1). These neurons can be used for electrophysiological or large-scale signaling analysis (e.g., Ca^{2+}), or the study of human genetic disorders through loss-of-function studies (Zhang et al., 2013). Given such high

purity, this approach may permit the study of the role of glutamatergic neurons in SCZ etiology. However, a criticism of this approach is that induction, which bypasses neuronal development, may mask developmental cellular phenotypes that contribute to disease initiation.

Etiologically, most cases of SCZ are thought to result from the complex interplay of environmental risk factors and contributions of different genomic loci that converge onto distinct developmental neurocircuitry (Gulsuner et al., 2013). At the cellular level, a growing body of evidence links the abnormal functioning of glutamatergic, GABAergic, and midbrain dopaminergic neurons with SCZ. Although pharmacological modulation of dopamine transmission helps manage the positive symptoms of SCZ for some patients (Demjaha et al., 2014), emerging evidence indicates that aberrant dopamine transmission is most likely downstream from dysfunctional GABA or GLUT neurons of the prefrontal cortex (Schwartz, Sachdeva, & Stahl, 2012). As mentioned previously, hiPSCs can be differentiated into several neuronal populations as well as astrocytes, thus hiPSC-based studies might be help to identify the specific neuronal subtype(s) whose aberrant activity contributes to SCZ initiation and progression. Thus the next section will focus on studies to date that have used hiPSC sources to model cellular phenotypes of SCZ under in vitro conditions.

HUMAN-INDUCED PLURIPOTENT STEM CELL MODELS OF SCZ

Numerous successful reprogramming based models of neuronal diseases have been established to date (for review, see Marchetto, Brennand, Boyer, & Gage, 2011). These hiPSC-based models aim to capture the inherited component of disease to elucidate the genetic

TABLE 2 Reported Cellular Phenotypes from hiPSC Models of SCZ

hiPSC Source	Cell Type Modeled	Phenotype Reported	References
2 Patients, DISC1 mutation, chronic undifferentiated SCZ and chronic paranoid SCZ	hiPSC only	None	Chiang et al. (2011)
4 Patients, SCZ and schizoaffective disorder diagnosis; paranoid	Forebrain neurons, mix of Glut and GABA	Aberrant gene expression, reduced neuronal connectivity	Brennand et al. (2011)
1 Patient, SCZ diagnosis	NPCs	Elevated levels of reactive oxygen species, aberrant mitochondrial oxygen consumption	Paulsen Bda et al. (2012)
3 Patients, paranoid SCZ diagnosis	Glut and DAergic neurons	Differentiation into DAergic neurons inhibited, lack of maturity for GLUT neurons	Robicsek et al. (2013)
Brennand et al. (2011)	NPCs	Aberrant gene and protein expression related to cytoskeletal remodeling and oxidative stress, aberrant migration and increased oxidative stress	Brennand et al. (2014)
Brennand et al. (2011)	Forebrain neurons, mix of Glut and GABA	Elevated levels of secreted DA, NE, and Epi; increased TH positive neurons	Hook et al. (2014)
Brennand et al. (2011)	Forebrain neurons, mix of Glut and GABA	Deficits in the generation of DG granule neurons, lower levels of NEUROD1, PROX1, and TBR1, reduced neuronal activity, and reduced levels of spontaneous neurotransmitter release	Yu et al. (2014)
3 Patients, child-onset SCZ, 15q11.2 deletion	NPCs	Deficits in adherents junctions and apical polarity	Yoon et al. (2014)
4 Patients, DISC1 mutation	Forebrain neurons, mix of Glut and GABA	Aberrant gene regulation using RNA-seq, demonstrated synaptic vesicle release deficits, corrected using gene editing	Wen et al. (2014)

DA, dopamine; DAergic, dopaminergic; Epi, epinephrine; GABA, GABAergic, Glut, glutamatergic; NE, norepinephrine; NPCs, neural progenitor cells; TH, tyrosine hydroxylase.

contribution to disease initiation and progression as well as provide a platform for therapeutic target discovery. Because twin and family studies consistently demonstrate the risk of developing SCZ has a highly heritable component (Cross-Disorder Group of the Psychiatric Genomics et al., 2013), hiPSC-based models of SCZ represent an invaluable tool to model specific cellular phenotypes of SCZ and to validate causal genes or genomic loci that have been implicated by a current genome-wide association study (Schizophrenia Working Group of the Psychiatric Genomics, 2014).

Numerous groups, including our own, have published reports on the use of SCZ patient-derived hiPSC in the modeling of specific aspects of SCZ (Table 2). Given the nature of SCZ being a neuropsychiatric disorder, it is not possible to model the disease as a whole; rather, investigators attempt to model cellular phenotypes that arise from genotypic defects. The first report of SCZ hiP-SCs were from patients genotyped for a DISC1 mutation (Chiang et al., 2011) (Table 2); however, hiPSC-derived neuronal cell types were not described. Later, our group reported aberrant gene expression profiles, in addition to reduced neuronal connectivity, neurite number, and synaptic maturation from a group of patients with complex genetic forms of SCZ (Brennand et al., 2011) (Table 2).

A third report, focused on cellular functional phenotypes, demonstrated elevated levels of reactive oxygen species and aberrant mitochondrial oxygen consumption in NPCs derived from one patient suffering from SCZ (Paulsen Bda et al., 2012). Such observations have been independently verified by a third group, reporting both impaired synaptic maturation and mitochondrial dysfunction in SCZ patient-derived hiPSCs (Robicsek et al., 2013) (Table 2). This group also reported that the differentiation of dopaminergic neurons from SCZ–hiPSC was also impaired, whereas a contrary publication demonstrated increased levels of tyrosine hydroxylase positive neurons as well as elevated levels of secreted catecholaminergic neurotransmitters, dopamine, norepinephrine, and epinephrine (Hook et al., 2014) (Table 2). However, these two groups used vastly different neural differentiation protocols. Hook et al. relied on EB formation and subsequent default anterior neural patterning, which generates neurons with expression profiles similar to that of fetal forebrain tissue (Brennand et al., 2014) (Table 2), whereas Robicsek et al. used the monolayer differentiation protocol, via dual SMAD inhibition, and dopamine patterning with SHH and FGF8, which is thought to generate hypothalamic DA neurons (Kriks et al., 2011); thus, it is difficult to compare the results from these studies. Focusing on a more refined differentiation protocol that enriches for a population of neurons expressing markers of hippocampal dentate gyral neurons, deficits were observed in neuronal activity and levels of spontaneous neurotransmitter (Yu et al., 2014) (Table 2).

In an attempt to model predisposition of SCZ, two studies have recently focused on studying NPCs rather than neurons. Using unbiased discovery approaches, microarray gene expression and stable isotope labeling by amino acids in cell culture quantitative proteomic mass spectrometry, we were able to identify abnormal gene and protein expression related to cytoskeletal remodeling and oxidative stress (Brennand et al., 2014) (Table 2). The translation of this discovery was demonstrated by aberrant migration and oxidative stress in SCZ NPCS in scalable phenotypic assays (Brennand et al., 2014) (Table 2; Figure 5). The other, using an SCZ-associated copy number variant cohort, confirmed deficits in cell migration while also demonstrating defects with apical polarity and adherent junctions in NPCs derived from 15q11.2

patients (Yoon et al., 2014) (Table 2). Through biochemical analysis, the authors were able to demonstrate that the observed phenotypes result from haploinsufficiency of CYFIP1, a component of the WAVE signaling complex, which regulates cytoskeletal dynamics (Yoon et al., 2014). Building on this discovery, in SCZ hiPSC-derived NPCs, the authors demonstrated that CYFP1 deficiency in the developing mouse cortex leads to ectopic placement of radial glial cells outside of the ventricular zone (Yoon et al., 2014), reinforcing the utility of hiPSC-based models in the discovery of phenotypes relevant to SCZ. Most recently, it was demonstrated that neurons derived from hiPSC patients with a DISC1 frameshift mutation exhibit synaptic vesicle release deficits as well as aberrant gene expression by RNA-seq, which could correct following repair of the DISC1 frameshift using genomic editing technology (Wen et al., 2014) (Table 2).

Together, these studies validate hiPSC-based in vitro modeling of SCZ because many of the genes that exhibited altered expression had previously been implicated in genetic, postmortem, or animal models of SCZ.

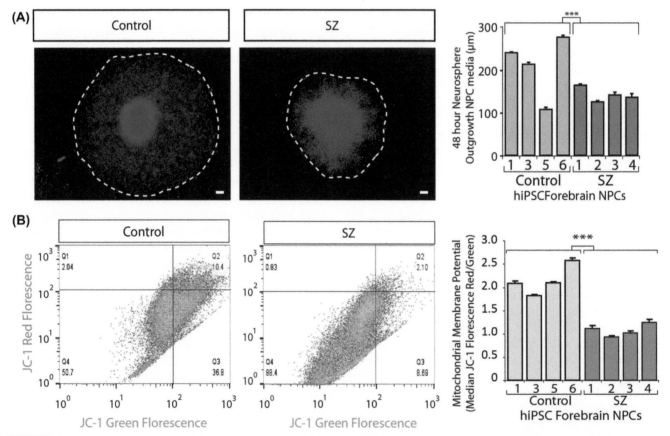

FIGURE 5　**Reported cellular phenotypes in hiPSC-based modeling of SCZ.** (A) Aberrant migration in SCZ-hiPSC–derived NPCs. Representative images of an NPC neurosphere outgrowth assay. The average distance between the radius of the inner neurosphere (dense aggregate of nuclei) and outer circumference of the neurosphere (white dashed line). Quantified for all cell lines in the right-hand panel. Cells stained with DAPI. (B) Mitochondrial damage and increased oxidative stress in SCZ–NPCs. Representative fluorescence-activated cell sorting (FACS) plots for JC-1 red/green fluorescence in control and SCZ hiPSC NPCs, quantified for all cell lines in the right-hand panel. hiPSC, human-induced pluripotent stem cell; NPC, neural progenitor cell; SCZ, schizophrenia. *Adapted from Brennand, K. J., Savas, J. N., Kim, Y., Tran, N. N., Simone, A., Hashimoto-Torii, K., et al. (2014). Phenotypic differences in hiPSC NPs derived from patients with. Molecular Psychiatry, 1–8.*

Moreover, the demonstration that cellular phenotypes can be replicated across numerous hiPSC-based studies, comprising independent patient cohorts, further validating and extending the promise of this technology in understanding the etiology behind SCZ disease initiation and progression.

Moving forward, regardless of whether they are directly differentiated from hiPSCs or induced, future in vitro cell-based models of SCZ will require cultures with improved regional patterning, cell-type specificity, and functional maturity. As mentioned previously, a recent protocol has been established that can yield pure cultures of excitatory neurons; it will be of utmost importance for similar protocols to come online for generating other neurotransmitter cell types in high purity to facilitate the understanding the role that particular neural subtypes have in SCZ disease initiation and progression. Moreover, because current hiPSC-based in vitro models of SCZ are small relative to genetic studies, either more genetically or clinically homogenous cohorts will be required. Additionally, to address issues of interpatient as well as intraexperiment variability, larger cohorts as well as scalable assays, are necessary. The next section will discuss steps required to move toward adapting in vitro based modeling of SCZ cellular phenotypes to a high-throughput arena.

ADAPTATION TO HIGH-THROUGHPUT TECHNOLOGIES

The sample size of current hiPSC-based models of SCZ remain extremely limited with respect to the size of other methodologies used to study etiology and disease risk, such as genome-wide association studies. Currently, numerous bottlenecks exist that greatly limit moving hiPSC-based cellular modeling toward realizing its full potential for cellular phenotyping and drug discovery. Technical constraints (listed in order of increasing difficulty) include patient identification and consent, derivation of hiPSC lines, differentiation of hiPSCs into NPCs, and neurons and cellular phenotyping; all affect the scalability of hiPSC based studies. As a consequence, published reports to date use small sample sizes, usually on the order of one to four SCZ patients, and thus raise a concern as to whether the findings translate to larger SCZ patient population.

The use of blood samples as an alternative somatic cell source in addition to fibroblasts, together with the improved efficacy of SeV or synthetic mRNA-based reprogramming, address the first bottleneck because these advances provide a more readily obtainable source of cells, although also permitting the adaptation of the reprogramming process to a high-throughput manner, as has been shown (Paull et al., 2014). This is not only important for expanding the repertoire of patient cell lines, but

also for expanding the number of control cell lines that are included in future studies to address issues of intrapatient and interpatient variability. Intrapatient variability arises because of the variation, either genetically or epigenetically, in individual hiPSC lines from the same person (Kim, Lee, et al., 2011). This type of variability might be unavoidable until the field better understands the effects on the epigenome that occur during the reprogramming process. Interpatient variability, on the other hand, is a result of the heterogeneity between patients with SCZ (or between healthy controls). Possible strategies for addressing interpatient variability include choosing a patient cohort on the basis of a shared clinical phenotype (e.g., child-onset schizophrenia), which would then be compared with age-matched individuals without the phenotype. Another, more focused approach relies on the use of genetically homogenous cohorts (e.g., patient with DISC1, NRG1, or NRNX1 lesions), whereby comparisons can be made to isogenic cell lines corrected by gene-targeting strategies such as CRISPR/Cas9 or TALEN based approaches (as demonstrated for DISC1 frameshift mutations (Wen et al., 2014)); this strategy limits "background genetic" effects that cannot currently be accounted for otherwise. The latter approach shares commonalties with traditional animal-based studies, which investigate the effects of rare but highly penetrant loci, although the former experimental design harnesses the full potential of hiPSC-based studies because it can investigate complex genetic disorders where the full knowledge of all loci involved is not annotated a priori. Regardless of the approach taken, either the use of clinically or genetically homogenous cohorts, the adaption of hiPSC derivation to a high-throughput setting will greatly facilitate this endeavor.

With respect to which neural subtype to model, no current differentiation protocols yield pure terminal cultures of particular neural subtypes. For adaptation to high-throughput screening, the use of a rapid induction protocol would be extremely advantageous because of its low cost and ease of use. The use of antibodies, or reporter-based systems, would facilitate either the purification or labeling of live human neurons or NPCs with particular regional or neurotransmitter phenotypes. Such an approach has already been demonstrated in a high-throughput–based study of familial dysautonomia, where neural crest progenitors where enriched before being adapted to a large-scale small molecule screen (Lee et al., 2012).

Cellular phenotyping on a large scale represents a novel challenge. Typically, investigators have used biased hypothesis driven approaches where one read out is usually undertaken per experiment, as has been the case for cell signaling assays in pharmacological studies. The past decade has witnessed the explosion of "omic" approaches that produce large volumes of data, and the study of cellular function both in normal and disease states has begun to move away from such traditional methodology. The application of unbiased DNA and RNA sequencing, together with higher throughput protein analysis and powerful biocomputation, is beginning to reveal information about some of the disease processes behind SCZ. As an example, both stable isotope labeling by amino acids in cell culture and microarray was able to predict aberrant cytoskeletal remodeling and oxidative stress in NPCs derived from SCZ hiPSC (Brennand et al., 2014). These predictions were subsequently confirmed in scalable assay, which demonstrates the amenability of hiPSC cellular models of SCZ to a high-throughput setting. With the advent of high throughput screening (HTS) systems, it is now possible to conduct assays on a multitude of samples, however typically the endpoint still consists of one read out of activity. Over recent years manufactures have begun to address the demand for high content screening systems, which in contrast to HTS allow investigators to measure many characteristics or features of individual cells within a culture at once. Such technology advances the ability to manipulate many variables in an experiment simultaneously in a highly controlled environment. With respect to SCZ in vitro modeling, one conceivable experiment would to study the effects of drugs on multiple therapeutic endpoints concurrently. For example, following the automation of hiPSC derivation and differentiation, assays could be conducted across several biological parameters, including the migration of neurons, the degree and morphology of axon and dendritic branching, as well as synaptic number and morphology, in response to particular drugs or dosages. Moreover, as the repertoire of genetically encoded biosensors expands the capabilities of these technologies, it will permit the ability to track many cellular endpoints in the same experiment across hundreds of cells in a well.

The adaptation of hiPSC derivation and differentiation as well as large-scale cellular phenotyping and drug library screening will allow hiPSC-based SCZ modeling to be conducted at unprecedented levels of complexity. Moreover, because this HTS space will require cooperation from across academic and industrial partners, we hope that the translational potential of hiPSC based in vitro studies of SCZ will more rapidly move therapeutics out of the discovery space and into patients.

References

Aasen, T., Raya, A., Barrero, M. J., Garreta, E., Consiglio, A., Gonzalez, F., et al. (2008). Efficient and rapid generation of induced pluripotent stem cells from human keratinocytes. *Nature Biotechnology, 26*, 1276–1284.

Ambasudhan, R., Talantova, M., Coleman, R., Yuan, X., Zhu, S., Lipton, S. A., et al. (2011). Direct reprogramming of adult human fibroblasts to functional neurons under defined conditions. *Cell Stem Cell, 9*, 113–118.

Anokye-Danso, F., Trivedi, C. M., Juhr, D., Gupta, M., Cui, Z., Tian, Y., et al. (2011). Highly efficient miRNA-mediated reprogramming of mouse and human somatic cells to pluripotency. *Cell Stem Cell, 8*, 376–388.

Bain, G., Kitchens, D., Yao, M., Huettner, J. E., & Gottlieb, D. I. (1995). Embryonic stem cells express neuronal properties in vitro. *Developmental Biology, 168*, 342–357.

Ban, H., Nishishita, N., Fusaki, N., Tabata, T., Saeki, K., Shikamura, M., et al. (2011). Efficient generation of transgene-free human induced pluripotent stem cells (iPSCs) by temperature-sensitive sendai virus vectors. *Proceedings of the National Academy of Sciences of the United States of America, 108*, 14234–14239.

Bar-Nur, O., Russ, H. A., Efrat, S., & Benvenisty, N. (2011). Epigenetic memory and preferential lineage-specific differentiation in induced pluripotent stem cells derived from human pancreatic islet beta cells. *Cell Stem Cell, 9*, 17–23.

Barberi, T., Klivenyi, P., Calingasan, N. Y., Lee, H., Kawamata, H., Loonam, K., et al. (2003). Neural subtype specification of fertilization and nuclear transfer embryonic stem cells and application in parkinsonian mice. *Nature Biotechnology, 21*, 1200–1207.

Beltrao-Braga, P. C., Pignatari, G. C., Maiorka, P. C., Oliveira, N. A., Lizier, N. F., Wenceslau, C. V., et al. (2011). Feeder-free derivation of induced pluripotent stem cells from human immature dental pulp stem cells. *Cell Transplantation, 20*, 1707–1719.

Bondy, B., Ackenheil, M., Birzle, W., Elbers, R., & Frohler, M. (1984). Catecholamines and their receptors in blood: evidence for alterations in schizophrenia. *Biological Psychiatry, 19*, 1377–1393.

Brandon, N. J., & Sawa, A. (2011). Linking neurodevelopmental and synaptic theories of mental illness through DISC1. *Nature Reviews Neuroscience, 12*(12), 707–722.

Brennand, K., Savas, J. N., Kim, Y., Tran, N., Simone, A., Hashimoto-Torii, K., et al. (2014). Phenotypic differences in hiPSC NPCs derived from patients with schizophrenia. *Molecular Psychiatry*.

Brennand, K. J., Simone, A., Jou, J., Gelboin-Burkhart, C., Tran, N., Sangar, S., et al. (2011). Modelling schizophrenia using human induced pluripotent stem cells. *Nature, 473*, 221–225.

Caiazzo, M., Dell'Anno, M. T., Dvoretskova, E., Lazarevic, D., Taverna, S., Leo, D., et al. (2011). Direct generation of functional dopaminergic neurons from mouse and human fibroblasts. *Nature, 476*, 224–227.

Campbell, K. H., McWhir, J., Ritchie, W. A., & Wilmut, I. (1996). Sheep cloned by nuclear transfer from a cultured cell line. *Nature, 380*, 64–66.

Carey, B. W., Markoulaki, S., Hanna, J., Saha, K., Gao, Q., Mitalipova, M., et al. (2009). Reprogramming of murine and human somatic cells using a single polycistronic vector. *Proceedings of the National Academy of Sciences of the United States of America, 106*, 157–162.

Catts, V. S., Catts, S. V., McGrath, J. J., Feron, F., McLean, D., Coulson, E. J., et al. (2006). Apoptosis and schizophrenia: a pilot study based on dermal fibroblast cell lines. *Schizophrenia Research, 84*, 20–28.

Chambers, S. M., Fasano, C. A., Papapetrou, E. P., Tomishima, M., Sadelain, M., & Studer, L. (2009). Highly efficient neural conversion of human ES and iPS cells by dual inhibition of SMAD signaling. *Nature Biotechnology, 27*, 275–280.

Chiang, C. H., Su, Y., Wen, Z., Yoritomo, N., Ross, C. A., Margolis, R. L., et al. (2011). Integration-free induced pluripotent stem cells derived from schizophrenia patients with a DISC1 mutation. *Molecular Psychiatry, 16*, 358–360.

Cross-Disorder Group of the Psychiatric Genomics Consortium, Lee, S. H., Ripke, S., Neale, B. M., Faraone, S. V., Purcell, S. M., Perlis, R. H., et al. (2013). Genetic relationship between five psychiatric disorders estimated from genome-wide SNPs. *Nature Genetics, 45*, 984–994.

Demjaha, A., Egerton, A., Murray, R. M., Kapur, S., Howes, O. D., Stone, J. M., et al. (2014). Antipsychotic treatment resistance in schizophrenia associated with elevated glutamate levels but normal dopamine function. *Biological Psychiatry, 75*, e11–13.

Ding, S., Wu, X., Li, G., Han, M., Zhuang, Y., & Xu, T. (2005). Efficient transposition of the piggyBac (PB) transposon in mammalian cells and mice. *Cell, 122,* 473–483.

Doi, A., Park, I. H., Wen, B., Murakami, P., Aryee, M. J., Irizarry, R., et al. (2009). Differential methylation of tissue- and cancer-specific CpG island shores distinguishes human induced pluripotent stem cells, embryonic stem cells and fibroblasts. *Nature Genetics, 41,* 1350–1353.

Domenici, E., Wille, D. R., Tozzi, F., Prokopenko, I., Miller, S., McKeown, A., et al. (2010). Plasma protein biomarkers for depression and schizophrenia by multi analyte profiling of case-control collections. *PLoS One, 5,* e9166.

Dowey, S. N., Huang, X., Chou, B. K., Ye, Z., & Cheng, L. (2012). Generation of integration-free human induced pluripotent stem cells from postnatal blood mononuclear cells by plasmid vector expression. *Nature Protocols, 7,* 2013–2021.

Egawa, N., Kitaoka, S., Tsukita, K., Naitoh, M., Takahashi, K., Yamamoto, T., et al. (2012). Drug screening for ALS using patient-specific induced pluripotent stem cells. *Science Translational Medicine 4,* 145ra104.

Elkabetz, Y., Panagiotakos, G., Al Shamy, G., Socci, N. D., Tabar, V., & Studer, L. (2008). Human ES cell-derived neural rosettes reveal a functionally distinct early neural stem cell stage. *Genes & Development, 22,* 152–165.

Espuny-Camacho, I., Michelsen, K. A., Gall, D., Linaro, D., Hasche, A., Bonnefont, J., et al. (2013). Pyramidal neurons derived from human pluripotent stem cells integrate efficiently into mouse brain circuits in vivo. *Neuron, 77,* 440–456.

Faisca, P., & Desmecht, D. (2007). Sendai virus, the mouse parainfluenza type 1: a longstanding pathogen that remains up-to-date. *Research in Veterinary Science, 82,* 115–125.

Fan, Y., Abrahamsen, G., McGrath, J. J., & Mackay-Sim, A. (2012). Altered cell cycle dynamics in schizophrenia. *Biological Psychiatry, 71,* 129–135.

Fan, Y., Abrahamsen, G., Mills, R., Calderon, C. C., Tee, J. Y., Leyton, L., et al. (2013). Focal adhesion dynamics are altered in schizophrenia. *Biological Psychiatry, 74,* 418–426.

Fasano, C. A., Chambers, S. M., Lee, G., Tomishima, M. J., & Studer, L. (2010). Efficient derivation of functional floor plate tissue from human embryonic stem cells. *Cell Stem Cell, 6,* 336–347.

Feron, F., Perry, C., Hirning, M. H., McGrath, J., & Mackay-Sim, A. (1999). Altered adhesion, proliferation and death in neural cultures from adults with schizophrenia. *Schizophrenia Research, 40,* 211–218.

Fusaki, N., Ban, H., Nishiyama, A., Saeki, K., & Hasegawa, M. (2009). Efficient induction of transgene-free human pluripotent stem cells using a vector based on sendai virus, an RNA virus that does not integrate into the host genome. *Proceedings of the Japan Academy Series B: Physical and Biological Sciences, 85,* 348–362.

Ganat, Y. M., Calder, E. L., Kriks, S., Nelander, J., Tu, E. Y., Jia, F., et al. (2012). Identification of embryonic stem cell-derived midbrain dopaminergic neurons for engraftment. *Journal of Clinical Investigation, 122,* 2928–2939.

Gonzalez, F., Boue, S., & Izpisua Belmonte, J. C. (2011). Methods for making induced pluripotent stem cells: reprogramming a la carte. *Nature Reviews Genetics, 12,* 231–242.

Gore, A., Li, Z., Fung, H. L., Young, J. E., Agarwal, S., Antosiewicz-Bourget, J., et al. (2011). Somatic coding mutations in human induced pluripotent stem cells. *Nature, 471,* 63–67.

Gulsuner, S., Walsh, T., Watts, A. C., Lee, M. K., Thornton, A. M., Casadei, S., et al. (2013). Spatial and temporal mapping of de novo mutations in schizophrenia to a fetal prefrontal cortical network. *Cell, 154,* 518–529.

Gurdon, J. B., Elsdale, T. R., & Fischberg, M. (1958). Sexually mature individuals of *Xenopus laevis* from the transplantation of single somatic nuclei. *Nature, 182,* 64–65.

Han, D. W., Tapia, N., Hermann, A., Hemmer, K., Hoing, S., Arauzo-Bravo, M. J., et al. (2012). Direct reprogramming of fibroblasts into neural stem cells by defined factors. *Cell Stem Cell, 10,* 465–472.

Han, S. S., Williams, L. A., & Eggan, K. C. (2011). Constructing and deconstructing stem cell models of neurological disease. *Neuron, 70,* 626–644.

Hook, V., Brennand, K. J., Kim, Y., Toneff, T., Funkelstein, L., Lee, K. C., et al. (2014). Human iPSC neurons display activity-dependent neurotransmitter secretion: aberrant catecholamine levels in schizophrenia neurons. *Stem Cell Reports, 3,* 531–538.

Hu, B. Y., Weick, J. P., Yu, J., Ma, L. X., Zhang, X. Q., Thomson, J. A., et al. (2010). Neural differentiation of human induced pluripotent stem cells follows developmental principles but with variable potency. *Proceedings of the National Academy of Sciences of the United States of America, 107,* 4335–4340.

Huangfu, D., Osafune, K., Maehr, R., Guo, W., Eijkelenboom, A., Chen, S., et al. (2008). Induction of pluripotent stem cells from primary human fibroblasts with only Oct4 and Sox2. *Nature Biotechnology, 26,* 1269–1275.

Hussein, S. M., Batada, N. N., Vuoristo, S., Ching, R. W., Autio, R., Narva, E., et al. (2011). Copy number variation and selection during reprogramming to pluripotency. *Nature, 471,* 58–62.

Ilani, T., Ben-Shachar, D., Strous, R. D., Mazor, M., Sheinkman, A., Kotler, M., et al. (2001). A peripheral marker for schizophrenia: increased levels of D3 dopamine receptor mRNA in blood lymphocytes. *Proceedings of the National Academy of Sciences of the United States of America, 98,* 625–628.

Israel, M. A., Yuan, S. H., Bardy, C., Reyna, S. M., Mu, Y., Herrera, C., et al. (2012). Probing sporadic and familial Alzheimer's disease using induced pluripotent stem cells. *Nature, 482,* 216–220.

Itskovitz-Eldor, J., Schuldiner, M., Karsenti, D., Eden, A., Yanuka, O., Amit, M., et al. (2000). Differentiation of human embryonic stem cells into embryoid bodies compromising the three embryonic germ layers. *Molecular Medicine, 6,* 88–95.

Jaaro-Peled, H., Ayhan, Y., Pletnikov, M. V., & Sawa, A. (2010). Review of pathological hallmarks of schizophrenia: comparison of genetic models with patients and nongenetic models. *Schizophrenia Bulletin, 36*(2), 301–313.

Kawasaki, H., Mizuseki, K., Nishikawa, S., Kaneko, S., Kuwana, Y., Nakanishi, S., et al. (2000). Induction of midbrain dopaminergic neurons from ES cells by stromal cell-derived inducing activity. *Neuron, 28,* 31–40.

Kim, D., Kim, C. H., Moon, J. I., Chung, Y. G., Chang, M. Y., Han, B. S., et al. (2009). Generation of human induced pluripotent stem cells by direct delivery of reprogramming proteins. *Cell Stem Cell, 4,* 472–476.

Kim, H., Lee, G., Ganat, Y., Papapetrou, E. P., Lipchina, I., Socci, N. D., et al. (2011). miR-371-3 expression predicts neural differentiation propensity in human pluripotent stem cells. *Cell Stem Cell, 8,* 695–706.

Kim, K., Zhao, R., Doi, A., Ng, K., Unternaehrer, J., Cahan, P., et al. (2011). Donor cell type can influence the epigenome and differentiation potential of human induced pluripotent stem cells. *Nature Biotechnology, 29,* 1117–1119.

Kiskinis, E., & Eggan, K. (2010). Progress toward the clinical application of patient-specific pluripotent stem cells. *Journal of Clinical Investigation, 120,* 51–59.

Kondo, T., Funayama, M., Tsukita, K., Hotta, A., Yasuda, A., Nori, S., et al. (2014). Focal transplantation of human iPSC-derived glial-rich neural progenitors improves lifespan of ALS mice. *Stem Cell Reports, 3,* 242–249.

Kriks, S., Shim, J. W., Piao, J., Ganat, Y. M., Wakeman, D. R., Xie, Z., et al. (2011). Dopamine neurons derived from human ES cells efficiently engraft in animal models of Parkinson's disease. *Nature, 480,* 547–551.

Ladewig, J., Mertens, J., Kesavan, J., Doerr, J., Poppe, D., Glaue, F., et al. (2012). Small molecules enable highly efficient neuronal conversion of human fibroblasts. *Nature Methods, 9,* 575–578.

Lamba, D. A., Karl, M. O., Ware, C. B., & Reh, T. A. (2006). Efficient generation of retinal progenitor cells from human embryonic stem cells. *Proceedings of the National Academy of Sciences of the United States of America, 103,* 12769–12774.

Lee, G., Ramirez, C. N., Kim, H., Zeltner, N., Liu, B., Radu, C., et al. (2012). Large-scale screening using familial dysautonomia induced pluripotent stem cells identifies compounds that rescue IKBKAP expression. *Nature Biotechnology, 30,* 1244–1248.

Lee, S. H., Lumelsky, N., Studer, L., Auerbach, J. M., & McKay, R. D. (2000). Efficient generation of midbrain and hindbrain neurons from mouse embryonic stem cells. *Nature Biotechnology, 18,* 675–679.

Lewis, D. A., Hashimoto, T., & Volk, D. W. (2005). Cortical inhibitory neurons and schizophrenia. *Nature Reviews Neuroscience, 6,* 312–324.

Li, J., Song, W., Pan, G., & Zhou, J. (2014). Advances in understanding the cell types and approaches used for generating induced pluripotent stem cells. *Journal of Hematology & Oncology, 7,* 50.

Li, W., Zhou, H., Abujarour, R., Zhu, S., Young Joo, J., Lin, T., et al. (2009). Generation of human-induced pluripotent stem cells in the absence of exogenous Sox2. *Stem Cells, 27,* 2992–3000.

Lister, R., Pelizzola, M., Kida, Y. S., Hawkins, R. D., Nery, J. R., Hon, G., et al. (2011). Hotspots of aberrant epigenomic reprogramming in human induced pluripotent stem cells. *Nature, 471,* 68–73.

Liu, X., Li, F., Stubblefield, E. A., Blanchard, B., Richards, T. L., Larson, G. A., et al. (2012). Direct reprogramming of human fibroblasts into dopaminergic neuron-like cells. *Cell Research, 22,* 321–332.

Loh, Y. H., Agarwal, S., Park, I. H., Urbach, A., Huo, H., Heffner, G. C., et al. (2009). Generation of induced pluripotent stem cells from human blood. *Blood, 113,* 5476–5479.

Lovell, M. A., Geiger, H., Van Zant, G. E., Lynn, B. C., & Markesbery, W. R. (2006). Isolation of neural precursor cells from Alzheimer's disease and aged control postmortem brain. *Neurobiology of Aging, 27,* 909–917.

Lu, J., Li, H., Hu, M., Sasaki, T., Baccei, A., Gilbert, D. M., et al. (2014). The distribution of genomic variations in human iPSCs is related to replication-timing reorganization during reprogramming. *Cell Reports, 7,* 70–78.

Lujan, E., Chanda, S., Ahlenius, H., Sudhof, T. C., & Wernig, M. (2012). Direct conversion of mouse fibroblasts to self-renewing, tripotent neural precursor cells. *Proceedings of the National Academy of Sciences of the United States of America, 109,* 2527–2532.

Ma, H., Morey, R., O'Neil, R. C., He, Y., Daughtry, B., Schultz, M. D., et al. (2014). Abnormalities in human pluripotent cells due to reprogramming mechanisms. *Nature, 511,* 177–183.

Mackay-Sima, A., & Chuahb, M. I. (2000). Neurotrophic factors in the primary olfactory pathway. *Progress in Neurobiology, 62,* 527–559.

Mahadik, S. P., Mukherjee, S., Laev, H., Reddy, R., & Schnur, D. B. (1991). Abnormal growth of skin fibroblasts from schizophrenic patients. *Psychiatry Research, 37,* 309–320.

Mahadik, S. P., Mukherjee, S., Wakade, C. G., Laev, H., Reddy, R. R., & Schnur, D. B. (1994). Decreased adhesiveness and altered cellular distribution of fibronectin in fibroblasts from schizophrenic patients. *Psychiatry Research, 53,* 87–97.

Maherali, N., Ahfeldt, T., Rigamonti, A., Utikal, J., Cowan, C., & Hochedlinger, K. (2008). A high-efficiency system for the generation and study of human induced pluripotent stem cells. *Cell Stem Cell, 3,* 340–345.

Mar, J. C., Matigian, N. A., Mackay-Sim, A., Mellick, G. D., Sue, C. M., Silburn, P. A., et al. (2011). Variance of gene expression identifies altered network constraints in neurological disease. *PLoS Genetics, 7,* e1002207.

Marchetto, M. C., Brennand, K. J., Boyer, L. F., & Gage, F. H. (2011). Induced pluripotent stem cells (iPSCs) and neurological disease modeling: progress and promises. *Human Molecular Genetics, 20,* R109–R115.

Mariani, J., Simonini, M. V., Palejev, D., Tomasini, L., Coppola, G., Szekely, A. M., et al. (2012). Modeling human cortical development in vitro using induced pluripotent stem cells. *Proceedings of the National Academy of Sciences of the United States of America, 109,* 12770–12775.

Maroof, A. M., Keros, S., Tyson, J. A., Ying, S. W., Ganat, Y. M., Merkle, F. T., et al. (2013). Directed differentiation and functional maturation of cortical interneurons from human embryonic stem cells. *Cell Stem Cell, 12,* 559–572.

Marro, S., Pang, Z. P., Yang, N., Tsai, M. C., Qu, K., Chang, H. Y., et al. (2011). Direct lineage conversion of terminally differentiated hepatocytes to functional neurons. *Cell Stem Cell, 9,* 374–382.

Matigian, N., Abrahamsen, G., Sutharsan, R., Cook, A. L., Vitale, A. M., Nouwens, A., et al. (2010). Disease-specific, neurosphere-derived cells as models for brain disorders. *Disease Models & Mechanisms, 3,* 785–798.

Mayshar, Y., Ben-David, U., Lavon, N., Biancotti, J. C., Yakir, B., Clark, A. T., et al. (2010). Identification and classification of chromosomal aberrations in human induced pluripotent stem cells. *Cell Stem Cell, 7,* 521–531.

McCurdy, R. D., Feron, F., Perry, C., Chant, D. C., McLean, D., Matigian, N., et al. (2006). Cell cycle alterations in biopsied olfactory neuroepithelium in schizophrenia and bipolar I disorder using cell culture and gene expression analyses. *Schizophrenia Research, 82,* 163–173.

Mei, L., & Xiong, W.-C. (2008). Neuregulin 1 in neural development, synaptic plasticity and schizophrenia. *Nature Reviews Neuroscience, 9*(6), 437–452.

Mekhoubad, S., Bock, C., de Boer, A. S., Kiskinis, E., Meissner, A., & Eggan, K. (2012). Erosion of dosage compensation impacts human iPSC disease modeling. *Cell Stem Cell, 10,* 595–609.

Meng, F., Chen, S., Miao, Q., Zhou, K., Lao, Q., Zhang, X., et al. (2012). Induction of fibroblasts to neurons through adenoviral gene delivery. *Cell Research, 22,* 436–440.

Miller, J. D., Ganat, Y. M., Kishinevsky, S., Bowman, R. L., Liu, B., Tu, E. Y., et al. (2013). Human iPSC-based modeling of late-onset disease via progerin-induced aging. *Cell Stem Cell, 13,* 691–705.

Murrell, W., Feron, F., Wetzig, A., Cameron, N., Splatt, K., Bellette, B., et al. (2005). Multipotent stem cells from adult olfactory mucosa. *Developmental Dynamics, 233,* 496–515.

Nakagawa, M., Koyanagi, M., Tanabe, K., Takahashi, K., Ichisaka, T., Aoi, T., et al. (2008). Generation of induced pluripotent stem cells without Myc from mouse and human fibroblasts. *Nature Biotechnology, 26,* 101–106.

Nazor, K. L., Altun, G., Lynch, C., Tran, H., Harness, J. V., Slavin, I., et al. (2012). Recurrent variations in DNA methylation in human pluripotent stem cells and their differentiated derivatives. *Cell Stem Cell, 10,* 620–634.

Nefzger, C. M., Su, C. T., Fabb, S. A., Hartley, B. J., Beh, S. J., Zeng, W. R., et al. (2012). Lmx1a allows context-specific isolation of progenitors of GABAergic or dopaminergic neurons during neural differentiation of embryonic stem cells. *Stem Cells, 30,* 1349–1361.

Nicholas, C. R., Chen, J., Tang, Y., Southwell, D. G., Chalmers, N., Vogt, D., et al. (2013). Functional maturation of hPSC-derived forebrain interneurons requires an extended timeline and mimics human neural development. *Cell Stem Cell, 12,* 573–586.

Nunes, M. C., Roy, N. S., Keyoung, H. M., Goodman, R. R., McKhann, G., 2nd, Jiang, L., et al. (2003). Identification and isolation of multipotential neural progenitor cells from the subcortical white matter of the adult human brain. *Nature Medicine, 9,* 439–447.

Okita, K., Ichisaka, T., & Yamanaka, S. (2007). Generation of germlinecompetent induced pluripotent stem cells. *Nature, 448,* 313–317.

Okita, K., Matsumura, Y., Sato, Y., Okada, A., Morizane, A., Okamoto, S., et al. (2011). A more efficient method to generate integration-free human iPS cells. *Nature Methods, 8,* 409–412.

Oliver-De La Cruz, J., Carrion-Navarro, J., Garcia-Romero, N., Gutierrez-Martin, A., Lazaro-Ibanez, E., Escobedo-Lucea, C., et al. (2014). SOX2+ cell population from normal human brain white matter is able to generate mature oligodendrocytes. *PLoS One, 9,* e99253.

Pagliuca, F. W., Millman, J. R., Gurtler, M., Segel, M., Van Dervort, A., Ryu, J. H., et al. (2014). Generation of functional human pancreatic beta cells in vitro. *Cell, 159,* 428–439.

Palmer, T. D., Schwartz, P. H., Taupin, P., Kaspar, B., Stein, S. A., & Gage, F. H. (2001). Cell culture. Progenitor cells from human brain after death. *Nature, 411,* 42–43.

Pang, Z. P., Yang, N., Vierbuchen, T., Ostermeier, A., Fuentes, D. R., Yang, T. Q., et al. (2011). Induction of human neuronal cells by defined transcription factors. *Nature, 476,* 220–223.

Paull, D., Sevilla-Hernandez, A., Zhou, M., Hahn, A., Kim, H., Napolitano, C., et al. (2014). A fully automated system for large-scale induced pluripotent stem cell production and differentiation. *ISSCR Poster Abstracts 12th Annual,* 83.

Paulsen Bda, S., de Moraes Maciel, R., Galina, A., Souza da Silveira, M., dos Santos Souza, C., Drummond, H., et al. (2012). Altered oxygen metabolism associated to neurogenesis of induced pluripotent stem cells derived from a schizophrenic patient. *Cell Transplantation, 21,* 1547–1559.

Pavon, L. F., Marti, L. C., Sibov, T. T., Malheiros, S. M., Brandt, R. A., Cavalheiro, S., et al. (2014). In vitro analysis of neurospheres derived from glioblastoma primary culture: a novel methodology paradigm. *Frontiers in Neurology, 4,* 214.

Perrier, A. L., Tabar, V., Barberi, T., Rubio, M. E., Bruses, J., Topf, N., et al. (2004). Derivation of midbrain dopamine neurons from human embryonic stem cells. *Proceedings of the National Academy of Sciences of the United States of America, 101,* 12543–12548.

Pfisterer, U., Kirkeby, A., Torper, O., Wood, J., Nelander, J., Dufour, A., et al. (2011). Direct conversion of human fibroblasts to dopaminergic neurons. *Proceedings of the National Academy of Sciences of the United States of America, 108,* 10343–10348.

Ring, K. L., Tong, L. M., Balestra, M. E., Javier, R., Andrews-Zwilling, Y., Li, G., et al. (2012). Direct reprogramming of mouse and human fibroblasts into multipotent neural stem cells with a single factor. *Cell Stem Cell, 11,* 100–109.

Robicsek, O., Karry, R., Petit, I., Salman-Kesner, N., Muller, F. J., Klein, E., et al. (2013). Abnormal neuronal differentiation and mitochondrial dysfunction in hair follicle-derived induced pluripotent stem cells of schizophrenia patients. *Molecular Psychiatry, 18,* 1067–1076.

Ruiz, S., Diep, D., Gore, A., Panopoulos, A. D., Montserrat, N., Plongthongkum, N., et al. (2012). Identification of a specific reprogramming-associated epigenetic signature in human induced pluripotent stem cells. *Proceedings of the National Academy of Sciences of the United States of America, 109,* 16196–16201.

Ruiz, S., Gore, A., Li, Z., Panopoulos, A. D., Montserrat, N., Fung, H. L., et al. (2013). Analysis of protein-coding mutations in hiPSCs and their possible role during somatic cell reprogramming. *Nature Communications, 4,* 1382.

Sandoe, J., & Eggan, K. (2013). Opportunities and challenges of pluripotent stem cell neurodegenerative disease models. *Nature Neuroscience, 16,* 780–789.

Schizophrenia Working Group of the Psychiatric Genomics Consortium. (2014). Biological insights from 108 schizophrenia-associated genetic loci. *Nature, 511,* 421–427.

Schwartz, T. L., Sachdeva, S., & Stahl, S. M. (2012). Glutamate neurocircuitry: theoretical underpinnings in schizophrenia. *Frontiers in Pharmacology, 3,* 195.

Schwarz, E., Guest, P. C., Rahmoune, H., Harris, L. W., Wang, L., Leweke, F. M., et al. (2012). Identification of a biological signature for schizophrenia in serum. *Molecular Psychiatry, 17,* 494–502.

Schwarz, E., Izmailov, R., Spain, M., Barnes, A., Mapes, J. P., Guest, P. C., et al. (2010). Validation of a blood-based laboratory test to aid in the confirmation of a diagnosis of schizophrenia. *Biomarker Insights, 5,* 39–47.

Shi, Y., Kirwan, P., Smith, J., Robinson, H. P., & Livesey, F. J. (2012). Human cerebral cortex development from pluripotent stem cells to functional excitatory synapses. *Nature Neuroscience 15,* 477–486, S471.

Soldner, F., Hockemeyer, D., Beard, C., Gao, Q., Bell, G. W., Cook, E. G., et al. (2009). Parkinson's disease patient-derived induced pluripotent stem cells free of viral reprogramming factors. *Cell, 136,* 964–977.

Sommer, C. A., Sommer, A. G., Longmire, T. A., Christodoulou, C., Thomas, D. D., Gostissa, M., et al. (2009). Excision of reprogramming transgenes improves the differentiation potential of iPS cells generated with a single excisable vector. *Stem Cells, 28,* 64–74.

Son, E. Y., Ichida, J. K., Wainger, B. J., Toma, J. S., Rafuse, V. F., Woolf, C. J., et al. (2011). Conversion of mouse and human fibroblasts into functional spinal motor neurons. *Cell Stem Cell, 9,* 205–218.

Song, H., Chung, S. K., & Xu, Y. (2010). Modeling disease in human ESCs using an efficient BAC-based homologous recombination system. *Cell Stem Cell, 6,* 80–89.

Takahashi, K., Tanabe, K., Ohnuki, M., Narita, M., Ichisaka, T., Tomoda, K., et al. (2007). Induction of pluripotent stem cells from adult human fibroblasts by defined factors. *Cell, 131,* 861–872.

Takahashi, K., & Yamanaka, S. (2006). Induction of pluripotent stem cells from mouse embryonic and adult fibroblast cultures by defined factors. *Cell, 126,* 663–676.

Thier, M., Worsdorfer, P., Lakes, Y. B., Gorris, R., Herms, S., Opitz, T., et al. (2012). Direct conversion of fibroblasts into stably expandable neural stem cells. *Cell Stem Cell, 10,* 473–479.

Tropepe, V., Hitoshi, S., Sirard, C., Mak, T. W., Rossant, J., & van der Kooy, D. (2001). Direct neural fate specification from embryonic stem cells: a primitive mammalian neural stem cell stage acquired through a default mechanism. *Neuron, 30,* 65–78.

Vierbuchen, T., Ostermeier, A., Pang, Z. P., Kokubu, Y., Sudhof, T. C., & Wernig, M. (2010). Direct conversion of fibroblasts to functional neurons by defined factors. *Nature, 463,* 1035–1041.

Villegas, J., & McPhaul, M. (2005). Establishment and culture of human skin fibroblasts. In F. M. Ausubel, et al. (Ed.), *Current protocols in molecular biology.* Chapter 28, Unit 28.23.

Wang, L., Lockstone, H. E., Guest, P. C., Levin, Y., Palotas, A., Pietsch, S., et al. (2010). Expression profiling of fibroblasts identifies cell cycle abnormalities in schizophrenia. *Journal of Proteome Research, 9,* 521–527.

Warren, L., Manos, P. D., Ahfeldt, T., Loh, Y. H., Li, H., Lau, F., et al. (2010). Highly efficient reprogramming to pluripotency and directed differentiation of human cells with synthetic modified mRNA. *Cell Stem Cell, 7,* 618–630.

Watanabe, K., Ueno, M., Kamiya, D., Nishiyama, A., Matsumura, M., Wataya, T., et al. (2007). A ROCK inhibitor permits survival of dissociated human embryonic stem cells. *Nature Biotechnology, 25,* 681–686.

Wen, Z., Nguyen, H. N., Guo, Z., Lalli, M. A., Wang, X., Su, Y., et al. (2014). Synaptic dysregulation in a human iPS cell model of mental disorders. *Nature, 515*(7527), 414–418.

Wilmut, I., Schnieke, A. E., McWhir, J., Kind, A. J., & Campbell, K. H. (1997). Viable offspring derived from fetal and adult mammalian cells. *Nature, 385,* 810–813.

Woltjen, K., Michael, I. P., Mohseni, P., Desai, R., Mileikovsky, M., Hamalainen, R., et al. (2009). piggyBac transposition reprograms fibroblasts to induced pluripotent stem cells. *Nature, 458,* 766–770.

Xue, Y., Ouyang, K., Huang, J., Zhou, Y., Ouyang, H., Li, H., et al. (2013). Direct conversion of fibroblasts to neurons by reprogramming PTB-regulated microRNA circuits. *Cell, 152,* 82–96.

Ying, Q. L., Nichols, J., Chambers, I., & Smith, A. (2003). BMP induction of Id proteins suppresses differentiation and sustains embryonic stem cell self-renewal in collaboration with STAT3. *Cell, 115,* 281–292.

Ying, Q. L., Stavridis, M., Griffiths, D., Li, M., & Smith, A. (2003). Conversion of embryonic stem cells into neuroectodermal precursors in adherent monoculture. *Nature Biotechnology, 21,* 183–186.

Yoo, A. S., Sun, A. X., Li, L., Shcheglovitov, A., Portmann, T., Li, Y., et al. (2011). MicroRNA-mediated conversion of human fibroblasts to neurons. *Nature, 476,* 228–231.

Yoon, K.-J., Nguyen, H. N., Ursini, G., Zhang, F., Kim, N.-S., Wen, Z., et al. (2014). Modeling a genetic risk for schizophrenia in iPSCs and mice reveals neural stem cell deficits associated with adherens junctions and polarity. *Cell Stem Cell, 15,* 79–91.

II. NEUROBIOLOGY OF PSYCHOTIC DISORDERS

Yu, D. X., Di Giorgio, F. P., Yao, J., Marchetto, M. C., Brennand, K., Wright, R., et al. (2014). Modeling hippocampal neurogenesis using human pluripotent stem cells. *Stem Cell Reports, 2*, 295–310.

Yu, J., Chau, K. F., Vodyanik, M. A., Jiang, J., & Jiang, Y. (2011). Efficient feeder-free episomal reprogramming with small molecules. *PLoS One, 6*, e17557.

Yu, J., Vodyanik, M. A., Smuga-Otto, K., Antosiewicz-Bourget, J., Frane, J. L., Tian, S., et al. (2007). Induced pluripotent stem cell lines derived from human somatic cells. *Science, 318*, 1917–1920.

Zhang, S. C., Wernig, M., Duncan, I. D., Brustle, O., & Thomson, J. A. (2001). In vitro differentiation of transplantable neural precursors from human embryonic stem cells. *Nature Biotechnology, 19*, 1129–1133.

Zhang, Y., Pak, C., Han, Y., Ahlenius, H., Zhang, Z., Chanda, S., et al. (2013). Rapid single-step induction of functional neurons from human pluripotent stem cells. *Neuron, 78*, 785–798.

Zhong, X., Gutierrez, C., Xue, T., Hampton, C., Vergara, M. N., Cao, L. H., et al. (2014). Generation of three-dimensional retinal tissue with functional photoreceptors from human iPSCs. *Nature Communications, 5*, 4047.

Zhou, T., Benda, C., Duzinger, S., Huang, Y., Li, X., Li, Y., et al. (2011). Generation of induced pluripotent stem cells from urine. *Journal of the American Society of Nephrology, 22*, 1221–1228.

24

Alternative Human Cell Models for Neuropsychiatric Research: Induced Neuronal Cells, Olfactory Epithelium, and Related Resources

Brian Lo, Daniel Chang, Shin-ichi Kano

Department of Psychiatry and Behavioral Sciences, The Johns Hopkins University School of Medicine, Baltimore, MD, USA

INTRODUCTION

The ultimate goal of research on neuropsychiatric disorders is to understand the clinical and pathological features of disorders and to develop novel therapeutic strategies. Because the brain is the primary organ affected in these disorders, investigating human brains is essential to achieve this goal. Indeed, studies on patient postmortem brain samples have revealed key pathological changes in schizophrenia, such as synaptic deficits in cortical pyramidal neurons, decreased levels of parvalbumin expression in cortical interneurons, and altered expression of myelin-related genes (Benes & Berretta, 2001; Davis et al., 2003; Jarskog, Miyamoto, & Lieberman, 2007; Lewis, Glantz, Pierri, & Sweet, 2003; Tkachev et al., 2003). Recent advances in genetics studies have also provided valuable information about common and rare genetic variations potentially involved in the pathology of schizophrenia (Fromer et al., 2014; International Schizophrenia et al., 2009; Purcell et al., 2014; Ripke et al., 2013; Schizophrenia Working Group of the Psychiatric Genomics, 2014; Shi et al., 2009; Stefansson et al., 2014, 2009). Furthermore, brain imaging studies, such as magnetic resonance imaging and positron emission tomography, have revealed both structural and functional alterations in the brains of patients with schizophrenia and related disorders (Fitzsimmons, Kubicki, & Shenton, 2013; Poels et al., 2014; Vita, De Peri,

Deste, & Sacchetti, 2012; Wong, Grunder, & Brasic, 2007). Nonetheless, none of these approaches possesses the capacity to address the molecular and functional alterations of live patient brain cells at the cell-level resolution.

Although studies on postmortem brains have provided many key findings in schizophrenia and related disorders, they have several major limitations (Lewis, 2002; McCullumsmith & Meador-Woodruff, 2011). First, cells in postmortem brains are not alive and thus functional alterations of brain cells cannot be addressed. Second, long-term use of medication may have modified the primary pathological changes because patients usually suffer from schizophrenia for many years before they die. Third, smoking habits or use of illicit drugs may have caused additional changes in the brain. Finally, postmortem changes by themselves may have masked or altered pathological changes that exist in live brains. To complement these limitations, rodent models have been extensively used to examine the roles of genes and neural circuits responsible for schizophrenia and related disorders (Arguello & Gogos, 2006; Insel, 2007). It needs to be acknowledged, however, that there is a huge gap between human and rodent brains both at the structural and functional levels (Geschwind & Rakic, 2013; Insel & Landis, 2013; Lui, Hansen, & Kriegstein, 2011). Research on primates has shown some promise as an alternative methodology that could be used in the future (Sasaki et al., 2009; Simen, DiLeone, & Arnsten, 2009), but it may take years for primate studies on mental illness to reach its premier stage (Garbarini, 2010). Thus, many experts in the field turn to *in vitro* human cell culture as a method to investigate the phenotypes of live human brain cells relevant for neuropsychiatric disorders.

The idea of using human cell culture as a model to understand brain disorders is not at all new. It is challenging, however, to obtain a brain biopsy from living individuals except in certain diseases in which surgical treatments are feasible (e.g., epilepsy). Thus, many researchers sought for alternative resources from which neuronal cells can be generated. These efforts have recently culminated in several culture protocols to generate patient-derived neuronal cells from tissues such as olfactory epithelium (OE) (Hahn, Han, et al., 2005; Kano et al., 2013; Morrison & Costanzo, 1990; Murrell et al., 2005; Roisen et al., 2001).

Meanwhile, a breakthrough in the field of stem cells and regenerative medicine has enabled researchers to generate pluripotent stem cells, called induced pluripotent stem (iPS) cells, from peripheral tissues such as skin fibroblasts (Takahashi et al., 2007; Takahashi & Yamanaka, 2006; Yu et al., 2007). As described in the previous chapter, iPS cells are generated from fibroblasts or other peripheral cells by forced expression of several sets of transcription factors (e.g., Oct3/4, Sox2, Klf4, c-Myc). The approach is reminiscent of earlier studies on cell fate conversion using transcription factors, such as changing fibroblasts into myoblasts by forced expression of the transcription factor MyoD (Davis, Weintraub, & Lassar, 1987; Lassar, Paterson, & Weintraub, 1986; Tapscott et al., 1988). Inspired by the success of iPS cell technology, some stem cell researchers and disease-oriented neurobiologists subsequently established methods to generate neuronal cells using cell fate conversion (or direct reprogramming) methods (Caiazzo et al., 2011; Pang et al., 2011; Pfisterer et al., 2011; Vierbuchen et al., 2010; Yoo et al., 2011; Kano et al., 2015).

These efforts are reaching a stage where the application to disease research is feasible. Together with iPS cell technology, cell models based on cell fate conversion (or direct reprogramming) and reprogramming-free methods (e.g., neuronal cells from OE) will serve as precious tools for research on neuropsychiatric disorders to gain insight directly from human cases. In the following sections, we will review the representative methodologies, applications to disease research, and limitations of these human cell models.

CELL MODELS BASED ON CELL FATE CONVERSION: INDUCED NEURONAL CELLS AND THEIR RELATIVES

Cell fate conversion is a phenomenon whereby certain cells such as fibroblasts are converted into another cell type. This same phenomenon is also called direct reprogramming or transdifferentiation. Cell fate conversion can be experimentally induced by forced expression of one or several transcription factors in target cells. Thus, technologies to induce cell fate conversion can serve as important tools to generate relevant brain cells from more accessible cells both *in vitro* and *in vivo*.

One of the pioneering efforts in which mammalian cells were converted from one cell type to another through the modulation of expression levels of certain transcription factors was reported in the late 1980s when researchers successfully converted fibroblasts into myoblasts by forced expression of the transcription factor MyoD (Davis et al., 1987; Lassar et al., 1986; Tapscott et al., 1988). Since then, cell conversion using transcription factors has been used as a technique to understand cell differentiation and development (Graf, 2011). The use of cell fate conversion, however, has not been highlighted as a methodology to generate brain-relevant cells from patients with brain disorders until recently.

Cell fate conversion with transcription factors has been revived by a breakthrough in the successful generation of iPS cells (Takahashi et al., 2007; Takahashi & Yamanaka, 2006; Yu et al., 2007). In this novel method, the idea of cell fate conversion using transcription factors was adopted to reprogram fibroblasts into pluripotent stem cells through the overexpression of several transcription factors such as a combination of Oct3/4, Sox2, Klf4, and c-Myc (Takahashi et al., 2007). A series of subsequent studies that demonstrated the generation of functional neuronal cells from iPS cells have prompted many investigators to work on iPS cells to obtain human relevant cells for research on brain disorders such as neuropsychiatric disorders and neurodegenerative diseases (Dolmetsch & Geschwind, 2011; Marchetto, Brennand, Boyer, & Gage, 2011). Recently, the overexpression of three transcription factors, Ascl1, Brn2, and Myt1 was shown to successfully convert mouse fibroblasts into functional neurons, induced neuronal (iN) cells, in 2010 (Vierbuchen et al., 2010). This study opened a new window for cell fate conversion method to be used for disease-oriented studies. In this section, we review advances in cell fate conversion research in neuroscience, including iN cells, induced neuronal stem (iNS) cells, and other central nervous system (CNS)-relevant induced cells, and discuss their utilities and limitations for neuropsychiatric research.

Methods

Induced Neuronal Cells

In 2010, it was reported that the expression of three transcription factors, Ascl1, Brn2, and Myt1, could convert mouse embryonic fibroblasts into postmitotic functional neurons, iN cells, without generating pluripotent

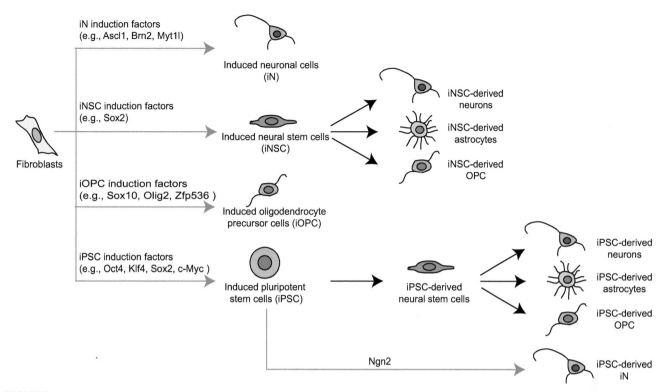

FIGURE 1 **Methods to generate human neuronal/glial cells using cell fate conversion techniques.** Red arrows indicate cell fate conversion steps; black arrows indicate in vitro differentiation steps. Shown above the arrows are representative sets of transcription factors that enable cell fate conversion. iN, induced neuronal; iNS cells, induced neural stem cells; iOPC, induced oligodendrocyte precursor cells.

stem cells and neural stem cells (Figure 1) (Vierbuchen et al., 2010). It was also shown later that the expression of these transcription factors, together with other factors, converted human fibroblasts into functional iN cells, most of which showed features of glutamatergic neurons (Pang et al., 2011). At least four different types of neuronal cells have been generated by iN cell techniques: glutamatergic neurons, gamma-aminobutyric acid (GABA) ergic interneurons, dopaminergic neurons, and spinal motor neurons (Table 1).

The overexpression of the transcription factors Ascl1, Brn2, and Myt1l was shown to successfully convert mouse fibroblasts or hepatocytes into functional neurons, mostly glutamatergic excitatory neurons (Marro et al., 2011; Vierbuchen et al., 2010). These mouse iN cells could be produced in a few weeks and exhibited synaptic activity as well as action potential spikes. Subsequently, the overexpression of a combination of either Ascl1, Pouf3f2, and Myt1l or Ascl1, Pou3f2, Myt1l, and NeuroD1 was shown to successfully convert human fibroblasts into iN cells that express markers for glutamatergic neurons and cortical identities, and elicit action potential spikes and synaptic activity (Pang et al., 2011; Pfisterer et al., 2011). Other approaches to generate iN cells used microRNAs that are known to be involved in neuronal development (Ambasudhan et al., 2011; Yoo et al., 2011). The expression of miR-9/9* and miR-124, together with NeuroD2, Ascl1, and Myt1l, was shown

to convert human fibroblasts into induced neurons with glutamatergic phenotypes (Yoo et al., 2011). Similarly, miR-124, together with Pou3f2 and Myt1l, successfully converted human fibroblast into glutamatergic iN cells (Ambasudhan et al., 2011).

Although there are no specific strategies currently available to directly generate GABAergic interneurons, most of the previously mentioned studies reported the presence of GABAergic interneurons in their converted cell lineages. For example, human iN cells generated by the overexpression of miR-9/9*, miR-124, NeuroD2, Ascl1, and Myt1l included neuronal cells expressing GABA and exhibited evoked inhibitory postsynaptic currents (Yoo et al., 2011). Although relatively small in population, other human iN cells generated by the overexpression of either transcription factors or microRNA also contained GABA expressing neurons (Ambasudhan et al., 2011; Pang et al., 2011; Pfisterer et al., 2011).

For creating induced dopaminergic neurons, at least two methodologies have been used. The first method involved the expression of Ascl1, Brn2, and Myt1l along with two genes, Lmx1a and FoxA2, or a set of 10 transcription factors involved in midbrain patterning and dopaminergic lineage differentiation, in human fibroblasts (Pfisterer et al., 2011). The resulting iN cells expressed tyrosine hydroxylase and had electrophysiological properties reminiscent of midbrain dopaminergic neurons (Pfisterer et al., 2011). The second method

TABLE 1   Representative Reports on iN Cells and Other Induced CNS Cells

Type	Species	Exogenous Factors	Original Cells	Resulting Cells	Disease Application	References
iN cells	Mouse	Ascl1, Pou3f2, Myt1l	Fibroblasts	Glutamatergic GABAergic neurons	None	Vierbuchen et al. (2010)
	Mouse	Ascl1, Pou3f2, Myt1l	Hepatocytes	Glutamatergic neurons	None	Marro et al. (2011)
	Human	Ascl1, Pouf3f2, Myt1l, NeuroD1	ES cells Fibroblasts	Glutamatergic GABAergic neurons	None	Pang et al. (2011)
	Mouse Human	miR-9/9*, miR-124, NeuroD2, Ascl1, Myt1l	Fibroblasts	Glutamatergic GABAergic neurons	None	Yoo et al. (2011)
	Human	miR-124, Pou3f2, Myt1l	Fibroblasts	Glutamatergic GABAergic neurons	None	Ambasudhan et al. (2011)
	Human	Ascl1, Pou3f2, Myt1ll	Fibroblasts	Glutamatergic neurons	Tay–Sachs disease, Dravet syndrome	Kano et al. (2015)
	Human	Ascl1, Pou3F2, Myt1l, Lmx1a, FoxA2	Fibroblasts	Glutamatergic GABAergic Dopaminergic neurons	None	Pfisterer et al. (2011)
	Mouse Human	Ascl1, Nurr1, Lmx1a	Fibroblasts	Dopaminergic neurons	Parkinson's disease (no characterization) L-ferritin deficiency	Caiazzo et al. (2011) and Cozzi et al. (2013)
	Mouse Human	Ascl1, Pou3f2, Myt1l, Lhx3, Hb9, Isl1, Ngn2	Fibroblasts	Spinal motor neurons	None	Son et al. (2011)
iNSCs	Mouse	Oct4, Sox2, Klf4, c-Myc	Fibroblasts	NSCs neurons, astrocytes	None	Kim, Efe, et al. (2011)
	Mouse	Sox2, FoxG1, Pou3f2	Fibroblasts	NSCs neurons, astrocytes oligodendrocytes	None	Lujan et al. (2012)
	Mouse	Pou3f4, Sox2, Klf4, c-Myc, E47/Tcf3	Fibroblasts	NSCs neurons, astrocytes oligodendrocytes	None	Han et al. (2012)
	Mouse	Sox2, Klf4, c-Myc, Oct4	Fibroblasts	NSCs neurons, astrocytes oligodendrocytes	None	Thier et al. (2012)
	Mouse Human	Sox2	Fibroblasts	NSCs neurons, astrocytes oligodendrocytes	None	Ring et al. (2012)
	Human	Sox2, Klf4, Oct3/4, c-Myc	Fibroblasts	NSC, astrocytes	Amyotrophic lateral sclerosis	Meyer et al. (2014)
iOPCs	Mouse	Sox10, Olig2, Nkx6.2	Fibroblasts	OPC, oligodendrocytes	Transplantation	Najm et al. (2013)
	Mouse Rat	Sox10, Olig2, Zfp536	Fibroblasts	OPC, oligodendrocytes	None	Yang et al. (2013)
iPSC-iN cells	Human	Ngn2	Pluripotent stem cells	Glutamatergic neurons	None	Zhang et al. (2013)

CNS, central nervous system; ES, embryonic stem; GABA, gamma-aminobutyric acid; iN, induced neuronal; iNSCs, induced neuronal stem cells; iPSC, induced pluripotent stem cell; NSCs, neuronal stem cells; OPC, oligodendrocyte precursor cell.

involved using a different set of three transcription factors: Ascl1, Nurr1, and Lmx1a (Caiazzo et al., 2011). This method produced iN cells that released dopamine and had electrophysiological properties similar to normal mouse dopaminergic neurons.

In addition to these brain neurons, spinal motor neurons were generated through a slightly more complicated conversion method—the expression of seven transcription factors: Ascl1, Brn2, Myt1l, Lhx3, Hb9, Isl1, and Ngn2 (Son et al., 2011). These motor neurons were characterized through electrophysiology tests and gene expression signatures, and were functionally similar to those motor neurons derived from embryos (Son et al., 2011).

Despite these successful examples of cell fate conversion, the underlying mechanisms have not been fully understood. Extensive gene expression and epigenetic profiling analysis during the course of direct conversion of mouse embryonic fibroblasts into iN cells has been performed using RNA sequencing (RNA-seq) and chromatin immunoprecipitation sequencing (ChIP-seq) techniques (Wapinski et al., 2013). They revealed a hierarchical mechanism in which Ascl1 acts as a pioneer transcription factor to first access the chromatin through its cognate binding sites on the genome in fibroblasts and then recruits another factor Pou3f2 to the sites occupied by Ascl1. They also found a unique "trivalent" chromatin signature comprising three different modifications for histone3 tails (H3K4me1, H3K27ac, and H3K9me3), which predicts permissiveness for Ascl1 occupancy and iN cell reprogramming among various nonneuronal cell types. Furthermore, the study identified critical downstream mediators that exert iN cell conversion downstream of Ascl1, Brn2, and Myt1l. Although this research has provided a systematic view on iN cell conversion at the molecular level for the first time, the core mechanisms that directly exert the conversion from nonneuronal to neuronal cells by changing the entire epigenetic status of the cells in different lineages, such as chromatin conformational changes and addition/removal of DNA methylation, are still not clear. It is also not fully understood how these epigenetic and gene expression changes smoothly alter the expression patterns of various proteins in an entire cell in such a short period. It is currently unknown whether there are any deleterious side effects on a cell that has undergone a conversion process compared to cells that have gone through physiological differentiation. Further research will be necessary to address these remaining issues and enable us to fully control specific cell fate conversions between two distinct cells.

Because the conversion of iN cells does not require an intermediate step, they have been successfully used in in vivo experiments as well (De la Rossa et al., 2013; Rouaux & Arlotta, 2010, 2013; Torper et al., 2013). For example, one group used doxycycline-inducible lentiviruses encoding Ascl1, Pou3f2, and Myt1l (Torper et al., 2013). Mouse fibroblasts and astrocytes were infected with these lentiviruses and transplanted into the striatum of mice. Then, the presence of doxycycline in the drinking water caused the activation of the encoded factors and resulted in cellular conversion into iN cells in living mice. This in vivo cell fate conversion may be therapeutically important for brain injuries or disorders such as Parkinson's disease, in which transplantation is considered to be a viable option to attenuate symptoms (Torper et al., 2013). The activation of the transcription factor Fezf2 in vivo was also shown to reprogram postmitotic neurons in layer II/III into layer V/VI corticofugal projection neurons (Rouaux & Arlotta, 2013). It was also discovered that the function, morphology, and fate of layer IV neurons could be changed during the first week after mitosis; for example, the expression of Fezf2 could convert progenitors that were destined to become spiny neurons into corticofugal neurons (De la Rossa et al., 2013; Rouaux & Arlotta, 2010). Taken together, these results provide evidence that not only fibroblasts, but also neurons and astrocytes in vivo, can be phenotypically changed by cell conversion (or direct reprogramming).

iNS cells

Beyond conversion into neurons, fibroblasts have also been able to be reprogrammed into iNS cells (Figure 1). iNS cells can self-renew and differentiate into more mature CNS cells such as neurons, astrocytes, or oligodendrocytes. Compared with iPS cells that require both reprogramming and differentiation, iNS cells bypass the pluripotent state and thus offer a faster and simpler way to make relevant CNS cells (Kim, Efe, et al., 2011).

Until now, mouse and human fibroblasts have successfully been converted into iNS cells through the expression of a variety of transcription factors and culture in specific media with various supplements (Table 1). Initially, overexpression of Oct4, Sox2, Klf4, and c-Myc in mouse fibroblasts in a medium with specific external signaling conditions was shown to convert mouse fibroblasts into iNS cells, and eventually into neurons and astrocytes (Kim, Efe, et al., 2011). Subsequently, it was reported that the overexpression of Sox2, FoxG1, and Pou3f2 in mouse fibroblasts induced tripotent iNS cells that can differentiate into neurons, astrocytes, and oligodendrocytes (Lujan, Chanda, Ahlenius, Sudhof, & Wernig, 2012). Although seemingly successful, these iNS cells had limitations such as poor expansion capacity or instability of cell fate. To overcome these limitations, additional efforts were made to generate iNS cells that are more similar to neural stem cells found in mice. First, the expression of Pou3f4, Sox2, Klf4, c-Myc, and E47/Tcf3 were able to convert mouse fibroblasts into iNS cells with a large capacity to differentiate into neurons, astrocytes, and oligodendrocytes (Han et al., 2012). Second, the expression of Sox2, Klf4, c-Myc, and the transient expression of Oct4 during the initial phase of reprogramming were also able to convert mouse fibroblasts into iNS cells with further differentiation capacity into neurons, astrocytes, and oligodendrocytes (Thier et al., 2012). Finally, the expression of only one transcription factor, Sox2, was discovered to be sufficient to elicit the formation of iNS cells from both mouse and human fibroblasts (Ring et al., 2012). These iNS cells were differentiated into neurons, astrocytes, and oligodendrocytes *in vitro* and also shown to differentiate into functioning neurons *in vivo* without generating tumors.

Induced Oligodendrocyte Precursor Cells

Oligodendrocyte precursor cells (OPCs) were also reported to be generated directly from fibroblasts by cell fate conversion in mice (Najm et al., 2013; Yang et al., 2013). Mouse embryonic and lung fibroblasts can be reprogrammed into OPCs through the expression of a set of three transcription factors (Sox10, Olig2, and Nkx6.2) (Najm et al., 2013). Successful generation of OPCs from mouse and rat fibroblasts through the overexpression of Sox10, Olig2, and Zpf536 was also reported (Yang et al., 2013). When such induced oligodendrocyte progenitor cells (iOPCs) were transplanted into the cortex of dysmyelinated shiverer mice, they helped ensheath axons with myelin to improve the conduction of impulses (Najm et al., 2013; Yang et al., 2013). Thus, iOPCs can be very useful in diseases relating to myelin deficits. For example, the implementation and use of iOPCs may serve as possible therapeutic options to attenuate or recover myelin deficits underlying the disorders. iOPCs can also be used to investigate the mechanisms underlying altered integrity in the white matter in patients with schizophrenia. Because oligodendrocytes form myelin sheaths around axons in the white matter, the altered function of oligodendrocytes can directly impact the axonal networks, which form the basis for various brain activities. Thus, biological understanding of such alterations in patient-derived iOPCs may provide further insight into the mechanisms underlying schizophrenia and can lead to the development of new therapeutic strategies by which myelin deficits and white matter changes in the disease can be attenuated or recovered. Collectively, iOPCs may allow us to investigate the cell-intrinsic pathology related to oligodendrocytes in neuropsychiatric disorders.

Disease Application

Induced cells obtained by cell fate conversion can be used for the characterization of the pathological phenotypes of live neurons and glia in many brain disorders as well as for therapeutic autologous transplantation.

Although technical advances in recent years are remarkable, reports on the application of induced cells to disease characterization or therapeutic transplantation are still limited.

A recent report successfully showed that the use of iN cells could help to recapitulate key pathological phenotypes and discover novel pathological phenotypes in several brain disorders (Kano et al., 2015). In this report, iN cells from patients with Tay–Sachs disease, a lysosomal storage disease mainly affecting the CNS, recapitulated a hallmark phenotype of the disease, accumulation of GM2 gangliosidosis. The study further showed that the GM2 accumulation phenotype was rescued pharmacologically by an inhibitor of GlyCer synthesis, suggesting the feasibility of using iN cells for the screening of therapeutic compounds. iN cells were also used to characterize electrophysiological properties of Dravet syndrome, leading to an unexpected finding that glutamatergic neuronal cells from patients have altered patterns of action potentials, which may add to the known phenotype of GABAergic interneurons in the disease. iN cells have also aided in characterizing the pathology and consequences of human L-ferritin deficiency, which is a disease characterized by seizures and restless leg syndrome (Cozzi et al., 2013). Patient fibroblasts were reprogrammed into dopaminergic neurons through the overexpression of Ascl1, Nurr1, and Lmx1. These iron-deficient cells exhibited both higher reactive oxygen species and oxidized protein levels, but similar mitochondrial membrane resting potential compared with control neurons. This was one of the first studies to describe the phenotype and the biological consequences of L-ferritin deficiency in live human neuronal cells.

The use of iNS cells can further aid in the characterization of the pathology of neuropsychiatric disorders. By allowing for a variety of cell lines to be used and created, each brain cell type can be analyzed through their developmental stages. A recent study converted fibroblasts from patients with amyotrophic lateral sclerosis into iNS cells, which were then further differentiated into astrocytes (Meyer et al., 2014). These amyotrophic lateral sclerosis patients' iNS cell–derived astrocytes were shown to be toxic to cocultured motor neurons, illustrating an intrinsic defect of astrocytes obtained from amyotrophic lateral sclerosis patients (Meyer et al., 2014). Unfortunately, beyond this study, there is still very limited research in the application of iNS cells in neuropsychiatric disorders.

The transplantation of induced cells into animals with certain diseases has been successful as a potential therapeutic strategy. Parkinson's disease, for example, is a disorder that causes dopaminergic neurons to degenerate, resulting in certain motor deficits. Dopaminergic iN cells have been successfully transplanted into a mouse model of Parkinson's disease, and have resulted in functional recovery

(Kim, Su, et al., 2011). Although cell transplantation is currently not an option in therapeutic strategies against neuropsychiatric disorders such as schizophrenia, the concept of transplanting normal neurons or glia into the brain, or even *in vivo* cell fate conversion of defective cells into recovered cells may be used as potential solutions to alleviate problems caused by the altered functions of local neural circuits that underlie neuropsychiatric disorders.

Limitations

Although iN cells and iNS cells have shown some promise in their use for the characterization of brain disorders, there are several limitations and challenges that need to be overcome.

First, iN cell methodologies resulted in a low reprogramming efficiency. One of the attempts to solve this problem has been through the use of small molecules, instead of transcription factors, in reprogramming cells. By using a set of small molecules that inhibit both glycogen synthase kinase-3B and smad signaling, conversion efficiency and purity can be drastically improved (Ladewig et al., 2012). Another solution may involve changing the oxygen concentration during cell fate conversion. It was shown that iN cell conversion was more efficient and gave rise to more functional neurons under hypoxic conditions (Davila, Chanda, Ang, Sudhof, & Wernig, 2013). Very recently, it has been shown that pluripotent stem cells can be rapidly converted into neurons by cell fate conversion technique, without generating neuronal stem cells and differentiating them into neurons (Zhang et al., 2013). The overexpression of one transcription factor, Ngn2, in pluripotent stem cells resulted in the generation of iN cells with nearly a 100% yield and 100% purity (Zhang et al., 2013). These newer methods may help improve the conversion rate and the reprogramming efficiency of cells.

Second, it must be taken into account that whenever overexpression of exogenous factors by lentivirus or retrovirus is used, there is a possibility of transgenic insertions into the genome, leading to gene disruption or silencing. Sendai virus has recently been used to solve this problem and generate integration-free iPS cell lines. Similar strategies can also be used in the generation of iN cells, iNS cells, and iOPCs by replacing lentivirus with Sendai virus. Another alternative may involve the development of new conversion protocols using only small molecules. Indeed, a recent study successfully reprogrammed mouse somatic cells into pluripotent stem cells through the use of seven small molecules in place of transcription factors (Hou et al., 2013). In the near future, the use of these small molecules may serve as a more efficient and safer alternative to transcription factors, and their use in cell fate conversion experiments may eventually contribute to genetic damage-free generation of brain-relevant cells for research on neuropsychiatric disorders.

Third, the number of original fibroblasts or unsuccessfully converted cells present in culture may hamper *in vitro* disease characterization and therapeutic transplantation by altering neuronal function or modifying the primary disease-associated phenotypes. This is particularly a problem for iN cells that cannot easily be separated from those original cells because iN cells are postmitotic. Further exploration of useful cell surface markers on neurons will help enrich iN cells from those unwanted contaminating cells in culture. It is also necessary to determine the optimal combination of transcription factors that will efficiently and successfully convert fibroblasts into neurons. Once very efficient conversion methods are established, the contamination of original fibroblasts or unsuccessfully converted cells may not hinder iN cell use.

Fourth, as with all transcription factor-based methods of reprogramming, there is still a risk for the formation of tumors. The overexpression or inactivation of certain transcription factors such as Oct-3/4 can result in the formation of malignant tumors (Gidekel, Pizov, Bergman, & Pikarsky, 2003). Sox2, one of the transcription factors necessary in the reprogramming of iNS cells, is a lineage-dependent oncogene (Bass et al., 2009). Beyond using transcription factors with oncogenic properties, the process of reprogramming cells using transcription factors can result in the formation of tumors. The creation of iPS cells, for example, is tumorigenic by nature as sequencing has showed that they contain approximately six point mutations per exome (Gore et al., 2011). Although, tumor formation may not be a primary concern in the characterization of brain disorders, alterations of genomic architecture resulting from tumorigenic changes can be a limitation to the detailed analysis of complex neuropsychiatric disorders.

Finally, limited knowledge is available for the mechanisms underlying cell conversion. Indeed, most of the previously mentioned limitations are associated with our poor understanding of the biological mechanisms. It is important to note that this problem is not limited to induced cells, but is also a common problem in iPS cells and other transcription factor–based reprogramming methods. To efficiently use these cell fate conversion-based methods, we have to focus our efforts on further understanding of the mechanisms.

OE AND DERIVED CELLS: CELL MODELS FREE FROM GENETIC MANIPULATION

OE is located in the nasal cavity and one of the few areas in the CNS where neurogenesis continues throughout life. Human OE contains several cell types: olfactory

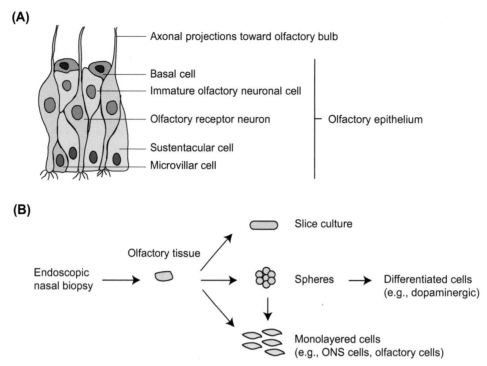

FIGURE 2   **Human olfactory epithelium (OE) and OE-derived cells/tissues.** (A) Schematic drawings of human OE. (B) Generation of OE slice, spheres, and monolayer cells from a tissue piece of OE collected by an endoscopic nasal biopsy.

receptor neurons that sense odor and transmit signals to olfactory bulb, basal cells that contain putative neuronal precursors, sustentacular cells (supporting cells) that provide structural and functional support to olfactory sensory neurons, and microvillar cells (Figure 2) (Morrison & Costanzo, 1990; Trojanowski, Newman, Hill, & Lee, 1991). Prior research in schizophrenia and other brain disorders revealed altered olfactory function that is widely involved from the level of olfactory receptor neurons in OE to higher order olfactory centers in the cortex (Sawa & Cascella, 2009; Turetsky, Hahn, Arnold, & Moberg, 2009). For example, in schizophrenia, olfactory deficits have been reported in odor detection threshold, sensitivity, odor identification, and odor memory (Dunn & Weller, 1989; Houlihan, Flaum, Arnold, Keshavan, & Alliger, 1994; Isseroff, Stoler, Ophir, Lancet, & Sirota, 1987; Kopala, Clark, & Hurwitz, 1993; Kopala, Clark, & Bassett, 1991; Malaspina et al., 1994; Seidman et al., 1991; Serby, Larson, & Kalkstein, 1990). Altered cellular and morphological characteristics of olfactory neurons were also reported in schizophrenia and Alzheimer's disease by histological examinations (Arnold, Smutzer, Trojanowski, & Moberg, 1998). Notably, evidence for dysregulated development of olfactory receptor neurons was shown in research on OE tissues from patients with schizophrenia (Arnold et al., 2001). OE tissue was also studied in the context of regenerative medicine because the tissue was easily accessible by nasal biopsy in living individuals. In particular, olfactory ensheathing cells

were shown to have therapeutic potentials for cellular and functional recovery in CNS injuries of animal models (Barnett & Riddell, 2007). In this section, we review historical advances in the use of OE-derived cells/tissues in neuropsychiatric research and discuss their utilities and limitations.

Methods

Because OE tissue contains neural stem cells that give rise to neurons, efforts have been made to establish live neuronal cell cultures from OE tissues. Earlier studies used slice cultures from human OE to recapitulate neuronal differentiation *in vitro* (Féron, Perry, Hirning, McGrath, & Mackay-Sim, 1999; Féron, Perry, McGrath, & Mackay-Sim, 1998; Hahn, Han, et al., 2005; McCurdy et al., 2006; Murrell et al., 1996). These explant (slice) cultures were used to examine cell adhesion capacity, cell proliferation and mitosis, and functional response to a neurotransmitter (Féron et al., 1999; Hahn, Han, et al., 2005). OE tissue slice cultures were also used to investigate changes in cell cycle by immunohistochemistry and microarray-based gene expression profiling (McCurdy et al., 2006).

In addition to OE slice cultures, dissociated cell cultures were established by various ways to explore morphological and functional alterations of neuronal cells from patients with psychiatric disorders (Table 2). Sphere forming cells from human OE were shown

TABLE 2   Representative Reports on Dissociated Cells Derived from Human Olfactory Epithelium

Type	Description	Characteristics	Disease Application	References
OE-derived sphere forming cells	Neurosphere forming cells	Expression of both neuronal and glial markers Capacity to differentiate into neuronal cells with dopaminergic and motoneuron markers	Transplantation (animal models of neuronal injury)	Roisen et al. (2001), Xiao et al. (2007), Xiao et al. (2005), Zhang, Cai, et al. (2006), Zhang, Klueber, et al. (2006), and Zhang et al. (2004)
	Olfactory neurospheres	Capacity to differentiate into neuronal cells with dopaminergic markers	Transplantation (animal models of Parkinson's disease)	Murrell et al. (2005) and Murrell et al. (2008)
OE-derived monolayer cells	Olfactory cell culture	Live olfactory neurons in heterogeneous cell populations	Bipolar disorder	Borgmann-Winter et al. (2009) and Hahn, Gomez, et al. (2005)
	ONS cells	Similar to mesenchymal stem cells	Parkinson's disease Ataxia telangiectasia Hereditary spastic paraplegia Schizophrenia	Abrahamsen et al. (2013), Matigian et al. (2010), Murrell et al. (2008), and Stewart et al. (2013)
	Olfactory cells	Immature neuronal phenotype Homogeneous populations	Schizophrenia	Horiuchi et al. (2013) and Kano et al. (2013)

OE, olfactory epithelium; ONS, olfactory neurosphere derived.

to be useful for autologous transplantation therapies and *in vitro* modeling of neuropsychiatric disorders (Murrell et al., 2005). These OE-derived neurospheres proliferated and generated dopaminergic cells *in vitro* and *in vivo* upon transplantation into rodent brains (Murrell et al., 2005, 2008). Another group also described *ex vivo* expansion of heterogeneous cell populations, including neuronal and glial cells in the form of neurospheres from OE tissues of cadavers (Roisen et al., 2001). They established a method to prepare neurospheres from OE tissues of living individuals and showed their characteristics as stem cells (Roisen et al., 2001; Xiao et al., 2007, 2005; Zhang, Cai, et al., 2006; Zhang, Klueber, et al., 2006; Zhang, Klueber, Guo, Lu, & Roisen, 2004). They also reported that application of retinoic acids, forskolin, and sonic hedgehog to neurosphere forming cells resulted in the expression of motoneuronal transcription factors, tyrosine hydroxylase, an indicator of dopamine production, and neurite formation (Zhang, Klueber, et al., 2006). These OE-derived neurospheres showed a promising potential as a resource for therapeutic transplantation in animal models of brain disorders such as Parkinson's disease (Murrell et al., 2008).

Monolayer cell cultures from OE tissues, derived by nasal biopsy, were also generated for functional and molecular characterization of neuropsychiatric disorders (Borgmann-Winter et al., 2009; Hahn, Gomez, et al., 2005; Hahn, Han, et al., 2005). Olfactory neurons recovered in dissociated cell culture from OE tissue were first used to characterize functional response to a mixture of odorants by calcium imaging with Fura-2/AM indicator (Hahn, Gomez, et al., 2005). Then, proliferating cells

in dissociated culture from OE tissues were also shown to express functional *N*-methyl-D-aspartate receptors and were predicted as a useful tool to address the functional and molecular features of neural cells in patients with neuropsychiatric disorders (Borgmann-Winter et al., 2009). Extensive molecular characterization of OE-derived dissociated cells by high-throughput profiling methods has recently been demonstrated in several studies (Kano et al., 2013; Matigian et al., 2010). In one study, olfactory neurospheres were dissociated and cultured in the presence of serum to expand as proliferating cells, olfactory neurosphere-derived (ONS) cells (Matigian et al., 2010). Flow cytometric analysis showed that the majority of these cells expressed CD105 and CD73, which are markers for mesenchymal stem cells. Fewer cells expressed Nestin (a marker for neural stem cells), OCT4 (a marker for ES cells), and β-tubulin III (a marker for neuronal cells) (Matigian et al., 2010). These cells were analyzed for messenger RNA and protein expression profiles by gene expression microarray and proteomic analysis using two-dimensional dye-in-gel-electrophoresis (Matigian et al., 2010). In addition, various biochemical and functional measures such as glutathione content, Caspase-3/7 activity, and MTS metabolism were taken using these ONS cells (Matigian et al., 2010). In another study, a protocol that can enrich cells with immature neuronal characteristics directly from OE tissue has been established. These olfactory cells showed homogeneous appearance and expressed β-tubulin III, a marker for neuronal cells. Systematic microarray gene expression profiling analysis of these olfactory cells with other resources including brains, peripheral blood–derived cells, and stem cells has revealed the close relationship between olfactory cells and mesenchymal stem cells as well as distinct features between olfactory cells and blood-derived cells (Horiuchi et al., 2013). These olfactory cells were used to explore epigenetic changes affecting gene expression by a combined analysis of ChIP-seq and gene expression microarray (Kano et al., 2013).

In parallel to the development of the live OE-derived cell/tissue culture method, a new technology was employed to explore the molecular signatures of olfactory neurons in OE tissue. In particular, laser capture microdissection technique, which allows the enrichment of a certain portion of tissues, has been successfully used to enrich olfactory neuronal layers where olfactory neurons are located (Tajinda et al., 2010). Availability of these homogenous cell populations from living human individuals will help high-throughput profiling studies using gene expression microarray, RNA-seq and various epigenetic sequencing, in which cellular heterogeneity can undermine a detection threshold.

Disease Application

Because olfactory functional deficits were known from earlier studies, OE-derived cells/tissues have been widely used in research on psychiatric and neurological diseases. Studies using OE slice cultures observed a significantly higher proportion of proliferating cells in cultures from patients with schizophrenia compared with controls (Féron et al., 1999; McCurdy et al., 2006). They also observed opposite effects of dopamine on dying cells between cultures from patients with schizophrenia and controls; dopamine decreased the proportion of dying cells in patients' cultures, whereas it increased the proportion in control cultures (Féron et al., 1999). In addition, OE slice cultures from patients with bipolar I disorder revealed significantly more cell death compared with those from controls (McCurdy et al., 2006).

Dissociated OE-derived cells have also contributed a lot to research on psychiatric diseases. Olfactory neurons in dissociated cultures from patients with bipolar disorder showed altered functional responses to a mixture of odorants in calcium imaging with Fura-2/AM indicator (Hahn, Gomez, et al., 2005). High-throughput molecular approaches using gene expression, protein expression, and cell function in patients with neuropsychiatric disorders have also been performed using dissociated OE-derived cells (Kano et al., 2013; Matigian et al., 2010). A study using ONS cells has revealed dysregulated neurodevelopmental pathways in schizophrenia and dysregulated mitochondrial function, oxidative stress, and xenobiotic metabolism in Parkinson's disease, all of which are not observed in patient-derived fibroblasts (Matigian et al., 2010). Another study using homogenous

olfactory cells with immature neuronal characteristics, which are directly derived from OE tissues, identified epigenetic alterations in schizophrenia including synaptogenesis, inflammatory cytokine signaling, and cellular defense system against oxidative stress (Kano et al., 2013).

In addition to neuropsychiatric disorders, dissociated OE-derived cells, in particular ONS cells, have been used in research on other hereditary brain disorders including ataxia telangiectasia (AT) and hereditary spastic paraplegia (Abrahamsen et al., 2013; Stewart et al., 2013). In AT, patient-derived ONS cells successfully modeled AT-relevant cellular phenotypes such as hypersensitivity to radiation, defects in radiation-induced signaling, and dysregulated cell cycle checkpoint regulation (Stewart et al., 2013). Notably, analysis of AT patient–derived ONS cells under a neuronal differentiation condition in vitro showed the reduced development of neurites, such as the number of neurites per cell and neurite length, suggesting that these cells have an impaired differentiation capacity in vitro into immature neuronal progenitors (Stewart et al., 2013). In hereditary spastic paraplegia, ONS cells showed changes in gene expression for microtubule dynamics, accompanied by altered intracellular distributions of peroxisomes and mitochondria as well as slower moving peroxisomes (Abrahamsen et al., 2013).

ONS cells have also been successfully used in transplantation therapies for animal models of Parkinson's disease (Murrell et al., 2008). When transplanted into the brain, ONS cells gave rise to dopaminergic cells and attenuated the behavioral asymmetry in the rat model of hemiparkinsonian induced by the injection of the selective neurotoxin, 6-hydroxydopamine, into the striatum (Murrell et al., 2008). Although psychiatric diseases are not generally accompanied by extensive loss of cells or tissues, the success in these transplantation therapies may pave the way for future consideration of functional correction by autologous transplantation of neuronal or glial cells into the brains of patients with psychiatric diseases.

Limitations

OE-derived cells have advantages over iPS cell–derived neuronal cells or iN cells in that no genetic engineering such as overexpression of complementary DNA by lentivirus vector is necessary. They can also be prepared relatively easily compared with iPS or iN cells. In addition, OE tissues provide an opportunity to perform longitudinal studies of disease progression or the effects of medication. For example, by collecting OE tissues at multiple time points, it can be possible to address how neuronal or glial status (or differentiation) is affected by the disease progress or medication. Thus, OE-derived cells/tissues can be widely used in translational research on neuropsychiatric disorders.

One major limitation in research using OE-derived cells/tissues is that few studies have comprehensively characterized postmitotic neurons obtained from olfactory spheres or other OE-derived immature neuronal cells. Indeed, apart from research studying human olfactory neurons in dissociated cell cultures by calcium imaging, there has been no clear demonstration that OE-derived postmitotic neurons show functional responses to their cognate stimulation such as depolarization or odorants. Although many studies rely on molecular and cellular methods to characterize OE-derived cells such as gene expression or immunocytochemistry, further validation of neuronal characteristics by electrophysiology is usually missing. Although OE-derived cells, in particular sphere-forming cells, are promising in that they may possess multipotency to be differentiated to a variety of neurons and glia, detailed functional characterization should be performed before we discuss them as alternative approaches to iPS cell–derived neurons/glia or iN cells/other induced brain cells.

Another limitation is the requirement of a nasal biopsy to obtain OE tissues. Although the surgical procedure is very simple and does not cause any side effects on olfactory function, it is more invasive than a simple blood draw. This is especially important when one designs a longitudinal collection of OE tissues. Notably, recent studies reported a method to collect OE tissue–derived cells by a simple brushing instead of performing an endoscopic nasal biopsy (Benitez-King et al., 2011). With the advance of culture techniques to recover a small number of OE-derived cells, this limitation may be solved in the near future.

FUTURE PERSPECTIVES

Use of Different Human Cell Models

With the advances in cell-culture technologies, there are now several different human CNS cell models available for research on schizophrenia and related disorders. These CNS cell models offer an opportunity to directly address the phenotypes of neuronal and glial cells in patients with neuropsychiatric disorders, which was not possible with previously available cell models, such as blood-derived cells or fibroblasts. They can also complement postmortem brain studies by providing phenotypic information of live brain cells. How should we use these various cells models? Here we compare major advantages and disadvantages of iN cells, iNS cells, and OE-derived cells and discuss their utilities (Table 3).

A key advantage of iN cells is that functional postmitotic neurons are obtained in a very short period of 2–3 weeks. Studies so far provided evidence that at least four types of neurons (glutamatergic, GABAergic, dopaminergic, and spinal motor neurons) can be directly generated from fibroblasts through cell fate conversion techniques using exogenous factors. Most of the studies also reported that these iN cells were electrophysiologically active and showed action potential spikes and, in some cases, synaptic activities. Although these features hold a high promise for iN cells' potential to be used for a variety of experiments on neuropsychiatric disorders, there are several shortcomings that must be reconciled. First, iN cells cannot be expanded or stored in a freezer for future use because they are already postmitotic neurons. Thus, iN cells need to be generated from fibroblasts for each experiment. Second, it is not clear at this moment whether iN cell techniques can be used to efficiently generate neuronal subtypes such as GABAergic interneurons or cholinergic neurons. Third, because iN cells bypass the developmental steps from neural stem cells, studies focusing on developmental alterations may not be feasible.

Notably, iNS cells can complement some of the shortcomings of iN cells. iNS cells proliferate effectively *in vitro* and thus can be expanded and stored in a freezer for future use. iNS cells can generate not only neurons, but also glia such as astrocytes and oligodendrocytes, providing greater opportunities to study disease-associated phenotypes in a wide range of CNS cells. Because iNS cells can be differentiated into neurons and glia, studies on disease-associated developmental alterations are also feasible. Another benefit is that iNS cells bypass the state of pluripotent stem cells and can also reduce the total costs and time needed for the generation of relevant CNS cells. Currently, a major shortcoming of iNS cells is that limited data is currently available on the characterization of human diseases. Although iNS cell–derived astrocytes were successfully used in a study on amyotrophic lateral sclerosis (Meyer et al., 2014), there have been no demonstrations that iNS cell–derived neurons or oligodendrocytes model the pathological features of human CNS disorders.

It is not completely understood yet whether cell fate conversion may leave any characteristics of original cells (e.g., fibroblasts) in iN cells and iNS cells. In fact, a very recent report has revealed that even iPS cells retain residual epigenetic patterns typical of original somatic cells (Ma et al., 2014). Thus, the effects of cell fate conversion should be carefully examined through cross comparison among iN cells, iNS cell–derived neurons, iPS cell–derived neurons, embryonic stem cell–derived neurons, and brain-derived neurons.

OE-derived cells are unique compared with iN cells, iNS cells, and iPS cell–derived neurons/glia in that cell fate conversion is not required. Accumulating evidence demonstrates that OE-derived cells are useful for both molecular and functional assays. In addition, OE-derived cells can be expanded and stored for future use. Because of these advantages, OE-derived cells have been used widely in research on schizophrenia and related disorders. A major drawback in OE-derived cell culture is that

TABLE 3   Basic Features of Currently Available Human Cell Models

Samples	Advantages	Disadvantages
iN cells	Very rapid generation of postmitotic neuronal cells	No expansion or storage
	Feasible for functional assays	Limited types of neurons can be generated
		Reprogramming with exogenous transcription factors required
iNS cells	Rapid generation of neural stem cells by bypassing iPS cell generation	Reprogramming with exogenous transcription factors required
	Feasible for expansion and storage Feasible for functional assays	Fewer data on applications to human diseases
	Feasible for study on neuronal and glial development	
iPS cells	Feasible for expansion and storage Feasible for functional assays	Requires long-term in vitro culture to generate neurons/glia
	Feasible for study on neuronal and glial development	Reprogramming with exogenous transcription factors required
	Abundant data on application to human diseases	
OE-derived cells/tissues	No requirement of reprogramming with exogenous transcription factors	May not recapitulate brain neuronal cells
	Feasible for expansion and storage Feasible for functional assays	Fewer data on well-characterized postmitotic neurons
Blood-derived cells	Easy to collect and analyze	May not reflect neuronal phenotype
	Feasible for expansion and storage Feasible for functional assays	
Postmortem brains	Neurons and glia in intact brain structures	No viable cells available No functional assays available
		Pathologies may be modified by medication, compensatory changes, substance abuse or smoking, and manner of death

iN, induced neuronal; iNS, induced neuronal stem; OE, olfactory epithelium.

neuronal cells may not reflect the phenotype of brain neurons. Further efforts are essential to improve cell culture methods and extend the utilities of OE-derived cells as alternatives to cell fate conversion-based methods.

Based on the pros and cons for each cell model as mentioned above, we propose a two-step strategy to use human CNS cell models in research on psychiatric disorders. During the initial phase of exploring potential new phenotypes or mechanisms, rapid generation of neuronal and glial cells offers greater advantages and is a higher priority. Thus, direct generation of neurons, glia, and neural progenitors (e.g., iN cells, iOPCs, iNS cells) can serve as beneficial tools. OE-derived cells can also be used for this purpose. Once the phenotypes or mechanisms of interest are found, additional detailed characterization can be performed with well-characterized iPS cells, which can be differentiated into desired cell types. In a more clinical study in which the longitudinal effects of medication or other interventions are tested, OE-derived cells may be a first choice because they can be collected multiple times during the course of study and quickly examined for any disease-associated phenotypes.

Back to the Brain

Although human cell models hold a promise for further development of research on schizophrenia and related disorders, they are still merely "cells on a culture dish." The behaviors of the cells on a dish may be totally different from those in intact brains. How should we fill this gap? There are multiple approaches. First, once cellular phenotypes are established in human cell models, new rodent models can be generated to find out the impact of such phenotypes on the brain. Analysis of such rodents will provide the opportunity to address the effects of cellular phenotypes on the network and tissue-level phenotypes of the brain. Second, brain imaging data from the individuals who provided the samples for human cell models can be analyzed to study the impact of cellular phenotypes on live brain activities. In particular, magnetic resonance spectroscopy or positron emission tomography can provide molecule-specific information that may be linked to cellular dysfunction of those individuals (Lukas, 2014). Finally, in vivo transplantation of human cell models into rodent brains may be used as "humanized" rodent brains. "Humanized" mice generally refer to the mice whose hematopoietic system is replaced with that of humans by bone marrow (or hematopoietic stem cell) transplantation after whole-body irradiation (Shultz, Ishikawa, & Greiner, 2007). Humanized mice have been widely used in research on blood disorders, immune diseases, and cancers. Although *in vivo* transplantation of human CNS cells have been attempted in many studies, its grafting efficiency is generally poor. As in the case of hematopoietic transplantation, removing target cell populations may increase grafting efficiency for the transplantation of human CNS cells into rodent brains. If successful, such approaches will bridge the gap of knowledge between *in vitro* cultured cells and *in vivo* brain cells.

CONCLUSIONS

With recent technological advances in cell culture of human neuronal and glial cells, research on neuropsychiatric disorders is entering a new era in which disease pathology can be directly studied in live patient cells. These new approaches have great potentials in identifying novel biological insights into brain disorders. Functional characterization of accumulating number of genetic variations associated with neuropsychiatric disorders will be facilitated by the use of those human cell models. In addition, combining human cell models with rodent models or brain imaging will enable us to address the impact of cellular phenotypes on the changes at the brain level. *In vivo* transplantation of human CNS cell models may also serve as a platform for generating humanized rodent brains. It needs to be emphasized that no single model can fulfill all the necessity in the field. Rather, different human cell models need to be used in parallel to complement each other's disadvantages and explore novel disease phenotypes. By integrating the findings from human cell models with other modalities such as genetics, neuropsychology, brain imaging, and model animal studies, we will be able to have a better picture of the pathological changes in the brains of patients with neuropsychiatric disorders and contribute to the development of novel therapeutic strategies.

Acknowledgments

S.K. is supported by a grant from National Institute of Mental Health (R00MH093458).

References

Abrahamsen, G., Fan, Y., Matigian, N., Wali, G., Bellette, B., Sutharsan, R., et al. (2013). A patient-derived stem cell model of hereditary spastic paraplegia with SPAST mutations. *Disease Models and Mechanisms, 6,* 489–502.

Ambasudhan, R., Talantova, M., Coleman, R., Yuan, X., Zhu, S., Lipton, S. A., et al. (2011). Direct reprogramming of adult human fibroblasts to functional neurons under defined conditions. *Cell Stem Cell, 9,* 113–118.

Arguello, P. A., & Gogos, J. A. (2006). Modeling madness in mice: one piece at a time. *Neuron, 52,* 179–196.

Arnold, S. E., Han, L. Y., Moberg, P. J., Turetsky, B. I., Gur, R. E., Trojanowski, J. Q., et al. (2001). Dysregulation of olfactory receptor neuron lineage in schizophrenia. *Archives of General Psychiatry, 58,* 829–835.

Arnold, S. E., Smutzer, G. S., Trojanowski, J. Q., & Moberg, P. J. (1998). Cellular and molecular neuropathology of the olfactory epithelium and central olfactory pathways in Alzheimer's disease and schizophrenia. *Annals of the New York Academy of Sciences, 855,* 762–775.

Barnett, S. C., & Riddell, J. S. (2007). Olfactory ensheathing cell transplantation as a strategy for spinal cord repair–what can it achieve? *Nature Clinical Practice Neurology, 3,* 152–161.

Bass, A. J., Watanabe, H., Mermel, C. H., Yu, S., Perner, S., Verhaak, R. G., et al. (2009). SOX2 is an amplified lineage-survival oncogene in lung and esophageal squamous cell carcinomas. *Nature Genetics, 41,* 1238–1242.

Benes, F. M., & Berretta, S. (2001). GABAergic interneurons: implications for understanding schizophrenia and bipolar disorder. *Neuropsychopharmacology, 25,* 1–27.

Benitez-King, G., Riquelme, A., Ortiz-Lopez, L., Berlanga, C., Rodriguez-Verdugo, M. S., Romo, F., et al. (2011). A non-invasive method to isolate the neuronal linage from the nasal epithelium from schizophrenic and bipolar diseases. *Journal of Neuroscience Methods, 201,* 35–45.

Borgmann-Winter, K. E., Rawson, N. E., Wang, H. Y., Wang, H., Macdonald, M. L., Ozdener, M. H., et al. (2009). Human olfactory epithelial cells generated in vitro express diverse neuronal characteristics. *Neuroscience, 158,* 642–653.

Caiazzo, M., Dell'Anno, M. T., Dvoretskova, E., Lazarevic, D., Taverna, S., Leo, D., et al. (2011). Direct generation of functional dopaminergic neurons from mouse and human fibroblasts. *Nature, 476,* 224–227.

Cozzi, A., Santambrogio, P., Privitera, D., Broccoli, V., Rotundo, L. I., Garavaglia, B., et al. (2013). Human L-ferritin deficiency is characterized by idiopathic generalized seizures and atypical restless leg syndrome. *The Journal of Experimental Medicine, 210,* 1779–1791.

Davila, J., Chanda, S., Ang, C. E., Sudhof, T. C., & Wernig, M. (2013). Acute reduction in oxygen tension enhances the induction of neurons from human fibroblasts. *Journal of Neuroscience Methods, 216,* 104–109.

Davis, K. L., Stewart, D. G., Friedman, J. I., Buchsbaum, M., Harvey, P. D., Hof, P. R., et al. (2003). White matter changes in schizophrenia: evidence for myelin-related dysfunction. *Archives of General Psychiatry, 60,* 443–456.

Davis, R. L., Weintraub, H., & Lassar, A. B. (1987). Expression of a single transfected cDNA converts fibroblasts to myoblasts. *Cell, 51,* 987–1000.

De la Rossa, A., Bellone, C., Golding, B., Vitali, I., Moss, J., Toni, N., et al. (2013). In vivo reprogramming of circuit connectivity in postmitotic neocortical neurons. *Nature Neuroscience, 16,* 193–200.

Dolmetsch, R., & Geschwind, D. H. (2011). The human brain in a dish: the promise of iPSC-derived neurons. *Cell, 145,* 831–834.

Dunn, T. P., & Weller, M. P. (1989). Olfaction in schizophrenia. *Perceptual and Motor Skills, 69,* 833–834.

Féron, F., Perry, C., Hirning, M. H., McGrath, J., & Mackay-Sim, A. (1999). Altered adhesion, proliferation and death in neural cultures from adults with schizophrenia. *Schizophrenia Research, 40,* 211–218.

Féron, F., Perry, C., McGrath, J. J., & Mackay-Sim, A. (1998). New techniques for biopsy and culture of human olfactory epithelial neurons. *Archives of Otolaryngology Head and Neck Surgery, 124,* 861–866.

Fitzsimmons, J., Kubicki, M., & Shenton, M. E. (2013). Review of functional and anatomical brain connectivity findings in schizophrenia. *Current Opinion in Psychiatry, 26,* 172–187.

Fromer, M., Pocklington, A. J., Kavanagh, D. H., Williams, H. J., Dwyer, S., Gormley, P., et al. (2014). De novo mutations in schizophrenia implicate synaptic networks. *Nature, 506,* 179–184.

Garbarini, N. (2010). Primates as a model for research. *Disease Models and Mechanisms, 3*, 15–19.

Geschwind, D. H., & Rakic, P. (2013). Cortical evolution: judge the brain by its cover. *Neuron, 80*, 633–647.

Gidekel, S., Pizov, G., Bergman, Y., & Pikarsky, E. (2003). Oct-3/4 is a dose-dependent oncogenic fate determinant. *Cancer Cell, 4*, 361–370.

Gore, A., Li, Z., Fung, H. L., Young, J. E., Agarwal, S., Antosiewicz-Bourget, J., et al. (2011). Somatic coding mutations in human induced pluripotent stem cells. *Nature, 471*, 63–67.

Graf, T. (2011). Historical origins of transdifferentiation and reprogramming. *Cell Stem Cell, 9*, 504–516.

Hahn, C. G., Gomez, G., Restrepo, D., Friedman, E., Josiassen, R., Pribitkin, E. A., et al. (2005). Aberrant intracellular calcium signaling in olfactory neurons from patients with bipolar disorder. *American Journal of Psychiatry, 162*, 616–618.

Hahn, C. G., Han, L. Y., Rawson, N. E., Mirza, N., Borgmann-Winter, K., Lenox, R. H., et al. (2005). In vivo and in vitro neurogenesis in human olfactory epithelium. *The Journal of Comparative Neurology, 483*, 154–163.

Han, D. W., Tapia, N., Hermann, A., Hemmer, K., Höing, S., Araúzo-Bravo, M. J., et al. (2012). Direct reprogramming of fibroblasts into neural stem cells by defined factors. *Cell Stem Cell, 10*, 465–472.

Horiuchi, Y., Kano, S., Ishizuka, K., Cascella, N. G., Ishii, S., Talbot, C. C., Jr., et al. (2013). Olfactory cells via nasal biopsy reflect the developing brain in gene expression profiles: utility and limitation of the surrogate tissues in research for brain disorders. *Neuroscience Research, 77*, 247–250.

Houlihan, D. J., Flaum, M., Arnold, S. E., Keshavan, M., & Alliger, R. (1994). Further evidence for olfactory identification deficits in schizophrenia. *Schizophrenia Research, 12*, 179–182.

Hou, P., Li, Y., Zhang, X., Liu, C., Guan, J., Li, H., et al. (2013). Pluripotent stem cells induced from mouse somatic cells by small-molecule compounds. *Science, 341*, 651–654.

Insel, T. R. (2007). From animal models to model animals. *Biological Psychiatry, 62*, 1337–1339.

Insel, T. R., & Landis, S. C. (2013). Twenty-five years of progress: the view from NIMH and NINDS. *Neuron, 80*, 561–567.

International Schizophrenia Consortium, Purcell, S. M., Wray, N. R., Stone, J. L., Visscher, P. M., O'Donovan, M. C., et al. (2009). Common polygenic variation contributes to risk of schizophrenia and bipolar disorder. *Nature, 460*, 748–752.

Isseroff, R. G., Stoler, M., Ophir, D., Lancet, D., & Sirota, P. (1987). Olfactory sensitivity to androstenone in schizophrenic patients. *Biological Psychiatry, 22*, 922–925.

Jarskog, L. F., Miyamoto, S., & Lieberman, J. A. (2007). Schizophrenia: new pathological insights and therapies. *Annual Review of Medicine, 58*, 49–61.

Kano, S., Colantuoni, C., Han, F., Zhou, Z., Yuan, Q., Wilson, A., et al. (2013). Genome-wide profiling of multiple histone methylations in olfactory cells: further implications for cellular susceptibility to oxidative stress in schizophrenia. *Molecular Psychiatry, 18*, 740–742.

Kano, S., Yuan, M., Cardarelli, A. R., Maegawa, G., Higurashi, N., Gaval-Cruz, M., et al. (2015). Clinical utility of neuronal cells directly converted from fibroblasts of patients for neuropsychiatric disorders: studies of lysosomal storage diseases and channelopathy. *Current Molecular Medicine, 15*, 138–145.

Kim, J., Efe, J. A., Zhu, S., Talantova, M., Yuan, X., Wang, S., et al. (2011). Direct reprogramming of mouse fibroblasts to neural progenitors. *Proceedings of the National Academy of Sciences of the United States of America, 108*, 7838–7843.

Kim, J., Su, S. C., Wang, H., Cheng, A. W., Cassady, J. P., Lodato, M. A., et al. (2011). Functional integration of dopaminergic neurons directly converted from mouse fibroblasts. *Cell Stem Cell, 9*, 413–419.

Kopala, L. C., Clark, C. C., & Bassett, A. (1991). Olfactory deficits in schizophrenia and chromosome 5. *Biological Psychiatry, 29*, 732–733.

Kopala, L. C., Clark, C., & Hurwitz, T. (1993). Olfactory deficits in neuroleptic naive patients with schizophrenia. *Schizophrenia Research, 8*, 245–250.

Ladewig, J., Mertens, J., Kesavan, J., Doerr, J., Poppe, D., Glaue, F., et al. (2012). Small molecules enable highly efficient neuronal conversion of human fibroblasts. *Nature Methods, 9*, 575–578.

Lassar, A. B., Paterson, B. M., & Weintraub, H. (1986). Transfection of a DNA locus that mediates the conversion of 10T1/2 fibroblasts to myoblasts. *Cell, 47*, 649–656.

Lewis, D. A. (2002). The human brain revisited: opportunities and challenges in postmortem studies of psychiatric disorders. *Neuropsychopharmacology, 26*, 143–154.

Lewis, D. A., Glantz, L. A., Pierri, J. N., & Sweet, R. A. (2003). Altered cortical glutamate neurotransmission in schizophrenia: evidence from morphological studies of pyramidal neurons. *Annals of the New York Academy of Sciences, 1003*, 102–112.

Lui, J. H., Hansen, D. V., & Kriegstein, A. R. (2011). Development and evolution of the human neocortex. *Cell, 146*, 18–36.

Lujan, E., Chanda, S., Ahlenius, H., Sudhof, T. C., & Wernig, M. (2012). Direct conversion of mouse fibroblasts to self-renewing, tripotent neural precursor cells. *Proceedings of the National Academy of Sciences of the United States of America, 109*, 2527–2532.

Lukas, S. E. (2014). New perspectives on using brain imaging to study CNS stimulants. *Neuropharmacology, 87*, 104–114.

Malaspina, D., Wray, A. D., Friedman, J. H., Amador, X., Yale, S., Hasan, A., et al. (1994). Odor discrimination deficits in schizophrenia: association with eye movement dysfunction. *The Journal of Neuropsychiatry and Clinical Neurosciences, 6*, 273–278.

Ma, H., Morey, R., O'Neil, R. C., He, Y., Daughtry, B., Schultz, M. D., et al. (2014). Abnormalities in human pluripotent cells due to reprogramming mechanisms. *Nature, 511*, 177–183.

Marchetto, M. C., Brennand, K. J., Boyer, L. F., & Gage, F. H. (2011). Induced pluripotent stem cells (iPSCs) and neurological disease modeling: progress and promises. *Human Molecular Genetics, 20*, R109–R115.

Marro, S., Pang, Z. P., Yang, N., Tsai, M. C., Qu, K., Chang, H. Y., et al. (2011). Direct lineage conversion of terminally differentiated hepatocytes to functional neurons. *Cell Stem Cell, 9*, 374–382.

Matigian, N., Abrahamsen, G., Sutharsan, R., Cook, A. L., Vitale, A. M., Nouwens, A., et al. (2010). Disease-specific, neurosphere-derived cells as models for brain disorders. *Disease Models and Mechanisms, 3*, 785–794.

McCullumsmith, R. E., & Meador-Woodruff, J. H. (2011). Novel approaches to the study of postmortem brain in psychiatric illness: old limitations and new challenges. *Biological Psychiatry, 69*, 127–133.

McCurdy, R. D., Féron, F., Perry, C., Chant, D. C., McLean, D., Matigian, N., et al. (2006). Cell cycle alterations in biopsied olfactory neuroepithelium in schizophrenia and bipolar I disorder using cell culture and gene expression analyses. *Schizophrenia Research, 82*, 163–173.

Meyer, K., Ferraiuolo, L., Miranda, C. J., Likhite, S., McElroy, S., Renusch, S., et al. (2014). Direct conversion of patient fibroblasts demonstrates non-cell autonomous toxicity of astrocytes to motor neurons in familial and sporadic ALS. *Proceedings of the National Academy of Sciences of the United States of America, 111*, 829–832.

Morrison, E. E., & Costanzo, R. M. (1990). Morphology of the human olfactory epithelium. *The Journal of Comparative Neurology, 297*, 1–13.

Murrell, W., Bushell, G. R., Livesey, J., McGrath, J., MacDonald, K. P., Bates, P. R., et al. (1996). Neurogenesis in adult human. *Neuroreport, 7*, 1189–1194.

Murrell, W., Féron, F., Wetzig, A., Cameron, N., Splatt, K., Bellette, B., et al. (2005). Multipotent stem cells from adult olfactory mucosa. *Developmental Dynamics, 233*, 496–515.

Murrell, W., Wetzig, A., Donnellan, M., Féron, F., Burne, T., Meedeniya, A., et al. (2008). Olfactory mucosa is a potential source for autologous stem cell therapy for Parkinson's disease. *Stem Cells, 26*, 2183–2192.

Najm, F. J., Lager, A. M., Zaremba, A., Wyatt, K., Caprariello, A. V., Factor, D. C., et al. (2013). Transcription factor-mediated reprogramming of fibroblasts to expandable, myelinogenic oligodendrocyte progenitor cells. *Nature Biotechnology, 31*, 426–433.

Pang, Z. P., Yang, N., Vierbuchen, T., Ostermeier, A., Fuentes, D. R., Yang, T. Q., et al. (2011). Induction of human neuronal cells by defined transcription factors. *Nature, 476*, 220–223.

Pfisterer, U., Kirkeby, A., Torper, O., Wood, J., Nelander, J., Dufour, A., et al. (2011). Direct conversion of human fibroblasts to dopaminergic neurons. *Proceedings of the National Academy of Sciences of the United States of America, 108*, 10343–10348.

Poels, E. M., Kegeles, L. S., Kantrowitz, J. T., Slifstein, M., Javitt, D. C., Lieberman, J. A., et al. (2014). Imaging glutamate in schizophrenia: review of findings and implications for drug discovery. *Molecular Psychiatry, 19*, 20–29.

Purcell, S. M., Moran, J. L., Fromer, M., Ruderfer, D., Solovieff, N., Roussos, P., et al. (2014). A polygenic burden of rare disruptive mutations in schizophrenia. *Nature, 506*, 185–190.

Ring, K. L., Tong, L. M., Balestra, M. E., Javier, R., Andrews-Zwilling, Y., Li, G., et al. (2012). Direct reprogramming of mouse and human fibroblasts into multipotent neural stem cells with a single factor. *Cell Stem Cell, 11*, 100–109.

Ripke, S., O'Dushlaine, C., Chambert, K., Moran, J. L., Kahler, A. K., Akterin, S., et al. (2013). Genome-wide association analysis identifies 13 new risk loci for schizophrenia. *Nature Genetics, 45*, 1150–1159.

Roisen, F. J., Klueber, K. M., Lu, C. L., Hatcher, L. M., Dozier, A., Shields, C. B., et al. (2001). Adult human olfactory stem cells. *Brain Research, 890*, 11–22.

Rouaux, C., & Arlotta, P. (2010). Fezf2 directs the differentiation of corticofugal neurons from striatal progenitors in vivo. *Nature Neuroscience, 13*, 1345–1347.

Rouaux, C., & Arlotta, P. (2013). Direct lineage reprogramming of postmitotic callosal neurons into corticofugal neurons in vivo. *Nature Cell Biology, 15*, 214–221.

Sasaki, E., Suemizu, H., Shimada, A., Hanazawa, K., Oiwa, R., Kamioka, M., et al. (2009). Generation of transgenic non-human primates with germline transmission. *Nature, 459*, 523–527.

Sawa, A., & Cascella, N. G. (2009). Peripheral olfactory system for clinical and basic psychiatry: a promising entry point to the mystery of brain mechanism and biomarker identification in schizophrenia. *American Journal of Psychiatry, 166*, 137–139.

Schizophrenia Working Group of the Psychiatric Genomics Consortium. (2014). Biological insights from 108 schizophrenia-associated genetic loci. *Nature, 511*, 421–427.

Seidman, L. J., Talbot, N. L., Kalinowski, A. G., McCarley, R. W., Faraone, S. V., Kremen, W. S., et al. (1991). Neuropsychological probes of fronto-limbic system dysfunction in schizophrenia. Olfactory identification and Wisconsin Card Sorting performance. *Schizophrenia Research, 6*, 55–65.

Serby, M., Larson, P., & Kalkstein, D. (1990). Olfactory sense in psychoses. *Biological Psychiatry, 28*, 830.

Shi, J., Levinson, D. F., Duan, J., Sanders, A. R., Zheng, Y., Pe'er, I., et al. (2009). Common variants on chromosome 6p22.1 are associated with schizophrenia. *Nature, 460*, 753–757.

Shultz, L. D., Ishikawa, F., & Greiner, D. L. (2007). Humanized mice in translational biomedical research. *Nature Reviews Immunology, 7*, 118–130.

Simen, A. A., DiLeone, R., & Arnsten, A. F. (2009). Primate models of schizophrenia: future possibilities. *Progress in Brain Research, 179*, 117–125.

Son, E. Y., Ichida, J. K., Wainger, B. J., Toma, J. S., Rafuse, V. F., Woolf, C. J., et al. (2011). Conversion of mouse and human fibroblasts into functional spinal motor neurons. *Cell Stem Cell, 9*, 205–218.

Stefansson, H., Meyer-Lindenberg, A., Steinberg, S., Magnusdottir, B., Morgen, K., Arnarsdottir, S., et al. (2014). CNVs conferring risk of autism or schizophrenia affect cognition in controls. *Nature, 505*, 361–366.

Stefansson, H., Ophoff, R. A., Steinberg, S., Andreassen, O. A., Cichon, S., Rujescu, D., et al. (2009). Common variants conferring risk of schizophrenia. *Nature, 460*, 744–747.

Stewart, R., Kozlov, S., Matigian, N., Wali, G., Gatei, M., Sutharsan, R., et al. (2013). A patient-derived olfactory stem cell disease model for ataxia-telangiectasia. *Human Molecular Genetics, 22*, 2495–2509.

Tajinda, K., Ishizuka, K., Colantuoni, C., Morita, M., Winicki, J., Le, C., et al. (2010). Neuronal biomarkers from patients with mental illnesses: a novel method through nasal biopsy combined with laser-captured microdissection. *Molecular Psychiatry, 15*, 231–232.

Takahashi, K., Tanabe, K., Ohnuki, M., Narita, M., Ichisaka, T., Tomoda, K., et al. (2007). Induction of pluripotent stem cells from adult human fibroblasts by defined factors. *Cell, 131*, 861–872.

Takahashi, K., & Yamanaka, S. (2006). Induction of pluripotent stem cells from mouse embryonic and adult fibroblast cultures by defined factors. *Cell, 126*, 663–676.

Tapscott, S. J., Davis, R. L., Thayer, M. J., Cheng, P. F., Weintraub, H., & Lassar, A. B. (1988). MyoD1: a nuclear phosphoprotein requiring a Myc homology region to convert fibroblasts to myoblasts. *Science, 242*, 405–411.

Thier, M., Worsdorfer, P., Lakes, Y. B., Gorris, R., Herms, S., Opitz, T., et al. (2012). Direct conversion of fibroblasts into stably expandable neural stem cells. *Cell Stem Cell, 10*, 473–479.

Tkachev, D., Mimmack, M. L., Ryan, M. M., Wayland, M., Freeman, T., Jones, P. B., et al. (2003). Oligodendrocyte dysfunction in schizophrenia and bipolar disorder. *Lancet, 362*, 798–805.

Torper, O., Pfisterer, U., Wolf, D. A., Pereira, M., Lau, S., Jakobsson, J., et al. (2013). Generation of induced neurons via direct conversion in vivo. *Proceedings of the National Academy of Sciences of the United States of America, 110*, 7038–7043.

Trojanowski, J. Q., Newman, P. D., Hill, W. D., & Lee, V. M. (1991). Human olfactory epithelium in normal aging, Alzheimer's disease, and other neurodegenerative disorders. *The Journal of Comparative Neurology, 310*, 365–376.

Turetsky, B. I., Hahn, C. G., Arnold, S. E., & Moberg, P. J. (2009). Olfactory receptor neuron dysfunction in schizophrenia. *Neuropsychopharmacology, 34*, 767–774.

Vierbuchen, T., Ostermeier, A., Pang, Z. P., Kokubu, Y., Südhof, T. C., & Wernig, M. (2010). Direct conversion of fibroblasts to functional neurons by defined factors. *Nature, 463*, 1035–1041.

Vita, A., De Peri, L., Deste, G., & Sacchetti, E. (2012). Progressive loss of cortical gray matter in schizophrenia: a meta-analysis and meta-regression of longitudinal MRI studies. *Translational Psychiatry, 2*, e190.

Wapinski, O. L., Vierbuchen, T., Qu, K., Lee, Q. Y., Chanda, S., Fuentes, D. R., et al. (2013). Hierarchical mechanisms for direct reprogramming of fibroblasts to neurons. *Cell, 155*, 621–635.

Wong, D. F., Grunder, G., & Brasic, J. R. (2007). Brain imaging research: does the science serve clinical practice? *International Review of Psychiatry, 19*, 541–558.

Xiao, M., Klueber, K. M., Guo, Z., Lu, C., Wang, H., & Roisen, F. J. (2007). Human adult olfactory neural progenitors promote axotomized rubrospinal tract axonal reinnervation and locomotor recovery. *Neurobiology of Disease, 26*, 363–374.

Xiao, M., Klueber, K. M., Lu, C., Guo, Z., Marshall, C. T., Wang, H., et al. (2005). Human adult olfactory neural progenitors rescue axotomized rodent rubrospinal neurons and promote functional recovery. *Experimental Neurology, 194*, 12–30.

Yang, N., Zuchero, J. B., Ahlenius, H., Marro, S., Ng, Y. H., Vierbuchen, T., et al. (2013). Generation of oligodendroglial cells by direct lineage conversion. *Nature Biotechnology, 31*, 434–439.

Yoo, A. S., Sun, A. X., Li, L., Shcheglovitov, A., Portmann, T., Li, Y., et al. (2011). MicroRNA-mediated conversion of human fibroblasts to neurons. *Nature, 476*, 228–231.

Yu, J., Vodyanik, M. A., Smuga-Otto, K., Antosiewicz-Bourget, J., Frane, J. L., Tian, S., et al. (2007). Induced pluripotent stem cell lines derived from human somatic cells. *Science, 318*, 1917–1920.

Zhang, X., Cai, J., Klueber, K. M., Guo, Z., Lu, C., Winstead, W. I., et al. (2006). Role of transcription factors in motoneuron differentiation of adult human olfactory neuroepithelial-derived progenitors. *Stem Cells, 24*, 434–442.

Zhang, X., Klueber, K. M., Guo, Z., Cai, J., Lu, C., Winstead, W. I., et al. (2006). Induction of neuronal differentiation of adult human olfactory neuroepithelial-derived progenitors. *Brain Research, 1073-1074*, 109–119.

Zhang, X., Klueber, K. M., Guo, Z., Lu, C., & Roisen, F. J. (2004). Adult human olfactory neural progenitors cultured in defined medium. *Experimental Neurology, 186*, 112–123.

Zhang, Y., Pak, C., Han, Y., Ahlenius, H., Zhang, Z., Chanda, S., et al. (2013). Rapid single-step induction of functional neurons from human pluripotent stem cells. *Neuron, 78*, 785–798.

Astrocytes as Pharmacological Targets in the Treatment of Schizophrenia: Focus on Kynurenic Acid

Ana Pocivavsek, Francesca M. Notarangelo*, Hui-Qiu Wu*,
John P. Bruno§,¶, Robert Schwarcz**

*Department of Psychiatry, Maryland Psychiatric Research Center, University of Maryland School of Medicine,
Baltimore, MD, USA; §Department of Psychology, The Ohio State University, Columbus, OH, USA; ¶Department of
Neuroscience, The Ohio State University, Columbus, OH, USA

INTRODUCTION

Mounting evidence indicates that an imbalance in glutamatergic neurotransmission contributes to the pathophysiology of schizophrenia (SZ). The glutamate hypothesis originated from the observation that the psychotomimetic drugs phencyclidine and ketamine, which induce positive and negative symptoms as well as cognitive impairments reminiscent of SZ in healthy individuals (Javitt & Zukin, 1991; Krystal et al., 1994), inhibit N-methyl-D-aspartate (NMDA) receptor function (Anis, Berry, Burton, & Lodge, 1983; Coyle, 2012), and that both drugs exacerbate psychotic symptoms in patients with SZ (Lahti, Koffel, LaPorte, & Tamminga, 1995; Luby, Cohen, Rosenbaum, Gottlieb, & Kelley, 1959). These clinical insights have since been corroborated using postmortem human brain tissue and by comparing healthy subjects and patients using a variety of in vivo imaging methods. Together with the identification of genetic links and numerous supportive studies in experimental animals, there is little doubt that glutamatergic abnormalities are indeed associated with disease symptoms and may play a role in the etiology of the disorder. Primary data, along with implications for disease progression and therapeutic strategies, have recently been summarized and discussed in several authoritative review articles (Coyle, Basu, Benneyworth, Balu, & Konopaske, 2012; Gonzalez-Burgos & Lewis, 2012; Poels et al., 2014).

Astrocytes, which are abundant in the mammalian brain, are increasingly understood to serve critical roles in brain function and dysfunction (Clarke & Barres, 2013; Sofroniew & Vinters, 2010; Takahashi & Sakurai, 2013), and, in particular, can influence and control a number of dynamic processes involved in glutamatergic neurotransmission (Bouzier-Sore & Pellerin, 2013; Schousboe, Bak, & Waagepetersen, 2013). Abnormal expression of astrocytic proteins that determine glutamate function has been repeatedly reported in SZ, and these changes have been considered as causative factors in pathophysiology (Katsel et al., 2011; Matute, Melone, Vallejo-Illarramendi, & Conti, 2005; Steffek, McCullumsmith, Haroutunian, & Meador-Woodruff, 2008). Notably, malfunction of astrocytes not only interferes with glutamatergic enzymes, receptors, and transporters directly, but is also associated with anomalous behavior of several small molecules, which have metabolic links to astrocytes and affect extracellular glutamate levels and/or glutamate receptors. This growing list of endogenous neuromodulators includes the dipeptide N-acetylaspartylglutamate (Bergeron & Coyle, 2012; Gehl, Saab, Bzdega, Wroblewska, & Neale, 2004), the glycine_B/NMDA receptor agonist D-serine (Bergersen et al., 2012; Martineau et al., 2013), and kynurenic acid (KYNA), a product of tryptophan degradation. Because of KYNA's unique neurobiological properties and demonstrated links to SZ, the following review and discussion will focus specifically on the possible role of this metabolite in brain physiology and pathology, paying special attention to the possibility that inhibition of astrocytic KYNA synthesis may alleviate cognitive impairments in SZ and, perhaps, other major psychiatric diseases.

KYNURENIC ACID IN THE BRAIN: MULTIPLE RECEPTOR TARGETS

The neuroinhibitory properties of KYNA were first recognized in the early 1980s, when the compound was found to be a broad-spectrum, competitive antagonist of ionotropic glutamate receptors at high micromolar concentrations (Perkins & Stone, 1982). This ability to inhibit the activity of NMDA, kainate, and α-amino-3-hydroxy-5-methyl-4-isoxazolepropionic acid receptors alike soon made KYNA a formidable and widely used tool in experimental situations that required elimination of glutamatergic neurotransmission. In line with this ability to neutralize the central effects of glutamate and other excitatory amino acids, KYNA was soon shown to have anticonvulsant and neuroprotective properties (Foster, Vezzani, French, & Schwarcz, 1984). It also turned out that KYNA has a preferential affinity to the NMDA receptor (Ganong, Lanthorn, & Cotman, 1983)—especially to the obligatory glycine coagonist (glycine$_B$) site of the receptor, which KYNA inhibits *competitively* with a median inhibition concentration (IC$_{50}$) of approximately 10 μM (Birch, Grossman, & Hayes, 1988; Kessler, Terramani, Lynch, & Baudry, 1989). Because the glycine$_B$ receptor is not saturated by glycine or its endogenous congener D-serine under physiological conditions (Thomson, Walker, & Flynn, 1989; Wood, 1995), KYNA became recognized as an excellent agent for studying the role(s) of glycine and D-serine in central nervous system function experimentally. Interest in KYNA was further increased when it was realized that it is present in the mammalian brain, albeit at submicromolar concentrations (Moroni, Russi, Lombardi, Beni, & Carlà, 1988; Turski et al., 1988). Unexpectedly, and for reasons that are still not understood, KYNA concentrations in the human brain are 20–50 times higher than in the rodent brain, and prenatal levels greatly exceed levels in adulthood (Beal, Swartz, & Isacson, 1992; Cannazza, Chiarugi, Parenti, Zanoli, & Baraldi, 2001; Ceresoli-Borroni & Schwarcz, 2000; Pocivavsek, Thomas, Elmer, Bruno, & Schwarcz, 2014). These findings increased the likelihood that endogenous KYNA, by serving as a direct modulator of glutamatergic neurotransmission, is involved in myriads of brain functions at all stages of the life cycle (Schwarcz et al., 1992).

As demonstrated in numerous in vivo microdialysis studies in rats and mice, KYNA is present in the brain's extracellular milieu and therefore has ready access to membrane receptor targets on any of a variety of brain cells. Basal extracellular KYNA concentrations in the rodent brain are in the low nanomolar range and do not vary substantially between brain regions (Swartz, During, Freese, & Beal, 1990; Wu et al., 2010; Wu, Ungerstedt, & Schwarcz, 1992). Although these concentrations may be sufficient to influence glycine$_B$ receptor function, especially when extracellular glycine or D-serine levels are low, endogenous KYNA probably targets other receptors preferentially in vivo. These include the G protein–coupled receptor 35, which, when activated by KYNA (Wang et al., 2006), affects cyclic adenosine monophosphate production, Ca^{2+} fluxes in astrocytes and secondarily reduces glutamatergic neurotransmission (Berlinguer-Palmini et al., 2013) and, as discovered more recently, the aryl hydrocarbon receptor (DiNatale et al., 2010).

Most evidence suggests, however, that the α7 nicotinic acetylcholine receptor (α7nAChR) is the preferred target of endogenous KYNA in the mammalian brain (Table 1). Originally observed in electrophysiological studies using cultured neurons and intact brain slices, KYNA inhibits the α7nAChR *noncompetitively* with an IC$_{50}$ of approximately 10 μM (Hilmas et al., 2001). A number of subsequent studies, mostly using KYNA concentrations in the mid-nanomolar range, indicated that α7nAChRs are the likely initial sites of KYNA action in the brain in vivo, and that this α7nAChR inhibition causes a series of functionally relevant effects downstream. More specifically, KYNA acts as an antagonist of an allosteric site located in the extracellular domain of the α7nAChR, which, interestingly, overlaps with a site that is activated by the cognition-enhancing drug galantamine (Lopes et al., 2007).

THE KYNURENINE PATHWAY OF TRYPTOPHAN METABOLISM

Approximately 5% of dietary tryptophan is degraded to serotonin, whereas the kynurenine pathway (KP), which is responsible for the neosynthesis of KYNA, accounts for the vast majority of catabolism of this essential amino acid (Leklem, 1971) (Figure 1). For decades, while the individual enzymes of the KP were identified and the metabolic relationships between their enzymatic products ("kynurenines") were established, tryptophan catabolism through the KP was regarded mainly as an endogenous route for vitamin B3 (nicotinic acid, nicotinamide, or niacin) production and a source of the coenzyme NAD$^+$, which is critically involved in numerous essential cellular functions. However, probably because of the many remarkable discoveries related to the function and dysfunction of serotonin in the brain, only sporadic attention was paid to a possible role of cerebral

TABLE 1   Receptors and Targets for the Actions of KYNA

Receptor or Binding Site	Site on Receptor	Action	EC$_{50}$ (μM)	References
AMPA/NMDA/Kainate	Glutamate	Antagonism (competitive)	100–400	Perkins and Stone (1982) and Ganong et al. (1983)
NMDA	Glycine	Antagonism (competitive)	10–30	Birch et al. (1988) and Kessler et al. (1989)
NMDA autoreceptor	Glutamate/glycine	Antagonism (competitive)	0.01–1	Luccini, Musante, Neri, Raiteri, and Pittaluga (2007)
α7nAChR	Allosteric potentiating site	Antagonism (noncompetitive)	1–8	Hilmas et al. (2001)
AMPA	Glutamate	Agonism	10	Prescott, Weeks, Staley, and Partin (2006)
G protein–coupled receptor 35	Unknown	Agonism	0.1–30	Wang et al. (2006)
Aryl hydrocarbon receptor	Unknown	Agonism	1–2	DiNatale et al. (2010)

References are limited to original and early publications. α7nAChR, α7 nicotinic acetylcholine receptor; AMPA, α-amino-3-hydroxy-5-methyl-4-isoxazolepropionic acid; EC$_{50}$, half maximal effective concentration; KYNA, kynurenic acid; NMDA, N-methyl-D-aspartate.

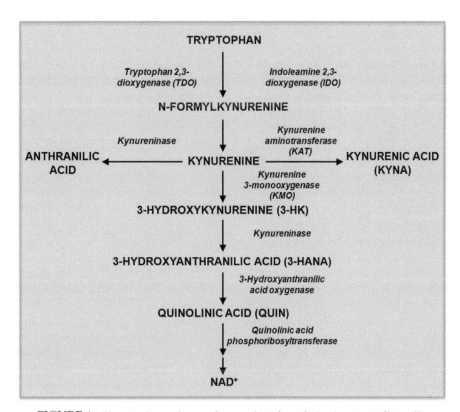

FIGURE 1   **Kynurenine pathway of tryptophan degradation in mammalian cells.**

kynurenines until the end of the 1970s (Gál & Sherman, 1978; Gál, Young, & Sherman, 1978; Green & Curzon, 1970; Joseph, 1978).

The situation changed with the discovery of the convulsant properties of the KP metabolite quinolinic acid (QUIN) (Lapin, 1978) and, soon thereafter, the demonstration that QUIN can function as an NMDA receptor agonist in the rat cerebral cortex (Stone & Perkins, 1981). In relatively rapid succession, with evidence for the neuroactive properties of KYNA (see previous section) and the demonstration that both QUIN and KYNA are normally present in the mammalian brain (Moroni et al., 1988; Turski et al., 1988; Wolfensberger et al., 1983), it became apparent that endogenous kynurenines may participate actively in a variety of brain functions. This insight and the realization that dysfunctions in brain QUIN or KYNA may play a causative role in neurodegenerative and seizure disorders (Schwarcz, Foster, French, Whetsell, & Köhler, 1984) and in neurovirological diseases such as AIDS dementia (Heyes, Brew, et al., 1992; Heyes, Saito, et al., 1992) stimulated a large number of studies, which were designed to uncover the features of cerebral KP metabolism in greater detail. Because the results of these investigations have been thoroughly reviewed in recent years (Schwarcz, Bruno, Muchowski, & Wu, 2012; Stone, Stoy, & Darlington, 2013; Vécsei, Szalardy, Fülop, & Toldi, 2013), we will limit our comments here mainly to the fundamental principles that govern the formation and function of brain kynurenines under physiological conditions.

As illustrated schematically in Figure 1, the KP is initiated by the oxidative opening of tryptophan's indole ring by indoleamine-2,3-dioxygenase (IDO) 1 and 2, and tryptophan-2,3-dioxygenase (TDO). All three of these enzymes, which are readily upregulated by various cytokines and hormones, produce N-formylkynurenine. This labile intermediate, the substrate of formamidase, is then rapidly converted to L-kynurenine ("kynurenine"), the pivotal metabolite of the KP, which is further degraded by either of three catabolic enzymes: (1) kynureninase, which forms anthranilic acid; (2) kynurenine 3-monooxygenase (KMO), which produces 3-hydroxykynurenine (3-HK); and (3) kynurenine aminotransferases (KATs), which synthesize KYNA. Of these three primary breakdown products of kynurenine, only 3-HK is situated in a major branch of the KP, successively yielding 3-hydroxyanthranilic acid via kynureninase and QUIN via 3-hydroxyanthranilic acid 3,4-dioxygenase, and eventually forming NAD$^+$.

Whereas, the biochemical characteristics of most individual KP enzymes are well-understood and their crystal structure has been elucidated in some cases (Amaral et al., 2013; Han, Robinson, & Li, 2008; Malik, Patterson, Ncube, & Toth, 2014; Meng et al., 2014; Phillips, 2014; Rafice, Chauhan, Efimov, Basran, & Raven, 2009; Rossi, Han, Li, Li, & Rizzi, 2004; Rossi et al., 2010), the complexity of the KP as a whole is staggering. Thus, as noted previously, three different enzymes are capable of catalyzing identical reactions at the beginning of the cascade, kynurenine can serve as a substrate of multiple KP enzymes, and several enzymes (kynureninase, KATs) recognize more than one KP metabolite as substrates. Translating isolated in vitro findings to a comprehensive in vivo scenario has therefore remained a challenging task, especially when considering the often dramatic changes seen under pathological conditions.

Although no major qualitative differences appear to exist between individual KP enzymes in peripheral organs and the brain, neurobiologists studying the KP face another major challenge because events in the periphery do not necessarily reflect or predict phenomena that occur in the central nervous system. The problem is at least two-pronged. First, only some KP metabolites, namely kynurenine and 3-HK, enter the brain readily from the circulation, whereas others, such as QUIN and KYNA (i.e., the most prominent neuroactive compounds) do not (Fukui, Schwarcz, Rapoport, Takada, & Smith, 1991). Under physiological conditions, cerebral IDO and TDO activity are very low, so that only very little kynurenine is produced locally from tryptophan. It follows that brain KP metabolism, including the neosynthesis of neuroactive kynurenines, is mainly driven by peripherally derived kynurenine and, possibly, 3-HK (Gál & Sherman, 1978; Reinhard, Erickson, & Flanagan, 1994; Swartz et al., 1990). Peripheral changes in KP metabolism downstream of kynurenine and 3-HK may therefore not be a good indicator of changes occurring in the brain.

Second, KP metabolism within the brain is segregated between various cell types. Notably, although neurons do have the ability to synthesize kynurenines (Guillemin et al., 2007), the local production of kynurenines in the mammalian brain takes place largely in nonneuronal cells. Of these, microglial cells, which lack KATs but contain all enzymes that are involved in the successive conversion of kynurenine to QUIN, are believed to normally account for the local neosynthesis of 3-HK, 3-hydroxyanthranilic acid, and QUIN. Moreover, microglia are responsible for the substantial upregulation of this major KP branch that is observed when the immune system is stimulated (Saito, Markey, & Heyes, 1992). KYNA synthesis, on the other hand, appears to occur almost exclusively in astrocytes, which lack KMO (Guillemin et al., 2001).

BRAIN KYNURENIC ACID SYNTHESIS: FOCUS ON ASTROCYTES AND KAT II

Competing with tryptophan and other neutral amino acids such as phenylalanine and leucine, blood-derived kynurenine enters the brain through the large neutral amino acid transporter (Fukui et al., 1991). Within the brain, kynurenine is then rapidly, and sodium-independently, taken up by astrocytes for further sequestration (Speciale, Hares, Schwarcz, & Brookes, 1989) and, though this has not been tested directly so far, is likely also actively transported into microglial cells. Moreover, kynurenine can enter neurons through a comparatively slow, sodium-dependent process (Speciale & Schwarcz, 1990). Intracellularly, kynurenine is then enzymatically degraded to KYNA, 3-HK, or anthranilic acid (Figure 1). Notably, in the mammalian brain the irreversible transamination of kynurenine to KYNA can be catalyzed by several enzymes. These enzymes were originally named for their ability to use glutamine, α-aminoadipate, and aspartate, respectively, as their primary substrate, but have been renamed KATs in the context of KP biology (Cooper, 2004; Guidetti, Hoffman, Melendez-Ferro, Albuquerque, & Schwarcz, 2007; Han, Cai, Tagle, Robinson, & Li, 2008; Okuno, Nakamura, & Schwarcz, 1991). Although the relative contributions of these KATs to cerebral KYNA biosynthesis have not been rigorously elaborated to date and may vary with physiological requirements and under pathological conditions, studies from our laboratories have provided evidence for a major role of KAT II. This was initially proposed theoretically on the basis that the enzyme's classic substrate, the lysine metabolite α-aminoadipate, is present in the brain at relatively low concentrations (Guidetti & Schwarcz, 2003), and that no competing endogenous substrate other than kynurenine had been described. In marked contrast, other KATs recognize and use far more abundant amino acids as their substrate and, in the case of KAT I and KAT III, have a pH optimum in the alkaline range (~9.0–9.5; Guidetti, Okuno, & Schwarcz, 1997; Han, Cai, et al., 2008). Direct support for a functionally significant role of KAT II in cerebral KYNA formation has come from mice with a targeted deletion of KAT II (Yu et al., 2004). These knockout mice display a variety of phenotypic and molecular alterations as a result of decreased KYNA formation in the brain, including increased α7nAChR function in the hippocampus (Alkondon et al., 2004), enhanced cognition (Potter et al., 2010), and increased vulnerability to QUIN-induced excitotoxicity (Sapko et al., 2006). These findings, together with the more recent advent and use of selective KAT II inhibitors, show that functional disinhibition occurs in the brain when KAT II activity is compromised.

KAT II, which is primarily expressed in astrocytes (Guidetti, Hoffman, et al., 2007), has a high K_m for kynurenine (Guidetti, Amori, Sapko, Okuno, & Schwarcz, 2007) (i.e., KYNA production increases linearly until the concentration of its bioprecursor, kynurenine, reaches millimolar concentrations). This is in line with other KATs but in marked contrast to other kynurenine-metabolizing enzymes, namely KMO and kynureninase (Figure 1), which have much lower K_m values (Bender & McCreanor, 1982) and are therefore much easier saturated when kynurenine concentrations rise. These biochemical considerations are of functional significance under conditions that favor brain influx of kynurenine, but appear to be less relevant when kynurenine synthesis from tryptophan is upregulated within microglia or in other brain cells that are involved in local neuroinflammatory phenomena (Heyes et al., 1996; Saito et al., 1993). Notably, the close apposition of KYNA-producing astrocytes to capillary walls and to pericytes of the blood–brain barrier places these glial cells in an excellent position to accumulate kynurenine from the circulation and to respond preferentially to fluctuations in peripheral kynurenine concentrations (Gál & Sherman, 1978; Gál et al., 1978; Owe-Young et al., 2008; Swartz et al., 1990).

Brain KYNA levels are reliably increased when circulating kynurenine concentrations are elevated, for example, by non-brain-penetrant KMO inhibitors. By attenuating degradation along the QUIN branch of the KP, systemic administration of these pharmacological agents cause the accumulation of blood kynurenine. This results in enhanced brain influx of kynurenine and, in turn, prompts astrocytes to produce more KYNA (see previous section). Interestingly, such a shift in KP metabolism is less evident in the early stages following an intracerebral injection of a selective KMO inhibitor, indicating a degree of functional, in addition to the anatomical, segregation of the two KP branches within the brain (Amori, Guidetti, Pellicciari, Kajii, & Schwarcz, 2009).

Mice with a targeted deletion of the Kmo gene have recently provided additional valuable information regarding the effects of selective KMO manipulation on KYNA (Giorgini et al., 2013). Extensive biochemical analysis of homozygous knockout mice confirmed the absence of KMO activity in both brain and peripheral organs, demonstrating that a single gene/enzyme accounts for the conversion of kynurenine to 3-HK. In these animals, 3-HK levels were dramatically reduced in all tissues, with the remaining amounts probably originating from food or bacterial sources. In line with the results obtained following the acute, systemic administration of selective KMO inhibitors (Carpenedo et al., 1994; Röver, Cesura, Huguenin, Kettler, & Szente, 1997; Speciale et al., 1996), mutant mice showed sustained elevations of KYNA levels. Importantly, the KYNA increase in the brain's extracellular compartment, assessed by in vivo microdialysis, was approximately five-fold compared with wild-type animals.

CAUSES AND EFFECTS OF KYNA FLUCTUATIONS IN THE BRAIN

Although critically relevant, increases or reductions in kynurenine levels are not the only mechanisms that determine the disposition of endogenous KYNA in the brain. Because catabolic enzymes for KYNA are not present in the mammalian brain (Turski & Schwarcz, 1988)—and in fact have only been observed to exist in prokaryotic organisms (Taniuchi & Hayaishi, 1963)—and because the metabolite is remarkably stable chemically speaking, no specific processes are available to degrade cerebral KYNA intracellularly or extracellularly under biological conditions. Thus, in the extracellular compartment, KYNA must compete with other acidic endogenous compounds for reuptake by organic anion transporters

(Uwai, Honjo, & Iwamoto, 2012) or for removal from the brain by a probenecid-sensitive process (Moroni et al., 1988). Of note, newly formed KYNA enters the extracellular milieu very rapidly (i.e., its release is not controlled by Ca^{2+} or other conventional mechanisms) (Turski, Gramsbergen, Traitler, & Schwarcz, 1989). To assure cerebral KYNA homeostasis in vivo as needed, several distinct mechanisms regulate the formation of endogenous KYNA from kynurenine. Although none of those mechanisms is believed to affect KYNA levels specifically, their ability to control KYNA neosynthesis may have significant ramifications for brain physiology and pathology.

Some of these regulatory processes are readily understood and have been verified in experimental paradigms ranging from cell-free preparations to in vivo protocols. This includes the ability of endogenous 2-oxoacids like pyruvate and 2-oxoglutarate, which act as cosubstrates/amino acceptors of the aminotransferase reaction, to stimulate KAT activity (Hodgkins & Schwarcz, 1998; Hodgkins, Wu, Zielke, & Schwarcz, 1999), and the ability of endogenous pro-oxidants (e.g., peroxynitrite and hydroxyl radicals) to promote the nonenzymatic conversion of kynurenine to KYNA (Lugo-Huitron et al., 2011; Blanco-Ayala et al., 2015). Moreover, by competing with kynurenine for transamination by KAT II, α-aminoadipate interferes readily with the production of KYNA, thus possibly linking lysine and tryptophan metabolism to KYNA function and dysfunction (Fukuwatari, Sekine, Higashiyama, Sano, & Shibata, 2013; Wu & Schwarcz, 1996). Notably, because of their simple and straightforward action, all these processes can operate in every tissue, even though they may have special consequences in the brain.

Other regulatory mechanisms are brain-specific, are only observed in intact tissue (i.e., in slice preparations or in vivo), and are less well-understood. For example, and apparently irrespective of the brain area, KYNA formation from kynurenine is greatly reduced under depolarizing conditions induced by veratridine or high concentrations of potassium (Turski et al., 1989; Wu et al., 1992). This effect is dependent on the presence of intact neurons because it is abolished when neurons are ablated experimentally (Gramsbergen et al., 1997; Wu et al., 1992). Interestingly, de novo synthesis of KYNA in the brain is also strongly influenced by cellular energy metabolism. Specifically, KYNA formation is substantially lower in the absence of glucose, perhaps because of the reduction in pyruvate formation (Gramsbergen et al., 1997; Turski et al., 1989), and this effect can be neutralized by lactate, which does not affect KYNA synthesis on its own (Hodgkins & Schwarcz, 1998). These and similar findings, including the substantial decline in extracellular KYNA levels following selective astrocytic poisoning with fluorocitrate (Wu, Rassoulpour, & Schwarcz, 2007), confirm that astrocytes play a central role in cerebral KYNA

production. At the same time, these studies highlight the complexity of KYNA neurobiology and, in particular, demonstrate that neuronal activity plays an active role in glial KYNA synthesis in the brain. Alone or together, impairments in any of these regulatory mechanisms may be responsible for the very rapid increases in extracellular KYNA, which occur in response to an excitotoxic insult (Wu et al., 1992) or seizure activity (Wu & Schwarcz, 1996). Moreover, they may underlie the slow dysregulation of cerebral KYNA levels, which is seen in several major human brain diseases and their animal models (see also the following section) (Schwarcz et al., 2012).

Fluctuations in brain KYNA levels have remarkable consequences on classic neurotransmitters, supporting the classification of the metabolite as an endogenous neuromodulator (Table 2). Thus, local perfusion of nanomolar concentrations of KYNA itself, or relatively modest stimulation of cerebral KYNA neosynthesis by kynurenine administration or systemic KMO inhibition, reliably result in substantial (30–50%) reductions in extracellular glutamate levels in several brain areas, including the striatum, the hippocampus, and the prefrontal cortex. Notably, although most of these studies were performed by in vivo microdialysis (Carpenedo et al., 2001; Pocivavsek et al., 2011; Rassoulpour, Wu, Ferré, & Schwarcz, 2005; Wu et al., 2010), the decrease in glutamate can also be readily detected using a glutamate-sensitive microelectrode array, which allows for a much higher temporal resolution of the effect (Konradsson-Geuken et al., 2010). Conversely, extracellular glutamate levels in the brain rise promptly when KYNA synthesis is compromised by the local application of a KAT II inhibitor. Attesting to the specificity of this phenomenon, the elevation in glutamate is not seen when minute amounts of KYNA are coadministered to offset the effect of KAT II inhibition (Konradsson-Geuken et al., 2010; Pocivavsek et al., 2011; Wu et al., 2010).

Experimental manipulations of brain KYNA not only influence glutamate but have qualitatively and quantitatively very similar effects on the extracellular levels of dopamine (Rassoulpour, Wu, Ferré, et al., 2005; Wu et al., 2007), gamma-aminobutyric acid (GABA) (Beggiato et al., 2013; Beggiato, Tanganelli, et al., 2014) and, as demonstrated by upregulation after KAT II inhibition, acetylcholine (Zmarowski et al., 2009). Although not as thoroughly investigated as the link between KYNA and glutamate, these effects similarly do not appear to be brain region-specific (see Figure 2 for an illustration of the inverse relationship of KYNA and dopamine in the rat prefrontal cortex). Moreover, they are clearly not limited to acute events since KYNA-deficient KAT II knockout mice show significant increases in extracellular dopamine levels in the striatum (Wu et al., 2007) and elevated extracellular glutamate levels in the hippocampus (Potter et al., 2010).

TABLE 2   Effects of KYNA Fluctuations on Extracellular Neurotransmitter Levels

	Neurotransmitter	Brain Area	References
Increased KYNA	↓ Glutamate	Caudate	Carpenedo et al. (2001)
		Striatum	Rassoulpour, Wu, Ferré, et al. (2005)
		PFC	Wu et al. (2010) and Konradsson-Geuken et al. (2010)
		Hippocampus	Pocivavsek et al. (2011) See Figure 3
	↓ GABA	Striatum	Beggiato et al. (2013)
		PFC	Beggiato, Tanganelli, et al. (2014)
	↓ Dopamine	Striatum	Rassoulpour, Wu, Ferré, et al. (2005)
		PFC	See Figure 2
Reduced KYNA	↑ Glutamate	PFC	Wu et al. (2010) and Konradsson-Geuken et al. (2010)
		Hippocampus	Pocivavsek et al. (2011)
		Striatum	Beggiato et al. (2013)
	↑ GABA	Striatum	Beggiato et al. (2013)
		PFC	Beggiato, Tanganelli, et al. (2014)
	↑ Dopamine	Striatum	Amori, Wu, et al. (2009)
		PFC	See Figure 2
	↑ Acetylcholine	PFC	Zmarowski et al. (2009)

GABA, gamma-aminobutyric acid; KYNA, kynurenic acid; PFC, prefrontal cortex.

The bidirectional actions of endogenous KYNA on classic neurotransmitter systems are likely initiated by α7nAChRs (Albuquerque & Schwarcz, 2013). Thus, KYNA-induced decreases in the extracellular levels of glutamate, GABA, and dopamine are readily prevented by low doses of galantamine, a drug that directly counteracts KYNA at an allosteric potentiating site of the receptor (Beggiato et al., 2013; Beggiato, Tanganelli, et al., 2014; Konradsson-Geuken et al., 2010; Lopes et al., 2007; Wu et al., 2010, 2007), or, shown in the case of dopamine, the α7nAChR agonist choline (Rassoulpour, Wu, Albuquerque, & Schwarcz, 2005). The involvement of α7nAChRs is also supported by the fact that the receptor antagonist methyllycaconitine duplicates, but is not additive with, the effects of KYNA (Carpenedo et al., 2001; Rassoulpour, Wu, Albuquerque, et al., 2005). In contrast, and arguing against the proposition that the effects of (fluctuations in) endogenous brain KYNA are mediated by NMDA receptors, the effects of KYNA on extracellular neurotransmitter levels are neither reproduced nor influenced by the potent and selective glycine$_B$ receptor antagonist 7-chloro-KYNA (Beggiato et al., 2013; Beggiato, Tanganelli, et al., 2014; Rassoulpour, Wu, Ferré, et al., 2005) and are not affected by co-perfusion with D-serine, a selective endogenous agonist of the glycine$_B$ site (Wu et al., 2007).

Interestingly, extracellular KYNA levels in the brain are in turn rapidly reduced by glutamate (Wu et al., 1992) and by various pharmacological agents that stimulate dopaminergic neurotransmission (Poeggeler, Rassoulpour, Guidetti, Wu, & Schwarcz, 1998; Rassoulpour, Wu, Poeggeler, & Schwarcz, 1998; Wu, Rassoulpour, & Schwarcz, 2002), and are also dysregulated by continuous nicotine administration (Rassoulpour, Wu, Albuquerque, et al., 2005). All these effects are in line with the presence of appropriate neurotransmitter receptors on astrocytes (Conti, DeBiasi, Minelli, & Melone, 1996; Duffy et al., 2011; Khan, Koulen, Rubinstein, Grandy, & Goldman-Rakic, 2001; Sharma & Vijayaraghavan, 2001) and highlight the functional complexity of the tripartite synapse (Perea, Navarrete, & Araque, 2009). Possible roles of these neurotransmitter effects on astrocytic KYNA formation, and especially possible implications for the pathophysiology of SZ and other brain diseases, have so far not been examined.

BEHAVIORAL EFFECTS OF MODERATE KYNA FLUCTUATIONS IN THE BRAIN

In adult rodents, nanomolar or low micromolar concentrations of KYNA itself, or stimulation of KYNA synthesis with kynurenine, causes a spectrum of cognitive deficits,

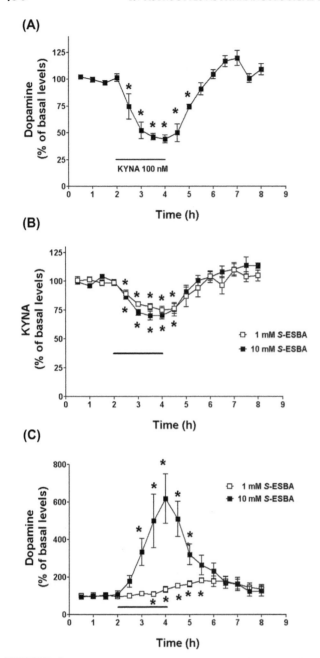

FIGURE 2   **Kynurenic acid (KYNA) reduces the extracellular concentration of dopamine in the rat prefrontal cortex.** (A) KYNA, applied for 2 h by reverse dialysis (bar), reversibly decreases dopamine levels (baseline: 1.3 nM). *$p < 0.05$ versus baseline value. The kynurenine aminotransferase II (KAT II) inhibitor, S-ESBA (1 or 10 mM), was applied for 2 h by reverse microdialysis (bar). (B, C) Extracellular levels of KYNA (baseline: 2.9 nM) and dopamine (baseline: 1.3 nM) were determined in the same microdialysate. Data are the mean ± standard error of the mean (SEM) (n = 4 per group). *$p < 0.05$ versus the respective baseline (two-way ANOVA with Bonferroni's posthoc test).

which are readily translatable to the human condition. Specifically, these relatively moderate elevations in cerebral KYNA levels result in disruptions in auditory sensory gating (Shepard, Joy, Clerkin, & Schwarcz, 2003) and prepulse inhibition (Erhardt, Schwieler, Emanuelsson, &

Geyer, 2004), and induce impairments in prefrontal-mediated cognitive flexibility (Alexander, Wu, Schwarcz, & Bruno, 2012; Hightower & Rodefer, 2011), hippocampus-mediated contextual learning and memory (Pocivavsek et al., 2011) (Figure 3), and working memory and contextual fear memory (Chess, Landers, & Bucci, 2009; Chess, Simoni, Alling, & Bucci, 2007; Vunck, Supe, Schwarcz, & Bruno, 2013) (see Table 3). Confirming the central role of α7nAChRs in KYNA function in the rat brain, several of these deficits are effectively neutralized by the administration of an α7nAChR agonist (Alexander et al., 2012; Phenis, Vunck, Schwarcz, & Bruno, 2014; Vunck et al., 2013). Moreover, again supporting a functional link between KYNA and cognitive processes, deficits in contextual memory and increased anxiety are seen in KMO knockout animals, which show a several-fold elevation in brain KYNA levels (Giorgini et al., 2013). These impairments may be causally related to a malfunction in dopaminergic neurotransmission (Schwieler et al., 2014).

Conversely, decreases in brain KYNA levels are associated with pro-cognitive effects. Thus, KAT II knockout mice display enhanced performance in a number of exemplary cognitive processes (Potter et al., 2010), and an acute reduction of brain KYNA significantly improves performance in a hippocampus-based cognitive task in rats (Pocivavsek et al., 2011) (see the following section for details). Taken together, these findings provide a strong rationale for considering KYNA as a possible etiological factor in the cognitive impairments seen in individuals with SZ and for inhibiting KYNA biosynthesis for therapeutic purposes.

KYNURENIC ACID AND COGNITIVE DEFICITS IN SCHIZOPHRENIA

Cognitive dysfunctions, including deficits in working memory, verbal and visual learning and memory, attention and vigilance, reasoning and problem-solving, processing speed, and social cognition, are a core domain of the psychopathology of SZ (Green et al., 2008; McKibbin, Brekke, Sires, Jeste, & Patterson, 2004; Nuechterlein et al., 2004). These deficits, which do not improve with antipsychotic treatment, are seen in the majority of patients and originate in early adolescence—preceding the onset of psychotic and negative symptoms in young adulthood or later in life (Gold, 2004; Heinrichs, 2005).

Studies in humans and animals have provided support for the hypothesis that an elevation in brain KYNA levels may be causally involved in cognitive impairments seen in SZ. We first articulated this idea more than two decades ago based on KYNA's ability to function as a preferential NMDA receptor antagonist (Ganong et al., 1983) and the emerging realization that NMDA receptor hypofunction plays a central role in several aspects of SZ pathology

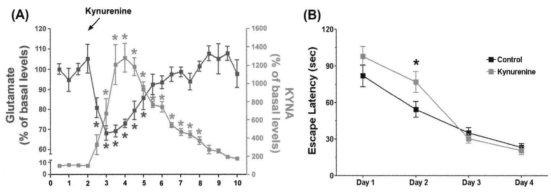

FIGURE 3   **Acute elevation of kynurenic acid (KYNA) by systemic injection of kynurenine reduces extracellular glutamate and impairs hippocampal-dependent learning in rats.** (A) Intraperitoneal (i.p.) injection of kynurenine (100 mg/kg) increases extracellular KYNA levels (baseline: 2.8 nM) and decreases extracellular glutamate (baseline: 2.0 μM) in the dorsal hippocampus. Data are the mean ± standard error of the mean (SEM) (n = 4, *$p < 0.05$ vs baseline, two-way ANOVA with Bonferroni's posthoc test). (B) Kynurenine (100 mg/kg; i.p.) was applied daily 90 min before testing in the Morris water maze. Data are the mean ± SEM (n = 12 per group, *$p < 0.05$ vs control, two-way repeated measures ANOVA with Bonferroni's posthoc test).

TABLE 3   Acute Stimulation of KYNA Synthesis: Behavioral Effects in Rats

Kynurenine Administration	Behavioral Task	Outcome	References
IP	Auditory sensory gating	Impairment	Shepard et al. (2003)
IP	Prepulse inhibition	Impairment	Erhardt et al. (2004)
IP	Spatial working memory	Impairment	Chess et al. (2007)
IP	Contextual fear conditioning	Impairment	Chess et al. (2007)
IP	Attentional set-shifting	Impairment	Hightower and Rodefer (2011)
ICV	Spatial learning and reference memory	Impairment	Pocivavsek et al. (2011)
IP	Spatial learning and reference memory	Impairment	See Figure 3
IP	Social behavior	No effect	Trecartin and Bucci (2011)
IP	Attentional set-shifting	Impairment	Alexander et al. (2012)
IP	Delayed nonmatch to position working memory	Impairment	Vunck et al. (2013) and Phenis et al. (2014)

ICV, intracerebroventricular administration; IP, intraperitoneal injection; KYNA, kynurenic acid.

(Coyle, 1996; Olney, Newcomer, & Farber, 1999; Schwarcz et al., 1992). The hypothetical link between KYNA and cognitive dysfunction in SZ was then reinforced by the discovery of KYNA's ability to noncompetitively inhibit α7nAChRs (Hilmas et al., 2001), which are critical for several cognitive processes (Levin, 2002) and believed to be impaired in SZ (Leonard et al., 1996; Sarter, Nelson, & Bruno, 2005).

Measurements in postmortem brain tissue and cerebrospinal fluid (CSF) consistently demonstrate significant increases in the levels of both KYNA and kynurenine in SZ, and these changes do not appear to affect 3-HK levels and are unrelated to prolonged treatment with antipsychotic drugs (Ceresoli-Borroni, Rassoulpour, Wu, Guidetti, & Schwarcz, 2006; Erhardt et al., 2001; Linderholm et al., 2012; Miller, Llenos, Dulay, & Weis, 2006; Nilsson et al., 2005; Sathyasaikumar et al., 2011; Schwarcz et al., 2001).

These elevations in both kynurenine and KYNA levels may result from enzymatic changes, in particular an increase in TDO and a reduction in KMO, which may jointly account for an increase in kynurenine production and a shift of KP metabolism toward enhanced KYNA formation (Figure 1). Gene expression studies (Miller et al., 2004, 2006; Sathyasaikumar et al., 2011; Wonodi et al., 2011) and, in the case of KMO, measurements of enzyme activity (Sathyasaikumar et al., 2011; Wonodi et al., 2011), have demonstrated qualitatively similar impairments of these enzymes in various regions of the cerebral cortex of persons with SZ. Notably, the tissue KYNA concentrations reached in these cases are in the high nanomolar range, sufficient to inhibit α7nAChRs and to subsequently impact glutamatergic, GABAergic, dopaminergic, and cholinergic systems, all of which have been implicated in the psychopathology of SZ (Carlsson & Carlsson, 1990; Carlsson, Carlsson, & Nilsson,

2004; Coyle et al., 2012; Gonzalez-Burgos & Lewis, 2012; Sarter et al., 2005).

In further support of the KYNA hypothesis, a single nucleotide polymorphism in the KMO gene has been identified in the brain of SZ patients (Aoyama et al., 2006). The same polymorphism (rs2275163) was subsequently linked to impairments in smooth pursuit eye movement and visuospatial working memory (Wonodi et al., 2011) and increased KYNA levels in CSF (Holtze et al., 2012). Although the connection between KMO single nucleotide polymorphisms and (a reduction in) KMO activity has not been verified so far, these studies suggest that the investigation of KP metabolism in SZ may be particularly informative using distinct subdomains of psychopathology (endophenotypes). A recent study demonstrating that SZ patients with distress intolerance show an especially pronounced stress-induced elevation in salivary KYNA levels support this general notion (Chiappelli et al., 2014).

Clinical studies (Borovcanin et al., 2012; Chittiprol et al., 2009; Nawa, Takahashi, & Patterson, 2000; Severance et al., 2012; Sirota, Schild, Elizur, Djaldetti, & Fishman, 1995), assessments of human postmortem brain tissue (Arion, Unger, Lewis, Levitt, & Mirnics, 2007; Busse et al., 2012; Saetre et al., 2007), genetic analyses and considerations (Michel, Schmidt, & Mirnics, 2012; Stefansson et al., 2009), and corresponding work in experimental animals (Behrens, Ali, & Dugan, 2008; Bergink, Gibney, & Drexhage, 2014) strongly indicate an etiologically significant connection between the immune system and various domains of SZ pathology, including cognitive impairments. As cytokines, including interferon-γ, interleukin-1β, and interleukin-6, stimulate several KP enzymes, most prominently IDO and KMO (Kiank et al., 2010; Saito, Markey, & Heyes, 1991; Widner, Ledochowski, & Fuchs, 2000), it is not surprising that KYNA and other kynurenines have been considered to be active participants in this process. Indeed, stress, viral, or microbial infections as well as direct cytokine administration cause increases in the formation of KP metabolites in the periphery, in the CSF, and in the brain, with larger effects in the QUIN branch of the pathway in many but not all cases (Chiarugi & Moroni, 1999; Heyes, Brew, et al., 1992; Heyes, Saito, et al., 1992; Laugeray et al., 2010; Miura, Shirokawa, Isobe, & Ozaki, 2009; Notarangelo et al., 2014; Pawlak, Takada, Urano, & Takada, 2000; Raison et al., 2010). Notably, infections in humans can result in long-lasting KYNA elevations in the CSF, as documented, for example, after tick-borne and herpes simplex virus type 1–induced encephalitis (Atlas et al., 2013; Holtze et al., 2012). However, evidence supporting the idea that immune activation *in adulthood* leads to stimulation of KP metabolism in SZ remains quite speculative (Bechter et al., 2010; Johansson et al., 2013; Schwieler et al., 2015).

The most compelling arguments favoring a role of immune-related KP impairments in SZ come from data in experimental animals that experience stress or other immune challenges early in life. This focus on immunological abnormalities in the immature brain, which is based on epidemiological and other studies in humans (Brown, 2011; Brown & Susser, 2002; Hornig & Lipkin, 2001; Rapoport, Giedd, & Gogtay, 2012; van Os & Selten, 1998; Volk & Lewis, 2013; Wright, Gill, & Murray, 1993), has led to a plethora of converging preclinical findings and the rather unambiguous conclusion that stress, bacterial, or viral infections in utero or during the early postnatal period cause structural changes as well as neurochemical and cognitive impairments in adulthood, which are reminiscent of those seen in SZ (see, e.g., Abazyan et al., 2010; Fatemi et al., 2002; Fortier, Luheshi, & Boksa, 2007; Markham & Koenig, 2011; McAllister, 2014; Meyer & Feldon, 2009; Piontkewitz, Arad, & Weiner, 2012; Shi, Fatemi, Sidwell, & Patterson, 2003). Notably, though these consequences of early immune abnormalities have been mostly described in mice and rats so far, they are also observed in nonhuman primates (Bauman et al., 2014; Willette et al., 2011).

Stress or infections affect KP metabolism and elevate brain KYNA levels not only in adulthood but also prenatally (Notarangelo & Schwarcz, 2014) and in the early postnatal period (Asp, Holtze, Powell, Karlsson, & Erhardt, 2010; Holtze, Asp, Schwieler, Engberg, & Karlsson, 2008; Zavitsanou et al., 2014). This made it possible to study the hypothetical connection between perinatal activation of the immune system, early stimulation of KP metabolism, and the emergence of SZ-like phenomena later in life directly by experimentally increasing KYNA levels in the immature rodent brain (Table 4). In one approach, pregnant rats were continuously fed KYNA's brain-penetrant bioprecursor kynurenine from embryonic day (ED) 15 to weaning (i.e., postnatal day 21). This protocol assures chronic elevation of brain KYNA levels during the entire treatment period. Upon termination of the treatment, all offspring were fed normal rodent chow until biochemical and behavioral testing in adulthood. As adults, animals exposed to high brain KYNA levels during early development show remarkable biochemical abnormalities reminiscent of SZ, namely increased extracellular KYNA and parallel reductions in extracellular glutamate levels in the prefrontal cortex and in the hippocampus. These biochemical changes may explain the pronounced deficits in hippocampal memory, learning and spatial memory, contextual memory, and executive function in these animals (Alexander et al., 2013; Pocivavsek, Wu, Elmer, Bruno, & Schwarcz, 2012). Follow-up studies revealed that an increase in fetal brain KYNA during the last week of gestation (ED–22) (i.e., at a time when ambient cerebral KYNA levels in the mammalian brain are already exceptionally high normally) (Beal et al., 1992; Cannazza et al.,

TABLE 4   Prolonged Systemic Kynurenine Administration: Behavioral Effects

Systemic Administration	Age of Manipulation	Testing	Behavioral Assessment	Outcome	Species	References
Laced food	ED15–22	PD56	Spatial learning and reference memory	Impairment	Rat	Pocivavsek, Thomas, et al. (2014)
			Passive avoidance contextual learning	Impairment		
Laced food	ED15–22	PD56	Attentional set-shifting	Impairment	Rat	Pershing et al. (2015)
Laced food	ED15–22	PD35	Trace fear conditioning	No effect	Rat	Pershing et al. (2014)
		PD56		Impairment		
Laced food	ED15–22	PD56	Delayed nonmatch to position working memory	Impairment	Rat	Vunck, Phenis, Tseng, Schwarcz, and Bruno (2014)
Laced food	ED15–PD21	PD56	Spatial learning and reference memory	Impairment	Rat	Pocivavsek et al. (2012)
			Passive avoidance contextual learning	Impairment		
Laced food	ED15–PD21	PD56	Attentional set-shifting	Impairment	Rat	Alexander et al. (2013)
IP	PD7–10	PD70	Social behavior	Impairment	Rat	Iaccarino et al. (2013)
IP	PD7–16	PD90	Amphetamine-induced locomotor activity	Impairment	Mouse	Liu et al. (2014)
IP	PD27–35	PD61	Social behavior	Impairment	Rat	Trecartin and Bucci (2011)
	PD61	PD84		No effect		
IP	PD27–35	PD61	Novel object recognition memory	Impairment	Rat	Akagbosu et al. (2012)
			Contextual fear memory	Impairment		
			Cue-specific fear memory	No effect		
IP	PD27–35	PD61	Motivational value by sign tracking	Increased	Rat	DeAngeli et al. (2015)
Laced food	PD42–49	PD85	Spatial learning and reference memory	No effect	Rat	Pocivavsek, Thomas, et al. (2014)
			Passive avoidance contextual learning	No effect		
IP	Adulthood	Adulthood	Prepulse inhibition	Impairment	Rat	Nilsson, Linderholm, and Erhardt (2006)
IP	Adulthood	Adulthood	Amphetamine-induced locomotor activity	Impairment	Mouse	Olsson, Larsson, and Erhardt (2012)

ED, embryonic day; IP, intraperitoneal injection; PD, postnatal day.

2001; Ceresoli-Borroni & Schwarcz, 2000), is sufficient to induce these biochemical and behavioral abnormalities in adulthood (Pershing et al., 2015; Pocivavsek, Thomas, et al., 2014). Interestingly, rats exposed to elevated KYNA during the final week of embryonic development also show a delayed decrease in the expression of α7nAChRs as well as reductions in dendritic spine density and subsensitivity to mesolimbic stimulation of glutamate release in the prefrontal cortex (Pershing et al., 2015).

KYNA levels in the fetal brain can also be elevated pharmacologically, using the systemic administration of the KMO inhibitor Ro 61-8048 (Röver et al., 1997) during the late gestational period. Applied three times (i.e., on ED 14, ED 16, and ED 18), this agent leads to long-lasting deficits in adult offspring, including a reduction in hippocampal long-term potentiation and structural changes in hippocampus and cortex (Forrest, Khalil, Pisar, Darlington, & Stone, 2013; Forrest, Khalil,

Pisar, McNair, et al., 2013; Khalil et al., 2014; Pisar et al., 2014). Jointly, these studies highlight the relevance of KP metabolism in fetal brain development and emphasize the importance of maintaining normal KP homeostasis in the maturing brain. The concept that hyperphysiological levels of KYNA in the fetal brain cause untoward consequences in adulthood is also indirectly supported by the recent demonstration that prenatal activation of α7nAChRs, possibly by counteracting the elevation in KYNA levels (Albuquerque & Schwarcz, 2013), effectively downregulates inflammatory responses in the fetal brain, and ameliorates the detrimental long-term effects of maternal infection (Wu et al., 2015). Further evaluation of the implications of all these findings for the pathophysiology of SZ, and the design of successful follow-up studies, will require detailed insights into the mechanisms, which normally control the presence, formation, and function of KYNA and other KP metabolites in the fetal brain. Unfortunately, these mechanisms are still only poorly understood.

KP manipulations during the early postnatal period or in adolescence also influence translationally relevant behavioral performances in adult animals. Thus, in mice, repeated systemic kynurenine injections on postnatal days 7–16 (Liu et al., 2014) or postnatal days 7–10 (Iaccarino, Suckow, Xie, & Bucci, 2013) enhance sensitivity to amphetamine-induced increases in locomotor activity and deficits in social behavior. In rats, intermittent exposure to kynurenine during adolescence causes impairments in two hippocampus-dependent cognitive processes (i.e., novel object recognition and contextual fear memory) as well as a deficit in social behavior, in adulthood (Akagbosu, Evans, Gulick, Suckow, & Bucci, 2012; Trecartin & Bucci, 2011). Moreover, kynurenine-treated rats show increased incentive salience of cues associated with reward, perhaps informing about the heightened sensitivity to drug-related cues seen in persons with SZ. Very interestingly, early exposure to kynurenine also prevents long-term potentiation after a burst of high-frequency stimulation that is sufficient to produce a robust effect in vehicle-treated rats (DeAngeli et al., 2014). Taken together, all these results reinforce the hypothesis that developmental events resulting in the increased presence and function of KYNA in the brain have significant construct validity for the study of cognitive deficits in persons with SZ.

PHARMACOLOGICAL APPROACHES TO REDUCE EXCESSIVE KYNA FUNCTION IN THE BRAIN

The idea that elevated KYNA concentrations are causally related to cognitive impairments in SZ immediately suggests possible clinical benefits of interventions that lower brain KYNA levels. Unfortunately, no degradative

enzymes or reuptake sites can be targeted to specifically promote the removal of excess KYNA from its effector site(s) in the brain, nor is it feasible to exploit the ability of depolarizing events or cellular energy deprivation to downregulate cerebral KYNA production (Gramsbergen et al., 1997; Turski et al., 1989). Efforts to reduce KYNA formation in the brain have therefore focused mostly on pharmacological KAT inhibition. Feasibility of this approach is demonstrated by the fact that the nonspecific aminotransferase inhibitor aminooxyacetic acid readily blocks cerebral KYNA neosynthesis in vivo (Speciale et al., 1990; Swartz et al., 1990). Because KAT II does not recognize abundant endogenous amino acids as competitors of its substrate kynurenine, this enzyme was soon regarded as the preferential target to effect KYNA synthesis inhibition in the brain (Schwarcz et al., 2012).

Development of (S)-4-(ethylsulphonyl)benzoylalanine (ESBA), the first selective KAT II inhibitor synthesized (Pellicciari et al., 2006), was delayed because other compounds with comparable inhibitory potency (Varasi et al., 1996) also attenuated KMO activity and therefore failed to lower KYNA levels in the rat brain in vivo (H.-Q. W and R.S., unpublished data; cf. Figure 1). However, ESBA rapidly reduces extracellular KYNA levels (Amori, Wu, et al., 2009; Pellicciari et al., 2006; Pocivavsek et al., 2011; Wu et al., 2010).

The use of ESBA, the structurally distinct inhibitor BFF-122 (Amori, Guidetti, et al., 2009) or the endogenous substrate α-aminoadipate (Wu, Ungerstedt, & Schwarcz, 1995), also revealed that KAT II preferentially controls a pool of KYNA that can be rapidly mobilized in the brain. Independent of brain region, this pool accounts for not more than 30–40% of extracellular KYNA levels in vivo. The relatively small reduction in KYNA caused by acute KAT II inhibition is sufficient, however, to increase the extracellular concentrations of glutamate (Pocivavsek et al., 2011; Wu et al., 2010), dopamine (Figure 2) (Amori, Wu, et al., 2009), and GABA (Beggiato et al., 2013; Beggiato, Tanganelli, et al., 2014) (i.e., the same neurotransmitters that are decreased when KYNA levels are moderately elevated). These studies, as well as the fact that selective KAT II inhibition results in an increase in extracellular acetylcholine levels in the medial prefrontal cortex (Zmarowski et al., 2009), establish that astrocyte-derived KYNA serves as a bidirectional neuromodulator in the rat brain.

A causal connection between a reduction in KYNA synthesis and cognitive enhancement was first demonstrated using KAT II knockout mice. These mutant animals exhibit significantly improved performance in three hippocampus-dependent behavioral paradigms, namely object exploration and recognition, passive avoidance, and spatial discrimination. Moreover, compared with wild-type controls, hippocampal slices from KAT II–deficient mice show an impressive increase in the amplitude of long-term potentiation in vitro (Potter et al., 2010).

A subsequent first proof-of-concept study in rats revealed that ESBA administration improves performance in the Morris water maze (Pocivavsek et al., 2011). Because of its inability to penetrate the blood–brain barrier to a significant extent, ESBA had to be applied intracerebroventricularly in this experiment, emphasizing the need to develop systemically active KAT II inhibitors. Two compounds with high specificity for KAT II are now available and have been successfully used in experimental animals. Both PF-04859989 (Dounay et al., 2012; IC_{50}: 263 nM), administered subcutaneously, and BFF-816 (Wu et al., 2014; IC_{50}: 14 µM), which is orally active, rapidly reduce extracellular KYNA levels in various regions of the rat brain. As anticipated from studies with focally applied KAT II inhibitors, oral BFF-816 at the same time increases both extracellular glutamate and dopamine. Remarkably, no tolerance is seen when animals are treated daily for five consecutive days (Wu et al., 2014). PF-04859989, too, boosts glutamatergic function, demonstrated by reversal of KYNA-induced attenuation of nicotine-evoked glutamatergic transients (Koshy Cherian et al., 2014), but unexpectedly does not affect extracellular dopamine levels (Kozak et al., 2014).

Behavioral tests have revealed remarkable pro-cognitive effects of both agents. Thus, in rodents, PF-04859989 prevents amphetamine- and ketamine-induced disruption of auditory gating as well as ketamine-induced disruption of performance in a working memory task and a spatial memory task, and improves performance in a sustained attention task (Kozak et al., 2014). Notably, the compound, which has especially high potency as an inhibitor of human KAT II (IC_{50}: 23 nM), also readily antagonizes ketamine-induced working memory deficits in nonhuman primates (Kozak et al., 2014). In excellent conceptual agreement, daily injections of BFF-816 significantly improve performance in spatial and reference memory in rats (Wu et al., 2014), and pretreatment with BFF-816 attenuates the contextual memory deficit exhibited in the offspring of kynurenine-treated dams (see the previous section; Pocivavsek, Wu, et al., 2014).

The use of α7nAChR agonists constitutes an alternative strategy to limit the actions of KYNA in the brain, and this approach has been validated to overcome KYNA-induced cognitive impairments in rats. Thus, the positive allosteric modulator galantamine effectively prevents KYNA-induced deficits in attentional set-shifting (Alexander et al., 2012) and working memory (Phenis et al., 2014), and the α7nAChR partial agonist SSR180711 restores conditioned freezing to control levels in the offspring of kynurenine-fed dams (Pershing et al., 2014).

Taken together, these results support the notion that KAT II inhibitors or pharmacological agents that attenuate the function of KYNA at its receptor(s), hold promise for cognitive enhancement in healthy people and especially for overcoming cognitive deficits in SZ and, possibly, other psychiatric disorders. In principle, because of KYNA's ability to effectively decrease the extracellular concentrations of several neurotransmitters known to play critical roles in cognitive processes, *any* pharmacological or other intervention that reduces the levels of KYNA or otherwise interferes with its function in the brain may show pro-cognitive effects. Antioxidants (Lugo-Huitron et al., 2011; Blanco-Ayala et al., 2015) and stimulants such as amphetamine (Rassoulpour et al., 1998) appear to constitute interesting leads in this context.

FUTURE PERSPECTIVES

In spite of the remarkable convergence of experimental data supporting a neuromodulatory role of KYNA in the mammalian brain, many fundamental issues of KYNA neurobiology continue to be unresolved. The understanding of the physiological function of KYNA in the brain may help to identify and reconcile the roles of the ever-expanding number of potential receptor targets (Stone et al., 2013, Table 1). These investigations are still in the very early phases, and it remains unknown if and under which conditions all these sites are directly affected by endogenous KYNA in vivo. Several unanswered questions also relate to physiological events upstream from KYNA. In other words, we need to focus on the mechanisms that normally link fluctuations in both peripheral and central KP metabolism to KYNA formation in the brain. Of critical importance in this regard would be, for example, a thorough examination of the possible functional relationship between the KP and the serotonin branch of tryptophan degradation. Other topics, such as the chronic effects of (changes in) dietary tryptophan or metabolic malfunction, possible sex differences, and circadian or seasonal phenomena, have so far not been investigated with regard to brain KYNA. Of more immediate significance, the recent emphasis on a possible role of KYNA in early brain development (see previously) and maturation (Thomases, Flores-Barrera, Bruno, Schwarcz, & Tseng, 2014) has highlighted the need to better understand the ontogenetic trajectory of the KP. Although relevant prior studies have been published in this area (Manuelpillai et al., 2005; Nicholls, Nitsos, Smythe, & Walker, 2001), the prenatal dynamics between mother, placenta, and fetus, in particular, are poorly understood (Beggiato, Sathyasaikumar, et al., 2014; Notarangelo & Schwarcz, 2014), yet must hold the key to the exceptionally high levels of KYNA in the fetal brain (Beal et al., 1992; Cannazza et al., 2001; Ceresoli-Borroni & Schwarcz, 2000; Pocivavsek, Thomas, et al., 2014). Complementary research with far-reaching implications should explore the possibility that tryptophan originating from the gut microbiome influences KYNA levels and function in the brain both pre- and postnatally. Because the production of tryptophan by microbiota is not enantioselective (Kolodkin-Gal et al., 2010; Lam et al., 2009; Yamada, Yoshida, Nakazawa, & Kumagai, 1975), these studies should include the assessment of D-tryptophan, which has recently been shown to raise brain KYNA levels in the rat following peripheral administration (Ishii, Iizuka, Ogaya, Song, & Fukushima, 2011; Notarangelo et al., 2013).

As reviewed here, the possible role of the KP, and KYNA in particular, in SZ has gained significant traction during the past decade. Because it appears that KP impairments in utero and/or later in life may be causally linked to cognitive and other abnormalities in persons with the disease, both genetic and environmental causes of cerebral KYNA malfunction will need to be examined longitudinally and in depth. These studies should include an evaluation of the involvement of KP metabolism and brain KYNA in "double-hit" phenomena, which are increasingly viewed to be etiologically significant in SZ (Bayer, Falkai, & Maier, 1999; Giovanoli et al., 2013).

In the clinical realm, it remains to be seen if measurements of KYNA and other KP metabolites in the serum or other peripheral compartments provide data that can be used as biomarkers for diagnostic and treatment purposes. In preparation of clinical applications, there is also a pressing need to develop new methodologies for specifically monitoring the effects of pharmacological KYNA manipulations in the *human* brain. Challenges include the distinct structure of human KAT II, which needs to be taken into consideration when attempting to tag the enzyme directly with a radiolabeled tracer (Pellicciari et al., 2008), and the multitude of potential receptor sites (see Table 1) for which no in vivo imaging techniques are available to verify target engagement of KYNA. Together with the availability of pharmacological agents that can predictably influence KYNA levels in the human brain, successful resolution of these methodological challenges will provide investigators with the tools that are necessary to test the KYNA hypothesis in persons with SZ and, it is hoped, help to attenuate the cognitive deficits that are associated with the disease.

Acknowledgments

Studies described in this review were in part supported by NIH grants P50MH103222 and RO1MH083729.

References

Abazyan, B., Nomura, J., Kannan, G., Ishizuka, K., Tamashiro, K. L., Nucifora, F., et al. (2010). Prenatal interaction of mutant DISC1 and immune activation produces adult psychopathology. *Biological Psychiatry, 68*(12), 1172–1181. http://dx.doi.org/10.1016/j.biopsych.2010.09.022.

Akagbosu, C. O., Evans, G. C., Gulick, D., Suckow, R. F., & Bucci, D. J. (2012). Exposure to kynurenic acid during adolescence produces memory deficits in adulthood. *Schizophrenia Bulletin, 38*(4), 769–778. http://dx.doi.org/10.1093/schbul/sbq151.

Albuquerque, E. X., & Schwarcz, R. (2013). Kynurenic acid as an antagonist of alpha7 nicotinic acetylcholine receptors in the brain: facts and challenges. *Biochemical Pharmacology, 85*(8), 1027–1032. http://dx.doi.org/10.1016/j.bcp.2012.12.014 pii:S0006-2952(12)00800-3.

Alexander, K. S., Pocivavsek, A., Wu, H.-Q., Pershing, M. L., Schwarcz, R., & Bruno, J. P. (2013). Early developmental elevations of brain kynurenic acid impair cognitive flexibility in adults: reversal with galantamine. *Neuroscience, 238,* 19–28. http://dx.doi.org/10.1016/j.neuroscience.2013.01.063.

Alexander, K. S., Wu, H.-Q., Schwarcz, R., & Bruno, J. P. (2012). Acute elevations of brain kynurenic acid impair cognitive flexibility: normalization by the alpha7 positive modulator galantamine. *Psychopharmacology, 220*(3), 627–637. http://dx.doi.org/10.1007/s00213-011-2539-2.

Alkondon, M., Pereira, E. F., Yu, P., Arruda, E. Z., Almeida, L. E., Guidetti, P., et al. (2004). Targeted deletion of the kynurenine aminotransferase ii gene reveals a critical role of endogenous kynurenic acid in the regulation of synaptic transmission via alpha7 nicotinic receptors in the hippocampus. *The Journal of Neuroscience, 24*(19), 4635–4648. http://dx.doi.org/10.1523/JNEUROSCI.5631-03.2004.

Amaral, M., Levy, C., Heyes, D. J., Lafite, P., Outeiro, T. F., Giorgini, F., et al. (2013). Structural basis of kynurenine 3-monooxygenase inhibition. *Nature, 496*(7445), 382–385. http://dx.doi.org/10.1038/nature12039.

Amori, L., Guidetti, P., Pellicciari, R., Kajii, Y., & Schwarcz, R. (2009). On the relationship between the two branches of the kynurenine pathway in the rat brain in vivo. *Journal of Neurochemistry, 109*(2), 316–325. http://dx.doi.org/10.1111/j.1471-4159.2009.05893.x.

Amori, L., Wu, H.-Q., Marinozzi, M., Pellicciari, R., Guidetti, P., & Schwarcz, R. (2009). Specific inhibition of kynurenate synthesis enhances extracellular dopamine levels in the rodent striatum. *Neuroscience, 159*(1), 196–203. http://dx.doi.org/10.1016/j.neuroscience.2008.11.055.

Anis, N. A., Berry, S. C., Burton, N. R., & Lodge, D. (1983). The dissociative anaesthetics, ketamine and phencyclidine, selectively reduce excitation of central mammalian neurones by N-methyl-aspartate. *British Journal of Pharmacology, 79*(2), 565–575.

Aoyama, N., Takahashi, N., Saito, S., Maeno, N., Ishihara, R., Ji, X., et al. (2006). Association study between kynurenine 3-monooxygenase gene and schizophrenia in the Japanese population. *Genes Brain and Behavior, 5*(4), 364–368. http://dx.doi.org/10.1111/j.1601-183X.2006.00231.x.

Arion, D., Unger, T., Lewis, D. A., Levitt, P., & Mirnics, K. (2007). Molecular evidence for increased expression of genes related to immune and chaperone function in the prefrontal cortex in schizophrenia. *Biological Psychiatry, 62*(7), 711–721. http://dx.doi.org/10.1016/j.biopsych.2006.12.021.

Asp, L., Holtze, M., Powell, S. B., Karlsson, H., & Erhardt, S. (2010). Neonatal infection with neurotropic influenza A virus induces the kynurenine pathway in early life and disrupts sensorimotor gating in adult Tap1$^{-/-}$ mice. *International Journal of Neuropsychopharmacology, 13*(4), 475–485. http://dx.doi.org/10.1017/S1461145709990253.

Atlas, A., Franzen-Rohl, E., Söderlund, J., Jonsson, E. G., Samuelsson, M., Schwieler, L., et al. (2013). Sustained elevation of kynurenic Acid in the cerebrospinal fluid of patients with herpes simplex virus type 1 encephalitis. *International Journal of Tryptophan Research, 6,* 89–96. http://dx.doi.org/10.4137/IJTR.S13256.

Bauman, M. D., Iosif, A. M., Smith, S. E., Bregere, C., Amaral, D. G., & Patterson, P. H. (2014). Activation of the maternal immune system during pregnancy alters behavioral development of rhesus monkey offspring. *Biological Psychiatry, 75*(4), 332–341. http://dx.doi.org/10.1016/j.biopsych.2013.06.025.

Bayer, T. A., Falkai, P., & Maier, W. (1999). Genetic and non-genetic vulnerability factors in schizophrenia: the basis of the "two hit hypothesis". *Journal of Psychiatric Research, 33*(6), 543–548.

Beal, M. F., Swartz, K. J., & Isacson, O. (1992). Developmental changes in brain kynurenic acid concentrations. *Developmental Brain Research, 68*(1), 136–139.

Bechter, K., Reiber, H., Herzog, S., Fuchs, D., Tumani, H., & Maxeiner, H. G. (2010). Cerebrospinal fluid analysis in affective and schizophrenic spectrum disorders: identification of subgroups with immune responses and blood-CSF barrier dysfunction. *Journal of Psychiatric Research*, 44(5), 321–330. http://dx.doi.org/10.1016/j.jpsychires.2009.08.008.

Beggiato, S., Antonelli, T., Tomasini, M. C., Tanganelli, S., Fuxe, K., Schwarcz, R., et al. (2013). Kynurenic acid, by targeting alpha7 nicotinic acetylcholine receptors, modulates extracellular GABA levels in the rat striatum in vivo. *European Journal of Neuroscience*, 37(9), 1470–1477. http://dx.doi.org/10.1111/ejn.12160.

Beggiato, S., Sathyasaikumar, K. V., Notarangelo, F. M., Giorgini, F., Muchowski, P. J., & Schwarcz, R. (2014). Prenatal kynurenine treatment in mice: effects on placental and fetal brain kynurenines. *Society for Neuroscience Abstract*, 39 51.05.

Beggiato, S., Tanganelli, S., Fuxe, K., Antonelli, T., Schwarcz, R., & Ferraro, L. (2014). Endogenous kynurenic acid regulates extracellular GABA levels in the rat prefrontal cortex. *Neuropharmacology*, 82, 11–18. http://dx.doi.org/10.1016/j.neuropharm.2014.02.019.

Behrens, M. M., Ali, S. S., & Dugan, L. L. (2008). Interleukin-6 mediates the increase in NADPH-oxidase in the ketamine model of schizophrenia. *The Journal of Neuroscience*, 28(51), 13957–13966. http://dx.doi.org/10.1523/JNEUROSCI.4457-08.2008.

Bender, D. A., & McCreanor, G. M. (1982). The preferred route of kynurenine metabolism in the rat. *Biochimica et Biophysica Acta*, 717(1), 56–60.

Bergeron, R., & Coyle, J. T. (2012). NAAG, NMDA receptor and psychosis. *Current Medicinal Chemistry*, 19(9), 1360–1364.

Bergersen, L. H., Morland, C., Ormel, L., Rinholm, J. E., Larsson, M., Wold, J. F., et al. (2012). Immunogold detection of L-glutamate and D-serine in small synaptic-like microvesicles in adult hippocampal astrocytes. *Cerebral Cortex*, 22(7), 1690–1697. http://dx.doi.org/10.1093/cercor/bhr254.

Bergink, V., Gibney, S. M., & Drexhage, H. A. (2014). Autoimmunity, inflammation, and psychosis: a search for peripheral markers. *Biological Psychiatry*, 75(4), 324–331. http://dx.doi.org/10.1016/j.biopsych.2013.09.037.

Berlinguer-Palmini, R., Masi, A., Narducci, R., Cavone, L., Maratea, D., Cozzi, A., et al. (2013). GPR35 activation reduces Ca^{2+} transients and contributes to the kynurenic acid-dependent reduction of synaptic activity at CA3-CA1 synapses. *PLoS One*, 8(11), e82180. http://dx.doi.org/10.1371/journal.pone.0082180.

Birch, P. J., Grossman, C. J., & Hayes, A. G. (1988). Kynurenic acid antagonises responses to NMDA via an action at the strychnine-insensitive glycine receptor. *European Journal of Pharmacology*, 154(1), 85–87.

Blanco Ayala, T., Lugo Huitron, R., Carmona Aparicio, L., Ramirez Ortega, D., Gonzalez Esquivel, D., Pedraza Chaverri, J., Perez de la Cruz, G., Rios, C., Schwarcz, R., & Perez de la Cruz, V., et al. (2015). Alternative kynurenic acid synthesis routes studied in the rat cerebellum. *Frontiers in Cell Neuroscience*, 9, 178. http://dx.doi.org/10.3389/fncel.2015.00178.

Borovcanin, M., Jovanovic, I., Radosavljevic, G., Djukic Dejanovic, S., Bankovic, D., Arsenijevic, N., et al. (2012). Elevated serum level of type-2 cytokine and low IL-17 in first episode psychosis and schizophrenia in relapse. *Journal of Psychiatric Research*, 46(11), 1421–1426. http://dx.doi.org/10.1016/j.jpsychires.2012.08.016.

Bouzier-Sore, A. K., & Pellerin, L. (2013). Unraveling the complex metabolic nature of astrocytes. *Frontiers in Cellular Neuroscience*, 7, 179. http://dx.doi.org/10.3389/fncel.2013.00179.

Brown, A. S. (2011). The environment and susceptibility to schizophrenia. *Progress in Neurobiology*, 93(1), 23–58. http://dx.doi.org/10.1016/j.pneurobio.2010.09.003.

Brown, A. S., & Susser, E. S. (2002). In utero infection and adult schizophrenia. *Mental Retardation and Developmental Disabilities Research Reviews*, 8(1), 51–57. http://dx.doi.org/10.1002/mrdd.10004.

Busse, S., Busse, M., Schiltz, K., Bielau, H., Gos, T., Brisch, R., et al. (2012). Different distribution patterns of lymphocytes and microglia in the hippocampus of patients with residual versus paranoid schizophrenia: further evidence for disease course-related immune alterations? *Brain Behavior and Immunity*, 26(8), 1273–1279. http://dx.doi.org/10.1016/j.bbi.2012.08.005.

Cannazza, G., Chiarugi, A., Parenti, C., Zanoli, P., & Baraldi, M. (2001). Changes in kynurenic, anthranilic, and quinolinic acid concentrations in rat brain tissue during development. *Neurochemical Research*, 26(5), 511–514.

Carlsson, M., & Carlsson, A. (1990). Schizophrenia: a subcortical neurotransmitter imbalance syndrome? *Schizophrenia Bulletin*, 16(3), 425–432.

Carlsson, M. L., Carlsson, A., & Nilsson, M. (2004). Schizophrenia: from dopamine to glutamate and back. *Current Medicinal Chemistry*, 11(3), 267–277.

Carpenedo, R., Chiarugi, A., Russi, P., Lombardi, G., Carlà, V., Pellicciari, R., et al. (1994). Inhibitors of kynurenine hydroxylase and kynureninase increase cerebral formation of kynurenate and have sedative and anticonvulsant activities. *Neuroscience*, 61(2), 237–243.

Carpenedo, R., Pittaluga, A., Cozzi, A., Attucci, S., Galli, A., Raiteri, M., et al. (2001). Presynaptic kynurenate-sensitive receptors inhibit glutamate release. *European Journal of Neuroscience*, 13(11), 2141–2147.

Ceresoli-Borroni, G., Rassoulpour, A., Wu, H.-Q., Guidetti, P., & Schwarcz, R. (2006). Chronic neuroleptic treatment reduces endogenous kynurenic acid levels in rat brain. *Journal of Neural Transmission*, 113(10), 1355–1365. http://dx.doi.org/10.1007/s00702-005-0432-z.

Ceresoli-Borroni, G., & Schwarcz, R. (2000). Perinatal kynurenine pathway metabolism in the normal and asphyctic rat brain. *Amino Acids*, 19(1), 311–323.

Chess, A. C., Landers, A. M., & Bucci, D. J. (2009). L-kynurenine treatment alters contextual fear conditioning and context discrimination but not cue-specific fear conditioning. *Behavioural Brain Research*, 201(2), 325–331. http://dx.doi.org/10.1016/j.bbr.2009.03.013.

Chess, A. C., Simoni, M. K., Alling, T. E., & Bucci, D. J. (2007). Elevations of endogenous kynurenic acid produce spatial working memory deficits. *Schizophrenia Bulletin*, 33(3), 797–804. http://dx.doi.org/10.1093/schbul/sbl033.

Chiappelli, J., Pocivavsek, A., Nugent, K. L., Notarangelo, F. M., Kochunov, P., Rowland, L. M., et al. (2014). Stress-induced increase in kynurenic acid as a potential biomarker for patients with schizophrenia and distress intolerance. *JAMA Psychiatry*, 71(7), 761–768. http://dx.doi.org/10.1001/jamapsychiatry.2014.243.

Chiarugi, A., & Moroni, F. (1999). Quinolinic acid formation in immune-activated mice: studies with (m-nitrobenzoyl)-alanine (mNBA) and 3,4-dimethoxy-[-N-4-(-3-nitrophenyl)thiazol-2yl]-benzenesul fonamide (Ro 61-8048), two potent and selective inhibitors of kynurenine hydroxylase. *Neuropharmacology*, 38(8), 1225–1233.

Chittiprol, S., Venkatasubramanian, G., Neelakantachar, N., Allha, N., Shetty, K. T., & Gangadhar, B. N. (2009). Beta2-microglobulin abnormalities in antipsychotic-naive schizophrenia: evidence for immune pathogenesis. *Brain Behavior and Immunity*, 23(2), 189–192. http://dx.doi.org/10.1016/j.bbi.2008.08.007.

Clarke, L. E., & Barres, B. A. (2013). Emerging roles of astrocytes in neural circuit development. *Nature Reviews Neuroscience*, 14(5), 311–321. http://dx.doi.org/10.1038/nrn3484.

Conti, F., DeBiasi, S., Minelli, A., & Melone, M. (1996). Expression of NR1 and NR2A/B subunits of the NMDA receptor in cortical astrocytes. *Glia*, 17(3), 254–258. http://dx.doi.org/10.1002/(SICI)1098-1136(199607)17 3<254::AID-GLIA7>3.0.CO;2-0.

Cooper, A. J. (2004). The role of glutamine transaminase K (GTK) in sulfur and alpha-keto acid metabolism in the brain, and in the possible bioactivation of neurotoxicants. *Neurochemistry International*, 44(8), 557–577. http://dx.doi.org/10.1016/j.neuint.2003.12.002.

Coyle, J. T. (1996). The glutamatergic dysfunction hypothesis for schizophrenia. *Harvard Review of Psychiatry, 3*(5), 241–253.

Coyle, J. T. (2012). NMDA receptor and schizophrenia: a brief history. *Schizophrenia Bulletin, 38*(5), 920–926. http://dx.doi.org/10.1093/schbul/sbs076.

Coyle, J. T., Basu, A., Benneyworth, M., Balu, D., & Konopaske, G. (2012). Glutamatergic synaptic dysregulation in schizophrenia: therapeutic implications. *Handbook of Experimental Pharmacology, 213*, 267–295. http://dx.doi.org/10.1007/978-3-642-25758-2_10.

DeAngeli, N. E., Todd, T. P., Chang, S. E., Yeh, H. H., Yeh, P. W., & Bucci, D. J. (2014). Exposure to kynurenic acid during adolescence increases sign-tracking and impairs long-term potentiation in adulthood. *Frontiers in Behavioral Neuroscience, 8*, 451. http://dx.doi.org/10.3389/fnbeh.2014.00451.

DiNatale, B. C., Murray, I. A., Schroeder, J. C., Flaveny, C. A., Lahoti, T. S., Laurenzana, E. M., et al. (2010). Kynurenic acid is a potent endogenous aryl hydrocarbon receptor ligand that synergistically induces interleukin-6 in the presence of inflammatory signaling. *Toxicological Sciences, 115*(1), 89–97. http://dx.doi.org/10.1093/toxsci/kfq024.

Dounay, A. B., Anderson, M., Bechle, B. M., Campbell, B. M., Claffey, M. M., Evdokimov, A., et al. (2012). Discovery of brain-penetrant, irreversible kynurenine aminotransferase II inhibitors for schizophrenia. *ACS Medicinal Chemistry Letters, 3*(3), 187–192. http://dx.doi.org/10.1021/ml200204m.

Duffy, A. M., Fitzgerald, M. L., Chan, J., Robinson, D. C., Milner, T. A., Mackie, K., et al. (2011). Acetylcholine alpha7 nicotinic and dopamine D2 receptors are targeted to many of the same postsynaptic dendrites and astrocytes in the rodent prefrontal cortex. *Synapse, 65*(12), 1350–1367. http://dx.doi.org/10.1002/syn.20977.

Erhardt, S., Blennow, K., Nordin, C., Skogh, E., Lindstrom, L. H., & Engberg, G. (2001). Kynurenic acid levels are elevated in the cerebrospinal fluid of patients with schizophrenia. *Neuroscience Letters, 313*(1–2), 96–98.

Erhardt, S., Schwieler, L., Emanuelsson, C., & Geyer, M. (2004). Endogenous kynurenic acid disrupts prepulse inhibition. *Biological Psychiatry, 56*(4), 255–260. http://dx.doi.org/10.1016/j.biopsych.2004.06.006.

Fatemi, S. H., Earle, J., Kanodia, R., Kist, D., Emamian, E. S., Patterson, P. H., et al. (2002). Prenatal viral infection leads to pyramidal cell atrophy and macrocephaly in adulthood: implications for genesis of autism and schizophrenia. *Cellular and Molecular Neurobiology, 22*(1), 25–33.

Forrest, C. M., Khalil, O. S., Pisar, M., Darlington, L. G., & Stone, T. W. (2013). Prenatal inhibition of the tryptophan-kynurenine pathway alters synaptic plasticity and protein expression in the rat hippocampus. *Brain Research, 1504*, 1–15. http://dx.doi.org/10.1016/j.brainres.2013.01.031.

Forrest, C. M., Khalil, O. S., Pisar, M., McNair, K., Kornisiuk, E., Snitcofsky, M., et al. (2013). Changes in synaptic transmission and protein expression in the brains of adult offspring after prenatal inhibition of the kynurenine pathway. *Neuroscience, 254*, 241–259. http://dx.doi.org/10.1016/j.neuroscience.2013.09.034.

Fortier, M. E., Luheshi, G. N., & Boksa, P. (2007). Effects of prenatal infection on prepulse inhibition in the rat depend on the nature of the infectious agent and the stage of pregnancy. *Behavioural Brain Research, 181*(2), 270–277. http://dx.doi.org/10.1016/j.bbr.2007.04.016.

Foster, A. C., Vezzani, A., French, E. D., & Schwarcz, R. (1984). Kynurenic acid blocks neurotoxicity and seizures induced in rats by the related brain metabolite quinolinic acid. *Neuroscience Letters, 48*(3), 273–278.

Fukui, S., Schwarcz, R., Rapoport, S. I., Takada, Y., & Smith, Q. R. (1991). Blood–brain barrier transport of kynurenines: implications for brain synthesis and metabolism. *Journal of Neurochemistry, 56*(6), 2007–2017.

Fukuwatari, T., Sekine, A., Higashiyama, S., Sano, M., & Shibata, K. (2013). High leucine and lysine diet shows additive effects on suppression of kynurenic acid production in rat brain. *Society for Neuroscience Abstract, 38* 152.16.

Gál, E. M., & Sherman, A. D. (1978). Synthesis and metabolism of L-kynurenine in rat brain. *Journal of Neurochemistry, 30*(3), 607–613.

Gál, E. M., Young, R. B., & Sherman, A. D. (1978). Tryptophan loading: consequent effects on the synthesis of kynurenine and 5-hydroxyindoles in rat brain. *Journal of Neurochemistry, 31*(1), 237–244.

Ganong, A. H., Lanthorn, T. H., & Cotman, C. W. (1983). Kynurenic acid inhibits synaptic and acidic amino acid-induced responses in the rat hippocampus and spinal cord. *Brain Research, 273*(1), 170–174.

Gehl, L. M., Saab, O. H., Bzdega, T., Wroblewska, B., & Neale, J. H. (2004). Biosynthesis of NAAG by an enzyme-mediated process in rat central nervous system neurons and glia. *Journal of Neurochemistry, 90*(4), 989–997. http://dx.doi.org/10.1111/j.1471-4159.2004.02578.x.

Giorgini, F., Huang, S. Y., Sathyasaikumar, K. V., Notarangelo, F. M., Thomas, M. A., Tararina, M., et al. (2013). Targeted deletion of kynurenine 3-monooxygenase in mice: a new tool for studying kynurenine pathway metabolism in periphery and brain. *Journal of Biological Chemistry, 288*(51), 36554–36566. http://dx.doi.org/10.1074/jbc.M113.503813.

Giovanoli, S., Engler, H., Engler, A., Richetto, J., Voget, M., Willi, R., et al. (2013). Stress in puberty unmasks latent neuropathological consequences of prenatal immune activation in mice. *Science, 339*(6123), 1095–1099. http://dx.doi.org/10.1126/science.1228261.

Gold, J. M. (2004). Cognitive deficits as treatment targets in schizophrenia. *Schizophrenia Research, 72*(1), 21–28. http://dx.doi.org/10.1016/j.schres.2004.09.008.

Gonzalez-Burgos, G., & Lewis, D. A. (2012). NMDA receptor hypofunction, parvalbumin-positive neurons, and cortical gamma oscillations in schizophrenia. *Schizophrenia Bulletin, 38*(5), 950–957. http://dx.doi.org/10.1093/schbul/sbs010.

Gramsbergen, J. B., Hodgkins, P. S., Rassoulpour, A., Turski, W. A., Guidetti, P., & Schwarcz, R. (1997). Brain-specific modulation of kynurenic acid synthesis in the rat. *Journal of Neurochemistry, 69*(1), 290–298.

Green, A. R., & Curzon, G. (1970). The effect of tryptophan metabolites on brain 5-hydroxytryptamine metabolism. *Biochemical Pharmacology, 19*(6), 2061–2068.

Green, M. F., Nuechterlein, K. H., Kern, R. S., Baade, L. E., Fenton, W. S., Gold, J. M., et al. (2008). Functional co-primary measures for clinical trials in schizophrenia: results from the MATRICS psychometric and standardization study. *American Journal of Psychiatry, 165*(2), 221–228. http://dx.doi.org/10.1176/appi.ajp.2007.07010089.

Guidetti, P., Amori, L., Sapko, M. T., Okuno, E., & Schwarcz, R. (2007). Mitochondrial aspartate aminotransferase: a third kynurenate-producing enzyme in the mammalian brain. *Journal of Neurochemistry, 102*(1), 103–111. http://dx.doi.org/10.1111/j.1471-4159.2007.04556.x.

Guidetti, P., Hoffman, G. E., Melendez-Ferro, M., Albuquerque, E. X., & Schwarcz, R. (2007). Astrocytic localization of kynurenine aminotransferase II in the rat brain visualized by immunocytochemistry. *Glia, 55*(1), 78–92. http://dx.doi.org/10.1002/glia.20432.

Guidetti, P., Okuno, E., & Schwarcz, R. (1997). Characterization of rat brain kynurenine aminotransferases I and II. *Journal of Neuroscience Research, 50*(3), 457–465.

Guidetti, P., & Schwarcz, R. (2003). Determination of alpha-aminoadipic acid in brain, peripheral tissues, and body fluids using GC/MS with negative chemical ionization. *Molecular Brain Research, 118*(1–2), 132–139.

Guillemin, G. J., Cullen, K. M., Lim, C. K., Smythe, G. A., Garner, B., Kapoor, V., et al. (2007). Characterization of the kynurenine pathway in human neurons. *The Journal of Neuroscience, 27*(47), 12884–12892. http://dx.doi.org/10.1523/JNEUROSCI.4101-07.2007.

Guillemin, G. J., Kerr, S. J., Smythe, G. A., Smith, D. G., Kapoor, V., Armati, P. J., et al. (2001). Kynurenine pathway metabolism in human astrocytes: a paradox for neuronal protection. *Journal of Neurochemistry, 78*(4), 842–853.

Han, Q., Cai, T., Tagle, D. A., Robinson, H., & Li, J. (2008). Substrate specificity and structure of human aminoadipate aminotransferase/kynurenine aminotransferase II. *Bioscience Reports, 28*(4), 205–215. http://dx.doi.org/10.1042/BSR20080085.

Han, Q., Robinson, H., & Li, J. (2008). Crystal structure of human kynurenine aminotransferase II. *Journal of Biological Chemistry, 283*(6), 3567–3573. http://dx.doi.org/10.1074/jbc.M708358200.

Heinrichs, R. W. (2005). The primacy of cognition in schizophrenia. *American Psychologist, 60*(3), 229–242. http://dx.doi.org/10.1037/0003-066X.60.3.229.

Heyes, M. P., Achim, C. L., Wiley, C. A., Major, E. O., Saito, K., & Markey, S. P. (1996). Human microglia convert l-tryptophan into the neurotoxin quinolinic acid. *Biochemical Journal, 320*(Pt 2), 595–597.

Heyes, M. P., Brew, B. J., Saito, K., Quearry, B. J., Price, R. W., Lee, K., et al. (1992). Inter-relationships between quinolinic acid, neuroactive kynurenines, neopterin and beta 2-microglobulin in cerebrospinal fluid and serum of HIV-1-infected patients. *Journal of Neuroimmunology, 40*(1), 71–80.

Heyes, M. P., Saito, K., Crowley, J. S., Davis, L. E., Demitrack, M. A., Der, M., et al. (1992). Quinolinic acid and kynurenine pathway metabolism in inflammatory and non-inflammatory neurological disease. *Brain, 115*(Pt 5), 1249–1273.

Hightower, B. G., & Rodefer, J. S. (2011). Investigation of kynurenic acid as a possible biomarker for cognitive impairment associated with schizophrenia. *Society for Neuroscience Abstract, 36* 163.19.

Hilmas, C., Pereira, E. F., Alkondon, M., Rassoulpour, A., Schwarcz, R., & Albuquerque, E. X. (2001). The brain metabolite kynurenic acid inhibits alpha7 nicotinic receptor activity and increases non-alpha7 nicotinic receptor expression: physiopathological implications. *The Journal of Neuroscience, 21*(19), 7463–7473.

Hodgkins, P. S., & Schwarcz, R. (1998). Interference with cellular energy metabolism reduces kynurenic acid formation in rat brain slices: reversal by lactate and pyruvate. *European Journal of Neuroscience, 10*(6), 1986–1994.

Hodgkins, P. S., Wu, H.-Q., Zielke, H. R., & Schwarcz, R. (1999). 2-Oxoacids regulate kynurenic acid production in the rat brain: studies in vitro and in vivo. *Journal of Neurochemistry, 72*(2), 643–651.

Holtze, M., Asp, L., Schwieler, L., Engberg, G., & Karlsson, H. (2008). Induction of the kynurenine pathway by neurotropic influenza A virus infection. *Journal of Neuroscience Research, 86*(16), 3674–3683. http://dx.doi.org/10.1002/jnr.21799.

Holtze, M., Saetre, P., Engberg, G., Schwieler, L., Werge, T., Andreassen, O. A., et al. (2012). Kynurenine 3-monooxygenase polymorphisms: relevance for kynurenic acid synthesis in patients with schizophrenia and healthy controls. *Journal of Psychiatry and Neuroscience, 37*(1), 53–57. http://dx.doi.org/10.1503/jpn.100175.

Hornig, M., & Lipkin, W. I. (2001). Infectious and immune factors in the pathogenesis of neurodevelopmental disorders: epidemiology, hypotheses, and animal models. *Mental Retardation and Developmental Disabilities Research Reviews, 7*(3), 200–210. http://dx.doi.org/10.1002/mrdd.1028.

Iaccarino, H. F., Suckow, R. F., Xie, S., & Bucci, D. J. (2013). The effect of transient increases in kynurenic acid and quinolinic acid levels early in life on behavior in adulthood: Implications for schizophrenia. *Schizophrenia Research, 150*(2–3), 392–397. http://dx.doi.org/10.1016/j.schres.2013.09.004.

Ishii, K., Iizuka, H., Ogaya, T., Song, Z., & Fukushima, T. (2011). Comparative study on kynurenic acid production in the rat striatum by tryptophan enantiomers: an in vivo microdialysis study. *Chirality, 23*(Suppl. 1), E12–E15. http://dx.doi.org/10.1002/chir.20938.

Javitt, D. C., & Zukin, S. R. (1991). Recent advances in the phencyclidine model of schizophrenia. *American Journal of Psychiatry, 148*(10), 1301–1308.

Johansson, A. S., Owe-Larsson, B., Asp, L., Kocki, T., Adler, M., Hetta, J., et al. (2013). Activation of kynurenine pathway in ex vivo fibroblasts from patients with bipolar disorder or schizophrenia: cytokine challenge increases production of 3-hydroxykynurenine. *Journal of Psychiatric Research, 47*(11), 1815–1823. http://dx.doi.org/10.1016/j.jpsychires.2013.08.008.

Joseph, M. H. (1978). Determination of kynurenine by a simple gas-liquid chromatographic method applicable to urine, plasma, brain and cerebrospinal fluid. *Journal of Chromatography, 146*(1), 33–41.

Katsel, P., Byne, W., Roussos, P., Tan, W., Siever, L., & Haroutunian, V. (2011). Astrocyte and glutamate markers in the superficial, deep, and white matter layers of the anterior cingulate gyrus in schizophrenia. *Neuropsychopharmacology, 36*(6), 1171–1177. http://dx.doi.org/10.1038/npp.2010.252.

Kessler, M., Terramani, T., Lynch, G., & Baudry, M. (1989). A glycine site associated with N-methyl-D-aspartic acid receptors: characterization and identification of a new class of antagonists. *Journal of Neurochemistry, 52*(4), 1319–1328.

Khalil, O. S., Pisar, M., Forrest, C. M., Vincenten, M. C., Darlington, L. G., & Stone, T. W. (2014). Prenatal inhibition of the kynurenine pathway leads to structural changes in the hippocampus of adult rat offspring. *European Journal of Neuroscience, 39*(10), 1558–1571. http://dx.doi.org/10.1111/ejn.12535.

Khan, Z. U., Koulen, P., Rubinstein, M., Grandy, D. K., & Goldman-Rakic, P. S. (2001). An astroglia-linked dopamine D2-receptor action in prefrontal cortex. *Proceedings of the National Academy of Sciences of the United States of America, 98*(4), 1964–1969. http://dx.doi.org/10.1073/pnas.98.4.1964.

Kiank, C., Zeden, J. P., Drude, S., Domanska, G., Fusch, G., Otten, W., et al. (2010). Psychological stress-induced, IDO1-dependent tryptophan catabolism: implications on immunosuppression in mice and humans. *PLoS One, 5*(7), e11825. http://dx.doi.org/10.1371/journal.pone.0011825.

Kolodkin-Gal, I., Romero, D., Cao, S., Clardy, J., Kolter, R., & Losick, R. (2010). D-amino acids trigger biofilm disassembly. *Science, 328*(5978), 627–629. http://dx.doi.org/10.1126/science.1188628.

Konradsson-Geuken, A., Wu, H.-Q., Gash, C. R., Alexander, K. S., Campbell, A., Sozeri, Y., et al. (2010). Cortical kynurenic acid bi-directionally modulates prefrontal glutamate levels as assessed by microdialysis and rapid electrochemistry. *Neuroscience, 169*(4), 1848–1859. http://dx.doi.org/10.1016/j.neuroscience.2010.05.052.

Koshy Cherian, A., Gritton, H., Johnson, D. E., Young, D., Kozak, R., & Sarter, M. (2014). A systemically-available kynurenine aminotransferase II (KAT II) inhibitor restores nicotine-evoked glutamatergic activity in the cortex of rats. *Neuropharmacology, 82*, 41–48. http://dx.doi.org/10.1016/j.neuropharm.2014.03.004.

Kozak, R., Campbell, B. M., Strick, C. A., Horner, W., Hoffmann, W. E., Kiss, T., et al. (2014). Reduction of brain kynurenic acid improves cognitive function. *The Journal of Neuroscience, 34*(32), 10592–10602. http://dx.doi.org/10.1523/JNEUROSCI.1107-14.2014.

Krystal, J. H., Karper, L. P., Seibyl, J. P., Freeman, G. K., Delaney, R., Bremner, J. D., et al. (1994). Subanesthetic effects of the noncompetitive NMDA antagonist, ketamine, in humans. Psychotomimetic, perceptual, cognitive, and neuroendocrine responses. *Archives of General Psychiatry, 51*(3), 199–214.

Lahti, A. C., Koffel, B., LaPorte, D., & Tamminga, C. A. (1995). Subanesthetic doses of ketamine stimulate psychosis in schizophrenia. *Neuropsychopharmacology, 13*(1), 9–19. http://dx.doi.org/10.1016/0893-133X(94)00131-I.

Lam, H., Oh, D. C., Cava, F., Takacs, C. N., Clardy, J., de Pedro, M. A., et al. (2009). D-amino acids govern stationary phase cell wall remodeling in bacteria. *Science, 325*(5947), 1552–1555. http://dx.doi.org/10.1126/science.1178123.

Lapin, I. P. (1978). Stimulant and convulsive effects of kynurenines injected into brain ventricles in mice. *Journal of Neural Transmission, 42*(1), 37–43.

Laugeray, A., Launay, J. M., Callebert, J., Surget, A., Belzung, C., & Barone, P. R. (2010). Peripheral and cerebral metabolic abnormalities of the tryptophan-kynurenine pathway in a murine model of major depression. *Behavioural Brain Research*, 210(1), 84–91. http://dx.doi.org/10.1016/j.bbr.2010.02.014.

Leklem, J. E. (1971). Quantitative aspects of tryptophan metabolism in humans and other species: a review. *American Journal of Clinical Nutrition*, 24(6), 659–672.

Leonard, S., Adams, C., Breese, C. R., Adler, L. E., Bickford, P., Byerley, W., et al. (1996). Nicotinic receptor function in schizophrenia. *Schizophrenia Bulletin*, 22(3), 431–445.

Levin, E. D. (2002). Nicotinic receptor subtypes and cognitive function. *Journal of Neurobiology*, 53(4), 633–640. http://dx.doi.org/10.1002/neu.10151.

Linderholm, K. R., Skogh, E., Olsson, S. K., Dahl, M. L., Holtze, M., Engberg, G., et al. (2012). Increased levels of kynurenine and kynurenic acid in the CSF of patients with schizophrenia. *Schizophrenia Bulletin*, 38(3), 426–432. http://dx.doi.org/10.1093/schbul/sbq086.

Liu, X. C., Holtze, M., Powell, S. B., Terrando, N., Larsson, M. K., Persson, A., et al. (2014). Behavioral disturbances in adult mice following neonatal virus infection or kynurenine treatment–role of brain kynurenic acid. *Brain Behavior and Immunity*, 36, 80–89. http://dx.doi.org/10.1016/j.bbi.2013.10.010.

Lopes, C., Pereira, E. F., Wu, H.-Q., Purushottamachar, P., Njar, V., Schwarcz, R., et al. (2007). Competitive antagonism between the nicotinic allosteric potentiating ligand galantamine and kynurenic acid at alpha7* nicotinic receptors. *Journal of Pharmacology and Experimental Therapeutics*, 322(1), 48–58. http://dx.doi.org/10.1124/jpet.107.123109.

Luby, E. D., Cohen, B. D., Rosenbaum, G., Gottlieb, J. S., & Kelley, R. (1959). Study of a new schizophrenomimetic drug; sernyl. *AMA Archives of Neurology and Psychiatry*, 81(3), 363–369.

Luccini, E., Musante, V., Neri, E., Raiteri, M., & Pittaluga, A. (2007). N-methyl-D-aspartate autoreceptors respond to low and high agonist concentrations by facilitating, respectively, exocytosis and carrier-mediated release of glutamate in rat hippocampus. *Journal of Neuroscience Research*, 85(16), 3657–3665. http://dx.doi.org/10.1002/jnr.21446.

Lugo-Huitron, R., Blanco-Ayala, T., Ugalde-Muniz, P., Carrillo-Mora, P., Pedraza-Chaverri, J., Silva-Adaya, D., et al. (2011). On the antioxidant properties of kynurenic acid: free radical scavenging activity and inhibition of oxidative stress. *Neurotoxicology and Teratology*, 33(5), 538–547. http://dx.doi.org/10.1016/j.ntt.2011.07.002.

Malik, S. S., Patterson, D. N., Ncube, Z., & Toth, E. A. (2014). The crystal structure of human quinolinic acid phosphoribosyltransferase in complex with its inhibitor phthalic acid. *Proteins*, 82(3), 405–414. http://dx.doi.org/10.1002/prot.24406.

Manuelpillai, U., Ligam, P., Smythe, G., Wallace, E. M., Hirst, J., & Walker, D. W. (2005). Identification of kynurenine pathway enzyme mRNAs and metabolites in human placenta: up-regulation by inflammatory stimuli and with clinical infection. *American Journal of Obstetrics and Gynecology*, 192(1), 280–288. http://dx.doi.org/10.1016/j.ajog.2004.06.090.

Markham, J. A., & Koenig, J. I. (2011). Prenatal stress: role in psychotic and depressive diseases. *Psychopharmacology (Berl)*, 214(1), 89–106. http://dx.doi.org/10.1007/s00213-010-2035-0.

Martineau, M., Shi, T., Puyal, J., Knolhoff, A. M., Dulong, J., Gasnier, B., et al. (2013). Storage and uptake of D-serine into astrocytic synaptic-like vesicles specify gliotransmission. *The Journal of Neuroscience*, 33(8), 3413–3423. http://dx.doi.org/10.1523/JNEUROSCI.3497-12.2013.

Matute, C., Melone, M., Vallejo-Illarramendi, A., & Conti, F. (2005). Increased expression of the astrocytic glutamate transporter GLT-1 in the prefrontal cortex of schizophrenics. *Glia*, 49(3), 451–455. http://dx.doi.org/10.1002/glia.20119.

McAllister, A. K. (2014). Major histocompatibility complex I in brain development and schizophrenia. *Biological Psychiatry*, 75(4), 262–268. http://dx.doi.org/10.1016/j.biopsych.2013.10.003.

McKibbin, C. L., Brekke, J. S., Sires, D., Jeste, D. V., & Patterson, T. L. (2004). Direct assessment of functional abilities: relevance to persons with schizophrenia. *Schizophrenia Research*, 72(1), 53–67. http://dx.doi.org/10.1016/j.schres.2004.09.011.

Meng, B., Wu, D., Gu, J., Ouyang, S., Ding, W., & Liu, Z. J. (2014). Structural and functional analyses of human tryptophan 2,3-dioxygenase. *Proteins*, 82(11), 3210–3216. http://dx.doi.org/10.1002/prot.24653.

Meyer, U., & Feldon, J. (2009). Prenatal exposure to infection: a primary mechanism for abnormal dopaminergic development in schizophrenia. *Psychopharmacology*, 206(4), 587–602. http://dx.doi.org/10.1007/s00213-009-1504-9.

Michel, M., Schmidt, M. J., & Mirnics, K. (2012). Immune system gene dysregulation in autism and schizophrenia. *Developmental Neurobiology*, 72(10), 1277–1287. http://dx.doi.org/10.1002/dneu.22044.

Miller, C. L., Llenos, I. C., Dulay, J. R., Barillo, M. M., Yolken, R. H., & Weis, S. (2004). Expression of the kynurenine pathway enzyme tryptophan 2,3-dioxygenase is increased in the frontal cortex of individuals with schizophrenia. *Neurobiology of Disease*, 15(3), 618–629. http://dx.doi.org/10.1016/j.nbd.2003.12.015.

Miller, C. L., Llenos, I. C., Dulay, J. R., & Weis, S. (2006). Upregulation of the initiating step of the kynurenine pathway in postmortem anterior cingulate cortex from individuals with schizophrenia and bipolar disorder. *Brain Research*, 1073–1074, 25–37. http://dx.doi.org/10.1016/j.brainres.2005.12.056.

Miura, H., Shirokawa, T., Isobe, K., & Ozaki, N. (2009). Shifting the balance of brain tryptophan metabolism elicited by isolation housing and systemic administration of lipopolysaccharide in mice. *Stress*, 12(3), 206–214. http://dx.doi.org/10.1080/10253890802252442.

Moroni, F., Russi, P., Lombardi, G., Beni, M., & Carlà, V. (1988). Presence of kynurenic acid in the mammalian brain. *Journal of Neurochemistry*, 51(1), 177–180.

Nawa, H., Takahashi, M., & Patterson, P. H. (2000). Cytokine and growth factor involvement in schizophrenia–support for the developmental model. *Molecular Psychiatry*, 5(6), 594–603.

Nicholls, T., Nitsos, I., Smythe, G., & Walker, D. W. (2001). Kynurenine production and catabolism in fetal sheep with embolized or nonembolized placentas. *American Journal of Obstetrics and Gynecology*, 185(4), 988–995. http://dx.doi.org/10.1067/mob.2001.117969.

Nilsson, L. K., Linderholm, K. R., Engberg, G., Paulson, L., Blennow, K., Lindstrom, L. H., et al. (2005). Elevated levels of kynurenic acid in the cerebrospinal fluid of male patients with schizophrenia. *Schizophrenia Research*, 80(2–3), 315–322. http://dx.doi.org/10.1016/j.schres.2005.07.013.

Nilsson, L. K., Linderholm, K. R., & Erhardt, S. (2006). Subchronic treatment with kynurenine and probenecid: effects on prepulse inhibition and firing of midbrain dopamine neurons. *Journal of Neural Transmission*, 113(5), 557–571. http://dx.doi.org/10.1007/s00702-005-0343-z.

Notarangelo, F. M., & Schwarcz, R. (2014). Restraint stress during pregnancy raises kynurenic acid levels in placenta and fetal brain. *Society for Neuroscience Abstract*, 39 348.16.

Notarangelo, F. M., Wang, X.-D., Horning, K. J., & Schwarcz, R. (2013). Role of D-amino acid oxidase in the production of kynurenine pathway metabolites from D-tryptophan in mice. Society for Neuroscience-Abstracts, 38, 344.307.

Notarangelo, F. M., Wilson, E. H., Horning, K. J., Thomas, M. A., Harris, T. H., Fang, Q., et al. (2014). Evaluation of kynurenine pathway metabolism in Toxoplasma gondii-infected mice: implications for schizophrenia. *Schizophrenia Research*, 152(1), 261–267. http://dx.doi.org/10.1016/j.schres.2013.11.011.

Nuechterlein, K. H., Barch, D. M., Gold, J. M., Goldberg, T. E., Green, M. F., & Heaton, R. K. (2004). Identification of separable cognitive factors in schizophrenia. *Schizophrenia Research*, 72(1), 29–39. http://dx.doi.org/10.1016/j.schres.2004.09.007.

Okuno, E., Nakamura, M., & Schwarcz, R. (1991). Two kynurenine aminotransferases in human brain. *Brain Research*, 542(2), 307–312.

Olney, J. W., Newcomer, J. W., & Farber, N. B. (1999). NMDA receptor hypofunction model of schizophrenia. *Journal of Psychiatric Research, 33*(6), 523–533.

Olsson, S. K., Larsson, M. K., & Erhardt, S. (2012). Subchronic elevation of brain kynurenic acid augments amphetamine-induced locomotor response in mice. *Journal of Neural Transmission, 119*(2), 155–163. http://dx.doi.org/10.1007/s00702-011-0706-6.

van Os, J., & Selten, J. P. (1998). Prenatal exposure to maternal stress and subsequent schizophrenia. The May 1940 invasion of The Netherlands. *British Journal of Psychiatry, 172,* 324–326.

Owe-Young, R., Webster, N. L., Mukhtar, M., Pomerantz, R. J., Smythe, G., Walker, D., et al. (2008). Kynurenine pathway metabolism in human blood-brain-barrier cells: implications for immune tolerance and neurotoxicity. *Journal of Neurochemistry, 105*(4), 1346–1357. http://dx.doi.org/10.1111/j.1471-4159.2008.05241.x.

Pawlak, D., Takada, Y., Urano, T., & Takada, A. (2000). Serotonergic and kynurenic pathways in rats exposed to foot shock. *Brain Research Bulletin, 52*(3), 197–205.

Pellicciari, R., Rizzo, R. C., Costantino, G., Marinozzi, M., Amori, L., Guidetti, P., et al. (2006). Modulators of the kynurenine pathway of tryptophan metabolism: synthesis and preliminary biological evaluation of (S)-4-(ethylsulfonyl)benzoylalanine, a potent and selective kynurenine aminotransferase II (KAT II) inhibitor. *ChemMedChem, 1*(5), 528–531. http://dx.doi.org/10.1002/cmdc.200500095.

Pellicciari, R., Venturoni, F., Bellocchi, D., Carotti, A., Marinozzi, M., Macchiarulo, A., et al. (2008). Sequence variants in kynurenine aminotransferase II (KAT II) orthologs determine different potencies of the inhibitor S-ESBA. *ChemMedChem, 3*(8), 1199–1202. http://dx.doi.org/10.1002/cmdc.200800109.

Perea, G., Navarrete, M., & Araque, A. (2009). Tripartite synapses: astrocytes process and control synaptic information. *Trends in Neuroscience, 32*(8), 421–431. http://dx.doi.org/10.1016/j.tins.2009.05.001.

Perkins, M. N., & Stone, T. W. (1982). An iontophoretic investigation of the actions of convulsant kynurenines and their interaction with the endogenous excitant quinolinic acid. *Brain Research, 247*(1), 184–187.

Pershing, M. L., Bortz, D. M., Pocivavsek, A., Fredericks, P. J., Jorgensen, C. V., Vunck, S. A., et al. (2015). Elevated levels of kynurenic acid during gestation produce neurochemical, morphological, and cognitive deficits in adulthood: implications for schizophrenia. *Neuropharmacology, 90,* 33–41. http://dx.doi.org/10.1016/j.neuropharm.2014.10.017.

Pershing, M. L., Lindquist, D. H., Pocivavsek, A., Tseng, K. Y., Schwarcz, R., & Bruno, J. P. (2014). Prenatal kynurenine exposure alters maturation of the conditioned fear response: normalization with an alpha7nAChR partial agonist. *Society for Neuroscience Abstract, 36* 51.09.

Phenis, D., Vunck, S. A., Schwarcz, R., & Bruno, J. P. (2014). Acute elevations of brain kynurenic acid induce working memory deficits: relative contributions of alpha7 nicotinic and NMDA receptor activity. *Society for Neuroscience Abstract, 39* 51.10.

Phillips, R. S. (2014). Structure and mechanism of kynureninase. *Archives of Biochemistry and Biophysics, 544,* 69–74. http://dx.doi.org/10.1016/j.abb.2013.10.020.

Piontkewitz, Y., Arad, M., & Weiner, I. (2012). Tracing the development of psychosis and its prevention: what can be learned from animal models. *Neuropharmacology, 62*(3), 1273–1289. http://dx.doi.org/10.1016/j.neuropharm.2011.04.019.

Pisar, M., Forrest, C. M., Khalil, O. S., McNair, K., Vincenten, M. C., Qasem, S., et al. (2014). Modified neocortical and cerebellar protein expression and morphology in adult rats following prenatal inhibition of the kynurenine pathway. *Brain Research, 1576,* 1–17. http://dx.doi.org/10.1016/j.brainres.2014.06.016.

Pocivavsek, A., Thomas, M. A., Elmer, G. I., Bruno, J. P., & Schwarcz, R. (2014). Continuous kynurenine administration during the prenatal period, but not during adolescence, causes learning and memory deficits in adult rats. *Psychopharmacology, 231*(14), 2799–2809. http://dx.doi.org/10.1007/s00213-014-3452-2.

Pocivavsek, A., Wu, H.-Q., Okuyama, M., Kajii, Y., Elmer, G. I., Bruno, J. P., et al. (2014). The systemically active kynurenine aminotransferase II inhibitor BFF816 attenuates contextual memory deficit induced by chronic prenatal kynurenine elevation in rats. *Society for Neuroscience Abstract, 39,* 707.07.

Pocivavsek, A., Wu, H.-Q., Elmer, G. I., Bruno, J. P., & Schwarcz, R. (2012). Pre- and postnatal exposure to kynurenine causes cognitive deficits in adulthood. *European Journal of Neuroscience, 35*(10), 1605–1612. http://dx.doi.org/10.1111/j.1460-9568.2012.08064.x.

Pocivavsek, A., Wu, H.-Q., Potter, M. C., Elmer, G. I., Pellicciari, R., & Schwarcz, R. (2011). Fluctuations in endogenous kynurenic acid control hippocampal glutamate and memory. *Neuropsychopharmacology, 36*(11), 2357–2367. http://dx.doi.org/10.1038/npp.2011.127.

Poeggeler, B., Rassoulpour, A., Guidetti, P., Wu, H.-Q., & Schwarcz, R. (1998). Dopaminergic control of kynurenate levels and N-methyl-D-aspartate toxicity in the developing rat striatum. *Developmental Neuroscience, 20*(2–3), 146–153.

Poels, E. M., Kegeles, L. S., Kantrowitz, J. T., Slifstein, M., Javitt, D. C., Lieberman, J. A., et al. (2014). Imaging glutamate in schizophrenia: review of findings and implications for drug discovery. *Molecular Psychiatry, 19*(1), 20–29. http://dx.doi.org/10.1038/mp.2013.136.

Potter, M. C., Elmer, G. I., Bergeron, R., Albuquerque, E. X., Guidetti, P., Wu, H.-Q., et al. (2010). Reduction of endogenous kynurenic acid formation enhances extracellular glutamate, hippocampal plasticity, and cognitive behavior. *Neuropsychopharmacology, 35*(8), 1734–1742. http://dx.doi.org/10.1038/npp.2010.39.

Prescott, C., Weeks, A. M., Staley, K. J., & Partin, K. M. (2006). Kynurenic acid has a dual action on AMPA receptor responses. *Neuroscience Letters, 402*(1–2), 108–112. http://dx.doi.org/10.1016/j.neulet.2006.03.051.

Rafice, S. A., Chauhan, N., Efimov, I., Basran, J., & Raven, E. L. (2009). Oxidation of L-tryptophan in biology: a comparison between tryptophan 2,3-dioxygenase and indoleamine 2,3-dioxygenase. *Biochemical Society Transactions, 37*(Pt 2), 408–412. http://dx.doi.org/10.1042/BST0370408.

Raison, C. L., Dantzer, R., Kelley, K. W., Lawson, M. A., Woolwine, B. J., Vogt, G., et al. (2010). CSF concentrations of brain tryptophan and kynurenines during immune stimulation with IFN-alpha: relationship to CNS immune responses and depression. *Molecular Psychiatry, 15*(4), 393–403. http://dx.doi.org/10.1038/mp.2009.116.

Rapoport, J. L., Giedd, J. N., & Gogtay, N. (2012). Neurodevelopmental model of schizophrenia: update 2012. *Molecular Psychiatry, 17*(12), 1228–1238. http://dx.doi.org/10.1038/mp.2012.23.

Rassoulpour, A., Wu, H.-Q., Albuquerque, E. X., & Schwarcz, R. (2005). Prolonged nicotine administration results in biphasic, brain-specific changes in kynurenate levels in the rat. *Neuropsychopharmacology, 30*(4), 697–704. http://dx.doi.org/10.1038/sj.npp.1300583.

Rassoulpour, A., Wu, H.-Q., Ferré, S., & Schwarcz, R. (2005). Nanomolar concentrations of kynurenic acid reduce extracellular dopamine levels in the striatum. *Journal of Neurochemistry, 93*(3), 762–765. http://dx.doi.org/10.1111/j.1471-4159.2005.03134.x.

Rassoulpour, A., Wu, H.-Q., Poeggeler, B., & Schwarcz, R. (1998). Systemic D-amphetamine administration causes a reduction of kynurenic acid levels in rat brain. *Brain Research, 802*(1–2), 111–118.

Reinhard, J. F., Jr., Erickson, J. B., & Flanagan, E. M. (1994). Quinolinic acid in neurological disease: opportunities for novel drug discovery. *Advances in Pharmacology, 30,* 85–127.

Rossi, F., Han, Q., Li, J., Li, J., & Rizzi, M. (2004). Crystal structure of human kynurenine aminotransferase I. *Journal of Biological Chemistry, 279*(48), 50214–50220. http://dx.doi.org/10.1074/jbc.M409291200.

Rossi, F., Valentina, C., Garavaglia, S., Sathyasaikumar, K. V., Schwarcz, R., Kojima, S., et al. (2010). Crystal structure-based selective targeting of the pyridoxal 5′-phosphate dependent enzyme kynurenine aminotransferase II for cognitive enhancement. *Journal of Medicinal Chemistry, 53*(15), 5684–5689. http://dx.doi.org/10.1021/jm100464k.

Röver, S., Cesura, A. M., Huguenin, P., Kettler, R., & Szente, A. (1997). Synthesis and biochemical evaluation of N-(4-phenylthiazol-2-yl) benzenesulfonamides as high-affinity inhibitors of kynurenine 3-hydroxylase. *Journal of Medicinal Chemistry*, 40(26), 4378–4385. http://dx.doi.org/10.1021/jm970467t.

Saetre, P., Emilsson, L., Axelsson, E., Kreuger, J., Lindholm, E., & Jazin, E. (2007). Inflammation-related genes up-regulated in schizophrenia brains. *BMC Psychiatry*, 7, 46. http://dx.doi.org/10.1186/1471-244X-7-46.

Saito, K., Markey, S. P., & Heyes, M. P. (1991). Chronic effects of gamma-interferon on quinolinic acid and indoleamine-2,3-dioxygenase in brain of C57BL6 mice. *Brain Research*, 546(1), 151–154.

Saito, K., Markey, S. P., & Heyes, M. P. (1992). Effects of immune activation on quinolinic acid and neuroactive kynurenines in the mouse. *Neuroscience*, 51(1), 25–39.

Saito, K., Nowak, T. S., Jr., Suyama, K., Quearry, B. J., Saito, M., Crowley, J. S., et al. (1993). Kynurenine pathway enzymes in brain: responses to ischemic brain injury versus systemic immune activation. *Journal of Neurochemistry*, 61(6), 2061–2070.

Sapko, M. T., Guidetti, P., Yu, P., Tagle, D. A., Pellicciari, R., & Schwarcz, R. (2006). Endogenous kynurenate controls the vulnerability of striatal neurons to quinolinate: Implications for Huntington's disease. *Experimental Neurology*, 197(1), 31–40. http://dx.doi.org/10.1016/j.expneurol.2005.07.004.

Sarter, M., Nelson, C. L., & Bruno, J. P. (2005). Cortical cholinergic transmission and cortical information processing in schizophrenia. *Schizophrenia Bulletin*, 31(1), 117–138. http://dx.doi.org/10.1093/schbul/sbi006.

Sathyasaikumar, K. V., Stachowski, E. K., Wonodi, I., Roberts, R. C., Rassoulpour, A., McMahon, R. P., et al. (2011). Impaired kynurenine pathway metabolism in the prefrontal cortex of individuals with schizophrenia. *Schizophrenia Bulletin*, 37(6), 1147–1156. http://dx.doi.org/10.1093/schbul/sbq112.

Schousboe, A., Bak, L. K., & Waagepetersen, H. S. (2013). Astrocytic control of biosynthesis and turnover of the neurotransmitters glutamate and GABA. *Frontiers in Endocrinology (Lausanne)*, 4, 102. http://dx.doi.org/10.3389/fendo.2013.00102.

Schwarcz, R., Bruno, J. P., Muchowski, P. J., & Wu, H.-Q. (2012). Kynurenines in the mammalian brain: when physiology meets pathology. *Nature Reviews Neuroscience*, 13(7), 465–477. http://dx.doi.org/10.1038/nrn3257.

Schwarcz, R., Du, F., Schmidt, W., Turski, W. A., Gramsbergen, J. B., Okuno, E., et al. (1992). Kynurenic acid: a potential pathogen in brain disorders. *Annals of the New York Academy of Sciences*, 648, 140–153.

Schwarcz, R., Foster, A. C., French, E. D., Whetsell, W. O., Jr., & Köhler, C. (1984). Excitotoxic models for neurodegenerative disorders. *Life Sciences*, 35(1), 19–32.

Schwarcz, R., Rassoulpour, A., Wu, H.-Q., Medoff, D., Tamminga, C. A., & Roberts, R. C. (2001). Increased cortical kynurenate content in schizophrenia. *Biological Psychiatry*, 50(7), 521–530.

Schwieler, L., Larsson, M. K., Skogh, E., Kegel, M. E., Orhan, F., Abdelmoaty, S., et al. (2015). Increased levels of IL-6 in the cerebrospinal fluid of patients with chronic schizophrenia - significance for activation of the kynurenine pathway. *Journal of Psychiatry and Neuroscience*, 40(2), 126–133.

Schwieler, L., Pocivavsek, A., Liu, X., Giorgini, F., Muchowski, P. J., Engberg, G., et al. (2014). Behavioral and electrophysiological abnormalities in mice deficient in kynurenine 3-monooxygenase: relevance to schizophrenia. *Society for Neuroscience Abstract*, 39 51.18.

Severance, E. G., Alaedini, A., Yang, S., Halling, M., Gressitt, K. L., Stallings, C. R., et al. (2012). Gastrointestinal inflammation and associated immune activation in schizophrenia. *Schizophrenia Research*, 138(1), 48–53. http://dx.doi.org/10.1016/j.schres.2012.02.025.

Sharma, G., & Vijayaraghavan, S. (2001). Nicotinic cholinergic signaling in hippocampal astrocytes involves calcium-induced calcium release from intracellular stores. *Proceedings of the National Academy of Sciences of the United States of America*, 98(7), 4148–4153. http://dx.doi.org/10.1073/pnas.071540198.

Shepard, P. D., Joy, B., Clerkin, L., & Schwarcz, R. (2003). Micromolar brain levels of kynurenic acid are associated with a disruption of auditory sensory gating in the rat. *Neuropsychopharmacology*, 28(8), 1454–1462. http://dx.doi.org/10.1038/sj.npp.1300188.

Shi, L., Fatemi, S. H., Sidwell, R. W., & Patterson, P. H. (2003). Maternal influenza infection causes marked behavioral and pharmacological changes in the offspring. *The Journal of Neuroscience*, 23(1), 297–302.

Sirota, P., Schild, K., Elizur, A., Djaldetti, M., & Fishman, P. (1995). Increased interleukin-1 and interleukin-3 like activity in schizophrenic patients. *Progress in Neuropsychopharmacology and Biological Psychiatry*, 19(1), 75–83.

Sofroniew, M. V., & Vinters, H. V. (2010). Astrocytes: biology and pathology. *Acta Neuropathologica*, 119(1), 7–35. http://dx.doi.org/10.1007/s00401-009-0619-8.

Speciale, C., Hares, K., Schwarcz, R., & Brookes, N. (1989). High-affinity uptake of L-kynurenine by a Na+-independent transporter of neutral amino acids in astrocytes. *The Journal of Neuroscience*, 9(6), 2066–2072.

Speciale, C., & Schwarcz, R. (1990). Uptake of kynurenine into rat brain slices. *Journal of Neurochemistry*, 54(1), 156–163.

Speciale, C., Wu, H.-Q., Cini, M., Marconi, M., Varasi, M., & Schwarcz, R. (1996). (R,S)-3,4-dichlorobenzoylalanine (FCE 28833A) causes a large and persistent increase in brain kynurenic acid levels in rats. *European Journal of Pharmacology*, 315(3), 263–267.

Speciale, C., Wu, H.-Q., Gramsbergen, J. B., Turski, W. A., Ungerstedt, U., & Schwarcz, R. (1990). Determination of extracellular kynurenic acid in the striatum of unanesthetized rats: effect of aminooxyacetic acid. *Neuroscience Letters*, 116(1–2), 198–203.

Stefansson, H., Ophoff, R. A., Steinberg, S., Andreassen, O. A., Cichon, S., Rujescu, D., et al. (2009). Common variants conferring risk of schizophrenia. *Nature*, 460(7256), 744–747. http://dx.doi.org/10.1038/nature08186.

Steffek, A. E., McCullumsmith, R. E., Haroutunian, V., & Meador-Woodruff, J. H. (2008). Cortical expression of glial fibrillary acidic protein and glutamine synthetase is decreased in schizophrenia. *Schizophrenia Research*, 103(1–3), 71–82. http://dx.doi.org/10.1016/j.schres.2008.04.032.

Stone, T. W., & Perkins, M. N. (1981). Quinolinic acid: a potent endogenous excitant at amino acid receptors in CNS. *European Journal of Pharmacology*, 72(4), 411–412.

Stone, T. W., Stoy, N., & Darlington, L. G. (2013). An expanding range of targets for kynurenine metabolites of tryptophan. *Trends in Pharmacological Sciences*, 34(2), 136–143. http://dx.doi.org/10.1016/j.tips.2012.09.006.

Swartz, K. J., During, M. J., Freese, A., & Beal, M. F. (1990). Cerebral synthesis and release of kynurenic acid: an endogenous antagonist of excitatory amino acid receptors. *The Journal of Neuroscience*, 10(9), 2965–2973.

Takahashi, N., & Sakurai, T. (2013). Roles of glial cells in schizophrenia: possible targets for therapeutic approaches. *Neurobiology of Disease*, 53, 49–60. http://dx.doi.org/10.1016/j.nbd.2012.11.001.

Taniuchi, H., & Hayaishi, O. (1963). Studies on the metabolism of kynurenic acid. III. Enzymatic formation of 7,8-dihydroxykynurenic acid from kynurenic acid. *Journal of Biological Chemistry*, 238, 283–293.

Thomases, D. R., Flores-Barrera, E., Bruno, J. P., Schwarcz, R., & Tseng, K. Y. (2014). Contribution of alpha-7 nAChR tone in sustaining the gain of GABAergic transmission in the adult prefrontal cortex. *Society for Neuroscience Abstract*, 39 33.02.

Thomson, A. M., Walker, V. E., & Flynn, D. M. (1989). Glycine enhances NMDA-receptor mediated synaptic potentials in neocortical slices. *Nature*, *338*(6214), 422–424. http://dx.doi.org/10.1038/338422a0.

Trecartin, K. V., & Bucci, D. J. (2011). Administration of kynurenine during adolescence, but not during adulthood, impairs social behavior in rats. *Schizophrenia Research*, *133*(1–3), 156–158. http://dx.doi.org/10.1016/j.schres.2011.08.014.

Turski, W. A., Gramsbergen, J. B., Traitler, H., & Schwarcz, R. (1989). Rat brain slices produce and liberate kynurenic acid upon exposure to L-kynurenine. *Journal of Neurochemistry*, *52*(5), 1629–1636.

Turski, W. A., Nakamura, M., Todd, W. P., Carpenter, B. K., Whetsell, W. O., Jr., & Schwarcz, R. (1988). Identification and quantification of kynurenic acid in human brain tissue. *Brain Research*, *454*(1–2), 164–169.

Turski, W. A., & Schwarcz, R. (1988). On the disposition of intrahippocampally injected kynurenic acid in the rat. *Experimental Brain Research*, *71*(3), 563–567.

Uwai, Y., Honjo, H., & Iwamoto, K. (2012). Interaction and transport of kynurenic acid via human organic anion transporters hOAT1 and hOAT3. *Pharmacological Research*, *65*(2), 254–260. http://dx.doi.org/10.1016/j.phrs.2011.11.003.

Varasi, M., Della Torre, A., Heidempergher, F., Pevarello, P., Speciale, C., Guidetti, P., et al. (1996). Derivatives of kynurenine as inhibitors of rat brain kynurenine aminotransferase. *European Journal of Medicinal Chemistry*, *31*(1), 11–21.

Vécsei, L., Szalardy, L., Fülop, F., & Toldi, J. (2013). Kynurenines in the CNS: recent advances and new questions. *Nature Reviews Drug Discovery*, *12*(1), 64–82. http://dx.doi.org/10.1038/nrd3793.

Volk, D. W., & Lewis, D. A. (2013). Prenatal ontogeny as a susceptibility period for cortical GABA neuron disturbances in schizophrenia. *Neuroscience*, *248*, 154–164. http://dx.doi.org/10.1016/j.neuroscience.2013.06.008.

Vunck, S. A., Phenis, D., Tseng, K. Y., Schwarcz, R., & Bruno, J. P. (2014). Rats exposed to elevated brain levels of kynurenic acid during the prenatal period exhibit an enhanced vulnerability to working memory deficits as adults. *Society for Neuroscience Abstract*, *39* 51.11.

Vunck, S. A., Supe, K., Schwarcz, R., & Bruno, J. P. (2013). Working memory deficits in adult rats after acute elevation of brain kynurenic acid are alleviated by co-administration of the alpha7 nicotinic positive modulator galantamine. *Society for Neuroscience Abstract*, *38* 255.09.

Wang, J., Simonavicius, N., Wu, X., Swaminath, G., Reagan, J., Tian, H., et al. (2006). Kynurenic acid as a ligand for orphan G protein-coupled receptor GPR35. *Journal of Biological Chemistry*, *281*(31), 22021–22028. http://dx.doi.org/10.1074/jbc.M603503200.

Widner, B., Ledochowski, M., & Fuchs, D. (2000). Interferon-gamma-induced tryptophan degradation: neuropsychiatric and immunological consequences. *Current Drug Metabolism*, *1*(2), 193–204.

Willette, A. A., Lubach, G. R., Knickmeyer, R. C., Short, S. J., Styner, M., Gilmore, J. H., et al. (2011). Brain enlargement and increased behavioral and cytokine reactivity in infant monkeys following acute prenatal endotoxemia. *Behavioural Brain Research*, *219*(1), 108–115. http://dx.doi.org/10.1016/j.bbr.2010.12.023.

Wolfensberger, M., Amsler, U., Cuénod, M., Foster, A. C., Whetsell, W. O., Jr., & Schwarcz, R. (1983). Identification of quinolinic acid in rat and human brain tissue. *Neuroscience Letters*, *41*(3), 247–252.

Wonodi, I., Stine, O. C., Sathyasaikumar, K. V., Roberts, R. C., Mitchell, B. D., Hong, L. E., et al. (2011). Downregulated kynurenine 3-monooxygenase gene expression and enzyme activity in schizophrenia and genetic association with schizophrenia endophenotypes. *Archives of General Psychiatry*, *68*(7), 665–674. http://dx.doi.org/10.1001/archgenpsychiatry.2011.71.

Wood, P. L. (1995). The co-agonist concept: is the NMDA-associated glycine receptor saturated in vivo? *Life Sciences*, *57*(4), 301–310.

Wright, P., Gill, M., & Murray, R. M. (1993). Schizophrenia: genetics and the maternal immune response to viral infection. *American Journal of Medical Genetics*, *48*(1), 40–46. http://dx.doi.org/10.1002/ajmg.1320480110.

Wu, W. L., Adams, C. E., Stevens, K. E., Chow, K. H., Freedman, R., & Patterson, P. H. (2015). The interaction between maternal immune activation and alpha 7 nicotinic acetylcholine receptor in regulating behaviors in the offspring. *Brain, Behavior, and Immunity*, *46*, 192–202. http://dx.doi.org/10.1016/j.bbi.2015.02.005.

Wu, H.-Q., Okuyama, M., Kajii, Y., Pocivavsek, A., Bruno, J. P., & Schwarcz, R. (2014). Targeting kynurenine aminotransferase II in psychiatric diseases: promising effects of an orally active enzyme inhibitor. *Schizophrenia Bulletin*, *40*(Suppl 2), S152–S158. http://dx.doi.org/10.1093/schbul/sbt157.

Wu, H.-Q., Pereira, E. F., Bruno, J. P., Pellicciari, R., Albuquerque, E. X., & Schwarcz, R. (2010). The astrocyte-derived alpha7 nicotinic receptor antagonist kynurenic acid controls extracellular glutamate levels in the prefrontal cortex. *Journal of Molecular Neuroscience*, *40*(1–2), 204–210. http://dx.doi.org/10.1007/s12031-009-9235-2.

Wu, H.-Q., Rassoulpour, A., & Schwarcz, R. (2002). Effect of systemic L-DOPA administration on extracellular kynurenate levels in the rat striatum. *Journal of Neural Transmission*, *109*(3), 239–249. http://dx.doi.org/10.1007/s007020200020.

Wu, H.-Q., Rassoulpour, A., & Schwarcz, R. (2007). Kynurenic acid leads, dopamine follows: a new case of volume transmission in the brain? *Journal of Neural Transmission*, *114*(1), 33–41. http://dx.doi.org/10.1007/s00702-006-0562-y.

Wu, H.-Q., & Schwarcz, R. (1996). Seizure activity causes elevation of endogenous extracellular kynurenic acid in the rat brain. *Brain Research Bulletin*, *39*(3), 155–162.

Wu, H.-Q., Ungerstedt, U., & Schwarcz, R. (1992). Regulation of kynurenic acid synthesis studied by microdialysis in the dorsal hippocampus of unanesthetized rats. *European Journal of Pharmacology*, *213*(3), 375–380.

Wu, H.-Q., Ungerstedt, U., & Schwarcz, R. (1995). L-alpha-aminoadipic acid as a regulator of kynurenic acid production in the hippocampus: a microdialysis study in freely moving rats. *European Journal of Pharmacology*, *281*(1), 55–61.

Yamada, H., Yoshida, H., Nakazawa, H., & Kumagai, H. (1975). Microbiological synthesis of L-tryptophan and its related amino acids. *Acta Vitaminology and Enzymology*, *29*(1–6), 248–251.

Yu, P., Di Prospero, N. A., Sapko, M. T., Cai, T., Chen, A., Melendez-Ferro, M., et al. (2004). Biochemical and phenotypic abnormalities in kynurenine aminotransferase II-deficient mice. *Molecular Cell Biology*, *24*(16), 6919–6930. http://dx.doi.org/10.1128/MCB.24.16.6919-6930.2004.

Zavitsanou, K., Lim, C. K., Purves-Tyson, T., Karl, T., Kassiou, M., Banister, S. D., et al. (2014). Effect of maternal immune activation on the kynurenine pathway in preadolescent rat offspring and on MK801-induced hyperlocomotion in adulthood: amelioration by COX-2 inhibition. *Brain Behavior and Immunity*, *41*, 173–181. http://dx.doi.org/10.1016/j.bbi.2014.05.011.

Zmarowski, A., Wu, H.-Q., Brooks, J. M., Potter, M. C., Pellicciari, R., Schwarcz, R., et al. (2009). Astrocyte-derived kynurenic acid modulates basal and evoked cortical acetylcholine release. *European Journal of Neuroscience*, *29*(3), 529–538. http://dx.doi.org/10.1111/j.1460-9568.2008.06594.x.

Molecular Studies

26

Dimensions of GSK3 Monoamine-Related Intracellular Signaling in Schizophrenia

Gohar Fakhfouri*,§,a, Jivan Khlghatyan*,§,a, Ilya Sukhanov¶,
Raul R. Gainetdinov¶,||,#, Jean-Martin Beaulieu*,§

*Department of Psychiatry and Neuroscience, Faculty of Medicine, Laval University, Québec City, QC, Canada; §Institut universitaire en santé mentale de Québec, Québec City, QC, Canada; ¶Department of Neuroscience and Brain Technologies, Istituto Italiano di Tecnologia, Genova, Italy; ||Institute of Translational Biomedicine, St. Petersburg State University, St. Petersburg, Russia; #Skolkovo Institute of Science and Technology (Skoltech), Skolkovo, Moscow Region, Russia

INTRODUCTION

Schizophrenia is one of the most devastating mental disorders, affecting about 1% of the general population worldwide. The clinical picture of the disease has been traditionally seen to embrace three major groups of symptoms (positive, negative, and cognitive symptoms) in various combinations. Positive symptoms include such prominent manifestations as hallucinations, delusions, and disordered thoughts and speech. A variety of emotional and social deficits are related to negative symptoms. Memory, attention, and learning deficits represent cognitive symptoms of schizophrenia that are notoriously difficult to treat.

Since the 1970s, when Seeman, Snyder, and others have shown that typical antipsychotics selectively block dopamine (DA) D2 receptors (Feinberg & Snyder, 1975; Seeman & Lee, 1975), the DA/monoamine theory of schizophrenia has been one of the principal frameworks to explain pathogenesis. Increased dopaminergic tone or sensitivity of D2 DA receptors resulting in dysregulation of intracellular signaling mechanisms would underlie manifestations of schizophrenia, particularly those related to positive symptoms. Most importantly, this theory still has strong predictive validity, because all of the clinically effective antipsychotics are D2 DA receptors antagonists.

All DA receptors, including D2 DA receptors, are members of the G protein-coupled receptor (GPCR) superfamily. Each of them possesses seven membrane-spanning domains and is able to activate G proteins to transduce signals to intracellular molecules. There are two major types of intracellular signaling mechanisms that can be triggered by the activation of D2 DA receptors. A first type is G protein-dependent and results in a negative regulation of cAMP and intracellular calcium levels by activation of ion channels or by release of calcium from intracellular depots (Nishi, Snyder, & Greengard, 1997; Missale, Nash, Robinson, Jaber, & Caron, 1998). A second type is G protein-independent and involves the formation of a protein complex composed of β-arrestin 2, Akt should be written in capitals (AKT), and protein phospholipase 2A (PP2A) (Beaulieu et al., 2005). Both mechanisms are believed to be involved in regulation of DA-associated behaviors.

Despite providing a good correlation between antipsychotic drug action, the monoamine theory of schizophrenia has received relatively poor support from genetic evidence. However, one major exception to this is the identification of a mechanism for the regulation of AKT and Glycogen synthase kinase 3 (GSK3) by D2 dopamine receptors. GSK3 is a highly conserved serine threonine kinase critically involved in D2R/β-arrestin 2/ AKT/PPA2 intracellular signaling downstream of AKT.

---

[a] These authors contributed equally to this work.

Handbook of Behavioral Neuroscience
http://dx.doi.org/10.1016/B978-0-12-800981-9.00026-2

There are two isoforms of GSK3: GSK3α (51 kDa) and GSK3β (47 kDa), which are coded by two separate gene loci. It was shown that several schizophrenia risk genes (such as AKT1, Neuregulin 1, and Disc1) directly interact with or contribute to cascades signaling through GSK3. Furthermore, this kinase also plays a role in neurodevelopment. GSK3 may, thus, be located at a crossroads of pathways that modulate development, behaviors, and cognition. Intriguingly, both psychomimetics and antipsychotics affect GSK3 activity (Beaulieu, 2012). Here, we discuss the involvement of GSK3 in DA-related intracellular signal cascades believed to be involved in different behavioral dimensions schizophrenia with a particular emphasis on the results of human and animal studies.

GSK3 REGULATING PATHWAYS

Regulation of GSK3 by AKT

AKT is a versatile serine/threonine kinase implicated in numerous cellular processes in neurons ranging from monoamine transporter trafficking and synaptic plasticity to morphology and metabolism. AKT, also termed protein kinase B (PKB), comprises three closely related isoforms (AKT1, 2, and 3), with distinct and specific functions. AKT is a major signal transducer downstream of phosphatidylinositol 3-kinase (PI3K) activation in response to cell surface receptor stimulation. PI3K activity produces phosphatidylinositol (3,4)-biphosphate (PIP2) and phosphatidylinositol (3,4,5)-trisphosphate (PIP3), which binds the pleckstrin homology (PH) domain of AKT, thereby recruiting AKT to the cell membrane where it is activated (Gonzalez &

McGraw, 2009). To be activated, AKT1undergoes sequential phosphorylation in the catalytic domain (Thr308) and carboxy terminal (Ser473) by intracellular kinases 3-phosphoinositide-dependent protein kinase 1 (PDK1) and rictor-mammalian target of rapamycin complex 2 (mTORC2), respectively (de Bartolomeis, Buonaguro, & Iasevoli, 2013). Following activation, AKT phosphorylates a number of downstream signaling molecules. GSK3 isoforms are phosphorylated by AKT at N-terminal serine residues, Ser21 (GSK3α) and Ser9 (GSK3β). This event results in the inhibition of both GSK3 isoforms. (Cross, Alessi, Cohen, Andjelkovich, & Hemmings, 1995) (Figure 1). Such inhibitory phosphorylation can also be catalyzed by other serine threonine kinases including p70 ribosomal S6 kinase (Sutherland, Leighton, & Cohen, 1993), p90 ribosomal S6 kinase (p90rsk-1) (Stambolic & Woodgett, 1994), AGC kinase, p38 mitogen-activated protein kinase (MAPK) (Cohen & Frame, 2001), protein kinase C, and phospholipase Cγ1 (Shin, Yoon, Kim, Kim, & Lee, 2002).

Regulation of GSK3 by Wnt

Wnt pathway, a prominent modulator of a plethora of cellular events also incorporates GSK3. In neurons, the processes governed by this cascade include but are not limited to synapse formation and specificity, synaptic plasticity, and neural development (Okerlund & Cheyette, 2011; Wu & Pan, 2010). In 1995, different groups showed for the first time that expression of a dominant negative mutant of GSK3 in the ventral side of *Xenopus* embryo could imitate Wnt-induced formation of an ectopic dorsal axis (Dominguez, Itoh, & Sokol, 1995; He, Saint-Jeannet, Woodgett, Varmus, & Dawid, 1995; Pierce & Kimelman,

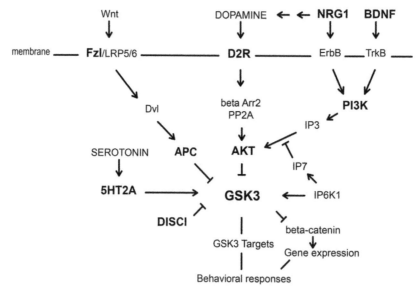

FIGURE 1   GSK3 signaling networks. Proteins represented in bold are encoded by genes conferring susceptibility to schizophrenia, arrows denote activation, and T-shaped arrows denote inhibition.

1995). Further investigation revealed that β-catenin, the key effector of the canonical Wnt system, is indeed a GSK3 substrate, the phosphorylation of which by GSK3 renders it unstable and subject to ubiquitination (Yost et al., 1996). This phenomenon occurs in the "β-catenin destruction complex" formed by interaction of the scaffolding protein AXIN with its partners and stabilized by phosphorylation of GSK3 and casein kinase I-alpha (CKIα). Other components include adenomatous polyposis coli (APC) and WTX. When the Wnt pathway is inactive, interplay with AXIN and APC brings cytoplasmic β-catenin to the complex, leading to its sequential phosphorylation by CKIα and GSK3 and resultant proteasomal degradation (Wu & Pan, 2010).

The canonical Wnt pathway is activated upon binding of Wnt ligands to seven transmembrane-domain protein frizzled (Fzd) and its co-receptors low-density lipoprotein receptor-related proteins 5 and 6 (LRP5/6). This event results in the mobilization of dishevelled (Dvl) and subsequently GSK3-associated AXIN to membrane, culminating in dissociation of GSK3 from β-catenin (Sutton & Rushlow, 2011). Stabilized β-catenin accumulates in the cytoplasm and translocates to the nucleus, where it forms a complex with co-transcription factors T cell factor/lymphoid enhancer factor (TCF/LEF) and initiates the transcription of Wnt-target genes (Wu & Pan, 2010) (Figure 1). Of note, activation of the Wnt cascade, as opposed to PI3K signaling pathway, does not affect the phosphorylation status and, therefore, kinase activity of GSK3 (Ding, Chen, & McCormick, 2000).

Regulation of GSK3 by Disc1

Disrupted-in-schizophrenia 1 (DISC1) is a scaffolding protein that interacts with several protein partners and modulates various signaling cascades in the brain and participates in neuronal development and synaptic functions (Johnstone et al., 2011). Recent findings have indicated that DISC1 binds and regulates GSK3β activity (Figure 1) (Mao et al., 2009). Using specific shRNAs against endogenous DISC1 in adult hippocampal progenitors (AHPs) or in E13 mouse brains, Mao et al. demonstrated that DISC1 promotes both embryonic and adult neural progenitor proliferation and that this effect is exerted through modulation of the canonical Wnt pathway (Mao et al., 2009). DISC1 KO decreased the number of proliferative neural progenitors in an embryonic mouse brain, abolished Wnt3a-induced AHP proliferation, reduced β-catenin amount, and specifically curtailed LEF/TCF transcriptional activity. The deficits were restored by expression of either DISC1 or a degradation-resistant β-catenin. Negative regulation of GSK3β activity, either directly or indirectly, by DISC1 was suggested by the observation that a decrease in β-catenin level was associated by increases in its phosphorylation

at Ser33/37 and Thr41, motifs known to be phosphorylated by GSK3.

More direct evidence for an inhibition of GSK3 by DISC1 came from the findings that DISC1 abrogation induced, while its overexpression precluded, GSK3β autophosphorylation at Tyr216, a step crucial for GSK3 activity (Lochhead et al., 2006). In contrast, Ser9 phosphorylation was unaltered by disc1 KO, excluding the involvement of AKT in regulation of GSK3β by DISC1. In an attempt to dissect the mechanism, DISC1 was found to inhibit GSK3β activity through a direct physical interaction of its N-terminal region (aa 1–220).

In adult mouse hippocampus, DISC1 has been shown to sequester an AKT activity enhancer called KIAA1212, leading to inhibition of AKT and one of its downstream kinases mTOR (Anai et al., 2005). Over the course of adult neurogenesis, a finely tuned stage-dependent role has been proposed for GSK3 and DISC1 (Kim et al., 2009). According to the findings of Ishizuka et al., during mid-embryonic stages when progenitor cell proliferation is prominent, unphosphorylated DISC1 binds GSK3β to promote cell proliferation. However, later in embryonic stages when neuronal migration predominates, phosphorylated DISC1 dissociates from GSK3β and switches its role to activating neuronal migration (Ishizuka et al., 2011). DISC1 also forms a complex with DIXDC1, and the resulting complex can potentiate the canonical Wnt pathway (Singh et al., 2010). Apart from β-catenin, phosphorylation of two other known substrates of GSK3β, namely Ngn2 (Ma et al., 2008) and C/EBPa (Ross, Erickson, Hemati, & MacDougald, 1999), is not affected by either DISC1 knockout or overexpression.

Regulation of GSK3 by IP6K1

Inositol hexakisphosphate kinases (IP6Ks) have been also implicated in regulating GSK3 activity. The inositol pyrophosphate IP7 (5-diphosphoinositol pentakisphosphate), produced by this kinase family, acts as a physiologic inhibitor of AKT signaling (Figure 1) through binding the PH domain of AKT, thereby preventing it from membrane translocation and subsequent PDK1-induced activatory phosphorylation at Thr308. Corroborating this finding, AKT activity and phospho-GSK3β are drastically augmented in hepatic, muscular, and adipose tissues from Ip6k1-KO mice (Chakraborty et al., 2010). Furthermore, GSK3 activity is considerably diminished in different brain regions of Ip6k1-KO mice. At the behavioral level, these mice perform similarly to WT animals treated with GSK3 inhibitors and to different transgenic mouse models of GSK3 deficiency. Reduced exploratory locomotor activity of Ip6k1-KO mice in a novel environment mimics that of Gsk3a-KO mice (Kaidanovich-Beilin et al., 2009), while their reduced amphetamine-induced hyperlocomotion is reminiscent of Gsk3β haploinsufficient mice (Beaulieu et al., 2004). Regarding sociability, Gsk3a-KO mice display a defective trait, while complete ablation of forebrain Gsk3β contrarily facilitates social interactions (Latapy, Rioux, Guitton, & Beaulieu, 2012), indicating distinct roles of GSK3 isoforms on social behavior. In the case of Ip6k1-KO mice, they manifest impaired social interaction that mimics WT mice receiving TDZD-8 (a general GSK3 inhibitor). Such an observation suggests that inhibition of both GSK3 isoforms adversely affects social interactions (Chakraborty, Latapy, Xu, Snyder, & Beaulieu, 2014). In addition to regulating GSK3 activity through AKT, we have recently demonstrated that IP6K1 directly interacts and potentiates GSK3α/β in mouse cortex. It is noteworthy that such potentiation is noncatalytic and occurs via physical binding of IP6K1 to the N-terminal domain of active GSK3 and hinders AKT-mediated inhibitory phosphorylation at this site (Chakraborty et al., 2014).

β-Arrestin-2-Mediated Regulation of GSK3 by Dopamine

Recent investigations indicate regulation of the AKT-GSK3 pathway by DA as well as involvement of this signaling pathway in DA-related behaviors and antipsychotic drug response (Beaulieu, 2012; Beaulieu, Gainetdinov, & Caron, 2009). It all started with a pioneering work on DA transporter knockout (DAT-KO) mice, a model, where DA reuptake was inhibited and mice exhibited almost fivefold increase of extracellular DA levels (Gainetdinov et al., 1999; Giros, Jaber, Jones, Wightman, & Caron, 1996; Sotnikova et al., 2005). Elevated levels of DA result in inactivation of AKT1 and, as a consequence, activation of GSK3α and GSK3β (Beaulieu et al., 2004). In agreement with previous phenomenon, amphetamine, methamphetamine, or apomorphine, known DA receptor agonists, decrease AKT1 activity and increase GSK3α and GSK3β activity when administered to wild-type mice (Beaulieu et al., 2004; Bychkov, Ahmed, Dalby, & Gurevich, 2007; Chen, Lao, & Chen, 2007). DA-mediated regulation of AKT-GSK3 signaling was also validated in a paradigm of DA depletion in the striatum by administration of DA synthesis inhibitor (Beaulieu et al., 2004; Bychkov et al., 2007; Chen, Lao, & Chen, 2007). By knockout of DA receptors and use of various receptor agonists, it was possible to show that the main receptor regulating DA-mediated AKT-GSK3 signaling is D2R. While being a D2 subtype, D3 DA receptor seems to function as an enhancer of D2R action on this signaling (Beaulieu et al., 2007).

When investigating involvement of D2R subtypes in regulation of AKT-GSK3 signaling, it was found that despite presence of DA D2RS splice variant in both pre- and postsynaptic neurons, D2RL-KO mice exhibited elevated AKT1 phosphorylation (Beaulieu et al., 2007).

This sets D2RL splice variant of D2R as a critical regulator of AKT and GSK3 by DA. However, there is a lack of studies exploring the effect of D2R receptor agonists on AKT and GSK3 phosphorylation in D2RL-KO mice, which leaves the specific contribution of D2RL to this modality of DA receptor signaling yet to be further investigated.

While D2R signals to cAMP, regulation of AKT1 was found not to be mediated by canonical signaling, but instead by involvement of the scaffolding protein β-Arrestin-2 (βArr2) (Beaulieu et al., 2005). It was observed that DA receptor agonists could not achieve to the AKT inhibition anymore when mice were lacking βArr2 (βArr2-KO) (Beaulieu et al., 2005). Formation of a novel complex consisting of βArr2, AKT1, and PP2A was found in response to D2R receptor activation. DA receptor stimulation facilitates complex formation and AKT1 dephosphorylation/inactivation by PP2A (Figure 1) (Beaulieu et al., 2005). And as a result of decreased AKT1 activity, GSK3 is dephosphorylated and activated. Moreover, GSK3, in turn, may contribute to regulation of this signaling by facilitating the formation of the βArr2/PP2A/AKT1 complex, as it was shown in genetic mouse models (O'Brien et al., 2011; Urs, Snyder, Jacobsen, Peterson, & Caron, 2012)

Regulation of D2R-mediated behaviors adds an extra importance to βArr2-AKT1-GSK3 signaling pathway. βArr2-KO mice exhibit decreased activity and diminished responsiveness to DA agonists compared to wild type littermates. (Beaulieu et al., 2005). In addition, hyperactive phenotype of DAT-KO mice is diminished by the lack of βArr2 (Beaulieu et al., 2005). Furthermore, hyperactivity of DAT-KO and amphetamine-treated normal mice can be reduced by administration of GSK3 inhibitors (Beaulieu et al., 2004; Gould, O'Donnell, Picchini, & Manji, 2007).

Decreased locomotion in response to amphetamine treatment was also documented in D2 neuron-specific GSK3β-KO and Gsk3b haploinsufficient mice (Beaulieu et al., 2004; Urs et al., 2012).

Regulation of GSK3 by Serotonin

Modulation of GSK3 function is not limited to DA, and several lines of evidence now point at another monoamine player, serotonin (Figure 1) (Polter & Li, 2011). The notion was driven from the observation that GSK3β was inactivated in vivo by various classes of serotonergic agents, including selective serotonin reuptake inhibitors, monoamine oxidase inhibitors, and tricyclic antidepressants (Li et al., 2004). Furthermore, administration of D-fenfluramine, an enhancer of serotonergic tone, to mice dramatically changes phosphorylated GSK3β levels in different brain regions (Li et al., 2004). The physiological importance of serotonin-dependent regulation of GSK3 was verified in a knock-in mouse model harboring a mutant form of tryptophan hydroxylase 2 (*Tph2*), the rate-limiting enzyme in brain serotonin biosynthesis (Walther et al., 2003; Zhang, Beaulieu, Sotnikova, Gainetdinov, & Caron, 2004). Deficient serotonin transmission in these mice is accompanied by anxiogenic- and depressive-like behavior. Interestingly, pharmacological or genetic inactivation of GSK3β substantially restored the phenotypes, implicating GSK3β as an important effector of serotonin-mediated behavioral responses (Beaulieu, Zhang, et al., 2008). When agonists and antagonists specific to a single serotonergic receptor were employed, it was shown that activation of 5HT1A receptors increase, while that of 5HT2 subtypes decrease phospho-GSK3β levels (Li et al., 2004). However, mechanisms contributing to serotonin-evoked GSK3β alterations remain to be elucidated.

GSK3 Regulation, a Final Remark

As one can realize, both GSK3 isoforms can be regulated by several converging mechanisms involving protein:protein interactions and/or the modulation of protein phosphorylation. Of interest, the regulation of AKT and GSK3 by D2R provides a unique mechanism by which an extracellular messenger molecule, in this case DA, can regulate the inactivation of AKT-mediated signaling. Furthermore, in view of the central role that DA and serotonin have been thought to play in the etiology and treatment of schizophrenia (Sawa & Snyder, 2002; Seeman, 2002), this pathway may also provide important cues on how pharmacological treatments acting on DA receptors may compensate for genetic deficits that are not obviously associated with the modulation of dopaminergic or serotonergic neurotransmission.

GSK3 IN SCHIZOPHRENIA

AKT-GSK3 Pathway in Biology of Schizophrenia

Progress in genetics sheds light on involvement of AKT in schizophrenia. Genetic studies of schizophrenic patients revealed several single nucleotide polymorphisms (SNPs) of the Akt gene to be associated with schizophrenia risk in patients with Northern European origin (Emamian, Hall, Birnbaum, Karayiorgou, & Gogos, 2004).

In addition, analyses of protein extracts of lymphocyte-derived cell lines (LDCs) obtained from schizophrenic patients revealed that AKT1 expression is decreased in diseased samples compared to control. Data got strengthened by the fact that a similar decrease of AKT1 is also observed in the postmortem cortex and hippocampus of patients with schizophrenia. Expression changes were specific to AKT1, and no differences were found in expression of AKT2 and AKT3 isoforms (Emamian et al., 2004). All these observations were very much in line with genetic studies. Since then, a plethora of investigations conclude in support of Akt1 gene variants as a risk factor of schizophrenia in Iranian (Bajestan et al., 2006), Japanese (Ikeda et al., 2004), Chinese (Xu et al., 2007), European (Karege et al., 2010; Schwab et al., 2005), and British (Mathur, Law, Megson, Shaw, & Wei, 2010; Norton et al., 2007) populations. There are also studies that failed to show the association of Akt1 haplotypes with schizophrenia in Japanese (Ide et al., 2006; Ohtsuki, Inada, & Arinami, 2004), Taiwanese (Liu et al., 2006, 2009), Finnish (Turunen et al., 2007), and Korean (Lee et al., 2010) samples. It is worth mentioning that there may be several reasons for inconsistencies between these results, and several factors can contribute, such as ethnic origins of analyzed subjects, size of selected cohorts, as well as the type of analyses performed (Emamian et al., 2004; Ohtsuki et al., 2004).

Regarding expression levels of total and phosphorylated AKT1 (pAKT1) in the frontal cortex of schizophrenic patients, there are also some studies bringing controversy to the field (Ide et al., 2006). One important aspect of these kinds of studies is to obtain high-quality postmortem samples. It has been shown that pH can influence greatly the phosphorylation of AKT1; a terminal medical state of the patient and the storage conditions after death should be considered as well (Ide et al., 2006). In addition, inconsistent results may stem from the fact that different brain regions have been examined over a wide range of studies.

Importantly, studies of recent years support AKT1 as a risk factor for schizophrenia. Decrease in AKT1 levels as well as pAKT1/AKT1 ratio in postmortem brains of schizophrenic patients was confirmed in various independent studies (Karege et al., 2010; Szamosi, Kelemen, & Keri, 2012). Although in other studies, decrease of AKT1 was not detected, and pAKT (S473) levels were significantly lower in dentate gyrus of schizophrenic patients compared to control individuals, indicating an overall decreased AKT1 activity (Balu et al., 2012).

A study found five new genetic loci significantly associated with schizophrenia risk (Schizophrenia Psychiatric Genome-Wide Association Study (GWAS) Consortium, 2011). An intriguingly low pAKT1/AKT1 ratio and diminished AKT1 activity were detected in all risk allele carriers, suggesting that proteins encoded by genes that are affected in schizophrenia may converge on a common pathway, having AKT1 as a shared component (Balog, Kiss, & Keri, 2012). One study addressed the question from different point of view by analyzing a complete set of genes affected in schizophrenia, and it found AKT1 among many other genes that are differentially expressed in schizophrenic patients. Metabolic and signaling pathways were reconstructed based on the discovered genes, and AKT1 appeared to be involved in 20 out of 35 deregulated pathways (van Beveren et al., 2012).

As mentioned, GSK3 is one of the substrates of AKT1; therefore, studies were conducted to explore its involvement in pathophysiology of the disease.

Several GSK3b gene variants are found to be associated with schizophrenia risk (Scassellati et al., 2004; Souza et al., 2008; Tang et al., 2013). A particular SNP located in the promoter region of GSK3b affects transcription factor binding, and it leads to an increased expression of GSK3β (Li et al., 2011). Association of Gsk3b polymorphisms with schizophrenia was confirmed by several studies; however, reporting decreased in GSK3 mRNA levels (Blasi et al., 2013; Kozlovsky, Shanon-Weickert, et al., 2004). Interestingly, decreased GSK3 mRNA levels were paradoxically accompanied by a reduction in β-catenin, which is suggestive of enhanced GSK3 activity.

Data regarding GSK3 protein levels and activity in schizophrenia is less conclusive. Unaltered expression of GSK3 in LDCs or in frontal cortex lysates of schizophrenic patients were found to be accompanied by decreased relative phosphorylation of GSK3β at Ser9, indicating an increased activity of GSK3β. The change in GSK3 phosphorylation could be the result of regulation by AKT1, since no difference was observed in its phosphorylation at Tyr216, while AKT1-dependant phosphorylation of GSK3β at Ser9 was decreased. These data are suggestive of a relationship between AKT1 and GSK3 in schizophrenia (Emamian et al., 2004). That being said, several studies have reported decreased protein levels and activity of GSK3 in schizophrenic patients (Beasley et al., 2001; Kozlovsky, Belmaker, & Agam, 2000, 2001; Kozlovsky, Regenold, et al., 2004). Since decreased immunoreactivity of GSK3 was detected along with unchanged levels of its direct substrate β-catenin, one may conclude increased GSK3 activity (Beasley et al., 2001).

AKT-GSK3 and the Pathophysiology of Schizophrenia

Several brain regions are known to be structurally and functionally altered in schizophrenic patients. Structural magnetic resonance imaging (sMRI) identified gray matter deficits that correlate with SNPs of 16 schizophrenia risk genes including Akt1, Pi3k, and Drd2 (Jagannathan et al., 2010). Reduction in hippocampal volume of schizophrenic patients is also found to correlate with decreased pAKT1/AKT1 ratio (Szamosi, Kelemen, & Keri, 2012). Akt1-deficient mice exhibit several hippocampal abnormalities including alterations in synaptic plasticity and impaired neurogenesis (Balu et al., 2012).

In addition to structural changes, Akt1 variants seem to also affect brain function of schizophrenic patients, since patients with a genetic variant of Akt1 exhibit poorer memory performance, particularly in attention/concentration compared to patients devoid of the variant. Akt1 variants also correlate with several brain morphological vulnerabilities and deficits in sustained attention and vigilance (Ohi et al., 2013). These data are supported by behavioral studies on Akt1-deficient mice. These mice exhibit deficiencies in spatial memory and attenuated PPI response, along with modest anxiety and a decrease in fear-conditioned learning (Balu et al., 2012).

In addition, AKT1 variants may epistatically interact with other risk genes to contribute to schizophrenia risk as well as to cognition and brain volume of affected individuals (Tan et al., 2012, 2008).

Gsk3b polymorphisms affect the temporal lobe gray matter, a region with the most consistently documented morphometric abnormalities in schizophrenia (Benedetti et al., 2010). Gsk3b SNPs correlate with reduced thickness of the dorsolateral prefrontal cortex (DLPFC) and are associated with attenuated activity of DLPFC and decreased cognitive performance and working memory as measured by functional magnetic resonance imaging (fMRI) (Blasi et al., 2013). In a wide range of neurological disorders such as bipolar disorder, Alzheimer's disease, and Fragile X syndrome, pharmacological and genetic inhibition of GSK3 has been associated with cognitive improvements in mice and human. Modulation of synaptic plasticity, neurogenesis, and neuroprotection by GSK3 are the most plausible underlying mechanisms (King et al., 2014). Altogether, data indicate that changes in the AKT-GSK3 pathway may contribute to behavioral manifestations of schizophrenia.

Wnt-GSK3 Pathway in Schizophrenia

Numerous alterations occur in the GSK3-regulating Wnt pathway in schizophrenia. Postmortem brains of schizophrenic patients display diminished β-catenin levels in the CA3 and CA4 hippocampal subregions (Cotter et al., 1998), which could possibly be a consequence of aberrant β-catenin instability due to unrestraint GSK3 activity. In the same brain regions, Wnt1 content has also been found elevated in schizophrenic subjects (Miyaoka, Seno, & Ishino, 1999). It is, therefore, conceivable that such upregulation occurs as part of an endogenous compensatory mechanism to abate the detrimental effects of increased GSK3-mediated β-catenin degradation. Association studies have identified a number of members of the Wnt cascade, namely Fzd3, Apc, and Tcf4 as schizophrenia susceptibility genes (Cui, Jiang, Jiang, Xu, & Yao, 2005; Katsu et al., 2003; Stefansson et al., 2009; Steinberg et al., 2011; Yang et al., 2003), and transgenic mice mimic certain schizophrenia-like phenotypes. TCF4 gain-of-function in the brain leads to impaired PPI but normal locomotor activity (Brzozka, Radyushkin, Wichert, Ehrenreich, & Rossner, 2010), while mice with partial KO of Apc display normal PPI but working memory deficit in adulthood and reduced locomotion (Koshimizu et al., 2011). DIX domain containing 1 (DIXDC1) is a positive regulator of Wnt that enhances TCF-dependent transcription through interaction with Dvl and AXIN (Shiomi et al., 2005; Shiomi, Uchida, Keino-Masu, & Masu, 2003). DIXDC1 knockout in mice generates a complex phenotype reminiscent of schizophrenia-like behavior in certain aspects (Kivimae et al., 2011). Dvl1-KO results in disrupted PPI and social interaction, which are typical endophenotypes of schizophrenia (Lijam et al., 1997). Given the role of Dvl1 in GSK3 inhibition, it is plausible that GSK3 overactivation underlies the defective sensorimotor gating and social behavior in Dvl1 loss of function.

NRG1-GSK3 and BDNF-GSK3 in Schizophrenia

Neuregulins (NRGs) constitute a family of growth factor-encoding genes (Nrg1–4). NRG1 is the best characterized member, and in humans, it occurs in more than 30 isoforms, all of which share an epidermal growth factor (EGF)-like domain. Upon binding of NRG1 to its receptors ERBB4, the latter forms a homo- or heterodimer with other ERBB subtypes (Pan, Huang, & Deng, 2011). As growth factors, both NRG1 and BDNF (brain-derived neurotrophic factor) activate receptor-type tyrosine kinases (Ogata et al., 2004) that transduce signals mainly through the MAPK pathway consisting of Ras-Raf-MAPK kinase (Mek)-extracellular signal-regulated kinase (Erk) and the PI3K pathway comprising PI3K (with its adaptor subunit p85 and the catalytic subunit p110)-AKT-GSK3 and other downstream molecules (Figure 1) (Hunter, 1997).

NRG1-ERBB4 signaling plays key roles in neurodevelopmental phenomena including neuronal migration, radial glia formation, dendritic development, axon myelination, and guidance (Deng, Pan, Engel, & Huang, 2013). Nrg1 and Erbb4 have been strongly associated with schizophrenia, and several studies have pinpointed them as susceptibility genes (Harrison & Law, 2006; Stefansson et al., 2003, 2002). Neurons derived from induced pluripotent stem cells of schizophrenic individuals manifest NRG1 and ERBB4 overexpression (Law et al., 2012). This finding has been corroborated by independent studies on postmortem brains from schizophrenic subjects (Law, Kleinman, Weinberger, & Weickert, 2007; Law et al., 2006; Silberberg, Darvasi, Pinkas-Kramarski, & Navon, 2006). Risk polymorphisms in *ERBB4* are also associated with increases in ERBB4 CYT-1 isoform in lymphoblastoid B-cell lines from schizophrenia patients (Law et al., 2012). ERBB4 CYT-1 possesses a binding site for PI3K through which it can activate the PI3K pathway (Junttila, Sundvall, Maatta, &

Elenius, 2000). Intriguingly, the same *ERBB4* genotype is also linked with elevated p110δ PIK3CD expression but paradoxically decreased PIP3 generation in schizophrenia (Law et al., 2012). Of importance, suppression of p110δ PIK3CD with a small molecule (IC87114) counteracts amphetamine-evoked hyperactivity in mice, increases brain Thr308 phospho-AKT levels, and corrects PPI defects in a rat neonatal ventral hippocampal lesion model of schizophrenia. Rats receiving the antipsychotic haloperidol chronically display a specific diminution in PIK3CD isoform expression in the brain (Law et al., 2012). Furthermore, in both first-episode unmedicated and chronic medicated schizophrenia, but not other psychotic disorders, NRG1-induced PI3K-mediated AKT phosphorylation at Ser473 is reduced (Keri, Beniczky, & Kelemen, 2010; Keri, Seres, Kelemen, & Benedek, 2009). Together, these findings conform to deregulation of AKT signaling in schizophrenia (Emamian et al., 2004) and point at augmented GSK3 activity as a pivotal element in the aberrations that engender or perpetuate the schizophrenic state.

Of great relevance to schizophrenia, NRG1 also affects both the function and neurodevelopment of the dopaminergic system (Pan et al., 2011). Indeed, central or peripheral administration of NRG1β enhances DA release in brain regions involved in dopaminergic transmission (Carlsson et al., 2011; Kwon et al., 2008; Yurek, Zhang, Fletcher-Turner, & Seroogy, 2004). How such modification could influence behavior was the subject of an elegant study (Kato et al., 2011); systemic administration of NRG1 to neonatal mice led to midbrain ERBB4 activation, enhanced expression, phosphorylation, and enzyme activity of tyrosine hydroxylase, all of which culminated in a hyperdopaminergic state in the medial prefrontal cortex that continued to persist through adulthood. In addition, once reaching adulthood, these mice manifested schizophrenia-related behaviors, that is, namely impaired social behaviors, PPI, latent inhibition (LI), and hypersensitivity to methamphetamine (Kato et al., 2011). Considering the relevance of βArr-mediated D2R signaling in schizophrenia and its pathophysiology, one can envisage that augmented NRG1-ERBB4 signaling confers susceptibility to schizophrenia through adversely affecting the dopaminergic transmission and AKT/GSK3 as its integral signaling modality.

As for BDNF, an intricate correlation exists between BDNF and GSK3β. Chronic administration of lithium, an established inhibitor of GSK3β, induces BDNF expression both in vitro (Hashimoto et al., 2002) and in vivo (Fukumoto, Morinobu, Okamoto, Kagaya, & Yamawaki, 2001). A more direct evidence comes from the work on dopaminergic human neuron-like cells, where protracted inhibition of GSK3β either genetically or pharmacologically was found to augment BDNF secretion (Gimenez-Cassina,

Lim, & Diaz-Nido, 2012). Phencyclidine (PCP) has long been associated with induction of a psychotomimetic state reminiscent of schizophrenia incorporating both positive and negative symptoms (Javitt & Zukin, 1991). Perinatal exposure of mice to PCP evokes a schizophrenia-like phenotype in later life that has been associated with apoptosis. BNDF-induced protection of corticostriatal cultures against PCP-evoked apoptosis involved inhibition of GSK3β downstream of the PI3K/AKT signaling cascade (Xia, Wang, Liu, Anastasio, & Johnson, 2010).

DISC1-GSK3 in Schizophrenia

DISC1 was first identified in a large Scottish pedigree in which a translocation in the Disc1 gene segregates with schizophrenia, bipolar disorder, and major depression (Margolis & Ross, 2010; Millar et al., 2000; St Clair et al., 1990). Through several postmortem, genetic association, and linkage studies in various ethnic groups, it is now well established that Disc1 is a bona fide risk gene for schizophrenia (Callicott et al., 2005; Cannon et al., 2005; Ekelund et al., 2004, 2001; Hennah et al., 2003; Hwu, Liu, Fann, Ou-Yang, & Lee, 2003; Nakata et al., 2009; Schumacher et al., 2009; Thomson et al., 2005; Zhang et al., 2006). Although the functional outcome of *DISC1* variants in psychiatric illnesses is elusive, gathering evidence on the roles of DISC1 within the brain networks has provided some valuable mechanistic insights. One hypothesis is that haploinsufficiency can result from Disc1 polymorphisms (Millar et al., 2005). This theory is supported by the finding that (1) mRNA levels of DISC1 were decreased in lymphocytes from 57 bipolar pedigrees, (2) a higher load of manic symptoms were associated with lower levels of DISC1 expression (Maeda et al., 2006), and (3) when mice are chronically treated with atypical antipsychotics olanzapine and risperidone, DISC1 mRNA is upregulated in the frontal cortex (Chiba et al., 2006), possibly as part of their therapeutic effects. Another theory, as corroborated by animal findings, states that the product of the mutation in Disc1 acts a dominant negative, disrupting the function of wild-type protein. For a detailed discussion of DISC1 in schizophrenia, the reader is referred to elegant reviews published elsewhere (Johnstone et al., 2011; Mackie, Millar, & Porteous, 2007). A missense L100P mutation gives rise to typical schizophrenia-like behavior, that is, hyperactivity, a dramatic decline in working memory, PPI, and LI, all of which can be can be abated by administration of typical or atypical antipsychotics. The anatomical findings of the brain also resemble those reported in schizophrenic patients (Clapcote et al., 2007) and, therefore, substantiate the implication of DISC1 in schizophrenia and establish a reliable animal model for this disorder.

With regard to the putative role of GSK3, treatment of Disc1 KO mice with GSK3β inhibitors offsets the novelty-induced hyperlocomotion, a murine equivalent of positive symptoms of schizophrenia and corrects impaired LEF/TCF-dependent neural progenitor proliferation (Lochhead et al., 2006). In DISC-1-L100P mutant mice, *Gsk3a* knockdown rescues dendritic spine defects of the frontal cortex neurons (Lee, Kaidanovich-Beilin, Roder, Woodgett, & Wong, 2011). As with antipsychotics, pharmacological or genetic inhibition of GSK3 suffices to offset the behavioral phenotypes of these mice (Lipina et al., 2011; Lipina, Palomo, Gil, Martinez, & Roder, 2013; Lipina, Wang, Liu, & Roder, 2012), verifying the significance of GSK3-incorporating pathways as a promising therapeutic target in schizophrenia.

REGULATION OF GSK3 BY ANTIPSYCHOTICS

The fact that the AKT-GSK3 pathway is involved in the pathophysiology of schizophrenia makes this pathway an attractive target for drug development. Most antipsychotics have the ability to act as D2R receptor antagonists with second-generation antipsychotics also antagonizing 5HT2A serotonin receptors. Since the AKT-GSK3 pathway is involved in signaling of DA and 5HT receptors, it is not surprising that most existing antipsychotics have been shown to affect AKT-GSK3 signaling either directly or indirectly.

Studies in mice show that first-generation antipsychotic haloperidol increases AKT1 and GSK3β phosphorylation without affecting their expression levels (Emamian et al., 2004). Chronic and subchronic but not acute treatment with several antipsychotics also caused increases in β-catenin, GSK3β, and pGSK3β levels in the striatum, prefrontal cortex (PFC), hippocampus, and ventral midbrain of rats (Alimohamad, Rajakumar, Seah, & Rushlow, 2005; Alimohamad, Sutton, Mouyal, Rajakumar, & Rushlow, 2005). In SH-SY5Y cells, clozapine increases Ser9 phosphorylation of GSK3β along with accumulation of β-catenin and its migration to the nucleus. Interestingly, this effect is resistant to the inhibition of the PI3K pathway, suggesting a possible involvement of other pathways such as Wnt (see above) in GSK3β regulation in response to clozapine (Kang et al., 2004). However, there is a lack of in vivo studies for involvement of other PI3K-independent mechanisms, such as the inactivation of AKT by PP2A and βArr2 or by 5HT receptors.

Using a bioluminescence resonance energy transfer method, an elegant study demonstrated that various antipsychotics, such as haloperidol, clozapine, aripiprazole, chlorpromazine, quetiapine, olanzapine, risperidone, and ziprasidone, all share the common ability to antagonize DA-mediated recruitment of βArr2 to D2LR (Masri et al., 2008). Further research led to the generation of βArr2-biased compounds that would selectively target βArr2-mediated D2R signaling. Newly synthetized aripiprazole derivatives UNC9975, UNC0006, and UNC9994 displayed antipsychotic-like activity in rodents (Allen et al., 2011). These three compounds act as partial agonists for βArr2 recruitment to D2R in the absence of a full agonist, while leaving cAMP signaling unaltered. It is worthy to point out that aripiprazole behaves as a partial agonist for βArr2 recruitment, since it is applied alone in in vitro assays (Allen et al., 2011); however, it acts as an antagonist of βArr2 recruitment when simultaneously applied with quinpirole (Masri et al., 2008). Thus, interpretation of the pharmacological properties of different UNC compounds should be approached carefully by taking in account whether applied alone in vitro or in the context of an active DA tone in vivo.

Further investigations of these compounds, including a characterization or their pharmacological profile in the presence of full D2R agonists, may constitute an important first step toward the development of a new class of antipsychotics targeting GSK3-mediated signaling.

HOW GSK3 AFFECTS BEHAVIOR

There are over 100 known substrates, which can be phosphorylated and regulated in different fashions by GSK3 (Sutherland, 2011). To date, little is known about the mechanisms by which GSK3 activity does contribute to the regulation of behavior. However, several GSK3 substrates might be implicated in neurological functions, and their dysregulation by GSK3 may contribute to pathological conditions (Figure 2). Below, we will discuss some of the GSK3 substrates and their possible

role in processes underlying neurological function and regulation of behaviors.

Circadian Rhythms

Circadian rhythms are periodic processes orchestrated by the suprachiasmatic nucleus (SCN) and are important for organisms to adapt to environmental changes. Circadian rhythms are tightly regulated on a molecular level by several factors and genes called clock genes (Gachon, Nagoshi, Brown, Ripperger, & Schibler, 2004). Being highly expressed in SCN, GSK3 exerts its effect on circadian rhythms by regulating its components. First, it has been shown that the nonselective GSK3 inhibitor lithium lengthens the period of circadian rhythms in vitro *and* in vivo (Abe, Herzog, & Block, 2000; Iwahana et al., 2004) and that GSK3 haploinsufficiency lengthens the circadian locomotor activity in mice (Lavoie, Hebert, & Beaulieu, 2013b). GSK3 is able to regulate clock genes PER2 and CRY2 by direct phosphorylation that promotes nuclear translocation (Iitaka, Miyazaki, Akaike, & Ishida, 2005) or degradation (Harada, Sakai, Kurabayashi, Hirota, & Fukada, 2005), accordingly. GSK3 also phosphorylates and stabilizes the negative component of the circadian clock Rev-erbα and lithium treatment results to its rapid proteasomal degradation and the activation of Rev-erbα repressed gene *Bmal1* as a result of GSK3 inhibition (Yin, Wang, Klein, & Lazar, 2006). Finally, GSK3 is crucial for maintaining the robustness of the circadian clock since phosphorylation of BMAL1 stabilizes this protein and controls the amplitude of the circadian oscillation (Sahar, Zocchi, Kinoshita, Borrelli, & Sassone-Corsi, 2010).

β-Catenin

As described above, GSK3 regulates β-catenin downstream of Wnt signaling. In addition to acting as a transcription factor when translocated to the nucleus, β-catenin can also interact with the cytoskeletal network. It has been shown that β-catenin is recruited to dendritic spines following depolarization, indicating that it may be involved in synaptic plasticity (Murase, Mosser, & Schuman, 2002). Since GSK3 can phosphorylate β-catenin, which directs it for degradation, it is possible that GSK3 may influence gene expression and synaptic plasticity via regulation of β-catenin levels. In support of this notion, β-catenin overexpression mimics the GSK3-dependent effect of lithium on locomotor hyperactivity (Gould et al., 2007). However, the role of β-catenin in regulation of normal behaviors is less prominent, since forebrain-specific *β-catenin*-KO mice exhibit little behavioral phenotype (Gould et al., 2008).

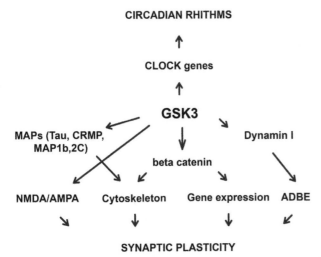

FIGURE 2 Involvement of GSK3 and its putative targets in neurological functions.

Microtubules

Microtubule-associated proteins (MAPs) regulate assembly and stability of microtubules. Microtubules constitute a major part of the cytoskeleton and are important in cytoskeletal rearrangements during neuronal growth, axon guidance, and synapse formation. Several MAPs are substrates of GSK3. GSK3 can phosphorylate and regulate Tau protein (Sutherland, 2011), collapsin response mediator proteins (Alabed, Pool, Ong, Sutherland, & Fournier, 2010; Cole et al., 2004; Yoshimura et al., 2005), MAP 1B (Lucas, Goold, Gordon-Weeks, & Salinas, 1998; Trivedi, Marsh, Goold, Wood-Kaczmar, & Gordon-Weeks, 2005), and MAP2C (Sanchez, Perez, & Avila, 2000). And as a result, they can regulate microtubule assembly and stability, axon growth, dendritic development, and axonal remodeling. Although the exact mechanism by which GSK3-mediated phosphorylation of microtubules can give rise to behavioral changes is not clear, we speculate that by doing so, GSK3 may regulate neurodevelopment and synaptic plasticity, which can result in modulation of behavioral responses.

AMPA and NMDA Receptors

GSK3 can act on ionotropic glutamate receptors AMPA and NMDA. This may be one of the mechanisms underlying the acute modulation of behavior by GSK3. AMPA and NMDA are known to be important for synaptic plasticity; in accordance, it has been shown that activation of GSK3 inhibits long-term potentiation, while its inhibition prevents development of long-term depression (Peineau et al., 2007; Zhu et al., 2007). Trafficking and cell surface expression of NMDA receptor subunits are also the subject of GSK3 regulation (Chen, Gu, Liu, & Yan, 2007; Zhu et al., 2007). Since glutamate receptors could potentially be involved in the etiology of psychiatric disorders, their regulation by GSK3 may be implicated in the pathophysiology of many diseases including schizophrenia.

Dynamin I

Dynamin I is a large GTPase and can serve as a GSK3 substrate. The phosphorylated form of dynamin I is involved in activity-dependent bulk endocytosis (ADBE), but not in clathrin-mediated endocytosis. The activity of GSK3-dependent phosphorylation of dynamin I is necessary and sufficient for ADBE to take place. Thus, GSK3 may also play an important role in preparing synaptic vesicles for retrieval during elevated neuronal activity (Clayton et al., 2010).

BIOMARKERS

Although at the beginning of the twentieth century the term schizophrenia was coined and its symptoms defined, diagnosis has conventionally relied on symptoms (Stefansson et al., 2009). A main obstacle in psychiatric research is how to obtain measurable biological information from a living brain (Lavoie, Maziade, & Hebert, 2014). Therefore, to improve diagnosis and facilitate monitoring of response to therapy, development of valuable and highly discriminating noninvasive biomarkers presents a priority in psychiatry.

Peripheral Blood Cells

Collection and further processing of peripheral blood cells for biochemical analyses represent a rapid and noninvasive method for data acquisition from individuals. mRNA and protein expression profiling in the peripheral blood can provide useful information about alterations in disease-related signaling networks. Individuals with schizophrenia demonstrate diminished AKT1 and phospho-GSK3β protein levels in their peripheral lymphocytes that mirror similar alterations in the brain (Emamian et al., 2004). Moreover, stimulation of B lymphoblasts from schizophrenic subjects with NRG1a leads to a prominent reduction in pAKT (Sei et al., 2007) that is specific to schizophrenia and not shared by other psychiatric disorders (Keri et al., 2009).

Olfactory Epithelium

A solution to overcome the limitations of using postmortem brain and nonneural tissues is to analyze olfactory epithelium (OE) collected from subjects. OE possesses the distinctive feature of being a neuronal tissue with safe accessibility in live human subjects (Mor et al., 2013). The gene expression pattern of these cells also resembles that of the central nervous system (CNS) (Arnold et al., 2001). What makes OE especially attractive for schizophrenia is the correlation of negative symptoms with the structural and functional olfactory deficits (Corcoran et al., 2005). However, expression studies are lacking on GSK3 and its signaling partners in OE obtained from diseased versus healthy individuals.

Electroretinogram

The activity of retina, as part of the CNS, can be utilized as a biomarker for the assessment of brain disorders since it reflects certain aspects of brain neurochemistry. The retinal functions can be monitored using the noninvasive flash electroretinogram (ERG) method. Interestingly, patients with schizophrenia display ERG abnormalities, namely a reduction in cone a-wave and rod a- and b-waves. In the same vein, young mice at high genetic risk (HR) for schizophrenia and bipolar disorder also manifest reduced rod b-wave amplitude at Vmax as a biological endophenotype (Lavoie et al., 2014a, 2014b, 2014c). In line with the putative role of increased GSK3 activity in schizophrenia, the ERG of mice with GSK3β overexpression in neurons (prpGsk3b mice) shows the same pattern reported in the ERG of HRs, that is, a longer rod b-wave implicit time at Vmax and decreased rod b-wave amplitude. Alteration in the opposite direction was detected in GSK3β haploinsufficient mice. Cone a-wave alterations consistent with those of schizophrenic patients were also seen in GSK3α-KO mice. These observations link the GSK3 expression or activity profile with certain ERG anomalies in HRs and patients, thus highlighting the relevance of ERG assessments as a potentially reliable biomarker for psychiatric research (Lavoie, Hebert, & Beaulieu, 2014a).

Magnetic Resonance Imaging

Schizophrenia is associated with a multitude of functional and structural and anomalies that could be detected by noninvasive imaging techniques such as MRI. Using sMRI, structural changes in cerebral white matter and gray matter thickness, the hippocampal and subcortical volumes were traced in patients with schizophrenia (van Erp et al., 2014; Ledoux et al., 2014; Suzuki et al., 2002). Furthermore, cognitive abnormalities including perturbations in working memory and attention as well as aberrant activity of various brain regions were detected by fMRI in schizophrenic subjects (Bittner et al., 2014). In order to assess the predictability power of MRI data, its correlation with the presence of risk gene polymorphisms was studied (Bittner et al., 2014). Of interest, gray matter deficits seen with sMRI in thalamus, frontal, and temporal lobes were associated with polymorphisms in Akt, Pi3k, D2dr (Jagannathan et al., 2010), and GSk3β Gsk3 (Benedetti et al., 2010) loci. In addition, decreased PFC thickness and activity in schizophrenic subjects were strongly correlated with the Gsk3b polymorphisms (Blasi et al., 2013). The potential utility of noninvasive imaging techniques for early diagnosis will foster effective treatment.

CONCLUSIONS

Schizophrenia is the most chronic and disabling of the major mental illnesses. It is a life-long disease with largely unmet therapeutic needs. Understanding the intricate regulation of GSK3 in schizophrenia and its involvement in different, behavioral, metabolic, and developmental dimensions of mental illnesses may pave the way to the development of better therapies. Current medications include two generations of antipsychotics: typical (first generation) blocking D2 DA receptors and atypical (second generation) modulating both DA and serotoninergic neurotransmission. However, schizophrenia cannot be cured but can only be controlled with proper treatment, with so-called positive symptoms being predominantly amenable. Furthermore, antipsychotics of both generations have propensity to generate significant motor and/or metabolic side effects. These reasons and growing evidence on the involvement of abnormalities in intracellular signaling mechanisms in schizophrenia have brought to focus the signaling cascades mediated by D2 DA receptors. For future antipsychotic drug discovery, the strategy aimed at targeting these cascades may represent a more "soft" and effective approach than targeting receptors themselves.

While there is no specific pharmacological agent in clinical practice – with exception of lithium (Beaulieu, Marion, et al., 2008) – that modulates intercellular signaling mechanisms of DA receptors, the recent research in this field demonstrate intensive progress. Several lines of research, both in experimental animals and humans, overviewed here indicate that dysregulation of AKT-GSK3 might be a cardinal signaling event in pathogenesis and/or manifestations of schizophrenia. However, growing understanding of the complex and broad array of AKT-GSK3 regulation pathways impedes direct aiming at AKT and/or GSK3 as targets of pharmacological intervention, rather suggesting potential utility of downstream signaling targets. One of the future directions for antipsychotic drug discovery might involve regulation of βArr2/AKT/GSK3 intracellular signaling by biased antagonists of D2 DA receptors favoring one signaling modality over another (Masri et al., 2008). It is expected that biased antagonists should provide unique pharmacological profile of action: these hypothetical agents might block only the βArr2/AKT/GSK3 signaling transduction pathway while leaving other intracellular signaling routes unaffected. These and other directions based on the idea of targeting DA-related intracellular signaling cascades involved in psychosis could eventually result in the development of a new generation of antipsychotic agents with unprecedented specificity to certain symptoms and minimal side effects.

References

Abe, M., Herzog, E. D., & Block, G. D. (2000). Lithium lengthens the circadian period of individual suprachiasmatic nucleus neurons. *Neuroreport, 11*, 3261–3264.

Alabed, Y. Z., Pool, M., Ong, T. S., Sutherland, C., & Fournier, A. E. (2010). GSK3β regulates myelin-dependent axon outgrowth inhibition through CRMP4. *Journal of Neuroscience, 30*, 5635–5643.

Alimohamad, H., Rajakumar, N., Seah, Y. H., & Rushlow, W. (2005). Antipsychotics alter the protein expression levels of β-catenin and GSK-3 in the rat medial prefrontal cortex and striatum. *Biological Psychiatry, 57*, 533–542.

Alimohamad, H., Sutton, L., Mouyal, J., Rajakumar, N., & Rushlow, W. J. (2005). The effects of antipsychotics on β-catenin, glycogen synthase kinase-3 and dishevelled in the ventral midbrain of rats. *Journal of Neurochemistry, 95*, 513–525.

Allen, J. A., Yost, J. M., Setola, V., Chen, X., Sassano, M. F., Chen, M., et al. (2011). Discovery of β-arrestin-biased dopamine D2 ligands for probing signal transduction pathways essential for antipsychotic efficacy. *Proceedings of the National Academy of Sciences of the United States of America, 108*, 18488–18493.

Anai, M., Shojima, N., Katagiri, H., Ogihara, T., Sakoda, H., Onishi, Y., et al. (2005). A novel protein kinase B (PKB)/AKT-binding protein enhances PKB kinase activity and regulates DNA synthesis. *Journal of Biological Chemistry, 280*, 18525–18535.

Arnold, S. E., Han, L. Y., Moberg, P. J., Turetsky, B. I., Gur, R. E., Trojanowski, J. Q., et al. (2001). Dysregulation of olfactory receptor neuron lineage in schizophrenia. *Archives of General Psychiatry, 58*, 829–835.

Bajestan, S. N., Sabouri, A. H., Nakamura, M., Takashima, H., Keikhaee, M. R., Behdani, F., et al. (2006). Association of AKT1 haplotype with the risk of schizophrenia in Iranian population. *American Journal of Medical Genetics Part B: Neuropsychiatric Genetics, 141B*, 383–386.

Balog, Z., Kiss, I., & Keri, S. (2012). Five new schizophrenia loci may converge on the same cellular mechanism: the AKT pathway. *American Journal of Psychiatry, 169*, 335.

Balu, D. T., Carlson, G. C., Talbot, K., Kazi, H., Hill-Smith, T. E., Easton, R. M., et al. (2012). Akt1 deficiency in schizophrenia and impairment of hippocampal plasticity and function. *Hippocampus, 22*, 230–240.

de Bartolomeis, A., Buonaguro, E. F., & Iasevoli, F. (2013). Serotonin-glutamate and serotonin-dopamine reciprocal interactions as putative molecular targets for novel antipsychotic treatments: from receptor heterodimers to postsynaptic scaffolding and effector proteins. *Psychopharmacology (Berl), 225*, 1–19.

Beasley, C., Cotter, D., Khan, N., Pollard, C., Sheppard, P., Varndell, I., et al. (2001). Glycogen synthase kinase-3β immunoreactivity is reduced in the prefrontal cortex in schizophrenia. *Neuroscience Letters, 302*, 117–120.

Beaulieu, J. M. (2012). A role for Akt and glycogen synthase kinase-3 as integrators of dopamine and serotonin neurotransmission in mental health. *Journal of Psychiatry & Neuroscience, 37*, 7–16.

Beaulieu, J. M., Gainetdinov, R. R., & Caron, M. G. (2009). Akt/GSK3 signaling in the action of psychotropic drugs. *Annual Review of Pharmacology and Toxicology, 49*, 327–347.

Beaulieu, J. M., Marion, S., Rodriguiz, R. M., Medvedev, I. O., Sotnikova, T. D., Ghisi, V., et al. (2008). A β-arrestin 2 signaling complex mediates lithium action on behavior. *Cell, 132*, 125–136.

Beaulieu, J. M., Sotnikova, T. D., Marion, S., Lefkowitz, R. J., Gainetdinov, R. R., & Caron, M. G. (2005). An Akt/β-arrestin 2/PP2A signaling complex mediates dopaminergic neurotransmission and behavior. *Cell, 122*, 261–273.

Beaulieu, J. M., Sotnikova, T. D., Yao, W. D., Kockeritz, L., Woodgett, J. R., Gainetdinov, R. R., et al. (2004). Lithium antagonizes dopamine-dependent behaviors mediated by an AKT/glycogen synthase kinase 3 signaling cascade. *Proceedings of the National Academy of Sciences of the United States of America, 101*, 5099–5104.

Beaulieu, J. M., Tirotta, E., Sotnikova, T. D., Masri, B., Salahpour, A., Gainetdinov, R. R., et al. (2007). Regulation of Akt signaling by D2 and D3 dopamine receptors in vivo. *Journal of Neuroscience, 27*, 881–885.

Beaulieu, J. M., Zhang, X., Rodriguiz, R. M., Sotnikova, T. D., Cools, M. J., Wetsel, W. C., et al. (2008). Role of GSK3β in behavioral abnormalities induced by serotonin deficiency. *Proceedings of the National Academy of Sciences of the United States of America, 105*, 1333–1338.

Benedetti, F., Poletti, S., Radaelli, D., Bernasconi, A., Cavallaro, R., Falini, A., et al. (2010). Temporal lobe grey matter volume in schizophrenia is associated with a genetic polymorphism influencing glycogen synthase kinase 3-β activity. *Genes, Brain and Behavior, 9*, 365–371.

van Beveren, N. J., Buitendijk, G. H., Swagemakers, S., Krab, L. C., Roder, C., de, H. L., et al. (2012). Marked reduction of AKT1 expression and deregulation of AKT1-associated pathways in peripheral blood mononuclear cells of schizophrenia patients. *PLoS One, 7*, e32618.

Bittner, R. A., Linden, D. E., Roebroeck, A., Hartling, F., Rotarska-Jagiela, A., Maurer, K., et al. (2014). The when and where of working memory dysfunction in early-onset schizophrenia – a functional magnetic resonance imaging study. *Cerebral Cortex* [Epub].

Blasi, G., Napolitano, F., Ursini, G., Di, G. A., Caforio, G., Taurisano, P., et al. (2013). Association of GSK-3β genetic variation with GSK-3β expression, prefrontal cortical thickness, prefrontal physiology, and schizophrenia. *American Journal of Psychiatry, 170*, 868–876.

Brzozka, M. M., Radyushkin, K., Wichert, S. P., Ehrenreich, H., & Rossner, M. J. (2010). Cognitive and sensorimotor gating impairments in transgenic mice overexpressing the schizophrenia susceptibility gene Tcf4 in the brain. *Biological Psychiatry, 68*, 33–40.

Bychkov, E., Ahmed, M. R., Dalby, K. N., & Gurevich, E. V. (2007). Dopamine depletion and subsequent treatment with L-DOPA, but not the long-lived dopamine agonist pergolide, enhances activity of the Akt pathway in the rat striatum. *Journal of Neurochemistry, 102*, 699–711.

Callicott, J. H., Straub, R. E., Pezawas, L., Egan, M. F., Mattay, V. S., Hariri, A. R., et al. (2005). Variation in DISC1 affects hippocampal structure and function and increases risk for schizophrenia. *Proceedings of the National Academy of Sciences of the United States of America, 102*, 8627–8632.

Cannon, T. D., Hennah, W., van Erp, T. G., Thompson, P. M., Lonnqvist, J., Huttunen, M., et al. (2005). Association of DISC1/TRAX haplotypes with schizophrenia, reduced prefrontal gray matter, and impaired short- and long-term memory. *Archives of General Psychiatry, 62*, 1205–1213.

Carlsson, T., Schindler, F. R., Hollerhage, M., Depboylu, C., Arias-Carrion, O., Schnurrbusch, S., et al. (2011). Systemic administration of neuregulin-1β1 protects dopaminergic neurons in a mouse model of Parkinson's disease. *Journal of Neurochemistry, 117*, 1066–1074.

Chakraborty, A., Koldobskiy, M. A., Bello, N. T., Maxwell, M., Potter, J. J., Juluri, K. R., et al. (2010). Inositol pyrophosphates inhibit Akt signaling, thereby regulating insulin sensitivity and weight gain. *Cell, 143*, 897–910.

Chakraborty, A., Latapy, C., Xu, J., Snyder, S. H., & Beaulieu, J. M. (2014). Inositol hexakisphosphate kinase-1 regulates behavioral responses via GSK3 signaling pathways. *Molecular Psychiatry, 19*, 284–293.

Chen, P., Gu, Z., Liu, W., & Yan, Z. (2007). Glycogen synthase kinase 3 regulates N-methyl-D-aspartate receptor channel trafficking and function in cortical neurons. *Molecular Pharmacology, 72*, 40–51.

Chen, P. C., Lao, C. L., & Chen, J. C. (2007). Dual alteration of limbic dopamine D1 receptor-mediated signalling and the Akt/GSK3 pathway in dopamine D3 receptor mutants during the development of methamphetamine sensitization. *Journal of Neurochemistry, 100*, 225–241.

Chiba, S., Hashimoto, R., Hattori, S., Yohda, M., Lipska, B., Weinberger, D. R., et al. (2006). Effect of antipsychotic drugs on DISC1 and dysbindin expression in mouse frontal cortex and hippocampus. *Journal of Neural Transmission, 113*, 1337–1346.

Clapcote, S. J., Lipina, T. V., Millar, J. K., Mackie, S., Christie, S., Ogawa, F., et al. (2007). Behavioral phenotypes of Disc1 missense mutations in mice. *Neuron, 54*, 387–402.

Clayton, E. L., Sue, N., Smillie, K. J., O'Leary, T., Bache, N., Cheung, G., et al. (2010). Dynamin I phosphorylation by GSK3 controls activity-dependent bulk endocytosis of synaptic vesicles. *Nature Neuroscience, 13*, 845–851.

Cohen, P., & Frame, S. (2001). The renaissance of GSK3. *Nature Reviews Molecular Cell Biology, 2*, 769–776.

Cole, A. R., Knebel, A., Morrice, N. A., Robertson, L. A., Irving, A. J., Connolly, C. N., et al. (2004). GSK-3 phosphorylation of the Alzheimer epitope within collapsin response mediator proteins regulates axon elongation in primary neurons. *Journal of Biological Chemistry, 279,* 50176–50180.

Corcoran, C., Whitaker, A., Coleman, E., Fried, J., Feldman, J., Goudsmit, N., et al. (2005). Olfactory deficits, cognition and negative symptoms in early onset psychosis. *Schizophrenia Research, 80,* 283–293.

Cotter, D., Kerwin, R., al-Sarraji, S., Brion, J. P., Chadwich, A., Lovestone, S., et al. (1998). Abnormalities of Wnt signalling in schizophrenia–evidence for neurodevelopmental abnormality. *Neuroreport, 9,* 1379–1383.

Cross, D. A., Alessi, D. R., Cohen, P., Andjelkovich, M., & Hemmings, B. A. (1995). Inhibition of glycogen synthase kinase-3 by insulin mediated by protein kinase B. *Nature, 378,* 785–789.

Cui, D. H., Jiang, K. D., Jiang, S. D., Xu, Y. F., & Yao, H. (2005). The tumor suppressor adenomatous polyposis coli gene is associated with susceptibility to schizophrenia. *Molecular Psychiatry, 10,* 669–677.

Deng, C., Pan, B., Engel, M., & Huang, X. F. (2013). Neuregulin-1 signalling and antipsychotic treatment: potential therapeutic targets in a schizophrenia candidate signalling pathway. *Psychopharmacology (Berl), 226,* 201–215.

Ding, V. W., Chen, R. H., & McCormick, F. (2000). Differential regulation of glycogen synthase kinase 3β by insulin and Wnt signaling. *Journal of Biological Chemistry, 275,* 32475–32481.

Dominguez, I., Itoh, K., & Sokol, S. Y. (1995). Role of glycogen synthase kinase 3β as a negative regulator of dorsoventral axis formation in *Xenopus* embryos. *Proceedings of the National Academy of Sciences of the United States of America, 92,* 8498–8502.

Ekelund, J., Hennah, W., Hiekkalinna, T., Parker, A., Meyer, J., Lonnqvist, J., et al. (2004). Replication of 1q42 linkage in Finnish schizophrenia pedigrees. *Molecular Psychiatry, 9,* 1037–1041.

Ekelund, J., Hovatta, I., Parker, A., Paunio, T., Varilo, T., Martin, R., et al. (2001). Chromosome 1 loci in Finnish schizophrenia families. *Human Molecular Genetics, 10,* 1611–1617.

Emamian, E. S., Hall, D., Birnbaum, M. J., Karayiorgou, M., & Gogos, J. A. (2004). Convergent evidence for impaired AKT1-GSK3β signaling in schizophrenia. *Nature Genetics, 36,* 131–137.

van Erp, T. G., Greve, D. N., Rasmussen, J., Turner, J., Calhoun, V. D., Young, S., et al. (2014). A multi-scanner study of subcortical brain volume abnormalities in schizophrenia. *Psychiatry Research, 222*(1-2), 10–16.

Feinberg, A. P., & Snyder, S. H. (1975). Phenothiazine drugs: structure-activity relationships explained by a conformation that mimics dopamine. *Proceedings of the National Academy of Sciences of the United States of America, 72,* 1899–1903.

Fukumoto, T., Morinobu, S., Okamoto, Y., Kagaya, A., & Yamawaki, S. (2001). Chronic lithium treatment increases the expression of brain-derived neurotrophic factor in the rat brain. *Psychopharmacology (Berl), 158,* 100–106.

Gachon, F., Nagoshi, E., Brown, S. A., Ripperger, J., & Schibler, U. (2004). The mammalian circadian timing system: from gene expression to physiology. *Chromosoma, 113,* 103–112.

Gainetdinov, R. R., Wetsel, W. C., Jones, S. R., Levin, E. D., Jaber, M., & Caron, M. G. (1999). Role of serotonin in the paradoxical calming effect of psychostimulants on hyperactivity. *Science, 283,* 397–401.

Gimenez-Cassina, A., Lim, F., & Diaz-Nido, J. (2012). Chronic inhibition of glycogen synthase kinase-3 protects against rotenone-induced cell death in human neuron-like cells by increasing BDNF secretion. *Neuroscience Letters, 531,* 182–187.

Giros, B., Jaber, M., Jones, S. R., Wightman, R. M., & Caron, M. G. (1996). Hyperlocomotion and indifference to cocaine and amphetamine in mice lacking the dopamine transporter. *Nature, 379,* 606–612.

Gonzalez, E., & McGraw, T. E. (2009). The Akt kinases: isoform specificity in metabolism and cancer. *Cell Cycle, 8,* 2502–2508.

Gould, T. D., O'Donnell, K. C., Picchini, A. M., Dow, E. R., Chen, G., & Manji, H. K. (2008). Generation and behavioral characterization of β-catenin forebrain-specific conditional knock-out mice. *Behavioural Brain Research, 189,* 117–125.

Gould, T. D., O'Donnell, K. C., Picchini, A. M., & Manji, H. K. (2007). Strain differences in lithium attenuation of *d*-amphetamine-induced hyperlocomotion: a mouse model for the genetics of clinical response to lithium. *Neuropsychopharmacology, 32,* 1321–1333.

Harada, Y., Sakai, M., Kurabayashi, N., Hirota, T., & Fukada, Y. (2005). Ser-557-phosphorylated mCRY2 is degraded upon synergistic phosphorylation by glycogen synthase kinase-3β. *Journal of Biological Chemistry, 280,* 31714–31721.

Harrison, P. J., & Law, A. J. (2006). Neuregulin 1 and schizophrenia: genetics, gene expression, and neurobiology. *Biological Psychiatry, 60,* 132–140.

Hashimoto, R., Takei, N., Shimazu, K., Christ, L., Lu, B., & Chuang, D. M. (2002). Lithium induces brain-derived neurotrophic factor and activates TrkB in rodent cortical neurons: an essential step for neuroprotection against glutamate excitotoxicity. *Neuropharmacology, 43,* 1173–1179.

He, X., Saint-Jeannet, J. P., Woodgett, J. R., Varmus, H. E., & Dawid, I. B. (1995). Glycogen synthase kinase-3 and dorsoventral patterning in *Xenopus* embryos. *Nature, 374,* 617–622.

Hennah, W., Varilo, T., Kestila, M., Paunio, T., Arajarvi, R., Haukka, J., et al. (2003). Haplotype transmission analysis provides evidence of association for DISC1 to schizophrenia and suggests sex-dependent effects. *Human Molecular Genetics, 12,* 3151–3159.

Hunter, T. (1997). Oncoprotein networks. *Cell, 88,* 333–346.

Hwu, H. G., Liu, C. M., Fann, C. S., Ou-Yang, W. C., & Lee, S. F. (2003). Linkage of schizophrenia with chromosome 1q loci in Taiwanese families. *Molecular Psychiatry, 8,* 445–452.

Ide, M., Ohnishi, T., Murayama, M., Matsumoto, I., Yamada, K., Iwayama, Y., et al. (2006). Failure to support a genetic contribution of AKT1 polymorphisms and altered AKT signaling in schizophrenia. *Journal of Neurochemistry, 99,* 277–287.

Iitaka, C., Miyazaki, K., Akaike, T., & Ishida, N. (2005). A role for glycogen synthase kinase-3β in the mammalian circadian clock. *Journal of Biological Chemistry, 280,* 29397–29402.

Ikeda, M., Iwata, N., Suzuki, T., Kitajima, T., Yamanouchi, Y., Kinoshita, Y., et al. (2004). Association of AKT1 with schizophrenia confirmed in a Japanese population. *Biological Psychiatry, 56,* 698–700.

Ishizuka, K., Kamiya, A., Oh, E. C., Kanki, H., Seshadri, S., Robinson, J. F., et al. (2011). DISC1-dependent switch from progenitor proliferation to migration in the developing cortex. *Nature, 473,* 92–96.

Iwahana, E., Akiyama, M., Miyakawa, K., Uchida, A., Kasahara, J., Fukunaga, K., et al. (2004). Effect of lithium on the circadian rhythms of locomotor activity and glycogen synthase kinase-3 protein expression in the mouse suprachiasmatic nuclei. *European Journal of Neuroscience, 19,* 2281–2287.

Jagannathan, K., Calhoun, V. D., Gelernter, J., Stevens, M. C., Liu, J., Bolognani, F., et al. (2010). Genetic associations of brain structural networks in schizophrenia: a preliminary study. *Biological Psychiatry, 68,* 657–666.

Javitt, D. C., & Zukin, S. R. (1991). Recent advances in the phencyclidine model of schizophrenia. *American Journal of Psychiatry, 148,* 1301–1308.

Johnstone, M., Thomson, P. A., Hall, J., McIntosh, A. M., Lawrie, S. M., & Porteous, D. J. (2011). DISC1 in schizophrenia: genetic mouse models and human genomic imaging. *Schizophrenia Bulletin, 37,* 14–20.

Junttila, T. T., Sundvall, M., Maatta, J. A., & Elenius, K. (2000). Erbb4 and its isoforms: selective regulation of growth factor responses by naturally occurring receptor variants. *Trends in Cardiovascular Medicine, 10,* 304–310.

Kaidanovich-Beilin, O., Lipina, T. V., Takao, K., van, E. M., Hattori, S., Laliberte, C., et al. (2009). Abnormalities in brain structure and behavior in GSK-3α mutant mice. *Molecular Brain, 2,* 35.

Kang, U. G., Roh, M. S., Jung, J. R., Shin, S. Y., Lee, Y. H., Park, J. B., et al. (2004). Activation of protein kinase B (Akt) signaling after electroconvulsive shock in the rat hippocampus. *Progress in Neuro-Psychopharmacology & Biological Psychiatry, 28*, 41–44.

Karege, F., Perroud, N., Schurhoff, F., Meary, A., Marillier, G., Burkhardt, S., et al. (2010). Association of AKT1 gene variants and protein expression in both schizophrenia and bipolar disorder. *Genes, Brain and Behavior, 9*, 503–511.

Kato, T., Abe, Y., Sotoyama, H., Kakita, A., Kominami, R., Hirokawa, S., et al. (2011). Transient exposure of neonatal mice to neuregulin-1 results in hyperdopaminergic states in adulthood: implication in neurodevelopmental hypothesis for schizophrenia. *Molecular Psychiatry, 16*, 307–320.

Katsu, T., Ujike, H., Nakano, T., Tanaka, Y., Nomura, A., Nakata, K., et al. (2003). The human frizzled-3 (FZD3) gene on chromosome 8p21, a receptor gene for Wnt ligands, is associated with the susceptibility to schizophrenia. *Neuroscience Letters, 353*, 53–56.

Keri, S., Beniczky, S., & Kelemen, O. (2010). Suppression of the P50 evoked response and neuregulin 1-induced AKT phosphorylation in first-episode schizophrenia. *American Journal of Psychiatry, 167*, 444–450.

Keri, S., Seres, I., Kelemen, O., & Benedek, G. (2009). Neuregulin 1-stimulated phosphorylation of AKT in psychotic disorders and its relationship with neurocognitive functions. *Neurochemistry International, 55*, 606–609.

Kim, J. Y., Duan, X., Liu, C. Y., Jang, M. H., Guo, J. U., Powanpongkul, N., et al. (2009). DISC1 regulates new neuron development in the adult brain via modulation of AKT-mTOR signaling through KIAA1212. *Neuron, 63*, 761–773.

King, M. K., Pardo, M., Cheng, Y., Downey, K., Jope, R. S., & Beurel, E. (2014). Glycogen synthase kinase-3 inhibitors: rescuers of cognitive impairments. *Pharmacology & Therapeutics, 141*, 1–12.

Kivimae, S., Martin, P. M., Kapfhamer, D., Ruan, Y., Heberlein, U., Rubenstein, J. L., et al. (2011). Abnormal behavior in mice mutant for the Disc1 binding partner, Dixdc1. *Translational Psychiatry, 1*, e43.

Koshimizu, H., Fukui, Y., Takao, K., Ohira, K., Tanda, K., Nakanishi, K., et al. (2011). Adenomatous polyposis coli heterozygous knockout mice display hypoactivity and age-dependent working memory deficits. *Frontiers in Behavioral Neuroscience, 5*, 85.

Kozlovsky, N., Belmaker, R. H., & Agam, G. (2000). Low GSK-3β immunoreactivity in postmortem frontal cortex of schizophrenic patients. *American Journal of Psychiatry, 157*, 831–833.

Kozlovsky, N., Belmaker, R. H., & Agam, G. (2001). Low GSK-3 activity in frontal cortex of schizophrenic patients. *Schizophrenia Research, 52*, 101–105.

Kozlovsky, N., Regenold, W. T., Levine, J., Rapoport, A., Belmaker, R. H., & Agam, G. (2004). GSK-3β in cerebrospinal fluid of schizophrenia patients. *Journal of Neural Transmission, 111*, 1093–1098.

Kozlovsky, N., Shanon-Weickert, C., Tomaskovic-Crook, E., Kleinman, J. E., Belmaker, R. H., & Agam, G. (2004). Reduced GSK-3β mRNA levels in postmortem dorsolateral prefrontal cortex of schizophrenic patients. *Journal of Neural Transmission, 111*, 1583–1592.

Kwon, O. B., Paredes, D., Gonzalez, C. M., Neddens, J., Hernandez, L., Vullhorst, D., et al. (2008). Neuregulin-1 regulates LTP at CA1 hippocampal synapses through activation of dopamine D4 receptors. *Proceedings of the National Academy of Sciences of the United States of America, 105*, 15587–15592.

Latapy, C., Rioux, V., Guitton, M. J., & Beaulieu, J. M. (2012). Selective deletion of forebrain glycogen synthase kinase 3β reveals a central role in serotonin-sensitive anxiety and social behaviour. *Philosophical Transactions of the Royal Society of London Series B: Biological Sciences, 367*, 2460–2474.

Lavoie, J., Hebert, M., & Beaulieu, J. M. (2014a). Glycogen synthase Kinase-3 overexpression replicates electroretinogram anomalies of offspring at high genetic risk for schizophrenia and bipolar disorder. *Biological Psychiatry, 76*(2), 93–100.

Lavoie, J., Hebert, M., & Beaulieu, J. M. (2013b). Glycogen synthase kinase-3β haploinsufficiency lengthens the circadian locomotor activity period in mice. *Behavioural Brain Research, 253*, 262–265.

Lavoie, J., Illiano, P., Sotnikova, T. D., Gainetdinov, R. R., Beaulieu, J. M., & Hebert, M. (2014b). The electroretinogram as a biomarker of central dopamine and serotonin: potential relevance to psychiatric disorders. *Biological Psychiatry, 75*, 479–486.

Lavoie, J., Maziade, M., & Hebert, M. (2014c). The brain through the retina: the flash electroretinogram as a tool to investigate psychiatric disorders. *Progress in Neuro-Psychopharmacology & Biological Psychiatry, 48*, 129–134.

Law, A. J., Kleinman, J. E., Weinberger, D. R., & Weickert, C. S. (2007). Disease-associated intronic variants in the ErbB4 gene are related to altered ErbB4 splice-variant expression in the brain in schizophrenia. *Human Molecular Genetics, 16*, 129–141.

Law, A. J., Lipska, B. K., Weickert, C. S., Hyde, T. M., Straub, R. E., Hashimoto, R., et al. (2006). Neuregulin 1 transcripts are differentially expressed in schizophrenia and regulated by 5′ SNPs associated with the disease. *Proceedings of the National Academy of Sciences of the United States of America, 103*, 6747–6752.

Law, A. J., Wang, Y., Sei, Y., O'Donnell, P., Piantadosi, P., Papaleo, F., et al. (2012). Neuregulin 1-ErbB4-PI3K signaling in schizophrenia and phosphoinositide 3-kinase-p110delta inhibition as a potential therapeutic strategy. *Proceedings of the National Academy of Sciences of the United States of America, 109*, 12165–12170.

Ledoux, A. A., Boyer, P., Phillips, J. L., Labelle, A., Smith, A., & Bohbot, V. D. (2014). Structural hippocampal anomalies in a schizophrenia population correlate with navigation performance on a wayfinding task. *Frontiers in Behavioral Neuroscience, 8*, 88.

Lee, K. Y., Joo, E. J., Jeong, S. H., Kang, U. G., Roh, M. S., Kim, S. H., et al. (2010). No association between AKT1 polymorphism and schizophrenia: a case-control study in a Korean population and a meta-analysis. *Neuroscience Research, 66*, 238–245.

Lee, F. H., Kaidanovich-Beilin, O., Roder, J. C., Woodgett, J. R., & Wong, A. H. (2011). Genetic inactivation of GSK3β rescues spine deficits in Disc1-L100P mutant mice. *Schizophrenia Research, 129*, 74–79.

Lijam, N., Paylor, R., McDonald, M. P., Crawley, J. N., Deng, C. X., Herrup, K., et al. (1997). Social interaction and sensorimotor gating abnormalities in mice lacking Dvl1. *Cell, 90*, 895–905.

Li, M., Mo, Y., Luo, X. J., Xiao, X., Shi, L., Peng, Y. M., et al. (2011). Genetic association and identification of a functional SNP at GSK3β for schizophrenia susceptibility. *Schizophrenia Research, 133*, 165–171.

Li, X., Zhu, W., Roh, M. S., Friedman, A. B., Rosborough, K., & Jope, R. S. (2004). In vivo regulation of glycogen synthase kinase-3β (GSK3β) by serotonergic activity in mouse brain. *Neuropsychopharmacology, 29*, 1426–1431.

Lipina, T. V., Kaidanovich-Beilin, O., Patel, S., Wang, M., Clapcote, S. J., Liu, F., et al. (2011). Genetic and pharmacological evidence for schizophrenia-related Disc1 interaction with GSK-3. *Synapse, 65*, 234–248.

Lipina, T. V., Palomo, V., Gil, C., Martinez, A., & Roder, J. C. (2013). Dual inhibitor of PDE7 and GSK-3-VP1.15 acts as antipsychotic and cognitive enhancer in C57BL/6J mice. *Neuropharmacology, 64*, 205–214.

Lipina, T. V., Wang, M., Liu, F., & Roder, J. C. (2012). Synergistic interactions between PDE4B and GSK-3: DISC1 mutant mice. *Neuropharmacology, 62*, 1252–1262.

Liu, Y. L., Fann, C. S., Liu, C. M., Wu, J. Y., Hung, S. I., Chan, H. Y., et al. (2006). Absence of significant associations between four AKT1 SNP markers and schizophrenia in the Taiwanese population. *Psychiatric Genetics, 16*, 39–41.

Liu, Y. C., Huang, C. L., Wu, P. L., Chang, Y. C., Huang, C. H., & Lane, H. Y. (2009). Lack of association between AKT1 variances versus clinical manifestations and social function in patients with schizophrenia. *Journal of Psychopharmacology, 23*, 937–943.

Lochhead, P. A., Kinstrie, R., Sibbet, G., Rawjee, T., Morrice, N., & Cleghon, V. (2006). A chaperone-dependent GSK3β transitional intermediate mediates activation-loop autophosphorylation. *Molecular Cell, 24*, 627–633.

Lucas, F. R., Goold, R. G., Gordon-Weeks, P. R., & Salinas, P. C. (1998). Inhibition of GSK-3β leading to the loss of phosphorylated MAP-1B is an early event in axonal remodelling induced by WNT-7a or lithium. *Journal of Cell Science, 111*(Pt 10), 1351–1361.

Mackie, S., Millar, J. K., & Porteous, D. J. (2007). Role of DISC1 in neural development and schizophrenia. *Current Opinion in Neurobiology, 17*, 95–102.

Maeda, K., Nwulia, E., Chang, J., Balkissoon, R., Ishizuka, K., Chen, H., et al. (2006). Differential expression of disrupted-in-schizophrenia (DISC1) in bipolar disorder. *Biological Psychiatry, 60*, 929–935.

Mao, Y., Ge, X., Frank, C. L., Madison, J. M., Koehler, A. N., Doud, M. K., et al. (2009). Disrupted in schizophrenia 1 regulates neuronal progenitor proliferation via modulation of GSK3β/β-catenin signaling. *Cell, 136*, 1017–1031.

Margolis, R. L., & Ross, C. A. (2010). Neuronal signaling pathways: genetic insights into the pathophysiology of major mental illness. *Neuropsychopharmacology, 35*, 350–351.

Ma, Y. C., Song, M. R., Park, J. P., Henry Ho, H. Y., Hu, L., Kurtev, M. V., et al. (2008). Regulation of motor neuron specification by phosphorylation of neurogenin 2. *Neuron, 58*, 65–77.

Masri, B., Salahpour, A., Didriksen, M., Ghisi, V., Beaulieu, J. M., Gainetdinov, R. R., et al. (2008). Antagonism of dopamine D2 receptor/β-arrestin 2 interaction is a common property of clinically effective antipsychotics. *Proceedings of the National Academy of Sciences of the United States of America, 105*, 13656–13661.

Mathur, A., Law, M. H., Megson, I. L., Shaw, D. J., & Wei, J. (2010). Genetic association of the AKT1 gene with schizophrenia in a British population. *Psychiatric Genetics, 20*, 118–122.

Millar, J. K., Pickard, B. S., Mackie, S., James, R., Christie, S., Buchanan, S. R., et al. (2005). DISC1 and PDE4B are interacting genetic factors in schizophrenia that regulate cAMP signaling. *Science, 310*, 1187–1191.

Millar, J. K., Wilson-Annan, J. C., Anderson, S., Christie, S., Taylor, M. S., Semple, C. A., et al. (2000). Disruption of two novel genes by a translocation co-segregating with schizophrenia. *Human Molecular Genetics, 9*, 1415–1423.

Missale, C., Nash, S. R., Robinson, S. W., Jaber, M., & Caron, M. G. (1998). Dopamine receptors: from structure to function. *Physiological Reviews, 78*, 189–225.

Miyaoka, T., Seno, H., & Ishino, H. (1999). Increased expression of Wnt-1 in schizophrenic brains. *Schizophrenia Research, 38*, 1–6.

Mor, E., Kano, S., Colantuoni, C., Sawa, A., Navon, R., & Shomron, N. (2013). MicroRNA-382 expression is elevated in the olfactory neuroepithelium of schizophrenia patients. *Neurobiology of Disease, 55*, 1–10.

Murase, S., Mosser, E., & Schuman, E. M. (2002). Depolarization drives β-Catenin into neuronal spines promoting changes in synaptic structure and function. *Neuron, 35*, 91–105.

Nakata, K., Lipska, B. K., Hyde, T. M., Ye, T., Newburn, E. N., Morita, Y., et al. (2009). DISC1 splice variants are upregulated in schizophrenia and associated with risk polymorphisms. *Proceedings of the National Academy of Sciences of the United States of America, 106*, 15873–15878.

Nishi, A., Snyder, G. L., & Greengard, P. (1997). Bidirectional regulation of DARPP-32 phosphorylation by dopamine. *Journal of Neuroscience, 17*, 8147–8155.

Norton, N., Williams, H. J., Dwyer, S., Carroll, L., Peirce, T., Moskvina, V., et al. (2007). Association analysis of AKT1 and schizophrenia in a UK case control sample. *Schizophrenia Research, 93*, 58–65.

O'Brien, W. T., Huang, J., Buccafusca, R., Garskof, J., Valvezan, A. J., Berry, G. T., et al. (2011). Glycogen synthase kinase-3 is essential for β-arrestin-2 complex formation and lithium-sensitive behaviors in mice. *Journal of Clinical Investigation, 121*, 3756–3762.

Ogata, T., Iijima, S., Hoshikawa, S., Miura, T., Yamamoto, S., Oda, H., et al. (2004). Opposing extracellular signal-regulated kinase and Akt pathways control Schwann cell myelination. *Journal of Neuroscience, 24*, 6724–6732.

Ohi, K., Hashimoto, R., Yasuda, Y., Fukumoto, M., Nemoto, K., Ohnishi, T., et al. (2013). The AKT1 gene is associated with attention and brain morphology in schizophrenia. *World Journal of Biological Psychiatry, 14*, 100–113.

Ohtsuki, T., Inada, T., & Arinami, T. (2004). Failure to confirm association between AKT1 haplotype and schizophrenia in a Japanese case-control population. *Molecular Psychiatry, 9*, 981–983.

Okerlund, N. D., & Cheyette, B. N. (2011). Synaptic Wnt signaling-a contributor to major psychiatric disorders? *Journal of Neurodevelopmental Disorders, 3*, 162–174.

Pan, B., Huang, X. F., & Deng, C. (2011). Antipsychotic treatment and neuregulin 1-ErbB4 signalling in schizophrenia. *Progress in Neuro-Psychopharmacology & Biological Psychiatry, 35*, 924–930.

Peineau, S., Taghibiglou, C., Bradley, C., Wong, T. P., Liu, L., Lu, J., et al. (2007). LTP inhibits LTD in the hippocampus via regulation of GSK3β. *Neuron, 53*, 703–717.

Pierce, S. B., & Kimelman, D. (1995). Regulation of Spemann organizer formation by the intracellular kinase Xgsk-3. *Development, 121*, 755–765.

Polter, A. M., & Li, X. (2011). Glycogen synthase kinase-3 is an intermediate modulator of serotonin neurotransmission. *Frontiers in Molecular Neuroscience, 4*, 31.

Ross, S. E., Erickson, R. L., Hemati, N., & MacDougald, O. A. (1999). Glycogen synthase kinase 3 is an insulin-regulated C/EBPα kinase. *Molecular and Cellular Biology, 19*, 8433–8441.

Sahar, S., Zocchi, L., Kinoshita, C., Borrelli, E., & Sassone-Corsi, P. (2010). Regulation of BMAL1 protein stability and circadian function by GSK3β-mediated phosphorylation. *PLoS One, 5*, e8561.

Sanchez, C., Perez, M., & Avila, J. (2000). GSK3β-mediated phosphorylation of the microtubule-associated protein 2C (MAP2C) prevents microtubule bundling. *European Journal of Cell Biology, 79*, 252–260.

Sawa, A., & Snyder, S. H. (2002). Schizophrenia: diverse approaches to a complex disease. *Science, 296*, 692–695.

Scassellati, C., Bonvicini, C., Perez, J., Bocchio-Chiavetto, L., Tura, G. B., Rossi, G., et al. (2004). Association study of -1727 A/T, -50 C/T and (CAA)n repeat GSK-3β gene polymorphisms with schizophrenia. *Neuropsychobiology, 50*, 16–20.

Schizophrenia Psychiatric Genome-Wide Association Study (GWAS) Consortium. (2011). Genome-wide association study identifies five new schizophrenia loci. *Nature Genetics, 43*, 969–976.

Schumacher, J., Laje, G., Abou, J. R., Becker, T., Muhleisen, T. W., Vasilescu, C., et al. (2009). The DISC locus and schizophrenia: evidence from an association study in a central European sample and from a meta-analysis across different European populations. *Human Molecular Genetics, 18*, 2719–2727.

Schwab, S. G., Hoefgen, B., Hanses, C., Hassenbach, M. B., Albus, M., Lerer, B., et al. (2005). Further evidence for association of variants in the AKT1 gene with schizophrenia in a sample of European sib-pair families. *Biological Psychiatry, 58*, 446–450.

Seeman, P. (2002). Atypical antipsychotics: mechanism of action. *Canadian Journal of Psychiatry, 47*, 27–38.

Seeman, P., & Lee, T. (1975). Antipsychotic drugs: direct correlation between clinical potency and presynaptic action on dopamine neurons. *Science, 188*, 1217–1219.

Sei, Y., Ren-Patterson, R., Li, Z., Tunbridge, E. M., Egan, M. F., Kolachana, B. S., et al. (2007). Neuregulin1-induced cell migration is impaired in schizophrenia: association with neuregulin1 and catechol-o-methyltransferase gene polymorphisms. *Molecular Psychiatry, 12*, 946–957.

Shin, S. Y., Yoon, S. C., Kim, Y. H., Kim, Y. S., & Lee, Y. H. (2002). Phosphorylation of glycogen synthase kinase-3β at serine-9 by phospholipase Cgamma1 through protein kinase C in rat 3Y1 fibroblasts. *Experimental & Molecular Medicine, 34*, 444–450.

Shiomi, K., Kanemoto, M., Keino-Masu, K., Yoshida, S., Soma, K., & Masu, M. (2005). Identification and differential expression of multiple isoforms of mouse Coiled-coil-DIX1 (Ccd1), a positive regulator of Wnt signaling. *Brain Research Molecular Brain Research, 135,* 169–180.

Shiomi, K., Uchida, H., Keino-Masu, K., & Masu, M. (2003). Ccd1, a novel protein with a DIX domain, is a positive regulator in the Wnt signaling during zebrafish neural patterning. *Current Biology, 13,* 73–77.

Silberberg, G., Darvasi, A., Pinkas-Kramarski, R., & Navon, R. (2006). The involvement of ErbB4 with schizophrenia: association and expression studies. *American Journal of Medical Genetics Part B: Neuropsychiatric Genetics, 141B,* 142–148.

Singh, K. K., Ge, X., Mao, Y., Drane, L., Meletis, K., Samuels, B. A., et al. (2010). Dixdc1 is a critical regulator of DISC1 and embryonic cortical development. *Neuron, 67,* 33–48.

Sotnikova, T. D., Beaulieu, J. M., Barak, L. S., Wetsel, W. C., Caron, M. G., & Gainetdinov, R. R. (2005). Dopamine-independent locomotor actions of amphetamines in a novel acute mouse model of Parkinson disease. *PLoS Biology, 3,* e271.

Souza, R. P., Romano-Silva, M. A., Lieberman, J. A., Meltzer, H. Y., Wong, A. H., & Kennedy, J. L. (2008). Association study of GSK3 gene polymorphisms with schizophrenia and clozapine response. *Psychopharmacology (Berl), 200,* 177–186.

StClair, D., Blackwood, D., Muir, W., Carothers, A., Walker, M., Spowart, G., et al. (1990). Association within a family of a balanced autosomal translocation with major mental illness. *Lancet, 336,* 13–16.

Stambolic, V., & Woodgett, J. R. (1994). Mitogen inactivation of glycogen synthase kinase-3β in intact cells via serine 9 phosphorylation. *Biochemical Journal, 303*(Pt 3), 701–704.

Stefansson, H., Ophoff, R. A., Steinberg, S., Andreassen, O. A., Cichon, S., Rujescu, D., et al. (2009). Common variants conferring risk of schizophrenia. *Nature, 460,* 744–747.

Stefansson, H., Sarginson, J., Kong, A., Yates, P., Steinthorsdottir, V., Gudfinnsson, E., et al. (2003). Association of neuregulin 1 with schizophrenia confirmed in a Scottish population. *American Journal of Human Genetics, 72,* 83–87.

Stefansson, H., Sigurdsson, E., Steinthorsdottir, V., Bjornsdottir, S., Sigmundsson, T., Ghosh, S., et al. (2002). Neuregulin 1 and susceptibility to schizophrenia. *American Journal of Human Genetics, 71,* 877–892.

Steinberg, S., de, J. S., Andreassen, O. A., Werge, T., Borglum, A. D., Mors, O., et al. (2011). Common variants at VRK2 and TCF4 conferring risk of schizophrenia. *Human Molecular Genetics, 20,* 4076–4081.

Sutherland, C. (2011). What are the bona fide GSK3 substrates? *International Journal of Alzheimer's Disease, 2011,* 505607.

Sutherland, C., Leighton, I. A., & Cohen, P. (1993). Inactivation of glycogen synthase kinase-3β by phosphorylation: new kinase connections in insulin and growth-factor signalling. *Biochemical Journal, 296*(Pt 1), 15–19.

Sutton, L. P., & Rushlow, W. J. (2011). The effects of neuropsychiatric drugs on glycogen synthase kinase-3 signaling. *Neuroscience, 199,* 116–124.

Suzuki, M., Nohara, S., Hagino, H., Kurokawa, K., Yotsutsuji, T., Kawasaki, Y., et al. (2002). Regional changes in brain gray and white matter in patients with schizophrenia demonstrated with voxel-based analysis of MRI. *Schizophrenia Research, 55,* 41–54.

Szamosi, A., Kelemen, O., & Keri, S. (2012). Hippocampal volume and the AKT signaling system in first-episode schizophrenia. *Journal of Psychiatric Research, 46,* 279–284.

Tan, H. Y., Chen, A. G., Chen, Q., Browne, L. B., Verchinski, B., Kolachana, B., et al. (2012). Epistatic interactions of AKT1 on human medial temporal lobe biology and pharmacogenetic implications. *Molecular Psychiatry, 17,* 1007–1016.

Tang, H., Shen, N., Jin, H., Liu, D., Miao, X., & Zhu, L. Q. (2013). GSK-3β polymorphism discriminates bipolar disorder and schizophrenia: a systematic meta-analysis. *Molecular Neurobiology, 48,* 404–411.

Tan, H. Y., Nicodemus, K. K., Chen, Q., Li, Z., Brooke, J. K., Honea, R., et al. (2008). Genetic variation in AKT1 is linked to dopamine-associated prefrontal cortical structure and function in humans. *Journal of Clinical Investigation, 118,* 2200–2208.

Thomson, P. A., Wray, N. R., Millar, J. K., Evans, K. L., Hellard, S. L., Condie, A., et al. (2005). Association between the TRAX/DISC locus and both bipolar disorder and schizophrenia in the Scottish population. *Molecular Psychiatry, 10,* 657–668, 616.

Trivedi, N., Marsh, P., Goold, R. G., Wood-Kaczmar, A., & Gordon-Weeks, P. R. (2005). Glycogen synthase kinase-3β phosphorylation of MAP1B at Ser1260 and Thr1265 is spatially restricted to growing axons. *Journal of Cell Science, 118,* 993–1005.

Turunen, J. A., Peltonen, J. O., Pietilainen, O. P., Hennah, W., Loukola, A., Paunio, T., et al. (2007). The role of DTNBP1, NRG1, and AKT1 in the genetics of schizophrenia in Finland. *Schizophrenia Research, 91,* 27–36.

Urs, N. M., Snyder, J. C., Jacobsen, J. P., Peterson, S. M., & Caron, M. G. (2012). Deletion of GSK3β in D2R-expressing neurons reveals distinct roles for β-arrestin signaling in antipsychotic and lithium action. *Proceedings of the National Academy of Sciences of the United States of America, 109,* 20732–20737.

Walther, D. J., Peter, J. U., Bashammakh, S., Hortnagl, H., Voits, M., Fink, H., et al. (2003). Synthesis of serotonin by a second tryptophan hydroxylase isoform. *Science, 299,* 76.

Wu, D., & Pan, W. (2010). GSK3: a multifaceted kinase in Wnt signaling. *Trends in Biochemical Sciences, 35,* 161–168.

Xia, Y., Wang, C. Z., Liu, J., Anastasio, N. C., & Johnson, K. M. (2010). Brain-derived neurotrophic factor prevents phencyclidine-induced apoptosis in developing brain by parallel activation of both the ERK and PI-3K/Akt pathways. *Neuropharmacology, 58,* 330–336.

Xu, M. Q., Xing, Q. H., Zheng, Y. L., Li, S., Gao, J. J., He, G., et al. (2007). Association of AKT1 gene polymorphisms with risk of schizophrenia and with response to antipsychotics in the Chinese population. *Journal of Clinical Psychiatry, 68,* 1358–1367.

Yang, J., Si, T., Ling, Y., Ruan, Y., Han, Y., Wang, X., et al. (2003). Association study of the human FZD3 locus with schizophrenia. *Biological Psychiatry, 54,* 1298–1301.

Yin, L., Wang, J., Klein, P. S., & Lazar, M. A. (2006). Nuclear receptor Rev-erbα is a critical lithium-sensitive component of the circadian clock. *Science, 311,* 1002–1005.

Yoshimura, T., Kawano, Y., Arimura, N., Kawabata, S., Kikuchi, A., & Kaibuchi, K. (2005). GSK-3β regulates phosphorylation of CRMP-2 and neuronal polarity. *Cell, 120,* 137–149.

Yost, C., Torres, M., Miller, J. R., Huang, E., Kimelman, D., & Moon, R. T. (1996). The axis-inducing activity, stability, and subcellular distribution of β-catenin is regulated in *Xenopus* embryos by glycogen synthase kinase 3. *Genes & Development, 10,* 1443–1454.

Yurek, D. M., Zhang, L., Fletcher-Turner, A., & Seroogy, K. B. (2004). Supranigral injection of neuregulin1-β induces striatal dopamine overflow. *Brain Research, 1028,* 116–119.

Zhang, X., Beaulieu, J. M., Sotnikova, T. D., Gainetdinov, R. R., & Caron, M. G. (2004). Tryptophan hydroxylase-2 controls brain serotonin synthesis. *Science, 305,* 217.

Zhang, F., Sarginson, J., Crombie, C., Walker, N., St, C. D., & Shaw, D. (2006). Genetic association between schizophrenia and the DISC1 gene in the Scottish population. *American Journal of Medical Genetics Part B: Neuropsychiatric Genetics, 141B,* 155–159.

Zhu, L. Q., Wang, S. H., Liu, D., Yin, Y. Y., Tian, Q., Wang, X. C., et al. (2007). Activation of glycogen synthase kinase-3 inhibits long-term potentiation with synapse-associated impairments. *Journal of Neuroscience, 27,* 12211–12220.

27

Hormones and Schizophrenia

Jayashri Kulkarni, Emmy Gavrilidis, Roisin Worsley

The Monash Alfred Psychiatry Research Centre, The Alfred and Monash University Central Clinical School, Monash University, Melbourne, VIC, Australia

INTRODUCTION

The interrelationships between the endocrine system and the nervous system are intricate and complex. Important connections between hormones and mental health have been observed and studied for centuries, in both the basic and applied research areas as well as in clinical practice. Pituitary disorder such as Cushing's disease, Sheehan's syndrome, and acromegaly are associated with a wide variety of psychiatric symptoms. Psychotic symptoms can be induced by the administration of high doses of steroids. Abnormalities of the thyroid, adrenal, or pituitary can result in psychotic symptoms. Hence, there is a great deal of clinical evidence linking endocrine (hormone) changes to mental disorders.

HISTORY

In 1891, Emil Kraepelin postulated links between hormones and dementia precox (Kendler & Jablensky, 2011). He undertook extensive endocrine reviews of his patients. Kretschrner observed "insufficient functions of the sexual glands" and "chronic hypoestrogenism" in women with schizophrenia (Kretschmer, 1922). Between 1940 and 1970, many researchers looked for evidence of endocrine dysfunction in people with schizophrenia.

Hoskins further examined the link between hormones and dementia precox in postmortem studies in 1929 and conducted case study experiments using "glandular extracts" to treat schizophrenia (Hoskins, 1929).

The discovery of major hypothalamic hormones in the early 1970s (Besser & Mortimer, 1974) excited researchers and formally confirmed psychoneuroendocrinology as a legitimate area for research in schizophrenia. The hormones discovered were growth hormone (GH), lutenizing hormone, follicle-stimulating hormone-releasing hormone (LH/FSH-RH now known as gonadotrophin-releasing hormone (GnRH)), thyrotrophin-releasing hormone (TRH), and corticotrophin-releasing factor (CRF). Prolactin release-inhibiting factor (PIF, now known as dopamine/somatostatin) and prolactin-releasing factor (PRF) had been shown to control prolactin release in the 1950s (Desclin, 1950; Everett, 1954).

Critically important in the history of hormones and schizophrenia was the development of the dopamine (DA) hypothesis in schizophrenia. The DA hypothesis is the oldest and most established of the schizophrenia hypotheses, with some empirical validation from antipsychotic drug action. Arvid Carlsson (Carlsson & Lindqvist, 1963) is credited with describing the DA hypothesis of schizophrenia in 1963, further highlighting the interrelationship between neurotransmitters, hormones, and schizophrenia. Between 1900 and 1960, endocrinology was pursued at the physiological level, and 25 hormones were identified.

Brambilla and Penati in 1978 reviewed the evidence for abnormal functioning of the pituitary, adrenal, gonads, and thyroid glands in people with schizophrenia (Brambilla & Penati, 1978). They reported that there were no true organic endocrinopathies, so that the disease processes of schizophrenia appear to be causing endocrine changes, rather than diseased endocrine organs causing schizophrenia.

The 1980s heralded an era of further considering the role of neurotransmitters in the regulation of pituitary hormone release via hypothalamic hormones. New neuroendocrine studies of schizophrenia aimed toward using pituitary hormones as markers of function of neurotransmitters (Meltzer, 1984). George Fink coined the phrase "the pituitary is the window to the brain," and a number of clinical neuroendocrine studies in schizophrenia measured pituitary hormones as markers of central nervous system CNS functioning (Fink, 2012).

As of 2015, we know of the existence of over 130 hormones, and the sphere of influence and mode of action of each hormone remains to be determined. Schizophrenia is a severe, complex, multidimensional illness with largely unknown etiology. The role of some hormones that have been studied with respect to schizophrenia etiology or impact will now be discussed.

Brief Definitions and Classification of Hormones

Hormones are signaling molecules that are synthesized in endocrine glands, travel through the circulation, and have actions in distant target tissues. Hormones have diverse chemical structures. Originally, there were thought to be three major classes of hormones based on their structures. As new hormones are discovered, this simple classification system has become inadequate (Carson-Jurica, Schrader, & O'Malley, 1990) (Table 1).

Basic Hormone Actions

Over the past decade, many neurotransmitters have been considered to operate in similar ways to hormones, in that neurotransmitters act like chemical messengers. Colloquially, the steroid class of hormones dominate discussion about hormones, and in particular in schizophrenia, this is the most widely studied class of hormones, along with the specific neurotransmitters such as DA, serotonin, acetylcholine, and glycine. Classical biochemical cascade mechanisms are generated by hormone actions acting at cell membranes to alter cell metabolism and ultimate cellular responses (Norman & Litwack, 1997). Within the CNS, the hormone cascade systems are generated in the hypothalamus to the pituitary to distal endocrine glands to target tissues. Feedback loops and circuits regulate hormone production. Electrical or chemical signals originating in the limbic system are sent to the hypothalamus to initiate CNS endocrine cascade systems (Norman & Litwack, 1997). Hormones deliver their "message" to target cells by interacting with cell receptors that are largely proteins and specifically bind with their correct hormone. Peptide hormones tend to bind with receptors present in the outer membrane of the cell, while steroid hormone receptors are usually present in the nuclear compartments of the cell and interact with DNA. The hormone–receptor complex physically interacts with other cellular constituents such as G proteins or ion channels (Norman & Litwack, 1997). The nervous systems and endocrine systems are closely integrated with hormonal actions influencing neurogenesis, apoptosis, synaptogenesis, and other neuromodulatory roles.

TABLE 1   Some Examples of Hormones and Their Classification (Norman & Litwack, 1997)

Hormone Function	Name	Type
Hypothalmic regulation	Thyrotropin-releasing hormone (TRH)	Peptide-protein
	Gonadotropin releasing hormone (GnRH)	Peptide-protein
	Corticotropin releasing hormone (CTH)	Peptide-protein
	Prolactin-releasing factor (PRF)	Peptide-protein
	Growth hormone-releasing hormone (GHRH)	Peptide-protein
Anterior pituitary functions	Prolactin (PRL)	Peptide-protein
	Growth hormone (GH)	Peptide-protein
	Lutenizing hormone (LH)	Peptide-protein
	Follicle-stimulating hormone (FSH)	Peptide-protein
	Thyroid-stimulating hormone (TSH)	Peptide-protein
Posterior pituitary functions	Oxytocin	Peptide-protein
	Vasopressin	Peptide-protein
Thyroid regulation	Thyroxine (T_4)	Amino acid derived
	Triiodothyronine (T_3)	Amino acid derived
Pancreas function	Insulin	Peptide-protein
Adrenal cortex	Cortisol	Steroid
	Aldosterone	Steroid
Adrenal medulla	Adrenalin	Amino acid derived
	Noradrenalin	Amino acid derived
Gonadal reproduction	Estradiol	Steroid
	Progesterone	Steroid
	Testosterone	Steroid
	Dehydroepiandrosterone (DHEA)	Steroid

Hormones are also secreted by neurons that are known as neurosecretory cells. This integral relationship between the nervous system and hormonal systems provides a key to the understanding of the hormonal influences on wide ranging and complex behaviors, including expression of mental illness symptoms such as those seen in schizophrenia.

It is beyond the scope of this chapter to provide a comprehensive review on all or even many of the hormone interactions and influences on schizophrenia. This review will summarize and appraise recent work on specific hormone impacts in schizophrenia. This includes the HPG axis effects in schizophrenia, the hypothalamic-pituitary-adrenal axis (HPA axis) prolactin effects and the hypothalamic-pituitary-thyroid (HPT) axis in schizophrenia.

THE HPG AXIS AND SCHIZOPHRENIA

The hormones of the HPG axis include gonadotropin-releasing hormone from the hypothalamus (GnRH), LH and FSH from the pituitary, and the steroid hormones estrogen, progesterone, and testosterone from ovaries and testes (Figure 1).

The link between estrogen and mental illness was recognized more than a century ago (Riecher-Rossler & Hafner, 1993), but the effects of estrogen and other hormones of the HPG axis in the CNS have really only been studied for the past 20 years. Although more research is needed, there is accumulating evidence for the complex interactions between gonadal hormones, particularly estrogen, and neurotransmitters of the CNS. This evidence includes epidemiological, clinical, and preclinical research data.

Epidemiological observations of sex differences in the onset and course of schizophrenia reveal that schizophrenia is a sexually dimorphic disease (Hafner, 2003; Hafner & an der Heiden, 1997). Women with schizophrenia present with their first episode about 5 years later than men (Angermeyer & Kuhn, 1988; Hafner, Riecher-Rossler, Maurer, Fatkenheuer, & Loffler, 1992; Jablensky et al., 1992; Loffler et al., 1994).

Life cycle studies describe increased risk of first episode or relapse of schizophrenia in women during times of decreasing or changing estrogen production such as premenstrually, in the postpartum phase, and during menopause (Kendell & Chalmers, Seeman cited in Kulkarni, de Castella, et al., 2008). In particular, epidemiological evidence reveals a second spike in the incidence of schizophrenia onset for women at age 45–50 (Rossler & Seeman, as cited in Kulkarni, de Castella, et al., 2008). This is associated with falling levels of estrogen during menopause. In essence, estrogen has a protective role against psychosis during reproductive years (Chavez et al., 2010).

Preclinical evidence has revealed that estrogen has significant actions in the CNS beyond its primary endocrine and reproductive functions (Fink, Sumner, Rosie, Grace, & Quinn, 1996). Estrogen receptors are found in abundance in the limbic system including the hippocampus and amygdala as well as the basal ganglia and cerebral cortex (ter Horst, 2010; Hughes et al., 2009). In classical genomic and rapid nongenomic interactions with these receptors, estrogen functions as a neuroactive steroid, influencing signaling pathways and neurodegenerative

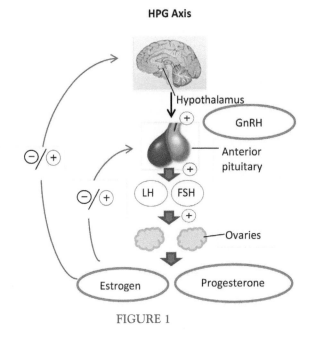

HPG Axis

FIGURE 1

processes with the CNS (Cosimo Melcangi & Garcia-Segura, 2010).

Estrogen: A Potent Neurotransmitter Modulator in Schizophrenia

There are three main forms of estrogen found in women: estradiol, the predominant hormone in reproductive years; estrone, the predominant form after menopause, and estriol, synthesized mainly in pregnancy. Estradiol has the highest affinity for estrogen receptors and is the focus of most studies of the influence of estrogen on psychosis.

DA, serotonin, and glutamate are widely accepted as key neurotransmitter systems involved in the pathophysiology of schizophrenia (Gonzalez-Maeso et al., 2008). Most antipsychotic drugs antagonize D2 (Dopamine) receptors, but the newer antipsychotics also interact with serotonin receptors (5-H2A and 5-HT1A) (Horacek et al., 2006).

Estradiol interacts significantly with dopaminergic, serotonergic, and glutaminergic systems and has properties similar to the newer antipsychotic drugs (Adams, Fink, Janssen, Shah, & Morrison, 2004; Hughes et al., 2009). Estrogen–dopamine interactions are complex and still not fully understood. Estrogen treatment has been found to increase the D2 receptor density in the striatum of ovariectomized rats (Sanchez, Bourque, Morissette, & Di Paolo, 2010). Estrogen also affects the serotonergic system (Lokuge, Frey, Foster, Soares, & Steiner, 2010) in many ways. Estradiol decreases the activity of monoamine oxidase, manipulates expression of the serotonin transporter, increased tryptophan activity, downregulates 5HT1A receptors, and upregulates 5HT2A receptors.

N-methyl-D-aspartate (NMDA) receptor antagonists such as phencyclidine (PCP) produce psychotic symptoms (Bubenikova-Valesova, Horacek, Vrajova, & Hoschl, 2008). This observation provides a basis for the role of hypoglutamatergic neurotransmission in the frontal cortex and hippocampus in the pathogenesis of schizophrenia. Estradiol upregulates NMDA receptors and increases NMDA agonist binding in the rat brain (Kulkarni, de Castella, et al., 2008), which could help to improve hypoactive glutamatergic functioning in schizophrenia.

Clinical Trials Using Estradiol as a Treatment in Schizophrenia

Estrogen supplementation appears to be a useful method for reducing psychotic symptoms associated with schizophrenia. Early work in this area showed that in an open label placebo, controlled pilot study using 2mg of adjunctive oral estradiol valerate, the women with schizophrenia receiving estradiol had a more rapid improvement in symptoms compared to women with schizophrenia receiving adjunctive placebo (Kulkarni et al., 1996). Subsequent early clinical trials including a dose-finding pilot study of transdermal estradiol (Kulkarni et al., 2001) and a second trial of 100mcg transdermal estradiol (Kulkarni, de Castella, et al., 2008) showed efficacy of adding estradiol to antipsychotic treatment in women with schizophrenia. A subsequent large clinical trial in 102 women provided further evidence for the efficacy of adjunctive transdermal estradiol (Kulkarni et al., 2014). Replication of these positive findings that adjunctive estradiol is effective in improving psychotic symptoms has been provided by Akhondzadeh et al. (Akhondzadeh et al., 2003). A meta-analysis performed in 2012 before the large trial of 102 women was published in 2014 (Kulkarni et al., 2014) of all estradiol treatment trials in schizophrenia concluded "Estrogens, especially estradiol, could be an effective augmentation strategy in the treatment of women with schizophrenia" (Begemann, Dekker, van Lunenburg, & Sommer, 2012). Estradiol treatment in men with schizophrenia is more difficult to trial with respect to the feminization side effects for men. In a short 14-day trial of 53 men with schizophrenia, the estradiol treatment group who had higher serum estradiol levels made a quicker recovery from psychotic symptoms (Kulkarni et al., 2011). This suggests that estradiol has a positive impact regardless of gender.

Estrogens and Neuroprotection

As well as the neurochemical impact of estrogens, schizophrenia is a disease with numerous brain anatomical abnormalities. Reduced gray matter volume has been reported in temporal, limbic, frontal, striatal, thalamic, and vestibular enlargement plus abnormalities in the prefrontal cortex (Fornito, Yucel, & Pantelis, 2009; Shenton, Dickey, Frumin, & McCarley, 2001). Changes in cytoarchitecture have also been described with abnormalities in neuropil volume, neuronal soma, irregular synaptic organization, and ectopic neurons (Flashman & Green, 2004; Iritani, 2007). Estrogen is known to have diverse neurotrophic properties that could be part of its ability to mediate the course and onset of brain disorder in schizophrenia. Estrogenic compounds can protect brain cells against injury from excitotoxicity, oxidative stress, inflammation, and apoptosis (Arevalo, Santos-Galindo, Bellini, Azcoitia, & Garcia-Segura, 2010; Bryant & Dorsa, 2010). Estrogens can enhance neurogenesis, angiogenesis, synaptic density, plasticity, connectivity, axonal sprouting, and remyelination (Li et al., 2011; Liu, Kelley, Herson, & Hurn, 2010). These neuroprotective actions are mediated by neuronal estrogen receptor alpha. Psychoprotective properties of estrogens are thought to originate from preservation and enhancement of neuronal mitochondrial functioning (Simpkins, Yi, Yang, & Dykens, 2010).

Selective Estrogen Receptor Modulators

Adjunctive estradiol treatment has been shown to improve psychotic symptoms (Akhondzadeh et al., 2003; Begemann et al., 2012; Kulkarni, de Castella, et al., 2008; Kulkarni et al., 2011, 1996, 2014, 2001) through a number of neuroprotective actions. However, the longer term use of unopposed estradiol can have a number of serious side effects because of estrogenic stimulation of breast, uterine, and gonadal tissue (Chlebowski et al., 2009). These concerns drive exploration of the selective estrogen receptor modulators (SERMs) (Chlebowski et al., 2009). SERMs such as raloxifene hydrochloride stimulate CNS and bone estrogen receptors, while having an inhibitory effect on uterine, breast, and gonadal tissue (Chan, Leung, et al., 2007; Kulkarni, Gurvich, et al., 2008). Raloxifene is a second generation SERM that is approved for use in the treatment of osteoporosis in postmenopausal women, and it has been shown to have a positive effect on memory (Yaffe et al., 2005).

The first dose-finding clinical trial using adjunctive raloxifene in schizophrenia (Kulkarni et al., 2010) demonstrated that in a dose of 120mg/day, positive and negative symptoms improved in a group of postmenopausal women with schizophrenia.

Subsequent studies using 60mg/day raloxifene adjunct showed some improvement in negative symptoms and cognition but not positive psychotic symptoms in postmenopausal women with schizophrenia (Usall et al., 2011).

Therefore, raloxifene hydrochloride 120 mg/day appears to be a useful adjunct in the treatment of older women with schizophrenia. However, further clinical trials are required to confirm this finding.

Other Sex Steroids and Schizophrenia

Androgens impact the mental state in a complex and poorly understood fashion. Testosterone may be implicated in the development of positive psychotic symptoms. However, a recent study has shown a negative correlation between plasma testosterone levels and the severity of negative symptoms of schizophrenia (Akhondzadeh et al., 2006).

Animal evidence suggests that testosterone may be propsychotic given that the administration of testosterone significantly enhanced NMDA antagonist-induced disruption in ovariectomized rats (Gogos, Kwek, & van den Buuse, 2012). High-dose androgenic steroids can induce psychotic symptoms (Talih, Fattal, & Malone, 2007), although most of this work has focussed on DHEA (dehydroepiandrosterone) and DHEA-S (DHEA Sulfate). DHEA-S has been shown to be a neuroprotective agent in some animal studies, but the results are inconsistent (Ritsner, 2011).

Pregnenolone and its metabolites, especially allopregnanolone, also seem to be promising hormone treatments in schizophrenia. Serum pregnenolone levels have been found to be lower in people with schizophrenia (Ritsner, 2011). Antipsychotic medications raise pregnenolone levels, and a recent review of three small pilot studies showed improvement in psychotic symptoms with pregnenolone treatment (Marx et al., 2011).

Sex steroids, in particular, estrogen, appear to have an important role in the treatment and understanding of the etiology of schizophrenia. Further clinical trials and etiological research are needed in this promising area.

PROLACTIN AND SCHIZOPHRENIA

Prolactin (PRL) is a single chain 199 amino acid polypeptide hormone secreted by the lactotroph cells of the anterior pituitary. It has a plasma half-life of 20–30 min and is responsible for the initiation and maintenance of lactation by direct action on mammary tissue. PRL secretion is under predominantly inhibitory hypothalamic control. PRL is released in a pulsatile manner with 13–14 peaks per day and has a circadian rhythm with a maximum level reached about 4 h after the onset of sleep, and a minimum level reached about 6 h after waking (Frantz, 1978). PRL levels are impacted by many factors such as stress, eating, sexual activity, menstrual cycle phase, pregnancy, and lactation frequency. The catecholamine

DA is considered to be a major physiological hypothalamic PRL-inhibiting factor. DA exerts a tonic inhibitory effect on lactotroph PRL secretion. PRL release increases as the DA available to the lactotroph is reduced. Estrogen, TRH, and vasoactive intestinal peptide all impact the pulsatile release of PRL (Moult, Dacie, Rees, & Besser, 1981).

DA is synthesized by tuberoinfundibular dopaminergic neurons that have their cell bodies in the arcuate and periventricular nuclei of the medial basal hypothalamus with terminals ending on the hypothalamic-hypophyseal portal capillaries at the median eminence (Gudelsky, 1981). DA is secreted by these neurons and transported by the portal system to the anterior pituitary, where it binds to the DA D2 receptor on the membrane of the lactotroph cells (Gudelsky, 1981). Serotonin may also stimulate PRL secretion (Tuomisto & Mannisto, 1985).

Since the DA excess theory remains a compelling neurotransmitter hypothesis in the development of schizophrenia, and DA is intricately related to PRL secretion, it is important to understand and study the role of PRL in schizophrenia. All antipsychotic drugs have the capacity to block DA D2 receptors in the mesolimbic and mesocortical areas. PRL response to even a single dose of antipsychotic medication is largely determined by pituitary DA mechanisms. Hence, PRL has been studied as a marker of DA systems in people with schizophrenia (Langer, Sachar, Gruen, & Halpern, 1980; Rubin & Hays, 1980). Using haloperidol as a challenge test to assay PRL levels, Keks et al. (1990) utilized the concept of the pituitary gland being a "window to the brain." Further symptom analysis revealed that there was a correlation between PRL/ DA levels and delusional symptoms (Kulkarni et al., 1990).

Antipsychotics and Prolactin

PRL elevation by antipsychotic drugs is a common side effect. There is some variation between the second generation antipsychotics (SGAs) in their propensity to elevate PRL. The first-generation antipsychotics have been shown to elevate PRL up to 10 times normal non-breast-feeding levels, with a correlation of elevation to antipsychotic dose (Smith, Wheeler, Murray, & O'Keane, 2002). Within the SGA group, quetiapine has negligible effect on PRL elevation (Arvanitis & Miller, 1997), while olanzapine elevates PRL in a dose-dependent fashion. PRL elevations appear to be present with over 40% of patients treated with ziprasidone (Grootens et al., 2011) and 60% treated with olanzapine (Grootens et al., 2011).

Risperidone and paliperidone have the greatest association with hyperprolactinaemia, and this is related to medication dose (Skopek & Manoj, 2010). Risperidone and paliperidone elevate PRL even more than the first-generation antipsychotics (Skopek & Manoj, 2010). It is important to note that female patients experience greater PRL elevation in response to antipsychotics, particularly in response to risperidone (Kinon, Gilmore, Liu, & Halbreich, 2003). Aripiprazole has also been associated with decreased PRL levels (Chan, Lin, et al., 2007), which may be explained by the action of aripiprazole. This action includes partial agonism at D2 receptors with subsequent activation of the DA autoreceptor systems (Aihara et al., 2004). A newer antipsychotic, asenapine, did not cause PRL elevation in comparison to placebo and risperidone treatment of patients with acute schizophrenia (Potkin, Cohen, & Panagides, 2007).

Elevated Prolactin Issues

Elevated PRL levels can often be asymptomatic, therefore, often undetected until laboratory investigation is performed (Kelly et al., 2013). Hyperprolactinaemia symptoms such as sexual dysfunction can be easily missed (Barnes cited in Riley, Peet, & Wilson, 1993) but are often a major reason for nonadherence to antipsychotic medication regimens. Symptomatic presentations of elevated PRL levels include galactorrhea, menstrual abnormality in women, and changes in bone density.

Galactorrhea due to antipsychotic-induced PRL elevation is more common in women than men (Kelly et al., 2013). Some studies have linked hyperprolactinaemia to an increased risk of breast cancer in women (Halbreich, Kinon, Gilmore, & Kahn, 2003; Hankinson et al., 1999). The mechanisms suggested to explain this possible link include the increased synthesis and expression of PRL receptors in breast cancer tissue and PRL-induced increase in DNA synthesis in breast cancer cells (Vyas, 2012). Epidemiological studies investigating a link between antipsychotic use in women and breast cancer have not produced clear findings. However, a recent retrospective cohort study (Wang et al., 2002) compared women who took PRL elevating antipsychotics with age-matched healthy controls. A small but significant increased incidence of breast cancer was found in the antipsychotic taking group. Another study (Cohen, Cohen, Maislos, & Buskila, 2000) did not find a correlation between hyperprolactinaemia and breast cancer. Menstrual cycle abnormalities are common in women taking PRL-elevating antipsychotics. Amenorrhea, anovulatory cycles, and long cycles are common (Kulkarni, de Castella, & Thompson) and can be related to the inverse relationship between PRL and estrogen.

Hypoestrogenism is commonly seen in women with amenorrhea and can increase the risks of osteoporosis and cardiovascular ischemic heart disease. Infertility is common in women who have prolonged hyperprolactinaemia (McIver, Romanski, & Nippoldt, 1997). As per the described work on estrogen providing neuroprotection in women with schizophrenia (Riecher-Rossler & Hafner, 1993), PRL-induced hypoestrogenism can also lead to worse outcomes in psychotic symptoms. The SOHO study (Brugnoli et al., 2012) described an increased risk of suicide by 64%, in women who had amenorrhea, related to hyperprolactinaemia. Although the SOHO study did not examine estradiol levels in the amenorrheic patients, it could be speculated that a decrease in circulating estradiol resulted in loss of neuroprotection in the affected women.

Osteoporosis is a significant problem of degeneration of the skeletal system, and people with schizophrenia have a high risk of developing osteoporosis because of PRL-elevating antipsychotics over a long period of time, plus the nature of schizophrenia as a chronic illness, with associated poor general health (Meaney et al., 2004).

Treatments for PRL elevation generally involve reducing the dose of the medication, if possible. The more potent D2 antagonist medications usually have the associated hyperprolactinaemia. Switching medications to a PRL-sparing antipsychotic is a treatment option, if lowering the dose is ineffective. However, the impact on treating psychosis symptoms can be detrimental if the patient was stable on high-potency antipsychotics. Direct PRL antagonists such as bromocryptine have been studied (Yuan et al., 2008), but there is an associated risk of worsening psychosis. Adjunctive estradiol if used with concurrent progesterone may be useful in women (Kulkarni et al., 2014), provided medical safety with respect to screening for breast, uterine, and ovarian tumors with longer term use. Overall, the importance of testing serum PRL in patients who need long-term antipsychotic treatment is often ignored by clinicians. Patients who are symptomatic need action to rectify the hyperprolactinaemia before longer-term side effects occur.

The HPA Axis and Schizophrenia

The hypothalamic-pituitary-adrenal axis (HPA or HTPA axis) is also known as the limbic-hypothalamic-pituitary-adrenal axis and is a complex set of interactions between the hypothalamus, the pituitary gland, and the adrenal (also called "suprarenal") glands (Figure 2).

The HPA axis is closely regulated by central mechanisms involving the limbic system and hypothalamus. Signals reach the paraventricular nucleus (PVN) of the hypothalamus from limbic structures. Secretion of

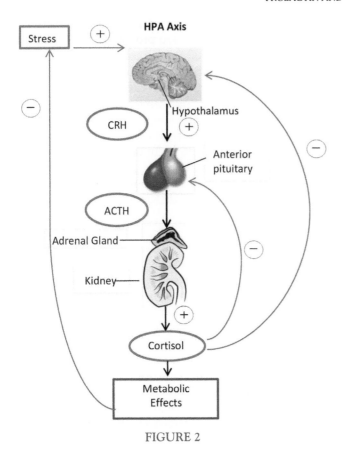

FIGURE 2

zona reticularis, which secrete glucocorticoids (cortisol and corticosterone), androgens (DHEA), and estrogens, is controlled primarily by ACTH (Mitrovic cited in Boron & Boulpaep, 2002).

Glucocorticoids and Mineralocorticoids

Steroids such as corticosterone and cortisol, elaborated in the zona fasciculate of the adrenal glands, cause glycogen production at the expense of protein breakdown, hence the term "glucocorticoid" (Sayers & Sayers, 1948).

Several decades later, the term "mineralocorticoid" was coined to explain the salt-conserving action of aldosterone produced in the adrenal zona glomerulosa (Herman et al., 2005). While there is a categorical distinction made between the two steroid groups, their actions are interdependent (Grundy, Simpson, & Tait, 1952).

Mineralocorticoid receptors (MRs) and glucocorticoid receptors (GRs) are present throughout the limbic and paralimbic regions, including the hippocampus, amygdala, and prefrontal cortex (Agarwal & Mirshahi, 1999; Oitzl, Champagne, van der Veen, & de Kloet, 2010).

Cortisol

Cortisol is one of the few hormones essential for life. It is termed as "glucocorticoid" and regulates the activity of the hypothalamus and pituitary by negative feedback effects (Mitrovic cited in Boron & Boulpaep, 2002). Peripheral cortisol levels have a circadian rhythm peaking in the morning and decreasing in the evening, with the lowest levels during early sleep cycles. Stress of various types causes activation of PVN, resulting in peaks of cortisol levels superimposed on the usual rhythm (Herman, Flak, & Jankord, 2008). Approximately 75% of the cortisol in the circulation is bound to a plasma protein named transcortin or corticosteroid-binding globulin. Another 15% is bound to albumin, and the remaining 10% is "free." It is the free cortisol that is biologically active. Transcortin is produced by the liver and stimulated by estrogens.

Plasma transcortin levels increase during pregnancy. As a result, more cortisol is bound, free cortisol concentration decreases, and ACTH secretion increases. Cortisol production then increases until the free cortisol concentration returns to normal. For this reason, pregnant women have elevated blood cortisol levels but do not have symptoms of glucocorticoid excess. The same phenomenon occurs in women taking estrogen-containing oral contraceptives (Mitrovic cited in Boron & Boulpaep, 2002).

Cortisol has many effects including anabolic effects on the liver and catabolic effects (proteolysis and lipolysis)

corticotrophin-releasing hormone (CRH) and arginine vasopressin from neurons of the PVN triggers release of adrenocorticotrophic hormone (ACTH) from the anterior pituitary (Mitrovic cited in Boron & Boulpaep, 2002). In addition to CRH, ACTH, cortisol, and numerous other messengers are involved in the HPA axis. For example, pro-opiomelanocortin (POMC), a prohormone, is the precursor for many bioactive peptides, including ACTH. ACTH is derived from POMC in the anterior pituitary (Stevens & White, 2010). ACTH travels in the blood and stimulates the adrenal gland.

The Adrenal Gland

The adrenal gland consists of two distinct endocrine glands: the adrenal medulla, which secretes catecholamines; and the adrenal cortex, which secretes steroid hormones. The adrenal medulla releases catecholamines (such as adrenalin and noradrenalin) directly into the blood. Adrenal medullary secretion is under sympathetic control (Herman, Ostrander, Mueller, & Figueiredo, 2005).

The adrenal cortex is divided into three zones: the zona glomerulosa, zona fasciculata, and zona reticularis. The zona glomerulosa, which secretes aldosterone, is controlled primarily by the reninangiotensin system, ACTH, and other factors, while the zona fasciculata and at several sites including muscle, adipose tissue, connective tissue, and lymphoid tissue. Cortisol increases glucose output by the liver, and glucose uptake by muscle, adipose, and other tissues decreases. As a result, blood glucose increases. These actions are mechanisms to mobilize energy sources (amino acids, fatty acids, and glycerol) from some tissues to provide energy, particularly glucose, for the brain and heart. Other hormones, particularly insulin, may counterbalance the metabolic effects of glucocorticoids. Insulin secretion is stimulated by the rise in blood glucose (Herman et al., 2008).

Cortisol inhibits ACTH secretion both at the hypothalamus and at the pituitary levels. It is the free cortisol that is responsible for the inhibition. In addition to its effects on the organs and tissues directly involved in metabolic homeostasis, cortisol influences a number of other organs and systems. Cortisol maintains the responsiveness of vascular smooth muscle to catecholamines and, therefore, participates in blood pressure regulation. Glucocortoicoids inhibit the inflammatory response to tissue injury. For example, cortisol (and all known glucocorticoids) suppresses synthesis and decreases the release of arachnidonic acid, the key precursor for a number of mediators of inflammation (e.g., prostaglandins and leucotrienes). It also decreases circulating T_4 lymphocytes, proliferation of local mast cells, stabilizes lysosomes, and decreases production of platelet-activating factor and nitric oxide. All of these effects suppress local inflammatory response (Spiga, Walker, Terry, & Lightman, 2011).

Cortisol and the CNS

In the CNS, cortisol can directly modulate electrical activity of the neurons via type I and type II GRs that are expressed particularly in the limbic system and hippocampus. Cortisol's ability to decrease hippocampal volume as well as memory has also been demonstrated. Cortisol decreases REM sleep but increases both slow-wave sleep and time spent awake. Excessive concentrations of cortisol in blood can cause insomnia and strikingly increase or decrease mood (Brown, Rush, & McEwen, 1999).

ACTH and cortisol secretion are increased by stressful stimuli including surgery, trauma, pain, apprehension, infection, hypoglycemia, and hemorrhage. GRs have a higher affinity for synthetic glucocorticoids (e.g., dexamethasone (DEX) or prednisone) and are activated by higher levels of endogenous glucocorticoids in times of stress or pharmacologic challenge (Jankord & Herman, 2008). In the hippocampus, GRs are primarily expressed in the dentate gyrus and CA1 and CA2 subregions, which are critical for cognitive function (DeRijk & de Kloet, 2005; Walker, Mittal, & Tessner, 2008). GRs are also present in the thalamus, septum, and PVN, as well as broadly throughout the prefrontal cortex and other cortical areas.

The increase in cortisol production is necessary for survival in times of stress. During stress or at the peak of the circadian cortisol rhythm (i.e., morning), MRs are saturated (unlike the 10% occupancy during rest), and increasing proportions of GRs become occupied (Silverman & Sternberg, 2012; Stevens & White, 2010). Both animal and human studies suggest that the relative proportion of MR to GR activation may be an important moderating factor in multiple brain processes, with the relation of receptor activation to brain function constituting an "inverted U" such that too much or too little can impair cognitive processes (de Kloet, Oitzl, & Joels, 1999; Lupien et al., 1998, 2002).

The reason that an increase in circulating glucocorticoid level is needed to resist stress is not well understood particularly in the context of the inhibitory effects of glucocorticoids on the immune system. It has been suggested that basal (or slightly elevated) levels of cortisol have permissive action that is critical for initial metabolic response to stress (and even immune response-glucocorticoids mobilize neutrophils from the bone marrow). Conversely, the immunosuppressive effects of glucocorticoids are supposed to protect the organism from an overactive immune system. As with other steroid hormones, the multiple effects of glucocorticoids result from stimulation of DNA-dependent mRNA synthesis in the cells of the target tissues (Herman et al., 2008; Spiga et al., 2011).

Aldosterone

Aldosterone is the major mineralocorticoid and the main hormone responsible for regulating the reabsorption of sodium and excretion of potassium, thereby regulating arterial pressure and electrical excitability of nerve and muscle, which critically affect a number of vital body functions. Aldosterone secretion generally is regulated by the level of pituitary ACTH, kidney angiotensin II, and plasma ions (especially sodium and potassium) (Agarwal & Mirshahi, 1999). Aldosterone secretion is sensitive to smaller amounts of ACTH than the GRs, so that feedback inhibition of aldosterone secretion is possible even in the presence of high levels of plasma glucocorticoids (Blair West et al., 1963; Ganong, Biglieri, & Mulrow, 1966). The increase in aldosterone secretion due to an excess of ACTH during stress is accompanied by an elevation in urinary mineralocorticoids (Melby, 1989). Aldosterone secretion is inhibited by atrial natriuretic peptide (ANP) (Ganguly, 1992), cortisol, testosterone (Emeric-Blanchouin, Zenatti, Vonarx, Schaison, & Aupetit-Faisant, 1992), and diabetes (Shimada et al., 1993). ACTH increases aldosterone acutely, but chronic exposure to ACTH can suppress aldosterone production (Hattangady, Olala, Bollag, & Rainey, 2012).

DA and somatostatin specifically impede the stimulatory effect of angiotensin II, whereas the ANP blocks the action of all stimulators of steroidogenesis in zona glomerulosa (Muller, 1995). Aldosterone secretion is stimulated by a large number of substances, including progesterone (Braley, Menachery, Yao, Mortensen, & Williams, 1996), DA agonists and H2 receptor antagonists (Garcia-Robles & Ruilope, 1987), spironolactone (Tsai, Davis, & Morris, 1980), and the pituitary adenylate cyclase-activating peptide (Bodart, Babinski, Ong, & De Lean, 1997). These suggest that zona glomerulosa activity is controlled by many factors.

The HPA Axis and Schizophrenia

There is a growing literature on the relationship between the HPA axis and schizophrenia. Two excellent recent reviews of this literature, Walker et al. (2008) and Holtzman et al. (2013), summarize several trends in the body of research findings in this area.

Patients with psychosis, especially nonmedicated patients, have higher baseline cortisol levels (Garner et al., 2011; Kale et al., 2010; Venkatasubramanian, Chittiprol, Neelakantachar, Shetty, & Gangadhar, 2010).

ACTH has also been found to be elevated in psychotic patients (Brunelin et al., 2008; Ryan, Sharifi, Condren, & Thakore, 2004). In fact, both ACTH and the DA metabolite homovanillic acid (HVA) response to metabolic stressor are also elevated in psychotic patients relative to controls (Brunelin et al., 2008). Further studies of ACTH are required to validate these findings since there are not many ACTH studies, largely due to the limitations in assaying ACTH in saliva and urine. A recent postmortem study of pituitary glands from schizophrenia patients and controls revealed that the level of proACTH was elevated, and the POMC level showed a trend toward elevation in pituitaries from schizophrenia patients (Krishnamurthy et al., 2013).

Antipsychotic medications reduce cortisol and ACTH secretion, in addition to decreasing positive symptoms, and findings published subsequent to the above review support this effect as well (Venkatasubramanian et al., 2010).

Psychotic patients show HPA axis dysfunction in response to pharmacologic challenge, such as the dexamethasone suppression test (DST). For example, administration of DEX, an exogenous glucocorticoid, typically leads to cortisol suppression due to the HPA axis negative feedback loop. DEX binds to GRs that, in turn, inhibit the expression of the POMC gene and, subsequently, the secretion of ACTH and cortisol. Thus, cortisol nonsuppression after the DST is an index of HPA axis dysfunction. In the DEX/CRH test, a more sensitive measure of HPA function, DEX is administered, then the following day, CRH is administered, and ACTH and cortisol responses are measured. More pronounced ACTH and cortisol secretion in response to CRH reflects reduced glucocorticoid feedback regulation. Higher post-DST and DEX/CRH levels of cortisol and ACTH were described in patients with schizophrenia and affective psychoses than in healthy and depressed comparison groups (Owashi et al., 2008; Walker et al., 2008). In many patients, this response is reversible with antipsychotic treatment (Ceskova, Kasparek, Zourkova, & Prikryl, 2006).

There are consistent reports of an inverse correlation between baseline cortisol and hippocampal volume in psychosis (Mondelli, Pariante, et al., 2010). The hippocampus exerts considerable influence on the HPA axis, and neuroimaging studies have consistently described decreased hippocampal volume reductions in patients with schizophrenia, so the link between hypercortisolaemia and schizophrenia is strengthened (Shepherd, Laurens, Matheson, Carr, & Green, 2012).

Recent studies of first episode psychotic patients revealed significant associations of positive and negative symptom severity with cortisol levels (Belvederi Murri et al., 2012; Garner et al., 2011).

The magnitude of symptom severity reduction in response to antipsychotic medications is well correlated with a decrease in serum cortisol (Mondelli, Dazzan, et al., 2010).

Hypercortisolemia may precipitate or exacerbate psychotic symptoms. Further evidence for this comes from studies involving the administration of exogenous corticosteroids in high doses and causing psychotic symptoms (Buchman, 2001; Warrington & Bostwick, 2006). Symptoms of hypercortisolemia-induced psychosis include pressured speech, hallucinations, delusions, and disorganized thought, which are often indistinguishable from the symptoms of psychotic disorders (Ling, Perry, & Tsuang, 1981; Wada et al., 2001).

Although there is relatively consistent evidence for elevated baseline HPA activity in psychosis, especially in nonmedicated patients, findings from investigations of psychosocial stress-induced cortisol are mixed. Some studies using laboratory psychosocial stressors have found that psychotic patients show no difference or less cortisol increase after stress induction, both on (Brenner et al., 2009; Jansen, Gispen-de Wied, & Kahn, 2000) and off (van Venrooij et al., 2012) antipsychotic medications. The absence of an enhanced psychosocial stress-induced cortisol increase in psychosis, despite evidence for baseline elevations, may reflect several factors. First, there are ceiling effects on cortisol increments beyond heightened baseline levels (Crowley, Hindmarsh, Honour, & Brook, 1993). Second, and perhaps more salient, after the onset of psychosis, the stress generated by the symptoms, especially distressing perceptions and ideations, may diminish the effect of any external psychosocial stress. Also, the psychosocial events that have the capacity for generating stress may become idiosyncratic. As discussed earlier, psychosis patients subjectively experience daily events as more distressing than healthy controls, even in the absence of increased stressor frequency.

Stress-sensitization may play a role in the elevated "set point" of HPA activity observed in some psychotic patients. For example, Bennett (2008) reviews the neural mechanisms through which early stressful experiences can alter the set point of the HPA axis and lead to chronically higher glucocorticoid activity, abnormalities in neuronal connectivity, and increased risk for subsequent psychosis. It has been shown that HPA set point is influenced by environmental factors such as prenatal maternal stress and early postnatal stress (Maccari et al., 2003), and it is also moderately heritable (Van Hulle, Shirtcliff, Lemery-Chalfant, & Goldsmith, 2012). Thus, as described below, genetic factors may also modulate biobehavioral sensitivity to stress.

Considerable research supports an association between HPA axis function and schizophrenia. In particular, elevated cortisol secretion in some patients with schizophrenia may be, in part, the trigger for illness onset and may determine the severity of symptoms and the course of illness.

More recently, the focus of some investigators has shifted to studies of the HPA axis in "ultra-high-risk" subjects, with the goal of addressing the critical question of whether abnormalities in HPA function precede the onset of psychosis. The studies here report conflicting results with some researchers (Garner et al., 2005) reporting that people at "ultra-high risk" (UHR) of developing psychosis, who went on to develop psychosis, had an enlarged pituitary gland at baseline, suggesting overactivity of the HPA axis. Mixed results of altered HPA axis function in people at risk of developing psychosis have been reported with the inconsistency in results being due to various methodological limitations. A recent study (Day et al., 2014) showed that UHR participants displayed a blunted cortisol awakening response compared with HC participants. No group difference in daytime cortisol levels was found, nor were any associations between cortisol measures and symptoms.

Unfortunately, most of the HPA axis studies do not separate male and female patients in the analysis and reporting of psychoneuroendocrine data. The HPA axis set points may be different for men and women, with known increased sensitivity to stress in women (Kelly et al., 2013).

Also, the methodologies employed in the UHR studies understandably need to accommodate noninvasive techniques for young people who do not have clear

symptoms, which further flaw the results. Also, since the majority of UHR people do not go on to develop schizophrenia (Fusar-Poli, Byrne, Badger, Valmaggia, & McGuire, 2013), it is difficult to draw generalizable conclusions about the HPA axis and its role in triggering schizophrenia.

However, the overall body of evidence in established schizophrenia that strongly suggests the HPA axis plays a role in the precipitation and perpetuation of schizophrenia is a compelling area of further investigation and underlines the impact of hormones in the development and expression of schizophrenia.

THYROID HORMONES AND SCHIZOPHRENIA

William Gull first described adult hypothyroidism in 1874 during an address to the Clinical Society of London (Gull, 1874). A few years later, William Ord coined the term "myxedema" to describe the nonpitting edema he observed in some patients with hypothyroidism (Ord, 1878). A Committee on Myxedema of the Clinical Society of London first linked hypothyroidism with psychosis and reported that in 109 patients with myxedema, "delusions and hallucinations occur in nearly half the cases, mainly where the disease is advanced" (Doyle, 1991; Ord, 1888). The relationship between psychosis and hypothyroidism was reported in 1949 (Asher, 1949), and the term "myxedema madness" was added to the literature (Asher, 1949; Heinrich & Grahm, 2003) (Figure 3).

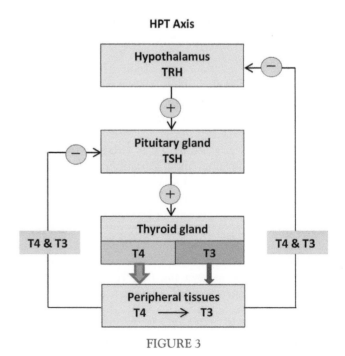

FIGURE 3

THE HYPOTHALAMIC-PITUITARY-THYROID AXIS

The pituitary regulates the synthesis and secretion of thyroid hormones (THs) through the release of thyrotropin—also known as thyroid-stimulating hormone (TSH)—from the anterior pituitary. The hypothalamus, in turn, stimulates the release of TSH through TRH. Finally, circulating THs (T_3, T_4) exert feedback control on both TRH and TSH secretion (Guyton & Hall, 1996). The two primary THs, thyroxine (T_4) and tri-iodothyronine (T_3), are labeled with the numbers 3 and 4 that refer to the number of atoms of iodine in the hormones. Iodine is essential for the production of THs. Low iodine diets lead to cell hyperplasia, known as goiter. The thyroid gland plays an important role in regulating the body's metabolism. The T_4 and T_3 hormones stimulate every tissue in the body to produce proteins and increase the amount of oxygen used by cells (Guyton & Hall, 1996).

Thyrotropin-Releasing Hormone

TRH is a tripeptide pyro-Glu-His-Pro containing the modified amino acid pyro-Glu. It is found in the cerebral cortex, the gastrointestinal tract, and the β cells of the pancreas. The major sources of the TRH that stimulates TSH synthesis and secretion are located in the arcuate nucleus and the median eminence of the hypothalamus.

In the anterior pituitary thyrotrophs, TRH binds to the TRH receptor, a G protein-coupled receptor on the cell membranes of the thyrotrophs. TRH binding triggers the phospholipase C pathway. Administering TRH also raises plasma PRL by stimulating lactotrophs in the anterior pituitary (Guyton & Hall, 1996).

Thyroid-Stimulating Hormone

TSH released by the thyrotrophs in the anterior pituitary is a 28-kDa glycoprotein with α and β chains. The α chain of TSH is identical to that of the other glycoprotein hormones such as the gonadotropins luteinizing hormone (LH) and FSH. The β chain is unique to TSH. Once secreted, TSH acts on the thyroid follicular cell through a specific receptor (Boron, Myers, Scarpa & Boulpaep cited in Boron & Boulpaep, 2011).

Circulating free T_4 and T_3 negatively feed back to both the hypothalamus and anterior pituitary and inhibit both the synthesis of TRH by hypothalamic neurons and the release of TSH by the thyrotrophs in the anterior pituitary. Plasma TSH is very sensitive to alteration in the levels of free T_4 and T_3. An excess of thyroid hormone leads to a decrease in plasma TSH (Guyton & Hall, 1996).

The sensor in this feedback system monitors the concentration of T_3 inside the thyrotroph. T_3 can enter directly from the blood plasma or form inside the thyrotroph by deiodination of T_4. The negative feedback of T_4 and T_3 on TSH release occurs at the level of the pituitary thyrotroph by both indirect and direct mechanisms. In the indirect feedback pathway, intracellular T_3 decreases the number of TRH receptors on the surface of the thyrotroph. THs indirectly inhibit TSH release by reducing the sensitivity of the thyrotrophs to TRH. In the direct feedback pathway, intracellular T_3 inhibits the synthesis of both the α and the β chains of TSH. Free T_4 and T_3 concentrations in the plasma are relatively constant over the course of 24h, and they have long half-lives. The feedback regulation of TSH secretion by THs is a slow process. T_3 feeds back on the thyrotroph by modulating gene transcription, which is a slow process (Boron, Myers, Scarpa & Boulpaep cited in Boron & Boulpaep, 2011).

The feedback of T_4 and T_3 on the release of TSH may also be under the control of somatostatin and DA from the hypothalamus. Somatostatin and DA both inhibit TSH secretion, apparently by making the thyrotroph more sensitive to inhibition by intracellular T_3. Thus, somatostatin and DA appear to counterbalance the stimulatory effect of TRH (Boron, Myers, Scarpa, & Boulpaep cited in Boron & Boulpaep, 2011).

The HPT Axis and Schizophrenia

There are many well-described cases of psychosis and depression described in patients with hyperthyroidism or hypothyroidism (Fountoulakis et al., 2006; Hickie, Bennett, Mitchell, Wilhelm, & Orlay, 1996; Snabboon, Khemkha, Chaiyaumporn, Lalitanantpong, & Sridama, 2009). There is considerable literature on the role of the THs on mood regulation, including the use of augmentation strategies with thyroid hormone treatments for depression (Abraham, Milev, & Lawson, 2006; Abulseoud et al., 2007). The link between THs and schizophrenia is also noted. Several groups have measured TH levels, and other thyroid-related parameters, in patients with schizophrenia, and found several abnormalities (Palha & Goodman, 2006; Sim, Chong, Chan, & Lum, 2002). In a recent review of thyroid abnormalities in schizophrenia (Santos et al., 2012), 15 independent studies of human population cohorts addressing the role of TH function in patients with schizophrenia were reported. Prior to the mid-1980s, the lack of high-sensitivity assays for measurement of TH, specifically for free TH, was a handicap. From the review of studies, a complex relationship emerged between psychiatric symptoms and fluctuations in TH. In an important study of war veterans (Southwick, Mason, Giller, & Kosten, 1989), a highly significant relationship between the range (maximum minus minimum value) of the BPRS sum and the range of free thyroxine levels was found, possibly indicating that clinical improvement may be associated with falling thyroxine levels in some patients and rising thyroxine levels in other patients.

A study by Roca and colleagues (Roca, Blackman, Ackerley, Harman, & Gregerman, 1990) showed that 49% of psychiatric patients, in their study, had significant changes in TH levels, with a significant positive correlation between severity of illness and elevations of TH levels. There are clinical case reports describing psychotic symptoms in people with hyperthyroidism (Benvenga, Lapa, & Trimarchi, 2003; Marian, Nica, Ionescu, & Ghinea, 2009; Snabboon et al., 2009).

A number of studies described above were done in patients with chronic schizophrenia who had received many years of antipsychotic medication. In a thorough study (Seeman cited in Kulkarni, de Castella, et al., 2008) of 31 acutely ill in-patients with schizophrenia before and after 4 weeks of treatment with perazine, T_4, T_3, reverseT$_3$ (rT$_3$), and TSH were measured in a further 19 patients with schizophrenia in remission on no medication, 20 schizophrenia patients in remission taking antipsychotics drugs, plus 24 patients with residual-type schizophrenia were tested.

The serum levels of T_4 of acutely ill schizophrenic patients were elevated, while those of T_3, rT$_3$, and TSH were normal. Their T_4 levels showed a positive correlation with the severity of illness and the degree of clinical response to antipsychotic treatment. There was a significant fall in serum concentrations of T_4 and rT$_3$ during 4 weeks of drug treatment, and the decrease was significantly correlated to clinical response. No abnormalities in the serum concentrations of any of the hormones measured were found in schizophrenic patients in remission or in residual-type schizophrenia (Baumgartner, Pietzcker, & Gaebel, 2000).

The authors concluded that their results indicated that elevated serum levels of T_4 with normal T_3 and TSH levels may be specific for acutely ill schizophrenia patients and that antipsychotic medication may affect thyroid hormone metabolism, this interaction being involved in the mechanism of action of these drugs (Baumgartner et al., 2000).

Mechanisms of Interaction between the HPT Axis and Schizophrenia

Either by direct action of the hormones of the HPT axis on neurotransmitters implicated in the formation of psychosis symptoms, or by an interaction on antipsychotic drug metabolism, there appears to be a close connection between the HPT axis and schizophrenia.

Dopamine and the HPT Axis

THs have been shown to regulate the levels of DA receptors (Crocker & Overstreet, 1984; Crocker, Overstreet, & Crocker, 1986) and the activity of tyrosine hydroxylase (Chaube & Joy, 2003; Diarra, Lefauconnier, Valens, Georges, & Gripois, 1989; Shikaeva & Koreneva, 1987), a critical enzyme of the cathecolaminergic pathway. DA may inhibit TSH secretion (Rao et al., 1990), and treatment with DA blockers leads to increased TSH level or subclinical hypothyroidism (Magliozzi, Gold, & Laubly, 1989). Conversely, hypothyroidism has been described as increasing DA receptor sensitivity (Crocker et al., 1986). In support of this, early animal studies showed that serum concentrations of T_4 and fT$_4$ declined after treatment with chlorpromazine and clozapine (Rinieris, Christodoulou, Souvatzoglou, Koutras, & Stefanis, 1980) and also after haloperidol treatment (Baumgartner, Graf, Kurten, & Meinhold, 1988). Subchronic treatment with haloperidol or clozapine induced specific changes in deiodinase activities in rat brains (Baumgartner et al., 1988) Alpha 1- and Beta-adrenergic catecholamines are involved in maintaining deiodinase activity, and thus brain thyroid status (Barnes cited in Riley et al., 1993). In this way, the impact of elevated DA due to schizophrenia would have a major impact on the HPT axis and vice versa.

Serotonin and the HPT Axis

Serotonin is a key neurotransmitter in the development of psychosis symptoms as well as depression. The SGA medications are also known as "atypical" antipsychotics mainly because of their actions on the serotonin systems as well as dopaminergic systems (Meltzer & Massey, 2011).

There are studies that show decreased serotonin activity in hypothyroid patients (Cleare, McGregor, Chambers, Dawling, & O'Keane, 1996; Cleare, McGregor, & O'Keane, 1995).

Work done by Strawn et al. (Strawn, Ekhator, D'Souza, & Geracioti, 2004) showed that CSF levels of the major metabolites of serotonin and dopamine-5-hydroxy indoleacetic acid and HVA were negatively correlated with plasma TSH, T_3, and FT$_3$. There does appear to be a significant interaction between the HPT and schizophrenia—although this connection is not as well studied as in mood disorders.

Glutamate and the HPT Axis

The glutamatergic hypothesis of schizophrenia posits that there is dysfunction of corticolimbic glutamatergic neurotransmission that may contribute to or account for the manifestations of schizophrenia. The hypothesis is based upon the observation that psychotomimetic agents, such as ketamine and PCP, induce neurocognitive deficiencies and psychotic symptoms, similar to those of schizophrenia, through blockage of the neurotransmission at NMDA- type glutamate receptors (Coyle, 1996).

NMDA receptors are colocated on brain circuits that regulate DA release, lending support to the notion that the two neurotransmitter systems are interlinked (Spiga et al., 2011). The role of T_3 in the CNS, specifically on regulation of glutamate uptake has begun to be studied (Mendes-de-Aguiar et al., 2008). This study described that T_3 modulates the astrocytic glutamate transporters and is thereby capable of regulating extracellular glutamate levels. The overall impact of adequate T_3 production appears to be to promote neuronal development and neuroprotection.

Glutamate receptor agonist administration in male rats has been found to increase TSH concentrations (Arufe, Duran, Perez-Vences, & Alfonso, 2002), while antagonists decreased TSH and TH serum levels.

The role of the HPT axis in glutamate regulation in schizophrenia appears to be a significant one, but further study is needed to ascertain the mechanisms and clinical impact of hypo- or hyperthyroidism on glutamate regulation and the phenotypic expression of this in schizophrenia.

CONCLUSION

Multiple hormones interact with neurotransmitters, neural regulators, and other systems within the CNS to cause the development of schizophrenia. The impact of hormone regulation through the pituitary gland and on to target organs with significant feedback loops to the CNS and the entire body is immense. The intricate balance of hormone regulation with environmental triggers, such as stress, provides a rich source for explanation of clinical phenomena seen in schizophrenia—such as the early onset of illness being triggered by sexual abuse or other external threats. The impact of hormonal imbalances appears to promote ongoing illness, for example, in people with long-term, persistent schizophrenia suffering from hyperprolactinemia leading to osteoporosis or other effects of hypoestrogenism. Hypothyroidism is known from historical times to cause psychosis, and recent exciting work exploring the impact of TH on key neurotransmitter systems is promising in understanding more about the etiological mechanisms leading to the development of schizophrenia. In this way, study of the pituitary and its products really is a "window to the brain" in schizophrenia.

While there is a great deal of research to be done in the area of endocrinology providing etiological answers to the development of schizophrenia, there is another burgeoning area of research that is about the use of hormones as innovative treatments for schizophrenia. The imbalances in various hormone systems, whether as direct cause or effect of schizophrenia, can be addressed with hormone administration with resultant improvement in the symptoms of schizophrenia. The role of adjunctive estrogen treatment is an excellent example of this. Since there are a significant number of people with intractable schizophrenia, new treatment approaches are vital. Hormone augmentation, particularly when schizophrenia has been noted to begin with major endocrine life events (e.g., postnatally) is an exciting area for research into the development of new, effective treatments.

Importantly, the clinical impacts of hormone imbalances due to existing treatments with antipsychotic medications need to be managed well by all clinicians involved in patient care. It is important for mental health clinicians to adopt a holistic approach. Examples include the consideration of the effect of menopause on their patients' existing or new psychosis, monitoring for diabetes in people who take weight gaining medication, and being aware of insidious onset of hypothyroidism if medications such as lithium carbonate are used to treat affective symptoms within the schizophrenia spectrum. There are many intricate interactions between medications, illness, hormones, and lifestyle factors that clinicians need to understand better and manage.

Hormones play a huge role in the development, perpetuation, and prognosis of people with schizophrenia. A broad approach to the etiological and treatment research paradigms as well as in the clinical management of schizophrenia is an important step toward better outcomes for patients.

References

Abraham, G., Milev, R., & Lawson, S. J. (2006). T_3 augmentation of SSRI resistant depression. *Journal of Affective Disorders, 91*(2–3), 211–215.

Abulseoud, O., Sane, N., Cozzolino, A., Kiriakos, L., Mehra, V., Gitlin, M., et al. (2007). Free T_4 index and clinical outcome in patients with depression. *Journal of Affective Disorders, 100*(1–3), 271–277.

Adams, M. M., Fink, S. E., Janssen, W. G., Shah, R. A., & Morrison, J. H. (2004). Estrogen modulates synaptic N-methyl-D-aspartate receptor subunit distribution in the aged hippocampus. *Journal of Comparative Neurology, 474*(3), 419–426.

Agarwal, M. K., & Mirshahi, M. (1999). General overview of mineralocorticoid hormone action. *Pharmacology & Therapeutics, 84*(3), 273–326.

Aihara, K., Shimada, J., Miwa, T., Tottori, K., Burris, K. D., Yocca, F. D., et al. (2004). The novel antipsychotic aripiprazole is a partial agonist at short and long isoforms of D2 receptors linked to the regulation of adenylyl cyclase activity and prolactin release. *Brain Research, 1003*(1–2), 9–17.

Akhondzadeh, S., Nejatisafa, A. A., Amini, H., Mohammadi, M. R., Larijani, B., Kashani, L., et al. (2003). Adjunctive estrogen treatment in women with chronic schizophrenia: a double-blind, randomized, and placebo-controlled trial. *Progress in Neuro-Psychopharmacology & Biological Psychiatry, 27*(6), 1007–1012.

Akhondzadeh, S., Rezaei, F., Larijani, B., Nejatisafa, A. A., Kashani, L., & Abbasi, S. H. (2006). Correlation between testosterone, gonadotropins and prolactin and severity of negative symptoms in male patients with chronic schizophrenia. *Schizophrenia Research, 84*(2–3), 405–410.

Angermeyer, M. C., & Kuhn, L. (1988). Gender differences in age at onset of schizophrenia. An overview. *European Archives of Psychiatry and Neurological Sciences, 237*(6), 351–364.

Arevalo, M. A., Santos-Galindo, M., Bellini, M. J., Azcoitia, I., & Garcia-Segura, L. M. (2010). Actions of estrogens on glial cells: implications for neuroprotection. *Biochimica et Biophysica Acta, 1800*(10), 1106–1112.

Arufe, M. C., Duran, R., Perez-Vences, D., & Alfonso, M. (2002). Endogenous excitatory amino acid neurotransmission regulates thyroid-stimulating hormone and thyroid hormone secretion in conscious freely moving male rats. *Endocrine, 17*(3), 193–197.

Arvanitis, L. A., & Miller, B. G. (1997). Multiple fixed doses of "Seroquel" (quetiapine) in patients with acute exacerbation of schizophrenia: a comparison with haloperidol and placebo. The Seroquel Trial 13 Study Group. *Biological Psychiatry, 42*(4), 233–246.

Asher, R. (1949). Myxoedematous madness. *British Medical Journal, 2*(4636), 1112.

Baumgartner, A., Graf, K. J., Kurten, I., & Meinhold, H. (1988). The hypothalamic-pituitary-thyroid axis in psychiatric patients and healthy subjects: Part II: repeated measure-ments of thyroxine, free thyroxine, triidothyronine, free triidothyronine and reverse triidothyronine in patients with major depressive disorder and schizophrenia and healthy subjects. *Psychiatry Research, 24*(3), 283–305.

Baumgartner, A., Pietzcker, A., & Gaebel, W. (2000). The hypothalamic-pituitary-thyroid axis in patients with schizophrenia. *Schizophrenia Research, 44*(3), 233–243.

Begemann, M. J., Dekker, C. F., van Lunenburg, M., & Sommer, I. E. (2012). Estrogen augmentation in schizophrenia: a quantitative review of current evidence. *Schizophrenia Research, 141*(2–3), 179–184.

Belvederi Murri, M., Pariante, C. M., Dazzan, P., Hepgul, N., Papadopoulos, A. S., Zunszain, P., et al. (2012). Hypothalamic-pituitary-adrenal axis and clinical symptoms in first-episode psychosis. *Psychoneuroendocrinology, 37*(5), 629–644.

Bennett, A. O. M. (2008). Stress and anxiety in schizophrenia and depression: glucocorticoids, corticotropin-releasing hormone and synapse regression. *Australian and New Zealand Journal of Psychiatry, 42*(12), 995–1002.

Benvenga, S., Lapa, D., & Trimarchi, F. (2003). Don't forget the thyroid in the etiology of psychoses. *American Journal of Medicine, 115*(2), 159–160.

Besser, G. M., & Mortimer, C. H. (1974). Hypothalamic regulatory hormones: a review. *Journal of Clinical Pathology, 27*(3), 173–184.

Blair West, J. R., Coghlan, J. P., Denton, D. A., Goding, J. R., Wintour, M., & Wright, R. D. (1963). The control of aldosterone secretion. *Recent Progress in Hormone Research, 19*, 311–383.

Bodart, V., Babinski, K., Ong, H., & De Lean, A. (1997). Comparative effect of pituitary adenylate cyclase-activating polypeptide on aldosterone secretion in normal bovine and human tumorous adrenal cells. *Endocrinology, 138*(2), 566–573.

Boron, F., & Boulpaep, E. (2002). *Medical physiology* (1st ed.).

Boron, W. F., & Boulpaep, E. L. (2011). *Medical physiology* (2nd ed.). Elsevier.

Braley, L. M., Menachery, A. I., Yao, T., Mortensen, R. M., & Williams, G. H. (1996). Effect of progesterone on aldosterone secretion in rats. *Endocrinology, 137*(11), 4773–4778.

Brambilla, F., & Penati, G. (1978). *Perspectives in endocrine psychobiology.* Wiley.

Brenner, K., Liu, A., Laplante, D. P., Lupien, S., Pruessner, J. C., Ciampi, A., et al. (2009). Cortisol response to a psychosocial stressor in schizophrenia: blunted, delayed, or normal? *Psychoneuroendocrinology, 34*(6), 859–868.

Brown, E. S., Rush, A. J., & McEwen, B. S. (1999). Hippocampal remodeling and damage by corticosteroids: implications for mood disorders. *Neuropsychopharmacology, 21*(4), 474–484.

Brugnoli, R., Novick, D., Haro, J. M., Rossi, A., Bortolomasi, M., Frediani, S., et al. (2012). Risk factors for suicide behaviors in the observational schizophrenia outpatient health outcomes (SOHO) study. *BMC Psychiatry, 12*, 83.

Brunelin, J., d'Amato, T., van Os, J., Cochet, A., Suaud-Chagny, M. F., & Saoud, M. (2008). Effects of acute metabolic stress on the dopaminergic and pituitary-adrenal axis activity in patients with schizophrenia, their unaffected siblings and controls. *Schizophrenia Research, 100*(1–3), 206–211.

Bryant, D. N., & Dorsa, D. M. (2010). Roles of estrogen receptors alpha and beta in sexually dimorphic neuroprotection against glutamate toxicity. *Neuroscience, 170*(4), 1261–1269.

Bubenikova-Valesova, V., Horacek, J., Vrajova, M., & Hoschl, C. (2008). Models of schizophrenia in humans and animals based on inhibition of NMDA receptors. *Neuroscience & Biobehavioral Reviews, 32*(5), 1014–1023.

Buchman, A. L. (2001). Side effects of corticosteroid therapy. *Journal of Clinical Gastroenterology, 33*(4), 289–294.

Carlsson, A., & Lindqvist, M. (1963). Effect of chlorpromazine or haloperidol on formation of 3methoxytyramine and normetanephrine in mouse brain. *Acta Pharmacologica et Toxicologica (Copenhagen), 20*, 140–144.

Carson-Jurica, M. A., Schrader, W. T., & O'Malley, B. W. (1990). Steroid receptor family: structure and functions. *Endocrine Reviews, 11*(2), 201–220.

Ceskova, E., Kasparek, T., Zourkova, A., & Prikryl, R. (2006). Dexamethasone suppression test in first-episode schizophrenia. *Neuro Endocrinology Letters, 27*(4), 433–437.

Chan, H. Y., Lin, W. W., Lin, S. K., Hwang, T. J., Su, T. P., Chiang, S. C., et al. (2007). Efficacy and safety of aripiprazole in the acute treatment of schizophrenia in Chinese patients with risperidone as an active control: a randomized trial. *Journal of Clinical Psychiatry, 68*(1), 29–36.

Chan, Y. C., Leung, F. P., Yao, X., Lau, C. W., Vanhoutte, P. M., & Huang, Y. (2007). Raloxifene modulates pulmonary vascular reactivity in spontaneously hypertensive rats. *Journal of Cardiovascular Pharmacology, 49*(6), 355–361.

Chaube, R., & Joy, K. P. (2003). Thyroid hormone modulation of brain in vivo tyrosine hydroxylase activity and kinetics in the female catfish *Heteropneustes fossilis. Journal of Endocrinology, 179*(2), 205–215.

Chavez, C., Hollaus, M., Scarr, E., Pavey, G., Gogos, A., & van den Buuse, M. (2010). The effect of estrogen on dopamine and serotonin receptor and transporter levels in the brain: an autoradiography study. *Brain Research, 1321*, 51–59.

Chlebowski, R. T., Kuller, L. H., Prentice, R. L., Stefanick, M. L., Manson, J. E., Gass, M., et al. (2009). Breast cancer after use of estrogen plus progestin in postmenopausal women. *New England Journal of Medicine, 360*(6), 573–587.

Cleare, A. J., McGregor, A., Chambers, S. M., Dawling, S., & O'Keane, V. (1996). Thyroxine replacement increases central 5-hydroxytryptamine activity and reduces depressive symptoms in hypothyroidism. *Neuroendocrinology, 64*(1), 65–69.

Cleare, A. J., McGregor, A., & O'Keane, V. (1995). Neuroendocrine evidence for an association between hypothyroidism, reduced central 5-HT activity and depression. *Clinical Endocrinology (Oxford), 43*(6), 713–719.

Cohen, A. D., Cohen, Y., Maislos, M., & Buskila, D. (2000). Prolactin serum level in patients with breast cancer. *Israel Medical Association Journal, 2*(4), 287–289.

Cosimo Melcangi, R., & Garcia-Segura, L. M. (2010). Sex-specific therapeutic strategies based on neuroactive steroids: in search for innovative tools for neuroprotection. *Hormones and Behavior, 57*(1), 2–11.

Coyle, J. T. (1996). The glutamatergic dysfunction hypothesis for schizophrenia. *Harvard Review of Psychiatry, 3*(5), 241–253.

Crocker, A. D., & Overstreet, D. H. (1984). Modification of the behavioural effects of haloperidol and of dopamine receptor regulation by altered thyroid status. *Psychopharmacology (Berl), 82*(1–2), 102–106.

Crocker, A. D., Overstreet, D. H., & Crocker, J. M. (1986). Hypothyroidism leads to increased dopamine receptor sensitivity and concentration. *Pharmacology Biochemistry and Behavior, 24*(6), 1593–1597.

Crowley, S., Hindmarsh, P. C., Honour, J. W., & Brook, C. G. (1993). Reproducibility of the cortisol response to stimulation with a low dose of ACTH(1-24): the effect of basal cortisol levels and comparison of low-dose with high-dose secretory dynamics. *Journal of Endocrinology, 136*(1), 167–172.

Day, F. L., Valmaggia, L. R., Mondelli, V., Papadopoulos, A., Papadopoulos, I., Pariante, C. M., et al. (2014). Blunted cortisol awakening response in people at ultra high risk of developing psychosis. *Schizophrenia Research, 158*(1–3), 25–31.

DeRijk, R., & de Kloet, E. R. (2005). Corticosteroid receptor genetic polymorphisms and stress responsivity. *Endocrine, 28*(3), 263–270.

Desclin, L. (1950). Mechanism effect of estrogens on the anterior lobe of the pituitary body of the rat. *Annales d'Endocrinologie (Paris), 11*(6), 656–659.

Diarra, A., Lefauconnier, J. M., Valens, M., Georges, P., & Gripois, D. (1989). Tyrosine content, influx and accumulation rate, and catecholamine biosynthesis measured in vivo, in the central nervous system and in peripheral organs of the young rat. Influence of neonatal hypo- and hyperthyroidism. *Archives Internationales de Physiologie et de Biochimie, 97*(5), 317–332.

Doyle, L. (1991). Myxoedema: some early reports and contributions by British authors, 1873–1898. *Journal of the Royal Society of Medicine, 84*(2), 103–106.

Emeric-Blanchouin, N., Zenatti, M., Vonarx, V., Schaison, G., & Aupetit-Faisant, B. (1992). Cortisol and testosterone: inhibitory agents of the mineralocorticoid pathway. Is there a physiopathological meaning in adrenal tumors? *Journal of Steroid Biochemistry and Molecular Biology, 41*(3–8), 823–826.

Everett, J. W. (1954). Luteotrophic function of autografts of the rat hypophysis. *Endocrinology, 54*(6), 685–690.

Fink, G. (2012). Chapter 5-Neural control of the anterior lobe of the pituitary gland (pars distalis). In G. F. W. P. E. Levine (Ed.), *Handbook of neuroendocrinology* (pp. 97–137). San Diego: Academic Press.

Fink, G., Sumner, B. H., Rosie, R., Grace, O., & Quinn, J. (1996). Estrogen control of central neurotransmission: effect on mood, mental state, and memory. *Cellular and Molecular Neurobiology, 16*(3), 325–344.

Flashman, L. A., & Green, M. F. (2004). Review of cognition and brain structure in schizophrenia: profiles, longitudinal course, and effects of treatment. *Psychiatric Clinics of North America, 27*(1), 1–18, vii.

Fornito, A., Yucel, M., & Pantelis, C. (2009). Reconciling neuroimaging and neuropathological findings in schizophrenia and bipolar disorder. *Current Opinion in Psychiatry, 22*(3), 312–319.

Fountoulakis, K. N., Kantartzis, S., Siamouli, M., Panagiotidis, P., Kaprinis, S., Iacovides, A., et al. (2006). Peripheral thyroid dysfunction in depression. *World Journal of Biological Psychiatry, 7*(3), 131–137.

Frantz, A. G. (1978). Prolactin. *New England Journal of Medicine, 298*(4), 201–207.

Fusar-Poli, P., Byrne, M., Badger, S., Valmaggia, L. R., & McGuire, P. K. (2013). Outreach and support in South London (OASIS), 2001–2011: ten years of early diagnosis and treatment for young individuals at high clinical risk for psychosis. *European Psychiatry, 28*(5), 315–326.

Ganguly, A. (1992). Atrial natriuretic peptide-induced inhibition of aldosterone secretion: a quest for mediator(s). *American Journal of Physiology, 263*(2 Pt 1), E181–E194.

Ganong, W. F., Biglieri, E. G., & Mulrow, P. J. (1966). Mechanisms regulating adrenocortical secretion of aldosterone and glucocorticoids. *Recent Progress in Hormone Research, 22*, 381–430.

Garcia-Robles, R., & Ruilope, L. M. (1987). Pharmacological influences on aldosterone secretion. *Journal of Steroid Biochemistry, 27*(4–6), 947–951.

Garner, B., Pariante, C. M., Wood, S. J., Velakoulis, D., Phillips, L., Soulsby, B., et al. (2005). Pituitary volume predicts future transition to psychosis in individuals at ultra-high risk of developing psychosis. *Biological Psychiatry, 58*(5), 417–423.

Garner, B., Phassouliotis, C., Phillips, L. J., Markulev, C., Butselaar, F., Bendall, S., et al. (2011). Cortisol and dehydroepiandrosterone-sulphate levels correlate with symptom severity in first-episode psychosis. *Journal of Psychiatric Research, 45*(2), 249–255.

Gogos, A., Kwek, P., & van den Buuse, M. (2012). The role of estrogen and testosterone in female rats in behavioral models of relevance to schizophrenia. *Psychopharmacology (Berl), 219*(1), 213–224.

Gonzalez-Maeso, J., Ang, R. L., Yuen, T., Chan, P., Weisstaub, N. V., Lopez-Gimenez, J. F., et al. (2008). Identification of a serotonin/glutamate receptor complex implicated in psychosis. *Nature, 452*(7183), 93–97.

Grootens, K. P., van Veelen, N. M., Peuskens, J., Sabbe, B. G., Thys, E., Buitelaar, J. K., et al. (2011). Ziprasidone vs olanzapine in recent-onset schizophrenia and schizoaffective disorder: results of an 8-week double-blind randomized controlled trial. *Schizophrenia Bulletin, 37*(2), 352–361.

Grundy, H. M., Simpson, S. A., & Tait, J. F. (1952). Isolation of a highly active mineralocorticoid from beef adrenal extract. *Nature, 169*(4306), 795–796.

Gudelsky, G. A. (1981). Tuberoinfundibular dopamine neurons and the regulation of prolactin secretion. *Psychoneuroendocrinology, 6*(1), 3–16.

Gull, W. W. (1874). *On cretinoid state supervening in adult life in women* (Vol. 7). Trans Clinical Society of London.

Guyton, A. C., & Hall, J. E. (1996). *Textbook of medical physiology* (9th ed.). Philadelphia: WB Saunders.

Hafner, H. (2003). Gender differences in schizophrenia. *Psychoneuroendocrinology, 28*(Suppl. 2), 17–54.

Hafner, H., & an der Heiden, W. (1997). Epidemiology of schizophrenia. *Canadian Journal of Psychiatry, 42*(2), 139–151.

Hafner, H., Riecher-Rossler, A., Maurer, K., Fatkenheuer, B., & Loffler, W. (1992). First onset and early symptomatology of schizophrenia. A chapter of epidemiological and neurobiological research into age and sex differences. *European Archives of Psychiatry and Clinical Neuroscience, 242*(2–3), 109–118.

Halbreich, U., Kinon, B. J., Gilmore, J. A., & Kahn, L. S. (2003). Elevated prolactin levels in patients with schizophrenia: mechanisms and related adverse effects. *Psychoneuroendocrinology, 28*(Suppl. 1), 53–67.

Hankinson, S. E., Willett, W. C., Michaud, D. S., Manson, J. E., Colditz, G. A., Longcope, C., et al. (1999). Plasma prolactin levels and subsequent risk of breast cancer in postmenopausal women. *Journal of the National Cancer Institute, 91*(7), 629–634.

Hattangady, N. G., Olala, L. O., Bollag, W. B., & Rainey, W. E. (2012). Acute and chronic regulation of aldosterone production. *Molecular and Cellular Endocrinology, 350*(2), 151–162.

Heinrich, T. W., & Grahm, G. (2003). Hypothyroidism presenting as psychosis: myxedema madness revisited. *Primary Care Companion to the Journal of Clinical Psychiatry, 5*(6), 260–266.

Herman, J. P., Flak, J., & Jankord, R. (2008). Chronic stress plasticity in the hypothalamic paraventricular nucleus. *Progress in Brain Research, 170*, 353–364.

Herman, J. P., Ostrander, M. M., Mueller, N. K., & Figueiredo, H. (2005). Limbic system mechanisms of stress regulation: hypothalamo-pituitary-adrenocortical axis. *Progress in Neuro-Psychopharmacology & Biological Psychiatry, 29*(8), 1201–1213.

Hickie, I., Bennett, B., Mitchell, P., Wilhelm, K., & Orlay, W. (1996). Clinical and subclinical hypothyroidism in patients with chronic and treatment-resistant depression. *Australian and New Zealand Journal of Psychiatry, 30*(2), 246–252.

Holtzman, C. W., Trotman, H. D., Goulding, S. M., Ryan, A. T., Macdonald, A. N., Shapiro, D. I., et al. (2013). Stress and neurodevelopmental processes in the emergence of psychosis. *Neuroscience, 249*, 172–191.

Horacek, J., Bubenikova-Valesova, V., Kopecek, M., Palenicek, T., Dockery, C., Mohr, P., et al. (2006). Mechanism of action of atypical antipsychotic drugs and the neurobiology of schizophrenia. *CNS Drugs, 20*(5), 389–409.

ter Horst, G. J. (2010). Estrogen in the limbic system. *Vitamins and Hormones, 82*, 319–338.

Hoskins, R. G. (1929). Endocrine factors in dementia precox. *New England Journal of Medicine, 200*(8), 361–369.

Hughes, Z. A., Liu, F., Marquis, K., Muniz, L., Pangalos, M. N., Ring, R. H., et al. (2009). Estrogen receptor neurobiology and its potential for translation into broad spectrum therapeutics for CNS disorders. *Current Molecular Pharmacology, 2*(3), 215–236.

Iritani, S. (2007). Neuropathology of schizophrenia: a mini review. *Neuropathology, 27*(6), 604–608.

Jablensky, A., Sartorius, N., Ernberg, G., Anker, M., Korten, A., Cooper, J. E., et al. (1992). Schizophrenia: manifestations, incidence and course in different cultures. A World Health Organization ten-country study. *Psychological Medicine Monograph Supplement, 20*, 1–97.

Jankord, R., & Herman, J. P. (2008). Limbic regulation of hypothalamo-pituitary-adrenocortical function during acute and chronic stress. *Annals of the New York Academy of Sciences, 1148*, 64–73.

Jansen, L. M., Gispen-de Wied, C. C., & Kahn, R. S. (2000). Selective impairments in the stress response in schizophrenic patients. *Psychopharmacology (Berl), 149*(3), 319–325.

Kale, A., Naphade, N., Sapkale, S., Kamaraju, M., Pillai, A., Joshi, S., et al. (2010). Reduced folic acid, vitamin B12 and docosahexaenoic acid and increased homocysteine and cortisol in never-medicated schizophrenia patients: implications for altered one-carbon metabolism. *Psychiatry Research, 175*(1–2), 47–53.

Keks, N. A., Copolov, D. L., Kulkarni, J., Mackie, B., Singh, B. S., McGorry, P., et al. (1990). Basal and haloperidol-stimulated prolactin in neuroleptic-free men with schizophrenia defined by 11 diagnostic systems. *Biological Psychiatry, 27*(11), 1203–1215.

Kelly, D. L., Wehring, H. J., Earl, A. K., Sullivan, K. M., Dickerson, F. B., Feldman, S., et al. (2013). Treating symptomatic hyperprolactinemia in women with schizophrenia: presentation of the ongoing DAAMSEL clinical trial (Dopamine partial Agonist, Aripiprazole, for the Management of Symptomatic ELevated prolactin). *BMC Psychiatry, 13*, 214.

Kendler, K. S., & Jablensky, A. (2011). Kraepelin's concept of psychiatric illness. *Psychologie Medicale, 41*(6), 1119–1126.

Kinon, B. J., Gilmore, J. A., Liu, H., & Halbreich, U. M. (2003). Prevalence of hyperprolactinemia in schizophrenic patients treated with conventional antipsychotic medications or risperidone. *Psychoneuroendocrinology, 28*(Suppl. 2), 55–68.

de Kloet, E. R., Oitzl, M. S., & Joels, M. (1999). Stress and cognition: are corticosteroids good or bad guys? *Trends in Neurosciences, 22*(10), 422–426.

Kretschmer, E. (1922). Körperbau und Charakter. Untersuchungen zum Konstitutionsproblem und zur Lehre von den Temperamenten. *Zeitschrift für Induktive Abstammungs- und Vererbungslehre, 30*(1), 139–144.

Krishnamurthy, D., Harris, L. W., Levin, Y., Koutroukides, T. A., Rahmoune, H., Pietsch, S., et al. (2013). Metabolic, hormonal and stress-related molecular changes in post-mortem pituitary glands from schizophrenia subjects. *World Journal of Biological Psychiatry, 14*(7), 478–489.

Kulkarni, J., de Castella, A., Fitzgerald, P. B., Gurvich, C. T., Bailey, M., Bartholomeusz, C., et al. (2008). Estrogen in severe mental illness: a potential new treatment approach. *Archives of General Psychiatry, 65*(8), 955–960.

Kulkarni, J., de Castella, A., Headey, B., Marston, N., Sinclair, K., Lee, S., et al. (2011). Estrogens and men with schizophrenia: is there a case for adjunctive therapy? *Schizophrenia Research, 125*(2–3), 278–283.

Kulkarni, J., de Castella, A., Smith, D., Taffe, J., Keks, N., & Copolov, D. (1996). A clinical trial of the effects of estrogen in acutely psychotic women. *Schizophrenia Research, 20*(3), 247–252.

Kulkarni, J., de Castella, A., & Thompson, K. (1998). Menstrual cycle changes in schizophrenia. *Schizophrenia Research, 29*(1), 188.

Kulkarni, J., Gavrilidis, E., Wang, W., Worsley, R., Fitzgerald, P. B., Gurvich, C., et al. (2014). Estradiol for treatment-resistant schizophrenia: a large-scale randomized-controlled trial in women of child-bearing age. *Molecular Psychiatry, 20*(6), 695–702.

Kulkarni, J., Gurvich, C., Gilbert, H., Mehmedbegovic, F., Mu, L., Marston, N., et al. (2008). Hormone modulation: a novel therapeutic approach for women with severe mental illness. *Australian and New Zealand Journal of Psychiatry, 42*(1), 83–88.

Kulkarni, J., Gurvich, C., Lee, S. J., Gilbert, H., Gavrilidis, E., de Castella, A., et al. (2010). Piloting the effective therapeutic dose of adjunctive selective estrogen receptor modulator treatment in postmenopausal women with schizophrenia. *Psychoneuroendocrinology, 35*(8), 1142–1147.

Kulkarni, J., Keks, N. A., Stuart, G., Mackie, B., Minas, I. H., Singh, B. S., et al. (1990). Relationship of psychotic symptoms to haloperidol-stimulated prolactin release. *Acta Psychiatrica Scandinavica, 82*(4), 271–274.

Kulkarni, J., Riedel, A., de Castella, A. R., Fitzgerald, P. B., Rolfe, T. J., Taffe, J., et al. (2001). Estrogen - a potential treatment for schizophrenia. *Schizophrenia Research, 48*(1), 137–144.

Langer, G., Sachar, E., Gruen, P., & Halpern, F. (1980). The prolactin model in schizophrenic patients: further studies on the psychodynamics of neuroleptic drugs. *Advances in Biological Psychiatry, 5*, 58.

Li, J., Siegel, M., Yuan, M., Zeng, Z., Finnucan, L., Persky, R., et al. (2011). Estrogen enhances neurogenesis and behavioral recovery after stroke. *Journal of Cerebral Blood Flow & Metabolism, 31*(2), 413–425.

Ling, M. H., Perry, P. J., & Tsuang, M. T. (1981). Side effects of corticosteroid therapy. Psychiatric aspects. *Archives of General Psychiatry, 38*(4), 471–477.

Liu, M., Kelley, M. H., Herson, P. S., & Hurn, P. D. (2010). Neuroprotection of sex steroids. *Minerva Endocrinologica, 35*(2), 127–143.

Loffler, W., Hafner, H., Fatkenheuer, B., Maurer, K., Riecher-Rossler, A., Lutzhoft, J., et al. (1994). Validation of Danish case register diagnosis for schizophrenia. *Acta Psychiatrica Scandinavica, 90*(3), 196–203.

Lokuge, S., Frey, B. N., Foster, J. A., Soares, C. N., & Steiner, M. (2010). The rapid effects of estrogen: a mini-review. *Behavioural Pharmacology, 21*(5–6), 465–472.

Lupien, S. J., de Leon, M., de Santi, S., Convit, A., Tarshish, C., Nair, N. P., et al. (1998). Cortisol levels during human aging predict hippocampal atrophy and memory deficits. *Nature Neuroscience, 1*(1), 69–73.

Lupien, S. J., Wilkinson, C. W., Briere, S., Menard, C., Ng Ying Kin, N. M., & Nair, N. P. (2002). The modulatory effects of corticosteroids on cognition: studies in young human populations. *Psychoneuroendocrinology, 27*(3), 401–416.

Maccari, S., Darnaudery, M., Morley-Fletcher, S., Zuena, A. R., Cinque, C., & Van Reeth, O. (2003). Prenatal stress and long-term consequences: implications of glucocorticoid hormones. *Neuroscience & Biobehavioral Reviews, 27*(1–2), 119–127.

Magliozzi, J. R., Gold, A., & Laubly, J. N. (1989). Effect of oral administration of haloperidol on plasma thyrotropin concentrations in men. *Psychoneuroendocrinology, 14*(1–2), 125–130.

Marian, G., Nica, E. A., Ionescu, B. E., & Ghinea, D. (2009). Hyperthyroidism–cause of depression and psychosis: a case report. *Journal of Medicine and Life, 2*(4), 440–442.

Marx, C. E., Bradford, D. W., Hamer, R. M., Naylor, J. C., Allen, T. B., Lieberman, J. A., et al. (2011). Pregnenolone as a novel therapeutic candidate in schizophrenia: emerging preclinical and clinical evidence. *Neuroscience, 191*, 78–90.

McIver, B., Romanski, S. A., & Nippoldt, T. B. (1997). Evaluation and management of amenorrhea. *Mayo Clinic Proceedings, 72*(12), 1161–1169.

Meaney, A. M., Smith, S., Howes, O. D., O'Brien, M., Murray, R. M., & O'Keane, V. (2004). Effects of long-term prolactin-raising antipsychotic medication on bone mineral density in patients with schizophrenia. *British Journal of Psychiatry, 184*, 503–508.

Melby, J. C. (1989). Clinical review 1: endocrine hypertension. *Journal of Clinical Endocrinology and Metabolism, 69*(4), 697–703.

Meltzer, H. (1984). *Neuroendocrine abnormalities in schizophrenia: Prolactin, growth hormone and gonadatrophins.* New York: Raven Press.

Meltzer, H. Y., & Massey, B. W. (2011). The role of serotonin receptors in the action of atypical antipsychotic drugs. *Current Opinion in Pharmacology, 11*(1), 59–67.

Mendes-de-Aguiar, C. B., Alchini, R., Decker, H., Alvarez-Silva, M., Tasca, C. I., & Trentin, A. G. (2008). Thyroid hormone increases astrocytic glutamate uptake and protects astrocytes and neurons against glutamate toxicity. *Journal of Neuroscience Research, 86*(14), 3117–3125.

Mondelli, V., Dazzan, P., Hepgul, N., Di Forti, M., Aas, M., D'Albenzio, A., et al. (2010). Abnormal cortisol levels during the day and cortisol awakening response in first-episode psychosis: the role of stress and of antipsychotic treatment. *Schizophrenia Research, 116*(2–3), 234–242.

Mondelli, V., Pariante, C. M., Navari, S., Aas, M., D'Albenzio, A., Di Forti, M., et al. (2010). Higher cortisol levels are associated with smaller left hippocampal volume in first-episode psychosis. *Schizophrenia Research, 119*(1–3), 75–78.

Moult, P. J., Dacie, J. E., Rees, L. H., & Besser, G. M. (1981). Prolactin pulsatility in patients with gonadal dysfunction. *Clinical Endocrinology (Oxford), 14*(4), 387–394.

Muller, J. (1995). Aldosterone: the minority hormone of the adrenal cortex. *Steroids, 60*(1), 2–9.

Norman, A. W., & Litwack, G. (1997). *Chapter 1-General considerations of hormones.* San Diego: Academic Press.

Oitzl, M. S., Champagne, D. L., van der Veen, R., & de Kloet, E. R. (2010). Brain development under stress: hypotheses of glucocorticoid actions revisited. *Neuroscience & Biobehavioral Reviews, 34*(6), 853–866.

Ord, W. M. (1878). On myxoedema. *R Royal Medical and Chirurgical Society Transcripts, 61,* 57–781.

Ord, W. M. (1888). Report of a committee of the Clinical Society of London nominated December 14, 1883, to investigate the subject of myxoedema. *Transactions of the Clinical Society of London, 21*(Suppl.).

Owashi, T., Otsubo, T., Oshima, A., Nakagome, K., Higuchi, T., & Kamijima, K. (2008). Longitudinal neuroendocrine changes assessed by dexamethasone/CRH and growth hormone releasing hormone tests in psychotic depression. *Psychoneuroendocrinology, 33*(2), 152–161.

Palha, J. A., & Goodman, A. B. (2006). Thyroid hormones and retinoids: a possible link between genes and environment in schizophrenia. *Brain Research Reviews, 51*(1), 61–71.

Potkin, S. G., Cohen, M., & Panagides, J. (2007). Efficacy and tolerability of asenapine in acute schizophrenia: a placebo- and risperidone-controlled trial. *Journal of Clinical Psychiatry, 68*(10), 1492–1500.

Rao, M. L., Gross, G., Strebel, B., Braunig, P., Huber, G., & Klosterkotter, J. (1990). Serum amino acids, central monoamines, and hormones in drug-naive, drug-free, and neuroleptic-treated schizophrenic patients and healthy subjects. *Psychiatry Research, 34*(3), 243–257.

Riecher-Rossler, A., & Hafner, H. (1993). Schizophrenia and oestrogens–is there an association? *European Archives of Psychiatry and Clinical Neuroscience, 242*(6), 323–328.

Riley, A., Peet, M., & Wilson, C. (1993). *Sexual pharmacology.* Clarendon Press.

Rinieris, P., Christodoulou, G. N., Souvatzoglou, A., Koutras, D. A., & Stefanis, C. (1980). Free-thyroxine index in schizophrenic patients before and after neuroleptic treatment. *Neuropsychobiology, 6*(1), 29–33.

Ritsner, M. S. (2011). The clinical and therapeutic potentials of dehydroepiandrosterone and pregnenolone in schizophrenia. *Neuroscience, 191,* 91–100.

Roca, R. P., Blackman, M. R., Ackerley, M. B., Harman, S. M., & Gregerman, R. I. (1990). Thyroid hormone elevations during acute psychiatric illness: relationship to severity and distinction from hyperthyroidism. *Endocrine Research, 16*(4), 415–447.

Rubin, R. T., & Hays, S. E. (1980). The prolactin secretory response to neuroleptic drugs: mechanisms, applications and limitations. *Psychoneuroendocrinology, 5*(2), 121–137.

Ryan, M. C., Sharifi, N., Condren, R., & Thakore, J. H. (2004). Evidence of basal pituitary-adrenal overactivity in first episode, drug naive patients with schizophrenia. *Psychoneuroendocrinology, 29*(8), 1065–1070.

Sanchez, M. G., Bourque, M., Morissette, M., & Di Paolo, T. (2010). Steroids-dopamine interactions in the pathophysiology and treatment of CNS disorders. *CNS Neuroscience & Therapeutics, 16*(3), e43–71.

Santos, N. C., Costa, P., Ruano, D., Macedo, A., Soares, M. J., Valente, J., et al. (2012). Revisiting thyroid hormones in schizophrenia. *Journal of Thyroid Research, 2012,* 569147.

Sayers, G., & Sayers, M. A. (1948). The pituitary-adrenal system. *Recent Progress in Hormone Research, 2*(1 Vol.), 81–115.

Shenton, M. E., Dickey, C. C., Frumin, M., & McCarley, R. W. (2001). A review of MRI findings in schizophrenia. *Schizophrenia Research, 49*(1–2), 1–52.

Shepherd, A. M., Laurens, K. R., Matheson, S. L., Carr, V. J., & Green, M. J. (2012). Systematic meta-review and quality assessment of the structural brain alterations in schizophrenia. *Neuroscience & Biobehavioral Reviews, 36*(4), 1342–1356.

Shikaeva, F. V., & Koreneva, G. P. (1987). Functional interrelations of monoamines, thyrotropic hormone and thyroid hormones in hyperprolactinemia. *Problemy Endokrinologii (Moskva), 33*(4), 27–30.

Shimada, T., Yasuda, K., Mori, A., Ni, H., Mercado-Asis, L. B., Murase, H., et al. (1993). Aldosterone binding to mineralocorticoid receptors of mononuclear leukocytes in diabetic subjects. *Acta Endocrinologica (Copenhagen), 128*(6), 529–535.

Silverman, M. N., & Sternberg, E. M. (2012). Glucocorticoid regulation of inflammation and its functional correlates: from HPA axis to glucocorticoid receptor dysfunction. *Annals of the New York Academy of Sciences, 1261,* 55–63.

Sim, K., Chong, S. A., Chan, Y. H., & Lum, W. M. (2002). Thyroid dysfunction in chronic schizophrenia within a state psychiatric hospital. *Annals of the Academy of Medicine, Singapore, 31*(5), 641–644.

Simpkins, J. W., Yi, K. D., Yang, S. H., & Dykens, J. A. (2010). Mitochondrial mechanisms of estrogen neuroprotection. *Biochimica et Biophysica Acta, 1800*(10), 1113–1120.

Skopek, M., & Manoj, P. (2010). Hyperprolactinaemia during treatment with paliperidone. *Australasian Psychiatry, 18*(3), 261–263.

Smith, S., Wheeler, M. J., Murray, R., & O'Keane, V. (2002). The effects of antipsychotic-induced hyperprolactinaemia on the hypothalamic-pituitary-gonadal axis. *Journal of Clinical Psychopharmacology, 22*(2), 109–114.

Snabboon, T., Khemkha, A., Chaiyaumporn, C., Lalitanantpong, D., & Sridama, V. (2009). Psychosis as the first presentation of hyperthyroidism. *Internal and Emergency Medicine, 4*(4), 359–360.

Southwick, S., Mason, J. W., Giller, E. L., & Kosten, T. R. (1989). Serum thyroxine change and clinical recovery in psychiatric inpatients. *Biological Psychiatry, 25*(1), 67–74.

Spiga, F., Walker, J. J., Terry, J. R., & Lightman, S. L. (2011). *HPA Axis-Rhythms.* John Wiley & Sons, Inc.

Stevens, A., & White, A. (2010). ACTH: cellular peptide hormone synthesis and secretory pathways. *Results and Problems in Cell Differentiation, 50,* 63–84.

Strawn, J. R., Ekhator, N. N., D'Souza, B. B., & Geracioti, T. D., Jr. (2004). Pituitary-thyroid state correlates with central dopaminergic and serotonergic activity in healthy humans. *Neuropsychobiology, 49*(2), 84–87.

Talih, F., Fattal, O., & Malone, D., Jr. (2007). Anabolic steroid abuse: psychiatric and physical costs. *Cleveland Clinic Journal of Medicine, 74*(5), 341–344 346, 349–352.

Tsai, R., Davis, R. P., & Morris, D. J. (1980). The effect of the antimineralocorticoid, spironolactone on the hepatic synthesis of polar metabolites of aldosterone in male rats. *Journal of Steroid Biochemistry, 13*(5), 481–487.

Tuomisto, J., & Mannisto, P. (1985). Neurotransmitter regulation of anterior pituitary hormones. *Pharmacological Reviews, 37*(3), 249–332.

Usall, J., Huerta-Ramos, E., Iniesta, R., Cobo, J., Araya, S., Roca, M., et al. (2011). Raloxifene as an adjunctive treatment for postmenopausal women with schizophrenia: a double-blind, randomized, placebo-controlled trial. *Journal of Clinical Psychiatry*, *72*(11), 1552–1557.

Van Hulle, C. A., Shirtcliff, E. A., Lemery-Chalfant, K., & Goldsmith, H. H. (2012). Genetic and environmental influences on individual differences in cortisol level and circadian rhythm in middle childhood. *Hormones and Behavior*, *62*(1), 36–42.

Venkatasubramanian, G., Chittiprol, S., Neelakantachar, N., Shetty, T., & Gangadhar, B. N. (2010). Effect of antipsychotic treatment on Insulin-like Growth Factor-1 and cortisol in schizophrenia: a longitudinal study. *Schizophrenia Research*, *119*(1–3), 131–137.

van Venrooij, J. A., Fluitman, S. B., Lijmer, J. G., Kavelaars, A., Heijnen, C. J., Westenberg, H. G., et al. (2012). Impaired neuroendocrine and immune response to acute stress in medication-naive patients with a first episode of psychosis. *Schizophrenia Bulletin*, *38*(2), 272–279.

Vyas, U. (2012). Risk of breast Cancer due to hyperprolactinemia caused by antipsychotics (Neuroleptics). *British Journal of Medical Practitioners*, *5*(4a), 534.

Wada, K., Yamada, N., Sato, T., Suzuki, H., Miki, M., Lee, Y., et al. (2001). Corticosteroid-induced psychotic and mood disorders: diagnosis defined by DSM-IV and clinical pictures. *Psychosomatics*, *42*(6), 461–466.

Walker, E., Mittal, V., & Tessner, K. (2008). Stress and the hypothalamic pituitary adrenal axis in the developmental course of schizophrenia. *Annual Review of Clinical Psychology*, *4*, 189–216.

Wang, P. S., Walker, A. M., Tsuang, M. T., Orav, E. J., Glynn, R. J., Levin, R., et al. (2002). Dopamine antagonists and the development of breast cancer. *Archives of General Psychiatry*, *59*(12), 1147–1154.

Warrington, T. P., & Bostwick, J. M. (2006). Psychiatric adverse effects of corticosteroids. *Mayo Clinic Proceedings*, *81*(10), 1361–1367.

Yaffe, K., Krueger, K., Cummings, S. R., Blackwell, T., Henderson, V. W., Sarkar, S., et al. (2005). Effect of raloxifene on prevention of dementia and cognitive impairment in older women: the multiple outcomes of raloxifene evaluation (MORE) randomized trial. *American Journal of Psychiatry*, *162*(4), 683–690.

Yuan, H. N., Wang, C. Y., Sze, C. W., Tong, Y., Tan, Q. R., Feng, X. J., et al. (2008). A randomized, crossover comparison of herbal medicine and bromocriptine against risperidone-induced hyperprolactinemia in patients with schizophrenia. *Journal of Clinical Psychopharmacology*, *28*(3), 264–370.

28

Role of Redox Dysregulation in White Matter Anomalies Associated with Schizophrenia

Aline Monin,§,#, Margot Fournier*,§,#, Philipp S. Baumann*,§,¶,
Michel Cuénod*,§, Kim Q. Do*,§*

*Center for Psychiatric Neuroscience, Centre Hospitalier Universitaire Vaudois and University of Lausanne
(CHUV-UNIL), Prilly-Lausanne, Switzerland; §Department of Psychiatry, Centre Hospitalier Universitaire Vaudois
and University of Lausanne (CHUV-UNIL), Prilly-Lausanne, Switzerland; ¶Service of General Psychiatry, Centre
Hospitalier Universitaire Vaudois and University of Lausanne (CHUV-UNIL), Prilly-Lausanne, Switzerland

INTRODUCTION

Schizophrenia is a neurodevelopmental disorder appearing in adolescence or early adulthood resulting from both genetic and environmental risk factors. Despite a high heritability (estimations range between 40% and 60%), monogenic causes cannot account for the cases, leading to the hypothesis of an interaction between genes and environment. Adverse events during prenatal life, perinatal life, childhood, or adolescence have been associated with the illness (Brown, 2011; van Os, Rutten, & Poulton, 2008; Schmitt, Malchow, Hasan, & Falkai, 2014). The delay between occurrence of these events and illness onset has led to the concept of a neurodevelopmental disorder (Catts et al., 2013; Insel, 2010; Weinberger, 1987). Interestingly, schizophrenia coincidentally develops with maturation of the prefrontal cortex (Fuster, 2002; Hoistad et al., 2009): volume of white matter in this region progresses through adolescence to reach a maximal volume in the third decade of life (Bartzokis et al., 2001; Lenroot & Giedd, 2006).

Imaging studies implicated anomalies of the prefrontal cortex in schizophrenia. Clinical manifestations of the illness, including cognitive symptoms, are hypothesized to reflect abnormal brain connectivity. This disconnectivity can result from disturbances of long-range neuronal circuits (i.e., white matter tracts) or of local circuits (i.e., GABAergic and glutamatergic system) (Ruiz, Birbaumer, & Sitaram, 2013; Schmitt, Hasan, Gruber, & Falkai, 2011; Steullet et al., 2014), both of which have been involved in schizophrenia. At the neuropathological level, alterations of oligodendrocytes and myelin appear as clear findings in schizophrenia. Because myelin influences conduction velocity, an impairment of myelination process would disrupt temporal coordination between distant brain regions, affect their synchrony, and thus lead to disconnectivity (Whitford, Ford, Mathalon, Kubicki, & Shenton, 2012).

Current works from our laboratory and others suggest that interactions of genes and environment during neurodevelopment converge to induce redox dysregulation and oxidative stress in schizophrenia (Do, Cabungcal, Frank, Steullet, & Cuenod, 2009; Steullet et al., 2014). In the present review, we will focus on evidences of redox dysregulation and myelin anomalies in patients with schizophrenia as well as in early psychotic patients. Finally, we review data from human studies and rodent models of schizophrenia showing that known genetic and environmental risk factors of schizophrenia induce redox dysregulation/oxidative stress and myelin anomalies. We suggest that oxidative stress during key periods of brain maturation interferes with myelin development thus leading to disconnectivity and schizophrenia symptoms.

Co-first authors.

IMBALANCE OF REDOX HOMEOSTASIS IN SCHIZOPHRENIA

Key Players of Redox Homeostasis

Redox state is a regulatory system of posttranslational modifications that controls cellular signalization in response to oxidants and free radicals. Oxidative stress is defined as an imbalance between prooxidants and antioxidants, which results in macromolecular damages (lipid peroxidation, protein carbonylation, and DNA oxidation) and in dysregulation of the redox system. Major prooxidants are free radicals, that is, reactive oxygen species (ROS; superoxide anion radicals $O_2 \cdot^-$, hydrogen peroxide H_2O_2, and hydroxyl radicals $OH \cdot$) and reactive nitrogen species (nitric oxide $NO \cdot$ and peroxynitrite $ONOO^-$) (Do, Bovet, et al., 2009; Valko et al., 2007). $NO \cdot$ is produced by the NO synthase in mitochondria and peroxisomes (Szibor, Richter, & Ghafourifar, 2001;

Valko et al., 2007). It diffuses through cytoplasm and plasma membranes, and plays signaling roles in various processes such as synaptic plasticity, immune response, or regulation of blood pressure. $NO \cdot$ toxicity is mainly linked to its reaction with $O_2 \cdot^-$ that forms $ONOO^-$, a strong oxidant inducing lipid oxidation and DNA fragmentation (Figure 1(A)) (Bergendi, Beneš, Ďuračková, & Ferenčik, 1999; Valko et al., 2007). In physiological conditions, $O_2 \cdot^-$ is produced within the cell by mitochondria and, to a lower extent, by endoplasmic reticulum. $O_2 \cdot^-$ is reduced by the superoxide dismutase (SOD) into H_2O_2 (Figure 1(A)). Moreover, peroxides are generated at high rates by anabolic and catabolic reactions ongoing in peroxisomes (Schrader & Fahimi, 2006), where catalase catalyzes their decomposition into water. In a reaction catalyzed by iron, peroxides may form $OH \cdot$ radicals, which are highly reactive and thus can lead to lipid peroxidation, protein carbonylation, and DNA oxidation (Figure 1(A)).

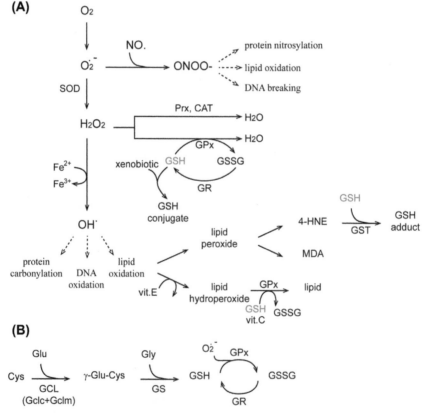

FIGURE 1   Antioxidant system (A) and glutathione (GSH) metabolism (B). (A) Free radicals such as $O_2 \cdot^-$ are catalyzed to hydrogen peroxide (H_2O_2) through superoxide dismutase (SOD). H_2O_2 can be detoxified to water via peroxiredoxin (Prx) or catalase (CAT). Glutathione peroxidase (GPx) also catalyzes the same reaction, using GSH as a reductant. H_2O_2 can be converted into hydroxyl radical $\cdot OH$ (Fenton reaction), which induces macromolecular damages: protein carbonylation, DNA oxidation, and lipid oxidation. Lipid oxidation generates end products such as 4-hydroxynonenal (4-HNE) and malondialdehyde (MDA), which are indirect oxidative stress markers. Lipids can be restored via vitamin E and GPx reactions using GSH as reductant. GSH acts as reductant to detoxify ROS or lipid via GPx, and is used as substrate by GSH transferase (GST) to detoxify xenobiotics. (B) GSH is synthesized by two consecutive enzymes: glutamine-cysteine ligase (GCL) and glutathione synthetase (GS). GCL has two subunits, the catalytic and the modulatory, coded by GCLC and GCLM. GCL combines cysteine to glutamate to form γ-glutamylcysteine. The second enzyme (GS) catalyzes the final step of GSH synthesis by adding glycine to γ-glutamylcysteine. Reduced GSH can react directly with ROS, generating oxidized GSH (GSSG). Reduced GSH can be recycled via the activity of glutathione reductase (GR).

Recent advances show that redox systems are regulated under dynamic, nonequilibrium conditions. "Redox signaling" is used to describe signaling processes in which a specific oxidative signal is conveyed through a specific redox element to direct a specific cellular response (i.e., Nrf2 redox-signaling pathway). Nrf2, a transcription factor that induces the expression of an array of antioxidant enzymes, is regulated by redox-sensitive proteins. Indeed, in conditions of redox dysregulation, the inhibitor of Nrf2, KEAP1, is oxidized on its cysteine residues, leading to the release of Nrf2 and its translocation to the nucleus (Kensler, Wakabayashi, & Biswal, 2007). Many signaling systems including kinase, phosphatase, and transmembrane ionic signaling (e.g., N-methyl-D-aspartate(NMDA)receptor) can also be regulated by "redox sensing" thiols of critical proteins in the pathways (Jones, 2008). Both redox sensing and redox signaling use thiol switches, especially cysteine residues in proteins which are sensitive to covalent or noncovalent modifications (i.e., reversible oxidation, nitrosylation, and glutathionylation), leading to structural and functional alterations of target protein. This has led to the concept of "orthogonal control of signal transduction systems by redox-sensing mechanisms" (Jones, 2010). Moreover, because redox potentials are differently controlled in subcellular compartments, the same signaling mechanism can be differentially regulated by the local redox environment. At present, there is no methodology to monitor these highly dynamic and unstable dithiol/disulfide switches neither in real-time nor in space (i.e., targeted to specific proteins, cells, and brain regions). Recent proteomics-based approaches are efficient but they assess the endpoint. Indeed, the effects cannot be localized to cell type/structure and artifactual oxidation/reduction can occur during isolation and fixation.

Redox regulators and endogenous antioxidants encompass a variety of enzymatic and nonenzymatic defenses. The nonenzymatic redox regulation is a multipartite system relying mainly on glutathione (GSH), thioredoxin (Trx), and cysteine. The tripeptide GSH is synthesized into two steps, the first and limiting one being catalyzed by the glutamate-cysteine ligase (GCL) (Figure 1(B)) (Lu, 2013). GSH can react with free radicals via a nonenzymatic reaction. This oxidation of GSH generates disulfides (GSSG), which can be restored by GSH reductase (Figure 1(B)). Moreover, many enzymatic reactions use GSH to detoxify ROS or regenerate oxidized molecules. Two main families of enzymes use GSH as a substrate: (1) the GSH peroxidase (GPx), which reduces peroxides or peroxidized lipids, and (2) the GSH transferase (GST), a superfamily of enzymes catalyzing the conjugation of GSH, with mixed functions, such as the detoxification of xenobiotics and the synthesis of steroid hormones (reviewed by Board & Menon, 2013) (Figure 1(A)). In addition, GSH can regenerate other antioxidants such as vitamin C, vitamin E, and glutaredoxin (Grx). Grx, Trx, and peroxiredoxin (Prx) are three families of thiol-dependant antioxidant proteins that can function independently of GSH. Prx catalyze the reduction of peroxides (Figure 1(A)). Grx and Trx reduce protein disulphide and mixed GSH disulphide (in the case of Grx). They are reduced back to their initial state by Trx reductase as well as by GSH in the case of Grx. Both GSH and Trx systems are dependent on reduced nicotinamide adenine dinucleotide phosphate–reducing potential. The very reducing redox state of reduced nicotinamide adenine dinucleotide phosphate/nicotinamide adenine dinucleotide phosphate + makes it the primary source of electrons for redox pathways.

Production of ROS is localized to specific part of the cell and, conversely, redox potential and its regulators are not evenly distributed (Table 1) (Go & Jones, 2008). This distribution has crucial importance in nervous tissues known to present complex compartmentalization. Mitochondria, the main source of $O_2\cdot^-$, contain GSH-dependent as well as GSH-independent enzymes (Trx2, TR2 and the manganese SOD, SOD2). In peroxisomes, high producers of H_2O_2, catalase is very active, as well as Prx and GPx (Go & Jones, 2008). GSH and Trx1 both regulate redox potential in the cytoplasm; however, they may vary independently. The nucleus constitutes an isolated environment protecting DNA from chemicals. Few antioxidant proteins are specifically addressed to the nucleus (Table 1), but oxidative stress and a large range of stressors induce translocation of cytoplasmic redox regulators as Trx1 and TR1 (Go & Jones, 2008). The extracellular space has a more oxidized state than the cytoplasm and the major redox couple is cysteine/cystine in contrast with other compartments where GSH/GSSG is main redox regulator (Go & Jones, 2008).

Redox Anomalies in Schizophrenia

Measurements of free radicals and nonradicals oxidants per se remain difficult because of their highly reactive nature. Similarly, redox homeostasis owing to its multipartite nature is not often assessed. Thus, evidences of oxidative stress and redox dysregulation in schizophrenia are mostly based on lowered antioxidant defenses and accumulation of oxidation end products such as 8-oxo-deoxyguanosine (8-oxodG, formed by oxidation of DNA), protein carbonylation, and lipid peroxidation (malondialdehyde, MDA; 4-hydroxynonenal, HNE; thiobarbituric acid reactive substances, TBARS).

Peripheral Marks of Oxidative Stress in Schizophrenia Patients

Marks of oxidative stress have been repeatedly reported in peripheral samples of schizophrenia patients, suggesting a systemic implication of the stress.

TABLE 1 Subcellular Localization of the Major Antioxidant Players According to Gene Ontology Annotations in the Uniprot Database (uniprot.org)

Subcellular Localization	Major ROS	SOD	Peroxiredoxin and Catalase	Thioredoxin and Glutaredoxin	Glutathione System		
					GSH Synthesis and Recycling	GPx	GST
Cytoplasm		SOD1	PRX1 PRX2 PRX4 PRX5 PRX6*	TXN TXNRD1 GRX1	GCLC GCLM GSS GR	GPX1 GPX2 GPX4	GSTA1-5 GSTM1-4 GSTO1 GSTP1 GSTT1, 2, 2B
Mitochondria	$O_2\bullet^-$	SOD2	PRX3 PRX5	TXN2 TXNRD2 GRX2 GRX5	GR	GPX4	GSTP1
Peroxisomes	H_2O_2, NO•		PRX5 CAT	GRX5			GSTK1
Nucleus		SOD1		TXN (see note 1) TXNRD1 (see note 2) TXNRD3 (see note 3) GRX2			GSTP1
Secreted		SOD3	PRX4			GPX3 GPX5 GPX6* GPX7*	
Others	H_2O_2: ER		PRX6*: Lysosomes	TXNRD3: Microsome, ER (see note 3)		GPX8*: ER lumen	GSTCD, exosomes

In the Grx family, the protein coded by GRX3 is probably enzymatically inactive and thus was not included. Note 1: The protein Trx1, coded by TXN, is nuclear after ultraviolet irradiation, but is mainly cytoplasmic otherwise. Note 2: Only a splicing variant of TXNRD1 (coding TR1) is reported to be nuclear. Note 3: TXNRD3 (coding TR3) is specifically expressed in testis. ER, endoplasmic reticulum. *: Putative subcellular localization.

In the urine of patients, reports indicate accumulation of 8-oxodG (Jorgensen et al., 2013), lipid peroxides (Anna Dietrich-Muszalska & Olas, 2009), and bilirubin oxidation (Miyaoka et al., 2005).

Increased lipid peroxidation (MDA or TBARS levels) might be the most robust result in blood of patients. Despite some negative studies, plasmatic amounts of MDA are mostly reported to be increased in schizophrenia patients. Consistently, results of two meta-analyses indicate that this increase is present in first episode as well as in chronic patients (Flatow, Buckley, & Miller, 2013; Grignon & Chianetta, 2007). In contrast, some oxidation markers as nitrite are accumulating only in chronic patients (Flatow et al., 2013).

Altogether, these data indicate an ongoing oxidative stress in schizophrenia patients. However, deficiencies of the antioxidant system are more controversial, as detailed in the next section.

Peripheral Levels of Antioxidant Defenses in Schizophrenia Patients

Mirroring the accumulation of oxidation products, the total antioxidant capacity is deficient in blood of schizophrenia patients (Dietrich-Muszalska & Kontek, 2010; Yao, Reddy, McElhinny, & van Kammen, 1998). Although there are negative findings (Sarandol et al., 2007; Sofic, Rustembegovic, Kroyer, & Cao, 2002), it remains significant in a recent meta-analysis (Flatow et al., 2013). The decrease of total antioxidant capacity might be due to lowered levels of GSH in blood, which was reported in schizophrenia patients as early as 1934 (Looney & Childs, 1934) and subsequently in early psychosis patients (Altuntas, Aksoy, Coskun, Caykoylu, & Akcay, 2000; Mico et al., 2011; Raffa et al., 2009).

Data on enzymatic activity are more contrasted, with increase, decrease and no change being reported for SOD, catalase, and GPx. Ruiz-Litago et al. conducted a 1-year follow-up of young drug-naive patients following their hospitalization (mean age at inclusion: 23.1 years) (Ruiz-Litago et al., 2012). They could show the transient nature of some antioxidant defects in plasma: GSH, total antioxidant defenses, as well as SOD and GPx activities were decreased 1 and 6 months after the first episode while TBARS were increased. After 1 year, they were all normalized. Interestingly, a similar study, but with less power, was performed on older patients in acute phase of illness (mean age at inclusion: 36.5 years) (Tsai, Liou, Lin, Lin, & Huang, 2013). This study did not reveal any change for TBARS, SOD, or GPx at 1 month of follow-up, suggesting that the deficits in antioxidant system reported by Ruiz-Litago et al. are specific of disease onset and might be suitable as early prognosis markers in at-risk individuals (Ruiz-Litago et al., 2012). Longitudinal assessment of redox markers on the long

term is necessary to characterize their progression and potential phase specific evolution.

Limits and Best Practices for Future Studies

Heterogeneity between studies is concerning, the impact of medication is controversial and the source of variability remains unclear. As suggested by Grignon et al. for MDA levels, heterogeneity of the results might be linked to the variable proportion of drug-free patients (Grignon & Chianetta, 2007). A good example of variability concerns data on SOD activity: the type of sample (plasma, serum, or red blood cells) and smoking status may change the picture completely (Flatow et al., 2013). Moreover, genetic background may account for some differences in the pattern of antioxidant response between individuals. Additional covariates as type of antipsychotic treatment, disease duration, disease phase (acute or not, early or chronic), body mass index, cotinine, glucose levels, and genotyping of key genes of the antioxidant systems are required in future studies. However, recent data noted the absence of exogenous factor contributions (e.g., antipsychotic, diet, and smoke) to blood GSH levels (Ballesteros et al., 2013). In addition, GSH can undergo artifactual oxidation and thus it might be difficult to setup optimal conditions for its measurement in clinical settings.

The complexity of the antioxidant system is also linked to the compartmentalization of the different players. One concern regarding the previously mentioned studies is the lack of discrimination between subcellular compartments. A more detailed characterization of the defects within different organelles and of GSH-independent systems would greatly help to pinpoint the defective systems.

Finally, an important point is also the lack of data to relate anomalies reported in periphery to their potential impact on the central nervous system. Nevertheless, and as detailed later, there are evidences of anomalies in redox homeostasis in the brain of schizophrenia patients.

Evidence for Disrupted Redox Homeostasis in the Brain of Schizophrenia Patients

Postmortem studies revealed increased lipid peroxidation (4-HNE) in the anterior cingulate cortex (Wang, Shao, Sun, & Young, 2009) but TBARS decreased in cerebrospinal fluid. SOD1 (Cu-Zn SOD) is decreased in cerebrospinal fluid of recent-onset schizophrenia patients (Coughlin et al., 2013), but SOD1 and SOD2 (Mn SOD) are increased in chronic patients' brains (Michel et al., 2004). GSH deficits are reported in caudate nucleus and prefrontal cortex of patients (Gawryluk, Wang, Andreazza, Shao, & Young, 2011; Yao, Leonard, & Reddy, 2006). Moreover, GSH levels are found to be reduced by 27% in cerebrospinal fluid of drug-naive chronic patients and by 40% in the prefrontal cortex in a group of patients as assessed by magnetic resonance spectroscopy (MRS) (Do et al., 2000). Matsuzawa et al. report no change in GSH levels in the posterior medial frontal cortex in chronic patients compared with healthy subjects, although low GSH levels are associated with more severe negative symptoms (Matsuzawa & Hashimoto, 2011). GSH quantification by MRS is a challenging approach and many technical issues may contribute to variability in the results reported previously (Poels et al., 2014). Moreover, recent observations from our group point to a crucial contribution of genotypes to brain GSH levels: indeed, polymorphisms associated with abnormal regulation of GCL and of GSH levels in periphery ("high-risk" genotypes, see Genetic Susceptibility to Oxidative Stress in Schizophrenia Patients Section) predict low GSH levels in prefrontal cortex (Xin et al., 2014). Thus, variability of genotype distribution of this polymorphism in the different relatively small studied samples may explain discrepancies between reports.

Genetic Susceptibility to Oxidative Stress in Schizophrenia Patients

What may cause oxidative stress and redox dysregulation in schizophrenia patients? Genetic factors, as *NRG1*, *PRODH*, and *DISC1*, may lead to oxidative stress via an indirect and yet unclear pathway (see Contribution of Genetic Factors Section). Other rare variants that have been associated with schizophrenia using linkage analysis approaches may directly impact on GSH metabolism. Indeed, copy number variation of genes coding for members of the GST family have been associated with schizophrenia—*GSTT1* (Saadat, Mobayen, & Farrashbandi, 2007), *GSTT2* (Rodriguez-Santiago et al., 2010), and *GSTM1* (Gravina et al., 2011; Harada, Tachikawa, & Kawanishi, 2001)—however, there is one negative report in the Japanese population (*GSTT1*, *GSTT2*, and *GSTM1*) (Matsuzawa et al., 2009). *SOD1* was associated with schizophrenia in a Turkish study (Akyol et al., 2005), but was not replicated (Hori et al., 2000; Pae et al., 2007; Ventriglia et al., 2006). Finally, different polymorphisms of the NOS have been associated with the disease in various ethnic groups (Fallin et al., 2005; Reif et al., 2006; Tang et al., 2008), including in the Japanese population for which there is also one negative report (Okumura et al., 2009). Moreover, polymorphisms in *GCLM* and in the 5′ noncoding region of *GCLC*, which code for the modulatory (GCLM) and catalytic (GCLC) subunit of the rate-limiting enzyme for GSH synthesis (GCL), have been associated with schizophrenia (Gysin et al., 2007; Ma et al., 2010; Tosic et al., 2006). These gene associations were not reproduced in studies of Japanese population (Hanzawa et al., 2011; Kishi et al., 2008; Matsuzawa et al., 2009). However, there are technical issues: *GCLC* polymorphism is a tri-nucleotide repeat of usually seven,

eight, or nine repeats. No good surrogate single-nucleotide polymorphism could be identified for any of the repeat lengths (Kulak et al., 2013); therefore, genotypes cannot be derived from available single-nucleotide polymorphisms, for instance, in genome-wide association studies. *GCLC* tri-nucleotide genotypes that are more frequent in patients than control individuals are associated with a decrease in plasma thiol levels (Gysin et al., 2007), impaired regulations of metabolism and of GCL activity following oxidative stress (Fournier et al., 2014; Gysin et al., 2007), and low GSH levels in the anterior cingulate cortex as assessed by MRS (Xin et al., 2014).

Contribution of NMDA Hypofunction and Inflammation to Oxidative Stress

At the molecular level, redox dysregulation may also arise following the impairments of other pathways involved in schizophrenia: NMDA receptor hypofunction and inflammation. Redox pathways present numerous reciprocal interactions with the glutamatergic and immune systems. Indeed, activation of synaptic NMDA receptors strengthens neuronal antioxidant defense mechanisms (Hardingham & Bading, 2010) and NMDA receptor hypofunction increases oxidative stress levels (Jiang, Cowell, & Nakazawa, 2013). In contrast, redox state modulates NMDA receptor function (Aizenman, Lipton, & Loring, 1989; Talukder, Kazi, & Wollmuth, 2011). Likewise, oxidative stress is tightly linked to inflammation. Many inflammatory mediators are activated by oxidative molecules, whereas activated immune cells such as microglia generate ROS/reactive nitrogen species (Buelna-Chontal & Zazueta, 2013; Dwir et al., 2014). These three systems are closely interacting and potentiating each other and a dysregulation within any of these factors can lead to disturbances of the others. It is proposed that dysregulations of redox homeostasis, neuroimmune, and glutamatergic systems induced by interaction between genetic and environmental risk factors during neurodevelopment, constitute one "central hub" contributing to schizophrenia pathophysiology. An imbalance within any of these "hub" systems would affect the excitatory/inhibitory balance of local neuronal circuits (microcircuits) and the connections between distant brain areas (macrocircuits) (Do, Cabungcal, et al., 2009; Kulak et al., 2013; Steullet et al., 2014).

In summary, these data indicate that there are abnormal oxidation levels in the periphery (blood) and in the central nervous system of schizophrenia patients. These redox anomalies are present early in the course of the disease and might be driven by an interaction between genetic and environment risk factors as well as by defects in other molecular pathways involved in schizophrenia (NMDA receptor hypofunction and neuroinflammation). The following sections aim at summarizing the impact of redox homeostasis imbalance on white matter integrity and connectivity in schizophrenia context.

WHITE MATTER IMPAIRMENTS IN SCHIZOPHRENIA

Connectivity abnormalities have been well-established in schizophrenia. Connectomic studies, mapping neuronal connections based on functional magnetic resonance imaging, revealed abnormal functional connectivity of the prefrontal cortex in first-episode patients. Functional connectivity is enhanced between prefrontal cortex and temporal lobe, and reduced between prefrontal cortex and parietal lobe, posterior cingulate cortex, thalamus, and striatum of patients (Zhou et al., 2007). Hypo- and hyperconnectivity in parietal, occipital lobe, and prominently in frontal and temporal lobe indicate a diffuse functional disconnectivity in schizophrenia (Fornito, Zalesky, Pantelis, & Bullmore, 2012).

Brain regions are wired through white matter tracts, whose development and integrity are essential for the flow of information and synchronization of distant brain regions, and thus for connectivity. Myelination starts before birth, continues through childhood and adolescence and even adulthood for long association tracts (Peters & Karlsgodt, 2014). Neuroimaging and postmortem studies highlighted white matter abnormalities in schizophrenia patients, which may participate to disconnectivity.

Evidences of White Matter Abnormalities in Imaging Studies

The noninvasive properties of magnetic resonance imaging have made it possible to address key questions in regards of timing of brain changes. Diffusion tensor imaging (DTI) is used to probe diffusion of water molecules, and thus reflects the underlying structure of the brain. Fractional anisotropy (FA), a frequently used metric, describes the degree of anisotropy of water diffusion: low FA values are often interpreted as impairment of myelin integrity although it is acknowledged that other factors influence FA as well (fiber coherence and axon diameter for instance) (Beaulieu, 2002).

Despite some discrepancies among studies, low FA has been repeatedly reported in frontal and temporal brain regions of schizophrenia patients (Fitzsimmons, Kubicki, & Shenton, 2013; Kanaan et al., 2005; Kyriakopoulos, Bargiotas, Barker, & Frangou, 2008). Bundle tracts connecting these regions (uncinate fasciculus, cingulum bundle, and arcuate fasciculus) have disrupted integrity, which emphasize frontotemporal circuitry abnormalities in the illness (Takahashi, Sakurai, Davis, & Buxbaum, 2011). To disentangle from other factors the

contribution of myelin abnormalities to FA, Du and Ongür propose to combine different imaging methods. Diffusion tensor spectroscopy and magnetization transfer ratio can be used to assess axonal integrity and myelin volume, respectively (Du & Ongur, 2013).

From a functional point of view, there may be a relation between lost white matter integrity and psychopathology. Indeed, more severe cognitive symptoms are associated with greater deficits in the volume of the frontal white matter (Ho, Alicata, et al., 2003; Ren, Wang, & Xiao, 2013).

To summarize, imaging studies indicate disruption of frontotemporal tracts in schizophrenia patients. These anomalies may reflect myelin impairments as suggested by transcriptomics and neurocytochemical findings described in the following section.

Evidences of Oligodendrocyte Disruption in Postmortem Studies

Postmortem studies and histological characterization of patients' brain support the view of altered white matter in schizophrenia patients. Indeed, structural alterations of myelinated fibers are reported in gray and white matter of prefrontal cortex and caudate nucleus of patients (Uranova, Vikhreva, Rachmanova, & Orlovskaya, 2011). Most studies report a decrease in oligodendrocyte density in thalamic nuclei and in prefrontal cortex (Byne et al., 2006; Hof, Haroutunian, Copland, Davis, & Buxbaum, 2002; Uranova, Vostrikov, Orlovskaya, & Rachmanova, 2004; Vostrikov, Uranova, & Orlovskaya, 2007). In prefrontal cortex, the age-related increase in number of mature oligodendrocytes normally observed in control subjects is absent in schizophrenia patients (Vostrikov & Uranova, 2011). Microarray analysis of prefrontal and anterior cingulate cortex of schizophrenia patients indicate a reduced expression of several genes related to myelin and oligodendrocytes (Dracheva et al., 2006; Hakak et al., 2001; Tkachev et al., 2003) and an altered expression of genes coding for cell-cycle maintenance or arrest (Katsel et al., 2008). Altogether, these findings point to impairment of oligodendrocyte maturation and of myelination.

Abnormalities of White Matter at Early Stages of Schizophrenia

Many studies revealed impairment of white matter integrity in tracts connecting frontal and temporal regions already at early stages of schizophrenia (reviewed in Samartzis, Dima, Fusar-Poli, & Kyriakopoulos, 2014), and even at illness onset for the frontal lobe (Hao et al., 2006; Samartzis et al., 2014; Witthaus et al., 2008; Yao et al., 2013). Voxel-based morphometry of structural magnetic images revealed smaller white matter volumes in temporal gyrus, frontal gyrus, and cingulum of first-episode patients compared with healthy subjects (Witthaus et al., 2008). In addition, early psychosis patients have a reduced progression of frontal white matter volume over time compared with control subjects (Ho, Andreasen, et al., 2003). Based on a recent meta-analysis study, FA values are decreased in two main clusters of the brain in first-episode patients: the right anterior cingulum (uncinate fasciculus and cingulum bundle) and the left temporal deep white matter (longitudinal fasciculus, fornix, fronto-occipital fasciculus, and interhemispheric fibers) (Yao et al., 2013). Furthermore, ultra-high-risk individuals with attenuated positive symptoms (i.e., at risk of developing psychosis) display a reduced volume of white matter in temporal lobe when compared with healthy subjects (Witthaus et al., 2008). Supporting these results, DTI analyses of ultra-high-risk individuals revealed alterations of white matter integrity in various brain regions (Karlsgodt et al., 2008; Peters et al., 2009; Samartzis et al., 2014), the superior and middle frontal lobe as well as the major frontoparietal connecting tract (Carletti et al., 2012). Also in line with these data, ultra-high-risk individuals present abnormal functional connectivity between frontal and temporal regions (Crossley et al., 2009). Interestingly, transition to psychosis in ultra-high-risk subjects is associated with a progressive decrease of white matter integrity in frontal and temporal lobes (Bloemen et al., 2010; Carletti et al., 2012).

In summary, imaging data indicate that white matter deficits are present before onset of illness, at illness onset, and persist in chronic schizophrenia patients. Additional observations suggest that white matter of patients fails to undergo normal myelination. Structural abnormalities in myelin and oligodendrocytes can interfere with long-range neuronal circuitry (Takahashi et al., 2011), and may disrupt synchronization across brain regions (Whitford et al., 2012), leading to complex symptoms in schizophrenia. In the somatosensory system, myelination is an important process to close the critical period of brain plasticity during which the neural circuits are shaped by experiences (Bavelier, Levi, Li, Dan, & Hensch, 2010; Morishita & Hensch, 2008; Takesian & Hensch, 2013). The notion of critical period for brain plasticity could be extended in other systems, including cognition (Barkat, Polley, & Hensch, 2011; Bavelier et al., 2010; Gogolla, Caroni, Luthi, & Herry, 2009). The consequences of delayed myelination on brain maturation remain to be explored in the context of schizophrenia. We will discuss next the evidence in human and animal models suggesting that oxidative stress and redox dysregulation underlie the impaired maturation of white matters and oligodendrocytes in frontal cortex.

ROLE OF REDOX IMBALANCE IN MYELIN IMPAIRMENTS ASSOCIATED WITH SCHIZOPHRENIA

Oligodendrocyte Development and Maturation

To understand how redox dysregulation and oxidative stress affect oligodendrocyte maturation, a description of oligodendrocyte development stages is first needed. Oligodendrocytes undergo a series of maturation stages, which are characterized by the expression of specific cellular surface and myelin component proteins (Figure 2(A)) (Baumann & Pham-Dinh, 2001). Oligodendrocyte progenitor cells (OPC) proliferate in response to growth factors such as platelet-derived growth factors (PDGF) throughout PDGF receptor-signaling pathway. At this stage, OPC present the markers A2B5, NG2, and PDGF receptor. OPC differentiate into preoligodendrocyte cells, which are characterized by multiple processes, a reduced motility, and a decreased sensitivity to growth factors as PDGF. Preoligodendrocytes present typical sulfated glycolipids that are recognized by the O4 antibody. Although preoligodendrocyte branches become more complex throughout development, the transition into immature oligodendrocytes is accompanied by a complete cell-cycle arrest. At this stage, expression of galactocerebroside and 2′,3′-cyclic nucleotide 3′-phosphodiesterase (CNP) begins. After a complete differentiation into mature oligodendrocytes, specific markers such as myelin-associated protein (MAG), myelin oligodendrocyte glycoprotein (MOG), proteolipid protein (PLP), and myelin basic protein (MBP) are present.

Sensitivity of Oligodendrocyte to Redox State

Oligodendrocytes are sensitive to redox dysregulation and oxidative stress because of their intrinsic properties and functions. During myelination process, oligodendrocytes have a high metabolic rate to produce and maintain membranes (Bradl & Lassmann, 2010; Cammer, 1984; El Waly, Macchi, Cayre, & Durbec, 2014). High metabolic activity is known to generate large amount of ROS (Dringen, 2000). Moreover, oligodendrocytes are the predominant iron storing cells in the brain, as it is a required cofactor for myelin synthesis (Thorburne & Juurlink, 1996). Iron catalyzes the formation of oxygen radicals (Figure 1(A)). In addition, myelin sheaths are enriched in polyunsaturated fatty acids (Baumann & Pham-Dinh, 2001), which are vulnerable to radical attacks. Surprisingly, oligodendrocytes display a low activity of GPx and low endogenous GSH levels (Baud et al., 2004; Juurlink, Thorburne, & Hertz, 1998). Data available online indicate that messenger RNA

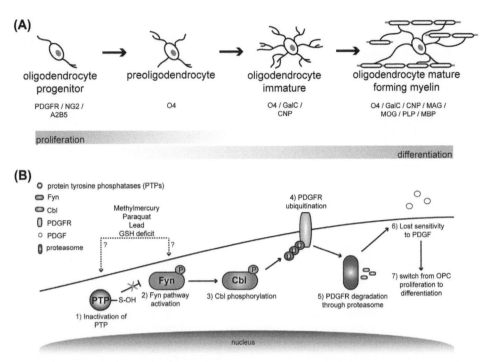

FIGURE 2   Regulation of oligodendrocyte maturation. (A) Oligodendrocyte maturation and markers used to characterize each step of oligo-dendrocyte development. PDGFR, receptor of platelet-derived growth factors; GalC, galactocerebroside; CNP, 2′,3′-cyclic nucleotide 3′-phospho-diesterase; MAG, myelin associated protein; MOG, myelin oligodendrocyte glycoprotein; PLP, proteolipid protein; MBP, myelin basic protein. (B) Redox state influences the switch between proliferation and differentiation of oligodendrocytes via the modulation of Fyn kinase. (1) In conditions of low GSH levels or oxidative stress, protein tyrosine phosphatases (PTPs) may be oxidized to sulfenic acid (S-OH), inactivating PTPs. (2) Via other signaling pathways or through the inactivation of PTP, Fyn kinase may be activated via autophosphorylation of Fyn activation loop. (3) Fyn kinase phosphorylates Cbl ubiquitin ligase, which (4) ubiquitinylates PDGFR. (5) Tagged PDGFR is targeted and degraded by the proteasome. (6) In response to PDGFR degradation, OPC lost sensitivity to growth factors and (7) switch to early differentiation.

expression of genes related to antioxidant capacity (GCLC) in the prefrontal cortex follow the same expression profile than myelin-related genes (e.g., MAG, PLP, http://braincloud.jhmi.edu/) (Kang et al., 2011). Expression of these genes peaks at late childhood and early adolescence period. Consistently, the most expressed genes in the prefrontal cortex at adolescence are related to myelin, lipid synthesis, the antioxidant system, and energy metabolism (Harris et al., 2009).

In schizophrenia patients, the direct role of redox control for myelin is supported by the positive correlation found between prefrontal cortex GSH levels and FA along the cingulum bundle, which connects the anterior cingulate to limbic structures (Monin et al., 2014). Interestingly, this correlation is present only in individuals younger than age 30 years and is lost when older subjects are included (Monin et al., 2014). The third decade of life corresponds to the final stage of prefrontal cortex maturation and cingulum myelination (Bartzokis et al., 2001; Lebel & Beaulieu, 2011; Lenroot & Giedd, 2006).

The importance of redox control for white matter integrity and oligodendrocyte development is further supported by animal models and in vitro research. Redox state

controls oligodendrocyte maturation as well as the switch between proliferation and differentiation (Monin et al., 2014; Noble, Smith, Power, & Mayer-Proschel, 2003). In reduced state, oligodendrocytes proliferate while they differentiate in oxidized state (Noble et al., 2003). Abnormal redox control would interfere with oligodendrocyte development. Consistently, *GCLM*-deficient mice, which present a 70% GSH deficit within the brain and an increase in oxidative stress marks in prefrontal cortex and ventral hippocampus (Cabungcal, Steullet, Kraftsik, Cuenod, & Do, 2013; Steullet et al., 2010), have reduced levels of mature oligodendrocytes and of myelin in the prefrontal cortex at peripubertal period (Monin et al., 2014). Although myelination reaches similar levels in adult *GCLM*-deficient and wild-type mice, DTI study shows persistent impairment of white matter integrity in fornix and anterior commissure (Corcoba et al., 2014). At functional levels, conduction velocity is reduced in both white matter tracts (Corcoba et al., 2014). Therefore, a delay in oligodendrocyte maturation and myelination generated by a redox dysregulation may induce permanent disturbance of FA values. At the cellular level, GSH deficiency in oligodendrocyte progenitors leads to cell-cycle arrest and reduces proliferation that can be reversed by the antioxidant N-acetylcysteine (Monin et al., 2014; Noble et al., 2003). In presence of growth factors, GSH depletion favors the early differentiation of oligodendrocytes as indicated by the increase of O4 and CNP markers (Monin et al., 2014; Noble et al., 2003) but, in presence of differentiating factor, a deficit in GSH prevents full oligodendrocyte maturation (Monin et al., 2014). Consistently, pharmacological inhibition of GCL decreases the expression of genes that promote oligodendrocyte differentiation and increases expression of those that inhibit differentiation (French, Reid, Mamontov, Simmons, & Grinspan, 2009). At the molecular level, the switch from proliferation to early differentiation is controlled by the PDGFR-Fyn pathway (Figure 2(B)) (Li, Dong, Proschel, & Noble, 2007; Monin et al., 2014). Indeed, redox dysregulation induced by a GSH deficit or oxidative stress generated by toxicants (methylmercury, paraquat, and lead) activates Fyn pathway. Activation of Fyn, a nonreceptor tyrosine kinase, induces phosphorylation of the ubiquitin ligase Cbl known to target PDGFR degradation through proteasome (Figure 2(B)) (Li et al., 2007). The mechanisms underlying the activation of Fyn remain elusive. Phosphorylation and dephosphorylation of Fyn at different tyrosine residues are needed to drive its activity, which could be regulated by protein tyrosine phosphatases (PTPs). PTPs can either negatively or positively modify tyrosine kinases (Ostman & Bohmer, 2001). Although it has been shown that PTPα member activates Fyn (Ponniah, Wang, Lim, & Pallen, 1999), other members of PTPs family could, in contrast, inactivate Fyn. Interestingly, these PTPs have a cysteine residue on their active site, which is sensitive to oxidation (Salmeen & Barford, 2005). In conditions of redox dysregulation or oxidative stress, the inactivation of PTPs via their redox-sensitive site could trigger the activity of tyrosine kinases as Fyn (Figure 2(B)). Interestingly, regulation of Fyn expression is impaired in early psychosis patients associated with a vulnerability to redox dysregulation (Monin et al., 2014). Postmortem studies in prefrontal cortex of schizophrenia patients also reveal abnormal expression of Fyn (Stanley database) (Ohnuma, Kato, Arai, McKenna, & Emson, 2003).

In conclusion, a proper timing of redox regulation is crucial to control the proliferation and differentiation of oligodendrocyte. Oxidative stress or abnormal redox control during the development could therefore contribute to myelin disruptions associated with schizophrenia.

Role of Nonredox Risk Factors in Oxidative Stress and Myelin Impairment

Contribution of Genetic Factors

NRG1

Genetic association studies of schizophrenia identified several alleles of *NRG1* as risk factors for the disease (Mei & Nave, 2014). Specifically, the C allele at rs35753505 and the T allele at rs6994992 were widely associated with the disease (Mei & Nave, 2014). Few studies investigate the relation between NRG1 and oxidative stress in brain. However NRG1 is known to regulate the level of ROS in vitro (Goldshmit, Erlich, & Pinkas-Kramarski, 2001) and several evidences indicate a protective role of NRG1 against oxidative stress by regulating endoplasmic reticulum stress in myocardial cells (Xu et al., 2014).

In schizophrenia patients, carriers of C allele at rs35753505 present a reduction in white matter volume within tracts binding frontal to posterior areas (Cannon et al., 2012). In contrast, T carrier patients have a lower FA in the anterior cingulum (Wang, Jiang, et al., 2009). The relation between *NRG1* risk variants and microstructural integrity was further investigated in healthy subjects to avoid bias because of antipsychotic drugs. White matter integrity in the subcortical white matter of the medial frontal and in the anterior thalamic radiation is reduced in carriers of the schizophrenia risk allele C at rs35753505 (Sprooten et al., 2009; Winterer et al., 2008). In addition, healthy subjects with the risk-associated T variant of *NRG1* at rs6994992 display a decreased FA in thalamic connecting tracts and in the fornix (Douet et al., 2014; McIntosh et al., 2008; Sprooten et al., 2009). Moreover, this T allele is associated with differential developmental trajectories of frontal, temporal, and parietal lobes (Douet et al., 2014). At the molecular level, *NRG1* gene is required to promote specification of oligodendrocyte lineage (Wood, Bonath, Kumar, Ross, & Cunliffe, 2009). *NRG1*-deficient mice are hypomyelinated in the prefrontal cortex (Makinodan, Rosen, Ito, & Corfas, 2012). NRG1, which is axonally bound or secreted, promotes oligodendrocyte survival and modulates myelin thickness through ErbB signaling (Mitew et al., 2013).

DISC1

DISC1 has been associated with various psychiatric conditions, including with schizophrenia (Blackwood et al., 2001; Millar et al., 2000). A missense variant of *DISC1* linked to schizophrenia is associated with low white matter integrity in fiber tracts interconnecting frontal to posterior areas (Sprooten et al., 2011). DISC1 is a multifunctional protein known to be involved in the neurodevelopment, cortical thickness, gray matter, and white matter control (Hikida, Gamo, & Sawa, 2012). DISC1 also plays a role in mitochondria fusion and fission (Park et al., 2010). A reduction in its function impairs mitochondrial dynamic, which leads to enhanced production of ROS and redox dysregulation (Park et al., 2010). In transgenic mice expressing a dominant negative variant of *DISC1*, levels of carbonylated proteins and of 8-oxodG are increased in the prefrontal cortex (Johnson et al., 2013). Moreover, these transgenic mice, which display phenotypes associated with schizophrenia, are characterized by disturbances in oligodendrocyte differentiation markers (CNP, MAG, PLP, and PDGFR) (Katsel et al., 2011). Indeed, DISC1 is known to be crucial for oligodendrocyte development (Wood et al., 2009). At molecular levels, *DISC1* variant may induce impairment of oligodendrocyte development via NRG1/ErbB signaling pathway (Katsel et al., 2011). These data also suggest a relationship between DISC1 and NRG1 for oligodendrocyte function.

Together, these data support the notion that schizophrenia involves several genetic loci that are indirectly associated with both disruption of oxidative stress and oligodendrocyte maturation.

Contribution of Environmental Factors

Environmental factors may also lead to redox dysregulation, oxidative stress, and myelination defect. To date, few studies have focused on the relation between early-life adversity and the impairment of white matter integrity in schizophrenia patients. However, several evidences in healthy subjects and other myelin-associated disorders suggest that environmental stress or childhood trauma alter white matter tracts.

Inflammation

Inflammation and oxidative stress widely influence each other (Bitanihirwe & Woo, 2011; Kirkpatrick & Miller, 2013; Steullet et al., 2014). Infection induces the formation of cytokines, inflammatory agents associated with free radical production that in turn promote inflammation. Little is known about the impact of pre- or postnatal inflammation on white matter in schizophrenia patients, but diseases with a prominent inflammatory component (such as multiple sclerosis and periventricular leukomalacia) are accompanied with disruption of white matter and marks of oxidative stress (Ferreira et al., 2013; Gironi et al., 2014; Haynes, Folkerth, Trachtenberg, Volpe, & Kinney, 2009). Multiple sclerosis is an autoimmune disease with abnormal integrity of white matter and demyelinating lesions mainly in the spinal cord, in addition to immune cell infiltration (El Waly et al., 2014; Roosendaal et al., 2009). Patients also display increased lipid peroxidation and impairment of GSH and of antioxidant enzymatic defenses (Ferreira et al., 2013; Pasichna, Morozova, Donchenko, Vinychuk, & Kopchak, 2007; Seven, Aslan, Incir, & Altintas, 2013). Interestingly, recent data strongly associate infectious agents such as Epstein-Barr virus and human herpes virus 6A to multiple sclerosis (El Waly et al., 2014).

In rodent, prenatal immune challenge with synthetic analog of double-stranded RNA (polyriboinosinic-polyribocytidilic acid (poly I:C)) has been used to mimic viral infection. Injected in dams, this inflammatory agent generates behavioral deficits reminiscent of schizophrenia in the offsprings (Bitanihirwe, Peleg-Raibstein, Mouttet, Feldon, & Meyer, 2010; Meyer & Feldon, 2012). Moreover, poly I:C prenatal administration decreases GSH

levels in the whole brain (Makinodan et al., 2009) and induces a delay in myelination (Makinodan et al., 2008). Indeed, myelin thickness and myelin protein levels such as MBP are reduced in 14-day-old mice but not in adult animals (Makinodan et al., 2008). Myelin impairments were specifically reported within the hippocampus and absent for the prefrontal cortex. In culture, poly I:C treatment promotes oligodendrocyte apoptosis and drastically reduces the number of the mature oligodendrocytes (Bsibsi, Nomden, van Noort, & Baron, 2012; Steelman & Li, 2011).

Obstetric Complications

Oxidative stress may play a role in obstetric complications such as preeclampsia and preterm birth because these events are associated with inflammation and marks of oxidation in the placenta. Moreover, hypoxia and hyperoxia are reported in preterm infants (Burton & Jauniaux, 2011). Premature babies present reduced volumes of white matter compared with term children (Back & Rosenberg, 2014; Salmaso, Jablonska, Scafidi, Vaccarino, & Gallo, 2014) and abnormal white matter integrity persists in adulthood (Eikenes, Lohaugen, Brubakk, Skranes, & Haberg, 2011). White matter injury, including the periventricular leukomalacia, is the major cause of brain injury in preterm birth (Back & Rosenberg, 2014; Chew, Fusar-Poli, & Schmitz, 2013). This disease with problems of motor control is characterized by periventricular white matter injuries and periventricular necrosis (Haynes et al., 2003). Interestingly, lipid peroxidation and nitrosative stress marks are present in oligodendrocytes of patients (Haynes et al., 2003).

In rodents, hypoxia or hyperoxia exposure, which are used to model the consequences of preterm birth, induce aberrant myelination process. Mice exposed to chronic hypoxia specifically present a delay in oligodendrocyte differentiation leading to abnormal myelin structure as demonstrated by electron microscopy (Jablonska et al., 2012). Consistently, hyperoxia exposure between 6 and 8 postnatal days generates ROS and triggers a delay in white matter and oligodendrocyte maturation in the corpus callosum (Gerstner et al., 2008; Schmitz et al., 2011). Interestingly, the number of oligodendrocyte labeled with CC1 marker returns to normal levels by 15 days (Schmitz et al., 2011). Hyperoxia exposure transiently disrupts development of myelin and generates persistent impairment in white matter integrity along corpus callosum as indicated by a low FA value in young adult rodents (Ritter et al., 2013; Schmitz et al., 2011).

Early-Life Trauma

Clinical evidences associate early trauma such as emotional abuse to schizophrenia. Emotional abuses encompass several forms, including physical and sexual abuse, verbal aggression, and social neglect. Early-life adversity deregulates the control of reaction to stress by the hypothalamic-pituitary-adrenal (HPA) axis and therefore may contribute to oxidative stress (Schiavone, Jaquet, Trabace, & Krause, 2013). Indeed, several evidences showed a role of the oxidative stress in the control of HPA axis. After psychosocial stress conditions, reduced nicotinamide adenine dinucleotide phosphate oxidase, which generates ROS, is increased in the hypothalamus and consequently disturbs HPA axis (Colaianna et al., 2013). In addition, oxidative stress reduces glucocorticoids negative feedback loop through nuclear translocation of glucocorticoid receptors (Asaba et al., 2004). Moreover, in the serum, oversecretion of glucocorticoids induces ROS (Sato, Takahashi, Sumitani, Takatsu, & Urano, 2010). In the brain, glucocorticoids also reduce the activities of antioxidant defenses (SOD, catalase, and GST) and the level of GSH (Zafir & Banu, 2009). Thus, oxidative stress affects HPA axis that further induces redox dysregulation and oxidative stress.

Posttraumatic stress disorder (PTSD) is commonly reported in maltreated children who suffered of emotional abuse. Maltreated children and adolescents diagnosed with PTSD present a reduction of the white matter volume in the superior temporal gyrus and the prefrontal cortex compared with nonmaltreated control subjects (De Bellis, Keshavan, Frustaci, et al., 2002; De Bellis, Keshavan, Shifflett, et al., 2002). Interestingly, brain volume negatively correlates with the duration of abuse (De Bellis, Keshavan, Shifflett, et al., 2002). Because these studies do not include subjects with maltreatments and without PTSD, consequences of maltreatment and/or the presence of PTSD on white matter cannot be distinguished. In young adults without PTSD, DTI analysis reveals a negative correlation between FA value within the inferior fronto-occipital fasciculus and early-life adversity (Frodl et al., 2012). Individuals exposed to early traumatic experiences also present a reduction in white matter integrity in the corpus callosum compared with nonexposed group (Lu et al., 2013; Paul et al., 2008). In young adults, subjects exposed to parental verbal abuse display reduced microstructural integrity in the arcuate fasciculus, and around the cingulum bundle and the fornix (Choi, Jeong, Rohan, Polcari, & Teicher, 2009). Consequently, parental verbal abuse is associated with alteration of the white matter integrity in tracts connecting parts of the limbic systems, including the prefrontal cortex (Choi et al., 2009). Early neglect is one type of trauma that has been considerably studied in the past few decades (Eluvathingal et al., 2006; Govindan, Behen, Helder, Makki, & Chugani, 2010; Hanson et al., 2013). Children who experienced early neglect in orphanage have a decrease volume of total white matter (Hanson et al., 2013). Despite a greater FA in the anterior thalamic radiation and the forceps minor, lower FA in early-deprived children has been underlined in a number of white matter tracts connecting the temporal lobe to the prefrontal cortex (Hanson et al., 2013). In addition, adopted children present a decreased FA in pathways of the limbic system, including the uncinate fasciculus (Eluvathingal et al., 2006; Govindan et al., 2010). Such disruption of the structural integrity was negatively associated with the duration of stay in the orphanage (Govindan et al., 2010).

In adult rodents, social isolation compromises the activity of GSH-related antioxidant defenses in blood and liver, and increases oxidation marks such as lipid peroxidation (Djordjevic, Djordjevic, Adzic, & Radojcic, 2010; Goncalves, Dafre, Carobrez, & Gasparotto, 2008). Social isolation of adult mice reduces myelin thickness in the prefrontal cortex (Liu et al., 2012). Early social isolation endured during juvenile and early adolescent periods specifically impairs oligodendrocyte maturation and myelination in the prefrontal cortex (Makinodan et al., 2012). Indeed, levels of MBP and MAG messenger RNA expression are reduced in socially deprived animals (Makinodan et al., 2012). In contrast, social deprivation endured after adolescent period, when oligodendrocyte development is completed, does not alter myelin contents. At the molecular level, the NRG1/ErbB signaling pathway has been proposed to contribute to such oligodendrocyte maturation impairments (Makinodan et al., 2012).

Altogether, these data suggest that oligodendrocyte maturation and myelination are particularly sensitive to oxidative stress generated by trauma endured during childhood or adolescence, and may lead to white matter anomalies in adulthood.

CONCLUSIONS AND PERSPECTIVES

Marks of oxidation and lowered antioxidant defenses are repeatedly associated with schizophrenia, thus tightening the link between redox dysfunction and illness physiopathology. We suggest that redox imbalance in tight interaction with NMDA receptor hypofunction and neuroinflammation constitutes a hub on which converge genetic and environmental risk factors, leading to brain disconnectivity (Figure 3(A)). Evidence from the literature indicates that risk factors for schizophrenia are associated with both oxidative stress and myelin defects in human. The sensitivity of oligodendrocytes to redox changes is well-demonstrated in vitro because dysregulation of redox homeostasis affects the balance between proliferation and differentiation of precursor cells. Therefore, a proper redox control is essential during periods of myelination that close window of plasticity in brain development. Because dynamics of maturation vary across brain regions, we propose that environmental

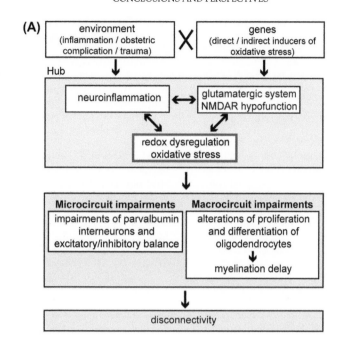

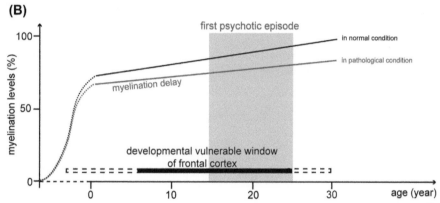

FIGURE 3 Potential mechanism underlying macrocircuit impairments in schizophrenia. (A) Redox dysregulation and oxidative stress, neuroinflammation, and glutamatergic system constitute one hub on which converge environmental and genetic factors. Redox dysregulation and oxidative stress are known to impair parvalbumin interneurons and excitatory/inhibitory balance of local neuronal circuits, and alter proliferation and differentiation of oligodendrocytes. Together, they may lead to microcircuit and macrocircuit disconnectivity. (B) The sensitivity of oligodendrocytes to redox dysregulation is specific to their maturation stage. The coincidence of schizophrenia onset with late prefrontal cortex development and the several evidences of structural abnormalities in prefrontal cortex support the hypothesis of a vulnerability window, during which stress would induce a myelination delay.

insults would preferentially impair myelin within maturing regions rather than in those fully developed. Different timing of environmental insults could thus lead to clinically heterogeneous symptoms. This model raises the hypothesis of a time window during which individuals with predisposition for redox dysfunction would be primed to develop schizophrenia by environmental factors that occurred during key periods of brain development (Figure 3(B)).

This model highlights the need for early interventions that prevent or limit the disruption of white matter integrity. Fyn, which participates to the switch of oligodendrocyte precursor proliferation to differentiation (Monin et al., 2014), is an interesting drug target. Broader antioxidants are already tested in clinical trials: some studies report positive effects of vitamins C and E, omega-3 fatty acid, and N-acetylcysteine on schizophrenia symptoms and even on psychosis prevention. Exploring the effect of these add-on therapies on white matter parameters and on disconnectivity in early stages of the disease should clarify their mode of action and, in the long term, help avoiding transition to psychosis and reducing the disabilities associated with the illness chronicity.

References

Aizenman, E., Lipton, S. A., & Loring, R. H. (1989). Selective modulation of NMDA responses by reduction and oxidation. *Neuron*, 2(3), 1257–1263.

Akyol, O., Yanik, M., Elyas, H., Namli, M., Canatan, H., Akin, H., et al. (2005). Association between Ala-9Val polymorphism of Mn-SOD gene and schizophrenia. *Progress in Neuro-Psychopharmacology & Biological Psychiatry*, 29(1), 123–131. http://dx.doi.org/10.1016/j.pnpbp.2004.10.014.

Altuntas, I., Aksoy, H., Coskun, I., Caykoylu, A., & Akcay, F. (2000). Erythrocyte superoxide dismutase and glutathione peroxidase activities, and malondialdehyde and reduced glutathione levels in schizophrenic patients. *Clinical Chemistry and Laboratory Medicine*, 38(12), 1277–1281. http://dx.doi.org/10.1515/CCLM.2000.201.

Asaba, K., Iwasaki, Y., Yoshida, M., Asai, M., Oiso, Y., Murohara, T., et al. (2004). Attenuation by reactive oxygen species of glucocorticoid suppression on proopiomelanocortin gene expression in pituitary corticotroph cells. *Endocrinology*, 145(1), 39–42. http://dx.doi.org/10.1210/en.2003-0375.

Back, S. A., & Rosenberg, P. A. (2014). Pathophysiology of glia in perinatal white matter injury. *Glia*. http://dx.doi.org/10.1002/glia.22658.

Ballesteros, A., Jiang, P., Summerfelt, A., Du, X., Chiappelli, J., O'Donnell, P., et al. (2013). No evidence of exogenous origin for the abnormal glutathione redox state in schizophrenia. *Schizophrenia Research*, 146(1–3), 184–189. http://dx.doi.org/10.1016/j.schres.2013.02.001.

Barkat, T. R., Polley, D. B., & Hensch, T. K. (2011). A critical period for auditory thalamocortical connectivity. *Nature Neuroscience*, 14(9), 1189–1194. http://dx.doi.org/10.1038/nn.2882.

Bartzokis, G., Beckson, M., Lu, P. H., Nuechterlein, K. H., Edwards, N., & Mintz, J. (2001). Age-related changes in frontal and temporal lobe volumes in men: a magnetic resonance imaging study. *Archives of General Psychiatry*, 58(5), 461–465.

Baud, O., Greene, A. E., Li, J., Wang, H., Volpe, J. J., & Rosenberg, P. A. (2004). Glutathione peroxidase-catalase cooperativity is required for resistance to hydrogen peroxide by mature rat oligodendrocytes. *Journal of Neuroscience*, 24(7), 1531–1540. http://dx.doi.org/10.1523/JNEUROSCI.3989-03.2004.

Baumann, N., & Pham-Dinh, D. (2001). Biology of oligodendrocyte and myelin in the mammalian central nervous system. *Physiological Reviews*, 81(2), 871–927.

Bavelier, D., Levi, D. M., Li, R. W., Dan, Y., & Hensch, T. K. (2010). Removing brakes on adult brain plasticity: from molecular to behavioral interventions. *Journal of Neuroscience*, 30(45), 14964–14971. http://dx.doi.org/10.1523/JNEUROSCI.4812-10.2010.

Beaulieu, C. (2002). The basis of anisotropic water diffusion in the nervous system – a technical review. *NMR in Biomedicine*, 15(7–8), 435–455. http://dx.doi.org/10.1002/nbm.782.

Bergendi, L., Beneš, L., Ďuračková, Z., & Ferenčik, M. (1999). Chemistry, physiology and pathology of free radicals. *Life Sciences*, 65(18–19), 1865–1874. http://dx.doi.org/10.1016/S0024-3205(99)00439-7.

Bitanihirwe, B. K., Peleg-Raibstein, D., Mouttet, F., Feldon, J., & Meyer, U. (2010). Late prenatal immune activation in mice leads to behavioral and neurochemical abnormalities relevant to the negative symptoms of schizophrenia. *Neuropsychopharmacology*, 35(12), 2462–2478. http://dx.doi.org/10.1038/npp.2010.129.

Bitanihirwe, B. K., & Woo, T. U. (2011). Oxidative stress in schizophrenia: an integrated approach. *Neuroscience & Biobehavioral Reviews*, 35(3), 878–893. http://dx.doi.org/10.1016/j.neubiorev.2010.10.008.

Blackwood, D. H., Fordyce, A., Walker, M. T., St Clair, D. M., Porteous, D. J., & Muir, W. J. (2001). Schizophrenia and affective disorders—cosegregation with a translocation at chromosome 1q42 that directly disrupts brain-expressed genes: clinical and P300 findings in a family. *American Journal of Human Genetics*, 69(2), 428–433.

Bloemen, O. J., de Koning, M. B., Schmitz, N., Nieman, D. H., Becker, H. E., de Haan, L., et al. (2010). White-matter markers for psychosis in a prospective ultra-high-risk cohort. *Psychological Medicine*, 40(8), 1297–1304. http://dx.doi.org/10.1017/S0033291709991711.

Board, P. G., & Menon, D. (2013). Glutathione transferases, regulators of cellular metabolism and physiology. *Biochimica et Biophysica Acta (BBA) – General Subjects*, 1830(5), 3267–3288. http://dx.doi.org/10.1016/j.bbagen.2012.11.019.

Bradl, M., & Lassmann, H. (2010). Oligodendrocytes: biology and pathology. *Acta Neuropathologica*, 119(1), 37–53. http://dx.doi.org/10.1007/s00401-009-0601-5.

Brown, A. S. (2011). The environment and susceptibility to schizophrenia. *Progress in Neurobiology*, 93(1), 23–58. http://dx.doi.org/10.1016/j.pneurobio.2010.09.003.

Bsibsi, M., Nomden, A., van Noort, J. M., & Baron, W. (2012). Toll-like receptors 2 and 3 agonists differentially affect oligodendrocyte survival, differentiation, and myelin membrane formation. *Journal of Neuroscience Research*, 90(2), 388–398. http://dx.doi.org/10.1002/jnr.22767.

Buelna-Chontal, M., & Zazueta, C. (2013). Redox activation of Nrf2 & NF-kappaB: a double end sword? *Cell Signal*, 25(12), 2548–2557. http://dx.doi.org/10.1016/j.cellsig.2013.08.007.

Burton, G. J., & Jauniaux, E. (2011). Oxidative stress. *Best Practice & Research Clinical Obstetrics & Gynaecology*, 25(3), 287–299. http://dx.doi.org/10.1016/j.bpobgyn.2010.10.016.

Byne, W., Kidkardnee, S., Tatusov, A., Yiannoulos, G., Buchsbaum, M. S., & Haroutunian, V. (2006). Schizophrenia-associated reduction of neuronal and oligodendrocyte numbers in the anterior principal thalamic nucleus. *Schizophrenia Research*, 85(1–3), 245–253. http://dx.doi.org/10.1016/j.schres.2006.03.029.

Cabungcal, J. H., Steullet, P., Kraftsik, R., Cuenod, M., & Do, K. Q. (2013). Early-life insults impair parvalbumin interneurons via oxidative stress: reversal by N-acetylcysteine. *Biological Psychiatry*, 73(6), 574–582. http://dx.doi.org/10.1016/j.biopsych.2012.09.020.

Cammer, W. (1984). Carbonic anhydrase in oligodendrocytes and myelin in the central nervous system. *Annals of the New York Academy of Sciences*, 429, 494–497.

Cannon, D. M., Walshe, M., Dempster, E., Collier, D. A., Marshall, N., Bramon, E., et al. (2012). The association of white matter volume in psychotic disorders with genotypic variation in NRG1, MOG and CNP: a voxel-based analysis in affected individuals and their unaffected relatives. *Translational Psychiatry*, 2, e167. http://dx.doi.org/10.1038/tp.2012.82.

Carletti, F., Woolley, J. B., Bhattacharyya, S., Perez-Iglesias, R., Fusar Poli, P., Valmaggia, L., et al. (2012). Alterations in white matter evident before the onset of psychosis. *Schizophrenia Bulletin*, 38(6), 1170–1179. http://dx.doi.org/10.1093/schbul/sbs053.

Catts, V. S., Fung, S. J., Long, L. E., Joshi, D., Vercammen, A., Allen, K. M., et al. (2013). Rethinking schizophrenia in the context of normal neurodevelopment. *Frontiers in Cellular Neuroscience*, 7, 60. http://dx.doi.org/10.3389/fncel.2013.00060.

Chew, L. J., Fusar-Poli, P., & Schmitz, T. (2013). Oligodendroglial alterations and the role of microglia in white matter injury: relevance to schizophrenia. *Developmental Neuroscience*, 35(2–3), 102–129. http://dx.doi.org/10.1159/000346157.

Choi, J., Jeong, B., Rohan, M. L., Polcari, A. M., & Teicher, M. H. (2009). Preliminary evidence for white matter tract abnormalities in young adults exposed to parental verbal abuse. *Biological Psychiatry*, 65(3), 227–234. http://dx.doi.org/10.1016/j.biopsych.2008.06.022.

Colaianna, M., Schiavone, S., Zotti, M., Tucci, P., Morgese, M. G., Backdahl, L., et al. (2013). Neuroendocrine profile in a rat model of psychosocial stress: relation to oxidative stress. *Antioxidants & Redox Signaling*, 18(12), 1385–1399. http://dx.doi.org/10.1089/ars.2012.4569.

Corcoba, A., Steullet, P., Duarte, J. M., van de Looij, Y., Gruetter, R., & Do, K. Q. (2014). Impaired white matter integrity in fornix and anterior commissure in a schizophrenia mouse model of redox dysregulation. *Biological Psychiatry*, 75(9S), 175S.

Coughlin, J. M., Ishizuka, K., Kano, S. I., Edwards, J. A., Seifuddin, F. T., Shimano, M. A., et al. (2013). Marked reduction of soluble superoxide dismutase-1 (SOD1) in cerebrospinal fluid of patients with recent-onset schizophrenia. *Molecular Psychiatry*, 18(1), 10–11. http://dx.doi.org/10.1038/mp.2012.6.

Crossley, N. A., Mechelli, A., Fusar-Poli, P., Broome, M. R., Matthiasson, P., Johns, L. C., et al. (2009). Superior temporal lobe dysfunction and frontotemporal dysconnectivity in subjects at risk of psychosis and in first-episode psychosis. *Human Brain Mapping, 30*(12), 4129–4137. http://dx.doi.org/10.1002/hbm.20834.

De Bellis, M. D., Keshavan, M. S., Frustaci, K., Shifflett, H., Iyengar, S., Beers, S. R., et al. (2002). Superior temporal gyrus volumes in maltreated children and adolescents with PTSD. *Biological Psychiatry, 51*(7), 544–552.

De Bellis, M. D., Keshavan, M. S., Shifflett, H., Iyengar, S., Beers, S. R., Hall, J., et al. (2002). Brain structures in pediatric maltreatment-related posttraumatic stress disorder: a sociodemographically matched study. *Biological Psychiatry, 52*(11), 1066–1078.

Dietrich-Muszalska, A., & Kontek, B. (2010). Lipid peroxidation in patients with schizophrenia. *Psychiatry and Clinical Neurosciences, 64*(5), 469–475. http://dx.doi.org/10.1111/j.1440-1819.2010.02132.x.

Dietrich-Muszalska, A., & Olas, B. (2009). Isoprostenes as indicators of oxidative stress in schizophrenia. *The World Journal of Biological Psychiatry, 10*(1), 27–33. http://dx.doi.org/10.1080/15622970701361263.

Djordjevic, J., Djordjevic, A., Adzic, M., & Radojcic, M. B. (2010). Chronic social isolation compromises the activity of both glutathione peroxidase and catalase in hippocampus of male wistar rats. *Cellular and Molecular Neurobiology, 30*(5), 693–700. http://dx.doi.org/10.1007/s10571-009-9493-0.

Do, K. Q., Bovet, P., Cabungcal, J. H., Conus, P., Gysin, R., Lavoie, S., et al. (2009). Redox dysregulation in schizophrenia: genetic susceptibility and pathophysiological mechanisms. In (3rd ed.) *Handbook of neurochemistry and molecular neurobiology* (vol. 2) (p. 27).

Do, K. Q., Cabungcal, J. H., Frank, A., Steullet, P., & Cuenod, M. (2009). Redox dysregulation, neurodevelopment, and schizophrenia. *Current Opinion in Neurobiology, 19*(2), 220–230. http://dx.doi.org/10.1016/j.conb.2009.05.001.

Do, K. Q., Trabesinger, A. H., Kirsten-Kruger, M., Lauer, C. J., Dydak, U., Hell, D., et al. (2000). Schizophrenia: glutathione deficit in cerebrospinal fluid and prefrontal cortex in vivo. *European Journal of Neuroscience, 12*(10), 3721–3728.

Douet, V., Chang, L., Pritchett, A., Lee, K., Keating, B., Bartsch, H., et al. (2014). Schizophrenia-risk variant rs6994992 in the neuregulin-1 gene on brain developmental trajectories in typically developing children. *Translational Psychiatry, 4*, e392. http://dx.doi.org/10.1038/tp.2014.41.

Dracheva, S., Davis, K. L., Chin, B., Woo, D. A., Schmeidler, J., & Haroutunian, V. (2006). Myelin-associated mRNA and protein expression deficits in the anterior cingulate cortex and hippocampus in elderly schizophrenia patients. *Neurobiology of Disease, 21*(3), 531–540. http://dx.doi.org/10.1016/j.nbd.2005.08.012.

Dringen, R. (2000). Metabolism and functions of glutathione in brain. *Progress in Neurobiology, 62*(6), 649–671.

Du, F., & Ongur, D. (2013). Probing myelin and axon abnormalities separately in psychiatric disorders using MRI techniques. *Frontiers in Integrative Neuroscience, 7*, 24. http://dx.doi.org/10.3389/fnint.2013.00024.

Dwir, D., Cabungcal, J.-H., Steullet, P., Fournier, M., Tirouvanziam, R., & Do, K. Q. (2014). Involvement of the receptor for advanced glycation end-product (RAGE) in redox dysregulation and neuroinflammation in an animal model of schizophrenia. *Biological Psychiatry, 75*(9).

Eikenes, L., Lohaugen, G. C., Brubakk, A. M., Skranes, J., & Haberg, A. K. (2011). Young adults born preterm with very low birth weight demonstrate widespread white matter alterations on brain DTI. *NeuroImage, 54*(3), 1774–1785. http://dx.doi.org/10.1016/j.neuroimage.2010.10.037.

El Waly, B., Macchi, M., Cayre, M., & Durbec, P. (2014). Oligodendrogenesis in the normal and pathological central nervous system. *Frontiers in Neuroscience, 8*, 145. http://dx.doi.org/10.3389/fnins.2014.00145.

Eluvathingal, T. J., Chugani, H. T., Behen, M. E., Juhasz, C., Muzik, O., Maqbool, M., et al. (2006). Abnormal brain connectivity in children after early severe socioemotional deprivation: a diffusion tensor imaging study. *Pediatrics, 117*(6), 2093–2100. http://dx.doi.org/10.1542/peds.2005-1727.

Fallin, M. D., Lasseter, V. K., Avramopoulos, D., Nicodemus, K. K., Wolyniec, P. S., McGrath, J. A., et al. (2005). Bipolar I disorder and schizophrenia: a 440-single-nucleotide polymorphism screen of 64 candidate genes among Ashkenazi Jewish case-parent trios. *American Journal of Human Genetics, 77*(6), 918–936. http://dx.doi.org/10.1086/497703.

Ferreira, B., Mendes, F., Osorio, N., Caseiro, A., Gabriel, A., & Valado, A. (2013). Glutathione in multiple sclerosis. *British Journal of Biomedical Science, 70*(2), 75–79.

Fitzsimmons, J., Kubicki, M., & Shenton, M. E. (2013). Review of functional and anatomical brain connectivity findings in schizophrenia. *Current Opinion in Psychiatry, 26*(2), 172–187. http://dx.doi.org/10.1097/YCO.0b013e32835d9e6a.

Flatow, J., Buckley, P., & Miller, B. J. (2013). Meta-analysis of oxidative stress in schizophrenia. *Biological Psychiatry, 74*(6), 400–409. http://dx.doi.org/10.1016/j.biopsych.2013.03.018.

Fornito, A., Zalesky, A., Pantelis, C., & Bullmore, E. T. (2012). Schizophrenia, neuroimaging and connectomics. *NeuroImage, 62*(4), 2296–2314. http://dx.doi.org/10.1016/j.neuroimage.2011.12.090.

Fournier, M., Ferrari, C., Baumann, P. S., Polari, A., Monin, A., Bellier-Teichmann, T., et al. (2014). Impaired metabolic reactivity to oxidative stress in early psychosis patients. *Schizophrenia Bulletin*. http://dx.doi.org/10.1093/schbul/sbu053.

French, H. M., Reid, M., Mamontov, P., Simmons, R. A., & Grinspan, J. B. (2009). Oxidative stress disrupts oligodendrocyte maturation. *Journal of Neuroscience Research, 87*(14), 3076–3087. http://dx.doi.org/10.1002/jnr.22139.

Frodl, T., Carballedo, A., Fagan, A. J., Lisiecka, D., Ferguson, Y., & Meaney, J. F. (2012). Effects of early-life adversity on white matter diffusivity changes in patients at risk for major depression. *Journal of Psychiatry Neuroscience, 37*(1), 37–45. http://dx.doi.org/10.1503/jpn.110028.

Fuster, J. M. (2002). Frontal lobe and cognitive development. *Journal of Neurocytology, 31*(3–5), 373–385.

Gawryluk, J. W., Wang, J. F., Andreazza, A. C., Shao, L., & Young, L. T. (2011). Decreased levels of glutathione, the major brain antioxidant, in post-mortem prefrontal cortex from patients with psychiatric disorders. *International Journal of Neuropsychopharmacology, 14*(1), 123–130. http://dx.doi.org/10.1017/S1461145710000805.

Gerstner, B., DeSilva, T. M., Genz, K., Armstrong, A., Brehmer, F., Neve, R. L., et al. (2008). Hyperoxia causes maturation-dependent cell death in the developing white matter. *Journal of Neuroscience, 28*(5), 1236–1245. http://dx.doi.org/10.1523/JNEUROSCI.3213-07.2008.

Gironi, M., Borgiani, B., Mariani, E., Cursano, C., Mendozzi, L., Cavarretta, R., et al. (2014). Oxidative stress is differentially present in multiple sclerosis courses, early evident, and unrelated to treatment. *Journal of Immunology Research, 2014*, 961863. http://dx.doi.org/10.1155/2014/961863.

Go, Y. M., & Jones, D. P. (2008). Redox compartmentalization in eukaryotic cells. *Biochimica et Biophysica Acta, 1780*(11), 1273–1290. http://dx.doi.org/10.1016/j.bbagen.2008.01.011.

Gogolla, N., Caroni, P., Luthi, A., & Herry, C. (2009). Perineuronal nets protect fear memories from erasure. *Science, 325*(5945), 1258–1261. http://dx.doi.org/10.1126/science.1174146.

Goldshmit, Y., Erlich, S., & Pinkas-Kramarski, R. (2001). Neuregulin rescues PC12-ErbB4 cells from cell death induced by H(2)O(2). Regulation of reactive oxygen species levels by phosphatidylinositol 3-kinase. *Journal of Biological Chemistry, 276*(49), 46379–46385. http://dx.doi.org/10.1074/jbc.M105637200.

Goncalves, L., Dafre, A. L., Carobrez, S. G., & Gasparotto, O. C. (2008). A temporal analysis of the relationships between social stress, humoral immune response and glutathione-related antioxidant defenses. *Behavioural Brain Research*, 192(2), 226–231. http://dx.doi.org/10.1016/j.bbr.2008.04.010.

Govindan, R. M., Behen, M. E., Helder, E., Makki, M. I., & Chugani, H. T. (2010). Altered water diffusivity in cortical association tracts in children with early deprivation identified with Tract-Based Spatial Statistics (TBSS). *Cerebral Cortex*, 20(3), 561–569. http://dx.doi.org/10.1093/cercor/bhp122.

Gravina, P., Spoletini, I., Masini, S., Valentini, A., Vanni, D., Paladini, E., et al. (2011). Genetic polymorphisms of glutathione S-transferases GSTM1, GSTT1, GSTP1 and GSTA1 as risk factors for schizophrenia. *Psychiatry Research*, 187(3), 454–456. http://dx.doi.org/10.1016/j.psychres.2010.10.008.

Grignon, S., & Chianetta, J. M. (2007). Assessment of malondialdehyde levels in schizophrenia: a meta-analysis and some methodological considerations. *Progress in Neuro-Psychopharmacology & Biological Psychiatry*, 31(2), 365–369. http://dx.doi.org/10.1016/j.pnpbp.2006.09.012.

Gysin, R., Kraftsik, R., Sandell, J., Bovet, P., Chappuis, C., Conus, P., et al. (2007). Impaired glutathione synthesis in schizophrenia: convergent genetic and functional evidence. *Proceedings of the National Academy of Sciences of the United States of America*, 104(42), 16621–16626. http://dx.doi.org/10.1073/pnas.0706778104.

Hakak, Y., Walker, J. R., Li, C., Wong, W. H., Davis, K. L., Buxbaum, J. D., et al. (2001). Genome-wide expression analysis reveals dysregulation of myelination-related genes in chronic schizophrenia. *Proceedings of the National Academy of Sciences of the United States of America*, 98(8), 4746–4751. http://dx.doi.org/10.1073/pnas.081071198.

Hanson, J. L., Adluru, N., Chung, M. K., Alexander, A. L., Davidson, R. J., & Pollak, S. D. (2013). Early neglect is associated with alterations in white matter integrity and cognitive functioning. *Child Development*, 84(5), 1566–1578. http://dx.doi.org/10.1111/cdev.12069.

Hanzawa, R., Ohnuma, T., Nagai, Y., Shibata, N., Maeshima, H., Baba, H., et al. (2011). No association between glutathione-synthesis-related genes and Japanese schizophrenia. *Psychiatry and Clinical Neurosciences*, 65(1), 39–46. http://dx.doi.org/10.1111/j.1440-1819.2010.02157.x.

Hao, Y., Liu, Z., Jiang, T., Gong, G., Liu, H., Tan, L., et al. (2006). White matter integrity of the whole brain is disrupted in first-episode schizophrenia. *NeuroReport*, 17(1), 23–26.

Harada, S., Tachikawa, H., & Kawanishi, Y. (2001). Glutathione S-transferase M1 gene deletion may be associated with susceptibility to certain forms of schizophrenia. *Biochemical and Biophysical Research Communications*, 281(2), 267–271. http://dx.doi.org/10.1006/bbrc.2001.4347.

Hardingham, G. E., & Bading, H. (2010). Synaptic versus extrasynaptic NMDA receptor signalling: implications for neurodegenerative disorders. *Nature Reviews Neuroscience*, 11(10), 682–696. http://dx.doi.org/10.1038/nrn2911.

Harris, L. W., Lockstone, H. E., Khaitovich, P., Weickert, C. S., Webster, M. J., & Bahn, S. (2009). Gene expression in the prefrontal cortex during adolescence: implications for the onset of schizophrenia. *BMC Medical Genomics*, 2, 28. http://dx.doi.org/10.1186/1755-8794-2-28.

Haynes, R. L., Folkerth, R. D., Keefe, R. J., Sung, I., Swzeda, L. I., Rosenberg, P. A., et al. (2003). Nitrosative and oxidative injury to premyelinating oligodendrocytes in periventricular leukomalacia. *Journal of Neuropathology & Experimental Neurology*, 62(5), 441–450.

Haynes, R. L., Folkerth, R. D., Trachtenberg, F. L., Volpe, J. J., & Kinney, H. C. (2009). Nitrosative stress and inducible nitric oxide synthase expression in periventricular leukomalacia. *Acta Neuropathologica*, 118(3), 391–399. http://dx.doi.org/10.1007/s00401-009-0540-1.

Hikida, T., Gamo, N. J., & Sawa, A. (2012). DISC1 as a therapeutic target for mental illnesses. *Expert Opinion on Therapeutic Targets*, 16(12), 1151–1160. http://dx.doi.org/10.1517/14728222.2012.719879.

Ho, B. C., Alicata, D., Ward, J., Moser, D. J., O'Leary, D. S., Arndt, S., et al. (2003). Untreated initial psychosis: relation to cognitive deficits and brain morphology in first-episode schizophrenia. *American Journal of Psychiatry*, 160(1), 142–148.

Ho, B. C., Andreasen, N. C., Nopoulos, P., Arndt, S., Magnotta, V., & Flaum, M. (2003). Progressive structural brain abnormalities and their relationship to clinical outcome: a longitudinal magnetic resonance imaging study early in schizophrenia. *Archives of General Psychiatry*, 60(6), 585–594. http://dx.doi.org/10.1001/archpsyc.60.6.585.

Hof, P. R., Haroutunian, V., Copland, C., Davis, K. L., & Buxbaum, J. D. (2002). Molecular and cellular evidence for an oligodendrocyte abnormality in schizophrenia. *Neurochemical Research*, 27(10), 1193–1200.

Hoistad, M., Segal, D., Takahashi, N., Sakurai, T., Buxbaum, J. D., & Hof, P. R. (2009). Linking white and grey matter in schizophrenia: oligodendrocyte and neuron pathology in the prefrontal cortex. *Frontiers in Neuroanatomy*, 3, 9. http://dx.doi.org/10.3389/neuro.05.009.2009.

Hori, H., Ohmori, O., Shinkai, T., Kojima, H., Okano, C., Suzuki, T., et al. (2000). Manganese superoxide dismutase gene polymorphism and schizophrenia: relation to tardive dyskinesia. *Neuropsychopharmacology*, 23(2), 170–177. http://dx.doi.org/10.1016/S0893-133X(99)00156-6.

Insel, T. R. (2010). Rethinking schizophrenia. *Nature*, 468(7321), 187–193. http://dx.doi.org/10.1038/nature09552.

Jablonska, B., Scafidi, J., Aguirre, A., Vaccarino, F., Nguyen, V., Borok, E., et al. (2012). Oligodendrocyte regeneration after neonatal hypoxia requires FoxO1-mediated p27Kip1 expression. *Journal of Neuroscience*, 32(42), 14775–14793. http://dx.doi.org/10.1523/JNEUROSCI.2060-12.2012.

Jiang, Z., Cowell, R. M., & Nakazawa, K. (2013). Convergence of genetic and environmental factors on parvalbumin-positive interneurons in schizophrenia. *Frontiers in Behavioral Neuroscience*, 7, 116. http://dx.doi.org/10.3389/fnbeh.2013.00116.

Johnson, A. W., Jaaro-Peled, H., Shahani, N., Sedlak, T. W., Zoubovsky, S., Burruss, D., et al. (2013). Cognitive and motivational deficits together with prefrontal oxidative stress in a mouse model for neuropsychiatric illness. *Proceedings of the National Academy of Sciences of the United States of America*, 110(30), 12462–12467. http://dx.doi.org/10.1073/pnas.1307925110.

Jones, D. P. (2008). Radical-free biology of oxidative stress. *American Journal of Physiology Cell Physiology*, 295(4), C849–C868. http://dx.doi.org/10.1152/ajpcell.00283.2008.

Jones, D. P. (2010). Redox sensing: orthogonal control in cell cycle and apoptosis signalling. *Journal of Internal Medicine*, 268(5), 432–448. http://dx.doi.org/10.1111/j.1365-2796.2010.02268.x.

Jorgensen, A., Broedbaek, K., Fink-Jensen, A., Knorr, U., Greisen Soendergaard, M., Henriksen, T., et al. (2013). Increased systemic oxidatively generated DNA and RNA damage in schizophrenia. *Psychiatry Research*, 209(3), 417–423. http://dx.doi.org/10.1016/j.psychres.2013.01.033.

Juurlink, B. H., Thorburne, S. K., & Hertz, L. (1998). Peroxide-scavenging deficit underlies oligodendrocyte susceptibility to oxidative stress. *Glia*, 22(4), 371–378.

Kanaan, R. A., Kim, J. S., Kaufmann, W. E., Pearlson, G. D., Barker, G. J., & McGuire, P. K. (2005). Diffusion tensor imaging in schizophrenia. *Biological Psychiatry*, 58(12), 921–929. http://dx.doi.org/10.1016/j.biopsych.2005.05.015.

Kang, H. J., Kawasawa, Y. I., Cheng, F., Zhu, Y., Xu, X., Li, M., et al. (2011). Spatio-temporal transcriptome of the human brain. *Nature*, 478(7370), 483–489. http://www.nature.com/nature/journal/v478/n7370/abs/nature10523.html#supplementary-information.

Karlsgodt, K. H., van Erp, T. G., Poldrack, R. A., Bearden, C. E., Nuechterlein, K. H., & Cannon, T. D. (2008). Diffusion tensor imaging of the superior longitudinal fasciculus and working memory in recent-onset schizophrenia. *Biological Psychiatry*, 63(5), 512–518. http://dx.doi.org/10.1016/j.biopsych.2007.06.017.

Katsel, P., Davis, K. L., Li, C., Tan, W., Greenstein, E., Kleiner Hoffman, L. B., et al. (2008). Abnormal indices of cell cycle activity in schizophrenia and their potential association with oligodendrocytes. *Neuropsychopharmacology, 33*(12), 2993–3009. http://dx.doi.org/10.1038/npp.2008.19.

Katsel, P., Tan, W., Abazyan, B., Davis, K. L., Ross, C., Pletnikov, M. V., et al. (2011). Expression of mutant human DISC1 in mice supports abnormalities in differentiation of oligodendrocytes. *Schizophrenia Research, 130*(1–3), 238–249. http://dx.doi.org/10.1016/j.schres.2011.04.021.

Kensler, T. W., Wakabayashi, N., & Biswal, S. (2007). Cell survival responses to environmental stresses via the Keap1-Nrf2-ARE pathway. *Annual Review of Pharmacology and Toxicology, 47*(1), 89–116. http://dx.doi.org/10.1146/annurev.pharmtox.46.120604.141046.

Kirkpatrick, B., & Miller, B. J. (2013). Inflammation and schizophrenia. *Schizophrenia Bulletin, 39*(6), 1174–1179. http://dx.doi.org/10.1093/schbul/sbt141.

Kishi, T., Ikeda, M., Kitajima, T., Yamanouchi, Y., Kinoshita, Y., Kawashima, K., et al. (2008). Glutamate cysteine ligase modifier (GCLM) subunit gene is not associated with methamphetamine-use disorder or schizophrenia in the Japanese population. *Annals of the New York Academy of Sciences, 1139*, 63–69. http://dx.doi.org/10.1196/annals.1432.022.

Kulak, A., Steullet, P., Cabungcal, J. H., Werge, T., Ingason, A., Cuenod, M., et al. (2013). Redox dysregulation in the pathophysiology of schizophrenia and bipolar disorder: insights from animal models. *Antioxidants & Redox Signaling, 18*(12), 1428–1443. http://dx.doi.org/10.1089/ars.2012.4858.

Kyriakopoulos, M., Bargiotas, T., Barker, G. J., & Frangou, S. (2008). Diffusion tensor imaging in schizophrenia. *European Psychiatry, 23*(4), 255–273. http://dx.doi.org/10.1016/j.eurpsy.2007.12.004.

Lebel, C., & Beaulieu, C. (2011). Longitudinal development of human brain wiring continues from childhood into adulthood. *Journal of Neuroscience, 31*(30), 10937–10947. http://dx.doi.org/10.1523/JNEUROSCI.5302-10.2011.

Lenroot, R. K., & Giedd, J. N. (2006). Brain development in children and adolescents: insights from anatomical magnetic resonance imaging. *Neuroscience & Biobehavioral Reviews, 30*(6), 718–729. http://dx.doi.org/10.1016/j.neubiorev.2006.06.001.

Li, Z., Dong, T., Proschel, C., & Noble, M. (2007). Chemically diverse toxicants converge on Fyn and c-Cbl to disrupt precursor cell function. *PLoS Biology, 5*(2), e35. http://dx.doi.org/10.1371/journal.pbio.0050035.

Liu, J., Dietz, K., DeLoyht, J. M., Pedre, X., Kelkar, D., Kaur, J., et al. (2012). Impaired adult myelination in the prefrontal cortex of socially isolated mice. *Nature Neuroscience, 15*(12), 1621–1623. http://dx.doi.org/10.1038/nn.3263.

Looney, J. M., & Childs, H. M. (1934). The lactic acid and glutathione content of the blood of schizophrenic patients. *Journal of Clinical Investigation, 13*(6), 963–968. http://dx.doi.org/10.1172/JCI100639.

Lu, S., Wei, Z., Gao, W., Wu, W., Liao, M., Zhang, Y., et al. (2013). White matter integrity alterations in young healthy adults reporting childhood trauma: a diffusion tensor imaging study. *Australian & New Zealand Journal of Psychiatry, 47*(12), 1183–1190. http://dx.doi.org/10.1177/0004867413508454.

Lu, S. C. (2013). Glutathione synthesis. *Biochimica et Biophysica Acta (BBA) – General Subjects, 1830*(5), 3143–3153. http://dx.doi.org/10.1016/j.bbagen.2012.09.008.

Ma, J., Li, D. M., Zhang, R., Yang, X. D., Gao, C. G., Lu, S. M., et al. (2010). Genetic analysis of glutamate cysteine ligase modifier (GCLM) gene and schizophrenia in Han Chinese. *Schizophrenia Research, 119*(1–3), 273–274. http://dx.doi.org/10.1016/j.schres.2009.12.017.

Makinodan, M., Rosen, K. M., Ito, S., & Corfas, G. (2012). A critical period for social experience-dependent oligodendrocyte maturation and myelination. *Science, 337*(6100), 1357–1360. http://dx.doi.org/10.1126/science.1220845.

Makinodan, M., Tatsumi, K., Manabe, T., Yamauchi, T., Makinodan, E., Matsuyoshi, H., et al. (2008). Maternal immune activation in mice delays myelination and axonal development in the hippocampus of the offspring. *Journal of Neuroscience Research, 86*(10), 2190–2200. http://dx.doi.org/10.1002/jnr.21673.

Makinodan, M., Yamauchi, T., Tatsumi, K., Okuda, H., Noriyama, Y., Sadamatsu, M., et al. (2009). Yi-gan san restores behavioral alterations and a decrease of brain glutathione level in a mouse model of schizophrenia. *Journal of Brain Disease, 1*, 1–6.

Matsuzawa, D., & Hashimoto, K. (2011). Magnetic resonance spectroscopy study of the antioxidant defense system in schizophrenia. *Antioxidants & Redox Signaling, 15*(7), 2057–2065. http://dx.doi.org/10.1089/ars.2010.3453.

Matsuzawa, D., Hashimoto, K., Hashimoto, T., Shimizu, E., Watanabe, H., Fujita, Y., et al. (2009). Association study between the genetic polymorphisms of glutathione-related enzymes and schizophrenia in a Japanese population. *American Journal of Medical Genetics Part B: Neuropsychiatric Genetics, 150B*(1), 86–94. http://dx.doi.org/10.1002/ajmg.b.30776.

McIntosh, A. M., Moorhead, T. W., Job, D., Lymer, G. K., Munoz Maniega, S., McKirdy, J., et al. (2008). The effects of a neuregulin 1 variant on white matter density and integrity. *Molecular Psychiatry, 13*(11), 1054–1059. http://dx.doi.org/10.1038/sj.mp.4002103.

Mei, L., & Nave, K. A. (2014). Neuregulin-ERBB signaling in the nervous system and neuropsychiatric diseases. *Neuron, 83*(1), 27–49. http://dx.doi.org/10.1016/j.neuron.2014.06.007.

Meyer, U., & Feldon, J. (2012). To poly(I: C) or not to poly(I: C): advancing preclinical schizophrenia research through the use of prenatal immune activation models. *Neuropharmacology, 62*(3), 1308–1321. http://dx.doi.org/10.1016/j.neuropharm.2011.01.009.

Michel, T. M., Thome, J., Martin, D., Nara, K., Zwerina, S., Tatschner, T., et al. (2004). Cu, Zn- and Mn-superoxide dismutase levels in brains of patients with schizophrenic psychosis. *Journal of Neural Transmission, 111*(9), 1191–1201. http://dx.doi.org/10.1007/s00702-004-0160-9.

Mico, J. A., Rojas-Corrales, M. O., Gibert-Rahola, J., Parellada, M., Moreno, D., Fraguas, D., et al. (2011). Reduced antioxidant defense in early onset first-episode psychosis: a case-control study. *BMC Psychiatry, 11*, 26. http://dx.doi.org/10.1186/1471-244X-11-26.

Millar, J. K., Wilson-Annan, J. C., Anderson, S., Christie, S., Taylor, M. S., Semple, C. A., et al. (2000). Disruption of two novel genes by a translocation co-segregating with schizophrenia. *Human Molecular Genetics, 9*(9), 1415–1423.

Mitew, S., Hay, C. M., Peckham, H., Xiao, J., Koenning, M., & Emery, B. (2013). Mechanisms regulating the development of oligodendrocytes and central nervous system myelin. *Neuroscience.* http://dx.doi.org/10.1016/j.neuroscience.2013.11.029.

Miyaoka, T., Yasukawa, R., Yasuda, H., Shimizu, M., Mizuno, S., Sukegawa, T., et al. (2005). Urinary excretion of biopyrrins, oxidative metabolites of bilirubin, increases in patients with psychiatric disorders. *European Neuropsychopharmacology, 15*(3), 249–252. http://dx.doi.org/10.1016/j.euroneuro.2004.11.002.

Monin, A., Baumann, P. S., Griffa, A., Xin, L., Mekle, R., Fournier, M., et al. (2014). Glutathione deficit impairs myelin maturation: relevance for white matter integrity in schizophrenia patients. *Molecular Psychiatry.* http://dx.doi.org/10.1038/mp.2014.88.

Morishita, H., & Hensch, T. K. (2008). Critical period revisited: impact on vision. *Current Opinion in Neurobiology, 18*(1), 101–107. http://dx.doi.org/10.1016/j.conb.2008.05.009.

Noble, M., Smith, J., Power, J., & Mayer-Proschel, M. (2003). Redox state as a central modulator of precursor cell function. *Annals of the New York Academy of Sciences, 991*, 251–271.

Ohnuma, T., Kato, H., Arai, H., McKenna, P. J., & Emson, P. C. (2003). Expression of Fyn, a non-receptor tyrosine kinase in prefrontal cortex from patients with schizophrenia and its correlation with clinical onset. *Brain Research. Molecular Brain Research, 112*(1–2), 90–94.

Okumura, T., Okochi, T., Kishi, T., Ikeda, M., Kitajima, T., Yamanouchi, Y., et al. (2009). No association between polymorphisms of neuronal oxide synthase 1 gene (NOS1) and schizophrenia in a Japanese population. *NeuroMolecular Medicine, 11*(2), 123–127. http://dx.doi.org/10.1007/s12017-009-8068-z.

van Os, J., Rutten, B. P., & Poulton, R. (2008). Gene-environment interactions in schizophrenia: review of epidemiological findings and future directions. *Schizophrenia Bulletin, 34*(6), 1066–1082. http://dx.doi.org/10.1093/schbul/sbn117.

Ostman, A., & Bohmer, F. D. (2001). Regulation of receptor tyrosine kinase signaling by protein tyrosine phosphatases. *Trends in Cell Biology, 11*(6), 258–266.

Pae, C. U., Kim, T. S., Patkar, A. A., Kim, J. J., Lee, C. U., Lee, S. J., et al. (2007). Manganese superoxide dismutase (MnSOD: Ala-9Val) gene polymorphism may not be associated with schizophrenia and tardive dyskinesia. *Psychiatry Research, 153*(1), 77–81. http://dx.doi.org/10.1016/j.psychres.2006.04.011.

Park, Y. U., Jeong, J., Lee, H., Mun, J. Y., Kim, J. H., Lee, J. S., et al. (2010). Disrupted-in-schizophrenia 1 (DISC1) plays essential roles in mitochondria in collaboration with Mitofilin. *Proceedings of the National Academy of Sciences of the United States of America, 107*(41), 17785–17790. http://dx.doi.org/10.1073/pnas.1004361107.

Pasichna, E. P., Morozova, R. P., Donchenko, H. V., Vinychuk, S. M., & Kopchak, O. O. (2007). Lipid peroxidation and antioxidant defence enzyme activity in multiple sclerosis. *Ukrainskiĭ Biokhimicheskiĭ Zhurnal, 79*(5), 165–174.

Paul, R., Henry, L., Grieve, S. M., Guilmette, T. J., Niaura, R., Bryant, R., et al. (2008). The relationship between early life stress and microstructural integrity of the corpus callosum in a non-clinical population. *Neuropsychiatric Disease and Treatment, 4*(1), 193–201.

Peters, B. D., & Karlsgodt, K. H. (2014). White matter development in the early stages of psychosis. *Schizophrenia Research.* http://dx.doi.org/10.1016/j.schres.2014.05.021.

Peters, B. D., Schmitz, N., Dingemans, P. M., van Amelsvoort, T. A., Linszen, D. H., de Haan, L., et al. (2009). Preliminary evidence for reduced frontal white matter integrity in subjects at ultra-high-risk for psychosis. *Schizophrenia Research, 111*(1–3), 192–193. http://dx.doi.org/10.1016/j.schres.2009.03.018.

Poels, E. M., Kegeles, L. S., Kantrowitz, J. T., Slifstein, M., Javitt, D. C., Lieberman, J. A., et al. (2014). Imaging glutamate in schizophrenia: review of findings and implications for drug discovery. *Molecular Psychiatry, 19*(1), 20–29. http://dx.doi.org/10.1038/mp.2013.136.

Ponniah, S., Wang, D. Z., Lim, K. L., & Pallen, C. J. (1999). Targeted disruption of the tyrosine phosphatase PTPalpha leads to constitutive downregulation of the kinases Src and Fyn. *Current Biology, 9*(10), 535–538.

Raffa, M., Mechri, A., Othman, L. B., Fendri, C., Gaha, L., & Kerkeni, A. (2009). Decreased glutathione levels and antioxidant enzyme activities in untreated and treated schizophrenic patients. *Progress in Neuro-Psychopharmacology & Biological Psychiatry, 33*(7), 1178–1183. http://dx.doi.org/10.1016/j.pnpbp.2009.06.018.

Reif, A., Herterich, S., Strobel, A., Ehlis, A. C., Saur, D., Jacob, C. P., et al. (2006). A neuronal nitric oxide synthase (NOS-I) haplotype associated with schizophrenia modifies prefrontal cortex function. *Molecular Psychiatry, 11*(3), 286–300. http://dx.doi.org/10.1038/sj.mp.4001779.

Ren, Y., Wang, H., & Xiao, L. (2013). Improving myelin/oligodendrocyte-related dysfunction: a new mechanism of antipsychotics in the treatment of schizophrenia? *International Journal of Neuropsychopharmacology, 16*(3), 691–700. http://dx.doi.org/10.1017/S1461145712001095.

Ritter, J., Schmitz, T., Chew, L. J., Buhrer, C., Mobius, W., Zonouzi, M., et al. (2013). Neonatal hyperoxia exposure disrupts axon-oligodendrocyte integrity in the subcortical white matter. *Journal of Neuroscience, 33*(21), 8990–9002. http://dx.doi.org/10.1523/JNEUROSCI.5528-12.2013.

Rodriguez-Santiago, B., Brunet, A., Sobrino, B., Serra-Juhe, C., Flores, R., Armengol, L., et al. (2010). Association of common copy number variants at the glutathione S-transferase genes and rare novel genomic changes with schizophrenia. *Molecular Psychiatry, 15*(10), 1023–1033. http://dx.doi.org/10.1038/mp.2009.53.

Roosendaal, S. D., Geurts, J. J., Vrenken, H., Hulst, H. E., Cover, K. S., Castelijns, J. A., et al. (2009). Regional DTI differences in multiple sclerosis patients. *NeuroImage, 44*(4), 1397–1403. http://dx.doi.org/10.1016/j.neuroimage.2008.10.026.

Ruiz, S., Birbaumer, N., & Sitaram, R. (2013). Abnormal neural connectivity in schizophrenia and fMRI-brain-computer interface as a potential therapeutic approach. *Frontiers in Psychiatry, 4*, 17. http://dx.doi.org/10.3389/fpsyt.2013.00017.

Ruiz-Litago, F., Seco, J., Echevarria, E., Martinez-Cengotitabengoa, M., Gil, J., Irazusta, J., et al. (2012). Adaptive response in the antioxidant defence system in the course and outcome in first-episode schizophrenia patients: a 12-months follow-up study. *Psychiatry Research, 200*(2–3), 218–222. http://dx.doi.org/10.1016/j.psychres.2012.07.024.

Saadat, M., Mobayen, F., & Farrashbandi, H. (2007). Genetic polymorphism of glutathione S-transferase T1: a candidate genetic modifier of individual susceptibility to schizophrenia. *Psychiatry Research, 153*(1), 87–91. http://dx.doi.org/10.1016/j.psychres.2006.03.024.

Salmaso, N., Jablonska, B., Scafidi, J., Vaccarino, F. M., & Gallo, V. (2014). Neurobiology of premature brain injury. *Nature Neuroscience, 17*(3), 341–346. http://dx.doi.org/10.1038/nn.3604.

Salmeen, A., & Barford, D. (2005). Functions and mechanisms of redox regulation of cysteine-based phosphatases. *Antioxidants & Redox Signaling, 7*(5–6), 560–577. http://dx.doi.org/10.1089/ars.2005.7.560.

Samartzis, L., Dima, D., Fusar-Poli, P., & Kyriakopoulos, M. (2014). White matter alterations in early stages of schizophrenia: a systematic review of diffusion tensor imaging studies. *Journal of Neuroimaging, 24*(2), 101–110. http://dx.doi.org/10.1111/j.1552-6569.2012.00779.x.

Sarandol, A., Kirli, S., Akkaya, C., Altin, A., Demirci, M., & Sarandol, E. (2007). Oxidative-antioxidative systems and their relation with serum S100 B levels in patients with schizophrenia: effects of short term antipsychotic treatment. *Progress in Neuro-Psychopharmacology & Biological Psychiatry, 31*(6), 1164–1169. http://dx.doi.org/10.1016/j.pnpbp.2007.03.008.

Sato, H., Takahashi, T., Sumitani, K., Takatsu, H., & Urano, S. (2010). Glucocorticoid generates ROS to induce oxidative injury in the Hippocampus, leading to impairment of cognitive function of rats. *Journal of Clinical Biochemistry and Nutrition, 47*(3), 224–232. http://dx.doi.org/10.3164/jcbn.10-58.

Schiavone, S., Jaquet, V., Trabace, L., & Krause, K. H. (2013). Severe life stress and oxidative stress in the brain: from animal models to human pathology. *Antioxidants & Redox Signaling, 18*(12), 1475–1490. http://dx.doi.org/10.1089/ars.2012.4720.

Schmitt, A., Hasan, A., Gruber, O., & Falkai, P. (2011). Schizophrenia as a disorder of disconnectivity. *European Archives of Psychiatry and Clinical Neurosciences, 261*(Suppl. 2), S150–S154. http://dx.doi.org/10.1007/s00406-011-0242-2.

Schmitt, A., Malchow, B., Hasan, A., & Falkai, P. (2014). The impact of environmental factors in severe psychiatric disorders. *Frontiers in Neuroscience, 8*, 19. http://dx.doi.org/10.3389/fnins.2014.00019.

Schmitz, T., Ritter, J., Mueller, S., Felderhoff-Mueser, U., Chew, L. J., & Gallo, V. (2011). Cellular changes underlying hyperoxia-induced delay of white matter development. *Journal of Neuroscience, 31*(11), 4327–4344. http://dx.doi.org/10.1523/JNEUROSCI.3942-10.2011.

Schrader, M., & Fahimi, H. D. (2006). Peroxisomes and oxidative stress. *Biochimica et Biophysica Acta, 1763*(12), 1755–1766. http://dx.doi.org/10.1016/j.bbamcr.2006.09.006.

Seven, A., Aslan, M., Incir, S., & Altintas, A. (2013). Evaluation of oxidative and nitrosative stress in relapsing remitting multiple sclerosis: effect of corticosteroid therapy. *Folia Neuropathologica, 51*(1), 58–64.

Sofic, E., Rustembegovic, A., Kroyer, G., & Cao, G. (2002). Serum antioxidant capacity in neurological, psychiatric, renal diseases and cardiomyopathy. *Journal of Neural Transmission, 109*(5–6), 711–719. http://dx.doi.org/10.1007/s007020200059.

Sprooten, E., Lymer, G. K., Munoz Maniega, S., McKirdy, J., Clayden, J. D., Bastin, M. E., et al. (2009). The relationship of anterior thalamic radiation integrity to psychosis risk associated neuregulin-1 variants. *Molecular Psychiatry, 14*(3), 237–238. http://dx.doi.org/10.1038/mp.2008.136 233.

Sprooten, E., Sussmann, J. E., Moorhead, T. W., Whalley, H. C., Ffrench-Constant, C., Blumberg, H. P., et al. (2011). Association of white matter integrity with genetic variation in an exonic DISC1 SNP. *Molecular Psychiatry, 16*(7)(685), 688–689. http://dx.doi.org/10.1038/mp.2011.15.

Steelman, A. J., & Li, J. (2011). Poly(I: C) promotes TNFalpha/TNFR1-dependent oligodendrocyte death in mixed glial cultures. *Journal of Neuroinflammation, 8*, 89. http://dx.doi.org/10.1186/1742-2094-8-89.

Steullet, P., Cabungcal, J. H., Kulak, A., Kraftsik, R., Chen, Y., Dalton, T. P., et al. (2010). Redox dysregulation affects the ventral but not dorsal hippocampus: impairment of parvalbumin neurons, gamma oscillations, and related behaviors. *Journal of Neuroscience, 30*(7), 2547–2558. http://dx.doi.org/10.1523/JNEUROSCI.3857-09.2010.

Steullet, P., Cabungcal, J. H., Monin, A., Dwir, D., O'Donnell, P., Cuenod, M., et al. (2014). Redox dysregulation, neuroinflammation, and NMDA receptor hypofunction: a "central hub" in schizophrenia pathophysiology? *Schizophrenia Research.* http://dx.doi.org/10.1016/j.schres.2014.06.021.

Szibor, M., Richter, C., & Ghafourifar, P. (2001). Redox control of mitochondrial functions. *Antioxidants & Redox Signaling, 3*(3), 515–523. http://dx.doi.org/10.1089/15230860152409149.

Takahashi, N., Sakurai, T., Davis, K. L., & Buxbaum, J. D. (2011). Linking oligodendrocyte and myelin dysfunction to neurocircuitry abnormalities in schizophrenia. *Progress in Neurobiology, 93*(1), 13–24. http://dx.doi.org/10.1016/j.pneurobio.2010.09.004.

Takesian, A. E., & Hensch, T. K. (2013). Balancing plasticity/stability across brain development. *Progress in Brain Research, 207*, 3–34. http://dx.doi.org/10.1016/B978-0-444-63327-9.00001-1.

Talukder, I., Kazi, R., & Wollmuth, L. P. (2011). GluN1-specific redox effects on the kinetic mechanism of NMDA receptor activation. *Biophysical Journal, 101*(10), 2389–2398. http://dx.doi.org/10.1016/j.bpj.2011.10.015.

Tang, W., Huang, K., Tang, R., Zhou, G., Fang, C., Zhang, J., et al. (2008). Evidence for association between the 5′ flank of the NOS1 gene and schizophrenia in the Chinese population. *International Journal of Neuropsychopharmacology, 11*(08), 1063–1071. http://dx.doi.org/10.1017/S1461145708008924.

Thorburne, S. K., & Juurlink, B. H. (1996). Low glutathione and high iron govern the susceptibility of oligodendroglial precursors to oxidative stress. *Journal of Neurochemistry, 67*(3), 1014–1022.

Tkachev, D., Mimmack, M. L., Ryan, M. M., Wayland, M., Freeman, T., Jones, P. B., et al. (2003). Oligodendrocyte dysfunction in schizophrenia and bipolar disorder. *Lancet, 362*(9386), 798–805. http://dx.doi.org/10.1016/S0140-6736(03)14289-4.

Tosic, M., Ott, J., Barral, S., Bovet, P., Deppen, P., Gheorghita, F., et al. (2006). Schizophrenia and oxidative stress: glutamate cysteine ligase modifier as a susceptibility gene. *American Journal of Human Genetics, 79*(3), 586–592. http://dx.doi.org/10.1086/507566.

Tsai, M. C., Liou, C. W., Lin, T. K., Lin, I. M., & Huang, T. L. (2013). Changes in oxidative stress markers in patients with schizophrenia: the effect of antipsychotic drugs. *Psychiatry Research, 209*(3), 284–290. http://dx.doi.org/10.1016/j.psychres.2013.01.023.

Uranova, N. A., Vikhreva, O. V., Rachmanova, V. I., & Orlovskaya, D. D. (2011). Ultrastructural alterations of myelinated fibers and oligodendrocytes in the prefrontal cortex in schizophrenia: a postmortem morphometric study. *Schizophrenia Research and Treatment, 2011,* 325789. http://dx.doi.org/10.1155/2011/325789.

Uranova, N. A., Vostrikov, V. M., Orlovskaya, D. D., & Rachmanova, V. I. (2004). Oligodendroglial density in the prefrontal cortex in schizophrenia and mood disorders: a study from the Stanley Neuropathology Consortium. *Schizophrenia Research, 67*(2–3), 269–275. http://dx.doi.org/10.1016/S0920-9964(03)00181-6.

Valko, M., Leibfritz, D., Moncol, J., Cronin, M. T., Mazur, M., & Telser, J. (2007). Free radicals and antioxidants in normal physiological functions and human disease. *International Journal of Biochemistry & Cell Biology, 39*(1), 44–84. http://dx.doi.org/10.1016/j.biocel.2006.07.001.

Ventriglia, M., Scassellati, C., Bonvicini, C., Squitti, R., Bevacqua, M. G., Foresti, G., et al. (2006). No association between Ala9Val functional polymorphism of MnSOD gene and schizophrenia in a representative Italian sample. *Neuroscience Letters, 410*(3), 208–211. http://dx.doi.org/10.1016/j.neulet.2006.10.009.

Vostrikov, V., & Uranova, N. (2011). Age-related increase in the number of oligodendrocytes is dysregulated in schizophrenia and mood disorders. *Schizophrenia Research and Treatment, 2011,* 174689. http://dx.doi.org/10.1155/2011/174689.

Vostrikov, V. M., Uranova, N. A., & Orlovskaya, D. D. (2007). Deficit of perineuronal oligodendrocytes in the prefrontal cortex in schizophrenia and mood disorders. *Schizophrenia Research, 94*(1–3), 273–280. http://dx.doi.org/10.1016/j.schres.2007.04.014.

Wang, F., Jiang, T., Sun, Z., Teng, S. L., Luo, X., Zhu, Z., et al. (2009). Neuregulin 1 genetic variation and anterior cingulum integrity in patients with schizophrenia and healthy controls. *Journal of Psychiatry & Neuroscience, 34*(3), 181–186.

Wang, J. F., Shao, L., Sun, X., & Young, L. T. (2009). Increased oxidative stress in the anterior cingulate cortex of subjects with bipolar disorder and schizophrenia. *Bipolar Disorder, 11*(5), 523–529. http://dx.doi.org/10.1111/j.1399-5618.2009.00717.x.

Weinberger, D. R. (1987). Implications of normal brain development for the pathogenesis of schizophrenia. *Archives of General Psychiatry, 44*(7), 660–669.

Whitford, T. J., Ford, J. M., Mathalon, D. H., Kubicki, M., & Shenton, M. E. (2012). Schizophrenia, myelination, and delayed corollary discharges: a hypothesis. *Schizophrenia Bulletin, 38*(3), 486–494. http://dx.doi.org/10.1093/schbul/sbq105.

Winterer, G., Konrad, A., Vucurevic, G., Musso, F., Stoeter, P., & Dahmen, N. (2008). Association of 5′ end neuregulin-1 (NRG1) gene variation with subcortical medial frontal microstructure in humans. *NeuroImage, 40*(2), 712–718. http://dx.doi.org/10.1016/j.neuroimage.2007.12.041.

Witthaus, H., Brune, M., Kaufmann, C., Bohner, G., Ozgurdal, S., Gudlowski, Y., et al. (2008). White matter abnormalities in subjects at ultra high-risk for schizophrenia and first-episode schizophrenic patients. *Schizophrenia Research, 102*(1–3), 141–149. http://dx.doi.org/10.1016/j.schres.2008.03.022.

Wood, J. D., Bonath, F., Kumar, S., Ross, C. A., & Cunliffe, V. T. (2009). Disrupted-in-schizophrenia 1 and neuregulin 1 are required for the specification of oligodendrocytes and neurones in the zebrafish brain. *Human Molecular Genetics, 18*(3), 391–404. http://dx.doi.org/10.1093/hmg/ddn361.

Xin, L., Mekle, R., Ferrari, C., Baumann, P. S., Alameda, L., Moser, H., et al. (2014). Genetic association with prefrontal glutathione deficit: a 3T 1H MRS study in early psychosis. *Biological Psychiatry, 75*(9), 108S.

Xu, M., Wu, X., Jie, B., Zhang, X., Zhang, J., Xin, Y., et al. (2014). Neuregulin-1 protects myocardial cells against H_2O_2-induced apoptosis by regulating endoplasmic reticulum stress. *Cell Biochemistry and Function, 32*(5), 464–469. http://dx.doi.org/10.1002/cbf.3038.

Yao, J. K., Leonard, S., & Reddy, R. (2006). Altered glutathione redox state in schizophrenia. *Disease Markers, 22*(1–2), 83–93.

Yao, J. K., Reddy, R., McElhinny, L. G., & van Kammen, D. P. (1998). Reduced status of plasma total antioxidant capacity in schizophrenia. *Schizophrenia Research, 32*(1), 1–8.

Yao, L., Lui, S., Liao, Y., Du, M. Y., Hu, N., Thomas, J. A., et al. (2013). White matter deficits in first episode schizophrenia: an activation likelihood estimation meta-analysis. *Progress in Neuro-Psychopharmacology & Biological Psychiatry, 45*, 100–106. http://dx.doi.org/10.1016/j.pnpbp.2013.04.019.

Zafir, A., & Banu, N. (2009). Modulation of in vivo oxidative status by exogenous corticosterone and restraint stress in rats. *Stress, 12*(2), 167–177. http://dx.doi.org/10.1080/10253890802234168.

Zhou, Y., Liang, M., Jiang, T., Tian, L., Liu, Y., Liu, Z., et al. (2007). Functional dysconnectivity of the dorsolateral prefrontal cortex in first-episode schizophrenia using resting-state fMRI. *Neuroscience Letters, 417*(3), 297–302. http://dx.doi.org/10.1016/j.neulet.2007.02.081.

Role of Immune and Autoimmune Dysfunction in Schizophrenia

Emily G. Severance, Robert H. Yolken

Department of Pediatrics, Johns Hopkins University School of Medicine, Baltimore, MD, USA

INTRODUCTION

Schizophrenia is a debilitating and complex brain disorder of unknown etiology. Complicating our understanding of the causes and pathophysiology of schizophrenia is the likelihood that what we call schizophrenia is actually a heterogeneous assemblage of etiological conditions across a broad spectrum (Arnedo et al., 2014). Reigning evidence supports a schizophrenia etiopathogenesis arising from and perpetuated by a multi-sourced genetic by environmental interaction (Demjaha, MacCabe, & Murray, 2012; Modinos et al., 2013; van Os et al., 2014; Tsuang, 2000). Although schizophrenia is highly heritable, the disease is polygenic, and gene studies to date have identified an enormous number of susceptibility loci (Kavanagh, Tansey, O'Donovan, & Owen, 2014; Schizophrenia Working Group of the Psychiatric Genomics Consortium, 2014). Thus, the disease is thought to manifest when one or more of many possible genetic predispositions co-occurs with exposure to one or more of many possible environmental factors. Relevant environmental factors can derive from a diversity of sources including exposures to infection, food-derived antigens, stress, smoking, cannabinoids, pollutants, and other toxins (Allen, Liu, Pelkowski, et al., 2014; Allen, Liu, Weston, et al., 2014; Fine, Zhang, & Stevens, 2014; Fineberg & Ellman, 2013; Fraga et al., 2011; Severance, Yolken, & Eaton, 2014; Suarez-Pinilla, Lopez-Gil, & Crespo-Facorro, 2014; Yolken & Torrey, 2008; Zhang et al., 2014). If these exposures coincide with critical periods of fetal and neonatal brain maturation, there is the potential to aberrantly impact important brain processes including neural migration, synaptogenesis, myelination, and synaptic pruning. Coinciding with these neurodevelopmental landmarks are events crucial for the instigation and maturation of innate and adaptive immunity.

A possible role for immune system dysregulation in schizophrenia etiopathogenesis would reconcile both genetic and environmental hypotheses. A number of genetic loci found to associate with schizophrenia involve immune functions directly or implicate biological pathways that can influence immune function. For example, a consistently replicated locus for association with schizophrenia is the 6p22 chromosomal region that houses the major histocompatibility (MHC) locus and human leukocyte antigens (Corvin & Morris, 2014; Purcell et al., 2009; Shi et al., 2009; Stefansson et al., 2009). The MHC/human leukocyte gene family functions to identify self and nonself entities and any dysfunction of these genes can render susceptibility to infectious disease, graft rejection, cancer, and autoimmunity. Environmental triggers that show consistently replicated associations with schizophrenia are also those that result in immune activation. Exposures to infectious pathogens, food antigens, and autoantigens have been especially well-studied risk factors for the development of schizophrenia, and special consideration is afforded to the timing, intensity, and type of immune activation elicited by these exposures (Jones, Mowry, Pender, & Greer, 2005; Kirch, 1993; Knuesel et al., 2014; Meyer, 2013; Muller, 2014; Rothermundt, Arolt, & Bayer, 2001; Severance, Yolken, et al., 2014; Torrey & Peterson, 1976; Yolken & Torrey, 2008).

The focus of this chapter is to review some of the evidence in support of an immune and autoimmune dysfunction in the etiology, pathogenesis, and pathophysiology of schizophrenia. From a historical perspective, a recurrent immune theme predominated the early literature with a particular emphasis on schizophrenia-associated immunoglobulins and antibrain antibodies. These ideas still formulate the basis of current immune topics in schizophrenia, but over the years the scope has widened beyond the adaptive immune system to encompass also innate immunity. Advances in our understanding of inflammation and mediators of both the adaptive and innate immune system and their functional roles in standard brain physiology provide an important context by which schizophrenia might arise as the result of the coupling of immune and neurodevelopmental dysregulation.

PRIMER ON BASIC IMMUNOLOGY

The focus of this review on immune system aberrations in schizophrenia requires a review of basic knowledge of the major molecules and cells involved in the highly regulated balance of interacting innate and adaptive immune pathways. The function of the immune system is to protect the organism from disease and allow distinction between self and nonself entities, a process that is generally classified into the innate (nonspecific, always present) and adaptive (specific, triggered) immune systems. The innate immune system is composed of physical epithelial barriers, monocytes/macrophages, dendritic cells, natural killer cells, and circulating plasma proteins. Microbial invaders or compromised cells interact with recognition receptors found on monocytes/macrophages and dendritic cells. Pattern recognition receptors can be cytoplasmic, membrane-bound, and secreted and include Toll-like receptors, complement receptors, nucleotide-binding oligomerization domain (NOD)-like receptors, pentraxins, and C-reactive protein. The adaptive immune system is composed of two immune response types: humoral (antibody) immunity and T-lymphocyte-mediated immunity. During activation of the adaptive immune system, binding of the invading antigen to B lymphocytes precipitates its differentiation into plasma cells that produce immunoglobulin antibodies specifically targeted to the invading antigen (Alberts, 2008; Rothermundt et al., 2001). The complement system acts in conjunction with the humoral immune system to form immune complexes with the antibody bound antigens and clear these from the body (Walport, 2001a, 2001b). Upon binding to monocytes/macrophages, pathogenic and other antigens also trigger the T-cell cascade, where T cells differentiate into cytotoxic T cells, T-helper cells, and natural killer cells. The lysis of cells containing the invading antigen is accompanied by the production of pro- and anti-inflammatory cytokines, signaling

proteins that function in immune regulation (Alberts, 2008; Rothermundt et al., 2001).

Dysregulation of any of these molecules, proteins, or cells at any stage of these pathways irrespective of a genetic or environmental origin can result in disorders of the immune system, which generally can take the form of inflammatory diseases, immunodeficiency, autoimmunity, or some forms of neoplasia. For complex psychiatric disorders such as schizophrenia, it is also necessary to understand how perturbations of these immune processes might impact the brain. Because schizophrenia is thought to originate as a result of aberrant neurodevelopment, it is important to note that for a number of these classic immune factors, including complement, MHC, Toll-like receptors, and pentraxins, additional functions in the developing brain are continuously being identified (Benoit & Tenner, 2011; Bialas & Stevens, 2013; Boulanger, 2009; Fourgeaud & Boulanger, 2007; Frodl & Amico, 2014; Garate et al., 2013; Nagyoszi et al., 2010; Pribiag & Stellwagen, 2014; Stephan et al., 2013; Stevens et al., 2007; Trotta, Porro, Calvello, & Panaro, 2014). It is also becoming increasingly evident that circulating endogenous peripheral immune entities may directly access the central nervous system (CNS) as a result of directed regulation or compromised endothelial barriers. At the same time, it is possible that invading or resident pathogens or their products could directly exert detriment to the CNS by similarly penetrating these barriers. As such, the spectrum of psychiatric dysfunctions known as schizophrenia may be the compilation of different stages of an immunoneurological intersection gone awry from both external and internal pathological molecules and pathways.

HISTORICAL PERSPECTIVE OF THE IMMUNE–SCHIZOPHRENIA ASSOCIATION

Early observations prepared a foundation for the studies of today where the role of immune activation is no longer questioned but understood to be the most parsimonious etiological explanation that encompasses a gene by environment landscape of schizophrenia. In this section, we will review the history of these immune associations and especially illuminate adaptive humoral immune system dysregulation because immunoglobulin abnormalities were the focus of early investigations (Kirch, 1993; Rothermundt et al., 2001). Although many of these early studies are inconsistent regarding the impact of any single infectious pathogen or autoimmune reaction against brain tissue, these investigations offer snapshots of how the immune process might be relevant to and influence brain function. Importantly, they bring to light issues that are still relevant today and that are now studied without previous restrictions such as unrecognized disease heterogeneity, constricted study designs, and limited laboratory technologies.

Activation of the adaptive immune system and specifically of humoral immunity generally is manifested by changes in the levels of immunoglobulin antibodies with respect to the disease state. Schizophrenia-associated changes in the levels of plasma and cerebrospinal fluid (CSF) proteins were repeated findings that implicated immunoglobulins and solidified the idea that in schizophrenia, either an infectious or an autoimmune process might be occurring (Amkraut, Solomon, Allansmith, McClellan, & Rappaport, 1973; Bock & Rafaelsen, 1974; Burian, Kubikova, & Krejcova, 1964; Durell & Archer, 1976; Fessel, 1962a, 1962b; Gammack & Hector, 1965; Hendrie, Paraskevas, & Varsamis, 1972; Selecki, Todd, Westwood, & Kraus, 1964; Solomon, Allansmith, McCellan, & Amkraut, 1969; Strahilevitz & Davis, 1970). Of particular interest were reports that people with schizophrenia who had elevated immunoglobulin levels were also the least likely to show clinical improvement over the course of hospitalization compared with those with lower immunoglobulin levels (Amkraut et al., 1973).

An infectious disease component contribution to psychotic mental disorders is often first attributed to Esquirol (1845), who suggested that the dissemination of psychoses unfolds similarly to an epidemic-like process (Esquirol, 1845). This observation was followed by other reports of psychotic epidemics in the decades following World War I and the 1918 influenza epidemic (Kirch, 1993; Menninger, 1919, 1926; Torrey & Peterson, 1973, 1976). The possible role of an antigen derived from a pathogenic organism such as a virus or bacteria took root in various forms and the early years of the viral hypothesis of schizophrenia is well-reviewed by Torrey and Peterson (1973, 1976) and Kirch (1993), with exposures to neurotropic viruses such as herpes simplex virus 1, measles, and rubella figuring prominently (Kirch, 1993; Torrey & Peterson, 1973, 1976).

There was also an extensive literature base primarily from the 1940s to 1950s that describe a variety of antibody reactions in people with schizophrenia including the Rosenow antibody–antigen skin reaction. This reaction was based on a hypothesis that several brain diseases such as epilepsy and schizophrenia were the result of alpha-hemolytic streptococci as measured by a cutaneous reaction to a streptococcal antibody or antigen that was obtained and cultured from nasopharynx samples (Rosenow, 1948). Results from these studies were varied, with some showing greater immune response (cutaneous reaction) associated with schizophrenia and others showing no difference (Gurassa & Fleischhacker, 1958; Rosenow, 1948). We will revisit this idea of a pathogen-derived viral or bacterial source of immune activation in schizophrenia in its current form in a later

section, because it is still a relevant hypothesis that is being explored with the benefit of modern tools such as high throughput sequencing.

Meanwhile, early literature on the topic of autoimmunity received similar effort and attention. One very early study of postmortem brain tissue identified the presence of autoantibodies to brain proteins and launched the idea that schizophrenia and other psychoses may have an autoimmune basis (Lehmann-Facius, 1937). This theme continued in later decades when the role of autoantibodies to brain proteins was actively studied and disputed (Boehme, Cottrell, Dohan, & Hillegass, 1973; Durell & Archer, 1976; Fessel, 1962a, 1962b; Heath, 1967; Heath & Krupp, 1967; Heath, Krupp, Byers, & Lijekvist, 1967a, 1967b; Jones et al., 2005; Kirch, 1993; Mellsop, Whittingham, & Ungar, 1973). In some of these studies, the observation again came that levels of antibrain antibodies seemed to correlate with the intensity of psychotic symptoms and were generally higher during the early disease state and during acute attacks (Glebov, 1972; Gurevich, 1969; Stamboliev, 1970; Stoimenov, 1969).

WHERE ARE WE TODAY WITH THE ADAPTIVE IMMUNE HYPOTHESES?

Dysregulation of the adaptive immune system and especially of humoral immunity still figures prominently in today's literature examining immune-based hypotheses for schizophrenia. Speculation that medication is behind changes in immune marker levels is unavoidable; however, studies of patients who are antipsychotic naive or who have a recent onset of the disease support specific immune activation early in the course of disease, even before medication is administered (Beumer et al., 2012; Drexhage et al., 2010; Drexhage et al., 2011; Leonard, Schwarz, & Myint, 2012; Miller, Mellor, & Buckley, 2012; Mondelli & Howes, 2014; Severance, Alaedini, et al., 2012; Severance, Gressitt, et al., 2012; Severance et al., 2013b; Steiner et al., 2012; Stojanovic et al., 2014). Next we describe some current evidence available regarding schizophrenia-specific immune responses to external antigens and autoantigens.

Pathogens

Exposure to infectious disease pathogens during the pre- and postnatal period as defined by an antibody response is significantly associated with the future development of or current status of schizophrenia (Arias et al., 2012; Brown & Derkits, 2010; Buka, Cannon, Torrey, & Yolken, 2008; Fellerhoff, Laumbacher, Mueller, Gu, & Wank, 2007; Mortensen et al., 2010; Niebuhr et al., 2008; Xiao et al., 2009; Yolken et al., 2001; Yolken & Torrey, 2008). We include both pre- and postnatal exposure references in this section and in a later section will review the implications on neurodevelopment of strictly maternal-occurring immune activation from a variety of sources including pathogens. Pathogenic microorganisms are relevant to schizophrenia pathophysiology because they or their products can be neurotropic as well as cytotoxic or because the process of immune system activation is pathogenic in schizophrenia. Certain viruses known to be neurotropic include the herpes simplex viruses, cytomegalovirus, and Epstein–Barr virus; these viruses are also of interest because their life cycle can contain a latent state from which they can be periodically reactivated (Kirch, 1993; Torrey & Peterson, 1973, 1976). To date, the strongest association of an infectious disease agent with schizophrenia is *Toxoplasma gondii*, a neurotropic parasite, and this relationship is well-reviewed in numerous analyses and meta-analyses (Arias et al., 2012; Monroe, Buckley, & Miller, 2014; Torrey, Bartko, Lun, & Yolken, 2007; Torrey, Bartko, & Yolken, 2012). Other pathogens that have shown significant associations with schizophrenia and psychoses also include Epstein–Barr virus, measles, polio, influenza, coronaviruses, human herpesvirus 2, Borna disease virus, human endogenous retrovirus, and Chlamydophila spp (Arias et al., 2012; Brown, Begg, et al., 2004; Dickerson, Stallings, Origoni, Copp, et al., 2010; Karlsson et al., 2001; Karlsson, Schroder, Bachmann, Bottmer, & Yolken, 2004; Khandaker, Stochl, Zammit, Lewis, & Jones, 2014; Mednick, Machon, Huttunen, & Bonett, 1988; Perron et al., 2012; Prasad, Shirts, Yolken, Keshavan, & Nimgaonkar, 2007; Severance et al., 2011; Suvisaari, Haukka, Tanskanen, Hovi, & Lonnqvist, 1999).

Of note, exposure to the process of infection may be as or more important than the virulence or neurotropism of any single pathogen. A large study of the Swedish national birth registry suggested that exposure to viral CNS infections during childhood could result in the later development of schizophrenia (Dalman et al., 2008). Unlike other investigations, this study did not support a link of bacterial infections with the development of subsequent psychoses. A different study, however, found that urinary tract infections (likely of bacterial origin) were found to occur with increased prevalence in schizophrenia and associated with acute relapse of psychosis (Graham, Carson, Ezeoke, Buckley, & Miller, 2014; Miller et al., 2013). Other conditions typically characterized by bacterial infection (sinusitis, tonsillitis, and pneumonia) were associated with the development of schizophrenia in the prenatal exposure scenario, as were genital and other reproductive infections (Babulas, Factor-Litvak, Goetz, Schaefer, & Brown, 2006; Sorensen, Mortensen, Reinisch, & Mednick, 2009).

It is expected that if schizophrenia in some people is the result of a specific virus or parasite, then evidence in the form of DNA sequences would be found in the brain. These data, however, have thus far been elusive. The ability to efficiently search for this needle in a haystack came several years ago with the advent of high-throughput sequencing. The infancy of this field has not yet uncovered evidence for a causative pathogen, but ongoing investigations have brought about findings in unexpected places, including microbes associated with the gut microbiome.

Food Antigens

The connection between food sensitivity and propensity for schizophrenia was pioneered by F. Curtis Dohan, who hypothesized that wheat glutens and bovine milk caseins were broken down into bioactive exorphins that could penetrate through gut barriers, enter systemic circulation, and have access to the CNS. His work was based on observations of celiac disease overlap with schizophrenia, with strong correlations of hospitalization rates for schizophrenia with wheat availability during wartime and improvement of psychotic symptoms following removal of wheat and dairy products from the diet (Dohan, 1969, 1970, 1973, 1980; Dohan, Harper, Clark, Rodrigue, & Zigas, 1984). A recent resurgence in this field is exemplified by the numerous antibody studies that confirm an increased immune response directed at these food antigens, including a role for maternal antibodies to food antigens and the possible presence of an antigen-specific immune reaction up to 2 years before diagnosis of the disease (Cascella et al., 2011; Dickerson, Stallings, Origoni, Vaughan, et al., 2010; Jackson et al., 2012; Karlsson et al., 2012; Lachance & McKenzie, 2014; Niebuhr et al., 2011; Samaroo et al., 2010; Severance et al., 2010; Severance, Gressitt, et al., 2012). The presence of food-derived exorphins or antibodies against them have been documented in the CSF of individuals with a variety of psychoses including schizophrenia and coupled with a propensity for blood–brain and CSF–brain barrier defects might implicate a neurotropic role of these peptides in the etiology or pathophysiology of the disease (Axelsson, Martensson, & Alling, 1982; Bauer & Kornhuber, 1987; Kirch et al., 1992; Lindstrom, Besev, Gunne, & Terenius, 1986; Lindstrom et al., 1984).

Autoantigens

Autoimmune disease epidemiology and schizophrenia have been strongly linked for some time, with the first vestiges of the association coming in the form of findings suggestive of an inverse correlation between rheumatoid arthritis and schizophrenia (Benros, Eaton, & Mortensen, 2014; Eaton, Hayward, & Ram, 1992; Torrey & Yolken, 2001). Observations of a co-occurring psychosis with a number of autoimmune diseases including celiac disease, multiple sclerosis, systemic lupus erythematosus, autoimmune thyrotoxicosis, autoimmune hepatitis, and psoriasis also lent credence to the idea of an interrelated component of autoimmunity and the brain (Benros et al., 2014; Eaton et al., 2006). Celiac disease perhaps provides the strongest association with schizophrenia and reinforces the idea that for some, immune activation and autoimmunity have roots in the gut (Baldwin, 1980; Dohan, 1970, 1973, 1980; Eaton et al., 2004). Celiac disease is a disease whereby the ingestion of wheat gluten launches an immune reaction that damages the epithelial lining of the small intestine through an autoimmune attack on tissue transglutaminase that breaks down the gluten peptide (Alaedini & Green, 2008; Green et al., 2005; Guandalini & Assiri, 2014).

In the same way that the type of pathogen infection is probably not as important as the infectious process itself in causing brain pathologies such as schizophrenia, the specific type of autoimmune disease may not be the primary determinant of brain pathology. Instead, the occurrence of a state of autoimmunity and its association with schizophrenia is rather likely to be a suggestion of the pathophysiology or faulty mechanism that is at work, perhaps as a disjunctive operation of an immune system pathway that has failed to function. Large Danish population-based studies, in fact, confirm that individuals or first-degree family members who had any history of an autoimmune disease have a 45% increased relative risk for schizophrenia (Eaton et al., 2006). The autoimmune link with schizophrenia was further solidified in an even larger investigation of this registry, and interestingly, this risk was further elevated in those with a history of an infection (Benros et al., 2011). This finding is not surprising given the fairly established literature base supporting the idea that exposure to infectious agents generates an autoimmune response (Ercolini & Miller, 2009).

As mentioned in a previous section, documenting and characterizing autoantibodies directed at brain proteins has been intriguing researchers for decades with generally mixed results. Among the many autoantigens analyzed for an association with schizophrenia and psychosis are N-methyl-D-aspartate (NMDA) receptors (Deakin, Lennox, & Zandi, 2014; Ezeoke, Mellor, Buckley, & Miller, 2013; Jones et al., 2005; Masdeu et al., 2012; Muller, 2014; Pearlman & Najjar, 2014; Steiner et al., 2014; Steiner et al., 2013). This NMDA receptor antibody quest was fueled by findings that antibodies to the NMDA receptor were elevated in women with ovarian teratoma and psychoses-related encephalitis (Dalmau et al., 2007). Other targets of autoimmune investigations include Neuregulin-2, human endogenous retroviruses, cholinergic muscarinic receptors, nicotinic acetylcholine receptors, dopamine D2 receptors, mu-opioid receptors, serotonin receptors, α-amino-3-hydroxy-5-methyl-4-isoxazolepropionic acid receptors, gamma-aminobutyric acid receptors, glutamic acid decarboxylase, potassium

channel receptors, cardiolipin, DNA, histones, and mitochondria (Deakin et al., 2014; Ezeoke et al., 2013; Jones et al., 2005; Masdeu et al., 2012). An increased understanding of the underlying immunopathological processes and an improved characterization of reactive epitopes involved in disease pathogenesis might improve the predictive value of autoantibody assays and provide for reliable markers of disease susceptibility.

MOVING TOWARD INNATE IMMUNITY AND "THE PROCESS OF IMMUNE ACTIVATION"

The Gut, Inflammation, and Endothelial Barrier Dysfunction

A movement away from schizophrenia as a solely brain-centric disease is an active one in psychiatric research circles where an increasing awareness of the importance of the gastrointestinal (GI) tract, the body's largest immune organ, may share a bidirectional pathway with the brain. The strong association between food-based sensitivities and schizophrenia implicates the GI tract as an important site to search for immunological dysfunction. Food antigen sensitivity is but one of a number of risk factors for schizophrenia that are related to gut inflammation, and this immunoglobulin G (IgG) sensitivity joins other gut-related risk factors such as endothelial barrier defects, celiac disease, and exposure to T. gondii (Severance, Yolken, et al., 2014). Research at this interface has shown in translational models that intestinal inflammation is a significant comorbidity of schizophrenia, and markers of this inflammation correlate with antibodies to food antigens such as gluten and casein at heightened rates in people with schizophrenia (Severance, Alaedini, et al., 2012; Severance, Yolken, et al., 2014). It has been demonstrated in rodent models that the schizophrenia-associated pathogen T. gondii has many effects on the gut and during infection allows the passage of gluten peptides to translocate into circulation and provoke an antibody response (Severance, Kannan, et al., 2012). In the presence of compromised epithelial and endothelial barriers, not only do food-based peptides but also bacteria and other related harmful substances cross into the systemic circulation and generate more inflammation and propagate autoimmunity. Markers of bacterial translocation are elevated in schizophrenia and also found to correlate with the antibody response to food antigens (Severance et al., 2013a). Thus gut-based inflammation can be added to the growing list of studies that implicate both peripheral and CNS inflammatory pathways associated with schizophrenia (Dickerson et al., 2013; Drexhage et al., 2010; Fillman et al., 2013; Fillman, Sinclair, Fung, Webster, & Shannon

Weickert, 2014; Gibney & Drexhage, 2013; Leonard et al., 2012; Linderholm et al., 2012; Miller, Buckley, Seabolt, Mellor, & Kirkpatrick, 2011; Miller et al., 2012; Monji et al., 2013; Muller, 2014; Muller, Myint, & Schwarz, 2012; Torrey et al., 2012; Yolken & Torrey, 2008).

The burgeoning field of gut brain axis analyses is the subject of investigations directed at the understanding of how gut microbes might impact neuronal connections in the CNS. Importantly, the gut microbiome functions to regulate the immune system. The ability of intestinal epithelial cells to actively respond to microbes is mediated by innate immune pattern recognition receptors (Toll-like receptors), NOD-like receptors, and helicases expressed on cell surfaces. During times of mucosal stress, gut homeostasis becomes disrupted (Stockinger, Hornef, & Chassin, 2011). Although there are numerous reports of autism-related altered communities of the intestinal microbiome (Adams, Johansen, Powell, Quig, & Rubin, 2011; Finegold et al., 2010; Finegold, Downes, & Summanen, 2012; Kang et al., 2013; Parracho, Bingham, Gibson, & McCartney, 2005; Williams et al., 2011; Williams, Hornig, Parekh, & Lipkin, 2012), studies of the microbiome in schizophrenia are scant. Preliminary clinical studies report altered pharyngeal and intestinal microbiomes in individuals with schizophrenia as compared to controls (Yolken & Dickerson, 2014). Some insight can be gleaned from rodent studies, where manipulations of gut microbiota do in fact result in behavioral, biochemical, and molecular changes (Collins, Surette, & Bercik, 2012; Foster & McVey Neufeld, 2013; Hsiao et al., 2013; Stilling, Dinan, & Cryan, 2014). Diaz-Heijtz et al. (2011), for example, illustrated that behavioral effects accompanied changes in synaptic markers, synaptophysin and PSD95, in the striatum (Diaz Heijtz et al., 2011). In these rodent studies, animal phenotypes were recovered with manipulations of gnotobiotic (germ-free) animals, vagotomy, probiotics, and/or antibiotics.

The ability of an extrinsically or intrinsically derived microbe, cell, protein, or other product normally found in peripheral circulation to enter to the CNS renders discussion of epithelial and endothelial barriers an important topic. Barrier permeability of the gut, blood–brain barrier, or blood–CSF barrier (Axelsson et al., 1982; Bauer & Kornhuber, 1987; Kirch et al., 1992) can arise from a variety of environmental factors or from genetic mutations in the many biological pathways that impact this cellular architecture. Barrier structures are composed of tight junctions (zonula occludens) that occur between the epithelial cells of the GI lumen of the GI tract; similar tight junction structures comprise the blood–brain barrier (Deli, 2009; Jong & Huang, 2005). The CSF–brain and CSF–blood barrier are slightly different, but these interfaces at the choroid plexus and arachnoid membrane are also relevant areas of access to the brain from the CSF (Laterra, Keep, Betz, & Goldstein, 1999). For schizophrenia, CNS barrier dysfunction has been evaluated

in studies of CSF dynamics and is often attributed to a low-grade, systemic inflammation (Bauer & Kornhuber, 1987; Bechter, 2013; Bechter et al., 2010; Kirch et al., 1992; Severance, Gressitt, Alaedini, et al., 2015). In conjunction with analyses of plasma and CSF protein dynamics, it has been possible to detect evidence for barrier defects or restricted flow, as is particularly evident by the high prevalence of plasma-derived albumin. Abnormal measures of plasma-derived albumin in the CSF are noteworthy because the CNS does not synthesize albumin and its elevation would require transport across the blood–brain or blood–CSF barrier (Tibbling, Link, & Ohman, 1977). An increased albumin ratio can be indicative of either an anatomical barrier defect or a decreased CSF flow rate, a dysfunction with numerous physiological causes (Reiber, 1994; Whedon & Glassey, 2009). The presence of pathological CNS structures such as choroid plexus calcification, arachnoid cysts, and decreased brain volume all can disrupt CSF flow patterns and all of these conditions have been previously associated with psychoses and schizophrenia (Arango et al., 2012; Kuloglu, Caykoylu, Yilmaz, & Ekinci, 2008; Laterra et al., 1999; Marinescu, Udristoiu, & Marinescu, 2013; Narr et al., 2003; Reiber, 1994; Rimol et al., 2012; Sandyk, 1993; Shiga et al., 2012; Veijola et al., 2014; Whedon & Glassey, 2009).

Although a systemic state of inflammation that might impact barrier integrities is most likely the result of immune activation from an environmental source, cellular barrier proteins and related biological pathways may also be the result of genetic associations. Specific barrier-related genes that have been significantly associated with schizophrenia include the tight junction protein claudin-5, cytoskeletal elements such as actin, haptoglobin, and nitric oxide synthetase (Burghardt, Grove, & Ellingrod, 2014; Hall, Trent, Thomas, O'Donovan, & Owen, 2014; Horvath & Mirnics, 2014; Maes et al., 2001; Sun et al., 2004; Wan et al., 2007; Wei & Hemmings, 2005; Yang et al., 2006; Ye et al., 2005; Zhao et al., 2014).

The Maternal–Fetal Environment

The etiology and pathogenesis of schizophrenia likely stem from aberrant neurodevelopment (Lewis & Levitt, 2002; Piper et al., 2012; Rapoport, Giedd, & Gogtay, 2012). Perinatal-occurring environmental disturbances such as maternal stress, infection, or obstetric complications may interact adversely in genetically predisposed offspring to impact neural migration, synaptogenesis, myelination, and synaptic pruning (Knuesel et al., 2014). Epidemiological and preclinical studies clearly indicate that exposure to maternal immune activity is associated with pathological brain development and thus maternal immune activation has become a strong risk factor for the development of schizophrenia (Bauman et al., 2014; Brown & Derkits, 2010; Canetta et al., 2014; Garbett, Hsiao, Kalman, Patterson, & Mirnics, 2012; Meyer, 2013;

Shi, Smith, et al., 2009). Specifically, maternal exposure to cytomegalovirus, herpes simplex virus type 2, influenza, rubella, *T. gondii*, and wheat glutens have all been documented to increase the risk of development of psychosis or schizophrenia (Blomstrom et al., 2012; Brown, Begg, et al., 2004; Brown, Cohen, Greenwald, & Susser, 2000; Brown, Hooton, et al., 2004; Buka et al., 2008; Ellman, Yolken, Buka, Torrey, & Cannon, 2009; Karlsson et al., 2012; Mortensen et al., 2010; Pedersen, Stevens, Pedersen, Norgaard-Pedersen, & Mortensen, 2011; Xiao et al., 2009). This repertoire was recently expanded to include exposure to general inflammation and innate immunity based on measures of C-reactive protein and complement C1q (Canetta et al., 2014; Severance, Gressitt, Buka, Cannon, & Yolken, 2014). In this section, we will review the timelines of brain and immune development and review the evidence where these trajectories might intersect and result in brain disorders (Figure 1).

Neural development is a highly regulated process and since molecules and proteins of the immune system are continually being found to participate in mechanisms of normal brain development, any immune overactivation, or failure of the immune system to activate will impact brain circuitry. The immune environment during pregnancy is a complex balance aimed at preserving immune protection of both sides of the maternal–fetal interface. Several good reviews are available of how this interface is skewed maternally toward inhibiting fetal immunity and regulating and maintaining a protective Th2 environment over the pro-inflammatory cytotoxic Th1 immune response needed to fight infectious disease (Belderbos, Levy, Meyaard, & Bont, 2013; Morein, Blomqvist, & Hu, 2007). Maternal immunity is antibody based and functions to maintain immune tolerance in the fetus and breast-feeding neonate. As a result, all antibodies including autoantibodies are passed to the offspring during this period. Furthermore, while under maternal immune protection, the antigen recognition system of the fetus is immature. Once maternal-derived immune factors are depleted, the immune system of the neonate must be redirected to become competent, including a more active Th1 component. Maturation of the innate and adaptive immune systems is a process that occurs from the fetal stage through adulthood (Belderbos et al., 2013; Knuesel et al., 2014; Morein et al., 2007).

Molecules and proteins of the immune system are intrinsically intertwined with important brain processes during development. These processes include initial proliferation of glia and neurons, consequent migration, programmed cell death, formation of synapses,

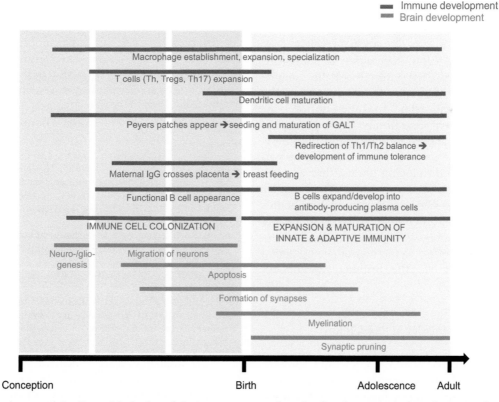

FIGURE 1 Developmental timelines of the brain and the immune system. Complex disorders such as schizophrenia are thought to arise when one or more neurodevelopmental processes are interrupted because of genetic and/or environmental factors. Various immune molecules, proteins, and cells such as C1q and major histocompatibility complex function in the brain during neurodevelopment, suggesting that any disruption in the immune system during pregnancy or postnatally has the ability to compound synaptic misconnections. *Compiled from Belderbos et al. (2013), Dietert et al. (2010), Kneusel et al. (2014), and Morein et al. (2007).*

myelination, and synapse pruning with the overall end-point to establish functional neuronal circuits (Knuesel et al., 2014). Here, we present the case of complement C1q as an example of an immune molecule that is highly active in the developing brain and that is also implicated in schizophrenia-associated gene and environmental studies. In the developing immune system, relevant processes include immune cell appearance, colonization, expansion, and maturation. Complement C1q and MHC1 were some of the first immune molecules identified to function in synapse development and pruning in the brain (Boulanger, 2009; Fourgeaud & Boulanger, 2007; Huh et al., 2000; Shatz, 2009; Stevens et al., 2007). Complement pathway-related genes that have been associated with schizophrenia include the C1QB gene, complement control-related genes, and complement surface receptor gene CD46 (Havik et al., 2011; Zakharyan et al., 2011). Biologically, complement-containing circulating immune complexes were elevated in individuals with schizophrenia compared to controls and a primary antigenic component of these immune complexes was often found to be casein or gluten (Arakelyan et al., 2011; Boyajyan, Khoyetsyan, Tsakanova, & Sim, 2008; Mailian, Boiadzhian, Sogoian, Sim, & Manukian, 2005; Mayilyan, Weinberger, & Sim, 2008; Severance, Gressitt, et al., 2012; Vetlugina, Logvinovich, Maslennikova, & Vasil'eva, 1984). Finally, elevated levels of maternal C1q IgG have been found to increase the odds for psychosis in offspring (Severance, Gressitt, Buka, et al., 2014). Given that maternal IgG antibodies begin transfer to the fetus at 13 weeks' gestation and approach maternal levels at time of birth (Malek, Sager, Kuhn, Nicolaides, & Schneider, 1996; Simister, 2003), this study introduces the interesting possibility that autoantibodies to C1q present in the mother might interact with fetal C1q during critical periods of brain development. Specifically, if the process of normal C1q-mediated synapse formation and pruning is interrupted, synaptic connections will presumably be permanently altered in the developing brain either through overpruning or through underpruning. Other studies have connected the presence of maternal autoantibodies and with the development of autism spectrum disorders where maternal autoantibodies have been found to recognize brain proteins critical to the neurodevelopmental process (Braunschweig et al., 2013; Brimberg, Sadiq, Gregersen, & Diamond, 2013).

CONCLUDING REMARKS

This chapter provides an introduction into some of the mechanisms by which the immune system might be involved in the development of schizophrenia. If schizophrenia has an immune component, and if evidence indicates a primary rather than secondary role in disease pathogenesis, then interventions that target the immune system are warranted. Toward this end, one purpose of this review was to emphasize the very diverse and multiple ways in which the immune system might impact schizophrenia. Its etiology, pathogenesis, and pathophysiology may not just be a function of exposure to an infectious agent or food antigen or dysfunctional innate immunity. Therefore, designing a treatment strategy to an extraordinarily heterogeneous disease is difficult. It is extremely important to be able to identify the subsets of people who have immune-related conditions and fully characterize what kind of immune anomaly is present. Only in this manner can tailored treatments be evaluated. In the future, therapeutic strategies might involve monoclonal or monospecific antibodies to antagonize or inactivate antigenic or other protein targets or use of other immunosuppressive treatments. The rapid advance in the use of monoclonal antibodies for the treatment of autoimmune disorders provides hope that such therapies can also have a major impact on schizophrenia as well. Dietary interventions have been successful in some instances clinically, and developmental compounds aimed to normalize gut function and endothelial barriers in other capacities appear promising (Freeman, 2013; Jackson et al., 2012; Kristoff et al., 2014; Whiteley et al., 2010, 2012). An improved understanding of the role of immune activation in schizophrenia may lead, not only to an improved understanding of disease pathogenesis but also to a new methods for the prevention and treatment of this devastating disorder.

Acknowledgments

This work was supported by National Institute of Mental Health P50 Silvio O. Conte Center at Johns Hopkins (grant #MH-94268) and by the Stanley Medical Research Institute.

References

Adams, J. B., Johansen, L. J., Powell, L. D., Quig, D., & Rubin, R. A. (2011). Gastrointestinal flora and gastrointestinal status in children with autism – comparisons to typical children and correlation with autism severity. *BMC Gastroenterology, 11*, 22. http://dx.doi.org/10.1186/1471-230X-11-22.

Alaedini, A., & Green, P. H. (2008). Autoantibodies in celiac disease. [Review] *Autoimmunity, 41*(1), 19–26. http://dx.doi.org/10.1080/08916930701619219.

Alberts, B. (2008). *Molecular biology of the cell* (5th ed.). New York: Garland Science.

Allen, J. L., Liu, X., Pelkowski, S., Palmer, B., Conrad, K., Oberdorster, G., et al. (2014). Early postnatal exposure to ultrafine particulate matter air pollution: persistent ventriculomegaly, neurochemical disruption, and glial activation preferentially in male mice. [Research Support, N.I.H., Extramural] *Environmental Health Perspectives, 122*(9), 939–945. http://dx.doi.org/10.1289/ehp.1307984.

Allen, J. L., Liu, X., Weston, D., Prince, L., Oberdorster, G., Finkelstein, J. N., & Cory-Slechta, D. A. (2014). Developmental exposure to concentrated ambient ultrafine particulate matter air pollution in mice results in persistent and sex-dependent behavioral neurotoxicity and glial activation. [Research Support, N.I.H., Extramural] *Toxicological Sciences: An Official Journal of the Society of Toxicology, 140*(1), 160–178. http://dx.doi.org/10.1093/toxsci/kfu059.

Amkraut, A., Solomon, G. F., Allansmith, M., McClellan, B., & Rappaport, M. (1973). Immunoglobulins and improvement in acute schizophrenic reactions. *Archives of General Psychiatry, 28*(5), 673–677.

Arakelyan, A., Zakharyan, R., Khoyetsyan, A., Poghosyan, D., Aroutiounian, R., Mrazek, F., et al. (2011). Functional characterization of the complement receptor type 1 and its circulating ligands in patients with schizophrenia. *BMC Clinical Pathology, 11*, 10. http://dx.doi.org/10.1186/1472-6890-11-10.

Arango, C., Rapado-Castro, M., Reig, S., Castro-Fornieles, J., Gonzalez-Pinto, A., Otero, S., et al. (2012). Progressive brain changes in children and adolescents with first-episode psychosis. [Comparative Study Multicenter Study Research Support, Non-U.S. Gov't] *Archives of General Psychiatry, 69*(1), 16–26. http://dx.doi.org/10.1001/archgenpsychiatry.2011.150.

Arias, I., Sorlozano, A., Villegas, E., de Dios Luna, J., McKenney, K., Cervilla, J., et al. (2012). Infectious agents associated with schizophrenia: a meta-analysis. [Meta-Analysis Review] *Schizophrenia Research, 136*(1–3), 128–136. http://dx.doi.org/10.1016/j.schres.2011.10.026.

Arnedo, J., Svrakic, D. M., Del Val, C., Romero-Zaliz, R., Hernandez-Cuervo, H., Fanous, A. H., et al. (2014). Uncovering the hidden risk architecture of the schizophrenias: confirmation in three independent genome-wide association studies. *American Journal of Psychiatry.* http://dx.doi.org/10.1176/appi.ajp.2014.14040435.

Axelsson, R., Martensson, E., & Alling, C. (1982). Impairment of the blood–brain barrier as an aetiological factor in paranoid psychosis. [Research Support, Non-U.S. Gov't] *The British Journal of Psychiatry: The Journal of Mental Science, 141*, 273–281.

Babulas, V., Factor-Litvak, P., Goetz, R., Schaefer, C. A., & Brown, A. S. (2006). Prenatal exposure to maternal genital and reproductive infections and adult schizophrenia. [Research Support, N.I.H., Extramural Research Support, Non-U.S. Gov't] *American Journal of Psychiatry, 163*(5), 927–929. http://dx.doi.org/10.1176/appi.ajp.163.5.927.

Baldwin, J. (1980). Schizophrenia and physical disease: a preliminary analysis of the data from the Oxford Record Linkage Study. In G. Hemmings (Ed.), *Biochemistry of schizophrenia and addiction.* Lancaster, England: MTP Press. (Reprinted from: Not in File).

Bauer, K., & Kornhuber, J. (1987). Blood-cerebrospinal fluid barrier in schizophrenic patients. *European Archives of Psychiatry and Neurological Sciences, 236*(5), 257–259.

Bauman, M. D., Iosif, A. M., Smith, S. E., Bregere, C., Amaral, D. G., & Patterson, P. H. (2014). Activation of the maternal immune system during pregnancy alters behavioral development of rhesus monkey offspring. [Research Support, N.I.H., Extramural Research Support, Non-U.S. Gov't] *Biological Psychiatry, 75*(4), 332–341. http://dx.doi.org/10.1016/j.biopsych.2013.06.025.

Bechter, K. (2013). Updating the mild encephalitis hypothesis of schizophrenia. [Review] *Progress in Neuro-Psychopharmacology & Biological Psychiatry, 42*, 71–91. http://dx.doi.org/10.1016/j.pnpbp.2012.06.019.

Bechter, K., Reiber, H., Herzog, S., Fuchs, D., Tumani, H., & Maxeiner, H. G. (2010). Cerebrospinal fluid analysis in affective and schizophrenic spectrum disorders: identification of subgroups with immune responses and blood-CSF barrier dysfunction. [Research Support, Non-U.S. Gov't] *Journal of Psychiatric Research, 44*(5), 321–330. http://dx.doi.org/10.1016/j.jpsychires.2009.08.008.

Belderbos, M. E., Levy, O., Meyaard, L., & Bont, L. (2013). Plasma-mediated immune suppression: a neonatal perspective. [Review] *Pediatric Allergy and Immunology: Official Publication of the European Society of Pediatric Allergy and Immunology, 24*(2), 102–113. http://dx.doi.org/10.1111/pai.12023.

Benoit, M. E., & Tenner, A. J. (2011). Complement protein C1q-mediated neuroprotection is correlated with regulation of neuronal gene and microRNA expression. [Comparative Study Research Support, N.I.H., Extramural Research Support, Non-U.S. Gov't Research Support, U.S. Gov't, Non-P.H.S.] *The Journal of Neuroscience: The Official Journal of the Society for Neuroscience, 31*(9), 3459–3469. http://dx.doi.org/10.1523/JNEUROSCI.3932-10.2011.

Benros, M. E., Eaton, W. W., & Mortensen, P. B. (2014). The epidemiologic evidence linking autoimmune diseases and psychosis. [Research Support, N.I.H., Extramural Research Support, Non-U.S. Gov't] *Biological Psychiatry, 75*(4), 300–306. http://dx.doi.org/10.1016/j.biopsych.2013.09.023.

Benros, M. E., Nielsen, P. R., Nordentoft, M., Eaton, W. W., Dalton, S. O., & Mortensen, P. B. (2011). Autoimmune diseases and severe infections as risk factors for schizophrenia: a 30-year population-based register study. [Research Support, N.I.H., Extramural Research Support, Non-U.S. Gov't] *American Journal of Psychiatry, 168*(12), 1303–1310. http://dx.doi.org/10.1176/appi.ajp.2011.11030516.

Beumer, W., Drexhage, R. C., De Wit, H., Versnel, M. A., Drexhage, H. A., & Cohen, D. (2012). Increased level of serum cytokines, chemokines and adipokines in patients with schizophrenia is associated with disease and metabolic syndrome. [Research Support, Non-U.S. Gov't] *Psychoneuroendocrinology, 37*(12), 1901–1911. http://dx.doi.org/10.1016/j.psyneuen.2012.04.001.

Bialas, A. R., & Stevens, B. (2013). TGF-beta signaling regulates neuronal C1q expression and developmental synaptic refinement. [Research Support, N.I.H., Extramural Research Support, Non-U.S. Gov't] *Nature Neuroscience, 16*(12), 1773–1782. http://dx.doi.org/10.1038/nn.3560.

Blomstrom, A., Karlsson, H., Wicks, S., Yang, S., Yolken, R. H., & Dalman, C. (2012). Maternal antibodies to infectious agents and risk for non-affective psychoses in the offspring – a matched case-control study. [Research Support, Non-U.S. Gov't] *Schizophrenia Research, 140*(1–3), 25–30. http://dx.doi.org/10.1016/j.schres.2012.06.035.

Bock, E., & Rafaelsen, O. J. (1974). Schizophrenia: proteins in blood and cerebrospinal fluid. A review. [Review] *Danish Medical Bulletin, 21*(3), 93–105.

Boehme, D. H., Cottrell, J. C., Dohan, F. C., & Hillegass, L. M. (1973). Fluorescent antibody studies of immunoglobulin binding by brain tissues. Demonstration of cytoplasmic fluorescence by direct and indirect testing in schizophrenic and nonschizophrenic subjects. *Archives of General Psychiatry, 28*(2), 202–207.

Boulanger, L. M. (2009). Immune proteins in brain development and synaptic plasticity. *Neuron, 64*(1), 93–109. http://dx.doi.org/10.1016/j.neuron.2009.09.001 pii:S0896-6273(09)00678-3.

Boyajyan, A., Khoyetsyan, A., Tsakanova, G., & Sim, R. B. (2008). Cryoglobulins as indicators of upregulated immune response in schizophrenia. *Clinical Biochemistry, 41*(6), 355–360. http://dx.doi.org/10.1016/j.clinbiochem.2007.11.014 pii:S0009-9120(07)00478-X.

Braunschweig, D., Krakowiak, P., Duncanson, P., Boyce, R., Hansen, R. L., Ashwood, P., et al. (2013). Autism-specific maternal autoantibodies recognize critical proteins in developing brain. *Translational Psychiatry, 3*, e277. http://dx.doi.org/10.1038/tp.2013.50.

Brimberg, L., Sadiq, A., Gregersen, P. K., & Diamond, B. (2013). Brain-reactive IgG correlates with autoimmunity in mothers of a child with an autism spectrum disorder. *Molecular Psychiatry.* http://dx.doi.org/10.1038/mp.2013.101.

Brown, A. S., Begg, M. D., Gravenstein, S., Schaefer, C. A., Wyatt, R. J., Bresnahan, M., et al. (2004). Serologic evidence of prenatal influenza in the etiology of schizophrenia. [Comparative Study] *Archives of General Psychiatry, 61*(8), 774–780. http://dx.doi.org/10.1001/archpsyc.61.8.774.

Brown, A. S., Cohen, P., Greenwald, S., & Susser, E. (2000). Nonaffective psychosis after prenatal exposure to rubella. [Research Support, Non-U.S. Gov't Research Support, U.S. Gov't, P.H.S.] *The American Journal of Psychiatry, 157*(3), 438–443.

Brown, A. S., & Derkits, E. J. (2010). Prenatal infection and schizophrenia: a review of epidemiologic and translational studies. [Research Support, N.I.H., Extramural Review] *The American Journal of Psychiatry, 167*(3), 261–280. http://dx.doi.org/10.1176/appi.ajp.2009.09030361.

Brown, A. S., Hooton, J., Schaefer, C. A., Zhang, H., Petkova, E., Babulas, V., et al. (2004). Elevated maternal interleukin-8 levels and risk of schizophrenia in adult offspring. [Research Support, Non-U.S. Gov't Research Support, U.S. Gov't, P.H.S.] *The American Journal of Psychiatry, 161*(5), 889–895.

Buka, S. L., Cannon, T. D., Torrey, E. F., & Yolken, R. H. (2008). Maternal exposure to herpes simplex virus and risk of psychosis among adult offspring. [Multicenter Study Research Support, N.I.H., Extramural Research Support, Non-U.S. Gov't] *Biological Psychiatry*, 63(8), 809–815. http://dx.doi.org/10.1016/j.biopsych.2007.09.022.

Burghardt, K., Grove, T., & Ellingrod, V. (2014). Endothelial nitric oxide synthetase genetic variants, metabolic syndrome and endothelial function in schizophrenia. [Research Support, N.I.H., Extramural Research Support, Non-U.S. Gov't Research Support, U.S. Gov't, Non-P.H.S.] *Journal of Psychopharmacology*, 28(4), 349–356. http://dx.doi.org/10.1177/0269881113516200.

Burian, L., Kubikova, A., & Krejcova, O. (1964). Human antiglobulins in the serum of schizophrenic patients. *Ceskoslovenska Psychiatrie*, 60, 26–29.

Canetta, S., Sourander, A., Surcel, H. M., Hinkka-Yli-Salomaki, S., Leiviska, J., Kellendonk, C., et al. (2014). Elevated maternal C-reactive protein and increased risk of schizophrenia in a national birth cohort. *American Journal of Psychiatry*. http://dx.doi.org/10.1176/appi.ajp.2014.13121579.

Cascella, N. G., Kryszak, D., Bhatti, B., Gregory, P., Kelly, D. L., Mc Evoy, J. P., et al. (2011). Prevalence of celiac disease and gluten sensitivity in the United States clinical antipsychotic trials of intervention effectiveness study population. *Schizophrenia Bulletin*, 37(1), 94–100. http://dx.doi.org/10.1093/schbul/sbp055.

Collins, S. M., Surette, M., & Bercik, P. (2012). The interplay between the intestinal microbiota and the brain. [Research Support, Non-U.S. Gov't Review] *Nature Reviews Microbiology*, 10(11), 735–742. http://dx.doi.org/10.1038/nrmicro2876.

Corvin, A., & Morris, D. W. (2014). Genome-wide association studies: findings at the major histocompatibility complex locus in psychosis. *Biological Psychiatry*, 75(4), 276–283. http://dx.doi.org/10.1016/j.biopsych.2013.09.018.

Dalman, C., Allebeck, P., Gunnell, D., Harrison, G., Kristensson, K., Lewis, G., et al. (2008). Infections in the CNS during childhood and the risk of subsequent psychotic illness: a cohort study of more than one million Swedish subjects. [Comparative Study Research Support, Non-U.S. Gov't] *American Journal of Psychiatry*, 165(1), 59–65. http://dx.doi.org/10.1176/appi.ajp.2007.07050740.

Dalmau, J., Tuzun, E., Wu, H. Y., Masjuan, J., Rossi, J. E., Voloschin, A., et al. (2007). Paraneoplastic anti-N-methyl-D-aspartate receptor encephalitis associated with ovarian teratoma. [Clinical Trial Comparative Study Research Support, N.I.H., Extramural] *Annals of Neurology*, 61(1), 25–36. http://dx.doi.org/10.1002/ana.21050.

Deakin, J., Lennox, B. R., & Zandi, M. S. (2014). Antibodies to the N-methyl-D-aspartate receptor and other synaptic proteins in psychosis. [Review] *Biological Psychiatry*, 75(4), 284–291. http://dx.doi.org/10.1016/j.biopsych.2013.07.018.

Deli, M. A. (2009). Potential use of tight junction modulators to reversibly open membranous barriers and improve drug delivery. *Biochimica et Biophysica Acta-Biomembranes*, 1788(4), 892–910. http://dx.doi.org/10.1016/j.bbamem.2008.09.016.

Demjaha, A., MacCabe, J. H., & Murray, R. M. (2012). How genes and environmental factors determine the different neurodevelopmental trajectories of schizophrenia and bipolar disorder. *Schizophrenia Bulletin*, 38(2), 209–214. http://dx.doi.org/10.1093/schbul/sbr100.

Diaz Heijtz, R., Wang, S., Anuar, F., Qian, Y., Bjorkholm, B., Samuelsson, A., et al. (2011). Normal gut microbiota modulates brain development and behavior. *Proceedings of the National Academy of Sciences of the United States of America*, 108(7), 3047–3052. http://dx.doi.org/10.1073/pnas.1010529108. Epub 2011 Jan 31. PMID: 21282636.

Dickerson, F., Stallings, C., Origoni, A., Copp, C., Khushalani, S., & Yolken, R. (2010). Antibodies to measles in individuals with recent onset psychosis. [Research Support, Non-U.S. Gov't] *Schizophrenia Research*, 119(1–3), 89–94. http://dx.doi.org/10.1016/j.schres.2009.12.010.

Dickerson, F., Stallings, C., Origoni, A., Vaughan, C., Khushalani, S., Leister, F., et al. (2010). Markers of gluten sensitivity and celiac disease in recent-onset psychosis and multi-episode schizophrenia. *Biological Psychiatry*, 68(1), 100–104. http://dx.doi.org/10.1016/j.biopsych.2010.03.021 pii:S0006-3223(10)00250-7.

Dickerson, F., Stallings, C., Origoni, A., Vaughan, C., Khushalani, S., Yang, S., et al. (2013). C-reactive protein is elevated in schizophrenia. [Research Support, Non-U.S. Gov't] *Schizophrenia Research*, 143(1), 198–202. http://dx.doi.org/10.1016/j.schres.2012.10.041.

Dietert, R. R., DeWitt, J. C., Germolec, D. R., & Zelikoff, J. T. (2010). Breaking patterns of environmentally influenced disease for health risk reduction: immune perspectives. *Environmental Health Perspectives*, 118(8), 1091–1099. http://dx.doi.org/10.1289/ehp.1001971. Epub 2010 May 18. Review. PMID: 20483701.

Dohan, F. C. (1969). Is celiac disease a clue to the pathogenesis of schizophrenia? *Mental Hygiene*, 53(4), 525–529.

Dohan, F. C. (1970). Coeliac disease and schizophrenia. *Lancet*, 1(7652), 897–898.

Dohan, F. C. (1973). Coeliac disease and schizophrenia. *British Medical Journal*, 3(5870), 51–52.

Dohan, F. C. (1980). Celiac disease and schizophrenia. *The New England Journal of Medicine*, 302(22), 1262.

Dohan, F. C., Harper, E. H., Clark, M. H., Rodrigue, R. B., & Zigas, V. (1984). Is schizophrenia rare if grain is rare? *Biological Psychiatry*, 19(3), 385–399.

Drexhage, R. C., Knijff, E. M., Padmos, R. C., Heul-Nieuwenhuijzen, L., Beumer, W., Versnel, M. A., et al. (2010). The mononuclear phagocyte system and its cytokine inflammatory networks in schizophrenia and bipolar disorder. *Expert Review of Neurotherapeutics*, 10(1), 59–76. http://dx.doi.org/10.1586/ern.09.144.

Drexhage, R. C., Weigelt, K., van Beveren, N., Cohen, D., Versnel, M. A., Nolen, W. A., et al. (2011). Immune and neuroimmune alterations in mood disorders and schizophrenia. [Research Support, Non-U.S. Gov't Review] *International Review of Neurobiology*, 101, 169–201. http://dx.doi.org/10.1016/B978-0-12-387718-5.00007-9.

Durell, J., & Archer, E. G. (1976). Plasma proteins in schizophrenia: a review. [Research Support, U.S. Gov't, Non-P.H.S. Review] *Schizophrenia Bulletin*, 2(1), 147–159.

Eaton, W., Hayward, C., & Ram, R. (1992). Schizophrenia and rheumatoid arthritis: a review. *Schizophrenia Research*, 6, 181–192.

Eaton, W., Mortensen, P. B., Agerbo, E., Byrne, M., Mors, O., & Ewald, H. (2004). Coeliac disease and schizophrenia: population based case control study with linkage of Danish national registers. [Research Support, Non-U.S. Gov't Research Support, U.S. Gov't, P.H.S.] *British Medical Journal*, 328(7437), 438–439. http://dx.doi.org/10.1136/bmj.328.7437.438.

Eaton, W. W., Byrne, M., Ewald, H., Mors, O., Chen, C. Y., Agerbo, E., et al. (2006). Association of schizophrenia and autoimmune diseases: linkage of Danish national registers. [Comparative Study Research Support, N.I.H., Extramural Research Support, Non-U.S. Gov't] *The American Journal of Psychiatry*, 163(3), 521–528. http://dx.doi.org/10.1176/appi.ajp.163.3.521.

Ellman, L. M., Yolken, R. H., Buka, S. L., Torrey, E. F., & Cannon, T. D. (2009). Cognitive functioning prior to the onset of psychosis: the role of fetal exposure to serologically determined influenza infection. [Research Support, N.I.H., Extramural Research Support, Non-U.S. Gov't] *Biological Psychiatry*, 65(12), 1040–1047. http://dx.doi.org/10.1016/j.biopsych.2008.12.015.

Ercolini, A. M., & Miller, S. D. (2009). The role of infections in autoimmune disease. [Review] *Clinical & Experimental Immunology*, 155(1), 1–15. http://dx.doi.org/10.1111/j.1365-2249.2008.03834.x.

Esquirol, J. E. (1845). *Mental maladies, a treatise on insanity*. Philadelphia, PA: Lea and Blanchard.

Ezeoke, A., Mellor, A., Buckley, P., & Miller, B. (2013). A systematic, quantitative review of blood autoantibodies in schizophrenia. [Review] *Schizophrenia Research*, 150(1), 245–251. http://dx.doi.org/10.1016/j.schres.2013.07.029.

Fellerhoff, B., Laumbacher, B., Mueller, N., Gu, S., & Wank, R. (2007). Associations between Chlamydophila infections, schizophrenia and risk of HLA-A10. [Comparative StudyResearch Support, Non-U.S. Gov't] *Molecular Psychiatry*, 12(3), 264–272. http://dx.doi.org/10.1038/sj.mp.4001925.

Fessel, W. J. (1962a). Autoimmunity and mental illness. A preliminary report. *Archives of General Psychiatry*, 6, 320–323.

Fessel, W. J. (1962b). Blood proteins in functional psychoses. A review of the literature and unifying hypothesis. *Archives of General Psychiatry*, 6, 132–148.

Fillman, S. G., Cloonan, N., Catts, V. S., Miller, L. C., Wong, J., McCrossin, T., et al. (2013). Increased inflammatory markers identified in the dorsolateral prefrontal cortex of individuals with schizophrenia. *Molecular Psychiatry*, 18(2), 206–214. http://dx.doi.org/10.1038/mp.2012.110.

Fillman, S. G., Sinclair, D., Fung, S. J., Webster, M. J., & Shannon Weickert, C. (2014). Markers of inflammation and stress distinguish subsets of individuals with schizophrenia and bipolar disorder. *Translational Psychiatry*, 4, e365. http://dx.doi.org/10.1038/tp.2014.8.

Fine, R., Zhang, J., & Stevens, H. E. (2014). Prenatal stress and inhibitory neuron systems: implications for neuropsychiatric disorders. [Research Support, N.I.H., Extramural Research Support, Non-U.S. Gov't] *Molecular Psychiatry*, 19(6), 641–651. http://dx.doi.org/10.1038/mp.2014.35.

Fineberg, A. M., & Ellman, L. M. (2013). Inflammatory cytokines and neurological and neurocognitive alterations in the course of schizophrenia. [Research Support, N.I.H., Extramural Research Support, Non-U.S. Gov't Review] *Biological Psychiatry*, 73(10), 951–966. http://dx.doi.org/10.1016/j.biopsych.2013.01.001.

Finegold, S. M., Dowd, S. E., Gontcharova, V., Liu, C., Henley, K. E., Wolcott, R. D., et al. (2010). Pyrosequencing study of fecal microflora of autistic and control children. *Anaerobe*, 16(4), 444–453. http://dx.doi.org/10.1016/j.anaerobe.2010.06.008.

Finegold, S. M., Downes, J., & Summanen, P. H. (2012). Microbiology of regressive autism. [Review] *Anaerobe*, 18(2), 260–262. http://dx.doi.org/10.1016/j.anaerobe.2011.12.018.

Foster, J. A., & McVey Neufeld, K. A. (2013). Gut-brain axis: how the microbiome influences anxiety and depression. [Research Support, Non-U.S. Gov't] *Trends in Neurosciences*, 36(5), 305–312. http://dx.doi.org/10.1016/j.tins.2013.01.005.

Fourgeaud, L., & Boulanger, L. M. (2007). Synapse remodeling, compliments of the complement system. [Comment] *Cell*, 131(6), 1034–1036. http://dx.doi.org/10.1016/j.cell.2007.11.031.

Fraga, D. B., Deroza, P. F., Ghedim, F. V., Steckert, A. V., De Luca, R. D., Silverio, A., et al. (2011). Prenatal exposure to cigarette smoke causes persistent changes in the oxidative balance and in DNA structural integrity in rats submitted to the animal model of schizophrenia. [Research Support, Non-U.S. Gov't] *Journal of Psychiatric Research*, 45(11), 1497–1503. http://dx.doi.org/10.1016/j.jpsychires.2011.06.007.

Freeman, H. J. (2013). Non-dietary forms of treatment for adult celiac disease. [Review] *World Journal of Gastrointestinal Pharmacology and Therapeutics*, 4(4), 108–112. http://dx.doi.org/10.4292/wjgpt.v4.i4.108.

Frodl, T., & Amico, F. (2014). Is there an association between peripheral immune markers and structural/functional neuroimaging findings? *Progress in Neuropsychopharmacology & Biological Psychiatry*, 48, 295–303. http://dx.doi.org/10.1016/j.pnpbp.2012.12.013.

Gammack, D. B., & Hector, R. I. (1965). A Study of Serum Proteins in Acute Schizophrenia. *Clinical Science*, 28, 469–475.

Garate, I., Garcia-Bueno, B., Madrigal, J. L., Caso, J. R., Alou, L., Gomez-Lus, M. L., et al. (2013). Stress-induced neuroinflammation: role of the Toll-like receptor-4 pathway. [Research Support, Non-U.S. Gov't] *Biological Psychiatry*, 73(1), 32–43. http://dx.doi.org/10.1016/j.biopsych.2012.07.005.

Garbett, K. A., Hsiao, E. Y., Kalman, S., Patterson, P. H., & Mirnics, K. (2012). Effects of maternal immune activation on gene expression patterns in the fetal brain. [Research Support, N.I.H., Extramural Research Support, Non-U.S. Gov't] *Translational Psychiatry*, 2, e98. http://dx.doi.org/10.1038/tp.2012.24.

Gibney, S. M., & Drexhage, H. A. (2013). Evidence for a dysregulated immune system in the etiology of psychiatric disorders. *Journal of Neuroimmune Pharmacology: The Official Journal of the Society on NeuroImmune Pharmacology*, 8(4), 900–920. http://dx.doi.org/10.1007/s11481-013-9462-8.

Glebov, V. S. (1972). Clinico-immunologic correlations in the period of development of therapeutical remissions in continuous forms of schizophrenia. *Zhurnal nevropatologii i psikhiatrii imeni S.S. Korsakova*, 72(8), 1191–1195.

Graham, K. L., Carson, C. M., Ezeoke, A., Buckley, P. F., & Miller, B. J. (2014). Urinary tract infections in acute psychosis. [Research Support, Non-U.S. Gov't] *The Journal of Clinical Psychiatry*, 75(4), 379–385. http://dx.doi.org/10.4088/JCP.13m08469.

Green, P. H., Alaedini, A., Sander, H. W., Brannagan, T. H., 3rd, Latov, N., & Chin, R. L. (2005). Mechanisms underlying celiac disease and its neurologic manifestations. [Review] *Cellular and Molecular Life Sciences*, 62(7–8), 791–799. http://dx.doi.org/10.1007/s00018-004-4109-9.

Guandalini, S., & Assiri, A. (2014). Celiac disease: a review. [Review] *JAMA Pediatrics*, 168(3), 272–278. http://dx.doi.org/10.1001/jamapediatrics.2013.3858.

Gurassa, W. P., & Fleischhacker, H. H. (1958). An investigation of the Rosenow antibody antigen skin reaction in schizophrenia. *Journal of Neurology, Neurosurgery, and Psychiatry*, 21(2), 141–145.

Gurevich, Z. P. (1969). Incomplete anti-tissue autoantibodies in schizophrenia. *Zhurnal nevropatologii i psikhiatrii imeni S.S. Korsakova*, 69(11), 1683–1687.

Hall, J., Trent, S., Thomas, K. L., O'Donovan, M. C., & Owen, M. J. (2014). Genetic risk for schizophrenia: convergence on synaptic pathways involved in plasticity. [Review] *Biological Psychiatry*. http://dx.doi.org/10.1016/j.biopsych.2014.07.011.

Havik, B., Le Hellard, S., Rietschel, M., Lybaek, H., Djurovic, S., Mattheisen, M., et al. (2011). The complement control-related genes CSMD1 and CSMD2 associate to schizophrenia. *Biological Psychiatry*, 70(1), 35–42. http://dx.doi.org/10.1016/j.biopsych.2011.01.030 pii:S0006-3223(11)00122-3.

Heath, R. G. (1967). Schizophrenia: pathogenetic theories. *International Journal of Psychiatry*, 3(5), 407–410.

Heath, R. G., & Krupp, I. M. (1967). Schizophrenia as an immunologic disorder. I. Demonstration of antibrain globulins by fluorescent antibody techniques. *Archives of General Psychiatry*, 16(1), 1–9.

Heath, R. G., Krupp, I. M., Byers, L. W., & Lijekvist, J. I. (1967a). Schizophrenia as an immunologic disorder. 3. Effects of antimonkey and antihuman brain antibody on brain function. *Archives of General Psychiatry*, 16(1), 24–33.

Heath, R. G., Krupp, I. M., Byers, L. W., & Liljekvist, J. I. (1967b). Schizophrenia as an immunologic disorder. II. Effects of serum protein fractions on brain function. *Archives of General Psychiatry*, 16(1), 10–23.

Hendrie, H. C., Paraskevas, F., & Varsamis, J. (1972). Gamma globulin levels in psychiatric patients. *Canadian Psychiatric Association Journal*, 17(2), 93–97.

Horvath, S., & Mirnics, K. (2014). Immune system disturbances in schizophrenia. [Research Support, N.I.H., Extramural Review] *Biological Psychiatry*, 75(4), 316–323. http://dx.doi.org/10.1016/j.biopsych.2013.06.010.

Hsiao, E. Y., McBride, S. W., Hsien, S., Sharon, G., Hyde, E. R., McCue, T., et al. (2013). Microbiota modulate behavioral and physiological abnormalities associated with neurodevelopmental disorders. [Research Support, N.I.H., Extramural Research Support, Non-U.S. Gov't Research Support, U.S. Gov't, Non-P.H.S.] *Cell*, 155(7), 1451–1463. http://dx.doi.org/10.1016/j.cell.2013.11.024.

Huh, G. S., Boulanger, L. M., Du, H., Riquelme, P. A., Brotz, T. M., & Shatz, C. J. (2000). Functional requirement for class I MHC in CNS development and plasticity. [Research Support, Non-U.S. Gov't Research Support, U.S. Gov't, P.H.S.] *Science*, 290(5499), 2155–2159.

Jackson, J., Eaton, W., Cascella, N., Fasano, A., Warfel, D., Feldman, S., et al. (2012). A gluten-free diet in people with schizophrenia and anti-tissue transglutaminase or anti-gliadin antibodies. [Letter] *Schizophrenia Research*, 140(1–3), 262–263. http://dx.doi.org/10.1016/j.schres.2012.06.011.

Jones, A. L., Mowry, B. J., Pender, M. P., & Greer, J. M. (2005). Immune dysregulation and self-reactivity in schizophrenia: do some cases of schizophrenia have an autoimmune basis? [Review] *Immunology and Cell Biology*, 83(1), 9–17. http://dx.doi.org/10.1111/j.1440-1711.2005.01305.x.

Jong, A., & Huang, S. H. (2005). Blood–brain barrier drug discovery for central nervous system infections. *Current Drug Targets – Infectious Disorders*, 5(1), 65–72.

Kang, D. W., Park, J. G., Ilhan, Z. E., Wallstrom, G., Labaer, J., Adams, J. B., et al. (2013). Reduced incidence of Prevotella and other fermenters in intestinal microflora of autistic children. [Research Support, Non-U.S. Gov't] *PLoS One*, 8(7), e68322. http://dx.doi.org/10.1371/journal.pone.0068322.

Karlsson, H., Bachmann, S., Schroder, J., McArthur, J., Torrey, E. F., & Yolken, R. H. (2001). Retroviral RNA identified in the cerebrospinal fluids and brains of individuals with schizophrenia. [Research Support, Non-U.S. Gov't] *Proceedings of the National Academy of Sciences of the United States of America*, 98(8), 4634–4639. http://dx.doi.org/10.1073/pnas.061021998.

Karlsson, H., Blomstrom, A., Wicks, S., Yang, S., Yolken, R. H., & Dalman, C. (2012). Maternal antibodies to dietary antigens and risk for nonaffective psychosis in offspring. *The American Journal of Psychiatry*. http://dx.doi.org/10.1176/appi.ajp.2012.11081197.

Karlsson, H., Schroder, J., Bachmann, S., Bottmer, C., & Yolken, R. H. (2004). HERV-W-related RNA detected in plasma from individuals with recent-onset schizophrenia or schizoaffective disorder. [Letter] *Molecular Psychiatry*, 9(1), 12–13. http://dx.doi.org/10.1038/sj.mp.4001439.

Kavanagh, D. H., Tansey, K. E., O'Donovan, M. C., & Owen, M. J. (2014). Schizophrenia genetics: emerging themes for a complex disorder. *Molecular Psychiatry*. http://dx.doi.org/10.1038/mp.2014.148.

Khandaker, G. M., Stochl, J., Zammit, S., Lewis, G., & Jones, P. B. (2014). Childhood Epstein-Barr Virus infection and subsequent risk of psychotic experiences in adolescence: a population-based prospective serological study. [Research Support, Non-U.S. Gov't] *Schizophrenia Research*, 158(1–3), 19–24. http://dx.doi.org/10.1016/j.schres.2014.05.019.

Kirch, D. G. (1993). Infection and autoimmunity as etiologic factors in schizophrenia: a review and reappraisal. [Review] *Schizophrenia Bulletin*, 19(2), 355–370.

Kirch, D. G., Alexander, R. C., Suddath, R. L., Papadopoulos, N. M., Kaufmann, C. A., Daniel, D. G., et al. (1992). Blood-CSF barrier permeability and central nervous system immunoglobulin G in schizophrenia. *Journal of Neural Transmission. General Section*, 89(3), 219–232.

Knuesel, I., Chicha, L., Britschgi, M., Schobel, S. A., Bodmer, M., Hellings, J. A., et al. (2014). Maternal immune activation and abnormal brain development across CNS disorders. [Review] *Nature Reviews. Neurology*, 10(11), 643–660. http://dx.doi.org/10.1038/nrneurol.2014.187.

Kristoff, J., Haret-Richter, G., Ma, D., Ribeiro, R. M., Xu, C., Cornell, E., et al. (2014). Early microbial translocation blockade reduces SIV-mediated inflammation and viral replication. *The Journal of Clinical Investigation*, 124(6), 2802–2806. http://dx.doi.org/10.1172/JCI75090.

Kuloglu, M., Caykoylu, A., Yilmaz, E., & Ekinci, O. (2008). A left temporal lobe arachnoid cyst in a patient with schizophrenia-like psychosis: a case report. [Case Reports Letter] *Progress in Neuro-Psychopharmacology & Biological Psychiatry*, 32(5), 1353–1354. http://dx.doi.org/10.1016/j.pnpbp.2008.04.014.

Lachance, L. R., & McKenzie, K. (2014). Biomarkers of gluten sensitivity in patients with non-affective psychosis: a meta-analysis. *Schizophrenia Research*, 152(2–3), 521–527. http://dx.doi.org/10.1016/j.schres.2013.12.001.

Laterra, J., Keep, R., Betz, L. A., & Goldstein, G. (1999). *Blood-cerebrospinal fluid barrier*. Philadelphia: Lippincott-Raven.

Lehmann-Facius, H. (1937). Über die Liequordiagnose der Schizophrenien. *Klinische Wochenschrift*, 16, 1646–1648.

Leonard, B. E., Schwarz, M., & Myint, A. M. (2012). The metabolic syndrome in schizophrenia: is inflammation a contributing cause? [Review] *Journal of Psychopharmacology*, 26(5 Suppl.), 33–41. http://dx.doi.org/10.1177/0269881111431622.

Lewis, D. A., & Levitt, P. (2002). Schizophrenia as a disorder of neurodevelopment. [Research Support, U.S. Gov't, P.H.S. Review] *Annual Review of Neuroscience*, 25, 409–432. http://dx.doi.org/10.1146/annurev.neuro.25.112701.142754.

Linderholm, K. R., Skogh, E., Olsson, S. K., Dahl, M. L., Holtze, M., Engberg, G., et al. (2012). Increased levels of kynurenine and kynurenic acid in the CSF of patients with schizophrenia. [Research Support, U.S. Gov't, Non-P.H.S.] *Schizophrenia Bulletin*, 38(3), 426–432. http://dx.doi.org/10.1093/schbul/sbq086.

Lindstrom, L. H., Besev, G., Gunne, L. M., & Terenius, L. (1986). CSF levels of receptor-active endorphins in schizophrenic patients: correlations with symptomatology and monoamine metabolites. [Research Support, Non-U.S. Gov't] *Psychiatry Research*, 19(2), 93–100.

Lindstrom, L. H., Nyberg, F., Terenius, L., Bauer, K., Besev, G., Gunne, L. M., et al. (1984). CSF and plasma beta-casomorphin-like opioid peptides in postpartum psychosis. [Comparative Study Research Support, Non-U.S. Gov't] *The American Journal of Psychiatry*, 141(9), 1059–1066.

Maes, M., Delanghe, J., Bocchio Chiavetto, L., Bignotti, S., Tura, G. B., Pioli, R., et al. (2001). Haptoglobin polymorphism and schizophrenia: genetic variation on chromosome 16. *Psychiatry Research*, 104(1), 1–9.

Mailian, K. R., Boiadzhian, A. S., Sogoian, A. F., Sim, R. B., & Manukian, L. A. (2005). Concentration and protein composition of circulating immune complexes in the blood of patients with schizophrenia and subjects with positive familial history of disease. *Zhurnal nevrologii i psikhiatrii imeni S.S. Korsakova*, 105(4), 55–60.

Malek, A., Sager, R., Kuhn, P., Nicolaides, K. H., & Schneider, H. (1996). Evolution of maternofetal transport of immunoglobulins during human pregnancy. [Research Support, Non-U.S. Gov't] *American Journal of Reproductive Immunology*, 36(5), 248–255.

Marinescu, I., Udristoiu, I., & Marinescu, D. (2013). Choroid plexus calcification: clinical, neuroimaging and histopathological correlations in schizophrenia. *Romanian Journal of Morphology and Embryology = Revue Roumaine de Morphologie et Embryologie*, 54(2), 365–369.

Masdeu, J. C., Gonzalez-Pinto, A., Matute, C., Ruiz De Azua, S., Palomino, A., De Leon, J., et al. (2012). Serum IgG antibodies against the NR1 subunit of the NMDA receptor not detected in schizophrenia. [Letter] *American Journal of Psychiatry*, 169(10), 1120–1121. http://dx.doi.org/10.1176/appi.ajp.2012.12050646.

Mayilyan, K. R., Weinberger, D. R., & Sim, R. B. (2008). The complement system in schizophrenia. *Drug News & Perspectives*, 21(4), 200–210. http://dx.doi.org/10.1358/dnp.2008.21.4.1213349.

Mednick, S. A., Machon, R. A., Huttunen, M. O., & Bonett, D. (1988). Adult schizophrenia following prenatal exposure to an influenza epidemic. [Research Support, U.S. Gov't, P.H.S.] *Archives of General Psychiatry*, 45(2), 189–192.

Mellsop, G., Whittingham, S., & Ungar, B. (1973). Schizophrenia and autoimmune serological reactions. *Archives of General Psychiatry*, 28(2), 194–196.

Menninger, K. A. (1919). Psychoses associated with influenza. *Journal of the American Medical Association*, 72, 235–241.

Menninger, K. A. (1926). Influenza and schizophrenia: an analysis of post-influenza "dementia praecox" as of 1918 and five years later. *American Journal of Psychiatry, 5,* 469–529.

Meyer, U. (2013). Developmental neuroinflammation and schizophrenia. [Research Support, Non-U.S. Gov't Review] *Progress in Neuro-Psychopharmacology & Biological Psychiatry, 42,* 20–34. http://dx.doi.org/10.1016/j.pnpbp.2011.11.003.

Miller, B. J., Buckley, P., Seabolt, W., Mellor, A., & Kirkpatrick, B. (2011). Meta-analysis of cytokine alterations in schizophrenia: clinical status and antipsychotic effects. [Meta-Analysis Research Support, N.I.H., Extramural Research Support, Non-U.S. Gov't] *Biological Psychiatry, 70*(7), 663–671. http://dx.doi.org/10.1016/j.biopsych.2011.04.013.

Miller, B. J., Graham, K. L., Bodenheimer, C. M., Culpepper, N. H., Waller, J. L., & Buckley, P. F. (2013). A prevalence study of urinary tract infections in acute relapse of schizophrenia. [Research Support, Non-U.S. Gov't] *The Journal of Clinical Psychiatry, 74*(3), 271–277. http://dx.doi.org/10.4088/JCP.12m08050.

Miller, B. J., Mellor, A., & Buckley, P. (2012). Total and differential white blood cell counts, high-sensitivity C-reactive protein, and the metabolic syndrome in non-affective psychoses. *Brain, Behavior, and Immunity, 31,* 82–89. http://dx.doi.org/10.1016/j.bbi.2012.08.016.

Modinos, G., Iyegbe, C., Prata, D., Rivera, M., Kempton, M. J., Valmaggia, L. R., et al. (2013). Molecular genetic gene-environment studies using candidate genes in schizophrenia: a systematic review. [Research Support, Non-U.S. Gov't] *Schizophrenia Research, 150*(2–3), 356–365. http://dx.doi.org/10.1016/j.schres.2013.09.010.

Mondelli, V., & Howes, O. (2014). Inflammation: its role in schizophrenia and the potential anti-inflammatory effects of antipsychotics. [Editorial] *Psychopharmacology, 231*(2), 317–318. http://dx.doi.org/10.1007/s00213-013-3383-3.

Monji, A., Kato, T. A., Mizoguchi, Y., Horikawa, H., Seki, Y., Kasai, M., et al. (2013). Neuroinflammation in schizophrenia especially focused on the role of microglia. [Review] *Progress in Neuro-Psychopharmacology & Biological Psychiatry, 42,* 115–121. http://dx.doi.org/10.1016/j.pnpbp.2011.12.002.

Monroe, J. M., Buckley, P. F., & Miller, B. J. (2014). Meta-analysis of Anti-*Toxoplasma gondii* IgM antibodies in acute psychosis. *Schizophrenia Bulletin.* http://dx.doi.org/10.1093/schbul/sbu159.

Morein, B., Blomqvist, G., & Hu, K. (2007). Immune responsiveness in the neonatal period. [Review] *Journal of Comparative Pathology, 137*(Suppl. 1), S27–S31. http://dx.doi.org/10.1016/j.jcpa.2007.04.008.

Mortensen, P. B., Pedersen, C. B., Hougaard, D. M., Norgaard-Petersen, B., Mors, O., Borglum, A. D., & Yolken, R. H. (2010). A Danish National Birth Cohort study of maternal HSV-2 antibodies as a risk factor for schizophrenia in their offspring. [Research Support, Non-U.S. Gov't] *Schizophrenia Research, 122*(1–3), 257–263. http://dx.doi.org/10.1016/j.schres.2010.06.010.

Muller, N. (2014). Immunology of schizophrenia. [Review] *Neuroimmunomodulation, 21*(2–3), 109–116. http://dx.doi.org/10.1159/000356538.

Muller, N., Myint, A. M., & Schwarz, M. J. (2012). Inflammation in schizophrenia. [Review] *Advances in Protein Chemistry and Structural Biology, 88,* 49–68. http://dx.doi.org/10.1016/B978-0-12-398314-5.00003-9.

Nagyoszi, P., Wilhelm, I., Farkas, A. E., Fazakas, C., Dung, N. T., Hasko, J., et al. (2010). Expression and regulation of toll-like receptors in cerebral endothelial cells. [Research Support, Non-U.S. Gov't] *Neurochemistry International, 57*(5), 556–564. http://dx.doi.org/10.1016/j.neuint.2010.07.002.

Narr, K. L., Sharma, T., Woods, R. P., Thompson, P. M., Sowell, E. R., Rex, D., et al. (2003). Increases in regional subarachnoid CSF without apparent cortical gray matter deficits in schizophrenia: modulating effects of sex and age. [Research Support, U.S. Gov't, P.H.S.] *The American Journal of Psychiatry, 160*(12), 2169–2180.

Niebuhr, D. W., Li, Y., Cowan, D. N., Weber, N. S., Fisher, J. A., Ford, G. M., et al. (2011). Association between bovine casein antibody and new onset schizophrenia among US military personnel. [Research Support, Non-U.S. Gov't Research Support, U.S. Gov't, Non-P.H.S.] *Schizophrenia Research, 128*(1–3), 51–55. http://dx.doi.org/10.1016/j.schres.2011.02.005.

Niebuhr, D. W., Millikan, A. M., Cowan, D. N., Yolken, R., Li, Y., & Weber, N. S. (2008). Selected infectious agents and risk of schizophrenia among U.S. military personnel. [Comparative Study Research Support, Non-U.S. Gov't Research Support, U.S. Gov't, Non-P.H.S.] *The American Journal of Psychiatry, 165*(1), 99–106. http://dx.doi.org/10.1176/appi.ajp.2007.06081254.

Parracho, H. M., Bingham, M. O., Gibson, G. R., & McCartney, A. L. (2005). Differences between the gut microflora of children with autistic spectrum disorders and that of healthy children. [Comparative Study Research Support, Non-U.S. Gov't] *Journal of Medical Microbiology, 54*(Pt 10), 987–991. http://dx.doi.org/10.1099/jmm.0.46101-0.

Pearlman, D. M., & Najjar, S. (2014). Meta-analysis of the association between N-methyl-D-aspartate receptor antibodies and schizophrenia, schizoaffective disorder, bipolar disorder, and major depressive disorder. *Schizophrenia Research, 157*(1–3), 249–258. http://dx.doi.org/10.1016/j.schres.2014.05.001.

Pedersen, M. G., Stevens, H., Pedersen, C. B., Norgaard-Pedersen, B., & Mortensen, P. B. (2011). Toxoplasma infection and later development of schizophrenia in mothers. [Research Support, Non-U.S. Gov't] *The American Journal of Psychiatry, 168*(8), 814–821. http://dx.doi.org/10.1176/appi.ajp.2011.10091351.

Perron, H., Hamdani, N., Faucard, R., Lajnef, M., Jamain, S., Daban-Huard, C., et al. (2012). Molecular characteristics of Human Endogenous Retrovirus type-W in schizophrenia and bipolar disorder. [Research Support, Non-U.S. Gov't] *Translational Psychiatry, 2,* e201. http://dx.doi.org/10.1038/tp.2012.125.

Piper, M., Beneyto, M., Burne, T. H., Eyles, D. W., Lewis, D. A., & McGrath, J. J. (2012). The neurodevelopmental hypothesis of schizophrenia: convergent clues from epidemiology and neuropathology. [Review] *The Psychiatric Clinics of North America, 35*(3), 571–584. http://dx.doi.org/10.1016/j.psc.2012.06.002.

Prasad, K. M., Shirts, B. H., Yolken, R. H., Keshavan, M. S., & Nimgaonkar, V. L. (2007). Brain morphological changes associated with exposure to HSV1 in first-episode schizophrenia. [Research Support, N.I.H., Extramural Research Support, Non-U.S. Gov't] *Molecular Psychiatry, 12*(1), 105–113, 101. http://dx.doi.org/10.1038/sj.mp.4001915.

Pribiag, H., & Stellwagen, D. (2014). Neuroimmune regulation of homeostatic synaptic plasticity. [Research Support, Non-U.S. Gov't] *Neuropharmacology, 78,* 13–22. http://dx.doi.org/10.1016/j.neuropharm.2013.06.008.

Purcell, S. M., Wray, N. R., Stone, J. L., Visscher, P. M., O'Donovan, M. C., Sullivan, P. F., et al. (2009). Common polygenic variation contributes to risk of schizophrenia and bipolar disorder. *Nature, 460*(7256), 748–752. http://dx.doi.org/10.1038/nature08185.

Rapoport, J. L., Giedd, J. N., & Gogtay, N. (2012). Neurodevelopmental model of schizophrenia: update 2012. [Review] *Molecular Psychiatry, 17*(12), 1228–1238. http://dx.doi.org/10.1038/mp.2012.23.

Reiber, H. (1994). Flow rate of cerebrospinal fluid (CSF) – a concept common to normal blood-CSF barrier function and to dysfunction in neurological diseases. *Journal of the Neurological Sciences, 122*(2), 189–203.

Rimol, L. M., Nesvag, R., Hagler, D. J., Jr., Bergmann, O., Fennema-Notestine, C., Hartberg, C. B., et al. (2012). Cortical volume, surface area, and thickness in schizophrenia and bipolar disorder. [Research Support, Non-U.S. Gov't] *Biological Psychiatry, 71*(6), 552–560. http://dx.doi.org/10.1016/j.biopsych.2011.11.026.

Rosenow, E. C. (1948). Bacteriologic, etiologic, and serologic studies in epilepsy and schizophrenia; cutaneous reactions to intradermal injection of streptococcal antibody and antigen. *Postgraduate Medicine, 3*(5), 367–376.

Rothermundt, M., Arolt, V., & Bayer, T. A. (2001). Review of immunological and immunopathological findings in schizophrenia. [Research Support, Non-U.S. Gov't Review] *Brain, Behavior, and Immunity*, 15(4), 319–339. http://dx.doi.org/10.1006/brbi.2001.0648.

Samaroo, D., Dickerson, F., Kasarda, D. D., Green, P. H., Briani, C., Yolken, R. H., et al. (2010). Novel immune response to gluten in individuals with schizophrenia. *Schizophrenia Research*, 118(1–3), 248–255. http://dx.doi.org/10.1016/j.schres.2009.08.009 pii:S0920-9964(09)00385-5.

Sandyk, R. (1993). Choroid plexus calcification as a possible marker of hallucinations in schizophrenia. *The International Journal of Neuroscience*, 71(1–4), 87–92.

Schizophrenia Working Group of the Psychiatric Genomics Consortium. (2014). Biological insights from 108 schizophrenia-associated genetic loci. [Research Support, N.I.H., Extramural Research Support, Non-U.S. Gov't] *Nature*, 511(7510), 421–427. http://dx.doi.org/10.1038/nature13595.

Selecki, B. R., Todd, P., Westwood, A. P., & Kraus, J. A. (1964). Cerebrospinal fluid and serum protein profiles in deteriorated epileptics, mental defectives with epilepsy, and schizophrenics. *The Medical Journal of Australia*, 2, 751–753.

Severance, E. G., Alaedini, A., Yang, S., Halling, M., Gressitt, K. L., Stallings, C. R., et al. (2012). Gastrointestinal inflammation and associated immune activation in schizophrenia. [Research Support, Non-U.S. Gov't] *Schizophrenia Research*, 138(1), 48–53. http://dx.doi.org/10.1016/j.schres.2012.02.025.

Severance, E. G., Dickerson, F. B., Halling, M., Krivogorsky, B., Haile, L., Yang, S., et al. (2010). Subunit and whole molecule specificity of the anti-bovine casein immune response in recent onset psychosis and schizophrenia. *Schizophrenia Research*, 118(1–3), 240–247. http://dx.doi.org/10.1016/j.schres.2009.12.030 pii:S0920-9964(09)00621-5.

Severance, E. G., Dickerson, F. B., Viscidi, R. P., Bossis, I., Stallings, C. R., Origoni, A. E., et al. (2011). Coronavirus immunoreactivity in individuals with a recent onset of psychotic symptoms. *Schizophrenia Bulletin*, 37(1), 101–107. http://dx.doi.org/10.1093/schbul/sbp052.

Severance, E. G., Gressitt, K. L., Alaedini, A., Rohleder, C., Enning, F., Bumb, J. M., et al. (2015). IgG dynamics of dietary antigens point to cerebrospinal fluid barrier or flow dysfunction in first-episode schizophrenia. *Brain, Behavior, and Immunity*, 44, 148–158. http://dx.doi.org/10.1016/j.bbi.2014.09.009. Epub 2014 Sep 20. PMID: 25241021.

Severance, E. G., Gressitt, K. L., Buka, S. L., Cannon, T. D., & Yolken, R. H. (2014). Maternal complement C1q and increased odds for psychosis in adult offspring. [Research Support, N.I.H., Extramural Research Support, Non-U.S. Gov't] *Schizophrenia Research*, 159(1), 14–19. http://dx.doi.org/10.1016/j.schres.2014.07.053.

Severance, E. G., Gressitt, K. L., Halling, M., Stallings, C. R., Origoni, A. E., Vaughan, C., et al. (2012). Complement C1q formation of immune complexes with milk caseins and wheat glutens in schizophrenia. *Neurobiology of Disease*, 48(3), 447–453. http://dx.doi.org/10.1016/j.nbd.2012.07.005.

Severance, E. G., Gressitt, K. L., Stallings, C. R., Origoni, A. E., Khushalani, S., Leweke, F. M., et al. (2013a). Discordant patterns of bacterial translocation markers and implications for innate immune imbalances in schizophrenia. [Multicenter Study Research Support, N.I.H., Extramural Research Support, Non-U.S. Gov't] *Schizophrenia Research*, 148(1–3), 130–137. http://dx.doi.org/10.1016/j.schres.2013.05.018.

Severance, E. G., Gressitt, K. L., Stallings, C. R., Origoni, A. E., Khushalani, S., Leweke, F. M., et al. (2013b). Discordant patterns of bacterial translocation markers and implications for innate immune imbalances in schizophrenia. *Schizophrenia Research*. http://dx.doi.org/10.1016/j.schres.2013.05.018.

Severance, E. G., Kannan, G., Gressitt, K. L., Xiao, J., Alaedini, A., Pletnikov, M. V., & Yolken, R. H. (2012). Anti-gluten immune response following *Toxoplasma gondii* infection in mice. [Research Support, N.I.H., Extramural Research Support, Non-U.S. Gov't] *PLoS One*, 7(11), e50991. http://dx.doi.org/10.1371/journal.pone.0050991.

Severance, E. G., Yolken, R. H., & Eaton, W. W. (2014). Autoimmune diseases, gastrointestinal disorders and the microbiome in schizophrenia: more than a gut feeling. [Review] *Schizophrenia Research*. http://dx.doi.org/10.1016/j.schres.2014.06.027.

Shatz, C. J. (2009). MHC class I: an unexpected role in neuronal plasticity. [Research Support, N.I.H., Extramural Research Support, Non-U.S. Gov't] *Neuron*, 64(1), 40–45. http://dx.doi.org/10.1016/j.neuron.2009.09.044.

Shi, J., Levinson, D. F., Duan, J., Sanders, A. R., Zheng, Y., Pe'er, I., et al. (2009). Common variants on chromosome 6p22.1 are associated with schizophrenia. *Nature*, 460(7256), 753–757. http://dx.doi.org/10.1038/nature08192.

Shi, L., Smith, S. E., Malkova, N., Tse, D., Su, Y., & Patterson, P. H. (2009). Activation of the maternal immune system alters cerebellar development in the offspring. [Research Support, N.I.H., Extramural Research Support, Non-U.S. Gov't] *Brain, Behavior, and Immunity*, 23(1), 116–123. http://dx.doi.org/10.1016/j.bbi.2008.07.012.

Shiga, T., Wada, A., Kunii, Y., Itagaki, S., Sakuma, J., Yabe, H., et al. (2012). Effective surgical intervention for schizophrenia-like symptoms and low event-related potentials caused by arachnoid cyst. [Case Reports Letter] *Psychiatry and Clinical Neurosciences*, 66(6), 536–537. http://dx.doi.org/10.1111/j.1440-1819.2012.02371.x.

Simister, N. E. (2003). Placental transport of immunoglobulin G. [Research Support, U.S. Gov't, P.H.S. Review] *Vaccine*, 21(24), 3365–3369.

Solomon, G. F., Allansmith, M., McCellan, B., & Amkraut, A. (1969). Immunoglobulins in psychiatric patients. *Archives of General Psychiatry*, 20(3), 272–277.

Sorensen, H. J., Mortensen, E. L., Reinisch, J. M., & Mednick, S. A. (2009). Association between prenatal exposure to bacterial infection and risk of schizophrenia. [Research Support, N.I.H., Extramural Research Support, Non-U.S. Gov't] *Schizophrenia Bulletin*, 35(3), 631–637. http://dx.doi.org/10.1093/schbul/sbn121.

Stamboliev, P. N. (1970). Immunoelectrophoretic analysis of serum during development of schizophrenia. *Zhurnal nevropatologii i psikhiatrii imeni S.S. Korsakova*, 70(9), 1339–1343.

Stefansson, H., Ophoff, R. A., Steinberg, S., Andreassen, O. A., Cichon, S., Rujescu, D., et al. (2009). Common variants conferring risk of schizophrenia. *Nature*, 460(7256), 744–747. http://dx.doi.org/10.1038/nature08186.

Steiner, J., Bernstein, H. G., Schiltz, K., Muller, U. J., Westphal, S., Drexhage, H. A., et al. (2012). Immune system and glucose metabolism interaction in schizophrenia: a chicken-egg dilemma. *Progress in Neuropsychopharmacology & Biological Psychiatry*, 48, 287–294. http://dx.doi.org/10.1016/j.pnpbp.2012.09.016.

Steiner, J., Teegen, B., Schiltz, K., Bernstein, H. G., Stoecker, W., & Bogerts, B. (2014). Prevalence of N-methyl-D-aspartate receptor autoantibodies in the peripheral blood: healthy control samples revisited. *JAMA Psychiatry*, 71(7), 838–839. http://dx.doi.org/10.1001/jamapsychiatry.2014.469.

Steiner, J., Walter, M., Glanz, W., Sarnyai, Z., Bernstein, H. G., Vielhaber, S., et al. (2013). Increased prevalence of diverse N-methyl-D-aspartate glutamate receptor antibodies in patients with an initial diagnosis of schizophrenia: specific relevance of IgG NR1a antibodies for distinction from N-methyl-D-aspartate glutamate receptor encephalitis. *JAMA Psychiatry*, 70(3), 271–278. http://dx.doi.org/10.1001/2013.jamapsychiatry.86.

Stephan, A. H., Madison, D. V., Mateos, J. M., Fraser, D. A., Lovelett, E. A., Coutellier, L., et al. (2013). A dramatic increase of C1q protein in the CNS during normal aging. [Research Support, N.I.H., Extramural Research Support, Non-U.S. Gov't] *The Journal of Neuroscience: The Official Journal of the Society for Neuroscience*, 33(33), 13460–13474. http://dx.doi.org/10.1523/JNEUROSCI.1333-13.2013.

Stevens, B., Allen, N. J., Vazquez, L. E., Howell, G. R., Christopherson, K. S., Nouri, N., et al. (2007). The classical complement cascade mediates CNS synapse elimination. *Cell*, 131(6), 1164–1178. http://dx.doi.org/10.1016/j.cell.2007.10.036 pii:S0092-8674(07)01355-4.

Stilling, R. M., Dinan, T. G., & Cryan, J. F. (2014). Microbial genes, brain & behaviour – epigenetic regulation of the gut-brain axis. [Research Support, Non-U.S. Gov't] *Genes, Brain, and Behavior, 13*(1), 69–86. http://dx.doi.org/10.1111/gbb.12109.

Stockinger, S., Hornef, M. W., & Chassin, C. (2011). Establishment of intestinal homeostasis during the neonatal period. [Research Support, Non-U.S. Gov't Review] *Cellular and Molecular Life Sciences, 68*(22), 3699–3712. http://dx.doi.org/10.1007/s00018-011-0831-2.

Stoimenov, I. A. (1969). Relationship between forms and symptoms of schizophrenia and the presence of brain antibodies in the blood serum. *Vestnik Akademii Meditsinskikh Nauk SSSR, 24*(4), 67–70.

Stojanovic, A., Martorell, L., Montalvo, I., Ortega, L., Monseny, R., Vilella, E., et al. (2014). Increased serum interleukin-6 levels in early stages of psychosis: associations with at-risk mental states and the severity of psychotic symptoms. *Psychoneuroendocrinology, 41*, 23–32. http://dx.doi.org/10.1016/j.psyneuen.2013.12.005.

Strahilevitz, M., & Davis, S. D. (1970). Increased IgA in schizophrenic patients. *Lancet, 2*(7668), 370.

Suarez-Pinilla, P., Lopez-Gil, J., & Crespo-Facorro, B. (2014). Immune system: a possible nexus between cannabinoids and psychosis. *Brain, Behavior, and Immunity, 40*, 269–282. http://dx.doi.org/10.1016/j.bbi.2014.01.018.

Sun, Z. Y., Wei, J., Xie, L., Shen, Y., Liu, S. Z., Ju, G. Z., et al. (2004). The CLDN5 locus may be involved in the vulnerability to schizophrenia. [Research Support, Non-U.S. Gov't] *European Psychiatry: The Journal of the Association of European Psychiatrists, 19*(6), 354–357. http://dx.doi.org/10.1016/j.eurpsy.2004.06.007.

Suvisaari, J., Haukka, J., Tanskanen, A., Hovi, T., & Lonnqvist, J. (1999). Association between prenatal exposure to poliovirus infection and adult schizophrenia. [Research Support, Non-U.S. Gov't] *American Journal of Psychiatry, 156*(7), 1100–1102.

Tibbling, G., Link, H., & Ohman, S. (1977). Principles of albumin and IgG analyses in neurological disorders. I. Establishment of reference values. [Clinical Trial Comparative Study] *Scandinavian Journal of Clinical and Laboratory Investigation, 37*(5), 385–390. http://dx.doi.org/10.1080/00365517709091496.

Torrey, E. F., Bartko, J. J., Lun, Z. R., & Yolken, R. H. (2007). Antibodies to *Toxoplasma gondii* in patients with schizophrenia: a meta-analysis. [Meta-Analysis] *Schizophrenia Bulletin, 33*(3), 729–736. http://dx.doi.org/10.1093/schbul/sbl050.

Torrey, E. F., Bartko, J. J., & Yolken, R. H. (2012). *Toxoplasma gondii* and other risk factors for schizophrenia: an update. *Schizophrenia Bulletin, 38*(3), 642–647. http://dx.doi.org/10.1093/schbul/sbs043.

Torrey, E. F., & Peterson, M. R. (1973). Slow and latent viruses in schizophrenia. *Lancet, 2*(7819), 22–24.

Torrey, E. F., & Peterson, M. R. (1976). The viral hypothesis of schizophrenia. *Schizophrenia Bulletin, 2*(1), 136–146.

Torrey, E. F., & Yolken, R. H. (2001). The schizophrenia-rheumatoid arthritis connection: infectious, immune, or both? *Brain, Behavior, and Immunity, 15*(4), 401–410.

Trotta, T., Porro, C., Calvello, R., & Panaro, M. A. (2014). Biological role of Toll-like receptor-4 in the brain. [Review] *Journal of Neuroimmunology, 268*(1–2), 1–12. http://dx.doi.org/10.1016/j.jneuroim.2014.01.014.

Tsuang, M. (2000). Schizophrenia: genes and environment. [Review] *Biological Psychiatry, 47*(3), 210–220.

van Os, J., Rutten, B. P., Myin-Germeys, I., Delespaul, P., Viechtbauer, W., van Zelst, C., & Mirjanic, T. (2014). Identifying gene-environment interactions in schizophrenia: contemporary challenges for integrated, large-scale investigations. [Research Support, Non-U.S. Gov't] *Schizophrenia Bulletin, 40*(4), 729–736. http://dx.doi.org/10.1093/schbul/sbu069.

Veijola, J., Guo, J. Y., Moilanen, J. S., Jaaskelainen, E., Miettunen, J., Kyllonen, M., et al. (2014). Longitudinal changes in total brain volume in schizophrenia: relation to symptom severity, cognition and antipsychotic medication. *PLoS One, 9*(7), e101689. http://dx.doi.org/10.1371/journal.pone.0101689.

Vetlugina, T. P., Logvinovich, G. V., Maslennikova, S. N., & Vasil'eva, O. A. (1984). Circulating immune complexes in the serum of mental patients and healthy subjects. *Zhurnal nevrologii i psikhiatrii imeni S.S. Korsakova, 84*(3), 422–426.

Walport, M. J. (2001a). Complement. First of two parts. [Review] *The New England Journal of Medicine, 344*(14), 1058–1066. http://dx.doi.org/10.1056/NEJM200104053441406.

Walport, M. J. (2001b). Complement. Second of two parts. [Research Support, Non-U.S. Gov't Review] *The New England Journal of Medicine, 344*(15), 1140–1144. http://dx.doi.org/10.1056/NEJM200104123441506.

Wan, C., La, Y., Zhu, H., Yang, Y., Jiang, L., Chen, Y., et al. (2007). Abnormal changes of plasma acute phase proteins in schizophrenia and the relation between schizophrenia and haptoglobin (Hp) gene. [Clinical Trial Research Support, Non-U.S. Gov't] *Amino Acids, 32*(1), 101–108. http://dx.doi.org/10.1007/s00726-005-0292-8.

Wei, J., & Hemmings, G. P. (2005). A study of the combined effect of the CLDN5 locus and the genes for the phospholipid metabolism pathway in schizophrenia. *Prostaglandins, Leukotrienes, and Essential Fatty Acids, 73*(6), 441–445. http://dx.doi.org/10.1016/j.plefa.2005.08.003.

Whedon, J. M., & Glassey, D. (2009). Cerebrospinal fluid stasis and its clinical significance. [Review] *Alternative Therapies in Health and Medicine, 15*(3), 54–60.

Whiteley, P., Haracopos, D., Knivsberg, A. M., Reichelt, K. L., Parlar, S., Jacobsen, J., et al. (2010). The ScanBrit randomised, controlled, single-blind study of a gluten- and casein-free dietary intervention for children with autism spectrum disorders. *Nutritional Neuroscience, 13*(2), 87–100. http://dx.doi.org/10.1179/1476830 10X12611460763922.

Whiteley, P., Shattock, P., Knivsberg, A. M., Seim, A., Reichelt, K. L., Todd, L., et al. (2012). Gluten- and casein-free dietary intervention for autism spectrum conditions. *Frontiers in Human Neuroscience, 6*, 344. http://dx.doi.org/10.3389/fnhum.2012.00344.

Williams, B. L., Hornig, M., Buie, T., Bauman, M. L., Cho Paik, M., Wick, I., et al. (2011). Impaired carbohydrate digestion and transport and mucosal dysbiosis in the intestines of children with autism and gastrointestinal disturbances. [Research Support, N.I.H., Extramural Research Support, Non-U.S. Gov't Research Support, U.S. Gov't, Non-P.H.S.] *PLoS One, 6*(9), e24585. http://dx.doi.org/10.1371/journal.pone.0024585.

Williams, B. L., Hornig, M., Parekh, T., & Lipkin, W. I. (2012). Application of novel PCR-based methods for detection, quantitation, and phylogenetic characterization of Sutterella species in intestinal biopsy samples from children with autism and gastrointestinal disturbances. [Research Support, N.I.H., Extramural Research Support, U.S. Gov't, Non-P.H.S.] *mBio, 3* (1). http://dx.doi.org/10.1128/mBio.00261-11.

Xiao, J., Buka, S. L., Cannon, T. D., Suzuki, Y., Viscidi, R. P., Torrey, E. F., et al. (2009). Serological pattern consistent with infection with type I *Toxoplasma gondii* in mothers and risk of psychosis among adult offspring. *Microbes and Infection, 11*(13), 1011–1018. http://dx.doi.org/10.1016/j.micinf.2009.07.007 pii:S1286-4579(09)00165-8.

Yang, Y., Wan, C., Li, H., Zhu, H., La, Y., Xi, Z., et al. (2006). Altered levels of acute phase proteins in the plasma of patients with schizophrenia. [Research Support, Non-U.S. Gov't] *Analytical Chemistry, 78*(11), 3571–3576. http://dx.doi.org/10.1021/ac051916x.

Ye, L., Sun, Z., Xie, L., Liu, S., Ju, G., Shi, J., et al. (2005). Further study of a genetic association between the CLDN5 locus and schizophrenia. [Letter Research Support, Non-U.S. Gov't] *Schizophrenia Research, 75*(1), 139–141. http://dx.doi.org/10.1016/j.schres.2004.11.003.

Yolken, R., & Dickerson, F. (2014). The microbiome – the missing link in the pathogenesis of schizophrenia. *Schizophrenia Research, 153*(Suppl. 1), S16.

Yolken, R.H., Bachmann, S., Ruslanova, I., Lillehoj, E., Ford, G., Torrey, E.F., et al. (2001). Antibodies to *Toxoplasma gondii* in individuals with first-episode schizophrenia. *Clinical Infectious Diseases*, 32(5), 842–844. http://dx.doi.org/10.1086/319221 pii:CID000667.

Yolken, R. H., & Torrey, E. F. (2008). Are some cases of psychosis caused by microbial agents? A review of the evidence. *Molecular Psychiatry*, 13(5), 470–479. http://dx.doi.org/10.1038/mp.2008.5.

Zakharyan, R., Khoyetsyan, A., Arakelyan, A., Boyajyan, A., Gevorgyan, A., Stahelova, A., et al. (2011). Association of C1QB gene polymorphism with schizophrenia in Armenian population. [Research Support, Non-U.S. Gov't] *BMC Medical Genetics*, 12, 126. http://dx.doi.org/10.1186/1471-2350-12-126.

Zhang, C., Xu, D., Luo, H., Lu, J., Liu, L., Ping, J., et al. (2014). Prenatal xenobiotic exposure and intrauterine hypothalamus-pituitary-adrenal axis programming alteration. [Review] *Toxicology*, 325C, 74–84. http://dx.doi.org/10.1016/j.tox.2014.08.015.

Zhao, Z., Xu, J., Chen, J., Kim, S., Reimers, M., Bacanu, S. A., et al. (2014). Transcriptome sequencing and genome-wide association analyses reveal lysosomal function and actin cytoskeleton remodeling in schizophrenia and bipolar disorder. *Molecular Psychiatry*. http://dx.doi.org/10.1038/mp.2014.82.

30

Future Directions

Mikhail V. Pletnikov*, John L. Waddington§,¶

Department of Psychiatry and Behavioral Sciences, Johns Hopkins University School of Medicine, Baltimore, MD, USA; §Molecular and Cellular Therapeutics, Royal College of Surgeons in Ireland, Dublin, Ireland; ¶Jiangsu Key Laboratory of Translational Research & Therapy for Neuro-Psychiatric-Disorders and Department of Pharmacology, College of Pharmaceutical Sciences, Soochow University, Suzhou, China

OVERVIEW

The chapters in this volume indicate clearly the extent to which the field of models for schizophrenia and related psychotic disorders has advanced over the past decade. This field was born to meet a growing demand for behavioral assays to investigate the "new" pharmacological agents, discovered essentially by serendipity, which entered psychiatric practice in the late 1950s through to the 1970s for the treatment of schizophrenia. At that time, the main goal was to develop one or more models with high predictive validity to facilitate the search for new antipsychotics.

Subsequently, progress in behavioral neuroscience during the 1980s/1990s facilitated the emergence of numerous models based on various approaches to manipulating brain integrity and having the aim of recapitulating behavioral changes observed in patients. Hyperactivity produced by psychotomimetics such as amphetamine was complemented by lesion-induced hyperactivity as models of positive, psychotic symptoms. These models were subsequently elaborated to involve lesion- and chemically induced disruption of early brain development, consequent to strong evidence that abnormalities of brain development were an important, even fundamental, component of the pathobiology of schizophrenia. However, though important and heuristic, these lesion- and chemically induced models were viewed more skeptically by many clinicians, who questioned both the etiological validity of such models and the behavioral isomorphism of hyperactivity and positive symptoms. In counterpoint, it remained evident that antipsychotics had similar effects on behavior in both psychotic patients and hyperactive rodents, with little effect on elements of behavior equated with other aspects of schizophrenia symptomatology.

It was not until the early 2000s that fundamental advances in animal models emerged. This happened for two main reasons: first, mouse genetics had come of age and was now able to reliably generate various genetically modified (mutant) lines, and second, novel findings from linkage and association studies had identified several candidate risk genes for schizophrenia. Some of those genes became celebrities (e.g., DISC1) as, in addition to these clinical findings, they were found to be involved in the regulation of brain development. There was widespread expectation that candidate risk factor models, both environmental and, particularly, genetic, would provide new insights into pathophysiological mechanisms and would lead to identification of new therapeutic targets. However, while genetic models were grouped depending on what diagnostic population was associated with a particular candidate gene, for example, genetic models for schizophrenia *or* for affective disorder, application of the "retrospectoscope" emphasizes ab initio that DISC1 is associated not only with schizophrenia but also with affective and other disorders.

CONFRONTING THE CHALLENGES

Concerns relating to model systems are heightened by additional complexities:

1. There is increasing recognition of the breadth of psychopathology manifested in psychotic illness, which involves at least five domains: positive (psychotic) symptoms, negative symptoms, cognitive dysfunction, depression, and mania. Furthermore,

psychosis can be manifested in 11 DSM-IV diagnostic categories in addition to schizophrenia, and there is emerging, though less extensive, evidence that the pathophysiology-neuropathology of psychotic illness may generalize across such diagnoses. Therefore, these aspects of psychopathology and pathophysiology-neuropathology should be reflected in our models, so that they can evolve beyond simplistic relationships to "schizophrenia" that are not in accordance with the clinical reality of psychotic illness.

2. There is increasing evidence from Genome-wide association study (GWAS) that many genes associated with risk for schizophrenia (both common genes of small effect and rare genes (copy number variations) of large effect) are associated also, to varying degrees, with risk for other neuropsychiatric disorders, including bipolar disorder, major depressive disorder, autism spectrum disorder, attention deficit-hyperactivity disorder, learning disability, and epilepsy. Thus, these aspects of genetics should also be incorporated into our models, so that they can further evolve beyond simplistic relationships to "schizophrenia."

3. There are continually evolving concepts and evidence that genes, which constitute our most substantive clues to the pathobiology of psychotic illness and tractable antipsychotic drug targets, do not operate in isolation; rather, they interact not only with environmental risk factors (gene–environment interactions), but also with other risk genes (gene–gene interactions; epistasis) in a manner complementary to evidence for interactions between environmental risk factors. Therefore, such interactions also require incorporation and interrogation in our models.

4. While early models were focused primarily on behavioral indices, increasing understanding of the pathobiology of psychosis has resulted in broader indices that now extend to brain structure, neuronal cytoarchitecture, molecular and cellular neurobiology, and neurophysiology. Furthermore, models are now being extended to include novel cellular systems and processes that allow interrogation of specific mechanisms implicated in the pathobiology of psychotic illness.

In summary, both the psychopathology and genetics of psychosis are disrespectful to our current nosology. This is, to some extent, both already evident but underappreciated in current models based on diagnostic categories. For example, some models of the positive symptoms of psychotic illness, such as hyperactivity, are used also by investigators in affective disorder as models of mania; some models of negative symptoms, such as anhedonia, are used also by investigators in affective disorder as models of depression; some models of negative symptoms, such as abnormalities of social behavior, arose from and were applied initially by investigators in autism spectrum disorder. Importantly, the complexities considered above emphasize that not every model should be expected to recapitulate every aspect of the psychopathology and pathobiology of psychotic illness; when juxtaposed with the clinical reality that patients show considerable clinical diversity, a model recapitulating only one domain may be more informative on an underlying "core" pathobiological process than a model recapitulating multiple or indeed "all" domains.

Evidence increasingly suggests that we are dealing with a milieu of neurodevelopmental outcomes that are in continuity with one another, with the boundaries that we impose and label as diagnostic categories being substantially arbitrary. While this is at least in part reflected in contemporary dimensional concepts of psychotic illness and research domain criteria, this evolution does not yet warrant abandonment of current clinical diagnostic structures: psychiatrists still need to care for a patient with a specific diagnosis; family members still want to know what illness their loved one has; last but not least, insurance companies still reimburse the cost of treatment on the basis of a particular diagnostic category.

Nevertheless, the dawn of a new era of animal models of psychotic illness and related psychiatric disorders has arrived, and the field appears to be ready to embrace these perspectives. There is new realization that animal models do not serve to recapitulate schizophrenia in its entirety but, rather, should focus on specific dimensions or domains that transgress existing diagnostic boundaries to become truly translational. Furthermore, this changing landscape of psychiatric illness, with attendant advances in neurobiology and neuroimaging, emphasizes measurement of neurobiological entities that are thought to be closer to genetic mechanisms (i.e., the concept of endophenotypes). Animal models are increasingly incorporating neurobiological indices that can be much more readily translated to similar measures in patients. We are now witnessing the emergence of many of these new directions. Animal models are here to stay and will continue to help progress across psychiatry in general and, particularly, for understanding and alleviating the debilities of psychotic illness.

Acknowledgments

The authors' studies were supported by MH-083728, MH-094268 Silvo O. Conte center, the Brain and Behavior Research Foundation, the Stanley Medical Research Institute, Tabakman Trust Gift Grant (MVP), and Science Foundation Ireland Principal Investigator Grant 07/IN.1/B960 (JLW).

Index